Dictionary of Literary Biography

Dictionary of Literary Biography Documentary Series

Dictionary of Literary Biography Yearbooks

1980 edited by Karen L. Rood, Jean W. Ross, and Richard Ziegfeld (1981)

1981 edited by Karen L. Rood, Jean W. Ross, and Richard Ziegfeld (1982)

1982 edited by Richard Ziegfeld; associate editors: Jean W. Ross and Lynne C. Zeigler (1983)

1983 edited by Mary Bruccoli and Jean W. Ross; associate editor Richard Ziegfeld (1984)

1984 edited by Jean W. Ross (1985)

1985 edited by Jean W. Ross (1986)

1986 edited by J. M. Brook (1987)

1987 edited by J. M. Brook (1988)

1988 edited by J. M. Brook (1989)

1989 edited by J. M. Brook (1990)

1990 edited by James W. Hipp (1991)

1991 edited by James W. Hipp (1992)

1992 edited by James W. Hipp (1993)

1993 edited by James W. Hipp, contributing editor George Garrett (1994)

1994 edited by James W. Hipp, contributing editor George Garrett (1995)

1995 edited by James W. Hipp, contributing editor George Garrett (1996)

1996 edited by Samuel W. Bruce and L. Kay Webster, contributing editor George Garrett (1997)

1997 edited by Matthew J. Bruccoli and George Garrett, with the assistance of L. Kay Webster (1998)

1998 edited by Matthew J. Bruccoli, contributing editor George Garrett, with the assistance of D. W. Thomas (1999)

1999 edited by Matthew J. Bruccoli, contributing editor George Garrett, with the assistance of D. W. Thomas (2000)

2000 edited by Matthew J. Bruccoli, contributing editor George Garrett, with the assistance of George Parker Anderson (2001)

2001 edited by Matthew J. Bruccoli, contributing editor George Garrett, with the assistance of George Parker Anderson (2002)

Concise Series

Concise Dictionary of American Literary Biography, 7 volumes (1988–1999): *The New Consciousness, 1941–1968; Colonization to the American Renaissance, 1640–1865; Realism, Naturalism, and Local Color, 1865–1917; The Twenties, 1917–1929; The Age of Maturity, 1929–1941; Broadening Views, 1968–1988; Supplement: Modern Writers, 1900–1998.*

Concise Dictionary of British Literary Biography, 8 volumes (1991–1992): *Writers of the Middle Ages and Renaissance Before 1660; Writers of the Restoration and Eighteenth Century, 1660–1789; Writers of the Romantic Period, 1789–1832; Victorian Writers, 1832–1890; Late-Victorian and Edwardian Writers, 1890–1914; Modern Writers, 1914–1945; Writers After World War II, 1945–1960; Contemporary Writers, 1960 to Present.*

Concise Dictionary of World Literary Biography, 4 volumes (1999–2000): *Ancient Greek and Roman Writers; German Writers; African, Caribbean, and Latin American Writers; South Slavic and Eastern European Writers.*

Dictionary of Literary Biography® • Volume Two Hundred Seventy-Seven

Russian Literature in the Age of Realism

Dictionary of Literary Biography® • Volume Two Hundred Seventy-Seven

Russian Literature in the Age of Realism

Edited by
Alyssa Dinega Gillespie
University of Notre Dame

GALE®

THOMSON
GALE

Detroit • New York • San Diego • San Francisco • Cleveland • New Haven, Conn. • Waterville, Maine • London • Munich

Dictionary of Literary Biography
Volume 277: Russian Literature
in the Age of Realism
Alyssa Dinega Gillespie

Advisory Board
John Baker
William Cagle
Patrick O'Connor
George Garrett
Trudier Harris
Alvin Kernan
Kenny J. Williams

Editorial Directors
Matthew J. Bruccoli and Richard Layman

LIBRARY OF CONGRESS CATALOGING-IN-PUBLICATION DATA

Russian literature in the Age of Realism / edited by Alyssa Dinega Gillespie.
p. cm. — (Dictionary of literary biography ; v. 277)
"A Bruccoli Clark Layman book."—CIP t.p.
Includes bibliographical references and index.
ISBN 0-7876-6021-3
1. Russian literature—19th century—Bio-bibliography—Dictionaries.
2. Authors, Russian—19th century—Biography—Dictionaries.
3. Realism in literature. I. Dinega, Alyssa W. II. Series.

PG3012.R78 2003
891.709'003—dc21
2003004002

Printed in the United States of America
10 9 8 7 6 5 4 3 2 1

Contents

Contents

Plan of the Series

. . . Almost the most prodigious asset of a country, and perhaps its most precious possession, is its native literary product—when that product is fine and noble and enduring.

Mark Twain*

The advisory board, the editors, and the publisher of the *Dictionary of Literary Biography* are joined in endorsing Mark Twain's declaration. The literature of a nation provides an inexhaustible resource of permanent worth. Our purpose is to make literature and its creators better understood and more accessible to students and the reading public, while satisfying the needs of teachers and researchers.

To meet these requirements, *literary biography* has been construed in terms of the author's achievement. The most important thing about a writer is his writing. Accordingly, the entries in *DLB* are career biographies, tracing the development of the author's canon and the evolution of his reputation.

The purpose of *DLB* is not only to provide reliable information in a usable format but also to place the figures in the larger perspective of literary history and to offer appraisals of their accomplishments by qualified scholars.

The publication plan for *DLB* resulted from two years of preparation. The project was proposed to Bruccoli Clark by Frederick G. Ruffner, president of the Gale Research Company, in November 1975. After specimen entries were prepared and typeset, an advisory board was formed to refine the entry format and develop the series rationale. In meetings held during 1976, the publisher, series editors, and advisory board approved the scheme for a comprehensive biographical dictionary of persons who contributed to literature. Editorial work on the first volume began in January 1977, and it was published in 1978. In order to make *DLB* more than a dictionary and to compile volumes that individually have claim to status as literary history, it was decided to organize volumes by topic, period, or

From an unpublished section of Mark Twain's autobiography, copyright by the Mark Twain Company

genre. Each of these freestanding volumes provides a biographical-bibliographical guide and overview for a particular area of literature. We are convinced that this organization—as opposed to a single alphabet method—constitutes a valuable innovation in the presentation of reference material. The volume plan necessarily requires many decisions for the placement and treatment of authors. Certain figures will be included in separate volumes, but with different entries emphasizing the aspect of his career appropriate to each volume. Ernest Hemingway, for example, is represented in *American Writers in Paris, 1920–1939* by an entry focusing on his expatriate apprenticeship; he is also in *American Novelists, 1910–1945* with an entry surveying his entire career, as well as in *American Short-Story Writers, 1910–1945, Second Series* with an entry concentrating on his short fiction. Each volume includes a cumulative index of the subject authors and articles.

Since 1981 the series has been further augmented by the *DLB Yearbooks,* which update published entries, add new entries to keep the *DLB* current with contemporary activity, and provide articles on literary history. There have also been nineteen *DLB Documentary Series* volumes, which provide illustrations, facsimiles, and biographical and critical source materials for figures, works, or groups judged to have particular interest for students. In 1999 the *Documentary Series* was incorporated into the *DLB* volume numbering system beginning with *DLB 210: Ernest Hemingway.*

We define literature as the *intellectual commerce of a nation:* not merely as belles lettres but as that ample and complex process by which ideas are generated, shaped, and transmitted. *DLB* entries are not limited to "creative writers" but extend to other figures who in their time and in their way influenced the mind of a people. Thus the series encompasses historians, journalists, publishers, book collectors, and screenwriters. By this means readers of *DLB* may be aided to perceive literature not as cult scripture in the keeping of intellectual high priests but firmly positioned at the center of a nation's life.

DLB includes the major writers appropriate to each volume and those standing in the ranks behind them. Scholarly and critical counsel has been sought in deciding which minor figures to include and how full their entries should be. Wherever possible, useful references are made to figures who do not warrant separate entries.

Each *DLB* volume has an expert volume editor responsible for planning the volume, selecting the figures for inclusion, and assigning the entries. Volume editors are also responsible for preparing, where appropriate, appendices surveying the major periodicals and literary and intellectual movements for their volumes, as well as lists of further readings. Work on the series as a whole is coordinated at the Bruccoli Clark Layman editorial center in Columbia, South Carolina, where the editorial staff is responsible for accuracy and utility of the published volumes.

One feature that distinguishes *DLB* is the illustration policy–its concern with the iconography of literature. Just as an author is influenced by his surroundings, so is the reader's understanding of the author enhanced by a knowledge of his environment. Therefore *DLB* volumes include not only drawings, paintings, and photographs of authors, often depicting them at various stages in their careers, but also illustrations of their families and places where they lived. Title pages are regularly reproduced in facsimile along with dust jackets for modern authors. The dust jackets are a special feature of *DLB* because they often document better than anything else the way in which an author's work was perceived in its own time. Specimens of the writers' manuscripts and letters are included when feasible.

Samuel Johnson rightly decreed that "The chief glory of every people arises from its authors." The purpose of the *Dictionary of Literary Biography* is to compile literary history in the surest way available to us–by accurate and comprehensive treatment of the lives and work of those who contributed to it.

The *DLB* Advisory Board

Introduction

The second half of the nineteenth century was a turbulent and momentous time in Russian history, during which were sown the seeds of the brutal revolution that would rout the monarchy and transform Russian society in the next century. In literature, this was the age of the great Realist novel, the age of Leo Tolstoy and Fyodor Dostoevsky, of *Voina i mir* (War and Peace, 1875–1877) and *Brat'ia Karamazovy* (The Brothers Karamazov, 1879–1880)–of the novelists and novels that first put Russian literature on the map of European culture. Indisputably, the novel was the crowning literary achievement of the age. Its most talented practitioners far exceeded the boundaries of the genre as it had been conceived in western Europe, imbuing their works with profound, wide-ranging moral, spiritual, philosophical, and political content that untidily but dramatically spilled across the divide between fiction and nonfiction, projecting a vision of an idealized future for humanity even as it grappled with the topical questions of the present day. Under a system of strict state censorship of the written word, the novel garnered the right to speak more frankly than any other literary form about Russians' hopes, fears, and struggles against injustices of all kinds, becoming, in the words of critic Richard Freeborn in *The Cambridge History of Russian Literature* (1992), "a surrogate parliament, second government, open university, academy of sciences, forum of public opinion and national conscience."

However, on the fringes of the novel, a multitude of other literary genres flourished throughout the age of Realism. Short fiction, philosophy, journalistic essays, literary criticism, drama, poetry, memoirs, and travel sketches were printed in periodicals amid the latest installments of the great novels. In most cases, the authors of the minor genres were lesser literary talents than the novelists, but they nevertheless set forth the terms of the cultural debates and literary polemics of the day. Their works can thus shed light upon the ideological foundations of the great novels, but these works are also interesting in their own right: as documents of thought and experience during a particularly restless time in Russian history and, sometimes, as literary experiments that suffered from their mismatch with the spirit of the age. Not all authors of the secondary genres were themselves second-rate, however. In some cases, these authors were–if not

quite giants in the international arena like the major novelists–hugely talented creative artists. Such, for example, were the dramatist Aleksandr Nikolaevich Ostrovsky, poets Afanasii Afanas'evich Fet and Nikolai Alekseevich Nekrasov, journalist Aleksandr Ivanovich Gertsen (Herzen), and short-story writer and dramatist Anton Pavlovich Chekhov.

This introduction seeks to place the minor genres of the Russian age of Realism in historical and literary-historical context. The second half of the nineteenth century can be divided into two periods, each of which corresponded to the reign of a single tsar–Alexander II (reigned 1855–1881) and his son Alexander III (reigned 1881–1894), respectively–and each of which was characterized by a distinct literary and political ethos. The former period was a time of revolutionary fervor, of radicalism, of Populism, of demands that art serve a social purpose. The latter period, on the contrary, was an era of quiet tension, of *malye dela* (small deeds), of trepidation and anticipation of changes soon to come. In political terms, the former period was a time of social and economic reforms that, ultimately, failed to satisfy either the Right or the Left and led to an escalation of disaffection and violence; the latter period was a time of cruel reaction, chauvinism, and tight government control of all cultural production.

The forerunner of Alexander II was Tsar Nicholas I, who died in 1855 at the height of the Crimean War (1855–1856). Nicholas had reigned since 1825, when his coronation was marred by the Decembrist Revolt, an abortive attempt led by liberal figures of the cultural elite to institute a constitutional government in Russia. The attempted coup was brutally crushed; five of its leaders, including the poet Kondratii Fedorovich Ryleev, were hanged, and more than a hundred other participants in the conspiratorial societies that had planned the rebellion, most of them members of the nobility, were exiled for life to the wastelands of Siberia. This outcome set a tone of disappointment and resentment that colored the entire reign of Nicholas I, who continued the oppressive policies of the previous regime. Russian literature came into its full flower during this period, in the person of Aleksandr Sergeevich Pushkin, whose youthful writings about freedom had inspired the Decembrists and who went on to become the progenitor of modern Russian literature through his creation of masterpiece after masterpiece in every conceivable genre, including lyric and narrative poetry, short fiction, long fiction, drama, and nonfiction. Ultimately, Pushkin fell victim to the stifling censorship, court intrigues, and bureaucratic strictures of his era; he perished in a senseless duel at the age of thirty-seven.

Despite the censorship, writing had become, by the time of Pushkin's death, a viable profession and even an industry. The first copyright laws had been drafted in Russia. So-called *tolstye zhurnaly* (thick journals) that published an eclectic mixture of fiction, poetry, opinion pieces, humor, and fashion proliferated. The monthly *Biblioteka dlia chteniia* (A Reading Library), a moderately conservative journal that introduced its readers to the work of many of the foremost Russian and European writers of the time, together with the more liberal *Otechestvennye zapiski* (Notes of the Fatherland), were the first of these journals to become hugely popular with the reading public. All these developments were facilitated by the growth of the *raznochintsy,* a motley middle class of intellectuals who emanated from various professions, including the urban artisans and shopkeepers, the minor civil servants, the provincial clergy, and the merchantry.

The decisive and humiliating defeat of Russia by France and Britain in the Crimean War followed shortly upon the debut of Tsar Alexander II's reign. National pride and confidence were at a nadir; the new emperor and his administration recognized that profound social and economic changes were imperative. Accordingly, in the postwar decade, sweeping reforms were enacted in the judicial system, local governments, universities, and the military in what came to be known as the epoch of Great Reforms (roughly 1855–1865). Perhaps the most significant of these reforms was the Emancipation Act of 1861, which abolished the feudal system that had crippled the socio-economic development of Russia and held her captive in a state of medieval stagnation. The serfs were freed from bondage and given an allotment of land; they were now made subject to the authority of their communes, which in turn were governed by newly created local councils that had the oversight of schools, hospitals, libraries, charities, and roads. The emancipation was disastrous for landowning gentry and peasants alike. Many former serfs could not afford the redemption payments for their land, and a massive migration of the impoverished peasantry to the cities was set in motion. Bankruptcy ravaged the gentry, who were devoid of the business acumen required to insure the survival of their country estates in an increasingly market-driven economy. Agriculture, too, was failing as years of inefficient cultivation of the soil led to poor harvests and widespread famine.

Meanwhile, the appetite for change on the part of liberals was not appeased but further stimulated by the reforms already enacted, which they viewed as impotent half measures that created more problems than they solved. Critics of the policy of limited social and political reforms particularly noted the stark contrast between the growing system of independent, elected local governing bodies and the continued unyielding autocratic rule of the central government. With the exiling of the influential radical critic Nikolai Gavrilovich Chernyshevsky in 1864 and the tsar's refusal to grant a liberal constitution in the mid 1860s, the political discontent that gradually had been mounting–fueled, in part, by open criticism of the regime from Nekrasov's leading journal *Sovremennik* (The Contemporary)–reached a fever pitch. In 1866 a student radical of noble descent named Dmitrii Vladimirovich Karakozov attempted to assassinate Alexander II. Although his shots failed to reach their mark, they effectively ended the era of reform.

As might be expected, political allegiances were closely intertwined with artistic credos during those years of great change, and an appreciation of the literature of the period is impossible without some understanding of the topical questions and movements through which intellectuals defined both themselves and their ideological opponents. The majority of public opinion during the era of the Great Reforms was generally liberal and Westward-leaning. Universities became hotbeds of political activism, even as Russian science and medicine began to rival western European accomplishments in these fields, and Russian artists and composers created world-class masterpieces that soared to new heights of originality. *Sovremennik,* founded by Pushkin in 1836, was the most popular journal during the early years of Alexander II's reign. The journal had been transformed into a forum for revolutionary-democratic thought when it came under Nekrasov's editorship in 1847; until it was shut down by the authorities in 1866, it was known as the chief organ of the Westernizer critics, including Vissarion Grigor'evich Belinsky, Vasilii Petrovich Botkin, Pavel Vasil'evich Annenkov, Aleksandr Vasil'evich Druzhinin, and Chernyshevsky. *Sovremennik* also published works by the leading writers of the day, including Tolstoy, Ivan Aleksandrovich Goncharov, Ivan Sergeevich Turgenev, Ostrovsky, and Nekrasov himself. However, when Chernyshevsky's controversial appointment to the editorial staff of *Sovremennik* in 1856 was followed shortly by the appointment of his fellow radical Nikolai Aleksandrovich Dobroliubov in 1857, many of the politically moderate contributors to the journal defected to *Vestnik Evropy* (The European Messenger), edited by the liberal historian Mikhail Matveevich Stasiulevich.

Indeed, beginning in the late 1850s, rifts among various political factions on the Left began to deepen. The radical critics Chernyshevsky, Dobroliubov, and Dmitrii Ivanovich Pisarev went well beyond Belinsky's injunctions that literature should reflect, and reflect upon, social reality when they professed the nihilist doctrine that the only worthwhile art is a utilitarian art, that aesthetic criteria merit no attention, and that a sociological approach is the only legitimate method of literary interpretation. The quintessentially Realist poetry of Nekrasov, which took as its themes the plight of the urban poor and the hard lot of the Russian peasantry, exemplified this civic trend. Meanwhile, Annenkov and Botkin remained political moderates; they traveled widely in western Europe, and both evaluated literary works according to traditional aesthetic categories, continued to revere Pushkin, and remained sponsors of the cause of "art for art's sake." Another branch of Leftist criticism in these years was represented by Herzen and his friend the poet and critic Nikolai Platonovich Ogarev, who had become voluntary exiles to western Europe (specifically, London and later Geneva) and who collaborated on two publications, the annual almanac *Poliarnaia zvezda* (The North Star) and the newspaper *Kolokol* (The Bell), which published a mixture of literary and political works that had been suppressed by the censorship in Russia together with works by European writers. Herzen and Ogarev were the forerunners of an ever-growing community of Russian émigré writers who doubled as revolutionary activists, including the anarchists Mikhail Aleksandrovich Bakunin and Petr Alekseevich Kropotkin.

There was no shortage of conservative political thought in mid-nineteenth-century Russia, either. Although noble ancestry was no guarantee of allegiance to the political Right (the civic writer Vasilii Alekseevich Sleptsov was of aristocratic birth, as were the Westernizer dramatist Aleksandr Vasil'evich Sukhovo-Kobylin and the radical critic Pisarev), some scions of the nobility remained faithful to their origins and championed the monarchic doctrine "Orthodoxy, Autocracy, and Nationality." Such, for instance, was the writer Konstantin Nikolaevich Leont'ev, whose religious faith and philosophical writings were founded upon strict Byzantine hierarchies; Leont'ev firmly opposed social egalitarianism, but he cannot finally be assigned to any particular political camp. Other writers began as progressives but became gradually more conservative and even reactionary; poet Nikolai Fedorovich Shcherbina and critic Mikhail Nikiforovich Katkov, publisher of the journal *Russkii vestnik* (The Russian Messenger), followed this trajectory. By contrast, the Official Nationalists, at whose center were historian Mikhail Petrovich Pogodin and critic and poet Stepan Petrovich Shevyrev, were passionate supporters of autocracy and virulent denouncers of the West. These two thinkers were associated with the literary and historical monthly *Moskvitianin* (The Muscovite); they were joined between 1850 and 1856 by the *molodaia redaktsiia* (young editors), including critic Apollon

Aleksandrovich Grigor'ev, dramatist Ostrovsky, and novelist Aleksei Feofilaktovich Pisemsky. In the mid 1860s the journals of Dostoevsky and his brother Mikhail Mikhailovich Dostoevsky, *Vremia* (Time) and *Epokha* (The Epoch), espoused a brand of conservatism consonant with that of Grigor'ev and the political historian Nikolai Nikolaevich Strakhov; calling themselves *pochvenniki* (men of the soil), they argued that the educated classes should strive to recover their Russian roots and achieve a synthesis of Russian and Western culture.

The Slavophiles made up another important conservative movement during the years of the Great Reforms. Slavophilism had first arisen during the 1840s, as a reaction to the Westernizers' view that Russia was unique among the European nations only insofar as she was woefully backward in her development (this view had been voiced with particular acerbity in the writings of Petr Iakovlevich Chaadaev). Unlike the Westernizers who longed for the modernization of Russia according to the European model on the one hand, and the Official Nationalists who upheld the imperial dynasty as the prime mover of Russian history on the other hand, the Slavophiles looked back with nostalgia to the era that predated the dramatic Europeanizing reforms and consolidation of state powers under Tsar Peter the Great (ruled 1689–1725). Slavophile philosophers held that Russia had a unique destiny among the nations of the world and that Russian Orthodoxy and the communal traditions of the Russian peasant were key to the realization of the true identity and mission of Russia. Ivan Sergeevich Aksakov, along with his brother Konstantin, Aleksei Stepanovich Khomiakov, Iurii Fedorovich Samarin, and the brothers Ivan Vasil'evich and Petr Vasil'evich Kireevsky, were the chief ideologues of Slavophile thought in the mid nineteenth century. Slavophile sympathies can be detected in the works of several other writers covered in this volume, different though they are in other respects; the poet Lev Aleksandrovich Mei is one example. The first journal of the Slavophiles, published in Moscow between 1856 and 1860, was *Russkaia beseda* (Russian Colloquy).

Yet another strain of political conservativism was comprised by the late-Romantic poets Afanasii Afanas'evich Fet, Fedor Ivanovich Tiutchev, Apollon Nikolaevich Maikov, and Iakov Petrovich Polonsky. Polonsky and Grigor'ev for a brief period together edited the journal *Russkoe slovo* (The Russian Word), which published works by Grigor'ev himself as well as by Dostoevsky, Fet, Maikov, and Mei; however, the journal soon changed editors and was transformed into an organ of the radical opposition. Tiutchev, Maikov, and Polonsky served together on the state committee for censorship of foreign literature in the early 1860s; Fet was the victim in the 1860s of a smear campaign mounted by the radical critics, his archenemies, in response to his political articles in which he expressed extremely conservative social views. All these poets worked in a political climate inimical to the Romantic aesthetics that formed their works; all of them were ostensibly apolitical poets, proponents of the doctrine of "art for art's sake." However, in an era of civic fervor in which any literary composition was by definition a political act and art was considered to be worthy of existence only to the extent that it served explicitly political ends, the refusal to write on topical issues of the day could be construed as treachery against the progressive cause.

The Franco-Prussian War of 1870 to 1871 provided a pretext for Russia to disregard the peace treaty that had ended the disastrous Crimean War fifteen years before and once again assert her influence over the eastern Mediterranean region. The Slavophile conviction that Russia should resist the path of capitalist development received encouragement from the spectacle of Europe tearing herself apart, and the new ideology of Pan-Slavism, which cherished the messianic dream of uniting all the Orthodox Slavs in a Russian-dominated utopia, soon led to a renewed conflict with Turkey in 1877 to 1878, which ended in military success, but at the cost of great carnage and later diplomatic losses. In a somewhat different vein, the intelligentsia's emphasis on the Russian peasant as the unspoiled conservator of the true Russian essence—an idea that was central not just to the conservative thought of the Slavophiles but also to the liberal philosophy of Herzen—rapidly gained ground in the 1870s, becoming the center of an agrarian socialist movement that in 1878 was dubbed *narodnichestvo* (Populism). This movement originated to a large extent in Herzen's idealization of the Russian peasant *mir* (commune), as well as in the anarchism of Bakunin and the civic thought of the radical critics including Chernyshevsky. The theoretical writings of Nikolai Konstantinovich Mikhailovsky and Petr Lavrovich Lavrov, who developed what they considered to be a scientific basis for social analysis and argued that Marxist theory was not valid in the economically backward context of Russian society, were also hugely influential. *Otechestvennye zapiski,* under the combined editorship of Nekrasov and satirist Mikhail Evgrafovich Saltykov since 1867, was transformed into the leading journal of the *narodniki* (Populists) in the 1870s. In later years *Russkaia mysl'* (Russian Thought) and *Russkoe bogatstvo* (Russian Wealth) also became important Populist venues.

The *narodniki* believed that the Russian intelligentsia, who had flourished thanks to the labors of the serfs, now had a moral obligation to make recompense by traveling to the countryside and spreading political enlightenment among the peasantry. Hence, beginning in the summer of 1873, a few *narodniki* of noble origin, including Kropotkin, led a massive Populist trek into the provinces that became known as *khozhdenie v narod* (going to the people). The Populist writer Gleb Nikolaevich Uspensky participated in one such pilgrimage in the summer of 1877, and Vladimir Galaktionovich Korolenko had been preparing to "go to the people" when he was arrested and exiled in 1876. The hope of these well-intentioned but naive activists was that a popular uprising would topple the despised institutions of the autocratic police state and rebuild a new, utopian society based around the communal traditions of the peasantry. Despite the Populists' initial adoption of democratic principles as a means to achieving this ideal, *narodnichestvo* was not just a political project but an encompassing creed; as Marc Slonim explains in *From Chekhov to the Revolution* (1962): "Russians brought to their political struggle a religiosity, an all-embracing spirit of total and self-annihilating devotion, an enthusiastic sharing of a doctrine, extremism in action, and often a Byzantine rigidity of thought and ritual unknown to Western tradition." When it became clear that the *khozhdenie v narod* movement had failed miserably in the face of the conservative peasantry's incomprehension, unreceptivity, and even open hostility—many frightened peasants informed on the propagandists, resulting in widespread arrests and ultimately in the mass trials of 1877—the *narodniki* regrouped, forming *Zemlia i volia* (Land and Freedom), the first organized political party in Russia, in 1876. In 1879 *Zemlia i volia* split into the short-lived *Chernyi peredel* (Black Partition), led by Marxist theorist Georgii Valentinovich Plekhanov, and the terrorist faction *Narodnaia volia* (The People's Will).

Members of *Narodnaia volia* plotted and carried out several terrorist attacks against Tsar Alexander II and his administration. In February 1880 a bomb exploded in the Winter Palace in St. Petersburg, killing ten officers of the guard. Shortly after, the tsar granted dictatorial powers to Count Mikhail Tarielovich Loris-Melikov, who revived the policy of gradual reform, even admitting the need for a constitution, but who simultaneously initiated a harsh crackdown against the socialist factions. His efforts, however, were insufficient. On 1 March 1881 the second of two bombs hurled at the tsar's carriage fatally wounded him. The era of change and of intelligentsia influence on governmental policy ended with Alexander II's assassination; his son's ascension to the throne inaugurated a period of severe reaction and repression. Five of the leaders of *Narodnaia volia* were executed, and others died in prison, while the rest were exiled to penal colonies in Siberia for life. Alexander III appointed Konstantin Pobedonostsev, head of the Russian Orthodox Church, as his key adviser. An extreme reactionary and a callous, ambitious statesman who likely served as the model for Dostoevsky's terrifying Grand Inquisitor, Pobedonostsev launched a barrage of oppressive measures aimed at crushing the revolutionary elements in Russian society and, at least for the time being, was largely successful in this project. What remnants of the socialist movement survived the onslaught mostly retreated abroad; a few isolated Populist circles were still active, but only on a sporadic basis. Members of the intelligentsia no longer hotly defended the Slavophile or the Westernizer position; instead, the majority of public opinion shifted toward the conservative, while a small liberal minority were quietly divided in their allegiance to either the Marxists or the Populists.

By and large, Alexander III's reign was an era of disillusionment, political apathy, and boredom. Even writers such as Uspensky and Korolenko, who retained sympathies with the Populist movement, were far less single-minded in their treatment of civic themes than were their predecessors; Uspensky refused to idealize the peasantry in his stories, and Korolenko's Populist sympathies with his peasant heroes were balanced by lyrical descriptive passages that would have offended the radical critics of the 1860s. Indeed, pure utilitarianism in literature was a thing of the past, and as the generation of the 1880s matured, aestheticism once again gained ascendancy. As a result, older lyric poets such as Fet and Konstantin Konstantinovich Sluchevsky, who had been cruelly attacked and ridiculed by the nihilist critics and so had failed to publish their poetry for nearly twenty years, reappeared on the cultural scene. Fet's masterful late collection *Vechernie ogni* (Evening Lights) includes poems about nature and love, as well as meditative philosophical poetry; it underwent four editions in his lifetime. Aleksei Nikolaevich Apukhtin, a friend of composer Petr Il'ich Chaikovsky and a staunchly "pure art" poet who had likewise refused to publish his work during the preceding decades, issued a collection of his lyrics in 1886 that proved to be hugely popular. The strong Romantic tendencies of poets in this period hark back to the sensibilities of the Golden Age poets in Russia, including Pushkin and Mikhail Iur'evich Lermontov; at the same time, though, the post-Romantic poets were transitional figures who anticipated—and sometimes influenced directly—the Symbolist poets of the next generation, who ushered in the period commonly known as the Silver Age. Thus, for example, Sluchevsky ran a popular St. Petersburg literary salon attended by several budding Symbolists; his own poetry, with its jarring rhythms, tragic motifs, and attention to the dark underside of quotidian reality, was not only reminiscent of Dostoevsky's fiction but also influential for later poets such as Boris Leonidovich Pasternak and Aleksandr Aleksandrovich Blok. Konstantin Mikhailovich Fofanov's poetry similarly served as a bridge between the civic verse of Nekrasov and the modern sensibilities of the Symbolists. The poet Semen Iakovlevich Nadson, who became a celebrity and a kind of poetic cult figure in his time, began as a civic poet but combined this inclination with Romanticism; somber and pessimistic, his works concern mainly illness, death, and despair and

anticipate the literary decadence of older Symbolists such as Valerii Iakovlevich Briusov or Fedor Kuz'mich Sologub.

Russian prose and drama also changed dramatically as the era of the great Realist novel came to an end (Tolstoy experienced a religious conversion in the late 1870s and wrote primarily nonfiction, short fiction, and drama in his final years; Dostoevsky's last great novel, *Brat'ia Karamazovy,* was finished in 1880). Short fictional forms predominated during the 1880s and 1890s; in these works could be observed a blend of realistic style and themes with symbolic, allegorical, and lyrical elements anticipating modernism. Such was the case in the stories of Vsevolod Mikhailovich Garshin—who combined a fascination with human psychology with a sharp eye for detail—as well as in the tales of Chekhov, the preeminent writer of this transitional period. Chekhov chronicled the life of that peculiarly Russian type, the *lishnii chelovek* (superfluous man), whom the radical critics such as Dobroliubov in his scathing essay "Chto takoe Oblomovshchina?" (What is Oblomovitis? 1859) had abhorred. Chekhov's protagonists are never heroes; they come from every walk of life and a wide variety of professions, yet all of them are to a degree without moorings, drifting forlornly, always in the process either of degenerating into mindless automatism or of barely saving themselves from that fate. They are full of hopes and dreams, yet they have no specific plans for improvement of either their individual lot or that of society as a whole. Chekhov was a brilliant analyst of the afflictions of his culture, whose demise he chronicled in both his short stories and his plays. Yet, by stark contrast with the moral convictions of Tolstoy and Dostoevsky in an earlier period, Chekhov played the role of a sympathetic but unobtrusive observer of the ailing subjects of his own writing, knowing full well that he was powerless to prescribe a cure.

On this wistful note of wry humor, faltering hope, and uneasy expectation of change, the reign of Alexander III ended. In the waning years of the nineteenth century, the throne was occupied by Alexander's son Nicholas II, a decent man but an impotent and uninspired tsar who, failing to recognize that a new era was beginning, continued the reactionary policies set in place by his father. Nicholas was fated to be the last imperial ruler of Russia; he, his wife, and their five children were brutally murdered during the aftermath of the Bolshevik Revolution.

What remains to be discussed in the context of these historical events and political and cultural debates is the position of Russian women writers in the second half of the nineteenth century. The "woman question" was a primary focus of the radical critics. Chernyshevsky's politically influential, though literarily inferior, novel *Chto delat'?* (What Is to Be Done? 1863) takes as its heroine an emancipated woman who becomes a socialist and founds a women's dressmaking collective; Pisarev began his literary career by writing book reviews for a women's journal. Women such as Vera Ivanovna Zasulich and Vera Nikolaevna Figner were prominent in the radical movement and played key roles in Populist terrorist organizations (Figner was involved in the planning of the assassination of Alexander II; Zasulich herself assassinated the St. Petersburg chief of police). More and more, institutions of higher learning opened their doors to women during the epoch of the Great Reforms, producing the cultural type of the *institutka* (female student), who received no small degree of attention, much of it derogatory, in the male-authored literature of the time. Still, despite the nascent stirrings of a feminist sensibility, women's economic independence remained severely curtailed; even for educated women, the only really viable professional prospect was a position as a teacher or a governess. Furthermore, as Jane Costlow has shown in her contribution to *Women Writers in Russian Literature* (1994), the identities and concerns of women–including enlightened literary women–in this period were largely scripted by men: "Inherited plots of love acted as cultural texts, ascribing to women particular capacities for feeling." Women writers interrogated these inherited plots, searching for an escape from gender oppression and financial dependence. After the assassination of Tsar Alexander II, stringent new regulations that deprived universities of all autonomy and academic freedom in 1884 also effectively barred women from institutions of higher learning.

Because women, for the most part, were isolated from one another, as well as from the incubators of male intellectual culture such as discussion circles and universities, to speak of a "women's tradition" in Russian literature is impossible. The women of the age of Realism struggled to define a literary voice for themselves in the midst of cultural isolation and, often, personal loneliness. Nadezhda Stepanovna Sokhanskaia spent her adult life in the provincial solitude of her family home in the Ukrainian countryside and made only occasional forays into the high society of the capital. Sof'ia Vasil'evna Kovalevskaia, the first woman in the world to earn a doctorate in mathematics, was denied a university appointment in her native country. Iuliia Valerianovna Zhadovskaia, born without a left arm and with a severely disfigured right arm, was denied permission to marry the man she loved and lived out her life in the provinces. The original works of Sof'ia Vladimirovna Engel'gardt were never published under her own name in her lifetime, and she declined ever to assemble them into a collected volume; as a result, they soon fell into almost complete obscurity. Elisaveta Nikitichna Shakhova escaped her mother's despotic control by entering the oblivion of a monastery. Even women writers who were more closely aligned with the male concerns of their age were at a distinct disadvantage because

of their gender. Thus, Anna Pavlovna Barykova, who participated in the Populist movement in her younger years and later was an adherent of Tolstoyanism, was ridiculed by contemporary critics, while Mari'a Semenovna Zhukova, whose fictional tales received warm praise from a variety of critics, was nevertheless condescendingly classified by Belinsky as a member of the second rank of Russian writers.

Many of the writers included in this volume are largely neglected in literary scholarship even within Russia, and a good number of them are practically unknown outside their native culture. The selection of writers was at some level arbitrary; an attempt was made to represent figures associated with a variety of literary genres and with various positions on the cultural and political spectrum. Although their talents are uneven and the writings of many of them certainly pale beside the works of the great Realist novelists who were their contemporaries, these minor writers, critics, and poets are still fascinating both for their own sake and for what their lives and works reveal about the changing currents in Russian literary history.

–Alyssa Dinega Gillepsie

Note on Bibliography

The first bibliographic rubric in each entry is Books, which encompasses separately published books and pamphlets, as well as collected editions that included at least some material published in book format for the first time. Many of these works might, however, have been published first in periodicals, sometimes serially. The "Editions and Collections" (or "Editions" or "Collections") rubric that follows lists later important publications that may include new introductions and commentary but do not constitute a first publication in book format of any of the works contained therein. Important shorter works published in periodical form are found under the Selected Periodical Publications rubric; these might or might not later have been included in collected editions. In cases where only periodical publications *not* later collected into editions are listed, the rubric is titled "Selected Periodical Publications–Uncollected."

Contributors to the volume have provided the fullest bibliographical information available to them at the time of writing. Bibliographies have been checked when applicable against Kseniia Dmitrievna Muratova, ed., *Istoriia russkoi literatury XIX veka. Bibliograficheskii ukazatel'* (Leningrad: Akademiia nauk SSSR, 1962); Muratova, ed., *Istoriia russkoi literatury kontsa XIX – nachala XX veka. Bibliograficheskii ukazatel'* (Moscow & Leningrad: Akademiia nauk SSSR, 1963); Avgusta V. Mez'er, comp., *Russkaia slovesnost' s XI po XIX stoletiia vkliuchitel'no. Bibliograficheskii ukazatel' proizvedenii russkoi slovesnosti v sviazi s istoriei literatury i kritikoi. Knigi i zhurnalnye stat'i,* volume 2 (St. Petersburg: Altshuler, 1902); and P. A. Nikolaev, ed., *Russkie pisateli, 1800–1917. Biograficheskii slovar',* 4 volumes to date (Moscow: Bol'shaia Rossiiskaia entsiklopediia, 1992–). Readers are referred to these publications, as well as to S. A. Vengerov, *Istochniki slovaria russkikh pisatelei,* 4 volumes (St. Petersburg, 1900–1917), which includes entries through Nekrasov, for further bibliographic detail.

Note on Dates, Names, and Transliteration

Almost all dates in this volume appear according to the calendar in use in Russia at the time, which before 1918 was the Julian calendar (Old Style). To convert to the Gregorian calendar (New Style), add twelve days for dates in the nineteenth century, thirteen days for pre-1918 dates in the twentieth century. Events that occurred in western Europe, however, appear according to the Gregorian calendar.

Russian names, titles, and quotations are transliterated according to the standard Library of Congress transliteration system (without diacritics, but preserving hard and soft signs) with the following exceptions. Surnames with the adjectival ending -yi or -ii are changed to -y. This exception will be seen most frequently in the ending -sky (rather than -skii). Tsars are given anglicized names (Alexander, Nicholas); Gogol appears without his final soft sign; and Leo Tolstoy and Fyodor Dostoevsky appear in their commonly accepted forms. Moscow and St. Petersburg are given their English names.

In accordance with standard scholarly practice, prerevolutionary Russian orthography has been modernized. Readers should note, however, that listings for nineteenth-century books and periodicals in library catalogues usually preserve the peculiarities of prerevolutionary spelling. Thus, for example, our modern spellings *Rassvet, Vestnik Evropy,* and *Moskovskie vedomosti* correspond to prerevolutionary *Razsviet, Viestnik Evropy,* and *Moskovskiia viedomosti.*

Editor's Acknowledgments

In-house editor Patricia Hswe was a dedicated partner during the finishing stages of the volume; she met its many challenges with tireless enthusiasm and unflappable good humor. Russian series editors Judith Kalb and Alexander Ogden provided invaluable practi-

cal advice and moral support throughout this project. Thanks are due also to the contributing authors for their hard work and commitment to the volume. My husband and children have assisted me in seeing this project to fruition in more ways than they know.

Acknowledgments

This book was produced by Bruccoli Clark Layman, Inc. Patricia Hswe was the in-house editor.

Production manager is Philip B. Dematteis.

Administrative support was provided by Ann M. Cheschi and Carol A. Cheschi.

Accountant is Ann-Marie Holland.

Copyediting supervisor is Sally R. Evans. The copyediting staff includes Phyllis A. Avant, Caryl Brown, Melissa D. Hinton, Philip I. Jones, Rebecca Mayo, Nancy E. Smith, and Elizabeth Jo Ann Sumner.

Editorial associates are Amelia B. Lacey, Michael S. Martin, Catherine M. Polit, and William Mathes Straney.

In-house prevetting is by Nicole A. La Rocque.

Permissions editor and database manager is Amber L. Coker.

Layout and graphics supervisor is Janet E. Hill. The graphics staff includes Zoe R. Cook and Sydney E. Hammock.

Office manager is Kathy Lawler Merlette.

Photography supervisor is Paul Talbot. Photography editor is Scott Nemzek.

Digital photographic copy work was performed by Joseph M. Bruccoli.

Systems manager is Donald Kevin Starling.

Typesetting supervisor is Kathleen M. Flanagan. The typesetting staff includes Patricia Marie Flanagan, Mark J. McEwan, and Pamela D. Norton. Freelance typesetters are Wanda Adams and Rebecca Mayo.

Walter W. Ross did library research. He was assisted by Jo Cottingham and the following other librarians at the Thomas Cooper Library of the University of South Carolina: circulation department head Tucker Taylor; reference department head Virginia W. Weathers; reference department staff Brette Barron, Marilee Birchfield, Paul Cammarata, Gary Geer, Michael Macan, Tom Marcil, Rose Marshall, and Sharon Verba; interlibrary loan department head John Brunswick; and interlibrary loan staff Robert Arndt, Hayden Battle, Alex Byrne, Bill Fetty, Marna Hostetler, and Nelson Rivera.

Dictionary of Literary Biography® • Volume Two Hundred Seventy-Seven

Russian Literature in the Age of Realism

Dictionary of Literary Biography

Ivan Sergeevich Aksakov

(26 September 1823 – 27 January 1886)

Thomas P. Hodge
Wellesley College

BOOKS: *Issledovanie o torgovle na ukrainskikh iarmarkakh* (St. Petersburg: Akademiia nauk, 1858);

Sliianie soslovii ili dvorianstvo, drugie sostoianiia i zemstvo, by Aksakov, Aleksandr Ivanovich Koshelev, and Prince Aleksandr Illarionovich Vasil'chikov (St. Petersburg: A. K. Kirkor, 1870);

Fedor Ivanovich Tiutchev: Biograficheskii ocherk (Moscow: V. Got'e, 1874); republished as *Biografiia Fedora Ivanovicha Tiutcheva* (Moscow: M. G. Volchaninov, 1886);

Prisutstvennyi den' ugolovnoi palaty: Sudebnye stseny (Leipzig: E. L. Kasprovich, 1874);

Rech' I. S. Aksakova, proiznesennaia, 22-ogo iiunia 1878 v Moskovskom slavianskom blagotvoritel'nom obshchestve (Berlin: B. Behr & E. Bock, 1878);

Sbornik stikhotvorenii (Moscow: T. I. Gagen, 1886)—includes "Na Dunai! tuda, gde novoi slavy," "Posle 1848 goda," "S prestupnoi gordost'iu," and "Zhizn' chinovnika: Misteriia v trekh periodakh";

Sbornik stat'ei, napechatannykh v raznykh periodicheskikh izdaniiakh po sluchaiu konchiny Aksakova (Moscow: L. F. Snegirev, 1886);

Obshcheevropeiskaia politika (1887);

Ivan Sergeevich Aksakov v ego pis'makh, 4 volumes (Moscow: M. G. Volchaninov, 1888–1896)—includes "Capriccio," "Chto mne skazat' ei v uteshen'e," "Dozhd'," "Iazykovu," "Kleimo domashnego pozora," "Pesnia Marii egipetskoi," "Pri klikakh derzostno-pobednykh," "Pri posylke stikhotvorenii Iu. Zhadovskoi," "Sannyi beg, vecherom, v gorode," and "V tikhoi komnate moei";

Rannie slavanofily, by Aksakov, Konstantin Sergeevich Aksakov, Aleksei Stepanovich Khomiakov, and

Ivan Sergeevich Aksakov

Ivan Vasil'evich Kireevsky (Moscow: I. D. Sytin, 1910);

Stikhotvoreniia i poemy, with an introduction by Andrei Grigor'evich Dement'ev and Evgenii Solomonovich Kalmanovsky (Leningrad: Sovetskii pisatel', 1960)—includes "K. S. Aksakovu" and "N. N. N. Otvet na pis'mo".

Editions and Collections: *Sbornik Stikhotvorenni* (Moscow: Gagen, 1886);

Sochinenii, 1860–1886, 7 volumes (Moscow: M. G. Volchaninov, 1886–1887);

Russkoe pravoslavie i svoboda sovesti, by Aksakov and Iurii Fedorovich Samarin (Leipzig: Bär and Hermann, 1888);

O evreiskom voprose (Pochaev: E. De-Vitte, 1911);

Literaturnaia kritika, by Aksakov and Konstantin Sergeevich Aksakov, with an introduction by A. S. Kurilov (Moscow: Sovremennik, 1981);

"I slovo pravdy . . .": Stikhi, p'esy, stat'i, ocherki, with an introduction by Mikhail Andreevich Chvanov (Ufa, 1986);

Biografiia Fedora Ivanovicha Tiutcheva, edited by V. N. Kasatkina and G. V. Chagin (Moscow: Kniga i biznes, 1997).

OTHER: "26-e sentiabria," "Ocherk," "Noch'," and "Sredi udobnykh i lenivykh," in *Moskovskii literaturnyi i uchenyi sbornik* (Moscow: A. Semen, 1846);

"Zimniaia doroga. (Licentia poetica). Dramaticheskie stseny v stikhakh i proze," in *Moskovskii literaturnyi i uchenyi sbornik na 1847* (Moscow: A. Semen, 1847);

"Otdykh," in *Kievlianin,* book 3 (Moscow: Universitetskaia tipografiia, 1850);

"Neskol'ko slov o Gogole" and "Otryvki iz pervoi chasti *Brodiagi,* ocherka v stikhakh," in *Moskovskii sbornik,* edited by Aksakov, volume 1 (Moscow: A. Semen, 1852);

"Otryvok iz knigi: Samye dostovernye zapiski chinovnika ochevidtsa. Prisutstvennyi den' Ugolovnoi palaty," in *Poliarnaia zvezda na 1858* (London: Vol'noe russkoe knigopechatanie, 1858);

Polnoe sobranie sochinenii Konstantina Sergeevicha Aksakova, 3 volumes, edited by Aksakov (Moscow: P. Bakhmetev, 1861–1880);

"Zhizn' chinovnika: Misteriia v trekh periodakh," in *Russkaia potaennaia literatura XIX stoletiia,* edited by Aleksandr Ivanovich Hertzen, with a preface by Nikolai Platonovich Ogarev (London: Trübner, 1861);

"Dvorianskoe delo," in *Kakoi iskhod dlia Rossii iz nyneshnego ee polozheniia,* by Aleksandr Ivanovich Koshelev (Leipzig: F. Vagner, 1862);

"Stikhotvoreniia F. I. Tiutcheva," in *Novonaidennye stikhotvoreniia F. I. Tiutcheva* (Moscow: Lebedev, 1879), pp. 3–10;

Sergei Sharapov, *Teoriia gosudarstva i slavianofilov,* with contributions by Aksakov and others (St. Petersburg: A. Porokhovshchikov, 1898).

SELECTED PERIODICAL PUBLICATIONS:
"Khristofor Kolumb s priiateliami," *Moskvitianin,* 2 (1845);

"Ustalykh sil ia dolgo ne zhalel" and "Dobro b mechty, dobro by strasti," *Russkaia beseda,* 1 (1856);

"Otvet," *Russkaia beseda,* 1 (1857);

"Brodiaga: Otryvki," *Parus,* 10 January 1859;

"Iz stikhotvorenii prezhnego perioda," *Den',* 29 (28 April 1862);

"Varvarino: Poslanie E. F. Tiutchevoi," *Rus',* 4 (6 December 1880).

Ivan Aksakov was the scion of one of the most prominent families in Russia, and he achieved widespread fame in his lifetime as a poet, essayist, journalist, editor, critic, Slavophile, and Pan-Slavic activist. An erudite writer and fine speaker, he was also uncompromisingly self-righteous, zealous, and extremely hardworking. Early in his career he battled ceaselessly with governmental and social corruption—later with censorship in the publications he edited. Aksakov had a titanic compulsion for self-expression, which found its outlet in poetry, letters, editorials, civil-service reports, and speeches. His most important contribution to Russian thought was the promulgation of Slavophile, Pan-Slavic, and nationalist ideas devised chiefly by others. By far his most important contribution to Russian literature, however, was his poetry, which, though not copious, is of excellent quality.

Aksakov was born Ivan Sergeevich Aksakov on 26 September 1823 in the village of Nadezhino, Belebei district, in Orenburg province. He was the third son of renowned writer Sergei Timofeevich Aksakov and the younger brother of both the Slavophile theoretician Konstantin Sergeevich Aksakov and the memoirist Vera Sergeevna Aksakova. His mother was Ol'ga Semenovna (Zaplatina) Aksakova, daughter of a general who served under Aleksandr Vasil'evich Suvorov, the most illustrious Russian military commander of the eighteenth century. In 1826 the family moved to Moscow, where Aksakov received rigorous home tutoring until 1838. From the age of ten he read newspapers and closely followed the international political scene.

In April 1838 Aksakov entered the Imperial School of Jurisprudence in St. Petersburg, an institution founded in 1835 to prepare young men from aristocratic families for top posts in the vast bureaucracy of the Russian government, especially in the Ministry of Justice; his schoolmates included composer Aleksandr Nikolaevich Serov and music critic Vladimir Vasil'evich Stasov (composer Petr Il'ich Chaikovsky was an 1859 graduate). While at school, Aksakov distinguished himself academically and corresponded with his father's friend, the noted conservative historian and publisher Mikhail Petrovich Pogodin, about Russian history. The writer Ivan Ivanovich Panaev introduced Aksakov in the early summer of 1840 to the literary critic Vissarion Grigor'evich Belinsky, who, in an 1840 letter to Konstantin Sergeevich Aksakov, described the young man as having "a healthy nature and an authentic, sturdy and brave spirit." In 1842, at the age of nineteen, Aksakov finished school with the rank of collegiate secretary, which qualified him to hold junior managerial positions.

Aksakov's earliest extant poetry dates from 1841, though he had begun writing verse as early as the late 1830s; indeed, archival evidence, such as "Oda k Litsiniiu" (Ode to Licinius), dates from that time, although an exact date is not known. His poetry falls into five basic categories: reflective, civic, narrative, dramatic, and occasional. He wrote the vast majority of his verse during the 1840s and 1850s, but little of it was published in those years; not a single collected edition of his poetry appeared during his lifetime. Though written in 1841, "Prostaia istoriia" (A Simple Story) was not published until 1886, when it appeared in the journal *Russkaia starina* (Russian Antiquity) as "Istoriia staroi devushki: Predskazanie." The poetry of Aksakov's school days is witty, fluent, and technically polished. "Prostaia istoriia," for example, consists of nine humorously allegorical octaves in iambic pentameter and describes his brother Konstantin's exploits as a literature student at Moscow University from 1832 to 1835.

Shortly after graduation Aksakov began his civil-service career in Moscow in the Criminal Department (Sixth Section) of a branch of the Ministry of Justice known as the Senate, the tsar's highest institution charged with overseeing legislative and judicial affairs in Russia. In December 1843 he transferred to a commission that was carrying out an audit of Astrakhan' Province, where he worked until November 1844. Aksakov's colleagues remarked on his extraordinary energy and dedication to his work in Astrakhan'; one coworker noted that the young man voluntarily labored sixteen hours a day, only after which did he spend time writing poetry and letters. Such zealous devotion to the task at hand was typical for Aksakov all his life and vividly separated him from the mass of lazy and apathetic bureaucrats by whom he was constantly surrounded.

While still in Moscow in 1843 Aksakov had written his first well-known work in verse, "Zhizn' chinovnika: Misteriia v trekh periodakh" (Life of a Bureaucrat: A Mystery Play in Three Periods). A showcase for his skills in writing theatrical verse, this satiric work achieved tremendous popularity among civil servants and circulated widely in manuscript in Moscow and beyond; no complete autograph manuscript has survived, and numerous variants compete for authoritative status. Aksakov attempted to have the work published in 1846, but it was rejected by the censorship. "Zhizn' chinovnika" first appeared in print in Alexander Herzen's (Aleksandr Ivanovich Gertsen) *Russkaia potaennaia literatura XIX stoletiia* (The Secret Literature of Nineteenth-Century Russia, 1861); the many textual

oddities of that edition virtually rule out the theory that Aksakov himself supplied Herzen with the manuscript. The work had its Russian print debut in Aksakov's 1886 *Sbornik stikhotvorenii* (Collected Poems).

In "Zhizn' Chinovnika" the three periods of the *misteriia* (mystery play) depict a *chinovnik* (bureaucrat) just before his service begins, then fifteen years later, and finally thirty years after that. The jocularity of the play is well conveyed by its parodic opening line, spoken by the bureaucrat-to-be: "To enter the civil service or not to enter the civil service, that is the question!" The hero is advised by two opposing personages: the "Demon sluzhby" (Demon of Service) who encourages him to devote his life to the bureaucracy, and the "Tainstvennyi golos" (Mysterious Voice) that advises him to remain aloof from such a pedestrian career and to pursue higher goals. The bureaucrat ultimately decides to enlist in the civil service, and he and his office mates furnish humorous vignettes of bureaucratic life. Just before his death, however, the protagonist realizes the full meaning of the soulful life he chose not to pursue so long before. In a prose epilogue, citizens who attend his funeral discuss his ambiguous achievement. The play is a romp teeming with witty classical periphrasis, allusions to contemporaneous literature, and jokes about the Russian system of ranks; there is even a passage sung by a group of bureaucrats to the tune of the spirits' chorus from Giacomo Meyerbeer's opera *Robert le diable* (Robert the Devil, 1831). Perhaps most impressive, however, is Aksakov's skill in deploying a dizzying variety of verse forms for the multifarious characters of the play in the context of a satire that blends keen psychological insight with vaudeville.

The lyric verse that Aksakov wrote during his Astrakhan' period shows, too, a marked increase in sophistication. "K. S. Aksakovu" (To K. S. Aksakov, 1960), written in 1844 when Ivan learned of his brother Konstantin's newfound affection for the social whirl, is a typically rigid rejection of the shallow enticements of high society. A humorous variation on the same theme is presented by "Astrakhanskii beau monde" (The Beau Monde of Astrakhan', published in *Russkaia starina* in 1886), in which Aksakov mocks the ridiculous denizens of polite Astrakhan' society. Also published in *Russkaia starina,* his "Romans" (Romance, 1886), which includes a conventional but well-crafted expression of longing for a "daughter of the fiery South," is an early example of his treatment of the theme of passion. Aksakov's first published poem, "Khristofor Kolumb s priiateliami" (Christopher Columbus with His Friends), was written on 1 November 1844 and appeared in *Moskvitianin* (The Muscovite) in 1845. This short verse dialogue between Columbus and two comrades offers a declaration of the explorer's firmness of purpose in the face of

Aksakov in the uniform of the Imperial School of Jurisprudence,
where he was enrolled from 1838 to 1842 (drawing
by A. Vorob'ev; Ambramtsevo Museum, Moscow)

well-intentioned exhortations to abandon his dangerous convictions; the strong resemblance between Columbus's resolve and Aksakov's own inflexible dedication to his principles could not have been lost on his parents, to whom he sent the poem a few days after completing it. Nonetheless, he wrote to them in a letter during this period that he had originally intended to dedicate the work to Konstantin but changed his mind, because the poem "was not worthy of that man."

Traveling in the Russian hinterland during the winter of 1844 to 1845, Aksakov devised his next major verse drama, "Zimniaia doroga. (Licentia poetica). Dramaticheskie stseny v stikhakh i proze" (Winter Road [Poetic License]. Dramatic Scenes in Verse and Prose), which appeared, with several cuts imposed by the censorship, in the almanac *Moskovskii literaturnyi i uchenyi sbornik na 1847* (Moscow Literary and Scholarly Miscellany for 1847). "Zimniaia doroga" depicts the journey of two young noblemen—the Slavophile Arkhipov and the Westernizer Iashcherin. The two discuss their opposing views in verse (consisting chiefly of free iambs), with Arkhipov clearly voicing Aksakov's own views: "By the spark of an inner light, / By the warmth of a secret fire, / Warmed by eternal truth / It's the life of the people for me!" Whenever the men speak to peasants, however, or when the peasants speak with each other, Aksakov employs prose; in addition, Iashcherin frequently switches to French when he needs to comment on the serfs' lot in their presence. The final scene, at a shabby wayside inn, exposes both men to the grim realities of peasant life: dirt, poverty, ignorance, enserfment to absentee landlords, and conscription. In the end Aksakov portrays the Slavophile and the Westernizer, despite their elegantly argued, poetic abstractions, as utter aliens in a literally prosaic peasant universe. Aksakov cleverly uses the subtitle, "Licentia poetica," to remind the reader that the license belongs to those who speak in poetry—the gentry—while the slaves, whose fate is debated by the gentry, are confined to a prison of prose. "Zimniaia doroga" became quite popular even before it appeared in print. Three excerpts from the verse passages were set to music by two major composers of the day, Aleksandr Aleksandrovich Aliab'ev and Aleksandr L'vovich Gurilev. Nikolai Vasil'evich Gogol's curiosity was piqued by what he heard about the work, and Aksakov's father, Sergei Timofeevich, sent the writer several of his son's poems. Gogol especially prized the angry diatribe "Sredi udobnykh i lenivykh" (Among the Comfortable and Indolent), written in 1845 and published in *Moskovskii literaturnyi i uchenyi sbornik* (Moscow Literary and Scholarly Miscellany, 1846). The poem prompted him to make this assessment of Aksakov in his own *Polnoe sobranie sochinenii:* "The young man evinces a decisive talent and a striving to adapt poetry to action and to a legitimate influence on current events."

From June 1845 to April 1847 Aksakov worked as vice chairman of the Kaluga criminal chamber. In Kaluga he spent a great deal of time with Aleksandra Osipovna Smirnova-Rosset—wife of the governor of Kaluga, celebrated hostess, friend of the leading writers of her day, and a former lady-in-waiting to the empress. Belinsky visited Aksakov in Kaluga and wrote to Herzen that he was fond of the young civil servant. During his stay in Kaluga, Aksakov's lyric verse flowed more freely than at any other time in his life; this ease in writing seems to have been prompted in part by his strong feelings for Smirnova-Rosset, with whom he probably fell in love for a time. In the summer of 1846 Aksakov even attempted to publish a sizable collection of his poems but was so disgusted by the censor's cuts and alterations that he withdrew the submission, and the volume was never published.

Noteworthy among the impassioned poetry of this period is the jeremiad "26-e sentiabria" (26 September), which Aksakov wrote in the early autumn of 1845 (published in *Moskovskii literaturnyi i uchenyi sbornik*). The title of the poem is the date of his birthday, and the text—which he likened, as he said in a letter around this time, to "a kind of long moral ode precisely like Gavrila Romanovich Derzhavin's 'Bog' [God, 1784]"—effectively encapsulates its creator's severe worldview. A stanza about anti-Westernizers from "26-e sentiabria" merits quotation:

V chadu tshcheslavnykh iskushenii,
Kak dushu ty ni storozhi,
V nei malo chistykh pobuzhdenii,
V nei malo pravdy, mnogo lzhi!
Tak malo v nas liubvi i very,
Tak v serdtse malo teploty,
Tak my umny, umny bez mery,
Tak my boimsia prostoty!

(Amid the intoxication of vainglorious temptations,
No matter how well you guard your soul,
It will possess few pure incentives,
It will possess little truth, and much falsehood!
How little love and faith there are in us,
How little warmth in our hearts,
How clever we are, clever beyond measure,
How we fear simplicity!)

In "S prestupnoi gordost'iu" (With Criminal Pride, 1886) Aksakov rages against the same vices, but this poem is crafted in unmistakably biblical language; in the final line the poet compares Russia with ancient Sodom. The same stern moralism can be found in "Sovet" (Advice, 1846), written as an exhortation to Konstantin not to allow himself to grow arrogant because of the public accolades he was receiving and published in the journal *Sovremennik* (The Contemporary). One of the clearest expressions of Aksakov's revulsion at the ills of Russia occurs in the final sextet of "My vse stradaem i toskuem . . ." (We're All Suffering and Sick at Heart . . . , published in the periodical *Den'* [Day] in 1862):

Toska! . . . Ispolnennyi tomlen'ia,
Mir zhazhdet, zhazhdet obnovlen'ia,
Ego ne teshit zhizni pir!
Driakhleia, muchitsia i stynet . . .
Kogda zh spasenie nakhlynet
I vetkhii osvezhitsia mir?

(Heartsickness! . . . Filled with languor,
The world thirsts, thirsts for renewal;
Life's feast will give it no gratification!
Growing decrepit, it is tormented and freezes over . . .
When will salvation surge forth
And the dilapidated world be revived?)

Although Aksakov was considered the least religiously oriented of the major Slavophiles, the craving for a messianic deliverance frequently found in the writings of his brother Konstantin and of Aleksei Stepanovich Khomiakov is palpable here.

Not all of Aksakov's Kaluga verse is dedicated to moral anguish; some of his most serene poetry dates from this period as well. For instance, "Noch'" (Night, 1846), written in 1845, is an elegiac meditation on the permanence of nature that culminates in a moving apostrophe to the moon. Another poem, which begins

"V tikhoi komnate moei" (In my quiet room, 1888) and was probably written at around the same time as "Noch'," is a compact lyric reminiscent of the work of poet Fedor Ivanovich Tiutchev, in which the poet finds his greatest freedom in the paradoxically liberating confinement of his own chamber. In "Dozhd'" (Rain, 1888), written in 1846, Aksakov's narrator hurries along in a coach during a rainstorm while observing a wide spectrum of Russians—merchant's son, peasant, townswoman, dandy—and daydreaming about a beautiful but sorrowful young woman who stands by an open window. Written in the same year, "Sannyi beg, vecherom, v gorode" (Evening Sleigh-Ride, in Town, 1888) offers a similar reflection on the poet's delight in observing the people he passes and in breathing in the salutary winter chill. Music and its ability to act as a balm for the soul in a troubled world were important themes for Aksakov, and his "Capriccio" (1888), also written in 1846, is an affectionate, wistful tribute to the old-fashioned Russian *romansy* (art songs) and singers that he loved. Written the following year, "Pri klikakh derzostno-pobednykh . . ." (amid impudent, triumphant cries . . . , 1888) was one of his father's favorites. This poem, which Aksakov claimed was based on a true story of misfortune, is a simple statement of the poet's deep sympathy for an enigmatic young woman who suffers for a reason not specified. During this period Aksakov also entered into eloquent verse exchanges with the important poets Nikolai Mikhailovich Iazykov and Iuliia Valerianovna Zhadovskaia: "Iazykovu" (To Iazykov, 1888) in 1845 and "Pri posylke stikhotvorenii Iu. Zhadovskoi" (On Sending Verses to Iu. Zhadovskaia, 1888) in 1846.

The unfinished "Mariia egipetskaia" (Mary of Egypt), which Aksakov began in the mid 1840s—around the same time as "Zimniaia doroga"—was intended to be a "Christian epic" centering on the psychological portrait of a repentant sinner: the sixth-century Orthodox saint Mary of Egypt, a prostitute who chose an eremitic life after a transformative visit to Jerusalem. Aksakov based his story on Saint Sofronii's *vita* (life) of Mary in the *Chet'i minei* (Monthly Readings), a collection of medieval religious texts that were read in the Orthodox Church on feast days. "Mariia egipetskaia," unlike Aksakov's other extended works, is written squarely in the style of the early-nineteenth-century narrative poem: it consists of an introduction, numbered iambic tetrameter cantos, and an inserted trochaic song. The completed portion of the text encompasses a provocatively anachronistic debate between Mariia and the gnostic Clement of Alexandria (who died in the early third century). Only the introduction, four short cantos, and "Pesnia Marii egipetskoi" (Song of Mary of Egypt, 1888) were finished. In a letter published in *Ivan Sergeevich Aksakov v ego pis'makh* (Ivan Sergeevich Aksokov in

Aksakov and his wife, Anna Fedorovna, circa 1870 (from Aksakov, Pis'ma k rodnym, 1849–1856, *1994)*

His Letters, 1888–1896), Aksakov declared he would "have had to be a better Christian" if he were to complete the poem as he had originally planned it, and he abandoned the work.

During the course of his travels and in his various civil-service posts, Aksakov remained an astonishingly faithful correspondent who wrote home to his parents every three days almost without fail, regardless of the circumstances; he also maintained an active correspondence with many of the major intellectual figures of his day, especially the Moscow Slavophiles. Even in an age of sophisticated epistolary culture, his letters stand out for their length, detail, and quality of language. Aksakov candidly recorded his impressions of the people he met and of the many places he visited throughout the Russian provinces. He also discussed at length the genesis and development of his literary works as well as wrote candidly about his thoughts, feelings, aspirations, and social concerns. According to Aksakov, his letters took the place of his diaries, and his correspondence constitutes a richly detailed chronicle of mid-nineteenth-century Russian life. Only a fraction of it has been published, most notably in *Ivan Sergeevich Aksakov v ego pis'makh* and *Pis'ma k rodnym: 1844–1849* (Letters Home: 1844–1849, 1988).

Aksakov returned to the Moscow Senate to work from 1847 to 1848 as *ober-secretary* (chief secretary) of its

Criminal Department and hoped to conquer corruption. But Aksakov soon realized that his attempts to reform the system from within were useless. The members of his department routinely perpetrated legal fraud, and they now pressured him to sign the acquittal of a debauched young nobleman who had murdered his mistress while drunk. Utterly disgusted, Aksakov transferred in September 1848 to the Interior Ministry. He was immediately dispatched to Bessarabia with the mission of secretly monitoring Christian sects that refused to conform to the strictures of Orthodoxy. In Bessarabia he made his first extensive acquaintance with Ukrainians and Jews, and he expressed his intense dislike for both groups. He returned to St. Petersburg in January 1849, awaiting further advancement in the Interior Ministry. During this period he spent a great deal of time with Iurii Fedorovich Samarin, one of the chief Slavophiles and a close friend of the Aksakov family. Samarin and Aksakov honed their antiserfdom views together, and Aksakov even considered publishing a book incorporating his own firsthand descriptions of the abuses that he had seen landowners commit.

Aksakov's poetry of the late 1840s reverberates with the emotional turbulence of the disillusionment he encountered in government service. He later wrote in a letter, published in *Ivan Sergeevich Aksakov v ego pis'makh,* that the poem "Otdykh" (Rest, written 1847; collected in *Kievlianin* [The Kievan], 1850) expressed "an inner struggle, the struggle of the poetic and artistic calling with consciousness of one's civic duty. It must be remembered that I was in the service then; I considered it wrong to fold my hands and say, 'Well, I'm a poet, so I get to do nothing.'" "Otdykh" embodies Aksakov's struggle; its eleven quatrains are devoted to the opposition of day (bureaucratic toil) and night (quiet reflection). "A. P. Elaginoi" (To A. P. Elagina, published in the journal *Russkii arkhiv* in 1877), written in 1848 and addressed to Avdot'ia Petrovna Elagina, mother of the Slavophile Kireevsky brothers (Ivan Vasil'evich and Petr Vasil'evich), is a fascinating rationalization of self-effacement and a rejection of worldly praise. Aksakov's worsening pessimism is vividly recorded in "Pust' gibnet vse . . ." (Let everything perish . . . , published in the journal *Russkaia beseda* in 1859), written in February 1849; the poem angrily declares that "The stronghold of sheer evil stands; / Senseless Falsehood reigns!"

On 4 March 1849 Samarin was arrested and imprisoned for twelve days at the Peter-Paul Fortress in St. Petersburg. His crime had been the circulation of his manuscript for "Pis'ma iz Rigi" (Letters from Riga), in which he denounced German dominance in the Baltic region and criticized what he viewed as an inadequate response by the Russian government to the German persecution of Baltic Russians. In a letter to his parents around this time, Aksakov wrote of Samarin's detainment and urged them to be "very careful" in their letters to their son; he also dared to call St. Petersburg society "villainous." In the wake of the revolutions of 1848 these comments, coupled with certain implications in the replies from Aksakov's father, were enough to raise suspicions of the existence of a dangerous "secret organization" among the Slavophiles.

On 18 March 1849, the day after Samarin's release, Aksakov was arrested on a warrant issued by His Imperial Majesty's Third Section (the secret police). The young civil servant was held, like Samarin, in the Peter-Paul Fortress, though for only four days. He was given a twelve-point questionnaire and was required to write down responses explaining his literary activities and political views. In his answers he systematically lambasted the West and lauded the natural sense of faith and aversion to revolution in Russia. Tsar Nicholas I personally read, and made handwritten annotations on, Aksakov's replies; according to a letter later published in *Ivan Sergeevich Aksakov v ego pis'makh,* the tsar's advice to Aleksei Fedorovich Orlov, Director of the Third Section, was "Summon him, read this to him, teach him, let him go!" The prisoner was indeed released, but he remained under secret surveillance. Aksakov was then given a punitive Interior Ministry assignment consisting of two extremely complicated tasks: to make a detailed report on every aspect of the economy of Iaroslavl' Province, and to make a secret report on the activities of the *beguny* (runners)—considered by some to be the most radical and elusive schismatic sectarians in Russia at the time. Only the final chapter of his lengthy report, titled "O begunakh" (On the Runners, 1870), was published during his lifetime; it appeared in the journal *Russkii arkhiv.* Aksakov worked diligently on these torturous projects from May 1849 to March 1851.

The arrest of Samarin—and his own arrest—intensified the negativity of the verse Aksakov wrote during the *mrachnoe semiletie* (seven years of gloom), between the revolutions of 1848 and the death of Nicholas I. "N. N. N. Otvet na pis'mo" (To N. N. N.: An Answer to a Letter, 1960) was written in March 1849 as a defiant response to his imprisonment:

Net! slovom zlym i delom chernym
Do dna dushi potriaseny,
My vse vragov kleimom pozornym
Kleimit' bez ustali dolzhny!

(No! shaken to the depths of our souls
By evil word and black deed,
We must all tirelessly brand our enemies
With the brand of shame!)

Similar imagery is employed in reverse for "Kleimo domashnego pozora . . ." (The brand of domestic

shame . . . , 1888–1896), written in a December 1849 letter to his parents: "The brand of domestic shame / We wear, though we seem glorious from without." In sending this poem to his parents, Aksakov—who knew that the secret police were perusing his mail—took the precaution of calling it a translation from the Sanskrit. "Ustalykh sil ia dolgo ne zhalel" (I did not regret my wearied strength for long . . .), written in November 1850 and published in 1856 in the first issue of *Russkaia beseda,* was admired on the political left by both Nikolai Alekseevich Nekrasov and Nikolai Gavrilovich Chernyshevsky. On the last day of 1850 Aksakov completed his poetic reaction to the events of 1848 in "Posle 1848 goda" (After 1848, 1886); the work was published only posthumously. At sixteen quatrains, long by his standards, this poem is a searing expression of dejection in the wake of recent mass oppression in Europe. Aksakov gave the text to his father, who sternly warned him never to show it to anyone. Sergei Timofeevich, however, allowed Ivan Sergeevich Turgenev to read "Posle 1848 goda" and wrote about Turgenev's response in the journal *Russkaia mysl'* (Russian Thought) in 1915: "There is hardly a person who could feel this poem more deeply in every respect: it is the cry of his own soul, but expressed by another."

Aksakov's longest poem, "Brodiaga: Ocherk v stikhakh" (The Vagrant: An Essay in Verse), though never completed, may safely be regarded as the author's magnum opus. Part 1 was not published in its entirety until it appeared in volume two of the posthumous edition of his letters in 1888. Aksakov first conceived "Brodiaga" in late 1844 while in Astrakhan', where he took great interest in the many runaway serfs and wandering vagrants who took refuge there. By the autumn of 1846 he referred to the work as his most important poetic effort, and he labored slowly on the project in fits and starts until portions of it first appeared in print. According to Aksakov's *Stikhotvoreniia i poemy* (Poems and Long Narrative Poems, 1960), the censorship was displeased with "Brodiaga," holding that it offered "in vagrancy the promise of freedom and impunity." While under arrest in 1849 Aksakov was specifically asked why he had chosen a vagrant as the hero of his poem. He answered in a letter later published in *Ivan Sergeevich Aksakov v ego pis'makh:*

Because his image struck me as highly poetic; because this is one of the phenomena of our national life; because a vagrant who wanders the whole of Russia gives me the opportunity to create a poetic description of Russia's natural world and Russian daily life in its various forms; and, finally, because this type was well known to me, since I have worked for so many years on criminal matters.

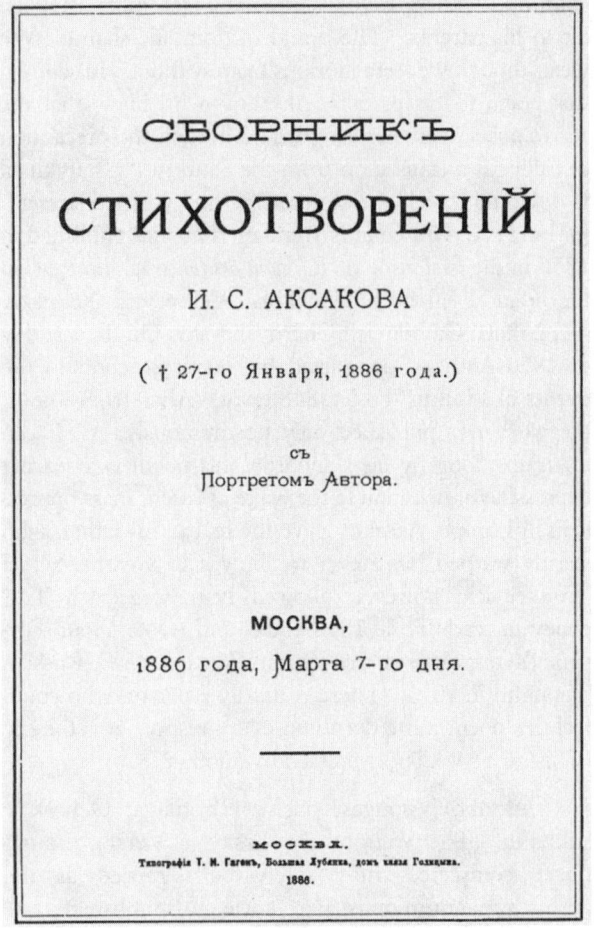

СБОРНИКЪ

СТИХОТВОРЕНІЙ

И. С. АКСАКОВА.

(† 27-го Января, 1886 года.)

съ
Портретомъ Автора.

МОСКВА,
1886 года, Марта 7-го дня.

МОСКВА.
Типографія Т. И. Гагенъ, Большая Лубянка, домъ князя Голицына.
1886.

Title page for the "mourning edition" of Aksakov's Sbornik
stikhotvorenii (Collected Poems), which came out
forty days after the poet died (Kilgour Collection
of Russian Literature, Harvard
University Library)

In part 1 of "Brodiaga" the reader meets the protagonist, Aleksei Matveevich (Aleshka), a young serf who flees his estate, leaving behind his beloved, the beautiful Parasha. The bailiff, Kornil Dem'ianich, takes the case to the *zemskii sud* (regional court), while Aleshka travels far, meeting a variety of colorful characters and finding work where he can. Part 2 has descriptions of autumn and winter and a lively account of the goings-on in a village tavern. Aksakov employs a wide variety of meters and line lengths to convey different moods and settings and to indicate the insertion of folk songs. There are extensive passages of deftly composed verse dialogue that occasionally drift into conventional dramatic form, with dialogue tags. Aksakov was clearly an expert on the subject of runaways, and the language of his descriptions is pithy and precise; the utterances of peasant characters are convincingly colloquial. The poem is credited as the first Russian attempt at a folk epic, and its structure and

style led directly to Nekrasov's famous "Komu na Rusi zhit' khorosho" (Who Can Live Well in Russia), which appeared serially between 1866 and 1881. Three excerpts from "Brodiaga" were eventually set to music by several composers.

In January 1851 Interior Minister Lev Alekseevich Perovsky received a denunciation of Aksakov for having read "Brodiaga" to his friends. In January and February 1851 Perovsky required Aksakov to account for the narrative poem. Satisfied, Perovsky nonetheless made the peremptory suggestion that the young civil servant "cease his authorial labors" in order to avoid future entanglements with the authorities. Outraged, the beleaguered writer tendered his resignation on 19 February 1851, and in April of that year he left Iaroslavl', never to undertake government service again, although he felt guilty about abandoning a salary to live off the work of his serfs.

In 1852 Aksakov edited and published the first volume of *Moskovskii sbornik* (Moscow Miscellany), a publication intended to unite Slavophiles both young and old. Besides excerpts from "Brodiaga," titled "Otryvki iz pervoi chasti *Brodiagi*, ocherka v stikhakh" (Excerpts from the First Part of *The Vagrant*, an Essay in Verse), volume one of *Moskovskii sbornik* included Aksakov's brief eulogy to Gogol, "Neskol'ko slov o Gogole" (A Few Words about Gogol). He calls Gogol "an artist-monk, a satirist-Christian, an ascetic and humorist, a martyr to lofty thought and an insoluble task" and declares him more significant than the great poets Aleksandr Sergeevich Pushkin, Aleksandr Sergeevich Griboedov, and Mikhail Iur'evich Lermontov. This eulogy violated the ban on discussing Gogol in print, and the authorities punished Aksakov swiftly: the manuscript for volume two of *Moskovskii sbornik* was confiscated, and contributors were required to submit their pieces directly to the Main Censorship Office in St. Petersburg rather than to the more pliant Moscow Censorship Committee; this requirement amounted to a ban on the publication. The coup de grâce was that Aksakov himself was deprived of the right to edit any future publications, a prohibition that remained in effect for the next seven years.

Finally giving free rein to his impulses as a playwright in 1853, Aksakov wrote *Prisutstvennyi den' ugolovnoi palaty: Sudebnye stseny* (A Workday in the Criminal Chamber: Judicial Scenes). The play was first published (anonymously) in London in *Poliarnaia zvezda* (The North Star) in 1858 by Herzen–who called the work "a thing of genius"–and came out in book form in 1874. A scathing attack on the entire tsarist legal system, *Prisutstvennyi den' ugolovnoi palaty* consists of twenty-six fully developed scenes centering on the middle-aged Semen Ivanovich Pososhkov and the dashing young Aleksei Aleksandrovich Zhabin. The play portrays the Russian legal system as utterly corrupt, and the plot consists of an unending parade of abuses large and small. In a *preduvedomlenie* (forewarning) to the piece, Aksakov shockingly advises readers that *Prisutstvennyi den' ugolovnoi palaty* fails even to come close to exhausting the store of incidents, such as those seen in the play, that he had gathered during his years of civil service.

After being rejected as "politically unreliable" when he applied to join a Russian circumnavigatory frigate expedition, in November 1852 Aksakov accepted a commission from the Russian Geographical Society to research the economics of Ukrainian fairs. Over the course of a year he visited every province of Ukraine and eventually produced *Issledovanie o torgovle na ukrainskikh iarmarkakh* (Study of Trade at Ukrainian Fairs), published as a book in 1858. The study received the Great Medal from the geographical society and the Demidov Prize from the Academy of Sciences.

The Crimean War broke out in August 1854, and on 18 February 1855 Aksakov volunteered to serve in the Serpukhov *druzhina* (detachment) of the Moscow *opolchenie* (home guard). In "Na Dunai! tuda, gde novoi slavy . . ." (To the Danube! There, where new glory . . . , 1886), written in April 1854, he had enthusiastically welcomed the war, but he soon grew disillusioned with Russia's chances for success. The Serpukhov *druzhina* made its way on foot to Odessa and into Bessarabia but failed to reach the front before the war ended in early 1856. Aksakov then served on a commission investigating abuses perpetrated by Russian quartermasters in Crimea during the war but returned to Moscow in December 1856, before the quartermaster case was finally adjudicated. In early 1857 he left Russia to travel throughout Europe and visited Munich, Paris, Rome, Naples, Berlin, and Zurich. He secretly made his way to London in order to meet with Herzen, who later wrote in his *Sobranie sochinenii* that he and Aksakov, despite their ideological differences, "got on very, very well." During this visit the two men agreed to have *Prisutstvennyi den' ugolovnoi palaty* published in London by the Free Russian Press (founded by Herzen in 1853). This meeting marked the start of Aksakov's clandestine collaboration—under the pseudonym "Kas'ianov"—with Herzen, who was by this time living in exile; more than thirty of Aksakov's articles and notices appeared in Herzen's publications through the early 1860s. These were mostly short pieces of political and social commentary on topics related to the sweeping reforms being pursued in Russia under Tsar Alexander II.

On his return to Russia in September 1857 Aksakov served as office director for the journal *Sel'skoe blagoustroistvo* (Rural Improvement) while secretly acting—beginning in the summer of 1858—as editor of *Russkaia beseda* (first published 1856); the nominal editor of the journal was Aleksandr Ivanovich Koshelev. At this time

Aksakov also helped found the Slavianskie blagotvoritel'nye komitety (Slavic Benevolent Committees), of which he became a key leader. After 29 March 1858, when he was officially allowed to resume his editing activities, he was granted permission to publish a newspaper called *Parus* (The Sail), which advocated the right of Russians and other Slavic peoples to develop autonomously. Aksakov promised to discuss in the second issue solutions to the problem of serfdom in Russia and ways to bring about its "annihilation"; this declaration prompted the authorities to shut down the newspaper at once, and Aksakov returned to *Russkaia beseda*.

His poetry once more became a critical forum for the airing of his social views. He wrote his poem "Dobro b mechty, dobro by strasti" (It would be a different matter if daydreams and passions, 1856) in April 1853 to attack the Russian liberal gentry for their devotion to dreamy abstractions on the eve of serious reforms. When the poem was published in *Russkaia beseda* in 1856, it touched off an illuminating exchange. Iakov Petrovich Polonsky replied with the verse "I. S. Aksakovu" (To I. S. Aksakov), suggesting that "to know good does not mean to ignore evil / And to love does not mean to pine away." In a letter, later published in *Ivan Sergeevich Aksakov v ego pis'makh,* he insightfully refers to Aksakov's "rigid, merciless" poetry with its testimony to the "cold truth," and compares him to a physician, scalpel at the ready, as he "studies the root of social ills." Although Aksakov claimed not to understand "exactly what Polonsky meant," he responded in early 1857 with "Otvet" (A Reply, 1857), in which he describes his indissoluble union with a "gnevnaia muza" (wrathful muse):

> Ne prelest' prazdnogo mechtan'ia,
> Ne nega sladostnykh molitv,
> No zloi poryv negodovan'ia,
> Zhestokii sud, prizyvy bitv,
> Otvaga derzko-molodaia
> V nei vdokhnovliali pesen stroi . . .

> (The structure of her songs was inspired
> Not by the charm of idle dreaming,
> Not by the languor of sweet prayers,
> But by the angry upsurge of indignation,
> By cruel judgment, by the call of battle,
> By daring and youthful bravery . . .)

In April 1859 Aksakov's father—one of the great patriarchs of traditional Russian society—died. The tubercular Konstantin, who had always been Sergei Timofeevich's clear favorite, fell ill with grief, while Ivan feigned indifference to the loss. In January 1860 Aksakov departed for a yearlong journey to Germany and various Slavic countries. In Belgrade he delivered Khomiakov's "K serbam: Poslanie iz Moskvy" (To the

Serbs: An Epistle from Moscow), which had been signed by all the leading Slavophiles. Though "K serbam" was greeted coolly by the Serbian press, Aksakov himself was received enthusiastically throughout the Balkans. He described his poem "Navstrechu veshchego proroka . . ." (To meet the sage prophet . . . , published in the journal *Russkaia beseda* in 1860) in a letter as a meditation on the way "we all frequently expect a historic event from the right, and it comes from the left; we expect it in a uniform, and it appears in something else, so we fail to recognize it."

Meanwhile, Konstantin's tuberculosis worsened, and he was sent to Europe by his doctors. Ivan met him in Germany, and the two brothers eventually decided to travel to the Greek island of Zante (Zákinthos) in the Ionian Sea. There, a fortnight later, on 19 December 1860 (New Style) Konstantin died. The Kireevsky brothers had both died in 1856, and Samarin was occupied with the drafting of documents enunciating the imminent emancipation of the Russian serfs. Aksakov had written "F. V. Chizhovu" (To F. V. Chizhov) in early May 1860 to Fedor Vasil'evich Chizhov, a Slavophile who, like Aksakov himself, sought to distill pragmatic lessons from the work of both Khomiakov and Aksakov's brother Konstantin, while rejecting their unattainable utopian visions. The chief themes of the epistle are the poet's weariness with his moral cargo and his need to concentrate his attention on a single goal. This poem is the last serious piece of verse that Aksakov wrote for nearly two decades. He became the sole spokesman for the Moscow Slavophiles and abandoned serious poetry for the rest of his life, with the exception of a small handful of poems dating from 1878. While Aksakov's ideological orientation had until this time been comparatively eclectic–Koshelev, for example, considered him in the 1840s and 1850s to be a Westernizer within the Slavophile tradition–he now took up the orthodox Slavophile positions of his brother Konstantin.

Aksakov next edited and published the newspapers *Den'* (1861–1865) and *Moskva* (Moscow, 1867–1868), writing the front-page editorial for each issue. The weekly *Den'*, which began publication in late 1861, was permitted to appear only if it lacked a section on politics. The censorship cracked down with particular severity as Aksakov's views on the Russian economy, Slavic peoples, and Baltic Germans–and his demands for full freedom of expression in Russia–became increasingly extreme; in a secret 1865 report titled *Epokha tsenzurnykh reform 1859–1865 godov* the censorship, led by novelist and civil servant Ivan Aleksandrovich Goncharov, described Aksakov as a "citizen-democrat with socialist tendencies." The first issue of *Moskva* appeared on 1 January 1867; before it was finally banned, this newspaper received nine warnings and was closed three times–for

three, four, and six months, respectively; during these intervals it was published under the title *Moskvich* (The Muscovite) by a figurehead editor. Aksakov was once again forbidden to work as an editor; this time the publishing ban lasted twelve years.

During the era of Tsar Aleksandr II's great reforms, Aksakov's ideological positions became harder and sharper. In advocating *obshchestvo* (society) as the bulwark that protected the *narod* (folk) from the onslaughts of the unnatural petrine state, Aksakov denounced the gentry as a class artificially created by Peter the Great to serve as a henchman for the state and suggested that the gentry be allowed to die out. Aksakov welcomed the zemstvo system (essentially a form of elective county government) in 1864 but was too skeptical to embrace immediately the sweeping legal reforms (such as jury trials, public trials, and courts of appeal) introduced in the 1860s, although by the mid 1870s he gave these his approval. His nationalist orientation in *Den'* and *Moskva* was virulently anti-Polish, anti-Baltic-German, anti-Catholic, and anti-Semitic. In 1863 he sharply criticized Herzen's support for the Poles during the Polish Uprising of 1863–1864, and relations between the two men were swiftly and permanently sundered. Though Aksakov had denounced published attacks on Jews early in his career, he later emerged–beginning in the early 1860s–as the most vociferously anti-Semitic of the Slavophiles, believing that Judaism represented a predatory negation of all that Christianity embodied.

After closing *Den'*, Aksakov married Anna Fedorovna Tiutcheva, daughter of poet and diplomat Tiutchev, on 12 January 1866. As a lady-in-waiting to the empress and a woman of fine intellect, Anna Fedorovna had exercised considerable influence at court–in spite of the imperfect command of Russian that her many years in the Francophilic court had bestowed upon her. Although precisely when Aksakov first made her acquaintance is not clear, she had interceded on behalf of *Den'* in 1862, when it was closed down after his refusal to divulge to the censorship the name of one of his correspondents. According to the memoirs of historian and political philosopher Boris Nikolaevich Chicherin, the marriage was a loving one, and although Anna Fedorovna disagreed with her husband's support for Pan-Slavism and autocracy, she and Aksakov found common ground in a deep sense of piety and reverence for the Orthodox Church.

From 1872 to 1874 Aksakov acted as chairman of the Obshchestvo liubitelei rossiiskoi slovesnosti (Society of Lovers of Russian Literature) at Moscow University. In 1874 he published the first edition of his *Fedor Ivanovich Tiutchev: Biograf'icheskii ocherk* (Fedor Ivanovich Tiutchev: A Biographical Sketch), which was confiscated and destroyed on the grounds that nationality was emphasized in the monograph more strongly than

Woodcut of Aksakov's grave in the cemetery at the Troitse-Sergieva Monastery in Zagorsk, outside Moscow
(Pushkin House, St. Petersburg)

was the official ideology of the Russian government. The biography, which revived Tiutchev's reputation, conceptualized his legacy in a way that influenced all future scholars of Tiutchev's work: "His is not *thinking* poetry, but rather poetic thought; not feeling that reasons and thinks, but thought that feels and is alive." Likewise, with his speech on Pushkin, Aksakov helped seal the reputation of the most significant nineteenth-century Russian poet; he gave this address at the 7 June 1880 meeting of the Obshchestvo liubitelei rossiiskoi slovesnosti, which was dedicated to the raising of the Pushkin statue in Moscow. Aksakov spoke immediately after Fyodor Dostoevsky's famous address. He declared that Dostoevsky had shown once and for all that Pushkin was a "national poet" in both senses—*narodnyi* (of the Russian people) as well as *natsional'nyi* (of the nation-state of Russia). As a result, Aksakov insisted, Pushkin was a figure on whom both Westernizers and Slavophiles could agree and who could heal the rift between those old ideological foes. For his part, Dostoevsky viewed Aksakov's speech on Pushkin as an historic event and saw Aksakov as his *edinomyshlennik* (ideological partner).

By the mid 1870s, under the influence of Tiutchev's writings and Nikolai Iakovlevich Danilevsky's *Rossiia i Evropa* (Russia and Europe, 1869),

Aksakov shifted his chief ideological focus from Slavophilism to Pan-Slavism. In 1875 he replaced Pogodin as president of the Moskovskoe slavianskoe blagotvoritel'noe obshchestvo (Moscow Slavic Benevolent Society) and held that position until the society closed in 1878. He led the effort in 1876 to provide material assistance to Serbia and Montenegro in their rebellion against the Turks, raising eight hundred thousand rubles and recruiting Russian volunteer soldiers. Similarly, when the Russo-Turkish War of 1877–1878 broke out, Aksakov was instrumental in expediting men and matériel to the Bulgarian detachments. Russia emerged victorious and negotiated an advantageous disposition of Slavic territory in the Treaty of San Stefano (March 1878). At the Congress of Berlin in June 1878, however, Russia—under threat of war from Britain—allowed greater Turkish control in the Balkans than had originally been agreed upon in the Treaty of San Stefano. Aksakov's Pan-Slavic dreams had been dashed by the foreign policy maneuvers of his own government. On 22 June 1878 he delivered an excoriating speech at the meeting of the Moskovskoe slavianskoe blagotvoritel'noe obshchestvo, in which he accused the Russian delegates to Berlin of participating in "an open conspiracy against the Russian people," of betraying the Serbs and Bulgarians, and of transforming Russia from victor to vanquished in the Russo-Turkish War. The sensational diatribe was met with great popularity and was immediately published in the right-wing newspaper *Grazhdanin* (The Citizen) and then in many European papers. Largely at the behest of Austria, the Russian government exiled Aksakov from Moscow to the Varvarino estate (Iur'ev District, Vladimir Province), which belonged to his wife's sister, Ekaterina Fedorovna Tiutcheva. The Moskovskoe slavianskoe blagotvoritel'noe obshchestvo was closed down permanently, and the Slavic benevolent societies in St. Petersburg, Kiev, and Odessa were taken over by the Ministry of Foreign Affairs.

After a hiatus from serious poetry of more than eighteen years, in the autumn of 1878 Aksakov wrote his five last poems, all of which were connected with his exile. In "Varvarino: Poslanie E. F. Tiutchevoi" (Varvarino: Epistle to E. F. Tiutcheva, published in *Rus'* in 1880) he asserts that "the whirlwind of an evil storm" has carried away his home. The poet thanks his hostess and praises the beauty of her estate. "Anne" (To Anna, published in the journal *Novoe vremia* in 1886) offers a comparison between Varvarino's refreshing natural beauty and the heart and soul of Aksakov's wife. A similarly pure lyricism characterizes the short, nostalgic "Sredi tsvetov pory osennei" (Among the flowers of autumn, published in *Novoe vremia* in 1886). This poem is the Aksakov text most attractive to musical transposition; it inspired five settings to music, one of which the nationalist composer Milii Alekseevich Balakirev wrote in the late 1890s. "29 noiabria" (29 November, published in *Rus'* in 1880), Aksakov's final poem, celebrates the day in 1878 when the poet learned he was permitted to pay a visit to Moscow.

In late 1880, after a two-year journalistic silence, Aksakov was finally allowed to return to Moscow. He received permission to edit and publish another newspaper, *Rus'* (Old Russia). The first issue appeared on 15 November 1880, and the newspaper continued to be published—with the exception of one six-month period in 1885 because of its editor's poor health—until the day of Aksakov's death. It came out weekly, save for a series of months between 1883 and 1885, when it appeared on a biweekly basis. *Rus'*, which had a small number of subscribers, continued to hold a Pan-Slavic editorial line. Opposed to the adoption of a constitutional monarchy in Russia, Aksakov advocated instead the resurrection of the *zemskii sobor*, an assembly of the various social estates convened by the tsar and dating back to the mid 1500s. He also wrote articles urging educational reforms and denouncing German and Austrian influence in eastern Europe. Employing *Rus'* as the vehicle, Aksakov was the first to publish in Russia the spurious "secret letter" attributed to Adolphe Crémieux, president of the Alliance Israélite Universelle (Universal Alliance of Israel) in France. This forgery, imported by Aksakov from France via Germany, was a direct precursor of the infamous anti-Semitic hoax known as the "Protokoly sionskikh mudretsov" (Protocols of the Elders of Zion), which appeared in Russia some two decades later.

Aksakov died suddenly of heart failure on 27 January 1886. The literary historian Semen Afanas'evich Vengerov claims that one hundred thousand people joined his funeral procession and that his widow received close to two hundred telegrams of sympathy from all over Russia and Europe. Aksakov was buried in the Troitse-Sergieva Monastery outside of Moscow.

Ivan Sergeevich Aksakov had his greatest literary success as a poet; yet, his Slavophile and Pan-Slavic essays are marked by the same zeal for attacking social ills that informs his poetry. These publicistic works were widely influential, even though they were rarely the product of creative or original thought. Especially in his later career Aksakov's nationalist writings and editorial projects were hamstrung by increasingly keen expressions of xenophobia and anti-Semitism. Regardless of the forum or the subject, however, one trait remained consistent in every aspect of his multifarious career: misguided or not, he was unfailingly courageous in his pursuit of what he considered to be right.

Letters:

Pis'ma k rodnym: 1844–1849, edited by Tatiana Fedorovna Pirozhkova (Moscow: Nauka, 1988);

Pis'ma iz provintsii; Prisutstvennyi den' v ugolovnoi palate, edited by Pirozhkova, (Moscow: Pravda, 1991);

Pis'ma k rodnym: 1849–1856, edited by Pirozhkova, (Moscow: Nauka, 1994).

Biographies:

Sergei Semenovich Trubachev, "Ivan Sergeevich Aksakov," in *Russkii biograficheskii slovar',* volume 1 (St. Petersburg, 1896), pp. 97–100;

Stephen Lukashevich, *Ivan Aksakov, 1823–1886: A Study in Russian Thought and Politics* (Cambridge, Mass.: Harvard University Press, 1965).

References:

Konstantin Sergeevich Aksakov, *Polnoe sobranie sochinenii,* 3 volumes (Zug, Switzerland: Inter Documentation, 1981);

Vera Sergeevna Aksakova, *Dnevnik, 1854–1855* (St. Petersburg: Ogni, 1913);

Elena Ivanovna Annenkova, *Gogol' i Aksakovy* (Leningrad: LGPI, 1983);

Konstantin Konstantinovich Arsen'ev, "I. S. Aksakov kak poet," in *Kriticheskie etiudy po russkoi literature,* volume 2 (St. Petersburg: M. M. Stasiulevich, 1888);

Vissarion Grigor'evich Belinsky, *Polnoe sobranie sochinenii,* volume 11 (Moscow: Akademiia Nauk SSSR, 1956), p. 534;

Natan Iakovlevich Eidel'man, *Tainye korrespondenty "Poliarnoi zvezdy"* (Moscow: Mysl', 1966);

Iuliia Ivanovna Gerasimova, *Iz istorii russkoi pechati i period revoliutsionnoi situatsii kontsa 1850-kh–nachala 1860-kh godov* (Moscow: Kniga, 1974);

A. I. Gertsen, *Sobranie sochinenii,* volume 26 (Moscow: Akademiia Nauk SSSR, 1963);

Nikolai Vasil'evich Gogol, *Polnoe sobranie sochinenii,* volume 13 (Moscow: Akademiia Nauk SSSR, 1952), p. 47;

Nikolai Vasil'evich Iakovlev, "Shchedrin i Aksakovy v 50-kh godakh," in *Trudy Otdela novoi russkoi literatury,* volume 1 (Moscow & Leningrad: Akademiia Nauk SSSR, 1948);

Vladimir Anatol'evich Kitaev, *Iz istorii ideinoi bor'by v Rossii v period pervoi revoliutsionnoi situatsii: Aksakov v obshchestvennom dvizhenii nachala 60-kh godov XIX veka* (Gor'ky: Gor'kovskii gosudarstvennyi universitet, 1974);

Kitaev, "Slavianofily v pervye poreformennye gody," *Voprosy istorii,* 6 (1977);

Viacheslav Anatol'evich Koshelev, *Esteticheskie i literaturnye vozzreniia russkikh slavianofilov: 1840–1850-kh godov* (Leningrad: Nauka, 1984);

Mikhail Konstantinovich Lemke, *Epokha tsenzurnykh reform 1859–1865 godov* (St. Petersburg: Gerol'd, 1904);

Konstantin Nikolaevich Lomunov, ed., *Literaturnye vzgliady i tvorchestvo slavianofilov: 1830–1850-e gg.* (Moscow: Nauka, 1978);

Sergei Aleksandrovich Nikitin, *Slavianskie komitety v Rossii v 1858–1876 godakh* (Moscow: Izdatel'stvo Moskovskogo universiteta, 1960);

Aleksandr L'vovich Ospovat, "Aksakov i *Russkii arkhiv:* K istorii izdaniia pervoi biografii F. I. Tiutcheva," *Fedorovskie chteniia 1979* (1982);

Vasili Igorevich Porokh, "Aksakov: Redaktor *Dnia,*" in *Osvoboditel'noe dvizhenie v Rossii,* vol. 5 (Saratov: Izdatel'stvo Saratovskogo universiteta, 1975);

Porokh, "Otnosheniia Aksakova k 'krest'ianskoi reforme' 1861 goda (po neopublikovannym pis'mam)," in *Nekotorye voprosy otechestvennoi i vseobshchei istorii,* edited by V. M. Gokhlerner (Saratov: Izdatel'stvo Saratovskogo universiteta, 1971);

Igor' Vasil'evich Porokh and Vasilii Igorevich Porokh, "Gertsen i Aksakov na rubezhe 50–60-kh godov XIX veka," in *Revoliutsionnaia situatsiia v Rossii v seredine XIX veka: Deiateli i istoriki,* edited by Militsa Vasil'evna Nechkina and others (Moscow: Institut istorii AN SSSR, 1986);

Mikhail Ivanovich Sukhomlinov, *Issledovaniia i stat'i po russkoi literature i prosveshcheniiu,* volume 2 (St. Petersburg, 1889);

Nikolai Ivanovich Tsimbaev, *I. S. Aksakov v obshchestvennoi zhizni poreformennoi Rossii* (Moscow: Izdatel'stvo Moskovskogo universiteta, 1978);

Tsimbaev, *Slavianofil'stvo: Iz istorii russkoi obshchestvennoi-politicheskoi mysli XIX veka* (Moscow: Izdatel'stvo Moskovskogo universiteta, 1986);

Semen Afanas'evich Vengerov, "Ivan Sergeevich Aksakov," in *Kritiko-biograficheskii slovar' russkikh pisatelei i uchenykh,* 6 volumes (St. Petersburg, 1889–1904), I;

Andrzej Walicki, *The Slavophile Controversy: History of a Conservative Utopia in Nineteenth-Century Russian Thought* (Oxford: Clarendon Press / New York: Oxford University Press, 1975);

M. N. Zubkov, "Predshestvenniki Nekrasova v sozdanii narodnoi geroicheskoi epopei (I. S. Aksakov, I. S. Nikitin)," in *Nekrasovskii sbornik,* 4 (1967).

Papers:

Ivan Sergeevich Aksakov's archival materials are held mainly at the Institute of Russian Literature (IRLI, Pushkin House), in St. Petersburg, in fond 3 (poetry, correspondence); at the Russian National Library (RNB), fond 14 (correspondence) and fond 696 (scrapbook on Aksakov, 1859–1910); and at the Russian State Historical Archive (RGIA), fond 772 (censored material). In Moscow, materials on Aksakov are held at the Russian State Archive of Literature and Art (RGALI), fond 10.

Pavel Vasil'evich Annenkov

(19 June 1813? – 20 March 1887)

John Mohan
Grinnell College

BOOKS: *Materialy dlia biografii Pushkina,* volume 1 of *Sochineniia,* by Aleksandr Sergeevich Pushkin, 7 volumes, edited by Annenkov (St. Petersburg, 1855); republished as *A. S. Pushkin. Materialy dlia ego biografii i otsenki proizvedenii* (St. Petersburg: Obshchestvennaia pol'za, 1873);

Nikolai Vladimirovich Stankevich. Biograficheskii ocherk (Moscow: Katkov, 1857);

Aleksandr Sergeevich Pushkin v Aleksandrovskuiu epokhu. 1799–1826 g. (St. Petersburg: M. Stasiulevich, 1874);

Vospominaniia i kriticheskie ocherki 1849–1868, 3 volumes (St. Petersburg: M. Stasiulevich, 1877–1881)–includes volume 1 (1877)–includes "N. V. Gogol' v Rime letom 1841 goda" and "Fevral' i mart v Parizhe 1848 goda"; volume 2 (1879)–includes "Zametki o russkoi literature 1848 goda," "Kharakteristiki: I. S. Turgeneva i gr. L. N. Tolstogo," "S. T. Aksakov i ego *Semeinaia khronika,*" "Literaturnyi tip slabogo cheloveka–Po povodu Turgenevskoi 'Asi,'" "Delovoi roman v nashei literature: *Tysiacha dush,* roman A. Pisemskogo," "Nashe obshchestvo v *Dvorianskom gnezde* Turgeneva," "*Groza* Ostrovskogo i kriticheskaia buria," "Russkaia belletristika v 1863 godu," "Russkaia sovremennaia istoriia v romane I. S. Turgeneva *Dym,*" and "Istoricheskie i esteticheskie voprosy v romane gr. L. N. Tolstogo *Voina i mir*"; and volume 3 (1881)–includes *Zamechatel'noe desiatiletie. 1838–1848 gg. Iz literaturnykh vospominanii;*

P. V. Annenkov i ego druz'ia: Literaturnye vospominaniia i perepiska 1835–1885 gg. (St. Petersburg: A. S. Suvorin, 1892)–includes "Idealisty tridtsatykh godov. Biograficheskii etiud," "Zapiska o N. P. Ogareve," "Pis'ma iz-za granitsy (1841–1847)," "Parizhskie pis'ma (1846–1847)," "Pis'mo iz Kieva," and "K istorii rabot nad Pushkinym";

Literaturnye vospominaniia (St. Petersburg, 1909)–includes "Molodost' I. S. Turgeneva: 1840–1856" and "Shest' let perepiski s I. S. Turgenevym: 1856–1862";

Literaturnye vospominaniia, with an introduction by V. P. Dorofeev (Moscow, 1960)–includes "Dve zimy v

Pavel Vasil'evich Annenkov

provintsii i derevne. S genvaria 1849 po avgust 1851 goda."

Editions: *Literaturnye vospominaniia,* with a preface by N. Piksanov and an introduction and notes by Boris Mikhailovich Eikhenbaum (Leningrad: Academia, 1928);

Literaturnye vospominaniia, with an introduction by Vasilii Ivanovich Kuleshov (Moscow: Khudozhestvennaia literatura, 1983);

Parizhskie pis'ma, edited and with essays by I. N. Konobeevskaia (Moscow: Nauka, 1983);

Materialy dlia biografii A. S. Pushkina, 2 volumes, with an introduction by K. V. Shilov and commentary by A. L. Ospovat and N. G. Okhotin (Moscow, 1985);

Pushkin v Aleksandrovskuiu epokhu, edited by A. I. Garusov (Minsk: Limarius, 1998);

Pushkin: Materialy dlia biografii Aleksandra Sergeevicha Pushkina (Moscow: TERRA-Knizhnyi klub, 1999);

Kriticheskie ocherki, edited by I. N. Sukhikh (St. Petersburg: Izdatel'stvo Russkogo khristianskogo gumanitarnogo instituta, 2000).

Edition in English: *The Extraordinary Decade,* translated by Irwin R. Titunik, edited and with an introduction by Arthur P. Mendel (Ann Arbor: University of Michigan Press, 1968)–includes "Two Winters in the Provinces and the Country."

OTHER: Aleksandr Sergeevich Pushkin, *Sochineniia,* 7 volumes, edited by Annenkov (St. Petersburg: Eduard Prats, 1855–1857).

SELECTED PERIODICAL PUBLICATIONS–UNCOLLECTED: *Provintsial'nye pis'ma,* in *Sovremennik,* 8 (1849), 10 (1849), 12 (1849), 1 (1850), 3 (1850), 5 (1850), 9 (1850), 1 (1851), 10 (1851);

"Iz perepiski s I. S. Turgenevym v 60-kh godakh," edited by Annenkov, *Vestnik Evropy,* 1–2 (1887);

"O M. E. Saltykove-Shchedrine," with an introduction by S. Makashin, *Literaturnoe nasledstvo,* 13–14 (1934): 505–508.

Pavel Annenkov won respect and a measure of fame as a journalistic observer of European culture and politics, as a memoirist and biographer, and as the first professional Pushkinist in Russia. In addition, his reviews of important literary works from the late 1840s to the late 1860s adhered to a fairly consistent set of aesthetic and civic standards and judgmental moderation. Yet, his complex and clumsy style made him no match for the fiery declarations of radical critics–such as Nikolai Gavrilovich Chernyshevsky, Nikolai Aleksandrovich Dobroliubov, and Dmitrii Ivanovich Pisarev–who militantly sought civic usefulness in literature.

Annenkov was born Pavel Vasil'evich Annenkov in Moscow into a prosperous gentry family of the Simbirsk region on 19 June 1813; some sources give 1812 as the year of his birth, but the consensus settles on the year 1813. His father was Vasilii Aleksandrovich Annenkov, his mother Agrapinna Fedorovna Annenkova (née Strekalova). Annenkov was slow in finding a constant path in life. He studied at the Mining Institute in St. Petersburg, leaving without a degree, and then audited courses in humanist studies at St. Petersburg University. In 1833 he began employment in the Ministry of Finances, but his duties there proved merely formal, and

he soon retired from the civil service in order to lead a broader and more interesting existence. From that time onward he pursued this goal through travel and through his acquaintances with eminent figures in Russian and European intellectual life.

Annenkov befriended Vissarion Grigor'evich Belinsky, the most influential literary critic of the time, and in 1840 the latter accompanied him as far as Kronstadt when Annenkov set sail for the first of two visits to Europe that he made in the course of the decade–the first from 1840 to 1843 and the second from 1846 to 1848. Belinsky invited Annenkov to send his travel letters to *Otechestvennye zapiski* (Notes of the Fatherland) and *Sovremennik* (The Contemporary), journals that Belinsky, headed. The principal works in Annenkov's travel genre are "Pis'ma iz-za granitsy" (Letters from Abroad, published in *Otechestvennye zapiski,* 1841–1843), his first publication, and the two series "Parizhskie pis'ma" (Parisian Letters, published in *Sovremennik,* 1847–1848) and "Fevral' i mart v Parizhe 1848 goda" (February and March in Paris in 1848, 1859–1862). Because of the tightened censorship prompted by the European revolutions of 1848, the third series of letters did not appear in the Russian periodical press until 1859. The letters at first show Annenkov to be an endlessly curious tourist–well-informed and fun-loving; then, as revolutionary forces gather in Europe, he becomes a sober, thoughtful analyst of the consequences that might result from revolution.

Two occurrences during Annenkov's sojourns in Europe had important later consequences for the author. He worked with Nikolai Vasil'evich Gogol in Rome in 1841, serving as a copyist for Gogol's novel *Pokhozhdenie Chichikova, ili Mertvye dushi. Poema* (The Adventures of Chichikov, or Dead Souls. A Narrative Poem, 1842). Years later, in 1857, for the journal *Biblioteka dlia chteniia* (A Reading Library), Annenkov wrote a reminiscence of this summer, "N. V. Gogol' v Rime letom 1841 goda" (N. V. Gogol in Rome in the Summer of 1841), which shed light on the art and vision of the mysterious Gogol. In 1847 Annenkov was with the dying Belinsky in Salzbrunn when the enraged critic wrote his well-known "Pis'mo k N. V. Gogoliu" (Letter to N. V. Gogol), an angry rejection of what Belinsky saw as Gogol's mystical retreat into the past and abandonment of a secular, progressive Russian future. Annenkov's mere presence at the creation of this document later caused him political difficulties in the reactionary atmosphere of Russia in the early 1850s.

After Belinsky's death in 1848 Annenkov replaced him at *Sovremennik* as the designated author of the annual review of literature from the past year. His one article in this capacity was "Zametki o russkoi literature 1848 goda" (Remarks on Russian Literature of the Year 1848, published in 1849). In this article he draws on his own aesthetics and Belinsky's statement that the main achievement of contemporary Russian literature was "its more and more intimate proximity to life, to reality." Accordingly, Annenkov deplores purely physiological or "daguerrotypical" portraits of life. He urges authors to get out of their rooms and depict the "life throbbing on the other side of the threshold." The novelist Ivan Sergeevich Turgenev is Annenkov's model of an author who strives to penetrate the husk of everyday life. Turgenev's *Zapiski okhotnika* (A Hunter's Sketches, 1847–1852) seeks out the beauty and variety of life that lie concealed beneath the drab outward appearance of the serf population.

The oppressive surveillance by the state and its virulent suspicion of the gentry intelligentsia caused Annenkov to retreat to his Simbirsk estate in 1849 and, for the most part, to remain there until 1851. He had reason to be fearful. In 1849 the writer Fyodor Dostoevsky was given a mock death sentence and ten years of hard labor and exile in Siberia for having circulated the letter from Belinsky to Gogol, and Annenkov had been with Belinsky during the composition of the letter. During these years, however, Annenkov managed to contribute his *Provintsial'nye pis'ma* (Provincial Letters, 1849–1851), letters that sympathetically describe peasant poverty on the banks of the Volga, to *Sovremennik*. These letters were later published as "Nakanune piatidesiatykh godov. Pis'ma iz provintsii" in volume one of *Vospominaniia i kriticheskie ocherki 1849–1868* (1877). Yet, the most important document that he produced during this self-imposed exile was a memoir written for the desk drawer. "Dve zimy v provintsii i derevne. S genvaria 1849 po avgust 1851 goda" (Two Winters in the Provinces and the Countryside: From January 1849 to August 1851) was not published until 1922, early in the Soviet era, in the journal *Byloe* (The Past); it was collected in book form only in 1960. The memoir is a blistering assault on the obtuse censorship of the time, on massive corruption in every branch of the economy, and on the pathological self-satisfaction and self-delusion of Tsar Nicholas I.

One bright event took place during Annenkov's sojourn at Chirikovo, his Simbirsk estate. Because of his brother Ivan's connections, he was approached by the widow of the great poet Aleksandr Sergeevich Pushkin and asked to consider editing a collection of her late husband's works. Natal'ia Nikolaevna Pushkina (née Goncharova; she became Lanskaia in her second marriage) sent trunks of the poet's papers to Annenkov. Greatly impressed by the value of these papers, he still felt trepidation at the complex and time-consuming burden to which he had been assigned. Capital was needed, and the political atmosphere had to change. Almost immediately, however, Annenkov produced a seven-volume *Sochineniia* (Works, 1855–1857), the first collection of Pushkin's materials and verses, which could be located previously only in various journals of Pushkin's time. Annenkov also wrote the introductory volume of the collection, *Materialy dlia biografii Pushkina* (Materials for a Biography of Pushkin, 1855). Focused on literary analysis and devoid of biographical information that might offend surviving members of the Pushkin family, *Materialy dlia biografii Pushkina* also reflects Annenkov's caution about the censorship in the final years of the reign of Tsar Nicholas I. When the rule of the censor waned under Alexander II, he returned to the archives in the 1870s and wrote more comprehensive studies of Pushkin.

Annenkov returned to literary criticism in the mid 1850s, by which time Chernyshevsky and, later, Dobroliubov had replaced Belinsky as the most influential sources of literary thought and journalistic writing. One strand of Belinsky's varied approaches to literature became the central passion in the writings of Chernyshevsky and Dobroliubov—namely, the conviction that literature should promote sociopolitical change, with the accompanying demands that authors in their works should favor the public sphere over the private sphere; that heroes and heroines should be exemplars of firm, progressive thinking and acting; and that thought and judgment should prevail over such literary considerations as imagination, subtle characterization, and love and longing. This cluster of beliefs formed the background against which Annenkov framed his most representative literary reviews between 1855 and 1868.

The title of Annenkov's mid-decade article expresses its guiding concern—"O mysli v proizvedeniiakh iziashchnoi slovesnosti" (On Thought in Works of Belles Lettres, published in *Sovremennik*, 1855). The article was republished as "Kharakteristiki: I. S. Turgeneva i gr. L. N. Tolstogo" (Characterizations: I. S. Turgenev and Count L. N. Tolstoy) in volume two of *Vospominaniia i kriticheskie ocherki 1849–1868*. The two works by Turgenev under review in this article are the stories "Dva priiatelia" (Two Friends, 1854) and "Zatish'e" (A Quiet Spot, 1854). Annenkov shows how Turgenev, without straying beyond the confines of literature, addresses a chronically recurrent figure in Russian literature—the *lishnii chelovek* (superfluous man), a literary character who thinks much but does little. The heroes of both stories fit this well-known type. According to Annenkov, in bodying forth such characters, Turgenev serves society in the sense that repeated exposure of them in literature will diminish their occurrence in life.

In the same article Annenkov expresses complete satisfaction with two of Leo Tolstoy's early works, *Detstvo* (Childhood, 1852) and *Otrochestvo* (Boyhood, 1854), which he likewise praises for their avoidance of explicit teachings. The child and boy constitute the central consciousness of both works, with only minimal interference by the adult narrator. In Annenkov's view the two stories organically reveal the measured growth of a young person, from vague early impressions of life through an uncertain awareness of family and society to, finally, a lucid perception of life and the world. He lauds the manner in which Tolstoy allows the "vital action of the narrative" to make the necessary revelations in this tales.

In his next article, "S. T. Aksakov i ego *Semeinaia khronika*" (S. T. Aksakov and His *Family Chronicle,* published in *Sovremennik,* 1856), Annenkov examines the distinction between reality and literary realism. In *Semeinaia khronika* (1856) Sergei Timofeevich Aksakov writes about his family and their way of life before he, the author, was born. Annenkov was the first to identify this work as a novel rather than a chronicle. For him, Aksakov—while drawing on family lore—is animated by purely creative impulses, and the author artistically liberates the novel from the distant reality that it depicts, cleansing the work of the "accidental features" and factual burdens that, though appropriate to a chronicle, weaken the novel as a genre. Aksakov adroitly uses selectivity and typicality to re-create, in a recognizable form, life on a remote eighteenth-century Russian estate.

The article on Aksakov in 1856 was Annenkov's last publication in *Sovremennik.* His subsequent writings appeared in several different journals, including *Atenei* (The Atheneum), *Biblioteka dlia chteniia,* and, most particularly, *Russkii vestnik* (The Russian Messenger) and *Vestnik Evropy* (The European Messenger). Annenkov's next critical article responded to an attack by Chernyshevsky—now the chief critic of *Sovremennik*—on Turgenev's story "Asia." In his critique of Turgenev's tale Chernyshevsky decrees that Hamlet-like characters are unnecessary, even dangerous, to the cause of transforming Russia. He first condemns love stories in general, insisting that the public has a greater interest in political reforms, and then deplores the hesitant romantic behavior of the hero: N.N. awakens love in Asia, a beautiful young woman, but flees the scene in the face of her love. In Chernyshevsky's view, if well-educated and moderate men cannot cope with love, they consequently lack the resolve needed to play important roles in public life. Annenkov's "Literaturnyi tip slabogo cheloveka–Po povodu Turgenevskoi 'Asi'" (The Weak Person as a Literary Type–On Turgenev's "Asia"), first published in *Atenei* (1858), responds to Chernyshevsky with the proposition that Turgenev's outwardly inactive characters are inwardly active; they shape themselves alone, without precedent models. Their "parents" and Russia have been unable to instill in them that self-governing ethic that—in Annenkov's idealized view of the West—every European nation begins to cultivate in children still in the cradle. In effect, these characters have been "orphaned." Turgenev's diffident personages may be divided, "weak" people, but Annenkov prefers them to the unreflective, "whole" peo-

ple who aspire to guide Russia. As a Westernizer, he sees long-bearded, pre-Petrine Russians lurking under Western dress and manners, just waiting for the opportunity to reclaim the nation, this time as despots of the left. Their opponents, Annenkov argues, should be a population of "weak" people, that is, people resistant to strident calls for action, since they are aware of the complexity of human beings and society. He asks in whose hands Asia would be safer, those of N.N. or those of a "whole" person. The subtextual implication is that Annenkov is really inquiring about the safety of Russia herself.

For Annenkov, the prerequisite for convincing literary realism is that the author have a deep understanding of the class and setting of the novel or tale. He approved of the way Turgenev had artistically entered the world of the enserfed peasantry in *Zapiski okhotnika.* In "Delovoi roman v nashei literature: *Tysiacha dush,* roman A. Pisemskogo" (The Novel of Public Life in Our Literature: A. Pisemsky's *One Thousand Souls,* published in *Atenei,* 1859), Annenkov praises novelist Aleksei Feofilaktovich Pisemsky for his persuasive representation of a provincial town and its inhabitants. However, as Pisemsky's hero ascends the bureaucratic ladder to a post in St. Petersburg and then becomes governor of his home province, the novel loses its moorings in realism because of "the writer's lack of access to the inner codes and workings of society's upper strata." By contrast, Annenkov's "Nashe obshchestvo v *Dvorianskom gnezde* Turgeneva" (Our Society in Turgenev's *A Nest of Gentry,* published in *Russkii vestnik,* 1859) declares that Turgenev has written a "large" and "calm" novel, made possible by his writing from the interior of gentry life. He also commends Turgenev for his "instinct for the most delicate poetic shades of life." Here he responds directly to Chernyshevsky's stated contempt for literary form ("Concern about form is concern about contrivances, mannerisms, about rouges and corsets").

A final example of Annenkov's conviction that authors must know their milieu can be found in his article "*Groza* Ostrovskogo i kriticheskaia buria" (Ostrovsky's *Storm* and the Critical Tempest, 1860). The tempestuous critical reaction to Aleksandr Nikolaevich Ostrovsky's play *Groza* (Storm, 1860) stemmed from one critic's insistence that, like the Russian peasantry, the "merchantry"—the subject of *Groza*—precludes literary understanding since its reality, folkways, and behavior resist the educated mind. Annenkov, by contrast, urges readers to attend to Ostrovsky's revelations of what lies beneath the surface of the merchant culture. Ostrovsky, he contends, has entered the literarily distant realm of the Russian merchant trade, has learned its language, and has replicated Turgenev's achievement in giving artistic life to a class little known to readers. A knowledge of merchant culture and language—together with the distinctive ways of life of every Russian class—will eventually bring about "a common Russian civilization."

In 1861 Annenkov married Glafira Aleksandrovna Rakovich (who, Annenkov acknowledged, had proposed to him herself) in a lavish wedding ceremony in St. Isaac's Cathedral in St. Petersburg. Two children were born to the marriage, Vera and Pavel. Annenkov's critical reviews of literature became less frequent and ultimately ended in the 1860s, and his work on Pushkin and memoirs took up much of the 1870s and 1880s. Marriage and family apparently caused him to prefer the latter genres as a liberation from the deadline pressures of literary criticism in the journals. As an illustration of these demands, his review of Russian literature in 1863 ran in eleven consecutive monthly editions of the journal *Sankt-Peterburgskaia gazeta* (St. Petersburg Gazette). From the mid 1860s the family lived abroad in Baden-Baden, Paris, Brussels, Milan, Zurich, Berlin, and Dresden. This lengthy residence in Europe should not be interpreted as government-decreed nor as a complete rejection of Russia on Annenkov's part. Like many members of the Russian gentry, Annenkov simply preferred the civilities of the West. In addition, he felt that the literary and political polemics in Russia had long since bypassed his generation. He and his family returned to Russia from time to time for visits to Chirikovo (Simbirsk), St. Petersburg, and Moscow. A particularly important visit to Moscow took place in 1880. During the special Pushkin celebrations of that year, Moscow University granted Annenkov and Turgenev honorary membership in its academic community.

Special attention must be given to Annenkov's assessments of Tolstoy and Turgenev in an 1863 survey of Russian literature, titled "Russkaia belletristika v 1863 godu" (Russian Belles Lettres in 1863, published in *Sankt-Peterburgskie vedomosti*, 1863), in which he reviewed Tolstoy's novel *Kazaki* (The Cossacks, 1863). Usually opposed to the incursions of other disciplines on literature, Annenkov hailed the marriage in *Kazaki* of ethnography and art, much in the spirit of his thoughts on Ostrovsky's *Groza*. Conscious of the growing "anti-civilization" sentiments in Tolstoy's writings, Annenkov cannot accept the validity of the hero Olenin's attempts to throw off civilization, nor can he view the Cossack village as a genuinely pastoral refuge from civilization. First of all, Olenin has not achieved the qualities of "a civilized Russian"; instead, he comes to the village suffering from the ills of a pseudocivilization, which life among the urban elite has inflicted upon him. Second, the poetic facade of the village prevents Olenin from seeing the brutal imperialistic function of the Cossacks on the Russian borderlands—a transient role, in Annenkov's opinion, and one that will change in response to an altered geopolitical situation in the Caucasus.

In the same 1863 article Annenkov battles with Pisarev, who in an article on Turgenev's novel *Ottsy i deti* (Fathers and Children, 1863) had proclaimed Bazarov, the nihilist hero of the novel, as worthy of emulation by radical youth. At first glance no one can deny Bazarov's power—which emanates from his negation of all received ideas, his determination to destroy the current structure of society, his absolute belief in science, and his contempt for art. Annenkov, however, sees in Bazarov an identical twin to Oblomov, the notoriously lazy hero of Ivan Aleksandrovich Goncharov's novel of the same name, who spends hours deciding whether to get out of bed: "Try to penetrate, through all his deceptive external activities, to Bazarov's soul—you will see that he is calm in a perfectly Oblomovian way; life's sufferings and the spiritual needs of the external world cost him nothing."

Generally reluctant to allow the macrocosm of nation and society to engulf the private, microcosmic realm of the novel, Annenkov had to perform intricate reversals in his critical standards when he wrote "Russkaia sovremennaia istoriia v romane I. S. Turgeneva *Dym*" (Russia's Contemporary History in I. S. Turgenev's Novel *Smoke*) for *Vestnik Evropy* in 1867. *Dym* is a direct and severe frontal assault on the Russian doctrinaires of the time—the unyielding aristocrats, the radical opponents of the existing order, and the Slavophiles. Since all three groups were hostile to Westernizers, like Annenkov and Turgenev, who advocated measured, evolutionary change, the critic suspends his preference for a many-sided literary representation of reality and praises the polemical vigor of the novel. In Annenkov's judgment the "needed word" had to be said, and Turgenev's bitter novel said it.

In "Istoricheskie i esteticheskie voprosy v romane gr. L. N. Tolstogo *Voina i mir*" (Historical and Aesthetic Questions in the Novel *War and Peace* by Count L. N. Tolstoy), first published in *Vestnik Evropy* (1868), Annenkov admires the seamless way Tolstoy joins history and art and the manner in which he sews the fates of empires together with the fates of both elite Russian families and simple peasants. The leading characters in the private spheres of the novel meet and interact with luminaries in the public sphere—the crowned heads of three empires and principal aides on both the French and Russian sides of the Napoleonic Wars. In addition, in this review of the first three volumes of *Voina i mir* (the six volumes of the novel appeared 1868–1869) Annenkov praises Tolstoy's characterization of people in the private circles of the narrative, so that his heroes and heroines confidently occupy the same ground as the Pan-European war. Yet, not all aspects of *Voina i mir* please Annenkov. For example, the episodic structure of the novel may ease its movement back and forth across a continent and between Moscow, St. Petersburg, and country estates, but this narrative device does not permit deep characterization. Annenkov pictures the main characters as changing behind the scenes of the narrative, in preparation for their next appearance in the expansive sweep of the novel. He claims that the reader sees "the characters and situations when the process of transformation has already been performed over them—we do not know the process itself." Annenkov's Westernizing orientation causes him to attack Natasha Rostova, one of the most beloved heroines in Russian literature. One cannot deny that Tolstoy locates in the Rostov family a positive embodiment of unlearned instinctual Russian values. By contrast, Annenkov scolds Natasha for her reliance on instinct—particularly in the first three volumes of the book, the limit of his review—to the exclusion of acquired knowledge, and he views her as "the poetic countess-child Natasha Rostova, who did not receive the least moral education in the home, subjected to all the temptations of her own organism and troubled thoughts, which forced her from childhood to fall in love left and right."

In the early 1870s Annenkov returned to the trunks of Pushkin materials left to him by the poet's widow. In a period of relaxed censorship he wrote *Aleksandr Sergeevich Pushkin v Aleksandrovskuiu epokhu. 1799–1826 g.* (Aleksandr Sergeevich Pushkin in the Age of Czar Alexander I, published in *Vestnik Evropy,* 1873–1874). In this biographical study of Pushkin, which is far more comprehensive than had been possible earlier, Annenkov portrays the poet as an orphaned child in a desert. His parents had shallow educational roots, with fluency in French and a good library as their only redemptive virtues. The renowned lycée at Tsarskoe Selo offered the young Pushkin only a sham education. After graduation from this hollow institution, Pushkin entered high society and found there only ruinous pastimes. Whatever passed for ideas in elite circles were imported and deformed. Only Arzamas, the loosely organized literary club, provided Pushkin with a sanctuary from the mindless society of the time. In opposition to Aleksandr Semenovich Shishkov's Beseda liubitelei russkogo slova (Colloquy of Lovers of the Russian Word), which prescribed conservative principles for the literary language, for literary topics, and, ultimately, for political life, Arzamas celebrated creative independence, reformist political goals, and irreverent humor.

During his Southern exile between 1820 and 1824 Pushkin embraced Byronism. Annenkov contends that the cult of the English poet may have had a true appeal in the time and place of its origins, but it did not arise from Russian conditions. Pushkin's unhappiness and wild behavior in the South derived from his rootless Byronic posturing. By contrast, his exile at Mikhailovskoe proved fruitful, largely because of his

study of William Shakespeare. From Shakespeare he borrowed certain devices in crafting *Boris Godunov* (1825)—for example, blank-verse iambic pentameter, stately poetic speeches, a sense of national history, and the use of folk humor and traditions. Yet, he absorbed as well Shakespeare's consciousness of the world and humanity as manifold, polyphonic, and complex.

Finally, Annenkov's study of Pushkin's papers calls into question the public view of Pushkin's creativity as spontaneous and effortless. Annenkov examined page after page of corrected and recorrected lyrics and prose, and he came to the conclusion that this toil paid moral and civic dividends. First, Pushkin's practice of his craft proved lifesaving: "It smoothed life's sharp manifestations, softened and ennobled all that was accidental, coarse, improper, and harsh in them." Second, readers preoccupied by the challenges of transforming Russia can draw strength from Pushkin's polished art and thought: "But who will not add to the list of *practically* useful subjects the science of thinking *nobly* and acting *nobly* in which Pushkin was a teacher still unsurpassed today?"

Much about Annenkov the person is revealed in his large memoir, *Zamechatel'noe desiatiletie. 1838–1848* (The Extraordinary Decade: 1838–1848, published in *Vestnik Evropy,* 1880). The author recalls and characterizes the remarkable people of those ten years, a period that gave birth to Russian social thought. He himself appears as a moderate man among immoderate men. Of the European luminaries whom Annenkov judges most severely, Karl Marx is first and foremost. He recalls attending a meeting over which Marx presided like a "democratic dictator incarnate." The charismatic Russian rebels of the decade dominate the memoir: Mikhail Aleksandrovich Bakunin, Alexander Herzen (Aleksandr Ivanovich Gertsen), and Belinsky. Annenkov suggests that Bakunin and Herzen became captives of the extreme idea and the extreme stance and that they clung to that idea and stance for purposes of self-dramatization, even when the reality around them no longer required their extremism. Nicknamed "neistovyi Vissarion" (the furious Vissarion) by friends and foes alike, Belinsky seemed the exact model of an immoderate man, but Annenkov describes him as both an intensively active and intensively reflective figure, one who resisted fixity or stasis in his convictions, even at the risk of seeming foolish and inconsistent.

When the seriously ill Turgenev in 1882 sensed his imminent death, he gave Annenkov permission to use his archives as he saw fit. In the years between Turgenev's death in 1882 and the end of Annenkov's own life in 1887, Annenkov published a three-part series consisting of two substantial biographical studies, "Molodost' I. S. Turgeneva, 1840–1856" (I. S. Turgenev's Youth, 1840–1856,

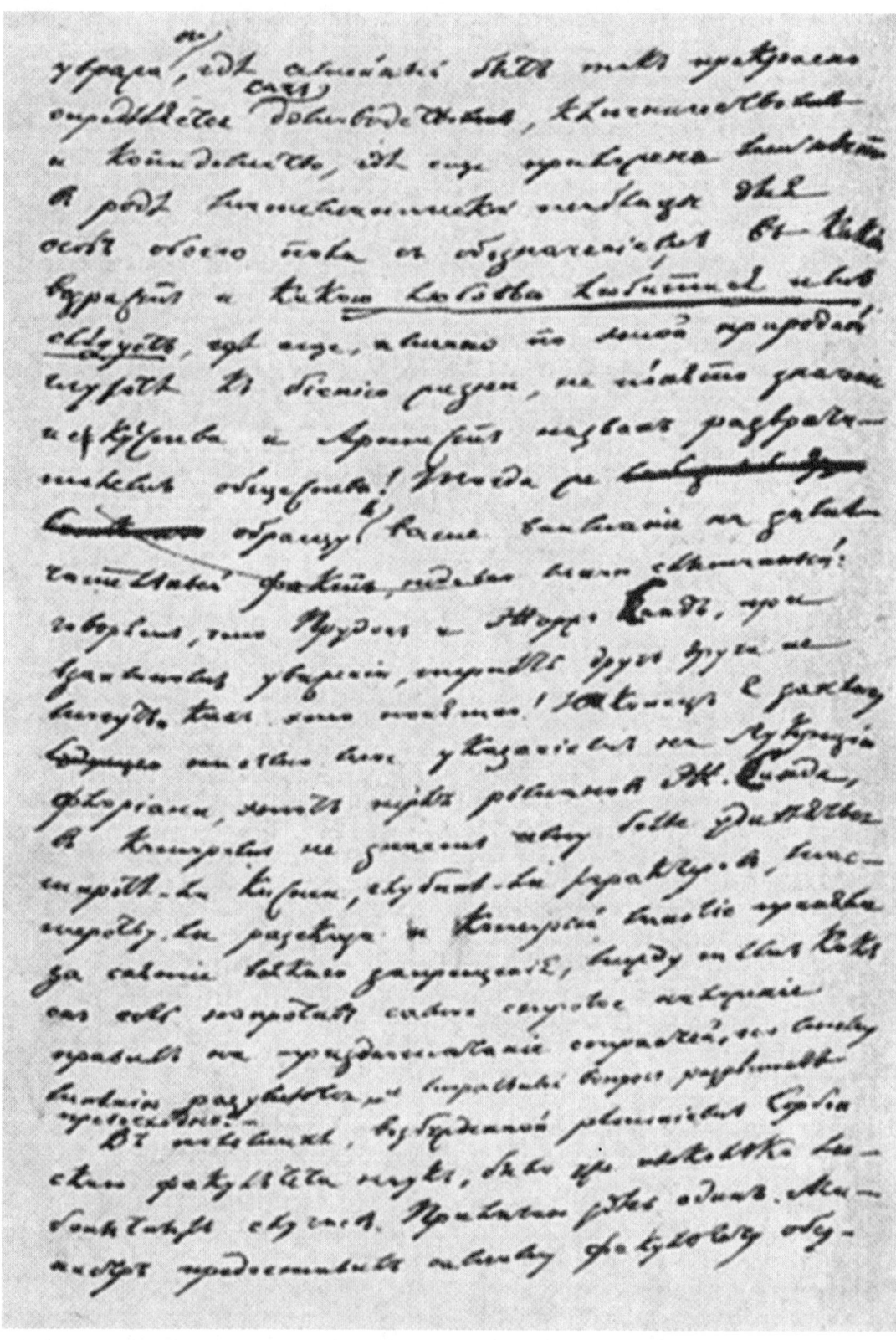

Page from the manuscript for Annenkov's Parizhskie pis'ma *(Parisian Letters), first published in the journal* Sovremennik
(The Contemporary) from 1847 to 1848 (from Annenkov, Parizhskie pis'ma, *1983)*

published in *Vestnik Evropy,* 1884) and "Shest' let perepiski s I. S. Turgenevym, 1856–1862" (Six Years of Correspondence with I. S. Turgenev, 1856–1862, published in *Vestnik Evropy,* 1885), as well as an annotated collection of Turgenev's letters, "Iz perepiski s I. S. Turgenevym v 60-kh godakh" (From Correspondence with I. S. Turgenev in the 1860s, published in *Vestnik Evropy,* 1887). In addition to insights into Turgenev's life and works, this series reveals the important services that Annenkov performed for Turgenev over many years–running errands in large and small matters, representing the author in legal affairs, and acting as the final authority on the readiness of Turgenev's novels and stories for publication. On one famous occasion Turgenev had summoned Annenkov to his home in order to determine whether the manuscript of his novel *Nakanune* (On the Eve) should be burned. "The fireplace," Annenkov wrote, "proved unnecessary." By the time Annenkov published the final installment of his three-part series on Turgenev, his health was failing. He died in Dresden on 20 March 1887 and was buried there.

To Annenkov's close circle of friends, he was a lovable man. In a letter to him in 1847 Belinsky concluded with a tribute to "my stout-bellied one, whom I adore, not mystically, but rationally." More than four decades later, when Turgenev's close friend the novelist Gustave Flaubert died in 1880, the Russian author wrote to his lifetime companion, Pauline Viardot: "Next to your family and Annenkov, this was, I believe, the man whom I loved above all others on earth." Not everyone, however, warmed to Annenkov's amiability. In a letter of 1857 Tolstoy granted that he was "happy and bright" but accused him of "foggy vaporizing and various insincere political effusions." While many commentators saw this latter trait reflected also in Annenkov's writing style, the secondary literature abounds in praise of his works. For example, commenting in "Nekrolog: Pavel Vasil'evich Annenkov" (Obituary: Pavel Vasil'evich Annenkov, published in *Vestnik Evropy,* 1887) on Annenkov's letters written from Europe in the 1840s, Aleksandr Nikolaevich Pypin characterized them as "those of a tourist who knew how to assess the broad phenomena of intellectual and literary life." In *A History of Russian Literature* (1955) Prince Dmitrii Petrovich Mirsky (who wrote as D. S. Mirsky) called *Aleksandr Sergeevich Pushkin v Aleksandrovskuiu epokhu* "a masterpiece of social history, indispensable to any student of Russian civilization." On the basis of *Zamechatel'noe desiatiletie* Leonard Schapiro named Annenkov "possibly the outstanding memoirist of the century" in *Turgenev: His Life and Times* (1978).

Evaluations of Pavel Vasil'evich Annenkov's literary criticism tend to be more mixed and qualified. In *Istoriia russkoi kritiki vosemnadtsatogo–deviatnadtsatogo vekov* (A History of Russian Criticism of the Eighteenth to Nineteenth Centuries, 1972) Vasilii Ivanovich Kuleshov, a

Soviet historian of Russian literary criticism, upbraided Annenkov for promoting "pure art," one who encouraged in literature "idleness and an apolitical quality." Kuleshov nevertheless advised readers that, under the layer of Annenkov's "wan style," one can find "a certain aesthetic acumen." American judgments of Annenkov's criticism are more positive. In his *Dictionary of Russian Literature* (1956) William E. Harkins grouped Annenkov, in an admiring way, among the few Russian critics who did not seek the importance of literature beyond the text itself. Viktor Terras praised Annenkov in *Belinskij and Russian Literary Criticism: The Heritage of Organic Aesthetics* (1974) for his "energetic insistency on the autonomy of art." And R. H. Stacy wrote in *Russian Literary Criticism: A Short History* (1974) that Annenkov "brought to bear on the books he read if not the acumen of genius, at least a cultivated and liberal taste." Indeed, Annenkov spent almost five decades in devoted, honest, and industrious labors on behalf of Russian literature.

Letters:

Letters to Aleksei Feofilaktovich Pisemsky, *Nov',* 20 (1888): 199–205;

Letters to Ivan Sergeevich Turgenev, with an introduction by L. Maikov, *Russkoe obozrenie,* 3–5 (1898);

M. M. Stasiulevich i ego sovremenniki v ikh perepiske, 5 volumes edited by Mikhail Konstantinovich Lemke (St. Petersburg, 1912), III: 292–451;

Letters to Turgenev, edited by M. Beliaev, *Literaturnaia mysl',* 1 (Petrograd, 1922): 188–207;

Letters to Turgenev, edited by N. M. Mendel'son, *Trudy Publichnoi biblioteki SSSR im. V. I. Lenina,* 3 (1934): 47–176, 275–279;

Letters to I. V. and F. V. Annenkov, *Literaturnoe nasledstvo,* 50 (1950): 182, 190–194.

Bibliographies:

Dmitrii Dmitr'evich Iazykov, "Literaturnye trudy P. V. Annenkova. (Bibliograficheskii ocherk)," *Istoricheskii vestnik,* 6 (1887): 656–659; republished in Iazykov's *Obzor zhizni i trudov pokoinykh russkikh pisatelei,* volume 7 (Moscow, 1892), pp. 5–7;

B. Koz'min, "Gertsen, Ogarev i ikh okruznie. Rukopisi, perepiska i dokumenty," *Biulleten' Goslitmuzeia,* 5 (Moscow, 1940): 5–9.

Biography:

Iu. V. Volodina, *Zhizn' i literaturno-kriticheskaia deiatel'nost' Annenkova* (Kuibyshev, 1973).

References:

Isaiah Berlin, "A Remarkable Decade," in *Russian Thinkers* (New York: Viking, 1978), pp. 114–209;

Boris Fedorovich Egorov, *Bor'ba esteticheskoi idei v Rossii serediny XIX v.* (Leningrad, 1982), pp. 212–258;

Egorov, "Esteticheskaia kritika bez laka i bez degtia," *Voprosy Literatury,* 5 (1965), pp. 142–160;

Egorov, "P. V. Annenkov–literator i kritik 1840-kh i 1850-kh gg.," *Trudy po russkoi i slavianskoi filologii,* volume 11 (Tartu, 1968): 51–108;

Vasilii Ivanovich Kuleshov, *Istoriia russkoi kritiki vosemnadtsatogo–deviatnadtsatogo vekov* (Moscow: Prosveshchenie, 1972), pp. 216, 225;

P. L. Lavrov, "Russkii turist 40-kh gg.," *Delo,* 8, part 2 (1877): 24–40;

Lavrov, "Turist-estetik," *Delo,* 10, part 2 (1879): 1–24;

John Michael Mohan, "The Literary Criticism of P. V. Annenkov," dissertation, Cornell University, 1981;

N. I. Prutskov, "'Esteticheskaia' kritika (Botkin, Druzhinin, Annenkov)," in *Istoriia russkoi kritiki,* 2 volumes, edited by Boris Pavlovich Gorodetsky and others (Moscow & Leningrad: AN SSSR, 1958), I: 450–469;

Aleksandr Nikolaevich Pypin, "Nekrolog: Pavel Vasil'evich Annenkov," *Vestnik Evropy,* 4 (1887): 884–891;

Leonard Schapiro, *Turgenev: His Life and Times* (New York: Random House, 1978), p. 105;

Viktor Terras, *Belinskij and Russian Literary Criticism: The Heritage of Organic Aesthetics* (Madison: University of Wisconsin Press, 1974), p. 231;

Iu. V. Volodina, "Annenkov–literaturnyi kritik," in *Russkaia kritika i istoriko-literaturnyi protsess,* edited by Viktor Alekseevich Bochkarev, Ivan Vladimirovich Popov, and M. S. Silina (Kuibyshev: Kuibyshevskii gosudarstvennyi pedagogicheskii institut imeni V. V. Kuibysheva, 1983).

Papers:
Pavel Vasil'evich Annenkov's papers are located in Moscow at the Russian State Archive of Literature and Art (RGALI), fond 7, and in St. Petersburg at the Institute of Russian Literature (IRLI, Pushkin House), fond 7 and fond 661, and at the Russian National Library (RNB), fond 23.

Aleksei Nikolaevich Apukhtin

(15 November 1840 – 17 August 1893)

Thomas P. Hodge
Wellesley College

BOOKS: *Stikhotvoreniia* (St. Petersburg: F. S. Sushchinsky, 1886); enlarged as *Sochineniia,* 2 volumes (St. Petersburg: M. M. Stasiulevich, 1895; enlarged edition, St. Petersburg: A. S. Suvorin, 1896; enlarged again, 1898; enlarged again, 1900)– *Stikhotvoreniia* (1886) includes "Minuty schast'ia," "Ni vesel'ia, ni sladkikh mechtanii . . . ," "Nochi bezumnye, nochi bessonnye . . . ," "O bud' moei zvezdoi . . . ," "Rekviem," and "Sud'ba: K 5-i simfonii Betkhovena"; *Sochineniia* (1895) includes "A. S. Dargomyzhskomu," "Dnevnik Pavlika Dol'skogo," "Iz arkhiva grafini D**: Povest' v pis'makh," "Grafu L. N. Tolstomu," "Kniaz' Tavrichesky," "Mezhdu smert'iu i zhizn'iu: Fantasticheskii rasskaz," "Pevets vo stane russkikh kompozitorov," and "Podrazhanie drevnim"; *Sochineniia* (1896) includes "Diletant" and "Ia zhdal tebia . . . Chasy polzli ynylo . . .";

Izbrannye stikhotvoreniia (New York: Rabochee knizhnoe izdatel'stvo, 1919);

Lirika (Berlin: Mysl', 1921);

Sochineniia A. N. Apukhtina, volume 1 (Berlin: Presse, 1924);

Sochineniia (Paris: Illiustrirovannaia Rossiia, 1936);

Stikhotvoreniia, edited, with an introduction, by Vsevolod Aleksandrovich Rozhdestvensky, Biblioteka poeta, Malaia seriia, no. 50 (Moscow & Leningrad: Sovetskii pisatel', 1938);

Stikhotvoreniia, compiled, with an introduction, by N. A. Kovarsky with notes by R. A. Shatseva, Biblioteka poeta, Bol'shaia seriia (Leningrad: Sovetskii pisatel', 1961)–includes "Dorógoi: P. I. Chaikovskomu," "K slavianofilam," "Kakoe gore zhdet menia?" "Mne bylo vcselo vchera na stsene shumnoi . . . ," and "P. Chaikovskomu";

Pesni moei otchizny. Stikhi. Proza, with an introduction by R. V. Iezuitova (Tula: Priokskoe knizhnoe izdatel'stvo, 1985);

Polnoe sobranie stikhotvorenii, edited by Iu. A. Andreev and others, with an introduction by M. V. Otradin

Aleksei Nikolaevich Apukhtin, 1880 (Museum of the Institute of Russian Literature, St. Petersburg)

(Leningrad: Sovetskii pisatel', 1991)–includes "Selo Kolotovka";

Stikhotvoreniia, compiled, with an introduction, by S. F. Dmitrenko (Moscow: Sovetskaia Rossiia, 1991).

Editions and Collections: *Sochineniia* (St. Petersburg: A. S. Suvorin, 1905);

Sochineniia (St. Petersburg: A. S. Suvorin, 1907);

Sochineniia (St. Petersburg: A. S. Suvorin, 1912);

Stikhotvoreniia, with an introduction by L. Afonin (Orel, 1959);

Sochineniia. Stikhotvoreniia. Proza, compiled by Andrei Fedorovich Zakharkin, with an introduction by M. V. Otradin (Moscow, 1985);

Stikhotvoreniia (Moscow: Gelikon, 1993);

Mezhdu smert'iu i zhizn'iu (Moscow: Rodnaia rech', 19–?);

Izbrannoe. Poeziia i proza (Moscow: Eksmo Press, 2000).

Editions in English: *From Death to Life,* translated by R. Frank and E. Huybers, in *Gems of Russian Literature* (New York: R. Frank, 1917);

"The Archive of Countess D–," in *Great Russian Short Stories,* edited by Stephen Graham (London: Benn, 1929), pp. 386–445;

"Between Life and Death," in *Russian Tales of the Fantastic,* translated by Marilyn Minto (London: Bristol Classical Press, 1994), pp. 141–171;

Three Tales, translated by Philip Taylor (Madison, N.J.: Fairleigh Dickinson University Press, 2002; London & Cranbury, N.J.: Associated University Presses, 2002)—comprises "The Papers of Countess D**: A Tale in Letters," "The Diary of Pavlik Dolsky," and "Between Life and Death: A Fantastic Story."

OTHER: *Skladchina,* with contributions by Apukhtin, Prince Petr Andreevich Viazemsky, and others, edited by Ivan Aleksandrovich Goncharov and others (St. Petersburg: A. M. Kotomin, 1874);

Gusliar: Sbornik stikhov, with contributions by Apukhtin (St. Petersburg: E. A. Evdokimov, 1887);

Para gnedykh (Stikhotvorenie), music by S. Donaurov, words by Apukhtin (St. Petersburg: M. Karlin, 1896);

Stikhotvoreniia A. Apukhtina, F. Tiutcheva i Golenishcheva-Kutuzova dlia detei, with contributions by Apukhtin (St. Petersburg: O. N. Polov, 1910);

Izbrannye stikhotvoreniia, with contributions by Apukhtin (Moscow, 1913);

"Iz Shillera," in *Fridrikh Shiller: Stat'i i materialy,* edited by R. M. Samarin and S. V. Turaev (Moscow: Nauka, 1966);

Izbrannoe, by Apukhtin, Ia. P. Polonsky, and A. K. Tolstoy (Moscow: Moskovskii rabochii, 1982).

Aleksei Apukhtin was a talented late-nineteenth-century poet who deserves credit as a gifted and witty litterateur; his lyric verse occasionally reaches the quality of that produced by his illustrious elder contemporaries, Afanasii Afanas'evich Fet and Fedor Ivanovich Tiutchev. A fundamentally apolitical person living in a fiercely politicized era, Apukhtin generally sought to distance himself from firm ideological stances in both his life and his art. While his poetic legacy is large and rich, his contemporaries felt that he failed to live up to the promise he had shown as a child prodigy. He wrote much fine lyric poetry,

but perhaps Apukhtin's most striking works are his dramatic first-person monologues, meant especially for declamation and aural pleasure.

Aleksei Nikolaevich Apukhtin was born the first child of Nikolai Fedorovich Apukhtin and Mar'ia Andreevna (Zheliabuzhskaia) Apukhtina on 15 November 1840 in the town of Bolkhovo, Orel Province. The registry of births gives the date as 16 November 1840, but all his life Apukhtin celebrated his birthday on the fifteenth. In an autobiographical note that he wrote to scholar Semen Afanas'evich Vengerov late in life, Apukhtin himself erroneously named the year as 1841, a mistake that has been repeated in many sources. His father was a retired major whose estate was located in the village of Pavlodar, in the Kozel'sk district of Kaluga Province. Apukhtin's family on both sides was descended from old gentry stock.

A weak and sickly boy, he received much attention from Mar'ia Andreevna, his doting mother. He later wrote in a letter (14 February 1856) to P. A. Valuev that she was "a woman of wonderful intelligence endowed with a warm and sympathetic heart and the most refined artistic taste. I . . . am indebted to her for the impulses in my heart to express my feelings." Mother and son formed an exceptionally close bond that lasted until she died in 1859. Mar'ia Andreevna arranged for an excellent domestic education for the young Apukhtin at Pavlodar, and he proved to be a precocious boy with a superb memory who learned by heart the verse of Aleksandr Sergeevich Pushkin and Mikhail Iur'evich Lermontov before the age of ten. In addition to declaiming the works of these and other Russian poets, Apukhtin was, as he himself recalled, composing his own poems by the age of nine (as noted in Modest Il'ich Chaikovsky's "Aleksei Nikolaevich Apukhtin" [1912]).

In 1852 Apukhtin entered the preparatory class of the elite Imperial School of Jurisprudence in St. Petersburg, an institution founded in 1835 to prepare young men from gentry families for top posts in the legal bureaucracy of Russia, especially in the Ministry of Justice. Famous alumni included composer Aleksandr Nikolaevich Serov (class of 1840), Slavophile poet Ivan Sergeevich Aksakov (class of 1842), and music critic Vladimir Vasil'evich Stasov (class of 1843). Because one of the most active participants in the 1849 Petrashevsky Affair (an anti-autocratic conspiracy of Russian radicals) had been a graduate of the school, by the time Apukhtin arrived the once cozy, family-like institution had been reorganized to impose near-military discipline on its pupils.

Future composer Petr Il'ich Chaikovsky had entered the school in 1850, but both he and Apukhtin graduated in 1859, since the latter's excellent preparation allowed him to advance a grade. Apukhtin and Chaikovsky were the same age, and they became close friends at school, where Apukhtin was given the nickname "Lëlia." On 15 June 1856 the poet wrote "Dorógoi: P. I. Chaikovskomu" (On the Way: To P. I. Chaikovsky, 1961), a reminiscence of a boat excursion that the two boys took on the Neva River:

> Vse zamolklo. Ne kolyshet
>   Sonnaia volna . . .
> Serdtse zhadno volei dyshit,
>   Negoi grud' polna,
> I pod mernoe kachan'e
>   Bleshchushchei lad'i
> My molchim, taia dykhan'e
>   V sladkom zabyt'i . . .
>
> (Everything has fallen silent. The sleepy water
>   Does not stir . . .
> My heart greedily breathes liberty,
>   My breast is full of languor,
> And amid the measured rocking
>   Of the sparkling boat
> We say nothing, holding our breath
>   In sweet oblivion . . .)

Apukhtin was from an early age exclusively homosexual, and he likely helped introduce Chaikovsky to gay social circles in St. Petersburg during and after their school years. The two remained friends for the rest of their lives—though with relatively frequent fallings-out for the rest of their lives—and six of Apukhtin's poems later served as vocal texts for the famous composer.

Apukhtin excelled in school, earning a reputation as a "future Pushkin" among his schoolmates; he was venerated by pupils and administrators alike for his sharp wit and intellectual brilliance. His earliest extant poem, "K rodine" (To My Homeland), was written on 15 June 1853 to celebrate his return home to Pavlodar after his first year at school. He wrote several more poems the following summer and autumn, including "Epaminond" (Epaminondas)—a tribute to the heroism of General Vladimir Alekseevich Kornilov, who had been killed earlier that month in the Crimean War. With the help of the school director, who greatly admired Apukhtin, this poem was published in the 6 November 1854 issue of *Russkii invalid* and signed "A. Apukhtin, pupil of the Imperial School of Jurisprudence, fifth grade, age 14." The same signature appeared below "Podrazhanie arabskomu: Oda na rozhdenie Velikoi Kniazhny Very Konstantinovny" (Imitation of the Arabic: Ode on the Birth of Grand Princess Vera Konstantinovna), published in *Russkii invalid* on 2 April 1855; the poem was received and acknowledged by the royal family. Apukhtin became renowned for his performances in amateur theatricals, Literaturnyi fond (The Literary Fund), a charity founded by distinguished men of letters to raise funds for needy writers and their families.

Apukhtin, circa 1855 (Museum of the Institute of Russian Literature, St. Petersburg)

Apukhtin registered his delight with thespianism in a poem written in 1859, "Mne bylo veselo vchera na stsene shumnoi . . ." (I had a merry time yesterday on the noisy stage . . . , published 1961). In spite of his academic and artistic triumphs his health was so poor that he was forced to delay his spring 1858 examinations until the following fall, and he spent his entire senior year (1858–1859) in the school infirmary.

Apukhtin soon made the personal acquaintance of many writers, including such major figures as Leo Tolstoy and Ivan Sergeevich Turgenev. In February 1858 he wrote a widely circulated parody of Fet's "Lesom my shli po tropichke edinstvennoi . . ." (We went through the woods on the only path . . . , published in *Russkii vestnik* [The Russian Messenger], 1858). When Fet and Turgenev paid a visit to the Apukhtin estate in July, Apukhtin quickly wrote a verse encomium by way of apology: "A. A. Fetu" (To A. A. Fet).

Apukhtin's glorious school days ended in tragedy; as he sat for his graduation examinations on 23 April 1859, his mother unexpectedly died. Devastated, the young poet wrote "Kakoe gore zhdet menia?" (What woe awaits me?, first published in 1961), one of five poems he composed that summer to commemorate her. Another of them, "Ni vesel'ia, ni sladkikh mechtanii . . ." (Neither merriment nor sweet daydreams . . . , 1886), includes this verse epitaph for Mar'ia Andreevna: "You died without growing old, / Because you loved too much, / Because you could not live!"

A bona fide prodigy, the prolific Apukhtin wrote more than 107 poems during his school years. He also made six translations of verse by German poets (Ludwig Rellstab, Friedrich Schiller, Nikolaus Lenau, and Heinrich Heine), two by French poets (André Chénier and Pierre-Jean de Béranger), and one by an English poet (George Gordon, Lord Byron); most of these were not published at the time and first appeared in his 1895 collection, *Sochineniia* (Works). Two of Apukhtin's original works were published, however, before he left school, while another twenty works appeared in various journals by the end of the year following his graduation. Because of Turgenev's mediation, ten of these poems appeared together in the September 1859 issue of Nikolai Alekseevich Nekrasov's influential left-leaning journal *Sovremennik* (The Contemporary) as a cycle titled "Derevenskie ocherki" (Country Sketches).

While some of the most politically oriented of his poems—for example, "K slavianofilam" (To the Slavophiles, 1961) and "Derevenskie ocherki"—date from this early period, Apukhtin mainly explored the themes of love, death, longing, memory, nostalgia, the countryside, the rhythms of nature, the arts (especially music and theater), biblical subjects, and antiquity; these subjects preoccupied him throughout his career. He deftly employed a wide variety of metrical forms—both binary and ternary—and verse genres, although his early poems tend to be short; the longest of these is "Segodnia mne ispolnilos' 17 let . . ." (Today I turned seventeen . . .), which totals 173 lines. His style is clear, forceful, and witty. His poetry from this period is often couched in classical periphrasis and at times contains suggestions of homoeroticism, as in "Podrazhanie drevnim" (Imitation of the Ancients, 1895), which he wrote in 1858.

Apukhtin's early verse displays impressive erudition and is saturated with references to, adaptations of, and quotations from Russian poets who preceded him, especially Lermontov, Pushkin, Vasilii Andreevich Zhukovsky, Evgenii Abramovich Baratynsky, Turgenev, Tiutchev, and Fet. This intertextuality is most often based on Lermontov's and Pushkin's works, but Pushkin occupied an especially exalted position for the young poet. Though many of Apukhtin's poems could be cited, perhaps he most clearly pays homage to Pushkin in "19 oktiabria 1858 goda" (19 October 1858), subtitled "Pamiati Pushkina" (In Memory of Pushkin), published as "Pamiati Pushkina. Stikotvorenie," in *Sovremennik* in 1859. Seniors from the School of Jurisprudence were invited to a commemorative ball at Pushkin's old school, the Lycée at Tsarskoe Selo, on the anniversary of its founding (19 October 1811). While his own schoolmates made merry, Apukhtin envisaged Pushkin's ghost seeking out his old comrades at the Lycée:

Uvy! gde te druz'ia? Uvy! gde tot poet?
Nevinnoi zhertvoiu pal trup ego krovavyi . . .
Piruite zh, iunoshi,—ego mezh vami net,
   On ne smutit vas derzkoi slavoi!

(Alas! Where are those friends? Alas! Where is that poet?
His bloody corpse fell as an innocent victim . . .
But enjoy your feast, young men–he's not here with you;
   He will not disturb you with his impudent fame!)

Pushkin remained a special figure for Apukhtin all his life–a sacred symbol of all that he valued and admired in Russian literature.

After earning a gold medal upon graduation from the School of Jurisprudence, Apukhtin–still grieving over the recent loss of his mother–began his service in the Ministry of Justice in May 1859. The poet never took his career as a civil servant seriously; instead, he devoted his energies to literature and the enticements of St. Petersburg high society. After his early association with radical journals, including *Sovremennik* and *Iskra* (The Spark), Apukhtin had by 1861 developed an antinihilist position, which he conveyed in "Sovremennym vitiiam" (To Our Contemporary Orators)–a poem first published in 1862 in *Vremia* (Time), a conservative journal edited by Fyodor Dostoevsky and his brother, Mikhail Mikhailovich Dostoevsky.

The ceaseless demands for social utility being made on Russian literature in the turbulent 1860s intimidated and repulsed Apukhtin, and during this decade there was a sharp drop in his artistic production: he wrote only sixty-nine lyric poems and one (fragmentary) narrative poem between 1860 and 1870. In an 1865 letter to Chaikovsky, Apukhtin proclaimed that nothing could force him "to go out into an arena crammed with dirty tricks, denunciations and . . . seminarists!" Between 1862 and 1872 Apukhtin published nothing, preferring to circulate his work in manuscript among a select group of friends.

Having attained the rank of junior assistant to a desk head in the Ministry of Justice, Apukhtin withdrew in late 1862 to his family estate in Orel Province. The poet then became senior official for special commissions and conducted legal investigations for the provincial governor. Returning to St. Petersburg in the spring of 1865, the independently wealthy Apukhtin abandoned for good his civil-service career, although he was thenceforth a nominal employee of the Interior Ministry. During this time he became extremely obese and of necessity led a sedentary life; memoirists frequently describe him as the embodiment of the corpulent, indolent Oblomov, the eponymous protagonist of Ivan Aleksandrovich Goncharov's 1859 novel. From this time forward Apukhtin left St. Petersburg only for short intervals.

He produced some significant verse in the early 1860s. Apukhtin's stay on his ancestral lands in Orel from 1863 to 1864 inspired his most ambitious attempt at a narrative poem up to that time, "Selo Kolotovka" (The Village of Kolotovka, 1991), of which only fragments remain. The 132 extant lines describe a bleak landscape and harsh conditions for the newly emancipated peasants; "Selo Kolotovka" has been described as the most Nekrasovian (after the poet Nikolai Alekseevich Nekrasov) of all Apukhtin's poems. Also written in 1863, "Sud'ba: K 5-i simfonii Betkhovena" (Fate: To Beethoven's Fifth Symphony, 1886)—dedicated to Chaikovsky in a manuscript copy—is a brilliant variation on Ludwig van Beethoven's programmatic concept of Fate knocking at the door. The short, bittersweet lyric "Minuty schast'ia" (Moments of Happiness) written in 1865, was one of the author's earliest poems to find exceptionally wide popularity with musicians; after its publication in 1886 the text was set to music by fourteen different composers. In the March 1865 issue of *Russkoe slovo,* nihilist critic Dmitrii Ivanovich Pisarev published his "Progulka po sadam rossiiskoi slovesnosti" (A Walk through the Gardens of Russian Literature), in which he attacked Pushkin as an outdated writer whose work lacked utility. In Orel an outraged Apukhtin responded by reading two public lectures on a theme, titled "O zhizni i sochineniiakh Pushkina" (On Pushkin's Life and Works), in which he explicitly defended his idol against Pisarev's critique.

The mid 1860s mark the low ebb of Apukhtin's productivity, but his prolific output of earlier years began to reappear in the second half of the decade. In 1867 he wrote "Niobeia" (Niobe), subtitled "Zaimstvovano iz *Metamorfoz* Ovidiia" (Borrowed from Ovid's *Metamorphoses*), which was first published in 1885 in *Russkaia mysl'* (Russian Thought). Apparently inspired by Fet's translation of Ovid, "Niobeia" is an amphibrachic retelling of the myth. In 1868 Apukhtin wrote "Noch' v Monplezire" (Night in Mon Plaisir, 1868) on the shore of the Gulf of Finland, in a seaside section of Peterhof known

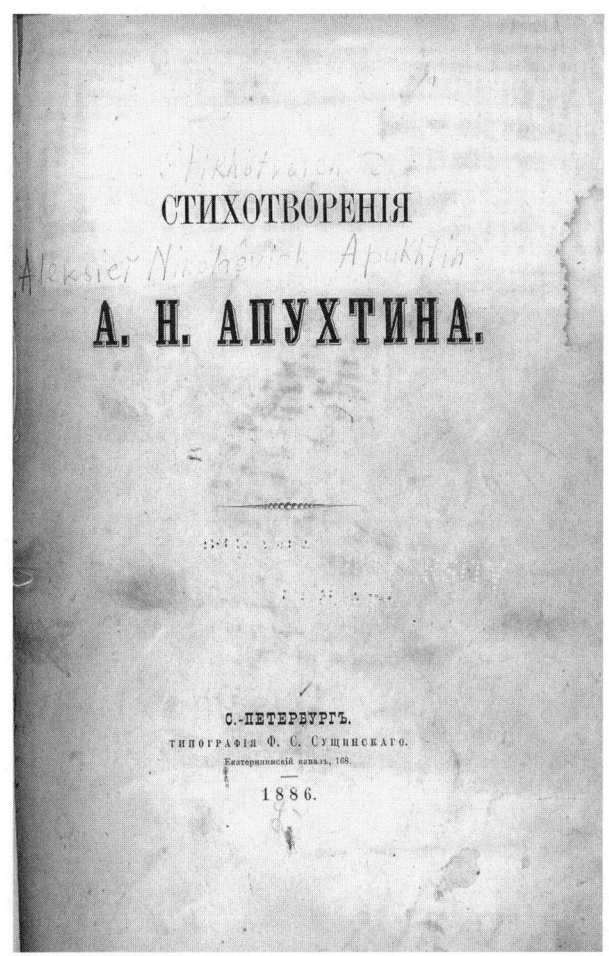

Paper cover for Apukhtin's first collection of poetry
(Main Library, Indiana University)

as Mon Plaisir; the poem compares the enigmatic movement of the dark sea to the stirring of emotion within the human soul. "Noch' v Monplezire" was first published in the journal *Grazhdanin* (The Citizen) in 1873. Also written at Peterhof that year and based on the Gospel of Matthew (chapter 26), "Molenie o chashe" (Prayer about the Cup), first published in *Russkaia mysl'* in 1885, reflects a deeply pious account of Jesus tormented by doubt in the Garden of Gethsemane.

The second half of the 1860s is a time of particular musical richness in Apukhtin's poetry. He wrote "A. S. Dargomyzhskomu" (To A. S. Dargomyzhsky, 1895) during this period, while composer Aleksandr Sergeevich Dargomyzhsky was at work on his opera *Kamennyi gost'* (The Stone Guest), based on Pushkin's tragedy of the same name; in the poem Apukhtin lauds the composer's ability to resurrect the great poet's work through music and even refers to Dargomyzhsky as Pushkin's brother. Apukhtin's "Rekviem" (Requiem, 1886), which also dates from the late 1860s, especially pleased poet and

Apukhtin in 1886 (drawing by V. A. Bobrov; from Petr Alekseevich Nikolaev, ed., Russkie pisateli, 1800–1917: *Biograficheskii slovar', 1989)*

Grand Prince Konstantin Konstantinovich Romanov, who recommended that Chaikovsky set the piece to music. Although the composer rejected it on the grounds that its philosophical passages made it antithetical to musical treatment, the poem is a powerful reconsideration of the Catholic requiem mass. At approximately the same time Apukhtin himself sent Chaikovsky his short poem "O, bud' moei zvezdoi . . ." (O, be my star and shine your quiet light on me . . . , 1886) in the hopes that it might serve as the text for an art song, but this text, too, the composer rejected. Once published, however, "O bud' moei zvezdoi" served as a song text for eighteen other composers, making it one of the most musically attractive of Apukhtin's poems. Even more alluring for musical transposition was the elegiac love song "Ia zhdal tebia . . . Chasy polzli ynylo . . ." (I waited for you . . . The hours crawled dolefully . . . , 1896), written in 1867

for a gypsy singer; the text was appropriated by twenty composers.

In the summer of 1870 Apukhtin made his long-awaited pilgrimage to Pushkin's grave at the monastery of Sviatye gory (Sacred Hills), south of Pskov. Later that summer he settled into an apartment in St. Petersburg on Italian Street where he remained for nearly two decades. Severely overweight and in poor health, Apukhtin rarely left his abode, though he made short trips to Moscow, Revel' (Tallinn), Kiev, and Orel Province. In spite of his steadfast indifference to the West throughout his life, Apukhtin made two visits to Europe. The first, on doctor's orders, was to Karlsbad to take the waters during May and June of 1872. The second, which took place in 1874, was a tour of northern Germany, southern France, Milan, and Venice.

While intended as a humorous jab at modern Russian society, Apukhtin's "Diletant" (Dilettante, 1896), which he wrote in the early 1870s, discusses the poet's real desire to remain aloof from the ideological fray. Apukhtin pointedly refers to himself as a dilettante in this poem and elsewhere and explicitly links himself to the early-nineteenth-century tradition of gentry litterateurs who independently indulged their art for reasons other than political exigency or monetary remuneration. In 1872, however, his old schoolmate Prince Vladimir Petrovich Meshchersky finally convinced him to begin publishing his works again. Apukhtin, who subsequently had a falling-out with Meshchersky, described the situation in a letter of 1885 to Chaikovsky, who had also been on friendly terms with the prince: "At one time Meshchersky, showering me with exaggerated praise, convinced me to contribute to *Grazhdanin,* which brought me nothing but unpleasantness." Meshchersky, who was an openly homosexual archconservative, later became a prominent friend and adviser to both Alexander III and Nicholas II. As editor and publisher of the right-wing weekly *Grazhdanin,* he brought out seven of Apukhtin's poems from 1872 to 1873.

In the 1870s Apukhtin essayed a wide range of themes—comedic, historical, martial, and exotic—in the sixty-eight poems he wrote over the course of that decade; several of these works contain his most important tributes to contemporaneous Russian writers. The humorous "Pevets vo stane russkikh kompozitorov" (A Singer in the Camp of the Russian Composers, 1895; written in 1875) bears a title that parodies Zhukovsky's famous "Pevets vo stane russkikh voinov" (A Singer in the Camp of the Russian Warriors, 1812); the poem effectively pokes fun at the nationalist composers of the Moguchaia kuchka (Mighty Handful). In 1876 Apukhtin wrote the text that became, thanks to Chaikovsky's 1886 setting, the poet's most famous song: "Nochi bezumnye, nochi bessonnye . . ." (Senseless nights, sleepless nights . . . , 1886). Tolstoy, who particularly admired that song, was one of Apukhtin's literary heroes. "In contemporary Russian literature," Apukhtin wrote in a letter to Chaikovsky in May 1866, "there is for me only one precious name: L. Tolstoy." Apukhtin's "Grafu L. N. Tolstomu" (To Count L. N. Tolstoy, 1895), written in 1877, was a laudatory assessment of the novelist's far-reaching vision of truth. Apukhtin enclosed his "P. Chaikovskomu" (To P. Chaikovsky, 1961) in a letter to his old friend in December 1877. The poem describes the composer's difficult rise to artistic greatness, then concludes with these four lines:

A ia, konchaia put' "nepriznannym" poetom,
Gorzhus', chto ugadal ia iskru bozhestva
V tebe, togda mertsavshuiu edva,
Goriashchuiu teper' takim moguchim svetom.

(While I, finishing my journey as an "unrecognized" poet,
Am proud that I discerned the spark of divinity
In you, which then was barely glimmering,
And which now burns with such powerful light.)

In a 21 December 1877 letter to his brother Anatolii, Chaikovsky confessed, "I received today a letter from Lëlia with a wondrous poem that made me shed many tears." One of Apukhtin's last poems from the 1870s, "Otchalila lodka. Chut' brezzhil rassvet . . ." (The boat set sail. The dawn was just breaking . . . , 1879)—set to music by nineteen composers (including Sergei Sergeevich Prokof'ev)—became a most successful song text. During this same period Apukhtin wrote his first and only dramatic fragment: "Kniaz' Tavrichesky" (The Prince of Tauris, 1895), an iambic pentameter rendition of Prince Grigorii Aleksandrovich Potemkin's death scene.

In 1880 the normally stingy and retiring Apukhtin energetically collected 500 rubles—100 of which were his own—to help fund the construction in Moscow of a statue in commemoration of Pushkin. He was devastated when those who organized the dedication of the monument failed to invite him to the celebratory event.

The first collection of Apukhtin's poetry was published in 1886 with a print run of three thousand copies; the book was republished three times during his life and seven times posthumously. In the 1880s, however, Apukhtin's productivity fell even further, and he produced only forty-six poems. The reasons seem to have been both ill health and artistic disillusionment, which he recorded in his bitter poem "Muze" (To My Muse) of February 1883:

Umolkni navsegda. Tosku i serdtsa zhar
Ne vystavliai vragam dlia uteshen'ia . . .
Prokliat'e vam, minuty vdokhnoven'ia,
Prokliatie tebe, nenuzhnyi pesen dar!
(Be silent forever. Do not display my pain and heart's fire
For the amusement of my enemies . . .
A curse upon you, O moments of inspiration,
And a curse upon you, O needless gift of song!)

Nonetheless, in the summer of 1883 Apukhtin created his most powerful work, "God v monastyre. Otryvki iz dnevnika" (A Year in a Monastery. Diary Excerpts, published in *Russkaia mysl'* in 1885). The poet himself referred to "God v monastyre" as a *poema* (narrative poem) and *kvazipoema* (quasi-narrative poem), but it can also be viewed as a cycle of twenty-three lyrics, each taking the form of a journal entry from a single year. The result is a dynamic monologue describing the thoughts and emotions of a thirty-year-old novice as he meditates on his new monastic life, questions his faith, recalls the beau monde, wrestles with illness, and agonizes over the woman he loved and with whom he parted. In the end, at the close of his novice year, the narrator decides to abandon the monastery on the eve of taking vows and plunge back into the secular world, leaving his diary behind to justify his decision to the monks whom he abandons. "God v monastyre" was Apukhtin's favorite text from among all his works, and he imbued it with great stylistic variety and adapted many autobiographical incidents for it. The entry for 2 May, "'Ona byla tvoia!' sheptal mne vecher maia . . ." ("She was yours!" the May evening whispered to me . . .), which also functions well as an autonomous lyric poem, attracted more composers than any other text in his career; it received twenty-two different musical settings. "God v monastyre" was adapted by composer Mariia Andreevna Danilevskaia into an opera called *Prizrak* (The Phantom), which premiered at the Mariinskii Theater in St. Petersburg on 13 April 1912.

In 1889, with his health continuing to decline, Apukhtin moved to an apartment on Kirochnaia Street in St. Petersburg. During the last years of his life he was forced to remain in a seated position, because lying down made breathing difficult; walking about his apartment for a mere twenty paces winded him and demanded several minutes' recuperation. Apukhtin's interest in prose increased sharply at this time, and he embarked on a long, untitled novel devoted to the transition from Nicholas I's rule to the era of "Great Reforms" under Alexander II, against the backdrop of the defeat of Russia in the Crimean War. He abandoned this project after completing approximately one-fourth of it and began working on *povesti* (long stories), eventually finishing three of them, each of which is narrated in the first person. In spite of the warm reception that these prose works received when he read them to friends, Apukhtin refused permission to have them published, and they did not appear until after his death, in his 1895 *Sochineniia*. "Iz arkhiva grafini D**: Povest' v pis'makh" (From the Archive of Countess D.: A Tale in Letters, 1895), is a distinctive epistolary work, because none of the letters is written by the central character (Countess Ekaterina Aleksandrovna D.); they come instead from nine of her correspondents. Her complicated personality and the events of one year of her life must be pieced together from her acquaintances' various accounts. In 1891 Apukhtin wrote his second *povest'*, "Dnevnik Pavlika Dol'skogo" (The Diary of Pavlik Dol'sky, 1895), which presents a protagonist descended from Chulkaturin in Turgenev's *Dnevnik lishnego cheloveka* (Diary of a Superfluous Man, 1850). Pavel Matveevich Dol'sky, taken ill in his late forties, begins to examine his life through a journal and narrate its various stages, including his quiet love for a seventeen-year-old girl—which in the end leads him to accept his old age. "Mezhdu smert'iu i zhizn'iu: Fantasticheskii rasskaz" (Between Death and Life: A Fantastic Story, 1895), Apukhtin's last prose work, was completed in 1892 and describes the supernatural events surrounding the death of Prince Dmitrii Aleksandrovich Trubchevsky. He dies after a long coma but remains conscious and is able to observe the repulsive histrionics of his mourners; in the end, Trubchevsky's spirit enters the body of a baby newly born to one of his servants.

In the autumn of 1891 the first signs of dropsy appeared in Apukhtin, but a course of therapy kept the malady at bay until it returned in February 1893. A superficial lessening of his symptoms in midsummer prompted him to move once more, to an apartment on Million Street. Soon thereafter, however, Apukhtin's condition drastically worsened. During the last few days of his life, one memoirist records, he desperately recited Pushkin's poetry whenever he regained consciousness, and spoke of nothing else. Apukhtin died at the age of fifty-two on 17 August 1893 and was buried in the Nikol'skoe kladbishche (Nikola Cemetery) in the Aleksandr Nevsky monastery in St. Petersburg. In the 1950s his grave was moved to the Literatorskie mostki (Writers' Platform) section of the Volkovskoe kladbishche (Volkovka Cemetery) in Leningrad, where his gravestone bears a long excerpt from his poem "Rekviem."

Aleksei Nikolaevich Apukhtin, who cultivated a reputation as a hedonistic aesthete, tends to be remembered today chiefly as the source of numerous art-song texts, especially for Chaikovsky. Ninety of Apukhtin's works—roughly one-third of all the poetry he wrote in his life—were set to music, most of them by more than one composer. Admittedly, he moved in musical circles and frequently submitted his poems to the attention of the composers he knew, and his contribution to Russian musical life in his day was profound. Nonetheless, he has been unjustly relegated to the ranks of third-rate lyricists who served as thralls to the burgeoning Russian art-song enterprise of the late 1800s. Apukhtin was instead one of the more important Russian poets active during the second half of the nineteenth century, and his verse stands on its own for its effortlessness, brilliance, technical ingenuity, and impressive thematic and stylistic variety. His erudition and aesthetic outlook also mark him as a significant transitional figure from the socially conscious poetry of Nekrasov to the "decadence" of Konstantin Dmitrievich Bal'mont and the renaissance of Russian verse ushered in by the symbolists during the first decade of the twentieth century.

Letters:

Modest Il'ich Chaikovsky, *Zhizn' Petra Il'icha Chaikovskogo,* volume 1 (Moscow: P. Iurgensen, 1900), pp. 241–243;

To Chaikovsky, *Golos minuvshego,* 1–4 (1919): 100;

L. N. Tolstoy, edited by E. Zaidenshnur, *Literaturnoe nasledstvo,* 37–38 (1939): 441–442;

Petr Il'ich Chaikovsky, *Pis'ma k rodnym,* volume 1 (Moscow: Muzgiz, 1940), p. 706.

Bibliographies:

Pamiatnaia knizhka pravovedov XX vypuska 1859, part 2 (St. Petersburg, 1894), pp. 8–14;

Kseniia D. Muratova and G. M. Sheveleva, eds., *Pisateli Orlovskogo kraia: Biobibliograficheskii slovar'* (Orel: Orlovskoe otdelenie Priokskogo knizhnogo izdatel'stva, 1981), pp. 20–21.

Biographies:

D. D. Iazykov, "A. N. Apukhtin. Nekrolog," *Moskovskie vedomosti,* 20 August 1893, p. 4;

Modest Il'ich Chaikovsky, "Aleksei Nikolaevich Apukhtin: Biograficheskii ocherk," in *Sochineniia,* by Apukhtin, volume 1 (St. Petersburg: M. M. Stasiulevich, 1895);

A. Skabichevsky, "Nechastnyi schastlivets," *Russkaia mysl',* 5 (1895);

M. Protopopov, "Pisatel'-diletant," *Russkoe bogatstvo,* 2 (1896);

A. V. Zhirkevich, "Poet milostiiu bozhiei," *Istoricheskii vestnik,* 11 (1906);

A. Raich, "K biografii Apukhtina," *Istoricheskii vestnik,* 2 (1907);

Modest Il'ich Chaikovsky, "Aleksei Nikolaevich Apukhtin," in *Sochineniia,* by Apukhtin (St. Petersburg: A. S. Suvorin, 1912);

Anatolii Fedorovich Koni, *Na zhiznennom puti,* volume 2 (St. Petersburg, 1913), pp. 125–129.

References:

V. G. Bertenson, "Za tridtsat' let," *Istoricheskii vestnik,* 6 (1912);

G. P. Blok, "Iz peterburgskikh vospominanii," *Tynianovskii sbornik,* 2 (1986): 161–162;

A. K. Borozdin, "Sovremennye literaturnye deiateli: A. N. Apukhtin," *Istoricheskii vestnik,* 5 (1895);

V. Burenin, "Kriticheskie ocherki," *Novoe vremia,* 3 (10 February 1895);

E. V. Ermilova, "Lirika 'bezvremen'ia' (Konets veka)," in *Kniga o russkoi liricheskoi poezii XIX veka: Razvitie stiliia i zhanra,* edited by Vadim Valieranovich Kozhinov (Moscow, 1978), pp. 269–277;

Pavel Petrovich Gromov, *A. Blok: Ego predshestvenniki i sovremenniki* (Leningrad: Sovetskii pisatel', 1966), pp. 31–52;

Vasilii Vasil'evich Iakovlev, "Chaikovsky i Apukhtin," in *Izbrannye trudy o muzyke,* volume 1 (Moscow, 1964);

I. Iampol'sky, "Sochineniia Apukhtina," *Literaturnoe obozrenie,* 13–14 (1938): 81–85;

N. Korobka, "Na poroge upadka," in *Ocherk literaturnykh nastroenii* (St. Petersburg, 1903), pp. 24–71;

P. Krechetov, "Orlovskie poety," *Orlovskii vestnik,* 21 April 1893;

A. Krukovsky, "Poeziia Apukhtina," *Filologicheskie zapiski,* 1 (1914);

K. P. Medvedsky as K. Govorov, "Prozaicheskie proizvedeniia Apukhtina," *Russkii vestnik,* 4 (1895);

Medvedsky as Govorov, *Sovremennye poety* (St. Petersburg, 1889);

Vladimir Petrovich Meshchersky, *Moi vospominaniia,* part 1 (St. Petersburg, 1897), pp. 33–34;

Meshchersky, Obituary on Apukhtin, *Grazhdanin,* 20 August 1893;

A. Narkevich, "Poety kontsa XIX veka v 'Biblioteke poeta,'" *Voprosy literatury,* 12 (1964): 200–205;

V. S. Nechaeva, "Epigony 'svetskogo stilia' v russkoi poezii kontsa XIX veka," *Literatura i marksizm,* 1 (1929);

Petr Alekseevich Nikolaev, ed., *Russkie pisateli, 1800–1917: Biograficheskii slovar',* 4 volumes (Moscow: Sovetskaia Entsiklopediia, 1989–);

P. Pertsov, *Filosofskoe techenie russkoi poezii* (St. Petersburg: M. Merkushev, 1896);

Alexander Poznansky, *Tchaikovsky: The Quest for the Inner Man* (New York: Maxwell Macmillan International, 1991);

A. Stolypin, "Ustritsy i stikhi v kabinete: Iz literaturnykh vospominanii," *Stolitsa i usad'ba,* 10 (1914): 8–9;

A. Volynsky, "Literaturnye zametki," *Severnyi vestnik,* 11 (1891);

Sergei Zalygin, *Literaturnye zaboty* (Moscow: Sovetskaia Rossiia, 1982), pp. 341–342.

Papers:

Aleksei Nikolaevich Apukhtin's archival materials are held mainly in St. Petersburg and may be found at the Russian State Historical Archive (RGIA), fond 1284 and fond 931; at the Institute of Russian Literature (IRLI, Pushkin House), fond 377; at the Russian National Library (RNB); and at the St. Petersburg State Historical Archive (SPbGIA), fond 355. In Moscow, Apukhtin's papers are housed at the Russian State Archive of Literature and Art (RGALI), fond 1002; and at the State Archive of the Russian Federation (GARF), fond 644 and fond 652.

Mikhail Aleksandrovich Bakunin

(18 May 1814 – 1 July 1876)

Marshall S. Shatz
University of Massachusetts–Boston

BOOKS: *17e anniversaire de la révolution polonaise* (Paris, 1847);

Aufruf an die Slaven (Köthen, 1848); Russian version published as *Vozzvanie k slavianam* (Berlin: G. Shteinits, 1904);

Narodnoe delo: Romanov, Pugachev, ili Pestel'? (London: Trübner, 1862);

K ofitseram russkoi armii (Geneva: Nechaevskaia organizatsiia, 1870);

Nauka i nasushchnoe revoliutsionnoe delo (Geneva: Czerniecki, 1870);

Vsesvetnyi revoliutsionnyi soiuz sotsial'noi demokratii. Russkoe otdelenie. K russkoi molodezhi (Geneva: Czerniecki, 1870);

L'Empire knouto-germanique et la révolution sociale, part 1 (Geneva, 1871); Russian version published as *Knuto-germanskaia imperiia i sotsial'naia revoliutsiia* (Moscow: Fraternité, 1907);

Gosudarstvennost' i anarkhiia, anonymous (Zurich & Geneva, 1873); translated by C. H. Plummer, edited by J. F. Harrison (New York: Revisionist Press, 1976);

Dieu et l'état, excerpt of *L'Empire knouto-germanique et la révolution sociale,* edited by Carlo Cafiero and Elisée Reclus (Geneva, 1882); Russian version published as *Bog i gosudarstvo* (Leipzig & St. Petersburg: Mysl', 1906); translated by Benjamin Tucker as *God and the State* (Boston, 1883; revised, London, 1910);

Parizhskaia kommuna i poniatie o gosudarstvennosti. S pis'mom P. A. Kropotkina k izdatelem Anarkhicheskoi biblioteki (Geneva: Novaia russkaia tipografiia, 1892); republished as *Pervyi opyt sotsial'noi revoliutsii = La commune de Paris et la notion d'état* (Moscow: Ravenstvo, 1906);

Oeuvres, 6 volumes, edited by Max Nettlau and James Guillaume (Paris: Stock, 1895–1913)–includes *L'Empire knouto-germanique et la révolution sociale,* part 2;

Rechi na kongresse Ligi mira i svobody (Berlin: G. Shteinits, 1904);

Mikhail Aleksandrovich Bakunin

Federalizm, sotsializm i antiteologizm (Leipzig & St. Petersburg: Mysl', 1906);

Politika Internatsionala, with an introduction by Petr Alekseevich Kropotkin (Moscow: Svoboda, 1906);

Usypiteli (St. Petersburg: Ravenstvo, 1906);

Ispoved' i pis'mo Aleksandru II, edited by Viacheslav Polonsky (Moscow: Gosudarstvennoe izdatel'stvo, 1921);

Materialy dlia biografii Bakunina, 3 volumes, edited by Polonsky (Moscow & Petrograd: Gosudarstvennoe izdatel'stvo, 1923–1933);

Neizdannye materialy i stat'i. Sbornik (Moscow: Izdatel'stvo Vsesoiuznogo obshchestva politichnykh katorzhan i ssyl'no-poselentsev, 1926);

Archives Bakounine, 8 volumes, edited by Arthur Lehning (Leiden: Brill, 1961–1981).

Collections: *Polnoe sobranie sochinenii,* 2 volumes, edited by A. I. Bakunin (St. Petersburg: I. Balashov, 1906);

Izbrannye sochineniia, 4 volumes (London: Khleb i volia, 1915);

Izbrannye sochineniia, 5 volumes (Petrograd & Moscow: "Golos truda," 1919–1922);

Sobranie sochinenii i pisem, 4 volumes, edited by Iurii Mikhailovich Steklov (Moscow: Izdatel'stvo Vsesoiuznogo obshchestva politichnykh katorzhan i ssyl'no-poselentsev, 1934–1935);

Izbrannye filosofskie sochineniia i pis'ma (Moscow: Mysl', 1987);

Filosofiia, sotsiologiia, politika, edited, with an introduction, by V. F. Pustarnakov (Moscow: Pravda, 1989).

Editions in English: *Marxism, Freedom and the State* (London: Freedom Press, 1950);

Bakunin on Anarchy, translated and edited by Sam Dolgoff (New York: Vintage, 1971); revised as *Bakunin on Anarchism* (Montreal: Black Rose Books, 1980);

Selected Writings, translated by Steven Cox and Olive Stephens, edited by Arthur Lehning (London: Cape, 1973);

The Confession of Mikhail Bakunin, translated by Robert C. Howes, edited by Lawrence D. Orton (Ithaca, N.Y., and London: Cornell University Press, 1977);

From Out of the Dustbin: Bakunin's Basic Writings, 1869–1871, translated and edited by Robert M. Cutler (Ann Arbor, Mich.: Ardis, 1985); republished as *The Basic Bakunin. Writings: 1869–1871* (Buffalo, N.Y.: Prometheus, 1992);

Statism and Anarchy, translated and edited by Marshall S. Shatz (Cambridge: Cambridge University Press, 1990).

OTHER: *Istoricheskoe razvitie Internatsionala. Sbornik,* part 1, by Bakunin and others (Zurich, 1873);

"Rechi i vozzvaniia," in *M. A. Bakunin* (St. Petersburg, 1906), pp. 113–281.

SELECTED PERIODICAL PUBLICATIONS: Johann Gottlieb Fichte, "O naznachenii uchenykh," translated by Bakunin, *Teleskop,* 25 (1835);

Georg Wilhelm Friedrich Hegel, "Gimnazicheskie rechi Gegelia," translated by Bakunin, *Moskovskii nabliudatel',* 16 (March 1838);

"O filosofii," *Otechestvennye zapiski,* 4 (1840);

"Die Reaktion in Deutschland," as Jules Elysard, in *Deutsche Jahrbücher für Wissenschaft und Kunst,* 5, nos. 247–251 (17–21 October 1842), pp. 985–1002; translated by Mary-Barbara Zeldin as "The Reaction in Germany," in *Russian Philosophy,* 4 volumes, edited by James M. Edie, James P. Scanlan, and Zeldin (Chicago: Quadrangle, 1965), I: 385–406.

Mikhail Bakunin was the foremost exponent of revolutionary anarchism in the nineteenth century. He was politically active from the 1840s to the 1870s, a turbulent period in European history in which efforts were made to extend the democratization begun by the French Revolution, industrial workers emerged as a significant social force, and movements arose for national unification or independence. Bakunin participated in all these developments. His most important writings elaborated the social and political principles of anarchism, and his organizational and propagandistic efforts laid the foundations of an international anarchist movement. His anarchist views were the product of a long intellectual and political evolution, however, and appeared in fully developed form only in the last decade of his life.

Bakunin was born Mikhail Aleksandrovich Bakunin, the son of a Russian noble landowner, on 18 May 1814 at Priamukhino, the family estate in Tver province. His father, Aleksandr Mikhailovich Bakunin, had been educated in Italy and served there in the Russian diplomatic corps. He retired to his estate, married a much younger woman, Varvara Aleksandrovna Murav'eva, and devoted himself to educating his ten children, inspired at least in part by the pedagogical principles of Jean-Jacques Rousseau. Bakunin, the eldest son, grew up well versed in the languages, literature, and philosophy of late-eighteenth- and early-nineteenth-century Europe. As he later acknowledged, his upbringing was idyllic but bore little relation to the actual conditions of Russian life.

At the age of fourteen Bakunin was sent to the Artillery School in St. Petersburg to train for a military career. Finding military life distasteful, he retired from the army in 1835 and over his father's opposition decided to devote himself to the study of philosophy. He settled in Moscow, where he led a bohemian existence and immersed himself in the intellectual life of the city, which was dominated in the 1830s by German Romantic literature and idealist philosophy, particularly the metaphysical doctrines of Friedrich Schelling, Johann Gottlieb Fichte, and Georg Wilhelm Friedrich

Priamukhino, Bakunin's birthplace, in Tver province (from Anthony Masters,
Bakunin: The Father of Anarchism, *1974)*

Hegel. He joined the philosophical circle of Nikolai Vladimirovich Stankevich and struck up various degrees of friendship with leading members of the early Russian intelligentsia, such as the literary critic Vissarion Grigor'evich Belinsky, the future radical journalists Alexander Herzen (Aleksandr Ivanovich Gertsen) and Nikolai Platonovich Ogarev, and, a bit later, the novelist Ivan Sergeevich Turgenev. His first published works, printed in Russian journals, were translations of Fichte's *Vorlesungen über die Bestimmung des Gelehrten* (Lectures on the Vocation of the Scholar, 1794) in 1835, and two of Hegel's five *Gymnasialreden* (Gymnasium Speeches, 1809–1815), which appeared along with a preface by Bakunin in 1838.

In 1840 Bakunin immigrated to Germany to pursue his philosophical studies at the University of Berlin. He was increasingly attracted to the so-called Left Hegelians, who were drawing radical conclusions from the philosophy of Hegel. In 1842 he published in a Left Hegelian journal his first major work, an article titled "Die Reaktion in Deutschland" (translated as "The Reaction in Germany," 1965), which he cautiously signed with the pseudonym Jules Elysard; "Reaktsiia v Germanii," a Russian translation of the article, was eventually collected in Bakunin's *Sobranie sochinenii i pisem* (Collected Works and Letters, 1934–1935). Though couched in the abstract philosophical language of the Hegelian dialectic, this article hints broadly at a renewal of the French Revolution for the purpose of bringing down the old order in Europe and even in Russia. It concludes with the words that, more than any others written and spoken by him, came to be associated with Bakunin: "The passion for destruction is also a creative passion."

As Bakunin began to consort with radicals and revolutionaries, the Russian government of Tsar Nicholas I grew alarmed and finally ordered him to return home. When he refused he was sentenced in absentia to hard labor in Siberia and deprived of his rights as a nobleman. For the next several years, with no reliable means of support, he wandered around Europe making the acquaintance of various figures whose ideas had a marked influence on him; they included Wilhelm Weitling, an early exponent of communism; Karl Marx, whom he met in Paris; and Pierre-Joseph Proudhon, the French anarchist, with whom he had lengthy conversations. In 1847 he made a fiery speech at a banquet of Polish émigrés in Paris, expressing solidarity with the efforts of the Poles to throw off Russian rule and urging Poles and Russians to join forces against the despotism of Nicholas I; in the same year, this speech was published as *17e anniversaire de la révolution polonaise*. At the behest of the Russian government he was deported from France.

The overthrow of the French king Louis-Philippe in early 1848 enabled Bakunin to return to Paris, where he found the revolutionary atmosphere exhilarating. With the support of the government of the new French republic, he set out for the Prussian part of Poland, intent on stirring up revolutionary sentiment against Russia. Instead, he ended up in Prague, in the Habsburg Empire, to attend a Slav Congress that had been called by Czech leaders to defend the rights of the Slavs against German and Hungarian nationalist claims. The congress was brought to an abrupt end when an armed insurrection broke out against Austrian rule; Bakunin participated in the insurrection but managed to elude capture when it was suppressed by the authorities. His political ideology at this point was revolutionary Pan-Slavism. At the end of 1848 he published a pamphlet titled *Aufruf an die Slaven* (Appeal to the Slavs), in which he urged the overthrow of the governments of Prussia, Russia, Turkey, and especially Austria and the formation of a free federation of Slavic peoples. The pamphlet was issued in German and Polish versions and was quickly translated into other languages and widely distributed, although the first Russian version, *Vozzvanie k slavianam,* was not published until 1904. It was the first of Bakunin's writings to reach a wide audience.

Bakunin then made his way to Dresden, the capital of Saxony (where he expounded his revolutionary theories to the composer Richard Wagner), and in May of 1849 he played a leading role in an unsuccessful insurrection against the Saxon monarchy. He was arrested, tried, and sentenced to death. He was then extradited from Saxony to Austria, where he was again tried and sentenced to death for his participation in the Prague uprising, only to be extradited once again to Russia in 1851. There he was placed in solitary confinement in the Peter-Paul Fortress in St. Petersburg, the main tsarist prison for those accused of political crimes. In 1854 he was transferred to the more remote Schlüsselburg Fortress, where he remained until 1857.

The harsh conditions of Bakunin's imprisonment in three different countries took a heavy toll on him both physically and psychologically. Enforced solitude and lack of activity were particular torments for so gregarious an individual. Hoping to ameliorate his situation, at Nicholas's invitation a few months after his incarceration in Russia he wrote one of the most controversial documents of his career, his *Ispoved'* (Confession), which was first published in book form in *Ispoved' i pis'mo Aleksandru II* in 1921. Addressed directly to Nicholas I, it recounts in considerable detail his activities and contacts in Europe since his departure from Russia, mingling attempts at explanation with expressions of repentance. The document, along with Nicholas's comments on it, was discovered in the tsarist archives only after the Russian Revolution of 1917. Some have viewed it as a humiliating apology to Nicholas I and therefore, at best, a reflection of Bakunin's desperation. Others, however, have interpreted it as a clever attempt on Bakunin's part to improve his lot by

Self-portrait of Bakunin in 1829 (from Natal'ia Mikhailovna Pirumova, Bakunin, *1970)*

telling Nicholas only what he already knew or could find out from other sources, a "confession" that concealed as much as it revealed. There are places in it where Bakunin even seems to be trying to educate Nicholas about conditions in Europe and possibly win him over to his Pan-Slavist views. In any case, when read carefully and in the light of the circumstances in which it was written, the confession provides a useful autobiographical account of Bakunin's intellectual and political development in the 1840s.

The confession evidently did not satisfy Nicholas, for it produced little improvement in Bakunin's prison conditions. On the other hand, those conditions failed to break him: a letter of February 1854, which he was able to smuggle out of prison to family members, shows that he never renounced his revolutionary ideas. Not until 1857, two years after Nicholas I was succeeded by his son Alexander II, was Bakunin allowed to trade prison for lifelong banishment to Siberia. There he met and married an eighteen-year-old Polish girl named Antonia Kwiatkowska. It was an odd match in several respects: Antonia was twenty-six years his junior, had little interest in politics, and in later years had three children by one of Bakunin's Italian followers, whom she married after Bakunin's death. The peculiarities of the marriage, along with the fact that Bakunin had previously displayed only fleeting romantic interests, have led several of his biographers to put forth psychological or even psychosexual explanations not only of his personal life but also of his commitment to revolutionary upheaval. These theories are highly speculative, however, and there is no reliable evidence for them. Much about Bakunin's inner life remains unexplained, but in this stormy era of European history extreme revolutionary views were not uncommon. Moreover, in radical circles of the day, bohemian lifestyles and a deliberate flouting of social norms frequently produced unconventional unions. Bakunin's marriage seems to have been founded on mutual affection, and it endured until his death in 1876.

In 1861 Bakunin managed to elude surveillance and boarded a vessel sailing from Siberia to Japan. There he took an American ship bound for San Francisco, made his way to New York, and after a side trip to Boston (where he dined with Henry Wadsworth Longfellow at his home in Cambridge) reached London at the end of 1861. He was welcomed by his old friends Herzen and Ogarev, now also émigrés from Russia, who published an influential Russian language newspaper, *Kolokol* (The Bell), which called for radical reform of the tsarist empire. Bakunin formed a collaboration with them, but—as became increasingly clear—his revolutionary zeal, undiminished by years of imprisonment and exile, was not shared by the more moderate and skeptical Herzen. In 1862 Bakunin published a pamphlet titled *Narodnoe delo: Romanov, Pugachev, ili Pestel'?* (The People's Cause: Romanov, Pugachev, or Pestel'?). It called on Alexander II, who had emancipated the serfs in 1861 but failed to satisfy the peasants' hunger for land, to place himself at the head of a bloodless national revolution. Otherwise, Bakunin warned, the tsar faced a repetition of the great peasant rebellion of the eighteenth century led by Emel'ian Ivanovich Pugachev during the reign of Catherine II. At the beginning of 1863 a Polish insurrection against Russian rule broke out, and in February of that year, despite Herzen's misgivings, Bakunin participated in an attempt to land a shipload of armed men on the Baltic coast in support of the Poles. The expedition foundered before it reached its goal. In 1864 Bakunin and his wife, who had joined him from Siberia, moved to Italy, where they lived for the next three years.

In Italy he began to formulate the anarchist ideas that he developed and refined over the next twelve years. He also drew up the statutes for a secret organization called the International Brotherhood. This was the first in a long series of conspiratorial revolutionary societies that he tried to create during the next several years. Some historians have found these secret circles

difficult to reconcile with Bakunin's repeated warnings about the dictatorial ambitions of revolutionary elites. None of these organizations ever engaged in actual revolutionary activity.

In 1867 he moved to Switzerland, a safer haven than Italy for a revolutionary, and began to compose works that expounded his anarchist ideology, most of them in French. Bakunin was a prolific but easily distracted writer. He typically set out to discuss a particular topic, digressed at length on various other themes, and never completed his original task, even as the manuscript grew longer and longer. As a result, most of his anarchist writings are in the form of disconnected fragments, many of which were published only years after his death. The central theme of these writings, and the defining principle of Bakunin's anarchism, is his unremitting hostility to the state, and to political organization itself as the source of oppression and exploitation. The first and immediate objective of revolution must be the destruction of the state, along with all other hierarchical authorities and institutions—religious, economic, and social. A system of free federations then replaces the state, whereby local communes and voluntary associations of economic producers federate into regional and ultimately national or even international organizations. In this way the hierarchical organization of the state "from above downward" will be replaced by the free organization of society "from below upward."

These ideas are spelled out in a major work, *L'Empire knouto-germanique et la révolution sociale* (The Knouto-Germanic Empire and the Social Revolution, 1871)—a sprawling though unfinished composition, the first part of which was published in 1871 and the second part only in 1908 in Bakunin's collected *Oeuvres* (Works, 1895–1913). A fragment of this work, found after his death, was published as *Dieu et l'état* (1882). Translated into many languages, *Dieu et l'état* became the best known of his writings. It attacks not only the state but also organized religion, which Bakunin regards as a vital pillar of support for the state. He calls on man to assert his innate freedom by throwing off the twin shackles of church and state, and it contains Bakunin's characterization of the devil as the exemplar of rebellion against authority. Reversing Voltaire's famous witticism about God, Bakunin declares that if Satan did not exist, he would have to be invented.

Bakunin wrote *L'Empire knouto-germanique et la révolution sociale* against the historical background of the Franco-Prussian War, which resulted in the defeat of France in September of 1870. Thenceforth he viewed the newly formed German Empire as the bastion of reaction in Europe, much as he had viewed Austria in 1848. Just after the French military defeat he traveled to Lyons, the second largest city in France, to participate

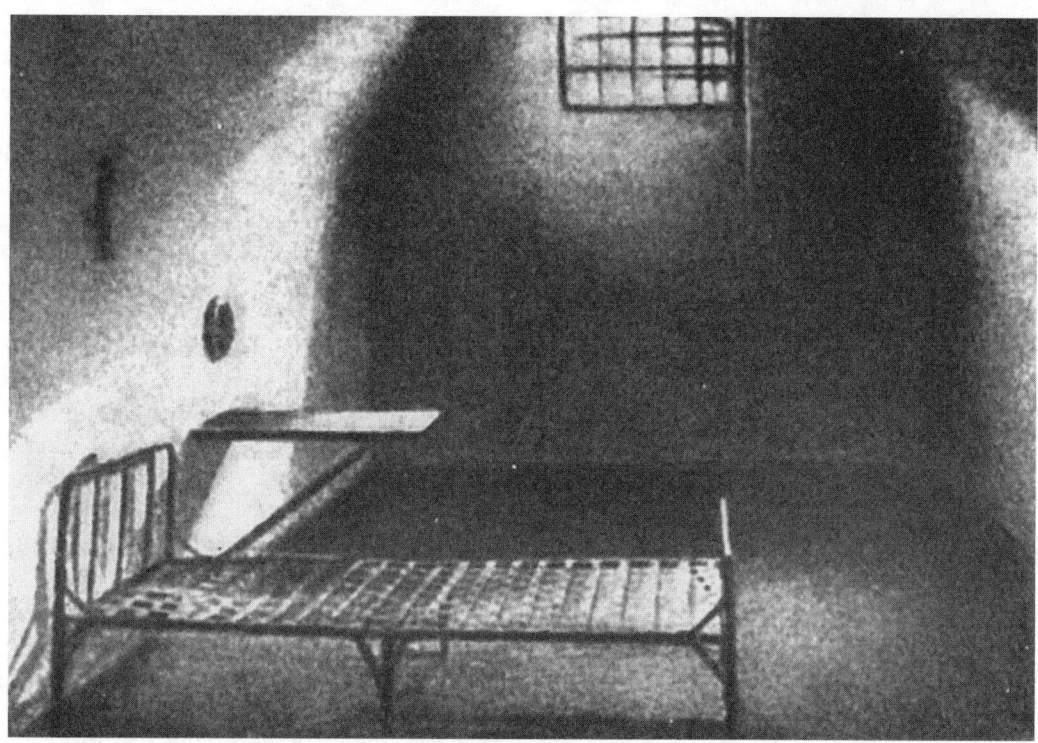

*Bakunin's cell at the Schusselburg Fortress, where he was imprisoned
from 1854 to 1857 (from Pirumova,* Bakunin, *1970)*

in an abortive socialist insurrection. After helping to seize the city hall, he was forced to flee and made his way back to Switzerland.

Meanwhile, he continued to take an interest in his homeland, which led him into an ill-fated collaboration with a young Russian named Sergei Gennadievich Nechaev. The long-awaited emancipation of the serfs in 1861, which disappointed many who had hoped for a more far-reaching reform, had the paradoxical effect of increasing antitsarist activity within the Russian empire. In 1869 Nechaev appeared in Switzerland claiming to head a far-flung network of revolutionary cells in Russia and sought to enlist Bakunin in his enterprise. As became apparent much later, Nechaev had in fact organized a small circle of radicals in Moscow. Having accused one of its members of planning to betray the group to the police, he persuaded the others to murder him and then fled the country to avoid arrest; Fyodor Dostoevsky subsequently used this episode as the basis for his novel *Besy* (The Devils, 1872). Bakunin, unaware of these events, was impressed by Nechaev's revolutionary claims and youthful energy and saw him as a link to the younger generation of revolutionaries that had grown up in Russia. The most notorious product of their partnership was a document called "Katekhizis revoliutsionera" (Catechism of the Revolutionary) of 1869, a cold-blooded statement of the rules of conduct

required of a revolutionary, who must renounce all the personal ties and moral standards that bind him to existing society and use any means available to extirpate it. This work was found written in code in Nechaev's papers when he was arrested and was published in a tsarist government journal during his trial. It was long considered a product largely of Bakunin's pen, but recently discovered evidence points to Nechaev as its principal, if not sole, author. Bakunin eventually broke with Nechaev and repudiated his unscrupulous practices, but not before considerable damage had been done to his reputation. Nechaev was ultimately extradited from Switzerland to Russia, where he was tried, convicted, and imprisoned for life.

In the early 1870s the growing antagonism between Bakunin and Marx came to a head. The two had first met in Paris in 1844 and again in London in 1864, and in the 1860s Bakunin joined the International Working Men's Association, which Marx and Friedrich Engels had formed. Bakunin respected Marx's erudition and shared his rejection of capitalism and commitment to socialism, but he regarded him as arrogant and authoritarian. Marx, who considered Russia the bulwark of European reaction, was suspicious of Russians and particularly of the undisciplined Bakunin. Underlying this personality clash were deep-seated ideological differences. As Bakunin's anarchist ideas developed, he

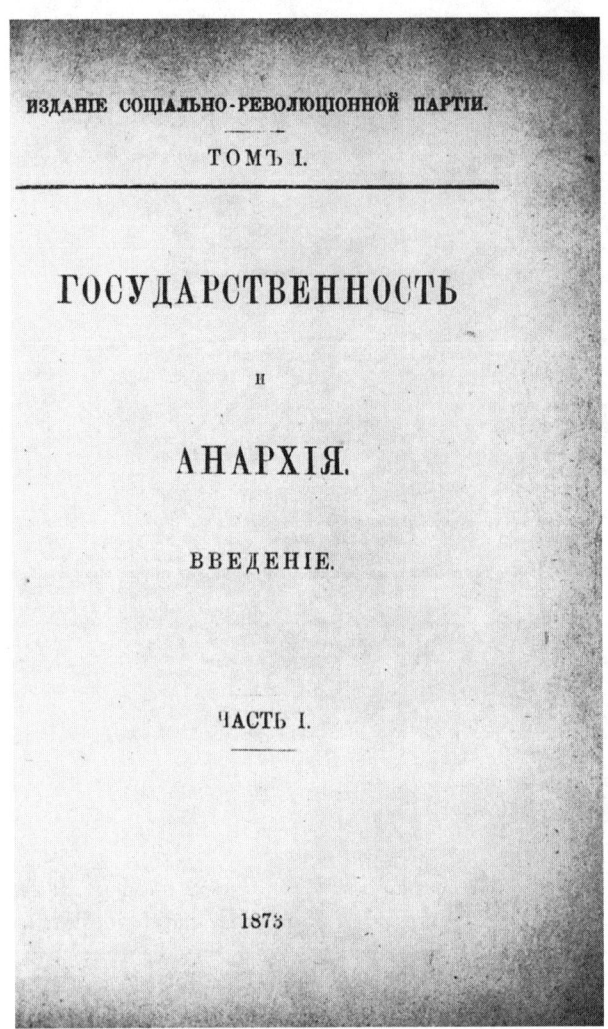

Title page for Bakunin's last significant work, Gosudarstvennost' i anarkhiia *(Statism and Anarchy), which greatly influenced the* narodnichestvo *(Populist movement) in Russia in the late nineteenth century (from Bakunin,* Gosudarstvennost' i anarkhiia, *1967)*

came to regard the immediate destruction of the state and its replacement by a federative system of social organization as the most important task of a revolution. Marx regarded the temporary seizure of the state by the workers and their creation of a "dictatorship of the proletariat" as the essential first step in the transition to a socialist society; only in a later phase of social and economic development could the state "wither away." Marxists therefore urged the proletariat of each country to organize itself for political purposes, while anarchists repudiated political activity altogether and called for the immediate transition to a stateless society. In addition, Marx relied on the "conscious," organized strata of the working class, in the most industrially advanced nations such as Germany and England, to carry out a socialist

revolution. Bakunin increasingly looked to the poorest, most downtrodden urban workers as well as the peasants in the more underdeveloped countries of Europe, such as Spain, Italy, and the Slavic lands, as the social base for revolution; he believed that these groups alone–with so little stake in the existing order–had the will to destroy it completely.

At the Hague Conference of the International in 1872 Marx succeeded in having Bakunin and his followers expelled from the organization, a move that destroyed the International itself. Bakunin's views, however, had taken root in parts of Europe. They found support especially in the workers' movements of Spain and Italy and among the watchmakers of the Jura region of Switzerland. Adherents of those views began to form their own international ties, and anarchism and Marxist socialism diverged from this point forward.

Bakunin's last important work was *Gosudarstvennost' i anarkhiia* (Statism and Anarchy, 1873); published anonymously, it summed up the conclusions that he had drawn from both the Franco-Prussian War and his clash with Marx. Like so many of his writings, this work is a tissue of digressions that was left unfinished, but it states his basic anarchist positions with particular clarity. Bakunin now sees Otto von Bismarck and the newly created German Empire as the foremost supporters in Europe of the centralized state against which anarchism has to struggle. Moreover, he equates Bismarck and Marx as kindred representatives of German authoritarianism. The work is most notable for his warning of the dangers posed by the Marxist notion of a dictatorship of the proletariat–a warning which has often been seen as a prophetic depiction of the path followed by the Soviet Union. He had already sounded this theme in *L'Empire knouto-germanique et la révolution sociale*, but now he expresses it even more directly. Such a dictatorship, Bakunin declares, will inevitably be exercised not by the proletariat itself but also by the self-proclaimed leaders of the proletariat–namely, Marx and his followers. They will seek to perpetuate their power, and the workers, as well as the peasants, will find themselves subjugated to a new class of rulers no better than the ones they have replaced. This vision now became the core of the unremitting hostility that anarchists harbored toward Marxists.

Unlike most of Bakunin's anarchist writings, *Gosudarstvennost' i anarkhiia* was written in Russian and was intended for underground circulation in Russia. In an appendix to the work he urges the revolutionaries of Russia to incite the peasants, whose rebellious instincts have prepared them to burst into open revolt. He idealizes the bandits of the Russian countryside as representatives of the peasants' rejection of established social arrangements, and he glorifies the leaders of the great peasant rebellions of the seventeenth and eighteenth centuries as models of antistate rebellion. Copies of *Gosudarstvennost' i anarkhiia* were smuggled into Russia and had an influence on the emerging *narodnichestvo* (Populist movement), which sought to create a distinctive form of Russian socialism based on peasant traditions.

Aging and increasingly ill, Mikhail Aleksandrovich Bakunin made one last effort to play a personal role in an insurrection. In the summer of 1874 he made his way to Bologna, Italy, to participate in a planned uprising. When the plans fell through, he returned to Switzerland and at last retired from revolution. He died in Berne on 1 July 1876. Soon, however, his writings were circulating more widely than they had during his lifetime. Some of his most significant anarchist works were published only in the decades after his death, and others came out in new editions. They gave anarchism a firm ideological foundation, which enabled it to present itself as an alternative to both liberal capitalism and Marxism and to play a notable role in subsequent historical events such as the Russian Revolution and the Spanish Civil War. Bakunin's ideas were rediscovered by the New Left in the 1960s, and his writings began to appear in new editions and translations. Their defense of the small voluntary community and their critique of "authoritarian socialism" came to be read with new appreciation a hundred years after his death.

Letters:

Pis'ma M. A. Bakunina k A. I. Gertsenu i N. P. Orgarevu, edited by Mikhail Petrovich Dragomanov (Geneva: Georg, 1896);

Sobranie sochinenii i pisem, 1828–1876, 4 volumes, edited by Iurii Mikhailovich Steklov (Moscow: Izdatel'stvo Vsesoiuznogo obshchestva politichnykh katorzhan i ssyl'no-poselentsev, 1934–1935).

Biographies:

Aleksandr Aleksandrovich Kornilov, *Molodye gody Mikhaila Bakunina* (Moscow: M. & S. Sabashnikovy, 1915);

Iurii Mikhailovich Steklov, *Mikhail Aleksandrovich Bakunin: Ego zhizn' i deiatel'nost' (1814–1876),* 4 volumes (Moscow: I. D. Sytin, 1920–1927);

Kornilov, *Gody stranstvii Mikhaila Bakunina* (Leningrad & Moscow: Gosudarstvennoe izdatel'stvo, 1925);

E. H. Carr, *Michael Bakunin* (London: Macmillan, 1937);

Natal'ia Mikhailovna Pirumova, *Bakunin* (Moscow: Molodaia gvardiia, 1970);

Anthony Masters, *Bakunin: The Father of Anarchism* (London: Sidgwick & Jackson, 1974; New York: Saturday Review, 1974);

Aileen Kelly, *Mikhail Bakunin: A Study in the Psychology and Politics of Utopianism* (Oxford: Clarendon Press, 1982; New York: Oxford University Press, 1982).

References:

Paul Avrich, "Bakunin and the United States," *International Review of Social History,* 24 (1979): 320–340;

Isaiah Berlin, "Herzen and Bakunin on Individual Liberty," in *Continuity and Change in Russian and Soviet Thought,* edited by Ernest J. Simmons (Cambridge, Mass.: Harvard University Press, 1955), pp. 473–499;

Canadian-American Slavic Studies, special Bakunin issue, 10 (Winter 1976);

Natal'ia Mikhailovna Pirumova, *Sotsial'naia doktrina M. A. Bakunina* (Moscow: Nauka, 1990);

T. R. Ravindranathan, *Bakunin and the Italians* (Kingston & Montreal: McGill-Queen's University Press, 1988);

Marshall S. Shatz, "Mikhail Bakunin and the Priamukhino Circle: Love and Liberation in the Russian Intelligentsia of the 1830s," *Canadian-American Slavic Studies,* 33 (Spring 1999): 1–29.

Papers:

The Bakunin family papers—as well as Mikhail Aleksandrovich Bakunin's letters and other material from his years in Russia—are located in the Priamukhino Archive, housed in the Institute of Russian Literature (IRLI, Pushkin House) in St. Petersburg. Other papers are located in the State Archive of the Russian Federation (GARF), fond 825; the Russian State Library (RGB, formerly the Lenin Library), fond 69; the Russian State Archive of Literature and Art (RGALI), fond 1328; the Saltykov-Shchedrin State Public Library, fond 629; and the Local History Museum of the Kalinin region. The principal collection of papers relating to his anarchist period is the Max Nettlau Archive in the International Institute for Social History in Amsterdam, The Netherlands.

Anna Pavlovna Barykova

(22 December 1839 – 31 May 1893)

Luc Beaudoin
University of Denver

BOOKS: *Stikhotvoreniia* (Piatigorsk: A. M. Baikov, 1878; enlarged edition, Moscow: I. D. Sytin, 1910);

Skazka pro to, kak Tsar' Akhreian khodil Bogu zhalovat'sia, anonymous (St. Petersburg: Narodnaia volia, 1883); translated by Christine D. Tomei as "The Tale of How Tsar Akhreian Went to God to Complain," in *Russian Women Writers,* 2 volumes, edited by Tomei (New York: Garland, 1999), I: 206–220;

Na pamiat' vnukam. Sbornik stikhotvorenii (Moscow: Posrednik, 1890);

Stikhotvoreniia i prozaicheskie proizvedeniia, with biographical comments by Vladimir Grigor'evich Chertkov and Anna Konstantinovna Chertkov (St. Petersburg: A. A. Porokhovshchikov, 1897);

Mat'-kormilitsa (St. Petersburg: Chetverikov, 1910);

Obrechennaia (St. Petersburg: Chetverikov, 1910).

Editions: *Skazka pro to, kak Tsar' Akhreian khodil Bogu zhalovat'sia,* anonymous (Geneva, 1896);

Kak Tsar' Akhreian khodil Bogu zhalovat'sia, anonymous (Paris: Sidoratsky, 1898);

Skazka pro to, kak Tsar' Akhreian khodil Bogu zhalovat'sia, anonymous (Geneva, 1901);

Skazka pro to, kak Tsar' Akhreian khodil Bogu zhalovat'sia (London: Zhizn', 1902);

Skazka pro to, kak Tsar' Akhreian khodil Bogu zhalovat'sia, anonymous (Berlin: G. Shteinits, 1903);

Skazka pro to, kak Tsar' Akhreian khodil Bogu zhalovat'sia (Petrograd: V. Vrublevsky, 1917);

Skazka pro to, kak Tsar' Akhreian khodil Bogu zhalovat'sia (St. Petersburg: El'zevir, 1922);

Skazka pro to, kak Tsar' Akhreian khodil Bogu zhalovat'sia (Moscow: Krasnaia nov', 1923).

OTHER: "Poet (Iz Zh. Rishpena)," in *Otklik,* edited by Petr Filippovich Iakubovich (St. Petersburg: A. S. Suvorin, 1881);

Alfred Tennyson, *Spasennyi,* translated by Barykova (Moscow: I. D. Sytin, 1888);

Anna Pavlovna Barykova

François Coppée, *Proshchenie: Drama v odnom deistvii v stikhakh,* translated by Barykova (Odessa, 1892);

Dozhdevaia volshebnitsa i drugie skazki, contributions by Barykova (Moscow: I. N. Kusherev, 1905);

Vol'naia russkaia poeziia vtoroi poloviny XIX veka, edited by Solomon Abramovich Reiser and Aleksei Alekseevich Shilov, contributions by Barykova (Leningrad: Sovetskii pisatel', 1959), pp. 404–405, 521;

Russkie poety XIX veka, compiled by Nikolai Matveevich Gaidenkov, contributions by Barykova (Moscow: Prosveshchenie, 1964), pp. 853–855;

Poety-demokraty 1870–1880kh godov, edited by V. G. Bazanov, B. L. Bessonov, and A. M. Bikhter, contributions by Barykova (Leningrad: Sovetskii pisatel', 1968), pp. 631–683;

Russkie poetessy XIX veka, compiled by Nikolai Vasilevich Bannikov, contributions by Barykova (Moscow: Sovetskaia Rossiia, 1979), pp. 146–157;

Tsaritsy muz: Russkie poetessy XIX–nachala XX veka, edited by V. Uchenova (Moscow, 1989).

Anna Pavlovna Barykova is a name unfamiliar even to most scholars of Russian literature. Her poetry was well regarded by some during her lifetime, derided by others as a poetry of low life and poverty–clearly a problem in a Russian culture steeped in the Romantic ethos of the poet as a leader of society who points the reader toward the beautiful and sublime. Barykova's poetry tends toward social critique. It unflinchingly identifies the flaws in the Russian Empire of the late 1800s and sympathizes with the plight of those who have no voice. Her goal was to advance progressive revolutionary causes through her work–a fact that made her best-known poem, *Skazka pro to, kak Tsar' Akhreian khodil Bogu zhalovat'sia* (1883; translated as "The Tale of How Tsar Akhreian Went to God to Complain," 1999), illegal in the empire.

Barykova was born Anna Pavlovna Kamenskaia on 22 December 1839 in St. Petersburg. She was the daughter of Pavel Pavlovich Kamensky, a nobleman and writer known at the time for his stories and plays, and Mariia Fedorovna Kamenskaia (née Tolstaia), likewise a writer and the daughter of sculptor and artist L. Fedor Tolstoy (Fedor Petrovich Tolstoy), the vice president of the Imperial Art Academy. The artistic and intellectual environment that surrounded Barykova in her childhood was formative. She was under the tutelage of her father and her governess until entering the Ekaterininskii Institute, which she completed in 1856, at the age of sixteen, with honors and a silver medal. Although the education she received at the institute covered, in her own words, "not a large stock of knowledge" (from *Stikhotvoreniia* [Poems]), she first wrote a selection of verse while a student there. Her initial attempt at publication during this early stage in her literary career was not poetry, however, but rather "Ptichnitsa" (The Little Bird), a prose work based on a Russian folktale. It was suppressed by the censor. This experience might have encouraged Barykova to turn her efforts henceforth more toward poetry than prose.

Little is known about Barykova's personal life. She had four children from two different marriages: a son and a daughter from her first marriage of 1857 to N. N. Karlinsky, an artillery officer, and two daughters from her second marriage of 1862 to S. L. Barykov, a barrister (the full names of Barykova's husbands remain unknown). Her marriages seem, overall, to have been inconsequential to her work, as she rarely mentions either her husbands or her children in her poetry and letters.

Barykova did not choose to publish her writing on her own for more than a decade after her marriage to Barykov, preferring to publish in the journal *Otechestvennye zapiski* (Notes of the Fatherland) beginning in 1872. Fluent in French, German, English, and Polish, she likewise published translations in *Severnyi vestnik* (The Northern Messenger), *Russkoe bogatstvo* (Russian Wealth), and other journals; these translations later appeared in *Stikhotvoreniia i prozaicheskie proizvedeniia* (Poetic and Prose Works), her posthumous 1897 collection. Her first independent collection of verse–the fruit of more than a decade of composing poems–appeared only in 1878 in Piatigorsk and was the only collection of Barykova's works published during her lifetime.

The poem "Krylia" (Wings), published in 1878 in *Otechestvennye zapiski,* conveys Barykov's poetic creed. In it, she recognizes that a poet can too easily lose sight of the importance of human suffering:

> Stradaniia liudei ottuda tak smeshny,
> Chto glazki zvezd bez vsiakogo uchast'ia
> Gliadiat na nikh iz sinei glubiny . . .
> No mne letat' tak skoro nadoelo,
> I s vysoty spustilas' ia opiat',
> Chtob vnov' nachat' svoe zemnoe delo:
> Skol'zit' v griazi–i padat', i stradat'!

> (From there people's sufferings are so funny,
> That the eyes of the stars look on
> Without any sympathy from the bluish depth . . .
> But flying there soon bored me,
> And from the heights I descended once more,
> In order to begin my earthly work anew:
> To slip in the mud–and to fall and suffer!)

Barykova makes a clear link between the work of the poet and the daily burdens of the masses. Although she is aware of the beauty of art, if it does not carry any importance in the earthly realm, it bores her. Perhaps this same need for artistic relevance drives her poem "V durnuiu pogodu" (In Bad Weather), which was first published in the 1878 Piatigorsk volume. Dedicated to Anna Pavlovna Filosofova, a liberal social activist for women's emancipation, the poem describes young prostitutes working in bad weather ("Business is bad: What's love for in such cold?"), while rich women race by in carriages to attend charity balls *"au profit de nos pauvres"* (for the benefit of the poor). Barykova contrasts the powerless poor–the "fallen women" of the streets–with the wealthy gentry. In this and other works she demonstrates a knack for unveiling the hypocrisy prevalent in society, whether among the upper or the lower classes.

In her poem "Liubimye kukly," (My Favorite Dolls) from the Piatigorsk volume one of her most frequently reprinted works, Barykova ruminates further on the role of women in Russian society. Observing a young girl at Christmas who, overtaken with rapture at her new Parisian doll, promises it undying love, the speaker reflects on the similarity between the girl and the doll:

> O sud'be obeikh dumalos' nevol'no.
> Devochka i kukla! Akh, kak vy pokhozhi!
> V zhizni ozhidaet vas odno i to zhe.
> . . . .
> Kto-nibud' obnimet, govoria, konechno,
> Chto liubit' nameren plamenno i vechno . . .
> Ch'ei-nibud' igrushkoi budesh' ty, naverno,–
> Tol'ko nenadolgo.

> (I unwittingly thought of the fates of both of them.
> The girl and the doll! Oh, how alike you are!
> The same awaits both of you in life.
> . . . .
> Someone will embrace you, saying, of course,
> That he's ready to love you passionately and eternally . . .
> You'll be someone's toy, indeed–
> Only not for long.)

Finally, Barykova relents and admits that perhaps she is too harsh: "Indeed, children don't break all these dolls . . . / And aren't there any happy women?" These final two lines of the poem only serve to reinforce the precarious nature of women's fates. The setting of the poem during the holidays, at the height of family giving, is striking.

Such radical views influenced Barykova's social standing, as well as the reaction of critics to her volume of poetry. As a rule her poetry treats those at the bottom of society with unabashed sympathy. Even the progressive critics turned this trait against her; for example, Viktor Petrovich Burenin called Barykova the "poetess of the dung heap," while Nikolai Alekseevich Liubimov, an aggressive editor who helped facilitate the publication of Leo Tolstoy's novels, nicknamed her the "washer girl." Such invective from critics earned them Barykova's scorn for life. The critics, for their part, were infuriated by her 1878 publication in *Otechestvennye zapiski* of a translation of a poem by Jean Richepin (a nihilist French writer of flamboyant verse) called "Oiseaux de passage" (Birds Flying By), in which Barykova describes an ordinary scene in a back courtyard:

> Vot griaznyi zadnii dvor, sovsem obyknovennyi:
> Koniushnia, khleb svinoi, korovnik i sarai.
> . . . .
> Tut vechno est i p'et bezdushnaia poroda;
> Na solnyshke blestit navoz, kak zolotoi.

> (There is the dirty back courtyard, quite ordinary:
> A stable, a pigsty, a cow shed and barn.
> . . . .
> There the airless race eternally eats and drinks;
> In the sun glistens manure, like gold.)

The passing birds are a mockery to those animals and flightless creatures that must live out their fates in the air-less courtyard. The birds–a metaphor for the rich, who are free to seek out new pleasures beyond their immediate confines–fully understand their freedom. The rich are not trapped by the limitations of poverty; they have a more spiritual vision and are able to transcend the necessities of carnal existence. The flightless animals, however, cannot understand what freedom means; they indulge their carnal needs (even their manure shines like gold) and are debased by their inability to rise above their physical natures. Here again, the contrast between the life of the privileged and that of the disadvantaged is a focal point of Barykova's lyric art.

Barykova's poem "Muchenitsa" (The Martyress, written in 1880) tells the story of a Christian martyr in the Roman Empire who is fed to the lions for her beliefs. Facing death, she continues to smile and remain calm, even addressing the crowd in the arena:

> "Ia veriu, ia znaiu–ono pobedit,
> Raspiatogo veshchee slovo!
> Ia vizhu: kumiry nechistykh bogov
> S litsa ischezaiut zemnogo . . .
> Moi bog votsaritsia na veki vekov,
> Bog ravenstva, bratstva sviatogo.
> Velikomu delu ia zhizn' otdala;
> Pobeda za nami–ia veriu!"

> ("I believe, I know that it will be victorious–
> The prophetic word of the crucifixion!
> I see the idols of the unclean gods
> Disappear from the face of the earth . . .
> My God will come to the throne for ever and ever,
> The God of equality, of holy brotherhood.
> I have given my life for a great thing;
> Victory is before us–I believe!")

Barykova similarly used her skill as a translator to convey her faith that those who are on the side of truth and right will ultimately achieve victory. For example, in her 1882 adaptation of Victor Hugo's poem "Il est des jours abjets . . ." (There are abject days . . .), which she retitled "Pered rassvetom" (Before Dawn), she writes that although there are times when evil seems to triumph and conscience disappears–when life "becomes an orgy"–these moments will pass. Barykova ends her reworking of "Il est des jours abjets . . ." with the following stanza:

> Takie vremena pozornye ne vechny.
> Prokhodit noch'; vstaet zaria na nebesakh . . .
> Tolpa nochnykh guliak! Ty skroesh'sia, konechno,
> Pri solnechnykh luchakh!

> (Such shameful times are not eternal.
> Night will pass; the morning will dawn in the heavens . . .
> Crowd of nocturnal idlers! You will hide, of course,
> From the sun's rays!)

In addition to the overtly captious message of this poem, Barykova's decision to translate Hugo carries an implicit message of republicanism, since by the 1870s he was admired as one of the leading Republican poets and writers in France. Because Barykova ostensibly remains the purveyor of someone else's thoughts in works such as "Il est des jours abjets . . . ," she is able to convey through the act of translation what are otherwise politically unacceptable messages.

Such strongly held views might inevitably and logically lead Barykova to some sort of political action. Indeed, her contributions to *Otechestvennye zapiski* produced connections with several liberal and progressive poets—among them Petr Filippovich Iakubovich, to whom she submitted a series of works for a collection he edited and published in 1881, titled *Otklik* (Echo). In the early 1880s Barykova lived in Rostov-on-Don, where she aided the revolutionary group Narodnaia volia (The People's Will), organized in 1879 and led by Andrei Ivanovich Zheliabov and Sofiia L'vovna Perovskaia. It proposed violent revolutionary upheaval and attempted to bomb government buildings such as the Winter Palace and kill highly placed officials. The group did succeed in assassinating Tsar Alexander II on 1 March 1881. Yet, the counterreaction to the tsar's assassination decimated Narodnaia volia and led to a remarkable decline of progressive sentiment in Russia.

While in Rostov-on-Don, however, Barykova sponsored covert meetings of Narodnaia volia in her home. One of the leaders of the group, German Aleksandrovich Lopatin, was arrested in 1884, and the discovery of Barykova's name among his papers led to her own arrest. She was imprisoned for one month and released on account of aggravated tuberculosis. While she was indeed involved with the terrorist revolutionary group, the authorities were never able to find any evidence to support their suspicions. Most striking, they were not able to ascribe to her the publication of *Skazka pro to, kak Tsar' Akhreian khodil Bogu zhalovat'sia.* Barykova's most famous work, it was first published anonymously in 1883 by the underground publishing house Narodnaia volia in St. Petersburg; it was later republished, again anonymously, in Geneva (1896 and 1901), and as *Kak Tsar Akhreian Bogu zhalovat'sia* in Paris (1898). The poem was circulated clandestinely in the Russian Empire and achieved quite a level of fame and popularity. Until its authorship by Barykova was established (when the social democratic organization Zhizn' published it in London in 1902), *Skazka pro to, kak Tsar' Akhreian khodil Bogu zhalovat'sia* was ascribed variously to Iakubovich (who was also arrested for involvement in Narodnaia volia) and to the poet and writer Aleksei Konstantinovich Tolstoy; subsequent editions of the work came out in 1903, 1917, 1922, and 1923.

Skazka pro to, kak Tsar' Akhreian khodil Bogu zhalovat'sia is, perhaps transparently, Aesopian in its use of symbols to convey its true meaning. It quickly betrays its folk origins as a *bylina* (tale in verse) as it describes the not-too-bright Tsar Akhreian and his decrepit kingdom. In his realm a struggle between good and evil forces has been unleashed, with the Tsar clearly in the camp of evildoers who are aligned with Falsehood. Mother-Truth rises against the Tsar, but she is defeated by Falsehood and imprisoned. The more Falsehood and the Tsar hound Mother-Truth, however, the greater are her power and moral authority, which she uses to urge the Tsar's subjects to rise up. Falsehood convinces the Tsar that he must complain to God about his situation. The Christian pantheon, though, does not cooperate with him: neither God nor Christ nor the Virgin Mary nor Saint Peter, nor even Saint Nicholas (Akhreian's escort in heaven) will help him. Barykova ends *Skazka pro to, kak Tsar' Akhreian khodil Bogu zhalovat'sia* with an evocation of its contemporaneity and a wish that the poem will one day become obsolete:

> Nashei skazke eshche ne konets prishel . . .
> A kogda nasha skazka konchitsia, Slava!
> Zapoem, bratsy, pesniu my novuiu, Slava!
> Chto veseluiu pesniu, svobodnuiu, Slava!
> Dukhu vechnomu Sveta i Istiny, Slava!
> Pravde-matushke, nashei zastupnitse, Slava!
> Vol'noi vole, narodu svobodnomu Slava!
>
> (The end has not yet come to our tale . . .
> And when our tale will end, Glory!
> We will sing, brothers, a new song, Glory!
> That is a happy song, and free, Glory!
> To the eternal spirit of Light and Truth, Glory!
> To Mother-Truth, our protector, Glory!
> To free will, to a free people, Glory!)

Ultimately, *Skazka pro to, kak Tsar' Akhreian khodil Bogu zhalovat'sia* is not only about the need to rise up against autocratic authority but also about the falsity of the doctrine that the tsar rules by divine right—the key to why the work is written in a folkloric style. Not surprisingly, Falsehood convinces Tsar Akhreian to turn to God for assistance against his people. God, however—while he should assist the Tsar if there is indeed such a thing as the divine right of kings—rages against him and states that he would never have anointed him with his holy myrrh. Barykova was compelled to hide her authorship of this work, as her progressive political leanings and her critique of the situation in late Imperial Russia were so boldly expressed in its lines.

Satire was another genre in which Barykova excelled. In two of her best-known satires, she returns to her favorite theme: namely, the mandate of art to express the suffering of the poor and to advocate social change. "Zhretsu estetiki" (To the Priest of Aesthetics, written in 1884) is a mocking invective against the poet Apollon Nikolaevich Maikov—whose award of the Pushkin Prize from the Academy of Sciences in 1882, for his poem "Dva Mira" (Two Worlds, 1872) was criticized for elevating the aesthetics of the pagan world above that of Christian idealism. Barykova scorns the idea of art elevated above the common person's woes:

> Ne znaiu ia tebia. Kakoi ty khochesh' slavy? . . .
> Skhodil li ty ko mne s vysokikh oblakov?
> Tvoi pevuchie krasivye "oktavy"
> Ia slyshala skvoz' ston golodnykh bedniakov;
> Kak iad nasmeshki zloi, kak zhguchaia otrava,
> Lilis' veselye melodii stikhov
> V isterzannuiu grud' . . . Primi zhe v nagrazhden'e
> Zabytoi materi prezren'e i zabven'e!

> (I do not know you. What kind of glory do you desire? . . .
> Have you come down to me from the elevated clouds?
> Your melodious, beautiful "octaves"
> I heard through the groans of the hungry poor;
> Like the poison of evil mockery, like a burning poison,
> The happy melodies of poems poured forth
> Into my tormented heart . . . Why don't you take as an award
> The contempt and oblivion of the forgotten mother!)

The poem "Pesn' torzhestvuiushchei svin'i" (Song of the Exultant Pig), written in the late 1880s, is modeled after a pamphlet by the satirist Mikhail Evgrafovich Saltykov. In this satirical verse Barykova lampoons those who are content to provide for themselves while others go without. In particular, she singles out those who prefer that poets ignore the suffering of the poor. In this respect Barykova takes ironic aim at her old enemy, the critic Burenin, even specifically referring to manure. This satire was never published in Barykova's lifetime but appeared in *Stikhotvoreniia i prozaicheskie proizvedeniia* in 1897.

Barykova's desire for political change was ultimately conflated with more spiritual goals. Beginning in the late 1880s she maintained an association with the thought and writing of Tolstoy and became familiar with his nonprofit publishing house, Posrednik (The Intermediary), founded in 1884 with the participation of Vladimir Grigor'evich Chertkov, Tolstoy's secretary, disciple, and executor of his last will and testament. Posrednik was explicitly conceived to bring Tolstoyan ideas of nonresistance to evil, vegetarianism, religion, and famine to the peasants in their own idiom. There are clear parallels between Barykova's revolutionary writings and Tolstoyanism—including her preoccupation with social injustice, her attention to the hypocrisy rampant in human society, her faith in the inevitable triumph of a just cause, and indeed the idiom of her own works.

One of Barykova's poems of her Tolstoyan period, "Sumasshedshaia" (Madwoman, written in 1878), begins with the description of a general's wife, who lives in luxury but is nonetheless overcome with grief for those who are not as fortunate. She finally asks a doctor whether there can be any relief from her tears. The doctor exclaims that she is mad; she continues her feelings of grief. The poem ends with her death:

> Gromko rydaia, rvalas' ona besheno:
> "Malo nas! Malo na svete pomeshannykh!
> Vsekh by spasli!"—i otkryla ob"iatiia,
> Slovno khotela vsiu nishchuiu bratiiu
> Razom obniat'. . . Pri poslednem dykhanii
> Slezy lilis' za chuzhie stradaniia . . .
> A khoronit' ee chinno prishedshie
> Dumali: eto byla sumasshedshaia!

> (Loudly sobbing, she exclaimed madly:
> "There are few of us! Few crazy people on the earth!
> You would have saved us all!" And she opened her arms
>   in an embrace,
> As if she wanted to embrace all the destitute brotherhood
> At once . . . With her last breath
> Tears flowed for the suffering of others . . .
> And those who had come dutifully to bury her
> Thought: this was a madwoman!)

Parallels to Tolstoy's own position as an aristocrat who strove unsuccessfully to alleviate the sufferings of others abound in Barykova's "Sumasshedshaia." She also discovered her Tolstoyan tendencies in translation. One of her better known translations of this period is "Spasennyi" (The Saved One)—from Alfred Tennyson's "Enoch Arden"—a fairly clichéd, sentimental poem about love and loss.

Anna Pavlovna Barykova died on 31 May 1893. Most critics agree that her revolutionary works, in particular *Skazka pro to, kak Tsar' Akhreian khodil Bogu zhalovat'sia,* are her best. Barykova seemed to have little concern for her literary legacy and chose, rather, to see her work as an agent of social change and self-improvement. She wrote in her autobiography (which appears in the 1910 *Stikhotvoreniia*): "So far I don't fear death; what will be after, I don't know. I would like to die somehow 'easily' and at the right time, not having outlived 'myself' nor having become, as a consequence of old age, an animal dimwittedly enamored with itself and its animal life." These harsh words exemplify Barykova's artistic credo. She was a woman who felt not only that a single life could change the world, but also that change, if just, would inevitably be victorious over evil. A poet in the age of realism, she tried to make the personal and effete lyricism of poetry fit the vulgarity and harshness of the world around her. She had a belief in the nobility of the human spirit, unshackled from the limitations of the animalistic world around it. A convert to Tolstoy's ideas of reforming the world, Barykova left behind a poetic legacy that has been largely overshadowed by the tumultuous events of the twentieth century. Despite her comparative obscurity, however, her works still speak to the fundamental social problems of today.

Letters:
"Otryvki iz pisem A. P. Barykovoi," in *Stikhotvoreniia* (Moscow: I. D. Sytin, 1910), pp. 5, 6, 15–35.

Biography:
A. V. Efremin, *A. P. Barykova (1839–1893)* (Moscow: Zhurnalnoe-gazetnoe ob"edinenie, 1934).

References:
K. N. Grigor'ian, "Poeziia semidesiatykh-vos'midesiatykh godov," in *Istoriia russkoi literatury,* volume 9, part 1 (Moscow & Leningrad: AN SSSR, 1956), pp. 428–429;

T. V. Krivoshchapova, "Russkaia stikhotvornaia skazka v kontse XIX – nachale XX v.," *Filologicheskie nauki,* 2 (1991): 28–35;

S. Liubimov, "Zapreshchennye stikhotvoreniia A. P. Barykovoi," *Krasnyi arkhiv,* 6 (1924);

Rimvydas Šilbajoris, "Anna Barykova," in *Russian Women Writers,* 2 volumes, edited by Christine D. Tomei (New York: Garland, 1999), I: 199–205.

Papers:

The papers of Anna Pavlovna Barykova are held in Moscow at the Russian State Archive of Literature and Art (RGALI), fond 46, fond 743, fond 1229, and fond 552 (letters written to Vladimir Grigor'evich Chertkov and Anna Konstantinovna Chertkov); the State Archive of the Russian Federation (GARF), fond 102; the State Historical Museum (GIM), fond 445; the Russian State Library (RGB, formerly the Lenin Library), fond 218; and the Central State Historical Archive (TsGIA), fond 418. Barykova's papers may also be found in St. Petersburg at the Institute of Russian Literature (IRLI, Pushkin House), fond 377.

Vasilii Petrovich Botkin

(27 December 1811 – 10 October 1869)

Derek Offord
University of Bristol

BOOKS: *Pis'ma ob Ispanii* (St. Petersburg: E. Prats, 1857);

Sochineniia, 3 volumes (St. Petersburg: Panteon Literatury, 1890–1893)—includes volume 1, *Puteshestviia*—includes "Russkii v Parizhe," "Otryvki iz dorozhnykh zametok po Italii," "Pis'mo iz Italii," "Dve nedeli v Londone"; and volume 2, *Stat'i po literature i iskusstvam;* "Priiuty dlia bezdomnykh nishchikh v Londone";

Literaturnaia kritika. Publitsistika. Pis'ma, with commentary by Egorov (Moscow: Sovetskaia Rossiia, 1984).

Edition: *Pis'ma ob Ispanii,* edited by Boris Fedorovich Egorov and A. Ia. Zvigil'sky (Leningrad: Nauka, 1976);

Edition in English: "A. A. Fet," translated by George Genereux, *Russian Literature Triquarterly,* 17 (1982): 23–60.

OTHER: "Literatura i teatr v Anglii do Shekspira," in *Polnoe sobranie dramaticheskikh proizvedenii Shekspira v perevode russkikh pisatelei,* volume 1 (St. Petersburg, 1865), pp. ix–xlvi.

Vasilii Petrovich Botkin

Vasilii Botkin is an important, if rather neglected, figure in the history of nineteenth-century Russian culture. He was the author of several pieces of travel writing. He also forcefully articulated a view of art as an end in itself that was widely held by leading Russian writers and literary critics in the late 1850s until utilitarian critics, such as Nikolai Gavrilovich Chernyshevsky and Nikolai Aleksandrovich Dobroliubov, succeeded in marginalizing it. Yet, Botkin's literary output was not voluminous, nor, for the most part, was it highly original. Apart from his travel writing and a small corpus of literary criticism, his output consists mainly of brief reviews of books and music, and translations and articles based on foreign works. Botkin's importance is therefore attributed to the centrality of his role in Russian intellectual life—in particular in the circle of the *zapadniki* (Westernizers)—from the late 1830s to the early 1860s, at the heart of the golden age of classical Russian literature and thought. His own development reflects the fancies of, and tensions within, the small educated class in Russia during that period, when it was assuming the character of what is known as an intelligentsia.

Born on 27 December 1811, Vasilii Petrovich Botkin was the eldest son of a wealthy Moscow tea merchant, Petr Kononovich Botkin. The name of Botkin's mother is unknown; after her death his father married Anna Ivanovna Posnikova, just six years Vasilii's senior. Botkin exercised a large cultural influence on his younger siblings, two of whom were also to achieve renown: Sergei as a major and influential clinician and Mikhail as a painter and art historian. Botkin was not a member of that class, the nobility, which dominated cultural life in the salons and *kruzhki* (circles) of the 1830s and 1840s but of a section of society, the *kupechestvo* (merchant class), which was generally treated with disdain by gentry intellectuals, irrespective of their philosophical or political leanings. Nor did he altogether desert the commercial class from which he came. He worked in the family business in the 1830s and 1840s and, after his father's death in 1853, for a while played a leading role in the management of its affairs.

Botkin mostly lacked formal education but read widely and voraciously of his own accord. Thanks to his own efforts and his appetite for study, he achieved a cultural breadth not usually associated with the *kupechestvo*. He acquired at least a reading knowledge of all the major European languages, particularly German and French. He taught himself English, Italian, and Spanish. His sufficiently passive knowledge of English enabled him to translate parts of the work *On Heroes, Hero-Worship and the Heroic in History* (1841) by the Victorian essayist and historian Thomas Carlyle as "O geroiakh i geroicheskom v istorii. Sochinenie T. Karleilia" in the October 1855, January 1856, and February 1856 editions of *Sovremennik* (The Contemporary). Botkin developed wide-ranging cultural tastes, including a capacity for the enjoyment of music and painting—of which he had a knowledge that was considered exceptional by his contemporaries—as well as of literature. Essentially, however, Botkin was a dilettante. He was also a *bon viveur* (a convivial companion who enjoys good food) and famously hedonistic. As the essayist, political thinker, and journalist Alexander Herzen (Aleksandr Ivanovich Gertsen) fondly recalled in his monumental memoir *Byloe i dumy* (written 1852–1868 and published in full in 1921; translated as *My Past and Thoughts: The Memoirs of Alexander Herzen*, 1924–1927), Botkin taught his contemporaries that one "may equally find 'pantheistic' enjoyment in contemplating the dance of the sea-waves and of Spanish maidens, in listening to the songs of Schubert, and scenting the aroma of a turkey stuffed with truffles" (from revised Higgens translation).

The burgeoning intellectual life in which Botkin began to participate in the mid 1830s was still conducted in close-knit literary *kruzhki,* whose members cherished friendship and shared their thoughts and impressions freely as they discussed the latest works of European culture and the writings—in the manuscript stage as well as following publication—of their compatriots. He describes the sense of excitement experienced by this small, beleaguered group as they struggled to promote an enlightened culture under the repressive regime of Nicholas I (who reigned as tsar from 1825 until 1855) in a country painfully aware of its backwardness by comparison with nations against which it now measured itself. In this environment, what originated in the mind of one person might quickly become common property. As a man who read voraciously and

was beginning to travel extensively—and who was good company, too—Botkin made a contribution to life in these circles that was greater than the corpus of his published work might suggest in retrospect.

In 1835 Botkin traveled to France and Italy and immediately tried his hand at the genre of the travel sketch. Three pieces arose out of his travels in that year: his first published article, "Russkii v Parizhe" (A Russian in Paris), published in 1836 in *Teleskop* (The Telescope); "Otryvki iz dorozhnykh zametok po Italii" (Fragments from Travel Notes about Italy), and "Pis'mo iz Italii" (A Letter from Italy). In 1837, after his return he participated in the discussions of German literature and philosophy by translating an article by the German critic Oswald-Gotthard Marbach, but publication was prohibited by the censor. An abridged, and imperfect, rendering by him of E. T. A. Hoffmann's *Kreisleriana* was published in *Moskovskii nabliudatel'* (The Moscow Observer) in 1838. In 1840 he translated an article on William Shakespeare by Heinrich Theodor Rötscher, a disciple of the philosopher Georg Wilhelm Friedrich Hegel and a major source of information for Russians on Hegel's aesthetic doctrines titled "Chetyre novye dramy, pripisyvaenye Shekspiru" for the journal *Otechestvennye zapiski.*

In any account of Botkin's impact on Russian intellectual life, mention must be made of his close relationship, starting in 1835, with the leading literary critic of Russia, Vissarion Grigor'evich Belinsky, who was central to the development of Russian literature during the 1830s and 1840s. The intensity of the bond between Botkin and Belinsky (from the time when they were introduced until Belinsky's premature death in 1848) is illustrated by their voluminous correspondence, particularly during the years from 1838 to 1843. To some extent the friendship—if "friendship" is not too restrained a word to describe the relationship—exemplified an attraction of opposites. Botkin's epicureanism and sensualism were quite foreign to the ascetic, almost self-punitive Belinsky, but Belinsky must have cherished in Botkin an equilibrium and constancy lacking in his own nature. Certainly, Belinsky was much indebted to Botkin, as he acknowledged in a letter of 1840. Botkin brought to the relationship a breadth of culture, linguistic expertise, and firsthand knowledge of Western life and culture that Belinsky, the untraveled son of a provincial doctor, did not have. In particular, in the late 1830s Botkin served as one of Belinsky's mentors in German philosophy, especially the philosophy of Hegel—of whom Botkin, like many of his contemporaries, was then a devotee. Botkin's research on and translations of Marbach and Rötscher are reflected in articles written by Belinsky in the period 1838 to 1840 in his own Hegelian mode. Belinsky's rejection of his accursed Hegelian "reconciliation with reality" from 1840 onward, however, did not diminish his dependency on Botkin; indeed, he seemed to need his friend even more. Botkin was the recipient of many of the prodigiously long letters in which Belinsky famously gave expression to the spiritual and intellectual crisis that he underwent in 1840.

In 1843 Botkin published three articles on German literature. In the first, "Germanskaia literatura v 1843 godu," published in the journal *Otechestvennye zapiski,* he incorporated a virtual translation of part of Friedrich Engels's pamphlet "Schelling und die Offenbarung" (Schelling and Revelation, 1842). He thereby helped to transmit the viewpoint of the so-called Young, or Left, Hegelians, who believed Hegel's dialectic could yield a politically radical interpretation and whose ideas gained currency in Russia in the 1840s. Then in September 1843 Botkin took a somewhat bizarre step, which is described with ironical wit by Herzen in *Byloe i dumy:* he married a French seamstress with whom he had had a brief affair. The wedding ceremony was conducted with pomp in the grand setting of the Kazan' Cathedral on Nevskii Prospekt in St. Petersburg. The relationship did not survive the couple's voyage from Russia to France, where they parted company on arrival. Botkin remained abroad, however, mainly in France, until 1846. This sojourn in the West helped to enlarge the pool of firsthand knowledge of Western life and culture that considerably enriched Russian thought and literature in the 1840s.

In the summer of 1845, during an intermission from his Parisian debauches–as described by the critic Pavel Vasil'evich Annenkov in his *Literaturnye vospominaniia* (Literary Reminiscences, 1960), Botkin's friend and fellow liberal Westernizer–Botkin undertook the journey to Spain that gave rise to his major literary work, *Pis'ma ob Ispanii* (Letters about Spain, 1857). Gastronomically, Spain left something to be desired for a gourmet like Botkin. Yet, in other respects Spain captivated him and appealed to both the carnal and spiritual sides of his nature. He was drawn to its exotic character, color, and vitality; the Spanish "worship of the body"; the seductiveness of the Andalusian women and the sensualism of their dance; and the religiosity of Spanish painting. The literary product of this journey, in the course of which Botkin visited Burgos, Madrid, Aranjuez, Córdoba, Seville, Cádiz, Málaga, and Granada, was published in the journal *Sovremennik.* Six of the letters came out between 1847 and 1849 and a seventh in 1851. In 1857 the whole series was collected as a separate edition. The work was highly acclaimed by critics at various points on the political spectrum.

Travel writing is a genre that has in general been somewhat neglected in the history of Russian letters, although it was popular in the nineteenth century and served important functions. Of particular appeal to writers during this period was the capacity of the genre both to inform their audience about foreign lands and, at least implicitly, to offer comparisons of those lands with Russia. Botkin's *Pis'ma ob Ispanii* performed the latter function as well as the former. In his account of Spain, Botkin discussed its landscape; its geographical isolation; its history of occupation in the distant past by alien infidels, the Moors; and the fact that it was relatively unknown to other Europeans. His commentary on Spain was bound to bring Russia herself–with her expanses of deserted territory, her marginal location in Europe, the legacy of occupation by infidels, and the cultural isolation that resulted from her relative inaccessibility–to the mind of the Russian reader.

Like Russia, Spain was engaged in an attempt both to "tear itself away from its past" and to "preserve all its old cherished traditions." It was refashioning its constitution "in a foreign manner"–as Westernizers, Botkin seems to imply, hoped Russia would refashion hers–but meanwhile it retained "all its old ghastly administration." The intellectual life of the country was conducted mainly in "political newspapers, divided into irreconcilably quarreling parties." (Intellectual life in Russia could not yet be described as overtly politicized, but it was increasingly conducted through journalism, and by the time Botkin wrote his *Pis'ma ob Ispanii,* the Westernist and Slavophile camps were irreconcilable.) As for the Spaniards themselves, they (like Russians, readers are no doubt intended to infer) have as many moral qualities as the next European people and all the attributes they need to become a nation of the first rank. Yet, Botkin intimates, they will not achieve this end through words alone, nor through comforting recollections of former glory. Instead they will have to educate their population, develop industry in the country, and accustom themselves to work.

The character and conduct of the Spanish people as they are depicted in *Pis'ma ob Ispanii* have an implicitly instructive and exemplary quality for Russians. In marveling at the "common sense, clear mind, ease, and freedom" with which the Spanish common people express themselves, Botkin is perhaps predicting what might be expected of a people emancipated from serfdom. At the same time, he sees the Spanish upper class, at the other end of the social spectrum, as endowed with a chivalric temperament (a quality for which the Russian Westernizers repeatedly expressed admiration). He extols the virtues of the *caballero* (a Spanish gentleman)–politeness, naturalness, and hospitality–and commends the strict code of honor that is reflected in the bullfight, a phenomenon that Botkin describes at length and with enthusiasm. He thinks he observes in Spain, finally, a sense of national unity that overrides class distinctions: the nobleman does not consider mingling with the crowd beneath his dignity, nor is the common man envious of the noble or obsequious toward him. Social intercourse between

Spaniards is honorable and free, and, Botkin suggests, Russians ought to strive for an equality of personal status similar to that which one encounters in Spain.

Botkin's contribution to the formation of the *zapadnichestvo* (Westernism) of the 1840s is apt for consideration at this point. His published writings do not explicitly argue what might be called a Westernist case, but then identifying the writings that do so is difficult, since Westernism is a mentality rather than an organized body of thought. On the other hand, Botkin's writings—particularly *Pis'ma ob Ispanii*—do reflect the respectful sympathetic attitude toward European culture and a willingness to embrace it that characterized the Westernist intelligentsia. His surviving private correspondence also reveals the degree to which he shared the hostility to Slavophilism that helped to shape Westernism and lend some coherence to it. In his letters Botkin describes the Slavophiles—whose main representatives were Aleksei Stepanovich Khomiakov, Ivan Vasil'evich Kireevsky, and Konstantin Sergeevich Aksakov—as "the most abstract theoreticians," men who were intolerant obscurantists and poorly schooled in economics. They preached narrow-mindedness and ignorance and defended a patriarchal social order and national prejudices. At bottom Slavophilism represented a vote for "ignorance" as opposed to "civilization." What precisely "civilization" signified, and what were therefore the contours of Westernism, is not so easy to define. However, Westernism as represented by Botkin certainly included respect for the rational knowledge derived from the intellectual labor of the West since the Renaissance; a commitment to economic progress, as promoted by the discipline of political economy, whose basic laws Botkin praised Adam Smith for discovering; and the erosion of social barriers, at least on the legal and moral planes if not on the material plane.

Shared attitudes toward the West in general, however, could not disguise differences among the Westernizers. During the 1840s disagreements arose among them over such matters as the relative merits of the Jacobins and the more moderate Girondins during the French Revolution, the immortality of the soul, and the philosophical materialism encouraged by the German philosopher Ludwig Feuerbach's work *Das Wesen des Christentums* (The Essence of Christianity, 1841), in which divinity is interpreted as merely a projection of human consciousness. In some respects Botkin became more radical in the 1840s, as did the Westernizers in general. For example, together with the revolutionary agitator and future anarchist Mikhail Aleksandrovich Bakunin, he represented the antitsarist forces of Russia at an evening meeting in Paris in 1844. In a letter of 1845 he subscribed to the view of religion as a convenient means of explaining away all that is unacceptable in human life and endorsed Feuerbach's treatment of religion. He also cooled now toward

German culture; warmed to French culture, which furnished more radical ideas at this time; and, like Belinsky in his post-Hegelian phase, accepted the need for a literature that did not exclude the harsher aspects of reality.

Yet, in other significant respects Botkin's allegiance to what later became the more moderate wing of Westernism was becoming clear. First, like his contemporary and fellow Westernizer the historian Timofei Nikolaevich Granovsky, but unlike the uncompromising Belinsky, he urged toleration of opposing views. Second, in contrast to Belinsky, who by the mid 1840s insisted that art should serve a civic purpose, Botkin reemphasized the paramount importance of artistry in creative work; he praised Ivan Sergeevich Turgenev's *Zapiski okhotnika* (A Hunter's Sketches), which began to appear in 1847, on the grounds of artistry, rather than for any sociopolitical content, real or imagined. Third, Botkin took a balanced view in a controversy of the late 1840s about the historical role of the bourgeoisie. Exhibiting an independent, tolerant perspective, he not only voiced his sympathy with the working class but also expressed the hope that Russia too might one day have a bourgeoisie.

In the repressive climate in Russia that followed the outbreak of revolutionary uprisings in the West in 1848, any boldness Botkin might once have felt evaporated. He moved from Moscow to St. Petersburg, where he sensed he might be safer. He wrote extremely little: only seven items by him, three of them about music, are known to have been published during this time, recognized historically as the *mrachnoe semiletie* (seven dismal years), the period of extreme political and repression reaction with which the reign of Tsar Nicholas I ended. What Botkin did write in those years indicates a withdrawal from the harsh reality of the everyday world. He now enjoyed the comic opera of the eighteenth-century Italian composer Domenico Cimarosa, for example, because he felt it reminded the careworn adult of a joyful childhood.

In the freer intellectual climate that followed the death of Nicholas I in 1855 and the humiliating defeat of Russia on its own territory in the Crimean War (1853–1856), the division that had begun to develop in the Westernist intelligentsia in the 1840s became more marked. A militant younger generation of thinkers, led by the socialist Chernyshevsky and emanating in the main from a more plebeian social background than the "men of the forties" such as Botkin, preached a crude philosophical materialism and a utilitarian ethical system. They propounded a view of beauty as rooted in everyday reality rather than on a transcendent plane, and they demanded that art, conceived as a surrogate of reality, serve socially useful ends. Chernyshevsky encouraged contemporary writers to emulate Gogol, whom he interpreted as a critic of Russian reality in the age of Nicholas. In opposition to this "Gogolian School," survivors of the Westernist camp of the 1840s now defended an essentially neo-Platonic view of art as embodying an eternal and more perfect beauty than could be present in the flawed material world. They exhorted artists not to serve the interests of any particular societal faction of their time and, while on the whole favoring social reform, urged a gradualism and political caution that could easily be construed as conservative in intention and effect. The literary model for these older men was the early-nineteenth-century poet Aleksandr Sergeevich Pushkin. The leading exponent of the "Pushkinian School" was the literary critic and, in the late 1850s, editor of the journal *Biblioteka dlia chteniia* (A Reading Library), Aleksandr Vasil'evich Druzhinin. Annenkov's acclaimed seven-volume edition of Pushkin's works (*Sochineniia*, 1855–1857) reflected the group's reverence for the great poet.

Botkin, after some expressions of support for Chernyshevsky and the Gogolian tendency in 1855 and 1856, soon aligned himself unequivocally with the Pushkinian School, agreeing in his correspondence with Druzhinin that "political ideas" were the "grave of art" and that a "blind passion for theories and systems" was eroding "poetic feelings." Botkin's allegiance to the moderate or "liberal" Westernism of the older generation (the "fathers" in the terminology of his close friend, Turgenev) is implicit in his decision in 1855 to translate Carlyle's lectures on Scandinavian mythology, Shakespeare, and Dante Alighieri that are included in *On Heroes, Hero-Worship and the Heroic in History*. Although they had first been published in 1841, Carlyle's lectures had a certain topicality for Russians in the post-Crimean intellectual climate. Carlyle attempts in this work to restore power and mystery to the natural world, which has been thus deprived by the tendency of the age to describe the world in scientific terms. He reveres the artist of genius who discerns the beauty of the world and sees the reality beyond the appearances of things, rather than the natural scientist who exercises his critical or logical intellect. Carlyle also propounds a view of history as the history of "Great Men"—the heroes to whom his title refers and whose supposed contribution to human history is in danger of being obscured in an age in which deterministic explanations of phenomena and democratic currents are in the ascendancy.

Botkin's translation of Carlyle was soon followed by an important explicit declaration of his commitment to the Pushkinian School in the form of an essay on the poetry of his close friend, Afanasii Afanas'evich Fet, titled "A. A. Feta," first published in 1857 in *Sovremennik* and translated in 1982 for *Russian Literature Triquarterly*. The importance that Botkin attached to both the translation of Carlyle and the essay on Fet is evident from the fact that he labored on these two pieces with uncharacteristic effort and urgency. Like Carlyle in his lectures—and like

Druzhinin in his criticism—Botkin sets out in "Stikhotvoreniia A. A. Feta" to defend poetry in an age that is primarily concerned with matters of apparently more immediate, practical significance. Art continues to answer a need for the expression of thoughts and feelings in images, Botkin argues, and almost all people have to some degree a poetic feeling that allows them to respond to it. Besides, the "human spirit" will never be willing to live on the material plane alone; in fact, human society is moved only by the "moral ideas" expressed in art. These ideas condition our view of life and leave their imprint on our everyday activity. Art may therefore have greater practical effect than phenomena that are more readily seen as practical, although it can only fulfill this practical function if the poet is left free to treat universally valid subject matter. Finally, Botkin applauds Fet, whose verse on the beauty of nature in the Russian countryside, devoid of topical significance, earned him the reputation of a quintessential exponent of the doctrine of "pure art," as a poetic talent who has preserved originality, independence, lyricism, sincerity, and serenity of vision—the materialistic nature of his age notwithstanding.

In spite of the efforts of Botkin and others to defend art as an end in itself, a sense of defeatism soon invaded the Pushkin camp. During the last twelve years of his life, which were punctuated by foreign trips, Botkin seemed more at home abroad than in Russia. In 1857 he went to Rome and became absorbed in medieval Christian art, a subject remote from contemporary concerns. In 1859 he visited England, and in two articles about his visit—"Dve nedeli v Londone" (Two Weeks in London) and "Priiuty dlia bezdomnykh nishchikh v Londone" (Refuges for London's Homeless Beggars), both collected in his *Sochineniia* (1890–1893)—he applauded England's order, stability, and political freedom; the social concern of its bourgeoisie; and the qualities of the English gentleman. In the 1860s Botkin's opposition to the radical wing of the intelligentsia became more vehement. He abandoned the liberal humanitarianism of contemporaries such as Turgenev, defended the brutal Russian suppression of the Polish revolt of 1863, and approved the shutdown by the government of certain journals, including *Sovremennik* in 1866. Former friends began to shun him, and he spent his last years in isolation, surrounded by luxuries that his health no longer permitted him to enjoy. He died in St. Petersburg on 10 October 1869 at the age of fifty-seven.

With the exception, arguably, of his *Pis'ma ob Ispanii*, Vasilii Petrovich Botkin did not produce writings of the first rank. His contribution to Russian culture needs to be seen, however, against the background of the age of Nicholas I in which, as Annenkov reminded his younger readers in an obituary to his friend, such "honest servants of knowledge" had had to "beat a track" through "jungles and thickets." In various ways—through published travel writing and criticism, published and unpublished translations, and private correspondence and participation in literary society–Botkin made a significant contribution to the dissemination of knowledge about European societies, philosophy, literature, music, and painting; to discussion of the role of art; and to the task of bringing Russian culture into full bloom in inhospitable conditions.

Letters:

Pavel Vasil'evich Annenkov, *P. V. Annenkov i ego druz'ia. Literaturnye vospominaniia i perepiska 1835–1885 godov* (St. Petersburg: A. S. Suvorin, 1892);

Vissarion Grigor'evich Belinsky, *Pis'ma,* edited by Evgenii Aleksandrovich Liatsky, volume 2 (St. Petersburg: M. M. Stasiulevich, 1914);

Turgenev i krug "Sovremennika": Neizdannye materialy, 1847–1861 (Moscow & Leningrad: Akademiia, 1930);

V. P. Botkin i I. S. Turgenev: Neizdannaia perepiska, 1851–1869 (Moscow & Leningrad: Akademiia, 1930);

"Pis'ma k M. A. Bakuninu," in *Ezhegodnik rukopisnogo otdela Pushkinskogo doma* (Leningrad: Nauka, 1980).

Bibliography:

Boris Fedorovich Egorov, Bibliography, in his "V. P. Botkin–literator i kritik," *Uchenye zapiski Tartuskogo gosudarstvennogo universiteta,* 139 (1963).

References:

Pavel Vasil'evich Annenkov, *The Extraordinary Decade. Literary Memoirs,* translated by Irwin Titunik, edited by Arthur Mendel (Ann Arbor: University of Michigan Press, 1968);

Annenkov, *Literaturnye vospominaniia* (Moscow: Khudozhestvennaia literatura, 1960);

Boris Fedorovich Egorov, *Bor'ba esteticheskikh idei v Rossii serediny XIX veka* (Leningrad: Iskusstvo, 1991);

Egorov, "V. P. Botkin–literator i kritik," *Uchenye zapiski Tartuskogo gosudarstvennogo universiteta,* 139 (1963): 20–81; 167 (1965): 81–122; 184 (1966): 33–43;

George Genereux, "Botkin's Collaboration with Belinsky on the Pushkin Articles," *Slavic and East European Journal,* 21 (1977): 470–482;

Genereux, "The Crisis in Russian Literary Criticism: 1856–The Decisive Year," *Russian Literature Triquarterly,* 17 (1982): 117–140;

Aleksandr Ivanovich Herzen, *My Past and Thoughts: The Memoirs of Alexander Herzen,* 4 volumes, translated by Constance Garnett, revised by Humphrey Higgens (London: Chatto & Windus, 1968), II: 420–425, 489–492, 630–638;

E. Kostka, "A Trailblazer of Russian Westernism," *Comparative Literature,* 18 (1966): 211–224;

Charles Moser, *Esthetics as Nightmare: Russian Literary Theory, 1855–1870* (Princeton: Princeton University Press, 1989);

George R. Motolanez, "Botkin as Literary Critic," dissertation, New York University, 1970;

Derek Offord, *Portraits of Early Russian Liberals: A Study of the Thought of T. N. Granovsky, V. P. Botkin, P. V. Annenkov, A. V. Druzhinin and K. D. Kavelin* (Cambridge: Cambridge University Press, 1985), pp. 79–105;

Andrzej Walicki, *A History of Russian Thought from the Enlightenment to Marxism,* translated by Hilda Andrews-Rusiecka (Stanford, Cal.: Stanford University Press, 1979), pp. 116–117, 144–147, 187, 194.

Papers:

Vasilii Petrovich Botkin's papers are held in the Russian State Archive of Literature and Art (RGALI), fond 54; the Russian State Library (RGB, formerly the Lenin Library), fond 178, fond 120 (letters to M. N. Katkov), and fond 315 (letters to A. A. and M. P. Fet); the State Tolstoy Museum (GMT); the Russian National Library (RNB), fond 391; the Institute of Russian Literature (IRLI, Pushkin House), fond 365 (letters to M. P. and D. P. Botkin and to K. A. Gorbunov) and fond 93 (letters to I. I. Panaev); the Scientific Library of Moscow State University; the State Historical Museum (GIM), fond 345 and fond 351 (letters to T. N. Granovsky and N. V. Stankevich); and the Russian State Historical Archive (RGIA), fond 869.

Anton Pavlovich Chekhov

(17 January 1860 – 2 July 1904)

Michael Finke
Washington University

BOOKS: *Skazki Mel'pomeny,* as A. Chekhonte (Moscow: A. Levenson, 1884);

Pestrye rasskazy, as Chekhonte (St. Petersburg: Oskolki, 1886; revised edition, St. Petersburg: A. S. Suvorin, 1891);

Ivanov, lithographic facsimile of manuscript (Moscow: Teatral'naia biblioteka E. N. Rassokhinoi, 1887; revised, first printed edition, St. Petersburg: V. Demakov, 1889);

Nevinnye rechi, as Chekhonte (Moscow: Sverchok, 1887);

O vrede tabaka, as Chekhonte, lithographic facsimile of manuscript (Moscow: Teatral'naia biblioteka S. I. Napoikina, 1887);

V sumerkakh. Ocherki i rasskazy (St. Petersburg: A. S. Suvorin, 1887)–includes "Panikhida" and "Sviatoiu noch'iu";

Lebedinnaia pesnia (Kalkhas), lithographic facsimile of manuscript (Moscow: Teatral'naia biblioteka E. N. Rassokhinoi, 1888);

Medved', lithographic facsimile of manuscript (Moscow: Teatral'naia biblioteka E. N. Rassokhinoi, 1888);

Predlozhenie. Shutka v odnom deistvii, lithographic facsimile of manuscript (Moscow: Teatral'naia biblioteka E. N. Rassokhinoi, 1888);

Rasskazy (St. Petersburg: A. S. Suvorin, 1888)–includes "Step'";

Detvora (St. Petersburg: A. S. Suvorin, 1889);

Tat'iana Repina (St. Petersburg: A. S. Suvorin, 1889);

Tragik po nevole (Iz dachnoi zhizni) (St. Petersburg: Teatral'naia biblioteka V. A. Bazarova, 1889; revised edition, lithographic facsimile of manuscript, Moscow: Teatral'naia biblioteka E. N. Rassokhinoi, 1889);

Khmurye liudi (St. Petersburg: A. S. Suvorin, 1890)–includes "Skuchnaia istoriia," "Spat' khochetsia," and "Pripadok";

Leshii, lithographic facsimile of manuscript (Moscow: Teatral'naia biblioteka E. N. Rassokhinoi, 1890);

Svad'ba, lithographic facsimile of manuscript (Moscow: S. F. Rassokhin, 1890);

Duel' (St. Petersburg: A. S. Suvorin, 1892);

Anton Pavlovich Chekhov

Iubilei (Moscow: S. F. Rassokhin, 1892);

Kashtanka (St. Petersburg: A. S. Suvorin, 1892);

Palata No. 6 (Moscow: Posrednik, 1893);

Palata No. 6 (i drugie rasskazy) (St. Petersburg: A. S. Suvorin, 1893)–includes "Baby," "Strakh," and "Gusev";

Zhena (Moscow: Posrednik, 1893);

Povesti i rasskazy (Moscow: I. D. Sytin, 1894)–includes "Bab'e tsarstvo," "V ssylke," "Poprygun'ia," "Chernyi monakh," and "Skripka Rotshil'da";

Ostrov Sakhalin (Moscow: Russkaia mysl', 1895);

P'esy (St. Petersburg: A. S. Suvorin, 1897)–includes *Chaika* and *Diadia Vania;*

Muzhiki (St. Petersburg: A. S. Suvorin, 1897);

Muzhiki i Moia zhizn' (St. Petersburg: A. S. Suvorin, 1897);

Mechty (Moscow: Moskovskoe obshchestvo gramotnosti, 1898);

Sochineniia, 6 volumes (St. Petersburg: A. F. Marks, 1899–1901);

Sochineniia, 15 volumes (St. Petersburg: A. F. Marks, 1901–1902);

Tri sestry (St. Petersburg: A. F. Marks, 1901);

Vishnevyi sad (St. Petersburg: A. F. Marks, 1904).

Collections: *Sochineniia,* 14 volumes (Berlin: Slovo, 1921–1922);

Polnoe sobranie sochinenii, 12 volumes, edited by Anatolii Vasil'evich Lunacharsky and Sergei Dmitrievich Balukhatyi (Moscow & Leningrad: Gosudarstvennoe izdatel'stvo khudozhestvennoi literatury, 1930–1933);

Polnoe sobranie sochinenii i pisem, 20 volumes, edited by Balukhatyi (Moscow: Gosudarstvennoe izdatel'stvo khudozhestvennoi literatury, 1944–1951);

Polnoe sobranie sochinenii i pisem, 30 volumes, edited by Nikolai Fedorovich Bel'chikov and others (Moscow: Nauka, 1974–1983);

Sobranie sochinenii, 15 volumes, compiled by O. Dorofeev (Moscow: TERRA, 1999).

Editions in English: *Plays by Anton Tchekoff,* 2 volumes, translated by Marian Fell and Julius West, with an introduction by Fell (New York: Scribners, 1912–1916)—includes *Uncle Vanya, Ivanoff, The Sea-Gull, The Swan Song, The Proposal, The Bear, A Tragedian in Spite of Himself, The Three Sisters,* and *The Cherry Orchard;*

Anton Tchekhov's Literary and Theatrical Reminiscences, translated and edited by S. S. Koteliansky (London: Routledge, 1925);

The Shooting Party, translated by A. E. Chamot (London: Stanley Paul, 1926); revised and edited, with an introduction, by Julian Symons (Chicago: University of Chicago Press, 1986);

The Portable Chekhov, edited by Avrahm Yarmolinsky (New York: Viking, 1947);

The Unknown Chekhov: Stories and Other Writings Hitherto Untranslated, translated by Yarmolinsky (New York: Noonday Press, 1954);

Selected Stories, translated by Ann Dunnigan (New York: New American Library, 1960);

Chekhov: The Major Plays, translated by Dunnigan (New York: Dutton, 1964);

Lady with Lapdog, and Other Stories, translated, with an introduction, by David Magarshack (Harmondsworth, U.K. & Baltimore: Penguin, 1964);

Ward Six and Other Stories, translated by Dunnigan (New York: New American Library, 1965);

The Oxford Chekhov, 9 volumes, translated by Ronald Hingley (Oxford: Oxford University Press, 1965–1975);

The Island: A Journey to Sakhalin, translated by Luba Terpak and Michael Terpak, introduction by Robert Payne (New York: Washington Square Press, 1967);

Anton Chekhov's Short Stories: Texts of the Stories, Background, Criticism, selected and edited by Ralph Matlaw (New York: Norton, 1979);

Chekhov, the Early Stories, 1883–1888, introduction, translation, and notes by Patrick Miles and Harvey Pitcher (New York: Macmillan, 1982); republished as *The Early Stories* (Oxford: Oxford University Press, 1994);

The Duel and Other Stories, translated and introduced by Ronald Wilks (Harmondsworth, U. K. & New York: Penguin, 1984);

The Comic Stories, translated and introduced by Pitcher (Chicago: Ivan R. Dee, 1999);

Stories, translated by Richard Pevear and Larissa Volokhonsky, introduction by Pevear (New York: Bantam, 2000);

The Undiscovered Chekhov: Fifty-One New Stories, translated by Peter Constantine (London: Duck Editions, 2001).

PLAY PRODUCTIONS: *O vrede tabaka,* Moscow, Korsh Theater, 1886;

Ivanov, Moscow, Korsh Theater, 1887;

Lebedinaia pesnia, Moscow, Korsh Theater, 1888;

Predlozhenie, St. Petersburg, Krasnoe Selo Theater, 1888;

Medved', Moscow, Korsh Theater, 1888;

Ivanov, revised, St. Petersburg, Aleksandrinskii Theater, 1889;

Leshii, Moscow, Abramova Theater, 1889;

Chaika, St. Petersburg, Aleksandrinskii Theater, 1896; revised, Moscow, Moscow Art Theater, 1898;

Diadia Vania, Nizhnyi Novgorod, Nizhnyi Novgorod Dramatic Theater, 1898;

Iubilei, Moscow, Society of Art and Literature, 1900;

Tri sestry, Moscow, Moscow Art Theater, 1901;

Vishnevyi sad, Moscow, Moscow Art Theater, 1904;

Svad'ba, St. Petersburg, Komissarzhevskaia Theater, 1904;

Platonov/Bezotstovshchina, Pskov, Pushkin Dramatic Theater, 1957;

Tatiana Repina, Scotland, Mull Little Theatre, 1974.

OTHER: "Shvedskaia spichka. Ugolovnyi rasskaz," in *Al'manakh "Strekozy"* (St. Petersburg, 1884).

Anton Chekhov is today one of the most widely known authors of nineteenth-century Russian literature. Appreciated not only in Russia and the West but also in Asia, he was a master of the short story, and his innovations in the poetics of short prose fiction served as models for the finest American and European short-story writers throughout the twentieth century. His slim output of four major dramatic works sufficed to play an influential role in launching a new era in European theater and—in the exaggerated view of some critics—to earn him the title of "Shakespeare of the twentieth century." In this respect, his success went hand-in-hand with that of the Moskovskii Khudozhestvennyi Akademicheskii Theater (MKhAT, Moscow Art Theater), organized by Konstantin Sergeevich Stanislavsky (pseudonym of K. S. Alekseev) and Vladimir Ivanovich Nemirovich-Danchenko.

Chekhov was of a social class far different from that of the major Russian authors before him. Born into a family only one generation removed from serfdom, he wrote his publisher and friend Aleksei Sergeevich Suvorin on 7 January 1889 of the difficult process by which he "squeezed the slave's blood out of himself" to attain self-respect and independence as a man and an author. Educated as a physician, Chekhov practiced only sporadically, though at times intensively and for the most part without remuneration. His identity as a physician remained strong throughout his short life, however, and his education in medicine and the sciences, together with the insights derived from clinical experience, is frequently credited with conditioning his authorial point of view. Without a doubt Chekhov's social consciousness and intensely ethical personal stance owe much to his identification with the progressive, self-sacrificing image of the zemstvo (rural district council) physician. An author of "good works" in every sense of the term, he was a relentless philanthropist whose contributions in labor and cash loomed huge in relation to his resources.

Anton Pavlovich Chekhov was born on 17 January 1860 in what was then the rather cosmopolitan port city of Taganrog. He was the third son of Pavel Egorovich Chekhov and Evgeniia Iakovlevna Morozova; the other siblings in this remarkably close-knit and talented family were Aleksandr (born 1855), Nikolai (born 1858), Ivan (born 1861), Mariia (born 1863), and Mikhail (born 1865). Chekhov's grandfather had been a serf who managed to purchase his whole family's freedom when Pavel Egorovich was already a teenager. By the time Chekhov was born, his father had become an independent merchant in Taganrog, the owner of a small general store, and an upstanding member of the religious community of the city. According to his brother Aleksandr (in *Shekhov v vospominaniiakh sovremennikov* [Chekhov in the Recollections of His Contemporaries], 1954), the mature Chekhov told close friends and family that "in my childhood there was no childhood." He and his elder brothers were pressed into long and late hours of service at their father's store. They were compelled to participate in pedantic family prayer sessions and to sing in their father's church choir; as a result the music and liturgy, which Chekhov knew so well and loved, later aroused other, much more

negative associations for him throughout his life. Worst of all, perhaps, the older Chekhov children were subjected to severe and arbitrary discipline. Chekhov later remarked that he could not help believing in progress because he had experienced in his own life the "terrible difference" between the time when he suffered beatings and the time when the abuses stopped. Nevertheless, his early years had their lighter and brighter side: family theatricals, theatergoing (as soon as the underage Chekhov could get away with it), a manuscript literary magazine edited by him, and an intense connection with the sea that showed itself in both his life and works.

While some disagreement regarding the character of Chekhov's father is reflected in the memoirs of the elder and younger Chekhov siblings, all evidence suggests that in the Taganrog years Pavel Egorovich was a petty tyrant who grounded his authority in a rote and pedantic religious sensibility. In the years to come both Chekhov and his eldest brother Aleksandr, a brilliant but troubled individual and a minor author, honed their considerable skills at verbal mimicry by parodying their father's rhetoric in their fascinating correspondence. The material was rich, as verified by this astonishing incident: when a dead rat was fished out of a barrel of cooking oil for sale at his store, Pavel Egorovich had the oil "purified" and so rehabilitated for sale by the singular method of having a priest bless it. Such practices could not have been good for business, and the combination of a failing business and the debt incurred to build a new house resulted, in 1876, in Pavel Egorovich fleeing Taganrog and the possibility of debtors' prison for Moscow, where his two eldest sons were then living. He was soon joined by the rest of his family, with the exception of Chekhov and, for a shorter period, Ivan, who both remained in Taganrog to finish their secondary education. Ivan lived with relatives, while Chekhov was left to fend for himself by giving private lessons and living as a boarder in what had been his family home. After a visit to Moscow in the spring of 1877, when he saw the poverty in which his family was living, Chekhov began sending a portion of his slim earnings to Moscow.

During this "exile" from his family Chekhov subscribed to the Taganrog public library, and the succor provided by that institution was richly repaid decades later. Library records show that he began his serious reading "career" with travel accounts, an early sign of the passion for travel that possessed him in his mature years. Meanwhile, Chekhov's elder brothers were already breaking into the *malaia pressai* (small press)—Aleksandr as an author, Nikolai as an illustrator—and, under the mentorship of Aleksandr, Chekhov tried his own hand at short humorous tales. He also wrote at least three plays. One was the lengthy *Bezotsovshchina* (Fatherlessness), which most Chekhov scholars believe is the play that was discovered after his death and known (and occasionally performed) as *Platonov* (first published as "Neizdannaia p'esa," 1923); Chekhov had destroyed the manuscript, but a copy was saved by his brother Mikhail. The other two are works that have become lost—*Nashla kosa na kamen'* (Scythe against Rock, which is idiomatic for "He's Met His Match") and *Ne darom kuritsa pela* (It's Not for Nothing the Hen Was Singing).

Chekhov's academic record was not particularly distinguished: as a youngster he wasted a year in a private Greek school, where—because of the wealth of the Greek community in Taganrog—his father had sent him and his brothers in pursuit of a well-paying job and social status; later he was held back in the gymnasium for failing Greek. Nevertheless, his comportment and industriousness appear to have impressed his teachers quite favorably, and after completing his secondary education in 1879, he was awarded a town scholarship in support of higher education. Chekhov joined his family in their damp, dark, and crowded basement apartment in Moscow and enrolled in the medical faculty of Moscow University. Although Pavel Egorovich was not immune from displays of paternal authority, such as posting rules and regulations on the wall and occasionally beating the younger children, his loss of status outside the family (because of his business failures) had severely undermined his position as a father; eventually he took a job that offered room and board apart from the family. Whereas the elder brothers Aleksandr and Nikolai in essence fled the family circle—Aleksandr went so far as to leave Moscow—Chekhov shouldered the responsibility of holding the family together. When he arrived in Moscow, he brought a boarder and his stipend from Taganrog to enhance family finances; soon he added his literary earnings to the kitty, and as the family's chief breadwinner and moral authority, he began taking over the position of his father—becoming, in short, father to his father.

In January 1880, after many attempts at publishing his work, Chekhov learned that the journal *Strekoza* (Dragonfly) planned to feature a short piece that he had submitted the previous December. "Pis'mo donskogo pomeshchika Stepan Vladimirovich N k uchenomu sosedu d-ru Fridrikhu" (A Letter from the Don Landowner Stepan Vladimirovich N. to His Learned Neighbor Dr. Fridrikh) appeared in March under the signature ". . . v"; and so began Chekhov's professional writing career—at the rate of 5.00 kopecks per line. The style of the story was apparently inspired by a letter to Chekhov's father from his grandfather, Egor Mikhailovich. The pompous, ignorant, and patently ridiculous pseudoscientific arguments—against, for instance, the theory of evolution—that the fictional letter- writer Stepan

Vladimirovich addresses to his educated neighbor in semi-illiterate language dramatize the educational and ideological gap between the younger Chekhovs and their parents; they also assert the superiority of the younger generation to, and their independence from, their elders. In addition, the genesis of the story (particularly in Chekhov's use of material close to home) sets a pattern that annoyed and offended many of his friends and family throughout his career.

Chekhov was soon publishing regularly in the "small press": anecdotes, stylized letters, dialogues, spoofs on authors of romance and adventure, captions to accompany the humorous illustrations of his brother Nikolai, and odd and incongruous lists. He published anything that could generate a laugh. In addition to appearing in *Strekoza,* his works were featured in *Budil'nik* (Alarm Clock), *Zritel'* (The Spectator), *Russkie vedomosti* (Russian News), *Moskva* (Moscow), and *Mirskoi tolk* (Worldly Chatter). Chekhov published under pseudonyms, the most famous and frequently utilized of which was "Antosha Chekhonte"; this name and its variations, such as "A. Chekhonte" and "Chekhonte," were based on a nickname given him by his teacher of religion at the gymnasium. By the time of his death, Chekhov had used a host of such pseudonyms—more than fifty if one counts all variations—including "Brother of My Brother," "Doctor without Patients," and "Man without a Spleen." While employing pseudonyms was customary among contributors to the small press, to attribute this use of pseudonyms entirely to convention would be facile. Chekhov stated in a letter that he planned to use his true family name only for his future scientific writings. There was more at stake for him in how he signed his works than obeying the customs of the small press. This complex question remains open to psychobiographical exploration.

Chekhov's first major break came in the fall of 1882, when he was introduced to the publisher of the St. Petersburg humor magazine *Oskolki* (Fragments), Nikolai Aleksandrovich Leikin, who invited him to collaborate with the journal. Leikin was himself a prolific master of the genre of the *stsenka* (little scene), and his publications were enormously popular among the burgeoning lower middle-class and (literate) urban population. He was somewhat ruthless as an editor; Chekhov, who never trusted the "lame devil," was often piqued by Leikin's rigid adherence to a poetics of brevity and simplicity that was proved to keep up circulation. Yet, arguably, these exact features had an enormously beneficent effect on Chekhov's mature poetics, and Chekhov himself became a no less ruthless editor of his own and others' writings later in life. In addition to the laconicity that he learned in the "small press," other features of his poetics probably derive from this apprenticeship—in particular, his pen-

and then rose to approximately 125 in 1885. This output occurred while he was proceeding with his medical studies and private practice, in which–if he was not proving himself outstanding–he was by all accounts competent and assiduous. When compiling his first collected works, Chekhov omitted all his pre-*Oskolki* production. Especially in the West, common practice among scholars has been to follow Chekhov's own indications and discount the early writings as hackwork. Nevertheless, some of his works from 1883 can already be considered among his masterpieces of biting irony; these include, for example, "Smert' chinovnika" (Death of a Government Clerk), "Doch' Albiona" (A Daughter of Albion), and "Tolstyi i tonkii" (Fat and Thin), all of which first appeared in *Oskolki*. Among other noteworthy works of this period are two spoofs of the detective genre: the intelligent and amusing "Shvedskaia spichka. Ugolovnyi rasskaz" (The Swedish Match: A Crime Tale, published in the anthology *Al'manakh "Strekozy,"* 1884), Chekhov's second longest story to date; and *Drama na okhote* (A Drama during the Hunt, published in *Novosti dnia* [News of the Day], 1884–1885; translated as *The Shooting Party,* 1926), which appeared serially and was the longest work of fiction that he ever published. The latter work evinced a stroke of genius, emulated by Agatha Christie much later (in *The Murder of Roger Ackroyd,* 1926), in which Chekhov's unreliable narrator, the investigating magistrate, turns out to be the murderer in the case he is investigating. "Shvedskaia spichka" and *Drama na okhote,* as well as many of Chekhov's earliest trifles, display an originality that bursts through the most hackneyed forms via parody and a sometimes subtle undermining of convention.

In the spring of 1883 Chekhov wrote Aleksandr a long letter in which he outlined a research project for a doctoral dissertation in medicine and invited his brother to collaborate. Provisionally titled "Istoriia polovogo avtoriteta" (A History of Sexual Dominance), the work was to employ the Darwinian theory of evolution in investigating why, in the human species, males had developed further than females. Most important, once this phenomenon was understood, corrective measures could be taken: "Nature must be helped," wrote Chekhov, who indeed envisioned utilizing his new-felt scientific powers to assist nature in raising women to an intellectual level on a par with that of men. Although the project never developed beyond this prospectus, it is a key manifestation of Chekhov's professional and emotional investment in the scientific theories of his time. The planned dissertation project, which alternately cites Henry Buckle, Herbert Spencer, and Charles Darwin, bespeaks an entanglement of the biological with the social-historical entirely in the spirit of the second half of the nineteenth century. Above all, Chekhov's letter demonstrates the seriousness of his ambitions in the medical field, a nearly euphoric confidence in his new knowledge,

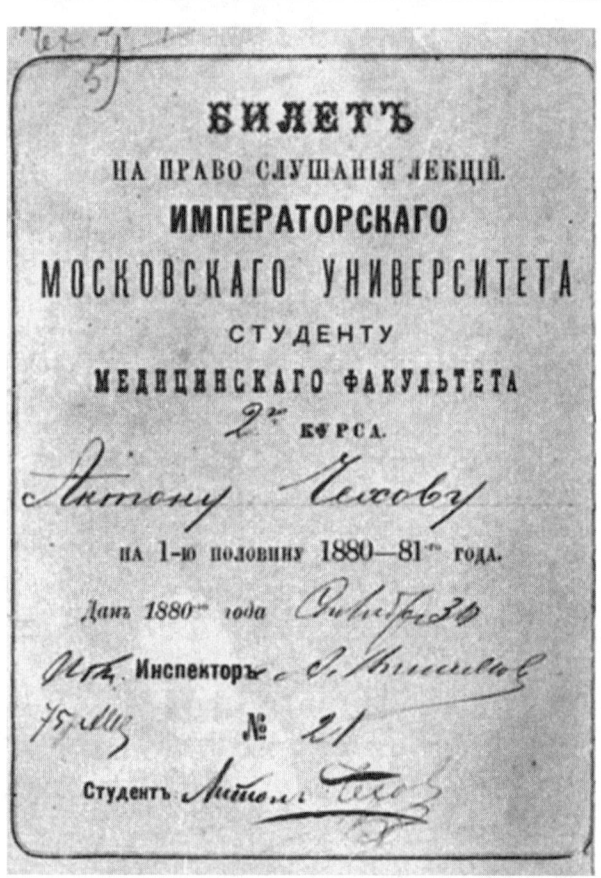

Chekhov's student card, which permitted him to take courses in medicine at Moscow University (from Ronald Hingley, Russian Writers and Society, 1825–1904, *1967)*

chant for structuring the temporal dimension of his works in accordance with seasons and holidays. When writing for small-press publications in Chekhov's day, one provided material in association with the time of the year: for example, the summer journals published tales of dacha (country home) romances; in the spring, features about the start of the hunting or fishing season typically appeared; and holiday-themed stories came out during the winter months. Such subgeneric categories were often indicated in subtitles. Chekhov also contributed a regular feuilleton column, "Oskolki moskovskoi zhizni" (Fragments of Moscow Life) under the psedonym of Ulysses.

By now Chekhov's earnings had risen significantly, even if his family's standard of living always tended to outpace his income (the Chekhovs changed apartments frequently in these years). His confidence was reaching a peak as well: he edited the writings of his eldest brother (and, later, those of many young literary protégés), laid down rules of poetics, and occasionally boasted of his earnings. His production in these years was enormous: from some 30 items in 1882 his list of publications increased to more than 100 in 1883, fell slightly in 1884, and, correspondingly, how little he expected from his literary activities, which still did not merit signature with his proper name. This project for a dissertation in medicine was followed by two others: in the year after his graduation from the university (1884–1885) and occasionally afterward, too, Chekhov gathered materials for an unrealized "Vrachebnoe delo v Rossii" (History of Medicine in Russia), which was to include the medieval period and folk practices; roughly a decade later he also explored the possibility of submitting as the dissertation his book on the Far East prison island of Sakhalin, which had been written at least in part to "pay his debt" to medicine.

In the early part of 1884 Chekhov compiled a selection of his stories, including the first one he ever published, for a volume illustrated by his brother Nikolai. Titled "Na dosuge" (Free Time), the collection remained unpublished because of a lack of funds. Later that year Chekhov did succeed in bringing out his first collection of stories, *Skazki Mel'pomeny* (Tales of Melpomene), under the pseudonym of A. Chekhonte. He financed this business venture himself (with credit extended by the publisher), and his family helped in distribution and marketing. In June, the same month that *Skazki Mel'pomeny* was published, Chekhov completed his course of studies at the medical faculty of Moscow University.

Chekhov's brother Ivan had taken a position in a parochial school in the town of Voskresensk, west of Moscow, in fall 1880, and for the next four years the Chekhov family took advantage of Ivan's location and vacationed there during the summer. During these holidays Chekhov had become acquainted with the director of a nearby hospital and other medical personnel in the area, and he was able to gain practical experience by assisting them. In the summer of 1884, now that he had finished his medical education, he worked in an official capacity substituting for the zemstvo doctor in nearby Zvenigorod—his first professional position as a physician. In September, after returning to Moscow, he hung out his shingle and embarked on a private practice. In writings about Chekhov one often encounters the mistaken assertion that he never actually practiced medicine. Admittedly, he was not able to support himself and his family through the practice of medicine; by the time he graduated, his literary earnings had outstripped what he could earn by working as a doctor, and he was always willing to administer his medical expertise as a favor to friends and colleagues in literature and the arts, as well as to others who could not afford to pay for his services. Nevertheless, Chekhov did set himself up in private practice at the start of his career, and he continued to practice the healing arts until his health no longer permitted him to do so. Indeed, Chekhov remained solidly attached to his identity as a physician until the end of his life.

If 1884 marks the start of Chekhov's career as a physician, then it also inaugurates his life as a consumptive. In the fall of that year he was serving as a court reporter on assignment for *Petersburgskaia gazeta* (The Petersburg Gazette) when he suffered his first pulmonary hemorrhage, a clear symptom of the tuberculosis that eventually killed him. More accurately, in 1884 Chekhov's vocation as a patient manqué commenced, for from this time until 1897, when a devastating hemorrhage nearly killed him, he did not allow himself to be examined by another physician. Chekhov's handling of his disease receives widely varying interpretation by scholars and memoirists: some read it as a form of psychopathological denial; others view it as the levelheaded stoicism of a physician who knew there was no reliable course of therapy. Marginal finances and familial obligations also rendered unthinkable the most likely prescriptions of more leisure and relocation to a warmer and drier climate. As with his use of pseudonyms, Chekhov's approach to his illness appears far more complex than any one of the standard critical hypotheses might allow, although there is surely an element of truth in each.

In the spring of 1885 Chekhov received his next major break as an author. Leikin, who could be quite jealous of his protégé's relations with other publishers, nevertheless could not resist boasting of having discovered "a new Saltykov-Shchedrin," in the words of Ronald Hingley in *A New Life of Anton Chekhov* (1976). On Leikin's recommendation Chekhov became a regular contributor of fiction to the *Petersburgskaia gazeta,* where he had much more freedom in regard to genre and tone than Leikin allowed at *Oskolki*. His submissions to *Petersburgskaia gazeta* in 1885 included stylistically complex and far from lighthearted pieces, such as "Eger'" (The Huntsman), "V apteke" (In the Pharmacy), "Zloumyshlennik" (The Malefactor), "Mertvoe telo" (The Corpse), and "Gore" (Grief). Often anthologized in collections of Chekhov's fiction, these stories not only owe much to Leikin's formula of *stsenka* but also show Chekhov in transition to his "serious" phase.

By the end of 1885 Chekhov had acquired a reputation among St. Petersburg insiders as a bright, talented, promising literary newcomer. Not until his first visit to St. Petersburg, as Leikin's guest that December, was Chekhov aware of his own public image. He was shocked to learn that the literary elite was reading him and that he was considered a major emerging talent. After returning to Moscow he wrote his brother Aleksandr on 4 January 1886 that he had been "stunned by the reception in Peter" (short for "St. Petersburg"), that he "became terrified," and that "Had I known they were reading me, I wouldn't have written like that, to order." Similar remarks can be found in other letters following Chekhov's return.

New developments were fast, furious, and significant. In January of 1886 Chekhov was invited to become a regular contributor to the St. Petersburg daily *Novoe vre-*

mia (New Times); the newspaper was owned by the conservative publisher and author Suvorin, a self-made man of wealth who soon became one of Chekhov's closest associates. After Chekhov submitted the story "Panikhida" (Requiem) under the pseudonym of A. Chekhonte, he was asked for permission to publish the tale under his real surname, and he consented. The appearance of "Panikhida" in *Novoe vremia* in February 1886 thus marks the start of Chekhov's regular publication under his own proper name (although four pieces had appeared under the name of Chekhov in the past—some by his own choice, others not). In less distinguished venues he continued to publish pseudonymously.

In March 1886 Chekhov received a letter of both admiration and rebuke from a respected elder of Russian literature, Dmitrii Vasil'evich Grigorovich, once a roommate of Fyodor Dostoevsky. Grigorovich told Chekhov that for the past year he had been reading "everything signed *Chekhonte,* though he was inwardly made angry by a man who valued himself so little that he considers it necessary to have recourse to a pseudonym"; he urged Chekhov to "respect his talent," to sign his forthcoming collection of stories with his real name, and to take more time when writing. In his effusive answer to Grigorovich's missive, which, Chekhov said, had "struck me like lightening," Chekhov excused his practices to date—indeed, he had always written quickly and avoided deploying his most cherished material; only now was he daring to believe that he had talent. He needed some time to free himself from writing on deadline. He explained that he was a doctor, occupied "up to his ears" in his practice, and having a tough time chasing "two hares" at once. Last, he said it was too late to have his next volume of stories published under his own name. Yet, soon after receiving Grigorovich's letter, Chekhov instructed the publisher of his second collection of stories, *Pestrye rasskazy* (Motley Tales, 1886), to add "A. P. Chekhov" in brackets to the second title page of the book.

Meanwhile, a change was taking place in Chekhov's medical practice as well. Over the winter he had been treating the three sisters and the mother of his friend, the artist Aleksandr Stepanovich Ianov, for typhus; the mother and one of the sisters died—the latter while holding Chekhov's hand. According to Chekhov's brother Mikhail, this event affected the writer so deeply that he took down his shingle and in essence ceased his private practice. While there is no reason to doubt Mikhail's characterization of this episode as traumatic, it may be inexact in the details: rather than taking down his sign immediately following his patients' deaths, Chekhov appears to have decided not to rehang it when he moved at the end of the summer. Even if one accepts Mikhail's chronology, the timing of Chekhov's decision to scale back his medical activities—following the trip to St. Petersburg and a dramatically expanding horizon for his literary efforts—suggests that he did so less as a defensive reaction to failure than as a positive step reflecting a new awareness of his literary potential. In any case, this episode by no means marks the end of Chekhov's practice of medicine: in the summer of 1886, for instance, he spent a short term in Zvenigorod substituting for the zemstvo physician there, and over the next decade he did much more medical work, keeping up with professional journals (as well as editing medical material for Suvorin) and attending professional meetings. He served his profession however he could: when in 1895 he learned that the recently founded *Khirurgicheskaia letopis'* (Surgical Chronicle) was failing, he solicited support for the journal from his own publishers; the following year, after the collapse of the journal, he helped obtain permission and financial support for the publication of a new periodical, *Khirurgiia* (Surgery).

In January of 1886 Chekhov informed the editorial secretary of *Oskolki,* Viktor Viktorovich Bilibin (with whom, to judge by the correspondence, he felt rather close at this time), that he had proposed to a certain young lady. This was Evdokiia (Dunia) Isaakovna Efros, a friend of Chekhov's sister and the daughter of a prosperous Jewish merchant. Chekhov's letter is not optimistic: the relationship has been stormy, and Efros refuses to convert to Orthodoxy; even if they do marry, an early divorce is likely. This engagement produced a few joking comments in letters to Bilibin, but otherwise fizzled out rather quickly—if, that is, it ever actually existed. The demand that Efros should assume Russian Orthodoxy strikes one as odd coming from Chekhov: he showed no particular concern when his older brothers were involved with Jewish women (according to one biographer, he himself had a two-year affair with the Jewess who, years later, became Aleksandr's second wife); he criticized his brother Aleksandr when the latter was troubled by the Chekhov family's opinion of his domestic affairs; he was not a pedantically religious man, if he had faith at all (a point of some contention nowadays); and he had many Jewish friends. Indeed, as a gymnasium student in Taganrog, Chekhov had organized a successful protest against the expulsion of a Jewish student who had slapped the face of a boy who had called him a "yid." Scholars have suggested that Chekhov's story "Tina" (Mire, published in *Novoe vremia,* 1886), about a Jewish seductress and loan shark who charms and ruins fine Russian men, was inspired by the Efros affair. The opposite extreme of Chekhov's handling of the Jewish leitmotiv may be found in the later masterpiece "Skripka Rotshil'da" (Rothschild's Fiddle, published in *Russkie vedomosti,* 1894), in which a Jew and his music become associated with memory and conscience.

After returning from their summer holiday, the Chekhov family moved into lodgings they were to occupy for the next four years—a comfortable house on the Sadovaia-Kudrinskaia Boulevard, which is today the Chekhov Museum in Moscow. Thanks mainly to Chekhov's literary earnings, his family had risen in status quite a bit since their flight from Tuganrog, but his own financial situation always remained stressful.

The increased public attention that Chekhov was receiving had its negative side as well. In June of 1886 a review of *Pestrye rasskazy* in the major Petersburg journal *Severnyi vestnik* (The Northern Messenger) accused Chekhov of "wasting his talent on trifles" and writing "the first thing that comes into his head, without thinking"; "writing himself out," Chekhov was bound to end up like a "squeezed out lemon," expiring "forgotten, under a wall somewhere." He referred to this offensive review years later in conversations with Ivan Alekseevich Bunin, Maksim Gor'ky, and others. Chekhov himself could hardly believe his sudden popularity, and in years to come he had cause also to complain of his contemporaries' envy and backbiting. When he and his sister, Mariia, returned from a visit to St. Petersburg toward the end of 1886, Chekhov compared the path of his career to the comet-like trajectory of Emile Zola's fictional actress and courtesan, writing in a letter to Mariia Kiseleva on 13 December 1886 that "In Peter I am becoming as fashionable as Nana." He lamented the public's lack of interest in more worthy authors, such as Vladimir Galaktionovich Korolenko, and predicted in the same letter that "not a single dog will recognize me when I begin working seriously." Nevertheless, he took pride when a serious review of his work (comparing him to Korolenko) appeared in *Russkoe bogatstvo* (Russian Wealth), for he was the only writer of "newspaper garbage"—his work had not yet been published in the more distinguished *tolstye zhurnaly* (thick journals)—to have ever merited such attention. Now that his work was, as he wrote in a letter to his uncle Mitrofan Egorovich Chekhov on 14 January 1887, "public and answerable, that makes it doubly difficult." Chekhov increasingly felt the demand that he write "seriously," which, above all, meant writing a novel—the challenge that, Chekhov had felt for several years, lay before him along the road to becoming a genuine Russian author. Meanwhile, in February 1887 he was elected a member of Obshchestvo dlia posobiia nuzhdaiushchimsia literatoram i uchenym (Society for Assistance to Needy Writers and Scholars), otherwise known as Literaturnyi fond (The Literary Fund).

In the spring of 1887 he took a six-week trip to Southern Russia, revisiting his hometown of Taganrog, as well as Novocherkassk, and staying with his old friend Gavril Pavlovich Kravtsov in an area known as the "Don Switzerland." He continued to send stories back while traveling and collecting material for future works. His visit to the monastery at Sviatye Gory, for instance, resulted in the story "Perkati-pole (Putevoi nabrosok)" (A Rolling Stone [A Travel Sketch], published in *Novoe vremia*, 1887). After this sojourn he joined his family in their current vacation retreat at the Kiselev estate of Babkino, developed his idea for a novel, and read the proofs of his colleague the physician Pavel Arsen'evich Arkhangel'sky's study of psychiatric institutions. That summer Suvorin published Chekhov's third collection of stories, *V sumerkakh. Ocherki i rasskazy* (In the Twilight. Sketches and Stories, 1887), which consisted of pieces written for *Novoe vremia*. Chekhov also agreed to the proposal of the publisher of *Sverchok* (Cricket) to bring out another collection of early humor; at this point in his career he preferred to leave such material behind (and later did), but 150 rubles in cash made such a "deal with the devil" irresistible. When the stories came out in October under the title *Nevinnye rechi* (Guiltless Utterances, 1887), he experienced acute seller's remorse.

In the autumn of 1887 Chekhov began working on the new full-length play that became *Ivanov* (1887, published 1887). He asked the prominent actor Vladimir Nikolaevich Davydov (pseudonym of Ivan Nikolaevich Gorelov) for an evaluation of the piece, and Davydov urged Chekhov to have the play staged. The play was produced in Moscow in November 1887 at the Korsh Theater with Davydov in the title role. *Ivanov*, whose eponymous hero is a tapped-out member of the intelligentsia tormented by guilt and rage over a wasted life and unhappy marriage with a tubercular Jewess, was extremely well received by the audience—Chekhov was summoned to the stage for applause after only the second act—and the following month the play was published in a lithographic facsimile edition.

Chekhov responded to his Moscow theatrical success by leaving town. He spent the first few weeks in St. Petersburg, where among the literary figures he met was the venerable liberal poet Aleksei Nikolaevich Pleshcheev, who had been arrested with Dostoevsky and the other members of the Petrashevsky circle in 1848. This association proved to be important for Chekhov. Pleshcheev edited one of the *tolstye zhurnaly*, in which Chekhov's writings had yet to appear. Soon Chekhov was working on his first serious long narrative, "Step'" (The Steppe), to be published in Pleshcheev's *Severnyi vestnik*. Letters show the author highly conscious of this turning point in his career and laboring intensively on a story that, as he wrote to Kiseleva on 3 February 1888, "cost me so much juice and energy." He had to struggle with the form of a work that ran approximately one hundred pages long, although during the remarkably short month when he wrote it, he

Paper cover for an issue of the journal Oskolki *(Fragments),*
which published Chekhov's early work (from
Liudmila Danilovna Mikitich, Literaturnyi
Peterburg, Petrograd, *1991)*

still found the time to dash off "Spat' khochetsia"
(Sleepy), a masterpiece of psychopathography; because
it came out in *Peterburgskaia gazeta,* Chekhov signed the
often anthologized "Spat' khochetsia" with a pseudonym rather than his proper name. "Step'" made use of
both the material that he had gathered during his recent
trip to Southern Russia and the recollections from his
travels through the steppe as a youngster. A tale of a
seven-year-old child's journey after he is taken from his
hometown (Taganrog) to a larger city (Rostov-on-Don),
where he will be schooled, "Step'" marks one of Chekhov's most poetic prose works. Full of nature
descriptions, it is a genuine hymn to the steppe, and
as a story about a rite of passage, it is also a profound study in child psychology.

According to legend, the enormously talented but
troubled storywriter Vsevolod Mikhailovich Garshin
became ecstatic and somewhat obsessed by "Step'" after
reading it. He proclaimed the appearance of a "new
first-class writer" and a short time later committed sui-

cide by throwing himself down the stairwell of his
apartment building. Chekhov, who had attempted to
call on Garshin twice when in St. Petersburg "but saw
only the staircase," contributed "Pripadok" (An Attack
of Nerves) to *Pamiati V. M. Garshina* (In Memory of V.
M. Garshin, 1889), edited by Pleshcheev. Like more
than a few stories by Chekhov, "Pripadok" makes
explicit use of his medical knowledge and, especially,
his interest in psychiatry.

In the period after finishing "Step'," to which critics
on the whole responded well, Chekhov contemplated a
sequel and continued planning his novel. Although neither conception was realized, these would have been the
logical next steps for an up-and-coming prose author.
Readers today often view the last twenty years of the
nineteenth century as an era in which the heyday of the
great realistic novel had passed and the short form
gained preeminence in Russian literature—a perspective
that renders Chekhov the leading figure of the period.
Yet, for an author living at that time and aspiring to join
the pantheon, which included Dostoevsky, Nikolai
Gogol, Leo Tolstoy, and Ivan Sergeevich Turgenev, a
successful full-length novel seemed a basic requirement.
Meanwhile, Surovin published another collection of
Chekhov's short fiction, *Rasskazy* (Stories, 1888).

The next story of significance that Chekhov wrote
was "Ogni" (Lights, 1888), published in *Severnyi vestnik.*
Quite unhappy with this piece, which indulged in "philosophizing" and received poor reviews, he later omitted
"Ogni" from the first complete collection of his works—a
rare outcome for his mature writings. When a literary
friend, however, took him to task for the last line of the
story ("Nichego ne razberesh' na etom svete" [You can't
figure anything out in this world]), arguing that "it is precisely the business of an author to figure things out, especially as regards the psyche of his character," Chekhov
defended himself and his poetics in a letter to Suvorin on
30 May 1888: "It seems to me that it's not belles-lettres
that should be resolving such questions as God, pessimism, and so on. The business of belles-lettres is to
depict only who, how, and under what conditions, was
talking or thinking about God or pessimism. The artist
should not be the judge of his characters and what they
talk about, but only an impartial witness."

During the summer of 1888 Chekhov vacationed
with his family in their new preferred site, Sumy (in
Khar'kov province). From Sumy he set out on his own
for travels through Ukraine. This journey was followed
by a visit to the Crimea and Suvorin's dacha at Feo-
dosiia and then a trip through the Caucasus with
Suvorin's son Aleksei. In the fall of 1888 Chekhov
revised *Ivanov,* which the Aleksandrinskii Theater in St.
Petersburg planned to stage. Letters of this time show
that while Chekhov was increasingly concerned about

censorship, he also acted more boldly and independently on behalf of his writing. He offered "Pripadok" for the Garshin volume on the condition that neither the censors nor the editors "cross out *a single word*" (Chekhov's italics), and he sent "Imeniny" (The Name Day Party) to *Severnyi vestnik* with a note insisting that nothing be removed from the text. Chekhov was sharply sensitive not only to the meddling of the governmental censors but also to the imperatives of a fashionable and unthinking "political correctness"—to use an anachronistic term—which he feared would be imposed on his text by the liberal editorial board of *Severnyi vestnik*. In an October 1888 letter to Pleshcheev, Chekhov made one of his most famous statements about the relationship between politics and literature:

> I'm afraid of those who search between the lines for tendentiousness and want to see me as absolutely a liberal or absolutely a conservative. I am neither a liberal, nor a conservative, nor a gradualist, nor a monk, nor an indifferentist. I would like to be a free artist, and regret only that God did not give me the strength to be one. I hate lies and violence in all their forms. . . . I consider tags and labels a prejudice. My holy of holies are the human body, health, intelligence, talent, inspiration, love, and absolute freedom, freedom from force and from lies, however these are expressed. That is the program I would follow if I were an important artist.

Chekhov was under personal attack for his "incorrect" associations: left-leaning literary associates could not understand why, now that he had gained entry into the *tolstye zhurnaly* and could publish virtually wherever he wanted, he maintained his close personal and professional connection with the reactionary and unscrupulous Suvorin and *Novoe vremia*. Chekhov was genuinely attached to Suvorin, however, and apparently found him intellectually stimulating; moreover, he owed Suvorin too much to abandon him now. For his part, Suvorin appears to have loved Chekhov like a son (or better than his own sons): he offered jobs and other assistance to Chekhov's siblings, and he even proposed, perhaps not entirely in jest, that Chekhov marry his minor-aged daughter. Politics eventually divided the two, though not for another decade and never with the finality asserted by some biographers.

In October, Chekhov also learned that *V sumerkakh* had won him the prestigious Pushkin Prize, awarded by the Otdelenie russkogo iazyka i slovesnosti imp. Akademii nauk (Division of Russian Language and Letters of the Imperial Academy of Sciences). This good news came in a letter from Grigorovich, who was a member of the award committee; the same letter also had words of rebuke both for the lack of esteem in which Chekhov had hitherto held his own talent and

for his lowbrow publishing venues. The prize entailed a five-hundred-ruble award, which was only half the usual premium—the remainder went to another writer, Korolenko, on whose behalf Chekhov had himself been agitating. Chekhov's letters regarding the prize are both ecstatic and humble: he would not have gotten the prize, he says, but for the inside help of Grigorovich, Suvorin, and other patrons of his talent; all he has written will be forgotten in five or ten years; and what really matters about this award is that he has "blazed a trail" from the "small press" to the legitimate—indeed, Parnassian—heights of Russian literature, a trail that others might follow.

The metaphorical phrase "blazing a trail" appears to have held deep meaning for Chekhov. Left alone in Taganrog, years before, he had read travel accounts; now he wrote an obituary (published in *Novoe vremia* on 26 October 1888) for the great explorer of Central Asia, Nikolai Mikhailovich Przhalevsky, whom he lauded as an inspiration and example. He wrote that Przhalevsky's life was a

> living document, demonstrating to society that besides people who argue about optimism and pessimism, and write, out of boredom, insignificant tales, useless plans, and cheap dissertations; besides people who live in debauchery in the name of negating life and lie for a piece of bread; besides skeptics, mystics, psychopaths, jesuits, philosphers, liberals, and conservatives, there are still people of another order, people of great feats of sacrifice, belief, and a clear, deliberate goal.

Chekhov's admiration for Przhalevsky's life of *podvig* (feats of self-sacrifice) helps clarify what impelled him to the most challenging voyage in his own life, the scientific expedition to Sakhalin in 1890. Interestingly, the Przhalevsky obituary and other pieces of *publitsistika* (editorial writing) that Chekhov published—essays that ostensibly expressed directly his personal opinion on matters such as the ethics of almsgiving or the abysmal conditions at the "research station" of the Moscow Zoo—appeared either without signature or under a pseudonym; one exception was his obituary in December 1891 for his friend and physician colleague Zinaida Mikhailovna Lintvareva.

In January 1889 a reworked *Ivanov* was staged with spectacular success by the Aleksandrinskii Theater in St. Petersburg. Chekhov had been heavily involved in preparing the play for production: he expressed his preferences regarding the assignment of roles, interpreted the play for members of the cast, provided lengthy explanations of his intentions in letters, and even offered to give a talk before the Russkoe literaturnoe i teatral'noe obshchestvo (Russian Literary and Theatrical Society) of St. Petersburg. In his subsequent

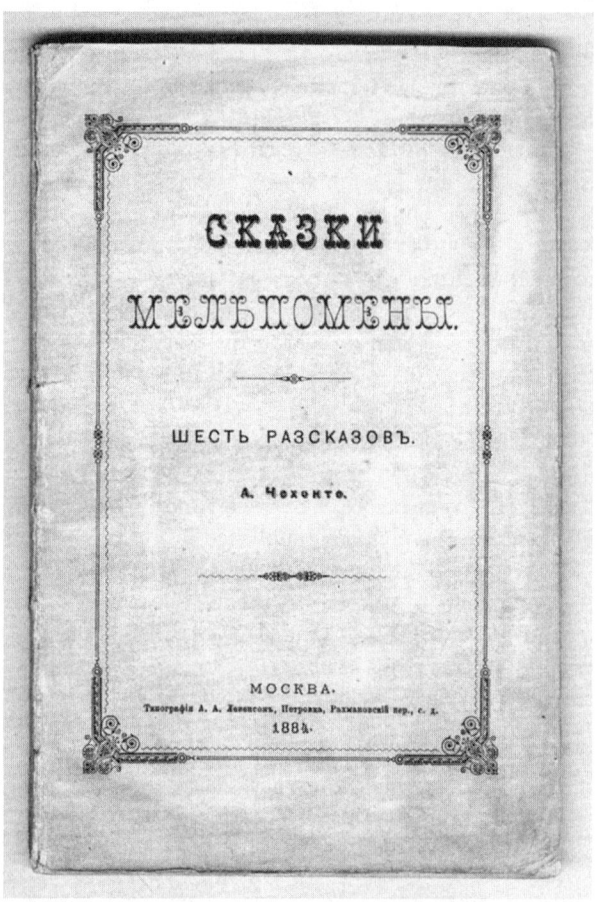

Paper cover for Chekhov's first book, Skazki Mel'pomeny
*(Tales of Melpomene), published at his own expense and
distributed and marketed with his family's help (from*
James S. Jaffe Rare Books, *catalogue 22)*

involvement with the MKhAT, by contrast, Chekhov was much more cautious, even enigmatic, in his pronouncements about the staging of his plays. While he continued to designate roles for particular actors, and he was not particularly shy about expressing dissatisfaction, he never again went to such lengths to explain his intentions as he did in this staging of *Ivanov.*

With success and visibility came new professional associations and duties. Chekhov began refereeing and editing the fiction that other writers submitted to *Novoe vremia,* an activity that consumed more and more of his time as the years progressed. In late February he was proposed as a full member of the Obshchestvo liubitelei rossiiskoi slovesnosti (Society of Lovers of Russian Literature), and in March he was elected a member of a committee of the Obshchestvo russkikh dramaticheskikh pisatelei i opernykh kompozitorov (Society of Russian Playwrights and Opera Composers). Meanwhile, his novel, provisionally titled "Rasskazy iz zhizni moikh druzei" (Stories from the Lives of My Friends), was beginning to take shape. He told Suvorin that he

was glad he had not tried to write a novel a few years earlier when urged by Grigorovich. Only now did Chekhov feel the "virility" and "personal freedom" to attempt it—only now had he overcome his demoralizing upbringing. He spoke of himself (indirectly, in the third person) as having "squeezed the slave's blood" from his veins drop by drop and "awakened one fine morning" with "real human blood flowing in his veins rather than a slave's." Chekhov's novel was never written, although its conception is reflected in the 1898 cycle of stories known as the "little trilogy" ("Chelovek v futliare" [The Man in a Case], "Kryzhovnik" [Gooseberries], and "O liubvi" [About Love]), published in *Russkaia mysl'* (Russian Thought); true liberation came when he felt free to abandon the novel altogether.

In the spring of 1889 Chekhov cared for his brother Nikolai, ill with typhoid fever, tuberculosis, and the ravages of alcoholism. Chekhov took him to the family's current summer retreat at the Lintvarev estate near Sumy, where he also worked on his next major play, *Leshii* (The Wood Demon, 1899; published 1890). In mid June, Chekhov took advantage of his brother Aleksandr's arrival and (as a respite from nursing Nikolai) departed for the estate of friends in Poltava province; on 17 June, however, the day after he left, Nikolai died. In a letter, written after the funeral to their father, Aleksandr reported that only Anton had not cried—"a eto—skverno" (and that's awful); both Chekhov's mother and his sister later alleged that the writer never cried in his life.

After Nikolai's burial in Sumy, Chekhov spent a month in the Crimea apart from his family. Deeply affected by Nikolai's death, he wrote one of his bleakest long stories, "Skuchnaia istoriia" (A Boring Story, published in *Severnyi vestnik* in 1889), originally conceived under the title "Moe imia i ia" (My Name and Me). The story, often associated with Tolstoy's "Smert' Ivana Il'icha" (Death of Ivan Il'ich, 1886), is narrated by a professor of medicine who is terminally ill and suffering alienation from his family, profession, and friends. Indeed, his own name has become foreign to him, representing a public persona utterly separate from his lived experience. The notes of loneliness and acute forebodings of death at the end of "Skuchnaia istoriia" worried Chekhov's friends, and although he objected vigorously to any identification of himself with the professor, the story is still seen generally as an expression of the author's mood at the time.

In the fall Chekhov had a setback with the finished draft of *Leshii.* He had offered the actor Pavel Matveevich Svobodin (pseudonym of P. M. Kozienko) the play for the latter's benefit at the Aleksandrinskii Theater, but an unofficial committee, which included Grigorovich, deemed the work unfit for the stage: it was odd and drawn out, they said, and it lacked action; moreover, the theater director feared that members of the imperial family would not like it. Lectured by his friends on the necessity of respect for theatrical conventions, Chekhov withdrew the play and swore (as he often did in his career) never again to write a full-length play. Yet, he was soon persuaded to allow the staging of a revised version at the Abramova Theater in Moscow, where the play premiered at the end of December. While *Leshii* subsequently did well in provincial theaters, it did not draw favorable reviews from its first run.

In letters to close friends and family Chekhov had been expressing a need to get away and "start over"—to give his life and work a more serious direction. Sometime toward the end of 1889, perhaps stimulated by his youngest brother Mikhail's studies of the penal system, he came upon the idea of visiting Sakhalin, and in the new year he traveled to St. Petersburg to obtain the required permissions for a full survey. Although he did receive a letter from the prison directorate authorizing all assistance necessary for accomplishment of his scientific and literary goals, a secret order prohibiting contact between Chekhov and certain political exiles and convicts was also sent to the administrator of Sakhalin Island. Chekhov's preparations were characteristically systematic: he composed a bibliography of sixty-five titles to read before his departure, and he studied topics ranging from the criminal-justice system to the history of the Far Eastern exploration—including the geology, ethnography, and meteorology of the region. Family and friends were enlisted to make notes from library books.

His motivations for this ambitious project were multifold and complex. While in letters he warned that he was not undertaking the journey for literary material, impressions from the trip did inspire or enrich subsequent works such as the stories "Gusev" (*Novoe vremia,* 1890) "V ssylke" (In Exile, published in *Vsemirnaia illustratsiia* [World Illustrated], 1892), and even "Palata No. 6" (Ward No. 6, published in *Russkaia mysl',* 1892). Chekhov also arranged to send back travel sketches during the voyage east for immediate publication in *Novoe vremia.* He wrote in a letter to Suvorin on 9 March 1890 that the trip and resulting study would "pay a little of my debt to medicine"; his later attempt to have his Sakhalin book accepted as a dissertation at the Faculty of Medicine, however, was only investigatory and indirect, and its rejection left him nonchalant. In one letter he wrote that he was merely seeking diversion from his accustomed pattern of life; in another he insisted on the great social value of visiting and publicizing this site of "unbearable suffering." Many scholars have speculated on various reasons for the sojourn to

Sakhalin: Chekhov sought to accomplish a *podvig* like those he had extolled in his obituary for Przhalevsky; he wanted to escape the inauthentic existence that fame had brought him; he was fleeing the depression caused by Nikolai's death; and, finally, he undertook a katabatic journey to the island of the damned—to hell itself—so as to return renewed and at terms with the death from consumption that awaited him as surely as it had taken Nikolai.

In the spring of 1890, before Chekhov's departure, another collection of his stories was published by Suvorin. The title, *Khmurye liudi* (Gloomy People), may have helped subsequent critics typecast Chekhov's works. The volume was dedicated to the composer Petr Il'ich Chaikovsky, whom Chekhov had met a year and a half previously; until Chaikovsky's death in 1893 the two maintained warm, mutually admiring relations.

Fewer than two weeks before setting out for Sakhalin, Chekhov sent an uncharacteristically angry and unrestrained letter to Vukol Mikhailovich Lavrov, editor and publisher of *Russkaia mysl',* where a review article had listed Chekhov among the "priests of unprincipled writing." Because he is about to leave Russia, perhaps never to return, Chekhov writes, he cannot restrain himself from answering a slander. He attaches no great value to most of what what he has published, but he refuses to be ashamed of his writings. Moreover, he is above all a doctor and primarily known as such to his acquaintances. Not surprisingly, Chekhov was extremely riled at this critical moment, when he was about to embark on a truly ambitious, difficult, and even dangerous voyage—a voyage that also manifested incredible social commitment. A few years later Lavrov made amends, the two became close, and Chekhov subsequently placed important works in *Russkaia mysl'.*

Chekhov departed Moscow on 21 April 1890, accompanied by family and friends during the first short rail stage to Yaroslavl. From there he traveled by river steamer to Perm', by rail to Ekaterinburg and Tiumen', and then by light horse-drawn carriages through Omsk, Tomsk, Krasnoiarsk, and on to Irkutsk. There were abysmal roads, torturous cold, and truly harrowing moments such as the crossing of flooded rivers and a collision with a government troika, its driver asleep, speeding in the opposite direction. In the end he traveled by horse-drawn carriage more than 4,000 versts (2,667 miles, or the rough equivalent of crossing the United States from coast to coast); the entire round-trip voyage covered 10,000 miles. From the Trans-Baikal city of Sretensk he was able to steam the rest of the way, first along the Amur River to the eastern shore of Siberia, the port town of Nikolaevsk, and from there across the Tartar Straits to Sakhalin where, when Chekhov arrived, many fires were burning in the taiga, rendering

Prisoners being put into shackles on Sakhalin Island during the 1880s. The island and its penal community were the subject of Chekhov's longest work, Ostrov Sakhalin *(Sakhalin Island), published as a book in 1895 (from Georgii Petrovich Berdnikov,* Chekhov, *1978).*

his final destination uncanny and hellish. Meanwhile, Chekhov's series of travel sketches had begun appearing in *Novoe vremia* before he reached Sakhalin.

While in Tiumen', Chekhov sent a letter to the chairman of the Taganrog city council, informing him about books he had arranged for the city library to receive and promising more such gifts in the future. In an anonymous editorial on poverty Chekhov had remarked that the recipients of scholarships never gave a thought to repaying this debt once they had made their way in the world. He himself did not follow this behavior, however, and among his many philanthropic works was a continuing effort to expand and improve the collection of the Taganrog public library. Over the years he cajoled publishers into donating books, contributed valuable author-signed editions and some two thousand volumes from his own personal collection, and even persuaded a sculptor to create a statue of Peter the Great for the library grounds. When he returned from Sakhalin, having witnessed firsthand the neglect and abuse of children on the island, he also undertook to have thousands of books shipped to the schools and library on the island. Many of these books he bought himself, but he also used his name and personal connections to obtain far heftier support for his charitable projects.

Once on Sakhalin, Chekhov was taken under the wing of the Aleksandrovsk settlement doctor, and he was able to meet with the top administrators of the island, as well as with Baron Andrei Nikolaevich Korf, the governor-general of the entire Priamurskii (Far Eastern) region. Chekhov received promises of cooperation and assistance—he could do virtually anything he liked other than meet with political prisoners and exiles—and there were frank discussions about the penal colony. He soon arranged for the printing of approximately ten thousand census cards for registering information about place of settlement, address, title, name, age, religion, place of birth, year of arrival on Sakhalin, chief occupation, level of education, marital status, assistance received from authorities, and ailments. In the end, as Chekhov wrote in a letter to Suvorin on 11 September 1890, he had surveyed the entire population of the island, stopping in at virtually every hut. He claimed, with perhaps slight exaggeration, that "on Sakhalin there is not one convict or settler who wouldn't have talked with me," and he was particularly pleased with the data that he collected on children. Yet, challenged by the prospect of integrating all this disparate information, he felt he "had seen everything, but failed to notice the elephant."

In October he departed for home via Vladivostok, Singapore, Colombo, Hong Kong, the Suez Canal, Constantinople, and Odessa. In letters he speaks of having visited hell and, on Ceylon, a heaven that included erotic adventures: "The real charmers are colored women," he later told a friend. When he arrived in Odessa on 1 December, he had been gone for more than seven months, with more than three spent on Sakhalin. The strenuous voyage and frenetic pace of work on the island, where he rose daily at five A.M. and retired late, was damaging to Chekhov's precarious health. Back in Moscow, he reported to Leikin that his heartbeat was irregular and that sitting had become difficult (he had long complained of hemorrhoids, headaches, and flashing in his eyes).

In the spring he traveled to western Europe with Suvorin and saw Vienna, Venice, Bologna, Florence, Rome, Naples, Nice, Monte Carlo (where he gambled), and Paris. In May, Chekhov and his family took a new dacha on the Oka River; a few weeks later they moved to better lodgings on an estate called Bogimovo, where Chekhov became acquainted with fellow vacationer and zoologist Vladimir Aleksandrovich Vagner. The two carried on extensive discussions of the theories of evolution and degeneration. According to his brother Mikhail, Chekhov asserted that the taints of inheritance could be overcome by an individual's effort; this position held personal significance for a man suffering from tuberculosis, which was at that time still considered partly hereditary. Contemporary intellectual debates regarding science, materialism, and the theory of degeneration were central to the major work he was then composing, "Duel'" (The Duel, published in *Novoe vremia,* 1891). Set by the sea in the Caucasus, this lengthy story evokes several traditional themes of nineteenth- century Russian literature–for example, the duel, the superfluous man, and the Romantic South. When it was serialized in *Novoe vremia,* other contributors complained that Chekhov was monopolizing the newspaper.

By the end of 1891 his attention had turned to the countryside. He was actively involved in raising funds to assist peasant victims of famine in the Nizhegorod and Voronezh provinces (a chapter of the book he was writing about Sakhalin appeared in a benefit volume), and he was looking for a small estate to purchase. Chekhov not only hoped to escape the expense of living in Moscow but also believed that his declining health necessitated such a move. He complained of ever increasing demands on his time by the visitors who plagued him since his return from Sakhalin, and he felt that a change of environment would advance his writing, as he confided to Suvorin in a letter, dated 20 October 1891: "If I'm a doctor, I need patients and a hospital; if I'm a littérateur, I need to live among the folk, and not on Malaia Dmitrovka with a mongoose. . . . This life between four walls, without nature, without people, without a homeland, without health and an appetite–this isn't life"; Malaia Dmitrovka was where the Chekhov family had moved during his absence, and he had acquired a mongoose in India on his voyage home from Sakhalin. On 2 February 1892 he signed a

contract to purchase the 575-acre estate of Melikhovo, located in the Serpukhov district, fewer than 50 miles south of Moscow. He moved there with his extended family at the beginning of March and began work on his next major story, "Palata No. 6."

Toward the end of April 1892, in the journal *Sever* (The North), Chekhov published "Poprygun'ia" (Grasshopper), a story about a flighty, celebrity-crazed woman who fails to respect her dull but devoted and hardworking physician spouse and has an affair with a painter; she understands only when her husband dies that he was in fact an enormously talented researcher for whom his colleagues expected a brilliant future. Those in the know quickly identified the adulterous pair of the story as caricatures of Chekhov's friend, the artist Isaak Il'ich Levitan, and of the wife of another friend and colleague, Dmitrii Pavlovich Kuvshinnikov. All three members of this love triangle had seen Chekhov off on his trip to Sakhalin two years earlier, and Kuvshinnikov had presented Chekhov with a flask of cognac to drink when he reached the Pacific Ocean. While Chekhov had previously modeled characters in his fiction and drama after his friends and relatives (and did again in the future), his use in "Poprygun'ia" of people and situations from his life produced a most explosive response. His close relations with Levitan were broken off for several years, as was his friendship with an actor who found himself represented unflatteringly in a member of the heroine's circle. Chekhov always denied guilt in such cases, even to the point of disingenuousness. In this instance on 29 April 1892 he wrote to his acquaintance Lidiia Alekseevna Avilova, who herself later boasted dubiously of a romance with him and, not without imagination and self-flattery, found herself represented in his works, that "an acquaintance of mine, a 42-year-old woman, recognized herself in the 20-year-old heroine of my 'Poprygun'ia' . . . and all of Moscow accuses me of a pasquinade. The main evidence–a superficial similarity: the lady paints, her husband is a doctor, and she's living with an artist." Disavowals and the transformative powers of art notwithstanding, Chekhov did at times make callous use of the lives of his friends.

In the summer of 1892 Chekhov signed on with the Serpukhov District Committee as an unpaid zemstvo doctor and dedicated himself to battling the cholera epidemic threatening the area. In addition to the official medical station of Melikhovo, he had charge of twenty-five other villages. He traveled jolting roads to villages, factories, and a monastery in order to educate, supervise, stock supplies, arrange for temporary barracks where the stricken might be cared for, and beg for the money to fund all this from factory owners and landholders–all this effort after receiving patients in the morning. The exhausting work left no time to make progress on the Sakhalin book or on other projects until mid October, when the cholera danger abated. He served again the following summer.

That winter two lengthy works of fiction were published in *Russkaia mysl'*. Chekhov's extraordinarily powerful "Palata No. 6" came out toward the end of the year, creating a sensation. The tale of a physician and a hospital chief who acquiesces to corruption among his medical staff, foul conditions in his hospital, and, in the end, his own unmerited commitment to the psychiatric ward, was read as a critique of Tolstoy's philosophy of nonresistance to evil; the hospital has often been interpreted as a microcosm of Russia. Impressionable female readers reputedly fainted while reading the end of the work, and no less a figure than Vladimir Lenin found the story deeply disturbing. The other piece, "Rasskaz neizvestnogo cheloveka" (The Story of an Anonymous Man, 1893), was one of Chekhov's most politically daring works (and also one of his most overtly Turgenevan). The central hero and narrator is a conspirator in the underground revolutionary movement involved in an assassination plot; while this content made Chekhov anxious about censorship, there was also reason for him to fear the wrath of liberal critics, since the hero of the story becomes disillusioned and ill and abandons the cause. In this period, too, Chekhov broke off relations with Suvorin for a time after Suvorin's son Aleksei publicly slapped the face of Lavrov, publisher of *Russkaia mysl'*. Chekhov and Suvorin were reconciled, but the ideological differences between them and the unprincipled conduct of Suvorin's newspaper continued to create problems in their friendship.

In late 1893 Chekhov pursued his long-standing interest in psychiatry with intensive reading in the field. According to the minor author Ieronim Ieronimovich Iasinsky in his *Roman moei zhizni. Kniga vospominanii* (Novel of My Life. A Book of Recollections, 1926), Chekhov averred that, had he not succeeded as a writer, he probably would have become a psychiatrist; Chekhov told his new acquaintance and disciple Tat'iana L'vovna Shchepkina-Kupernik that a knowledge of psychiatry was "indispensable" for a real author. His own work had always shown keen psychological insight and an interest in psychopathology—which is quintessentially the case in "Chernyi monakh" (The Black Monk, published in *Artist*, 1894), a story he was writing around this time, about a young scholar who suffers delusions of grandeur. Although the black monk who visits the hallucinating hero was derived from a disturbing dream that Chekhov had reported to others, he nevertheless asserted that the story had nothing to do with himself (a position consistent with his view of the "Poprygun'ia" affair) and that there was no need to worry about his sanity.

Also at the end of 1893 Chekhov's book on Sakhalin began appearing in *Russkaia mysl'*, though not without censorship problems. While *Ostrov Sakhalin* (1895) is the longest work that Chekhov wrote and the one on which, arguably, he expended the greatest effort, it probably has received the least critical attention of all his major writings. Upon completing it he felt, as he wrote in a letter to Suvorin on 2 January 1894, that he had "paid his due" to medicine and science, and he was "glad that in my belletristic wardrobe will be hanging also this coarse convict's smock." A few years later Chekhov's friend and medical school classmate Grigorii Ivanovich Rossolimo made discrete inquiries regarding the possibility that Moscow University would accept Chekhov's work on Sakhalin as a dissertation. Such an action would give Chekhov the credentials necessary to teach medicine at the university, a prospect quite appealing to him. According to Rossolimo, Chekhov planned to bring pedagogic innovations to the field: he aimed above all to try to "draw my audience as deeply as possible into the realm of the subjective feelings of the patient." One can surmise that in order to accomplish this task, Chekhov would have relied upon precisely those techniques he had developed in representing the inner worlds of his fictional characters. The shocked dean rejected Rossolimo's unconventional proposal out of hand; and, hearing of the dean's reaction, Chekhov laughed. A century later the blossoming field of medical humanities in the United States made Chekhov appear far ahead of his time.

After a trip to western Europe in the fall of 1894 Chekhov returned to Melikhovo and finished his next long story, "Tri goda" (Three Years, published in *Russkaia mysl'*, 1895), a depressing depiction of the Moscow merchant milieu in which his father had worked until a few years earlier and a no less disturbing portrait of marriage and family life. He also threw himself into community service. He was appointed trustee of the nearby village school, where he first paid for new desks and soon began preparations for the construction of a new building for the school (it was finished in August 1895); in the next few years he erected a second school (largely at his own expense), supervised the establishment of libraries at two other area schools, and collected data for the first general census (1897) in Russia. He also served as a juror in Serpukhov.

At the beginning of 1895 Shchepkina-Kupernik brought Levitan with her to see Chekhov at Melikhovo, and the two old friends resumed their close relations as though nothing had happened. During this period Chekhov also had meetings and a romantic (non)involvement with Avilova; among memoirists and biographers only Bunin accepts Avilova's portrayal of Chekhov's attachment to her. Generally speaking, until recently the domi-

Playbill for the Moscow Art Theater (MKhAT) premiere of Chaika *(The Seagull) on 17 December 1898
(from Andrei Turkov, comp.,* Anton Chekhov and His Times, *1995)*

nant image of Chekhov was extraordinarily ascetic. Now that Russian archives are more open than before and scholars, unworried about censorship, are less reverent, the picture of a Chekhov who at times verged on "Don Juanism" has resulted. Nevertheless, his most important romantic relationship before his marriage remains the one about which scholars and memoirists have been most forthcoming–his romance with Lidiia Stakhievna Mizinova, a friend and colleague of his sister whom he had met toward the end of 1889. Their correspondence demonstrates that Chekhov was indeed capable of self-ishness and emotional cruelty: he prolongs the relationship exclusively on his own terms; he employs the rhetoric of intimacy only under accents of humor; and he alternately seduces and distances himself from a clearly hurt woman. By this point, however, Mizinova had given up on Chekhov; while he was in Vienna, she was living in Paris and entangled in a relationship with Chekhov's friend, the married writer Ignatii Nikolaevich Potapenko, by whom she was pregnant. At this time Chekhov wrote her: "Obviously, I've yawned away my health, just as I did you." To Suvorin, who was urging

him to get married, Chekhov conceded in March 1895 that he was willing to take a wife, on the condition that she remain in Moscow, and he in the country. He needed a wife "like the moon, who would not appear in my sky every day," and he predicted that getting married "won't make me write better."

In August, Chekhov finally met Tolstoy in person, visiting him at Iasnaia Poliana, the latter's estate. He made some helpful criticisms regarding Tolstoy's portrayal of the penal system in *Voskresenie* (Resurrection, 1899), the novel that Tolstoy was then writing. Chekhov had named Tolstoy as his favorite author in an autobiographical note, and he had enormous respect for the towering figure. Nevertheless, Chekhov could be quite critical: he particularly resented Tolstoy's representation of doctors and his disregard for scientific facts, and he was constitutionally incapable of aligning himself with any "-ism"–Tolstoyanism included. A year earlier he had written Suvorin that Tolstoy's philosophy had gripped him deeply for a period of six or seven years, but no longer: "Now something in me protests; my sense of fairness and economy tells me that there's more love for humanity in electricity and steam than in chastity and abstaining from meat." Yet, this changed outlook did not prevent him from admiring the power of Tolstoy's narrative art, the rhetorical brilliance of his nonfictional writings, and his "above-it-all" moral stance and contempt for governmental and religious authorities.

That fall Chekhov wrote *Chaika* (The Seagull, 1896; published in *Russkaia mysl'*, 1896)–the first of what scholars consider his four major dramatic pieces–in a small wooden studio that he had had built behind the Melikhovo house. At the beginning of December he traveled to Moscow, where he read the play to a group of literary and theatrical friends gathered at the home of the actress Lidiia Borisovna Iavorskaia (with whom Chekhov once had a short affair). He also solicited suggestions for revision from others whose opinions he respected, such as Nemirovich-Danchenko–a playwright and professor at the drama school of the Moscow Philharmonia–and Suvorin. Whereas he felt himself "at home" with stories, Chekhov told Suvorin that he "had no luck" as a playwright, and he felt out of sorts and vulnerable while writing. After much revision the play went into rehearsal at the Aleksandrinskii Theater in St. Petersburg in October 1896, with Chekhov in attendance. Although he was quite pleased with the penultimate rehearsal, and especially with the inspired performance of Vera Fedorovna Kommissarzhevskaia in the role of Nina, he grew desperately pessimistic after the final rehearsal and wished to cancel the staging of the play. His forebodings were not without foundation, for the premiere of *Chaika* on 17 October was a fiasco. Chekhov left his auditorium seat during the second act, hid in an actress's dressing room until the play was over, and then slipped out of the theater to wander the streets of St. Petersburg and contemplate his failure. Friends and relatives, unable to find him, feared the worst; he had the reputation of a proud man for whom such public humiliation might be devastating.

In fact, Chekhov regained his equilibrium fairly quickly. The next day, avoiding discussions and insufferable words of consolation and swearing to all, yet again, never to write another play, he left for home; he also attempted to withdraw the play from publication in *Russkaia mysl'*. He could soon take heart, however, because the subsequent four performances of *Chaika* at the Aleksandrinskii Theater were actually a critical success. Hindsight attributed the lion's share of the failure of the premiere to an extremely inappropriate audience, unwisely selected by Chekhov himself when he agreed to have the play staged as a benefit performance for the comic actress Elizaveta Ivanovna Levkeeva: her unsophisticated fans anticipated a buffoonish entertainment. Though the play was pulled from the Aleksandrinskii stage after five performances and Chekhov resisted subsequent efforts to stage it in Moscow, it was performed with great success in Kiev and lesser provincial cities.

Chekhov's next long story, "Moia zhizn'" (My Life), began appearing in October 1896 in *Ezhemesiachnye literaturnye prilozheniia k "Nive"* (Monthly Literary Supplement to "Niva"). The critics in large measure passed over this painful tale of a well-born provincial youth who–perhaps on the Tolstoyan model–"drops out" and becomes a house painter; a Freudian might call the character's attempt to live the moral life of a simple laborer moral masochism. Chekhov's next major story drew much attention. In March of the following year he sent "Muzhiki" (Peasants) to *Russkaia mysl'*. This highly controversial portrayal of peasant life was published only after considerable censorship, and because of it Chekhov could not be criticized for dodging the most important issues of the day; Russia faced no more important social and political problem than the condition and future of its peasantry. Populists were outraged–Tolstoy called the story a "sin against the folk" in a commentary–while others lauded its unsentimental approach. Chekhov's later and even more brutal story about the effects of capital on peasant life, "V ovrage" (In the Ravine, 1900), was much better appreciated by Tolstoy.

Chekhov wrote to Suvorin that "Muzhiki" had exhausted the literary usefulness of living in the country. He indeed planned to leave Melikhovo, but not for literary reasons: only a few days after finishing the story, while dining with Suvorin in Moscow, he began hemorrhaging from the lungs. When several days later he attempted to carry on as though nothing had happened, he was stricken again and then taken to the clinic of the physician Aleksei Alekseevich Ostroumov, where he stayed for more than two weeks. Among his many visitors was Tolstoy, who ignored the doctor's orders that Chekhov should remain quiet, drew him into a lengthy discussion about immortality, and quite nearly helped him gain firsthand experience of it, since another hemorrhage soon followed. Tolstoy admired Chekhov's talents greatly and read aloud to family and friends certain of Chekhov's stories, such as "Dushechka" (The Darling, published in *Sem'ia*, 1899). Several years later he wrote in his diary that Chekhov, "like Pushkin, advanced the form. And that's a great service." In conversation he called Chekhov a "Pushkin in prose," in whose writings all readers can find echoes of their experiences. Tolstoy disliked Chekhov's plays, however, and told him, to Chekhov's great amusement, that his plays were "even worse" than Shakespeare's. When Chekhov returned home to Melikhovo to recuperate, he found himself continuously beset by visitors, whom he was always too polite to turn away outright.

Postcards of scenes from act 3 of Diadia Vania *(Uncle Vania, 1897), staged by MKhAT in October 1899*
(from Laurence Senelick, The Chekhov Theatre, *1997)*

Thenceforth, Chekhov was an invalid; the years of denying his illness and carrying on as though it were not serious had definitively ended. His brother Mikhail and his sister attributed blame for the breakdown of his health to the trauma Chekhov experienced upon the failure of *Chaika,* but the writer had been suffering periodic episodes of blood spitting since 1884. In recent years he had complained of an irregular heartbeat, near fainting spells, migraines, ringing in his ears, and flashes in his eyes. Now the doctors were ordering Chekhov to change his mode of life, and he knew that he had to obey those orders. Still, during the summer of 1897 he was active again, visiting Moscow and St. Petersburg and assisting his brother Aleksandr's project of founding a therapeutic colony for alcoholics. Aleksandr had struggled with alcoholism all his adult life—indeed, his talents and intellect were such that he might well have surpassed Chekhov as an author had it not been for this disease—and he had written a book on the subject.

At the end of the summer Chekhov left for travel abroad, where after visits to Biarritz and Paris he spent the winter in Nice, a haven for consumptives from all over Europe; soon he was cultivating plans (never realized) to travel to Algeria with his new acquaintance, the exiled sociologist Maksim Maksimovich Kovalevsky. Chekhov had

been reviewing his French and, at one point, even considered translating the works of Guy de Maupassant. Now, following reports of the Dreyfus affair quite closely, he drew the obvious conclusion that the Jewish officer was innocent. Alfred Dreyfus had been convicted of espionage on the basis of forgeries, and the army, fearing embarrassment and supported by an atmosphere of anti-Semitic and xenophobic hysteria, was blocking a readdress of the case even after clear evidence of its injustice had surfaced. Chekhov responded admiringly to Zola's famous open letter in defense of Dreyfus, "J'accuse" (I Accuse), published 13 January 1898 in the newspaper *L'Aurore* (Dawn). He was in equal measure disgusted by the handling of the matter in the Russian press, among which there was no worse offender than the reactionary *Novoe vremia.* Suvorin apparently accepted Chekhov's version of the matter, yet did nothing to rein in his muckraking newspaper, and this inaction further outraged Chekhov. This new strain did not lead to the final break in relations that is sometimes claimed by biographers—they met in Paris in the spring of 1898, and their correspondence continued—but it did grave damage to their friendship.

While Chekhov's political sentiments were clearly left leaning, they remained for the most part private. His approach to suffering, injustice, and governmental brutishness probably owed more to the ethical imperatives of clinical medicine than it did to political ideology; this fact perhaps explains how he could have remained close with Suvorin for so long in spite of the ideological significance of *Novoe vremia*. Chekhov finally distanced himself from Suvorin not for ideological reasons but because he had become fed up with his friend's lack of character. In February 1899 Chekhov wrote in a letter to Ivan I. Orlov on 22 February 1989, "I don't believe in our intelligentsia, hypocritical, false, hysterical, uneducated, lazy . . . I believe in individual people, I see salvation in individual personalities, spread out all over Russia—whether they're members of the intelligentsia or peasants—there's strength in them, even if they are few in number." In times of student riots and strikes Chekhov was quite critical of the government in personal remarks, and he expressed ever greater disgust with Suvorin and *Novoe vremia* (where, to complicate matters, his brother Aleksandr was working); he did his part to create change through private acts of philanthropy and his unrecompensed medical practice but always avoided public statements, propagandistic art, and membership in any party.

In April 1898, shortly before his return to Russia, Chekhov received a letter that led to the last, and perhaps most important, turning point in both his literary career and his private life. His friend and advisor in theatrical matters, Nemirovich-Danchenko, wrote to tell him of the new "exclusively artistic" theater that he and Stanislavsky were creating and asked permission to stage *Chaika*. Chekhov at first refused, frankly admitting that he did not wish to suffer a repeat of his experience with the premiere of the play in St. Petersburg two years before. Though his plays were being successfully produced in the provinces, and he had warmly supported the staging of *Diadia Vania* (Uncle Vania, 1898; published 1897) by an amateur group close to home in Serpukhov (he even read the play aloud to them), he feared exposure in the two capitals. He eventually agreed, however, and through the performances at the MKhAT—which took the silhouette of a seagull as its emblem and became known as the Chekhov Theater—he achieved his great reputation as a playwright.

In September, Chekhov attended a rehearsal of the play in Mosow and met the actors and actresses of the MKhAT; among them was the woman who later became his wife, Ol'ga Leonardovna Knipper, who had the role of Arkadina. After watching the troupe rehearse its debut play, Aleksei Konstantinovich Tolstoy's *Tsar' Fedor Ioannovich* (Tsar Fedor Ivanovich, published in *Vestnik Evropy,* 1868), the extremely private Chekhov rather uncharacteristically revealed his infatuation with Knipper in a letter: if he stayed in Moscow, he wrote, he would fall in love. The MKhAT production of *Chaika* premiered on 17 December 1898 to triumphant success. Now wintering in the Crimea, Chekhov telegraphed his appreciation to Nemirovich-Danchenko and complained that in Yalta he felt like "Dreyfus on Devil's Island."

In October 1898 Chekhov's father was rushed to Moscow for surgery on an entrapped hernia and died following the operation. The loss was great. Pavel Egorovich had mellowed in his declining years. He had taken pride in, and helped run, his son's estate; he gardened, painted icons, and read holy texts with his wife in the evenings and had kept an invaluable chronicle of the comings and goings of family and friends. Chekhov wrote in letters that "the main gear in the Melikhovo mechanism" was now gone; his mother and sister no longer wished to live in the country. In fact, he had been contemplating a move even before his father's death and was shopping for a property in the Crimea. His health demanded changes in his own life, and his financial situation did not allow him to maintain two households. By the end of the month Chekhov had bought a piece of land in a suburb above Yalta and begun the process of building a house there. Meanwhile, he was financing and supervising from afar the construction of a third school near Melikhovo and collecting contributions for children suffering from famine in Samara province. Although he was often ill himself, he also occasionally practiced as a physician.

In January 1899 Chekhov signed (by proxy) a contract with the publisher Adol'f Fedorovich Marks that guaranteed the publication of a full collection of his works. Chekhov was to receive 75,000 rubles for all his writings, past and future, with additional payments for any new collections of his stories that Marks might publish; income from the production of his plays belonged to Chekhov so long as he lived. Chekhov's friends were appalled at these terms, and Suvorin in particular urged him not to act hastily: he offered a loan of 20,000 rubles if immediate needs were driving this deal. In addition to the anticipated infusion of cash, however, Chekhov was also seeking liberation from Suvorin, whose press had in fact already begun printing the collected works of the writer in an irritatingly disorganized fashion. Moreover, Chekhov likely knew quite well that he had but a short career ahead of him. In the coming years Gor'ky and other literary friends and associates urged Chekhov to renegotiate or break the contract, and at times lawyers were consulted; although Marks was probably making two or three rubles for every ruble that Chekhov himself received, Chekhov's sense of honor and abhorrence of conflict inhibited him from retracting his word.

The terms of the contract forced Chekhov to provide copies of every work that he had ever written, but he insisted on the right to deem a particular piece unworthy of the collection; he did so with all of his pre-*Oskolki* production. So much of his early work had been dashed off quickly, published under pseudonyms, and forgotten, that its collection was a considerable task. He asked for a great deal of assistance from friends and family. While he was collecting his own early works, many of them forgotten by him, he also decided to gather the published illustrations of his late brother Nikolai: he wished to compose an album and donate it to the Taganrog library for safekeeping.

From this point until the end of his life he expended an enormous amount of time and energy rereading and editing his earlier works. This "convict labor," as Chekhov called it, was a significant factor in Chekhov's decreasing production of new works—so, too, were the discomfort and low spirits caused by his sanitary "exile" in Yalta. By now, too, he had become teacher, editor, and patron for an ever increasing number of younger authors, whose manuscripts he handled with a great sense of responsibility and often helped publish. Among these was Gor'ky, whom Chekhov met in early spring 1899, after a correspondence of several months.

In April, Chekhov returned north and traveled first to Moscow, where he rented an apartment. The decision was finally made to sell Melikhovo. (The house there later burned down in the 1920s, but after World War II a facsimile was built and made into a museum with the help of Chekhov's sister.) Meanwhile, the first order of business in Moscow was to retract his play *Diadia Vania* from the Malyi Theater, to which it had long been promised. Nemirovich-Danchenko had also asked Chekhov for permission to stage *Diadia Vania,* and now that the literary-theatrical committee overseeing the repertoire of the state theater had insisted on a number of revisions, Chekhov decided to withdraw the play from the Malyi and give it to the MKhAT, where it premiered with moderate success at the end of October. In his memoirs Chekhov's younger brother Mikhail, who had labored to improve Melikhovo, saw himself in the character of Uncle Vania: the moment of crisis in the play occurs when Vania's brother-in-law, a bombastic and self-centered man of letters, proposes selling the estate of Vania's late sister and niece, which Vania has been managing. Chekhov's physician colleagues were particularly touched, too, by his depiction of the bodily and spiritual wear and tear suffered by Dr. Astrov after years of rural medical practice.

During this period Chekhov also courted Knipper. The two arranged a rendezvous in Novorossiisk in July 1899 and sailed together to Yalta, where Chekhov supervised the construction of his house in Autka. They returned to Moscow together two weeks later, after which Chekhov returned to Yalta to move into his new home. Toward the end of the year he published one of his finest stories—and certainly his most affirming love story—"Dama s sobachkoi" (Lady with the Lapdog, published in *Russkaia mysl',* 1899). While the tale of an adulterous summer fling that deepens into profound attachment has its genesis in notes preceding Chekhov's romance with Knipper, and scholars have identified other prototypes for its heroine, the sentiment behind the tale almost certainly derives chiefly from Chekhov's feelings for her. Knipper apparently saw herself in Anna, the "lady" of the story.

In his new home Chekhov occupied himself with gardening, a lifelong passion; even in the early years, when his family vacationed in Voskresensk, he had planted trees on the hospital grounds where he was working as a locum tenens. He also continued his good works: when a teacher from a Crimean school came to ask for his support in keeping the school open, Chekhov donated all the cash he had—500 rubles. Another charitable donation was his offer to pay room and board in Yalta for one member of an organization of primary-school teachers in the Serpukhov district in need of therapeutic rest, and he helped organize a sanitarium for the desperate tuberculars who came south to Yalta only to die, all too often alone. In 1900 he donated 5,000 rubles to establish a house with twenty beds for indigent consumptives in Yalta.

The last few years of Chekhov's life brought official recognition and rewards for both his philanthropic and his literary activities. In December 1899 he was awarded the Order of St. Stanislav for his efforts on behalf of popular education, and in January 1900 he learned of his selection as member of the Otdelenie russkogo iazyka i slovesnosti imp. Akademii nauk. In 1902, however, Chekhov and Korolenko together resigned from the academy to protest the annulment of Gor'ky's selection (because of the latter's revolutionary associations and arrest record).

In January 1900 Chekhov bought a dacha on the coast in the town of Gurzuf, a short distance south from Yalta. He was particularly proud of the fact that his property on a small bay also included the so-called Pushkin Rock, jutting out of the water a short distance from the shore, where Pushkin himself was supposed to have perched; today the dacha is an auxiliary of the Chekhov House-Museum in Yalta. In April, Chekhov was able to see *Diadia Vania* staged for the first time when the MKhAT, on tour in nearby Sevastopol', performed their Chekhov repertoire along with plays by Gerhart Hauptmann (whom Chekhov admired) and Henrik Ibsen (whom he did not). The theater company visited Yalta as well, and for a short time Chekhov's home became the gathering

Chekhov and Ol'ga Leonardovna Knipper, whom he married in 1901 (from Turkov, comp., Anton Chekhov and His Times, *1995)*

place for quite a large number of present and future literary and theatrical luminaries.

In spite of poor health, Chekhov continued to travel. After a short visit to Moscow in the summer of 1900, he joined Gor'ky and the artist Viktor Mikhailovich Vasnetsov on an expedition through the Caucasus. In July, Knipper came to Yalta for a lengthy, and apparently decisive, stay: the two were on "ty" terms (an intimate form of address) afterward. After her departure Chekhov began intensive efforts on *Tri sestry* (Three Sisters, 1901; published in *Russkaia mysl'*, 1901), the first play he wrote with the cast of the MKhAT specifically in mind; he read the play to the troupe in Moscow in October. That winter he again traveled abroad, visiting Vienna, Nice, Tuscany, and Rome; once again he aborted plans to sail to Algeria with Kovalevsky (this time because of the weather). When on 31 January 1901 *Tri sestry* premiered at the MKhAT, Chekhov could not be reached with news of the success of the play, as though he wanted to be out of touch at this critical moment in order to avoid experiencing the trauma that had resulted years earlier from the premiere of *Chaika*.

In May he left Yalta for Moscow, where, two weeks later, he and Knipper were married. Their separation had

been, and would continue to be, difficult for both. In the fall he had written her, "If we're not together now, then neither you nor I are guilty, but the demon who put, into me, a bacillus, and into you, a love of art." Chekhov's proposal was quite unromantic: in April, shortly after Knipper's two-week visit to Yalta, he wrote: "If you give your word that not a single soul in Moscow will know about our wedding until it's over, then we can get married even on the day I arrive. For some reason I'm horribly afraid of the wedding ceremony, and the congratulations, and the champagne that one has to hold in one's hand while smiling vaguely." Not only were Chekhov and Knipper married in secret (with the minimal necessary witnesses: her brother and uncle and two students); they also practiced, at Chekhov's insistence, a series of stunning deceptions. To his sister, Mariia, Chekhov wrote from Moscow that he might consider getting married if he had not left the necessary documents in Yalta. While the ceremony took place, a large group of family and friends, who had been called together by Chekhov for a dinner party far from where he and Knipper were wed, puzzled over the absence of the two. That is to say, Chekhov did not merely arrange an extremely private wedding; he at the same time staged a public event for those who had been expecting a wedding, and he deliberately absented himself from this gathering. After the ceremony he and his new wife briefly visited her mother, and Chekhov sent a telegram to his own mother informing her that he was married, asking for her blessing and promising that "all would remain as before." The two then set out for a sanitarium in Ufa province, where Chekhov took the kumiss (fermented milk) cure prescribed to him by the Moscow doctor that he had consulted a week earlier, for the bridegroom's health was clearly deteriorating.

The marriage created a great deal of turmoil in the Chekhov family. Chekhov's sister, in particular, was staggered: deeply devoted to her brother, Mariia had also become quite attached to Knipper; now she had been deceived by both and appeared to be losing the two people closest to her. Moreover, there had been several instances when she could have married, but after consulting Chekhov she had turned down her suitors. Now Mariia suggested in letters that she too might marry, and she went so far as to ask Bunin, who had become close to the Chekhov family, to find her a mate. Chekhov attempted to appease his sister by inviting her to join him and Knipper during their honeymoon, but Mariia declined. Above all, there were concerns for Chekhov's health: in his memoir Bunin called the marriage a "suicide."

Bored and uncomfortable in their primitive lodgings, Chekhov and Knipper returned to Yalta after only one of the two prescribed months had passed in Aksenova. At the beginning of August 1901, well aware of the precariousness of his health and most likely also wishing to clarify his respective financial ties to wife and family, Chekhov wrote a will. In it he left his Yalta house, savings, and earnings from the production of his plays to Mariia and his Gurzuf dacha and 5,000 rubles to Knipper, who–Chekhov had written to his sister–could be expected to support herself in the event of his death. There were bequests as well to brothers and cousins, but eventually, after the deaths of his mother and his siblings, Chekhov's estate went to the city of Taganrog, for "public education." The last words of the will, which was composed as a letter to his sister, were: "Help the poor. Take care of mother. Live in peace." Although this will was not legally valid, Chekhov's relations divided his estate amicably and in accordance with his wishes after he died.

In September, Chekhov attended a performance of *Tri sestry* in Moscow and was summoned to the stage for ovations. Back in Yalta for the winter, he made visits to Tolstoy, who was convalescing at nearby Gaspra at this time; joining him at times were Gor'ky, who stayed with Chekhov for a while, and the poet Konstantin Dmitrievich Bal'mont. When Knipper, on tour with the MKhAT in St. Petersburg, fell gravely ill following a miscarriage, she was brought to Yalta to convalesce. After a few weeks she and Chekhov traveled to Moscow, where she was seen by other physicians and diagnosed with peritonitis. Chekhov took pride in the fact that he alone among the physicians treating her had correctly ordered her not to eat solids. By June, Knipper had largely recovered, but Chekhov was himself utterly exhausted and much in need of recuperation. He thus accompanied the magnate Savva Timofeevich Morozov to the latter's estate near Perm'. Though ill at ease and uninspired in the provinicial empire of this "Russian Rockefeller," Chekhov nevertheless found ways to make his visit worthwhile: after touring a chemical factory owned by Morozov, Chekhov persuaded his host to shorten the workers' twelve-hour work day.

In July Chekhov became a shareholder in the MKhAT cooperative. Chekhov and Knipper vacationed and continued to recuperate at the Alekseev (Stanislavsky) estate of Liubimovka. There Chekhov drew some of the material for what turned out to be his last play, *Vishnevyi sad* (Cherry Orchard, 1904; first published in *Sbornik tovarishchestva "Znanie"* [Miscellany of the "Knowledge" Society], 1904). Illness and editing duties made progress on the play slow. During the last year of his life he agreed to serve as editor of the belles-lettres department for *Russkaia mysl';* Tolstoy, learning this, offered his novella "Khadzhi-Murat" to the journal. Even before officially assuming the position, he was refereeing and editing the fiction of others for Lavrov. He turned down other offers, however,

such as the editorship of the journal *Mir iskusstva* (World of Art) offered by Sergei Pavlovich Diaghilev. In addition, when he was elected chairman of Obshchestvo liubitelei rossiiskoi slovesnosti toward the end of 1903, an appreciative Chekhov explained that he would be unable to carry out the duties of the position, because of illness, for at least a few years.

In spring 1903, after a trip to St. Petersburg in hope of changing the terms of his contract with Marks, Chekhov took a dacha outside Moscow and looked for a small estate in the area to purchase. When the Yiddish author Sholem Aleichem requested a story for a volume in Yiddish benefiting Jewish victims of the Kishinev pogrom, Chekhov offered any of his previously published works that Aleichem might like, with "heartfelt satisfaction."

In July 1903 he was back in Yalta with Knipper. His wife's concern for his health did not keep her from prodding him to finish *Vishnevyi sad*. There was great anxiety about Chekhov's health in the MkhAT company; as Stanislavsky wrote to Knipper, "our theater is Chekhov's theater, and without him it will go badly for us." Nearly finished with the play, Chekhov wrote his wife with characteristic understatement: "it seems to me that in my play, boring as it is, there is something new. Not one gun-shot in the whole play, by the way." In mid October he finally sent *Vishnevyi sad* to Moscow. The play is the most vaudevillean of Chehkov's long dramatic works, and he gave it the subtitle "a comedy." Yet, *Vishnevyi sad* has most often been interpreted as a representation of the sociohistorical tragic drama of an entire class. In such readings the bankruptcy of the Ranevsky family and the clearing of their cherry orchard–the lumber will be sold and the land divided into small plots for the dachas of middle-class vacationers–reflect the decline of the gentry in the twilight of imperial Russia. *Vishnevyi sad* has also been read–like the last two stories Chekhov published (in *Zhurnal dlia vsekh* [Journal for Everyone]), "Arkhierei" (The Bishop, 1902) and "Nevesta" (The Fiancée, 1903)–as the autobiographical "last testament" of an author who was anticipating his own passing.

In Moscow the previous spring Ostroumov had told Chekhov that he should spend the following winter in or around the city. Although his Yalta physician, Isaak Naumovich Al'tshuller, begged him not to return to Moscow for the winter, Chekhov nonetheless followed his play there at the start of December. He had expressed his preferences regarding the distribution of roles, and now he attended rehearsals of the play nearly every day. Meanwhile, Chekhov's literary friends were preparing to celebrate the twenty-fifth anniversary of his literary career (a year early, as Chekhov himself pointed out). At this time a group of well-known

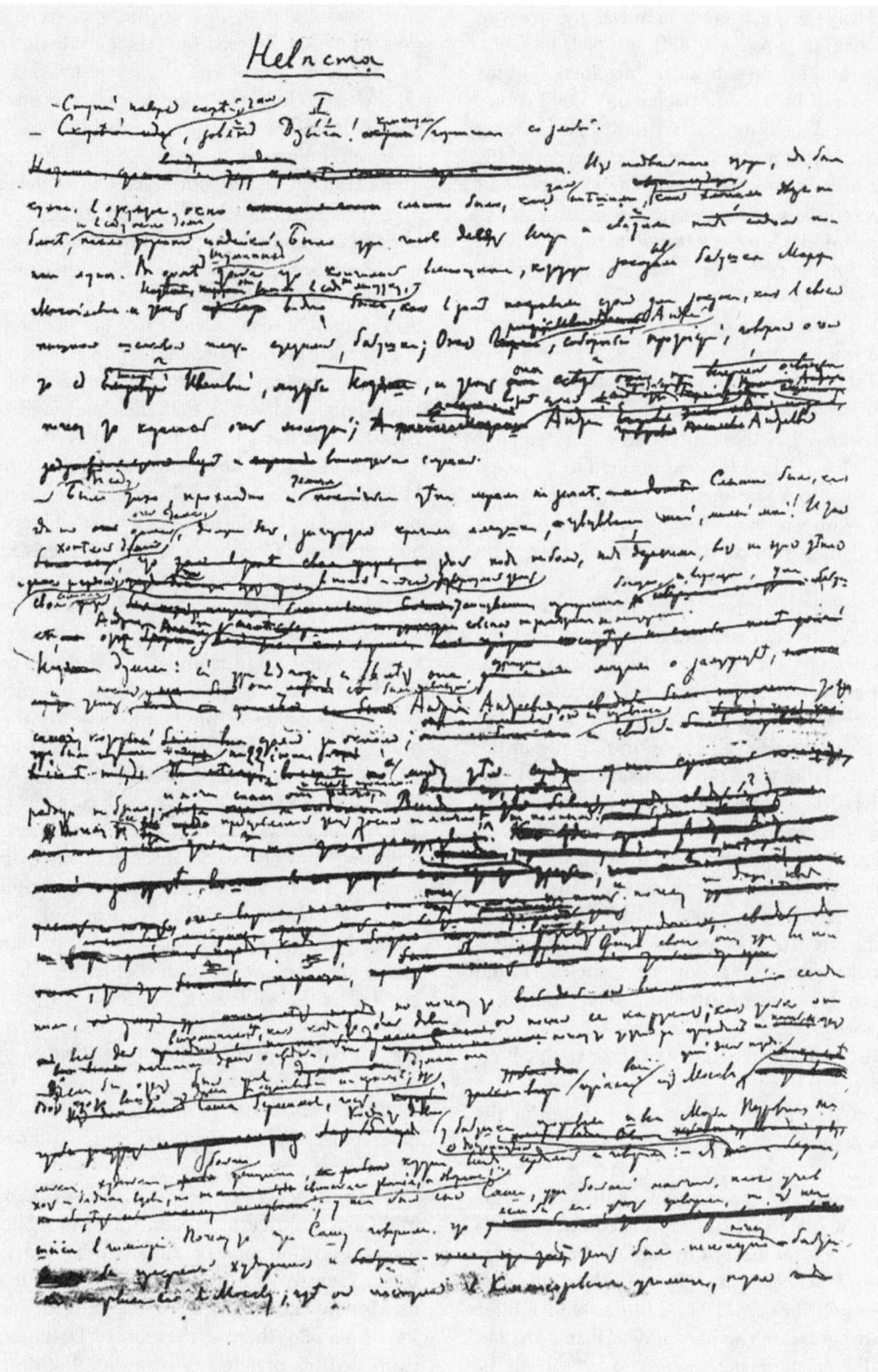

Page from the manuscript for Chekhov's last story, Nevesta *(The Fiancée), first published in* Zhurnal dlia vsekh
(Journal for Everyone) in 1903 (from Phillip Callow, Chekhov: The Hidden Ground, *1998)*

authors signed a petition meant for Marks, the publisher of Chekhov's collected works, and composed by Leonid Nikolaevich Andreev and Gor'ky, in which Marks was asked to change the terms of his contract with Chekhov, particularly in view of the upcoming jubilee. Chekhov asked them not to present the letter to Marks, however, and thus once again stopped the efforts of others to improve his contractual status.

On 17 January 1904—Chekhov's forty-fourth birthday—*Vishnevyi sad* premiered at the MKhAT. He was unaware that the evening had been dedicated to the celebration of his jubilee and had remained at home, continuing his policy of avoiding the premieres of his plays. After the second act, however, Nemirovich-Danchenko sent him a note asking him to come to the theater: the play was going well, the audience had called for the author, and the actors wanted to have him in the theater for the last intermission. Nemirovich-Danchenko also assured him that the audience, now believing that Chekhov was not in the building, would not try summoning him again. When he came to the theater, Chekhov found himself compelled to take the stage and remain standing—visibly uncomfortable, weak, and coughing—for a lengthy ceremony that at the least probably damaged his health as much as did the failure of *Chaika* some years before. Among the gifts presented to him was an antique laurel wreath with portraits of actors and students of the MkhAT, which, Nemirovich-Danchenko declared in his speech, Chekhov should consider "my theater"—that is, Chekhov's own. There was endless bombast, and telegrams sent from all over Russia were read aloud. This situation was precisely the kind that Chekhov had mocked all his life, but now he could only submit. Meanwhile, the performance of the play was less than a full success; he was particularly irritated by the troupe's unwillingness to take to heart his definition of its genre as comic.

The next month Chekhov left for Yalta; he returned to Moscow in May quite ill, and doctors ordered him to take a cure abroad. There are contradictory indications as to whether, toward the end, Chekhov fully understood his condition. In February he wrote to Obshchestvo liubitelei rossiiskoi slovesnosti that he planned to spend the next winter in Moscow and assume his chairmanship or other duties; in April he wrote the author and journalist Aleksandr Valentinovich Amfiteatrov that, if healthy, he intended to travel to the Far East and serve as a doctor in the war with Japan. Yet, reportedly, on the eve of his departure for the Black Forest resort town of Badenweiler, he stated frankly that he was leaving Russia to die. By the beginning of June he had regained enough strength to undertake the journey.

While abroad, during the last days of his life, he was confronted with the double-dealing of his publisher Marks, as well as reproaches from Gor'ky's publishing house Znanie (Knowledge), over the publication of *Vishnevyi sad*. Toward the end of the month Chekhov's heart began to give out. While he wrote home that his health was taking a dramatic turn for the better, he also arranged to have money available in Berlin in his wife's name, "just in case." A short time before dying he entertained Knipper with a story that he did not get the chance to write down: the wealthy patrons of a fashionable resort are stunned when they settle into their places in the dining hall, only to learn that the chef has abandoned them. Through this story Chekhov was joking at some level about the reaction that his own absence would soon cause; the comic plot and his own death—far removed from family, friends, and Moscow—are both reminiscent of the practical joke he carried out at the time of his wedding.

The final crisis occurred in the early morning hours of 2 July 1904. When the doctor attending him ordered a glass of champagne, Chekhov famously uttered, "Ich sterbe . . ." (I am dying); his last conscious words were, "It's a long time since I drank champagne." He died at three in the morning. Chekhovian incongruencies, which have become traditional to note in writings about him, characterized his return to Moscow and burial in the cemetery of the Novodevichii Monastery there: his body arrived at the train station in a refrigerated railway car labeled "for fresh oysters," and his funeral procession was confused with that of a general being buried at the same time. After his death his sister, Mariia, became the guardian of his reputation and personal effects. Throughout the Russian Revolution and the Russian Civil War, she maintained the Yalta home as it was when he died and lobbied to have it made into a museum (1921); the museum and Mariia survived both the Stalinist terror and Nazi occupation.

In most evaluations, Chekhov closes out the age of realism in this era of Russian literature. Gor'ky famously told him that he was "killing realism," and indeed, his final dramatic work, *Vishnevyi sad*, is awash with symbolic undercurrents. Nevertheless, Chekhov himself made quite negative remarks regarding the nascent symbolist or, as it was known then, "decadent" movement, and he predicted that the decadent authors coming into fashion in his last years would have short-lived reputations, whereas more traditional writers such as Gor'ky, Andreev, and Aleksandr Ivanovich Kuprin would be read for ages. Leaving aside the vicissitudes of the literary reputations of those authors, what Chekhov predicted for certain of his contemporaries has unquestionably proven true of himself.

Letters:

Pis'ma A. P. Chekhova, 6 volumes, edited by Mariia Pavlovna Chekhova (Moscow, 1912–1916);

Letters of Anton Chekhov to His Family and Friends, translated by Constance Garnett (New York: Macmillan, 1920);

Pis'ma A. P. Chekhova k O. L. Knipper–Chekhovoi (Berlin: Slovo, 1924);

The Life and Letters of Anton Tchekhov, translated and edited by S. S. Koteliansky and Philip Tomlinson (London: Cassell, 1925); translated by Garnett as *The Letters of Anton Pavlovitch Tchehov to Olga Leonardovna Knipper,* edited by Garnett (New York: B. Blom, 1966);

Perepiska A. P. Chekhova i O. L. Knipper, edited by A. B. Derman (Moscow: Mir, 1934);

Pis'ma A. P. Chekhovu ego brata Aleksandra Chekhova, edited by I. S. Ezhov and I. K. Luppol (Moscow: Gosudarstvennoe sotsial'no-ekonomicheskoe izdatel'stvo, 1939);

The Selected Letters of Anton Chekhov, translated by Sidonie Lederer, edited by Lillian Hellman (New York: Farrar, Straus & Young, 1955);

Letters of Anton Chekhov, translated by Michael Henry Heim in collaboration with Simon Karlinsky (New York: Harper & Row, 1973); republished as *Anton Chekhov's Life and Thought: Selected Letters and Commentary* (Berkeley: University of California Press, 1975);

Dear Writer–Dear Actress–: The Love Letters of Olga Knipper and Anton Chekhov, translated by Jean Benedetti (London: Methuen Drama, 1996);

Perepiska A. P. Chekhova, 3 volumes, edited by Vadim Erazmovich Vatsuro and others (Moscow: Nasledie, 1996).

Bibliographies:

Ivan Fillippovich Masanov, *Chekhoviana: Sistematicheskii ukazatel' literatury o Chekhove i ego tvorchestve* (Moscow: Gosudarstvennaia tsentral'naia knizhnaia palata RSFSR, 1929);

Kseniia Dmitrievna Muratova, comp., *A. P. Chekhov. Bibliografiia* (Leningrad: Leningradskaia knizhnaia lavka pisatelei, 1944);

I. E. Grudinina and A. I. Khvatov, eds., *A. P. Chekhov: Materialy Literaturnogo muzeia Pushkinskogo doma* (Leningrad: Nauka, 1982);

K. A. Lantz, *Anton Chekhov: A Reference Guide to Literature* (Boston: G. K. Hall, 1985);

Charles W. Meister, *Chekhov Bibliography: Works in English by and about Anton Chekhov: American, British and Canadian Performances* (Jefferson, N.C.: McFarland, 1985);

Savely Senderovich and Munir Sendich, *Anton Chekhov Rediscovered: A Collection of New Studies with a Comprehensive Bibliography* (East Lansing, Mich.: Russian Language Journal, 1987).

Biographies:

Ernest J. Simmons, *Chekhov: A Biography* (Boston: Little, Brown, 1962);

Ronald Hingley, *A New Life of Anton Chekhov* (Oxford: Oxford University Press, 1976; New York: Knopf, 1976);

Georgii Petrovich Berdnikov, *Chekhov* (Moscow, Molodaia gvardiia, 1978);

Carolina de Maegd-Soëp, *Chekhov and Women: Women in the Life and Work of Chekhov* (Columbus, Ohio: Slavica, 1987);

Andrei Turkov, comp., *Anton Chekhov and His Times,* translated by Cynthia Carlile (Fayetteville: University of Arkansas Press, 1995);

Donald Rayfield, *Anton Chekhov: A Life* (London: HarperCollins, 1997);

Phillip Callow, *Chekhov: The Hidden Ground* (Chicago: Ivan R. Dee, 1998).

References:

Jean-Pierre Barricelli, ed., *Chekhov's Great Plays: A Critical Anthology* (New York: New York University Press, 1981);

Petr Mikhailovich Bitsilli, *Chekhov's Art: A Stylistic Analysis,* translated by Toby W. Clyman and Edwina J. Cruise (Ann Arbor, Mich.: Ardis, 1983);

Harold Bloom, ed., *Anton Chekhov,* Modern Critical Views (Philadelphia: Chelsea House Publishers, 1999);

Aleksandr P. Chekhov (A. Sedoi), *V gostiakh u dedushki i babushki. Stranichka iz detstva Antona Pavlovicha Chekhova* (St. Petersburg: L. Ia. Ganzburg, 1912);

Mikhail P. Chekhov, *Anton Chekhov i ego siuzhety* (Moscow: "9-e Ianvaria," 1923);

Mikhail P. Chekhov, *Vokrug Chekhova; Vstrechi i vpechatleniia* (Moscow: Moskovskii rabochii, 1959);

Mariia P. Chekhova, *Iz dalekogo proshlogo* (Moscow: Gosudarstvennoe izdatel'stvo khudozhestvennoi literatury, 1960);

Aleksandr Pavlovich Chudakov, *Chekhov's Poetics,* translated by Cruise and Donald Dragt (Ann Arbor, Mich.: Ardis, 1983);

Clyman, ed., *A Chekhov Companion* (Westport, Conn.: Greenwood Press, 1985);

Michael Finke, "The Hero's Descent to the Underworld in Chekhov," *Russian Review,* 53, no. 1 (January 1994): 67–80;

Finke, *Metapoesis: The Russian Tradition from Pushkin to Chekhov* (Durham, N.C.: Duke University Press, 1995);

Richard Gilman, *Chekhov's Plays: An Opening into Eternity* (New Haven: Yale University Press, 1995);

N. I. Gitovich, ed., *A. P. Chekhov v vospominaniiakh sovremennikov* (Moscow: Khudozhestvennaia literatura, 1986);

Gitovich, *Letopis' zhizni i tvorchestva A. P. Chekhova* (Moscow: Gosudarstvennoe izdatel'stvo khudozhestvennoi literatury, 1955);

Maksim Gor'ky, Aleksander Kuprin, and Ivan Alekseevich Bunin, *Reminiscences of Anton Chekhov,* translated by Samuel Solomonovitch Koteliansky and Leonard Wolf (New York: B. W. Huersch, 1921);

Robert Louis Jackson, comp., *Chekhov: A Collection of Critical Essays* (Englewood Cliffs, N.J.: Prentice-Hall, 1967);

Jackson, ed., *Reading Chekhov's Text* (Evanston, Ill.: Northwestern University Press, 1993);

Vladimir Borisovich Kataev, *Literaturnye sviazi Chekhova* (Moscow: Izdatel'stvo Moskovskogo Universiteta, 1989);

Kataev, *Proza Chekhova: Problemy interpretatsii* (Moscow: Izdatel'stvo Moskovskogo Universiteta, 1979);

Daria A. Kirjanov, *Chekhov and the Poetics of Memory* (New York: Peter Lang, 2000);

Karl D. Kramer, *The Chameleon and the Dream: The Image of Reality in Cexov's Stories* (The Hague & Paris: Mouton, 1970);

Alevtina Pavlovna Kuzicheva, *A. P. Chekhov v russkoi teatral'noi kritike. Kommentirovannaia antologiia* (Moscow: Chekhovskii poligraficheskii kombinat, 1999);

Kuzicheva and Evgeniia Mikhailovna Sakharova, *Melikhovskii letopisets: Dnevnik Pavla Egorovicha Chekhova* (Moscow: Nauka, 1995);

R. E. Lapushin, *Ne postigaemoe bytie . . . Opyt prochteniia A. P. Chekhova* (Minsk: Propilei, 1998);

Liudmila Danilovna Mikitich, *Literaturnyi Peterburg, Petrograd* (Moscow: Sovetskaia Rossiia, 1991);

Natalia Pervukhina, *Anton Chekhov: The Sense and the Nonsense* (New York & Ottawa: Legas, 1993);

Harvey Pitcher, *The Chekhov Play: A New Interpretation* (London: Chatto & Windus, 1973);

Pitcher, *Chekhov's Leading Lady: A Portrait of the Actress Olga Knipper* (London: Murray, 1979);

Cathy Popkin, "Chekhov as Ethnographer: Epistemological Crisis on Sakhalin Island," *Slavic Review,* 51, no. 1 (1992): 36–51;

Popkin, *The Pragmatics of Insignificance: Chekhov, Zoshchenko, Gogol* (Stanford: Stanford University Press, 1993);

Donald Rayfield, *Understanding Chekhov: A Critical Study of Chekhov's Prose and Drama* (Madison: University of Wisconsin Press, 1999; London: Bristol Classical, 1999);

Marena Senderovich, "Chekhov's Name drama," in *Reading Chekhov's Text,* edited by Jackson (Evanston, Ill.: Northwestern University Press, 1993), pp. 31–48;

Savely Senderovich, *Chekhov–s glazu na glaz. Istoriia odnoi oderzhimosti A. P. Chekhova. Opyt fenomenologii tvorchestva* (St. Petersburg: Dmitrii Bulanin, 1994);

Senderovich, "*The Cherry Orchard:* Chechov's Last Testament," *Russian Literature,* 35 (1994): 223–242;

Senderovich, "O chekhovskoi glubine, ili iudofobskii rasskaz Chekhova v svete iudaisticheskoi ekzegezy," in *Avtor i tekst: Sbornik statei,* edited by V. M. Markovich and Wolf Schmid (St. Petersburg: Izdatel'stvo Sankt-Peterburgskogo universiteta, 1996), pp. 306–340;

Laurence Senelick, *The Chekhov Theatre: A Century of the Plays in Performance* (Cambridge: Cambridge University Press, 1997);

Julie de Sherbinin, *Chekhov and Russian Religious Culture: The Poetics of the Marian Paradigm* (Evanston, Ill.: Northwestern University Press, 1997);

Elena Tolstaya, *Poetika razdrazheniia: Chekhov v kontse 1880-kh nachale 1890-kh godov* (Moscow: Radkis, 1994);

Thomas Winner, *Chekhov and His Prose* (New York: Holt, Rinehart & Winston, 1966).

Papers:

Most of Anton Pavlovich Chekhov's archives are held in the Russian State Library (RGB, formerly the Lenin Library) in Moscow, although there are also some materials of interest at the Institute of Russian Literature (IRLI, Pushkin House) in St. Petersburg. The greatest quantity of authentic personal effects, including the books that were still in his possession at the time of his death, can be found in the Chekhov House-Museum in Yalta. Detailed information on Chekhov's archival holdings is also given in Donald Rayfield's *Anton Chekhov: A Life,* pp. 633–639.

Nikolai Aleksandrovich Dobroliubov

(24 January 1836 – 17 November 1861)

Donald Senese
University of Victoria

BOOKS: *Aleksei Vasil'evich Kol'tsov, ego zhizn' i sochineniia: Chteniia dlia iunoshestva* (Moscow: A. I. Glazunov, 1858);

Sochineniia, 4 volumes, edited, with an introduction, by Nikolai Gavrilovich Chernyshevsky (St. Petersburg: Ogrizko, 1862);

Pervoe polnoe sobranie sochinenii, 4 volumes, edited by Mikhail Konstantinovich Lemke (St. Petersburg: A. S. Panafidina, 1911);

Sobranie sochinenii, 8 volumes, edited by Vladimir Pavlovich Kranikhfel'd (St. Petersburg: Prosveshchenie, 1911);

Polnoe sobranie sochinenii, 9 volumes, edited by E. V. Anichkov (St. Petersburg: Deiatel', 1911–1913);

Dnevniki, 1851–1859 (Moscow, 1931, 1932);

Polnoe sobranie sochinenii, 6 volumes, edited by Pavel Ivanovich Lebedev-Poliansky (Moscow & Leningrad: GIKhL, 1934; Leningrad: Goslitizdat, 1935; Moscow: Goslitizdat, 1936–1941);

Stikhotvoreniia, edited by Boris Iakovlevich Bukhshtab, with an introduction by V. Kirpotin, Biblioteka poeta, Malaia seriia, no. 45 (Leningrad: Sovetskii pisatel', 1939);

Sobranie sochinenii, 9 volumes, edited by Boris Ivanovich Brusov and others (Moscow & Leningrad: Goslitizdat, 1961–1964);

Polnoe sobranie stikhotvorenii, edited by Bukhshtab, Biblioteka poeta, Bol'shaia seriia (Leningrad: Sovetskii pisatel', 1969).

Editions and Collections: *Literaturno-kriticheskie stat'i,* with an introduction by Valerian Poliansky (Moscow: Goslitizdat, 1935);

Izbrannye filosofskie sochineniia, 2 volumes, edited by Mikhail Trifonovich Iovchuk (Moscow: Gosudarstvennoe izdatel'stvo politicheskoi literatury, 1945); republished as *Izbrannye filosofskie proizvedeniia,* 2 volumes, edited by Iovchuk (Moscow: Gospolitizdat, 1948);

Stikhotvoreniia, edited, with an introduction, by Boris Iakovlevich Bukhshtab, Biblioteka poeta,

Nikolai Aleksandrovich Dobroliubov

Malaia seriia (Moscow: Sovetskii pisatel', 1948);

Izbrannye pedagogicheskie proizvedeniia (Moscow: Akademiia pedagogicheskikh nauk RSFSR, 1952);

Literaturnaia kritika, with an introduction by A. N. Dmitrieva (Moscow: Goslitizdat, 1961); enlarged edition, 2 volumes, with an introduction by N. I. Sokolov (Leningrad: Khudozhestvennaia literatura, 1984);

N. A. Dobroliubov o klassikakh russkoi literatury: Sbornik, edited by P. Tkachev (Minsk: Vysheishaia shkola, 1976);

Stikhotvoreniia. Rasskazy. Dnevniki, with an introduction by G. V. Krasnov (Gor'ky: Volgo-Viatskoe knizhnoe izdatel'stvo, 1986);

Sobranie sochineniia, 3 volumes, with an introduction by Iu. G. Burtin (Moscow, 1986–1987)–includes volume 1, *Stat'i, retsenzii i zametki, 1853-1858;* volume 2, *Stat'i i retsenzii, 1859;* and volume 3, *Stat'i i retsenzii, 1860-1861; Iz "Svistka"; Iz liriki.*

Editions in English: *Selected Philosophical Essays,* translated by J. Fineberg (Moscow: Foreign Languages Publishing House, 1956);

Belinsky, Chernyshevsky, and Dobrolyubov: Selected Criticism, edited and translated, with an introduction, by Ralph E. Matlaw (New York: Dutton, 1962)–includes "What Is Oblomovitis?" and "When Will the Real Day Come?";

The Indian National Uprising of 1857: A Contemporary Russian Account, translated by Harish C. Gupta (Calcutta: Nalanda Publications, 1988).

OTHER: "Neizdannye teksty N. A. Dobroliubova," with commentary by S. Reiser, *Literaturnoe nasledstvo,* 25–26 (1936): 243–245.

Nikolai Aleksandrovich Dobroliubov was one of the most influential Russian literary critics of the nineteenth century. His critical approach–which placed greater value on an accurate depiction of reality, rather than on any aesthetic consideration, and interpreted literature for its political or social message–was first developed by Vissarion Grigor'evich Belinsky in the preceding generation. Dobroliubov wrote at a time when censorship, though still harsh, was far less restrictive than in Belinsky's day, and he wrote as well for a far larger reading public. Between 1857 and 1861, as literary critic for the journal *Sovremennik* (The Contemporary), he exerted a profound influence over Russian letters. Fyodor Dostoevsky said of Dobroliubov that his reviews in *Sovremennik* were always the first thing people read at a time when hardly anyone bothered to read literary criticism. After Dobroliubov's early death in 1861 his writing continued to inspire successive generations of readers–especially the youth of Russia, for whom his angry and scarcely veiled denunciations of the evils of tsarism made him more a revolutionary tribune than a literary critic. His reputation, burnished by the favorable attention lavished on him by Soviet scholars, continued to grow throughout the twentieth century.

Dobroliubov was born on 24 January 1836 in Nizhnii Novgorod, a provincial capital and trading center at the confluence of the Volga and the Oka Rivers about 250 miles east of Moscow. His father, Aleksandr Ivanovich Dobroliubov, was archpriest of the Church of St. Nicholas. His mother, Zinaida Vasil'evna (Pokrovskaia) Dobroliubova, was the daughter of the priest who had held the parish before her marriage, and she effectively brought it to Aleksandr Ivanovich as her dowry. Dobroliubov was the firstborn of a family that eventually numbered eight children. He was always his mother's favorite, a fact noticed and commented on by his siblings. While the family was not poor, money was a constant concern, and Aleksandr Ivanovich had to supplement his church salary by teaching, by renting out rooms in the Dobroliubov home, and by various small entrepreneurial ventures. He was absent a good deal of the time and, even when home, was frequently distracted and remote. Not a domestic tyrant, he nonetheless inspired a degree of fear among the children. In these circumstances Zinaida Vasil'evna became the emotional anchor of the family. Her tenderness and solicitation compensated in part for the emotional void created by her husband. She was probably the most important personal influence in Dobroliubov's life. He idolized her, and her early death (in childbirth) when he was only eighteen was an emotional blow from which he never fully recovered.

From an early age Dobroliubov was recognized as a prodigy by his family and his teachers. He was taught at home first by his mother and subsequently by private tutors. His capacity for work, especially his ability to read and assimilate information at great speed, was remarkable. In 1847 he entered the senior class of the local parochial school and a year later graduated with distinction and transferred to the Nizhnii Novgorod seminary, where he remained until the summer of 1853. At the seminary he was recognized as a student of exceptional ability and, in the words of his tutor, M. A. Kostrov, "the most pious boy in all Nizhnii," as quoted in Pavel Ivanovich Lebedev-Poliansky's 1935 biography of Dobroliubov. In addition to his studies, he wrote much juvenile poetry, collected folk sayings and local songs, and contributed articles to a town newspaper. Most of all, he read. He compiled what he called "registers" in which he noted the books that he read and his evaluation of them–in effect, reviews. By the time he left the seminary he had recorded more than four thousand titles in these registers.

From 1852 until 1859 Dobroliubov kept diaries. He was not a conscientious or systematic diarist, and there are long breaks in the entries. Some years amount to only a few pages, and there are no entries at all for 1858. As a chronicle of his daily activities, the diaries are of limited value, but as a window into his inner life and the intellectual and moral struggles that marked it, they are an invaluable source. The diaries reveal, for instance, that by 1852 the pious sixteen-year-old was beginning to have doubts about his faith. Likewise, they disclose that on the eve of his departure to St. Petersburg in the summer of 1853, his first priority was not to profit from the superior educational opportunities that the capital provided but, rather, to have a chance to associate with journalists and writers—to become a writer himself.

His family sent him to St. Petersburg to finish his religious schooling at the St. Petersburg Theological Academy Central Pedagogical Institute. Shortly after his arrival in August 1853 Dobroliubov decided instead to enroll in the Pedagogical Institute—that is, the teachers' college of the capital—and his father reluctantly acquiesced. At the institute Dobroliubov quickly acquired the same reputation that he had established in school in Nizhnii Novgorod, for he was a top student—intimidating, precocious, and eager to display his ability and to claim the precedence that he thought was his due. In 1854 he suffered a double loss: his mother died in March after giving birth to her last child, Elizaveta, and his father succumbed to cholera in August. Dobroliubov's first concern was for his family. He prepared to leave the institute immediately and take a job as a schoolteacher in order to provide for his seven orphaned siblings. Family and friends persuaded him that other arrangements for their support could be worked out, but to the end of his life he considered them his responsibility and aided them as much as his always slender income permitted.

The death of Aleksandr Ivanovich, whose disapproval had made the renunciation of religion difficult for his son, removed a powerful barrier to Dobroliubov's definitive rejection of traditional religious beliefs. When he returned to the Pedagogical Institute in the autumn of 1854, he rather quickly transferred his spiritual allegiance to the radical secular beliefs of mid-nineteenth-century Europe—socialism and materialism. He organized a circle (*kruzhok*) among his fellow students where he led readings and discussions of forbidden works by Belinsky, Ludwig Feuerbach, and Alexander Herzen (Aleksandr Ivanovich Gertsen). Herzen was Dobroliubov's introduction to the application of socialist ideas to Russia, and he always retained the impress of this early exposure. Socialism, for Dobroliubov, was a comprehensive, vague, and idealistic notion. "I am a passionate socialist," he wrote in his diary in January 1854, "ready to enter, at once if you like, into a society of modest means that has equal laws and community of property for all its members."

A comprehensive philosophical matrix was provided to Dobroliubov by the materialist views of Feuerbach. Scholars often assert that Nikolai Gavrilovich Chernyshevsky first introduced Feuerbach to Dobro-

liubov and used the monistic and materialist worldview of the German theologian to wean him away from his early admiration for the idealist Herzen. In fact, Dobroliubov had studied Feuerbach two years before he met Chernyshevsky. In 1855 he had begun a translation of Feuerbach's *Das Wesen des Christentums* (The Essence of Christianity, 1841) into Russian. Like Chernyshevsky, Dobroliubov found in Feuerbach's thought a ready justification for abandoning his religious faith. Moreover, like many other midcentury radicals, he came to believe that if religion was basically the projection of humankind's own emotional and intellectual assumptions, as Feuerbach preached, then the same must be true of all human institutions and culture, including politics, the social order, and literature. He greeted enthusiastically Chernyshevsky's seminal thesis for St. Petersburg University, "Esteticheskie otnosheniia iskusstva k deistvitel'nosti" (The Aesthetic Relations of Art to Reality, 1853), precisely because his thoughts had already turned in the same direction.

During his last two years at the institute Dobroliubov increasingly played the role of troublemaker and agitator. He led deputations of student protestors and complained of the rigid discipline imposed by Ivan Ivanovich Davydov, the director of the institute. He published an illegal handwritten newsletter, *Slukhi* (Rumors). These were the years of Russian defeat in the Crimean War, the death of the authoritarian tsar Nicholas I, and the disquieting realization by the whole society that Russia was entering a period of rapid and open-ended change. Students felt these stirrings more keenly than any other segment of the society, and Dobroliubov was intimately attuned to their hopes and their impatience. During his career as a journalist and critic he impressed all with his mastery of a mature literary tradition that was already a century old and with an understanding of a culture that was far older than that, but his primary audience was always the "Youth" of Russia who, preeminently, had the daring to imagine a radically different order of things.

In December 1854 Dobroliubov's oppositional sentiments were broadcast beyond the walls of the institute. A celebration had been held to mark the fiftieth jubilee of the publisher Nikolai Ivanovich Grech. Dobroliubov composed a poem denouncing Grech, his reactionary views, and his collaboration with the Third Section (the secret police) and then mailed the poem to Grech and to the editors of several newspapers. Although the police could not prove Dobroliubov's authorship, a search of his rooms produced a quantity of illegal literature, and he was threatened with expulsion from the institute. Through the intercession of sympathetic faculty, he was spared this fate, and his punishment was no more than a period of house arrest in the institute infirmary. The incident was not forgotten, however, and resulted in his being denied the Gold Medal, which belonged rightly to him as the student with the best academic record in the graduating class of June 1857. This rejection was a palpable injustice, but Dobroliubov was able to shrug it off because by that time he was already becoming established in the literary career that eventually thrust him into national prominence.

In August 1856 *Sovremennik*, the leading monthly journal of the day, published an article, "Sobesednik liubitelei Rossiiskogo slova" (The Companion of Lovers of the Russian Word) by N. Laibov. Laibov was in fact Dobroliubov (the pseudonym was formed from the final syllables of his first and last names). The article was an impressively researched account of a short-lived eighteenth-century literary journal, but what made it a sensation was Dobroliubov's criticism of Catherine the Great, the sponsor of the journal and a frequent contributor. Dodging nimbly around the censor, Dobroliubov gave the reader his assessment of Catherine: as a writer she was untalented, and as a person she was devious and controlling. For the first time a national audience became exposed to Dobroliubov's trademark style—solid scholarship and a serious discussion of issues intercut with nervy irony and occasional bursts of sarcasm. Ivan Sergeevich Turgenev wrote from Paris to Ivan Ivanovich Panaev, an editor and part owner of *Sovremennik*, "That article of Laibov is very solid (Who is this Laibov?)."

As well as writing for *Sovremennik*, Dobroliubov contributed regularly to *Zhurnal dlia vospitaniia* (Journal for Education). Throughout his career he showed a special interest in the education of the young and reviewed children's books and magazines as seriously as pedagogical treatises. Drawing on the writings of Jean-Jacques Rousseau, he felt that education should be based on the natural inclinations of the child and that rigid discipline and proscriptive rules, both characteristics of Russian education at that time, not only taught nothing of value but also suppressed the child's natural abilities. The use of corporal punishment to enforce rote learning was an abomination against which he frequently railed.

Dobroliubov's name was forever associated, however, with *Sovremennik*. The journal was published by the poet Nikolai Alekseevich Nekrasov and boasted a stable of writers under exclusive contract—Turgenev, Ivan Aleksandrovich Goncharov, Aleksandr Nikolaevich Ostrovsky, and Leo Tolstoy. From 1856 onward the chief editor was Chernyshevsky, whose radical articles made the journal a leader in demands for more rapid and far-reaching changes than the government was willing to contemplate. The dominant voice in the literary world of its day, *Sovremennik* was a force with which to be reckoned in the influence of public opinion.

Dobroliubov's rise at *Sovremennik* was meteoric and, aside from his obvious talent, facilitated by his friendship with Chernyshevsky. The two first met in the spring of 1856, just before Dobroliubov entered his final year at the institute. Chernyshevsky encouraged him to send his manuscript of "Sobesednik liubitelei Rossiiskogo slova" to *Sovremennik*. The two men quickly became friends and in fact shared much in common. Both were the sons of priests. Both came from Volga River towns. Both were *raznochintsy* (nonnoble intellectuals). Both were passionate materialists. Most important, both were dedicated to revolutionary change for Russia, and Chernyshevsky recognized that Dobroliubov was an effective advocate for such change. He took him on as an editorial assistant and, upon Dobroliubov's graduation from the institute, promoted him to the editorial board. Then in September 1857 Chernyshevsky—who wished to devote himself full-time to writing on economic and social issues—proposed that Dobroliubov direct the literary section of the journal. This position was one of extraordinary influence for a young man of twenty-two, scarcely out of school.

Dobroliubov lived in a modest, not to say squalid, flat in St. Petersburg. He was paid for his work on *Sovremennik* and supplemented this income through private tutoring in the evenings, but the cost of living in the capital was high, and he regularly sent money home to his family. He was forced to draw advances and take loans from the cash fund of the journal. Nekrasov, the publisher, who had grown fond of his young colleague, freely advanced him money, and in September 1857 he induced Dobroliubov to take a small suite in the house where Nekrasov lived with his long-time mistress, Avdot'ia Iakovlevna Panaeva, a famous beauty and the wife of Ivan Panaev, Nekrasov's partner. Dobroliubov regularly took meals and tea with the couple and spent much time discussing editorial matters with Nekrasov.

A maternal relationship developed between Dobroliubov and Panaeva, who was only three years younger than his mother would have been. She scolded him for disregarding his health and for working too hard; "You can no more live without work than a drunk without vodka," she told him (quoted in *N. A. Dobroliubov v vospominaniakh sovremennikov* [N. A. Dobroliubov in the Recollections of His Contemporaries, 1961]). Dobroliubov, for his part, was more open and at ease with her than with any other woman.

As his diaries and letters suggest, Dobroliubov's relationships with women were his greatest torment. He suffered frequently from bouts of depression, which were marked by feelings of inadequacy and self-loathing. Almost inevitably, these episodes were brought on by a

Page from the "register" Dobroliubov kept as a youth, listing and evaluating books that he read (from Vladimir Viktorovich Zhdanov, Nikolai Aleksandrovich Dobroliubov, 1836–1861, *1951)* perceived failure or rejection in his love life. Since he made little effort to meet "respectable" women on his own, the successive objects of his affection tended to be the girls that he tutored or the female relatives of friends and colleagues. Fixing on someone new, he envisioned contradictory scenarios—seduction and abandonment one moment, marriage and lifelong bliss the next. In these musings he appeared more like a confused adolescent than the literary arbiter of Russia. He was searching for an intelligent, loving life companion yet could not believe that such a woman could love him. His constant idealization of women, or his tendency to place them on a pedestal, accounts in large part for the otherwise puzzling fact that almost all the "positive heroes" he identified in the books that he reviewed—the principled, strong, dedicated characters—were women.

Most of Dobroliubov's "relationships" existed, however, only in his imagination; whole romances were played out in his thoughts without the women ever being aware of it. An exception was his near engagement to Chernyshevsky's sister-in-law, Anna Sokratovna Vasil'eva (Aniuta). He had previously paid court to Chernyshevsky's wife, Ol'ga, a notorious coquette who only toyed with him. He then turned his attention to her sister, and in short order the couple presented themselves to Chernyshevsky for his blessing. Instead, prompted by Ol'ga, Chernyshevsky took the girl home to her family in Saratov.

Although all the photographs of Dobroliubov portray a prepossessing enough young man, descriptions of him by contemporaries convey an entirely different picture. He was quite tall and thin with sloping shoulders and a sunken chest; his skin had a gray-green tint; his lips were thick and his nose large. According to Lebedev-Poliansky, he was, in Chernyshevsky's words, "not really ugly, but quite unattractive." In the summer of 1858 he developed scrofula, a tubercular infection of the lymph nodes that produces lesions and subsequent scarring around the neck.

To satisfy his desire for intimacy, Dobroliubov often saw prostitutes. Most of these encounters were by definition transitory, but an important exception was his relationship with Theresa Grunwald, a German girl to whom he was extremely close from December 1856 until early 1860. His letters and diaries make frequent references to Theresa by name, and a prostitute named "Mashen'ka," also often mentioned, is now thought to be the same person. At one time he considered marrying her—to the consternation of Chernyshevsky, who described Theresa as not having the manners of a chambermaid. In August 1858 he literally dragged Dobroliubov from a railway station and forcibly prevented him from going to Theresa. Pressure from

Chernyshevsky was, in fact, the major reason Dobroliubov broke off the relationship. After Dobroliubov's death Chernyshevsky, perhaps conscience-stricken, took an interest in Theresa's welfare even after his own arrest and imprisonment.

In contrast to the lack of confidence and timidity he conveyed around women, Dobroliubov was perceived by the men of the St. Petersburg literary establishment as supercilious and arrogant. In social situations his frequent silences and distracted air were seen as signs of boredom, and his occasional dry observations were interpreted as ironic reproofs. He sometimes descended to sheer rudeness, telling Turgenev once that he was bored with his conversation and suggesting that they not talk further. Part of this behavior did reflect a defensive sensitivity to his status as a poor, provincial former seminarian; yet, in fact, he did believe that he was intellectually and morally superior to most of the writers that he met in the capital, and he was not shy in asserting this superiority. In late 1858 a banquet was organized to commemorate the tenth anniversary of Belinsky's death. Partway through the evening Dobroliubov thought that the proceedings were taking too jovial a turn for the solemnity of the occasion. He walked out and registered his protest in a poem, "Na tost v pamiat' Belinskogo" (For a Toast in Memory of Belinsky), which he distributed to the participants. Many of them had personally known and loved Belinsky and were deeply offended that this arrogant young man should presume to lecture them on what was the proper manner in which to honor his memory.

A satirical supplement to *Sovremennik* called *Svistok* (Whistle) was established early in 1859. Dobroliubov was not only its founding editor but also a frequent contributor, writing topical, satiric verses. He had composed poetry from quite an early age, in large part for his own personal gratification. More than three hundred of these poems, including juvenilia and translations, have been discovered and published, and many more are assumed to have been lost. Almost all of the poetry published during Dobroliubov's lifetime was in the form of satirical verses, most of which appeared in *Svistok*. Such poems attacked the same abuses in Russian life that he targeted in his articles and reviews. Although always marked by a latent bitterness, these squibs are, nonetheless, often genuinely funny. His send-ups of the works of "denunciatory" and official poets are particularly impressive, displaying great facility of language and a deadly talent for parody.

In contrast to the notoriety that Dobroliubov's satirical verse brought him, his lyric poetry was virtually unknown during his lifetime. He consented to publish just six of his lyric poems in 1858—and these only reluctantly, at the insistence of Nekrasov. After Dobroliubov's death a great store of lyric poetry was discovered among his papers and subsequently published. Although generally characterized as "civic poetry" because of its focus on social and political issues, his lyric verse is, in fact, largely personal and contemplative in nature. Its style and tone display the strong influences of both Nekrasov and the German poet Heinrich Heine. No scholar places Dobroliubov among the leading ranks of Russian poets, however, and his reluctance to publish his poetry attests to his honesty and critical discernment. The posthumous publication of so many of his poems owes less to their intrinsic merit than to his reputation as one of the greatest Russian literary critics.

An early target of Dobroliubov's satirical verse was the then current vogue of *oblichitel'naia* (denunciatory) literature. With the new tsar, Alexander II, came a gradual relaxation of censorship as the government began to show an increasing tolerance for criticism of the political system. This policy of acceptance was designed to accustom the society to the notion of political discourse and to prepare public opinion for the reforms that the government had already decided to undertake. The new tolerance encouraged the development of denunciatory literature, in which writers waxed indignant over specific examples of official arbitrariness and corruption. What Dobroliubov satirized wickedly in his poems was the insignificant nature of these denunciations—focused as they were on minor officials and trifling problems.

In the winter of 1859 *Sovremennik* published his "Literaturnye melochi proshlogo goda" (Literary Trifles of the Past Year), in which he explicitly spelled out his objections to this trend. Nothing and no one of any importance was ever criticized, and, far more important, no attempt was ever made to connect these minor abuses to a general pattern of misrule. Using Aesopian language—a mixture of allusion and code words which allowed writers of his day to elude the censorship and place forbidden ideas before their readers—Dobroliubov went on to imply that the whole interlocked system of autocracy and serfdom should be the appropriate target of attack, leaving no doubt of his own hatred for both. Clearly included in this programmatic statement was a rejection not only of denunciatory literature but also of any gradualist or reformist approach to solving the problems of Russia—the approach still favored by the majority of contemporary liberals, including liberal writers.

Herzen, publisher of the illegal but widely read London-based journal *Kolokol* (The Bell), condemned "Literaturnye melochi proshlogo goda" immediately in an article titled "Very Dangerous!" He argued that there was a real risk of dividing progressive opinion in Russia and implied that *Sovremennik* and *Svistok* might be consciously aiding the censorship. Herzen's article produced a crisis at *Sovremennik*. Circulation fell off and the

publisher, Nekrasov, came close to a nervous breakdown. Chernyshevsky even made a trip to London to attempt to smooth over the dispute. Dobroliubov, however, was able to maintain his customary sangfroid in the face of the storm. In 1859, when informed of Herzen's veiled accusations of collaboration with the censorship, he noted in his diary, "If that's true then Herzen is certainly not a serious person. To make thoughtless judgments about people in the press is really preposterous."

In 1859 and 1860 Dobroliubov was at the height of both his influence at *Sovremennik* and his popularity with the reading public. During this two-year span his reviews of the works of Goncharov, Turgenev, and Ostrovsky also appeared—reviews that have been universally acclaimed as his best work and upon which his reputation still rests largely. In these essays he developed not only the techniques of what he called "real criticism" but also the theoretical justification for that particular mode of interpreting and passing judgment upon literature. While other names have been given (both by contemporaries and by subsequent commentators) to his style of criticism, it is most often called "utilitarian," an approach to literature that tends to ignore or derogate aesthetic considerations yet insists upon a useful social message. Other terms used to describe it are "civic," which underlines its commitment to the common good, and "nihilist," which presumably emphasizes its radicalism and rejection of traditional values.

"Chto takoe oblomovshchina?" (translated as "What is Oblomovitis?" 1962), published in 1859 in *Sovremennik,* is a review of the novel *Oblomov* (1859) by Goncharov and Dobroliubov's best-known essay. Indeed, "Chto takoe oblomovshchina?" likely marks the one work for which Dobroliubov is remembered today, although serious students of Russian literature know him for many other writings as well. The word *oblomovshchina* was not Dobroliubov's invention but, rather, was first uttered by Stolz, one of the characters in the novel. Through his essay Dobroliubov did, however, give the term its meaning and make it an enduring and fascinating catchword for Russians. Tricky to translate, the word undoubtedly carries a negative connotation. "Oblomovism" is standard but too neutral, while "Oblomovitis," another common translation, is too clinical. An approximate definition is "the Oblomov problem." Goncharov's novel constitutes an enduring masterpiece of Russian literature, and the meaning of the peculiarly torpid behavior of Oblomov—the eponymous hero (who essentially does nothing but lie around in his dressing gown for the whole course of the book)—continues to be the subject of varied speculation.

Front page from an issue of Dobroliubov's handwritten newspaper, Slukhi *(Rumors), which he circulated illegally while studying at the Pedagogical Institute in St. Petersburg during the mid 1850s (from Zhdanov,*
Nikolai Aleksandrovich Dobroliubov, 1836–1861, *1951)*

For Dobroliubov, the interpretation was clear and immediate: Oblomov typified the "do-nothing" spirit that characterized all of Russian society. In Dobroliubov's view the whole of contemporary society—writers, artists, professors, and government officials—are Oblomovs, who

> only talk about higher strivings, about the consciousness of a moral obligation and the dedication to common interests, but it turns out that in fact all this is words, just words. Their most sincere and heartfelt striving is the striving for rest and for the dressing-gown with which they cover their emptiness and apathy. . . . everything they talk and dream about is alien and superficial to them; one dream, one ideal alone is rooted in the depths of their souls—the greatest possible undisturbed rest, quietism, *oblomovshchina*.

With this simple reductionist approach Dobroliubov transforms Oblomov into a "type," and a unique and fascinating creation of imaginative fiction becomes an analytical model for social criticism.

Dobroliubov finds a sufficient reason for Oblomov's inaction in the person of his serf and valet, Zakhar, who fulfills his master's needs in every way—down to the simplest tasks of life, such as getting dressed. Dobroliubov sees Zakhar as a representative of the hundreds of serfs on Oblomov's family estate, who since his birth have made possible his life of idle uselessness. *Oblomovshchina*—that is, the inability of educated Russians to bestir themselves to meaningful action—is directly linked to the institution of serfdom. Armed with this new understanding, the reader is able to appreciate the revolutionary appeal of Dobroliubov's ringing peroration: "Who now will budge them from the spot by that all-powerful word 'Forward!' which Gogol dreamed of and for which Rus' has so long and painfully waited?"

Fearlessly, Dobroliubov pushed his conception of *oblomovshchina* to comment on one of the most important recurrent themes of Russian literature—the "superfluous man," a tragic hero who can find no meaningful role in society. Aleksandr Sergeevich Pushkin's Onegin, Mikhail Iur'evich Lermontov's Pechorin, and Turgenev's Rudin are all examples of this type. Dobroliubov's analysis dismisses the usual explanations for the detached and alienated stance of these men—emotional trauma or a spirit too noble for this world—and provides his own. In his view their environment has deprived them of any capacity for useful activity; they are all Oblomovs. He claims, in fact, that Oblomov represents the last and most perfect example of the "superfluous man."

Dobroliubov finds that Stolz, Oblomov's energetic friend, does not possess the qualities that can show Rus-

sians the way out from stagnation and apathy. In the first place, Stolz's German name betrays the fact that he is in some sense not really Russian. Second, Goncharov declines to make clear exactly how Stolz's activity achieves its results; he appears more as a plot device and a foil for Oblomov's torpor than as a model for purposeful action. Instead, Dobroliubov finds that the positive hero of the book is Oblomov's fiancée, Ol'ga, who leaves him for Stolz: "She is ready for this fight, she yearns for it. . . . It is clear that she does not want to bow her head and peacefully endure the hard times in hopes that life will again smile. . . . She knows *oblomovshchina* very well, she knows how to recognize it in all its aspects, under all its masks, and she will always be able to find within herself the strength to pronounce a merciless judgment upon it." Looking to the example of women models is a recurrent theme in Dobroliubov's writings. In his long digression on the theme of the "superfluous man," he repeatedly stresses that the women in these men's lives are always their moral superiors.

Dobroliubov's critical values and assumptions are well illustrated in "Chto takoe oblomovshchina?" For him the characters of a story are not products of the author's imagination but of his experience. The true gift of a writer is the ability to describe people and situations that he has observed, consciously or not, in the society around him over the course of his life.

He also believed that once the writer captures the true image of reality, it is no longer his. Instead, it becomes the property of the critic, who is free to interpret it as he sees fit. In this instance two people who are more opposed in personality and politics than the writer and the critic are difficult to imagine. Goncharov was conservative, famously meek, and loyal to the system for which he served as a government bureaucrat. From 1855 to 1867 he was an official of the State censorship, that branch of government that continually tormented Dobroliubov and, in Chernyshevsky's view at least, drove him to an early grave. Nevertheless, Dobroliubov lavished praise on Goncharov because he created images that were not only true but also potentially useful to the critic. The most frequent observation about Dobroliubov's approach, voiced by contemporaries and subsequent generations alike, is that he "stole" characters from the writers whose work he analyzed. That is, he put his own interpretation upon the personality and actions of characters—interpretations that in many cases appear to diverge wildly from the manifest intention of the writers themselves. Dobroliubov never denied that he engaged in this reinterpretation, which he considered a critic's key function. If an author were aware of the social significance of the images he created, so much the better—but if not, then the critic was there to reveal it.

The most explicitly voiced of Dobroliubov's critical criteria was his insistence that writing have a social purpose. He argued vehemently against the belief that art by definition should be judged on its aesthetic, or artistic, merit. This point was never made with greater force than in "Chto takoe oblomovshchina?," where he writes:

> Here we part company with the adherents of so-called 'art for art's sake,' who maintain that an excellent description of a little tree leaf is as important as, for instance, an excellent description of a person's character. Perhaps, subjectively, that would be true. . . . But we will never agree that a poet who wastes his talent on perfect descriptions of little leaves and brooks can have the same significance as one who with equal talent knows how to reproduce, for instance, the phenomena of social life. . . . far more important than the scope and quality of an author's talent is the question of what is it used for, in what is it expressed.

Contemporaries dubbed this approach "utilitarian," and more than any other aspect of Dobroliubov's criticism it provoked opposition from writers and other critics alike.

In April 1860 *Sovremennik* ran Dobroliubov's review of Turgenev's short novel *Nakanune* (On the Eve, 1860). The review had been written several months previously but was held up for a particularly long time partly by the censor but, more significantly, by the bitter opposition of Turgenev, who was shown the galley proofs and demanded changes. In February, Turgenev gave an ultimatum to Nekrasov: "Choose: either me or Dobroliubov." Nekrasov wavered but in the end announced his intention of publishing the review. Turgenev carried through on his threat, stopped contributing to *Sovremennik,* and convinced several other "liberal" writers to do likewise. This famous cause célèbre (the capital was transfixed for weeks by rumors of what was going on) gives some indication of the importance that Dobroliubov had assumed in the literary life of the nation. It also marked the capture of *Sovremennik* by the radical editorial faction led by him and Chernyshevsky.

Dobroliubov's review of *Nakanune* was titled "Kogda zhe pridet nastoiashchii den'?" (translated as "When Will the Real Day Come?" 1962). The question has an impatient tone and is a direct response to the title of Turgenev's novel. The implied political meaning of this Aesopian wordplay is "You have imagined the eve of a better day, but you lack the courage to envision the day itself." This rebuke was merited in Dobroliubov's eyes, because Turgenev—who had in many of his works made clear his exasperation with contemporary Russia—continued to place his hopes for

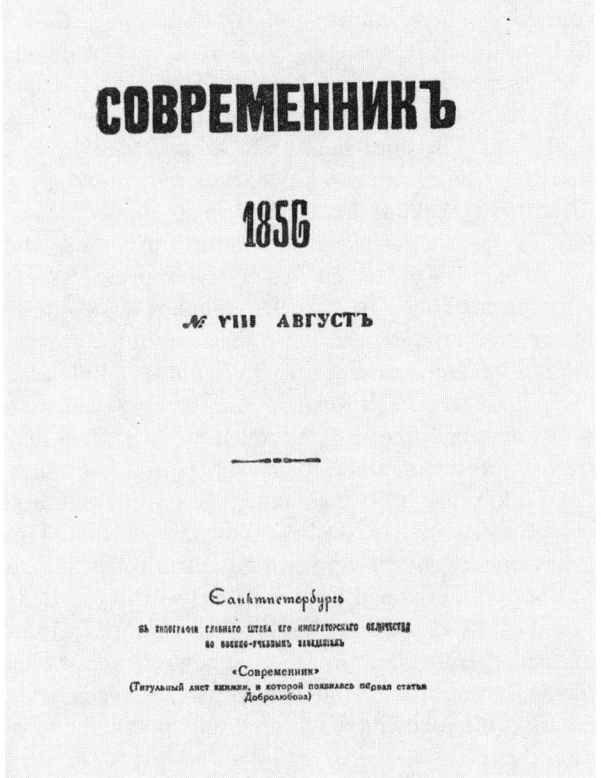

Paper cover for the issue of Sovremennik *(The Contemporary) in which Dobroliubov's article criticizing Catherine the Great appeared (from Zhdanov,* Nikolai Aleksandrovich Dobroliubov, 1836–1861, *1951)*

change in peaceful evolutionary development. Disagreement over the nature and scope of change was really the root cause of the crisis within *Sovremennik,* and it was precipitated by the publication of "Kogda zhe pridet nastoiashchii den'?"

"Kogda zhe pridet nastoiashchii den'?" is one of the best known, and certainly the most explicitly political, of Dobroliubov's reviews. As it unfolds, the essay passes smoothly between a conventional discussion of plot and character and a quite thinly veiled appeal to revolutionary action. The central figure of *Nakanune* was Elena Stakhova, who personifies for Dobroliubov the youth of contemporary Russia, as he describes in his review:

> She expressed that undefined yearning for something, that almost unconscious, but irresistible need for a new life, for new people which now grips all of Russian society. . . . The finest strivings of our contemporary life were so clearly reflected in Elena while everything inconsequential in that life appears so vividly in those around her that one is involuntarily seized with a desire to draw an allegorical parallel.

Over the course of a single summer Elena is courted by three suitors. Two, whom she rejects, are Russians, each representing a different facet of the clichéd "superfluous man." One is charming but frivolous—the other, decent and well-intentioned but ineffectual. The third suitor, who wins Elena's love, is Insarov, a Bulgarian revolutionary whose whole life is dedicated to ridding his country of its Turkish overlords. Insarov's passionate commitment to a cause and his willingness to act on behalf of his principles are what attract Elena to him. Dobroliubov asks querulously, "What, therefore, is the meaning of the appearance of a *Bulgarian* in this story? What does a Bulgarian mean here, why not a Russian? Are there no such characters among Russians?" As much as Bulgaria suffers from Turkish suzerainty, Russia suffers from the "internal Turk"; that is, its own autocratic government and feudal social system. Dobroliubov implies that Turgenev unconsciously expressed a sad truth—that Russia has not yet developed its own Insarovs who can dedicate themselves totally to freeing their country from its internal tyranny, but—in Dobroliubov's words—"That day will come at last! And, in any case, the eve is never far from the following day: in all only one night separates them."

Despite the best efforts of the tsarist police and the exhaustive research of Soviet historians, Dobroliubov has never been linked to any overt act of revolution. He was unquestionably, however, one of the great revolutionary influences of his century. Myriad sources speak to the inspiring and radicalizing impact of his articles, especially on the young people both of his own day and of subsequent generations. His writing seemed to breathe an air of expectancy and hope that a new and better Russia lay just over the horizon. Despite such an influential voice, however, his own vision of the future was remarkably vague. Two beliefs can be inferred from his writings: first, that the revolution—the overthrow of tsarism and serfdom—will be accomplished by a peasant revolt; and second, that the new Russia will be socialist. He was not, however, a *narodnik,* a nativist socialist who believed that the traditional values of peasant life would serve as a model for the new society. He loved the Russian peasants, agonized over their fate, worked for their education, and praised writers, such as Marko Vovchok, who wrote about them; yet, he believed that socialism was a world force, the logical culmination of universal hopes and values. The social order that he envisioned, it seems, owed more to the writing and example of European utopian socialists than to the collectivist folkways of the Russian masses.

Along with "Chto takoe oblomovshchina?" and "Kogda zhe pridet nastoiashchii den'?" Dobroliubov's

two reviews of Ostrovsky's plays are counted among his most significant works. During the summer of 1859 *Sovremennik* published his "Temnoe tsarstvo" (The Dark Kingdom), a review of a recently published collection of Ostrovsky's early plays, and in October 1860 there appeared "Luch sveta v temnom tsarstve" (A Ray of Light in the Dark Kingdom), a review of Ostrovsky's most recent play, *Groza* (The Thunderstorm, 1860).

"Temnoe tsarstvo" is Dobroliubov's longest review: it ran in three consecutive issues of *Sovremennik* and was more than fifty thousand words long. In it Dobroliubov considers six of Ostrovsky's plays in detail and touches on several more. The plays, which enjoyed great popularity on the stage, are about members of the traditional Russian merchant class, their way of life and values, especially the enormous emphasis placed on the related topics of family and money. Sifting through the body of Ostrovsky's work, Dobroliubov isolates the recurrent theme of *samodurstvo* (domestic tyranny), by which the *samodur* (tyrannical head of household) was able to dominate and control all members of the family. This world is the kingdom of darkness—a place of crude, and often cruel, men who destroy the lives of family members and employees alike out of greed or a perverted determination to be accorded respect.

As usual, Dobroliubov writes on two levels. Accepting Ostrovsky's plays as a genuine depiction of the lives of Russian merchant families, he catalogues a host of hateful practices revealed by the plays and the destructive effect of such practices both on the family members who bow to tyranny and on those who destroy themselves by opposing it. His Aesopian subtext is equally clear. The kingdom of darkness is Russia, the *samodur* is the government, and the tyrannized family is the nation. A good example of this two-track approach is Dobroliubov's discussion of why women are so often victimized in merchant families. The most important reason he finds is a lack of material security. Women have no access to property of their own and thus can be bullied at will by parents, guardians, and husbands. Dobroliubov treats this theme at length, drawing examples from several plays, and he evidently views it as a social wrong in and of itself. A perceptive reader, however, can see that he is discussing at the same time the future status of the Russian peasants, who were at this moment on the eve of emancipation from serfdom. The most hotly debated aspect of the emancipation settlement was the question of property: will the freed serfs be given enough land to become truly independent or will they be left so badly off that they continue in a de facto state of dependency on their former landlords?

Dobroliubov's most controversial review, "Luch sveta v temnom tsarstve," is a critique of *Groza*, one of Ostrovsky's darkest tragedies. Katerina, the heroine of the play, is crushed by the interference and bullying of her malicious mother-in-law, Kalbanova. The evils of *samodurstvo*, identified in "Temnoe tsarstvo," are reprised. At the climax of the play Katerina, her life in ruins, throws herself into the Volga. Ostrovsky—as well as the succession of actresses who played the role in this perennially popular drama—clearly saw her as a confused and tragic victim. Dobroliubov, however, celebrates her as a heroic rebel who chooses suicide over submission to injustice and so places herself beyond the power of any tyranny. She is the ray of light in the kingdom of darkness. Dobroliubov's message is that freedom is to be found in existential acts of self-sacrifice. Yet, most commentators have held that the play will simply not bear this interpretation. The critic René Wellek, for instance, cites the review as "the very height of what could be called 'loss of contact' with the text."

Dobroliubov's last literary essay was "Zabitye liudi" (Downtrodden People), which appeared in *Sovremennik* in October 1861 just a month before his death. It was, ostensibly, a review of two recent Dostoevsky publications: a collection of his early works published the previous year and a novel, *Unizhennye i oskorblennye* (The Insulted and Injured), which first appeared in Dostoevsky's journal *Vremia* (Time) in 1861. In fact, the review was meant to serve as a response to an attack, titled "G-n -bov i vopros ob iskusstve" (Mr. -bov and the Question of Art), which Dostoevsky had launched against Dobroliubov in the pages of *Vremia* that same year. Some have seen in this last literary essay of Dobroliubov signs of a turn away from "realistic criticism" and a recognition of the importance of aesthetic considerations in the judgment of literature. What these commentators have failed to note is the polemical context of this article and the obvious irony of Dobroliubov's strictures on the artistic shortcomings of Dostoevsky's work.

In "G-n -bov i vopros ob iskusstve" Dostoevsky had rather cruelly parodied Dobroliubov's critical approach and the materialist assumptions that underlie it. In "Zabitye liudi" Dobroliubov pays him back in kind, subjecting his works to the sort of "organic" criticism that Dostoevsky espoused and finding them, by that standard, seriously deficient. As Dobroliubov writes, the characters are unfinished (the women in particular are poorly drawn); the plots are convoluted; and the language is colorless and repetitious. In Dobroliubov's view Dostoevsky succeeds not when he is judged by his own critical standards but when he is judged by Dobroliubov's. "Even if he does not satisfy artistic demands, even if he sometimes is wide of the mark and expresses himself badly, we will not dwell on that and will be ready to talk about him at length and in depth, as long as the sense of his work is for some reason important to society."

Although Dobroliubov adroitly defended critical realism in his reply to Dostoevsky, he was silent on another issue raised in "G-n -bov i vopros ob iskusstve"—namely, Dostoevsky's accusation that there was an ominous element of prescription in Dobroliubov's advocacy of social relevance as the essential and legitimizing quality of literature. Through the enormous popularity and influence that he exerted in his reviews, Dobroliubov, in Dostoevsky's opinion, was trying to force writers to conform to his notion of what constituted literature. "People demand," Dostoevsky had written, "chiefly when they want to compel by force, while the first law in art is freedom of inspiration and creation. Everything that has been brought forth by demand, everything forced, from time immemorial has not succeeded, and instead of benefit has brought only harm." Here Dostoevsky's critique is not only valid but prescient. Dobroliubov himself could not compel conformity to his critical norms, but when these norms came to be incorporated into the officially sanctioned policy of a coercive state during the Soviet era, they were, in fact, forced upon all Russian writers.

In June 1858 Dobroliubov had gone to Staraia Russa, an ancient town near Novgorod, to have his scrofula treated by the mineral waters and mud baths of the local spa. Eager to get back to work, he returned to St. Petersburg in August before a complete cure had been achieved. His health continued to be precarious, and in early 1860 he began to exhibit symptoms of pulmonary tuberculosis. On the advice of his doctors and at the insistence of friends, he left Russia in May of that year to seek a cure abroad. He was to remain out of the country for thirteen months, returning in June 1861. Except for a stay in Nice around the turn of the year, he seems to have spent little of this period actively seeking a cure. Instead, he divided his time between touring and observing local politics.

From mid February of 1861 onward he restricted his traveling to Italy, moving from the north to Naples in March and then on to Sicily shortly before his return to Russia. During his stay in Italy he sent *Sovremennik* three long articles on the revolution that was just winding down there. These works were pure journalism that never touched on a literary theme, but Dobroliubov's technique of implied commentary on Russian affairs is manifest throughout. The charismatic Giuseppe Garibaldi, who had overthrown the reactionary rulers of Sicily and Naples, was an Italian Insarov; the Italian

СОЧИНЕНІЯ

Н. А. ДОБРОЛЮБОВА.

Милый другъ, я умираю,
Оттого, что былъ я честенъ;
Но за то родному краю
Вѣрно буду я извѣстенъ.

Милый другъ, я умираю,
Но спокоенъ я душою....
И тебя благословляю:
Шествуй тою же стезею.

Н. Добролюбовъ.

ТОМЪ I.

САНКТПЕТЕРБУРГЪ.
ВЪ ТИПОГРАФІИ ІОСАФАТА ОГРИЗКО.
1862.

Title page for volume one of Dobroliubov's posthumously published, four-volume Sochineniia (Works), *the first collection of his writings (from Dobroliubov,* Polnoe sobranie stikhotvorenii, *1969)*

and was back to work in St. Petersburg by mid August. He was grievously ill, although whether he realized yet that he was dying is unclear. As his condition steadily worsened, he continued to write, visit the office at *Sovremennik,* and fight with the censors against proposed cuts to his articles. His condition took a critical turn at the beginning of November, and he asked that Panaeva, who was then in Paris, be sent for. She nursed him in his final days; he died in her arms during the night of 17 November 1861.

What is most remarkable about Dobroliubov is that his writing never went out of style. In 1862, only a year after his death, the first collection of his works was published, in which many of the censor's cuts to his *Sovremennik* articles were restored. Four subsequent editions appeared before the end of the century, and a complete collection of his works, edited by Mikhail Konstantinovich Lemke, was published in 1911. Unlike the writings of Belinsky, whose famous letter to Gogol was required memorization for Russian schoolboys, Dobroliubov's reviews were available in print (though sometimes removed from public library shelves), and his daring sallies and sarcastic cadences continued to thrill Russian readers even during the periods of stronger censorship and repression that ensued after 1866. The memoirs of many participants in revolutionary activity from the 1870s through 1917 attest to the inspirational power of Dobroliubov's writings. For instance, Vladimir Lenin—who was born in 1870, nine years after Dobroliubov's death—as a boy apparently read his articles in old copies of *Sovremennik* that his father kept in the attic. Certainly, Lenin's works contain many references to Dobroliubov. He used the term *oblomovshchina* when he was exasperated by what he saw as his countrymen's reluctance to abandon old patterns of behavior. When he founded the first Bolshevik journal in 1904 he named it *Vpered* (Forward), as if to answer Dobroliubov's question from "Chto takoe oblomovshchina?": "Who then will pronounce that all-powerful word . . . for which Rus' has so long and so painfully waited?"

During the Soviet period Dobroliubov's popularity grew, at least among Russian scholars. His revolutionary sentiments and Lenin's imprimatur were helpful here, but most important was the linkage explicitly made between the official Soviet literary doctrine of Socialist Realism and Dobroliubov's critical theories—especially his insistence on making the depiction of reality the touchstone of literary worth and his view that this reality could be interpreted to serve progressive social ends. Yet, to make Dobroliubov a prophet of the stultifying doctrine that blighted Russian letters for half a century is patently absurd. This misconception ignores the rebellious spirit, the hatred of hypocrisy,

people responded to a populist appeal; and compromising middle-class politicians had thwarted the revolution.

In Italy, Dobroliubov had his last romance. He became engaged to Hildegonde Fiocchi, daughter of a Sicilian landowner. Unclear about how marriage would affect his life, he inquired of his uncle, Vasilii Dobroliubov, how much it would cost for a couple to live modestly in St. Petersburg; at the same time, he wrote to Chernyshevsky with a tentative proposal to reduce his writing commitments, learn a new trade, and stay on in Italy. Whatever his plan might have been, it came to naught when the girl's family forbade the marriage, either because they simply did not want to lose their daughter (the version related by the majority of contemporaries) or because a confidential medical report, which they commissioned, showed that Dobroliubov had only months to live.

Soon after his return to Russia, Dobroliubov paid a final visit to family members in Nizhnii Novgorod and the insistence on the worth of the individual that inform all of Dobroliubov's writings. Nevertheless, his canonization in the Soviet literary establishment made him a safe and popular subject for scholarly inquiry. Two superbly edited editions of Dobroliubov's complete works appeared, one in 1934 and another in 1961–1964. Separate collections of his writings on philosophy and pedagogy were also published. Even his poetry, which had never been thought to possess more than topical or historical significance, was edited and published. Most striking, hundreds of books and articles, both scholarly and popular, were devoted to his life and writings—a flood that abated only in the 1980s.

Letters:

Materialy dlia biografii N. A. Dobroliubova, sobrannye v 1861–1862 gg., volume 1, edited by Nikolai Gavrilovich Chernyshevsky (Moscow: K. T. Soldatenkov, 1890);

"Pis'ma," *Literaturnoe nasledstvo,* 67 (1949): 270–276;

Pis'ma, volume 9 of *Sobranie sochinenii* (Moscow & Leningrad: Goslitizdat, 1964).

Bibliographies:

D. P. Sil'chevsky, "Bibliograficheskii ukazatel' literatury o Dobroliubove za 1856–1911 gg.," in *Sobranie sochinenii,* edited by Vladimir Pavlovich Kranikhfel'd, volume 8 (St. Petersburg: Prosveshchenie, 1911);

E. A. Pavlovich and Solomon Abramovich Reiser, "Literatura o Dobroliubove (1917–1936)," *Izvestiia AN SSR. Otdelenie obshchestvennykh nauk,* 1–2 (1936);

N. Matsuev, "Iubileinaia literatura o Dobroliubove," *Literaturnyi kritik,* 7 (1936);

Iu. D. Ryskin, *N. A. Dobroliubov. Ukazatel' literatury. 1917–1960 gg.* (Moscow, 1961);

N. P. Zhuravlev, *Dobroliubov o russkikh pisateliakh: Seminarii* (Moscow: Izdatel'stvo Moskovskogo universiteta, 1971);

E. D. Lebedeva, "Literatura o N. A. Dobroliubove. Bibliograficheskii ukazatel'. 1961–1986," in *N. A. Dobroliubov i russkaia literaturnaia kritika,* edited by G. G. Elizavetina (Moscow: Nauka, 1988), pp. 206–229.

Biographies:

Aleksandr Mikhailovich Skabichevsky, *N. A. Dobroliubov: Ego zhizn' i literaturnaia deiatel'nost'* (St. Petersburg: Obshchestvennaia pol'za, 1894);

Pavel Ivanovich Lebedev-Poliansky, *N. A. Dobroliubov: Mirovozzrenie i literaturno-kriticheskaia deiatel'nost'* (Moscow: Khudozhestvennaia literatura, 1935);

Vladimir Viktorovich Zhdanov, *N. A. Dobroliubov: Kritiko-biograficheskii ocherk* (Moscow: Gosudarstvennoe izdatel'stvo khudozhestvennoi literatury, 1961);

Evgenii Lampert, "Nikolai Dobrolyubov," in his *Sons against Fathers: Studies in Russian Radicalism and Revolution* (Oxford: Clarendon Press, 1965);

Rufus W. Mathewson, "Dobrolyubov: Beyond the Superfluous Man," in *The Positive Hero in Soviet Literature* (Stanford, Cal.: Stanford University Press, 1975).

References:

Charles Corbet, "Principes esthétiques et réalités sentimentales dans la critique de Dobroljubov," *Revue des Etudes Slaves,* 29 (1952): 34–54;

G. G. Elizavetina, ed., *N. A. Dobroliubov i russkaia literaturnaia kritika* (Moscow: "Nauka," 1988);

Kamsar Nersesovich Grigor'ian, ed., *Nikolai Aleksandrovich Dobroliubov v portretakh, illiustratsiiakh, dokumentakh,* compiled by I. E. Grudinina (Leningrad: Prosveshchenie, 1969);

Vladimir Semenovich Kruzhkov, *N. A. Dobroliubov: Zhizn', deiatel'nost', mirovozzrenie* (Moscow: Nauka, 1976);

Mariia Alekseevna Naumova, *Sotsiologicheskie, filosofiskie i esteticheskie vzgliady N. A. Dobroliubova* (Moscow: Akademiia nauk SSR, 1960);

Solomon Abramovich Reiser, *Letopis' zhizni i deiatel'nosti N. A. Dobroliubova* (Moscow: Gosudarstvennoe izdatel'stvo Kulturno-prosvetitel'noi literatury, 1953);

Reiser, ed., *N. A. Dobroliubov v vospominaniiakh sovremennikov* (Leningrad: Khudozhestvennaia literatura, 1961);

R. H. Stacy, *Russian Literary Criticism: A Short History* (Syracuse, N.Y.: Syracuse University Press, 1974): 55–65;

René Wellek, *A History of Modern Criticism: 1750–1950,* 8 volumes (New Haven: Yale University Press, 1955–1992), IV: 245–253;

Vladimir Viktorovich Zhdanov, *Nikolai Aleksandrovich Dobroliubov, 1836–1861* (Moscow: Molodaiia gvardiia, 1951).

Papers:

Nikolai Aleksandrovich Dobroliubov's papers are held in Moscow at the Russian State Archive of Literature and Art (RGALI), fond 166; in St. Petersburg at the Institute of Russian Literature (IRLI, Pushkin House), fond 97; and the Russian National Library (RNB), fond 255. Additional materials can be found at the State House–Museum of Chernyshevsky in Saratov.

Sof'ia Vladimirovna Engel'gardt

(1828 – 1894)

Mary F. Zirin

BOOKS: *Ne soshlis',* as Ol'ga N. (Moscow: Universiteta tipografiia, 1867);

Krasnoe iachko, as Ol'ga N., Knizhki dlia shkol., no. 71 (Moscow: Obshchestvo rasprostraneniia poleznykh knig, 1873);

Rasskaz materi Margarity, as Ol'ga N., Knizhki dlia shkol., no. 73 (Moscow: Obshchestvo rasprostraneniia poleznykh knig, 1873);

Korobeinnik. Tri rasskaza, as Ol'ga N. (Moscow: Obshchestvo rasprostraneniia poleznykh knig, 1874)–includes "Zvezda," "Arapka," and "Petushok koldun";

Sof'ia Zakharovna Almazova. Nekrolog, with notes by B. Almazov (Moscow: V. Got'e, 1875);

Ottsovskii grekh. Rasskaz (Moscow: A. Gattsuk, 1878);

Klad. Rasskaz strannika (St. Petersburg: Dosug i delo, 1880);

Selekhonskie. Rasskaz, as Ol'ga N. (Moscow: A. Gattsuk, 1880);

Tsaritsyny rasskaz (Moscow: A. Gattsuk, 1880);

Sviatochnyi rasskaz, as Ol'ga N. (Moscow: A. A. Levenson, 1891);

Tak bog velel. Povesti, as Ol'ga N. (Universiteta tipografiia, 1907).

OTHER: Aleksandr Sergeevich Pushkin, *Oeuvres de Pouchkine* (Paris: Berger-Levrault, 1875)–includes *Boris Godounoff; Le Chevalier avare; Mozart et Saliéri;* and *Les Nuits d'Égypte.*

PERIODICAL PUBLICATIONS–UNCOLLECTED:

DRAMA

"Um priidet–pora proidet. Poslovitsa," *Otechestvennye zapiski,* 7 (1855): 199–224;

"Kon' i o chetyrekh nogakh spotykaetsia," *Otechestvennye zapiski,* 9 (1856): 270–312.

FICTION

"Derevnia," *Otechestvennye zapiski,* 9 (1853): 1–26;

"Utro vechera mudrenee," *Otechestvennye zapiski,* 11 (1853): 93–128;

"Suzhenogo konem ne ob"edesh'," *Otechestvennye zapiski,* 2 (1854): 387–458;

"Ne tak zhivi kak khochetsia, a tak kak Bog velit," *Sovremennik,* 12 (1854): 269–342;

"Na ves' svet ne ugodish'," *Otechestvennye zapiski,* 2 (1855): 297–368;

"Starik," *Biblioteka dlia chteniia,* 3 (1857): 25–49;

"Mirazh," *Russkii vestnik,* 5, part 1 (1859): 129–176; 5, part 2 (1859): 305–333;

"Sila solomu lomit," *Biblioteka dlia chteniia,* 1, part 2 (1859): 1–40;

"Obochlis'," *Biblioteka dlia chteniia,* 1 (1860): 1–34, 55–84;

"Kniazhny Troidenovy," *Russkii vestnik,* 2, part 1 (1860): 554–599;

"Skol'zkii shag," *Russkaia rech',* 83–89 (1861);

"Sud'ba ili kharakter?" *Russkii vestnik,* 11 (1861): 125–176;

"Kamen' pretknoveniia," *Russkii vestnik,* 12 (1862): 590–635;

"Semeistvo Tureninykh," *Otechestvennye zapiski,* 1 (1863): 296–413;

"Dva novosel'ia," *Russkii vestnik,* 7 (1864): 170–245;

"Liza," *Epokha,* 8 (1864): 1–26;

"Gde zhe schast'e?" as N.O., *Russkii vestnik,* 9 (1864): 80–154;

"Dva svidaniia," *Russkii vestnik,* 3 (1865): 216–276;

"Vrag gorami kachaet," as O.N. T-va, *Russkii vestnik,* 10 (1865): 727–770; 11 (1865): 71–144;

"Ne odnogo polia iagody," *Russkii vestnik,* 8 (1868): 485–549;

"Son babushki i vnuchki," *Vestnik Evropy,* 6 (1869): 647–690;

"Na rodine," *Russkii vestnik,* 8 (1870): 683–770;

"Vospominaniia na dache," *Russkii vestnik,* 7 (1874): 323–392;

"Chernyi surguch," *Gazeta A. Gatsuka,* 32–35 (1877);

"Staraia vera," *Russkii vestnik,* 3 (1879): 304–368;

"Zloba dnia," *Russkii vestnik,* 4 (1881): 748–831;

"Ne pervaia i ne posledniaia," *Russkii vestnik,* 9 (1883): 358–414;

"Byl' sorokovykh godov," *Russkii vestnik,* 12 (1884): 523–575;

"Petr Ivanovich Korondeev. Byl'," *Russkoe obozrenie*, 5 (1891): 181–196;

"Propazha. Rasskaz starosvetskogo pomeshchika," *Russkoe obozrenie*, 8 (1892): 562–575.

NONFICTION

"Zagranichnye pis'ma," as O.N., *Moskovskie vedomosti*, 162 (1860); 180 (1860); 199 (1860);

"Nikolai Fedorovich Shcherbina," as Ol'ga N., *Zaria*, 5 (1870): 67–93;

"Iz vospominanii," as Ol'ga T-va, *Russkii vestnik*, 10 (1887): 690–715; 11 (1887): 159–180;

"Iz proshlogo," as Ol'ga T-va, *Russkii vestnik*, 7 (1889): 25–58;

"Iz vospominanii," as Ol'ga T-va, *Russkoe obozrenie*, 11 (1890): 83–114.

Sof'ia Engel'gardt was a gifted storyteller who, in thirty-four short works of fiction published between 1853 and 1892, chronicled the dissolution of the patriarchal certainties of Tsar Nicholas I's reign and showed its effect on Moscow gentry of succeeding generations. The rise of Russian radicalism–beginning in the 1840s–the abolition of serfdom in 1861, and the resulting waves of reform and reaction in the ensuing decades furnish the background for her cogent observations of the society in which she spent her life.

Engel'gardt was born Sofiia Vladimirovna Novosil'tseva in 1828 (exact date of birth unknown), and what little has been revealed about her family comes from a memoir, "Semeinye zapiski" (Family Notes, 1862), written by her eldest sister, Ekaterina Vladimirovna Novosil'tseva, a prolific author of popular historical works, fiction, and memoirs under the pen name T. Tolycheva. Tolycheva describes the family (identified only as the Ns) as having served the Muscovite and Russian states well, roughly since the fourteenth century: "From the day of the Battle of Kulikovo to the Polish Campaign of 1830, more than twenty of our clan died in battle." The extensive properties with which they were rewarded gradually fell prey, in the eighteenth century, to bad management or lawsuits. By Engel'gardt's childhood, what remained to her family was a large home on the outskirts of Moscow and a few scattered estates.

After their marriage in the late 1810s Sof'ia's parents, Vladimir Vasil'evich Novosil'tsev and Avdot'ia Aleksandrovna (née Novikova) Novosil'tseva, settled in the country, where they produced one son, Aleksandr, and four daughters, Ekaterina, Nadezhda, Mariia, and Sof'ia. Vladimir Novosil'tsev died of cholera when Sof'ia was two, "bequeathing my poor mother eternal woe, eternal tears, and eternal mourning," as Tolycheva recalls in the memoir. After Avdot'ia Aleksandrovna's death six years later, rich relatives in Moscow took in the orphaned sisters. Aleksandr, then fourteen, went to live with a professor, to be tutored for admission to Moscow University. Tolycheva reports that after four years she and Nadezhda escaped to the house of their paternal grandmother and aunts: "We cried bitterly as we parted from our younger sisters; until our brother's marriage they remained in those gilded chambers, which none of us until the present day cannot, and never will, pass without a sinking heart." In several stories Sof'ia described with contempt the "decorous, cold, strait-laced" atmosphere of a similar mansion ruled by a living relic of despotic eighteenth-century patriarchal mores. The soul-warping effect of the girls' upbringing there underlies Engel'gardt's semi-autobiographical "Vospominaniia na dache" (Reminiscing at a Summer House, 1874), published in *Russkii vestnik*.

The girls were educated by governesses and grew up immersed in French culture. In one of Engel'gardt's stories the female narrator explains that "at seventeen I knew the name of Pushkin only by hearsay, and in our house Gogol was called an '*izba* [peasant-hut] writer.' . . . Our children's library comprised, as if selected on purpose, extemely boring books, mostly French. Particularly memorable to me is one entitled *Les annales de la vertu* (The Annals of Virtue). . . . Oh, virtue! how early our instructors, in all innocence, taught us to hate you." In "Vospominaniia na dache" Engel'gardt includes an anecdote about her young narrator's first encounter with Russian as a drawing-room language: after Iuliia sees a performance by the famous St. Petersburg–based actor Vasilii Andreevich Karatygin, she sneaks out to a neighbor's home to attend a soirée in his honor. To her horror she discovers that "Karatygin was speaking Russian, and I couldn't assemble two Russian phrases and, for the first time in my life, was vexed at my ignorance of my native tongue and realized that in Russia it might possibly be of use." Engel'gardt learned the Russian language rapidly once she set her mind to the task. Although editors had to correct her grammar at first, her fiction was packed with closely described realia and aphoristic turns of phrase, and she had a keen ear for adages, idioms, and colloquial speech. She continued including French passages in her stories to indicate the prevalence of that language in Moscow society; in a couple of tales, too, she poked fun at social climbers for their bad French. In 1860 Engel'gardt put her Francophilic upbringing to journalistic use and contributed three "Zagranichnye pis'ma" (Letters from Abroad) on current events in France to a Moscow newspaper. Her translation into French of Aleksandr Sergeevich Pushkin's dramatic works appeared in Paris in 1875.

When her brother married, he took the younger girls to live with him on his country estate, and soon afterward Nadezhda's marriage to the historian Dmitrii

Pavlovich Golokhvastov reunited all the sisters in Moscow. The status of Sof'ia's marriage to Vladimir Egorovich Engel'gardt, who rose to the rank of acting state councilor in the civil service, remains an enigma. Vladimir was from St. Petersburg, where his father, Egor Antonovich Engel'gardt, had been headmaster of the Alexander Lycée. By 1852 Sof'ia was using her married name, but her husband is not mentioned in her letters and memoirs. From the mid 1850s she apparently lived alone or, at times, with other members of the Novosil'tsev clan and earned at least a partial livelihood by writing. A confirmed Muscovite, she circulated both in aristocratic society and among the intelligentsia. "Iz vospominanii" (From Reminiscences, 1890) offers sometimes unflattering but fond sketches of the circle connected with the journal *Moskvitianin* (The Muscovite), to whom Sof'ia and her sisters played host in the early 1850s; the *Moskvitianin* circle included the poets Boris Nikolaevich Almazov, Nikolai Fedorovich Shcherbina, and Afanasii Afanas'evich Fet; the poet and critic Apollon Aleksandrovich Grigor'ev; the writers Nikolai Vasil'evich Berg and Nikolai Fedorovich Pavlov; the playwright Nikolai Alekseevich Ostrovsky; and the liberal intellectuals Timofei Nikolaevich Granovsky and Aleksandr Ivanovich Herzen. Sof'ia knew, yet was not particularly close to, other women writers living in Moscow–Karolina Karlovna Pavlova, Evdokiia Petrovna Rostopchina, and Evgeniia Tur.

In 1859 fellow writers elected Engel'gardt to membership in the recently revived Obshchestvo liubitelei rossiiskoi slovesnosti (Society of Lovers of Russian Literature), which was affiliated with Moscow University, and two of her works were read aloud by other members at meetings in the late 1870s. The Engel'gardt family archive includes letters written to Sof'ia in the 1860s by writers of varied political views based in St. Petersburg–among them Ivan Sergeevich Aksakov, Fyodor Dostoevsky, Nikolai Semenovich Leskov, Aleksei Feofilaktovich Pisemsky, and Ivan Sergeevich Turgenev. Despite these tantalizing indications that she remained active in literary society, however, she left no memoirs from her later life, and her own extant letters are uninformative. From her fiction one can deduce her growing disillusionment with pat answers to the intractable social dilemmas of her time.

In the early 1850s Engel'gardt began submitting works to major Petersburg journals–called *tolstye zhurnaly* (thick journals) because of their generous mixture of sociopolitical articles and belles lettres. Shcherbina chose "Ol'ga N." for Engel'gardt's pen name and often called her *krestnitsa* (goddaughter). He also advised her to send her first literary efforts to *Otechestvennye zapiski* (Notes of the Fatherland), and four of her fictional

works and two short plays appeared there in rapid succession between 1853 and 1856.

These early works, most of them labeled *povesti* (novellas) but varying in length and complexity, buff the Romantic sheen from the *svetskaia povest'* (society tale), a leading literary genre of the 1830s to 1840s that featured ironic portrayals of the mating rituals of the Russian upper classes. The balls, masquerades, and other outings prominent in society tales are absent from Engel'gardt's deglamorized variants: men and women cultivate their relationships through exchanges of opinions and sympathies in the drawing room and the garden. Her approach to character is taxonomic in its portrayal of a wide variety of psychological types and ethnographic in the specificity of the settings in which they live. The books that characters read and respond to are indicators of personality. In "Iz vospominanii" (1887) Engel'gardt recounts that in her youth Herzen urged her to read George Sand, whose works were just then becoming influential in Russian liberal society, and sent her one of the French author's novels: "Her influence is an essential counterweight to the dry and petty nature of the concepts they've tried to instill in you," he told her. Although she describes herself as too inexperienced at that point to appreciate what she calls Sand's doctrine of "freedom of emotions," varying attitudes to Sand's works serve as a touchstone of character in several of Engel'gardt's tales. Engel'gardt's narrative voice, however, is usually closer to Jane Austen's detached irony than to Sand's Romanticism. Her class-sensitive plots and their concern with money and status recall the fiction of Western writers such as Henry James and Edith Wharton. Striking epiphanies are rare, and while her heroines are independent in spirit, few of them defy their society, maneuvering instead to find an elusive happiness within it. Some of her female characters have escaped patriarchal domination by becoming conveniently orphaned or widowed. Several of her plots focus on a self-centered or ruthless woman who manipulates those around her, and households in which an older woman is raising a niece, a ward, or a goddaughter are more common than intact families. Among woman writers of that time Engel'gardt has a rare gift for the portrayal of men's psychology. She enriches her tales with engaging secondary characters and subsidiary plots.

In Engel'gardt's first work to appear in print, "Derevnia" (In the Country, 1853), an impressionable young nobleman from St. Petersburg, on a summer visit to his sister's estate, is unprepared for the assault on his emotions launched by her neighbors: a seductive countess–a "perfectly aristocratic young lady"–and a naive poor girl. Engel'gardt's next stories have titles drawn from proverbs. "Utro vechera mudrenee" (Morning Brings Counsel, 1853), "Suzhenogo konem ne ob"edesh'" (You Can't Escape Your Destined Mate, 1854), and "Na ves' svet ne ugodish'" (You Can't Please Everyone, 1855)—all published in *Otechestvennye zapiski*—concern passions that boil up under the exchange of social niceties. Untypically, in "Suzhenogo konem ne ob"edesh'," the narrator, Nastia, is a woman from the Tambov steppes ill at ease with Moscow ways. She never escapes the blight cast on her life by the continual bad advice offered by an eternally immature cousin, one Iurii Nagibin, with whom she remains hopelessly in love. The two short plays that Engel'gardt published in *Otechestvennye zapiski*, "Um priidet—pora proidet. Poslovitsa" (Wise After the Event. A Proverb, 1855) and "Kon' i o chetyrekh nogakh spotykaetsia" (Nobody's Perfect, 1856), which literally translates as, "A Horse Stumbles Even on Four Legs," are exercises in the colloquial dialogue that became an important facet of her fiction.

During this period Engel'gardt placed one story in the radical journal *Sovremennik* (The Contemporary). "Ne tak zhivi kak khochetsia, a tak kak Bog velit" (Live God's Way Not Your Own, 1854) portrays a frivolous, self-absorbed girl who happily goes her own way at the expense of principled people who become involved with her. After Engel'gardt had sought in vain to be paid for the story, Granovsky interceded with the editor of *Sovremennik*, Nikolai Alekseevich Nekrasov. Nekrasov sent her the money but asked her not to submit any more "dramatized proverbs." She never published another play and simplified her titles.

A cordial correspondence in French developed between Engel'gardt and the writer Aleksandr Vasil'evich Druzhinin in 1854, and three of her tales appeared in the Petersburg journal that he edited, *Biblioteka dlia chteniia* (A Reading Library). "Starik" (The Old Man, 1857) reflects the trauma of the Crimean War. Although the landowner to whom this title refers lives in provincial isolation, he is a passionate devotee of European culture. Voltaire; Jean-Jacques Rousseau; George Gordon, Lord Byron; and the Emperor Napoleon (despite his invasion of Russia) are the old man's "gods" until the siege of Sevastopol' in the Crimean War turns him into a Russian patriot. "Sila solomu lomit" (Might Makes Right, 1859) depicts a ward, the epitome of submissiveness in most Russian fiction, who manipulates, bullies, and thieves her way into a position of power over the son of her widowed benefactor. The essence of "Obochlis'" (They Miscalculated, 1860) is summed up in the title of the intricately plotted tale: family and neighbors alike are unsuccessful in their attempts to manipulate an unworldly widower in his mid thirties, either to further a loveless marriage to an unattractive heiress or to persuade him to make a more suitable match with a cousin who loves him.

Sof'ia Vladimirovna Engel'gardt's friend, the poet Nikolai Fedorovich Shcherbina, who selected her pen name, "Ol'ga N." (from Shcherbina, Stikhotvoreniia, 1937)

When Mikhail Nikiforovich Katkov established the moderate Moscow journal *Russkii vestnik* (The Russian Messenger) in 1856, he asked Engel'gardt to contribute, and seventeen of her tales appeared there between 1859 and 1884. "Mirazh" (Mirage, 1859) is the first to feature a situation that was later central to "Staraia vera" (The Old Faith, 1879) and "Ne pervaia i ne posledniaia" (Neither the First Woman nor the Last, 1883): the plight of a credulous gentry woman who falls under the influence of a radical ideologue. Despite her sympathy for the liberal ideals of the 1840s, Engel'gardt portrays the later generation of revolutionaries as cynical men who preach socialist ideals without living them. In "Mirazh" Vasilii Sergeev's pompous orations parody the rhetoric of left-wing journalists of the 1850s. He is influential in persuading his young private pupil, Masha, to defy her godmother's intention of marrying her to a rich but childish neighbor, who is described as "playing tag with the maids" on the sly. Seven years later, however, Masha is still in thrall to Sergeev's preachments at the cost of her capacity for love and her attachment to her family.

"Kniazhny Troidenovy" (The Princesses Troidenov, 1860) involves a family fortune hidden during the Napoleonic invasion and recovered too late to recompense the Troidenov sisters for decades spent living "skuchno, skudno, skupo" (monotonously, meagerly, meanly) in provincial isolation. The three, who resemble Engel'gardt's own aunts as Tolycheva describes them in "Semeinye zapiski," react according to their natures: aristocratic Nastas'ia, realizing that she is too old to glitter in drawing rooms, withers and dies; flighty Vera finds a retired general who marries her and introduces her into society; and practical Ekaterina remains in the country and uses her money to benefit the family's small village of serfs.

"Sud'ba ili kharakter?" (Fate or Character?, 1861), the interwoven stories of three women, suggests that the most idealistic and demanding women are the least likely to find happiness. In an article in *Rassvet* (Dawn)—a journal for "grown-up young ladies"—the minor writer Sof'ia Dmitrievna Bibikova used this story as the basis for a plea for equal opportunities for women. By offering women only inadequate education and limited possibilities for work, she wrote, Russian society dooms them to reliance on love for fulfillment, a chancy prospect at best. The conflict in Russian society between Westernizers, who hoped to see Russia develop along European lines, and Slavophiles, who emphasized the uniqueness of Russian culture, underlies the plot of "Kamen' pretknoveniia" (The Stumbling Block, 1862). Valentina Kolyvanova, a widow who has suffered from her Francophile husband's despotic caprices, realizes that a Slavophile suitor's idealization of her femininity masks expectations of meek submission that would make for no happier a marriage. She disillusions her suitor by letting him catch her reading a novel by Sand. "Skolz'kii shag" (A False Step), a tale that Engel'gardt published in Tur's short-lived biweekly newspaper *Russkaia rech'* (Russian Speech) in 1861, features one of her most Sandian heroines—a woman who fails in her quest to find a man who can share her capacity for all-encompassing love. Through an oration by Engel'gardt's sympathetic hero, the author inserts into the tale a tribute to the recently deceased Granovsky that praises his way of nurturing the ideals and intellects of his students at Moscow University.

After the emancipation of the serfs in 1861 Engel'gardt's works displayed an increased historicism: they contrasted past and present generations and more directly reflected the turbulent times. She toned down verbal display and used an impersonal, but still chatty,

voice more often than first-person narration. One last *povest'*, "Semeistvo Tureninykh" (The Turenin Family), appeared in *Otechestvennye zapiski* in 1863. The denouement of the ingeniously constructed plot is the extinction of a noble clan whose patriarch has squandered its fortune on one harebrained entrepreneurial scheme after another. In "Dva novosel'ia" (Two Housewarmings, 1864), Marfa Alekseevna loses her beloved estate of Dubrava when a careless relative fails to register a will but regains the estate when her niece and ward marries its inheritor for love. A subplot in the story involves the "woman question" of the 1860s: a young neighbor, Liza, has adopted the free-and-easy manners and slovenly appearance that were the parodic traits ascribed to the "new woman," but she does not have the moral underpinnings that make freedom from social strictures viable.

By contrast, "Liza," which was published in the Dostoevsky brothers' short-lived journal, *Epokha* (Epoch), that same year, is Engel'gardt's sympathetic depiction of a woman who lives by the essence rather than the appearance of emancipated principles. The structure of "Gde zhe schast'e?" (Where's Happiness Anyway? 1864) is—like its pseudonymous signature, "N.O."—exceptional among Engel'gardt's works. This tale is a throwback to the epistolary form and exalted rhetoric of late-eighteenth-century sentimentalism. The novelty of Engel'gardt's treatment of the clichéd plot—in which upright people suffer and die through betrayal by an amoral manipulator—is that the seductive villain is not a male but a woman aptly named Kleopatra. Dmitrii Ivanovich Pisarev's merciless lampoon of this story in his review signaled the radical critic's impatience with works that concerned romantic dilemmas rather than his sociopolitical agenda.

"Dva svidaniia" (Two Meetings, 1865) opens with a mordantly funny sketch of Moscow society in the late 1830s. Vera Vishnevskaia, bound by duty and religious principle to an elderly, frail husband, falls in love with Vasilii Vil'menev, a dashing hussar on his way to exile in the Caucasus for a duel over the honor of a woman from the demimonde. As expected, when Vil'menev reenters her life twenty-five years later, Vishnevskaia is disillusioned by "his entire banal way of life, his bureaucratic occupations, his after-dinner snoring, his habit of salacious dalliance." A fresh twist in this story is the older generation's generous acceptance of the younger one's mores—in particular, the unlikely love match between Mania (Vishnevskaia's forthright cousin) and Vil'menev's son. Engel'gardt later wrote that she drew the character of the younger Vil'menev, a dedicated naturalist who is awkward in society, from that of the explorer Nikolai Alekseevich Severtsov, who courted her sister in the 1850s.

"Vrag gorami kachaet" (The Devil Shakes Mountains, 1865) is an extended psychological portrait of Andrei Al'shansky, who thinks of himself as a principled liberal but who commits an act of bribery to inherit a fortune by a will written in his favor but left unsigned. Pursued by his own conscience and by rumors about this false step, he never recovers his moral equilibrium. Engel'gardt's signature for the tale, "O. N. T-va," suggests that she might have written it in collaboration with Novosil'tseva-Tolycheva. In *Ne soshlis* (They Didn't Connect, 1867) the narrator, Nastia, recalls the summer when she first experienced the force of passion. As she describes herself at seventeen, Nastia is still observing her governess's strictures against thinking for herself. At the behest of her elders she allows herself to become engaged to Vladimir Gornov, a suitable young man who respects her child-like nature. At their summer home her first spark of emotion is aroused by a female neighbor, Elena Vlas'eva, who has an ulterior motive for cultivating Nastia: she uses the younger girl's crush to manipulate her into renouncing Gornov, whom Vlas'eva wants for herself. Gornov's ardent reaction to Nastia's accusation that he loves her only platonically arouses her passion fully for the first time—yet too late.

In "Ne odnogo polia iagody" (Birds Not of a Feather, 1868) Engel'gardt's heroine, Zhenia, against the advice of her sensible elder sister, marries a man who, despite his resemblance to the medieval knight of her dreams, has mercenary designs on a fortune that he connives for her to inherit. Disabused of her illusions yet heartsick, Zhenia finally breaks with him, but the narrator notes that with her passionate nature she will probably make no better choice next time. Other disparate "birds" appear in a scene in which Engel'gardt mocks the utilitarian spirit of the times. At a "literary evening" a fictional civic poet suggests that threshing machines are a more suitable topic for poetry than private emotions, while the actual poet Fet is engrossed in a discussion of the latest agricultural machinery and recites his lyrics aloud. One of these is a poem, "Posle bala" (After the Ball), reproduced in full in the story and described as "translated by him the day before for the album of a woman friend."

"Son babushki i vnuchki" (A Great-Aunt's and Great-Niece's Dreams, 1869) was the only work that Engel'gardt published in the prestigious Moscow journal *Vestnik Evropy* (The European Messenger). It is a taut tale of the ways in which women use and abuse the instruments of power at their disposal: money and religiosity. Margarita Polibina's lifelong "dream" has been to save enough capital to build a church that she has promised to God, not in expiation of the sin of taking a lover outside of marriage, but in blasphemous hope of reunion with him in the afterlife. Her run-down house and neglected estate testify to her monomania. Polibina's dream is threatened when her ward and great-niece Elia falls mutually in love with an honorable young man, Gleb Matveev. His mother, who has three daughters for whom to provide dowries, flatly insists that her son must marry a woman with means greater than Polibina can provide, without sacrificing her secret hoard. In despair, Elia develops an insane obsession with winning the lottery. The problem is solved when Polibina's long-dead lover appears to her in a dream to reassure her that using the money for her niece will not imperil their reunion; a passage she picks at random from the Bible reinforces the message.

Engel'gardt's feverish pace of publication slowed in the 1870s. "Na rodine" (In Their Native Land, 1870) delineates the fate of two deracinated Russians. Brought up in Paris but imbued with his mother's idealized view of Russia, Dmitrii Opalev returns "home" in 1863 as the adult heir to a large estate. Unwittingly snobbish, he seeks intelligentsia ideals among aristocrats and fails to recognize the true idealists he meets—in particular, a brilliant young doctor—who could direct him in his goal of playing a useful role in Russian society. His sister Nelly, whose preferred milieu is the Faubourg St. Germain, fares no better with Russian nobles. Prince Lykov, a charming rake, "marries" her and takes her back to Paris. When Lykov turns out to have left a living wife behind in the Caucasus, Opalev kills him in a duel, and Nelly, her reputation destroyed, retreats to a nunnery. In *Tak Bog velel. Povesti* (As God Ordained, first published in *Russkii vestnik,* 1872) Mar'ia Obraztsova, who is bitter at her husband for deserting her in frustration that he could not counter her domineering mother's influence, is courted anew by him after her mother dies. A subplot traces the emotional arc of a Bourbonist French count during the Franco-Prussian War. The bitter, semi-autobiographical "Vospominaniia na dache" appeared in 1874, and in 1877 Engel'gardt published one story, "Chernyi surguch" (Black Sealing-Wax), in the minor newspaper *Gazeta A. Gattsuka* (A. Gattsuk's Gazette). In "Staraia vera" an egotistical revolutionary's plans to finance the cause and become a martyr by stealing a large sum of money and then confessing publicly, go awry. The woman who loves him, a true Christian occupied with furthering the welfare of the peasants on her godfather's estate, deserts them to follow him to Siberia, even after she finds out that the money he stole belonged to her benefactor.

"Zloba dnia" (News of the Day, 1881) is another portrait of an egotist, a young woman whose plans to conquer Moscow society are thwarted by its insularity. In a subplot another woman becomes obsessed with spiritualism in hopes of contacting her fiancé, who was killed in the Russo-Turkish War. "Ne pervaia i ne posledniaia" (1883) is a polemic, a denunciation of the increasingly violent revolutionary movement. The story is taken from the headlines, encompassing as it does the national euphoria at the consecration of the Pushkin monument in Moscow in 1880, the "catastrophe of March 1" (the assassination of Tsar Alexander II) in 1881, and the coronation of Alexander III in May 1883. Engel'gardt's last major work of fiction was "Byl' sorokovykh godov" (A True Tale of the '40s, 1884). Interwoven themes of Rousseauian fads in education, ill treatment of serfs, and the social position of illegitimate children lend historical resonance to this depiction of life on an isolated estate near Tambov.

After the death of her sister Tolycheva in 1885 Sof'ia Vladimirovna Engel'gardt published memoirs based on her Moscow life in the 1840s to 1850s. Two last anecdotal tales appeared in the conservative journal *Russkoe obozrenie* (Moscow Review) in the 1890s. Engel'gardt never took the final step toward professionalism by arranging to republish her works in collected editions. Left moldering in journals and slender volumes, her talented tales were soon forgotten, as was she: no obituaries marked her passing in 1894. Her exploration of individual psychology foreshadowed the preoccupations of the symbolist epoch, but her generally sympathetic picture of Moscow gentry life and her distaste for the excesses of the revolutionary movement were anathema to the Soviets. Today Engel'gardt's tales offer glimpses of a society that, with the 1917 revolution, perished more totally than she could ever have imagined.

Letters:

Neizdannye pis'ma k A. N. Ostrovskomu (Moscow & Leningrad: Academia, 1932), pp. 637–642;

Pis'ma k A. V. Druzhininu: 1850–1863, edited by Pavel Sergeevich Popov (Moscow, 1948), pp. 359–393;

". . . Ia tak davno privyk k vashim druzheskim pis'mam . . . ," edited by N. P. Generalova, in *A. A. Fet. Problemy izucheniia zhizni i tvorchestva,* edited by G. E. Golle (Kursk: Izdatel'stvo Kurskogo pedagogicheskogo universiteta, 1994), pp. 174–234.

References:

Sof'ia Bibikova, as Sof'ia B., "Mysli po povodu odnoi povesti Ol'gi N.," *Rassvet,* 13 (1862): 303–310;

"Engel'gardt (Ol'ga N.), Sof'ia Vladimirovna," edited by A. P. Dobryv, in his *Biografii russkikh' pisatelei sredniago i novago periodov* (St. Petersburg: Stolichnaia tipografiia, 1900), p. 325;

Vera Stepanovna Nechaeva, *Zhurnal M. M. i F. M. Dostoevskikh "Epokha" 1864–1865* (Moscow: Nauka, 1975), p. 132;

Ekaterina Vladimirovna Novosil'tseva, as T. Tolycheva, "Semeinye zapiski," *Russkii vestnik,* 10 (1862): 665–775;

Dmitrii Ivanovich Pisarev, *Literaturnaia kritika,* 3 volumes, edited, with an introduction and commentary, by Iurii Sergeevich Sorokin (Leningrad: Khudozhestvennaia literatura, 1981), II: 286–289;

Nikolai Fedorovich Shcherbina, *Stikhotvoreniia,* edited by I. Aizenshtok (Leningrad: Sovetskii pisatel', 1937);

Slovar' chlenov obshchestva liubitelei rossiiskoi slovesnosti pri Moskovskom universitetie, 1811–1911 (Moscow: Pechatiia A. Snegirevoi, 1911), p. 325.

Papers:

Sof'ia Vladimirovna Engel'gardt's papers are held, along with those of her husband and husband's father, at the Russian State Archive of Literature and Art (RGALI), fond 574.

Afanasii Afanas'evich Fet

(November 1820? – 21 November 1892)

Emily Klenin
University of California, Los Angeles

BOOKS: *Liricheskii Panteon,* as A. F. (Moscow: S. Selivanovsky, 1840);

Stikhotvoreniia A. Feta (Moscow: N. Stepanov, 1850);

Stikhotvoreniia A. A. Feta (St. Petersburg: E. Prats, 1856);

Stikhotvoreniia, 2 volumes (Moscow: Grachev, 1863);

Vechernie ogni. Sobranie neizdannykh stikhotvorenii (Moscow: A. Gattsuk, 1883);

Vechernie ogni. Vypusk vtoroi neizdannykh stikhotvorenii (Moscow: M. G. Volchaninov, 1885);

Vechernie ogni. Vypusk tretii neizdannykh stikhotvorenii (Moscow: E. Lissner & Iu. Roman, 1888);

Moi vospominaniia. 1848–1889, 2 volumes (Moscow: A. I. Mamontov, 1890);

Vechernie ogni. Vypusk chetvertyi neizdannykh stikhotvorenii (Moscow: A. I. Mamontov, 1891);

Rannie gody moei zhizni (Moscow: A. I. Mamontov, 1893);

Liricheskie stikhotvoreniia v dvukh chastiakh, with an introduction by Nikolai Nikolaevich Strakhov (St. Petersburg: Brat'ia Panteleevy, 1894);

Polnoe sobranie stikhotvorenii, edited, with an introduction, by Boris Vladimirovich Nikol'sky (St. Petersburg: A. F. Marks, 1901);

Polnoe sobranie stikhotvorenii, 3 volumes, edited by Boris Iakovlevich Bukhshtab, Biblioteka poeta (Leningrad: Sovetskii pisatel', 1937);

Sochineniia, 2 volumes, edited by Aleksandr Evgen'evich Tarkhov (Moscow: Khudozhestvennaia literatura, 1982);

Vospominaniia, edited by Tarkhov (Moscow: Pravda, 1983);

Afanasii Fet, edited by G. D. Aslanova, Proza poeta (Moscow: Vagrius, 2001);

Zhizn' Stepanovki, ili, Liricheskoe khoziastvo, edited, with an introduction, by Viacheslav Anatol'evich Koshelev (Moscow: Novoe literaturnoe obozrenie, 2001);

Stikhotvoreniia i poemy 1839–1863, edited by Aslanova, with commentary by N. P. Generalova, V. A. Koshelev, and G. V. Petrova (St. Petersburg: Akademicheskii proekt, 2002).

Afanasii Afanas'evich Fet

Editions and Collections: *Polnoe sobranie stikhotvorenii,* 2 volumes, edited by Boris Vladimirovich Nikol'sky (St. Petersburg: A. F. Marks, 1912);

Polnoe sobranie stikhotvorenii, edited by Boris Iakovlevich Bukhshtab, Biblioteka poeta (Leningrad: Sovetskii pisatel', 1959);

Vechernie ogni, edited by Dmitrii Dmitrievich Blagoi and M. A. Sokolova, Literaturnye pamiatniki (Moscow: Nauka, 1971);

Stikhotvoreniia i poemy, edited by Bukhshtab, Biblioteka poeta (Leningrad: Sovetskii pisatel', 1986);

Stikhotvoreniia. Proza. Pis'ma, edited by G. D. Aslanova, preface by Aleksandr Evgen'evich Tarkhov (Moscow: Sovetskaia Rossiia, 1988);

Stikhotvoreniia, poemy. Sovremenniki o Fete, edited by Aslanova and Tarkhov (Moscow: Pravda, 1989);

Vospominaniia, 3 volumes (Pushkino: Kul'tura, 1992)–comprises volume 1, *Moi vospominaniia, 1848–1863;* volume 2, *Moi vospominaniia, 1864–1889;* and volume 3, *Rannie gody moei zhizni;*

Stikhotvoreniia, edited by A. V. Uspenskaia, introduction by I. N. Sukhikh, Novaia biblioteka poeta, Malaia seriia (St. Petersburg: Gumanitarnoe agentstvo "Akademicheskii proekt," 2001).

Editions in English: "Three poems by Fet," translated by Vladimir Nabokov, *Russian Review,* 3, no. 1 (1943): 31–33;

Poems by Fet, translated by B. Raffel, in *Russian Poetry under the Tsars,* edited by Raffel (Albany: SUNY Press, 1971), pp. 145–152;

Poems by Fet, translated by Walter Arndt, *Russian Literature Triquarterly,* 11 (1975): 283–284;

I have come to you to greet you. Selected poems, translated by James Greene, introduction by Henry Gifford (London: Angel Books, 1982);

Twenty poems by Fet, translated by R. H. Morrison, *Russian Literature Triquarterly,* 23 (1990): 25–34;

"Fet on Tiutchev," in *Russian Writers on Russian Writers,* edited by Faith Wigzell (Oxford & Providence, R. I.: Berg, 1994), pp. 15–25;

Two poems by Fet, translated by Alyssa Dinega Gillespie, in *An Anthology of Jewish-Russian Literature: Two Centuries of a Dual Identity,* 2 volumes, edited by Maxim D. Shrayer (Armonk, N.Y.: M. E. Sharpe, forthcoming).

OTHER: "Po povodu statui g. Ivanova na vystavke Obshchestva Liubitelei Khudozhestv," in *Khudozhestvennyi sbornik* (Moscow: OLKh, 1866), pp. 75–92;

"Neizvestnoe stikhotvorenie A. A. Feta," published by A. I. Frumkina, in *A. A. Fet. Traditsii i problemy izucheniia. Sbornik nauchnykh trudov,* edited by N. N. Skatov (Kursk: Kurskii gosudarstvennyi pedagogicheskii institut, 1985), pp. 127–128.

TRANSLATIONS: Horace, *Ody, v chetyrekh knigakh* (St. Petersburg: Korolev, 1856);

Arthur Schopenhauer, *Mir, kak volia i predstavlenie* (N.p., 1881);

Johann Wolfgang von Goethe, *Faust,* 2 volumes (St. Petersburg: A. F. Marks, 1882, 1888);

Horace [Complete Works] (Moscow: Shchepkin, 1883);

Decimus Junius Juvenalis, *Satiry* (Moscow, 1885);

Tibullus, *Elegii* (Moscow: A. I. Mamontov, 1886);

Schopenhauer, *O chetveriakom korne zakona dostatochnogo osnovaiia. O vole v prirode* (Moscow: A. I. Mamontov, 1886);

C. Valerius Catullus, *Stikhotvoreniia* (St. Petersburg: A. I. Mamontov, 1886);

Ovid, *XV knig Prevrashchenii* (Moscow, 1887);

Sextus Propertius, *Elegii* (St. Petersburg: V. S. Balashev, 1888);

Virgil, *Eneida,* parts 1 and 2, with an introduction and notes by D. I. Naguevskogo (Moscow: A. I. Mamontov, 1888);

Persius, *Satiry* (St. Petersburg: V. S. Balashev, 1889);

Martial, *Epigrammy,* parts 1 and 2 (Moscow: A. I. Mamontov, 1891);

Plautus, *Gorshok. Komediia* (Moscow: A. I. Mamontov, 1891);

Ovid, *Skorbi* (Moscow: A. I. Mamontov, 1893).

SELECTED PERIODICAL PUBLICATIONS:

"Otvet na stat'iu Russkogo vestnika ob Odakh Goratsiia," *Otechestvennye zapiski,* 106, no.6, section 2 (1856): 27–44;

"Iz-za granitsy. Putevye vpechatleniia," *Sovremennik* (November 1856): 71–117;

"Pis'mo vtoroe," *Sovremennik* (February 1857): 237–271;

"Pis'mo tret'e," *Sovremennik* (August 1857): 81–128;

"O stikhotvoreniiakh F. Tiutcheva," *Russkoe slovo* (February 1859): 63–84;

"Zametki o vol'no-naemnom trude," *Russkii vestnik,* 38, no. 3 (1862): 358–379; 39, no. 5 (1862): 219–273;

"Iz derevni," *Russkii vestnik,* 43 (1863): 438–470; 44 (1863): 299–350; 50 (1864): 575–626;

"Dva pis'ma o znachenii drevnikh iazykov v nashem vospitanii," *Literaturnaia biblioteka* (April 1867): 48–69; (May 1867): 298–315;

"Zametka o vybore mirovykh sudei," *Literaturnaia biblioteka* (January 1868): 167–173;

"Iz derevni," *Literaturnaia biblioteka* (February 1868): 90–124;

"Iz derevni," *Zaria,* 6 (June 1871): 1–86;

"Otgolosok sel'skogo sud'i," *Russkii vestnik,* 113 (1874): 388–410;

"Po voprosu o lichnom naime," *Russkii vestnik,* 121 (1876): 408–441;

"Nashi korni," as Derevenskii zhitel', *Russkii vestnik,* 157 (1882): 485–538;

"Kormlenie v drevnei Rusi. Pis'mo v redaktsiiu," *Novoe vremia,* 5139 (1890): 3;

"O pomoshchi krest'ianam neurozhainykh mestnostei," *Moskovskie vedomosti,* 280 (10 October 1891): 5;

"Dva slova o zapasnykh magazinakh," *Moskovskie vedomosti,* 331 (30 November 1891): 3;

"Sovremenniki o potselue. Mnenie A. A. Feta," in *Potselui. Issledovaniia i nabliudeniia. Potselui s tochki zreniia fiziologicheskoi, gigienicheskoi, istoricheskoi, etnograficheskoi, iuridicheskoi, gipnoticheskoi, filologicheskoi i pr.,* edited by M. V. Shevliakov (St. Petersburg, 1892), pp. 183–189; reprinted in Boris Sadovskoi, *Ledokhod* (Petrograd, 1916), pp. 181–184 and in V. P. Shestakov, ed., *Russkii Eros ili filosofiia liubvi v Rossii* (Moscow: Progress, 1991), pp. 92–95;

"Neizdannaia stat'ia A. A. Feta o Romane N. G. Chernyshevskogo 'Chto delat'?,'" by Fet and V. P. Botkin, commentary by G. Volkov, *Literaturnoe nasledstvo,* 25–26 (1936): 485–544;

"Chto sluchilos' po smerti Anny Kareninoi v *Russkom vestnike,*" excerpt, *Literaturnoe nasledstvo,* special Tolstoy issue, 37–38 (1939): 231–238.

The best-known works of Afanasii Fet are short lyric poems on traditional themes. Most often on a miniature scale and in simple language, his work celebrated individual and private responses to the phenomenal world. Fet's contemporaries often failed to appreciate his work, and the poet himself met with rejection and abuse because of what is often considered his "art-for-art's-sake" aesthetics and his conservative social views. The finest Russian poet of his generation, he prided himself on keeping alive essential traditions of the earlier Golden Age of Russian poetry during an era largely inimical to them. Fet's pride in this role is all the more striking because his own life and work are rooted only partly within the Russian tradition. Born in Russia but of German heritage, Fet introduced into Russian poetry formal and aesthetic tendencies that he assimilated through his German-oriented schooling. He translated both poetry and prose—not only from German but also from several other languages, most notably Latin. His translations are far more extensive than his original poems, yet equally controversial. He was a colleague and sometimes intimate friend of several leading writers in Russia. His ambition to be a professional man of letters was to a great extent, however, defeated. He lived most of his life in the Russian countryside.

Afanasii Afanas'evich Fet was born in October or November 1820 in Novoselki, a country home in the Mtsensk region of Russia. Novoselki belonged to Afanasii Neofitovich Shenshin. He had brought Fet's mother there from her native Darmstadt, Germany, where the couple had met when he was a Russian army officer and she, born Charlotte Becker, was married to J. P. K. W. Foeth. Charlotte was pregnant with the future poet when she left Germany for Russia. Foeth, who seems to have taken no interest in the baby, remarried in 1824 and died in 1825. Afanasii Neofitovich, who married Fet's mother in 1822, registered the infant as his child and treated him as his own. However, the boy's legal status (was he a Foeth or a Shenshin?) remained uncertain throughout his childhood and early adolescence. The decision was important because it affected his nationality (German or Russian) and his social position (including his status as Afanasii Neofitovich's heir), as well as his name.

As was customary at the time in rural Russia, the boy acquired a basic education at home, reading in both Russian and German languages from an early age. According to Fet, his favorite early reading was poetry, and he began translating German poetry into Russian while still a young child. In January 1835 he entered a boarding school in Werro (now Võru), a town in Estonia, then part of the Russian Empire. That same January the legal question of his parentage was resolved in favor of Foeth's paternity, and Foeth's surname, in Russified form, became the poet's. He was, however, known at school under the family name Shenshin. In his memoirs Fet reports learning of his new status only after he had been at the school for some months. His parents likely had selected the school in anticipation of the legal decision: for someone making his way as a German in Russia, Estonia was the best place for an education. The Baltic region had become part of the Russian Empire only in the eighteenth century, and its population included a significant number of landowners of German origin. Baltic Germans enjoyed considerable autonomy, and the university at Dorpat (now Tartu, Estonia) was in practice a German university, the only one in the Russian Empire.

The boarding school that Fet attended was run mainly by German-born teachers trained by the Moravian Church based in Herrnhut, Germany, and most of the pupils there were Baltic Germans. Though rather new, the school had a fine reputation and successfully prepared boys to enter Dorpat University. At school Fet acquired excellent Latin and a good basic education in mathematics and the sciences, as well as various practical skills. In his published reminiscences of his school years he recalls the church music that he heard at school (he mentions organ and piano music as well as singing), reports on the devotion and pedagogical skill of his teachers, and even incorporates into the memoirs a *Schulrede* (school talk) by the headmaster, Heinrich Caspar Krümmer, who was a well-known pedagogue. In addition to German literature and the classical languages, Fet studied French and English as well as Russian. Taught only as a foreign language, Russian was obligatory in the school program because the school itself was in Russia, but this part of the program was poorly organized. Encouraged by Krümmer, Fet began writing original poetry in Russian. According to the poet, none of this early work was successful, and none is extant. Afanasii Neofitovich removed Fet from the school in Werro at the end of 1837

Fet's room at the home of his friend Apollon Aleksandrovich Grigor'ev's family,
with whom the poet lived during most of his university

or early 1838, probably because of changes in government educational policies.

Fet completed his formal education in Moscow. From February through the summer of 1838 he attended a preparatory boarding school run by the historian and editor Mikhail Petrovich Pogodin. Fet had little respect for his schoolmates or for the educational program, but he did become friends with the translator and critic Irinarkh Ivanovich Vvedensky, who taught for a time (1838–1840) at Pogodin's school, where Fet continued to board after he had ceased taking classes there. Vvedensky, later characterized by Pogodin as a wellspring of Russian nihilism, encouraged Fet's poetry. He was also, according to Fet, a model of irregular social behavior, and he provoked the younger man's commitment to potentially dangerous beliefs: Vvedensky and Fet drew up a "contract" on 1 December 1838 in which Fet (under a pseudonym) proclaims his atheism and declares his intention of maintaining it for the next twenty years, under penalty of a fine.

In August 1838 Fet was accepted at Moscow University, where he was a student from September 1838 to June 1844. He studied with several eminent professors: Ivan Ivanovich Davydov, Dmitrii L'vovich Kriukov, and Stepan Petrovich Shevyrev, who welcomed Fet into his home. Nevertheless, the university as such seems not to have played a strongly positive, or even important, role in Fet's development as a poet: he avoided classes, received mediocre grades, and had to repeat a year. Rather, his private relationships nurtured his talent, which began to manifest itself in poems that he willingly shared with friends and brought to the attention of established literary figures and eventually the public.

In the autumn of 1838 Fet met the writer Apollon Aleksandrovich Grigor'ev, and they soon began to exchange and compare the poems that they were writing. About a year later Fet submitted a notebook of his poems to Pogodin, who showed them to the writer Nikolai Vasil'evich Gogol. At that time (September to October 1839) Gogol was living at Pogodin's house–as was Fet himself, according to his memoirs.

Sometime in 1839 or 1840 Fet moved from Pogodin's home to that of Grigor'ev's family, with whom he lived for the rest of his university career. Grigor'ev's friendship was decisive for Fet's artistic development, and Grigor'ev also played an important role in the maturation of Fet's sensitive personality. Inclined to depression, Fet had a temperament that was often wearing for his intimates, and his early adulthood seems to have been a tempestuous emotional period. The rooms where Fet and Grigor'ev stayed became a meeting place for a circle of young students, aspiring intellectuals, and poets. One of the poets was Iakov Petrovich Polonsky, with whom Fet formed a close and lasting friendship. In addition to Fet's literary talent, his excellent German was an important contribution to their collective education, since the group read and discussed the works of Georg Wilhelm Friedrich Hegel and other German writers. Fet at the time was particularly enamored of Friedrich Schiller, but he also translated other works—including the long poem "Hermann und Dorothea" (1798) by Johann Wolfgang von Goethe. In addition, he translated Latin poetry (the Odes of Horace), and he enthusiastically read the works of current Russian poets such as Vladimir Grigor'evich Benediktov and Mikhail Iur'evich Lermontov. He also reports in his memoirs on other literary enthusiasms of his circle, notably William Shakespeare, Alphonse de Lamartine, and George Gordon, Lord Byron.

Fet also noted in his memoirs that at this time Grigor'ev began copying his friend's poems into a fresh notebook, which became the basis of a book. Fet spent the summer of 1840 on the Shenshin estate, where he became romantically involved with the Shenshin children's governess. She gave Fet three hundred rubles to finance publication of his book, and in November 1840 he made his literary debut with *Liricheskii Panteon* (The Lyrical Pantheon), published under the initials "A.F." Fet's relationship with the governess was terminated by Afanasii Neofitovich.

An eclectic work, *Liricheskii Panteon* features both original poems and translations of works by Horace, Lamartine, Schiller, and Goethe. Most of the book is of only historical interest, but Fet included two of the original poems—"Gretsiia" (Greece) and "Kogda petukh . . ." (When the cock . . .)—in his final collected works; the translations of Horace also appeared later in the Russian translation of his complete works that Fet published in 1883. Both of these original poems, which Fet retained afterward in his canon, represent his affinity for Hellenism, in particular as it was mediated by German literature, especially by Goethe. Fet's work in this Hellenistic and, more broadly, classicizing line met with a generally favorable critical response in its own day, although modern readers have been less enthusiastic.

Liricheskii Panteon was not only Fet's first book of poetry but also his first public appearance as a poet. Not until a full year later did his poetry first appear on the pages of a journal—*Moskvitianin* (The Muscovite), edited by Pogodin (issue 12 for the year 1841). Five of Fet's poems were published on this occasion, including three translations of poems by the German poet Heinrich Heine, whose verse he continued to translate throughout his career; during his lifetime the Heine translations were among his most widely appreciated works. They were part of a more general line in Fet's verse: he wrote many poems that became songs, and the Heine texts figure prominently in this category. Many of Fet's poems, both original and translated, were known at least as well from song performance as they were from their appearance on the printed page.

In 1842 Fet began to publish regularly—now under the name "Fet"—both in *Moskvitianin* and in the St. Peters-

burg journal *Otechestvennye zapiski* (Notes of the Fatherland). He also wrote for a student volume, *Podzemnye kliuchi* (Subterranean Springs). "Chudnaia Kartina . . ." (Magical picture . . .), one of his poems published in *Moskvitianin,* was the first of about half a dozen that became famous examples of an unusual syntactic practice associated with Fet—namely, the composition of entire poems without any overt personal verb forms. In Fet's day this practice was said to derive from Heine's influence; more recently, it has been seen as a precursor of a style favored by some twentieth-century poets, for example Aleksandr Aleksandrovich Blok. In 1842 Fet also published a long poem, "Talisman" (The Talisman), the first of five such long poems in the course of his career. Aesthetically less interesting, for the most part, than his short poems, these poems are of considerable biographical interest. In February 1844 Grigor'ev moved to St. Petersburg, where he became affiliated with the journal *Repertuar i Panteon* (Repertoire and Pantheon), and in late 1844 Fet also began to publish there instead of in *Moskvitianin.*

Many of the poems first published in journals in the early 1840s were included in Fet's later collections and are still reprinted. Among the characteristics of this verse were its psychologism and its exploitation of techniques and forms novel to Russian poetry, although these stylistic traits often had classical and German antecedents. Fet's early poems had a rich sound structure but were known for making less use of fully rhymed stanzas than was typical in Russian poetry of the time. Like his choice of meters and syntax, his early rhyme usage derives from German models. His early vocabulary is relatively close to contemporary post-Romantic norms but has peculiarities for which Fet became well known. An example is his unusually frequent mention of windows. In the Russian tradition Fet's references to windows mark an innovation that connects his poetry to the verse of twentieth-century poet Boris Leonidovich Pasternak, although in the broader Western tradition, windows play an important role much earlier. References to windows are more characteristic of Fet's poetry from the 1840s and are rare in his later works.

The poems that Fet published during his student years were on the whole well received, and he left the university with a reputation as a promising young poet. The years from November 1840 through mid 1844 thus constitute the first period in his active career. His publications had moved rapidly from juvenilia to mature lyric poems, and by the end of this period his work was no longer financed by personal enthusiasts but by professional honoraria. His profile as a writer of both original poetry and translations was clear from the beginning, as was his affinity for classicizing verse, on the one hand, and poetry evocative of song, on the other.

ЛИРИЧЕСКIЙ

ПАНТЕОНЪ.

Я. Ф.

Si tu pouvais jamais egaler, o ma lyre!
Le doux fremissement des ailes du zephire
A travers les rameaux

Ou l'onde qui murmure en caressant ses rives,
Ou le roucoulement des colombes plaintives
Jouant aux bords des eaux.

Lamartine.

МОСКВА.
Въ Типографіи С. Селивановскаго.
1840.

Title page for Fet's first book, Liricheskii Panteon
*(The Lyrical Pantheon), which includes both original
verse and his translations of Latin, French, and
German poetry (Kilgour Collection of Russian
Literature, Harvard University Library)*

Fet passed his last university examinations in the spring of 1844, and in May of that year he left Moscow so hastily that he asked that his diploma be entrusted to a friend. The preceding summer his mother, who suffered from psychiatric illness, had been hospitalized, and her psychiatric condition had apparently delayed diagnosis of her breast cancer. During the summer of 1844 Fet visited her family in Germany, where he received the inheritance owed her from her parents. She died in late 1844 or spring 1845. Around this time Fet also learned of the death of his father Afanasii Neofitovich's brother. He had expected to receive an inheritance from him (he was not legally heir to either Foeth or Shenshin), but he did not. Thus, Fet in 1845 found himself at the age of twenty-five with neither mother nor—in the eyes of the law—any father and with no financial resources.

In April 1845 he joined a cuirassier (cavalry) regiment in the Kherson region, in present-day Ukraine. At

the time commissioned officers were automatically granted hereditary nobility, and Fet might well have expected such a patent of nobility to help resolve his insecure social status. He lacked the money he needed to support himself in a prestigious unit, which might have offered more useful social and intellectual contacts, but he must have expected to serve for only a short time before returning to literary life. He had not yet received his officer's commission, however, when, in accordance with a decree of 11 June 1845, the law changed: nobility would be awarded only at the rank of major; Fet turned out to have embarked on a longer career in the army than he had thought. In February 1846, in connection with his army service, he took an oath of allegiance and became a naturalized Russian subject.

In the early years of Fet's army career his comrades were suspicious of his literary background, while Fet himself, although assiduous, privately characterized his army life as Gogolian and referred to the area where he was stationed as Kamchatka—the name of a Siberian peninsula known for, among other things, its penal colony. His surroundings were culturally bleak, and he was so isolated that he found it hard even to send out or receive his mail. Friends and relatives apparently tried to persuade him to give up this dreary career, but he was determined to pursue it; what practical alternatives he had at the time are unclear. Fet made a few good friends, notably Aleksei Fedorovich Brzhesky and his wife, Aleksandra L'vovna Brzheskaia. He also kept on writing: by the end of 1847 he had accumulated a significant number of poems, which he had not yet published because of the difficulty in communicating with editors based in Moscow and St. Petersburg.

In late 1847 Fet arranged a leave in Moscow, and there, with the editorial advice of Grigor'ev, he prepared the manuscript for a second book. It was approved by the censor in December 1847, while Fet was still in Moscow. A Moscow printer was hired; Pogodin helped arrange for distribution; and a prepublication book notice appeared. The book languished unpublished, however, for two more years, because the printer apparently did not get paid, and Fet, no longer in Moscow, could not resolve the problem. In 1848, instead of the expected second book, not a single poem by Fet appeared in print—the first such "barren" year since the appearance of *Liricheskii Panteon* in 1840.

Meanwhile, however, the revolutions of 1848 led to new military assignments: in June 1848, on the eve of Russian intervention in Romania, Fet's regiment was moved westward. While stationed at his new post, Fet experienced the great love of his life—his romance with Mariia Kuzminichna Lazich, who became his lifelong inspiration. In spite of his continued anxiety about his book, he experienced the early months of 1849 as a hopeful time. In January his translations once more appeared in *Moskvitianin,* and this literary success was followed in February by an advancement in his military career to the position of regimental adjutant. In the spring and summer of 1849, however, he became increasingly convinced that he had no prospect of enjoying the financial security required to propose marriage, and he began to withdraw from his relationship with Lazich. In July 1849 his unit again moved, this time in connection with the Russian intervention in Hungary, but he did not break completely with Lazich in spite of his effort to do so.

In early 1850 Fet's second book finally appeared, under the title *Stikhotvoreniia A. Feta* (Poems of A. Fet). The book collects the earliest mature works of the poet, from 1841 to 1847, alongside four poems that originally appeared in *Liricheskii Panteon.* In an arrangement inspired by Goethe's 1815 collected works, the 1850 *Stikhotvoreniia* is organized in sections with headings and ordering determined by Grigor'ev, who also wrote an important essay (actually a review) about the volume and emphasized the importance of Goethe as the model underlying it. The German orientation of the 1850 volume is also evident in the forms and themes of individual poems, as well as in the identification of certain types of poems by characteristic rubrics. For example, the poems called *Elegii* (Elegies) are clearly modeled on Goethe's *Römische Elegien* (Roman Elegies, 1795). This Germanophile quality is set off, however, by a specifically Russian nationalism, marked by the first poem, which begins with the words "Ia russkii . . ." (I am a Russian . . .). The 1850 *Stikhotvoreniia,* like Fet's previous volume, incorporates both original and translated texts, but here the most prominent translations are of works by Heine: they occupy a large section of the book. In addition the volume features translations from German, French (an imitation, by the French poet and Hellenist André Chénier, of a classical Greek work), English, and Polish. The cultural range is even more ambitious than is suggested by the list of languages from which Fet translated: one of his two translations from English is of a "Venetian song," actually a poem composed by the Irish poet Thomas Moore, while the other is "Sun of the sleepless! melancholy star! . . ." from the *Hebrew Melodies* (1815) of Byron. The Jewish connection in the Byron text is part of a pattern: Heine, with whose work Fet was closely associated by his nineteenth-century readers, was Jewish, and some of Fet's close friends believed him to be of Jewish origin also. While this perception has not usually been to the poet's advantage, in the 1850 edition he seems not to avoid but rather to embrace it as part of a more general appeal to a variety of national traditions and as an investigation of his own place at their intersection. The original poems in the 1850 book are also characterized by allusions to several cultures, as seen in the long "oriental" poem, called "Solovei i roza" (The Nightingale

Fet as an army officer in the 1850s

and the Rose), which—set in Kashmir—is formally evocative of Goethe and German orientalism.

The formal profile of the 1850 volume differs significantly from that of Fet's other books and from the conventions for Russian poetry at this time. Many of the poems in the 1850 volume still appear in modern collections of Fet's poetry, but not usually in their original form. They were changed during the 1850s at the insistence of Fet's editors, who shortened his early poems and brought his usage into conformity with contemporary norms. Fet's affinity for songs is shown by his unusually extensive use of meters that, in the Russian tradition, have associations with song forms. Conversely, iambic tetrameter, the most neutral of all Russian meters, does not even rank among the commonest meters used in the 1850 book (it had ranked fourth in *Liricheskii Panteon*). The 1850 collection also has some of the poet's finest works in what is termed the "anthological" style, which in Fet's case is verse of delicate workmanship inspired by classical models, often through the intermediary of the classical Goethe. For example, the book reprints some of Fet's best poems written in a metrically "freed" and rhymeless form that was quite daring (indeed unique in nineteenth-century Russian poetry) and not used even by Fet himself in his later original poetry.

The 1850 volume was generally well received, and Grigor'ev's review (written anonymously) is still one of the best appreciations ever written of Fet's work. In addition, Fet's poetry appeared in several journals early in 1850. The most noteworthy of these publications was "Shepot, robkoe dykhan'e . . ." (Whispering, timid breathing . . .), another poem famous for its nominal syntax but also much loved (though also much parodied) for the delicacy with which it presents a night of erotic passion, brought to its end in the blazing light of dawn. That summer the poet's relationship with Lazich came to an end in another sort of blaze: after a meeting in which Fet decisively rejected her, Lazich died in a fire, which started from a cigarette she dropped on her dress while reading. Her death might have been a suicide.

Unhappy love had not been an important element in Fet's earlier thematics, but it recurs in the few poems he wrote between 1850 and 1852, including several probably written and published before he learned of Lazich's death. These poems, few of which appear in the canon of Fet's poetry, are also different from his later love poems: they contain many references to death and mourning but only as metaphor, usually for the sorrow felt by the textual speaker. For instance, alluding to his tears, he writes in an 1850 poem "Sleza slezu s lanity zharkoi gonit . . ." (Tear chases tear from the hot cheek . . .): "Each moment inters the next, / And a shrine sparkles on the place of burial." Most of Fet's poetry is less gloomy, but when he wrote about death in subsequent years he usually meant it literally, insofar as he had in mind the death of specific people, most often himself.

Fet's correspondence from 1850 to 1852 shows the poet depressed and disgusted with his life. He also suffered serious illnesses during this period, some of which became chronic. Gradually, however, he returned to literature. In mid 1851 Grigor'ev slipped into *Moskvitianin* (to Pogodin's displeasure) a poem Fet had written in 1842, one of his finest erotic anthological poems: "Son i Pazifaia" (Sleep and Pasithea). In 1852 new work by Fet began to appear for the first time in *Sovremennik* (The Contemporary): his first publication there was "V dolgie nochi, kak vezhdy na son ne zamknuty . . ." (In the long nights, as my eyelids are not closed in sleeping . . .), which came out in the March issue. An autographed copy of the poem bears the title "Ne opravdanie" (Not a Justification), which apparently refers to the poet's relationship with Lazich.

In May 1853 Fet was reassigned to a guards unit near St. Petersburg. He had sought the new posting to gain access to literary circles in the capital. While en route there Fet stopped at his birthplace, Novoselki, and from Novoselki he made an excursion to Spasskoe, the

home of Ivan Sergeevich Turgenev, to whom Fet read some of his work. Turgenev responded with sympathetic interest, expressed both to Fet and, in letters, to others. Because Turgenev not only was a leading writer but also maintained a wide and dense network of contacts, Fet's acquaintance with Turgenev was extremely fruitful. Within six months, by January 1854, he was able to develop contacts with other literary figures in St. Petersburg, most notably the editors and contributors of *Sovremennik*. Besides Turgenev, Fet's new acquaintances included Nikolai Alekseevich Nekrasov, Ivan Ivanovich Panaev, Avdot'ia Iakovlevna Panaeva, Vasilii Petrovich Botkin, and Aleksandr Vasil'evich Druzhinin, to name only those whose connection with Fet left an enduring trace. Both individually and collectively, the circle of *Sovremennik* played a crucial role in Fet's career and personal life.

The Crimean War had begun in October 1853, with Turkey's declaration of war against Russia. Following an imperial decree of 10 February 1854 that warned of impending hostilities with England and France, Fet was posted to Estonia. He spent nearly all the rest of 1854 and 1855 in the Baltic region, mostly in the vicinity of Reval (now Tallinn), but also in other towns, including Dorpat. This might have been when he first read the work of the philosopher Arthur Schopenhauer and met the astronomer Johann Heinrich Mädler. Fet's conversations with Mädler contributed to important later poems with astral and cosmological themes, notably the famous "Izmuchen zhizn'iu, kovarstvom nadezhdy . . ." (Worn out by life, by the perfidy of hope . . .), written in the 1860s.

In 1854 and 1855 dozens of original poems by Fet appeared in *Sovremennik* and *Otechestvennye zapiski*. These poems to a great extent reflect the taste of his new associates, especially Turgenev, who had begun preparing a new edition of Fet's work. Throughout the period of Fet's association with them, Turgenev and the other editors of *Sovremennik* sifted out poems that they considered weak, and they encouraged and even forced revisions in poems that they liked but believed had flaws. They made a special point of repressing what they and others perceived as intrusive Germanisms. Although critics have often argued that Turgenev and his colleagues did not respect Fet's poetics properly, the poet himself adopted their taste. Not only did he change his style in the poetry that he wrote from then on, he also followed their judgments about his earlier poems, which he nonetheless reviewed again in his final years. In 1854, in addition to publishing original poetry, Fet also made plans to put out a book of translations of Horace's *Odes,* a project he had conceived in the 1840s. He obtained permission to dedicate the volume to Aleksandr Nikolaevich, heir to the Russian throne, who was the patron of Fet's military unit. The book was still in press, however, when Alexander became emperor in February 1855. Fet then had to petition for renewed permission to dedicate the book to him, and as a result its appearance was delayed. In addition to his other publications and projects, Fet also published his first stories in *Otechestvennye zapiski:* "Kalenik" appeared in 1854, and "Diadiushka i dvoiurodnyi bratets" (Uncle and Cousin) in 1855.

During the last days of the war, in late January 1856, Fet made the acquaintance of Leo Tolstoy, whose stories about the siege of Sevastopol' had just appeared in *Sovremennik.* Fet and Tolstoy later came to enjoy a close friendship. On 11 February, Fet's third collection of poetry, *Stikhotvoreniia A. A. Feta* (Poems of A. A. Fet), was approved by the censor and published in St. Petersburg soon afterward. It was the crowning achievement in this period of his career.

About two-thirds of the 1856 book consists of poems first printed in Fet's 1850 collection (these republished poems account for roughly half of the works featured in the 1850 book). The differences between the two books, however, are much greater than this fact suggests. Many of the repeated poems have been changed, often by the elimination of a final stanza. The 1856 book is about a third shorter than the edition of 1850, and the pruning affected not only individual poems but also the overall aesthetics of the volume. The anthological tendency, well represented earlier, is stronger than ever. Although Fet's talent for song form is still apparent in the 1856 book, the poems of that type conform more closely than before to contemporary norms and are technically more polished and less experimental. In addition, the division between the anthological poems and the song-form poems is now much clearer, because so much of the rich diversity of the earlier book has been swept away. Grigor'ev's organization of the 1850 collection also has been rejected in favor of a structure closer to the one familiar to modern readers; there is no separate section for translations, and the total number of translations has been reduced. Fet wrote many years later that the edition of 1856 had, even for him, completely replaced his earlier work, which he dismissed for more than thirty years.

The treaty ending the Crimean War was announced less than a week after the appearance of Fet's third book, and the poet immediately sought an extended leave from the army. While he waited for his leave, his literary reputation continued to grow, fostered in particular by a nearly ecstatic review by Druzhinin, published in the March issue of *Biblioteka dlia chteniia* (A Reading Library), which also began featuring Fet's work. In April, Fet read to a group of colleagues a draft of his second long poem. Druzhinin made extensive changes in it, and it was published in *Otechestvennye zapiski* later that year under the title "Son" (The Dream, 1856). In May, Fet's translations of Horace appeared. His work was reviewed in *Russkii vestnik*

СТИХОТВОРЕНIЯ

А. А. ФЕТА.

Санктпетербургъ.
—
1856.

Title page for Fet's well-received third poetry volume,
Stikhotvoreniia *(Poems), produced at the peak*
of his career (Kilgour Collection of Russian
Literature, Harvard University Library)

(The Russian Messenger) by Sergei Dmitrievich Shestakov, an adjunct of Moscow University, scholar of classical literature, and translator of the works of Sophocles and Plautus. Fet's response to Shestakov is the earliest of several essays in which the poet discusses translation technique and aesthetics; this work is also Fet's first extended published essay on any literary topic. That same year he also gained a reputation as a major translator of German poetry when his rendering of Goethe's *Hermann und Dorothea* appeared in *Sovremennik.* Fet had written the translation while a student.

On 23 June 1856, the same day that he obtained his leave, Fet set out for what turned into a six-month-long tour of Germany, France, and Italy. During this time he maintained contact with *Sovremennik*, two of whose editors (Turgenev and Nekrasov) he visited abroad. He sent travel notes to Russia and also wrote poetry. The impressions left by this trip–his only opportunity for extensive exploration of the major European museums–is shown in several descriptive poems about the works of art that he saw there (for example, the Sistine Madonna), as well as in poems, not usually characteristic of Fet, in which he presents his perception of national and political issues in the wake of the Crimean War; most of these poems were published between 1857 and 1859, after his return from Europe. On 9 December 1856, however, Alexander II raised the rank at which military service earned an award of hereditary nobility, and when Fet returned to Russia in early 1857 he had decided to retire from the army.

Fet's publications of early 1857 include not only short poems (some of them the fruit of his Italian journey, such as the well-received "U kamina" [By the Fireside], published that year in *Sovremennik*) but also the third of his long poems, "Dve lipki" (Two Lindens), which appeared in *Otechestvennye zapiski*. In the spring of 1857 he became engaged to Botkin's younger sister Mariia Petrovna Botkina, and they were married in Paris on 16 August. On their return to Russia, Fet and his wife settled in Moscow. At around this time his professional relationships also began to change, as he grew closer to Tolstoy and more distant from Nekrasov. By late 1857 Fet had ceased publishing in *Otechestvennye zapiski*, but both original and translated poems continued to come out in *Sovremennik* and *Biblioteka dlia chteniia* as well as in, for the first time, *Russkii vestnik*. A long essay, praising Fet's poetry and situating it in the best Russian and European poetic traditions, was written by Botkin and published in *Sovremennik* in early 1857. Unknown to Fet, however, Botkin's praise won the enmity of the radical critic Nikolai Aleksandrovich Dobroliubov, who wrote a vicious retort for *Otechestvennye zapiski*–which did not publish it. Private hostility toward Fet's poetry had been expressed even earlier by Nikolai Gavrilovich Chernyshevsky. Dobroliubov's and Chernyshevsky's attitudes toward Fet soon found public expression, as the radicals began to take control of the literary criticism sections in major journals.

Fet's extended military leave ended in his permanent discharge on 27 January 1858. Throughout 1858 and 1859 he continued to enjoy and even deepen some of the relationships most important for his writing–with Turgenev, for example, and especially Tolstoy. One of Fet's poems was published in German translation, and throughout the summer of 1859 he continued to publish original and translated poetry in *Sovremennik, Russkii vestnik,* and his other usual outlets. On the whole, however, his ties to literary circles were becoming increasingly unstable and unpleasant. His relationship with Nekrasov worsened, and Druzhinin complained about Fet's work, both to Fet and to others. In early 1859 Fet's essay on the poetry of Fedor Ivanovich Tiutchev appeared in *Russkoe slovo* (The Russian Word), with which Grigor'ev and Polonsky were then associated; the first part of Grigor'ev's essay "Vzgliad na russkuiu literaturu so

smerti Pushkina" (A Glance at Russian Literature since the Death of Pushkin) directly preceded the article on Tiutchev in the pages of the criticism section. Fet's essay is a valuable appreciation of the older poet, but its orientation toward beauty and its rejection of popular taste and practicality were out of step with the times. Soon thereafter, his translation of Shakespeare's *Julius Caesar* (performed 1599, published 1623) came out in *Biblioteka dlia chteniia,* then still edited by Druzhinin. That summer *Sovremennik* published one of Fet's most effective poems of this period, "Krichat perepela, treshchat korosteli . . ." (The quails cry, the corncrakes chatter . . .), in which he writes, "The youths go by me with a smile, and I hear their loud whisper: 'What is he looking for here . . . with his incomprehensible longing?'" The poem concludes, "My time will come . . . my rebirth . . . and, calm, reconciled, I shall become the eternal citizen of a new world."

This poem was prophetic. In the same issue of *Sovremennik* in which it was published, there appeared a pseudonymous review of Fet's translation of *Julius Caesar.* In addition to harsh, negative criticism, the review had a nasty personal tone, and it exploited certain unflattering information about Fet that was known only to an inner circle of his colleagues at *Sovremennik.* Using a quotation from Fet's article on Tiutchev as an epigraph to the review, the critic made even clearer that his attack was not against the poet's techniques of translation but, rather, his entire aesthetics. Fet broke with the journal after the review appeared–the effect intended by the critic and the editors who published the crude attack. Fet severed his ties with *Sovremennik* so quickly that he withdrew his "Dozhdlivoe leto" (The Rainy Summer), originally intended for an 1859 issue of the journal; the poem was not published until the next edition of his collected works (1863). Fet likewise ended his association with *Biblioteka dlia chteniia* in late 1859.

In the fall of 1859 he was still writing both original poetry ("Topol'" [The Poplar], "Zevs" [Zeus]) and translations of poems written in German by Georg Friedrich Daumer that were based on the work of the fourteenth-century Persian poet Hafis. He read some of this work at a meeting of the Obshchestvo liubitelei rossiiskoi slovesnosti (Society of Lovers of Russian Literature), of which he had become a member the preceding February. The Hafis translations were unenthusiastically received. Concluding that his career had come to a standstill, Fet began to plan a life removed from professional literary activity. During the first half of 1860 his poetry was still appearing in *Russkii vestnik* and *Russkoe slovo,* where most of his Hafis translations were published in the February issue. By mid 1860, however, the radical critics were taking over *Russkoe slovo.* Somewhat less explicably, Fet also ceased publishing even in *Russkii vestnik,* which was not radical at all. With one exception–the poignant short poem "Motylek mal'chiku" (A Moth to a Boy)–everything he published in 1860 had been written no later than the previous autumn.

In July 1860 Fet purchased Stepanovka, an undeveloped estate in the Mtsensk region familiar to him from boyhood, and he took up residence on the estate while fixing it up. In his memoirs Fet motivates the purchase by his need to earn a living outside literature, but his friends and relatives were unpleasantly surprised at his decision, since he had other possibilities. His marriage had brought him some modest means; his wife's family was prominent and well connected not only in the world of Russian culture but also commercially; and Fet himself was efficient and practical. His letters from the 1840s and many comments he published later show that he had no attachment to the country life of his childhood, and he had no illusions about the difficulty of taking over a country estate in the unstable situation of rural Russia in 1860, on the eve of the Great Reforms. Moreover, he had no experience running–much less developing–an estate, and he had selected his property badly and overpaid for it. Stepanovka was isolated and distant even from Novoselki, the Mtsensk family estate where Fet's close relatives still lived. Yet, its isolation might have been an attraction.

Fet did not stop writing poetry in 1860 entirely, although he wrote much less than when he had been surrounded by readers eager for his new work. The poems that he wrote that year are not generally inferior to his earlier work. With the exception of "Motylek mal'chiku," they did not, however, find ready outlets: one was published in 1865 in *Biblioteka dlia chteniia*, another in 1868 in *Russkii vestnik*, and the rest appeared only in Fet's collected works. In 1861 he apparently wrote no poetry, nor was any work published. He was intensively engaged in building up Stepanovka and had somewhat troubled relations with his friends. Yet, in February, in an article published in his journal *Vremia* (Time), Fyodor Dostoevsky offered a brilliant and sympathetic analysis of "Diana," one of Fet's best anthological poems (first published in 1850 and again in 1856).

Fet returned to the pages of *Russkii vestnik* in 1862, but not with poetry. Instead, the March issue featured the first of his agricultural essays, which delighted his enemies and disappointed his friends. More of his agricultural prose came out early in 1863, but he was at the same time making arrangements for the appearance of a new collection of his poetry, this one in two volumes. Volumes one and two were approved by the censor on 19 January and 21 February 1863, respectively. Fet maintained the same practice in this 1863 collection as he did in all his other books: he published a new book when, in his or his editors' opinion, he had accumulated enough previously uncollected material to warrant presenting it to the public.

The 1863 collection incorporates only a small number of works not previously published, but–in addition to works from the 1856 volume–it includes other works published in journals from 1856 onward. The second volume reprints virtually all the important translations that Fet had published since 1841 and constitutes the first such broad collection of his translations. Most significant, however, is what the book does not have: evidence that Fet in 1863 had any serious quarrel with Turgenev's approach to editing his poetry. The poems reprinted from the 1856 volume are nearly all kept exactly as they appear there.

The 1863 edition was poorly received. Copies remained unsold even at the end of Fet's life, and reviews mocked both his style and his social views. A famous review by Dmitrii Dmitrievich Minaev in *Russkoe slovo* suggested that one read the lines of a certain Fet poem in reverse order: the result, says Minaev, reads no worse than the lines in the order they were printed. This hostile response is only one example of many in an energetic and crude campaign against Fet during the 1860s. The hostility of the critics was only partly a reaction to his verse. At least as important were Fet's social and political views, expressed publicly in the agricultural essays. In 1863 he sought to publish a review criticizing Chernyshevsky's politically radical novel *Chto delat'?* (What Is to Be Done? 1863), which had just appeared, but his proposal was rejected. He did publish a translation of Horace's Epode XI from the *Iambi* (Epodes, 30 B.C.) Epode, but his translation of the *Ars Poetica* (Art of Poetry, 23–18 B.C. or 13–8 B.C.), also completed by 1863, was published only twenty years later in 1883.

In the mid 1860s Fet's literary and personal connections changed, as he suffered the loss of relatives, friends, and associates. In 1864 his former colleague Druzhinin died; his younger sister Nadezhda Afanas'evna Borisova was permanently hospitalized because of her mental illness; and, finally, in the autumn of that year Grigor'ev died. Around this time Fet began to be influenced increasingly by Tiutchev, and the two poets met privately on several occasions. Fet's friendship with Tolstoy also deepened, and the two writers visited one another, corresponded often, and exerted considerable influence on each other's views.

The pattern of Fet's publications continued as at the start of the decade: he wrote far fewer original poems than when he had enjoyed a more encouraging literary context, and his poems were sometimes published only with considerable delay. Thus, in 1864 he published only three poems, although he wrote more than a dozen. The published poems, moreover, were greeted without much enthusiasm even by those few colleagues, such as Turgenev, who paid attention to them. In 1865 Fet published nine poems, of which five appeared in *Russkii vestnik* and the rest in *Biblioteka dlia chteniia*. The only poetry by him to

Manuscript for "Alter Ego" (Another Self), one of Fet's best-known poems, written shortly after he moved to his new estate, Vorob'evka, and published in 1878 (from Fet, Vospominaniia, *1983)* appear in 1866 were four more poems published in *Russkii vestnik*. At this time he was also translating poetry by Friedrich Rückert and Eduard Mörike, although except for one Rückert translation published in 1866, most of these translations appeared in print only much later. He also continued to write prose, publishing essays on art (1866) and on the distinct roles of humanistic and scientific education in the growth of the human spirit (1867). In 1867 Fet published only one poem, again in *Russkii vestnik*. By now, he had nearly stopped not only publishing original poetry but also writing it. There is not one poem by him the composition of which can be dated to 1868, and only one short poem was published in each of the three years from 1867 to 1869. Two more essays appeared in *Literaturnaia biblioteka* (The Literary Library) in 1868, but their thematics were not literary. The dismal publication record of Fet's poetry in the 1860s continued into the following decade as well. More than a third of the poems that he wrote in the 1860s were unpublished at least until 1883, when his next collection appeared. About two-thirds of the poems that he wrote in the 1870s shared the same fate, and the total number of poems was smaller.

Nevertheless, the 1870s in some ways occasioned a turning point. As the decade opened Fet was continuing his futile attempt to establish himself as a prose writer: his story "Semeistvo Gol'ts" (The Hol'ts Family) appeared in 1870 in *Russkii vestnik* (The Russian Messenger). He wrote only two poems that year, both published in *Zaria* (The Dawn), and one of them, "Maiskaia noch'" (May Night), won Tolstoy's special approbation as a rare masterpiece and as a reminder of Fet's earlier poetic strength. In 1871 Fet's brother-in-law died, and he found himself the guardian of a niece and a nephew. That year his children's story, "Pervyi zaiats" (The First Rabbit), first appeared in print, although it had been written in 1864. In 1871 *Zaria* reprinted Fet's rural sketches of the 1860s, and it also published three new poems. The quantity of verse that Fet wrote and published remained small, however—at most, one or two poems appeared each year—throughout the first half of the decade. He continued to publish in *Zaria*, but beginning in 1873 he also returned to *Russkii vestnik*.

In December 1873 Tsar Alexander II granted Fet the right to take the name, and enjoy the status, of the Shenshin family. The decision was a source of great personal satisfaction to Fet (who continued to write under the name Fet), but his pleasure in the change and his profound gratitude toward the emperor became a source of mockery in literary circles. The change created friction even with friends, who were unsympathetic to the poet's need for this kind of social validation. His determination to change his name and social status was interpreted in the light of his extreme social conservatism, which he continued to manifest in political articles. In 1874 the long relationship between Fet and Turgenev broke down in recriminations, and Turgenev wrote in exasperation: "As Fet you had a name for yourself, as Shenshin all you have is a surname." Fet's old friend Polonsky had been involved in the quarrel, and after Turgenev broke off relations with Fet, Fet and Polonsky were also estranged until the 1880s–although Turgenev and Fet were, at least formally, reconciled by the end of August 1878. By the end of the 1870s Fet's friendship with Tolstoy also was cooling.

In the wake of the crisis of the mid 1870s, however, there followed a clear improvement in Fet's personal and professional situation. Through Tolstoy, in July 1877 Fet came to know the critic, essayist, and philosopher Nikolai Nikolaevich Strakhov, and Fet and Strakhov became warm friends. In autumn 1877 Fet sold the estate on which he had been living and moved to Vorob'evka, a much more attractive estate in the vicinity of Shchigry (Kursk). In this new environment he began to write more. He also continued to translate, and his work now encompassed both the German poets he had known since his early youth and other work of a different character. In late 1877 he wrote a translation of Goethe's "Grenzen der Menschheit" (The Limits of Mankind, 1789) and also started to translate the writings of the philosopher Immanuel Kant. The Goethe translation appeared in 1878, and that same year Fet turned again to Schiller, translating Schiller's *Die Götter Griechenlandes* (The Gods of Greece, 1788). Fet soon gave up his Kant project (a Russian translation already existed), but in January 1879 he undertook his translation of Schopenhauer's great work, *Die Welt als Wille und Vorstellung* (The World as Will and Representation, 1819).

Most important, at Vorob'evka, Fet once again was writing original Russian verse. He wrote several of his best-known later works in the late 1870s, and they were published in journals relatively quickly. Thus, for example, "Alter ego" ("Kak lileia gliaditsia v nagornyi ruchei . . ." [As the lily glances into the mountain stream . . .]) and the well-known verse epistle to his friend Aleksandra L'vovna ("Dalekii drug! Poimi moi rydan'ia . . ." [Distant friend! Comprehend my weeping . . .]) both appeared in 1879, relatively soon after he wrote them. The epistle to Aleksandra L'vovna is important not only for its artistic worth but also because, like the Schiller translation, it shows Fet revisiting in his late work the life experiences and artistic interests of his younger days. Such reminiscences increase in frequency in his work in the 1880s. In general, Fet in 1879 published more poems (seven) than at any time since his 1863 collection had come out, and those published represented only about half of what he wrote that year. His poetry, moreover, was now richly connected not only with reminiscences of earlier work but also with his current interest in philosophy. In December 1879 he wrote the poem "Ia

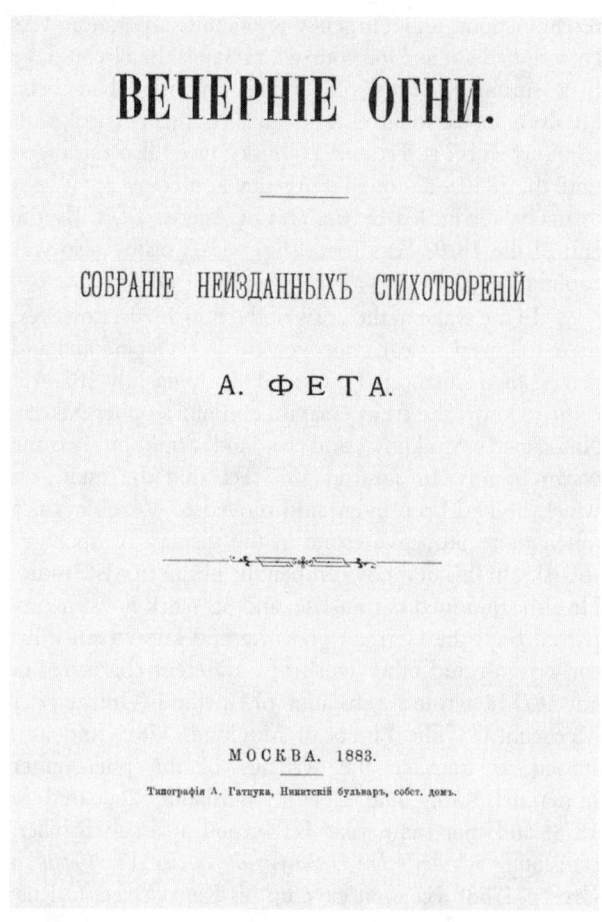

ВЕЧЕРНІЕ ОГНИ.

СОБРАНІЕ НЕИЗДАННЫХЪ СТИХОТВОРЕНІЙ

А. ФЕТА.

МОСКВА. 1883.

Типографія А. Гатцука, Никитскій бульваръ, собст. домъ.

Title page for the first edition of Fet's Vechernie ogni
*(Evening Lights), the last great poetic project of his
life (Kilgour Collection of Russian Literature,
Harvard University Library)*

rad, kogda s zemnogo lona . . ." (I am glad when from the bosom of the earth . . . , published 1880), the imagery of which derives from the Schopenhauer text that he was then translating. This translation itself was completed in 1880 and published in 1881. Fet's best-known short story, "Kaktus" (The Cactus), which also incorporates Schopenhauerian elements, appeared in *Russkii vestnik* in November 1881. He also produced important translations of German poetry around this same time: in December the censor approved Fet's translation of part 1 of Goethe's *Faust* (1808), and Fet then proceeded to translate part 2 (1832) as well. In 1881 he purchased a home in Moscow, and from then on he usually wintered there.

In the early 1880s Fet's name began to be mentioned again, but on the whole he seems to have been thought of as someone from a former age. In his "Skvernaia istoriia" (A Nasty Story, 1882) the young Anton Pavlovich Chekhov effectively orients Fet in a stereotypical romantic setting. The association of the poet with the world of the past was strengthened by his activities, which

then included his publication of conservative political prose such as "Nashi korni" (Our Roots, 1882). At the same time, however, his artistic powers were slowly being renewed. In the years 1880 through 1882 he began writing more new poems and was reviewing poetry that he had written in the 1860s and 1870s but had never published. With the help of new editors, he was organizing his return to the public arena.

The year 1883 marked both the culmination of much of Fet's earlier work and, at the same time, the beginning of his last and greatest period of creative activity. His lifelong devotion to Goethe was marked by the publication that year of his translation of *Faust,* now including part 2 (a second, corrected edition appeared in 1889). Fet afterward published other translations from German, but the greater part of his late translations were from Latin. In 1883 he published a volume containing his complete annotated Horace translations. In this book Fet reprints his translations of the *Carmina* (Odes, 23–13 B.C.), the *Carmen saeculare* (Secular Hymn, 17 B.C.), and the Epode XI, and he adds the remaining epodes, the satires, and the epistles, including the *Ars Poetica.* This monumental work was rewarded in 1884 with the Pushkin Prize, and it was followed nearly every year afterward by new books of Latin translations. Translations–from German, Latin, and French–were also included in 1883 in the first of the four volumes of poetry that he published under the common title *Vechernie ogni* (Evening Lights).

The character of each of the four volumes of *Vechernie ogni* is distinct. The first volume is shaped partly by its inclusion of a backlog of poems that had not been published in any previous collection and, in many cases, had never been published at all. The title of the collection corresponds to the changed persona that Fet presents to his readers. Whereas his early work is remembered for its delight in sensual pleasure, this book adopts the perspective of old age (Fet was sixty-two when the volume appeared). As always he relied greatly on editors for decisions about what should be published and how it should be arranged. The 1883 volume had two principal editors. The first was Strakhov, who had become a close friend and adviser to Fet; until his death Strakhov in 1896 continued to edit Fet's work. The other editor was the poet and philosopher Vladimir Sergeevich Solov'ev. Fet dedicated a copy of the 1883 *Vechernie ogni* to Solov'ev and characterized him as "the architect" of the book. For this reason, the arrangement of the poems in it is usually credited to Solov'ev; in fact, it is the volume of Fet's poetry that is architectonically best formed. Of all the published versions of *Vechernie ogni,* the first was the longest, and it was probably the only one long enough to warrant the arrangement of the poems in an elaborate structure.

Departing in structure from Fet's earlier books–although it retains many of the rubrics found as early as the 1850 collection—the 1883 volume starts with a single poem that serves as a preface, "Okna v reshetkakh, i sumrachny litsa . . ." (The windows are barred and the faces are gloomy . . .). The rest of the poems are divided among nine rubrics, the first five of which are thematically motivated, such as "More" (The Sea) and "Vesna" (Spring). The other four rubrics are miscellanies: for example, "Raznye stikhotvoreniia" (Various Poems) and "Dopolnenie" (Supplement). Translations occupy one such section, as do verse epistles, and the inclusion of these sections serves not only to acquaint readers with specific verses but also to present specific personae of the poet, who is renowned for his Goethe translations and can write friendly epistles to Tiutchev, Tolstoy, and Aleksei Konstantinovich Tolstoy.

The five groups of poems at the beginning of the book are arranged so that the pensive mood of the opening group, "Elegii i dumy" (Elegies and Thoughts), yields to the poetic ecstasy of the fifth group, "Melodii" (Melodies). The three groups in between—"More," "Snega" (Snows), and "Vesna"—portray the poet as situated in the external world. In each group the male poet-figure is joined by a female, who is more closely associated than he with intuition and nature. The central group, "Snega," is an interlude of "deathliness," which gives way to the reinvigoration of the natural world (hence "Vesna") and, finally, to the joyous mood of the poet. The whole structure thus resembles a ring, in which the interior world of the poet's thoughts is the focus of the exterior groups, and the exterior world appears within his perceptions. The themes of renewal and final awakening to new life are characteristic of Fet's individual poems. The grouping is of course on a larger scale, but its development is nonetheless similar. The "self-similarity" of poem and grouping is quite different from the more open, linear structure of, notably, the 1850 collection.

The second volume of *Vechernie ogni* was prepared immediately after the first; approved by the censor in October 1884, it was published in 1885. As might be expected, this second volume is much smaller (nearly all the poems in it were written in 1883 or 1884), and the structure is less elaborate than that found in the first volume of the series. In some respects, however, the 1885 volume is even more remarkable than the earlier book, because it represents Fet's creative energies during the time immediately preceding its publication. It includes such masterpieces as "Lastochki" (Swallows), "Babochka" (Butterfly), "Govorili v drevnem Rime . . ." (They used to say in ancient Rome . . .), and "Nyne pervyi my slyshali grom . . ." (Today we heard the first thunder . . .). Here, too, appears Fet's best-known long poem, "Student" (The Student), which is of considerable autobiographical interest, since it indubitably refers to the poet's own student

days and to events surrounding both his earliest work and his relationship with Grigor'ev.

In late 1886 Grand Duke Konstantin Konstantinovich Romanov, using the pseudonym K.R., published his first book of poetry, distributed only privately, however, by the author. In December he sent a copy to Fet, thus initiating a correspondence that continued until Fet's death. In his letters Fet attempts to guide the younger poet, and in so doing he sometimes talks about his own poetics. The correspondence became cordial (in 1887, the correspondents met for the first time and were mutually entranced), and the grand duke was helpful to Fet personally, involving himself in Fet's quest for recognition at court. The period after the appearance of the 1885 edition of *Vechernie ogni* was generally productive and rewarding. Besides continuing to write original poetry, Fet was active in translating more Latin authors. In addition to his warm correspondence with the grand duke, he enjoyed the company of other literary figures much younger than he. He also reconciled with Polonsky, with whom he enjoyed an intensive correspondence in his later years. Fet's health was declining, but his work was noted in the press; he was, if not popular, at least respected by those whose opinion he esteemed, and he saw that an appreciative younger generation would value his work after his death.

Fet expected the third volume of *Vechernie ogni* to be his last. Each of the preceding two volumes had been prefaced with a verse text, but the third volume—and after it the fourth—had forewords in prose. In the relatively long foreword to the third volume Fet speaks about his own aesthetics and a little about the history of his creative work. Characterizing poetry as a refuge from daily life, he describes his sense of injury at the hands of politically motivated critics, whose unfavorable reviews he could have understood, he says, if his poetry in any way had been attacking current trends, but it was not. Rather, it was rejected because of the purity of its vocation. He asserts that, despite what has been written about him, he has shared the sorrows of his country and commiserated with its people. Yet, poetry must bring people joy, and the poet must dwell in a different world, to which misery is not given access. How, Fet asks, is the poet to bring release from misery if he carries misery with him? Mentioning in addition the importance of his editors' roles in each of his books, he explains that Grigor'ev was responsible for the organization of the 1850 volume and that Turgenev had not only been the principal editor of the 1856 collection but had also written its preface. He reveals that this current volume of *Vechernie ogni* includes certain poems originally published in the 1850 collection, although the long poem "Solovei i roza" appears in a revised version, much shorter than the original. The poems from the 1850 volume are all texts that Turgenev had excluded from the collection of 1856, and Fet says that his later editors urged him to reprint these poems in *Vechernie ogni*.

In the 1888 edition, unlike the 1971 scholarly edition that includes it, the poems reprinted from the 1850 collection are actually demarcated in the table of contents with a distinct heading: "From the edition of 1850." This section is followed by memorial poems written in the 1860s in honor of the then recently deceased Druzhinin and Botkin. The group of poems from the 1850 edition is, moreover, preceded by two recent translations from Goethe. In the original publication Goethe's name does not appear either in the table of contents or together with the translations, which actually are not marked as translations. This choice is consonant with Fet's practice in his 1850 volume, in which by no means all of his translations were noted as such; his treatment of the translations in the 1888 publication is, therefore, another retrospective feature of the volume.

The first volume of *Vechernie ogni* embodied poems written much earlier, but the reason for their inclusion had been Fet's inability to produce a collection of his work in the meantime. The 1888 volume, by contrast, was the first one in which his decision to include early work clearly involves a reevaluation of earlier editors' decisions. The book reflects a more general habit of the poet in his final years to revisit his earliest poems and revise some of them significantly. Although Fet's vocabulary, syntax, and formal usage had changed considerably since his earlier collections, the late poetry also shows a partial return to the practices of his youth, even in new poems. The similarities, however, would not necessarily have been noticed by contemporary readers, because Fet's early work was no longer well known, and even for modern readers the expressive power and technical mastery exhibited in his late poems so greatly exceeds those of his early ones that the similarities are not always apparent. In addition, the later poems are truly different in important ways; for example, the later Fet often alludes to Tiutchev's later poetry, but Fet's early poetry is untouched by Tiutchev's work. More generally, his later persona as a poet of old age tended to connect his work with other poets' later writings; for instance, although Goethe was always important for Fet's poetry, the early Fet tended to evoke early Goethe, and the later Fet, later Goethe.

Fet's 1888 volume thus differs markedly from either of its predecessors in *Vechernie ogni*, and it is in some respects the purest representative of Fet's work in his last years. The volume features many well-known small masterpieces. Among them should be mentioned at least the following: "Kak beden nash iazyk!–Khochu i ne mogu . . ." (How impoverished our language!–I want, and I cannot . . .), "Chto za zvuk v polumrake vechernem? Bog vest' . . ." (What is that sound in the evening dusk? God knows . . .), "Dul sever. Plakala trava . . ." (The north was blowing. The grass cried . . .), "Kak bogat ia v bezumnykh stikhakh . . ." (How rich am I in senseless verses . . .), "Pamiati N. Ia. Danilevskogo" (In Memory of N. Ia. Danilevsky), "Svetil nam den', budia ogon' v krovi . . ." (The day shone, rousing fire in the blood . . .), "Ia tebe nichego ne skazhu . . ." (I'll tell you nothing . . .), "Kogda chitala ty muchitel'nye stroki . . ." (When you read the torturous lines . . .), "Ty vsia v ogniakh. Tvoikh zarnits . . ." (You are all in flames. Of your lightning flashes . . .), and "Moego tot bezumstva zhelal, kto smezhal . . ." (He wished for my madness who closed . . .).

The achievement represented in the 1888 collection was a culmination of Fet's work as an original poet and comparable to his 1883 achievement as a translator. Just as he brought to a close his life's work as a translator of Horace by publishing Horace's complete texts, and just as he had concluded his lifelong work as a Goethe translator by publishing the second part of *Faust*, so now he had published a book of original poems in which he had taken a look back at his entire production of original Russian verse. Correspondingly, just as one year after publishing the Horace translation Fet was awarded the Pushkin Prize, so now he promoted recognition for himself on the eve of his golden jubilee–fifty years of activity as a poet. Although his debut had been in 1840, not 1839, he was insistent on arranging his own jubilee early in 1889. In connection with the jubilee, moreover, he also sought for himself some token of recognition from the court, and in February 1889 he was made a court chamberlain. The honor delighted him, but it was inappropriate to the poet's age, and he was severely criticized by even his close friends for seeking it.

Fet continued to organize and memorialize in yet another way: he wrote a two-volume memoir more than eight hundred pages long. Often considered self-serving, *Moi vospominaniia. 1848–1889* (1890) is, in important ways, also unreliable. Although he makes occasional mention of earlier events, Fet really begins his narrative only in the 1850s, at the apogee of his early professional career, with his acquaintance with Turgenev. This period in Fet's personal life is also relatively glamorous, since he was serving as an officer in a respectable royal guards unit near the capital. The memoir thus achieves the poet's goal of offering his public a kind of final summation of his accomplishments, which are of some independent interest even today. He revisits his travels abroad, his experience of country living, and his family's psychiatric misfortunes, as well as all the ups and downs of his professional life and relationships with colleagues. The memoir also incorporates extracts from Fet's rich correspondence, which his wife had organized from the time of their marriage onward, and some of these letters are otherwise unknown.

*Fet with Iakov Petrovich Polonsky (left) and Nikolai Nikolaevich
Strakhov (center) at Vorob'evka in 1890*

The fourth and final volume of *Vechernie ogni,* published in 1891, is considered Fet's last public farewell, although he continued even afterward to publish new original poems and new translations. In this last collection to appear during his lifetime, however, the poet emphasizes as never before both his gratitude for the friendships that he has enjoyed and his awareness that his life and work are ending. Fet's foreword to the volume also affirms that he continued to be cognizant of the limited appeal of his poetry, which never became universally popular. Among the fine poems that appear in the 1891 edition of *Vechernie ogni* are "Odnim tolchkom sognat' lad'iu zhivuiu . . ." (To send off the living vessel with a single shove . . .), "Ustalo vse krugom, ustal i tsvet nebes . . ." (Everything around has tired, tired is even the color of the heavens . . .), "Na kacheliakh" (On the Swing), "Polurazrushennyi, poluzhilets mogily . . ." (Half fallen apart, halfway to the grave . . .), "Ugasshim zvezdam" (To the Extinguished Stars), "Vo sne" (In a Dream), "Byla pora i led potoka . . ." (There was a time, even the ice flow . . .), "V polunochnoi tishi bessonitsy moe . . ." (In the midnight quiet of my insomnia . . .), "Roiami podnialis' krylatye mechty . . ." (The winged dreams have risen up in swarms . . .), "Ot ognei, ot tolpy besposhchadnoi . . ."

(From the lights, from the merciless crowd . . .), and "Raketa" (The Rocket). Fet's perennial themes of love and nature remain, and although the poet now looks back ("My soul burned in vain," he writes in "Raketa"), he continues to aspire to what is presently beyond reach as in "Roiami podnialis' krylatye mechty . . . : "Tomorrow at dawn the wings will buzz again, to rush into what is unseen, unknown, where overnight it has blossomed, the first aroma, to get there and disappear in luxurious delight."

As was characteristic of the older Fet, the 1891 volume of his poetry represented only a relatively modest part of his publishing activities that year. Besides publishing a translation of Martial's *Epigrammaton Libri* (Books of Epigrams, A.D. 86–102) , he also continued to write prose essays—now on famine and the means of food production available to the peasantry. At the same time, he was writing privately as early as January 1891 about how bored he was with life: had he the strength, he wrote to Strakhov, he would travel to Japan so as to have at least some new experience in his life. In the following year Fet's generally gloomy frame of mind intensified. He continued to translate from Latin, work on his memoirs, plan future publications, and even write new poems and revise old ones. His health, however, was poor, and when, in early

October in Moscow, he became ill after overexposure to the cold, he apparently could not—nor perhaps did he hope to—recover.

Fet languished for weeks, unable to walk without assistance, his breathing so painful that he could not even lie down to sleep. His secretary Ekaterina Vladimirovna Kudriavtseva witnessed his death and described it in the document "O smerti A. A. Feta" (On the Death of A. A. Fet) published in the 1994 volume *Rossiiskii arkhiv: Istoriia otechestva v svidetel'stvakh i dokumentakh XVIII–XX* (Russian Archive: The History of the Fatherland in Testimonies and Documents from the Eighteenth to the Twentieth Centuries). According to her, in his last days Fet continued to translate Ovid and consult with visitors about his work, and he went on, as he had earlier, listening to her practice reading in French (in particular Gustave Flaubert's novel, *Madame Bovary,* published 1857). His death was so clearly imminent, however, that his wife was several times urged to send for a priest. This Mariia Petrovna declined to do: Fet was irreligious and even in the best of times irascible, and she feared a priest's arrival would set off a fatal scene.

On 21 November 1892 Fet arranged to be left alone briefly in his house with Kudriavtseva and two servants. He had Kudriavtseva help him to his study and, holding a metal knife used for opening letters, he began dictating a farewell note. The secretary belatedly realized that Fet intended to kill himself. There followed a struggle over the knife (Kudriavtseva was injured) and an exhausting flight through the rooms of the house that ended in the poet's collapse onto a chair and his final loss of consciousness. He was buried in the crypt of a new church on Shenshin family property in the village of Kleimenovo, in the Mtsensk district of Orlov guberniia. His wife was buried in the same church in 1894. Afanasii Neofitovich and the poet's mother had been buried in an older church nearby.

At his death Fet left behind a considerable quantity of work that either had not been published or was intended for republication in future collections. The Ovid translation on which he had been working came out in 1893, as did his last autobiographical memoir, *Rannie gody moei zhizni* (The Early Years of My Life). His widow and his friends, including most notably the grand duke and Strakhov, promoted the publication of his collected poetry. Fet's planned fifth volume of *Vechernie ogni* was reconstructed and published only in 1971. Yet, the 1894 collection of his work, edited by both the grand duke and Strakhov, was the first of a succession of collections that, as late as 1959, continued to offer previously unknown poems to readers as well as interpret in various ways the plan that Fet had left for organizing a final collection of poems written in the 1840s onward.

Although he was always a poet favored more by literary elites than by any larger public, Fet nonetheless was widely appreciated as a poet of song, and his poems were set to music throughout his career. Immediately upon his death there was a great increase in the production of songs using words by Fet, and the boom continued into the twentieth century. By 1917 some two hundred of his more than eight hundred original short poems had been set to music, one or two before they were published in any other form, and many of the poems have been set to music several times.

Afanasii Afanas'evich Fet was deeply appreciated, even revered, by succeeding generations of poets—in particular the Russian symbolists—and his work is of special importance in relation to the poetry of Blok. Others have pointed to the significance of Fet's verse for an understanding of the poetics of Boris Pasternak. Clearly imbued by Romantic and immediately post-Romantic aesthetics, Fet's poetry is sometimes viewed as a bridge spanning the age of Realism and connecting the Golden Age of Aleksandr Sergeevich Pushkin with the "Silver Age" of Blok. Fet's work also constitutes the best representative in Russian literature of "art for art's sake." Contemporary critics who cite Fet's close and fruitful interaction with Tolstoy have connected his poetry with the age of prose as well as with impressionism and even with the aesthetics of cinematography. A variety of readers continue to value his poetry and its contribution to the Russian literary tradition. Fet is generally agreed to be one of the great poets of his century, and this high status is unlikely ever to suffer revision.

Letters:

Iu. A. Nikol'sky, "Istoriia odnoi druzhby. Fet i Polonskii," *Russkaia mysl'* (1917): 82–127;

Georgy Petrovich Blok, "Fet i Brzheskaia," *Nachala. Zhurnal istorii literatury i istorii obshchestvennosti,* 2 (1922): 106–123;

Blok, "Fet v perepiske s I. P. Borisovym," edited by E. Pokrovskaia, *Literaturnaia mysl',* 1 (1922); 1 (1923);

Blok, *Rozhdenie poeta: Povest' o molodosti Feta: po neopublikovannym materialam* (Leningrad: Vremiia, 1924);

"Perepiska Tolstogo s A. A. Fetom," edited by N. Pokrovskaia, *Literaturnoe nasledstvo,* 37–38 (1939): 208–230;

"Pis'ma A. A. Feta k A. V. Zhirkevichu," edited by I. A. Pokrovskaia, *Russkaia literatura,* 3 (1971): 94–101;

Lev Tolstoy, *Perepiska s russkimi pisateliami,* 2 volumes, compiled by Susanna Abramovna Rozanova (Moscow: Khudozhestvennaia literatura, 1978);

"Pis'ma," edited by Aleksandr Evgen'evich Tarkhov, in *Sochineniia v dvukh tomakh,* volume 2 (Moscow: Khudozhestvennaia literatura, 1982), pp. 185–362;

Ivan Sergeevich Turgenev, *Perepiska I. S. Turgeneva,* 2 volumes (Moscow: Khudozhestvennaia literatura, 1986);

Fet, *Stikhotvoreniia. Proza. Pis'ma* (Moscow: Sovetskaia Rossiia, 1988), pp. 327–417;

"Ne stydilsia ia za sebia . . . ," edited by N. P. Generalova and A. Auer, *Literaturnaia Rossiia,* 49 (4 December 1992): 10;

"Pis'ma A. A. Feta k F. E. Korshu," edited by G. A. Kosmolinskaia, in *Iz Fonda redkikh knig i rukopisei Nauchnoi biblioteki Moskovskogo universiteta,* edited by Sigurd Ottovich Shmidt (Moscow: Izdatel'stvo Moskovskogo Universiteta, 1993), pp. 204–228;

"Perepiska A. A. Feta s A. Ia. Polonskim," edited by G. L. Medyntseva, in *Novye materialy po istorii russkoi literatury: Sbornik nauchnykh trudov,* edited by N. V. Shakhalova (Moscow: Gosudarstvennyi literaturnyi muzei, 1994), pp. 49–91;

"'Navstrechu serdtsem k vam lechu'. Istoriia zhenit'by A. A. Feta po arkhivnym dokumentam," edited by G. D. Aslanova, *Novyi mir,* 5 (1997): 197–210;

K. R. (Grand Duke Konstantin Konstantinovich Romanov), *Izbrannaia perepiska,* compiled by Liudmila Ivanovna Kuz'mina (St. Petersburg: D. Bulanin, 1999), pp. 239–392.

Bibliographies:

Georgii Konstantinovich Ivanov, "Fet, Afanasii Afanas'evich (1820–1892)," in his *Russkaia poeziia v otechestvennoi muzyke (do 1917 goda): Spravochnik,* volume 1 (Moscow: Muzyka, 1966), pp. 363–373;

Boris Iakovlevich Bukhshtab, "Sud'ba literaturnogo nasledstva A. A. Feta. Obzor," in his *Fet i drugie: Izbrannye raboty* (St. Petersburg: Akademicheskii proekt, 2000), pp. 150–200;

Emily Klenin, "Sources," in her *The Poetics of Afanasy Fet* (Köln: Böhlau, 2002), pp. 359–385.

Biographies:

Boris Iakovlevich Bukhshtab, *A. A. Fet: Ocherk zhizni i tvorchestva* (Leningrad: Nauka, 1974);

Lydia M. Lotman, *Afanasy Fet* (Boston: Twayne, 1976);

Georgy Petrovich Blok, ed., "Letopis' zhizni A. A. Feta. Publikatsiia B. Ia. Bukhshtaba," in *A. A. Fet: Traditsii i problemy izucheniia: Sbornik nauchnykh trudov,* edited by Nikolai Nikolaevich Skatov (Kursk: Kurskii gosudarstvennyi pedagogicheskii instit, 1985), pp. 129–182.

References:

G. D. Aslanova, ed., "O smerti A. A. Feta," in *Rossiiskii arkhiv: Istoriia otechestva v svidetel'stvakh i dokumentakh*

XVIII–XX (Moscow: Studiia TRITE, 1994), pp. 240–248;

Vasily Botkin, "A. A. Fet," translated by George Genereux, *Russian Literature Triquarterly,* 17 (1982): 23–63;

Rainer Goldt, "Bürde und Bindung. Afanasij Fet als Mittler und Kritiker deutscher Kultur," in *Russisches Denken im europäischen Dialog,* edited by Maria Deppermann (Innsbruck & Wien: Studien, 1998), pp. 72–120;

A. A. Grigor'ev, "Stikhotvoreniia A. Feta," *Otechestvennye zapiski,* 68, no. 5 (February 1850): 49–72;

Richard F. Gustafson, *The Imagination of Spring: The Poetry of Afanasy Fet* (New Haven: Yale University Press, 1966);

Emily Klenin, *The Poetics of Afanasy Fet* (Köln: Böhlau, 2002);

"O smerti A. A. Feta," in *Rossiiskii arkhiv: Istoriia obshchestva v svidetel'skvakh i dokumentakh* XVII–XX (Moscow: Studiia TRITE, 1994);

Boris Sadovskoi, *Ledokhod: Stat'i i zametki* (Petrograd, 1916);

Veronika Shenshina, *A. A. Fet-Shenshin. Poeticheskoe mirosozertsanie* (Moscow: Vek, 1998);

Rimvydas Silbajoris, "Dynamic Elements in the Lyrics of Fet," *Slavic Review,* 26 (1967): 217–226.

Papers:

Afanasii Afanas'evich Fet's personal archive was collected and organized by his wife Mariia Petrovna Botkina Fet-Shenshin, and few materials from before his marriage are extant. The most extensive Fet archives are housed in the Manuscript Division of the Institute of Russian Literature (IRLI, Pushkin House) in St. Petersburg and in the Russian State Library (RGB, formerly the Lenin Library) in Moscow. Fet saved no autographs of his work before 1854. Of Fet's work from 1854 onward, only two notebooks of autographic works are extant; these can be found in IRLI (fonds 14166 and 14167). RGB also has a book of notes by Fet (fond 315). An important source for information about the preparation of Fet's 1856 collection is the "Ostroukhov copy" (of the 1850 collection), archived at the Tret'iakov Gallery in Moscow. The location of some important papers is unknown, and some used by scholars in the early twentieth century have since been lost. Although a full listing of the papers is therefore impossible, those that were known in 1935 are described in Boris Iakovlevich Bukhshtab's authoritative (but now dated) bibliographic survey "Sud'ba literaturnogo nasledstva A. A. Feta. Obzor." Extensive references to archival sources are also provided in the collections and editions of Fet's works of 1937, 1959, 1971, and 1986.

Konstantin Mikhailovich Fofanov

(18 May 1862 – 17 May 1911)

Ludmila Shleyfer Lavine

Pennsylvania State University

BOOKS: *Stikhotvoreniia* (St. Petersburg: G. Goppe, 1887)—includes "Teni A. S. Pushkina";

Stikhotvoreniia (St. Petersburg: A. S. Suvorin, 1889);

Teni i tainy. Stikhotvoreniia (St. Petersburg: M. V. Popov, 1892);

Baron Klaks. Rasskaz v stikhakh (Moscow, 1892);

Stikhotvoreniia, 5 parts (St. Petersburg: A. S. Suvorin, 1896)—comprises part 1, *Malen'kie poemy;* part 2, *Etiudy v rifmakh;* part 3, *Snegurka;* part 4, *Maiskii shum;* and part 5, *Monologi;*

Illiuzii. Stikhotvoreniia (St. Petersburg: A. S. Suvorin, 1900);

Neobyknovennyi roman. (Povest' v oktavakh) (St. Petersburg: I. Fleitman, 1910);

Posle Golgofy. (Misteriia–poemy) (St. Petersburg: I. Fleitman, 1910);

Stikhotvoreniia, edited and with an introduction by M. Kleman (Leningrad: Sovetskii pisatel', 1939) [Biblioteka poeta, malaia seriia];

Stikhotvoreniia i poemy, edited by V. V. Smirensky, with an introduction by Galina Mikhailovna Tsurikova (Leningrad: Sovetskii pisatel', 1962).

Collections: *Izbrannye proizvedeniia* (Moscow: Dobroe utro, 1918);

Pod muzyku osennego dozhdia. Stikhotvoreniia i poemy, Mir poezii (Moscow: Letopis', 2000).

OTHER: [Poems], in *Poety 1880–1890-x godov,* with an introduction by G. A. Bialyi (Moscow & Leningrad, 1964).

SELECTED PERIODICAL PUBLICATIONS– UNCOLLECTED:
"Zlopoluchnaia. Iz zapisok Ogulina," *Vek,* 5 (1882);

"Chasy ukrali," *Vek,* 3 (1883);

"Pervye tsvety," *Russkoe bogatstvo,* 4 (1888);

"Pesni uznika," *Novaia illiustratsiia,* 2 (1907);

[Poems], in "Prints i nishchii (Iz vospominanii o K. M. Fofanove)," by A. Izmailov, *Istoricheskii vestik,* 144 (1916): 463, 464, 467, 471, 472;

"O golode," *Vestnik literatury,* 8 (1921);

Konstantin Mikhailovich Fofanov

"Lazurnym glazam," *Krasnaia gazeta,* 127 (1 June 1926);

"Nynche mesiats zazhegsia tak iasno," *Literaturnaia gazeta,* 60 (29 October 1935);

"Opiat' razognana svoboda," *Knizhnye novosti,* 19 (1936);

"Ia–ubezhdennyi demokrat," *Knizhnye novosti,* 11 (1937);

"Mironositsy," in "K istorii neizvestnogo stikhotvoreniia K. M. Fofanova," by I. Parkhomenko, *Moskovskii zhurnal,* 4 (1995).

Konstantin Fofanov wrote during one of the bleakest periods in Russian poetry, when poetic figures were largely eclipsed by giants of Russian prose such as Leo Tolstoy and Anton Pavlovich Chekhov. Although Fofanov's name fell into relative obscurity in subsequent years, an entire generation of late-nineteenth-century Russian poets was once referred to as belonging to the "Fofanov period." Fofanov was as prolific as some of the most active Russian poets. His total output exceeds two thousand works, consisting of lyric and narrative poetry as well as dramatic scenes and plays in verse. While his poetry was identified with different, often opposing, literary camps, he frequently wrote in the spirit of the civic poetry of the 1860s and 1870s. The majority of his verse, however, belongs to the school of "pure art," which arose in the 1880s and 1890s as a reaction to calls for social consciousness and utilitarianism in literature. During Fofanov's lifetime his work was attributed to two other, equally divergent, literary camps as well: the more mature tradition of realism and the emerging trend of modernism. While some critics accused Fofanov of drowning in Chekhovian minutiae, writer and religious philosopher Dmitrii Sergeevich Merezhkovsky, in his symbolist manifesto *O prichinakh upadka i o novykh techeniiakh sovremennoi russkoi literatury* (On the Reasons for the Decline of, and on New Trends in, Contemporary Russian Literature, 1893), hailed the poet as the closest precursor to modernism in Russia. Fofanov's subject matter was indeed appealing to both realists and modernists. His verse is characterized by a constant tension between the tedious details of life and a glorious, self-created world of dreams.

Fofanov's pedigree was more typical of a *raznochinets* (nonnoble intellectual) or a "democratic" poet for that period in Russia than of a practitioner of "pure poetry." He was born Konstantin Mikhailovich Fofanov on 18 May 1862 on Vasil'evskii ostrov (Vasil'ev Island), a lower-class section of St. Petersburg. Fofanov's father, Mikhail Petrovich Fofanov, was a merchant and an Old Believer who had dreamed in his youth of becoming a monk. Mikhail Petrovich owned a small house and forest in St. Petersburg and sold wood to support his family of twelve. When Fofanov was about ten years old, his father engaged in a risky business venture, went bankrupt, slipped into nostalgia for a spiritual way of life, and began to drink heavily. Extremely little is known about Fofanov's mother, Ekaterina Afanas'evna (Briukhanova) Fofanova, except that her family came from the Iaroslavl' district.

Fofanov was largely self-educated. Although he read a great deal, his studies were random and unsystematic. He was passionately interested in the lives of poets, who seemed to him supernatural beings. Aleksandr Sergeevich Pushkin was at the center of the young Fofanov's fascination with poets' biographies, and Pushkin's influence remained constant throughout Fofanov's life. The poem "Teni A. S. Pushkina" (The Shadows of A. S. Pushkin, 1887) is a particularly compelling tribute to his idol. Echoes from Pushkin's poetry, especially from the lyric "Ia pomniu chudnoe mgnoven'e . . ." (I recall a wondrous moment . . . , 1825), linger in Fofanov's poem in an intentionally half-conscious and illusive fashion. Fofanov's speaker attempts to

reconstruct from childhood memories the fateful moment of his own encounter with Pushkin himself. Fofanov's narrative poetry is often openly imitative of Pushkin's verse. At the age of fourteen Fofanov became influenced by Nikolai Alekseevich Nekrasov, a poet of the realist school in the 1850s through the 1870s, from whom Fofanov frequently borrowed folkloric meters and themes for his own verse. Nekrasov's notion of the poet as a singer of justice—mediated by Semen Iakovlevich Nadson, another poet close to Fofanov's heart, who came from the generation of writers that followed Nekrasov—played an important role in Fofanov's early development.

Between the ages of sixteen and eighteen Fofanov undertook a serious study of the Bible. He made his literary debut with a poem based on an episode from the Old Testament. "Iz bibleiskikh motivov" (From Biblical Motifs) appeared in 1881 in the journal *Russkii evrei* (The Russian Jew) under the pseudonym "Komifo" (composed of the first syllables of his first name, patronymic, and last name). The poem is a transparent political allegory on the impending doom of the Russian monarchy. Its Populist message is encoded in Fofanov's choice of the third chapter of Deuteronomy as his subject matter—a chapter in which God delivers his people to the Promised Land and annihilates the kings who do not allow the procession of Moses to pass through. The last lines of each stanza in Fofanov's poem read, respectively, "I brought justice," "I brought truth," and "I brought freedom." The use of biblical motifs as commentary on the current social condition in Russia was widespread among poets of the 1860s and 1870s, the height of *narodnichestvo* (Populism). As a result, the reading public became trained in detecting political unrest and revolutionary fervor in religious symbols. Hence, Fofanov's announcement to the world came in the language of civic poetry and in a manner that did not particularly distinguish him from literary vogues of the previous generation.

In the spring of 1881 Fofanov met his future wife, Lidiia Konstantinovna Tupylova, who was a fourteen-year-old schoolgirl at the time. Her family was vehemently against her friendship with the young man whose profession was less than reliable. She was forced to quit school that academic year to help the family weather a difficult financial situation. After her mother insisted that she reject the poet's marriage proposal, Lidiia Konstantinovna moved to Kronstadt (twenty kilometers west of St. Petersburg), where she worked as a teacher and planned to become a nun.

Fofanov continued to publish politically minded poetry in the mode of Nekrasov and Nadson, although his production of such verse diminished toward the end of the 1880s. In 1887 Fofanov wrote a versified fairy tale, "Ocharovannyi prints" (An Enchanted Prince), about a prince who rejects the throne after traveling beyond the walls of his castle and encountering the poverty-stricken

Fofanov in an 1888 portrait by Ili'a Efimovich Repin (from Fofanov's Stikhotvoreniia i poemy, *edited by V. V. Smirensky, 1962)*

people who supplied him with the comforts of life. Yet, however significant Fofanov's contributions to civic poetry were, contemporary democratic literary critics such as Petr Filippovich Iakubovich (pseudonym Grinevich) continuously declared him "bezprintsipnyi" (unprincipled) and "bezideinyi" (without ideals). Even though Nadson's socially minded lyrics served as a great inspiration to the young Fofanov, in radical literary circles Fofanov's work was constantly judged against Nadson's. While Nadson was viewed as a spokesman for social justice, Fofanov's poetic persona became synonymous with useless aestheticism; he was identified more with his nature poems and his poems about verse itself than with his civic poetry. In one of his programmatic verses on the poetic process, "Ne pravda l', vse dyshalo prozoi" (Isn't it true that everything breathed prose . . . , 1885), the speaker revels in his ability to transform the quotidian places where he meets with his beloved into spaces of white-foamed cliffs and golden palaces.

The year of Fofanov's first publications coincided with a great blow to the Populist movement in Russia. The 1881 assassination of Tsar Alexander II by members of Narodnaia volia led to the elimination of the group and severe policing of intellectual thought for the next decade and a half. In 1884 the government closed *Otechestvennye zapiski* (Notes of the Fatherland), which had been edited by

the satirist Mikhail Evgrafovich Saltykov (and formally by Nekrasov) and was the leading journal of *narodnichestvo*. Fofanov was among the first to express his outrage against this injustice. His archives include an unpublished note in which he bemoans the journal as the last organ of truth. The failure of *narodnichestvo* noticeably rearranged the Russian poetic landscape, as a general sense of disillusionment in the possibility of effecting social change took hold among the intelligentsia.

As a consequence the poetic emphasis in the 1880s and 1890s shifted away from social topics to aesthetic concerns. Models of late Russian Romanticism, such as the poets Fedor Ivanovich Tiutchev and Afanasii Afanas'evich Fet, were revisited with new vigor. Disengaged images of nature, a focus on the poetic muse and the creative process itself, and ultrasubjectivism became prominent. Poets of the aesthetic school include Apollon Nikolaevich Maikov, Iakov Petrovich Polonsky, Arsenii Arkad'evich Golenishchev-Kutuzov, and Dmitrii Nikolaevich Tsertelev. Konstantin Konstantinovich Sluchevsky and Aleksei Nikolaevich Apukhtin–whose lamentations on the themes of autumnal boredom, the dreariness of everyday existence, and lack of passion had been quite exceptional in the 1850s–resurfaced in the 1880s in the wake of the new literary trend. In the late 1880s Fofanov's name emerged at the head of this group of poets. Much of his poetry treats the theme of youthful ideals that are worn out by reality. General apathy, resignation, and melancholy resound, with poetry as one's only salvation in life. Galina Mikhailovna Tsurikova notes that his poetry was not as disengaged from his times as has commonly been thought: his works reflected contemporary reality, insofar as nothing of any social significance was happening in Russia during the final two decades of the nineteenth century.

In 1885 Fofanov's family relations became strained to the point that he had to leave home. Mikhail Petrovich in particular disapproved of his son's chosen profession. At this time writing indeed had become the sole source of income for the young man. For this reason he was forced to write an excessive amount and publish wherever he could, often producing only haphazard variations on the same theme. He even experimented with prose and published three sentimental, rather second-rate short stories that largely went unnoticed–"Zlopoluchnaia. Iz zapisok Ogulina" (An Ill-Fated Woman. From Ogulina's Notes, 1882), "Chasy ukrali" (They Stole the Watch, 1883), both published in the journal *Vek,* (Century), and "Pervye tsvety" (First Flowers, 1888), published in the journal *Russkoe bogatstvo* (Russian Wealth). Nevertheless, his level of production was peaking at this time. His works appeared in a wide variety of journals, including *Zhivopisnoe obozrenie* (Picturesque Review), *Literaturnyi zhurnal* (The Literary Journal), *Nabliudatel'* (The Observer), and *Vek,* as well as in newspapers such as *Moskovskaia gazeta* (The Moscow

Gazette), *Den'* (Day), and *Nedelia* (The Week). Yet, when Fofanov's name was mentioned in the press before 1887, it was mostly to complain about the current state of Russian poetry.

Fofanov was not widely recognized until 1886, when Nadson—a cult figure among the young generation of poetry patrons—brought Fofanov to the attention of the reading public. Nadson ended one literary overview in the journal *Rassvet* (Dawn) by asking readers to take note of a poet with "a great gift of a purely artistic nature." The following year the St. Petersburg publishing house of German Goppe (known as G. Goppe) published Fofanov's first book of verse, *Stikhotvoreniia*. The collection encompassed 207 poems, or almost everything he had written up to that year. Drawing mixed reviews, the book was criticized for repetitiveness and thus a poverty of images, derivative ultra-Romanticism, and carelessness on all levels, such as grammatical mistakes. The collection was also attacked for the author's indiscriminate inclusion of the bad along with the good. Even a critic of aesthetic leanings from *Novoe vremia* (New Time), a journal with which Fofanov was later professionally associated until the end of his life, suggested that one-third of the material should not have been published, and another third ought to have been drastically reworked. Vsevolod Mikhailovich Garshin, a Populist prose writer and critic, complained of the preoccupation in the book with poetic form and its utterly uninteresting content and lamented the passing of the brave participation of poetry in the cause of the *narod* (common people).

At the same time, the appearance of the 1887 *Stikhotvoreniia* encouraged litterateurs to take a closer look at Fofanov. Even those who severely criticized the book appreciated Fofanov's mastery of form. The lyric poem "Zvezdy iasnye, zvezdy prekrasnye . . ." (Clear stars, beautiful stars . . .) became extremely popular for its mellifluousness and was often set to music. It is Fofanov's programmatic statement of Romantic retreat into nature for poetic inspiration. Other works from the collection, such as the poem "Nevesta" (The Bride) and the fairy tales in verse "Kamenotes" (The Stone Mason) and "Triolet" (The Triolet), were praised for their elegant simplicity and originality. In a letter to D. V. Grigorovich, written on 12 January 1888, Chekhov wrote: "Among the poets, Fofanov is beginning to stand out. He is truly talented, while others are not worth anything as artists." According to Andrei Nikolaevich Leskov, Nikolai Semenovich Leskov described Fofanov as "a poet from head to foot, sincere, without affectation or artificiality." Years later, in a letter to Fofanov dated 11 September 1902, Tolstoy expressed a similar sentiment, claiming that Fofanov's verse was the one "natural" voice amid a sea of "intentionally constructed" poetry. Fofanov's book was even nominated for the prestigious Pushkin Prize awarded by the Academy of Sciences but was ultimately rejected because the Academy could not throw its support

behind such "excessive poetic liberties" and the multitude of incorrect grammatical usages. The general view of Fofanov in literary circles was that he possessed a God-given gift but that his social background and narrow worldview, due to his lack of education and travel, kept him from rising to a more refined level.

A year later Fofanov attracted another type of attention to himself. His poem "Tainstvo liubvi" (The Sacrament of Love), written in 1885 and published in 1888, was declared blasphemous by the church. The journal in which it had been published, *Nabliudatel'*, was subsequently closed for six months, and Fofanov was nearly excommunicated from the Russian Orthodox Church. Church officials found the poem heretical on the grounds that it allegedly perverted the idea of the sacrament in the Orthodox faith. The author did indeed experiment with several inflammatory ideas in "Tainstvo liubvi." The God of the Old Testament—whimsical, terrifying, and destructive—is purified of his violent tendencies only by coming in contact with earthly innocence in the form of the Virgin Mary: "Now He has been purified by sinless love / And enlightened by a dream of earthly innocence." The clerics' outrage was mostly directed at the concreteness with which the circumstances of the Immaculate Conception, the greatest religious sacrament, are presented in the poem: Mary's bedroom is complete with curtains, rugs, and frescoes, and the dove that circles above the Virgin's bed is God himself.

This incident had no serious repercussions for the poet. In fact, his popularity grew, as his circle of acquaintances expanded to include such a motley group of literary figures as Merezhkovsky, Leskov, Polonsky, and Maikov. The artist Il'ia Efimovich Repin, who became a close family friend for years to come, painted a famous portrait of Fofanov in 1888, depicting the poet as the quintessential Romantic, with long, flowing hair and an inspired gaze upward. Fofanov participated in readings at modernist gatherings in the presence of such rising stars of Russian symbolism as Zinaida Nikolaevna Gippius and Valerii Iakovlevich Briusov. He also frequented literary evenings in Repin's studio. In his reminiscences the artist describes Fofanov's appearances at these gatherings in a way that closely resembles Pushkin's depiction, in his *Egipetskie nochi* (Egyptian Nights, 1835), of a stereotypical Romantic in the figure of the improviser: though working in cramped and uncomfortable quarters, downtrodden by life and poverty, Fofanov was transformed beyond recognition once he began to read from his poetry.

With his financial and professional standing now improved, Fofanov's second proposal of marriage to Lidiia Konstantinovna was accepted, and the couple married in the summer of 1887. According to her memoirs, the late 1880s were the happiest years in the poet's life. In 1888 Aleksei Sergeevich Suvorin, a publishing magnate, invited Fofanov to become a collaborator on the journal *Novoe vre-*

I. I. Iasinsky's drawing of Fofanov, 1888 (from Fofanov's
Stikhotvoreniia i poemy, *edited by Smirensky, 1962)*

mia. For the first time in his life Fofanov received a respectable monthly salary. While the journal had a wide circulation, it also had a reputation of compromising its principles. Although he had been known as a liberal journalist in the 1860s, in the 1880s Suvorin became famous for pandering to the mass-market readership. One of his modes of profit was developing a monopoly on the sale of books in railway stations. More than a decade later Aleksandr Aleksandrovich Blok suggested in his article "Literaturnyi razgovor" (Literary Dialogue, 1910) that the decline in the quality of Fofanov's work of the latter years was a result of his association with Suvorin's journal. Fofanov's poetry appeared in an array of other thick journals with a variety of reputations. He published in *Russkoe bogatstvo,* which in the late 1880s became the main organ for *narodnichestvo; Russkaia mysl'* (Russian Thought), a moderate liberal journal with no regard for literary and political factions; and *Severnyi vestnik* (The Northern Messenger), one of the few journals of the early 1890s that published works by the emerging wave of Russian symbolists, including Konstantin Dmitrievich Bal'mont, Fedor Kuz'mich Sologub, Gippius, and Merezhkovsky.

In 1889 Suvorin published Fofanov's second volume of verse, featuring 125 works written since his first collection. In this second book titled *Stikhotvoreniia* the poet further distanced himself from the proponents of civic poetry, and it consequently was received with hostility in liberal circles. An anonymous critic rebuked the author for siding with an approach that postulated a certain level of unconsciousness inherent in the creative process—he likened Fofanov's poetry to a bird's singing. Fofanov was frequently criticized for his fascination with melody and form to the detriment of thought. In his second volume the author's creative vision was indeed beginning to take a direction away from the declamatory tone of civic poetry. The lyric hero's sphere of action in this collection shifts almost completely to his inner world. Evgenii Zamirovich Tarlanov, a prolific Fofanov scholar, argues that this publication marks Fofanov's new dedication to modernist trends in poetry. Furthermore, Fofanov's second *Stikhotvoreniia* suggests that the poet, for all the gaps in his formal education, was not uninformed by foreign models. Tarlanov observes that Fofanov was in fact one of the first in Russia to be influenced by the French poet of decadent leanings, Charles Baudelaire. There is reason to believe that Fofanov had a working knowledge of French: the concentration of images and ideas in his poems, echoing works of Baudelaire that had not yet been translated into Russian, is too high to be coincidental.

Shortly after the publication of his second book of poems, Fofanov developed a nervous condition, began to hallucinate, and was institutionalized for six months. In the hospital he attempted suicide several times. Upon his doctors' advice to move from St. Petersburg, the family relocated to Gatchina (about fifty kilometers south of the capital city), where they lived for the next thirteen years. Lidiia Konstantinovna opened a small preparatory school for boys and girls, which made a humble contribution to the family finances. Fofanov's distress was compounded by his feeling of being supplanted by the symbolists, in particular Briusov and Bal'mont, who made their literary debuts in the early 1890s.

Despite the onset of heavy alcoholism, Fofanov remained active throughout the 1890s. In 1892 he published his third volume of poetry, *Teni i tainy* (Shadows and Mysteries), through the bookseller Mikhail Vasil'evich Popov (known as M. V. Popov). Although the book was criticized in its time for vagueness and inconsistencies, in subsequent scholarship it is often considered Fofanov's most mature collection. *Teni i tainy* is characterized by an intensification of the subjective, irrational, impressionistic, and mystical tendencies that fermented in the poet's earlier works. The collision between the world of dreams and reality is the dominant principle, with a tragic note sounded by a resignation to the banalities of life. In this collection echoes of the religious and aesthetic philosophies that influenced the Russian symbolists, such as the philosophy of Vladimir Sergeevich Solov'ev, can be deciphered amid the light-and-shadow images in earthly life as a reflection of the otherworldly. As Tarlanov has observed, perceptions of beauty intuited through the mediation of female figures approximate Solov'ev's metaphysics of *vechnaia zhenstvennost'* (the eternal feminine), a universal feminine principle of reconciliation and harmony. In Fofanov's "Belaia zhenshchina" (A White Woman), for instance, an apparition of a woman made out of sea foam helps the speaker grasp inexplicable transcendental truths. The theme of duality, which later plays an important role in Blok's verse, is a constant presence in Fofanov's works, as seen by titles such as "Dva mira" (Two Worlds, 1886) and "Dvoinik" (The Double, 1887). In *Teni i tainy* the lyric hero's spiritual schism—into, on the one hand, a dweller of this earth and, on the other hand, an inhabitant of the shadowy realms of his alter ego—is developed further, as in, for instance, the 1892 poem "Kto on? Zachem? Otkuda etot gost'? . . ." (Who is he? Why is he? Where did this guest come from? . . .). Fofanov's next collection of verse, published by Suvorin in 1896, is close to the aesthetics of modernism in yet another way. In this collection he combined the poetry from his 1889 book with new works, arranging everything into five parts: *Malen'kie poemy* (Short Narrative Poems), *Etiudy v rifmakh* (Etudes in Verse), *Snegurka* (The Snow Maiden), *Maiskii shum* (May Bustle), and *Monologi* (Monologues). Each of these parts forms a new whole—distinct yet fragmented—and echoes a tendency toward lyric cycles, the main organizing principle in the poetry of the Silver Age.

Fofanov's level of creative output declined during the last decade of his life. The thin volume *Illiuzii* (Illusions), published in 1900, represents his last burst of activity before Blok and the symbolists took center stage. Although writer and critic Vasilii Vasil'evich Rozanov called Fofanov the "first Russian poet of modern times" in his review of *Illiuzii*, the book was generally censured for having too many contradictions, repetitions, and Romantic clichés. Fofanov's resentment of poetic circles, especially those of the symbolists, continued to grow. At one time a welcome presence, he now appeared provocatively coarse at literary gatherings. In 1900 Fofanov openly attempted to distance himself from the symbolists' cult of aesthetics and artificial posing through the poem "Dekadentam" (To the Decadents):

Proch', figliary! Masku donkikhotstva
Pust' sorvet s vas derzkaia ladon'!

. . . .

Vasha Muza—kak bol'noi urod,
Chto sebia soboiu uteshaet!"

(Away, buffoons! Let a daring hand
Tear away your mask of Don Quixoteism!

. . . .

Your Muse is like an ill freak
That comforts itself with its very self!)

In his last years Fofanov made a gesture toward the poetry of civil discontent once again and inserted revolutionary suggestions even into some of his more impressionistic nature poems. In his tale in verse "Poetessa" (The

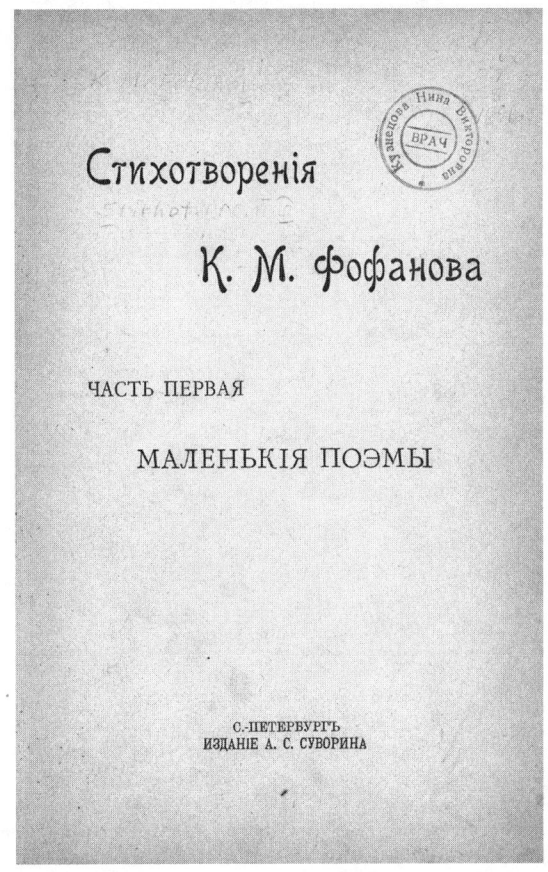

Title page for Malen'kie poemy *(Little Narrative Poems), part 1 of Fofanov's five-part* Stikhotvoreniia *(Poems), which consists largely of lyric cycles (Main Library, University of California, Irvine)*

Poetess, published in *Illiuzii*) Fofanov returned to *narodnichestvo*. In the spirit of Pushkin's poem "K Chaadaevu" (To Chaadaev, 1818), the final lines of the poem "Lomka" (The Breaking, 1906) read, "Russia will rise from sleep with new glory / In the morning hour of freedom and dawning." Fofanov's overt treatment of the revolutionary events of 1905, the four-act play "Zheleznoe vremia" (The Iron Age), was permanently shelved by the censors. His renewed interest in civic subject matter earned Fofanov an arrest for "political unreliability" in 1907. He spent two weeks in prison in Gatchina and recorded his prison impressions in a cycle of poems, some of which were included in "Pesni uznika" (Songs of a Prisoner, 1907); others were not published until the 1962 edition of his verse. In 1910 two small volumes appeared, *Posle Golgofy* (After Golgotha) and *Neobyknovennyi roman* (An Unusual Novel)—works that sealed the poet's reputation as a has-been among the circle of symbolists who had followed his earlier career with interest. After Fofanov read the latter at a literary evening, Briusov branded him a "galvanized corpse." It became increasingly difficult for Fofanov to publish his seemingly outdated poetry in the literary atmosphere of post-1905 Russia. He

*Fofanov in 1910, one year before his death
from malnutrition and pneumonia*

prepared two more collections of verse—"Efiry" (Ethers), which consisted of poems written between 1901 and 1906, and "Kryl'ia i slezy" (Wings and Tears), featuring poetry written between 1907 and 1911—but these works were never published.

During the last decade of Fofanov's life his lexicon expanded beyond the vocabulary of daydreams and visions. Elevated language from the Romantic canon becomes interlaced with banalities such as the word *musor* (trash) and even a rare profanity, such as *der'mo* (shit). Images from the realm of the everyday become more prominent. The poem "Vechernii chai" (An Evening Tea, 1898) masterfully celebrates the minutiae of life. A romance unfolds amid objects of everyday use—a table, a samovar, a squeaky gate—to the clinking of glasses and the barking of dogs. The poem ends with a rhyme that brings together "rai" (heaven) and "chai" (a quotidian ritual of tea-drinking). In other works, reality outweighs fantasy as Fofanov's beloved metonymies of the other world, such as the stars and the moon, are presented as reflections in "puddles on the street" ("Derevnia skrylasia . . . " [The village disappeared from view . . . , 1899]) and in "damp ditches" ("Ia idu, vokrug vse izby . . ." [I walk, village huts all around me . . . , 1907]). According to Briusov in his "K. M. Fofanov" (1995), Fofanov's ultimate failure lies in his inability to develop further this flirtation with reality. At the end of his article on Fofanov, Briusov laments the fact that the poet never completely accepted real life as subject matter worthy of poetry.

The constantly intensifying central idea of Fofanov's verse—namely, the victory of reality and prose over the enchanted world of poetic fancy—parallels the final years of Fofanov's biography especially closely. He found living on the income he received from his literary publications nearly impossible. For most of their life Fofanov and Lidiia Konstantinovna struggled in poverty, barely managing to support their nine children on the poet's small honoraria and Lidiia's meager teacher's salary. To make matters worse, Fofanov chronically struggled with severe outbursts of alcoholism, a disease that ran in his family. His archives include a newspaper advertisement, attributed to the year 1908, in which he offered his services as a doorman, a street sweeper, or a servant in a tavern. In 1909 he planned to place an ad in the newspaper alerting publishing houses that he was willing to sell fifteen volumes of his poetry for an insignificant sum of money. In 1911 Lidiia Konstantinovna went to one of the publishing houses in St. Petersburg to request help with medical expenses for her husband, who had fallen gravely ill. The family had no money to treat him. The funds were found, and the poet was taken to a reputable hospital, where he died on 17 May 1911 of pneumonia, complicated by malnutrition. In his autobiographical sketches Fofanov had declared: "My ancestors belong to the great family that is called humanity . . . their caskets are not sealed with the coat of arms of aristocracy." Fofanov's publisher, Suvorin, purchased a burial lot for him at a cemetery for nobility at the Novodevichii monastery in Moscow, next to the great neo-Romantic painter Mikhail Aleksandrovich Vrubel'.

Reactions to Konstantin Mikhailovich Fofanov's poetry by his contemporaries ranged from dismissing him as an epigone of German and Russian Romanticism to declaring him the first Russian neo-Romantic. The quality of Fofanov's verse that leads to these contradictory receptions is precisely what contemporary scholars find valuable about the poet and places special emphasis on his role as a connecting link between the Golden Age of Russian poetry (which peaked in the 1820s) and the poetic revival of the Silver Age (which peaked in the early twentieth century). In an obituary for Fofanov the Acmeist poet Nikolai Sergeevich Gumilev called him a "humble poet of quiet beauty." Fofanov's "quiet" talent reached, in its modest way, not only the Russian realists and symbolists but also participants of other poetic schools at the turn of the twentieth century. The Ego-Futurist Igor' Severianin, the father of Ego-Futurism (a modernist movement of the early teens of the twentieth century in Russia that believed poetic word was an end in itself) considered Fofanov his "king" and claimed to owe his indoctrination into poetry to Fofanov. At one point Anna Andreevna Akhmatova belonged to the Literaturnoe obshchestvo imeni Fofanova (Fofanov Literary Society), which was active in St. Petersburg in the 1920s. Blok, who considered Fofanov one of the most representative writers of his age, perhaps best characterizes the poet in his *Pis'ma o poezii* (Letters on Poetry, 1908), in which he observes that Fofanov, along with the symbolists Merezhkovsky and Gippius, scripted a "slogan for an entire enormous epoch," shaped by his "thirst for sacred things, which do not exist."

Letters:

"I. L. Shcheglovu," in *Chestvovanie 25-letiia literaturnoi deiatel'nosti I. L. Shcheglova,* by L. M. Shakh-Paroniants (Kronshtadt, 1902), pp. 32–34;

Letter to the editors, *Birzhevye vedomosti* (11 April 1906): 5;

Letter to the editors, *Birzhevye vedomosti, vechernii vypusk* (15 July 1906): 2;

Letter to the editors, *Golos pravdy,* 748 (13 March 1908): 3;

"N. I. Kareevu," *Iubileinyi sbornik Literaturnogo fonda, 1859–1909,* compiled and edited by S. A. Vengerov (St. Petersburg: Obshchestvennaia pol'za, 1909), p. 630;

"F. F. Fidleru," *Probuzhdenie,* 17 (1916): 524–525;

"P. P. Pertsovu," in *Literaturnye vospominaniia, 1890–1902 gg,* by Petr Petrovich Pertsov (Moscow: Academia, 1933), pp. 188–189.

Bibliographies:

Vladimir Smirensky, "Knigi K. M. Fofanova," *Knizhnye novosti,* no. 19 (1836): 25;

Cesare G. De Michelis, "Bibliografia," in his *Le illusioni e i simboli: K. M. Fofanov* (Venice: Marsilio, 1973), pp. 149–154.

Biographies:

A. Izmailov, "Prints i nishchii (Iz vospominanii o K. M. Fofanove)," *Istoricheskii vestnik,* 144 (1916): 459–478;

Evgenii Zamirovich Tarlanov, *Konstantin Fofanov: Legenda i deistvitel'nost'* (Petrozavodsk: Izdatel'stvo Petrozavodskogo universiteta, 1993);

Tarlanov, "Labirinty Konstantina Fofanova," *Russkii iazyk za rubezhom,* 1 (1995): 109–111.

References:

Aleksandr Aleksandrovich Blok, "Pis'ma o poezii" and "Literaturnyi razgovor," in his *Sobranie sochinenii v vos'mi tomakh,* 8 volumes, edited by V. N. Orlov, A. A. Surkov, and K. I. Chaikovsky (Moscow & Leningrad: Khudozhestvennaia literatura, 1962), V: 277–300, 437–441;

Valerii Iakovlevich Briusov, *The Diary of Valery Bryusov (1893–1905),* edited and translated by Joan Delaney Grossman (Berkeley: University of California Press, 1980), pp. 83–84;

Briusov, "K. M. Fofanov," in his *Izbrannye sochineniia,* 2 volumes, edited by N. M. Briusova (Moscow: Khudozhestvennaia literatura, 1955), II: 226–230;

Anton Pavlovich Chekhov, *Polnoe sobranie sochinenii i pisem,* 20 volumes, edited by Sergei Dmitrievich Balukhatyi (Moscow: Gos. izdatel'stvo khudozhestvennoi literatury, 1944–1951), XIV: 16;

Ingrid Fenner, *Zur Poetik des Lyrikers Konstantin M. Fofanov,* in the series *Slavistische Beiträge* (Munich: O. Sagner, 1998);

Evgenii Mikhailovich Garshin, "Voskhodiashchee svetilo poezii (Stikhotvoreniia g. Fofanova)," in his *Kriticheskie opyty* (St. Petersburg: Skorokhodov, 1888), pp. 246–251;

Nikolai Sergeevich Gumilev, "Dva nekrologa: K. M. Fofanov i V. V. Gofman," in his *Sobranie sochinenii v chetyrekh tomakh,* 4 volumes (Moscow: Terra, 1991), IV: 369;

P. F. Iakubovich [P. F. Grinevich], "K. M. Fofanov," in his *Ocherki russkoi poezii* (St. Petersburg: Tipografiia Pervoi Sankt-Peterburgskoi trudovoi arteli, 1911), pp. 301–311;

Kilgour Collection of Russian Literature, 1750–1920 (Cambridge, Mass.: Harvard College Library, 1959);

Andrei Nikolaevich Leskov, *Zhizn' Nikolaia Leskova,* 2 volumes (Moscow: Khudozhestvennaia literatura, 1984), I: 135;

Dmitrii Sergeevich Merezhkovsky, *O prichinakh upadka i o novykh techeniiakh sovremennoi russkoi literatury* (St. Petersburg: Vol'f, 1893), pp. 85–89;

Rainer Maria Rilke, *Briefe und Tagebücher aus der Frühzeit: 1899 bis 1902* (Leipzig: Insel-verlag, 1931);

V. Rozanov, "K. M. Fofanov. Illiuzii," *Novoe vremia,* 8960 (1901);

Evgenii Zamirovich Tarlanov, *Konstantin Fofanov: Legenda i deistvitel'nost* (Petrozavodsk: Izdatel'stvo Petrozavodskogo universiteta, 1993);

Leo Tolstoy, *Sobraniia sochinenii,* 20 volumes (Moscow: Khudozhestvennaia literatura, 1965), XVIII: 309;

S. A. Vengerov, *Ocherki po istorii russkoi literatury* (St. Petersburg: Obshchestvennaia Pol'za, 1907), pp. 139–143.

Papers:

Konstantin Mikhailovich Fofanov's papers (including the manuscripts of his unpublished works "Zheleznoe vremia," "Efiry," and "Kryl'ia i slezy") are located in the Russian State Archive of Literature and Art (RGALI) in Moscow. Information about his archive can be found in "Novye materialy o poete Fofanove," anonymous, *Literaturnaia gazeta,* 5 June 1938, p. 6.

Vsevolod Mikhailovich Garshin

(2 February 1855 – 24 March 1888)

John Givens
University of Rochester

BOOKS: *Rasskazy* (St. Petersburg: A. M. Kotomina, 1882);

Vtoraia knizhka rasskazov (St. Petersburg: Golike, 1885);

Tret'ia knizhka rasskazov (St. Petersburg: Literaturnyi fond, 1888);

Polnoe sobranie sochinenii V. M. Garshina (St. Petersburg: A. F. Marks, 1910);

Rasskazy (Moscow & Leningrad: Gosudarstvennoe izdatel'stvo, 1929); enlarged as *Sochineniia,* edited by Iu. G. Oksman (Moscow & Leningrad: GIKhL, 1934);

Polnoe sobranie sochinenii i pisem, 3 volumes, edited by Oksman (Moscow & Leningrad: Akademiia, 1934);

Sochineniia, edited by Grigorii Abramovich Bialyi (Moscow: Gostlitizdat, 1938).

Collections: *Sochineniia* (Moscow: Khudozhestvennaia literatura, 1983);

Sochineniia: Rasskazy, ocherki, stat'i, pis'ma, edited, with an introduction, by Vladimir I. Porudominsky (Moscow: Sovetskaia Rossiia, 1984).

Editions in English: "Wounded in Battle," in *The Saghalien Convict and Other Stories* (New York: Tait, 1892; London: Unwin, 1892);

Stories from Garshin, translated by E. L. Voynich (London: Unwin, 1893);

The Signal and Other Stories, translated by Rowland Smith (London: Duckworth, 1912);

"The Signal" and "The Red Flower," in *Selected Russian Short Stories,* translated by Alfred Edward Chamot (London & New York: Oxford University Press, 1925);

The Scarlet Flower, translated by Bernard Isaacs (Moscow: Foreign Languages Publishing House, 1959);

The Frog Went Travelling, translated by Olga Shartse (Moscow: Progress, 1975);

Last Translations. Three Stories, translated by Eugene M. Kayden (Boulder: Colorado Quarterly, 1979);

Stories, translated by Isaacs (Moscow: Progress, 1982);

From the Reminiscences of Private Ivanov and Other Stories, translated by Peter Henry, Liv Tudge, D. Ray-

Portrait by Il'ia Efimovich Repin, 1884
(Tretykov Gallery, Moscow)

field, and P. Taylor, with an introduction by Henry (London: Angel Books, 1988)–includes "From the Reminiscences of Private Ivanov."

OTHER: "Skazka o zhabe i roze (dlia detei)," in *Sbornik obshchestva dlia posobiia nuzhdaiushchimsia literatoram i uchenym* (St. Petersburg: Obshchestvo, 1884);

"V. M. Garshin: Otryvok iz neizdannoi povesti," edited by B. M. Engel'gardt, in *Raduga: Al'manakh Pushkinskogo Doma* (Petrograd: Kooperativnoe izdatel'stvo literatorov i uchenykh, 1922), pp. 278–286.

TRANSLATIONS: Prosper Mérimée, *Kolomba, Iziashchnaia literatura,* 10 (1883): 1–151;

Marie Louise de la Ramée Ouida, "Chestoliubivaia Roza," in *Skazki dlia detei* (St. Petersburg, 1883), pp. 199–218;

Ouida, "Niurenbergskaia pech'," in *Skazki dlia detei* (St. Petersburg, 1883), pp. 61–148;

Carmen de Silva, "Zamok ved'my," in *Tsarstvo skazok* (N.p., 1883), pp. 61–79;

De Silva, "Chakhlau," in *Tsarstvo skazok* (N.p., 1883), pp. 193–205.

SELECTED PERIODICAL PUBLICATIONS:
POETRY
"Na pervoi vystavke kartin Vereshchagina, *Den,* 39 (1888): 2;

"28 sentiabria 1883 g. (Na smert' Turgeneva)," *Russkoe slovo* (24 March 1913);

"Kogda nauki trudnyi put' proidetsia . . . ," *Russkaia mysl',* 1 (1917): 63;

"Piatnadtsat' let tomu nazad . . . ," 1 (1917): 63–64;

"Stikhotvorenie Garshina na smert' Nekrasova. Iz zapisnoi knizhki V. M. Garshina," edited by E. Bazilevskaia, *Literaturnoe nasledstvo,* 49–50 (1946): 636.

FICTION
"Chetyre dnia," *Otechestvennye zapiski,* 10 (October 1877);

"Proisshestvie," *Otechestvennye zapiski,* 3 (1878);

"Trus. Iz zapisnoi knizhki," *Otechestvennye zapiski,* 3 (March 1879);

"Vstrecha. Otryvok," *Otechestvennye zapiski,* 4 (April 1879);

"Khudozhniki," *Otechestvennye zapiski,* 9 (September 1879);

"Attalea princeps. Skazka," *Russkoe bogatstvo,* 1 (1880);

"Denshchik i ofitser," *Russkoe bogatstvo,* 1 (March 1880);

"Noch'. Rasskaz," *Otechestvennye zapiski,* 6 (1880);

"To, chego ne bylo," *Ustoi,* 3–4 (1882);

"Iz vospominanii riadovogo Ivanova," *Otechestvennye zapiski,* 1 (1883);

"Krasnyi tsvetok," *Otechestvennye zapiski,* 10 (October 1883);

"Medvedi. Rasskaz," *Otechestvennye zapiski,* 11 (1883);

"Dva otryvka iz neokonchennoi dramy (1884–85)," *Zhurnal Teatra literaturno-khudozhestvennogo obshchestva* (1910): 19–24;

"Nadezhda Nikolaevna. Rasskaz," *Russkaia mysl',* 2 (1885); 3 (1885);

"Skazanie o gordom Aggee. Starinnoe predanie," *Russkaia mysl',* 4 (1886);

"Signal," *Severnyi vestnik,* 1 (1887);

"Liagushka-puteshestvennitsa," *Rodnik,* 7 (1887);

"Tri neokonchennykh proizvedeniia V. M. Garshina," edited by M. Kostova, *Russkaia literatura,* 2 (1962): 180–189;

"Neizvestnye stranitsy tvorchestva Garshina," edited by V. Porudominskii, *Prometei,* 7 (1969): 260–265;

"Neizvestnyi fel'eton Vsevoloda Garshina," edited by G. D. Dzhavakhishvili, *Russkaia literatura,* 1 (1971): 99–101;

"Neizvestnaia zametka V. M. Garshina," edited by A. M. Berezkina, *Russkaia literatura,* 1 (1975): 163;

"Iz tvorcheskogo naslediia. Nedopisannye rasskazy. Pis'ma," *Literaturnoe nasledstvo,* 87 (1977): 159–257;

"Chetvertoe deistvie neokonchennoi dramy V. M. Garshina i N. A. Demchinskogo 'Den'gi,'" edited by P. V. Bekedina, *Russkaia literatura,* 1 (1991): 165–176.

NONFICTION
"Aiaslarskoe delo," *Novosti* (13 November 1877).

Vsevolod Garshin made his literary debut in the twilight decades of the nineteenth century, when Russian culture was at a crossroads. In Russia as in Europe, the era of the great realist novel was waning; Leo Tolstoy had essentially given up on the genre, while the other great novelists soon passed from the scene–Fyodor Dostoevsky in 1881 and Ivan Sergeevich Turgenev in 1883. The emphasis on utilitarian art in the 1860s and the Populists' idealization of the peasant in the 1870s gave way to a renewed interest in individual psychology and the cultivation of a personal style more suited to the climate of political reaction, anxiety, and social fragmentation that followed the 1881 assassination of Tsar Alexander II. Small genres–short stories, sketches, and novellas–became dominant, as writers turned increasingly toward concise depictions of personal experience and incident rather than broad canvases of family and social history. Garshin emerged from this environment an undisputed master of the small genre. His legacy of a mere handful of short stories constitutes a powerful creative response to moral and mental suffering and has gained him an important place in the literary canon as a key transitional figure between the realistic period in Russian literature and the rise of modernism. His laconic, impressionistic style; his attention to craft; his eye for symbolic imagery; his feeling for the uncanny; and his deft insights into the human psyche anticipate the mature stories of Anton Pavlovich Chekhov and the advent of the symbolist impulse in Russian culture.

Vsevolod Mikhailovich Garshin was born 2 February 1855 at the estate of his maternal grandmother in the Bakhmut District of the Ekaterinoslav province in Ukraine. His father, Mikhail Egorovich Garshin, was an army officer. His mother, Ekaterina Stepanovna (Akimova) Garshina, was the daughter of a Bakhmut landowner whom Mikhail Egorovich met while traveling with his regiment in Ukraine. They married in 1848. He was a mild-tempered, quiet man and content with the prospects that service in the army offered. She was, as Garshin later recollected in an autobiographical note (published in *Polnoe sobranie sochinenii i pisem* [Complete Collected Works and Letters], 1934), "a well-educated girl for that time" who thrived in the constantly changing environment of military life. While each move from province to province brought new acquaintances and distractions for Ekaterina Stepanovna, the uprootedness of army life and the constant parade of "huge horses and huge men" were especially upsetting for the young Garshin, the third of three sons born to the couple. His impressions as a three-year-old of regimental life were later the source of "many troubling memories."

When Garshin's paternal grandfather died, leaving a small inheritance, Mikhail Egorovich retired from the service early and settled on an estate near Starobelsk in 1858. This abrupt change in daily life brought drastic consequences. Garshin's mother, a progressive woman and follower of the socialist philosophy of Nikolai Gavrilovich Chernyshevsky, could not abide the stale routine of provincial life with a husband who was content with a quiet, unchanging daily routine. In 1860 she eloped with a radical student named Petr Vasil'evich Zavadsky, the tutor of Garshin's two brothers. Although she and her lover took her two eldest sons with them to St. Petersburg, the five-year-old Garshin was left behind in the care of his father. The trauma of separation and abandonment left a permanent mark on the writer, who later wrote in his *Polnoe sobranie sochinenii i pisem*: "The largely sad expression on my face doubtless dates from this time." After three years Garshin's mother brought him to St. Petersburg, where he attended a modern school and was exposed to the liberal views of his mother's radical friends. Soon, however, financial difficulties removed her to Khar'kov, and he began an unsettled existence living in boardinghouses and with distant relatives while completing his education. Little help—financial or emotional—came from his father, who was never mentally strong; hereditary insanity, alcoholism, and suicide haunted both sides of Garshin's family. Mikhail Egorovich died in 1870 and left little legacy. Garshin himself, probably because of the strain of his circumstances, suffered a nervous breakdown two years later, the first of three serious episodes of mental collapse in his life. He was hospitalized from December 1872 until the following summer, only to learn, upon his recovery, of his brother Viktor's suicide several months prior.

Garshin completed his high school education in 1874 and enrolled in the St. Petersburg Institute of Mining that fall, where he spent most of his time cultivating his interest in art and literature and fraternizing with artists. He also began to write—first poetry, much of which he burned, and later prose. Some thirty poems by Garshin are extant;

roughly half of them were composed between 1871 and 1877, before he seriously devoted himself to prose. None of Garshin's poetry was published during his lifetime. His poems are interesting mainly for the light they shed on his concerns as a prose writer. "Na pervoi vystavke kartin Vereshchagina" (At Vereshchagin's First Exhibition, 1874, published in the journal *Den'* in 1988), for instance, records Garshin's impressions of Vasilii Vasil'evich Vereshchagin's paintings, which depict the conquering of Turkistan and battle scenes from Asia. Where other exhibition goers see only excellent technique and verisimilitude ("How charming and realistic it is," they exclaim in Garshin's poem), Garshin perceives the horror of war, where death and destruction blur the distinction between conquered and conqueror. The poem gives a glimpse of Garshin's preoccupation—so prominent in his war stories—with the high moral cost and dehumanizing face of war. "Piatnadtsat' let tomu nazad . . ." (Fifteen years ago . . .), written in 1876 and published in the periodical *Russkaia mysl'* in 1917, is a meditation on the failures that followed the emancipation of the serfs in 1861 and reveals Garshin's populist proclivities. "Plennitsa" (The Prisoner, written 1876, published 1889) is a sketch in verse for the writer's 1880 story "Attalea princeps" (The Palm Tree, published in *Russkoe bogatstvo* [Russian Wealth]). Finally, "Druz'ia, my sobralis' pered razlukoi . . ." (Friends, we have gathered before parting . . . , 1876, published 1913) records Garshin's ardent sympathy for the Serbian war of independence against Turkey. An expression of unabashed Pan-Slavic pride and fraternity, the poem was turned down by the censors because of the line "We go not on the whim of a ruler . . . but because in every honest Russian breast the bidding of our native country beckons."

Garshin's interest in the events in the Balkans consumed him in 1876 and 1877 and quickly overshadowed the joy of his first prose publication, a satire on life in provincial Starobelsk titled "Podlinnaia istoriia Enskogo zemskogo sobraniia" (The True Story of the Zemstvo Meeting at N.). The piece appeared in the newspaper *Molva* (Rumor) on 11 April 1876 under the initials "R.A."—Raisa Vsevolodovna Aleksandrova, a woman to whom Garshin was all but engaged until 1879. In the spring of 1876 he tried to volunteer for the Serbian cause but was rejected, because he was of draft age and might be called up if Russia itself declared war on Turkey. When that eventuality came to pass on 12 April 1877, Garshin and a friend from the institute immediately volunteered. Garshin enlisted as a volunteer private in the 138th Bolkhov Infantry Regiment. He had no illusions about the war: the daily reports from the front had become for him far more than the story of Turkish atrocities and human carnage. The war took on a personal moral dimension. "I can't hide behind the walls of the Institute," he wrote in a letter to his mother on 12–13 April 1877, "when others my age are exposing their breasts to bullets."

The grueling march from Kishinev to the Danube took six months. Garshin saw his first action on 14 July. He was wounded a month later in his second engagement at Aiaslar on 11 August, the details of which are related in his autobiographical sketch "Aiaslarskoe delo" (The Action at Aiaslar), which was published in the periodical *Novosti* on 13 November 1877. This account of the war, however, was not the one that made Garshin famous. That distinction belonged to "Chetyre dnia." (Four Days.), which was published in the October 1877 issue of *Otechestvennye zapiski* (Notes of the Fatherland) and which marked Garshin's sensational entry onto the literary scene. Published within fourteen days of its receipt by Mikhail Evgrafovich Saltykov, the editor of the journal, the story instantly captivated readers by its interior monologue of a wounded Russian soldier lying for four days on an abandoned battlefield next to the Turkish soldier he has just killed. What begins in the story as a heroic act of uncommon bravery becomes, in its contemplation, nothing less than cold-blooded murder, and the narrator's despair over his deed only grows as he witnesses the rapid daily decomposition of his victim's body. Garshin's naturalistic depiction; the swift, episodic progression of the narrative; the perfect pitch of the narrator's tortured thoughts communicated in almost stream-of-consciousness fashion; and the antiwar sentiment of the story created a sensation among readers, who appreciated the ironies of "Chetyre dnia," one of which is that an act of valor is really an act of senseless brutality, and patriotism is really a betrayal of one's morals. The dead Turkish soldier becomes the means by which the narrator is saved, both physically and spiritually–through the water in the Turkish soldier's canteen and the truth that his death imparts. There had been nothing like this story written about war since Tolstoy's "Sevastopol'" stories (Sevastopol' v dekabre mesiatse," "Sevastopol' v mae," and "Sevastopol' v avguste 1855 goda," all published in 1855).

Garshin had composed "Chetyre dnia" while convalescing in Khar'kov, and its success took him off guard. As requests poured in from newspapers and journals for more stories, he took a step back and published one article on an art exhibit in December and only two stories–"Proisshestvie" (An Incident) and "Ochen' koroten'kii roman" (A Very Brief Romance)–in all of the following year. "I will now publish only in extreme cases," he declared, according to Edmund Yarwood's 1981 biography *Vsevolod Garshin*. The art exhibit review–"Imperatorskaia akademiia iskusstv za 1876–77 uchebnyi god" (The Imperial Academy of Art for the 1876–77 Academic Year)–continued Garshin's attack on the academy for its refusal to "paint real life" in its insistence that entries for its annual competition be based on biblical, classical, or mythological themes. As in his previous three reviews published in March and April of 1877, Garshin reveals his allegiance to the *Peredvizhniki* (Itinerants), a group of artists who broke away from the academy in 1863 and insisted that not only should art be brought to the common man in traveling exhibits but that it should also take up subjects that speak to the plight of the worker in the city or the peasant in the country. The social message and realistic style of the *Peredvizhniki* were important influences on Garshin's own art. Indeed, the writer became a close friend of one of the most famous artists associated with the group, Il'ia Efimovich Repin, and even posed as the son of Ivan the Terrible for Repin's painting *Ivan Groznyi s synom* (*Ivan IV with the Body of His Son,* 1885). Not surprisingly, artists and the theme of *ars poetica* occupy prominent places in several of Garshin's later stories.

"Proisshestvie" was published in March 1878. Garshin had doubts about its success: "I think *Otechestvennye zapiski* will turn it down," he wrote to his mother on 16 February 1878. "It has nothing to do with war or social, political or other questions. Simply the torments of two broken souls." Told through multiple viewpoints–the story includes an omniscient narrator as well as dueling first-person accounts–"Proisshestvie" relates how a young man commits suicide after he fails to save an articulate, strong-willed woman from a life of prostitution. This story is typical of Garshin's work in three ways: it uses sensationalist, even lurid material toward personal aesthetic purposes; it features a clash of subjective discourses to apprehend a higher truth; and it abounds in ironies. In this case the prostitute is an educated, knowing, and independent woman who balks at giving up her autonomy in exchange for the circumscribed role of a wife, while the respectable young man who tries to save her becomes a hopeless drunk. In a twist on a usual theme, the decent young man must be saved by the indecent whore. Her refusal to be saved, or to save another, subverts the image of the "good" prostitute popularized by Dostoevsky, and indeed the story parodies the excesses of Dostoevskian melodrama even as it exploits such melodrama for its own purposes: at one point the young man follows her as she walks the streets, then sits freezing in a hayloft, and watches her conduct her business through the lace curtains of her bedroom. Rather than making a moral point, this melodrama comments on gender roles and social stereotypes.

"Ochen' koroten'kii roman" continues Garshin's parodic engagement with Dostoevsky in the ironically told, first-person narrative of a young man who returns as an amputee from the war to his beloved, only to find her engaged to someone else. Crushed but not devastated, the amputee even agrees to serve as best man and accuses his incredulous reader-interlocutor of wishing to see three people unhappy rather than one. Published in the popular humor magazine *Strekoza* (Dragonfly) under the pseudonym "L'homme qui pleure" (The man who weeps), the story is clearly a spoof, whose source, according to Yarwood in *Vsevolod Garshin,* is Dostoevsky's *povest'* (novella) "Belye nochi" (White Nights, 1848).

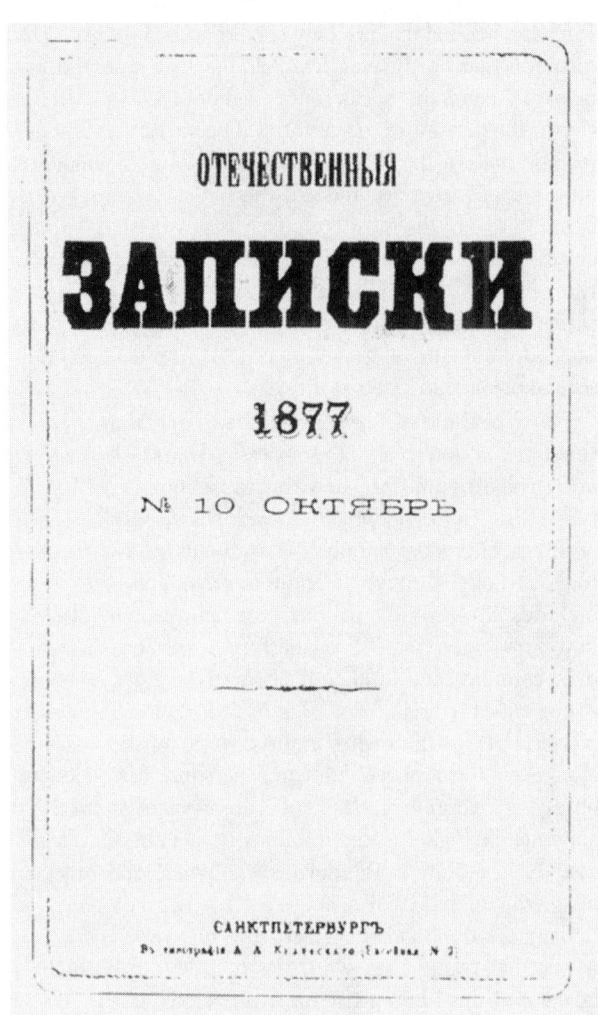

Cover for the issue of the journal Otechestvennye zapiski
*(Notes of the Fatherland) in which Garshin's war story
"Chetyre dnia" (Four Days) first appeared
(Bodleian Library, Oxford)*

In the meantime Garshin was promoted to ensign and recommended for a medal. The thought of active service again, however, filled the writer with dread. He spent the summer of 1878 in the countryside near Khar'kov, and in the autumn he attended lectures on history at St. Petersburg University. Most of November was spent in the Nikolaevskii hospital, where he underwent a series of medical tests to establish proof of his unfitness for service. There he met Nadezhda Mikhailovna Zolotilova, a medical student with whom he developed a close relationship. That December, with his disability confirmed, Garshin was able to resign his commission from the army. By the spring of 1879 his five-year relationship with Raisa Vsevolodovna had broken off (Garshin blamed her for the rupture). Free from the army and with a new love in his life, Garshin returned to his literary pursuits with renewed zeal.

Two new stories appeared in the March and April 1879 issues of *Otechestvennye zapiski:* "Trus. Iz zapisnoi knizhki" (The Coward) and "Vstrecha" (An Encounter). "Trus" marks a return to the war theme and is told in diary-entry form by a young man in despair at reports, received from the front, of daily casualties. Like the writer himself, he is torn: he holds war in contempt but agonizes over his guilty feeling that he should somehow share in the general suffering. The horror of the mounting, daily loss of life soon becomes embodied in the suffering of an acquaintance, stricken with gangrene, whose slow anguish and eventual death serve as a catalyst: the coward dons a uniform and heads to the front, where he stoically accepts the same fate as his friend–a premature death. "Vstrecha" makes use of the same device of contrasting two fates as a way of illuminating Garshin's theme. If human suffering is the central theme of "Trus," greed and dishonesty are taken up in "Vstrecha." Two former high school friends meet later in life just as one, Vasilii Petrovich, is about to take up a post as a teacher. The other, Nikolai Kudriashov, is already quite successful; he amassed a fortune as an engineer by swindling the government over a fraudulent breakwater project. The story, which at first seems a straightforward contrast between the virtuous teacher and the corrupt engineer, ends on an ambiguous note, as Vasilii Petrovich, once resentful but now overwhelmed by the well-appointed home of his friend and by the fabulous aquarium that Nikolai has built in his cellar, slowly withdraws his objections. Thus, Garshin subtly reveals the fine line between integrity and moral compromise.

Two other stories were finished and a *povest'*, "Nadezhda Nikolaevna" (1885), was begun by the end of 1879–despite another serious mental collapse in September. Garshin was then admitted to Dr. Aleksandr Iakovlevich Frei's psychiatric clinic in St. Petersburg, where he had been treated seven years earlier in 1872, and for the next two years he battled recurring bouts of dread and depression. His next story appeared in *Otechestvennye zapiski* the same month that he was institutionalized. "Khudozhniki" (Artists, 1879) is Garshin's most explicit treatment of the *ars poetica* theme. Two artists and their philosophies are contrasted in alternating diary entries from each that comprise both the separate chapters of the story and a larger dialogue on the nature of art. For one artist, Dedov, art is all about technique; it is supposed to soothe one's soul, and provide income for the painter. For the other, Riabinin, art is a pathogen–it should infect the viewer, disturb him, rouse him from his apathy, and change him and society for the better; here Garshin anticipates Tolstoy's views in his essay "Chto takoe iskusstvo?" (What is Art?, 1898) by nearly twenty years. The dramatic element of the story centers on Riabinin's decision to paint a *glukhar'* (human anvil), a worker whose job requires him to crawl inside a boiler and hold a rivet together with pincers while another worker strikes a head into it from the outside. Hellish and exhausting, the labor usually results in severe hearing impairment–

hence the Russian term *glukhar'*, which literally means "deaf person." Indeed, the mere act of painting causes a nervous breakdown in Riabinin, who thereafter gives up creating art and becomes a teacher. Dedov, in the meantime, wins the gold medal in the academy competition and is granted a trip abroad. While Garshin's endorsement of the Populist views of Riabinin is tempting to read in this conclusion, ultimately he does not side with either artist, and the story remains open-ended.

Winter 1879–1880 was as productive a time for Garshin professionally as it was traumatic personally. He completed three stories, which appeared in January, March, and June of 1880, as well as two more art reviews, both published in *Russkie vedomosti* (Russian News) in January and February. The first story, the fairy tale "Attalea princeps," was one of Garshin's most popular works, yet initially rejected for publication by Saltykov because of its pessimistic ending. Appearing in *Russkoe bogatstvo,* a journal that Garshin helped run at the time, "Attalea princeps" marks the first of his many fairy tales. It is about an exotic palm tree that seeks to escape its imprisoning urban greenhouse by growing up through the glass roof to freedom, only to discover, however, somber autumnal skies and the doleful warning from trees, stripped bare of their leaves, that the palm will freeze in the cold. "Is this all there is?" the palm asks, before it is hacked down and removed from the conservatory. An allegory on the human quest for freedom, "Attalea princeps" was also read as a tribute by Garshin to the indomitable will and determination of the Narodnaia volia (People's Will) movement, which sought political change at any cost, including through assassination and acts of terror.

Certainly Garshin admired the idealism of the men and women of Narodnaia volia. At the same time he abhorred "blood shed by whomsoever" and for whatever cause. When on 5 February 1880 an explosion at the Winter Palace planned by members of Narodnaia volia killed ten officers of the tsar's Finnish Life Guards while sparing the tsar himself, Garshin was haunted for days by visions of the victims. Two weeks later a young radical, Ippolit Osipovich Mlodetsky, made an attempt on the life of Count Mikhail Tarielovich Loris-Melikov, chairman of the Supreme Administration Commission. Mlodetsky was apprehended, tried, and sentenced to death. No longer could Garshin stand by idly. In a state of nervous agitation he wrote an impassioned letter to Loris-Melikov on 21 February 1880 and begged for an end to the cycle of violence: "Remember the lacerated corpses of February fifth, remember them! But also bear in mind that not with gallows and not with penal servitude, not with daggers, not with pistols and dynamite, can ideas either false or true be changed, but by an example of moral self-renunciation." Garshin delivered the letter personally and even obtained an audience with the count, during which he pleaded for Mlodetsky's

life. He left convinced that he had succeeded, but all in vain. Mlodetsky was hanged the next day.

Traumatized by the turn of events, Garshin sank deeper into mental crisis. He secretly left for Moscow, where he suddenly resolved to have an interview with the chief of police. After an incomprehensible conference (the chief realized Garshin was not in his right mind), Garshin left for Rybinsk, where his regiment was stationed, to collect the rest of the soldier's pay that was owed to him. From Rybinsk he intended to visit his mother in Khar'kov, but he inexplicably turned back instead to Moscow, where he passed two weeks of aimless existence. Deciding again to set out for his mother's home, Garshin found that he could afford a train ticket only as far as Tula. From there he conceived a desire to visit Tolstoy at his estate Iasnaia Poliana, where for several hours he discussed good and evil and the need to resist violence with the venerable writer, who remembered Garshin's "Chetyre dnia." Emboldened by the encounter, Garshin—in a state of intermittent insanity—roamed from town to village on a stolen horse, preaching the Gospel. He was ultimately found by his brother Evgenii and brought back to Khar'kov. For three weeks he lived with his brother in a state of extreme agitation and nervous exhaustion, then disappeared again only to turn up at an insane asylum in Orel. He was brought back to Khar'kov by train—bound and in a separate compartment—and placed in the Saburova Dacha psychiatric hospital, where patients were kept behind bars. Nadezhda Mikhailovna tried to visit him, but he was too violent to be seen. In September he was taken back to St. Petersburg and placed again under Frei's care before his maternal uncle Vladimir Stepanovich Akimov agreed to take him to his estate at Efimovka near the Black Sea to recuperate.

During this time the last two of the stories that he had completed over the winter were published—the noteworthy "Denshchik i ofitser" (Orderly and Officer, published in *Russkoe bogatstvo,* March 1880) and "Noch'. Rasskaz" (Night. A Story, published in *Otechestvennye zapiski,* 1880). "Denshchik i ofitser" won high praise from both Tolstoy and Turgenev, the latter of whom wrote Garshin a letter in which he identified the young writer as a worthy heir to the literary legacy of the older generation. This story was originally conceived as the first of several sketches on military life for a volume, to be titled "Liudi i voina" (People and War), a project that was never completed. "Denshchik i ofitser" is a masterpiece of understatement. As Peter Henry argues in his introduction to *From the Reminiscences of Private Ivanov and Other Stories* (1988), it "has the deceptive simplicity of an open-ended Chekovian tale: nothing dramatic happens, no problems are resolved, no one is morally reborn." Instead, the reader is left—as is often the case in a story by Garshin—with contrasting portraits of two men: Nikita, the retarded peasant orderly, who has been conscripted into the army and separated from his wife and family, for whom he was the main breadwinner, and Aleksandr Mikhailovich Stebelkov, the officer to whom Nikita is attached, an ensign fresh out of the military academy who dreams of promotions and glory. Though worlds apart in all respects, the fates of these two characters merge together by the end of the story, as each is shown to be similarly trapped in the tedium and shallowness of army life.

"Noch'," the last of the stories that Garshin wrote during winter 1879–1880, is an extended meditation on the meaning of life by a man, Aleksei Petrovich, contemplating suicide. It is told in a mixture of interior monologue, imagined dialogue, and third-person narrative. Infected by the modern sickness of self, Aleksei reflects upon his life story and confirms that he has squandered his life in thralldom to the petty, vain needs of his ego. Recollections of his childhood and a chance encounter with the New Testament, however, effect a sudden cure: to live life correctly, he must renounce his self, reject the needs of his ego, and live for "the truth common to all men and which exists in the world"–that is, for the service of others. Paradoxically, the story ends with his corpse lying peacefully on the floor, his pistol loaded and unused on the table next to him. Rather than despair and suicide, the overwhelming rapture of this biblical truth–likened to the pealing of a thousand church bells and the blinding flare-up of the sun–kills him in the end. His death is a literal realization of the central theme of the story: the need to "annihilate the self" in order to apprehend the greater truth of life.

From November 1880 to May 1882 Garshin lived at his uncle's estate and had almost no contact with his St. Petersburg friends. During the first few weeks he still suffered from frequent fits of violent weeping, but his uncle countered his depression by devising a strict regimen for him. He could receive letters from the outside world only from his mother, his brother Evgenii, and his closest friend, Viktor A. Fausek. The winter was passed in light physical exercise (ice-skating and activities with the children) and light mental occupations (transcribing legal reports for his uncle and playing chess in the evening). In such a way Garshin was shielded from the vicissitudes of life in the "real world." When Tsar Alexander II finally fell victim to an assassin's plot on 1 March 1881, Garshin was fortunately far from the capital and far from any thought of returning there. In time, however, the clouds began to pass. He even began to write again, initially at the request of the children of his friend Aleksandr Iakovlevich Gerd, who wrote to him at Efimovka asking for a fairy tale. In February 1882 he completed his second venture in the genre, "To, chego ne bylo" (What Never Was), a fable in the manner of Hans Christian Andersen that came out in the journal Ustoi (Foundations) that March. Taking place in a farmyard, it describes a spirited conversation about the purpose of life among a snail, a dung beetle, a lizard, a caterpillar, a grasshopper, a bay horse, and two flies. In discussing their particular perspective on the question, each inevitably reveals the narrowness of his worldview. The untimely arrival of the coachman Anton, however, puts an end to the philosophizing before any conclusion can be drawn, and half of the company is flattened under the sole of his boot. Only the flies, the horse, and the lizard escape, the latter losing half her tail for "daring to express my opinion," as she later says. While Garshin's readers were delighted, sensing a parody of current social theories laced with political allusions, he himself was flabbergasted. "It never occurred to me that these flies and Antons were anything but flies and Antons," he wrote in a letter dated 26 February 1882.

By May 1882 Garshin was well enough to return to St. Petersburg. One of the first things he did was to assemble everything that he had published into his first collection of stories, which came out later that year as Rasskazy (Stories). This volume helped considerably to secure his reputation as a writer. He also renewed his relationship with Nadezhda Mikhailovna, to whom he had not written in some two years and who was, by chance, in St. Petersburg on a visit. Separation had not quelled their affections, and by the time Nadezhda Mikhailovna left to resume her medical work on the Volga, Garshin had pledged his love to her. In July, Turgenev invited him to spend the summer at his estate at Spasskoe-Lutovinovo. Garshin's visit there was a satisfying and productive time, although Turgenev was unable to join him because of illness. Most of "Iz vospominanii riadovogo Ivanova" (published in Otechestvennye zapiski, 1883; translated as "From the Reminiscences of Private Ivanov," 1988), Garshin's finest povest', was composed there, and in general the atmosphere of rest and work completed his recovery. His only attempt at a newspaper feuilleton, "Peterburgskie pis'ma" (Letters from St. Petersburg), appeared in the Khar'kov newspaper Iuzhnyi krai (The South Country) later in 1882. In September he returned to St. Petersburg and obtained a minor post at the Annolovo paper warehouse. He resumed his contacts with the cultural elite of the capital, becoming friends at this time with the painter Repin, in whose apartment he spent many evenings discussing social and literary problems with other artists and writers.

The publication of "Iz vospominanii riadovogo Ivanova" marked a new plateau for the writer. In returning to his own experiences in the Russo-Turkish War, Garshin manages to achieve in the fictional tale of Private Ivanov a detached tone and epic sweep, as he depicts various scenes from the Russian peasant army's march from Kishinev to Bulgaria. The story encompasses several psychologically compelling portraits, in particular that of the first-person narrator Private Ivanov, who is a fictional alter ego of Garshin himself–an intellectual who has chosen to share the common lot and "expose his breast to the bullets"–and Captain Ventsel, a man of sensibility and culture who nevertheless frequently resorts to mercilessly beating the men

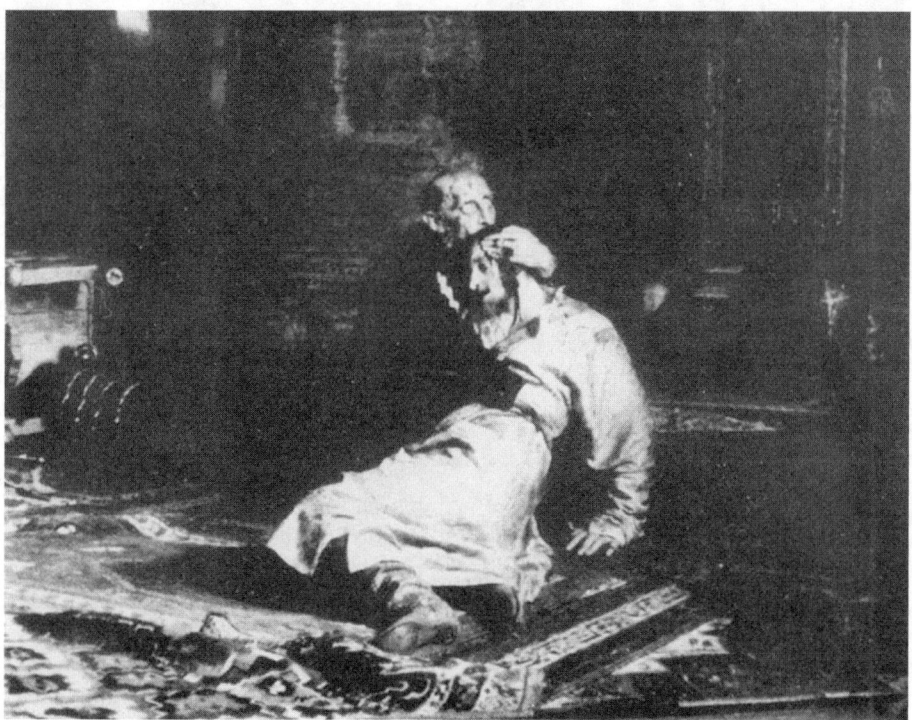

Ivan IV with the Body of His Son, *an 1885 painting by Repin for which Garshin posed as the*
model for the son (Tretyakov Gallery, Moscow)

under his charge. Although the story is mainly a loose narrative of the day-to-day events in the regiment, the contrast
between Ivanov, who is sympathetic to his peasant army
mates, and Ventsel, who berates and beats them, provides
an undercurrent of tension that pervades the story and
lends it one of its moral shadings. As is usually the case, this
Garshinian contrast produces an ambiguous outcome
when, in the last paragraph of the story, Ivanov glimpses
Ventsel alone in his tent, bitterly weeping over the men he
lost that day in battle—exactly the men whom he had been
abusing so relentlessly. While this epiphany is a fitting conclusion to the narrative, it is not, however, the main point of
the story, the focus of which has consistently been elsewhere, such as on the vivid details of camp life—communicated in flawless objective prose—as well as on the common
soldiers themselves, whose voices, personalities, and fears
are deftly caught in descriptions and dialogues that betray
Garshin's keen artistic eye and finely tuned ear. Turgenev
in particular praised "Iz vospominanii riadovogo Ivanova"
in a 2 February 1883 letter to the writer. Together with
Garshin's "Chetyre dnia" and "Denshchik i ofitser," this
story represents some of the finest writing in Russian literature on the experience of war.

On 11 February 1883 Garshin married Nadezhda
Mikhailovna, and the couple settled into a new life together.
In April he obtained a new post as secretary at the Congress
of Representatives of Russian Railways in St. Petersburg.
The work was light—a mere three hours or so a day—and he

was able to write and pursue other activities as he saw fit.
Although his reputation as a writer was secure, Garshin
nevertheless could not see making literature "the sole occupation" of his life. He wrote slowly and wrote what pleased
him, even starting work on a novel set in the time of Peter
the Great (a work he left uncompleted at his death). He was
quite happily married but still suffered from bouts of depression—attacks which, in Garshin's own words, were prevented from turning into full-blown crises only by the
loving presence of his wife. News of Turgenev's death
reached him in August 1883, just as he was finishing work
on a new story, which he promptly dedicated to Turgenev's
memory. "Krasnyi tsvetok" (The Red Flower), published in
Otechestvennye zapiski that October, stands beside "Chetyre
dnia" as Garshin's most frequently anthologized and widely
known story. Many critics view it as his masterpiece. In his
introduction to *The Reminiscences of Private Ivanov and Other Stories* Henry calls it "the artistic summit of his achievement, a
vibrant, image-rich, 'surrealist' narrative, a stylistic tour de
force." It is a taut third-person account of a violently mad
inmate of an insane asylum who believes all the evil in the
world is concentrated in the three red blooms of a poppy
flower growing on the asylum grounds. His struggle to
destroy these three blooms—thus saving the world from universal evil—makes up the central action of the story, which,
by Garshin's admission, relates to his time at the Saburova
Dacha psychiatric institute. In a letter to a friend on 9 July
1883 he described the story as "somewhat fantastic" yet

"strictly realistic"; the writer's negotiation of these extremes lends the story its peculiar surrealism.

Like many of Garshin's stories, "Krasnyi tsvetok" proceeds in swift, episodic fashion—now tense, now lax—as the narration alternates between dispassionate, almost clinical descriptions of the conditions and routines of the asylum and intensely subjective, inwardly focused passages in which one is privy to the thoughts and emotions of the nameless inmate. In this way the narration itself mirrors the madman's state of mind—now lucid, now delusional. His self-professed messianic mission is complicated by the fact that picking the flowers that grow rather luxuriantly in the asylum garden is strictly forbidden. He must plan his attempts carefully and repeat his feat three times, for he is able to pluck only one flower at a time. The number "3," the red crosses on the inmates' gardening caps, the white robes that they wear, and the madman's own dialogue with a "heavenly father" are obvious Christian associations, although the madman himself names not Satan but the Zoroastrian Lord of the Darkness, Ahriman, as his supreme foe in this battle. In the end he succeeds in his mission, despite both the fierce resistance of the asylum staff who try to prevent his seemingly irrational thefts and the nearly lethal "poison" that he must absorb into his body while clutching the red blossoms under his nightgown. The last blossom actually costs him his life, and he is buried with the scarlet flower still clutched in his mad grip, a typical Garshinian marker of narrative ambiguity: the flower apparently has not died—only the madman has. Responses to this story were overwhelmingly positive, with some critics viewing it as a classical depiction of mental illness, and others reading into it hidden social commentary.

Besides several translations from French—*Kolomba* (1883) by Prosper Mérimée, "Niurenbergskaia pech'" (The Nuremberg Stove, 1883) by Marie Louise de la Ramée Ouida, and "Zamok ved'my" (The Witch's Castle) and "Chakhlau" by Carmen de Silva—which all appeared in various venues that same year, Garshin's only other original work for 1883 was the story "Medvedi" (The Bears). Set in 1857 in the provincial city of Belsk, it tells of a government-mandated slaughter of performing bears owned by traveling gypsies. From its lyrical opening passages to its ironic conclusion, the influence of Nikolai Vasil'evich Gogol is everywhere felt, as the story lurches from pathos to bathos in the sort of "laughter through tears" style often associated with Gogol's mature work. As in Gogol's fiction, "Medvedi" depicts a stultifying sameness of provincial life, the same parade of grotesque provincial types, the same poeticizing of triviality by a playful narrator, and the same underlying sense of hopeless melancholy and moral emptiness that concludes many of Gogol's stories. In this instance the gypsies simply take to stealing horses when deprived of their main livelihood, an outcome foreseen by the townsfolk but deemed inevitable by them, as the gov-ernment edict can not be countermanded. The absurd implication—that the gypsies' horse thievery must be tolerated, because the government finds that activity an acceptable alternative to performing with their bears—is thick with irony.

"Medvedi" was the writer's last appearance in *Otechestvennye zapiski,* which was closed down by the authorities on 20 April 1884 for political reasons. The closure came as a harsh blow to Garshin, who was sympathetic with the Populist views of the journal, knew its editorial staff, and had published all of his most important works there. Already in a state of depression, Garshin slid deeper into illness upon hearing the news. He passed the spring and summer of 1884 in a state of total apathy, working sporadically on his *povest'* "Nadezhda Nikolaevna" before breaking off work on it that August. The only story by Garshin to appear in 1884 was his third fairy tale, "Skazka o zhabe i roze" (The Tale of the Toad and the Rose), composed on 1 January 1884 after a piano recital by Anton Grigor'evich Rubinshtein. According to Garshin's friend Fausek, Garshin conceived of the story after being struck by the disparity between Rubinshtein's beautiful playing and the unpleasant expression of a disagreeable elderly man of high rank sitting in the audience. In the story the offensive old man can be glimpsed in an ugly toad, who tries—out of sheer spite—to gobble up a beautiful rose which has just opened in the garden of an extremely sick little boy. The rose is saved from its fate, however, when the boy's sister plucks it at his request so that he may smell its perfume before he dies. Thus, beauty prevails over ugliness and cruelty, even in death.

In January 1885 Garshin traveled to Moscow, hoping (albeit in vain) to see Tolstoy. Though still fighting off attacks of melancholy, he managed to complete "Nadezhda Nikolaevna" early in the year and began an active association with Litfond (The Literary Fund), an organization that aided needy writers. Garshin's most ambitious work, yet also one of his least successful, "Nadezhda Nikolaevna" appeared that spring in the second and third issues of *Russkaia mysl'* (Russian Thought). One critic, Milton Ehre, in his section on Garshin for the *Handbook of Russian Literature* (1985), called it "a case of Dostoevsky undigested," and indeed its story of a doomed love triangle suffers from melodramatic excess, beginning with its cast of characters: a noble prostitute, a suffering artist and his hunchbacked colleague, a jealous writer, and a mysterious retired Polish captain who runs a boardinghouse. The story is simple. The artist Lopatin finds the perfect model for his painting of the French terrorist Charlotte Corday in the title character, Nadezhda Nikolaevna, a prostitute and one-time love object of Bessonov, the jealous writer. When Lopatin and Nadezhda Nikolaevna fall in love, Bessonov confronts the couple in a jealous rage, killing her before Lopatin strikes him down. Throughout, the hunchback wrings his hands and the enigmatic Pole makes mysterious appearances. In the end, Lopatin—stricken with remorse over the killing—awaits his own

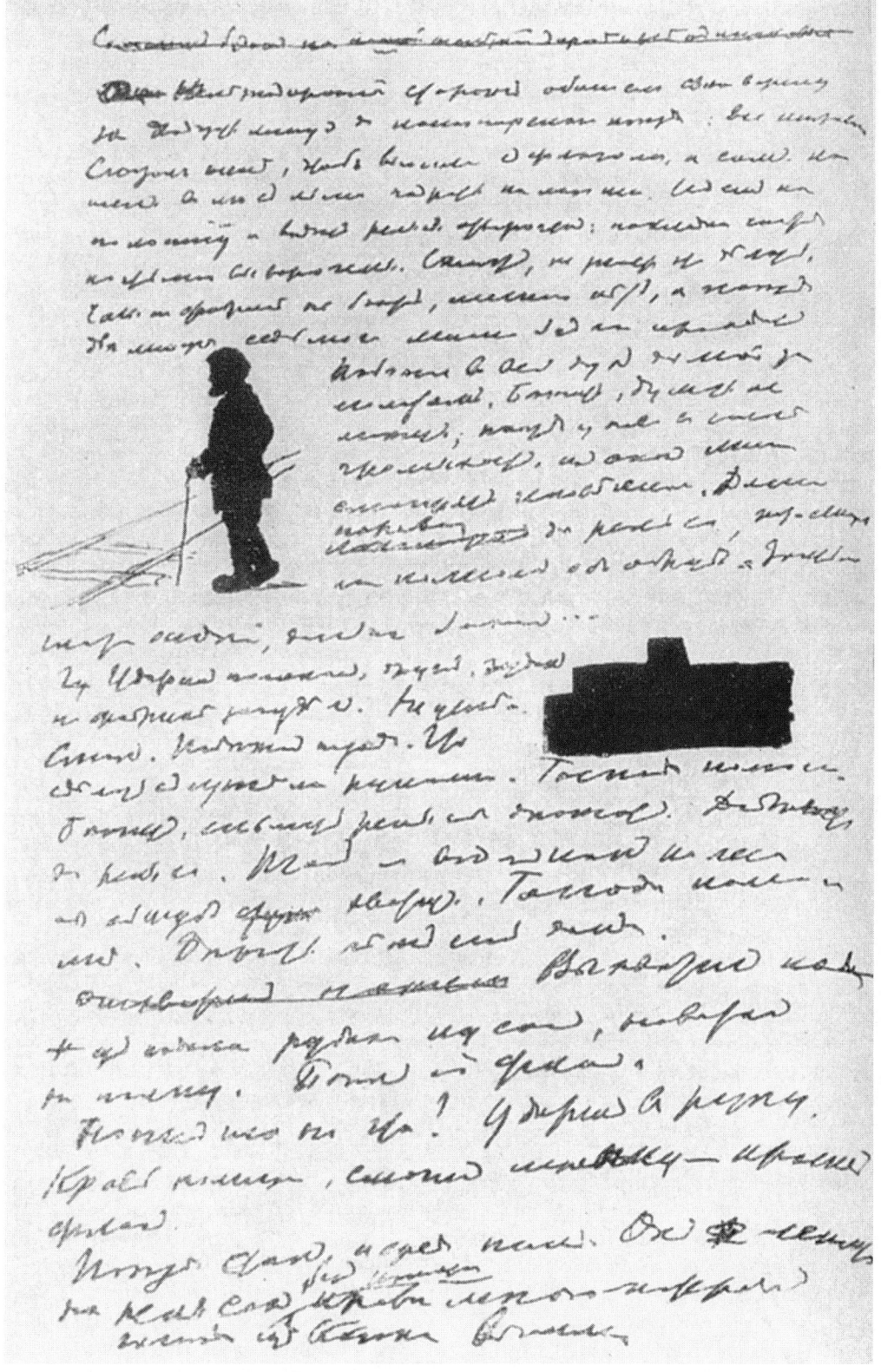

Page from the manuscript for Garshin's 1887 story "Signal" (from Porudominsky, Garshin, *1962)*

death from sheer grief and hopes to be reunited with Nadezhda Nikolaevna and Bessonov in the other world. The story, intended by Garshin as a continuation of the tale of the prostitute from "Proisshestvie," failed to create a stir among readers.

In August 1885 Garshin complained of depression again. He wrote to his friend Vladimir Mikhailovich Latkin on 29 September 1885, recalling the battle of Aiaslar, "I have often bitterly regretted that the bullet eight years ago did not turn a little more to the left." The writer's mood, however, improved the following spring, and he wrote to Fausek on 9 April 1886 that he felt like a normal person for the first time in years. His fourth fairy tale, "Skazanie o gordom Aggee" (The Legend of Aggei the Proud), came out in *Russkaia mysl'* at this time, his only publication in 1886. A retelling of the classic Russian tale of how a proud king is stripped of his wealth by God and is forced to live among the poor of his realm for three years, Garshin's version differs from its source only in its conclusion, in which Aggei refuses to retake the throne after his period of penance because he wishes to continue his life as a guide for twelve blind men. Tolstoy's teaching is discernible here, and indeed Tolstoy gave up working on his own variant when he heard of Garshin's story.

Tolstoy's influence is felt in Garshin's next story as well. "Signal" (The Signal) was published in the first issue of *Severnyi vestnik* (The Northern Messenger) in 1887. In this story Garshin returns to his favorite technique of contrasting two characters—in this case, two linemen: Semen Ivanov, an old-timer who served in the Russo-Turkish War and has finally carved out a piece of happiness with his new job for the railroads, and Vasilii Spiridov, a young malcontent who harbors a grudge against the authorities. Failing to gain satisfaction over his complaint of mistreatment, Spiridov pulls up a rail, intent on derailing a passenger train. Ivanov discovers the sabotage when the train is already nearing the spot, and in desperation bloodies his handkerchief to signal the train to stop, only to faint from loss of blood. Spiridov, who had been hiding nearby, picks up the flag, stops the train, and confesses to the deed. Although Ivanov seems cast here in the role of the simple Tolstoyan hero, the ending is actually more ambiguous. There are several textual indicators that argue for Garshin's submerged criticism of Ivanov and of Tolstoyan morality in the story, whose true yet unlikely hero is actually Spiridov, an "early model of the positive proletarian hero," according to Henry in his introduction to *Reminiscences*. As in many of his other stories, Garshin leaves the conclusion to this one open to interpretation.

Garshin was in sufficient good humor in March 1887 to join his friend Aleksandr Gerd and Gerd's family on Easter holiday in the Crimea, but the summer brought a sharp turn in his health. In the autumn he was forced to resign his position at the Congress of Representatives of Russian Railways. The death that year of his friend, the popular poet

Semen Iakovlevich Nadson, from consumption was also a blow. Besides "Signal," Garshin published only two other works before his death: an art exhibition review for *Severnyi vestnik*, which includes extended reflections on two paintings, Vasilii Dmitrievich Polenov's *Christ and a Sinner* (1888) and Vasilii Ivanovich Surikov's *Boyarina Morozova* (1887), and his last fictional work, "Liagushka-puteshestvennitsa" (The Traveling Frog), a lightly humorous, ironic fable, published in the children's journal *Rodnik* (The Spring) in July 1887, about how a frog goes for a ride with some ducks. In September he completed a story with an occultist theme, but he later destroyed it. Throughout the fall and winter Garshin was despondent. When a family scandal broke out in early 1888 over his brother Evgenii's short-lived marriage to the sister of his wife Nadezhda Mikhailovna, it proved too much for Garshin to take. A hostile letter from his mother, who blamed Nadezhda Mikhailovna for the fiasco, sent Garshin spiraling into mental collapse. Frei was consulted once more, and a trip out of town was prescribed. On the morning of his departure for the Caucasus, however, Garshin threw himself down a stairwell. He died several days later, on 24 March 1888, at the Red Cross Hospital and was buried on 26 March at Volkovo Cemetery in St. Petersburg.

A tormented soul who deeply felt the sufferings of others, Vsevolod Mikhailovich Garshin is at once a tragic and noble figure. Endearing him to the readers of his day, these qualities continue to influence how he is perceived. While he is sometimes characterized as the best of a group of second-rate writers, the continued interest in, and popularity of, his works are testimony to the lasting value, significance, and quality of his prose. Garshin's wide acquaintance with the important cultural figures of his day placed him at the center of cultural life in St. Petersburg; he knew the writers Tolstoy, Turgenev, and Uspensky; the editor and publicist Vladimir Grigor'evich Chertkov; the poets Nadson, Nikolai Maksimovich Minsky [Vilenkin], and Aleksei Nikolaevich Pleshcheev; and the painters Repin, Nikolai Aleksandrovich Iaroshenko, and Mikhail Egorovich Malyshev. Garshin was both importantly influenced and importantly influential, and to discuss those who came after him—Chekhov, Leonid Nikolaevich Andreev, and Maksim Gor'ky, to name only a few—is impossible without reference to Garshin. His finely crafted, innovative, and eclectic twenty-odd stories have earned him a secure place in Russian letters.

Letters:

"Pis'ma," in *Polnoe sobranie sochinenii V. M. Garshina* (St. Petersburg: A. F. Marks, 1910), pp. 481–505;

Polnoe sobranie sochinenii, edited by Iu. G. Oksman, volume 3 (Moscow & Leningrad: Academia, 1934);

"Pis'mo M. T. Loris-Melikovu, 25 fevralia 1880," *Krasnyi arkhiv*, 3 (1934): 143–144;

"Pis'ma V. M. Garshina k V. G. Chertkovu," *Zven'ia*, 5 (1935): 679–681;

"Dva neopublikovannykh pis'ma Garshina k I. T. Poliakovu," *Zven'ia*, 6 (1936): 799–803;

"Pis'mo ofitsial'nomu litsu, 1877–88," *Zvezda*, 2 (1945): 137;

"Pis'mo F. F. Pavlenkovu, 29 noiabria 1882," *Literaturnyi Saratov*, 14 (1956): 236;

Evgenii Dmitrievich Petriaev, ed., "Papka starogo khudozhnika," in his *Liudi, rukopisi, knigi: Literaturnye nakhodki* (Kirov: Kirovskoe otdelenie Volgo-Viatskogo knizhnogo izdatel'stva, 1970), pp. 155–170;

"Iz perepiski," *Literaturnoe nasledstvo*, 87 (1977): 198–239.

Bibliographies:

Edmund Yarwood, "A Bibliography of Works by and about Vsevolod Melvyl. Garshin," *Russian Literature Triquarterly*, 17 (1982): 227–241;

M. V. Brestkina and others, "A New Garshin Bibliography," in *Vsevolod Garshin at the Turn of the Century: An International Symposium in Three Volumes*, edited by Peter Henry, Vladimir Porudominsky, and Mikhail Girshman (Oxford: Northgate Press, 2000), pp. 119–191.

Biographies:

S. Durylin, "Vs. M. Garshin: Iz zapisok biografa," *Zven'ia*, 5 (1935): 571–676;

N. Z. Beliaev, *Garshin* (Moscow: Molodaia gvardiia, 1938);

Grigorii Abramovich Bialyi, *V. M. Garshin: Kritiko-biograficheskii ocherk* (Moscow: Gostlitizdat, 1955);

Vladimir Porudominsky, *Garshin* (Moscow: Molodaia gvardiia, 1962);

Bialyi, *Vsevolod Mikhailovich Garshin* (Leningrad: Prosveshchenie, 1969);

Edmund Yarwood, *Vsevolod Garshin* (Boston: Twayne, 1981);

Peter Henry, *A Hamlet of His Time. Vsevolod Garshin: The Man, His Works and His Milieu* (Oxford: Meeuws, 1983);

Porudominsky, *Grustnyi soldat, ili, Zhizn' Vsevoloda Garshina* (Moscow: Kniga, 1986).

References:

M. Artz, "'The Red Flower' of V. M. Garshin and 'The Black Monk' of A. P. Chekhov: A Survey of One Hundred Years of Literary Criticism," *Russian Literature*, 20, no. 3 (1986): 267–295;

G. Bernikov, "Problema pessimizma: Chekhov i Garshin," *Russkaia literatura*, 1 (1960): 3–25;

James Aaron Bezant, "Vsevolod Mikhailovitch Garshine," *Anglo-Russian Literary Society: Proceedings*, 105, no. 23 (6 December 1898): 23–45;

Grigorii Abramovich Bialyi, "Problemy obshchestvennogo pessimizma v tvorchestve V. M. Garshina,"

Izvestiia Akademii Nauk SSSR: Otdelenie obshchestvennykh nauk, 9, 10 (1935): 813–836, 1003–1038;

Bialyi, *V. M. Garshin i literaturnaia bor'ba vos'midesiatykh godov* (Moscow & Leningrad: Izdatel'stvo AN SSSR, 1937);

Jan Brodal, "Motiv samopozhertvovaniia v tvorchestve V. M. Garshina," *Scando-Slavica*, 30 (1984): 117–131;

Brodal, "The Pessimism of V. M. Garshin," *Scando-Slavica*, 19 (1973): 17–30;

Kornei Ivanovich Chukovsky, "O Vsevolode Garshine," *Russkaia mysl'*, 12 (1909): 117–141;

S. Durylin, *Repin i Garshin* (Moscow: Gosudarstvennaia akademiia khudozhestvennykh nauk, 1926);

Milton Ehre, "Garshin, Vsevolod Mikhailovich," in *Handbook of Russian Literature*, edited by Victor Terras (New Haven: Yale University Press, 1985);

Fedor Evnin, "F. M. Dostoevsky i V. M. Garshin," *Izvestiia Akademii Nauk SSSR: Otdelenie literatury i iazyka*, 4 (1962): 289–301;

Leland Fetzer, "Art and Assassination: Garshin's 'Nadezhda Nikolaevna,'" *Russian Review*, 34, no. 1 (1975): 55–65;

Peter Henry, "Image and Symbol in Garshin's 'The Red Flower,'" *Essays in Poetics*, 7, no. 1 (1982): 1–41;

Henry, "Imagery of *podvig* and *podvizhnichestvo* in the Works of Garshin and the Early Gorky," *Slavonic and East European Review*, 61, no. 1 (1983): 139–159;

Henry, "Vsevolod Garshin and the Early Gorky: Some Artistic and Cultural Links and Affinities," in *Fifty Years On: Gorky and His Time*, edited by Nicholas Luker (Nottingham: Astra, 1987), pp. 63–104;

Henry, Vladimir Porudominsky, and Mikhail Girshman, eds., *Vsevolod Garshin at the Turn of the Century: An International Symposium in Three Volumes* (Oxford: Northgate Press, 2000);

L. A. Iezuitova, "Leonid Andreev i Vsevolod Garshin," *Vestnik Leningradskogo universiteta: Seriia istoriia, iazyk i literatura*, 8 (1964): 87–109;

A. H. Keesman-Marwitz, "Ivanov's Race With Time (On V. Garšin's 'Cetyre dnja')," in *Semantic Analysis of Literary Texts: To Honour Jan van der Eng on the Occasion of his 65th Birthday*, edited by Eric De Haard, Thomas Langerak, and Willem G. Weststeijn (New York: Elsevier/Nelson, 1990), pp. 353–364;

Keesman-Marwitz, "'To, chego ne bylo': Some Thoughts on Garshin's First Animal Tale," *Russian Literature*, 37 (1995): 497–504;

V. Kostrica, "The Work of V. M. Garshin in the Context of Russian Literature," *Scottish Slavonic Review,* 11 (1988): 45–55;

Karl D. Kramer, "Impressionistic Tendencies in the Work of Vsevolod Garshin," in *American Contributions to the Seventh International Congress of Slavists, Warsaw, August 21–27, 1973: Literature and Folklore,* edited by Victor Terras, volume 2 (The Hague: Mouton, 1973), pp. 339–355;

Krasnyi tsvetok: Literaturnyi sbornik v pamiat' V. M. Garshina (St. Petersburg: I. N. Skorokhodov, 1889);

Hamilkars Lejins, "Suicide in Garshin's Life and Stories," *South Central Bulletin,* 4 (1967): 34–44;

Clarence Manning, "The Guilty Conscience of Garshin," *Slavonic Review,* 29 (1931): 285–292;

Iurii Gennad'evich Miliukov and others, eds., *Poetika V. M. Garshina: Uchebnoe posobie* (Cheliabinsk: Cheliabinskii universitet, 1990);

L. E. Obolensky, "V. M. Garshin," as Sozertsatel', *Russkoe bogatstvo,* nos. 3, 4 (1886): 227–241, 206–214;

Pamiati V. M. Garshina: Khudozhestvenno-literaturnyi sbornik (St. Petersburg: V. I. Shtein, 1889);

Fan Parker, *Vsevolod Garshin: A Study of a Russian Conscience* (Morningside Heights, N.Y.: King's Crown Press, 1946);

Bernard Penny, "Vsevolod Mikhaylovich Garshin: A Study of the Dynamics of Guilt," dissertation, Georgetown University, 1977;

G. F. Samosiuk, ed., *Sovremenniki o V. M. Garshine: vospominaniia* (Saratov: Izdatel'stvo Saratovskogo universiteta, 1977);

N. Shmakov, *Tipy Vsevoloda Garshina: Kriticheskii etiud* (Tver': Tipografiia F. S. Murav'eva, 1884);

George Siegel, "The Art of Vsevolod Garshin," dissertation, Harvard University, 1956;

Liv Tudge, "V. M. Garshin (1855–1888) and His Works in Russian and Soviet Literary Criticism," dissertation, Oxford University, 1974;

Vladimir Tumanov, "V. M. Garshin: A Pioneer of Direct Interior Monologue," *Wiener Slavistischer Almanach,* 30 (1992): 47–77;

Paul Varnai, "The Prose of V. Garshin," dissertation, University of Michigan, 1970;

Varnai, "Structure and Syntactic Devices in Garshin's Stories," *Russian Language Journal,* 94–95 (1972): 61–71;

Harry Weber, "Mithra and St. George: Sources of *Krasnyi tsvetok*," *Slavic Review,* 46, no. 2 (1987): 281–291;

Edmund Yarwood, "Hero and Foil: Structure in the Stories of V. Garshin," dissertation, University of North Carolina, 1974.

Papers:

Vsevolod Mikhailovich Garshin's papers are located at the Institute of Russian Literature (IRLI, Pushkin House) and the Russian National Library (RNB) in St. Petersburg, as well as the Russian State Library (RGB) and the Russian Literary Museum (RLM) in Moscow. A listing of archival holdings relevant to Garshin in IRLI can be found in L. P. Klochkova, "Rukopisi i perepiska V. M. Garshina," *Biulleten' Rukopisnogo otdela Pushkinskogo doma* (Moscow & Leningrad: AN SSSR, Institut russkoi literatury), 8 (1959): 45–114.

Apollon Aleksandrovich Grigor'ev
(July 1822 – 25 September 1864)

Robert Whittaker
Lehman College, City University of New York

BOOKS: *Stikhotvoreniia* (St. Petersburg: K. Krai, 1846);

Sochineniia, edited by Nikolai Nikolaevich Strakhov (St. Petersburg: Obshchestvennaia pol'za, 1876);

Moi literaturnye i nravstvennye skital'chestva, edited by Pavel Sukhotin (Moscow: K. F. Nekrasov, 1915);

Sobranie sochinenii, 14 volumes, edited by Vladimir Fedorovich Savodnik (Moscow: I. N. Kushnerev, 1915–1916);

Stikhotvoreniia, edited by Aleksandr Aleksandrovich Blok (Moscow: K. F. Nekrasov, 1916);

Polnoe sobranie sochinenii i pisem Apollona Grigor'eva v 12-i tomakh, edited by Vasilii Spiridonovich Spiridonov, volume 1 (Petrograd: P. P. Ivanov, 1918);

Vospominaniia, edited by Razumnik Vasil'evich Ivanov-Razumnik (Moscow & Leningrad: Academia, 1930);

Stikhotvoreniia, edited, with an introduction, by Nikolai Leonidovich Stepanov, Biblioteka poeta, Malaia seriia (Moscow: Sovetskii pisatel', 1937);

Izbrannye proizvedeniia, edited, with an introduction and notes, by Pavel Petrovich Gromov and Boris Osipovich Kostelianets, Biblioteka poeta, Bol'shaia seriia (Leningrad: Sovetskaia Rossiia, 1959);

Literaturnaia kritika, edited, with an introduction, by Boris Fedorovich Egorov (Moscow: Khudozhestvennaia literatura, 1967);

Sochineniia, edited by Victor S. Krupich (Villanova, Pa.: Villanova University Press, 1970).

Editions and Collections: *Stikhotvoreniia i poemy,* edited by Boris Fedorovich Egorov (Moscow: Sovetskaia Rossiia, 1978);

Estetika i kritika, edited, with an introduction, by Anna Ivanovna Zhuravleva (Moscow: Iskusstvo, 1980);

Vospominaniia, edited, with an introduction, by Egorov (Leningrad: Nauka, 1980);

Teatral'naia kritika, edited, with an introduction, by Anatolii Iakovlevich Al'tshuller and Egorov (Leningrad: Iskusstvo, 1985);

Apollon Aleksandrovich Grigor'ev

Iskusstvo i nravstvennost', edited, with an introduction, by Egorov (Moscow: Sovremennik, 1986);

Vospominaniia, edited, with an introduction, by Egorov (Leningrad: Nauka, 1987);

Odisseia poslednego romantika: Poemy. Stikhotvoreniia. Drama. Proza. Pis'ma. Vospominaniia ob Apollone Grigor'eve, edited, with an introduction, by Aleksandr L'vovich Ospovat (Moscow: Moskovskii rabochii, 1988);

Stikhotvoreniia i poemy, edited by Evgenii Lebedev (Moscow: Sovremennik, 1989);

141

Sochineniia, 2 volumes, edited, with an introduction, by Egorov and Ospovat (Moscow: Khudozhestvennaia literatura, 1990);

Stikhotvoreniia. Poemy. Dramy, edited, with an introduction and notes, by Egorov (St. Petersburg: Akademicheskii proekt, 2001).

Editions in English: *My Literary and Moral Wanderings and Other Autobiographical Material,* translated by Ralph Eugene Matlaw (New York: Dutton, 1962)–includes "A Hopeless Situation," "Sorrowful Thoughts about the Despotism and Voluntary Slavery of Thought," and "A Brief Record as a Keepsake for My Old and New Friends";

"*A Nest of Gentry* by Ivan Turgenev," in *Literature and National Identity,* edited by P. Debreczeny and J. Zeldin (Lincoln: University of Nebraska Press, 1970), pp. 65–118;

"The Literary Work of Count L. Tolstoi," translated by Paul Mitchell, *Russian Literature Triquarterly,* 17 (1982): 7–18.

OTHER: "Drugoi iz mnogikh," in *Proza russkikh poetov XIX v.* (Moscow, 1982).

TRANSLATIONS: William Shakespeare, *Son v letniuiu noch',* in *Biblioteka dlia chteniia,* 144, no. 8 (1857): 195–266;

Shakespeare, *Sheilok, venetsianskii zhid* (St. Petersburg: V. G. Avsenko, 1860);

Carlo Pepoli, *Puritane,* music by Vincenzo Bellini (St. Petersburg, 1861);

Francesco Maria Piave, *Ernani,* music by Giuseppe Verdi (St. Petersburg: F. Stellovsky, 1861);

Antonio Somma, *Bal-maskarad,* music by Verdi (St. Petersburg, 1862);

Eugène Scribe and Charles-Gaspar-Delestr-Poirson, *Graf Ori (Il conte Ory),* music by Gioacchino Rossini (St. Petersburg: F. Stellovsky, 1862);

Lorenzo Da Ponte [Emanuele Conigliano], *Don-Zhuan* (Don Giovanni), music by Wolfgang Amadeus Mozart (St. Petersburg: F. Stellovsky, 1862);

Josef Sonnleithner and Georg Friedrich Treitschke, *Fidelio,* music by Ludwig van Beethoven (St. Petersburg, 1862);

Gaetano Donizetti and Michele Accursi [Giacomo Ruffini], *Don Paskvale,* music by Donizetti (St. Petersburg: F. Stellovsky, 1863);

Jules Barbier and Michel Carré, *Faust,* music by Charles Gounod (St. Petersburg, 1863);

Carlo Pedrotti, *Fiorina, ili Shveitsarskaia devushka (La Fanciulla di Glaris)* (St. Petersburg: F. Stellovsky, 1863);

Salvatore Cammarano, *Luchiia di Lammermur (Lucia di Lammermoor),* music by Donizetti (St. Petersburg: F. Stellovskogo, 1863);

Felice Romani, *Somnambula,* music by Bellini (St. Petersburg, 1863);

W. Friedrich [Friedrich Wilhelm Riese], *Stradella,* music by Friedrich von Flotow (St. Petersburg, 1863);

Alphonse Royer and Gustav Vaëz, *Favoritka (La Favorita),* music by Donizetti (St. Petersburg: F. Stellovsky, 1863);

Giacomo Ferretti, *Chenerentola (La Cenerentola),* music by Rossini (St. Petersburg: F. Stellovsky, 1864);

Gaetano Rossi, *Linda di Shamuni,* music by Donizetti (St. Petersburg, 1864);

Shakespeare, "Romeo i Dzhul'etta," *Russkaia stsena,* 4, no. 8 (1864): 101–260;

Carl Beck, *Deti stepei, ili ukrainskie tsygane,* music by A. Rubinshtein (Moscow, 1867).

Apollon Grigor'ev, considered the best nineteenth-century Russian literary critic, was also a significant poet, memoirist, and translator. He was the first to appreciate Aleksandr Sergeevich Pushkin's universal genius, to recognize Aleksandr Nikolaevich Ostrovsky's creation of a Russian national theater, to appreciate Nikolai Vasil'evich Gogol's significance as a thinker, to understand Ivan Sergeevich Turgenev's idiosyncratic realism, and to appreciate Leo Tolstoy's uncompromising objectivity as seen in his early works. Although Grigor'ev died before the great novels of Fyodor Dostoevsky appeared, he recognized Dostoevsky's distinctive talent in *Zapiski iz podpol'ia* (Notes from Underground, 1864) and, as Dostoevsky recalled in an 1869 letter to Strakhov, Grigor'ev encouraged him, "Keep writing just this way!" Grigor'ev rejected the aesthetics and critical methods of the progressive Westernizers, or Revolutionary Democrats (Vissarion Grigor'evich Belinsky, Nikolai Aleksandrovich Dobroliubov, Nikolai Gavrilovich Chernyshevsky, Dmitrii Ivanovich Pisarev), and therefore has been viewed as conservative. But he also criticized the positions of the Slavophiles and aesthetic critics (the Kireevsky brothers Ivan and Petr Vasil'evich, Ivan Sergeevich Aksakov, Aleksei Stepanovich Khomiakov, Aleksandr Vasil'evich Druzhinin). Temperamentally and philosophically, Grigor'ev was a late Romantic. His early "historical" criticism developed later into a method he called *organicheskaia kritika* (organic criticism), which in the 1860s formed the theoretical basis for the *pochvennichestvo* (native soil) movement of Dostoevsky, his brother Mikhail Dostoevsky, and Nikolai Nikolaevich Strakhov. Grigor'ev's erudite criticism, grounded in the philosophy of Friedrich Wilhelm Joseph von Schelling and other German idealist philosophers, was, however, obscured by his unwillingness to simplify his views, and

The Grigor'ev family home on Malaia Polianka in Moscow, 1915
(from Grigor'ev, Pis'ma, 1999)

his effectiveness as a journalist and critic was undermined by disorder in his personal life and by drinking, debts, and dissolute tendencies.

Apollon Aleksandrovich Grigor'ev, whose exact date of birth remains unknown, was born the illegitimate son of a civil servant in July 1822. Grigor'ev later asserted the "legitimacy" of his democratic, nonnoble origins in a colorful memoir of his early years, *Moi literaturnye i nravstvennye skital'chestva* (My Literary and Moral Wanderings, 1915), which appeared first in *Vremia* (Time) in 1862 and then in *Epokha* (Epoch) in 1864. His mother, Tat'iana Andreevna (maiden name unknown) was the daughter of the Grigor'ev family coachman; Grigor'ev's father, Aleksandr Ivanovich Grigor'ev, had brought her to Moscow early in 1822 from the family home, Irinki (or Arinki), in Vladimir province. Five months after Apollon's birth his father and mother married, and four months later he was legally adopted. His early years were shaped by his surroundings in the merchant and clerk district of Moscow (Zamoskvorech'e), where the family moved in 1827. Schooled at home, Grigor'ev learned as much from the servants and popular street culture as he did from a series of tutors who developed his musical talent on the piano and managed to impart some Latin and an excellent command of French. In his memoir of growing up in Zamoskvorech'e, he describes the influence of the house serfs, of his father's sentimental literary tastes, and of the Romanticism of his last tutor, a former seminarian and university

student, Sergei Ivanovich Lebedev. Despite his lack of formal school education, Grigor'ev passed the university entrance examinations.

An exemplary student, Grigor'ev excelled in his studies in the Juridical Faculty of Moscow University between 1838 and 1842, which prepared him for a career as a civil servant (later he taught civil practice). More important, he came in contact with the German idealism of Westernizer historians (such as Timofei Nikolaevich Granovsky) and with Slavophile Moscow (through Mikhail Petrovich Pogodin, the nationalist historian and a mainstay of Moscow intellectual life). Pogodin, who was the editor of *Moskvitianin* (The Muscovite), gave Grigor'ev his start in journalism, at first by publishing his early verse, which was heavily influenced by the romantic lyrics of Mikhail Iur'evich Lermontov and Heinrich Heine and by Masonic mysticism. Grigor'ev's first publication was the poem "Dobroi nochi!" (Good night!), which came out in *Moskvitianin* in 1843. Distraught over a failed love affair with Antonina Fedorovna Korsh and suffocated by oppressive parental control, Grigor'ev escaped to St. Petersburg in 1844, where he found work as a civil servant and journalist. During this short interlude he published an ignored volume of verse, *Stikhotvoreniia* (Poems, 1846), romantic narrative poems, and prose. More significant were his early reviews and other brief articles, as well as some contacts with oppositional, socialist thinkers. Grigor'ev escaped arrest in the government repression of underground philosophical circles by virtue of his return to Moscow in 1847. The most lasting effect of this interlude was a deep antipathy for St. Petersburg and a renewed loyalty to the traditions and ideals of Moscow. In the summer of 1847 he married Lidiia Korsh, Antonina's sister, but the couple soon became estranged.

Back in Moscow, Grigor'ev began his career as a journalist and literary critic with a sympathetic review of Gogol's *Vybrannye mesta iz perepiski s druz'iami* (Selected Passages from Correspondence with Friends, 1847), which other critics unanimously condemned and about which the outraged Belinsky wrote his famous unpublished letter. Grigor'ev also wrote reviews and articles on the theater for *Otechestvennye zapiski* (Notes of the Fatherland) and thus began a career as one of the most important theater critics in Russia. His writings acquired greater significance in 1851 when he became the chief critic for a group of young journalists, gathered around Ostrovsky—who together took over the literature and criticism sections of the *Moskvitianin* and were called the *molodaia redaktsiia* (Young Editors) by Pogodin. In addition to journal reviews, Grigor'ev contributed annual surveys of literature published the previous year, thereby continuing and elaborating on a genre established by Belinsky. Grigor'ev's group of friends contributed vitality and innovation to popular culture in Moscow no less than to its journalism: they encouraged performers of folk songs and popular entertainment, which found expression in the colorful, democratic urban and merchant elements of Ostrovsky's plays, and they scandalized upper-class devotees of classical French theater in a campaign against performances by the actress Mademoiselle Rachel (as seen in Grigor'ev's 1854 poem "Iskusstvo i pravda': elegiia, oda, satira . . ." [Art and truth: elegy, ode, satire . . .]). Although the *molodaia redaktsiia* was disbanding, in 1855 Grigor'ev produced major statements on Ostrovsky's plays and the concept of *narodnost'* (national identity), on the nature and significance of national types, and on the "organic" relationship of art to life. The next year he published, in the periodical *Russkaia beseda,* a philosophical treatise on aesthetics, "O pravde i iskrennosti v iskusstve" (On Truth and Sincerity in Art), dedicated to Khomiakov, the leading Slavophile thinker, on whether an artist can transcend temporal and national boundaries.

During these Moscow years Grigor'ev acquired a deserved reputation for carousing and fast living: he drank heavily, dressed extravagantly, and partied with actors, writers, and merchants; he enjoyed wild visits to the gypsies; and he lived far beyond his means. He was perpetually in debt, even though he held teaching positions and did tutoring in addition to his journalism. As his family life disintegrated, he found himself desperately in love with a colleague's daughter, Leonida Iakovlevna

Vizard, who became the inspiration for "Bor'ba" (Struggle, 1857), published in installments in the periodical *Syn otechestva,* and "Venezia la bella" (Beautiful Venice, 1858), published in the journal *Sovremennik,* two magnificent cycles of lyrics. Infused with gypsy and folk elements, the first of these cycles includes a lyric that subsequently became a popular "anonymous" folk song, "Dve gitary za stenoi . . ." (Two guitars, heard through the wall . . .). At this time Grigor'ev also published *Son v letniuiu noch'* (in the periodical *Biblioteka dlia chteniia* [A Reading Library], 1857), a translation of William Shakespeare's *A Midsummer Night's Dream* (1600) that is considered remarkable for its use of Russian folk speech; he dedicated the translation to Leonida, whom he envisioned as Titania. In 1856 *Moskvitianin* ceased publication, Grigor'ev was unable to find another journal that would accept him as principal critic, and he was devastated when Leonida accepted the marriage proposal of another man. As he had done earlier, Grigor'ev escaped from Moscow—this time abroad, to Italy.

Although Grigor'ev wrote little criticism during this Italian interlude of fourteen months, beginning in July 1857 he threw himself into an intensive study of Western art and aesthetics and of the distinctions between European and Russian artistic traditions. This process of discovery and self-awareness is documented in his letters to friends in Russia, especially to former members of the *molodaia redaktsiia* and Leonida's confidante, Ekaterina Sergeevna Protopopova (who later married the composer Aleksandr Porfir'evich Borodin). He spent most of his time in Florence serving as tutor to the young Prince Ivan Iur'evich Trubetskoi. Yet, Grigor'ev had little patience for the aristocratic caprice of his charge and for other members of the family, and after his legendary carousing with friends in Paris in the summer of 1858, the family was quite willing to accept his resignation. Grigor'ev returned to Russia—this time to St. Petersburg and a position with a new journal, *Russkoe slovo* (The Russian Word).

Hired to edit the journal jointly with the poet Iakov Petrovich Polonsky, an old Moscow acquaintance, in 1859 Grigor'ev published a series of critical articles on Russian literature since Pushkin; another series on Turgenev and his recent novel, *Dvorianskoe gnezdo* (A Nest of Gentry); and a statement on the terms and concepts of his new *organicheskaia kritika,* which elaborated on his major statement of 1858, "Kriticheskii vzgliad na osnovy, znacheniia i priemy sovremennoi kritiki iskusstva" (A Critical View of the Bases, Meanings and Methods of Contemporary Art Criticism), published in *Biblioteka dlia chteniia.* Much as Ostrovsky had formed the center of Grigor'ev's *Moskvitianin* criticism, Pushkin now became the keystone of his *organicheskaia kritika* in St. Petersburg. Asserting that "Pushkin is our everything," he explained in "Vzgliad na russkuiu literaturu so smerti Pushkina"

(*Russkoe slovo,* 1859) that the poet was the fullest expression of Russia's national character and the guiding force of contemporary literature. Grigor'ev believed that he was continuing the work of Belinsky, whom he described as the conscience of his times. Turgenev had created the fullest expression of Pushkin's national type, Grigor'ev argued, and therefore had become the poet's most legitimate heir. Grigor'ev's unconventional critical style and extreme defensiveness led to a conflict with Polonsky and the owner of *Russkoe slovo,* with the result that he left the journal in the summer of 1859.

Grigor'ev continued publishing criticism in other St. Petersburg journals, first *Russkii mir* (The Russian World) and then *Svetoch* (The Torch). He also became editor of his own periodical, a monthly miscellany of dramatic works titled *Dramaticheskii sbornik* (Dramatic Miscellany), which he used as an outlet for his own work—such as a translation of Shakespeare's *The Merchant of Venice* (1600) in 1860—but which did not publish literary criticism. His "Posle *Grozy* Ostrovskogo" (After Ostrovsky's *Thunderstorm*) appeared in *Russkii mir* early in 1860 as a series of letters to Turgenev, in which Grigor'ev attacked the progressive Westernizer critics of *Sovremennik* (The Contemporary)—especially Dobroliubov—with polemics recalling that of the hero in *Zapiski iz podpol'ia from Underground,* even to the extent of insisting that "there are thought processes . . . in which 2 x 2 gives not 4 but a tallow candle." In his 1861 articles for *Svetoch,* Grigor'ev hardened his insistence on the absolute independence of art; in "Iskusstvo i nravstvennost'" (Art and Morality) he argued, using Ostrovsky and Turgenev as examples, that art does not reflect life but, rather, dictates morality (in other words, that life learns from art), and that the proper role of art is to protest against conventional morality. At this time, through the editor of *Svetoch,* Aleksandr Petrovich Miliukov, Grigor'ev met Strakhov and the Dostoevsky brothers, who admired his criticism. They brought him to work at their new journal, *Vremia,* as principal literary critic, and in 1861 he published a series of articles there on the evolution of *narodnost'* in Russian literature—"Narodnost' i literatura" (National Identity and Literature), "Zapadnichestvo i russkaia literatura" (Westernism and Russian Literature), "Belinsky i otritsatel'nyi vzgliad v literature" (Belinsky and the Negative View in Literature), and "Oppozitsiia zastoia" (Opposition to Stagnation)—continuing a series he had begun in *Russkoe slovo* and *Russkii mir.* He also continued to publish in *Svetoch,* where his "Realizm i idealizm" (Realism and Idealism) appeared in the same year.

While he was intensively publishing these explanations of *organicheskaia kritika,* Grigor'ev understood that his position was not as popular and influential as that of the progressive Westernizers, especially among students and

Antonina Fedorovna Korsh (married name Kavelina) in the 1850s, about a decade after Grigor'ev's relationship with her ended (from Grigor'ev, Pis'ma, *1999)*

the younger intelligentsia, and this awareness increased his feeling of being an outsider. For *Vremia* in 1861 he wrote a feuilleton titled "O postepennom no bystrom i povsemestnom rasprostranenii nevezhestva i bezgramotnosti v rossiiskoi slovesnosti" (On the Gradual, but Swift and Ubiquitous Spread of Ignorance and Illiteracy in Russian Literature), which he signed "Nenuzhnyi chelovek" (An Unnecessary Man). Grigor'ev's sense of exclusion from the intellectual mainstream was enhanced by his ongoing taste for social scandal. In addition to public drunkenness, he began living with a flamboyant former prostitute, Mariia Fedorovna Dubrovskaia, and continued extravagant living beyond his means. The Dostoevskys soon found their chief critic in debtors' prison, where he spent much of the spring of 1861; the orderly surroundings of the prison probably contributed to Grigor'ev's high level of productivity as a critic during this period. To escape from debt and the chaos of his life in St. Petersburg, Grigor'ev signed up as a teacher of Russian language and literature at the military school in Orenburg, a

Cossack outpost on the eastern frontier and a developing center of trade with Central Asia. In this way, Grigor'ev for the third time fled from domestic difficulties into what he called in an 1861 letter to Strakhov "voluntary exile." He described the events leading up to this exile in his last and greatest lyric cycle, "Vverkh po Volge" (Up the Volga, 1862), the title of which suggests his struggle to move against the current, yet ever closer to the origins of Russian national identity.

Disagreements with *Vremia* surface in Grigor'ev's letters from Orenburg: he disapproved of its conciliatory tone with Chernyshevsky and *Sovremennik,* its lack of a clear position on the importance of art, and what he considered its low editorial standards. He was particularly incensed by Dostoevsky's suggestion that *Vremia* publish his works anonymously. The journal managed to placate Grigor'ev sufficiently for him to send a major article, "Iavleniia sovremennoi literatury propushchennye nashei kritikoi: Graf L. Tolstoi i ego sochineniia" (Phenomena of Contemporary Literature Missed by Our Criticism: Count L. Tolstoy and His Works, 1862), in which he defined his own "organic" position vis-à-vis Slavophiles, Revolutionary Democrats (whom he called "theoreticians"), Westernizers, *Otechestvennye zapiski,* and the nationalists of another journal, *Russkii vestnik* (The Russian Messenger). In this statement, without naming it as such, Grigor'ev made his first contribution to the *pochvennichestvo* movement and provided its interpretation of the central figures of Russian literature—Pushkin, Lermontov, Gogol, and Ostrovsky.

Grigor'ev returned to St. Petersburg and *Vremia* in July 1862 and during the next six months published three sets of articles: he completed the cycle on Tolstoy, continued the cycle on national character with a series of three articles titled "Lermontov i ego napravlenie" (Lermontov and His Orientation, 1862), and began a series of theater reviews. He continued to develop the ideology of the journal: *pochvennichestvo* was a concrete metaphor for the *narodnost'* that he had begun writing about in Moscow. Here, too, he developed his theory of cultural and literary types: the negative type—first drawn by Pushkin in *Povesti pokoinogo Ivana Petrovicha Belkina* (Tales of the Deceased Ivan Petrovich Belkin, 1831)—now became the *smirnyi* (humble) type, while his opposite and antagonist was termed the *khishchnyi* (predatory) type. These two antithetical types appear, for example, in the characters of Maksim Maksimych and Pechorin, respectively, in Lermontov's *Geroi nashego vremeni* (A Hero of Our Time, 1840). In these articles Grigor'ev presented Tolstoy as a more thorough analyst of national types than Turgenev, and in a review of Nikolai Alekseevich Nekrasov's poetry he demonstrated that poet's deep bond with the *pochva* (native soil) as well as the profundity of Nekrasov's national

protest. Finally, in *Vremia* in the fall of 1862 Grigor'ev published the major explication of his own *pochva*—the first half of his memoir *Moi literaturnye i nravstvennye skital'chestva,* which he dedicated to Mikhail Dostoevsky.

Early in 1863 Grigor'ev left *Vremia* to head his own weekly journal, *Iakor'* (Anchor), just weeks before the Dostoevskys' journal was closed by the censorship. On the pages of *Iakor',* Grigor'ev proclaimed his belief in the central importance of *narodnost'* in literature and on the stage; at the same time, he vented his personal frustrations in ironic, paradoxical apologia on the state of being "unnecessary," as in his "Bezvykhodnoe polozhenie" (1863; translated as "A Hopeless Situation," 1962). The format of a weekly paper did not allow for lengthy critical articles—although he did publish one critical article on Aleksei Feofilaktovich Pisemsky's novel *Vzbalamuchennoe more* (Troubled Sea, 1863)—and so Grigor'ev wrote mostly reviews, enjoying great success. His reviews covered all aspects of the theater: dramatic literature, playwrights, actors, stage settings and design, and even music and lighting. He reviewed many playwrights, showing special favor for Pisemsky, Lev Aleksandrovich Mei, and Aleksandr Vasil'evich Sukhovo-Kobylin, but always reserved his highest respect for Ostrovsky. These reviews, together with his series of pieces on Russian actors, earned Grigor'ev his place as the foremost theatrical critic of nineteenth-century Russia.

When Mikhail Dostoevsky began a new journal in January 1864, Grigor'ev abandoned *Iakor'* and joined this new enterprise, *Epokha,* where he hoped to find more space to continue his cycle on the idea of *narodnost'.* His close friend, the young philosopher Strakhov, however, was given the role of principal critic, and Grigor'ev continued only his chronicles of the Russian theater. He renewed the cycle that he had begun in *Vremia* under the same title—"Russkii teatr" (Russian Theater)—and insisted on the same high standards for a national repertoire and for actors to create true national types. He applied the same rigorous demands to dramatic writing as he did to fiction and poetry: theatrical art was also the highest form of consciousness and no less a vehicle of everything new in life than were the other literary forms. He also published the continuation of his memoirs, *Moi literaturnye i nravstvennye skital'chestva,* in two final installments in *Epokha;* in these memoirs he provided an intellectual and literary history of his own evolution and of Moscow in the 1830s. His literary criticism per se in *Epokha* was limited to two open letters to Dostoevsky titled "Paradoksy organicheskoi kritiki" (Paradoxes of Organic Criticism, 1864).

Grigor'ev's profound impact on Dostoevsky and his contribution to the latter's *pochvennichestvo* ideology is generally acknowledged, as is his role as a model for several of Dostoevsky's characters. However, the personal

Grigor'ev's 23 August 1861 letter to his close friend Nikolai Nikolaevich Strakhov, written while Grigor'ev
was teaching Russian at a military school in Orenburg (from Grigor'ev, Pis'ma, 1999)

relations of the two writers were strained and even at times unpleasant. In the first of the "Paradoksy" letters Grigor'ev publicly blamed Dostoevsky for "the multitude of literary misunderstandings that had arisen" between them. Grigor'ev had written extensively on all the major writers and poets of his time, but never on Dostoevsky—and the reason for this omission seems to have been the personal disagreements between the two. Their differences concerned tactics and methods, however, more than principles or values: they could not agree how best to preserve what both agreed was true and essential to Russian literature and culture. Dostoevsky accepted many of Grigor'ev's views on national literary types, and he incorporated them into his famous speech at the Pushkin celebrations in Moscow in 1881. In his open "letters" to Dostoevsky, Grigor'ev attempted to explain the essence of his *organicheskaia kritika* and thereby show that its principles must not be compromised. The letters, in actual fact, contain no "paradoxes," but they do provide the most succinct, forceful explanation that Grigor'ev was ever to give of his critical ideals. The second letter, by way of illustrating the principles described in the first, details Grigor'ev's enthusiasm for Victor Hugo's critical essay *William Shakespeare* (1864). No third letter was published, although one was probably written and delivered to Dostoevsky just before Grigor'ev's death.

After Orenburg, Grigor'ev's personal life entered a downward spiral. He had returned to St. Petersburg without Dubrovskaia and carried on his extravagant habits, drinking excessively and sinking deeper into debt. In addition to his journalism, he published many translations of Italian opera librettos and completed a successful translation of Shakespeare's *Romeo and Juliet,* titled "Romeo i Dzhul'etta" and published in *Russkaia stsena* (The Russian Stage, 1864). Yet, this furious activity was not enough to keep him out of debtors' prison, where he found himself again in June 1864. After Mikhail Dostoevsky's death in July, Grigor'ev felt increasingly isolated, and in August he decided that he could no longer compromise his principles by publishing in *Epokha.* Grigor'ev's sudden death on 25 September, at the age of forty-two, occurred in obscure circumstances. He had been freed from debtors' prison by Anna Ivanovna Bibikova, who was apparently interested in his translation of *Romeo and Juliet,* and he died three days later from a stroke, during an argument with a publisher to whom he apparently owed money. One circumstance was clear: his health had been undermined by steady drinking since the spring of 1863. His funeral was sparsely attended by a few writers, critics, and journalists, and by his "colleagues" from the debtors' prison—a sad confirmation of his "unnecessariness."

Despite attempts by Strakhov to rescue the critic's reputation through the publication of his letters and the republication of a collection of his articles, Grigor'ev was soon forgotten. He was resurrected as a poet by Aleksandr Aleksandrovich Blok, who published an edition of Grigor'ev's poetry in 1916. This renewed interest led scholars to attempt to collect more of Grigor'ev's writings; Vasilii Spiridonovich Spiridonov tried again to collect Grigor'ev's articles, and Vladimir A. Kniazhnin worked on a collection of his letters. However, Grigor'ev again lapsed into obscurity during the Soviet period, during which cultural ideologues condemned him for his opposition to the Revolutionary Democrats. Only in the 1960s did a serious reconsideration of Grigor'ev's poetry and criticism begin, and by the end of the twentieth century all his poetry and most of his critical works had been republished, and a complete edition of his extant letters had appeared.

Grigor'ev was a late Romantic poet and critic, and his best lyrics survive because of their use of folk and gypsy motifs and an unrestrained passion intent on self-immolation. His critical works, although written with little discipline or regard for structure, reward the reader who is sufficiently patient to follow the twists and turns of his thought. Grigor'ev loved literature as he loved life, sincerely and passionately, and his insight into the finer details of the Russian creative spirit, intellect, and psyche are unrivaled for his time. Although he tended to repeat himself, he never oversimplified or talked down to his readers, and for this reason the vitality of his criticism survives better than that of his more popular contemporaries. Because of Grigor'ev's passion to explain the intricate evolution of Russian ideas and images, his readers today are rewarded with a deeper understanding of the drifts and currents of Russian art, literature, and life during the mid nineteenth century.

Apollon Aleksandrovich Grigor'ev is considered most significant for his impact on and contribution to the writings of his great contemporary, Dostoevsky. His *Moi literaturnye i nravstvennye skital'chestva* remains among the most colorful and readable of Russian memoirs, competing with those of Aleksandr Herzen. Some of his lyric verse has become a part of the national repertoire. Grigor'ev's contribution to the evolution of Russian theater and dramaturgy, however, has still to be fully appreciated. Likewise, his collected letters remain largely unknown, although they are among the most lively and unrestrained commentaries on the life and literature of their time. Grigor'ev's writings remain unchallenged by those of other nineteenth-century critics for their philosophical sophistication, absolute sincerity, passion for truth, and unfailing perceptiveness.

Letters:

Apollon Aleksandrovich Grigor'ev: Materialy dlia biografii, edited by Vladimir A. Kniazhnin, Izdanie Pushkinskogo doma pri Akademii nauk (Petrograd: Tipografiia Ministerstva Zemledeliia, 1917);

Pis'ma, edited by Robert Vittaker [Whittaker] and Boris Fedorovich Egorov, Literaturnye pamiatniki (Moscow: Nauka, 1999).

Bibliography:

Robert Whittaker, "Bibliography," in his *Russia's Last Romantic: Apollon Grigor'ev, 1822–1864* (Lewiston, N.Y.: Edwin Mellen Press, 1999), pp. 453–518.

Biographies:

Dmitrii Nikolaevich Mikhailov, *Apollon Grigor'ev: Zhizn' v sviazi s kharakterom literaturnoi dieiatel'nosti ego* (St. Petersburg: N. Gerasimov, 1900);

Mikhail Dmitrievich Beliaev and Vasilii Spiridonovich Spiridonov, comps., *A. A. Grigor'ev: Biografiia i putevoditel' po vystavke i zalakh Pushkinskogo Doma* (St. Petersburg: Pushkinskii dom, 1922);

Laura Satta Boschian, *Il regno oscuro: Vita e opere di A. Grigor'ev* (Naples: Morano, 1969);

Fyodor Dostoevsky, *Polnoe sobranie sochinenii,* 30 volumes, edited by V. G. Bazanov (Leningrad: Nauka, 1972–1988);

Sergei Nikolaevich Nosov, *Apollon Grigor'ev. Sud'ba i tvorchestvo* (Moscow: Sovetskii pisatel', 1990);

Wayne Dowler, *An Unnecessary Man: The Life of Apollon Grigor'ev* (Toronto: University of Toronto Press, 1995);

Vladimir Dmitrievich Glebov, *Apollon Grigor'ev. Kontseptsiia istoriko-literaturnogo protsessa 1830–1860-kh godov* (Moscow, 1996);

Andrzej Lazari, *"Ostatni romantyk" Apollon Grigorjew: Zarys monografii swiatopogladu* (Katowice: Ślask, 1996);

Robert Whittaker, *Russia's Last Romantic: Apollon Grigor'ev, 1822–1864* (Lewiston, N.Y.: Edwin Mellen Press, 1999); translated into Russian by M. A. Shereshevskaia as *Poslednii russkii romantik: Apollon Grigor'ev* (St. Petersburg: Akademicheskii proekt, 2000);

Boris Fedorovich Egorov, *Apollon Grigor'ev* (Moscow: Molodaia gvardiia, 2000).

References:

Boris Iakovlevich Bukhshtab, "Gimny Apollona Grigor'eva," in his *Bibliograficheskie razyskaniia po russkoi literature XIX veka* (Moscow: Izdatel'stvo Kniga, 1966);

Boris Fedorovich Egorov, "Apollon Grigor'ev–kritik," *Uchenye zapiski Tartuskogo gosudarstvennogo universiteta,* 98 (1960): 210–246; 104 (1961): 58–83;

Aleksandr Apollonovich Grigor'ev, "Odinokii kritik," *Knizhki "Nedeli,"* 8 (1895): 5–23; 9 (1895): 52–81;

Leonid Grossman, "Apollon Grigor'ev. Osnovatel' novoi kritiki," *Russkaia mysl',* 11, no. 2 (1914): 1–19;

Sophie Lafitte, "Apollon Grigor'ev et Dostoevskii," *Revue des Etudes slaves,* 43 (1964): 13–16;

Jürgen Lehmann, *Der Einfluß der Philosophie des deutschen Idealismus in der russischen Literaturkritik des 19. Jahrhunderts: Die "organische Kritik" Apollon A. Grigor'evs* (Heidelberg: Carl Winter, 1975);

Aleksandr L'vovich Ospovat, "K izucheniiu pochvennichestva (Dostoevskii i Ap. Grigor'ev)," in *Dostoevskii: Materialy i issledovaniia,* edited by Georgii Mikhailovich Fridlender, volume 3 (Leningrad: Nauka, 1978);

Liudmila Anatol'evna Rozanova, "K biografii Apollona Grigor'eva," *Uchenye zapiski Ivanovskogo gosudarstvennogo pedinstituta,* 115 (1973): 132–161;

Victor Terras, "Apollon Grigoriev's Organic Criticism and Its Western Sources," in *Western Philosophical Systems in Russian Literature: A Collection of Critical Studies,* edited by Anthony M. Mlikotin (Los Angeles: University of Southern California Press, 1979), pp. 71–88;

Tat'iana Borisovna Zabozlaeva, "A. A. Grigor'ev," in *Ocherki istorii russkoi teatral'noi kritiki: vtoraia polovina XIX veka,* edited by Anatolii Iakovlevich Al'tshuller (Leningrad: Iskusstvo, 1976), pp. 56–67;

Il'ia Samoilovich Zil'bershtein, "Apollon Grigor'ev i popytka vozrodit' 'Moskvitianin' (nakanune sotrudnichestva v zhurnale 'Vremia')," *Literaturnoe nasledstvo,* 86 (1973): 567–580.

Papers:

While the papers of Apollon Aleksandrovich Grigor'ev have yet to be located, if they exist at all, his letters have been discovered and can be found among the papers of his correspondents. The greatest number of such letters is found in the papers of Mikhail Petrovich Pogodin in the Russian State Library (RGB, formerly the Lenin Library) in Moscow. For details on other papers, see *Pis'ma.*

Alexander Herzen
(Aleksandr Ivanovich Gertsen)
(25 March 1812 – 21 January 1870)

University of Pittsburgh, Greensburg

BOOKS: *Kto vinovat? Roman v dvukh chastiakh,* as Iskander (St. Petersburg: Sovremennik, 1847); translated by M. Wettlin as *Who is to Blame?* (Moscow: Progress, 1978);

Vom anderen Ufer, as Ein Russe (Hamburg, 1850); Russian version published as *S togo berega,* as Iskander (London: Trübner, 1855);

Briefe aus Italien und Frankreich, as Ein Russe (Hamburg, 1850); Russian version published as *Pis'ma iz Frantsii i Italii (1847–1852),* as Iskander (London: Trübner, 1855); translated by Judith E. Zimmerman as *Letters from France and Italy, 1847–1851,* edited by Zimmerman (Pittsburgh, Pa.: University of Pittsburgh Press, 1995);

Du Développement des idées révolutionnaires en Russie, as A. Iskander (Paris: A. Franck, 1851);

Le Peuple russe et le socialisme: Lettre à Jules Michelet, as Iskander (Paris, 1852); translated as *The Russian People and Their Socialism. A Letter to M. Jules Michelet* (Brantwood, U.K., 1855); Russian version published as *Russkii narod i sotsializm. Pis'mo k I. Mishle,* as Iskander (London: Trübner, 1858);

Kreshchenaia sobstvennost' (London: Vol'noe russkoe knigopechatanie, 1853);

Vol'noe russkoe knigopechatanie v Londone (London: Free Russian Press, 1853);

Iur'ev den! Iur'ev den! Russkomu dvorianstvu (London: Vol'noe russkoe knigopechatanie, 1853);

Poliaki proshchaiut nas! (London: Vol'noe russkoe knigopechatanie, 1853);

Vol'naia russkaia obshchina v Londone. Russkomu voinstvu v Pol'she (London: Vol'noe russkoe knigopechatanie, 1854);

Imprimerie russe à Londres (London: Vol'noe russkoe knigopechatanie, 1854);

Prervannye rasskazy, as Iskander (London: Universal Library, 1854; revised edition, London: Trübner, 1857)–comprises "Dolg prezhde vsego," "Povrezhdennyi," "Mimoezdom," and "Doktor Krupov";

Alexander Herzen

Tiurma i ssylka. Iz zapisok Iskandera, as Iskander (London & Paris: Vol'noe russkoe knigopechatanie, 1854); translated as *My Exile in Siberia,* 2 volumes (London: Hurst & Blackett, 1855);

Poliarnaia zvezda: Tretnoi obozvenie osvobozhdainshcheisia Rus i (London: Vol'noe russkoe knigopechatanie, 1855);

La conspiration russe de 1825: Suivie d'une lettre sur L'émancipation des paysans en Russie, as Iskander (London: S. Tchorzewski, 1858);

150

La France ou l'Angleterre?: Variations sur le thême de l'attentat du 14 janvier, as Iskander (London: Trübner, 1858); Russian version published as *Frantsüa ili Anglüa? Russküa variatsü na temu 14 ianvaria 1858* (London: Trübner, 1858);

14 dekabria 1825 i Imperator Nikolai: Po povodu knigi Barona Korfa, by Herzen and the editorial staff of *Poliarnaia zvezda* (London: Trübner, 1858);

Byloe i dumy Iskandera, 4 volumes, 5 parts (London: Trübner, 1861–1867);

Sbornik posmertnykh statei (Geneva, 1870);

Sochineniia, 10 volumes (Geneva, Basel & Lyon: H. Georg, 1875–1879);

Polnoe sobranie sochinenii i pisem, edited by M. K. Lemke, 22 volumes (Petrograd: Literaturnoe izd. otd. Nar. kom. po prosveshcheniiu, 1919–1925);

Byloe i dumy, 5 volumes, first complete edition (Berlin: Slovo, 1921);

Sobranie sochinenii, 30 volumes, edited by Viacheslav Petrovich Volgin (Moscow: Izdatel'stvo Akademii nauk SSSR, 1954–1965).

Editions and Collections: *Desiatiletie Vol'noi russkoi tipografii v Londone. Sbornik ee pervykh listov,* edited by L. Chernetsky (London, 1863);

Povesti i rasskazy, edited by Ia. E. El'sberg (Moscow & Leningrad: "Academia," 1934; revised, 1936);

Khudozhestvennye proizvedeniia, edited by L. A. Plotkin (Leningrad: Khudozhestvennaia literatura, 1937);

Izbrannye filosofskie sochineniia, 2 volumes (Moscow: Gospolitizdat, 1948);

Izbrannye pedagogicheskie vyskazyvaniia, edited and with an introduction by M. F. Shabaeva (Moscow: Akademiia pedagogicheskikh nauk RSFSR, 1951);

Gertsen ob iskusstve, edited by V. A. Putintsev and El'sberg (Moscow: Iskusstvo, 1954);

Pis'ma izdaleka. (Izbrannye literaturno-kriticheskie stat'i i zametki) (Moscow, 1981);

14 dekabria 1825 goda i ego istolkovateli: Gertsen i Ogarev protiv barona Korfa, edited by Evgeniia Lvovna Rudnitskaia, with an introduction and commentary by Rudnitskaia and Aleksandr Georgievich Tartakovsky (Moscow: Nauka, 1994).

Editions in English: *The Memoirs of Alexander Herzen, Parts I and II,* translated by J. D. Duff (New Haven: Yale University Press, 1923); republished as *Childhood, Youth and Exile* (Oxford: Oxford University Press, 1979);

My Past and Thoughts: The Memoirs of Alexander Herzen, 6 volumes, translated by Constance Garnett (New York: Knopf, 1924–1927; London: Chatto & Windus, 1924–1927); revised by Humphrey Higgens, 4 volumes (London: Chatto & Windus, 1968);

Selected Philosophical Works, translated by L. Navrozov (Moscow: Foreign Languages Publishing House, 1956);

From the Other Shore. The Russian People and Socialism (New York: Braziller, 1956; London: Weidenfeld & Nicolson, 1956);

Who is to Blame? A Novel in Two Parts, translated by Michael Katz (Ithaca, N.Y.: Cornell University Press, 1984);

The Thieving Magpie: A Story, translated by Avril Pyman (Moscow: Raduga, 1986).

OTHER: Kniaz' Mikhail Mikhailovich Shcherbatov, *O povrezhdenii nravov v Rossii kniazia M. Shcherbatova i puteshchestvie [iz Peterburga v Moskvu] A. Radishcheva,* with a preface by Herzen as Iskander (London: Trübner, 1858);

Catherine II, Empress of Russia, *Mémoires de l'impératrice Catherine II,* with a preface by Herzen (London: Trübner, 1859); translated as *Memoirs of the Empress Catherine II* (London: Trübner, 1859);

George Sand, *Pokhozhdeniia Gribul'ia,* translated by V. T. Kel'sieva, with a preface by Herzen as Iskander (London: Trübner, 1860);

Ivan Vladimirovich Lopukhin, *Zapiski iz nekotorykh obstoiatel'stv zhizni i sluzhby,* with a preface by Herzen as Iskander (London: Trübner, 1860).

SELECTED PERIODICAL PUBLICATION: "Kontsy i nachala," *Kolokol,* 138 (1862), 140 (1862), 142 (1862), 144 (1862), 145 (1862), 148 (1862), 149 (1862), 154 (1862), 156 (1862).

Alexander Herzen was a prolific and varied writer. His collected works approach forty volumes in the standard Soviet edition and are dominated by his masterpiece—his memoirs, *Byloe i dumy* (first complete edition, 1921; translated as *My Past and Thoughts: The Memoirs of Alexander Herzen,* 1924–1927). Overall, he is probably best characterized as a radical journalist and essayist, and all his works, including the memoirs and his early fiction, are imbued with his political and social convictions. Despite shifts in his views over the years, his basic themes remained constant: hatred for the oppressive regime of Tsar Nicholas I; a demand for individual freedom; and anger at the injustice suffered by the enserfed peasant population in Russia. Herzen drew much early inspiration from western European "utopian" socialists, and like them he devoted much attention to issues of marriage, family life, and the position of women.

Herzen was born Aleksandr Ivanovich Gertsen (the Russian equivalent in pronunciation for "Herzen") in Moscow on 25 March 1812, the illegitimate son of a wealthy landowner, Ivan Alekseevich Iakovlev, and a middle-class German woman, Louisa Haag (known in Russian as Luiza Ivanova), whom Iakovlev met while in the diplomatic service and whom he brought back to Russia on his return. Although his unmarried father acknowledged Herzen and brought him up in luxurious surroundings in his home, he never made any effort to legitimize his son's birth. Ivan Alekseevich gave his son, a child of his heart, the last name "Herzen," which comes from *herz,* the German word for heart. As an illegitimate son, Herzen technically was not a member of the nobility and enjoyed none of the privileges of noble status. By the time Herzen was born, Ivan Alekseevich had withdrawn from government service into a reclusive existence, and his son grew up isolated from his peers and contemporaries, as well as from his remote father. Available evidence suggests that his mother also played a minor role in his life. He spent his time with his tutors and with the house serfs who cared for the family. His contacts with young people of his own class were limited to a few cousins and, rarely, the son of a friend of his father. The young Herzen learned about the injustices of Russian social life from the servants. He absorbed Enlightenment ideas from his father's library. His tutors, along with a Western education, inspired him with the ideals of the French Revolution. What he never absorbed was any sense of identification—national, religious, or class—with Russian traditions.

Herzen's rather free-floating sense of oppression and desire for freedom received a political focus in 1825 when Tsar Alexander I died suddenly. To the surprise of the public, he was succeeded by the younger and more reactionary of his brothers, Nicholas. The first ideologically motivated revolt in Russia, the Decembrist uprising (which took place on 14 December 1825), protested this succession. Failing to ignite a general mutiny, the uprising was quickly suppressed. The trial and punishment of the Decembrist leaders, men from families well known to Herzen's father, was astonishing; that five members of the aristocracy were executed shocked Moscow high society. In his later accounts Herzen might have exaggerated the consistency, clarity, and rapidity of his reaction to the events of 1825 to 1826 but not their impact on his outlook. For the next thirty years Tsar Nicholas I was the focus of Herzen's rage, and opposition to the political system over which Nicholas reigned was his goal. The Decembrists remained his models and ideals.

At about the same time, Herzen began to organize his outlook into an ideological position, based, in the first instance, on the works of the German dramatist Friedrich Schiller, whose works explored love, friendship, and freedom. Schiller's heroes provided images on which the teenage rebel could model himself as he struggled to find a usable ideal of freedom. At about the same time, Herzen was introduced to Nikolai Platonovich

Ogarev, a boy one year younger than himself who shared Herzen's sense of isolation from the Russian world into which he had been born. In addition to their personal compatibility, Herzen and Ogarev discovered a shared passion for Schiller, a hatred of paternal and paternalistic tyranny, and a longing for freedom. In 1826 or 1827 they stood on the Vorob'evye gory (Sparrow Hills) overlooking Moscow and swore an oath to sacrifice their lives in the struggle for the liberty of Russia. Like the memory of the Decembrist martyrs and his friendship with Ogarev, this oath on Sparrow Hills became part of the mythology by which Herzen would define the purpose of his life.

In 1829 Herzen and Ogarev became students at Moscow University, which, after their constricted childhoods and adolescence, seemed an oasis of freedom to them. For the first time they were free to come and go relatively unhampered, to choose their own friends, and to plunge into impassioned studies of the questions that moved them. Their education came less from the lecture hall than from their circle of friends; the *kruzhok* (circle), a small group of people passionately involved with each other and with intellectual and political issues, became yet another of Herzen's icons. Even after he had left Russia and had broken with most of his friends, the *kruzhok* continued to constitute his imaginary ideal audience, and the sociability of the *kruzhok* remained his ideal of community life. The earnest discussions of the circle were primarily about Friedrich Wilhelm Joseph von Schelling's nature philosophy. Herzen and Ogarev were also intrigued by their first contact with the ideas of Claude-Henri, comte de Saint Simon's French followers. Although the interests of the *kruzhok* tended to be abstract and philosophical, political reality intruded on university life. The outbreak of revolution in France in 1830 revived the sense of radical possibilities and might have spurred Herzen's and Ogarev's interest in French thought. The sympathy of the *kruzhok* members for the revolution in France also came to the attention of the authorities. The Warsaw uprising in 1832 quickened Herzen's interest in revolution still further.

Rather than obtaining jobs or entering government service, members of the *kruzhok* remained intact for a year after graduation. Not attracted by a career in government service, Herzen, Ogarev, and some of their friends from the *kruzhok* hoped to disseminate their ideas for a somewhat broader audience through a journal. By 1833 Ogarev had committed himself to being a poet, but Herzen had as yet written nothing for publication. His output consisted of university papers, including a dissertation that won the university's second, or silver, prize, and long letters to Ogarev in which he explored philosophical themes. In any case, their plans for a journal came to nothing. Instead, early in July 1834 Ogarev and other members of the *kruzhok* were arrested; at the end of the month Herzen suffered the same fate.

The period between Ogarev's arrest and Herzen's own were crucial for the latter's biography and self-image. He looked for help from the older generation of freer-thinking men of his acquaintance and found only disappointment. Consolation in his trouble came from his first cousin Natal'ia Aleksandrovna Zakhar'ina, or Natalie, as Herzen referred to her. The illegitimate daughter of Herzen's uncle and a peasant woman, Natalie was brought up by an unsympathetic aunt. Isolated and almost friendless, Natalie compensated with an intense religiosity and capacity for devotion. In the trials to come, she provided Herzen with unwavering support. Gratitude grew into friendship, which grew into love. The romance with Natalie became the final piece of the young Herzen's image of his place in the world. Love, friendship with Ogarev, and his circle of friends constituted the personal side of Herzen's persona. Ideologically, he demanded personal freedom and hatred of political despotism, and he had made a commitment to socialism. However vague the content of the latter, it implied a search for social justice.

Herzen's arrest led to ten months of solitary confinement, followed by exile first to Viatka, on the far eastern edge of European Russia, and later to Vladimir *guberniia* (province), close to Moscow. He was required to work for the provincial administration in both places. From Vladimir he was able to steal back to Moscow and elope with Natalie. During this period of exile Herzen expressed religious beliefs for the first and only time in his life. Yet, despite Natalie's influence, he showed little interest in Christian belief and doctrine. Rather, influenced by Schelling, Ogarev's interpretation of Schelling, and the architect Aleksandr Lavrent'evich Vitberg—a mystic Freemason who shared Herzen's living quarters in Viatka—he adopted a mystic pantheism. Also for the first time, during this period Herzen attempted to express his views through fiction and drama, since his primary audience was now the rather poorly educated Natalie instead of the philosophically sophisticated Ogarev. Not all of this material was preserved, and none of it was published during Herzen's life. In addition, exile gave him his first experience as a working journalist. In 1839 he was named one of two editors of the Vladimir provincial newspaper, *Vladimirskie vedomosti* (Vladimir News), just established by a government order creating provincial government magazines throughout the country.

Pardoned in 1839, Herzen moved to St. Petersburg to continue government service, this time in the central administration. The short period that he was in St. Petersburg marked the real beginning of his literary career. He moved in intellectual circles, became friends with Vissarion Grigor'evich Belinsky, who was at the time the most influential literary critic in Russia, and began writing for *Otechestvennye zapiski* (Notes of the Fatherland), where Belinsky was literary editor. Herzen's first significant piece in the journal was a fictionalized and bowdlerized autobiography, "Zapiski odnogo molodogo cheloveka" (Notes of a Certain Young Man), which appeared in two installments in 1839 and 1840 and was signed Iskander, as were all of the works that Herzen published in Russia. At the end of 1840 he was arrested again, and in 1841 he began a second term of exile, while still in government service, in Novgorod. Natalie was ill; Novgorod was oppressive; his arrest was arbitrary; and Herzen responded with rage and an intensified hatred for the regime of Nicholas I. As punishment he had to work for the government; once freed, he devoted himself to working against it. Finally in 1842 Herzen was allowed to return to Moscow with his family, although he remained under police surveillance until he left Russia for good in 1847.

Upon his return from Viatka to western Russia, Herzen had been disconcerted to discover a new enthusiasm among Russian intellectuals for the writings of Georg Wilhelm Friedrich Hegel; he was particularly distressed because Russians were interpreting Hegel's thought as a conservative doctrine. He took up the study of Hegel with the initial intention of refuting the Prussian philosopher. In the end, however, he accepted much of Hegel's philosophy of history but interpreted it as a doctrine of radical change rather than conservatism—a reading that Belinsky eventually found persuasive; Mikhail Aleksandrovich Bakunin, Herzen's acquaintance and a fellow student of Hegel who was living in western Europe, independently arrived at similar conclusions. Thus, a Russian Left Hegelianism evolved contemporaneously with that of the German Young Hegelians, but independent of it. Herzen's philosophical studies eventuated in two major cycles of articles, begun in Novgorod but published in *Otechestvennye zapiski* after his return to Moscow: "Diletantizm v nauke" (Dilettantism in Science, 1843), and "Pis'ma ob izuchenii prirody" (Letters on the Study of Nature, 1845–1846).

When Herzen returned at last to Moscow, he had already resigned from government service, and for the next five years he devoted himself to discussion and writing. The 1840s were a period of great intellectual ferment among the Moscow intellectuals. New circles formed, this time with an ideological cast, which had been largely lacking in the 1830s. The Slavophiles were the more coherent group; they were conservatives who found in Russian Orthodoxy and the *obshchina* (peasant commune) qualities of holiness and community superior to Western individualism. Their opponents, the Westernizers, were united more by friendship than ideology. Herzen, the leader of the group, was also its most radical member.

His friends did not share his rage at Russian despotism or his belief that Western liberalism merely shifted the locus of privilege from the aristocracy to the bourgeoisie. Since the Westernizers published rarely (and what they did publish was subjected to strict censorship), and since the few memoirs of the 1840s are not explicit on ideological issues, a reconstruction of their views with any specificity is not possible. Still, all of them considered western Europe a model in regard to personal freedom and economic development. Whereas the Slavophiles admired the eternal qualities that they perceived in Russia, the Westernizers were drawn to the dynamism of Western development, and although some of the Westernizers were personally religious, their outlook on historical and political issues was rationalist and secular.

Herzen expressed Westernizer views as clearly as the censorship allowed in the essays and feuilletons that he wrote during the 1840s. The witty "Moskva i Peterburg" (Moscow and St. Petersburg, *Kolokol* [The Bell] 1857), written in 1841 or 1842, could not be published right away but was circulated in manuscript; it expressed Herzen's preference for Western-oriented St. Petersburg. "Buddizm v nauke" (Buddhism in Science), part of the "Pis'ma ob izuchenii prirody" cycle, used the East-West dichotomy of the Slavophile-Westernizer debate to attack scientific obscurantism. Admiration for the medieval West and its developmental potential was expressed in a series of public lectures given by Herzen's friend and fellow *kruzhok* member Timofei Nikolaevich Granovsky in 1843; Herzen seconded this view in a critique of Granovsky's first lecture. Yet, his article on Granovsky's next lecture did not pass the censorship, and the series ended.

As young men, both Herzen and Ogarev had rejected prevailing sexual and marital mores. Neither a marriage of convenience nor the kind of free union that Herzen's father carried on with Louisa Haag—which left her almost a prisoner in a strange country—satisfied them. The sexual exploitation of serf women, in which the partners had no status and could make no claims, emotional or material, on their owners, was even less acceptable. Nothing less than a marriage of equals mattered to them, and they sought partners who would be friends, sisters, and soul mates. In reality, however, Ogarev's wife never accepted her husband's exalted views, and she longed for a life of societal frivolity. The marriage slowly came apart, causing Ogarev great embarrassment and excruciating pain. Herzen was more fortunate. Natalie, who was both intelligent and emotionally needy, eagerly took on the role of soul mate and moral anchor for the more volatile Herzen. External misfortunes wounded the partners, however, and endangered their relationship. Herzen suffered from his second exile, and his rage made him difficult to live with. Natalie suffered far more grievously from repeated failed preg-

nancies. The couple's first child, Aleksandr Aleksandrovich, was born in 1839. Later, however, during and after Herzen's Novgorod exile, she lost three infants. Natalie then became deeply depressed, and Herzen found consolation in other relationships. He confessed to her, which only intensified the misery that the couple inflicted on each other. After the Herzens moved back to the center of Moscow intellectual life, they had another son, Nikolai (Kolia), in 1843 and a daughter, Natal'ia (Tata), in 1844. This period was one of domestic calm for them.

Moved by the difficulties in his and Ogarev's marriages, Herzen was increasingly concerned with issues regarding women and marriage during his last years in Russia. A major intellectual influence was George Sand, whose novels he had been reading enthusiastically since the 1830s, but he also drew on the works of Charles Fourier and Johann Wolfgang von Goethe and the philosophy of the Saint-Simonians. He explored the problems surrounding relations between the sexes in both fiction and essays. He later grouped together three separately published articles under the title "Kaprizy i razdum'e" (Caprices and Reflections, 1843–1847). One of these articles, "Po povodu odnoi dramy" (On the Subject of a Certain Drama), examined M. Arnould's (Auguste Jean François Arnould) and Narcisse Fournier's play *Huit ans de plus* (Eight Years Older, 1837), whose plot—about the conflict between marriage (even a happy marriage) and the eruption of sexual passion—was reminiscent of Goethe's novella *Die Wahlverwandtschaften* (Elective Affinities, 1809). While expressing sympathy for all the characters in *Huit ans de plus,* Herzen refused to accept the notion that the marriage bond should be considered sacrosanct. He countered demands for self-restraint for the sake of an existing marriage with a Saint-Simonian *rehabilitation de la chair* (rehabilitation of the flesh). Another of the articles, "Po raznym povodam" (On Various Topics), uses a device to which Herzen resorted again later: an eccentric observer's inability to distinguish between the normal and the pathological in human activity points up the absurdity of conventional behavior. One of the three episodes in this segment addresses the mistreatment of women in marriage.

Herzen wrote extremely little fiction, almost all of it in the period shortly before he left Russia and almost all concerning women's issues. "Doktor Krupov" (Doctor Krupov), written in 1846 and published in *Sovremennik* (The Contemporary) in 1847, is a satirical survey of mores among both the common folk and the nobility. The narrator, an outsider like the observer of "Po raznym povodam," is a psychiatrist who uses his anecdotes to argue that the supposedly sane are at least as irrational as those whom society brands as mad. Written in 1846 and published in *Sovremennik* in 1848, "Soroka-vorovka" (translated as *The Thieving Magpie: A*

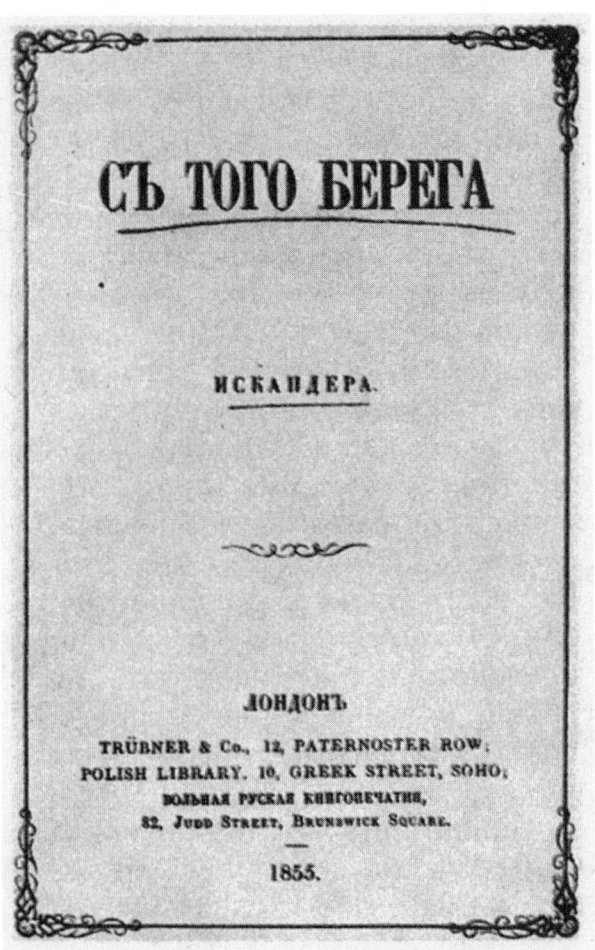

Title page for first Russian-language edition of S togo berega
(From the Other Shore), which Herzen wrote as Iskander
(*from Petr Alekseevich Niklaev, ed.,* Russkie pisateli,
1800–1917: Biograficheskii slovar', *1989)*

Story, 1986) tells the pathetic tale of a serf actress who commits suicide rather than become her owner's mistress. The story also includes an interesting discussion of women and their appropriate role in society by a Slavophile, a liberal Westernizer, and a radical Westernizer (all males).

Herzen's most substantial piece of fiction was the novella *Kto vinovat? Roman v dvukh chastiakh* (translated as *Who is to Blame?* 1978), published serially in *Otechestvennye zapiski* in 1845 and 1846 and issued as a separate volume in 1847. It is the most personal of Herzen's fiction. His wife Natalie's experiences are reflected in the character of the heroine, Liubov', the illegitimate child of a landowner who grows up tolerated but scorned in her father's family. In the main plot her happy marriage is destroyed by a stranger—young, educated, and rich, with no function in Russian society and no role to fill—whose frustrated talents and energy turn him into a destructive force. This character, Bel'tov, is a major link in the chain

of *lishnie liudi* (superfluous men) in nineteenth-century Russian literature, with connections to both Aleksandr Sergeevich Pushkin's *Evgeny Onegin* (1825–1932) in the past and Ivan Sergeevich Turgenev's *Rudin* (1856) in the future. Although Herzen was considered one of the leading literary lights of 1840s Moscow, his output from the Russian period of his life does not add up to a significant career. Of all his early work, only *Kto vinovat?* is available in a modern English translation. The rest is the province of scholars, not general readers.

Early in 1847 Herzen and his family left Russia for western Europe—never to return. They traveled overland, through Germany and Belgium, to Paris, where they rented an apartment on Avenue Marigny, located in the fashionable and expensive section of the Right Bank. Herzen attended sessions of Parliament, studied the newspapers, attended the theater, and patronized restaurants and cafés. Through his Moscow acquaintance Bakunin he became friendly with radical exiles from Germany and Poland who had found relative freedom in France. As he watched French life and participated in discussions about it, his initial excitement gave way to disillusionment, anger, and disgust. Seeking a warmer, drier climate for his wife's and older son's health and an escape from Parisian corruption and scandal, Herzen and his family left for Italy in the autumn of 1847.

Herzen had begun his journey with the intention of writing travel letters, hoping to slip a survey of Western radicalism past the censor. Originally titled "Pis'ma iz Avenue Marigny" (Letters from the Avenue Marigny, published in 1847 in *Sovremennik*), the work opens with a verve quite lacking in Herzen's earlier writings. In the first letter, which describes the journey from Moscow to Paris, Herzen is both excited about and critical of what he saw in the German-speaking lands. He also begins to develop the notion that Western culture could serve as the foundation for Russian development—that Russia was not the rival of western Europe but its successor. The tone of the letters, however, soon darkens; Herzen reserves his respect for the working classes, while expressing scorn for all the other strata of Western society. His intense involvement in the minutiae of current events in the French capital makes doubtful that many readers in Russia could follow his arguments. The fourth and final letter in "Pis'ma iz Avenue Marigny" is marked by extreme pessimism and a sense that the government and society in France are approaching a crisis. Despite censorship problems, the work was published in *Sovremennik,* where the letters met with his friends' disapproval because of their critical attitude toward western Europe. Herzen did not attempt publication of the subsequent series of letters in Russia, but manuscript copies were smuggled into the country and circulated among his friends. They continued to feel that he had become too extreme for their tastes, however, and their relations with him, already badly strained before his departure, deteriorated further. Eventually, the *kruzhok* remained a luminous memory for him, but one that belied his troubled relationship with his old companions.

Herzen and his family set out for the states of the Italian Peninsula at the end of the summer of 1847, just as revolutionary agitation was beginning there. By the time they arrived in Rome they had seen great popular celebrations, as the people of Savoy and Tuscany welcomed reforms granted by their rulers. Later, together with his family and friends Herzen participated in demonstrations in Rome and traveled to Naples to greet the new Sicilian constitution. The three letters in "Pis'ma s Via del Corso" (Letters from the Via del Corso) that Herzen wrote from his Rome address are essentially journalism, vivid accounts of events seen and emotions experienced in the springtime of the revolutions of 1848.

Simultaneously with the first letter of the "Pis'ma s Via del Corso," Herzen wrote a philosophical reflection on ideology and reality, "Pered grozoi" (Before the Storm), which became the introductory chapter to *S togo berega* (From the Other Shore, 1855); first published in German as *Vom anderen Ufer* (1850), it is Herzen's only theoretical work that continues to fascinate generations of readers. Just as Herzen's journalism came alive once he was free of censorship—and perhaps of a circle of readers who knew him only too well—so were his philosophical essays vivified. "Pered grozoi" abandons the heavy German philosophical terminology that he had used in the past and instead presents his argument as a series of dialogues between intelligent and committed people trying to orient themselves in the historical process. Herzen's old fascination with grand "historiosophical" schemes, whether presented by Hegel or the Saint-Simonians, is now decisively abandoned. The voice in the dialogue that approximates Herzen's own insists that development, historical and natural, is not constrained by human intellectual constructs and cannot legitimately be judged by them. He thus calls for the jettisoning of Romanticism, which he sees as an ideology no less oppressive than the medieval Catholicism it has replaced. He demands that every conscious individual orient himself in an indifferent universe and make his own decisions, neither constrained nor supported by abstract, arbitrary systems.

The Herzens remained in Italy until early 1848, by which time the revolutionary dynamism had come to a halt. King Charles Albert of Savoy had gone to war with Austria in an attempt to drive the Hapsburgs out of the peninsula and unify Italy under his own rule. He was thoroughly defeated, and with this loss the rulers of the states of Italy regained the initiative. Before Herzen's apprehension could give way to despair, however, news arrived in Rome of the February Revolution in Paris.

The changes in France were more thoroughgoing than the Italian reforms and constitutions, which had been granted more or less willingly by beleaguered rulers. King Louis Philippe had been forced to abdicate, and a republic had been declared. In the spring the Herzens headed back to France to see the new regime in action.

The enthusiastic beginning of the revolution had passed by the time they arrived in Paris. The new National Assembly had just convened; although elected by universal manhood suffrage, it was far more conservative than the provisional government that had directed the country since the end of February. A series of street demonstrations and clashes had polarized Paris and the country, and the elections showed that France as a whole had little sympathy with the radicalism of the Paris workers and the socialist journalists and politicians who had been active at the start of the revolution. In June a horrifying spectacle of bloody battles occurred in the streets of Paris between the army of the republican government and the workers. These violent days were followed by a repression of the Left: activists were arrested; working-class and radical clubs were closed; and many socialist leaders went into exile. For Herzen, this period—known historically as the June Days—was the ultimate political crisis that changed forever his perception of European society.

Once back in France, Herzen continued his letters with a cycle titled "Opiat' v Parizhe" (Again in Paris). It took the form of three long letters, which provided a narrative history of the revolution from February to the opening of the National Assembly at the time of Herzen's own arrival. A fourth letter, dated October 1848, closed the series with his initial impressions of the journey from Italy to France. He also continued to write the essays that eventually constituted *S togo berega,* and once the cycle of letters had closed, these essays began to combine narration with reflection. In the aftermath of the June catastrophe, Herzen refused ever again to countenance the least sentimentality or wishful thinking about political and social issues. In the later chapters of *S togo berega* he condemned the illusions of the republicans as obsolete and retrograde and began to argue that the entire civilization of the West was rotten and would be swept away by the triumph of proletarian "barbarians."

Herzen remained in Paris from May 1848 to June 1849. During this period he established ties with other foreigners in Paris, most particularly the Germans who returned to exile after the defeat of their efforts at home. His closest friend was the poet Georg Herwegh, whom he had met through his Russian contacts soon after his first arrival in Paris. Herwegh and Herzen were personally compatible, and their bleak analysis of the political prospects after June were quite similar. In one of the major dramas of Herzen's life, the two men became comrades and collaborators—and ultimately bitter enemies.

Following his participation in a demonstration in June 1849, Herzen was forced to flee Paris. He went to Geneva, where his wealth and generosity made him a major figure among the exile community. Although he soon became disenchanted with the exiles, who increasingly struck him as futile dreamers, his contacts among European radicals enabled him to take on a new role—as an interpreter of radical Russia for the West. Shortly after arriving in Geneva, he began negotiations that eventuated with his and Herwegh's participation in a new newspaper edited by the anarchist theorist and publicist Pierre Joseph Proudhon, *La Voix du peuple* (The Voice of the People), for which Herzen provided some needed funds. *La Voix du peuple* did not become the internationally oriented paper that Herzen had dreamed of, and his influence on it was far less than he liked. Nevertheless, the newspaper was the venue of his first Western publications. His essay "La Russie" (Russia, 1849), in the form of an open letter to Herwegh, informed Western readers for the first time of Herzen's view of the potential for socialist development in Russia. A more philosophical piece on the Spanish reactionary thinker Donoso Cortes, which also appeared in *La Voix du peuple*, ended up as part of *S togo berega*.

In addition to his work on Proudhon's paper, Herzen published several other important works aimed at Western audiences at this time. His longest and most sustained argument for the radical tradition and socialist potential of Russia was a French work, *Du Développement des idées révolutionnaires en Russie* (On the Development of Revolutionary Ideas in Russia), written in 1850 and published in 1851. He thoroughly reworked the letters (*pis'ma*) that he had been writing at intervals since 1847, added an additional letter (dated June 1849), and published them anonymously in book form as *Briefe aus Italien und Frankreich* (Letters from Italy and France; Russian version published as *Pis'ma iz Frantsii i Italii [1847–1852]*, 1855) in 1850. While the letters were well received in radical circles, Herzen's philosophical articles—also published anonymously the same year as *Vom anderen Ufer*—had a more mixed reception. German socialists criticized the pessimism of the essays, but the work made a considerable impact in circles where the author's identity was either known from the start or was soon revealed. Finally, Herzen wrote to the democratic French historian Jules Michelet to protest his portrayal of Russia in a work devoted to Polish martyrs to freedom, *Légendes démocratiques du nord* (Democratic Legends of the North). Michelet graciously invited Herzen to respond to the work, and this response, titled "Le Peuple russe et le socialisme" (The Russian People and Socialism), was appended to *Légendes démocratiques du nord* when it was brought out as a book in 1851. This essay became the most accessible and familiar of Herzen's Western works.

A fuller version was published separately in 1852 as *Le Peuple russe et le socialisme: Lettre à Jules Michelet*.

This flurry of major works published over quite a short period of time established Herzen's reputation as a left socialist with formidable skill in argument and with an attractive style, even in relatively crude translations. He had become a colleague of Proudhon, a friend of Michelet, an acquaintance of the Italian democratic revolutionary Giuseppe Mazzini, and a major presence among the non-Marxist German radicals. He had also come into his maturity as a social thinker. In effect, in the works he published during 1850 and 1851 he distilled four years of observation, experience, and reflection into an ideological position that he soon ceased to elaborate upon much in the future. He eventually changed his mind about the methods needed to achieve social change in Russia but not about the possibility of a Russian socialism based on popular institutions. Compared to the rest of the Westernizers, Herzen had never idealized the West; now he was farther than ever from seeing a model for Russian development there. The revolutionary experience had shattered whatever faith he might have had in liberal institutions; he had come to loathe the bourgeoisie; and he felt that the revolutionaries, however sincere they might be, were misguided and followed a futile course of action.

Herzen saw his role in the West as two-sided, but in these first years, while he was brilliantly successful in fulfilling one side—providing a Russian point of view to a Western audience—the other aspect of his intentions was only outlined, not fulfilled. In a farewell letter to his Russian friends, he had assumed the role of the émigré spokesman in regard to the movement for social and political change in Russia. From the West he could be the "uncensored voice" of Russia, and in so doing would be part of a revolutionary tradition: "In every country at the beginning of an upheaval, while thought is still feeble and material power unbridled, men of energy and devotion withdraw, their free speech rings out from the distance. . . . Emigration is the first symptom of approaching upheaval." There is evidence that in 1849, and again two years later, Herzen contemplated establishing a Russian press abroad through which he planned to publish his own works free of censorship, but for which he would also solicit manuscripts from Russia. These ephemeral designs accurately foreshadowed Herzen's mature career.

Ultimately, rather than combining the two roles of the émigré, Herzen shifted from a predominantly Western to a predominantly Russian orientation. The reorientation came as a by-product of the overwhelming crisis in his personal life that he endured between 1850 and 1852. Not only had Western revolutionaries betrayed the revolutionary hopes placed on them, but in the person of

Herwegh the West had committed a profound personal betrayal of Herzen himself.

In the summer of 1849 in Geneva, Natalie Herzen and Herwegh became involved in an intense love affair of which Herzen remained ignorant. The relationship was interrupted when Herzen, goaded by Herwegh's wife, summoned Natalie and the children to join him in Paris, while Herwegh, fearing for his safety, remained in Geneva. The affair was resumed when both families moved to Nice, where they shared a house, in the summer of 1850. By the end of the year Herzen had become suspicious, and Natalie confessed to him. There ensued a stormy period of recrimination and a temporary separation. At the end of the summer of 1851 the couple were finally reconciled, only to be struck by tragedy a few months later. In November their younger son and Herzen's mother were drowned in a shipwreck off the coast of southern France. Natalie, who was pregnant, became ill in her grief, and on May 2, after delivering a daughter who lived only a few days, she died.

Herzen's first thought was that he would avenge Natalie's death by attacking Herwegh. He rejected physical combat and indeed refused to fight a duel when Herwegh challenged him. Each man managed to humiliate the other publicly, to the embarrassment of the more established members of the radical community but to the delight of those who wished them ill. Herzen then arrived at the notion of having the radical community hold a "court of honor" and condemn Herwegh as unworthy of their company. To this end, he traveled to Italy, Switzerland, and finally London, soliciting support through a network of correspondence. He also undertook to write a "memoir" detailing what he perceived as Herwegh's violation of revolutionary morality. While many of Herzen's friends and acquaintances sympathized with his grief and anger, and indeed Herwegh's reputation was irredeemably damaged in the process, the kind of institutional action that Herzen envisioned did not take place. Moreover, when he went to work on the "memoir," he found, to his surprise and chagrin, that the indictment was turning into "memoirs," as *Byloe i dumy* came into being.

Just as Herzen's arrival in London marked the initiation of his most important single work, it was also the beginning of his mature political and journalistic career. A landowner's son, he had known of the peasants' condition all his life and frequently discussed it from 1848 to 1852 as he developed his theory of Russian socialism. Nonetheless, there is no foreshadowing of the statement that he made at the end of 1852: "An amazing project is turning around in my head—to undertake agitation for the liberation of the peasants." At the time he had just written a substantial piece, which was published in English as "Russian Serfdom" in the radical journal *The*

Leader in 1853. He also published a Russian pamphlet, *Kreshchenaia sobstvennost'* (Baptized Property, 1853), on the same theme.

Accompanying Herzen's new goal was the realization of an older project: the establishment of a Russian press abroad for the purpose of disseminating radical and reformist ideas in Russia. In England he quickly made contact with the radical wing of the Polish émigré population, the Polish Democratic Society, and its leader, Stanislas Worcell, a man he greatly admired. A collaboration between Herzen and the Poles was soon established. In return for Herzen's financial assistance, the Poles provided Herzen with Cyrillic fonts for his press and assistance in moving his publications into the Russian Empire, an activity with which they had long experience. For a time, the Poles' press and Herzen's Vol'noe russkoe knigopechatanie (Free Russian Press) shared the same facilities, but quarrels led to their separation at the end of 1854. The collaboration continued, however, and reinforced Herzen's association with the Polish cause, which dated back to his student days and had been strengthened by Bakunin's influence on him during his time in Paris. Ultimately, Herzen's loyalty to the Polish cause was extremely harmful to his own position.

In February 1853 Herzen published a brief pamphlet announcing the existence of his press. He called on his friends and other reform-minded Russians to supply him with material, so that the press could act as a forum for free thought. He also requested copies of manuscripts of banned poetry, so that it could finally be published. The results were disappointing; nothing arrived from Russia. Herzen published his new work, reprinted some older pieces, and solicited material from other Russian émigrés while waiting for a response from Russia. The wait was long, and the silence—and even the condemnation of his enterprise by his old friends—was particularly painful. The lack of activity at the press though, however dispiriting, gave Herzen time to work on his memoirs. He wrote fairly steadily between early 1852 and 1855 and completed what are now the first five sections of the work. These parts of *Byloe i dumy* are the most accessible and appealing; they tell Herzen's life story more or less chronologically from his infancy during the French occupation of Moscow until Natalie's death.

Although reasonably accurate, the material is shaped to create a mythic revolutionary, embodied by Herzen himself. He is linked directly to his country's history through his presence in Moscow during the occupation, and again during the coronation of Nicholas I; the Decembrist uprising stirs his demand for political change. His family exemplifies the old half-savage, half-epic nobility, now reduced to a decadent eccentricity by the bureaucratized modern despotism. The child's experience also reflects the relationship of the upper class

First page from the first issue of Kolokol *(The Bell), the biweekly newspaper Herzen founded in London to publish information he received from Russia (from Natal'ia Mikhailovna Pirumova,* Aleksandr Gertsen, *1989)* and the peasantry: on the one hand, the infant and child Herzen draws nurture and strength from his enserfed attendants; on the other, the oppression of the peasantry is described in telling anecdotes, as are the peasants' occasional outbursts of hatred and revenge against the landowning class. The three supports that enable Herzen to become a man committed to the struggle for freedom are his friendship with Ogarev, his love for Natalie, and the phalanx of young, educated graduates of Moscow University whom he befriends. His disillusionment with the West is embodied in Herwegh—the romantic revolutionary turned cynical and squalid seducer. Herzen wrote and edited the section of *Byloe i dumy* about Herwegh and Natalie but did not publish it. His daughter included it in an edition after his death. He was never able to come to terms with the nature of the relationship between his wife and Herwegh; not only did he avoid acknowledging that it was sexual, but he could never admit, even to himself, that Natalie had been a full participant and not an innocent victim.

Herzen was criticized in his own day for stylistic failings—such as a plethora of foreign words and many grammatical and linguistic infelicities. All this becomes irrelevant, however, as the reader is carried along by the acute character sketches, illuminating anecdotes, and often wicked wit. Separated from Russia forever, in these initial sections of *Byloe i dumy*, Herzen creates a vivid image of his native land compounded of nostalgia and political condemnation.

The outbreak of the Crimean War in 1853 further intensified Herzen's isolation. Still unable to make contact with his compatriots, he had now become suspect to the European radicals and fellow émigrés whose countries were fighting against Russia. He published extremely little new material during the war but used his enforced idleness to prepare Russian editions of the works he had published since his arrival in western Europe. *S togo berega* and the augmented and greatly revised *Pis'ma iz Frantsii i Italii* (Letters from France and Italy) appeared in 1855. A new French edition of *Le Peuple russe et le socialisme* came out the same year in the Isle of Jersey, as did an English translation. (Herzen brought out the first Russian edition only in 1858.) He also published an English translation of the section of *Byloe i dumy* that concerns his arrest and exile. Unfortunately, this piece appeared with the title "My Exile to Siberia," which led to charges that he exaggerated the punishment that he had suffered in Russia.

The death of Tsar Nicholas I in 1855 marked a major change in Herzen's life. Even as he celebrated the disappearance of his nemesis, a thaw began in his home country. Herzen began to receive visitors from Russia and was able to renew contact with the surviving members of the old *kruzhok*. After the long drought he now

started receiving manuscripts from Russia. Before the year was out he had embarked on a new venture—a journal, *Poliarnaia zvezda* (The North Star)—that printed substantial articles by him and other contributors from within and outside Russia. In 1856 chapters of *Byloe i dumy* began to appear in this journal.

In 1856 Ogarev was able to leave Russia and joined Herzen in emigration. Ogarev was accompanied by his wife, Natalie Alekseevna (née Tuchkova), who had been a close friend and admirer of Natalie Herzen. Soon after the Ogarevs arrived in London, Natalie Tuchkova and Herzen became intimate companions and eventually had children together (twins, a boy and a girl, born in 1861). Nonetheless, his collaboration and friendship with Ogarev continued, and although eventually the men were separated geographically and had political disagreements, their friendship lasted until Herzen's death.

When in 1856 Tsar Alexander II initiated the process of peasant emancipation, Herzen—still based in London—became a major participant. He published proposals and programs, provided commentary on statements by the government and the noble assemblies, and soon was receiving leaked information from St. Petersburg chancelleries, which he made available to the public. For the next five years Herzen enjoyed a celebrity and authority unrivaled by any of his countrymen. The volume of material he received from Russia soon overwhelmed *Poliarnaia zvezda*. He reserved his original journal for major pieces and in 1857 started a newspaper to publicize the items of information he had received—on political chicanery, noble brutality, clerical drunkenness, corruption by petty and great bureaucrats. *Kolokol* (The Bell) eventually appeared every two weeks and became his most popular and important outlet. For the most part, Herzen's writing for *Kolokol* consisted of summaries of information received, or of short introductions to reports, from Russia. His prose for *Kolokol* became an offensive weapon, characterized by invective, sarcasm, sardonic humor, and memorable phrases. The articles that he published in *Poliarnaia zvezda* shared his minimum program of calling for peasant emancipation with land. From time to time articles arrived from Russian correspondents that expressed a conservative, private-property-oriented liberalism or a Slavophile point of view that diverged too greatly from Herzen's own opinions for him to feel comfortable placing them in *Poliarnaia zvezda*. For these works he started yet another publication—an anthology series titled *Golosa iz Rossii* (Voices from Russia).

In the late 1850s, with the responsibility of putting out three journals as well as of writing much of the copy for *Kolokol*, Herzen had little time to write more extended works. He did, however, write several essays on English life and about the European émigrés who had participated in the failed revolutions of 1848 and whose London circles constituted Herzen's social environment in England. He first published these essays in *Poliarnaia zvezda;* later they were collected to constitute much of the second part of *Byloe i dumy.* Unlike the first part of the memoir, the second remains a collection of articles in which Herzen is largely an observer, and there is no narrative continuity. Little of his personal life is included—in this section of the memoir the memoirist almost disappears. The essays on western Europeans constitute the first section, while the second is concerned with Herzen's activity in regard to Russia and includes quite critical analyses of his collaborators. Finally, there is a set of impromptu sketches written in the last years of Herzen's life. There is no definitive version of part 2: although he made clear that his articles were part of *Byloe i dumy,* Herzen died before he could select articles for collection and choose the order of their presentation.

In addition to his accomplishments as a memoirist, journalist, political philosopher, and publisher, Herzen made quite important contributions as an historian. From the time he founded his press, he energetically collected and published materials documenting the past of Russia—especially those that provided radicalism with a useful historical tradition. That the first number of *Poliarnaia zvezda* printed Belinsky's "Pis'mo k Gogoliu" (Letter to Gogol, 1855)—perhaps the single most important statement of Westernism—shows that preserving the radical past was one of Herzen's major aims. He and Ogarev had been inspired by the Decembrists from the time of their oath and memorialized them by using an image of the five who were executed as the logo for *Poliarnaia zvezda* (which also repeated the title of a Decembrist publication). As publisher and editor, Herzen managed to collect a substantial amount of writing by and about the Decembrists, and he eventually published three volumes of material. Both Aleksandr Nikolaevich Radishchev's *Puteshestvie iz Peterburga v Moskvu* (Journey from St. Petersburg to Moscow), which was collected in 1858 with Kniaz' Mikhail Mikhailovich Shcherbatov's *O povrezhdenii nravov v Rossii kniazia M. Shcherbatova,* and Tsarina Catherine II's *Mémoires de l'impératrice Catherine II* (1859; translated as *Memoirs of the Empress Catherine II,* 1859) were brought out by Herzen, along with many more specialized plans and programs of reform devised in the eighteenth and early nineteenth centuries. Another area of interest for Herzen was censored poetry—that of Pushkin and many of his contemporaries as well. The Russian history studied in the twentieth century owes much of its structure to materials provided by Herzen.

The announcement of peasant emancipation in 1861 was the high point of Herzen's career. He had made his exile publications the focal point for discussions of the reform; his leaked information had helped nudge the government away from the most restrictive proposals; his demand that the peasants be emancipated with land had been at least partially realized. While the planning had been in progress, Herzen had achieved great renown in Russia, and visitors to western Europe made special efforts to seek him out. For Western radicals, he had become the Russian representative of their movement, and his participation was solicited for collective statements and actions. He had also, however, made enemies. Young men in Russia found him hesitant in recommending action, excessively concerned with style over substance, and altogether too aristocratic. Nikolai Gavrilovich Chernyshevsky, an editor of *Sovremennik* and a spokesman for Herzen's Russian critics, came to London in 1859 to attempt a reconciliation. The two men took an instant and intense dislike to each other, and henceforth Herzen's isolation and alienation from younger Russian radicals only intensified. Moreover, former collaborators who had left or been dismissed from Herzen's enterprise were often bitter and added their resentment to the growing distrust, and a severe factionalism among the Western émigrés could not fail to extend to Herzen, who was friend to some groups and thus foe to others. Karl Marx and Friedrich Engels loathed him, his aristocratic background, and all he appeared to represent. Herzen's collaboration with the Poles of the Polish Democratic Society was difficult in itself; the Poles were intensely nationalistic and not sympathetic to Herzen's socialism, while Herzen had the socialist's suspicion of intense nationalism. He became estranged from other Polish groups to the Left and the Right.

The Polish issue became acute almost immediately. Herzen had planned a major celebration to greet the emancipation proclamation. But news of the bloody suppression of a demonstration in Warsaw arrived just before the festivities, and Herzen canceled them. This event was symptomatic of the way in which his triumph in regard to Russian social and political developments later was undermined and destroyed by Polish issues. Finding a way through the conflicting loyalties raised by Russian conquest and control of Poland was not easy. Most thoughtful Russians, while perhaps feeling that Russian rule in Poland was too harsh, found their nationalism challenged by Polish demands for independence. Herzen tried to combine an advocacy of democracy and self-determination with Russian interests in a program that called for the thorough democratization of both societies and Polish independence. Then he hoped the Poles would join voluntarily with a free Russia in a Slavic federation. His lack of enthusiasm for the prospect of an aristocratic, independent Poland alienated him from the more conservative wing of the Polish movement. His support for Polish independence, even if it did not lead to union with Russia, angered nationalistic Russians who felt that Poland was part of their patrimony. His lack of enthusi-

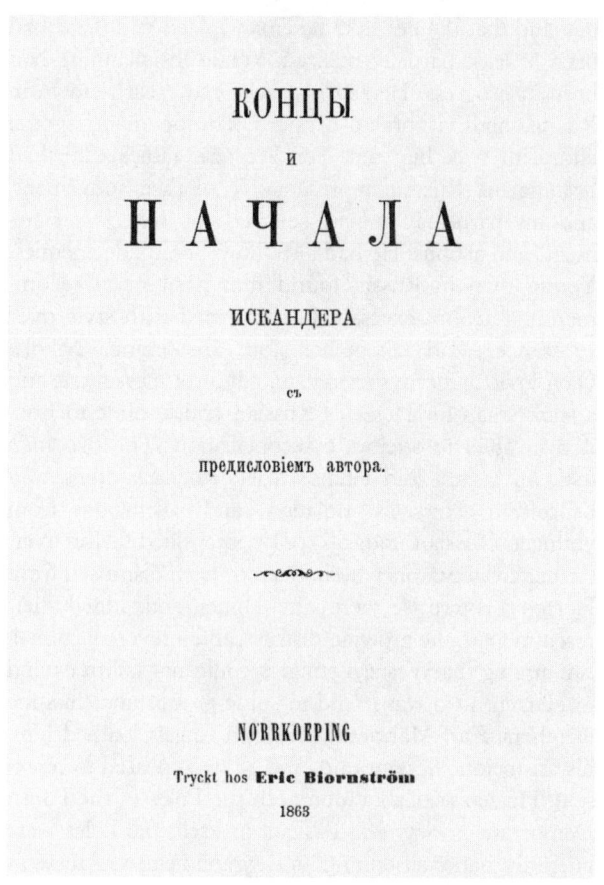

КОНЦЫ

и

НАЧАЛА

ИСКАНДЕРА

съ

предисловіемъ автора.

NORRKOEPING

Tryckt hos **Eric Biornström**

1863

Title page for Herzen's Kontsy i nachala *(Ends and Beginnings),*
a series of letters criticizing the West, first published in Kolokol
in 1862 (Kilgour Collection of Russian Literature,
Harvard University Library)

asm for violent revolution distressed the most radical Poles. After Worcell's death in 1857, none of the Polish political leaders inspired Herzen's affection and loyalty.

As demonstrations and repression continued in Russian Poland, and Poles abroad became more active in plotting an uprising, Herzen's position grew increasingly difficult. Bakunin, who had escaped from Siberian exile in 1860 and made his way to the London exiles, was an enthusiastic supporter of Polish action, and so, to a lesser extent, was Ogarev. In Herzen's certain opinion, any attempt at an uprising would be futile; he also knew that his Russian public would sympathize neither with a Polish revolt nor with a Russian émigré group that supported it. Yet, given his long-term support for the Polish cause, the extent to which his entire enterprise depended on Polish auxiliary personnel, his friends' enthusiasm, and his own commitments, he could not refrain from backing the Polish effort. As he expected, the effect came quickly and catastrophically. Circulation of his journals dropped precipitously, and Herzen and Ogarev found themselves increasingly isolated.

Herzen did not write anything major during his last years. There were travel impressions that ultimately went into *Byloe i dumy,* and he continuously strove to define himself in relation to other political tendencies in Russia, an effort that had begun in the 1850s. Over the years he wrote a series of substantial articles that could be read together as the political manifesto he never attempted. In 1858 and 1859 he responded to Polish criticism of him in *Kolokol* with a series of articles–later reprinted as "Rossiia i Pol'sha" (Russia and Poland). He defended his policy of concentrating his attention on the practical question of peasant emancipation with land, rather than on a full-scale political and social program, and reasserted his view that Poland had the right to independence, though he ultimately hoped for the federation of a free Poland with a free Russia.

Herzen's increasingly strained relations with the younger generation of radicals were also aired in 1859. His concentration on practical measures of reform as opposed to attempts to transform Russia completely; his advocacy of a broad coalition of reformers; and his open letters to Tsar Alexander II–which appeared to acknowledge Alexander's legitimacy as ruler–irritated the doctrinally more rigid young radicals. In an article aimed against the writers of *Sovremennik,* titled "Very Dangerous!" (*Kolokol,* 1859), Herzen defended his approach and rejected the young radicals' easy condemnation of the irresolution of the *lishnie liudi* (superfluous people) of his own generation. He defended the men of his own and earlier generations even more forcefully a year later, in "Lishnie liudi i zhelcheviki" (*Kolokol,* 1860), again directed against *Sovremennik.* These articles suggest that the differences between Herzen and the younger generation began as issues of style more than substance. In 1862 Herzen's criticism took on new content, when he responded to the appearance of an incendiary pamphlet, *Molodaia Rossiia* (Young Russia), in St. Petersburg. He regarded it as likely to provoke repression, rather than encourage revolution, and he expressly stated that he had lost any taste for violent methods of struggle.

Two other conflicts of the 1860s were less angry, since they involved personal friends. Herzen defined himself against the less political, more conservative Turgenev in a series of nine open letters, "Kontsy i nachala" (Ends and Beginnings, published in *Kolokol,* 1862). These letters criticized Western bourgeois society for its conservatism, charging that even liberals were more concerned with repressing the revolutionary forces of the working classes than with extending liberty. Finally, almost at the end of his life, Herzen wrote another cycle of letters criticizing the "revolutionism" of his old friend Bakunin. He argued that only gradual change could actually alter the mentality of the people and thus bring about a solid transformation not based on violence. This repudiation of revolutionary violence is Herzen's last word on revolutionary change, but hardly the only view he expressed during his lifetime.

The final years of Herzen's life are a depressing chronicle of decline. After his and Natalie Tuchkova's three-year-old twins died suddenly of diphtheria in 1864, the couple could no longer bear to remain in England. Herzen, Ogarev, and the press moved to Geneva—along with Ogarev's mistress, Herzen's son's illegitimate son, and the boy's mother—while Natalie eventually settled in Nice. Almost at once a fierce attack on Herzen by one of the younger, more radical Russians who had set up operations in Geneva soured him on his new home. Henceforth, Herzen led a peripatetic existence. He visited the members of his increasingly scattered family, closed his journals, and made attempts at refounding them, including a French version of *Kolokol*. In 1868 he was diagnosed with diabetes, and declining health became another motif in his existence, along with visits to spas and doctors. In 1870 Herzen was living in Paris when his older daughter had a breakdown in Italy. He rushed to help her and brought her back to Paris, but the strain turned out to be too much for him. He became ill on his return, rapidly developed pneumonia, and died a few days later on 21 January 1870. Despite its frustrations with Herzen of recent years, the international radical community reacted with shock at the disappearance of a figure who seemed to embody the Russian striving for personal and political liberation.

Herzen's fame rests above all on the persona that he presented for two decades. He was the rebel, the man who had sacrificed his homeland for his ideals and who, once in exile, worked to realize his ideals through practical activity, rather than languish in luxurious idleness as previous émigrés had done. Moreover, Herzen never allowed his rebellious nature to overshadow his attractive personal qualities: he was a man of learning and fellowship; the romantic lover of his wife, Natalie; and the cultivated promoter of a still young Russian cultural life. The only one of Herzen's literary works to enjoy and deserve a lasting reputation is the one that established and publicized his persona, *Byloe i dumy*. Other of his works, particularly those that predate the establishment of the Vol'noe russkoe knigopechatanie, are remarkable for their probing questions and their images of a Europe in crisis. *S togo berega* and *Pis'ma s Frantsii i Italii* are especially noteworthy. Finally, Herzen's work in recovering the Russian past has not been given its due. Because of Herzen the memoirs of Catherine II, much of the primary material created by the Decembrists and their friends, and some of the poetry of Pushkin and his contemporaries are all available. Furthermore, Herzen is largely responsible for the framework of Russian history still accepted in modern universities.

Ultimately, Alexander Herzen's personal qualities undermined his position in the radical movement. He was too rich, too genteel, and too concerned with the consequences of revolutionary action to function effectively in the harder world that emerged after the emancipation of the peasants. With the polarization of Russian public opinion, he was caught in the middle—too radical for liberal reformers of his own class and too cautious for the generation of radicals that drew its inspiration from Chernyshevsky. Repudiated in his own day, Herzen nonetheless stands as the image of what is most appealing in the Russian radical tradition.

Letters:

Neizdannye pis'ma A. I. Gertsena k N. I. i T. A. Astrakovym, edited by L. L. Domager (New York: Novyi zhurnal, 1957);

Sobranie sochinenii v tridtsati tomakh, volumes 21–30 (Moscow: Izdatel'stvo Akademii nauk SSSR, 1961–1965);

Lettres inédites à sa fille Olga, edited by Alexandre Zviguilsky (Paris: Librairie des cinq continents, 1970);

"Six lettres de Herzen à Proudhon," edited by Michel Mervaud, *Cahiers du monde russe et soviétiques,* 12, no. 3 (July–September 1971): 307–316;

Marc Vuilleumier, Michel Aucouturier, Sven Stelling-Michaud and Michel Cadot, eds., *Autour d'Alexandre Herzen* (Geneva: Librairie Droz, 1973);

Lettres inédites: Herzen, Ogarev, Bakounine, volume 7 of *Les inédits russes,* edited by Mervaud (Paris: Librairie des cinq continents, 1975).

Bibliographies:

A. G. Fomin, "Bibliografiia proizvedenii A. I. Gertsena i literatury o nem," in Ch. Vetrinsky [V. E. Cheshikhin], *Gertsen* (St. Petersburg, 1908), pp. 467–521;

L. E. Barsukova, comp., *Gertsen, Ogarev i ikh okruzhenie: Rukopisi, perepiska i dokumenty* (Moscow: Izdatel'stvo gosudarstvennogo literaturnogo muzeia, 1940);

Boris Iakovlevich Bukhshtab, *A. I. Gertsen. Ukazatel' osnovnoi literatury* (Leningrad: Leningradskoe gazetno-zhurnal'noe i knizhnoe izdatel'stvo, 1945);

A. V. Askariants and Z. V. Kemenova, *Opisanie rukopisei A. I. Gertsena* (Moscow, 1950);

Bibliografiia literatury ob A. I. Gertsene: 1917–1970 gg (Leningrad: Leningradskii gosudarstvennyi pedagogicheskii institut imeni A. I. Gertsena, 1978).

Biographies:

Mar'ia Kasparovna Reikhel, *Otryvki iz vospominanii M. K. Reikhel' i pis'ma k nei A. I. Gertsena* (Moscow: Izd. L. E. Bukhgeim, 1909);

Edward Hallett Carr, *The Romantic Exiles: A Nineteenth-Century Portrait Gallery* (New York: Stokes, 1933);

Henry Grosshans, "Alexander Herzen and the Free Russian Press in London, 1853–1865," *Research Studies,* 26 (1958): 17–36;

Tat'iana Petrovna Passek, *Iz dal'nykh let: Vospominaniia,* 2 volumes (Moscow: Gosudarstvennoe izdatelst'vo khudozhestvennoi literatury, 1963);

Martin Malia, *Alexander Herzen and the Birth of Russian Socialism: 1812–1855* (Cambridge, Mass.: Harvard University Press, 1963);

Monica Partridge, *Herzen. 1812–1870* (Paris: Unesco, 1984);

Judith E. Zimmerman, *Midpassage: Alexander Herzen and European Revolution, 1847–1852* (Pittsburgh, Pa.: University of Pittsburgh Press, 1989).

References:

Edward Acton, *Alexander Herzen and the Role of the Intellectual Revolutionary* (Cambridge: Cambridge University Press, 1979);

Isaiah Berlin, "Alexander Herzen," in his *Russian Thinkers* (New York: Viking, 1978), pp. 186–209;

Nadja Bontadina, *Alexander Herzen und die Schweiz: das Verhältnis des russischen Publizisten und Aristokraten zur einzigen Republik im Europa seiner Zeit* (Frankfurt am Main & New York: Peter Lang, 1999);

Lidiia Chukovskaia, *"Byloe i dumy" Gertsena* (Moscow: Khudozhestvennaia literatura, 1966);

Elena Dryzhakova, *Gertsen na Zapade: v labirinte nadezhd, slavy i otrechenii* (St. Petersburg: Akademicheskii proekt, 1999);

Natan Iakovlevich Eidel'man, *Gertsen protiv samoderzhaviia: Sekretnaia politicheskaia istoriia Rossii XVIII–XIX vekov i Vol'naia pechat'* (Moscow: Mysl', 1973);

Lidiia Iakovlevna Ginzburg, *"Byloe i dumy" Gertsena* (Leningrad: Gosudarstvennoe izdatel'stvo khudozhestvennoi literatury, 1957);

Abbott Gleason, *Young Russia: The Genesis of Russian Radicalism in the 1860s* (New York: Viking, 1980);

S. D. Gurvich-Lishchiner, *Gertsen i russkaia khudozhestvennaia kul'tura 1860-kh godov* (Tel Aviv: Tel Aviv University Press, 1997);

Gurvich-Lishchiner, *Tvorchestvo Gertsena v razvitii russkogo realizma serediny XIX veka* (Moscow: Nasledie, 1994);

Aileen M. Kelly, *Views from the Other Shore: Essays on Herzen, Chekhov, and Bakhtin* (New Haven & London: Yale University Press, 1999);

Monica Partridge, *Alexander Herzen: Collected Studies* (Nottingham, U.K.: Astra, 1993);

Partridge, ed., *Alexander Herzen and European Culture* (Nottingham, U.K.: Astra, 1984);

Lev Plotkin, *O russkoi literature: A. I. Gertsen, I. S. Nikitin, D. I. Pisarev* (Leningrad: Khudozhestvennaia literatura, 1986);

Ulrike Preissmann, *Alexander Herzen und Italien* (Mainz: Liber, 1989);

L. S. Radek, *Gertsen i Turgenev: Literaturno-esteticheskaia polemika* (Kishinev: "Shtiintsa," 1984);

Vladimir Artemovich Tunimanov, *A. I. Gertsen i russkaia obshchestvenno-literaturnaia mysl' XIX v.* (St. Petersburg: Nauka, 1994);

Franco Venturi, *Roots of Revolution: A History of the Populist and Socialist Movements in Nineteenth-Century Russia,* translated by Francis Haskell (London: Weidenfeld & Nicolson, 1960).

Papers:

The papers of Alexander Herzen are held in Moscow at the Russian State Archive of Literature and Art (RGALI), fond 129; the State Literary Museum (GLM), fond 22; and the Russian State Library (RGB, formerly the Lenin Library), fond 69; and in St. Petersburg at the Institute of Russian Literature (IRLI, Pushkin House); and the Russian National Library (RNB), fond 180. A description of the documents related to Herzen and archived in IRLI can be found in the article "Rukopisi Gertsena v Insitute russkoi literatury (Pushkinskom dome) AN SSSR," published in 1950 in the journal *Biulleten' Rukopisnogo otdela IRLI.*

Vladimir Galaktionovich Korolenko

(15 July 1853 – 25 December 1921)

Radha Balasubramanian
University of Nebraska, Lincoln

BOOKS: *Ocherki i rasskazy,* book 1 (Moscow, 1886)–comprises "V durnom obshchestve," "Son Makara," "Les shumit," "V noch' pod svetlyi prazdnik," "V podsledstvennom otdelenii," "Staryi zvonar'," "Ocherki sibirskogo turista," and "Sokolinets";

Ubivets. Rasskaz sibirskogo iamshchika (Moscow, 1887); republished as *Ubivets. (Ocherki sibirskogo turista). Rasskaz* (St. Petersburg: M. A. Kolomenkina, 1910);

Nevol'naia ubitsa (St. Petersburg: Sankt-Peterburgskii Komitet Gramotnosti, 1888);

Slepoi muzykant. (Etiud) (Moscow: Russkaia mysl', 1888); translated by Aline Delano as *The Blind Musician,* with an introduction by George Kennan (Boston: Little, Brown, 1890);

Ocherki i rasskazy, book 2 (Moscow: "Russkaia mysl'," 1893)–comprises "Reka igraet," "Na zatmenii," "At-Davan," "Cherkes," "Za ikonoi," "Noch'iu," "Teni," and "Sudnyi den' (Iom-Kipur)";

Deti podzemel'ia (Moscow: V. Ia. Murinov, 1894);

V golodnyi god (St. Petersburg: Russkoe bogatstvo, 1894);

V durnom obshchestve (Moscow: Posrednik, 1894);

Sudnyi den'. Malorusskaia skazka (St. Petersburg: Sankt-Peterburgskii Komitet Gramotnosti, 1895);

Teni. Fantaziia (Moscow: Posrednik, 1896);

Bez iazyka (St. Petersburg: Russkoe bogatstvo, 1902);

Ocherki i rasskazy, book 3 (St. Petersburg: Russkoe bogatstvo, 1903)–comprises "Ogon'ki," "Skazanie o Flore, Agrippe, i Menakheme, syne Iegudy," "Paradoks," "Gosudarevy iamshchiki," "Poslednii luch," "Marusina zaimka," "Mgnoven'e," "V oblachnyi den'";

Dom No. 13-yi (Berlin: H. Caspari, 1903–1904)–includes "Dom No. 13";

Vospominaniia o N. G. Chernyshevskom (Berlin: G. Shteinits, 1904);

Otoshedshie. Ob Uspenskom. O Chernyshevskom. O Chekhove (St. Petersburg: Russkoe bogatstvo, 1908);

Istoriia moego sovremennika, 2 volumes (St. Petersburg, 1909, 1919)–comprises volume 1, *Rannee detstvo i gody ucheniia* (1909); and volume 2, *Studencheskie gody i ssyl'nyia skitaniia* (1919); enlarged, 3 volumes (Moscow: Zadruga, 1921); enlarged, 5 volumes (Moscow & Berlin: Vozrozhdenie, 1922); translated and abridged by Neil Parsons as *The History of My Contemporary* (Oxford: Oxford University Press, 1972);

Polnoe sobranie sochinenii, 9 volumes (St. Petersburg: A. F. Marks, 1914)–includes volume 2–includes "Moe pervoe znakomstvo s Dikensom"; translated as "My First Encounter with Dickens," in *Russian Literature and Modern English Fiction,* edited by Donald Davie (Chicago: University of Chicago Press, 1965), pp. 107–116;

Voina, otechestvo i chelovechestvo. (Pis'ma o voprosakh nashego vremeni) (Moscow: Vserossiiskii tsentral'nyi soiuz potrebnykh obshchstv, 1917; enlarged, Moscow: Kooperatsiia izdatel'stva, 1917);

Padenie tsarskoi vlasti (Moscow: Narodopravstvo, 1917; Petrograd: Osvobozhdenaia Rossiia, 1917);

Pis'ma k Lunacharskomu (Paris: Zadruga, 1922);

Polnoe sobranie sochinenii. Posmertnoe izdanie, volumes 1–5, 7–8, 13, 15–22, 24, 50–51, edited by A. S. Korolenko, Sofiia Vladimirovna Korolenko, T. A. Bogdanovich, and others (Khar'kov & Poltava: Gosudarstvennoe izdatel'stvo Ukrainy, 1922–1929);

Dnevnik, volumes 1–4 of *Polnoe sobranie sochinenii* (Khar'kov & Poltava: Gosudarstvennoe izdatel'stvo Ukrainy, 1925–1928);

Zapisnaia knizhka 1879, with an introduction by S. Alekseev (Gor'ky: Kraevoe izdatel'stvo, 1933);

Vospominaniia o pisateliakh, edited by Sofiia Vladimirovna Korolenko and A. L. Krivinskaia (Moscow: Mir, 1934);

Zapisnye knizhki (1880–1900), edited by Sofiia Vladimirovna Korolenko and Krivinskaia (Moscow: Khudozhestvennaia literatura, 1935);

Vladimir Galaktionovich Korolenko, 1907

Sobranie sochinenii, 10 volumes (Moscow: Goslitizdat, 1953–1956);

Povesti i rasskazy, 2 volumes (Moscow: Goslitizdat, 1960);

Zemli! Zemli! Mysli, vospominaniia, kartiny, edited by P. I. Negretov and M. I. Perper (Moscow: Sovetskii pisatel', 1991)–includes "Pis'ma k Lunacharskomu";

Dnevnik 1917–1921, Pis'ma, edited by Viktora I. Losev (Moscow: Sovetskii pisatel', 2001).

Editions and Collections: *Sochineniia,* edited by Nikolai Kir'iakovich Piksanov, with an introduction by Anatolii Vasil'evich Lunacharsky (Moscow & Leningrad: Gosudarstvennoe izdatel'stvo, 1929);

Izbrannye sochineniia, edited by A. K. Kotov (Moscow: Academia, 1937);

Sibirskie ocherki i rasskazy, 2 parts, edited by Natal'ia Vladimirovna and Sofiia Vladimirovna Korolenko (Moscow: Goslitizdat, 1946);

Izbrannye proizvedeniia, edited by Natal'ia Vladimirovna and Sofiia Vladimirovna Korolenko, with an introduction by Kotov (Moscow: Goslitizdat, 1947, 1948);

Sobranie sochinenii, 8 volumes (Moscow: Pravda, 1953);

O literature, with an introduction by A. V. Khrabrovitsky (Moscow, 1957);

Sobranie sochinenii, 5 volumes, with an introduction by Khrabrovitsky and commentary by M. A. Sokolova and G. M. Mironov (Moscow: Molodaia gvardiia, 1960–1961);

Istoriia moego sovremennika, edited, with a commentary, by Khrabrovitsky (Moscow: Khudozhestvennaia literatura, 1965);

Vospominaniia. Stat'i. Pis'ma, edited by S. I. Timina (Moscow: Sovetskaia Rossiia, 1988);

Rasskazy i povesti, vospominaniia, kriticheskie stat'i, publitsistika, edited by I. E. Kaplan (Moscow: AST Olimp, 1997);

Reka igraet. Povesti, rasskazy, publitsistika (Voronezh: Izdatel'stvo im. E. A. Bolkhovitinova, 2000).

Editions in English: *The Vagrant and Other Tales,* translated by Aline Delano (New York: Crowell, 1887)–comprises "The Old Bell-Ringer," "The Forest Soughs," "A Forest Legend," "Easter Night," "A Sakhalinian," and "The Tale of a Vagrant";

The Murmuring Forest and Other Stories, translated by Marian Fell (London: Duckworth, 1916); republished as *Makar's Dream and Other Stories* (New York: Duffield, 1916)–comprises "Makar's Dream," "The Murmuring Forest," "In Bad Company," and "The Day of Atonement";

Birds of Heaven and Other Stories, translated by Clarence Augustus Manning (New York: Duffield, 1919)–

comprises "Birds of Heaven," "Isn't It Terrible?" "Necessity," "On the Volga," and "The Village of God";

In a Strange Land, translated by Gregory Zilboorg (New York: Richards, 1925);

"Makar's Dream," translated by Carl R. Proffer, in his *From Karamzin to Bunin,* edited by Proffer (Bloomington: Indiana University Press, 1969), pp. 300–327;

Selected Stories, with an introduction by R. Bobrova (Moscow: Progress, 1978)—comprises "In Bad Company," "The Blind Musician," "The Strange One," "Makar's Dream," "The Murmuring Forest," "The River at Dawn," and "Lights."

OTHER: "Reka igraet" and "Cherkes," in *Pomoshch' golodaiushchim: Nauchno-literaturnyi sbornik,* by Korolenko, Konstantin Dmitrievich Bal'mont, Anton Pavlovich Chekhov, and others (Moscow: Russkie vedomosti, 1892);

"Mgnoven'e," in *Na slavnom postu. (1860–1900). Literaturnyi sbornik,* by Korolenko, D. Mamin-Sibiriak, and others (St. Petersburg: N. N. Klobukov, 1900);

"Ogon'ki," in *Pomoshch' evreiam postradavshim ot neurozhaia. Literaturno-khudozhestvennyi sbornik* (St. Petersburg, 1901);

G. T. Khokhpov, *Puteshestvie uralskikh kazakov: V bielovodskoe tsarstvo,* with a preface by Korolenko (St. Petersburg: Gerol'd, 1903).

Vladimir Korolenko is remembered not only as a writer but also as a publicist and a humanitarian. He fought to defend the rights of the defenseless, and he came to be regarded as the conscience of the nation. During his lifetime he was highly respected as an original writer and characterized by his peers and the reading public as an unusual person of moral superiority who lived during a chaotic period in Russian history. In his writings he conveyed the struggles of ordinary people, who were distinguished by his portrayal of their convictions and steadfastness. Written between 1879 and 1919, Korolenko's fiction encompasses fifty-three short stories, the bulk of which date from the 1880s and 1890s. In the mid 1890s his focus shifted to editing a leading literary journal, *Russkoe bogatstvo* (Russian Wealth), and to writing his autobiography, begun in 1905, on which he worked until the end of his life.

Vladimir Galaktionovich Korolenko was born on 15 July 1853 in Zhitomir, in the province of Volyn', to Galaktion Afanas'evich Korolenko, a district judge who descended from Ukrainian gentry, and Evelina Iosifovna Skurevich, a cultured Polish woman. His father was an honest, straightforward man of astounding integrity. His mother was an affectionate and sensitive woman with a generous heart. Their son inherited Galaktion Afanas'evich's stubborn, decisive nature and Evelina Iosifovna's love for mankind, and this combination made him well suited to serve people in his later years. Until the insurrection of 1861, Polish was the primary language spoken in Korolenko's family. In 1866 the family moved to Rovno, where Galaktion Afanas'evich had just been appointed the district judge.

Korolenko had a stable family and a happy childhood. The children (five in all) knew no want until their father's death in 1868. Korolenko graduated from the gymnasium in 1871 and entered St. Petersburg Technological Institute, but instead of studying, as he had originally planned, he had to make a living. He tried to compensate by studying in the summers and working at various jobs—coloring atlases, proofreading, and translating—during the academic year. In 1874 he moved to Moscow to study at the Petrov Academy of Agriculture and Forestry. The new ideas of *narodnichestvo* (Populism), which hoped to transform social consciousness and spread democratic concepts in the countryside, captured the imagination of the intelligentsia in the 1870s. During the years 1874 to 1876 many young students, filled with populist fervor, gave up the Academy to go "to the people." Korolenko, wishing to follow the *narodniki* (Populists), prepared himself by attending student meetings in order to learn more about the movement. At one such meeting in 1875 he met Avdot'ia Semenovna Ivanovskaia, a female student who shared his views and whom he later married.

The *narodnichestvo* eventually collapsed under the pressures of mass arrests and persecution by the authorities in the late 1870s and early 1880s. Korolenko's first arrest came in 1876, when he and two others presented a collective declaration to the director of the Academy signed by more than ninety students. As a consequence, he was exiled to Ust-Sysol'sk in Vologda province. Before he reached his destination, however, he was freed and offered the chance to return to his native Volyn' province. Instead, he chose to go to Kronstadt, where his mother and sister lived. There, he tried to get reinstated at the Academy, but he was treated as if he had been expelled. In Kronstadt, Korolenko performed many odd jobs, one of which was proofreading for a small St. Petersburg newspaper, *Novosti* (News). During his time at the paper he wrote his first article on a brawl that he witnessed between two watchmen. The work of publishing attracted him, and he began to write fiction. His first attempt, "Epizody iz zhizni 'iskatelia'" (Episodes in the Life of a "Seeker"), was rejected by satirist Mikhail Evgrafovich Saltykov, editor of the journal *Otechestvennye zapiski* (Notes of the Fatherland), who said the story needed to be reworked. Korolenko eventually

Korolenko in 1879, the year in which he was exiled for suspected ties to the Populist movement in Russia

published "Epizody iz zhizni 'iskatelia'" in the journal *Slovo* (Word) in 1879 and included it in his 1914 *Polnoe sobranie sochinenii* (Complete Collected Works).

Russian society had begun to disintegrate in the wake of the emancipation of the serfs in 1861 by Tsar Alexander II. This extreme social change was reflected in the short fiction of the 1860s and 1870s. Fictive heroes broke away from their traditional roles: a peasant left his village and moved to another town to work in an industry, or a landed member of the gentry went to till his own land like a peasant. The presence of the author became more prominent in the person of the narrator as the narrator increasingly identified with the morals of this changing Russian society. Writers chose to depict minute and disparate scenes and portrayed characters who were moving, searching, and adapting to the new milieu in a collage of pictures and fragments, without any plotline but often with subtitles that referred to the state of the hero's physical or mental

condition. Character analysis, rather than plot development, inhabited the foreground, as writers searched for a new kind of hero and a new way to define that hero's responsibility to society. Often a protagonist was portrayed through a conflict between his or her personal desires and the hostile social forces of class prejudice, religious dogma, and ethical prohibitions. Such themes demanded authenticity and accuracy and resulted in a narrowing of differences between genres such as fiction, memoir, and publicism.

These trends are typical of Korolenko's writings as well, beginning with his earliest tales. The narrator and hero of "Epizody iz zhizni 'iskatelia'" is a young "seeker" who chooses to portray episodes from his own life. While visiting a friend's farm, he becomes acquainted with the servant, Iakub, who until now has been intractable because of his unwillingness to talk. The narrator's ability to spot spontaneous wisdom and moral strength in people such as Iakub becomes evident in the course of the story. The "seeker" is at a crossroads in his own life: he can either marry a young lady and settle down or undertake a journey to unknown places. He chooses the second path and thus becomes the prototype of Korolenko's narrator in later works—a traveler and a recorder of life who devotes himself to highlighting the significance of insignificant people.

Korolenko again was ordered into exile in 1879, as the *narodnichestvo* turned more militant. After activist Vera Ivanovna Zasulich, a militant revolutionary, shot the mayor of St. Petersburg, the administration decided to crack down on political suspects. The Korolenko household was searched, and although no incriminating documents were found, Korolenko and his elder brother were exiled to the town of Glazov in Viatka province, where they soon settled with the other political prisoners. Korolenko did not get along with the district police officer, who was quite suspicious of any correspondence that the exile received. Thus, he was transferred to Berezovye Pochinki, which was considered godforsaken by the Glazov residents. He did not stay there long. The authorities misconstrued a trip that he undertook to buy supplies, and Korolenko was moved to Vishnevolosk prison.

Korolenko wrote two of his most famous works in 1880—"Komandirovka" (The Trip, *Russkoe bogatstvo,* 1905), also called "Chudnaia" (The Strange One), and "Vremennye obitateli 'posledstvennogo otdaleniia'" (Temporary Residents of a "Trial Unit," *Slovo,* 1881), also known as "Iashka." Written during Korolenko's time at the Vishnevolosk prison, "Chudnaia" is narrated by a political prisoner who is headed for an exile camp because of his suspected involvement with *narodnik* circles. Accompanied by two gendarmes, he is on his way to an unknown destination when his journey is curtailed by a blizzard, and all three stop at an inn for the night. Trapped in this temporary shelter, the narrator and one of the policemen discover that they share similar thoughts of uncertainty and fear. These two "sworn enemies" strike up a conversation, and the policeman reminisces about a past situation that reminds him of the present incongruity. Previously, the policeman had accompanied a young female revolutionary whom he pitied as he now pities the narrator of the story. The revolutionary girl was not prepared to concede that the policeman could be genuinely concerned for her, however, and she stubbornly rejected his attention. Now, on the contrary, the narrator and he are "friendly" enough to chat and share thoughts. The policeman's ability to cross social boundaries and destroy circumstantial barriers reaffirms his real human emotions for the narrator.

In July 1880 Korolenko was to be sent into exile in east Siberia, but along the way he received permission to remain instead in Perm', where he lived until August 1881. During his time in Perm' he composed his story "Iashka." Sometimes Korolenko's narrator shows how his own life struggle parallels that of another human being in spirit and conviction, and this approach can be seen indeed in "Iashka." The eponymous hero of the story, Iashka, and the narrator occupy neighboring prison cells for nearly two weeks for violating a political code—the narrator for his alleged participation in the Populist movement and Iashka for being one of the stubborn "Old Believers" (called thus because of their rejection of the Moscovite Church during the Great Schism of the seventeenth century). Iashka is condemned as a madman and treated as such, but he shows his defiance by intermittently kicking the prison door. The narrator, being a rebel, understands Iashka's protest but is unable to help him in any way— even when Iashka is branded a madman and is carried away to a lunatic asylum. The narrator's encounter with Iashka shows him that Russia has men such as Iashka who will choose to die for their faith rather than bow down under pressure to the authorities.

The assassination of Tsar Alexander II in 1881 abruptly changed the atmosphere in Russia, ushering in a crackdown on radical activity and a general sense of despair. With the ascent of Alexander III to power, political prisoners were asked to sign an oath of allegiance to the new tsar. Korolenko's refusal to sign resulted in his exile to east Siberia. He spent the next three years (1882–1885) in the village of Amga in the Iakutsk region. His experiences there provided abundant material for his future writing. Subsequently, the tsarist administration boasted, "Had we not sent him to Siberia, he would not have written such a monumental story as 'Son Makara' [Makar's Dream] in 1885," as M.

Novorussky noted in his contribution to *V. G. Korolenko: Zhizn' i tvorchestvo* (1922).

"Son Makara," published in *Russkaia mysl'* (Russian Thought), concerns an insignificant hero, who—upon the narrator's persistent investigation—turns out to be noteworthy. The story became popular almost instantly, as it was written in the tradition of Nikolai Vasil'evich Gogol's "Shinel'" (The Overcoat, 1842) and Fyodor Mikhailovich Dostoevsky's "Bednye liudi" (Poor Folk, 1846). The hero's name, Makar (same as that of Dostoevsky's hapless hero, Makar Devushkin), and the quoted proverbs in the opening paragraph of the story bring Makar's helpless existence to the forefront. He is subjected to an extreme poverty and humiliation that force him to commit a few sins. His desire to escape from this drudgery is fulfilled in his dream, when he freezes and dies. While Makar is on his way to heaven, God confronts him and makes him answerable for the sins he committed in the world. He admits his sins but justifies himself, saying that he had no other recourse. Makar concludes his statement by stating that he is not guilty for his actions and asking, "Who then is guilty?" Makar's eloquent speech evokes pity in God, whose tears trickle down his cheeks. In this way Korolenko provides a hero who exhibits more latent strength than either of his predecessors, Gogol's Akakii Akakievich or Dostoevsky's Makar Devushkin. Korolenko's story touched the hearts of the reading public with its message that there is justice for everyone—if not in this world, then at least in the next.

Korolenko's period of exile ended in September 1884, and soon afterward he received permission from the authorities to leave Amga. He arrived as an unknown writer in Nizhnii Novgorod on 25 January 1885. In the years immediately following, he published some of his best works written during the previous five years of exile, including—apart from "Son Makara"— those that belong to his well-known Siberian cycle of stories: "Sokolinets" (The Man from Sakhalin), first published in 1885 in *Severnyi vestnik* (The Northern Messenger), and *Ubivets. Rasskaz sibirskogo iamshchika* (The Murderer. Story of a Siberian Coachman, 1887).

Korolenko's Siberian stories portray characters who live close to nature, in which they find the source and sustenance of life. The narrator's quest in these stories takes him to faraway places, where he looks among the simple people for protagonists who distinguish themselves by their humility, courage, or independent spirit. Once the narrator locates these heroes, in lyrical poetic prose he vividly portrays them in harmony with formidable, untamed nature and often draws a parallel between the lives of humans and the patterns of nature. Many of Korolenko's stories from 1881 through 1884 employ nature as a backdrop. "Sokolinets" opens with

Avdot'ia Semenovna Ivanovskaia in 1879, seven years before she married Korolenko

a description of restlessness, both in nature and in the characters' minds, that predicts a sudden change or a crisis. The narrator and the hero—an escaped convict—are trapped together in a temporary shelter, not knowing the outcome of the ominous snowstorm, as a similarity of hopes and fears emerges between them. They find themselves involuntarily reassessing their lives and remembering significant incidents from the past, when their courage and conviction were tested. Against the background of the storm, the tramp-convict recounts for the narrator his terrible escape from prison. Once the storm clears up and the sun emerges, the narrator discovers that he is alone.

The terrible story of Silin in *Ubivets. Rasskaz sibirskogo iamshchika* is similarly set against an appropriate natural backdrop. Silin drives the narrator through a pitch-dark forest at night. From a horse-driven coach they combat gangsters, robbers, and vagrants. This night with the narrator reminds Silin of the day when he killed bandits to save an innocent woman and her children. He tells the narrator his story and asks if he was justified in the killing. He finishes speaking just as the sun rises—as if nature has absolved him of his crime. The story ends with the narrator's journeying on the same route after an interval of time and discovering that Silin himself has been murdered. He becomes involved in the search for the right killers among the bandits and vagabonds who stand accused. The brutality of the murder—the body was butchered—uncovers the real killers, and the narrator now understands the different shades of right and wrong that "govern" the outlaws of society.

Also in 1885 Korolenko published "V durnom obshchestve" (In Bad Company), a timeless favorite of young readers. This story retells events of his own childhood through a fictitious narrator identified as "my friend from childhood." Growing up without a mother, the six-year-old narrator appears vulnerable and yearns for attention, especially since his father is stern and distant. The father is a well-respected judge but removed from the day-to-day life of his young son. The communication gap between the helpless boy and the strict father builds to a climax when the latter finds out that his son has befriended a family of social outcasts in the town. The narrator steals his sister's doll to give to the young daughter of this family in order to comfort her just before she dies. When the father questions the boy, he admits to the theft, which was done out of compassion for the poor girl. The father understands the sentiment behind his son's crime; yet, he condemns the theft and instills the correct values of right and wrong quite sternly in the mind of the impressionable young boy.

The following year Korolenko became more famous with the publication of "Slepoi muzykant (Etiud)" in *Russkie vedomosti* (Russian News). The hero of "Slepoi muzykant" is a child who is born blind. He begins to comprehend life and "see light and color" through sounds. His mother helps him to distinguish black and white by means of high and low tones played on the piano. The lower tones, heavy and dull, suggest dark colors, while the higher tones, light and flighty, impart a sense of brightness. The mother's instinctive ability to improve the quality of her son's life makes this tale a study of intuitive psychology, filled with Romantic and impressionistic imagery. This approach was later criticized by some for the lack of accurate, scientific description of a blind child's ordeal. Korolenko's story withstood such criticism, however, because it did not strive to depict a blind person's real struggle as much as it strove to show the natural attraction of a human to the mysterious and the unattainable. Korolenko's story admittedly lacks the psychological depth that some critics looked for, but it nonetheless boasts a fascinating plot, which is structured around the boy's reaction to light and darkness through his other senses. His keen sense of hearing compensates for his inability to see; music fills the void inside him as he grows up. Reading like a short story, the *povest'* does not describe the hero's development from childhood to adulthood, or his interaction with the world, in great depth. Instead, the narrator concentrates on certain aspects of his growing up and romanticizes the boy's struggle to overcome through music the darkness surrounding him. The touching, poetic narration helped the story to surpass its shortcomings and become one of Korolenko's most famous works.

In another remarkable story, "Les shumit. Polesskaia legenda" (The Forest Murmurs. A Woodlands Legend, *Russkaia mysl'*, 1886), there is complete fusion of sound and action. The short-story writer and dramatist Anton Pavlovich Chekhov admired "Les shumit" and made a careful study of its composition. It is a story of despotism, rape, and revenge told through an old man's nostalgic recollection of the events. The narrator meets the old man on a day when a storm hits the forest, and the storyteller recalls that on an identical windy night, the peasant Roman and the free-spirited Opanas killed their landowner for seducing Oksana, the woman they both loved. The characters give vent to their rage in the narration as the storm intensifies. The main story revives the legend of the past and brings it alive through the old man's narration. The ugliness of real-life tragedy is presented artistically through a description of nature, with expressive phrases repeated at frequent intervals as a musical refrain, by the narrator. The natural description, the old man's narration, and the story itself are woven together with sound, words, and phrases to re-create the tragedy of the past. The murderers stand vindicated as they defend themselves from their exploiter. According to Korolenko, force cannot be judged as good or bad without knowledge of the cause for which it was used. If force is intended to free the defenseless, then the story suggests that Korolenko advocates its use.

This same principle is at work in another story, "Skazanie o Flore, Agrippe, i Menakheme, syne Iegudy" (The Legend of Flohr, Agrippa, and Menakhem, the Son of Yehudah, first published in *Severnyi vestnik* as "Skazanie o Flore Rimlianine, ob Agrippe tsare i Menakheme, syne Iegudy," 1886), in which Korolenko argues against novelist Leo Tolstoy's advocacy of passive resistance to evil. This story is based on *The History of the Jewish Wars* (A.D. 75–79) by the ancient Jewish writer and statesman Flavius Josephus. Menakhem, a wise man and the son of the patriot Yehudah, who died fighting for the freedom of his people, argues that force can be used if justified by the cause. "Skazanie o Flore, Agrippe, i Menakheme, syne Iegudy" is made up of five parts: the Roman occupation of Judea; the

description of the Roman commanders; the battle between the Jews and the invading Roman army; the revelation of strife in the Jewish camps; and Menakhem's prayer for protection. Menakhem shares Korolenko's struggle to secure freedom for the people, while Agrippa's plea to acquiesce to the Romans represents Tolstoy's faith in peaceful surrender. Many minor details of the story—including the journalistic style of the introduction, the derogatory epithets for the evil leaders (for example, Flohr, who persecutes the Jews), a clear demarcation of good versus evil in the battle scenes, and the use of sermons and monologues—are reminiscent of military tales, such as the medieval Slavic epic *Slovo o polku Igoreve* (The Lay of Prince Igor's Campaign), composed circa 1187 and published in 1800 after its rediscovery in 1795. The final scene of the story describes the Jewish camps and details the arguments between the two Jewish factions. Menakhem pleads for the need to fight for a good cause and expose the futility of passive resistance to evil.

The year 1886 proved the happiest and most productive period in Korolenko's life. His family joined him in Nizhnii Novgorod; the first volume of his collection *Ocherki i rasskazy* (Sketches and Tales) was published; and he married Avdot'ia Semenovna, who fully shared his views and convictions. Korolenko and his wife had their first child, a daughter, this same year; they had three more daughters, the fourth born in 1895. He also began work as a newspaper correspondent for *Volzhskii vestnik* (The Volga Messenger) and *Russkie vedomosti* (Russian News) and exposed societal injustices and indiscretions. A small group of intellectuals in Nizhnii Novgorod, including Korolenko, frequently met and discussed the role and evolution of the *narodnichestvo*. In addition, in connection with his work on the Archives Committee of Nizhnii Novgorod, he published many historical essays. At the same time, he collected material for a novel about Emel'ian Ivanovich Pugachev, a Don Cossack who had led his people from the Urals to revolt against the authorities in 1773; Pugachev's character, mentality, and psychology fascinated the writer. In 1887 Korolenko was finally granted permission to visit Moscow and St. Petersburg. In Moscow he met Chekhov, and with his every visit to that city their friendship grew in warmth and closeness. (On Korolenko's advice, Chekhov undertook the writing of his first *povest'*, "Step'" [The Steppe, 1888].) In St. Petersburg later the same year, Korolenko met Gleb Ivanovich Uspensky, who turned out to be an important literary influence. Korolenko was also close to Nikolai Konstantinovich Mikhailovsky and was acquainted with Nikolai Fedorovich Annensky, Nikolai Gavrilovich Chernyshevsky, and Tolstoy. In 1889 Maksim Gor'ky, then a nascent writer, came to Korolenko's home to

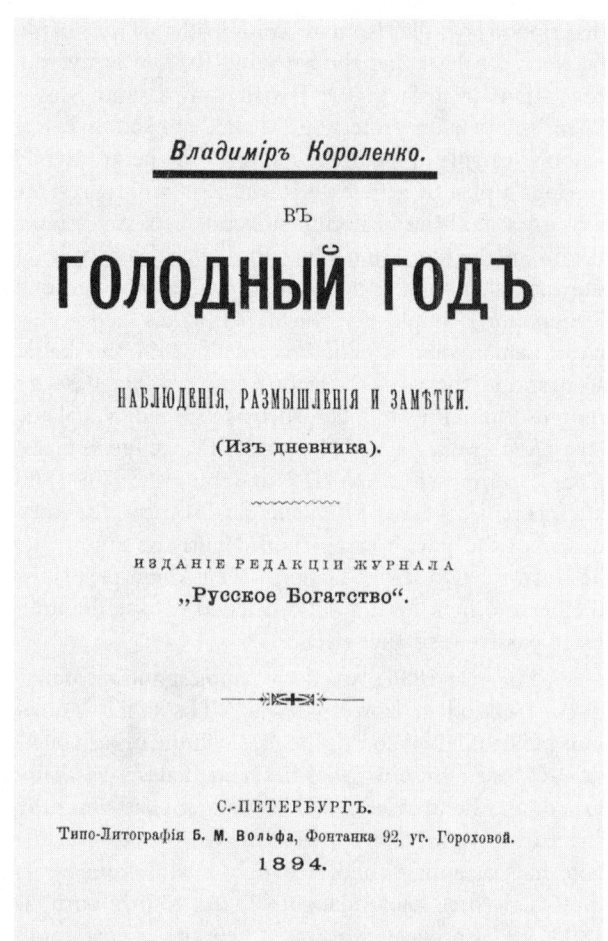

Title page for Korolenko's V golodnyi god *(In the Year of Famine), a collection of essays describing his participation in famine-relief efforts in Nizhnii Novgorod province (Kilgour Collection of Russian Literature, Harvard University Library)*

liar and his impressions of the woodlands, the blind, beggars, monks, and pilgrims are reflected in his sketches "Ptitsy nebesnye" (Birds of Heaven, 1889), "Ushel" (He Has Gone, written in 1902, published in *Polnoe sobranie sochinenii. Posmertnoe zidanie* [Complete Collected Works. Posthumous Edition], 1923), "Reka igraet" (The Playful River, 1893) and "V pustynnykh mestakh" (In Uninhabited Places, published in *Russkie vedomosti,* 1890). These sentimental works, written in the form of travelogues, recount the vivid perceptions of the narrator, who served as both a minor character and a witness.

The years 1888 through 1891 were comparatively quiet. In the fall of 1888, while sitting in a room beside his niece's corpse, Korolenko wrote "Noch'iu" (At Night, *Severnyi vestnik,* 1888), a story about the birth of a baby girl and the household activities surrounding that event as viewed by a young boy, Vasia. Vasia sits in a dimly lit room, listening to the nocturnal insects and the sound of raindrops on the roof and looking at the elongated shadows. The imaginative boy, who is nine or ten years old, wants to believe that girl babies are brought by the angels. The sound of carriages and the voices of visitors reassure him of his theory. In his naive understanding, girls have to be born, while boys have always existed. When he finds out that his mother has given birth to another girl, his faith that only girls are born is upheld. The story ends with a child's innocence preserved, which possibly was the reason for its great success.

Korolenko's several trips to the once prosperous village of Pavlovo gave rise to his "Pavlovskie ocherki" (Pavlovo Sketches, published in *Russkaia mysl',* 1890). With these essays taken directly from life and supported by case histories, he completely shattered the prevalent myth that the domestic industry sustaining the village was prosperous and independent. On the contrary, the craftsmen of Pavlovo lived in abject poverty, in constant fear of falling prices, and were entirely dependent on the selfish village buyers. Korolenko began to expose the activities of the local gentry in their manipulations of the town bank, court, and government. As a result of his articles in the newspapers, the functioning of the bank was straightened out. Millions of dollars were found to have been embezzled; several directors were indicted; the bank was taken into government receivership; and, thanks to Korolenko's vigilance, ordinary villagers were saved from losing their property.

Much like Socrates, Korolenko relied upon words and dialogue to elicit truth. In his story "Teni" (The Shadows, published in *Russkaia mysl',* 1891) both thinkers—Socrates and Korolenko—come together, as the latter reworks the dialogues of Socrates to discover a common search for Truth, symbolized here by light.

show him a poem he had written and seek an opinion on his writing. Gor'ky was grateful to Korolenko later for his sharp criticism and regarded him as his first teacher in the craft of writing.

Korolenko's stories, essays, and reports for newspapers were nurtured by his direct contact with the life of the people. Beginning in the summer of 1886, he took trips to outlying areas in the province of Nizhnii Novgorod. Traveling with a knapsack on his back and a notebook in his hand, he meticulously gathered materials for his works. One such visit, to the village Oranki, resulted in the composition of his story "Za ikonoi" (Before the Icon, published in *Severnyi vestnik,* 1887). Here he describes the mentality and psychology of peasants in the presence of an icon known for its miraculous power. Korolenko's visit to the city of Iurevits inspired his story "Na zatmenii" (During an Eclipse, *Russkie vedomosti,* 1887). His trip to Lake Sveto-

Ktezipp, the narrator of the story, recounts the trial and death of the philosopher in the first two chapters. As a former student of the philosopher, Ktezipp is able to relate Socrates' crimes authoritatively. These crimes amount to the renunciation of tradition, the denial of the existence of the Greek gods, and the corruption of youth with new ideas. They also include warning the public against harmful generals, philosophers, and "sophists" and preaching the search for truth. The figure of Socrates, who neither fears his accusers nor questions the law–for which he has the utmost respect–is reminiscent of Korolenko himself, who also faces arrests and imprisonment with total faith in the legal system.

Korolenko's story "Sudnyi den' (Iom-Kipur)" (The Day of Atonement [Yom Kippur], first published in *Russkie vedomosti*, 1891) presents a Ukrainian Jewish superstition that on Yom Kippur, the Day of Atonement, the devil comes to the earth and carries away a Jew with him. The story is filled with adventures, fantasies, and dreams that embellish its central romantic plot; its scenes move as if caused by an external force, which in the story is often attributed indirectly to the devil. The narrative action takes place on Yom Kippur in two consecutive years. In the first year the devil takes Iankel', a merciless moneylender and the owner of a pub, for his annual feast. Iankel' has few sympathizers, and since no one will ask for his release, he is bound to the devil, who carries him away for one whole year. A year later on the same day, the miller–who has taken over as owner of the pub–finds himself in an identical position. Yet, his unscrupulous acts over the past year far outweigh those of Iankel'. The devil brings Iankel' back and this time claims the miller for his feast. Realizing in a flash that there is no one in the village who will try to save him, the miller genuinely repents the hardships he has caused his young betrothed, Galia, and her mother and promises to mend his ways. When Galia hears the miller's faint plea, she takes pity on him and demands his release. Thus the miller, in a dazed state, finds himself back on Earth, a changed person.

In 1892 Korolenko was preoccupied with the famine in the Lukianov district of Nizhnii Novgorod province; during the previous summer, famine had become a frightening reality for the unfortunate peasants. He collected contributions of a thousand rubles and headed for the famine-stricken village, leaving his family to fend for themselves. At the village he set up dining halls and fed the hungry peasants and their families. With their pragmatic minds, they could not comprehend that Korolenko was helping them out of sheer altruism and his love and desire to help suffering humanity. His book that resulted from this experience, *V golodnyi god* (In the

Year of Famine, 1894), was published several times upon demand.

Also in 1892, with the publication of "At-Davan," Korolenko made his literary debut in the journal *Russkoe bogatstvo*. The story is a fictionalized retelling of an historical event: Alabin, a governor-general's aid, was sent to east Siberia with the news of the death of Tsar Alexander II. Unscrupulous and with scant regard for regulations, Alabin terrified the local people during his trip through small stations. One such station was At-Davan, where–according to legend–he coolly shot the postmaster. Korolenko became interested in this event when he happened to travel a route similar to the one that Alabin took; he first published articles about Alabin's ruthlessness in *Volzhskii vestnik*. Later, in Korolenko's fictionalized version of events, the little stationmaster stands up for his convictions and challenges the "god-like" Alabin.

In "At-Davan" the narrator is traveling along the frozen river Lena when he notices a small spot where the current boils so furiously that it resists the cold, even though there is thick ice all around it. Stranded, he decides to rest for the night at a stagecoach station located near the river. Here he meets the stationmaster, Kruglikov, who is small and insignificant in size but unrelenting and determined in combat against his "invincible" enemies. During the night the narrator learns that in his youth Kruglikov once confronted a general who stole his beloved. Now the narrator witnesses the stationmaster demanding money from Alabin, who habitually never pays for his horses at any of the other stations. The boiling, bubbling current in the river near this station becomes a metaphor for Kruglikov's righteous fury.

In 1893 Korolenko visited the World's Fair in Chicago as a correspondent for *Russkie vedomosti*. His itinerary included, among other places, Stockholm, Copenhagen, London, and Liverpool. Although he was initially excited about his visit to the Western nations, he was soon disillusioned when he observed how the rich and the poor lived side by side and how the poor in those nations were not that much different from the poor in Russia. Aside from his official duty as a correspondent, he wanted to meet and to converse "heart-to-heart" with the Russian émigrés in Europe and the United States. Korolenko describes his trip to Chicago via Niagara Falls in his story "Bez iazyka. Rasskaz iz zagranichnykh ocherkov" (Speechless. A Tale from Foreign Sketches, published in *Russkoe bogatstvo*, 1895; translated as *In a Strange Land*, 1925), in which he explores the issues of culture shock and miscommunication between peoples of the East and the West. He writes in the third person about a fictitious hero, Matvei Dyshlo, who travels to the United States ("Amerika" in

Korolenko's mother, Evelina Iosifovna, in the 1890s
(photograph by Korolenko)

incessant striving for happiness. He embodied this philosophy in his tiny sketch "Ogon'ki" (Flickers, 1901) and his brilliant story "Paradoks" (The Paradox, 1894).

In "Ogon'ki" the narrator and the oarsman, while sailing on the river, suddenly catch sight of lights and argue about the distance to shore. There is a strong contrast in the way the narrator, an inexperienced traveler, perceives the flickering light as they move forward, and how the more experienced oarsman knows that they are in reality still quite far away. Once the narrator is convinced that the oarsman is right, he realizes that one has to keep on plying the oars to reach the lights—or, metaphorically, to achieve one's happiness and life goal. In "Paradoks," Korolenko uncovers the illusory dreamworld of a child-narrator. The hero, a young boy, is distracted from playing with his brother by the appearance of the paraplegic Fenomen (Phenomenon), who is performing tricks for the people gathered around him. Fenomen writes the aphorism "Man is created for happiness, as a bird is for flight"; the paradoxical nature of his situation emerges in the realization that, though crippled and neither happy nor able to fly, the paraplegic arrives at this truth. The young hero comes to understand, however, that happiness always exists—despite occasions when we grow incapable of experiencing it.

From 1895 onward Korolenko became increasingly involved with *Russkoe bogatstvo*. In 1895 and 1896 he took up the defense of ten Udmurts (members of an indigenous Siberian tribe) of the Russian Orthodox faith, who were accused of a ritualistic murder. Seven of the Udmurts were pronounced guilty in two separate trials, but Korolenko, who witnessed the second trial and took meticulous notes, was convinced of their innocence. He vowed to save them. He personally visited the village of Old Multan, where the Udmurts lived, and after a painstaking investigation found out that the allegation of human sacrifice had been a setup, and the torture and killings had been fabricated. His article "Multanskoe zhertvoprinoshenie" (The Human Sacrifice of Old Multan, published in *Russkoe bogatstvo*, 1895) became the talk of the provincial towns and the capital. A third trial was held; Korolenko himself gave tireless speeches against a biased jury and was overcome by emotion during his final closing speech. At the same time, he received news of the death of his youngest daughter. He had to cope with a grave personal tragedy even as he achieved a moral victory: the Udmurts finally were found not guilty. These events took their toll, however, and he began to suffer from insomnia.

Korolenko's editorship of *Russkoe bogatstvo* took him to St. Petersburg in 1896, and he remained there until 1900. The city that had inspired Gogol and Dostoevsky to write masterpieces had the opposite influence

the story) in search of his sister's husband. Since the focus is on the hero's experiences and exploits in the huge city of New York, the conflict between natural man and the civilized world becomes an important theme. The narrator, through the hero's adventures, paints an unflattering picture of political, industrial, and labor institutions in the United States, which Korolenko saw as a land of contradictions. The emphasis on material benefits in the Western world did not impress him.

During this year of extensive travel, on his way to Paris, Korolenko learned of his daughter Elena's death; his third child, she was not yet a year old. He left for Romania, where the family grieved together for their loss. The year 1893 was not yet over when misfortune struck again: a bout of grippe left Korolenko with severely impaired hearing. He never became accustomed to his handicap, for the sounds of wind, snow, rain, and trees were an integral part of his descriptions of nature. Yet, despite his disillusionment and despair, he still held the view that life was a manifestation of a higher law, whose driving principles were happiness and goodness. For Korolenko, the goal of life lay in the on Korolenko. He wrote little during his St. Petersburg years, with the exception of a few stories, most of which were based on his diary entries of life in Amga. He was occupied primarily with editorial tasks, and this stressful work was worsened by his insomnia. Publication of *Russkoe bogatstvo* was suspended for three months when Korolenko refused to retract his article on Finland, written jointly with Annensky in 1898 ("Finlandskie dela," [Finnish Matters, 1899]). The suspension of the journal caused a loss of income for Korolenko, and consequently his family lost almost all of their possessions.

One story written in St. Petersburg that differed from the rest was "Neobkhodimost'" (Necessity, published in *Russkoe bogatstvo*, 1898). For this tale, in a continued search for truth and in answer to the question about responsibility for one's actions, Korolenko turns to Indian philosophy. A story within a story, "Neobkhodimost'" is about two Indian sages, Darnu and Purana, who go in search of ultimate truth. Darnu is stubborn and believes in finding the truth by himself, while Purana is lazy, satisfied just to witness the existence of truth. When the two go to the top of a mountain and fall into a state of deep meditation, they are confronted by the goddess Neobkhodimost' (Necessity); Darnu defies her, whereas Purana sits back and observes her. Neither of their attitudes helps them attain truth, however, and the wise men walk farther away and freeze in meditation. A young shepherdess, who decides that they are new statues for her to play with, washes and decorates them. An innocent kiss on Darnu's lips wakens him—a kiss that brings about the understanding that everything that has happened to him, including his meditation, was preordained by a power greater than himself. He finally learns to humble himself. He wakes Purana, and both of them realize that, although their actions are predestined, they cannot be complacent. They have to make a conscious choice at every crossroads and actively participate in life. Through this parable Korolenko provides an indirect answer to the irksome question, "Who is responsible for what happens?" He shows that although a person is not totally responsible for his fate, he can make a difference in the path his life takes by exercising proper judgment.

In 1899 Korolenko published his essay "Smirennye" (The Humble Ones, *Russkoe bogatstvo*) and wrote the fairytale "Stoi, solntse: ne dvizhis', luna" (Sun, Stop: Do Not Move, Moon), a satire on autocratic order in Russia, in the vein of Saltykov. In this allegorical tale the villain advises the king to reverse the natural flow of time in order to avoid the predicted downfall of the kingdom. Consequently, the public is confused by fictitious months and dates on newspapers that are printed dating backward. The fairy tale was not allowed to be published at the time; thus, it did not appear in print until collected into Korolenko's 1927 *Polnoe sobranie sochinenii*.

In honor of the one hundredth anniversary of poet Aleksandr Sergeevich Pushkin's birth, members were elected to the newly formed Academy of Sciences. Along with Tolstoy and Chekhov, Korolenko was elected in the first round. Korolenko proposed Gor'ky's election in 1902. The proposal was rejected by the tsar, however, and this circumstance brought about both Korolenko's and Chekhov's renunciation of their titles.

In 1900 Korolenko moved to Poltava, where he found relief after years of insomnia. As a result he plunged anew into the writing of fiction. He wrote a series of stories that are grouped together in his second Siberian cycle, published in *Russkoe bogatstvo* in 1901: "Gosudarevy iamshchiki" (His Majesty's Coachmen), "Moroz" (The Frost), and "Poslednii luch" (The Last Ray). "Gosudarevy iamshchiki" exposes the bureaucratic corruption existing in Siberian towns, while "Moroz" and "Poslednii luch" examine the influence of climatic changes on people's moods, thoughts, and actions. In "Moroz" two goats, stranded on a thick block of ice in biting, subzero cold, carefully orchestrate their jumps and escape the attack of a big shaggy dog; during the whole ordeal, the older goat protects the younger one. Sokolsky, who witnesses this event, recollects a similar situation, in which his friend Ignatovich could have accompanied another helpless human to safety—as the older goat did in the allegorical narrative—but ignored a plea for help. According to Sokolsky, however, Ignatovich could not have acted otherwise, because his conscience froze along with the atmosphere. This theory is substantiated by Ignatovich's realization of his failure to help another human being once he went inside a shelter and was warm—a realization that led him to plunge back into the cold in despair, never to return. Similarly, in the story "Poslednii luch" a grandfather and grandson bid farewell to the rays of the sun, which appear fleetingly on the mountaintops in extreme northern Siberia. According to the old man, the rays disappear in autumn as the axis of the earth shifts, and they reappear only in late spring or early summer. The fading of the sun symbolizes the grandfather's anticipation of the departure of his family from the face of the earth, as first he and then his grandson will pass away.

The cultural life in Poltava was rich. At the age of fifty, Korolenko was at the center of lively, stimulating conversations. He was now an author of considerable renown, a social activist, and a great humanitarian—and a man in midlife who had long since forgotten the days of his youth. Because the government, however, never forgot that he had once been a revolutionary, he was constantly watched by the secret police. Yet, this surveillance did not deter him from his good works. Once,

Corrected proof for the 1902 edition of Korolenko's story "Bez iazyka" (Speechless), originally published in 1895, about his travels in the United States in 1893 (from Georgii Mikhailovich Mironov, Korolenko, *1962)* when the peasants revolted and were faced with likely starvation, Korolenko–driven by his need to serve humanity–went to defend them.

Meanwhile, a scapegoat for all the existing evils in Russia had to be found, and the authorities embarked upon a policy of exploiting national prejudices and racial hatreds. On Easter Sunday in 1903 a pogrom, which was supposed to last two days, erupted in Kishinev. Approximately twenty-five to fifty Jews were killed, three hundred wounded, and thousands left destitute. Korolenko described the persecution of the Jews in his works *Dom No. 13–yi* (House #13, 1903–1904), "Pavlovskie ocherki," "Sudnyi den'," and "Bez iazyka."

The people of Polatava were preparing to celebrate Korolenko's fiftieth birthday on 15 July 1903, and to escape the festivities, he decided to go away on a trip. Upon his return he was pleasantly surprised to find about six hundred telegrams and two hundred letters. In the next two years Korolenko wrote no artistic works. Newspapers and periodicals defined his major sphere of activity, where he dominated the writing on social and political issues of the day–in particular the Russo-Japanese War, which he viewed as a grave misfortune. He became the sole editor of *Russkoe bogatstvo* in 1905, the same year that he began a work titled *Istoriia moego sovremennika* (A History of My Contemporary, initially published in *Sovremennye zapiski,* 1906), which he continued to write until his death. This fictionalized autobiography told the experiences of a person similar to himself who had spent his childhood in the 1850s. Korolenko did not strive to give a cohesive narrative of his hero's life but, rather, stressed the significance of his life against a broader historical background. During this period he also wrote several important essays, among them "Bytovoe iavlenie. (Zametki publitsista o smertnoi kazni" (An Everyday Occurrence. [A Publicist's Notes on the Death Penalty]), in which he bitterly describes the ineffectiveness of the government in defending the rights of individuals. This article became a favorite of Tolstoy's when it appeared in *Russkoe bogatstvo* in 1910.

At this time, in order to divert the attention of the masses from unrest and rebellion, the panic-stricken autocracy campaigned with ferocious intensity against the national minorities. The Jewish minority, a popular and easily accessible target, suffered savage assaults as the campaign of anti-Semitism reached its climax. Beginning in Kishinev, a tide of pogroms swept the country; the most notorious assaults occurred in Odessa, Belostok, Nikolaev, and Kiev. Korolenko worked relentlessly to protect the Jews of Poltava and avoid a pogrom there. Anti-Semitic feelings continued, and Mendel Beilis (a Jewish salesman in a brick manufacturing company) was accused of killing a Russian boy, Andrei Iushchinsky, in 1911. Discovering that Beilis had been framed, Korolenko published in the periodical *Rech'* (Speech) on 30 November 1911 an address, signed by well-known scholars and civil servants and titled "K russkomu obshchestvu (po povodu krovavogo naveta na evreev)" (To Russian Society [About the Bloody Calumny against the Jews]). Korolenko's health was deteriorating, and his doctor advised him against taking an active role in Beilis's defense. Nevertheless, he went to Kiev and observed the courtroom proceedings, in which it had been determined in advance that Beilis was guilty. Unable to watch silently this travesty of justice, Korolenko wrote fifteen articles under the title "Delo Beilisa" (The Beilis Case) in October 1913, becoming the most prominent of the journalists who reported on the trial. These articles, appearing in *Rech', Russkie vedomosti, Russkoe bogatstvo,* and *Kievskaia mysl'* (Kievan Thought), saved Beilis's life. When Korolenko appeared on the street after this outcome, his public appearance created a riot, and traffic came to a halt so that people could give him an ovation.

Korolenko's health improved somewhat, and he took a vacation with his family. They spent more than a year in France, returning in May 1915 in time to witness the collapse of the tsarist regime. Korolenko saw no new forces that could replace the autocracy. He could not support the Marxists; he feared that they were ignoring the peasants just as the *narodniki* had ignored the proletariat. Morever, as a liberal democrat, Korolenko felt that political changes should be brought about gradually and always within the framework of the law, rather than through revolutionary upheaval. Feeling the need to explain to the people the historical implications of current events in the political arena, Korolenko gave many speeches and wrote about fifty articles. The most important article at this time was "Padenie tsarskoi vlasti. (Rech' k prostym liudiam o sobytiiakh v Rossii)" (The Fall of Tsardom. [A Speech to the Common People about Events in Russia]), published in the May 1917 issue of *Russkie vedomosti.* In Poltava, during the years 1917 to 1919, when General Anton Denikin's White Volunteer Army and the Bolsheviks were struggling for power, Korolenko took upon himself the care of the most helpless victims, the children. In 1920 he wrote "Pis'ma k Lunacharskomu" (Letters to Lunacharsky), six open missives to Anatolii Vasil'evich Lunacharsky, the Minister of Education, in which Korolenko touches upon the pressing social, economic, and political problems of the day.

Privately owned newspapers and journals were closed in the wake of the Bolshevik Revolution. *Russkoe bogatstvo* ceased to exist, and Korolenko struggled to support himself and his family. The new government discovered his difficulties, however, and tried to ensure his well-being. Korolenko's birthdays in 1920 and 1921

*Korolenko in 1913, at the trial of Mendel Beilis, a Jew
who had been falsely accused of killing a Russian boy
(drawing by V. Koldun; from Petr Alekseevich
Nikolaev,* Russkie pisateli, 1800–1917:
Biograficheski slovar', *1989)*

were celebrated with gifts of flour, sugar, soap, grain, lard, meat, and firewood. His health declined drastically toward the end of 1920, when Konstantin Ivanovich Liakhovich–Korolenko's secretary and right-hand man–was imprisoned by the Bolsheviks for his Menshevik leanings. Liakhovich's death in prison was a terrible blow to Korolenko. His strength gave out, and he lost his voice and the ability to speak. He died on 25 December 1921 and was given a civil burial.

Vladimir Galaktionovich Korolenko's optimistic view of life, his search for moral strength in people, his nonjudgmental attitude, and his innate kindness made his stories extremely popular during his lifetime. He did not follow any school of writing, nor did he fashion his writing after the style of any of his predecessors. His aim was to portray a variety of people who live in the remote parts of Russia. The intricate process of coming to know and understand human character was the pervading theme of his stories. Critical opinion on Korolenko's talents has varied vastly. Some think that he is not a preeminent writer, because he does not explore deep, mystical, psychological issues, while others believe that Korolenko is a fine artist, whose masterpieces will always be read and discussed for their portrayal of spontaneous beauty and their lyrical descriptions of nature. Korolenko is often rightly char-

acterized as a "major minor writer," some of whose stories are published in anthologies and read widely even today. He occupies an important place in Russian literature as an author who both continued the classical traditions of the nineteenth century established by Tolstoy and Ivan Sergeevich Turgenev and foreshadowed the sensibilities of Gor'ky, Ivan Alekseevich Bunin, and socialist realist writers of the twentieth century.

Letters:

Pis'ma 1888–1921, edited by Boris L'vovich Modzalevskago (St. Petersburg: Vremia, 1922);

Pis'ma, in *Polnoe sobranie sochinenii. Posmertnoe izdanie* (Khar'kov & Poltava, 1922–1929)–includes volume 50, *1879–1887* (1923); and volume 51, *1888–1889* (1923);

Pis'ma k P. S. Ivanovskoi, edited by A. B. Derman, with a preface by Praskovia Semenova Ivanovskaia (Moscow: Politkatorzhan, 1930);

Izbrannye pis'ma, 3 volumes (Moscow: Kooperativnoe izdatel'stvo, 1932–1936);

"Pis'ma Korolenko raznym litsam," edited by I. A. Zhelvakova, in *Novoe i zabytoe,* edited by Nikolai Fedorovich Piiashev, volume 1 (Moscow: Nauka, 1966);

"Avtobiograficheskie pis'ma Korolenko," edited by A. V. Khrabrovitsky, *Literaturnoe nasledstvo,* 87 (1977);

"V. G. Korolenko i N. K. Mikhailovsky v ikh perepiske," edited by Grigorii Abramovich Bialyi, in *Ot Griboedova do Gor'kogo,* edited by Nikolai Ivanovich Sokolov (Leningrad: Izdatel'stvo Leningradskogo universiteta, 1979);

"4 pis'ma Gor'komu, 1921," *Rodina,* 3 (1989);

"Pis'ma k Kh. G. Rakovskomu," *Voprosy istorii,* 10 (1990);

"Pis'ma k A. G. Gornfel'du. 1918–1921," *Strannik,* 2 (1991);

"Skol'ko takikh tragicheskikh pisem chitaiu ia . . . ," edited by O. V. Shugan [Perepiska M. Gor'kogo s V. G. Korolenko 1920–1921 godov], in *Neizdannaia perepiska s Bogdanovym, Leninym, Stalinym, Zinov'evym, Kamenevym, Korolenko,* by Maksim Gor'ky, edited by Stanislav Vasil'evich Zaika, Gor'ky: Materialy i issledovaniia, issue 5 (Moscow: Nasledie, 1998), pp. 149–192.

Bibliographies:

E. V. Mokrshanskaia, *V. G. Korolenko. Bibliograficheskii ukazatel' sochinenii* (Moscow, 1953);

T. G. Morozova, *Literatura o Korolenko* (Moscow, 1953);

A. V. Khrabrovitsky, *Materialy k bibliografii proizvedenii Korolenko* (Moscow, 1975);

Khrabrovitsky, *Perepiska Korolenko. Bibliograficheskii ukazatel'* (Moscow, 1975).

Biographies:

Nataliia Dmitrievna Shakhovskaia, *V. G. Korolenko: Opyt biograficheskoi kharakteristiki* (Moscow: K. F. Nekrasov, 1912);

A. B. Derman, "V. G. Korolenko," *Ruskaia mysl',* 12 (1915): 1–24;

Fedor Dmitrievich Batiushkov, *V. G. Korolenko kak chelovek i pisatel'* (Moscow: Zadruga, 1922);

M. Tsetlin, "Korolenko: Chelovek i pisatel' (k semidesiatiletiiu so dnia rozhdeniia)," *Sovremennye zapiski,* 37 (1928): 472–481;

Georgii Mikhailovich Mironov, *Korolenko* (Moscow: Molodaia gvardiia, 1962);

Grigorii Abramovich Bialyi, *V. G. Korolenko* (Moscow: Gosudarstvennoe izdatel'stvo khudozhestvennoi literatury, 1949; Leningrad: Khudozhestvennaia literatura, 1983);

Nina Davydovna Petropavlovskaia, *Kak ia liubliu ee: iz zhizni V. G. Korolenko* (Moscow: Flinta, Nauka, 2000).

References:

Victoria Babenko, "Nature Descriptions and Their Function in Korolenko's Stories," *Canadian Slavonic Papers,* 16 (1974): 424–435;

Radha Balasubramanian, *The Poetics of Korolenko's Fiction* (New York: Peter Lang, 1997);

Grigorii Abramovich Bialyi, *Chekhov i russkii realizm: ocherki* (Leningrad: Sovetskii pisatel', 1981);

R. F. Christian, "V. G. Korolenko (1853–1921): A Centennial Appreciation," *Slavonic and East European Review,* 32 (1954): 449–463;

S. M. Gorodesky, "V. G. Korolenko i ego khudozhestvennyi metod," *Nashi Dni,* 2 (1922): 335–349;

Oskar Osipovich Gruzenberg, "V. G. Korolenko," in his *Yesterday: Memoirs of a Russian-Jewish Lawyer* (Berkeley & London: University of California Press, 1981), pp. 169–188;

Ruth Gordon Hastie, "Vladimir Galaktionovich Korolenko: The Writer and the Liberation Movement 1853–1907," dissertation, Washington University (St. Louis), 1979;

Vladimir Ivanovich Kaminsky, *Puti razvitiia realizma v russkoi literature kontsa XIX v.* (Leningrad: Nauka, 1979);

Nataliya M. Kolb-Seletsky, "Elements of Light in the Fiction of Korolenko," *Slavic and East European Journal,* 16 (1972): 173–183;

Larisa Semenovna Kulik, *Sibirskie rasskazy V. G. Korolenko* (Kiev: Akademii nauk Ukrainy SSR, 1961);

Lauren G. Leighton, "Korolenko's Stories of Siberia," *Slavonic and East European Review,* 49 (1971): 200–213;

Charles A. Moser, "Korolenko and America," *Russian Review,* 28 (1969): 303–314;

M. Novorussky, "Korolenko v Slissel'burge," in *V. G. Korolenko: Zhizn' i tvorchestvo,* edited by A. B. Petrishchev (St. Petersburg: Mysl', 1922), p. 138;

Lawrence Michael O'Toole, "Korolenko: 'Makar's Dream,'" in his *Structure, Style and Interpretation in the Russian Short Story* (New Haven & London: Yale University Press, 1982), pp. 84–98;

N. Piksanov, "Lirizm Korolenko," *Zhizn',* 2 (1922): 5–15;

Carl R. Proffer, "Makar's Dream," in his *From Karamzin to Bunin: An Anthology of Russian Short Stories* (Bloomington: Indiana University Press, 1969), pp. 32–34;

Vladimir Shub, "Lenin and Vladimir Korolenko," *Russian Review,* 25 (1966): 46–53.

Papers:

Vladimir Galaktionovich Korolenko's papers are held in Moscow at the Russian State Library (RGB, formerly the Lenin Library), fond 135; the State Literary Museum (GLM), fond 13; and the Central State Archive of Literature and Art (RGALI), fond 234. Additional materials can be found in St. Petersburg at the Institute of Russian Literature (IRLI, Pushkin House), and in Poltava at the Literary-Memorial Korolenko Museum. For descriptions of Korolenko's manuscripts and correspondence held at the RGB, see R. P. Matorina, *Opisanie rukopisei Korolenko* (Moscow, 1950) and V. M. Fedorova, *Opisanie pisem Korolenko* (Moscow: Gosudarstvennaia biblioteka SSSR imeni V. I. Lenina, 1961). For descriptions of holdings at RGALI, see *V. G. Korolenko. Opis' dokumental'nykh materialov lichnogo fonda* (Moscow, 1949). Descriptions of materials related to Korolenko in various archives at IRLI can be found in *Ezhegodnik Rukopisnogo otdela Pushkinskogo doma* (Leningrad: Nauka, 1970).

Sof'ia Vasil'evna Kovalevskaia

(3 January 1850 – 29 January 1891)

Ann Hibner Koblitz
Arizona State University

BOOKS: *Zur Theorie der partiellen Differential-gleichungen* (Berlin: G. Reimer, 1874);

Kampen för Lyckan. Två paralleldramer, by Kovalevskaia and Anne-Charlotte Leffler (Stockholm, 1887); Russian version by M. Luchitskaia published as *Bor'ba za schast'e. Dve parallel'nye dramy* (Kiev: F. A. Poganson, 1892)–comprises *Kak eto bylo* and *Kak ono moglo byt';*

Ur ryska lifvet. Systrarna Rajevski (Stockholm: Heggström, 1889); Russian version published as *Vospominaniia detstva, Vestnik Evropy,* 7 (1890): 55–98; 8 (1890): 584–640; translated by Isabel F. Hapgood and A. M. Clive Bayley as *Sonya Kovalevsky. Her Recollections of Childhood with a Biography by Anna Carlotta Leffler, Duchess of Cajanello* (New York: Century, 1895);

Vera Vorontzoff (Stockholm: Bonnier, 1892); Russian version published as *Nigilistka* (Geneva: Volnaia russkaia tipografiia, 1892); translated by Sergius Stepniak and William Westall as *Vera Barantzova* (London: Ward & Downey, 1895);

Literaturnye sochineniia, edited by Maksim Maksimovich Kovalevsky (St. Petersburg: M. Stasiulevich, 1893)–includes "Vae victus" and "Otryvok iz romana, proiskhodiashchego na Riv'ere";

Vospominaniia detstva i biograficheskie ocherki, edited by Solomon Iakovlevich Shtraikh (Moscow: AN SSSR, 1945); revised and enlarged as *Vospominaniia i pis'ma,* edited by Shtraikh (Moscow: AN SSSR, 1951; revised, 1961);

Nauchnye raboty, edited by Pelageia Iakovlevna Polubarinova-Kochina (Moscow: AN SSSR, 1948);

Vospominaniia. Povesti, edited by Polubarinova-Kochina (Moscow: Nauka, 1974)–includes "Nigilist" and *Na vystavke.*

Editions and Collections: *Nigilistka* (Moscow: Izdatel'stvo Kokhmanskogo, 1906);

Vospominaniia detstva. Nigilistka, edited, with an introduction, by V. A. Putintsev (Moscow: Khudozhestvennaia literatura, 1960);

Sof'ia Vasil'evna Kovalevskaia

Izbrannye proizvedeniia (Moscow: Sovetskaia Rossiia, 1982);

Vospominaniia. Povesti (Moscow, 1986).

Editions in English: *A Russian Childhood,* translated by Beatrice Stillman (New York: Springer, 1978);

Nihilist Girl, translated by Natasha Kolchevska and Mary Zirin (New York: Modern Language Association of America, 2001).

SELECTED PERIODICAL PUBLICATIONS: "Zur Theorie der partiellen Differentialgleichungen," *Crelle's Journal*, 80 (1875): 1–32;

"Uber die Reduction einer bestimmten Klasse von Abel'scher Integrale 3-en Ranges auf elliptische Integrale," *Acta Mathematica*, 4 (1884): 393–414;

"Sur la propagation de la lumière dans un milieu cristallisé," *Comptes rendus de l'Académie des Sciences*, 98 (1884): 356–357;

"Vospominaniia o Dzhorzhe Elliote," *Stockholms Dagblad*, 1885; *Russkaia mysl'*, 6 (1886);

"V bol'nitse La Charité. Gipnoticheskii seans u doktora Liuisa'," *Russkie vedomosti*, 28 October 1888;

"V bol'nitse La Salpêtrière. Klinicheskaia lektsiia doktora Sharko'," *Russkie vedomosti*, 1 November 1888;

"Sur le problème de la rotation d'un corps solide autour d'un point fixe," *Acta Mathematica*, 12 (1888–1889): 177–232;

[Eulogy to M. E. Saltykov], *Stockholms Dagblad*, June 1889; *Literaturnoe nasledie*, 13–14 (1934): 543–554;

"Tri dnia v krest'ianskom universitete v Shvetsii," *Severnyi vestnik*, 11 (1890);

"Avtobiograficheskii rasskaz," *Russkaia starina*, 72, no. 11 (1891): 449–463;

"Vae victis. Predislovie k neokonchennomu romanu," *Severnyi vestnik*, 4 (1892).

The mathematician, writer, and women's rights activist Sof'ia Kovalevskaia was the first woman in the world to receive a doctorate in mathematics and the first woman in nineteenth-century Europe to teach mathematics (or, indeed, any subject) at the university level. Kovalevskaia's work on the rotation of a solid body about a fixed point won a prize from the French Academy of Sciences; she was the first woman to serve on the editorial board of a major scientific journal and the first woman elected as a Corresponding Member of the Russian Imperial Academy of Sciences. Indeed, she was arguably the greatest woman scientist before Maria Sklodowska Curie. During the same time that Kovalevskaia achieved international fame because of her scientific accomplishments, she also attained recognition as a writer. She wrote a number of plays, novellas, poems, essays, and sketches, many of which were unfinished at the time of her death. Yet, enough of Kovalevskaia's work appeared during her lifetime to merit her significant literary reputation. Her much-acclaimed autobiographical work *Vospominaniia detstva*, first published in Swedish as *Ur ryska lifvet. Systrarna Rajevski* (From Russian Life: The Sisters Rajevski, 1889) and then in Russian (its original language) in *Vestnik Evropy* (The European Messenger) in 1890, was translated into many European languages. Several of her essays also garnered

popularity among Russians and western Europeans alike.

Kovalevskaia was born Sof'ia Vasil'evna Korvin-Krukovskaia in Moscow on 3 January 1850. Her father, Vasilii Vasil'evich Korvin-Krukovsky, was a landowner and military man; her mother, Elizaveta Fedorovna (Shubert) Korvin-Krukovskaia, was from a family of German scholars who had settled in Russia during the time of Catherine the Great. After the Crimean War and the accession to power of Tsar Alexander II, Vasilii Vasil'evich retired from the military with the rank of general and brought his family home to his estate at Palibino (now near the border between Russia, Lithuania, and Belarus).

In most respects Kovalevskaia enjoyed the usual upbringing for a girl of her class and time. Following the retirement of her Russian serf nanny, she had a succession of French, Swiss, and English governesses; she read voraciously in English and French as well as in Russian; and she took part in amateur theatricals and other amusements of the rural gentry. She was better educated than many of her gently bred peers, however, in part because her father allowed her to study advanced mathematics with a series of tutors. Moreover, Kovalevskaia grew to adulthood in the tumultuous intellectual atmosphere of the 1860s and was influenced in her educational development by the movements of the time. Many Russian radicals called themselves "nihilists" in half-mocking acknowledgment of the philosophy of the hero in Ivan Sergeevich Turgenev's novel *Ottsy i deti* (Fathers and Children, 1862). The nihilists believed in the power of education to improve the lot of humanity and felt that the most useful branches of knowledge were the natural sciences. For them, to become a scientist was to ally oneself with the forces of progress in the battle against superstition, backwardness, and autocracy. Moreover, the nihilists joined their faith in science and social revolution to a firm conviction about the equality of women. They taught that women of the privileged classes had a duty to educate themselves so that they could help the masses in Russia.

Kovalevskaia encountered nihilist ideas at a young age—ideas that proved crucial for her scientific and literary development. She found the philosophy congenial, with its emphasis on the natural sciences, revolutionary social change, and women's equality. Nihilism provided her with a framework in which her interests in mathematics, politics, women's rights, and literature were seen as harmonious with one another. She remained true to nihilist precepts throughout her life, and all of her nonmathematical writings are imbued with the spirit of the "new ideas" of the 1860s.

52   FÉVRIER   315
21. JEUDI. Saint Félix.

Page from Kovalevskaia's diary, dated 21 February 1884 (from Kovalevskaia, Vospominaniia i pis'ma, 1961)

An understanding of Kovalevskaia's work is impossible to attain without situating her in the nihilist context.

At the age of eighteen she married fellow nihilist, scientific translator, and book publisher Vladimir Onufrievich Kovalevsky, who later distinguished himself as a paleontologist. Their marriage was at first *fiktivnyi* (fictitious). That is, it was contracted to allow Kovalevskaia the possibility of studying in a university abroad and was not intended as a real union. With time, however, the couple grew close, and their marriage resulted in a daughter, Sof'ia Vladimirovna Kovalevskaia, born 17 October 1878. The story of the marriage between Kovalevskaia and Vladimir is long and complicated. The pair had different views on a range of subjects, including his get-rich-quick schemes and her research ambitions. More important, Vladimir experienced increasing mental problems as he grew older; he turned more and more capricious, moody, and paranoid. Life with her husband became steadily more difficult for Kovalevskaia, and in the three years before his death in 1883 the couple led largely separate lives.

From 1868 to 1874 Kovalevskaia devoted herself almost entirely to her university studies. In 1869 she persuaded the authorities at Heidelberg University to allow her to audit courses there. She worked with the famous researchers Paul DuBois-Reymond, Hermann Helmholtz, Gustav Kirchhoff, and Leo Königsberger, all of whom were impressed by her seriousness and preparation. In time, Königsberger persuaded her to move to Berlin to work with the great mathematical analyst Karl Weierstrass, and in 1871 she became the latter's pupil. After an unsuccessful attempt to convince the academic senate of Berlin University to open its doors to women, Weierstrass agreed to tutor Kovalevskaia privately. Under his direction she produced three dissertations, any one of which, in Weierstrass's opinion, merited the doctoral degree. Because Kovalevskaia was the first woman ever to apply for her degree in mathematics, however, Weierstrass wanted her case to be particularly strong.

Since the universities in both Heidelberg and Berlin proved reluctant to grant degrees to women, Weierstrass, DuBois-Reymond, and other mathematicians turned to Göttingen University, which had a long tradition of granting doctorates to foreigners in absentia. In August 1874 Kovalevskaia received her doctorate, summa cum laude, from Göttingen University, which did not require her to take oral examinations or meet the residency criterion. She was the first woman in the world to obtain a doctoral degree in mathematics in the modern sense of the term "degree"; before the late eighteenth to early nineteenth century doctorates were Latin philosophical disputations. Kovalevskaia was one of the first women to obtain a doctorate in any field.

Yet, her status as the first woman mathematician with a university degree did not result in job offers commensurate with her education. When she returned to St. Petersburg, she discovered that—despite the petitions of her mathematical colleagues—the tsarist government would not permit her to take the licensing examination necessary to obtain employment at the postsecondary level. She became somewhat discouraged and turned her attention to nonscientific pursuits.

From her return to Russia in the autumn of 1874 until she was pregnant with her daughter in 1878, Kovalevskaia immersed herself in the social whirl of St. Petersburg. She at first encouraged, and then merely tolerated, her husband's various plans to make them rich. She entertained Vladimir's business colleagues in a lavish manner and established a salon in which she mingled with luminaries of the Russian literary scene such as Fyodor Dostoevsky, Ivan Sergeevich Turgenev, Mikhail Evgrafovich Saltykov, and others.

Although Kovalevskaia had been writing poetry occasionally since the age of twelve, her first serious attempts at nonmathematical compositions appeared during this period. Through an old law-institute schoolmate, the jurist and financial speculator Vladimir Ivanovich Likhachev, Kovalevskaia's husband became acquainted with the journalist Aleksei Sergeevich Suvorin. In 1876 Likhachev and Suvorin proposed a joint newspaper venture to Vladimir. *Novoe vremia* (New Times) was intended to provide a progressive alternative to the progovernment paper *Golos* (Voice), which the liberal and radical intelligentsia viewed as sycophantic and unprincipled. Vladimir loved the idea. He invested heavily in the project (largely with Kovalevskaia's money), persuaded liberal literary figures to contribute, acted as night editor, and wrote unsigned articles as well as popular-science pieces under his own name. Kovalevskaia contributed at least four short items on scientific topics to *Novoe vremia* and probably several unsigned theater reviews as well. Her authorship of these reviews is not clearly established, although her Russian biographer Pelageia Iakovlevna Polubarinova-Kochina gives a list of articles probably written by Kovalevskaia in *Sof'ia Vasil'evna Kovalevskaia, 1850–1891* (1981). After fewer than two years, however, Kovalevskaia's and Vladimir's connections with *Novoe vremia* ended rather abruptly. Suvorin changed the political direction of the newspaper to such an extent that it ceased to have credibility with the radical intelligentsia. The Kovalevskys left the project, and their loan to Suvorin was never repaid.

During her pregnancy in 1878 Kovalevskaia had the leisure to contemplate her life since her return to St. Petersburg and came to the conclusion that she mostly had been wasting her time. According to Liubov Andreevna Vorontsova's biography *Sof'ia Kovalevskaia* (1959), she began to refer to her literary salon and her support of her husband's entrepreneurial endeavors as part of "the soft slime of bourgeois existence." As her friend and biographer, the mathematical pedagogue Elizaveta Fedorovna Litvinova, recalled in *S. V. Kovalevskaia: Ee zhizn' i nauchnaia deiatel'nost'* (S. V. Kovalevskaia: Her Life and Scientific Work, 1893), Kovalevskaia later said that the only good thing to come out of those years in St. Petersburg was her daughter (nicknamed "Fufa" to distinguish her from her mother).

Soon after Fufa's birth, the Kovalevskys' finances collapsed. Creditors began to demand repayment from Vladimir, who had spent not only all of his own money but also all of Kovalevskaia's inheritance from her father, as well as investment money entrusted to him by his brother Aleksandr and by several of the couple's friends. The situation had become so dire by the end of 1879 that the pair was forced to declare bankruptcy, and many of their possessions ended up being sold at public auction. Kovalevskaia and Vladimir each reacted quite differently to this financial catastrophe. He was unhinged by the disaster, became even more unstable than earlier, and committed suicide four years later in 1883. Kovalevskaia, on the other hand, was apparently relieved and interpreted their new lack of means as a sign that she needed to reestablish herself in the mathematical world. She renewed her contacts with Weierstrass and other mathematicians, revised her two unpublished doctoral dissertations, and was elected to membership in the Paris Mathematical Society.

Kovalevskaia let her mathematical colleagues know that she desired a professional position and was ready to travel to any country in Europe to teach at an institution willing to hire her. The Swedish mathematician Gösta Mittag-Leffler, also a former student of Weierstrass, tried to get her a post at Helsinki University, but her fame as a nihilist was too frightening for the Finnish university authorities. Finland was under the tsar's control, and administrators were afraid that Kovalevskaia's presence on the faculty might become a pretext for repression by the tsarist Ministry of Education. Mittag-Leffler abandoned his attempt in Helsinki, but when he moved to the newly created Stockholm University in 1882, he renewed his efforts on Kovalevskaia's behalf. In 1884 Kovalevskaia secured a position at Stockholm University and became the first woman in Europe at that time to teach university-level courses. The European and American presses heralded her for this achievement, and she became something of a celebrity. Driven by the urging of journal and newspaper editors, inspired by her nihilist zeal for popular enlightenment, and motivated by financial necessity (the university

Kovalevskaia in 1885 with her close friend Anne-Charlotte Leffler, sister of her Stockholm University colleague Gösta Mittag-Leffler

did not pay well), she began to write a series of essays in 1885.

In "Vospominaniia o Dzhorzhe Elliote" [sic] (Memories of George Eliot), which first appeared in 1885 in *Stockholms Dagblad* (Stockholm Daily News) and in 1886 in *Russkaia mysl'* (Russian Thought), Kovalevskaia describes her visits to George Eliot's salon in London in October 1869. The highlight of these visits was her encounter with the philosopher and social-Darwinist theorist Herbert Spencer, with whom Kovalevskaia debated women's capacity for scientific work for three hours, much to Eliot's amusement. This episode was perhaps not so firmly fixed in Eliot's mind as it was in Kovalevskaia's, although the former did note in a journal entry on 5 October 1869, which was later published in her *George Eliot's Life as Related in her Letters and Journals* (1895), that Kovalevskaia was "a pretty creature, with charming modest voice and speech, who is studying mathematics . . . at Heidelberg."

Kovalevskaia's second published piece was a collaborative effort. *Kampen för Lyckan. Två paralleldramer* (The Struggle for Happiness. Two Parallel Dramas,

1887) was written in Swedish in conjunction with Anne Charlotte Leffler, the sister of her Stockholm University colleague Mittag-Leffler. The Russian version was published as *Bor'ba za schast'e. Dve parallel'nye dramy* (The Struggle for Happiness. Two Parallel Dramas, 1892). The play is really two companion pieces with the same characters and prologue, but the action takes divergent paths. In the portion of *Bor'ba za schast'e* known as *Kak eto bylo* (How It Was), the characters lack the resolution and political commitment to go against convention and find happiness. In the second part, *Kak ono moglo byt'* (How It Might Have Been), on the other hand, the protagonists find the fortitude to break with tradition and achieve personal contentment for themselves as well as justice for their employees, with whom they establish a workers' cooperative. *Kampen för Lyckan* was Kovalevskaia's only attempt at a play and her only collaborative project. The characters lack depth, the speeches are stilted, and inconsistencies arise because the play was conceived by Kovalevskaia as a purely Russian story and then transferred by Leffler (herself a well-known author of novels, novellas, and later a biography of Kovalevskaia) to a Swedish locale.

Neither variant of *Kampen för Lyckan* was popular in Sweden. Each was too alien in both form and content for acceptance by the Swedes, and Scandinavian audiences were uninterested, for the most part, in the utopian socialism of the play. Moreover, the psychological theme of rebellion against convention had been treated more capably by Henrik Ibsen and even by Leffler, when she was not working in conjunction with Kovalevskaia. By contrast, in Russia the play enjoyed some success—though more for its progressive politics than for its artistry. In 1895 the actress Lidiia Borisovna Iavorskaia (Princess Bariatinskaia) chose *Kak ono moglo byt'* for her benefit performance at the Korsh Theater in Moscow. Reviewers noted that whenever key words such as "workers," "union," and "happiness for the majority" were uttered, the audience—composed mostly of students and young workers—burst into thunderous applause. Iavorskaia and the other actors sometimes had to wait several minutes for the noise to stop after the heroine's stirring declarations of solidarity with the workers.

The late 1880s were a time of unprecedented professional activity for Kovalevskaia. She was a respected member of the European mathematical community and was routinely ranked by her peers as one of the greatest mathematicians of her generation. She made significant progress on what is now regarded as one of her two most important mathematical works, the rotation of a solid body about a fixed point (the well-known "Kovalevskaia top"). In 1888 she won the Prix Bordin of the French Academy of Sciences, and in 1889 she was appointed for life to the Chair of Analysis at Stockholm University (in contemporary North American terms, she became a tenured full professor). That same year the Russian Imperial Academy of Sciences in St. Petersburg changed its rules so that Kovalevskaia could become the first female Corresponding Member.

In the late 1880s Kovalevskaia's personal life changed also. In 1887 the sociologist and jurist Maksim Maksimovich Kovalevsky (a distant relation of Kovalevskaia's late husband) gave a course of lectures in Stockholm. Kovalevskaia and Maksim Kovalevsky were drawn to one another. They began to live together whenever their respective schedules allowed, and there is some evidence that they were planning to marry in St. Petersburg in the spring of 1891.

These years of increasing fame as a mathematician were productive for Kovalevskaia from a literary standpoint as well. She wrote essays, novellas, memoirs, and poetry, most of which remained unfinished at the time of her death; the collected fragments appear in their fullest form in *Vospominaniia. Povesti* (Memoirs. Stories, 1974). Perhaps the most notable of Kovalevskaia's essays were "V bol'nitse 'La Charité'" (In La Charité Hospital) and "V bol'nitse 'La Salpêtrière'" (In La Salpêtrière Hospital), both published in *Russkie vedomosti* (Russian News) in 1888, in which she describes her visits to the hospital clinics of two of the most famous French alienists (psychiatrists) of the period. Jules-Bernard Luys and Jean Charcot were both avid proponents of hypnotism as a cure-all for disorders of the nervous system. They experimented with, and demonstrated their techniques primarily on, "subjects" (Kovalevskaia always puts the word in quotation marks, apparently to emphasize the callousness of the doctors) who submitted to the indignities visited upon them because they were destitute, homeless, and unfit for work.

The essays show throughout that Kovalevskaia was contemptuous of the doctors' methods, suspicious of their supposed results, and incensed by the pair's treatment of their mostly female "subjects." Luys addressed his patients as if they were simpleminded children, while Charcot acted as if they could not hear the hurtful remarks that he delivered to his interns in the women's presence. Both saw nothing unusual in ordering the women to disrobe, bark like dogs, or act the part of drunkards in order to "prove" that they were truly hypnotized. Kovalevskaia manages to convey her indignation with some subtlety. She does not claim that all doctor-hypnotists are frauds, nor does she accuse Luys and Charcot themselves of outright charlatanism. Rather, she calmly recounts her observations, carefully noting the elitism and sexism of the physicians and the economic and social powerlessness of their patients. In concluding the essays she leaves her reader with a feeling of pity and perhaps admiration for the "subjects," coupled with a firm dislike of Luys and Charcot.

Kovalevskaia also wrote a tribute to the eminent Russian satirist Saltykov on the occasion of his death on 28 April 1889. In this work she tried to explain to European readers Saltykov's great importance for Russians. Drama was the same everywhere, she reasoned, but satire was different for each country and each period. What made Saltykov so popular was his ability to satirize what most needed correction in the Russia of his day. The article was translated into Swedish and French and made its way into several European newspapers, including *Stockholms Dagblad,* in June of 1889.

Kovalevskaia also took the opportunity of a visit to a peasant school in rural Sweden to write an essay deploring the state of education in rural Russia. "Tri dnia v krest'ianskom universitete v Shvetsii" (Three Days in a Peasant University in Sweden), which first appeared in *Severnyi vestnik* (The Northern Messenger) in 1890, was ostensibly about the diligence and intelligence of the students in an adult-education program in the Swedish countryside. Kovalevskaia's Russian contemporaries, however, correctly read the piece as a criticism of the lack of similar educational opportunities for the Russian peasantry.

In a sense, the most popular and enduring of Kovalevskaia's literary works was her *Vospominaniia detstva,* the first translation of which (into Swedish) was a group effort. Kovalevskaia read the chapters aloud in her fractured Swedish, and her circle of Swedish friends—which included Leffler, the feminist writer Ellen Key, and the translator and writer Walborg Hedberg—as well as Kovalevskaia's daughter Fufa (who was now effectively bilingual) and others transformed the broken phrases into polished prose. After it appeared in English and French translations, the book met with universal praise, not only in Sweden but also all over Europe and North America. One London journalist, "T. P." of *The Weekly Sun,* even went so far as to compare Kovalevskaia's memoirs to Turgenev's great novel *Ottsy i deti* in his review of an English translation in 1894. *Vospominaniia detstva* stands out from Kovalevskaia's other works not only because of its beautiful lyricism but also because of the ways in which the account was fictionalized. Virtually all of her writings, including her poetry and political essays, incorporate autobiographical elements. In those pieces, however, she describes incidents in her life in a manner consonant with the information one can glean from other sources. *Vospominaniia detstva,* by contrast, seems to explore a sort of alternate self; it sketches a persona for the youthful Sof'ia, the heroine of the memoirs, that is internally consistent but not accurate in any historical sense of the word.

Kovalevskaia's fiancé, Maksim Maksimovich Kovalevsky, during the 1880s

In fact, the real heroine of *Vospominaniia detstva* is not the young Sof'ia at all but, rather, Kovalevskaia's actual older sister Aniuta (Anna Korvin-Krukovskaia Jaclard). Aniuta died a painful and lingering death from cancer just as Kovalevskaia was embarking on her memoirs, and Sof'ia seems to have intended *Vospominaniia detstva* as a sort of memorial to her sister's tragically brief life. For most of the book Aniuta takes center stage, and Sof'ia relegates herself to the role of worshipful acolyte and admirer. Absent from the narrative are oft-told family anecdotes illustrating Sof'ia's independence and initiative; gone also is any intimation of the fact that by all accounts (except this one) Sof'ia was her father's favorite child. What remains is a lovely tale of two gently bred Russian girls growing up on a country estate around the time of the emancipation of the serfs in 1861. Their experiences of name-day theatricals, mushroom-gathering expeditions, and the petty gossip and affairs of a large gentry and peasant household are carefully drawn, as is Aniuta's first exposure and eventual conversion to nihilist ideas. Kovalevskaia's *Vospominaniia detstva* has proved to be enduringly popular, and new translations and editions continue to appear to this day.

The last of Kovalevskaia's works to be completed was "Avtobiograficheskii rasskaz" (Autobiographical Sketch, 1891), which appeared in the journal *Russkaia starina* (The Russian Past) several months after her death. The essay is abrupt and matter-of-fact in tone and completely different from *Vospominaniia detstva*. Most notable are the pride with which Kovalevskaia recounts her mathematical achievements and discoveries and her genuine attempt to interest the reader in the joys of mathematics.

In late January 1891 Kovalevskaia contracted a bad cold while returning to Sweden from visiting Maksim Kovalevsky in the south of France. Despite her ill health and the awful weather, she stopped off in Paris and Berlin to see her mathematical colleagues. By the time she arrived in Stockholm she was seriously ill with pneumonia. She taught her first classes of the spring term and even went to a fund-raising party, but she took to her bed soon after, and five days later she was dead.

Upon Kovalevskaia's death, her friends discovered many literary projects in various stages of completion. The closest to being ready was a work originally titled *Nigilistka* (A Nihilist Woman, 1892), which was first published as *Vera Vorontzoff* (1892) in a futile attempt to deceive the censors about the nature of the novel; it was initially written in 1884 in Russian, French, and Swedish segments. Maksim Kovalevsky prepared the text for publication, but *Nigilistka* was repeatedly banned in Russia. It first appeared in 1892 in a Swedish translation and then in a Russian edition printed by Maksim Kovalevsky in Geneva in the same year. Yet, the novel was omitted from the first Russian edition of Kovalevskaia's collected (literary) works, *Literaturnye sochineniia* (Literary Works, 1893); reportedly, a line from Maksim Kovalevsky's introduction to this volume even had to be removed because it mentioned *Nigilistka*. Despite the attempts of the government to ban *Nigilistka,* however, the Russian intelligentsia was familiar with the book from its first appearance in 1892. German, French, Polish, and English translations were smuggled into St. Petersburg from abroad, as was Maksim Kovalevsky's Geneva edition. The plot and politics of the novel were open secrets. As a result, Kovalevskaia's reputation among the radical and liberal intelligentsia of the Russian Empire was enhanced even further.

Nigilistka is the story of a young woman, Vera Vorontsova, who sacrifices her own personal happiness to marry a condemned revolutionary, for—in accordance with tsarist practice—the marriage could cause his sentence to be reduced. The novel gives a sympathetic portrayal of the young people of the *V narod!* (Go to the People!) movement who were arrested in 1874. It also encompasses autobiographical material concerning Kovalevskaia's own return to St. Petersburg in 1874

after she had finished her doctoral studies in Germany. The last scene shows Kovalevskaia crying as she sees Vera off to Siberia to be with her exiled husband.

With the exception of *Vospominaniia detstva, Nigilistka* is the most beautifully crafted of Kovalevskaia's semifictionalized works. Kovalevskaia was at her best when writing fictionalized accounts of events through which she had lived. For this reason, both *Vospominaniia detstva* and *Nigilistka* are better written and more believable than *Bor'ba za schast'e*. Like *Vospominaniia detstva, Nigilistka* is of considerable historical interest. Besides the sympathetic portrayal of the radical movement of the 1870s, the novel gives a skillful depiction of a girl's childhood and adolescence in a noble household in mid-nineteenth-century Russia. Although ostensibly the girl is Vera, much of the picture fits the young Kovalevskaia equally well. Through *Nigilistka,* Kovalevskaia tells more of her own early childhood and further explains the development of her political ideas.

Unfinished at the time of her death, "Nigilist" (A Nihilist Man, written circa 1890), which was first published in book form in 1974, also marks a political statement. The novel was intended as a fictionalized biography of the radical publicist Nikolai Gavrilovich Chernyshevsky and his wife Ol'ga. The portion that Kovalevskaia finished before she died features fascinating descriptions of the political and intellectual circles of the 1860s. There are brief sketches of the leading literary figures of the early 1860s and portraits of the first women students—Nadezhda Prokof'evna Suslova, Natal'ia and Mariia Ieronimovna Korsini, and others. The manuscript breaks off in mid sentence. According to the Swedish writer Key, who was with Kovalevskaia during her last illness, Kovalevskaia had meant to end the novel with a midnight knock on Chernyshevsky's door signifying his arrest.

The main body of "Vae victis" (Woe to the Vanquished, 1892); a projected novel set on the Riviera, published as a fragment in *Literaturnye sochineniia* (Literary Works, 1893); a novella titled *Na vystavke* (At the Exhibition, published in 1974); and another novel to be called "Muzhi i zheny" (Husbands and Wives) are only some of the literary projects Kovalevskaia left unfinished. These works can be found in *Vospominaniia. Povesti;* the manuscript for the never published "Muzhi i zheny" is located in Sweden in the Institut Mittag-Leffler archives. All of Kovalevskaia's unfinished works are competently written and bear some historical interest because of their autobiographical elements. For example, the heroine of "Vae Victis" is a teacher of mathematics; the hero of the Riviera novel is a thinly disguised Maksim Kovalevsky; and Kovalevskaia's cousin Mikhail was to figure in *Na vystavke*. These and Kovalevskaia's other novels were broken off at an early

49 / 20

[illegible] 11/6 1891

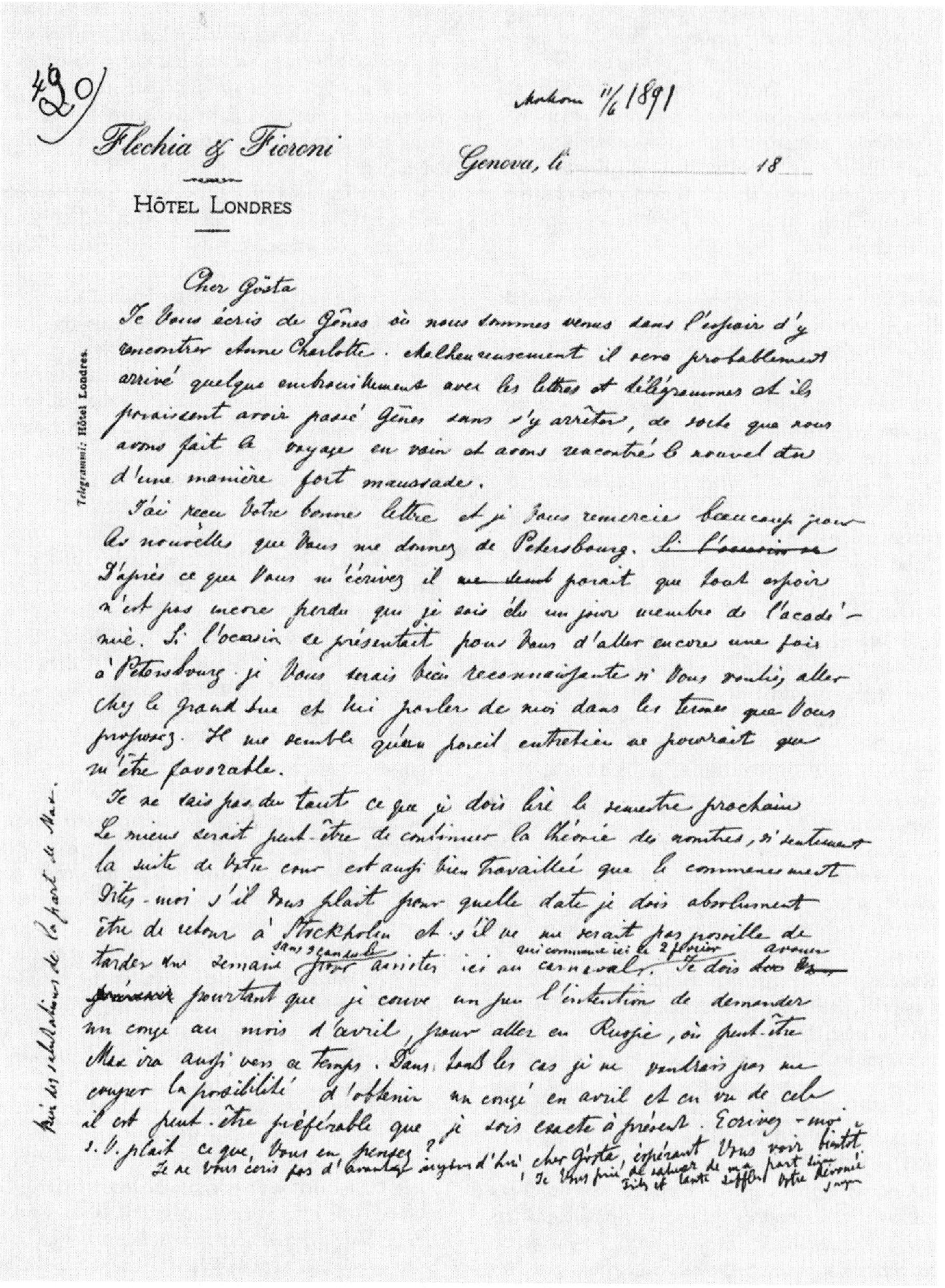

Flechia & Fioroni

HÔTEL LONDRES

Genova, li ______ 18__

Telegrammi: Hôtel Londres.

Cher Gösta

Je Vous écris de Gênes où nous sommes venus dans l'espoir d'y rencontrer Anne Charlotte. Malheureusement il sera probablement arrivé quelque embrouillement avec les lettres et télégrammes et ils paraissent avoir passé Gênes sans s'y arrêter, de sorte que nous avons fait le voyage en vain et avons rencontré le nouvel an d'une manière fort maussade.

J'ai reçu Votre bonne lettre et je Vous remercie beaucoup pour les nouvelles que Vous me donnez de Petersbourg. ~~Si l'occasion se~~ D'après ce que Vous m'écrivez il ~~me semble~~ paraît que tout espoir n'est pas encore perdu que je sois élu un jour membre de l'académie. Si l'occasion se présentait pour Vous d'aller encore une fois à Petersbourg je Vous serais bien reconnaissante si Vous vouliez aller chez le grand duc et lui parler de moi dans les termes que Vous proposez. Il me semble qu'un pareil entretien ne pourrait que m'être favorable.

Je ne sais pas du tout ce que je dois lire le semestre prochain. Le mieux serait peut-être de continuer la théorie des nombres, si seulement la suite de Votre cours est aussi bien travaillée que le commencement. Dites-moi s'il Vous plaît pour quelle date je dois absolument être de retour à Stockholm et s'il ne me serait pas possible de tarder une semaine sans scandale ~~pour~~ arriver ici au carnaval qui commence ici le 2 février avant. Je dois ~~[illegible]~~ pourtant que je couve un peu l'intention de demander un congé au mois d'avril, pour aller en Russie, où peut-être Max ira aussi vers ce temps. Dans tous les cas je ne voudrais pas me couper la possibilité d'obtenir un congé en avril et en vue de cela il est peut-être préférable que je sois exacte à présent. Écrivez-moi s.v. plaît ce que Vous en pensez?

Je ne Vous écris pas d'avantage aujourd'hui, cher Gösta, espérant Vous voir bientôt. Je Vous prie de saluer de ma part [illegible] et toute [illegible]. Votre dévouée [illegible]

Avec les salutations de la part de Max.

An 1891 letter from Kovalevskaia to Swedish mathematician Mittag-Leffler, one of her earliest supporters (from Kovalevskaia, Vospominaniia i pisma, *1961)* stage, however, so that in most of them even the main outline of the plot remains unclear.

Kovalevskaia's poetry has survived in a more complete form. One poem in particular, "Zhaloba muzha" (A Husband's Lament), probably written around 1870, is notable for its half-joking diatribe against educated wives. It is written from the point of view of the man, who complains that women's notions of equality have hurt men more than they have helped women. The narrator warns that men who try to flirt with women by humoring their ideas of equality risk being taken more seriously than they intend. The poem combines humor with irony and was probably written to amuse or goad Kovalevskaia's husband, Vladimir. It, like much of Kovalevskaia's poetry, was first published in *Vospominaniia i pis'ma* (Memoirs and Letters) in 1951.

At the time of their first appearance in Russia in the late 1880s and early 1890s, Kovalevskaia's writings were read with eagerness. Some reviewers liked her style, but for the most part they concentrated their attention on the political content of her works. Aleksandr Nikolaevich Pypin of *Vestnik Evropy*, for example, commented in a review of *Literaturnye sochineniia* that "however few her works, they constantly reflect the grand themes of social life." By this he meant to say that Kovalevskaia had progressive beliefs and that, compared to what he considered the frothy, trivial productions of many other belle-lettrists, her writings were worth reading. Kovalevskaia's works appealed to the liberal and radical intelligentsia and to those segments of the reading public who cherished hopes for reform of the tsarist government. Her readers ranged politically from the famous communist-feminist Aleksandra Mikhailovna Kollontai to at least one member of Tsar Nicholas II's own family. The wide acceptance of Kovalevskaia's writings partly resulted from the ambiguous way in which their messages were phrased. Her vague language often satisfied the tsarist censors and more than satisfied the public. People on the moderate-to-liberal side of the debate who read Kovalevskaia's writings could declare that she had meant nothing more than precisely what she had written: a mildly expressed hope for nonviolent change in the distant future. People of radical-to-revolutionary leanings could read between the lines of her works and assert that secretly Kovalevskaia was one of them.

Kovalevskaia herself appears to have seen her writings as part of her nihilism. Virtually everything she produced in her six-year career as an author—essays and reminiscences included—touched upon at least one of the following contemporary topics: rebellion against tradition, the deceptions of pseudoscience, public education, feminism, socialism, and communism. While her views were sometimes romantic and idealistic,

Kovalevskaia clearly intended that her work be taken as a political statement.

The early death of Sof'ia Vasil'evna Kovalevskaia shocked her contemporaries. Since she died just as her first full-length literary works were appearing, reviewers possibly assigned more importance to her talents as a writer than they would otherwise have done. One must remember that Kovalevskaia was already a celebrity in the entirely different field of mathematics. Thus, there was a curiosity value attached to all of her literary productions, regardless of their artistic merit. Yet, several of Kovalevskaia's literary publications, including *Vospominaniia detstva, Nigilistka,* and perhaps the two hospital essays, continue to attract interest to this day. Her work is among the best by the Russian nihilist women of her generation, and she has made a lasting contribution to Russian literary culture.

Letters:
Sophie Adelung, "Jugenderinnerungen an Sophie Kovalewsky," *Deutsche Rundschau,* 89 (1896): 394–425;

"Briefe von Sophie Kowalewska," edited by Marie Mendelson, *Neue Deutsche Rundschau,* 6 (1897): 589–614;

"Pis'ma S. V. Kovalevskoi 1868 g.," *Golos minuvshego,* 2 (1916): 226–240; 3 (1916): 213–231; 4 (1916): 77–94;

"Iz perepiski S. V. Kovalevskoi," edited by Pelageia Iakovlevna Polubarinova-Kochina, *Uspekhi matematicheskikh nauk,* 7, no. 4 (1952): 103–125;

Pis'ma Karla Veierstrassa k Sof'e Kovalevskoi. 1871–1891, edited by Polubarinova-Kochina (Moscow: Nauka, 1973);

Pis'ma S. V. Kovalevskoi ot inostrannykh korrespondentov, edited by Polubarinova-Kochina (Moscow: Institut problem mekhaniki AN SSSR, 1979);

Perepiska S. V. Kovalevskoi i G. Mittag-Lefflera, edited by Adol'f Pavlovich Iushkevich (Moscow: Nauka, 1984).

Biographies:
Elizaveta Fedorovna Litvinova, *S. V. Kovalevskaia: Ee zhizn' i nauchnaia deiatel'nost'* (St. Petersburg: Obshchestvennaia Pol'za, 1893);

Jella von Zednik, *Sophie Kowalewsky, ein weiblicher Professor* (Prague: Sammlung Gemeinnutziger Vorträge, 1898);

Solomon Iakovlevich Shtraikh, *S. Kovalevskaia* (Moscow: Zhurnal'no-gazetnoe Ob"edinenie, 1935);

Pelageia Iakovlevna Polubarinova-Kochina, *Zhizn' i deiatel'nost' S. V. Kovalevskoi: k 100-letiiu so dnia rozhdeniia* (Moscow: Izdatel'stvo Akademii nauk SSSR, 1950);

Ia. L. Geronimus, *Sofja Wassiljewna Kowalewskaja, 1850 bis 1891: Mathematische Berechnung der Kreiselbewegung* (Berlin: Verlag Technik, 1954);

Polubarinova-Kochina, *Sof'ia Vasil'evna Kovalevskaia: E zhizn' i deiatel'nost'* (Moscow: Gosudarstvennoe Izdatel'stvo Tekhnicheski-Teoreticheskoi Literatury, 1955);

Liubov Andreevna Vorontsova, *Sof'ia Kovalevskaia* (Moscow: Molodaia gvardiia, 1959);

Polubarinova-Kochina, *Sof'ia Vasil'evna Kovalevskaia, 1850–1891* (Moscow: Nauka, 1981);

Don H. Kennedy, *Little Sparrow: A Portrait of Sophia Kovalevsky* (Athens: Ohio University Press, 1983);

Ann Hibner Koblitz, *A Convergence of Lives: Sofia Kovalevskaia: Scientist, Writer, Revolutionary* (Boston: Birkhäuser, 1983; revised and enlarged edition, New Brunswick, N.J.: Rutgers University Press, 1993).

References:

Roger Cooke, *The Mathematics of Sonya Kovalevskaya* (New York: Springer-Verlag, 1984);

George Eliot, *George Eliot's Life as Related in her Letters and Journals,* edited by John Walter Cross, volume 3 (Boston: Estes & Lauriat, 1895), p. 78;

Laura Marholm Hansson, *Six Modern Women: Psychological Sketches,* translated by Hermione Ramsden (Boston: Roberts, 1896);

Isabel F. Hapgood, "Notable Women: Sonya Kovalevsky," *Century Magazine,* 50 (1895): 536–539;

Lars Hörmander, "The First Woman Professor and Her Male Colleague," in *Miscellanea mathematica,* edited by Peter Hilton, Friedrich Hirzebruch, and Reinhold Remmert (Berlin & London: Springer-Verlag, 1991), pp. 195–211;

E. Kannak, "S. Kovalevskaia i M. Kovalevskii," *Novyi zhurnal,* 39 (1954): 194–211;

Ellen Key, *Drei frauenschicksale* (Berlin: S. Fischer, 1908);

Ann Hibner Koblitz, *Science, Women and Revolution in Russia* (Amsterdam: Harwood Academic Publishers, 2000);

Koblitz, "Sofia Kovalevskaia and the Mathematical Community," *Mathematical Intelligencer,* 6, no. 1 (1984): 20–29;

L. Kronecker, "Sophie von Kowalevsky," *Crelle's Journal,* 108 (1891): 88;

Elizaveta Fedorovna Litvinova, as E. El', "Iz vremen moego studenchestva (Znakomstvo s S. V. Kovalevskoi)," *Zhenskoe delo,* 4 (1899): 34–63;

Gösta Mittag-Leffler, "Weierstrass et Sonja Kowalewsky," *Acta Mathematica,* 39 (1923): 133–198;

Pamiati S. V. Kovalevskoi: Sbornik statei, edited by Polubarinova-Kochina (Moscow: Izdatel'stvo Akademii nauk SSSR, 1951);

Solomon Iakovlevich Shtraikh, *Sem'ia Kovalevskikh* (Moscow: Sovetskii pisatel', 1948);

Shtraikh, *Sestry Korvin-Krukovskie* (Moscow: Mir, 1933);

N. Ia. Sonin, "Zametka po povodu pis'ma P. L. Chebysheva k S. V. Kovalevskoi," *Izvestiia Imperatorskoi akademii nauk,* 2, no. 1 (1895): 15–26;

Beatrice Stillman, "Sofya Kovalevskaya: Growing Up in the Sixties," *Russian Literature Triquarterly,* 9 (1974): 276–302;

A. G. Stoletov, N. E. Zhukovskii, and P. A. Nekrasov, "S. V. Kovalevskaia," *Matematicheskii sbornik,* 16 (1891–1892): 1–38.

Papers:

Collections of Sof'ia Vasil'evna Kovalevskaia's papers are located in the Archive of the Russian Academy of Science (AAN), fond 768 and fond 300 at the St. Petersburg branch, and fond 603 at the Moscow branch (Sof'ia Vladimirovna Kovalevskaia and Iuliia Vsevolodovna Lermontova collection). A part of the manuscript of *Nigilistka,* along with other materials, is held at the S. V. Kovalevskaia Local History Museum in Velikoluk, the location of her family estate. In addition, there are several cartons of uncatalogued papers in the Institut Mittag-Leffler in Djürsholm, Sweden.

Petr Alekseevich Kropotkin

(27 November 1842 – 8 February 1921)

George Crowder
Flinders University

BOOKS: *Gde luchshe? Skazka o chetyrekh brat'iakh i ob ikh prikliucheniiakh,* by Kropotkin and L. A. Tikhomirov (Geneva, 1873);

Emel'ian Ivanovich Pugachev, ili Bunt 1773 goda, by Kropotkin and Tikhomirov (Geneva, 1874);

Issledovaniia o lednikovom periode (St. Petersburg: M. Stasiulevich, 1876);

Le Procès de Solovieff (La Vie d'un socialiste russe) (Geneva: Imp. Jurassienne, 1879);

Aux jeunes gens (Geneva, 1881); translated by H. M. Hyndman as *An Appeal to the Young* (London: Modern, 1885);

La Vérité sur les exécutions en Russie, suivie d'une esquisse biographique sur Sophie Perovskaia (Geneva: Imp. Jurassienne, 1881);

La Guerre, excerpt of *Paroles d'un révolté* (Geneva: Le Révolté, 1882); translated as *War!* (London: Seymour, 1888);

Paroles d'un révolté (Paris: E. Flammarion, 1885); translated into Russian as *Rechi buntovshchika* (St. Petersburg: A. E. Beliaev, 1906); translated, with an introduction, by George Woodcock as *Words of a Rebel* (Montreal & Cheektowaga, N.Y.: Black Rose, 1992);

The Place of Anarchism in Socialist Evolution: An Address Delivered in Paris, translated by Henry Glasse (London: International, 1886);

Law and Authority: An Anarchist Essay (London: International, 1886);

In Russian and French Prisons (London: Ward & Downey, 1887); translated into Russian as *V russkikh i frantsuzskikh tiur'makh,* volume 4 of *Sochineniia* (St. Petersburg: Znanie, 1906–1907);

The Wage System, Freedom Pamphlets, no. 1 (London, 1889; revised, 1894);

Anarchist Communism: Its Basis and Principles (London: Freedom, 1891);

The Commune of Paris (London: New Fellowship, 1891; Columbus Junction, Iowa: E. H. Fulton, 1896);

La Conquête du pain (Paris: Tresse & Stock, 1892); translated into Russian as *Khleb i volia* (London:

Petr Alekseevich Kropotkin

Gruppa russkikh kommunistov-anarkhistov, 1902; St. Petersburg: Svobodnaia mysl', 1906); translated as *The Conquest of Bread* (London: Chapman & Hall, 1906; New York: Putnam, 1907);

Revolutionary Government (London: Freedom, 1892);

L'Agriculture (Paris, 1893); translated as *Agriculture* (London: J. Tochatti, 1896);

L'Anarchie: Sa philosophie, son idéal, Bibliothèque sociologique, no. 9 (Paris: P.-V. Stock, 1896); translated as *Anarchism: Its Philosophy and Ideal* (London: Freedom, 1897); translated into Russian as *Anarkhiia, ee filosofiia, ee ideal* (Geneva: E. Held, 1900; Leipzig & St. Petersburg: Mysl', 1906);

La Grande Grève des Docks, by Kropotkin and J. Burns (Paris: Bibliothèque des Temps Nouveaux, 1897);

L'état, son rôle historique (Paris, 1897); translated as *The State: Its Historic Role* (London: "Freedom" Office, 1898);

Fields, Factories and Workshops (London: Hutchinson, 1899; New York: Putnam, 1901; revised and enlarged edition, London: Nelson, 1912); translated into Russian by A. N. Konshin as *Zemledelie, fabrichno-zavodskaia i kustarnaia promyshlennost' i remesla* (Moscow, 1903); revised as *Polia, fabriki i masterskie* (Moscow: Posrednik, 1908);

Memoirs of a Revolutionist, 2 volumes, edited by George Morris Cohen Brandes (London: Smith Elder, 1899; Boston: Houghton, Mifflin, 1899); translated into Russian as *Zapiski revoliutsionera* (London: Fond vol'noi russkoi pressy, 1902);

Sovremennaia nauka i anarkhizm (London: Gruppa russkikh kommunistov-anarkhistov, 1901); translated by David A. Modell as *Modern Science and Anarchism* (Philadelphia: Social Science Club, 1903; London: Freedom, 1912);

Mutual Aid: A Factor of Evolution (London: Heinemann, 1902; revised, 1904); translated into Russian as *Vzaimnhpomoshch' sredi zhivotnykh i liudei* (St. Petersburg, 1904);

Russian Literature (London: Duckworth, 1905; New York: McClure, Phillips, 1905); translated into Russian as *Idealy i deistvitel'nost' v russkoi literature,* volume 5 of *Sochineniia* (St. Petersburg: Znanie, 1906–1907); translated as *Ideas and Realities in Russian Literature* (New York: Knopf, 1915);

Sochineniia, volumes 1, 2, 4, 5, and 7 (St. Petersburg: Znanie, 1906–1907);

Anarchist Morality (London: Freedom, 1909);

La Grande révolution 1789–1793, Bibliothèque historique, no. 3 (Paris: Stock, 1909); translated by N. F. Dryhurst as *The Great French Revolution 1789–1793* (London: Heinemann, 1909; New York: Putnam, 1909); translated into Russian as *Velikaia frantsuzskaia revoliutsiia. 1789–1793* (London, 1914; Moscow, 1918);

The Terror in Russia: An Appeal to the British Nation (London: Methuen, 1909);

Pis'ma o tekushchikh sobytiiakh (Moscow: Zadruga, 1917);

Sobranie sochinenii, 2 volumes (Moscow: I. D. Sytin, 1918);

Etika (St. Petersburg & Moscow: Golos truda, 1922); translated as *Ethics: Origin and Development by L.*

Friedland and J. Piroshnikoff (London: Harrap, 1924; New York: L. MacVeagh, 1924);

Dnevnik, edited by A. A. Bosovoi (Moscow & Petrograd: Gosundarstvennoe izdatel'stvo, 1923);

Dnevniki raznykh let, with an introduction by A. V. Anikin (Moscow: Sovetskaia Rossiia, 1992).

Editions: *Velikaia frantsuzskaia revoliutsiia. 1789–1793* (Moscow: Nauka, 1979);

Zapiski revoliutsionera, with an introduction and commentary by V. A. Tvardovskaia (Moscow: Moskovskii rabochii, 1988);

Khleb i volia; Sovremennaia nauka i anarkhiia (Moscow: Pravda, 1990);

Etika (Moscow: Politizdat, 1991);

Anarkhiia, ee filosofiia, ee ideal, edited and with an introduction by M. A. Timofeev (Moscow: Eksmo, 1999).

Editions in English: *Kropotkin's Revolutionary Pamphlets,* edited by R. N. Baldwin (New York: Vanguard, 1927); republished as *Anarchism: A Collection of Revolutionary Writings* (Mineola, N.Y.: Dover, 2002);

Kropotkin: Selections from His Writings, edited by H. Read (London: Freedom, 1942);

The State: Its Historic Role, Anarchist Classics (London: Freedom, 1969; revised, 1987);

Selected Writings on Anarchism and Revolution, edited, with an introduction, by Martin A. Miller (London & Cambridge, Mass.: MIT Press, 1970);

Fields, Factories and Workshops Tomorrow, edited, with an introduction, by Colin Ward (London: Allen & Unwin, 1974; New York: Harper & Row, 1975);

The Essential Kropotkin, edited by E. Capouya and K. Tompkins (New York: Liveright, 1975);

Anarchism and Anarchist Communism, edited by N. Walter (London: Freedom, 1987);

Act for Yourselves: Articles from Freedom 1886–1907, edited by Walter and H. Becker, Freedom Press Centenary Series, volume 1 (London: Freedom, 1988);

Fields, Factories and Workshops, with a new introduction by Yaacov Oved (New Brunswick, N.J.: Transaction, 1993);

The Conquest of Bread and Other Writings, edited by Marshall Shatz (Cambridge: Cambridge University Press, 1995);

Collected Works of Peter Kropotkin, 11 volumes, edited by George Woodcock (Montreal: Black Rose, 1996);

Prince Peter Alekseievich Kropotkin (1842–1921), edited by Subrata Mukherjee and Sushila Ramaswamy, World's Greatest Socialist Thinkers, no. 16 (New Delhi: Deep & Deep, 1998).

OTHER: "Anarchism," in *Encyclopaedia Britannica,* eleventh edition, edited by H. Chisholm (Cambridge: Cambridge University Press, 1910–1911).

Petr Kropotkin is chiefly remembered today as one of the great advocates of anarchism. For those who reject the state and look forward to the creation of a human society without a central, coercive government, Kropotkin's influence has been immense. His writings, along with those of Mikhail Aleksandrovich Bakunin and Pierre-Joseph Proudhon, have attained a canonical status among anarchists that is little short of holy writ. Writing fluently in French and English as well as Russian, Kropotkin produced a vast body of writing–books, articles, pamphlets, journals, and speeches–especially after his withdrawal from revolutionary activism in the 1880s. In works such as *Sovremennaia nauka i anarkhizm* (1901; translated as *Modern Science and Anarchism*, 1903) and *Mutual Aid: A Factor of Evolution* (1902), he sought to place anarchist principles on a scientific basis, drawing in particular on Charles Darwin's ideas of biological and social evolution. Two sides of Kropotkin's personality are evident here. An internationally respected geographer, he was a man of science and letters; at the same time, he was a revolutionary activist, deeply imbued with a sense of the injustices inflicted by modern societies on the working classes and those without property. *La Conquête du pain* (1892; translated as *The Conquest of Bread*, 1906) and *Fields, Factories and Workshops* (1899) together provide one of the most explicit attempts to imagine what an anarchist society might look like. In *Memoirs of a Revolutionist* (1899) Kropotkin leaves us a brilliantly vivid and humane record of Russia in the latter half of the nineteenth century, of the revolutionary currents flowing throughout Europe in that period, and of his personal evolution from privileged aristocrat to active revolutionary and thinker.

Petr Alekseevich Kropotkin, the youngest of four children, was born in Moscow on 27 November 1842 into a family of aristocratic landowners. Kropotkin's hereditary title was *kniaz'* (prince). The family traced their ancestry to the princes of Smolensk, and successive generations had served the Romanov tsars in various capacities, mostly military, since the sixteenth century. There was a similar tradition of military service on his mother's side of the family; his maternal grandfather served as governor-general of West Siberia and later East Siberia, where Kropotkin himself eventually served. The Kropotkins were relatively wealthy, with a house in the aristocratic Starokoniushenskii (Old Equerries) quarter of Moscow and three country estates. In *Memoirs of a Revolutionist* Kropotkin reports, using the word "souls" to mean "male serfs," that his father owned "nearly twelve hundred souls, in three different provinces."

Kropotkin's childhood was blighted by the death of his mother, Ekaterina Nikolaevna (née Sulima) Kropotkina, when he was three. His father, Aleksei Petrovich Kropotkin, a career army officer, was an aloof, authoritarian figure, and his stepmother, whom his father married in

1848, was preoccupied with her own child. The young Kropotkin's emotional support came chiefly from his brother Aleksandr, who was only one year older, and from the house serfs, of whom he writes in *Memoirs of a Revolutionist,* "I do not know what would have become of us if we had not found in our house, amidst the serf servants, that atmosphere of love which children must have around them." During this period the seeds of Kropotkin's lifelong sympathy with the common people were sown.

Initially educated by domestic tutors, Kropotkin enrolled in 1857 in the Corps of Pages, an elite military academy whose members served as pages to the royal family. At the top of his class in 1861, Kropotkin was duly selected to act as personal page to Tsar Alexander II. That same year Alexander II issued his proclamation emancipating the serfs, and Kropotkin was much affected by the atmosphere of reform, with which he found himself sympathetic. Increasingly, he experienced feelings of inner conflict between, on the one hand, his inherited social position and professional duties and, on the other, his growing passion for social change.

These feelings surfaced in his decision, upon graduation from the Corps of Pages in 1862, to join an unfashionable Cossack regiment in eastern Siberia and northern Manchuria, where there was greater scope, he believed, to work for social reform. In Siberia he sought ways to improve local administrative institutions, but his attempts were ultimately thwarted by official inaction. Such experiences persuaded Kropotkin that even the best of governments was not capable of producing genuine social progress. "Although I did not then formulate my thoughts in terms borrowed from political party struggles, I may now say that in Siberia I lost all faith in state discipline. I was prepared to become an anarchist," he later wrote in his *Memoirs of a Revolutionist.* Frustrated, he began to turn his attention toward geographical exploration, a field that indulged his love of nature and his commitment to scientific method. Later, in *Mutual Aid,* he looked back on his Siberian period as providing the first clues to his understanding of the laws of natural survival as cooperative rather than competitive within species–the foundation of his evolutionary defense of anarchism. Kropotkin's first literary publications were inspired by his Siberian travels; he published his series of ethnographic sketches titled "Na puti v Vostochnuiu Sibir'" (En Route to East Siberia, 1862) and "Iz Vostochnoi Sibiri" (From East Siberia, 1862, 1867) in the newspaper *Sovremennaia letopis'* (The Modern Chronicle).

A new phase of Kropotkin's life commenced in 1867, when he resigned from the army with the intention of pursuing both his reformist and scientific ambitions. He realized a long-standing desire by entering St. Petersburg University to study mathematics, which he regarded as an essential preparation for any scientific career. Soon, how-

Kropotkin at eighteen, when he was a pupil in the Corps of Pages,
the elite military academy he attended in 1857–1862
(from Viacheslav Alekseevich Markin,
Neizvestnyi Kropotkin, *2002)*

ever, his mathematical studies were eclipsed by his devotion to geography, in which he rapidly established a reputation for important and innovative work. In 1871 Kropotkin's success led to an invitation to become secretary of the Russian Geographical Society, and this event triggered a crisis of conscience that he describes in *Memoirs of a Revolutionist:*

> What right had I to these higher joys, when all around me was nothing but misery and struggle for a mouldy bit of bread; when whatsoever I should spend to enable me to live in that world of higher emotions must needs be taken from the very mouths of those who grew the wheat and had not bread enough for their children? . . . So I sent my negative reply to the Geographical Society.

Dedicated now to the cause of social and political reform, Kropotkin sought to expand his political education by traveling to western Europe in 1872. His special goal was Switzerland, a center of considerable Russian émigré activity as well as the headquarters at that time of the International Workingmen's Association (the "International"), the main agency of the international socialist movement. Most significant in Kropotkin's experiences

during this visit was his encounter with the watchmakers of the Jura Mountains, whose Jura Federation had become a rebel organization within the Marxist-dominated International. He found among the watchmakers a community that combined principles of personal and collective independence with egalitarianism imbibed in part from Bakunin. These principles appealed strongly to Kropotkin. Moreover, according to his *Memoirs,* the watchmakers convinced him that the state socialism advocated by Marx invited "an economic despotism far more dangerous than the merely political despotism" of the current tsarist regime. At the end of his weeklong stay in the Juras, he declared himself an anarchist.

Returning to St. Petersburg, Kropotkin joined the Chaikovsky circle, an intellectual center of *narodnichestvo* (Populism) that sought a non-Marxist path to socialism by way of the values embodied in the traditional Russian *mir* (peasant commune). But in 1874 the police crushed the Chaikovsky circle and arrested many of its members, including Kropotkin himself. Imprisoned for two years in the Fortress of St. Peter and St. Paul, he became increasingly ill, and only through family connections and good fortune was he transferred to a prison hospital where he could recover. From there, in 1876, he made a dramatic escape into exile in western Europe.

Kropotkin traveled again to Switzerland, where he reestablished his links with the Jura Federation, becoming an organizer and journalist for the international anarchist movement. In 1879 he founded the anarchist journal *Le Révolté* (The Rebel), whose title changed to *La Révolte* (Rebellion) when he moved to France and then later to *Les Temps nouveaux* (Modern Times). Several of his articles for *Le Révolté* were later collected as *Paroles d'un révolté* (1885; translated as *Words of a Rebel,* 1992), his first book-length work of political advocacy. In what is perhaps a sign of his complete dedication to the revolutionary cause, he makes only occasional mention in *Memoirs of a Revolutionist* of his wife, Sofiia Grigor'evna Anan'eva, whom Kropotkin married in 1879. Kropotkin and Sofiia, the daughter of a prosperous Polish-Jewish manufacturer, met in Geneva, where she had insisted on studying in defiance of her parents and where she had become involved in the revolutionary movement. Their only child, Aleksandra (Sasha), was born in 1887.

In 1881, following the assassination of Tsar Alexander II, Kropotkin was expelled from Switzerland as a result of Russian diplomatic pressure. The next year he was arrested in France and convicted of a fabricated offense. He was imprisoned at Clairvaux and remained there for three years. A long public campaign for his release, which attracted the support of some of the most distinguished intellectual and political figures of the period (including Georges Clemenceau, Victor Hugo, Algernon Swinburne, and William Morris), finally succeeded in 1886. Kropotkin's moving account of prison life, *In Russian and French Prisons,* was published the following year. He and his wife settled in London, where they were to live for the next thirty years.

Kropotkin's release from prison marked the end of his career as an activist. His failing health and relative isolation, in London, from the Continental mainstream of the anarchist movement increasingly impeded his direct engagement in the struggle against the state—in particular the Russian state, his main target. Yet, the close of Kropotkin's activism merely inaugurated his new devotion to the promotion of anarchism through the written and spoken word. He now became the most respected and prolific spokesman that the anarchist outlook has known. Kropotkin wrote, in French and English more often than in Russian, for as wide an audience as he could reach. A good example of his gifts in this regard is provided by his article on anarchism for the *Encyclopaedia Britannica* (1910–1911). In addition to ten major books published during his lifetime, he produced scores of shorter pieces and helped to found the British anarchist journal *Freedom* in 1886. He also became a successful speaker on the American lecture circuit and toured the United States from 1897 to 1898 and again in 1901. As a result of the first of these tours, Kropotkin was invited to write the series of autobiographical articles for the *Atlantic Monthly* that was expanded and republished in 1899 as *Memoirs of a Revolutionist.*

Kropotkin's case for anarchism can be divided into three main elements: a critique of the state, a vision of the stateless society of the future, and an account of the transition from the state to anarchism. The first of these elements, the attack on the modern state, is found throughout all of his anarchist writing, but the pamphlet *L'état, son rôle historique* (1897; translated as *The State: Its Historic Role,* 1898) is representative. There he refers to "the State, both in its present form, in its very essence, and in whatever guise it might appear" as "an obstacle to the social revolution, the greatest hindrance to the birth of a society based on equality and liberty." The state crushes human freedom not merely by direct coercion through the enforcement of law and the waging of war but also by encouraging the willing acceptance of authority through devices such as religion. For Kropotkin, the state is thus "the Triple Alliance, finally constituted, of the military chief, the Roman judge and the priest—the three constituting a mutual assurance for domination."

In place of state domination, Kropotkin insists on the possibility of a modern society without coercive government and characterized by freedom, equality, and solidarity. *La Conquête du pain* reflects his first major attempt to describe such a society. In this work Kropotkin advocates "anarchist-communism," under which necessities are distributed according to need rather than in accordance with the amount of labor performed as in the "mutualist" anarchism of Proudhon or the "collectivist" anarchism of Bakunin. Thus far, Kropotkin agrees with Karl Marx. He parts decisively with the "German state socialists," however, in his rejection of any revolutionary role for government or for a party led by an elite, both of which will simply reproduce the state and its problems. Rather, the model for social relations must be voluntary agreement, guaranteed by the innate good sense of the people. Later, focusing in particular on the nature of production, Kropotkin elaborates his vision of the future in *Fields, Factories and Workshops.* The anarchist-communist society, he argues, will be radically decentralized, both politically and industrially. People will live in small, self-governing communities, connected with one another by a loose system of federation in which authority will percolate from the lower levels to the upper, instead of being imposed from the top down. Each community will integrate both agriculture and industry, and individual citizens will engage in both hand and brain work.

Kropotkin makes several different suggestions as to how the desirable society of the future will be reached, given the current slavery of the people. One frequent theme is his faith in the basic goodness and intelligence of ordinary men and women. In *La Conquête du pain,* for example, he writes of "that admirable spirit of organization inherent in the people." Kropotkin is ambivalent toward the view that the social revolution can be made only through violence—a view that was widespread, although not universally accepted, among anarchists of the period. He tends to play down the role of violence, although he is reluctant to condemn even those anarchists engaged in the terrorist methods of "propaganda by deed." His more characteristic approach is to look to the guidance of science.

The attempt to ground anarchism in natural science is Kropotkin's most distinctive contribution to anarchist thought—and, more generally, to political theory. His outlook is summarized in *Modern Science and Anarchism:*

> Anarchism is a conception of the Universe based on the mechanical interpretation of phenomena, which comprises the whole of Nature, including the life of human societies and their economic, political, and moral problems. Its method is that of natural sciences, and every conclusion it comes to must be verified by this method if it pretends to be scientific.

Kropotkin appeals to science as a basis for anarchism in two senses, which may be labeled "internal" and "external." On the one hand, scientific enlightenment will lead people to internalize a true understanding of human morality (conceived as a form of natural law) and thereby create an unforced convergence of beliefs about the basic terms of right conduct. This convergence will belie any case for the alleged necessity of state coercion.

Kropotkin's drawing of Clairvaux, the French prison where he was confined in 1882–1885
(from Markin, Neizvestnyi Kropotkin, *2002)*

On the other hand, Kropotkin presents science as supportive of anarchism in an "external" sense, in that science provides an account of the coming of anarchism as inevitable and independent of the wills of individuals.

According to this latter view, anarchism is inevitable because it is ultimately required by the laws of nature as revealed by Darwin's theory of evolution. Kropotkin developed this argument in a series of articles for the journal *Nineteenth Century,* written between 1890 and 1896 and later collected under the title of *Mutual Aid,* his best-known work today. An enthusiast for Darwin's thought, Kropotkin takes from it quite a different message from that of the English and American "social Darwinists" who see in the natural "struggle for survival" a confirmation of the norms of unrestrained capitalist competition. In the introduction to *Mutual Aid,* Kropotkin looks back to his naturalist observations in Siberia and argues that although nature is indeed a theater of struggle for survival, the struggle is primarily between whole species and their environment rather than between individuals within the species: "I saw Mutual Aid and Mutual Support carried on to an extent which made me suspect in it a feature of the greatest importance for the maintenance of life, the preservation of each species, and its further evolution." The greater struggle is necessarily collective, and its success is dependent not on internecine competition but on cooperation. Kropotkin traces mutual aid through many aspects—first of the natural world and then of human social evolution. In the latter case he sees the tendency to mutual aid as natural to human beings yet obstructed in its operation by the divisive and oppressive hand of the state. The obvious logical problem with this view is that, if the evolution of mutual aid really is a law of nature, then how it can be impeded by an artificial institution is hard to see. Kropotkin seems to be aware of this difficulty, but his reply—that in modern times mutual aid is becoming more widespread but less intense—is not persuasive.

Not all of Kropotkin's published writings are explicitly concerned with anarchism, since he also found time to write about literature and history. *Russian Literature* was published in 1905, and *La Grande révolution 1789–1793* (translated as *The Great French Revolution 1789–1793,* 1909) came out four years later. Even in these works, however, anarchist themes are never far from the surface. In *Russian Literature* Kropotkin's survey of the leading Russian writers of the nineteenth century is oriented more toward social, rather than purely aesthetic, issues. He argues that literature is unusually influential in Russia during this period, because the absence of an "open political life" under the tsarist autocracy has made poetry, novels, and even literary criticism the chief vehicle for social criticism. *La Grande révolution 1789–1793* is notable for its emphasis on the economic distress of the common people as a factor that creates and drives the revolution, in contrast with the hitherto more conventional focus on the personalities and manipulations of political leaders. Kropotkin is concerned here not only with the course of the French Revolution itself but also with its implications for the success or failure of revolution in general.

Kropotkin's last years were also the final years of the anarchist movement as a major international political force. The anarchists found themselves squeezed between nationalism from one side and the statist socialism of Marxism-Leninism from the other. Nationalism confirmed its continuing influence in 1914 when millions of workers from all over Europe flocked eagerly to serve their respective nation-states in World War I. This outpouring of nationalist sentiment swept aside the mainstream anarchist view that all states are equally the enemy of ordinary people. Kropotkin himself departed from the standard anarchist line in this case, defending the cause of the Allies against that of the Central Powers on the grounds that the latter represented the forces of authoritarian reaction against the admittedly imperfect democracy of the former. As a result, he found himself at odds with many of his anarchist comrades.

The blow to anarchism from the direction of state socialism was still more crushing. In February 1917 the Russian tsar was overthrown, and a provisional government, of broadly constitutionalist outlook, was proclaimed. Throughout his years of exile Kropotkin had followed developments in Russia as well as he could; in 1909 he published *The Terror in Russia* to alert British opinion to the repression that ensued after the uprising of 1905. Now at last, with the end of tsarist autocracy, Kropotkin was able to return to his homeland with real hopes of contributing to the longed-for social revolution. By May 1917 he had arrived in the newly renamed city of Petrograd. Then in October the Bolsheviks seized power and began to suppress all political rivals, including the anarchists. Kropotkin, protected by his status as one of the great revolutionary figures of Russia, was left unharmed. He was also ignored. Settling with his wife in the village of Dmitrov near Moscow, he tried to exert some moderating influence on the Soviet government through letters and even an interview with Lenin, but apparently to little avail. His attitude toward the Soviet revolution was mixed: he was supportive of the overall goal of communist socialism but was also, in keeping with his anarchist ideals, opposed to the use of the state as the means for bringing about socialism.

Kropotkin's final writings of note are his two letters to Lenin (1920) and the unfinished *Etika* (1922; translated as *Ethics: Origin and Development* by L. Friedland and J. Piroshnikoff, 1924), published posthumously. The latter develops the evolutionary account of the moral sense that he began in *Mutual Aid*. Kropotkin died of pneumonia on 8 February 1921. At his funeral, twenty thousand mourners, many displaying anarchist banners, followed his coffin in the last great public statement of the anarchist movement in Russia. After the final suppression of the movement, Kropotkin's anarchist writings became unavailable in the Soviet Union, although the publication of a biography in 1972 signaled a thaw in official attitudes that continued under glasnost' (Soviet leader Mikhail Sergeevich Gorbachev's policy of increased openness) in the 1980s.

In the West, Petr Alekseevich Kropotkin was regarded in his own time as the acceptable face of anarchism, by contrast with the movement's contemporary reputation for terrorism. Indeed, he achieved the status of a kind of secular saint. Oscar Wilde's description in his *De Profundis* (1949) of him as "a man with a soul of that beautiful white Christ which seems coming out of Russia" is one of many similar portrayals. As a political thinker, Kropotkin is still regarded as the most systematic and accessible exponent of nineteenth-century classical anarchism. His arguments are widely seen as seriously flawed—in particular, his attempt to deduce prescriptive moral laws from descriptive laws of nature; his underestimation of the potential of the state for beneficial social action; and his overestimation of the virtues and capacity for harmonious cooperation of ordinary people. Although he presents himself as a scientist, his political views owe more to his moral convictions and faith in progress. Nevertheless, Kropotkin continues to be studied, and he is rightly celebrated as one of the greatest champions of human freedom.

Letters:

To Vladimir Il'ich Lenin, in Vladimir Bonch-Bruevich, "Moi vospominaniia o Peter Alekseeviche Kropotkine," *Zvezda*, 6 (1930): 186–187, 193–194;

Petr i Aleksandr Kropotkiny: Perepiska, edited by Nikolai Konstantinovich Lebedev, 2 volumes (Moscow & Leningrad: Academia, 1932, 1933);

Pis'ma iz Vostochnoi Sibiri, edited by A. I. Alekseev, compiled by V. A. Markin and Evgenii Vasil'evich Starostin (Irkutsk: Vostochno-Sibirskoe knizhnoe izdatel'stvo, 1983);

"Lettres de Pierre Kropotkine à James Guillaume sur les terres communales," edited by Max Nettlau, in *La Grande révolution 1789–1793* (Paris: Editions du Monde libertaire, 1989);

Anarchistes en exil: Correspondance inédite de Pierre Kropotkine à Marie Goldsmith, 1897–1917 (Paris: Institut d'études slaves, 1995).

Bibliographies:

Max Nettlau, *Bibliographie de l'Anarchie* (Brussels: Bibliothèque des Temps Nouveaux, 1897), pp. 72–86, 238–239;

Sbornik statei, posviashchennyi pamiati P. A. Kropotkina, edited by Aleksei Borovoi and Nikolai Konstantinovich Lebedev (Moscow & Petrograd: Golos truda, 1922), pp. 190–249;

Evgenii Vasil'evich Starostin, *P. A. Kropotkin (1842–1921): Bibliograficheskii ukazatel' pechatnykh trudov,* 2 volumes (Moscow: In-t istorii SSSR, 1980);

Heinz Hug and Heidi Grau, *Peter Kropotkin (1842–1921): Bibliographie* (Grafenau & Württ: Edition Anares im Trotzdem-Verlag, 1994).

Biographies:

Nikolai Konstantinovich Lebedev, *P. A. Kropotkin* (Moscow: Gosudarstvennoe izdatel'stvo, 1925);

George Woodcock and Ivan Avakumovic, *The Anarchist Prince: A Biographical Study of Peter Kropotkin* (London & New York: T. V. Boardman, 1950);

Natal'ia Mikhailovna Pirumova, *Petr Alekseevich Kropotkin* (Moscow: Nauka, 1972);

Martin A. Miller, *Kropotkin* (Chicago & London: University of Chicago Press, 1976).

References:

Paul Avrich, *Anarchist Portraits* (Princeton, N. J.: Princeton University Press, 1988);

Avrich, *The Russian Anarchists* (Princeton, N. J.: Princeton University Press, 1967);

Caroline Cahm, *Kropotkin and the Rise of Revolutionary Anarchism 1872–1886* (Cambridge: Cambridge University Press, 1989);

George Crowder, *Classical Anarchism: The Political Thought of Godwin, Proudhon, Bakunin, and Kropotkin* (Oxford: Clarendon Press, 1991);

James W. Hulse, *Revolutionists in London: A Study of Five Unorthodox Socialists* (Oxford: Clarendon Press, 1970);

Grigorii Petrovich Maksimov, ed., *Internatsional'nyi sbornik posviashchennyi desiatoi godovshchine smerti P. A. Kropotkina* (Chicago: Knigoizd-vo Fed. Russkikh Anarkho-Kommunisticheskikh Grupp Soed. Shtatov i Kanady, 1931);

Viacheslav Alekseevich Markin, *Neizvestnyi Kropotkin* (Moscow: OLMA-PRESS, 2002);

Peter Marshall, *Demanding the Impossible: A History of Anarchism* (London: HarperCollins, 1992);

David Miller, "Kropotkin," in *Rediscoveries,* edited by John Hall (Oxford: Clarendon Press, 1986);

Stephen Osofsky, *Peter Kropotkin* (Boston: Twayne, 1979);

Natal'ia Mikhailovna Pirumova, ed., "P. A. Kropotkin," *Voprosy filosofii,* 11 (1991): 38–71;

Raven (Anarchist Quarterly), special Kropotkin issue, 5, no. 4 (October–December 1992);

Sbornik statei, posviashchennyi pamiati P. A. Kropotkina, edited by Aleksei Borovoi and Nikolai Konstantinovich Lebedev (Moscow & Petrograd: Golos truda, 1922);

David Shub, "Kropotkin and Lenin," *The Russian Review,* 12 (October 1953): 227–234;

John Slatter, "P. A. Kropotkin on Legality and Ethics," *Studies in East European Thought,* 48, nos. 2–4 (September 1996): 255–276;

Slatter, "Peter Kropotkin's Literary Adviser: The Letters to Edward Garnett, 1897–1916," *Solanus: International Journal for Russia & East European Bibliographic, Library & Publishing Studies,* 12 (1998): 33–56;

Daniel P. Todes, *Darwin without Malthus: The Struggle for Existence in Russian Evolutionary Thought* (New York & Oxford: Oxford University Press, 1989);

Oscar Wilde, *De Profundis* (London: Methuen, 1949).

Papers:

Petr Alekseevich Kropotkin's papers are located in three archives in Moscow: the State Archive of the Russian Federation (GARF, formerly the Central State Archive of the October Revolution), fond R-7366; the Russian State Library (RGB, formerly the Lenin Library), fond 410; and the State Literary Museum (GLM), fond 108.

Konstantin Nikolaevich Leont'ev

(13 January 1831 – 12 November 1891)

Henrietta Mondry
University of Canterbury

BOOKS: *V svoem kraiu. Roman v dvukh chastiakh* (St. Petersburg: A. A. Kraevsky, 1864);

Pembe: Razskaz iz Epiro-albanskoi zhizni (Leipzig: V. Gergard, 1870);

Iz zhizni khristian v Turtsii, 3 volumes (Moscow: M. Katkov, 1876);

Vizantizm i slavianstvo (Moscow: Imp. Obshchestvo istorii i drevnostei rossiiskikh pri Moskovskom universite, 1876);

Pravoslavnyi nemets. Optinskii ieromonakh otets Kliment (Zedergol'm) (Warsaw: V. Istomin, 1880); republished as *Otets Kliment Zedergol'm, Ieromonakh Optinoi Pustyni* (Moscow: Moskovskoe tovarishchestvo, 1882);

Kak nado ponimat' sblizhenie s narodom? (Moscow: E. I. Pogodin, 1881);

Nashi novye khristiane (Moscow: E. I. Pogodin, 1882);

Vostok, Rossiia i slavianstvo, 2 volumes (Moscow: I. N. Kushnerev, 1885, 1886);

Natsional'naia politika, kak orudie vsemirnoi revoliutsii (Moscow: I. N. Kushnerev, 1889);

Analiz, stil' i veianie. O romanakh grafa L. N. Tolstogo. Kriticheskii etiud (St. Petersburg: Obshchestvennaia pol'za, 1890); republished as *O romanakh gr. L. N. Tolstogo. Analiz, stil' i veianie. Kriticheskii etiud* (Moscow: V. M. Sablin, 1911);

O Vladimire Solov'eve i estetike zhizni (Moscow: Tvorcheskaia mysl', 1912);

Sobranie sochinenii, 9 volumes, edited by Iosif Ivanovich Fudel' (Moscow & St. Petersburg: V. M. Sablin, 1912–1913)–includes volume 1 (1912), *Romany i povesti*–includes *Podlipki* and *Ispoved' muzha;*

Otshel'nichestvo, monastyr' i mir. Ikh sushchnost' i vzaimnaia sviaz'. (Chetyre pis'ma s Afona) (Sergiev Posad, 1913);

Stranitsy vospominanii, edited by P. K. Guber (St. Petersburg: Parfenon, 1922);

Moia literaturnaia sud'ba. Avtobiografiia (New York: Johnson Reprint, 1965).

Editions and Collections: *Egipetskii golub'; Ditia dushi* (New York: Chekhov, 1954);

Analiz, stil' i veianie: O romanakh grafa L. N. Tolstogo (Providence: Brown University Press, 1965);

Konstantin Nikolaevich Leont'ev

Sobranie sochinenii K. Leont'eva, 4 volumes, Analecta Slavica (Würzburg, Germany: Jal-reprint, 1975);

Egipetskii golub'. Roman, povesti, vospominaniia, with an introduction by V. A. Kotel'nikov (Moscow: Sovremennik, 1991);

Zapiski otshel'nika, edited by Viktor Kochetkov (Moscow: Russkaia kniga, 1992);

Tsvetushchaia slozhnost'. Izbrannye stat'i (Moscow: Molodaia gvardiia, 1992);

Izbrannoe, edited by Igor' Nikolaevich Smirnov (Moscow: Moskovskii rabochii, 1993);

K. Leont'ev, nash sovremennik: Sbornik, compiled by B. Adrianov and N. Mal'chevsky (St. Petersburg: Izdatel'stvo Chernysheva, 1993);

Pozdniaia osen' Rossii (Moscow: Agraf, 2000);

Polnoe sobranie sochinenii, 12 volumes, edited by Kotel'nikov and others (St. Petersburg: Vladimir Dal', 2000–).

Editions in English: "The Average European as an Ideal and Instrument of Universal Destruction," translated by W. Shafer and G. Kline, in *Russian Philosophy,* edited by J. Edie and others, volume 2 (Chicago: Quadrangle, 1965);

The Egyptian Dove: The Story of a Russian, translated by George Reavey (New York: Weybright & Talley, 1969);

Against the Current: Selections from the Novels, Essays, Notes and Letters of Konstantin Leontiev, translated by Reavey, edited by George Ivask (New York: Weybright & Talley, 1969);

"The Novels of Count L. N. Tolstoy," in *Essays in Russian Literature. The Conservative View: Leontiev, Rozanov, Shestov,* edited and translated by Spencer E. Roberts (Athens: Ohio University Press, 1969), pp. 225–356.

OTHER: *Dostoevsky i Pushkin: Rech' i stat'ia F. M. Dostoevskogo,* with contributions by Leont'ev, A. Volynsky, G. Uspensky, edited by Volynsky (St. Petersburg: Parfenon, 1921).

Konstantin Leont'ev is known as a philosopher of history and an author of novels about Russian life (for which he received praise from Ivan Sergeevich Turgenev), as well as the author of ethnographic novels about the life of Christians in Turkey. His reputation as an original thinker is based on his philosophy of history, which utilizes aesthetic, rather than ethic, principles. His aestheticism was linked not to an examination of art, however, but to an examination of life itself. Leont'ev is best known for his concept of transcendental egotism and his tripartite division of the historical process into periods of primeval simplicity, complex flowering, and resimplification. His religious and sociological views were based on a desire to propagate strict Byzantine principles. He did not accept the nationalistic principles of the Slavophilic doctrine; thus, his reputation as a Slavophile is a misconception. Leont'ev's view of the Slavs was as controversial as that of Petr Iakovlevich Chaadaev, and his faith lay in his strict adherence to the teachings of the Church Fathers and to Byzantine hierarchies.

Konstantin Nikolaevich Leont'ev was born on 13 January 1831 at Kudinovo, in the Kaluga province; Kudinovo was a not-too-large estate belonging to Leont'ev's father, Nikolai Borisovich Leont'ev. Premature at birth, the newborn Leont'ev was kept in an imitation womb—a rabbit-skin bag—that was placed in a basket in a Russian steam bath. His mother, Fedosia Petrovna

(Karabanova) Leont'eva, watched over her son during the critical first two months after he was born, a vigil that helped to ensure his survival in this imitation of uterine space. Leont'ev revered and adored his mother. She represented aristocratic refinement and high style for her son as well as the incarnation of aesthetic principles in her everyday life. A member of an old gentry family of Tartar origin, Fedosia Petrovna as a young woman received a polished education at the Catherine Institute in St. Petersburg, and she remained a faithful devotee of the Russian monarchy. Leont'ev's mother taught her son to love autocracy and to believe in the protective powers of the monarchy, which encompassed the gentry. Leont'ev's personal life bore features of the repressed and sublimated love that he harbored for Fedosia Petrovna. His bisexuality and religiosity manifested two aspects of his identification with—and narcissistic projection onto—his mother and reflected a sublimation of his libido into religious channels.

Leont'ev's esteem for his mother contrasted greatly with his feelings for his father. Nikolai Borisovich, a member of the gentry, had served in the army as a young man but was discharged because of his uncontrolled fits of anger. He spent the remainder of his life managing Kudinovo. Leont'ev disliked his father, and in later years, whenever Leont'ev reflected on his youth, he attempted to sever all ties and connections to his father and cherish and emulate his links to his mother. As a mature man he continued to cherish his fantasy of being the illegitimate son of his beloved mother. Nikolai Borisovich died in 1839, and neither Leont'ev nor Fedosia Petrovna attended the funeral.

Leont'ev received his primary education at home under his mother's supervision. In 1843 he entered a military school, Dvorianskii polk (Gentry Regiment), and prepared himself for a career typical of a member of the gentry; he had to leave the school, however, because of his poor health. He was then sent to the Kaluga gymnasium and graduated from there in 1849. Although he entered the Demidov Lycée in Iaroslavl' in the same year, his poor health was, yet again, the cause of his transfer to a new educational institution. Leont'ev entered the medical school at Moscow University in 1849 and graduated in 1854 with little enthusiasm for a career in medicine, which he had pursued at his mother's insistence—she wanted him to have a practical profession.

Leont'ev's proneness to psychosomatic illnesses surfaced during his years at the university. He complained of chest pains in 1851 and imagined himself dying from consumption. His ill health coincided with two consecutive love affairs: one with a young girl, Zinaida Kononova, and another with a fellow medical student, Aleksei Georgievsky. He relinquished his affair with Kononova because his mother persuaded him to do so; his love for Georgievsky came to an end, however, when he transferred his intellectual affection to Turgenev, whom he had met at the writer Evgeniia Tur's literary salon. Both Kononova and Georgievsky became prototypes for Leont'ev's comedy *Zhenit'ba po liubvi* (Married for Love)–the work that he showed to Turgenev. His alter ego in the play, Kireev, refuses to marry Zinaida because he is not sure whether he loves her, while his friend, Ianitsky, accuses him of being unable to love a woman. Leont'ev felt relief that was twofold from writing the play: first, the experience helped him learn to rationalize his psychological problems, and second, it derived from the encouraging remarks that Turgenev made about the quality of his work.

Turgenev's guidance turned out to be beneficial for Leont'ev, in terms of both his literary career and his personal life. Turgenev praised Leont'ev after reading the sequel to *Zhenit'ba po liubvi*, titled *Bulavinskii zavod* (Bulavin's Factory, 1851), and, once Turgenev became a mentor, Leont'ev was able to sever his ties with Georgievsky, whose intellectual guidance and approval he had sought for the previous three years. Turgenev also gave Leont'ev some valuable advice about his personal affairs, such as encouraging the young man to take a position as a military doctor in the Crimea in order to achieve financial independence. Leont'ev took such a position in 1854. That same year, his first literary publication appeared in the newspaper *Moskovskie vedomosti* (Moscow News): a *povest'* (novella) titled "Blagodarnost'" (Thankfulness), which the censor in St. Petersburg had earlier rejected. The following year in Feodosia, a town in the Crimea, Leont'ev became involved with Elizaveta Pavlovna Politova, the daughter of a wealthy Greek merchant. He married her six years later. At the end of the Crimean War in 1856 Leont'ev spent his six months' leave at a friend's estate in Tamak. There he started work on one of his major novels, *Podlipki. Roman* (The Estate under the Linden Trees. A Novel), which appeared in *Otechestvennye zapiski* (Notes of the Fatherland) in 1861.

The novel *Podlipki* provides valuable insights into the Leont'evian dialectic between morality and beauty, one of the fundamental points of Leont'ev's philosophy of history. In *Podlipki* the central conflict is manifested in the opposition between a romantic ideal and the harsh realities of life. The main characters, Ladnev and his friend, Iur'ev, are depicted as Platonic dreamers; for them, Grecian aesthetic ideals are linked with their understanding of physical beauty. Ladnev is Leont'ev's alter ego; the symbolism of this hero's surname indicates his narcissistic nature, because it signifies that he is *ladnyi* (handsome, harmonious) and thus perfect all around: in appearance, personality, and behavior. Ladnev expresses his need to experience all the delights of life–all of its

"vitality." He juxtaposes a life devoted to Grecian aesthetics with one governed by Christian ideas. The young hedonist cannot enjoy life fully because of his inner conflict between the quest for pagan aestheticism and the demands of Christian ethics. For Ladnev, the estate of Podlipki is a Russian Greece: the place where he enjoys life, but also the place where his fall occurs.

In many of his works Leont'ev develops the idea that class differences are a necessary source of diversity in life and, thus, of the aesthetic value of life. Egalitarianism destroys the social contrasts that are responsible for the development of a creative imagination. Two protagonists represent Leont'ev's aesthetic and historical ideal in his second important novel, *V svoem kraiu. Roman v dvukh chastiakh* (In My Own Land. A Novel in Two Parts, 1864). Both Milkeev and Rudnev rail against social egalitarianism and put out a "manifesto-like" pronouncement that beauty is an end in itself. In this novel Leont'ev conducts a full-scale polemic against the Chernyshevskian view that aesthetics is subordinate to realism in art and that representational beauty is inferior to reality. The opinions of Nikolai Gavrilovich Chernyshevsky and Nikolai Aleksandrovich Dobroliubov are satirized in a third character–the figure Aleksei Bogoiavlensky, a caricatured composite of Chernyshevsky and Dobroliubov. In fact, the materialist doctrine of "rational egotism" that Bogoiavlensky preaches (a mixture of the seminary and revolutionary rhetoric characteristic of Chernyshevsky) is the antithesis of Leont'ev's own principle of "transcendental egotism," which is based on the desire to gain a personal, transcendental salvation attainable only after death.

From 1864 to 1874 Leont'ev spent an exciting career in exotic locales. He joined the Ministry of Foreign Affairs in 1863 and was assigned to the Asiatic Department. On 1 January 1864 he arrived at his first post as a secretary and dragoman of the Russian consulate in Crete. His wife, Elizaveta Pavlovna, accompanied him to the place of his assignment but returned to Russia soon after their arrival. Leont'ev's use of his marriage to conceal his homosexuality led to a pattern of interruption in the couple's cohabitation. Six months after his arrival in Crete, he caused a diplomatic scandal during one of his violent outbursts of anger by attacking the French consul for making derogatory remarks about Russians. After his diplomatic mishap, Leont'ev was sent to Adrianople and remained there until 1866. According to his letters at the time, he sank into his most hedonistic behavior during this period. His unrestrained promiscuity manifested itself in his equal admiration of the beauty of the British consul's wife and that of Greek, Bulgarian, and Turkish girls, as well as in his organization of private wrestling contests between young Turkish boys.

Leont'ev was promoted to vice-consul in 1867 and assigned to Tulja, on the Danube. Also in 1867 his best story, *Ispoved' muzha* (A Husband's Confession, published in book form in 1912), was published as "Ai-Burun. Povest'" in the journal *Otechestvennye zapiski*. In an act indicative of the psychological growth that he experienced upon his religious awakening, Leont'ev forbade the posthumous publication of this novel. In "Gde razyskat' moi sochinenia posle moei smerti" (Where to Find My Literary Work after My Death, 1882), published in *Russkoe obozrenie* (Russian Review), he calls the novel sinful, but at the same time he says it was composed with the genuine feeling of a profoundly depraved heart.

Ispoved' muzha is set in the Crimea, an appropriate venue for the conflict—pagan versus Christian—that develops in the novel. An elderly, retired man marries a young, robust girl, Liza, in order to provide her with comfort and to save her from poverty. In order to satisfy her sexual needs, her husband chooses a lover for her. The lover is a young Greek man who wears a colorful ethnic costume and has the statuesque beauty of an ancient Greek god. In this novel Leont'ev breaks down barriers between the sexes by giving Liza a masculine beauty and the young Greek a feminine vanity. Liza has a strong, thick voice and hairy arms, while the Greek lover sports a white *fustanella* (jacket), blue tunic, and crimson embroidered boots with tassels on the upturned toes. Besides mixing conventions of gender and sexuality for two of the protagonists in his novel, Leont'ev also toys with the idea of marital boundaries. The husband fastens his narcissistic libido onto both of the young people, whose blurred gender and sexuality satisfy his own bisexual desires. Both young people answer the symbolic gaze fixed on them by the husband with all the physical beauty of their youth. The story has a tragic ending befitting a Greek love novel: after a peripeteia, the lovers perish in the Black Sea as a result of a shipwreck. Not only do Eros and Thanatos meet in this story, but also the suicide of the confessing husband brings his life, lived in transgression against the norms of Christianity, to its un-Christian end.

In his novel *Dve izbrannitsy* (Two Favorites), only the first part of which was accepted for publication in 1867 and finally published in 1885 in *Rossiia* (Russia), Leont'ev again returns to the theme of a love triangle in which a masculine woman plays the key role. This time the triangle is composed of the handsome Colonel Matveev, his Moldavian wife (who leaves him unfulfilled), and the young woman Sonia, a nihilist of masculine appearance and behavior. Leont'ev's personal search for sexual equilibrium compelled him to experiment with several scenarios in both his life and his novels—scenarios consisting of love triangles with people of indistinct sexuality. In *Dve izbrannitsy* Leont'ev's hope of abstaining from transgression, by falling in love with a masculine woman,

constitutes his most evident attempt to achieve a socially and religiously acceptable private life.

While on leave in St. Petersburg in 1868 Leont'ev learned of—and was disappointed by—his promotion to a consulship in Janina, in the Albanian Epirus; he had failed to receive the promotion that he had applied for—the rank of consul in Tulja. Despite this setback he used his stay in St. Petersburg to meet with prominent literary figures such as the critic Pavel Vasil'evich Annenkov and critic and philosopher Nikolai Nikolaevich Strakhov, to whom he showed his novel "Reka vremen" (The Stream of Time). Leont'ev intended this work as a monumental epic describing the life of his family.

In July 1871 Leont'ev became sick. While all his symptoms suggested cholera, his illness in fact turned out to be psychosomatic, for it had followed the news of his mother's death. In a letter written to Vasilii Vasil'evich Rozanov on 14 August 1891, the year that Leont'ev himself died, he claims that at the time of his 1871 illness he had a vision of a woman who stayed next to his bed, and he believed he was being visited by the Mother of God. During a two-hour-long ordeal, his repressed guilt found sublimation in the form of a religious prayer when he confessed his sins to the icon of the Holy Virgin. Before her Leont'ev promised to become a simple monk and refrain from all forms of indulgence. Rozanov maintains that, because he was a pathologist, Leont'ev saw visions of physical suffering and death—such as dissected corpses and decaying flesh—all of which evoked in him a natural fear of physical suffering. Leont'ev's concept of personal responsibility before God for sins committed was linked to his concept of transcendental egotism. According to Rozanov, Leont'ev saw himself in a one-on-one relationship with God—hence his low esteem for Slavophilic concepts of group responsibility and communal religion. His miraculous recovery from his cathartic illness, which occurred after he had taken a vow to become a monk, was in keeping with the psychological nature of his disorder.

After his recovery, as an impulsive gesture of sacrifice, Leont'ev threw the manuscript of "Reka vremen" into the fire. As an epic about his family and his childhood development, it might have also included traces of his admiration for, and attachment to, Fedosia Petrovna, as well as other personal psychological peculiarities—peculiarities that he often divulges in his novels. Therefore the manuscript likely contained compromising, self-analytical material that detailed his indulgences.

At this time, after resigning from his position in the Asiatic Department for health reasons, he started work on his major ideological tract, *Vizantizm i slavianstvo* (Byzantinism and Slavdom, 1876). Leont'ev's need to express a conservative and restrictive ideology was a manifestation of his Christian awakening. The elders at Mount Athos did not encourage his stay at the monastery, and he settled in Constantinople, living on a small pension from the Asiatic Department. He stayed in Constantinople from 1872 until 1874, during which time he finished his manifesto *Vizantizm i slavianstvo* and two important articles: "Panslavizm i greki" (Pan-Slavism and the Greeks) and "Panslavizm na Afone" (Pan-Slavism on Mount Athos), published in *Russkii vestnik* (The Russian Messenger) in 1873 and 1973, respectively. In both articles Leont'ev goes against the official Slavophilic sentiment and defends the Greek Church. The idea of Byzantium was, according to Leont'ev, a central idea of the Russian state. In Leont'evian formalist philosophy, an idea constitutes a basis for a form and gives a state its shape, not allowing its disintegration. In the sphere of politics the Byzantine idea translates into the form of an autocratic state; in the sphere of religion it represents the opposite of Western churches, which have been fractured by schisms throughout history. Byzantium, with its emphasis on personal faith, repudiates any hope of universal happiness and thus withstands the trend of panhumanism and political egalitarianism. Leont'ev considered Byzantium a non-Russian phenomenon, one particularly beneficial to the Russian nation. Like Chaadaev, he felt that Russians were rather colorless Europeans with imitative ideas and that they lacked creativity and an originality of thought and expression. He explained the lack of creativity in the national sense by asserting that the Russian aristocracy and peasantry were not sufficiently close to create the friction necessary for what Leont'ev termed the *slozhnoe tsvetenie* (complex flowering) of society, the result of which is the production of an original culture.

Throughout his work—and particularly in *Vizantizm i slavianstvo*—Leont'ev espoused the idea that the universe is governed by a *triedinyi* (triune) law of evolution. According to this idea, a life cycle consists of three stages: *pervichnaia prostota* (primeval simplicity), *slozhnoe tsvetenie*, and *vtorichnoe uproshchenie* (resimplification). Leont'ev pictured contemporary Europe in the third stage, which he believed was identical to an end. He wanted to freeze the development of Russia so that it did not reach this third stage of unification and *smeshenie* (fusion). For him the fundamental law of the beautiful existed in diversity within unity. Social diversity was needed to save society from the resimplification that in organic matter was synonymous with death. Freedom in nature destroyed life, as it allowed disintegration of form. Leont'ev thus identified freedom and egalitarianism as anti-aesthetical, ugly, and deadly. Consequently, he believed that during the reign of Tsar Nicholas I, Russia had undergone a period of cultural productivity, in which societal stagnation was stopped by measures of political control. Leont'ev, as a biologist, claimed that the preservation of Russia from stagnation could be achieved by freezing its organism, thereby stopping cultural rot and decay. He likewise

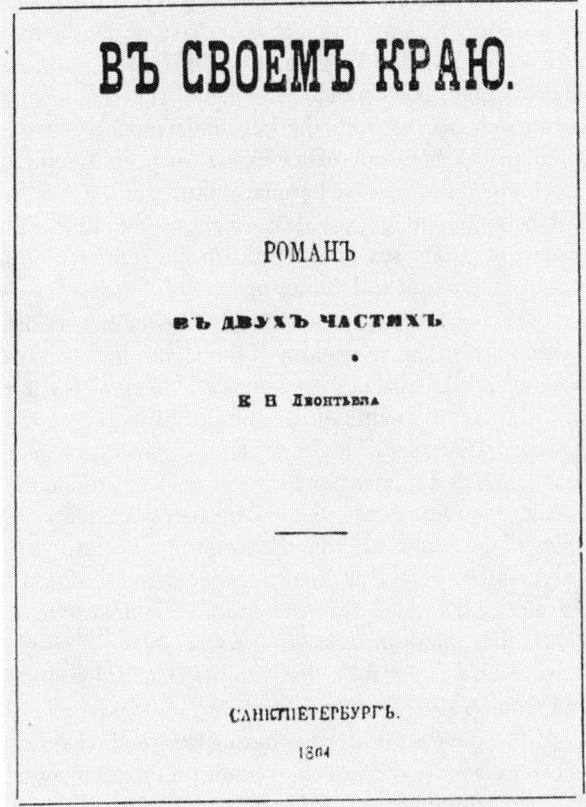

Title page for Leont'ev's novel V svoem kraiu *(In My Own Land), an expression of his anti-egalitarian, realist views on art (Leont'ev, Moia literaturnaia sud'ba. Avtobiografiia, 1965)*

used this biological metaphor to emphasize his understanding of the State as an organism composed of many human bodies. His aestheticism—the result of his repentant conversion from a life of debauchery—is manifested in this language of organic body politics.

Leont'ev returned to Russia from Greece in 1874. That same year, he lived for six months as a novice at the Nikolo-Ugresh monastery near Moscow, leaving when he became unable to withstand the hardships of monastic life, and settled on his estate at Kudinovo. From 1880 until 1887 he served on the Moscow censorship committee. Leont'ev's impressions of life in exotic locales continued to feed his artistic imagination. He published *Iz zhizni khristian v Turtsii* (The Lives of Christians in Turkey), his cycle of novels, in 1876, and his autobiographical novel, *Egipetskii golub'* (The Egyptian Dove), was serialized in *Russkii vestnik* (The Russian Messenger) in 1881 and 1882. In *Iz zhizni khristian v Turtsii* he provides colorful ethnographic descriptions of the lives of both Christians and Muslims in the Balkans. In *Egipetskii golub'* Leont'ev returns to the theme of a life lived for pleasure and aesthetic fulfillment. He relives his own experiences through the life of his long-standing autobiographical hero, Ladnev. Ladnev's passionate longing for the object of his desire, Masha Antoniadi, is understood by the narrator as a command from nature and thus as an inner state of being. His condition—a languid state of longing for an intimate act with the beautiful woman—is compared to the behavior of an exotic bird, an Egyptian dove. The dove, like the heroine, epitomizes the duality of Christian and pagan ideas, such as the torturous abstention from sex and eroticism and the conflict between the moral and the aesthetic.

This dichotomy, present in all of Leont'ev's works, is embodied in the symbolism of the names for both the heroine and the bird in *Egipetskii golub'*. "Masha" is short for "Mariia," the name of the Mother of God, but her surname, "Antoniadi," is Greek. The Egyptian dove likewise connotes a dual symbolism—the ancient Orient and its cult of fertility as well as the Christian symbol for the purity of the soul freed from the constraints of flesh; similarly, Andrei Belyi later used the dove to symbolize the castrates in his novel *Serebrianyi golub'* (The Silver Dove, 1909). The hero in *Egipetskii golub'* is himself caught between his longing for unity with the beautiful and elegant woman and his quest to renounce his sexuality.

The dove is described as having close anthropomorphic associations with human passions; it makes a sound that seems to signify the conflicted feelings of torment and joy that accompany the state of being in love. The degree of suffering embodied in the dove's cry parallels Ladnev's experience with Masha. The hero experiences a state of unsatisfied yearning, and he is able to cultivate this contradictory state by refraining from physical closeness with the heroine—although he discovers in the process many features about Masha, with which he delights to be afflicted. Fully aware of the subconscious complexities of feelings, Leont'ev depicts emotions in sets of contradictions. He chooses the parallelism between the hero and the Egyptian dove to express his understanding of love on both a symbolic level and on the level of organic similarities in nature. His worldview was built on the parallelism between biology and history; human emotions were manifestations of a state of complex flowering, which he considered the highest and most aesthetically valuable part of the life of an organism or of human society.

In his pamphlet *Nashi novye khristiane* (Our New Christians, 1882) Leont'ev condemns what he calls the "rosy Christianity" of Fyodor Dostoevsky and Leo Tolstoy, along with their hopes of an earthly Jerusalem. Leont'ev's faith, following his Christian awakening, was based on a fear of God's retribution for sins and transgressions committed; it was not unlike the faith of the writer Nikolai Gogol, who also burned the manuscript for the second part of his novel *Pokhozhdenie Chichikova, ili Mertvye dushi. Poema* (The Adventures of Chichikov, or Dead Souls. A Narrative Poem, 1842) in a gesture of sac-

rifice similar to Leont'ev's own. Leont'ev maintains in his essay that the forms of Christianity preached by Dostoevsky and Tolstoy lack the sobriety of real Christianity, which is a religion of strict observation of laws and everyday prayer and whose adherents fear God and abandon earthly pleasures for the sake of personal salvation. His characterization of Dostoevsky's Christianity as "rosy" was based on his personal monastic experience and his acquaintance with the elders of the Optina Pustyn' monastery, who together had ostensibly served as Dostoevsky's model for the all-loving and all-forgiving Father Zosima in *Brat'ia Karamazovy* (The Brothers Karamazov, 1880). Leont'ev had visited the monastery, which was located near Kaluga, in 1874 and claimed that the elders were somber and had nothing in common with Dostoevsky's depiction.

Leont'ev made his most programmatic pronouncements about Russian literature in the age of Realism in his essay, published as a book, *Analiz, stil' i veianie. O romanakh grafa L. N. Tolstogo. Kriticheskii etiud* (An Analysis, Style and Tendencies: On the Novels of Count L. N. Tolstoy, 1890). This work did not attract in vain the attention of formalist critic Boris Mikhailovich Eikhenbaum, who saw in it the first proper manifestations of an approach to literature based on the merits of literary devices rather than of ideological values. In *Analiz, stil' i veianie* Leont'ev declares that not only *what* is said but also *how* it is said is of equal importance to him; he thus proclaims the principle of the unity of form and content—the main principle of Russian formalist poetics. In this essay he makes harsh judgments against the neurotic nature of Dostoevsky's writing (he dislikes the intensity of Dostoevskian heroes) as well as against Tolstoy's excessive psychological detail. For Leont'ev, Gogol—the founding father of the *natural'naia shkola* (natural school) in Russian literature—was responsible for the distasteful literary practice of emphasizing the ugly and unhealthy side of life and promoting the purely aesthetic (amoral) value of narration. Leont'ev treated literary imitations of peasant speech and portrayals of the habits of the poorly educated Russian classes as an artificial and vulgar tool. He challenged the effectiveness of this method as a device for establishing authenticity in a work of literature.

Leont'ev's views on literature and Realism had a major impact on the writer, critic, and philosopher Rozanov. As Leont'ev's main admirer and disciple, Rozanov inherited a passionate hatred for the politically destructive role of literature in Russian society and for the style of narration belonging to the *natural'naia shkola*. Both dislikes are manifested in Rozanov's innovative approach to literature, called "parataxis," a disjointed form of narration that consists of seemingly unrelated pieces that nonetheless form a homogenous meaning—a narrative technique intended to negate and challenge both the style and content of traditional Russian literature. Leont'ev's *Pis'ma k Vasiliiu Rozanovu* (Letters to Vasilii Rozanov, 1981), written in the last year of his life, constitutes an important historical document that provides insight into Leont'ev's personal life and worldview. Also in 1891 Rozanov began writing an article about Leont'ev, titled "Esteticheskoe pominanie istorii" (An Aesthetic Approach to History), and he sent Leont'ev the first draft; the article remained unpublished. Leont'ev considered Rozanov, together with the priest and publicist Iosif Ivanovich Fudel', to be one of the few people who understood his ideas without distorting them. Rozanov states that he enjoyed a rapport with Leont'ev because of the similarity between their temperaments. He compares Leont'ev to the Old Testament prophets who had the courage to put up a fight with God. When, after Leont'ev's death, Rozanov looked through Leont'ev's personal library, he found a book on Alcibiades, the famous debaucher from ancient Athens. Comparing Leont'ev to this hero from pagan Greece, who, because of his courage, knew no inhibitions or restraints, Rozanov stresses Leont'ev's honesty and generosity; he claims—based on knowledge gained from private sources—that Leont'ev treated the people around him, including his servant, with kindness and respect. He reveals that, at the same time, this kind and noble man became enraged at the sight of disrespect shown by simple people toward authority. Rozanov's insight into Leont'ev's character remains an extremely valuable source of knowledge about a writer who was stigmatized by his contemporaries for his alleged immorality.

Leont'ev's characteristic refusal to belong to any group was expressed in a semiotic manner by the way he chose to live during the last years of his life. When he left his native Kudinovo and moved to the Optina Pustyn' monastery after retiring from his government post in 1887, he lived in a house on the border between the town and the monastery. He filled his relatively spacious abode with family furniture and ornaments that he brought with him from his estate. His wife, who had suffered from a psychological illness since the late 1860s, accompanied him there. During the last year of his life Leont'ev finally entered the monastic discipline and was assigned to the Trinity-Sergius monastery near Moscow. He had been under the aesthetic spell of his mother's house since he was a boy, and it remained an ideal of physical comfort and narcissistic pleasure for him. When he entered Trinity-Sergius, however, he cut off his link to the domestic microcosm that he had created in imitation of that feminine ideal and gave up for the first time his family belongings and his personal aesthetic comforts. He also orchestrated a symbolic rebirth by changing his name to Kliment, but the organic death that he so feared came nonetheless. There was little fresh air within the monastery walls, and his room did not provide him with the illusion of the comfort of uterine space that he so craved. He fell ill with a cold and died of pneumonia on 12 November 1891. His brethren at the monastery decided to bury him as a layman rather than as a monk, and the hybridism of the two vocations within Leont'ev himself might have been the reason why. Therefore, he was buried not in but near the Gethsemane hermitage of the Trinity-Sergius monastery. Rozanov, Leont'ev's talented disciple and loyal friend, was buried next to him upon his own death twenty-eight years later.

Just as Leont'ev was caught in life between his aesthetic and erotic needs on the one hand, and his desire to repress and sublimate these needs on the other, so too are his writings full of paradoxes and dualities. His need to reconcile those categories that were treated as binary by Christianity—aesthetics and ethics, life and death, transgression and punishment, and erotic love for both men and women—led him to create new categories. These categories, which are composed of paradoxes and a quest for holistic unity, became a subject of inquiry for his younger contemporaries.

Konstantin Nikolaevich Leont'ev was not a Pan-Slavist; he was interested in Christian Orthodoxy rather than in affinities by Slavic blood. The most telling example of his rejection of any racist and ethnic nationalism is found in his view that race is meaningless without its own system of religious and political ideas. In his correspondence with Rozanov he dismissed the notions of "pure blood" and "kinship by blood" as nonsense and maintained that all great nations are of mixed blood. Leont'ev's rejection of such nationalistic beliefs and his balanced treatment of the complex, multinational cultures of the Balkans effectively challenged the nationalism of the Slavophiles as well as the accepted boundary between the European self and the Oriental other. A victim of the cultural beliefs of his epoch, he left behind liberating fictional accounts of love, which for him transgressed the boundaries of both gender and religion. Leont'ev's main contribution to Russian literature was his attempt to free it from the clichés of the *natural'naia shkola*. Through *Analiz, stil' i veianie* he laid the groundwork for an analysis in which the meaning of a work of art is not separable from the form of its expression, and the essay is even today considered his most important work on the history of Russian literature.

Letters:

Pamiati K. N. Leont'a; Pis'ma K. N. Leont'eva k Anatoliiu Aleksandrovu, edited by Anatolii Aleksandrov (Sergiev Posad, 1915);

Iz neizdannykh pisem Konstantina Leont'eva, edited by Arkhimandrit Kiprian (Paris, 1959);

Pis'ma k Vasiliiu Rozanovu, edited by Vasilii Vasil'evich Rozanov (London: Nina Karsov, 1981);

"Kto pravee? Pis'ma k V. S. Solov'evu. Pis'mo tret'e," edited by G. Kremnev, *Nash sovremennik,* no. 12 (1991);

Izbrannye pis'ma: 1854–1891, edited by Damir Solov'ev (St. Petersburg: Pushkinskii fond, 1993).

Bibliography:

Iurii K. Ivask, [Bibliography], in *Konstantin Leont'ev: Zhizn' i tvorchestvo* (Bern: H. Lang, 1974).

Biographies:

Pamiati Konstantina Nikolaevicha Leont'eva. 1891. Literaturnyi sbornik (St. Petersburg: Sirius, 1911);

N. A. Berdiaev, *Konstantin Leont'ev: Ocherk iz istorii russkoi religioznoi mysli* (Paris: YMCA Press, 1926); translated by George Reavey as *Leontiev* (Orono, Me.: Academic International, 1968);

Stephen Lukashevich, *Konstantin Leontev (1831–1891): A Study in Russian "Heroic Vitalism"* (New York: Pageant Press, 1967);

Alexander Obolensky, "Konstantin Nikolaevic Leont'ev: An Expository Study and Analysis of His Thought as Reflected in His Life and His Writing," dissertation, University of Pennsylvania, 1967;

Iurii K. Ivask, *Konstantin Leont'ev: Zhizn' i tvorchestvo* (Bern: H. Lang, 1974);

D. M. Volodikhin, *"Vysokomernyi strannik": Filosofiia i zhizn' Konstantina Leont'eva* (Moscow: Manufaktura, 2000).

References:

S. G. Bocharov, "Esteticheskoe okhranenie' v literaturoi kritike (Konstantin Leont'ev o russkoi literature)," *Kontekst* (1977): 142–193;

Ioachim Diec, "Konstantin Leontiev and His Philosophical Counterparts," *Slavica Orientalis,* 43, no. 4 (1994): 447–455;

E. W. Dowler, "Two Conservative Views of Nationality and Personality: A. A. Grigor'ev and K. N. Leont'ev," *Studies in Soviet Thought,* 41, no. 1 (January 1991): 19–32;

Boris Mikhailovich Eikhenbaum, *Skvoz' literaturu: Sbornik statei* (The Hague: Mouton, 1962);

Semen Liudvigovich Frank, "Mirosozertsanie K. Leont'eva," in his *Filosofiia i zhizn': Etiudy i nabroski po filosofii kul'tury* (St. Petersburg: D. E. Zhukovsky, 1910), pp. 382–389;

P. Gaidenko, "Naperekor istoricheskomu protsesu (Konstantin Leont'ev–literaturnyi kritik)," *Voprosy literatury,* 18, no. 5 (1974): 159–205;

Dmitry Khanin, "What Was Leont'ev to Rozanov?" *Canadian Slavonic Papers,* 41, no. 1 (1999): 69–84;

G. Ivask, "Konstantin Leontiev's Fiction," *Slavic Review,* 20 (1961): 622–627;

K. N. Leont'ev–Pro et Contra: Lichnost' i tvorchestvo Konstantina Leont'eva v otsenke russkikh myslitelei i issledovatelei, 1891–1917 gg.: Antologiia, 2 volumes, edited by D. K. Burlaka (St. Petersburg: Khristianskii gumanitarnyi institut, 1995);

Glenn Kronin, "Konstantin Leont'ev: Creative Reaction," in *Ideology in Russian Literature,* edited by Richard Freeborn and Jane Grayson (New York: St. Martin's Press, 1990), pp. 99–115;

J. E. Kurland, "Leontiev's Views on the Course of Russian Literature," *American Slavic and East European Review,* 16 (1957): 260–274;

D. S. Mirsky, *A History of Russian Literature from Its Beginnings to 1900,* edited by Francis J. Whitfield (New York: Vintage, 1958), pp. 339–346;

Henrietta Mondry, "Another Literary Parody on Chernyshevsky in K. Leont'ev's *In My Own Land,*" *Die Welt Der Slaven,* 35, no. 2 (1990): 255–275;

Mondry and Sally Thompson, *Konstantin Leont'ev: An Examination of His Major Fiction* (Moscow: Nauka, 1993);

A. V. Repnikov, *"Esteticheskii amoralizm" v proizvedeniiakh K. N. Leont'eva* (Moscow, 1999);

Vasilii Vasil'evich Rozanov, "Teoriia istoricheskogo progressa i upadka," *Russkii vestnik,* 1 (1892): 156–188; 2 (1892): 7–35; 3 (1892): 281–327;

Nicholas Rzhevsky, *Russian Literature and Ideology: Herzen, Dostoevsky, Leontiev, Tolstoy, Fadeyev* (Urbana: University of Illinois Press, 1983).

Papers:

The papers of Konstantin Nikolaevich Leont'ev are held in Moscow at the Russian State Archive of Literature and Art (RGALI), fond 290, which includes the second part of *Dve izbrannitsy* (first part published 1867) and at the State Literary Museum (GLM), fond 196. In St. Petersburg Leont'ev's papers are housed at the Russian National Library (RNB) and the Russian State Historical Archive (RGIA), fond 776.

Aleksandr Ivanovich Levitov

(20 July 1835? – 4 January 1877)

Kenneth Lantz
University of Toronto

BOOKS: *Stepnye ocherki,* 3 volumes (St. Petersburg & Moscow: V. E. Genkel' & V. P. Plemiannikov, 1865–1867; revised and enlarged, 2 volumes, Moscow: A. I. Mamontov, 1874)–includes "Sapozhnik Shkurlan," translated by Leo Wiener as "Shoemaker Cock-of-the-Boots," in *Anthology of Russian Literature from the Earliest Period to the Present Time,* 2 volumes (New York & London: Putnam, 1903), II: 417–427;

Moskovskie nory i trushchoby, by Levitov and Mikhail Alekseevich Voronov, 2 volumes (St. Petersburg: N. G. Ovsianinkov, 1866; enlarged, St. Petersburg: V. E. Genkel', 1869); revised and enlarged as *Zhizn' moskovskikh zakoulkov* (Moscow: A. I. Mamontov, 1875);

Dvorianka. Vyselki (St. Petersburg, 1868);

Babushka Maslikha. Stepnye ocherki (St. Petersburg, 1868);

Sosedi. Stepnye ocherki (St. Petersburg, 1868);

Ulichnye kartinki. Ocherki (St. Petersburg, 1868);

Gore sel, dorog i gorodov. Povesti, rasskazy, ocherki i kartiny iz narodnogo byta (Moscow: F. Ioganson, 1874);

Akhovskii posad. Stepnye nravy starogo vremeni (Moscow, 1877);

Bezpriiutnyi (Moscow: Narodnaia biblioteka, 1883);

Sobranie sochinenii, 2 volumes (Moscow: K. T. Soldatenkov, 1884);

Polnoe sobranie sochinenii, 4 volumes, with an introduction by V. A. Nikol'sky (St. Petersburg: N. F. Mertts, 1905);

Sobranie sochinenii, 8 volumes, edited by A. A. Izmailov (St. Petersburg: Prosveshchenie, 1911);

Moia familiia; [Gorbun: Rasskazy] (Leningrad: Priboi, 1926).

Editions and Collections: *Akhovskii posad. (Stepnye nravy starogo vremeni)* (Moscow: Literaturno-izdatel'skii otdel Narodnogo komissariata po prosveshcheniiu, 1919);

Rasskazy (Moscow, 1919);

Skazka i pravda. Bespriiutnyi (Moscow: Literaturno-izdatel'skii otdel Narodnogo komissariata po prosveshcheniiu, 1919);

Aleksandr Ivanovich Levitov

Sochineniia, 2 volumes, edited by I. S. Ezhov (Moscow & Leningrad: Academia, 1932, 1933);

Sochineniia, with an introduction by N. I. Sokolov (Moscow: Goslitizdat, 1956);

"Rasprava" i drugie rasskazy, with an introduction by M. Blinchevskaia (Moscow: Goslitizdat, 1959);

Sochineniia (Moscow: Khudozhestvennaia literatura, 1977);

Izbrannoe (Moscow: Moskovskii rabochii, 1982);

Izbrannye proizvedeniia (Moscow: Khudozhestvennaia literatura, 1988).

OTHER: *Durochka. A. I. Levitova–Zhenskaia taina. Ezhena Bertuu.–Ottsy i deti. G. I. Uspenskogo.–Vishnia. N. F.*

Z–ia, with a contribution by Levitov (Moscow: Zritel', 1862);

Krym. Ivana Sizogo (A. Levitov)–Maskarad. Aleksandra Diuma–Abanskie vody. Emilia Suvestra–Pervaia kukharka. Ivana Sizogo (A. Levitov), with a contribution by Levitov (Moscow: Zritel', 1862).

The life of Aleksandr Levitov, in its bare outline, is typical of many of the *raznochintsy,* those young Russian intellectuals who were neither of the gentry nor the peasantry and who were struggling to make their mark on the cultural scene in Russia in the late 1850s and 1860s. Like his contemporaries, such as the critic Nikolai Aleksandrovich Dobroliubov and the writers Nikolai Gerasimovich Pomialovsky and Fedor Mikhailovich Reshetnikov, he was born into poverty; like them, he made a painful break with the clerical tradition of his family and struggled to acquire an education and gain entry into the world of literature. After a relatively brief career marked by more poverty and alcohol abuse, he died prematurely of tuberculosis without fully developing his potential. Levitov is known primarily for his sketches (short works straddling the boundary between reportage and fiction) that portray the lives of the Russian underclasses—the peasants and the slum dwellers of Moscow. He is often seen as a Populist, although his view of the peasantry and of peasant life is by no means an idealized or even an optimistic one. Whether portraying the rural or the urban poor, Levitov presents his characters with brutal honesty and often depressing detail.

Aleksandr Ivanovich Levitov was born in the summer of 1835 into a family of minor clergy in the village of Dobroe, in Tambov province, deep in the heart of the Russian hinterland. His father, Ivan Fedorovich Levitov, was a deacon in the village church who supplemented his meager income by keeping an inn and running a school in his home for peasant children. From the age of eight Levitov assisted his father in the school and eventually taught an elementary class; here he first became acquainted with the culture and way of life of Russian peasants. His mother, Praskov'ia Prokof'evna (née Kuz'mina) Levitova, also came from a clerical family; her brother Andrei Prokof'evich Kuz'min, who was studying in a seminary, was one of the strongest positive influences of Levitov's childhood. Something of a romantic and a writer of poetry, Kuz'min introduced Levitov to literature during the summers that he spent with the family. As was usual in Russia at the time, Levitov was marked to follow his father in a career in the Church.

In 1844 he was accepted into the third grade of a nearby school for children of the clergy. The recollections by one of Levitov's fictional characters (in the sketch "Peterburgskii sluchai" [A Petersburg Incident],

1869) of his school days convey the atmosphere in which Levitov received his own early education. In the sketch the central figure dreams of

> a scurfy herd of ill-assorted urchins, half-starved and so prepared to steal anything they could lay hands upon from anyone; raised without supervision and so covered with scrapes and scratches like animals; without any good examples to guide them and so already doomed in childhood to perish as do almost all people who have not from an early age been accustomed to a healthy understanding and relationship to life's realities. . . . The strident clanging of the bell drove this herd to a set of benches like stinking stalls where they were addressed for the most part in words that were not in accepted usage in any stratum of social intercourse. The swish of supple four-foot switches, the howling of a dozen children in various stalls whose skin bore the traces of those switches, the ringing of the bell and, finally, the inculcation of utter gibberish that never ceased despite all the other hubbub—all this combined into one general uproar full of the most hideous barbarism.

After a few months Levitov was allowed to continue his studies at home on condition that he return to the school to take examinations every four months. His father needed his help to run the school, so Levitov's own studies were scheduled around his teaching duties, which went on until ten o'clock each evening.

In 1850 Levitov was accepted into the Tambov Seminary. The anxiety that the fifteen-year-old felt upon leaving his close family was tempered by his eagerness to learn—now not independently or from ill-qualified tutors but from actual professors. He did quite well at his studies initially, but the dry scholasticism and rote learning that were the rule in the seminary gradually disillusioned the intellectually curious and impressionable youth.

Even before the seminary, Levitov had developed a passion for the works of Russian writers such as Aleksandr Sergeevich Pushkin, Nikolai Vasil'evich Gogol, and Mikhail Iur'evich Lermontov, along with Charles Dickens, William Makepeace Thackeray, and Friedrich Schiller. His enthusiasm was infectious, and soon a circle of students began meeting in the evenings to read and discuss literature. His literary interests ran counter, however, to the traditions of seminary education, for his professors frowned upon secular literature. This potential conflict came to a head in the second year of Levitov's studies with the arrival of a new inspector, responsible for discipline among the students. The inspector, a monk named Hieronymus, was a narrow-minded and harsh pedant who was determined to see that every aspect of the students' lives conformed to the strictest interpretation of Church teachings and that his charges not depart from the religious texts prescribed by the program. Levitov, who had written some comical and mildly satirical verses on seminary life, aroused the monk's attention as one whose attraction toward secular literature needed immediately to be curbed.

Hieronymus disciplined Levitov for reading Dickens and again for reading Gogol. In the third year of Levitov's studies, the monk burst into his room late one night and found him reading Gogol's *Pokhozhdenie Chichikova, ili Mertvye dushi. Poema* (The Adventures of Chichikov, or Dead Souls. A Narrative Poem, 1842), best known as *Mertvye dushi* (Dead Souls), aloud to a group of classmates. Levitov later recounted the incident to his friend and first biographer, the Populist writer and ethnographer Filipp Diomidovich Nefedov, as follows:

> I was accused, without any investigation or trial, of bringing women into my room and of making obscene remarks to my superior and was sentenced to be flogged. Hieronymus knew full well that I would find punishment of that sort much more painful than expulsion from the seminary. From the moment I was summoned, along with my whole class, for administration of the punishment, I lost consciousness . . . What happened later I do not know; I know only that I was sentenced to death: I fell into a nervous collapse and came to my senses only a month later, in the hospital.

This event proved to be the catalyst that ended Levitov's clerical career. By the time he came home for the Christmas holiday in 1854, a year before completing his studies, he had made up his mind never to return to the seminary. Shortly thereafter he and a friend made their way to Moscow, on foot and with scarcely any money between them, with the intent of enrolling in medical studies at Moscow University.

Levitov's parents were devastated at this sudden end to the career they had long cherished for their obviously talented son. His mother, in fact, was so shocked when she learned the news that she collapsed and, two days later, died. His father, utterly distraught over the loss of his wife and the virtual loss of his son, soon took to drink; before long he remarried and abandoned his offspring. What had been a close and united family (Levitov had a sister, Mariia, to whom he was devoted, as well as a younger brother, Aleksei) was now barely held together by Levitov's grandmother.

In Moscow in the summer of 1855 Levitov prepared for his entrance examinations to the university, attended some lectures, and made friends among student radicals. He passed the examinations but learned that he was unlikely to be considered for one of the few vacancies that came with scholarships. With no other means of supporting himself in Moscow, he decided to try his luck in the capital and made his way, on foot once more, to the Medical-Surgical Academy in St. Petersburg. Here, in the autumn of 1855, he was admitted and eventually awarded a small scholarship. He studied diligently and passed his first year, although it was one of struggle, as he tried to survive amid desperate poverty. At the same time, he was tormented by the fate of his younger siblings, whom their grandmother had inexplicably abandoned.

Not long after the beginning of his second year of studies, Levitov was abruptly expelled from the academy. Levitov himself never spoke about the cause of this drastic event, and even his beloved sister, Mariia, to whom he wrote regularly and with whom he shared his hopes and fears, was given no explanation. She told Levitov's biographer Nefedov: "Something compelled him to leave the academy. It is some sort of terrible secret. My brother never spoke to me about this, and I am sure that he himself tried to forget this terrible truth. This event broke his spirit completely, ruined his character, and cast a pall of gloom over his pure soul." The official reason given for Levitov's expulsion was unsatisfactory performance in his studies, but academic matters likely were not the real issue, since he had done well in his first-year examinations. A Soviet scholar, Boris Pavlovich Koz'min, has argued that the explanation for this sudden event has its roots in a report—on the expulsion of three students from the Medical-Surgical Academy—that appeared in Aleksandr Ivanovich Herzen's *Kolokol* (The Bell) on 10 October 1857. *Kolokol* states that several students had been delegated by their fellows to appeal directly to Tsar Alexander II about Academy policies and financial mismanagement that kept them in virtual starvation. Koz'min argues persuasively that Levitov was a part of this student delegation (which did, in fact, manage to pass a complaint to the tsar, leading eventually to a review that uncovered widespread bribery and embezzlement of Academy funds). Koz'min speculates that the authorities of the Academy compelled Levitov to keep silent about the real reason for this abrupt end to his studies.

To compound the injustice of Levitov's expulsion, he was obliged to repay through work the small scholarship he had managed to obtain. He was sent into virtual exile, first in Vologda and then even farther from the capital to the small, remote town of Shenkursk in Arkhangel'sk province. Extremely little is known of these years other than that he worked as a medical assistant. His few letters of this period are full of concern about the fate of his sister and brother but say little about his own activities. In later life he did not speak of his dark years in exile even to his closest friends. In Shenkursk, Levitov, nervous and impressionable by nature, succumbed to a passion for alcohol, one of the few distractions that the isolated town offered. Alcohol abuse dominated the remainder of his life. In 1857 he was transferred to the town of Vel'sk, a larger center some 150 miles southwest of Shenkursk, and in the following year back to Vologda, where his exile ended in 1859.

The single positive result of these years was the beginning of Levitov's literary career. Even during his student year in St. Petersburg he had begun work on some sketches of peasant life. His friends had recognized his talent and now wrote to encourage him to continue his literary efforts; they saw this activity also as a means of helping him to endure the boredom and isolation of exile. He worked on various sketches and recollections and assembled material that appeared in his later writings. His first literary work, "Iarmarochnye stseny" (Scenes from a Village Fair), was begun in Shenkursk and Vologda. His friends in St. Petersburg tried in vain to find a publisher, but the work was still uncompleted and appeared only in 1861. This first work, like almost everything Levitov wrote, with the exception of a few short stories, was in a genre that he later claimed as his own—the *ocherk* (sketch).

The *ocherk* in Russian literature is a fictional genre, although it is a form of documentary fiction that has strong elements of reportage. If not based specifically on an author's own experiences, it creates the impression of being so and is often presented as an eyewitness account. The narrator in Levitov's *ocherki* (sketches) is often his alter ego, a disillusioned and downtrodden *raznochinets* traveler who frequents inns and taverns along his route or who finds shelter for the night with anyone who will take him in. The people he encounters—peasants, minor clerks, retired soldiers, tradesmen, and children—are beset by problems and sorrows. Several of Levitov's works have a peasant narrator whose distinctive language and outlook are conveyed in detail. Levitov has a sharp ear for dialogue and uses it to help convey the characteristics of the particular social group to which each speaker belongs. His *ocherki* have scarcely any plot; their emphasis is on character and milieu, often presented through a series of episodes that illustrate a particular situation or problem. The works are filled with naturalistic details that create a picture of the grimness of life in impoverished villages or in the shabby tenements of Moscow slums. Levitov's characters are distinctly unheroic, and he in no way idealizes them; they are most often despondent victims—either of the injustice of the system in which they live or of their own flaws and weaknesses. Still, there is no overt protest in the *ocherki* against the injustice of the social order, although the effect of Levitov's works is to evoke sympathy for the sufferings of his characters. Alcohol is a factor in many of the *ocherki*: his characters of all social levels drink, not for pleasure but in a futile attempt to escape from the frustra-

tions and miseries of their lives. Levitov derives his *ocherki* from direct experience, a fact that accounts for both their strength and their weakness: the sketches have an air of authenticity and of the flavor of real life, but at the same time their effect is sometimes that of a photograph—they reproduce an unmediated reality in which the truly significant competes with the incidental.

When Levitov was allowed to leave his exile in 1859, he made his way, again on foot, to his home province and supported himself by whatever clerical work he could find in villages along the way. In August he arrived at the home of his sister, now married to a deacon and living in Lebedian', in Tambov province. Levitov was ill and wretched; his shoes had worn through, and his feet were bleeding. He found work as a tutor to the children of a German overseer of an estate and continued writing, but he was unable to settle for long. He still had hopes of entering the university, and in the spring of 1860 he again set off on foot for Moscow, earning enough money to survive by working along the way as a temporary clerk in local administrative offices. The impressions of these trips served him well as literary raw material for years thereafter.

Again, Levitov failed to gain admission to Moscow University, and he found himself living on the streets and spending his nights under overturned boats along the embankment of the Moscow River. During this period he made acquaintances with the tramps and displaced peasants who formed much of the Moscow underclass, and characters such as these appeared in his later sketches of Moscow life. By now he had managed to complete the work he had begun in exile, "Iarmarochnye stseny," and he had begun two others—the short stories "Tseloval'nichikha" (The Tavern Keeper's Wife, *Russkain rech'* [Russian Speech], 1861) and "Sladkoe zhit'e" (A Sweet Life, *Vremia* [Time], 1861). One of the few strokes of luck in Levitov's life of adversity came during the summer of 1860. By chance he made the acquaintance of a typesetter for the literary journal *Russkii vestnik* (The Russian Messenger). Learning that Levitov was writing stories, the man asked to read some of his work; he was so taken with "Iarmarochnye stseny" that he insisted on showing the story to the literary critic and poet Apollon Aleksandrovich Grigor'ev, who was then working for the journal. Grigor'ev recognized the worth of the story, summoned Levitov, and praised the originality of his writing. Learning of Levitov's desperate circumstances, he introduced him to Mikhail Nikiforovich Katkov, the editor of *Russkii vestnik,* who gave the aspiring writer a job as assistant to the editorial secretary. The salary, 360 rubles a year for the first steady employment that Levitov had ever had, was meager, but it allowed him to live better than he had ever lived before.

The three years that followed were the happiest and most productive of Levitov's career. Russian intellectual life during this time, the high point in the reform era of the 1860s, was in a state of generally optimistic anticipation of better things to come. Russian journalism, relieved from the worst burdens of censorship, was flourishing, and in St. Petersburg in particular a whole range of new periodicals appeared. In the late summer of 1861 Levitov met the single love of his life, a Moscow seamstress (Levitov's biographer Nefedov identifies her only as K.D.), who became his common-law wife. Not much is known about her other than that she was of peasant stock, an orphan, and barely literate; she shared the vagaries of Levitov's career for the rest of his life. His first publication (the third work he had written), an excerpt of "Sladkoe zhit'e," appeared in the journal *Moskovskii vestnik* (The Moscow Messenger) in January 1861, although the journal closed before the final part of the story could be published; it appeared in full in Fyodor Dostoevsky's journal *Vremia* in August of the same year. In the spring of 1861 the journal *Russkaia rech'* published not only "Tseloval'nichikha" but also "Proezzhaia stepnaia doroga" (The Road Across the Steppe), "Nakanune Khristova dnia" (Easter Eve), and several sketches of Moscow vagrants. The first work that Levitov had written, "Iarmarochnye stseny," appeared in *Vremia* in June 1861. The less prestigious journals *Zritel'* (The Spectator) and *Razvlechenie* (Entertainment) published several of Levitov's sketches in 1862. The proceeds from these writings allowed him to escape the poverty that had accompanied him through all his early years. He was able to moderate his drinking, and the relative stability in his life was reflected in a steady stream of publications.

Levitov's restlessness and lack of direction soon resurfaced, however. An illness, probably compounded by a drinking bout, and some differences with the editorial staff of *Russkii vestnik* led to his break with that journal after only some six months of employment. The publications that readily accepted his writings—*Razvlechenie, Zritel'*, and *Russkaia rech'*—were not literary journals of the first rank. When the latter two closed, Levitov decided to try his luck in the center of Russian cultural life, St. Petersburg—where, in contrast to Moscow, the periodical press was flourishing.

In St. Petersburg, Levitov not surprisingly gravitated toward the radical and "nihilist" circles that were making their presence increasingly felt. Although he himself had no particular interest in political or social movements, he found the most sympathetic reception from fellow writers and journalists who occupied the left of the political spectrum. Among his closest friends during this period were radicals such as the writer Vasilii Ivanovich

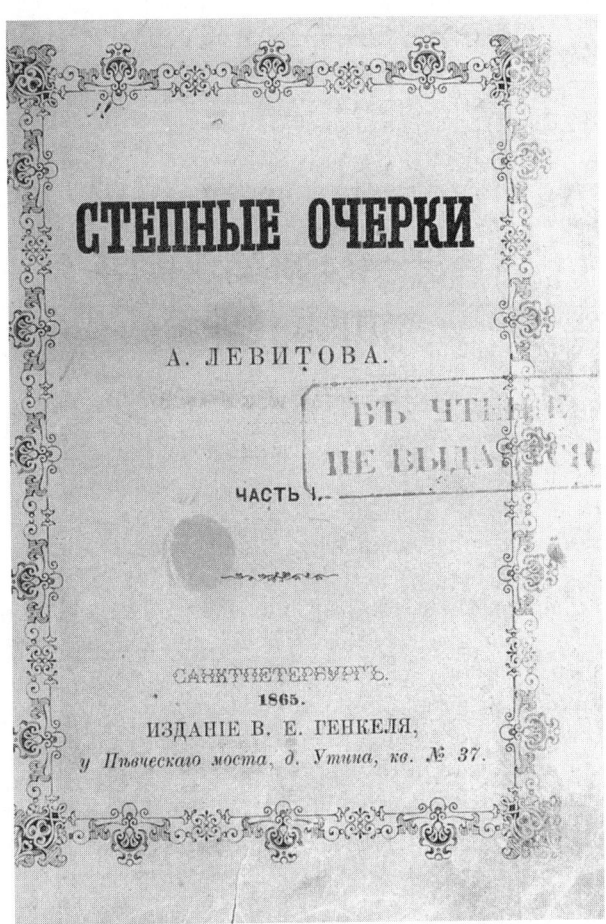

Paper cover for volume one of Levitov's well-received
Stepnye ocherki *(Sketches of the Steppe),*
considered his most significant
work (Library of Congress)

Kel'siev, the journalist and agitator Artur Benni, and the writer Vasilii Alekseevich Sleptsov. He also became acquainted with established writers such as Nikolai Alekseevich Nekrasov, Mikhail Evgrafovich Saltykov, Viktor Petrovich Burenin, and Gleb Ivanovich Uspensky. Levitov's writings appeared in *Iskra* (The Spark), the satirical supplement to *Sovremennik* (The Contemporary), the leading journal on the left; in *Biblioteka dlia chteniia* (A Reading Library); and later in *Sovremennik* itself. He also produced articles and feuilletons for many other newspapers and magazines. In all, he produced some thirty works during the first half of the 1860s. The initial publication in 1865 of a collection of Levitov's writings, *Stepnye ocherki* (Sketches of the Steppe), drew a favorable review from *Sovremennik* in April 1866; this review was the only one of Levitov's work to appear during his lifetime, and it marked the high point of his popularity. His greatest admirers were found among the younger generation and, in particular, among *raznochintsy* like himself.

Starting in the mid 1860s, Levitov increasingly turned his attention to the urban dwellers in Russia–specifically to the urban underclass. His own experiences in the cheap rooming houses of Moscow and St. Petersburg are reflected in *ocherki* such as "Moskovskie 'komnaty snebil'iu'" (Moscow "Furnished Rooms," *Biblioteka dlia chteniia*, 1863). "Nravy moskovskikh devstvennykh ulits" (The Ways of Moscow's Virgin Streets, *Moskovskie gubernskie vedomosti* [Moscow Provincial News], 1864). The lives of the people he describes–petty tradespeople, tenants of shabby rooming houses, and denizens of disreputable taverns–are beset by the same problems of grinding poverty, ignorance, and alcohol as are the figures of Levitov's peasant sketches.

Although Levitov had won himself at least a modest literary reputation, he was always plagued by a restlessness that never allowed him to stay for long in one place, even when the place happened to be a comfortable one. He also had little ability to manage his affairs, and the proceeds from his publications soon slipped through his fingers. His drinking bouts grew more frequent, and his health deteriorated. The damp cold of St. Petersburg also contributed to the advance of tuberculosis. In 1865 Levitov qualified himself at St. Petersburg University as an elementary school teacher, and in August he took a post teaching in a country school in Riazhsk, not far from his birthplace. After only a few months of teaching, however, he realized that he had made a mistake in fleeing the city and the literary life to isolate himself in the provinces. He abandoned his job and made his way back to Moscow, where he eked out a meager living by selling a few of his writings, giving private lessons, and taking short-lived teaching jobs. His literary output was scant, however, because the daily struggle to survive, coupled with his declining health, left him little time and energy for writing. He moved between Moscow and St. Petersburg several times, taught briefly in a Moscow school, and worked on the railway. His frequent drinking bouts, along with his congenital restlessness, made him an unreliable worker.

Finally, in 1868 Levitov moved to Sergiev, just outside St. Petersburg, and returned to writing. Once again the genre of the *ocherk* attracted him, and he managed to publish a few minor items in St. Petersburg magazines. These include not only more sketches of peasant life and of the Moscow slums but also autobiographical pieces such as "Moe detstvo" (My Childhood, 1870). His *ocherk* "Devichii greshok" (Maidenly Sin, 1874) concerns another of the unsavory phenomena in Russian society of the time–the social conditions that forced into prostitution innocent peasant girls who migrated to the city.

Although Levitov's literary output is predominantly in short works, during the last years of his life he was obsessed with writing a novel. In May 1870 he wrote to a friend: "I am now writing a large novel, and I have more than a hundred pages written. There's an enormous amount left to be done, but it will be finished by winter. It will be called 'Sny i fakty' (Dreams and Facts), I think, but perhaps 'Zatikhshaia buria' (The Calm after the Storm); I don't yet know for certain." He had promised the work to the liberal journal *Vestnik Evropy* (The European Messenger), but he never managed to complete it. Levitov's literary talent, as expressed in his published writings, had developed exclusively in the short form, and the rather different problems posed by the novel proved insoluble for him. In October 1870 he sent a chapter and the plan of the whole novel to Mikhail Matveevich Stasiulevich, the editor of *Vestnik Evropy*. According to the plan, Levitov's proposed novel was heavily autobiographical. The central figure was an artist who, through the frustrations of creativity and the ravages of alcohol, gradually sinks into madness. This artist had taken to drink after an exile in the far north; his life thereafter has been an unending battle against hostile circumstances. He is tormented both by his inability to create the kind of art he believes he is capable of creating and by the crushing poverty he sees around him in the Moscow slums where he spends his last days. The epilogue, as outlined by Levitov, depicts the artist lying drunk in a ditch by the highway, singing a song that none of the passersby can understand.

After many requests to the editor of the journal for advances, along with promises that the work would be completed soon, Levitov at last had to abandon the project. When he realized that he would probably never be able to complete his novel as planned, however, he did devote himself to writing an episode from it, which he hoped could be published as an independent work. He described it to Stasiulevich as follows: "This episode is called 'Govoriashchaia obez'iana' (The Talking Monkey) because the man introduced in the first chapter, in a moment of his madness when he has no one to talk to, buys a monkey that tells him things that gratify him completely and so allow him to die more or less happy." This chapter was eventually published in Svet (Light) in 1879, after Levitov's death. As an epigraph for the story Levitov chose a few lines from a poem by Aleksandr Ivanovich Polezhaev, "Providenie" (Providence, 1828): "I was perishing– / My evil genius / Was triumphant. . . ."

Levitov's own evil genius was clearly gaining the upper hand. As he wrote to a friend on 20 January 1871: "My dear friend! The drink is killing me. I try and I try to keep my courage up, but still I keep on drinking. Even when I'm absolutely sober I feel that I'm still drunk. It seems that Death is walking all around me. I summon up all my meager strength to keep myself out of the madhouse, but there's nothing that can be done." Levitov spent the last six years of his life restlessly moving between Moscow and St. Petersburg. He sought treatment for alcoholism from a specialist and managed to give up drinking for a time. In the mid 1870s his stories and sketches again began appearing in newspapers and journals. He taught school again briefly, and for six months in 1871 he served as the de facto editor of an illustrated magazine, *Sïanie* (Aurora). Yet, Levitov's total lack of business acumen left him ill-equipped for survival in the cutthroat world of Russian publishing at the time. His friend the writer and journalist Pavel Vladimirovich Zasodimsky notes in "Iz literaturnykh vospominanii" (From Literary Recollections, 1881):

> Levitov sometimes liked to pretend that he was a shrewd, practical person. . . . I think I have never, ever encountered anyone less practical. He had a childish naiveté and absolutely no ability to manage his affairs advantageously. His craftiness and guile were so artless and so transparent that they could not lead even a child astray. One could only laugh at his attempts at craftiness. . . . Money, it seemed, was a burden to him. It was not often in his life, however, that he had to bear this burden. . . . He had no idea of the value of money and didn't like it; money, it seemed, reciprocated and did not like him either.

Levitov's fragile emotional state and irritability–aggravated, no doubt, by the advance of his tuberculosis and efforts to abstain from alcohol–undermined his relations with others and alienated many who were well disposed to him and who were in a position to help him. Zasodimsky, who was then beginning his own literary career, worked with Levitov during his stint on the magazine *Sïanie* and noted how obviously Levitov's health had been shattered; despite Levitov's frailty and irascibility, however, Zasodimsky writes that his friend's essential goodness remained unspoiled: "Levitov had a heart of gold. He wanted to give all of himself to help those close to him, and he was sorry for the deficiencies in his knowledge only because they hindered him from serving people. . . . He lived, by the way, entirely in accordance with the teachings of Christ, in the sense that he would share the last of whatever he had with his brethren who had nothing." Indeed, all his life Levitov had been acutely sensitive to suffering, and even during the most desperate moments of his own tragic existence, he had agonized over the fates of his beloved sister and younger brother.

In the last five years of his life, from 1872 to 1877 (apart from a few months in 1875 as a village school teacher), Levitov lived in abject poverty in wretched hovels in Moscow or on the outskirts of the city. The ravages of tuberculosis, severely compounded by alcoholism, sapped his strength. As he wrote to an editor in 1872 to assure him that he was alive and not drunk, "lying in a ditch somewhere," Levitov continued: "I'm amazed that such a thing hasn't yet happened! But now my utter apathy is so deathly that it rules out even the thought of a drinking bout. I did go on a spree once and I got so ill that I gave it up; and now I sit like an owl, responding to no one, finding joy in nothing, thinking of nothing . . . "

Levitov was also in deep despair over the lack of attention to his published writings and the complete absence of critical response to them. The radical intelligentsia who in the 1860s had been eager to read his unvarnished truth about the peasantry were, with the growth of *narodnichestvo* (Populism) in the 1870s, much more inclined toward renewed idealization of the common people as the repository of strength and truth. Levitov did continue to write, however, and he published a few more *ocherki* in the early 1870s. A third edition of his first collection, *Stepnye ocherki*, appeared in 1874, as did another collection of his previously published work, *Gore sel, dorog i gorodov* (The Woes of Villages, Roads and Towns). *Zhizn' moskovskikh zakoulkov* (The Life of Moscow's Dark Alleys), the third enlarged edition of *Moskovskie nory i trushchoby*, appeared in 1875. The royalties from these editions–some 700.00 rubles– sustained him during his final years.

By 1875 Levitov's tuberculosis had advanced to a critical point, and his last months were spent in the clinic of Moscow University. In December 1876 he ventured into the winter cold, wearing only a light overcoat, to collect a 5.00-ruble royalty that a publisher owed him. He contracted a severe cold and died in the clinic in January 1877. His friends and students from the university had to take up a collection to cover his funeral expenses.

Levitov is often categorized as a Populist writer–a predecessor of Maksim Gor'ky. Yet, he is a *narodnik* (Populist) only in the limited sense that his subject is the life of the common people in Russia, and he is a predecessor of Gor'ky only in that both write about dwellers of the Russian "lower depths." Levitov's works reflect no idealization of popular life nor any romanticizing of characters; indeed, his writings evoke the darker sides of the people he portrays. What emerges from the works, however, is not condemnation or contempt for the characters in his *ocherki,* but rather a deep sorrow over the perversion of human qualities and the waste of human capital. Speaking of the downtrodden folk who populate his stories of the Moscow slums, he told a friend and admirer, the writer Nikolai Nikolaevich Zlatovratsky: "But what dear people live in these places! . . . You would think that they've long lost any image of God, that they've been worn away by life and tossed over the fence like some worn-out women's shoes. But when you live with them a while and talk to them heart to heart, suddenly you see it, deep down inside, glowing and winking like a firefly, the soul that's come from God himself. Indeed, the concern for maintaining and nourishing "the living soul" is present, either overtly or covertly, in almost all of Levitov's works.

Aleksandr Ivanovich Levitov is remembered as a masterful practitioner of the *ocherk,* a genre that has considerable importance in Russian literature. His sketches provide portraits of rural Russia before and during the period of the great reforms of the 1860s and of the urban underclass in the latter part of that decade. The documentary value of Levitov's writings lies in their illustration of the social forces at work during the period—such as the erosion of many traditional rural values caused by the penetration of urbanism into the countryside and the dilemma of uprooted peasants forced to make their way in the cities. The literary value of his works lies in their vivid, honest, and unflinching portrayal of a range of characters and milieus from both rural and urban Russia.

Letters:

Sobranie sochinenii A. I. Levitova, 2 volumes (Moscow: K. T. Soldatenkov, 1884), I: 28–132;

M. M. Stasiulevich i ego sovremenniki v ikh perepiskie, 5 volumes, edited by Mikhail Konstantinovich Lemke (St. Petersburg: M. Stasiulevich, 1913), V: 249–256;

Neizdannye pis'ma L.N. Tolstogo, I. A. Goncharova, M. A. Nekrasova, F. M. Dostoevskogo, A. F. Pisemskogo i dr. Iz arkhiva A. N. Ostrovskogo, edited by Mikhail Danilovich Prygunov, Iu. A. Bakhrushin, and N. A. Brodsky (Moscow: Academia, 1932), pp. 195–197;

Zven'ia, 2 (1933), pp. 658–673;

To N. A. Nekrasov, edited by V. E. Evgen'ev-Maksimov, *Literaturnoe nasledstvo,* 51–52 (1949): 373–374.

Bibliographies:

I. Gvozdev, "Bibliografiia sochinenii A. I. Levitova," *Russkii arkhiv,* 12 (1907): 465–470;

D. P. Sil'chevsky, "Bibliograficheskii ukazatel' k *Sobraniiu sochinenii* A. I. Levitova," in Levitov's *Sobranie sochinenii,* 8 volumes (St. Petersburg: Prosveshchenie, 1911), VIII: 393–401;

I. S. Ezhov, "Bibliografiia A.. Levitova," in Levitov's *Sochineniia,* 2 volumes, edited by Ezhov (Moscow & Leningrad: Academia, 1932, 1933), II: 721–731;

Pisateli Lipetskogo kraia. Kratkii ukazatel' literatury (Lipetsk, 1963);

Vasilii Vasil'evich Shakhov, *Pisatel'-demokrat Levitov. Bibliograficheskii ukazatel'* (Lipetsk: Lipetskaia oblastnaia universitetskaia nauchnaia biblioteka, 1985).

Biographies:

Pavel Vladimirovich Zasodimsky, "Iz literaturnykh vospominanii," *Russkoe bogatstvo,* 12 (1881): 99–128;

Filipp Diomidovich Nefedov, "Aleksandr Ivanovich Levitov," in Levitov's *Sobranie sochinenii,* 2 volumes (Moscow: K. T. Soldatenkov, 1884), I: iii-cxxxix;

Nikolai Nikolaevich Zlatovratsky, "A. I. Levitov," in his *Vospominaniia* (Moscow: Khudozhestvennaia literatura, 1956), pp. 289–302;

Andrei Fedovorich Strukov, *Aleksandr Ivanovich Levitov* (Lipetsk: Lipetskoe knizhnoe izdatel'stvo, 1960);

Aleksei Iakovlevich Silaev, *Liry zvon kandal'nyi: Ocherki zhizni i tvorchestva A. I. Levitova* (Lipetsk: Lipetskoe knizhnoe izdatel'stvo, 1963);

Mateja Matejić, "Aleksandr Ivanovich Levitov (1835–1877): Life and Works," dissertation, University of Michigan, 1967.

References:

Iulii Isaevich Aikhenval'd, *Siluety russkikh pisatelei,* volume 3 (Moscow: Nauchnoe slovo, 1913), pp. 81–88;

Rose Glickman, "An Alternative View of the Peasantry: The *Raznochintsy* Writers of the 1860s," *Slavic Review,* 32 (1973): 693–704;

Boris Pavlovich Koz'min, "'Uzhasnaia taina' A. I. Levitova," *Katorga i ssylka,* 91, no. 6 (1932): 193–198;

L. M. Lotman, "Levitov," in *Istoriia russkoi literatury,* edited by M. P. Alekseev and others, volume 8, part 1 (Moscow & Leningrad: Nauka, 1956), pp. 617–634;

Mateja Matejić, "Major Themes in the Prose of A. I. Levitov," *Slavic and East European Journal,* 15 (1971): 184–189;

Mikhas Vasil'evich Nekhai, *Russkii demokraticheskii ocherk 60-kh godov XIX stoletiia: N. Uspenskii, V. Sleptsov, A. Levitov* (Minsk: BGU, 1971);

A. Silaev and B. Shakhov, "Nekotorye novye dannye o zhizni A. I. Levitova (po materialam Tambovskogo oblastnogo arkhiva)," *Russkaia literatura,* 2 (1965): 166–167;

Aleksandr Mikhailovich Skabichevsky, *Belletristiki-narodniki: F. Rieshetnikov, A. Levitov, Gl. Uspensky, N. Zlatovratsky i dr.: Kriticheskie ocherki* (St. Petersburg: V. S. Balashev, 1888), pp. 127–217.

Papers:

The papers of Aleksandr Ivanovich Levitov are held in St. Petersburg at the Institute of Russian Literature (IRLI, Pushkin House); at the State Archive of the Vladimir region, fond 410 (including his letters to family members and to Filipp Diomidovich Nefedov); and at the State Archive of the Tambov region, fond 186.

Apollon Nikolaevich Maikov

(23 May 1821 – 8 March 1897)

Karen Evans-Romaine
Ohio University

BOOKS: *Stikhotvoreniia* (St. Petersburg: E. Prats, 1842; enlarged, 2 books, St. Petersburg: G. A. Kushelev-Bezborodko, 1858; enlarged, 3 parts, St. Petersburg: V. P. Meshchersky, 1872); revised and enlarged as *Polnoe sobranie sochinenii*, 3 volumes (St. Petersburg: A. F. Marks, 1884)–includes "Dva mira" (complete version) and "Otzyvy istorii"; revised and enlarged edition (St. Petersburg: A. F. Marks, 1888; revised and enlarged again, 1893; revised and enlarged again, 1901; revised and enlarged again, 4 volumes edited by Petr Vasil'evich Bykov, 1914)–includes "Orel";

Dve sud'by. Byl' (St. Petersburg: E. Prats, 1845);

Ocherki Rima (St. Petersburg: I. Glazunov, 1847);

1854 god. Riad stikhotvorenii po povodu vostochnoi voiny (St. Petersburg: Tipografiia Imperatorskoi Akademii nauk, 1855)–includes "Klermontovskii sobor";

Novye stikhotvoreniia (1858–1863) (St. Petersburg: Katkov, 1864)–includes "Neapolitanskii al'bom (Miss Meri)" and excerpts of "Novogrecheskie pesni";

"4-oe aprelia 1866 g." Dva stikhotvoreniia (St. Petersburg: V. Golovin, 1866);

Iz russkoi istorii (St. Petersburg: A. Transhel', 1877);

Iz-za chego poshli voiny Rossii s musul'manstvom, 3 books (St. Petersburg: Postaiannaia kommissiia po ustroistvu narodnykh chtenii, 1883);

Ivan Tretii Vasil'evich (St. Petersburg: Postaiannaia kommissiia po ustroistvu narodnykh chtenii, 1885);

"30 aprelia". Stikhotvoreniia (1883–1888) (St. Petersburg: A. F. Marks, 1888);

Izbrannye proizvedeniia, edited by L. S. Geiro, Biblioteka poeta, Bol'shaia seriia (Leningrad: Sovetskii pisatel', 1977);

Sochineniia, 2 volumes, edited by L. S. Geiro, with an introduction by Fedor Iakovlevich Priima (Moscow: Pravda, 1984).

Editions and Collections: *Stikhi* (Berlin: Mysl', 1921);

Stikhotvoreniia, edited, with an introduction, by Nikolai Leonidovich Stepanov, Biblioteka poeta, Malaia seriia (Moscow: Sovetskii pisatel', 1937); republished as *Izbrannoe*, edited by N. M. Gaidenkov,

Apollon Nikolaevich Maikov

Biblioteka poeta, Malaia seriia (Leningrad: Sovetskii pisatel', 1952); republished as *Izbrannye proizvedeniia*, edited by Stepanov, Biblioteka poeta, Malaia seriia (Leningrad: Sovetskii pisatel', 1957);

Lev Mei. Dramy.–A. Maikov. Dramaticheskie poemy, edited by E. I. Prokhorov (Moscow: Iskusstvo, 1961)–

includes "Tri smerti," "Smert' Liutsiia," "Dva mira," and "Strannik";

Stikhotvoreniia, edited by V. I. Ivashnev (Moscow: Sovetskaia Rossiia, 1980);

Stikhotvoreniia i poemy, edited by Geiro (Leningrad: Lenizdat, 1987);

Stikhotvoreniia (Stavropol': Knizhnoe izdatel'stvo, 1988)–includes *Bal'dur. Pesn' o solntse, po skazaniiam skandinavskoi Eddy.*

Edition in English: "Several Words about Dostoevsky," in *The Dostoevsky Archive: Firsthand Accounts of the Novelist from Contemporaries' Memoirs and Rare Periodicals,* compiled by Peter Sekirin, with an introduction by Igor Volgin (Jefferson City, N.C.: McFarland, 1997), pp. 287–290.

OTHER: "Son" and "Kartina vechera," as M., in *Odesskii al'manakh na 1840 god* (Odessa: Gorodskaia tipografiia, 1839);

"Mashen'ka," in *Peterburgskii sbornik,* edited by Nikolai Alekseevich Nekrasov, Fyodor Mikhailovich Dostoevsky, and Ivan Sergeevich Turgenev (St. Petersburg: Eduard Prats, 1846);

Anonymous, *Slovo o polku Igoreve. Neskol'ko predvaritel'nykh zamechanii ob etom pamiatnike,* translated by Maikov (St. Petersburg, 1870); republished as *Slovo o polku Igoreve,* edited by Dmitrii Sergeevich Likhachev, Biblioteka poeta, Malaia seriia (Leningrad: Sovetskii pisatel', 1949);

Anonymous, *Bal'dur. Pesn' o solntse, po skazaniiam skandinavskoi Eddy,* translated by Maikov (St. Petersburg, 1871);

"Dva mira," in *Sbornik "Grazhdanina,"* part 2 (St. Petersburg, 1872), pp. 1–56;

Literaturnyi sbornik proizvedenii studentov Imperatorskogo gosudarstvennogo Sankt-Peterburgskogo Universiteta, edited by Maikov, Dmitrii Vasil'evich Grigorovich, and Iakov Petrovich Polonsky (St. Petersburg, 1896).

SELECTED PERIODICAL PUBLICATIONS–
UNCOLLECTED: "Avtoram 'Pis'ma k Longinovu'" (1854), in S. Reisner and A. Maksimovich, "Dva stikhotvoreniia Ap. Maikova o Nekrasove. Iz istorii literaturnoi bor'by 1850-kh gg.," *Literaturnoe nasledstvo,* 49–50 (1946): 614–618;

"Neopublikovannye proizvedeniia," *Ezhegodnik Rukopisnogo otdela Pushkinskogo doma. 1974* (Leningrad, 1976);

"Neizdannye stikhotvoreniia," *Ezhegodnik Rukopisnogo otdela Pushkinskogo doma. 1976* (Leningrad, 1978);

"Neopublikovannaia stat'ia A. N. Maikova," edited by P. A. Gaponenko, *Russkaia literatura,* 2 (2001): 102–105.

Apollon Maikov is a significant figure among poets in the age of realism in Russia. Critics generally do not rank Maikov among the best poets of his generation, an honor reserved for Afanasii Afanas'evich Fet, Nikolai Alekseevich Nekrasov, and their older colleague Fedor Ivanovich Tiutchev; yet, Maikov was well respected during his time. He, Fet, and Iakov Petrovich Polonsky are often classified together as poets of "pure art" during an age when socially engaged prose dominated the Russian literary landscape. Maikov wrote little prose and established his career almost entirely on his poetry; he was especially admired for his anthological verse–short lyrics written in the classical Greek style on light or melancholy subjects. In addition, he wrote *poemy* (long narrative poems) and lyric dramas, most of which can be considered important milestones in his career. Maikov also translated the works of classical and modern poets. He is renowned for his 1870 translation of the medieval Russian epic *Slovo o polku Igoreve* (The Lay of Prince Igor's Campaign, written circa twelfth century and first published in 1800).

Apollon Nikolaevich Maikov was born in Moscow on 23 May 1821 into a well-educated and cultured noble family. His ancestors included scholars, writers, and enlightened noblemen since the era of Tsar Ivan IV (Ivan the Terrible). Maikov's great-great-uncle was Vasilii Ivanovich Maikov, the eighteenth-century poet and author of the long comic poem "Elisei, ili razdrazhennyi Vakkh" (Elisei, or Bacchus Enraged, 1771). Maikov's father, Nikolai Apollonovich Maikov, was a painter and academician. His mother, Evgeniia Petrovna (née Gusiatnikova) Maikova, was a highly educated noblewoman who wrote verse and prose published in the journal *Biblioteka dlia chteniia* (A Reading Library), both anonymously and under the pseudonym E. Podol'skaia. Thus, Maikov was born into an atmosphere that fostered a literary career. According to Petr Vasil'evich Bykov's introduction to the 1914 edition of Maikov's *Polnoe sobranie sochinenii,* family friend Ivan Aleksandrovich Goncharov, author of the novel *Oblomov* (1859), recalled that the household "bubbled with life"; Nikolai Ivanovich and Evgeniia Petrovna were hosts to scholars, writers, and artists of several generations and were fond of encouraging young talent.

Maikov was the eldest of four sons. The second son, Valerian, became well known as a literary critic and publicist. The third, Vladimir, also established a literary career as a writer, translator, and publisher of the children's journals *Podsnezhnik* (Snowdrop, 1858–1862) and *Semeinye vechera* (Family Evenings, 1864–1870). The youngest son, Leonid, became a literary historian, a scholar of the poet Aleksandr Sergeevich Pushkin, and an ethnographer; he was named vice president of the Academy of Sciences and assistant director of the Imperial Public Library in St. Petersburg. Maikov spent his childhood years both on his father's country estate, Nikol'skoe–located outside Moscow, not far from the Trinity and St. Sergius Monastery in Sergiev Posad– and on his grandmother's estate in the village of Chepchikho, in the Klin district, near Moscow. These bucolic surroundings, similar to those depicted in novels by his contemporaries–including Sergei Timofeevich Aksakov and Leo Tolstoy–later inspired Maikov's nature poems.

In 1833, when Maikov was twelve years old, he was sent to live with his uncle in St. Petersburg at a pension that prepared young men for higher education at military academies. The following year the Maikov family moved to the capital, and the boy rejoined his parents. The Maikov household became a literary and artistic salon visited by, among others, the Romantic poet Vladimir Grigor'evich Benediktov. Maikov was tutored at home by family friend Vladimir Andreevich Solonitsyn, a poet who worked with Osip Ivanovich Senkovsky at *Biblioteka dlia chteniia,* and by Goncharov, who had just graduated from Moscow University. While guiding Maikov through his gymnasium studies, Solonitsyn proposed the idea of a manuscript journal, *Podsnezhnik* (different from the children's journal of the same name), which appeared from 1835 until 1838 and was produced at the Maikov home; it was succeeded in 1839 by the manuscript almanac *Lunnye nochi* (Moonlit Nights). Contributors to these publications included well-known writers and poets such as Goncharov and Benediktov, as well as Maikov's mother and two of his brothers. Maikov's father provided illustrations. Maikov himself also published verse and articles in the journals; an article titled "Okhota za povestiami i anekdotami" (Hunt for Novellas and Anecdotes) in *Podsnezhnik* constituted his unofficial literary debut in 1835.

Maikov's first official appearance in print was also in 1835, with his poem "Orel" (Eagle), written that year and sent, probably by Solonitsyn, to the established journal *Biblioteka dlia chteniia.* This poem can be found in the four-volume 1914 complete edition of Maikov's works but does not appear in later scholarly editions. According to Vadim Solomonovich Baevsky's article in *Russkie Pisateli 1800–1917: Biograficheskii slovar',* Maikov wrote that he began to compose poetry at the age of fifteen, but this publication confirms that his literary career actually began when he was thirteen, since "Orel" passed censorship for publication in February 1835.

Maikov completed the equivalent of a gymnasium education in 1837 at the age of sixteen. He dreamed of becoming a painter like his father but, at the encouragement of Solonitsyn, instead entered the law faculty of St. Petersburg University that year. He later wrote in a letter to I. S. Remerov that he regretted

СТИХОТВОРЕНІЯ

АПОЛЛОНА МАЙКОВА.

Санктпетербургъ.
1842.

Title page for Maikov's first verse collection, featuring nature poetry, imitative classical verse, and poems inspired by Middle Eastern culture (Kilgour Collection of Russian Literature, Harvard University Library)

not having studied either philology or mathematics, particularly because he had impressed university faculty in both subjects at his entrance examinations. Apparently, he was indebted to his brother Valerian for his education in the humanities. Maikov attended lectures in Roman law with particular interest, as well as courses in general history, and also studied the Slavonic Bible. His fascination with Roman history led him to an intensive study of Latin and classical literature. He also read Greek classics in French translation; his study of Greek did not begin until the 1850s. Thus, the ground was laid for the historical and classical subjects of his later work.

According to Baevsky, Maikov's career began, by his own estimation, in 1838 while he was still a student. His professors, including Aleksandr Vasil'evich Nikitenko, Petr Aleksandrovich Pletnev, and Stepan Petrovich Shevyrev, supported his literary efforts; Nikitenko and Shevyrev read his verse that year to their students, and Pletnev later reviewed his work favorably in the press. During Maikov's university years his verse appeared in *Biblioteka dlia chteniia* and *Otechestvennye zapiski* (Notes of the Fatherland). The publication of his 1839 poems "Son" (Sleep) and "Kartina vechera" (Evening Picture)—submitted by Benediktov with the author's permission and signed "M."—in *Odesskii al'manakh na 1840 god* (Odessa Almanac for 1840) prompted the first critical response to his work. "Son" attracted the praise of critic Vissarion Grigor'evich Belinsky and quickly became one of Maikov's most anthologized works. Belinsky quoted "Son" in its entirety in *Otechestvennye zapiski* in 1841 and called the author an "unknown but talented poet." Thus, Maikov's literary career was publicly launched by the time he graduated from Moscow University in 1841. He completed his candidate's dissertation on Slavic law and graduated first in his class. Upon graduation he entered government service in the Department of the Treasury.

In St. Petersburg in 1842 the first collection of Maikov's verse appeared. Simply called *Stikhotvoreniia* (Poems), the book embodies both nature poetry and classically influenced verse in the Pushkinian tradition. The latter group consists of imitations of Sappho, Anakreon, Horace, Ovid, and others; elegies in the classical style; and Eastern-influenced verse, such as "Evreiskie pesni" (Jewish Songs) and "Molitva Beduina" (Bedouin's Prayer). The collection received favorable attention in the press and in both literary and ruling circles. Belinsky singled out "Son" in a review once again, ranking the poem on a level with Pushkin's best anthological verse. The book caught the attention of the minister of education, Sergei Semenovich Uvarov, who asked to meet the young poet and to show his verse to the emperor, Tsar Nicholas I. The positive reception of his debut collection set Maikov firmly on his literary path, for up to that time he was still deciding whether to devote his life to painting or to poetry.

The 1842 collection included Maikov's first attempt at a dramatic poem on a theme that was to occupy him his entire life—the clash between pagan and Christian cultures in Rome at the beginning of the Christian era. "Olinf i Esfir'. Rimskie tseny vremen piatogo veka khristianstva" (Olynthus and Esther: Roman Scenes from the Fifth Century A.D.) depicts this opposition through a love triangle. The pagan Olinf spurns the passionate love of the beautiful Aglaia for the Christian Esfir', who rejects his advances for the sake of her faith. The poem is written in a lofty tone stylizing both biblical language and that of Greek tragedy. Belinsky criticized the poem as shallow and weak, and Maikov himself later expressed dissatisfaction with it; however, many elements from the poem appeared in his subsequent work.

That year Maikov took his first trip abroad. He traveled to Italy with the support of Nicholas I, who was impressed by his debut collection and by one of his paintings, a depiction of the Crucifixion. On 29 June Maikov set off together with his father, to be joined later by his brother Valerian and Solonitsyn. The trip also included a visit to Paris, where the brothers attended lectures at the Sorbonne and the Collège de France and conducted research in the national library. While in Paris, Maikov wrote his first *poema,* "Dve sud'by" (Two Fates, published as a book in 1845). As he had in "Olinf i Esfir'," in this work he juxtaposed Russia and Italy through romantic rivalry, this time between Russian and Italian protagonists. His Russian hero, Vladimir, struck critics, including Nikolai Gavrilovich Chernyshevsky, as a continuation of the line of *lishnie liudi* (superfluous men) already well established in Russian literary tradition by 1843. The poem was censored before its 1845 publication for its implied social criticism. Upon its publication, nonetheless, it was praised in reviews by the liberals and Westernizers Belinsky, Chernyshevsky, and Alexander Herzen (Aleksandr Ivanovich Gertsen).

On the way back to Russia, Maikov traveled to Dresden and Prague. In Dresden he visited the national gallery. His interest in Slavic history and culture led him to Prague, then considered a center for Slavic studies, and he learned Czech in two months. The Prague stay had a strong impact on Maikov's later work with Slavic historical and folkloric themes. He returned to Russia in March 1844 and took a new post as assistant librarian at the Rumiantsev Museum, then located in St. Petersburg. He became acquainted with many leading literary figures of the day, particularly the realist writers grouped around Belinsky: Ivan Sergeevich Turgenev, Nekrasov, Dmitrii Vasil'evich Grigorovich, Ivan Ivanovich Panaev, and Andrei Aleksandrovich Kraevsky, publisher of *Otechestvennye zapiski*. Valerian, Maikov's politically liberal brother, headed the criticism section of that journal.

During this period, in 1845, Maikov wrote his second *poema,* "Mashen'ka," which was published in *Peterburgskii sbornik* (Petersburg Collection, 1846), a periodical of the *natural'naia shkola* (natural school). The poem is about a young noblewoman who is seduced and abandoned by her lover and cursed by her heartbroken father, a midlevel bureaucrat. It ends with a kind of reconciliation between the aged father and the prodigal daughter. Like "Dve sud'by," this work was subject both to censors' cuts and to self-censorship. Written in highly colloquial language, the poem reflects hints of two works by Pushkin. The lightly ironic, narratorial digressions in "Mashen'ka" recall Pushkin's novel in verse *Evgeny Onegin* (Eugene Onegin, 1833), and the plot of the *poema* is similar to that of Pushkin's story "Stantsionnyi smotritel'" (The Stationmaster, 1830). Maikov's tone is more melodramatic, however, and his irony weaker than Pushkin's. The *poema* was another landmark in Maikov's association with Belinsky, who praised the work in a review for *Peterburgskii sbornik*). Yet, critics Apollon Apollonovich Grigor'ev and Aleksandr Vasil'evich Druzhinin saw the poem as an unsuccessful foray into social writing.

In 1846 Maikov met Fyodor Dostoevsky. Dostoevsky supported Maikov's work and views as the poet turned increasingly conservative, beginning in the 1850s. The two remained lifelong friends.

In 1847, three years after his return to Russia, Maikov published the poetry collection *Ocherki Rima* (Roman Sketches), both as a separate book and in *Otechestvennye zapiski*. In this collection Maikov shows his talents as poet, painter, and historian in his depictions of Rome. He displays his poetic virtuosity in the variety of his forms; the frequency of poetic conceits from classical and Romantic verse; and the relative flexibility of stylistic registers, from the lofty to the colloquial. Through verse he paints Roman landscapes and character portraits, and the subjects of his poetic canvases are taken both from his personal observations and from myth, literature, or legend. The historian in Maikov brings ancient Rome to life, as in the poem "Drevnii Rim." This collection also displays his social conscience, for he condemns slavery in "Igry" (The Games) and depicts a beggar amid beautiful ruins in "Campagna di Roma" (The Roman Countryside). *Ocherki Rima* thus confirms the continuing influence of Belinsky and his circle and of Nekrasov's socially oriented verse. Yet, it also marks a new distance, since Belinsky was disappointed by Maikov's return to anthological verse, away from the *natural'naia shkola* poetics of his two *poemy*, "Dve sud'by" and "Mashen'ka."

In the late 1840s Maikov was still associated with Belinsky's literary politics, but this situation soon changed. Maikov frequented the radical Petrashevsky *kruzhok* (circle) in 1847 and 1848 and felt sympathy with the democratic political views of liberal writers in and outside that circle. During this period he published short prose sketches influenced by his Italian tour, as well as reviews of literary and artistic works, in the liberal journals *Otechestvennye zapiski* and *Sovremennik* (The Contemporary). When the authorities disbanded the Petrashevsky group in 1849, Maikov was interrogated but released and secretly observed until 1855. At about this time he made the acquaintance of Grigor'ev, a writer and poet of much more conservative political views than Maikov's own. Like the liberal Belinsky, however, Grigor'ev was interested in the historical destiny of Russia and in a writer's prophetic power.

ДВѢ СУДЬБЫ,

Быль.

АПОЛЛОНА МАЙКОВА.

Санктпетербургъ.

1845.

Title page for Maikov's first long narrative poem, Dve sud'by *(Two Fates), written during a visit to Paris (Kilgour Collection of Russian Literature, Harvard University Library)*

Grigor'ev and Maikov were both religious Orthodox Christians, and the combination of their religious and historical views encouraged their increasingly close association. Best known as a critic, Grigor'ev held Maikov's work in high esteem.

From 1845 until 1851 Maikov worked on his second dramatic poem, "Tri smerti" (Three Deaths), a work considered by critics as one of his best. The poem returns to the theme that he first addressed in "Olinf i Esfir'"–the decline of the Roman Empire. Maikov depicts the last day of three men ordered by Emperor Nero to commit suicide by midnight–the philosopher Seneka (Seneca), the poet Lukan (Lucanus), and the Epicurean philosopher Liutsii (Lucius), who together discuss their roles in changing Roman society and their varying attitudes to death. "Tri smerti" was completed at an inopportune time for publication. The period between 1848 and 1855 was one of particularly harsh censorship, and the possible parallel between Nero's suppression of poets and thinkers and the repressions of Nicholas I was too close to make the poem publishable under the Russian ruler. "Tri smerti" came out only in 1857 in

Biblioteka dlia chteniia, and then a year later, with corrections, in the second, enlarged edition of Maikov's *Stikhotvoreniia.* Before its publication, however, the dramatic poem was distributed in manuscript form and praised by Pletnev and the poet Vasilii Andreevich Zhukovsky. Druzhinin called the piece "the crown of Maikov's work in his *Sobranie sochinenii* (1865)." That assessment was echoed by later critics, including the Russian symbolist poet Innokentii Fedorovich Annensky and writer Dmitrii Sergeevich Merezhkovsky.

At the same time that Maikov was writing "Tri smerti," he also worked on his *poema* "Savonarola," completed in 1851. The work depicts the fate of a religious reformer (who lived from 1452 to 1498), the head of the Florentine republic, who was removed from his post by the pope and executed. "Savonarola," which Nikolai Vasil'evich Gogol greatly admired, is a condemnation of blind fanaticism and of faith based on fear rather than love. Like "Tri smerti," it was not published until 1857, first in *Biblioteka dlia chteniia,* and its theme was repeated in Maikov's later work.

In 1852 Maikov married Anna Ivanovna Stemmer, a Russian of German extraction and a Lutheran. The couple eventually had four children—three sons and a daughter. That year he also moved to a new professional position as a censor of foreign literature when the Rumiantsev Museum was transferred to Moscow, and remained in government service as a censor for the next forty-five years. In 1853 he was elected a corresponding member of the Imperial Academy of Sciences.

Maikov's next collection reflected contemporary rather than ancient historical events—namely, the Crimean War. *1854 god. Riad stikhotvorenii po povodu vostochnoi voiny* (The Year 1854. A Series of Poems on the Occasion of the Eastern War), published in 1855, grew out of the nationalistic mood that swept the country—as a result of Russian engagement in the war—and that embraced Maikov as well, as seen in the poems included in the series, such as "Klermontovskii sobor" (The Clermont Cathedral). The messianic message of "Klermontovskii sobor" appealed to Dostoevsky, and critics, including Chernyshevsky and Nekrasov, appreciated Maikov's effort to express public sentiment in the poem. In 1854 Maikov also composed a verse that seriously damaged his reputation in progressive circles. In "Koliaska" (The Carriage), his panegyric to Nicholas I, he portrayed the tsar as a conscientious public servant and a great autocrat and defended Nicholas against public "slander." Not impressed with the portrayal of himself as a victim, the tsar commanded that the poet be thanked and that the poem not be published. Liberal critics accused Maikov of sycophancy; he was called "Apollon Koliaskin" in the satirical press.

After the Crimean War, Maikov began to associate with more conservative literary and political circles, including the Slavophiles and the "molodaia redaktsiia" (Young Editors) connected with the journal *Moskvitianin* (The Muscovite), to which his professional and personal ties brought him closer. He was never an adherent of extreme views at either end of the political spectrum, however, and he maintained his independence. His high regard for Tsar Peter I (Peter the Great) and for Peter's reforms, for example, met with disagreement from the Slavophiles. Maikov's literary reputation had shifted by now as well, for by the late 1850s he was known as a poet who, along with his contemporaries Fet, Polonsky, and Aleksei Konstantinovich Tolstoy, believed in "art for art's sake."

Maikov's lyric poetry reached its peak during this period. In 1855 he produced one of his most famous poems, a pastoral piece titled "Rybnaia lovlia" (Fishing), which he dedicated to his father, to a series of writers—Sergei Aksakov, Goncharov, Aleksandr Nikolaevich Ostrovsky—and to "everyone who understands this matter." An idyll extolling the pleasures of country life and the beauty of nature, it is written in a mockingly lofty poetic style, combined with the conversational language of men fishing for pleasure. Soon after the composition of "Rybnaia lovlia," Maikov wrote many of the nature poems that secured his reputation as a poet of lasting significance, such as "Lastochki" (Swallows, 1856), "Vesna! Vystavliaetsia pervaia rama . . . " (Spring! The winter pane is taken out . . . , 1858), "Letnii dozhd'" (Summer Rain, 1858), and "Senokos" (Haymaking, 1858).

In 1858, on Maikov's recommendation, the great poet Tiutchev was appointed to the St. Petersburg censorship committee. Maikov treasured his professional relationship and friendship with Tiutchev for the rest of his life. That same year Maikov went abroad for a second time under the auspices of Grand Duke Konstantin Nikolaevich Romanov, who headed the Maritime Ministry. Maikov was sent to Greece, and in preparation for the trip he studied modern Greek. While he traveled to Nice, Palermo, Naples, and Spain, in the end he did not reach Greece. The journey is reflected in his poetic cycles "Neapolitanskii al'bom [Miss Meri]" (Neapolitan Album [Miss Mary], written from 1858 to 1859, published 1864) and "Novogrecheskie pesni" (Modern Greek Songs, written 1858–1860, published 1864).

After Maikov's return from abroad, Polonsky joined him on the St. Petersburg censorship committee in 1860. At this time Maikov returned to the theme of his "Tri smerti" in order to depict the death of Lucius in "Smert' Liutsiia" (The Death of Lucius). He completed the work in 1863 and published it that same year in conservative Mikhail Nikiforovich Katkov's *Russkii vestnik* (The Russian Messenger). In 1864 "Smert'

Liutsiia" was republished as the second part of the dramatic poem "Liutsii" in Maikov's collection *Novye stikhotvoreniia (1858–1863)* (New Poems [1858–1863], 1864); the first part of this poem was "Tri smerti." "Liutsii" never appeared again in print. Maikov reworked its second part, "Smert' Liutsiia," as part of his dramatic poem "Dva mira" (Two Worlds) in 1872. In "Smert' Liutsiia" Maikov juxtaposes Christian and pagan views of death and sacrifice through the deaths of the hero and those of Lucius's Christian acquaintances. He also reflects on the role of the poet in a declining society through the opening scene of the work, in which Lucius and the poet Juvenal have a conversation and lament the passing of the great literary heritage of Rome. Critical reaction from the left against this poem was strong. In 1863 the satirical journal *Iskra* (The Spark) published a parody of it by Dmitrii Dmitrievich Minaev. Titled "Smert' Maikova" (The Death of Maikov), this version mocked not only Maikov but also Fet and Polonsky.

During the period when he was producing dramatic poetry with Roman themes, Maikov wrote "Strannik" (The Wanderer, 1864), a dramatic poem devoted to a Russian historical topic–the Great Schism of the seventeenth century, in which some Russian Orthodox believers refused to follow the reforms instituted by Patriarch Nikon. Those who did not agree with the reforms were called Old Believers. "Strannik," which Dostoevsky considered Maikov's masterpiece, resumes the theme of fanaticism addressed previously in "Savonarola" and expresses the poet's dislike of all kinds of political or religious extremism. Maikov based the poem on his reading of Pavel Ivanovich Mel'nikov-Pechersky's tale "Grisha" (Grisha, 1861), on Petr Vasil'evich Kireevsky's collection of folk songs, and on other literary sources. In "Strannik" the fanatic Grisha is capable of blindly carrying out any orders–including commands for thievery and arson–given to him by the Wanderer, an ascetic who adopts Grisha as his apostle. Written in a way that stylizes seventeenth-century Russian language, the poem was later praised by Merezhkovsky as Maikov's "archaic verses."

In 1866 Maikov's only daughter, Vera, died at the age of eleven. He wrote a poem on her death, titled "Ne mozhet byt'! Ne mozhet byt'!" (It Can't Be! It Can't Be!), which he included in his cycle "Docheri" (To My Daughter), together with poems he had written about her during the first two years of her life. The combination of verses about early childhood with those about a child's death produces a stunning impression of paternal joy and grief.

Around this time Maikov also began a serious study of Slavic and western European folklore. His interest in these traditions reached its culmination in his trans-

lation of the medieval Russian epic poem *Slovo o polku Igoreve*, considered one of the best nineteenth-century renderings of the work. From 1866 until 1870 Maikov worked intently on the translation. Accompanied by his copious scholarly commentaries, it was first published in full in the journal *Zaria* (Dawn) in 1870. During this period he also wrote historical poems based on, and free adaptations of, folk songs and epics from the Slavic and west European traditions, including Serbian, Czech, and Scandinavian.

The final development of the Roman theme among Maikov's longer works can be seen in "Dva mira," written and published in 1872. The lyric tragedy first appeared in *Sbornik "Grazhdanina"* (The "Citizen" Collection) and almost simultaneously in the third edition of his poems. In this work Maikov returns to the conflict between pagan and Christian cultures. He explains in an afterword to "Dva mira" that his goal was to emphasize his Epicurean hero's positive traits and thus to convey what he himself admired in Roman society. In turn, the Christian world of "Dva mira" is further developed through the depiction of Christians hiding in the catacombs. The motif of fear and secrecy among the politically repressed poets and Christians is significant in this work as well. The language of "Dva mira" is more varied than in Maikov's previous works on this topic: Liutsii's feast is depicted in colloquial speech, which contrasts with the lofty, biblical style of the Christians. "Dva mira" is imbued with a lyricism lacking in "Smert' Liutsiia" and features symbolic oppositions of light and darkness, slavery and freedom, selfishness and sacrifice, and decay and eternity.

In the 1860s and 1870s Maikov began to write more poetry on Russian historical themes and figures, such as on the Mongol invasions of medieval Russia, Alexander Nevsky, Peter the Great and his sister Sophia, and the eighteenth-century poet Mikhail Vasil'evich Lomonosov. Maikov gathered these poems into a cycle titled "Otzyvy istorii" (Historical Judgments, published in 1884) for the next edition of his collected works. Written during the era of high realism in art, these poems feature striking visual images reminiscent of the historical compositions of the *Peredvizhniki* (Itinerants), a group of realist painters in the second half of the nineteenth century who were named for the moving exhibitions of their works in provincial Russian cities. Like many of the canvases of the *Peredvizhniki*, Maikov's historical poems often depict a critical moment in the career of a great leader.

In 1875 Maikov was promoted to head the St. Petersburg committee on the censorship of foreign literature, where he continued to work with Tiutchev and Polonsky. The Academy of Sciences awarded him its Pushkin Prize for "Dva mira" in 1882, and that year a second edition of the poem was published in *Russkii vestnik*. Two years later the fourth edition of Maikov's collected works, *Polnoe sobranie sochinenii* (Complete Collected Works), appeared in St. Petersburg; the first three editions had been titled *Stikhotvoreniia*. On 30 April 1888 the Literaturno-dramaticheskoe obshchestvo (Literary-Dramatic Society) celebrated the fiftieth anniversary of Maikov's career. A poem by Grand Duke Konstantin Konstantinovich Romanov (under the pseudonym K.R.) was read at the gathering, where poets Polonsky, Konstantin Konstantinovich Sluchevsky, and Count Arsenii Arkad'evich Golenishchev-Kutuzov were present. Fet also sent a poem for the occasion. Tsar Alexander III promoted Maikov to the rank of privy councillor.

Next, Maikov returned to folkloric themes and wrote the *poema* "Bringil'da" (Brynhild), which first came out in *Russkii vestnik* in 1888. Like his earlier folkloric stylizations, "Bringil'da" is based on his reading of the *Edda* (written in the thirteenth century) and other Scandinavian sagas. He also turned to more philosophical lyric poetry in the 1870s and 1880s. A characteristic work of this period is his 1887 poem "Ex tenebris lux" (Light from Darkness), from the cycle "Vechnye voprosy" (Eternal Questions, written in 1874–1888). "Ex tenebris lux" features the symbolic opposition of light and darkness prevalent in "Dva mira." Maikov's cycle "Iz Apollodora Gnostika" (From the Gnostic Apollodor, 1877–1893) includes reflections on poetry, faith, and existence.

On 26 February 1897 Maikov read his poem "20 oktiabria 1894" (20 October 1894) at a meeting in memory of Tsar Alexander III at the Obshchestvo revnitelei russkogo istoricheskogo prosveshcheniia (Society for the Support of Russian Historical Education). This reading was the poet's final public appearance. That winter he caught cold and contracted pneumonia, of which he died on 8 March 1897. He was buried in the cemetery at the Voskresenskii Novodevichii monastery in St. Petersburg.

The literary legacy of Apollon Nikolaevich Maikov must be viewed through the prism of subsequent changes in literary and cultural history. He died when literary tastes were changing; when the age of realism was coming to an end and the Russian symbolist movement was growing; and when Aleksandr Aleksandrovich Blok, the greatest symbolist in Russia, was writing his earliest verses. Maikov received considerable critical attention soon after his death from poets of the decadent and symbolist movements, most notably from Merezhkovsky and Annensky. Annensky in particular discussed Maikov from the point of view of the "pedagogical significance" of his work—its ability to develop a sense of beauty in the young reader. During the Soviet era Maikov was relegated to the position of a second-rate poet of dubious politics and therefore given relatively little attention. His work did, however, engage the attention of twentieth-century poets; for instance, a recent article on Boris Leonidovich Pasternak's reception of Maikov's poetry demonstrates that he influenced Pasternak greatly. The appearance of several new studies on Maikov in Russia in recent years also indicates the possibility of renewed interest in his work.

Letters:

[Letters], *Ezhegodnik Rukopisnogo otdela Pushkinskogo doma. 1975* (Leningrad, 1977);

[Letters], *Ezhegodnik Rukopisnogo otdela Pushkinskogo doma. 1978* (Leningrad, 1980);

"Neizvestnye poslaniia A. N. Maikova i P. A. Pletneva," edited by E. P. Gorbenko, *Russkaia literatura,* 2 (1984): 162–164;

"Pis'ma Maikova k F. M. Dostoevskomu, 1867–78," *Pamiatniki kul'tury, 1982* (1984).

Bibliography:

Dmitrii Dmitrievich Iazykov, [Bibliografiia], in his *Zhizn' i trudy A. N. Maikova* (St. Petersburg: V. Chicherin, 1898).

Biographies:

Mikhail Leont'evich Zlatkovsky, *Apollon Nikolaevich Maikov: Biograficheskii ocherk* (St. Petersburg: A. F. Marks, 1888); enlarged as *Apollon Nikolaevich Maikov, 1821–1897 g.: Biograficheskii ocherk* (St. Petersburg: P. P. Soikin, 1898);

Dmitrii Ivanovich Tikhomirov, *A. N. Maikov i Ia. P. Polonskii: Biografii i izbrannye stikhotvoreniia* (Moscow: K. L. Men'shov, 1909);

A. N. Maikov: Biografiia i kharakteristika, edited by Aleksandr Vasil'evich Kruglov (Moscow: A. S. Panafidina, 1914);

Petr Vasil'evich Bykov, "A. N. Maikov. Kritiko-biograficheskii ocherk," in Maikov's *Polnoe sobranie sochinenii,* 4 volumes, edited by Bykov (St. Petersburg: A. F. Marks, 1914), I: iii–xlvii;

Vadim Solomonovich Baevsky, "Maikov Apollon Nikolaevich," in *Russkie pisateli, 1800–1917: Biograficheskii slovar',* edited by Petr Alekseevich Nikolaev, volume 3 (Moscow: Sovetskaia entsiklopediia, 1994), pp. 453–458.

References:

Iulii Isaevich Aikhenval'd, "Maikov," in his *Siluety russkikh pisatelei,* volume 2 (The Hague & Paris: Mouton, 1969), pp. 55–68;

Innokentii Fedorovich Annensky, "Maikov i pedago-gicheskoe znachenie ego poezii," in his *Kniga otrazhenii,* edited by N. T. Ashimbaev (Moscow: Nauka, 1979), pp. 271–303, 619–626;

Apollon Nikolaevich Maikov: Ego zhizn' i sochineniia. Sbornik istoriko-literaturnykh statei, compiled by Vasilii Ivanovich Pokrovsky (Moscow: G. Lissner & A. Geshelii, 1904; enlarged edition, Moscow: V. Spiridonov and A. Mikhailov, 1911);

A. A. Asosian, *"Dve sud'by* Apollona Maikova i liro-epicheskaia poema sorokovykh godov XIX veka," *Filologicheskie nauki,* volume 122, no. 2 (1981): 31–36;

Nikolai Pavlovich Avtonomov, *Russkie motivy v tvorchestve A. N. Maikova* (Medford, Ore.: N. P. Avtonomoff, 1948);

Mikhail M. Borodkin, *Poeticheskoe tvorchestvo A. N. Maikova* (St. Petersburg: P. P. Soikin, 1900);

A. A. Divil'kovskii, "Apollon Nikolaevich Maikov," in *Istoriia russkoi literatury XIX veka,* 5 volumes, edited by Dmitrii Nikolaevich Ovsianiko-Kulikovskago, American Council of Learned Societies Reprints, Russian Series, no. 11 (Ann Arbor, Mich.: Edwards Brothers, 1949), III: 472–481;

Aleksander Vasil'evich Druzhinin, *Sobranie sochinenii,* volume 7 (St. Petersburg: Tipografiia Imperatorskoi Akademii nauk, 1865), p. 513;

P. A. Gaponenko, "Mozhno li 'shalit' kliatvoiu'? O poeticheskoi rechi A. N. Maikova," *Russkaia rech',* 6 (1994): 3–7;

Gaponenko, "Pis'mo A. A. Feta k A. N. Maikovu," *Russkaia literatura,* 4 (1988): 180–181;

Gaponenko, "Poetika dvukh stikhotvornykh poslanii A. Fetu," *Russkii iazyk v shkole,* 2 (1998): 64–68;

Iakov Karlovich Grot and Petr Aleksandrovich Pletnev, *Perepiska Ia. K. Grota s P. A. Pletnevym,* 3 volumes (St. Petersburg: Tipografiia Ministerstva Putei Soobshcheniia, 1896);

I. A. Gulova, "A. N. Maikov: 'Osennie list'ia po vetru kruzhat . . .'," *Russkii iazyk v shkole,* 3 (2001): 58–63;

J. A. Harvie, "Maykov's Masterpiece *Dva mira,*" *Melbourne Slavic Studies,* 16 (1982): 89–106;

Isaak Grigor'evich Iampol'sky, "Iz arkhiva Maikova," *Ezhegodnik Rukopisnogo otdela Pushkinskogo doma. 1974* (Leningrad, 1976): 24–52;

Iampol'sky, *Poety i prozaiki: stat'i o russkikh pisateliakh XIX–nachala XX v.* (Leningrad: Sovetskii pisatel', 1986), pp. 110–141;

Valentin Ivanovich Korovin, "Poet Apollon Maikov," in Maikov's *Stikhotvoreniia* (Moscow: Sovetskaia Rossiia, 1980), pp. 5–22;

Witold Kowalczyk, *Twórczosc Apollona Majkowa i jej konteksty kulturowe* (Lublin: Uniwersytet Marii Curie-Sklodowskiej, 1991);

L. Lanskoi, "Opisanie knig biblioteki Belinskogo," *Literaturnoe nasledstvo,* 55, no. 1 (1948): 474–476;

Dmitry Sergeyevich Merezhkovsky, *Vechnye sputniki: Portrety iz vsemirnoi istorii* (St. Petersburg: Obshchestvennaia pol'za, 1916);

D. S. Noskova, "A. N. Maikov: Posleslovie k tsiklu: Po arkhivnym materialam," *Russkaia literatura,* 2 (2000): 195–199;

Petr Pertsov, *Literaturnye vospominaniia 1890–1902 gg.,* foreword by B. F. Porshnev (Moscow & Leningrad: Academia, 1933), pp. 108–115;

Fedor Iakovlevich Priima, "Poeziia A. N. Maikova," in Maikov's *Sochineniia,* 2 volumes, edited by L. S. Geiro (Moscow: Pravda, 1984), pp. 3–40;

Konstantin Mikhailovich Polivanov, "Apollon Maikov i *Sestra moia–zhizn'* Borisa Pasternaka," in *Pasternakovskie chteniia,* edited by Mikhail Leonovich Gasparov, Irina Iur'evna. Podgaetskaia, and Konstantin Polivanov, volume 2 (Moscow: Nasledie, 1998), pp. 259–266;

E. I. Prokhorov, "Dramaticheskie poemy A. N. Maikova," in *Ler Mei. Dramy.–A. Maikov. Dramaticheskie poemy,* edited by Prokhorov (Moscow: Iskusstvo, 1961), pp. 341–356;

Barbara Stawarz, "O kontemplacji. Dzielo sztuki antycznej w poezji Mikolaja Szczerbiny i Apollona Majkowa," *Slavia Orientalis,* 44, no. 4 (1995): 473–483;

Nikolai Leonidovich Stepanov, "Apollon Maikov," in *Istoriia russkoi literatury,* edited by Mikhail Pavlovich Alekseev and others, volume 8 (Moscow: Akademii Nauk SSSR, 1956), pp. 284–301.

Papers:

Apollon Nikolaevich Maikov's papers are located in St. Petersburg at the Institute of Russian Literature (IRLI, Pushkin House), fond 168; the Russian National Library (RNB), fond 453; and the Dostoevsky Museum. In Moscow, Maikov's papers can be found at the Russian State Archive of Literature and Art (RGALI), fond 311.

Lev Aleksandrovich Mei

(13 February 1822 – 16 May 1862)

Karla Cruise

BOOKS: *Tsarskaia nevesta. Drama* (Moscow: Universitetskaia tipografiia, 1849; revised, St. Petersburg: F. Stellovsky, 1861);

Serviliia (St. Petersburg: Korolev, 1854);

Kirilych. Neskol'ko listkov iz zapisok. Povest' (St. Petersburg: A. Smirdin, 1856); republished as *Kirilych* (St. Petersburg: N. G. Martynov, 1887);

Stikhotvoreniia (St. Petersburg: A. Smirdin, 1857);

Pskovitianka (St. Petersburg: F. Stellovsky, 1860);

Sochineniia i perevody. Kniga I. Byliny i pesni (St. Petersburg: E. P. Pechatkin, 1861);

Sochineniia, 3 volumes (St. Petersburg: G. A. Kushelev-Bezborodko, 1862–1863);

Pervoe polnoe sobranie sochinenii, 5 volumes (St. Petersburg: N. G. Martynov, 1887);

Okhota (St. Petersburg: N. G. Martynov, 1887)—comprises "Sbornoe voskresen'e" and "Medvezh'ia travlia";

Sof'ia. Eshche neskol'ko listkov iz zapisok (St. Petersburg: N. G. Martynov, 1887);

Grivennik. (Nepravdopodobnoe sobytie) (St. Petersburg: N. G. Martynov, 1887);

Na paperti. (Iz dnevnika) (St. Petersburg: N. G. Martynov, 1887);

Chubuk (St. Petersburg: N. G. Martynov, 1887);

Batia. Pravdivyi rasskaz (St. Petersburg: N. G. Martynov, 1887);

Tri rasskaza (St. Petersburg: N. G. Martynov, 1887)—comprises "Kazus," "Lesnye dikovinki," and "Shveika";

Pesnia pro boiarina Evpatiia Kolovrata. Iz vremen tatarshchiny (St. Petersburg: N. G. Martynov, 1898);

Polnoe sobranie sochinenii, 3 volumes, edited by Petr Vasil'evich Bykov (St. Petersburg: A. F. Marks, 1910–1911; revised and enlarged, 2 volumes, 1911);

Dramy, edited by E. I. Prokhorov (Moscow: Iskusstvo, 1961)—includes Apollon Nikolaevich Maikov's *Dramaticheskie poemy.*

Editions and Collections: *Stikhotvoreniia,* with an introduction and commentary by Solomon Abramo-

Lev Aleksandrovich Mei

vich Reiser, Biblioteka poeta, Malaia seriia (Moscow & Leningrad: Sovetskii pisatel', 1937);

Stikhotvoreniia i dramy, edited by Reiser, Biblioteka poeta, Bol'shaia seriia (Leningrad: Sovetskii pisatel', 1947);

Stikhotvoreniia, edited by Reiser, Biblioteka poeta, Malaia seriia (Leningrad: Sovetskii pisatel', 1951);

Izbrannye proizvedeniia, with an introduction by G. M. Fridlender, Biblioteka poeta, Malaia seriia (Moscow & Leningrad: Sovetskii pisatel', 1962);

Izbrannye proizvedeniia, with an introduction by K. K. Bukhmeier, Biblioteka poeta, Bol'shaia seriia (Leningrad: Sovetskii pisatel', 1972);

Zabytye iamby (Moscow: Detskaia literatura, 1984);

Stikhotvoreniia, edited by Bukhmeier (Moscow: Sovetskaia Rossiia, 1985).

TRANSLATIONS: Anonymous, *Slovo o polku Igoreve* (St. Petersburg: Imperatorskaia Akademiia nauk, 1856);

Friedrich Schiller, *Dmitrii Samozvanets. Neokonchennaia tragediia* (St. Petersburg, 1860);

Schiller, *Lager' Vallenshteina. Dramaticheskoe stikhotvorenie* (St. Petersburg: F. Stellovsky, 1861);

Taras Shevchenko, *Batrachka. Povest' v stikhakh* (St. Petersburg: Kommissiia gramotnosti, 1881);

Pierre-Jean de Béranger, *Pesni* (St. Petersburg: N. G. Martynov, 1887);

Mastera russkogo stikhotvornogo perevoda, contributions by Mei, with an introduction by Efim Grigor'evich Etkind, volume 1, Biblioteka poeta, Bol'shaia seriia (Leningrad: Sovetskii pisatel', 1968).

PLAY PRODUCTIONS: *Tsarskaia nevesta,* Moscow, Malyi Theater, 1849;

Pskovitianka, St. Petersburg, Aleksandrinskii Theater, 1861.

Poet, dramatist, and translator Lev Mei drew his subjects from history, folklore, mythology, and the Bible. Mei's works were influenced by the early-nineteenth-century German and English Romantic writers Johann Wolfgang Goethe, Friedrich Schiller, and George Gordon, Lord Byron, as well as by Russian writers and poets such as Nikolai Mikhailovich Karamzin, Nikolai Mikhailovich Iazykov, Mikhail Iur'evich Lermontov, and Aleksandr Sergeevich Pushkin. Mei's lifelong efforts to create and promote a national literature organically rooted in the Russian experience have linked him with the Slavophile movement, whose chief objective was national self-definition. Though criticized by his contemporaries for his failure to address himself adequately to the important social questions of his day, he was admired by later critics for his virtuosic facility with Russian verse and the profoundly humane vision reflected in his works.

Lev Aleksandrovich Mei was born on 13 February 1822 in Moscow into an impoverished gentry family of German descent. His grandfather was a famous book dealer in Moscow, and his father, Aleksandr Il'ich Mei, was a retired officer who had been critically injured in the Battle of Borodino. When Mei's father died at age thirty-five, the family was left destitute. At four years of age Mei went with his mother, Ol'ga Ivanovna (née Shlykovaia) Mei, and two siblings to live in Moscow with his maternal grandmother, Agrafena Stanislavovna Shlykovaia. His early childhood years were spent with his grandmother, mother, and aunt, all of whom insisted on the strict observation of Orthodox religious holidays and ceremonies. In his 1855 story "Kirilych" (published as a book in 1856) Mei remembers the hours he spent listening to his house serf, Kirilych, tell folktales, fairy tales, proverbs, and legends. He especially marveled at the way Kirilych had built an entire "philosophy of life" from proverbs and sayings. Mei's interest in folklore and legend seems to date from these early childhood experiences. "Kirilych" is part of a cycle of autobiographical stories that includes "Sof'ia" (1856) and "Na paperti" (On the Church Porch, 1859), both published as books in 1887.

In 1831 the nine-year-old Mei was enrolled in a Moscow boarding school for the gentry; because of his exceptional work there, he was transferred, at public expense, to Tsarskoe Selo Lycée near St. Petersburg in 1836. Mei's attendance at the lycée coincided with the policy of "Official Nationality," ordered by Tsar Nicholas I, which forced all schools to promote "Orthodoxy, autocracy and nationality." Unlike the education of the young men of Pushkin's era, Mei's education was designed to render him an obedient servant of the empire rather than an informed citizen of a nation. Mei studied world history, ancient and modern languages, and Russian and European literature, but he was not encouraged to think about contemporary social or political issues. His lifelong friend, Vladimir Rafailovich Zotov, went to school with the poet and remembers that he was an excellent student, fond of making trouble and carousing.

One aspect of the lycée that had not changed since Pushkin's days was the importance attributed to literature, even to creative pieces written by the students themselves. While still at the lycée, Mei distinguished himself as a poet and contributed to the school literary journal *Voobshche* (In General) with verses celebrating love, wine, and parties. From 1839 to 1840 his poetry began to reflect some of the subject matter that fascinated him for the rest of his artistic career: history and the role of the poet. The most significant of Mei's poems written during his lycée years (1838–1841) was his "Vechevoi kolokol" (The *Veche* Bell of Novgorod, 1840), first published anonymously in Aleksandr Ivanovich Herzen's London journal *Golosa iz Rossii* (Voices from Russia) in 1857. The poem, set in the time of Ivan III (Ivan the Great), commemorates the doomed struggle of the free city of Novgorod against authoritarian control in Moscow. Specifically, it refers to the time in 1478 when Muscovites seized the bell that rang to assemble the *veche,* the democratic town council of Novgorod. The metrical patterns of the poem imitate those of the Russian *bylina,* a type of epic folk song. Thematically, the call for justice and freedom in "Vechevoi kolokol" echoes works by the Decembrist poets, who in the 1820s had also evoked Novgorod as the symbol of the stifled democratic spirit of the country.

Mei's other notable poems from his lycée years are "Lunatik" (The Sleepwalker) and "Gvanagani" (The Bahamas)—with which he debuted in 1840, when both works were published under the pseudonym Zelensky in the St. Petersburg journal *Maiak* (The Beacon). These poems, like "Vechevoi kolokol," are Romantic in sentiment and praise nature, freedom, and the exalted role of the poet. In "Lunatik" Mei develops the Romantic notion that the poet is an intermediary between heaven and earth. The poet is the "favored child of nature, an envoy of God" whose "spiritual eye" is open to everything "elevated and beautiful." In "Gvanagani" (an excerpt from the unfinished poem "Kolumb" [Columbus]), the poet idealizes the simple life of the "savage people," whose one law is freedom and whose one desire is peace. In this poem Mei exhibits his love for lush, colorful descriptions: a "golden pineapple" hangs in the treetops, a "multi-colored parrot" sings, and a cluster of overripe bananas bends a tree.

Mei's literary successes at the lycée no doubt suggested to him that his true vocation was writing, but he also knew that he did not have the means to pursue literature as a full-time occupation. After finishing his studies in 1841, he moved back to Moscow to take up a bureaucratic post at the Moscow governor-general's office. Few details are known about Mei's life or literary activities during the first half of the 1840s. He fulfilled his official duties faithfully in the daytime and spent his evenings at the home of his distant relatives, the Polianskys (Grigorii Mikhailovich Poliansky was a Smolensk landowner whom Mei first met in Moscow). He studied theology, ancient writers, and the Russian chronicles during this time and began to court the woman who later became his wife, Sof'ia Grigor'evna Polianskaia. Mei's poetry from this period is inspired by his emotion for Polianskaia and explores the complex, contradictory nature of a lover's feelings for his beloved—as, for example, in his 1844 poem "Kogda ty, sklonias' nad roial'iu . . ." (When you sit at the piano . . .). Mei's poem "Ne znaiu, otchego tak grustno mne pri nei? . . ." (Why am I so sad with her? . . . , 1844) clearly alludes to Lermontov's "Mne grustno, potomy chto ia tebia liubliu . . ." (I'm sad because I love you . . . , 1840). Yet, despite the

psychological complexity of these verses, Mei never echoes Lermontov's characteristic weltschmertz, or world-weariness; the persona remains idealistic and sincere throughout. Whereas the speakers in Romantic poems often treat their loved ones as naive and unthinking, Mei addresses his beloved as "a girl of intellect and soul" in his poem "Oktavy" (Octaves, 1844). In addition to writing love poetry to his future wife, Mei wrote poems describing the beauty of the Russian countryside: examples of these are "Sosna" (The Pine Tree, 1845) and "Derevnia" (The Countryside, 1847). He also began work on his translation of the medieval Slavic epic *Slovo o polku Igoreve* (The Lay of Prince Igor's Campaign, 1856) into contemporary Russian; the work, which he completed in 1850, six years before its publication as a book, was widely and universally acclaimed.

When in 1849 Mei started to publish regularly in the *Moskvitianin* (The Muscovite), a journal founded by the Slavophile historian Mikhail Petrovich Pogodin, he quit his job at the governor-general's office to devote himself entirely to literature. The journal was then being edited by the influential poet and critic Apollon Aleksandrovich Grigor'ev. To rekindle interest in *Moskvitianin,* whose subscriptions had recently declined, Pogodin had permitted the thirty-year-old Grigor'ev to enlist a group of young and talented writers. Mei was part of this group, which came to be known as the *molodaia redaktsiia* (Young Editors) and included the leading nineteenth-century playwright Aleksandr Nikolaevich Ostrovsky, as well as the poets and playwrights Boris Nikolaevich Almazov, Evgenii Nikolaevich Edel'son, and Tertii Ivanovich Filippov. Although the members of the *molodaia redaktsiia* had different backgrounds, interests, and styles of writing, most espoused some form of Slavophilism, which encouraged them to seek a distinctive and authentic Russian *narodnost'* (national identity) in literature. While both Slavophilism and *narodnost'* were variously defined, the *molodaia redaktsiia* considered *narodnost'* a more ethnographic than philosophical or political concern. Consequently, their interest in what was distinctly Russian centered on Russian history, folklore, and folk songs, which they mined for their quintessentially Russian language, imagery, and characterizations.

The influence of the Slavophile *molodaia redaktsiia* is evident in Mei's historical drama *Tsarskaia nevesta* (The Tsar's Bride), published in *Moskvitianin* in 1849. The female characters are patterned after the two most common feminine types depicted in Russian folk songs: the *udalaia* (daring), passionate woman and the woman who is resigned and *smirennaia* (meek). In the play Griaznoi, an *oprichnik* (a member of the brutal guard of Tsar Ivan IV [Ivan the Terrible]), is desperately in love with the meek Marfa. Liubasha, Griaznoi's daring mistress, substitutes poison for the love potion that Griaznoi plans to give Marfa. As a further complication in the plot, Marfa is chosen as a bride for Ivan the Terrible. In the end Griaznoi kills Liubasha, while Marfa goes mad and dies. Tsar Ivan never appears on stage. The plot of *Tsarskaia nevesta* is based in part on an historical legend about the poisoning and death of the tsar's third wife, Marfa Sobakina. Most of the plot was drawn, however, from the playwright's imagination. The language of *Tsarskaia nevesta* was a welcome contrast to the artificial, flowery rhetoric characteristic of historical plays of the 1830s and 1840s–particularly the propagandistic plays of Nestor Vasil'evich Kukol'nik, Platon Grigor'evich Obodovsky, Rafail Mikhailovich Zotov, and Nikolai Alekseevich Polevoi. Mei's simple, conversational, yet historically accurate dramatic dialogue won praise from critics inside his circle (Pogodin, Grigor'ev) and out (Aleksandr Vasil'evich Druzhinin, Anatolii Fedorovich Koni). Not all reviews of *Tsarskaia nevesta,* however, were positive. Some critics faulted the play for its many and unnecessary scenes, melodramatic denouement, and historical inaccuracies–such as the depiction of free mixing between the sexes (a cultural taboo in medieval Russia). Fifty years after its initial publication, Mei's play was adapted as an opera by the composer Nikolai Andreevich Rimsky-Korsakov; the opera, also called *Tsarskaia nevesta,* had its premiere in Moscow at the Solodovnikov Theater on 3 November 1899.

Mei married Sof'ia Polianskaia in April 1850, just after his debut as a dramatist in the pages of *Moskvitianin.* In the fall of that same year the couple traveled to St. Petersburg for the staging of *Tsarskaia nevesta* at the Aleksandrinskii Theater. After the play was successfully produced, they spent some time in the country on a friend's Smolensk estate, where Mei translated works by the nineteenth-century Polish Romantic poet Adam Mickiewicz and assembled local folklore and songs. In March 1852 Mei and his wife moved back to Moscow, where he began his new job as an inspector for the Second Moscow Gymnasium. He began this new job filled with humanitarian zeal: he worked to improve conditions for the students who boarded at the school; to make relations between students and their tutors more amicable; and to increase the financial support for able students from poor families. Unintentionally, however, he became a thorn in the side of the older, more conservative school administrators, who were apparently less than appreciative of the young poet's energy and generous spirit. Mei's position in Moscow became increasingly uncomfortable: disagreements at the gymnasium, friction with his colleagues at *Moskvitianin,* and limited possibilities for publishing his poetry led to his decision to leave the city where he had been born and for which he seems to have felt a special affinity. Another less overt but per-

Mei in 1836, while he was a student at the lycée (drawing by S. Ia. Golubtsov; from Mei, Stikhotvoreniia i dramy, *1947)*

haps more powerful incentive for leaving the city was that Mei had developed a serious drinking problem in Moscow, and his wife hoped to remove him from Grigor'ev's circle, where excessive drinking was the norm. Her fears seem well justified, given Grigor'ev's description, according to Richard Taruskin's *Opera and Drama in Russia: As Preached and Practiced in the 1860s,* of the members of the *molodaia redaktsiia* as "young, daring, honest, talented, and drunken."

In the spring of 1853 Mei and Sof'ia went to St. Petersburg to petition for a new appointment from the minister of education, Avram Sergeevich Norov. They requested a position somewhere in the south of Russia, ostensibly because of Sof'ia's health. Norov granted Mei a position as the inspector for the Second Gymnasium in Odessa. Yet, the demands of Mei's creditors as well as the onset of war in the Crimea delayed their departure from the capital, and–after the couple had successfully sent their furniture to Odessa–he was fired for failing to report to his post. As a consequence, he remained in St. Petersburg and from 1854 until 1859 worked regularly for *Biblioteka dlia chteniia* (A Reading Library), an influential journal that offered its readers both literary and scholarly works. In the 1850s Mei wrote, edited, and proofread for *Panteon* (Pantheon), *Russkoe slovo* (The Russian Word), *Iskra* (The Spark), *Otechestvennye zapiski* (Notes of the Fatherland), *Syn otechestva* (Son of the Fatherland), and other St. Petersburg journals. Despite the poet's hard work and frequently attested literary skills, however, the material conditions of his life did not improve. He and his wife lived a bohemian existence in a poorly heated, cheaply furnished small apartment with little money for food. In a letter Sof'ia wrote to her sister during the winter of 1854, she complains that "there is nothing to eat and no money to pay the postman." Dire need, however, did not seem to compromise Mei's generosity, as he gave money to anyone if their need seemed greater than his own. Mei was also fond of entertaining in the "Moscow style" and would encourage friends and acquaintances to stop by and enjoy food and drink, which he had gone into debt to provide. The material conditions of Mei's life no doubt encouraged him to seek oblivion in drunkenness, and these convivial bouts of drinking by the 1850s were fast becoming a fatal disease. Mei's deepening association with his former lycée classmate Grigorii Aleksandrovich Kushelev-Bezborodko, a wealthy patron of the arts known for his drinking parties, indirectly led to the poet's early death.

The clash between Mei's Romantic idealism and the everyday reality of poverty in the capital seemed to charge the poet's lyrics with greater depth and poignancy. Although in many respects the nadir of his personal life, the St. Petersburg years (1852–1862) were the height of his literary career. Less elevated, more contemporary issues find their way into his writing during this period. For instance, he writes about his problems with the censor in his poem "O gospodi, poshli dolgoterpen'e . . ." (Oh, God, send me long-sufferance . . . , 1855). In a style reminiscent of Nikolai Alekseevich Nekrasov, he follows with his imagination the city smoke that issues from the chimneys of the rich and poor alike in his poem "Dym" (Smoke, 1861). In "Sumerki" (Twilight, 1858) he expresses his bitterness at the injustices of life, his own weakness, and his lack of freedom. "Barashki" (Whitecaps, 1860) and "Spat' pora" (Time for Sleep, 1861) constitute his poetic response to the emancipation of the serfs in 1861 and express his hopes for a freer Russia. Though written slightly before his sojourn in St. Petersburg, some of Mei's prose also demonstrates the writer's desire to turn elements of everyday life into art. In 1850 he wrote his *Okhota* (The Hunt), consisting of two sketches that anticipated Ivan Sergeevich Turgenev's *Zapiski okhotnika* (A Hunter's Sketches, 1852)–"Sbornoe voskresen'e"

(Open Season) and "Medvezh'ia travlia" (Bear Hunting), both published in *Moskvitianin* in 1850. In these short works (his first published prose), Mei strives to create a feeling of simplicity and spontaneity while describing ordinary events.

Some of Mei's St. Petersburg poetry reflects his interest in the Bible. Unlike his lyrics of this period, which incorporate everyday realia, his biblical poems present a world that is remote and purely aesthetic. In "Otoidi ot menia, Satana! . . ." (Get thee behind me, Satan! . . . , 1852) a scene depicting Christ's temptation by earthly power is followed by a series of descriptive pictures of the peoples and cultures of ancient Palestine, Egypt, India, Greece, and Rome. At one point the speaker focuses on the image of a sleeping North (Russia)–a "colossus" waiting to leap up and shake off its fetters of ice. By depicting the seemingly arbitrary rise and fall of cultures and civilizations, Mei suggests the immutability of the central biblical drama that the poem depicts. Another of Mei's biblical poems is "Evreiskie pesni" (Hebrew Songs, 1856), a reworking of the Old Testament "Song of Songs" that replaces the sometimes inaccessible language of ancient oriental poetry with a simpler lexicon and more concise comparisons. Mei's "Evreiskie pesni" was favorably reviewed by contemporary critics–most notably, Nikolai Aleksandrovich Dobroliubov. In *History of Nineteenth-Century Russian Literature* (1974) Dmitrii Ivanovich Čiževskij, a twentieth-century critic and literary historian, notes that Mei "portrayed the ancient and biblical world with the same care as he did Russia and the Russians."

In addition to the Bible, classical antiquity also informed Mei's work in the 1850s and early 1860s. He saw ancient Rome not as a source of order and harmony but rather as a source of passion and conflict. Two of his works are set in Nero's Rome: the historical drama *Serviliia* (Servilia, 1850–1860) and the *poema* (long narrative poem) "Tsvety" (Flowers, 1855). Although it features a fictional love story, the plot of *Serviliia*–which is the name of a Roman senator's daughter–was based on Tacitus's and Svetonius's historical accounts of the persecution of the Christians by the Stoics. The play was faulted for lacking dramatic action and for being, in general, too cerebral. More than forty years later Rimsky-Korsakov created an opera based on *Serviliia;* it had its first performance on 1 October 1902 at the Mariinskii Theater in St. Petersburg. "Tsvety," Mei's next work based on Nero's Rome, met with a much more positive response from both experts and the general public. According to K. K. Bukhmeier's introduction to Mei's 1972 *Izbrannye proizvedeniia,* its epic grandeur and restraint and its abundant and striking geographical details prompted Grigor'ev to call it "a pearl in any language, a picture by a true master." Classical mythology and antiquity are also the subjects of Mei's much-admired poems "Galateia" (Galatea, 1858), "Frine" (Phryne, 1859)—which takes its title from the nickname of a fourth-century-B.C. Athenian courtesan who was the model for Appelles' picture of Aphrodite and also for Praxiteles' statue of Aphrodite—and "Obman" (The Deception, 1861).

Another of Mei's successful works from the 1850s is the historical drama *Pskovitianka* (The Maiden from Pskov, published 1860). *Pskovitianka* continues the tradition, established by Walter Scott's historical fiction and by Pushkin's historical drama *Boris Godunov* (1825), of intertwining the lives of the historically significant and insignificant. Like *Tsarskaia nevesta*, *Pskovitianka* recalls the "terrible" second half of the reign of Ivan the Terrible, particularly the tsar's efforts to bring formerly independent cities under the central authority of Moscow. Drawing on Karamzin's *Istoriia gosudarstva Rossiiskogo* (History of the Russian State, 1818–1826)—a work that Mei had loved and studied while still a child—and the ancient Russian *letopisi* (chronicles), the drama attempts to give an explanation for Tsar Ivan's unexpected leniency toward the people of Pskov after his cruel suppression of the city of Novgorod. To account for Ivan's change of heart, the play proposes a meeting between the tsar and his illegitimate daughter from Pskov, Ol'ga (whose existence is not supported by the historical record). This meeting reminds the tsar of his love for the girl's mother and softens his heart. Mei's vivid dramatization of a stormy meeting of the city *veche* as well as his psychologically complex portrait of Ivan the Terrible won immediate praise. Turgenev called *Pskovitianka* a "lofty artistic work," as quoted in *Russkie pisateli, 1800–1917: Biograficheskii slovar'* (Russian Writers, 1800–1917: A Biographical Dictionary, 1994). He wanted to publish it in *Sovremmenik* (The Contemporary), the most influential journal of nineteenth-century Russia; yet, Nikolai Gavrilovich Chernyshevsky, then editor of the journal, opposed the idea. The historical plays of both Ostrovsky and Aleksei Konstantinovich Tolstoy demonstrate the influence of *Pskovitianka*. In addition, the play inspired Rimsky-Korsakov's opera of the same name, which had its premiere on 13 January 1873 in St. Petersburg at the Mariinskii Theater.

In his lycée poem "Lunatik" Mei had described the poet as a loud and free singer of songs, and the number of songs he wrote during the 1850s and early 1860s demonstrates that he meant this description of the poet's task quite literally. More than thirty of Mei's works have been set to music by such notable composers as Mikhail Ivanovich Glinka, Petr Il'ich Chaikovsky, Aleksandr Porfir'evich Borodin, Rimsky-Korsakov, Cesar Antonovich Tsui, Modest Petrovich Mussorgsky, and Sergei Vasil'evich Rakhmaninov. *Tsarskaia nevesta*

Mei and his wife, Sof'ia Grigor'evna, early 1850s (portrait by an unknown artist; from Mei, Stikhotvoreniia i dramy, 1947)

and *Pskovitianka* were made into successful operas by Rimsky-Korsakov. Mei wrote numerous *pesni-zhaloby* (songs of complaint), a traditional folk-song genre in which a young peasant woman bemoans her bitter fate at being married to someone she does not love. He also wrote imitations of folk ballads and historical songs—"Oboroten'" (The Werewolf, 1859), "Leshii" (The Wood Goblin, 1861), and "Volkhv" (The Magician, 1861)—that reflect his interest in folkloric superstitions. Modeled after the unrhymed folk genre of the *bylina*, "Pesnia pro boiarina Evpatiia Kolovrata" (Song about the Boyar Evpatii Kolovrat, 1859) tells the story of the destruction of Riazan'. Other historical songs by Mei include "Pesnia pro kniaginiu Ul'ianu Andreevnu Viazemskuiu" (Song about the Princess Ul'iana Andreevna Viazemskaia, 1859) and "Aleksandr Nevsky" (1861). In these historical songs, Mei strives to revive the heroic aspects of the Russian past in the popular consciousness.

Mei's interest in and facility for the musical aspects of the Russian language—together with his impressive knowledge of German, French, Polish, English, classical Hebrew, and classical Greek—made him one of the best translators of his day. In addition to his translation of the Russian epic *Slovo o polku Igoreve,* he is known for his translations of the ancient poets Anacreon and Theocritus. His translations of works by Schiller, Heinrich Heine, Mickiewicz, Pierre-Jean de Béranger, and Ukrainian poet Taras Shevchenko garnered him particular praise. Mei's translations were published in book form in the five-volume collected edition of his works in 1887. According to G. M. Fridlender's introduction to the 1962 edition of Mei's *Izbrannye proizvedeniia,* though critical of Mei's original poetry and drama for its apparent lack of involvement with social issues, Chernyshevsky and Dobroliubov praised his translations, the latter calling them "irreproachable." In his translations Mei tries to render the author's creation as faithfully and precisely as possible—an ideal that was relatively new at the time to translators, who often felt free to personalize and reinvent the original.

All of Mei's feverish artistic activity during the 1850s and early 1860s rendered him neither healthy nor financially secure. As a member of the "literary proletariat," Mei worked long hours for which he was poorly paid; his alcoholism and selfless generosity made his already dismal financial situation even worse. Throughout his literary career he had dreamed of having his own journal, but it was his wife Sof'ia who actually realized those dreams in 1862 and began publishing an illustrated journal of women's fashions. The success of Sof'ia's venture improved the family's finances, but it was already too late for Mei, who had been sick for more than a year and finally died on 16 May 1862 of, according to Bukhmeier, "paralysis of the lungs." He was buried in the Mitrofan'evskoe cemetery in St. Petersburg.

The work of Lev Aleksandrovich Mei was Romantic in the sense that there was a typically Romantic division between a "pure" world of art and an unaesthetic world of everyday reality. (In particular, his lycée works and his poems based on classical and biblical themes evidence this division.) Yet, his lyric poetry clearly shows him aiming to integrate the two spheres. Mei's historical dramas *Tsarskaia nevesta* and *Pskovitianka* are also Romantic in that they feature the characters' tortured and often fatal passions. The realistic, historically accurate dramatic language and convincingly complex psychological portraiture (especially of Ivan the Terrible) in these plays, however, greatly influenced subsequent Russian historical dramas. Mei's bold and successful experiments with various poetic meters and his ability to invest folkloric images, subjects, and cadences with his own compelling vision have secured for him an important place in the history of Russian letters.

Letters:

Vladimir Rafailovich Zotov, *Lev Aleksandrovich Mei i ego znachenie v russkoi literature* (St. Petersburg: N. G. Martynov, 1887), pp. 29–30;

To Ia. I. Rostovtsev, *Russkaia starina,* no. 1 (1889): 194;

Vestnik literatury, nos. 11–12 (1916): 197–199;

Apollon Aleksandrovich Grigor'ev: Materialy dlia biografii, edited by Vladimir Kniazhnina (Petrograd: Akademiia nauk, 1917), p. 382;

Neizdannye pis'ma k A. N. Ostrovskomu L. N. Tolstogo, I. A. Goncharova, N. A. Nekrasova, F. M. Dostoevskogo, A. F. Pisemskogo, i drugie, edited by M. D. Prygunov, Iu. A. Bakhrushin and N. A. Brodsky (Moscow & Leningrad: Academia, 1932), pp. 220–222;

Pis'ma k A. V. Druzhininu (1850–1863), edited by Pavel Sergeevich Popov (Moscow: Gosudarstvennyi literaturnyi muzei, 1948), pp. 206, 214, 255.

Bibliographies:

N. V. Gerbel', "Bibliografiia sochinenii Meia," *Knizhnyi vestnik,* no. 19 (1865);

Petr Vasil'evich Bykov, *Bibliografiia sochinenii i perevodov L'va Aleksandrovicha Meia* (St. Petersburg: N. G. Martynov, 1887);

Bykov, "Bibliografiia sochinenii L. A. Meia," in Mei's *Polnoe sobranie sochinenii,* 3 volumes, edited by Bykov (St. Petersburg: A. F. Marks, 1911), III: 331–349.

Biographies:

Ia. P. Polonsky, "Mei kak chelovek i pisatel'," *Russkii vestnik,* no. 9 (1896);

Pasil Vasil'evich Bykov, "L. A. Mei. (Kritiko-biograficheskii ocherk)," in Mei's *Polnoe sobranie sochinenii,* edited by Bykov, volume 1 (St. Petersburg: A. F. Marks, 1910), pp. 5–40;

A. G. Polianskaia, "K biografii L. A. Meia," *Russkaia starina,* nos. 3–5, 10 (1911);

Solomon Abramovich Reiser, "L. A. Mei," in Mei's *Stikhotvoreniia i dramy,* edited by Reiser (Moscow: Sovetskii pisatel', 1947), pp. v–xxxi;

Reiser, "Mei," in *Istoriia russkoi literatury,* volume 8, part 2 (Moscow & Leningrad: AN SSSR, 1956), pp. 302–314.

References:

Tamara Andreevna Bakhor, *Stikhotvoreniia Meia i stikhovaia kul'tura serediny XIX v.* (Tartu, 1990);

Dmitrii Ivanovich Čiževskij, *History of Nineteenth-Century Russian Literature,* volume 2, translated by Richard Noel Porter, edited by Serge A. Zenkovsky (Nashville: Vanderbilt University Press, 1974), p. 126;

Nikolai Aleksandrovich Dobroliubov, "Stikhotvoreniia L. Meia," in his *Polnoe sobranie sochinenii: V shesti tomakh,* 6 volumes, edited by Pavel Ivanovich Lebedev-Poliansky (Leningrad: GIKhL, 1934), I: 300–303;

Viktor Evgen'evich Gusev, ed., *Pesni i romansy russkikh poetov* (Moscow & Leningrad: Sovetskii pisatel', 1963), p. 655;

A. A. Izmailov, "Baianovy gusli. (L. A. Mei i ego sochineniia)," *Literaturnoe i populiarno-nauchnoe prilozhenie k "Nive,"* 1 (1910): 467–494;

Petr Alekseevich Nikolaev, ed., *Russkie pisateli, 1800–1917: Biograficheskii slovar'* (Moscow: Sovetskaia entsiklopediia, 1994), pp. 565–568;

I. A. Ovchinina, *Dramaturgiia L. A. Meia* (Moscow, 1980);

Vladimir Alekseevich Piast, ed., *L. A. Mei i ego poeziia* (St. Petersburg: Parfenon, 1922);

Nikolai Nikolaevich Sergievsky, *Russkii poet L. A. Mei* (St. Petersburg: Sel'skii vestnik, 1913);

Richard Taruskin, *Opera and Drama in Russia: As Preached and Practiced in the 1860s* (Ann Arbor, Mich.: UMI Research Press, 1981), p. 143;

Margarita Mikhailovna Umanskaia, "Istoriko-bytovye p'esy L. A. Meia i A. N. Ostrovskogo," in her *Russkaia istoricheskaia dramaturgiia 60-kh godov XIX veka,* Uchenye zapiski Saratovskogo pedagogicheskogo instituta, no. 35 (Vol'sk, 1958), pp. 271–305;

Vladimir Rafailovich Zotov, *L. A. Mei i ego znachenie v russkoi literature* (St. Petersburg: N. G. Martynov, 1887);

Zotov, "Peterburg v sorokovykh godakh," *Istoricheskii vestnik,* 6 (1890): 536–537.

Papers:

The papers of Lev Aleksandrovich Mei are held in both Moscow and St. Petersburg. The principal collection, which includes manuscripts of his poetry and letters, is located in Moscow at the Russian State Archive of Literature and Art (RGALI), fond 310. His letters to M. P. Pogodin can be found as well at the Russian State Library (RGB, formerly the Lenin Library), fond 213. In St. Petersburg, Mei's papers are held among the papers of his wife, Sof'ia Grigor'evna Mei, at both the Russian National Library (RNB), fond 475, and the Institute of Russian Literature (IRLI, Pushkin House), fond 257.

Nikolai Konstantinovich Mikhailovsky

(15 November 1842 – 28 January 1904)

Wayne Dowler
University of Toronto

BOOKS: *Sochineniia,* 4 volumes (St. Petersburg: F. S. Sushchinsky, 1879–1885);

Kriticheskie opyty, 3 volumes (St. Petersburg: S. P. Iakovlev, 1887–1894);

Literatura i zhizn' (St. Petersburg: Novosti, 1892);

Sochineniia, 6 volumes (St. Petersburg: Russkoe bogatstvo, 1896–1897);

Literaturnye vospominaniia i sovremennaia smuta, 2 volumes (St. Petersburg: Russkoe bogatstvo, 1900);

Otkliki, 2 volumes (St. Petersburg: Russkoe bogatstvo, 1904);

Poslednie sochineniia, 2 volumes (St. Petersburg: Russkoe bogatstvo, 1905);

Iz romana "Kar'era Oladushkina" (St. Petersburg: Russkoe bogatstvo, 1906);

Polnoe sobranie sochinenii, volumes 1–8, 10 (St. Petersburg: Russkoe bogatstvo and N. N. Mikhailovsky, 1909–1914);

Chto takoe progress? (Petrograd: Kolos, 1922).

Editions and Collections: *Revoliutsionnye stat'i* (Berlin: G. Shteinits, 1906);

Literaturno-kriticheskie stat'i, edited, with an introduction, by G. A. Bialyi (Moscow: Goslitizdat, 1957);

Literaturnaia kritika. Stat'i o russkoi literature XIX–nachala XX veka, with an introduction by B. V. Averin (Leningrad: Khudozhestvennaia literatura, 1989);

Literaturnaia kritika i vospominaniia, with an introduction by M. G. Petrova and V. G. Khoros (Moscow: Iskusstvo, 1995);

Geroi i tolpa, edited by V. V. Kozlovsky (St. Petersburg: Aleteiia, 1998).

Editions in English: "What is Progress?" and "Darwin's Theory and Social Science" (excerpts), translated by James P. Scanlon, in *Russian Philosophy,* edited by Scanlon, James M. Edie, and Mary-Barbara Zeldin, with the collaboration of George L. Kline, volume 2 (Chicago: Quadrangle, 1965);

Dostoevsky: A Cruel Talent, translated by Spencer Cadmus (Ann Arbor, Mich.: Ardis, 1978).

Nikolai Konstantinovich Mikhailovsky

OTHER: P. J. Proudhon, *Frantsuzskaia demokratiia,* translated by Mikhailovsky (St. Petersburg, 1867);

John Stuart Mill, *Podchinennost' zhenshchiny,* with a preface by Mikhailovsky and others (St. Petersburg: S. V. Zvonareva, 1869);

Nikolai Vasil'evich Shelgunov, *Sochineniia,* with an introduction by Mikhailovsky (St. Petersburg, 1891);

Grigorii Zakharovich Eliseev, *Sochineniia,* 2 volumes, with an introduction by Mikhailovsky (St. Petersburg: K. T. Soldatenkov, 1894), I: 1–46;

Vissarion Grigor'evich Belinsky, *Sochineniia,* 4 volumes in 2 books, contribution by Mikhailovsky (St. Petersburg: F. Pavlenkov, 1896);

Gleb Ivanovich Uspensky, *Sochineniia,* 2 volumes, with an introduction by Mikhailovsky (St. Petersburg: Iu. N. Erlikh, 1896–1898);

V zashchitu slova. Sbornik, contributions by Mikhailovsky, A. V. Peshekhonov, and P. N. Miliukov (St. Petersburg: N. N. Klobukov, 1905).

Nikolai Mikhailovsky was one of the most influential and respected journalists in Russia in the second half of the nineteenth century. He was a *narodnik* (Populist) who believed that the autarkic Russian peasant commune contained the kernel of a future socialist society. The main purpose of thought and action for Mikhailovsky was to create the conditions for the flowering of the integral personality. Subjective sociology, of which he was a cofounder, obliged a person to oppose progress and the so-called objective course of events in the name of the subjective ideal of the well-rounded individual. A prolific literary critic, Mikhailovsky believed that art should serve social ideals. During his long career he pronounced his stern but entertaining judgments on most of the important writers of his day.

Nikolai Konstantinovich Mikhailovsky was born into the Russian nobility on 15 November 1842 to a Russianized German mother and a gentry landowner father in the provincial town of Meshchovsk in the province of Kaluga. His mother, Iuliia Vasil'evna (née Fisher) Mikhailovskaia, whom he did not remember, died in his early childhood; his father, Konstantin Pavlovich Mikhailovsky, took little interest in his son's upbringing. In the late 1840s Konstantin Pavlovich sold the estate and moved to Kostroma, where Mikhailovsky attended the gymnasium. When his father died in 1856, before Mikhailovsky graduated, his relatives sent him to the Institute of Mining Engineering in St. Petersburg. There he proved to be an able and diligent student. He soon acquired a lasting attachment to the *tolstye zhurnaly* (thick journals) that proliferated during the emancipation period. In April 1861 he debuted as a literary critic in *Rassvet* (The Dawn), a journal for young women, with a review of "Sof'ia Nikolaevna Belovodova" (1850), an excerpt from Ivan Aleksandrovich Goncharov's novel *Obryv* (The Precipice, 1869). The review, which focused on the "woman question," set out the main idea of all of Mikhailovsky's subsequent aesthetic criticism: art should serve a social purpose. Later in the decade he wrote a series on the emancipation of women and contributed a laudatory introduction to *Podchinennost' zhenshchiny* (1869),

the Russian translation of John Stuart Mill's *The Subjection of Women* (1869).

A lightning rod for student protest in the Mining Institute, Mikhailovsky organized a demonstration on behalf of student corporatism during the widespread student protests of 1861. He was expelled before sitting for the examinations in his specialist subjects. After a brief retreat to Kostroma he returned to the capital intent on studying law. But in December the authorities closed St. Petersburg University, and he was prevented from enrolling. Excited by the forthcoming judicial reforms of 1864, Mikhailovsky continued to pursue his interest in the law, and he read widely in Russian and European juridical literature. In 1862 he met the Populist publicist and editor Grigorii Zakorovich Eliseev, whose views on communalism influenced him deeply. Eliseev guided him to Pierre-Joseph Proudhon's *Système des contradictions économiques, ou Philosophie de la misère* (1846; translated as *System of Economic Contradictions: or, The Philosophy of Poverty,* 1888). This work convinced him of the futility of law as an instrument of deep social change. In 1863 Mikhailovsky put his meager inheritance into a cooperative bookbinding business according to plans advocated by Eliseev. The failing business soon swallowed his inheritance.

Mikhailovsky's links to the book trade brought him to the attention of Nikolai Stepanovich Kurochkin, editor of *Knizhnyi vestnik* (The Book Messenger). After struggling for a time to make his living by tutoring young foreigners, Mikhailovsky was relieved in 1865 to secure a permanent place as reviewer for *Knizhnyi vestnik*. His new collaborators encouraged his study of Proudhon, and in 1866 he wrote "Prudon i nashi publitsisty" (Proudhon and Our Publicists) for the journal. Proudhon's defense of the individual against all external authority was the touchstone of Mikhailovsky's later social thought. Equally important in the evolution of his "subjective sociology" was another collaborator, Nikolai Dmitrievich Nozhin, a marine biologist and disciple of the English social thinker Herbert Spencer, who coined the phrase "survival of the fittest."

Mikhailovsky's employment was short-lived. Kurochkin was implicated in Dmitrii Vladimirovich Karakozov's attempt to assassinate Tsar Alexander II in 1866; he was arrested and imprisoned for four months. Though questioned, Mikhailovsky was not charged and was left to edit the journal alone; it folded in autumn of 1866. Until spring of 1869 Mikhailovsky eked out a living by writing articles for several *tolstye zhurnaly*. Most promising was his association with *Sovremennoe obozrenie* (The Contemporary Review). Mikhailovsky had written the first part of a novel, "Bor'ba" (The Struggle), which Nikolai L'vovich Tiblen, the editor of *Sovremennoe obozrenie,* agreed to publish. Before the novel went to press, however, Tiblen fled abroad to escape his creditors, and the journal closed. Mikhailovsky never finished the novel, although he later used material from it in his series "Vperemezhku" (Alternatively) in the 1870s for the journal *Otechestvennye zapiski* (Notes of the Fatherland).

During Mikhailovsky's time of troubles, Eliseev had courted him on behalf of the newly formed *Otechestvennye zapiski,* led by the poet Nikolai Alekseevich Nekrasov and the novelist Mikhail Evgrafovich Saltykov. Nekrasov's reputation–sullied by his behavior during the Karakozov affair–was, for Mikhailovsky, an obstacle to joining the journal. Finally, on meeting Nekrasov in 1869, the force of the poet's personality overcame Mikhailovsky's scruples. In March he joined the journal that shaped the rest of his career. Nekrasov cherished him, and according to his *Polnoe sobranie sochinenii i pisem,* called Mikhailovsky in 1869 the "most gifted of the new men."

Between 1869 and 1871 Mikhailovsky wrote a series of articles for *Otechestvennye zapiski* in which he developed the principles of subjective sociology, his major contribution to Russian social thought. The series included "Chto takoe progress?" (What is Progress?), "Teoriia Darvina i obshchestvennaia nauka" ([Charles] Darwin's Theory and Social Science), and "Anologicheskii metod v obshchestvennoi nauke" (The Analogical Method in Social Science). Like Petr Lavrovich Lavrov, with whom he created "ethical sociology," Mikhailovsky took as his points of departure both the moral element and the individual. Both men disputed the inevitability of progress, and both believed that the educated elite owed a debt to the masses that had to be repaid in social action. On many subjects, however, their views diverged significantly.

The German embryologist Karl von Baer defined progress in the organic world as a movement from the simple (homogeneous) to the complex (heterogeneous). Spencer made this definition of progress a law in the social realm. Mikhailovsky accepted the definition but recognized an inevitable struggle between higher individualities, who seek to integrate their parts into the whole, and lower individualities, who seek to preserve their integrity against the whole. Organic society is inevitably in conflict with the many-sided personality. In Mikhailovsky's terms the *tsel'naia* (integral), or fully rounded, personality is the opposite of the integrated personality, which has been adapted as a specialized unit of the social whole. In his view the division of labor drives the process of social integration.

With an eye to the tripartite division of history proposed by Auguste Comte, the French sociologist and founder of positivism, Mikhailovsky, too, discerns three ages in social development. The first he calls "objectively simple cooperation." Early societies were homogeneous, but their members were highly heterogeneous in function

and personality. Division of labor produced the second, or "eccentric," age of development. It reached its apogee in the Middle Ages with the feudal estate structure. Capitalism, which rested on the highest degree of the division of labor and specialization, had subsequently destroyed the feudal estates but had also curtailed small units of economic self-sufficiency. Among the communal, self-sufficient survivors was the Russian *mir* (peasant commune), in which Mikhailovsky places his hopes for the third age, "subjectively simple cooperation." "Progress," Mikhailovsky concludes in *Chto tako progress?* (What Is Progress? 1922), "is the gradual realization of the integral individual, of the fullest and most diversified division of labor possible among human organs and the least possible division of labor among persons. Everything that stands in the way of this process is immoral, unjust, harmful, and irrational. Everything that reduces the heterogeneity of society and so increases the heterogeneity of its members is moral, just, rational, and useful." Lavrov replied that to end the divison of labor would produce a static society.

In 1873 Fyodor Dostoevsky called Mikhailovsky the "most sincere journalist" in the capital. Mikhailovsky repaid the compliment that year by attacking Dostoevsky's novel *Besy* (The Devils). The characters of the novel are pale figures, he says, who live on the border between reason and madness and who perform moral tasks artificially imposed on them by their creator. Neither their actions nor their feverish religious preoccupations are representative of Russian youth. "You focus your attention," he complains, "on a contemptible handful of madmen and malcontents." When, in 1873, Lavrov invited Mikhailovsky abroad to join the revolutionaries in exile, Mikhailovsky declined, declaring that he was not a revolutionary. He went on to say that he feared the reactionaries less than the revolutionaries.

Four years earlier, in 1869, Mikhailovsky had married Mariia Evgrafovna Pavlovskaia, a music student at the St. Petersburg Conservatory. Older than Mikhailovsky, she was more passionate and fun-loving than her staid husband. In 1873 Mikhailovsky formed a common-law relationship with Liudmila Nikolaevna (surname unknown), with whom he had two sons, Mark and Nikolai.

From 1875 to 1876 Mikhailovsky wrote a series of articles in *Otechestvennye zapiski* called "Bor'ba za individual'nost'" (The Struggle for Individuality). Building on his earlier ideas about the struggle between human individuality and social individuality, Mikhailovsky contends that the thinking person can and should oppose the objective course of social development with his subjective ideal of personal development. Individuals should judge both persons and social phenomena from the point of view of their subjective ideal. Since the conditions for the emergence of the subjective ideal were included in the objective course of events, the ideal was not arbitrary but appropriate to the current stage of historical development.

In "Desnitsa i shuitsa L'va Tolstogo" (The Right and Left Hands of Leo Tolstoy, published in *Otechestvennye zapiski*, 1875), a review of Tolstoy's article "O narodnom obrazovanii" (On Popular Education, published in his 1873 *Sochineniia*), Mikhailovsky treats Tolstoy as an ally in his critique of civilization. Tolstoy grasps that the progress of civilization matters less than the progress of human well-being. Like Mikhailovsky, he rejects the European path for Russia, believing that humans have a rational and moral right to oppose apparently inevitable historical phenomena because they are harmful and immoral. In "Desnitsa i shuitsa L'va Tolstogo" Mikhailovsky makes his well-known distinction between *degree* of development and *type* of development. England, he grants, has attained a much higher degree of development than has Russia. Russia, however, represents a higher type of development than does England because of the economic autarky of the *mir,* which promotes the many-sidedness of personality and function of the individual members in the commune. Mikhailovsky parts company with Tolstoy, though, over the latter's belief that the *narod* (common people) should set the school curriculum. In particular, Tolstoy believes that education should not try to form the character of the pupil. Mikhailovsky understands education as a relationship of two people or groups of people seeking an equality of knowledge, and the curriculum must reflect that reciprocity. Moreover, says Mikhailovsky, all knowledge carries with it convictions and values that inevitably shape the pupil.

Mikhailovsky's piece on Tolstoy belongs to a cycle of articles, titled "Zapiski profana" (Notes of a Layman, published in *Otechestvennye zapiski*, 1875–1877), in which he elaborates his views on art. By "layman" he means that, while recognizing art and science as the epitome of human creativity, he evaluates them to the extent that they work on behalf of society and the *narod.* A central article in the cycle was "O Shillere i o mnogom drugom" (On Schiller and Much Else, 1876). Mikhailovsky discovers his ideal of the artist in Friedrich Schiller, who, far from defending art for art's sake, seeks to place aesthetic enjoyment in the service of moral and political aims. He calls Schiller an unrivaled world genius who looks on art as a "powerful tool for the attainment of the highest goals." Schiller sees art as the means of restoring the harmony between reason and feeling that the advance of civilization has disrupted. Mikhailovsky, too, was deeply attached to the Romantics' desire to harmonize the knowledge of reason with the knowledge of intuition and emotion; he hoped that a return to simple cooperation in human society would achieve this end.

In 1877 Nekrasov died, and Mikhailovsky became co-editor and later a shareholder of *Otechestvennye zapiski.* The editors of the journal had an uneasy relationship with Populist revolutionaries. In 1871 Mikhailovsky had consulted with members of the Chaikovsky *kruzhok* (circle), the first of the revolutionary Populist groups. While he denied that revolution was necessary to achieving the social and moral ideals of *narodnichestvo* (Populism), he did not reject the use of force in defense of a moral social order. By 1878 he was advocating the establishment of a constitution and parliament in Russia as a necessary condition of social change. With that goal in mind he sought out allies among liberals of the zemstvo (an elected district or provincial council and a training ground for Russian liberals). Although willing to cooperate with liberals for interim goals, Mikhailovsky was never a liberal himself. He continued to distinguish between legal right and moral right and rejected private property and the contractual society advocated by liberals.

As revolutionary fervor grew in 1879, Mikhailovsky sought to deflect the young revolutionaries in the Populist terrorist group Narodnaia volia (The People's Will) away from terrorism and toward a constitutional struggle. He placed some hope in Count Mikhail Tarielovich Loris-Melikov, the minister of the interior, who was considering making concessions to appease liberal public opinion. The execution of a Polish student terrorist in February 1880, however, provoked Mikhailovsky to attack Loris-Melikov's duplicity in an article in June. A meeting in September with the minister only confirmed Mikhailovsky's low opinion of him. As repression of activist *narodniki* mounted, Mikhailovsky abandoned his opposition to revolutionary action. Following the assassination of Tsar Alexander II on 1 March 1881, he joined leaders of Narodnaia volia in sending a letter to the new tsar, Alexander III, asking him to forgive the six arrested assassins and to institute a constitutional regime. In December 1882 the authorities briefly exiled Mikhailovsky from the capital for his harsh criticism of government actions.

The first pogroms against Jews in Russia spurred Mikhailovsky in 1882 to begin a cycle of articles, which extended over twelve years, called "Geroi i tolpa" (Heroes and the Mob). The cycle explores the psychology of mass movements. Mikhailovsky attributes the sudden and unexpected coalescence of the mob around a heroic leader to imitation—the wish to emulate the attributes of the heroic that are absent from the one-sided and limited existence of ordinary people. Mob action provides brief revenge for the monotony and gloom of life, along with a fleeting sense of invincibility. Mikhailovsky idealizes neither the mob nor the hero. The mob is not the *narod;* mobs are unpredictable and changeable, a herd.

Heroes are often fanatics or sociopaths who can attract people both to good and to evil.

By 1882 Mikhailovsky was prepared to concede Dostoevsky's artistic genius but not the moral value of his work. In his article "Zhestokii talant" (A Cruel Talent), published in *Otechestvennye zapiski* that same year, he reviews the second and third volumes of Dostoevsky's recently published collected works. In his early work Mikhailovsky discerns the perennial subjects of Dostoevsky's whole opus: cruelty and tyranny, torment and suffering. Dostoevsky's characters form a menagerie encompassing varieties of wolves and lambs. His writings invariably portray unnecessary suffering, and only his vast talent prevents his works from falling into the sphere of the comic. In his literary criticism Mikhailovsky uses an author's works to reveal his character. Therefore, he makes no essential distinction between Dostoevsky's journalism and his creative writing, employing the former to cast light on the latter. In both the journalism and the novels, according to Mikhailovsky, Dostoevsky portrays the special capacity of Russians, especially the common people, for suffering. While Russians certainly suffer, Mikhailovsky ridicules the idea that they welcome their suffering as a means of redemption. On the one hand, says Mikhailovsky, Dostoevsky is motivated by cruelty, and on the other, by respect for the existing order. If he has an ideal at all, it lies in his declared belief that serfdom poses no obstacle to a moral relationship between serf and master.

Mikhailovsky was kinder to Ivan Sergeevich Turgenev. In "O Turgeneve" (About Turgenev), published in *Otechestvennye zapiski* on 3 September 1883, shortly after the novelist's death, he judges Turgenev to have been a "musical" talent, and "music, as is known, evokes undefined but good, agreeable, and bright emotions." Unlike Nikolai Vasil'evich Gogol, who created purely Russian types, Turgenev was a European writer who portrayed European types in the Russian context. After his novel *Otsy i deti* (Fathers and Children, 1862), according to Mikhailovsky, Turgenev became a victim of his readers' and, perhaps, his own expectation that he would always remain an artist of the present moment—the discoverer of new types. He failed, however, to fulfill that role. For instance, the character Nezhdanov of the late novel *Nov'* (Virgin Soil, 1877) is the same old superfluous man as Turgenev's characters of the early period. With each successive novel, Turgenev merely inserted the same type into new circumstances. Still, he was a genius at individualizing his characters. His strong heroes are invariably dull and without character; his weak heroes are always highly attractive figures around whom a poetic halo shines. Mikhailovsky is surprised that Turgenev showed no interest in the woman question in his novels, in spite of his great sensitivity to a woman's heart. He concludes

that Turgenev was alien in his art to precise thought or decisive action. He had not taken an active part in the struggle against the darkness in Russia but had always served the broad ideals of freedom and enlightenment.

In March 1884 the authorities closed *Otechestvennye zapiski* forever. A year later Mikhailovsky's common-law wife left him for a mining engineer. Mikhailovsky retained custody of his two sons. The following years were difficult, as he sought a new home for his vast journalistic talent. In 1885 he published "Povest' Tavolgina" (The Tale of Tavolgin) in the journal *Russkie vedomosti* (Russian News), an excerpt from an unfinished novel called "Kar'era Oladushkina" (Oladushkin's Career). The surviving fragments of the novel were published in an anthology in 1899 and separately in 1906 as *Iz romana "Kar'era Oladushkina"* (From the Novel *Oladushkin's Career*). The novel is about a "typical scoundrel," a false revolutionary drawn to *narodnichestvo* by ambition but who later abandons the cause. In 1886 Mikhailovsky joined *Severnyi vestnik* (The Northern Messenger) for a couple of years and also contributed to the Geneva-based Populist journal *Samoupravlenie* (Self-Government), which advocated political rights as a prerequisite to social change. He retained, however, his links to more-radical groups. Because of these associations, the authorities again banned him from St. Petersburg in 1891 until the spring of 1892.

In 1891 Mikhailovsky published his "Literaturnye vospominaniia" (Literary Memoirs) in *Russkaia mysl'* (Russian Thought). The memoirs furnish a self-conscious portrayal of the difficult position of the writer-publicist in tsarist Russia and the human costs of prolonged opposition to the regime. The work is spare in autobiographical detail but provides powerful portraits of people such as the Kurochkin brothers, Nekrasov, Saltykov, and Eliseev. Mikhailovsky's growing interest in psychology prompted him in the same year to write a psychological portrait of the Romantic poet Mikhail Iur'evich Lermontov. In 1892 Mikhailovsky became editor of *Russkoe bogatstvo* (Russian Wealth), his last literary home. He reassembled the surviving Populist forces on the journal, which exercised a strong influence on progressive public opinion until the end of the century. Although he wrote on many subjects in these years, including a loving and troubling portrait of the writer Gleb Ivanovich Uspensky in 1897, two themes stand out. The first was the fight against "decadence" in literature and literary criticism; the second was opposition to the rising tide of Marxism among the radical intelligentsia.

In an 1893 article called "Russkoe otrazhenie frantsuzskogo simvolizma" (A Russian Reflection of French Symbolism, published in *Russkoe bogatstvo* in 1893), Mikhailovsky replies to Dmitrii Sergeevich Merezhkovsky's October 1892 public lecture (and later book) titled "O prichinakh upadka i o novykh techeniiakh sovremennoi russkoi literatury" (On the Reasons for the Decline of and on New Trends in Contemporary Russian Literature, 1893). Against Merezhkovsky's assertion that words could never capture the essence of art, Mikhailovsky–while granting that the meanings of words shift according to changing circumstances–contends that all ideas could be expressed by the right choice of words. Mikhailovsky traces Merezhkovsky's mystical views about art to the French symbolists, who were reacting against the naturalism of Emile Zola and the positivism of Comte. He defends his favorite, Comte, who, he points out, had also criticized the aridity of scientific positivism. He argues that Merezhkovsky's concern for the decline of Russian literature is misplaced. Russian writers had never adopted Zola's naturalism and had retained a strong idealism. Although he agrees with Merezhkovsky on the need to unite moral feeling with scientific knowledge through religious feeling, he rejects Merezhkovsky's mysticism and defines religious feeling as the motive force without which both science and moral doctrine are moribund. In Mikhailovsky's view, Merezhkovsky is afraid of Russian reality and seeks refuge in a borrowed mysticism that has no roots in Russian life.

In Friedrich Nietzsche, Mikhailovsky discerned both the brightest light and darkest shadow of the age. In "I eshche o Nitsshe" (More on Nietzsche), published in *Russkoe bogatstvo* in 1894, he recognizes Nietzsche as an ally in his own struggle against historical facts and the tyranny of reality in the name of personality. He holds that for Nietzsche the human personality is the measure of all things, and the right of the personality to the fullest possible life is beyond dispute. Far from being an egoist and immoralist, Nietzsche appears to Mikhailovsky as an extreme idealist and a seeker after the highest morality. Mikhailovsky cannot, however, accept the Nietzschean aristocracy of supermen, contempt for ordinary people, and profound misogyny. He sees in Dostoevsky a precursor of Nietzsche's darker thoughts but is also aware of the many differences that separate the two writers.

In a cycle of articles called "Literatura i zhizn'" (Literature and Life), which he began in the 1890s, Mikhailovsky polemicizes against the surging forces of Marxism among Russian youth. His most determined foe was Georgii Valentinovich Plekhanov, the founder of Russian Marxism. Mikhailovsky had learned much from Marx's critique of capitalism, and his ideal of the integral personality closely resembled Marx's image of the liberated individual under communism. He disputes, however, the scientific claims of Marxism. Nothing about the Marxist historical stages is inevitable, and Russia need not pass through the school of capitalism as the Russian Marxists insist. Pointing to the ambition, aggressiveness, and theoretical dogmatism of Russian Marxists, he fights against their denial of free choice to the individual and

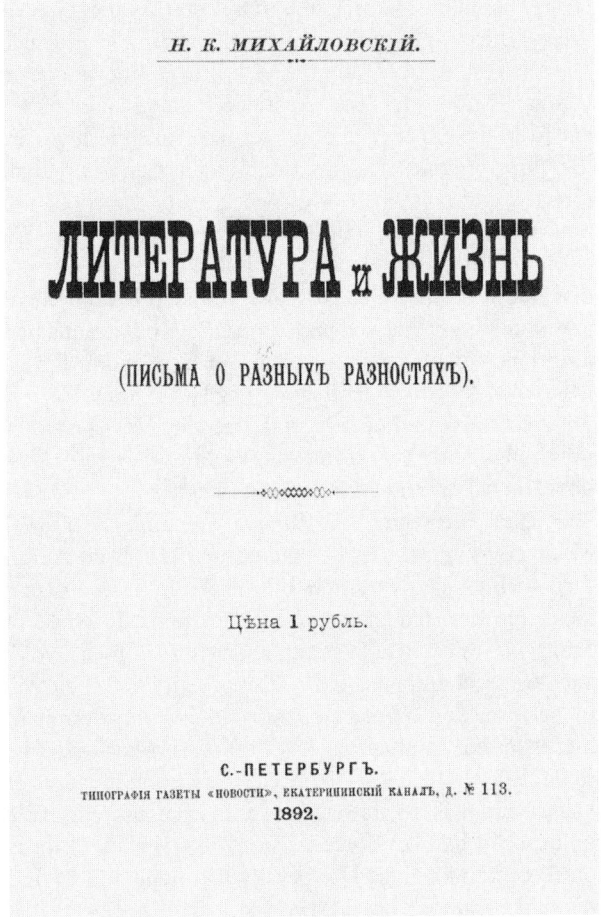

Title page for Mikhailovsky's Literatura i zhizn' *(Literature and Life), a collection of polemical, anti-Marxist articles (Kilgour Collection of Russian Literature, Harvard University Library)*

rejects the class struggle as the impetus for socialism. Instead, Mikhailovsky believes, the individual has to assert the ideals of socialism against all classes.

Mikhailovsky had much in common with Tolstoy. Both rejected progress as it was then generally understood, and both opposed ethics to the laws of history. They agreed as well that the social division of labor should be replaced by the division of each individual's labor. Mikhailovsky could not, however, accept Tolstoy's views in "Chto takoe iskusstvo?" (What is Art? 1897–1898). In his 1898 articles "O L. N. Tolstom i khudozhestvennykh vystavkakh" (About L. N. Tolstoy and Art Exhibitions) and "Eshche ob iskusstve i gr. Tolstom" (More About Art and Count Tolstoy), both published in *Russkoe bogatstvo*, Mikhailovsky disputes Tolstoy's separation of art from enjoyment and his insistence that art is necessary for the good of the individual and humanity because it joins people in a common feeling. Tolstoy sees art as the simple transference of feeling from artist to audience. Mikhailovsky discerns a more complex process. An actor, for example, portrays suffering, which the audience experiences. At the same time, however, the audience enjoys the portrayal. The experience of art is quite different from the experience of witnessing real suffering. Art, therefore, imitates feelings rather than expresses them directly, and enjoyment is as necessary to the contagion that Tolstoy correctly attributed to art as it is to procreation or eating. Mikhailovsky also dismisses Tolstoy's division of art into elite art that is founded in enjoyment and popular art that is founded on religion. Russians had long enjoyed art, both in secular and religious forms. Mikhailovsky concludes that although art is desirable, it is not necessary to human good. He deplores Tolstoy's preachings and finds in his latest works the "most despotic, merciless, and cruel capriciousness."

Not everything in Russian literature displeased Mikhailovsky at the end of the century. He liked Anton Pavlovich Chekhov's stories but missed in them a strong ideal. He detected great promise in the early work of Maksim Gor'ky, whose tramp characters—in their avoidance of social and personal obligations and ties, their will to perform some great act transcending the dominant moral order, and their love of tyrannizing others—reminded Mikhailovsky of Nietzsche's transvaluation of values and will to power. He suspected, however, the influence of Dostoevsky and warned Gor'ky not to focus on the exceptional, as Dostoevsky had done, but to find his subjects among normal people.

By the end of the century the influence of *Russkoe bogatstvo* had declined markedly among radical youth. Mikhailovsky's personal popularity, however, remained high. During the huge jubilee that celebrated his forty years in journalism in 1900, a festschrift in his honor quickly sold out—three thousand copies in all. More than twenty thousand people sent congratulations to him. The authorities forbade any mention in the press of the testimonial dinner on his birthday, but on that day hundreds joined the tribute.

Although Mikhailovsky denounced the new wave of terrorism that began at the turn of the century, he remained suspect to the police. After the assassination of the minister of the interior in 1902 the authorities banished Mikhailovsky from St. Petersburg late in the year. He returned to the capital toward the end of 1903, by then seriously ill. He died in the early morning of 28 January 1904 and was buried according to Orthodox rites. The crowd at Mikhailovsky's funeral apparently exceeded the one that had gathered at Turgenev's funeral years before. A student choir accompanied Mikhailovsky's coffin to the cemetery. So did the police, who were on the streets in large numbers for the occasion.

Nikolai Konstantinovich Mikhailovsky steered his own course through the dangerous currents of reaction and revolution in Russia. A man of vast integrity, an independent thinker, and a talented writer, Mikhailovsky challenged the system builders and the prophets of inevitable progress. With intelligence and wit he skewered hypocrisy and pomposity wherever he found it and gained the admiration of even his sternest critics. His hostility to Marxism and defense of agrarian socialism guaranteed that his legacy would be little known in his homeland. Editions of selections from Mikhailovsky's literary criticism as well as of his literary memoirs, published since the end of the Soviet Union, suggest a modest revival of interest in his literary activity. *Geroi i tolpa*, a 1998 edition of his study of mass psychology of the same title, indicates that at least some of Mikhailovsky's social thought retains its relevance, or at least has uses, in Russian politics today. His thought is scarcely known in the West, although a handful of international development specialists see some applicability of Populist thinking, including Mikhailovsky's, in Third World conditions.

Letters:

"'Politika' N. K. Mikhailovskogo: Iz vospominanii o nem i ego pisem," *Byloe,* 7 (1907): 124–138;

"P. L. Lavrovu," *Minuvshie gody,* 1 (1908): 125–128;

"Iz perepiski N. K. Mikhailovskogo (Otvet tolstovtsu)," *Russkoe bogatstvo,* 1 (1909): 225–231;

"V. A. Gol'tsevu," in *Pamiati Viktora Aleksandrovicha Gol'tseva,* edited by Aleksandr Aleksandrovich Kizevetter (Moscow: N. N. Klochkov, 1910), pp. 202–207;

"A. P. Chekhovu," in *Slovo. Sbornik vtoroi* (Moscow: Knizhestvo pisatelei, 1914), pp. 216–218;

"V. A. Gol'tsevu," in *Arkhiv V. A. Gol'tseva,* volume 1 (Moscow: Knizhestvo pisatelei, 1914), pp. 198–217;

"Iz pisem N. K. Mikhailovsogo (K 10-letiiu ego konchiny)," *Russkoe bogatstvo,* 1 (1914): 370–398;

V. E. Evgen'ev-Maksimov, *N. A. Nekrasov i ego sovremenniki: Ocherki* (Moscow: Federatsiia, 1930), pp. 315–320, 325–326;

"M. Gorkomu," in *M. Gor'ky. Materialy i issledovaniia,* edited by Vasilii Alekseevich Desnitsky, volume 2 (Leningrad: Akademii nauk SSSR, 1936), pp. 353–354;

"V. G. Korolenko," in *V. G. Korolenko. Izbrannye pis'ma,* edited by N. V. Korolenko and A. L. Krivinskaia, volume 3 (Moscow: Goslitizdat, 1936), pp. 149–150;

"N. Ia. Nikoladze," in *Pis'ma russkikh literaturno-obshchestvennykh deiatelei k N. Ia. Nikoladze,* edited by Vano Shaduri (Tbilisi: Zaria Vostoka, 1949), pp. 89–91;

Vasilii Alekseevich Desnitsky, "M. Gorkomu," in his *A. M. Gor'ky: Ocherki zhizni i tvorchestva* (Moscow: Khudozhestvennaia literatura, 1959), pp. 66–67.

Bibliographies:

D. P. Sil'chevsky, "K bibliografii sochinenii N. K. Mikhailovskogo (1860–1900)," in *Na slavnom postu. Literaturnyi sbornik, posviashchennyi N. K. Mikhailovskomu* (St. Petersburg: Knigoved, 1900), pp. 510–516;

"Bibliografiia," in Mikhailovsky's *Polnoe sobranie sochinenii*, volume 10 (St. Petersburg: Russkoe bogatstvo and N. N. Mikhailovsky, 1913), pp. 1087–1144.

Biographies:

Viktor Mikhailovich Chernov, *Pamiati N. K. Mikhailovskago* (Geneva: Partiia sotsialistov-revoliutsionerov, 1904);

James H. Billington, *Mikhailovsky and Russian Populism* (Oxford: Clarendon Press, 1958);

Anatolii Aleksandrovich Slin'ko, *N. K. Mikhailovsky i russkoe obshchestvenno-literaturnoe dvizhenie vtoroi poloviny XIX–nachala XX veka* (Voronezh: Izdatel'stvo Voronezhskogo universiteta, 1982);

Guilia Lami, *Un ribelle "legale": N. K. Michajlovskij (1842–1904): Contributi per una biografia intellectuale* (Milan: Unicopli, 1990).

References:

Vladimir Alexeyev, "Nikolai Mikhailovsky," in *A History of Russian Philosophy: From the Tenth through the Twentieth Centuries*, edited by Valery A. Kuvakin, 2 volumes (Buffalo, N.Y.: Prometheus Books, 1994), I: 325–335;

Nikolai Berdiaev, *Sub"ektivizm i individualizm v obshchestvennoi filosofii: Kriticheskii etiud o N. K. Mikhailovskom* (Moscow: Kanon+, 1999);

Isaiah Berlin, *Russian Thinkers* (London: Penguin, 1979);

Marina Kanevskaya, *N. K. Mikhailovsky's Criticism of Dostoevsky: The Cruel Critic* (Lewistown, N.Y.: Edwin Mellen Press, 2001);

Anatolii Pavlovich Kazakov, *Teoriia progressa v russkoi sotsiologii kontsa XIX veka* (Leningrad: Izdatel'stvo Leningradskogo universiteta, 1969);

Arthur P. Mendel, *Dilemmas of Progress in Tsarist Russia: Legal Marxism and Legal Populism* (Cambridge, Mass.: Harvard University Press, 1961);

Nikolai Alekseevich Nekrasov, *Polnoe sobranie sochinenii i pisem*, 12 volumes, edited by Vladislav Evgen'evich Evgen'ev-Maksimov, Aleksandr Mikhailovich Egolin, and Kornei Ivanovich Chukovsky (Moscow: Goslitizdat, 1948–1953), IV: 147;

Philip Pomper, *The Russian Revolutionary Intelligentsia* (New York: Crowell, 1970);

Francis B. Randall, "The Major Prophets of Russian Peasant Socialism: A Study in the Social Thought of N. K. Mikhailovskii and V. M. Chernov," dissertation, Columbia University, 1961;

Alexander Vucinich, *Social Thought in Tsarist Russia. The Quest for a General Science of Society, 1861–1917* (Chicago & London: University of Chicago Press, 1976);

Andrzej Walicki, *The Controversy over Capitalism: Studies in the Social Philosphy of the Russian Populists* (Oxford: Clarendon, 1969);

Walicki, *A History of Russian Social Thought from the Enlightenment to Marxism* (Stanford, Cal.: Stanford University Press, 1979);

Richard Wortman, *The Crisis of Russian Populism* (Cambridge: Cambridge University Press, 1967).

Papers:

Nikolai Konstantinovich Mikhailovsky's papers are located in Moscow at the Russian State Archive of Literature and Art (RGALI), fond 280, fond 308, and fond 452. Letters to various correspondents are held in St. Petersburg at the Institute of Russian Literature (IRLI, Pushkin House), fond 181, and in Moscow at the Russian State Library (RGB, formerly the Lenin Library), fond 135, fond 178, fond 358, and fond 578. A description of Mikhailovsky's correspondence, with excerpts, can be found in N. S. Rusanov, "Arkhiv N. K. Mikhailovskogo," *Russkoe bogatstvo*, 1 (1914): 129–164.

Semen Iakovlevich Nadson

(14 December 1862 – 19 January 1887)

Robert D. Wessling
Stanford University

BOOKS: *Stikhotvoreniia* (St. Petersburg: A. S. Suvorin, 1885; revised and enlarged, 1886);

Literaturnye ocherki (1883–1886) (St. Petersburg: I. N. Skorokhodov, 1887);

S. Ia. Nadson i Grafinia Lida (St. Petersburg, 1888);

Nedopetye pesni. (Iz posmertnykh bumag) (St. Petersburg: I. N. Skorokhodov, 1902);

Proza. Dnevniki. Pis'ma, edited by Mariia Valentinovna Vatson (St. Petersburg: M. A. Aleksandrov, 1912);

Polnoe sobranie sochinenii, 2 volumes, edited by Vatson (Petrograd: A. F. Marks, 1917).

Editions and Collections: *Proza. Dnevniki. Pis'ma,* edited by Mariia Valentinovna Vatson (St. Petersburg: M. A. Aleksandrov, 1913);

Izbrannye stikhotvoreniia, edited by Grigorii Dmitrievich Deev-Khomiakovsky (Moscow: Dobroe utro, 1918);

S. Ia. Nadson i Grafinia Lida (St. Petersburg, 1921);

Stikhi (Berlin: Mysl', 1921);

Stikhotvoreniia, edited, with an introduction, by Aleksandr L'vovich Dymshits, Biblioteka poeta, Malaia seriia, no. 48 (Leningrad: Sovetskii pisatel', 1937);

Polnoe sobranie stikhotvorenii, edited by F. A. Shushkovsky, with an introduction by G. A. Bialyi, Biblioteka poeta, Bol'shaia seriia (Moscow & Leningrad: Sovetskii pisatel', 1962);

Stikhotvoreniia, with an introduction by E. V. Ivanova (Moscow: Sovetskaia Rossiia, 1987);

Stikhotvoreniia (Moscow: Kniga Printshop, 1990);

Izbrannoe, compiled by Liobov' Semenovna Pustil'nik (Moscow: Terra, 1994);

Akkord eshche rydaet (Moscow: EKSMO-Press, 1998);

Polnoe sobranie sochinenii (St. Petersburg: Akademicheskii proekt, 2001).

Edition in English: "Selected Translations of S. Ja. Nadson's Poetry," in *The Chord Resounds Still. A Study for the Centennial of Semjon Nadson,* edited by Alexander N. Konrad (Cleveland: Press of Case Western Reserve University, 1963), pp. 15–23.

Semen Iakovlevich Nadson

OTHER: *Izbrannye stikhotvoreniia,* contributions by Nadson and others (Rostov-on-Don: Donskaia rech', 1904);

K svetu, contributions by Nadson, Ivan Alekseevich Bunin, N. B. Khvostov, and others (Moscow: P. K. Prianishnikov, 1905);

Izbrannye stikhotvoreniia, contributions by Nadson, Aleksei Nikolaevich Pleshcheev, and Iakov Petrovich Polonsky (Moscow: Rus. t-va, 1912).

On the merits of his only book of poems, first published in 1885, Semen Nadson is generally accepted as the defining Russian poet of the 1880s. Nadson, moreover, has secured a lasting reputation among a devoted readership whose cult-like veneration of the poet–initiated during his lifetime–is still practiced today. Despite this success, critics have long considered Nadson a minor poet of questionable aesthetic significance. In its didacticism and social idealism Nadson's poetry belongs to the nineteenth-century tradition of Russian civic verse, but it also displays the important influence of an earlier lyric tradition of Romantic agony. The facts of the poet's biography (he was a tubercular who died at the age of twenty-four) instilled Nadson's readership with an unswerving faith in the mimetic realism of his lyrics devoted to personal suffering, in spite of their dependence on poetic clichés. Since his death, Nadson's poetry and popular cult have sometimes been viewed as a native precursor to decadence, a cultural tendency that originated in France and entered Russian literature in the 1890s. His poetry and its admirers have also been interpreted as signposts of Russian literary *poshlost'* (kitsch).

Although Nadson wrote critical prose, short stories, and narrative poems, his reputation is based on the short lyrics that predominate his output. His most typical poems present the speaker writing in his lyrical diary on a sleepless night in the sickroom, as in "Opiat' vokrug menia nochnaia tishina . . ." His most typical poems present the speaker writing in his lyrical diary on a sleepless night in the sickroom, as in "Opiat' vokrug menia nochnaia tishina . . ." (The stillness of the night surrounds me again . . .), written in 1883 and first published in the journal *Ezheldel'noe obozrenie* (Daily Survey) in 1885, or as in "Otryvok" (Fragment), written in 1884 and first published in Nadson's *Stikhotvoreniia* (Poems) in 1885. Nadson's most famous poem, "Drug moi, brat moi, ustalyi stradaiushchii brat . . ." (My friend, my brother, tired, suffering brother . . .), written in 1880 and first published in the journal *Slovo* (Word) in 1881, offers an inspirational anthem of compassion for the oppressed. Such lyrics make use of the intelligentsia sickroom as the setting for an elegiac lament for lost youth, sanity, and health. As first-person testimonies of suffering, Nadson's poems are often interpreted as a faithful representation of the agony experienced en masse by the intelligentsia in the 1880s–a decade of intense political repression in tsarist Russia. In this context Nadson has been called a *poet bezvremen'ia* (poet of social stagnation) and a *poet bol'nogo pokoleniia* (poet of the sick generation).

Semen Iakovlevich Nadson was born in St. Petersburg on 14 December 1862. A series of formative events in his early childhood, spent in St. Petersburg and Kiev, contributed to the development of the pessimistic outlook that would dominate his poetry. His father, Iakov Semenovich Nadson, the son of a Jewish merchant who had converted to Russian Orthodox Christianity, died in a mental hospital in 1864 shortly after moving from St. Petersburg to begin work in a bureaucratic office in Kiev. The poet's mother, Antonina Stepanovna (Mamantova) Nadson, the descendant of a celebrated family of the Russian aristocracy, gave birth to Nadson's sister, Anna, in 1865; worked as a governess on a family estate near Kiev until 1870; and then married Nikolai Gavrilovich Fomin–a psychologically unstable government bureaucrat who hanged himself the following year in a summer house outside Kiev. Antonina Stepanovna died of tuberculosis in 1873, leaving Nadson and his sister orphans in the guardianship of their uncle Il'ia Stepanovich Mamantov, an influential St. Petersburg bureaucrat.

Nadson received his earliest education in classical gymnasiums in Kiev and St. Petersburg but entered a boarding school for military cadets in 1872 after securing a government scholarship. At school he began keeping a diary (first published in 1912 in *Proza. Dnevniki. Pis'ma* [Prose. Diaries. Letters]), a kind of literary laboratory in which he developed a poetic self-image on the basis of his childhood experiences. The trope of the "sad childhood" held a double cachet for Nadson during these early years. On the one hand, it signaled the return to favor in intelligentsia culture of the Russian Romantics and sentimentalists, such as Vasilii Andreevich Zhukovsky, whom Nadson frequently cited in the pages of his adolescent diary. The young diarist also wrote about the sorrows of childhood as the consequence of a congenital nervous disorder. Nadson thus began an aesthetic project that consumed him during the rest of his life: he couched epigonic Romantic experiences, such as the sad childhood of an orphaned poet, in the idiom of the diagnostic realism that had become popular among the Russian intelligentsia in the 1850s and 1860s. This mixed cultural idiom, present in his diary and later in his poetry, brought a physiological language of the body to the poetic discourse of spiritual suffering.

During the years 1878 to 1880 Nadson engaged in the self-conscious project of establishing a poetic identity and a readership for his verse. He found a muse in Natal'ia Mikhailovna Deshevova, the sister of a classmate at military school. After Deshevova's untimely death from tuberculosis in 1879 Nadson devoted poems to her that were later published in the first edition of his book, *Stikhotvoreniia* (Poems, 1885). In St. Petersburg, as word spread of the young cadet's talent for poetry, Nadson found publication outlets in minor literary journals. Nikolai Petrovich Vagner, an influential zoologist, author, and editor of the journal *Svet* (Light), was an early sponsor responsible for Nadson's first publication: a poem titled "Na zare" (At Sunset), which appeared in *Svet* in 1878. During the autumn of 1879, shortly after entering the Pavlovsk military academy in St. Petersburg, Nadson was stricken with pneumonia; this experience of illness further motivated his interest in the poetry of personal suffering.

Nadson spent most of 1880 in Tbilisi on a medical leave that included limited military training. He wrote poems, semi-autobiographical short stories, and diary entries in which he alluded to Romantic literary sources that emphasized the spiritual dimensions of suffering. Drawing on contemporary notions about nervous physiology found in abundance in Russian journals since the emergence of psychiatry as a distinct branch of medical science, he reevaluated the Romantic malaise called *splin* (spleen)—most notably as experienced by the Byronic heroes in the poetry and prose of Mikhail Iur'evich Lermontov. In an important biographical convergence Lermontov, like Nadson, served a tour of military duty in the southern reaches of the Russian Empire. In his reevaluation of Romantic pathology Nadson turned to another Russian source, Nikolai Vasil'evich Gogol's short story "Zapiski sumasshedshego" (Notes of a Madman, 1835). Nadson also titled his diary "Zapiski sumasshedshego," thereby asserting the larger literary significance of his personal testimony of nervous exhaustion—a pathology in keeping with contemporary psychiatric theories. This self-diagnosis was confirmed by a memoirist who recalled that the teenage Nadson looked like a "second Lermontov" with the premature wrinkles caused by nervous exhaustion. Nadson extended the theme of juvenile exhaustion to all the *vos'midesiatniki* (generation of the 1880s) in his poem "Nashe pokolen'e iunosti ne znaet . . ." (Our generation knows not youth . . . , written in 1884 and published in the journal *Zhivospisnoe obozrenie* [Pictorial Survey] the same year):

Chut' ne s kolybeli serdtsem my driakhleem,
Nas tomit bezver'e, nas gryzet toska . . .

(Hardly out of the cradle and our hearts become decrepit,
We have been exhausted by our lack of faith, harassed by
 boredom . . .)

Nadson's social typology of the *vos'midesiatniki* draws on a Romantic literary subtext, Lermontov's poem "Duma" (Melancholy Meditation, 1838), and a contemporary scientific concept—the urban epidemic of nervous exhaustion.

In late 1880 Nadson returned to his military studies in St. Petersburg, graduating from the Pavlovsk military academy in 1882. He then began the obligatory service required of recipients of a state-financed military education and was stationed in Kronshtadt as an officer in the Second Caspian Regiment. During his three years of service as a second lieutenant in the Russian army, Nadson became a poet of national significance. He was accepted into the prestigious *pushkinskii kruzhok* (Pushkin circle) led by Aleksei Nikolaevich Pleshcheev, the poetry editor of *Otechestvennye zapiski* (Notes of the Fatherland), an important intelligentsia journal with wide distribution throughout Russia. Pleshcheev actively promoted Nadson's poetry for print in this and other *tolstye zhurnaly* (thick journals) read voraciously by members of the intelligentsia. As the base of Nadson's readership expanded, he began receiving the first of hundreds of letters from fans of his poetry.

Military physicians diagnosed Nadson with pulmonary tuberculosis in 1882, and this diagnosis became the mainstay of a poetic identity that initially tied Nadson to the Romantic tradition of poet-tuberculars. In his diary and poetry he entertained fantasies about the "sweet illness" of consumption—an obvious allusion to the Romantic interpretation of tuberculosis as an edifying disease that sublimely wastes away the sufferer's body by a consuming fever, as seen in this diary fragment dated 8 October 1882: "I'd like to fall ill, though not with a laborious illness, but rather with a sweet one. . . . I would like to lie in bed with fever, delirious, with my forehead burning—motionless, without a thought. I would like to lie in bed feeling the cold, tender hand of a woman dotingly brushing back the hair that has fallen from my feverish forehead and feel her dear lips, chapped after the sleepless night, touching my brow with a hardly audible, tender kiss." Nadson's approach to illness changed dramatically in June 1883, when he was bedridden in excruciating pain for nearly two months with a fistula, a festering wound that is a common complication of tuberculosis. By bringing Romantic fantasies of tubercular elegance to the medical reality of its fleshly unsightliness, he achieved an aesthetic breakthrough: he composed poetry glamorizing literary figures of bodily decay, as in the poem "Gasnet zhizn', razrushaetsia zazhivo telo . . ." (Life is expiring, my body decomposing alive . . .), written in 1883 and first published in the journal *Den* (The Day) in 1887:

Skoro trup moi zaroiut mogil'noi zemleiu,
Skoro vysokhnet mozg moi i serdtse zamret,
I podnimetsia gusto trava nado mnoi,
I po mertvym glazam moim cherv' popolzet . . .

(Soon my corpse will be buried in a grave plot,
Soon my brain will dry up and my heart stop beating,

And above me grass will grow thick,
A worm crawling about my lifeless eyes . . .)

These images prepared a terrain onto which the Russian literary elite of the 1890s earnestly imported cultural decadence from French sources.

From 1883 to 1884 Nadson conducted a correspondence with the poet Dmitrii Sergeevich Merezhkovsky, who became a central figure of Russian decadence in the 1890s. The content of this correspondence alluded to ongoing debates about civic verse—the dominant mode of poetic expression that invoked the Russian intelligentsia to combat social injustice. Merezhkovsky argued that a sickly poet such as Nadson was simply too unfit to assume the collective burden of the suffering Russian people. He implored Nadson to concentrate on his own physical recuperation and discontinue writing any further poetry promoting an illness "chic." Nadson countered by championing a predecadent aesthetic in his letters as well as in his verse. In the poem "Muza" (Muse), dedicated to Merezhkovsky in 1883 and first published in the journal *Illiustrirovannyi mir* (Illustrated World) in 1884, the muse disrobes at the poet's request, exposing the sickly glamour of her suffering body.

Nadson's aesthethics of illness also displayed the influential legacy of the greatest Russian civic poet, Nikolai Alekseevich Nekrasov, whose *Poslednie pesni* (Last Songs, 1877) articulates the poet's final agonizing gasps of "civic sorrow" (Nekrasov composed these lyrics during the months before his death from stomach cancer in 1878). Following Nekrasov's example, Nadson identified the poet's deathbed suffering and lament as the central concern of civic verse, as in these lines from "Net, muza, ne zovi! . . . Ne uvlekai mechtami . . . " (Don't summon me, muse! . . . Don't enthrall me with dreams . . .), written in 1884 and published in the St. Petersburg newspaper *Nedelia* (The Week) later that year:

Put' slishkom byl tiazhel . . . Somnen'ia i trevogi
Na chasti rvali grud' . . . Ustalyi piligrim
Ne vynes vsekh pregrad muchitel'noi dorogi
I gibnet, porazhen nedugom rokovym . . .

(Too arduous the path . . . Anxieties and doubts
Have torn my chest to pieces. This tired pilgrim
Could not surmount every obstacle agonizing him on the
    way.
Smitten by a fatal disease, he is dying . . .)

In other works Nadson's lyric persona painstakingly reiterates the idea that the sick poet fulfills a pressing civic duty. He is consumed by illness—which metaphorically afflicts his poetic body—and asks for the reader's

Nadson as an officer in the Second Caspian Regiment in the early 1880s

compassion, as in this poem written and published in the journal *Delo* (The Deed) in 1882:

Milyi drug, ia znaiu, ia gluboko znaiu,
Chto bessilen stikh moi, blednyi i bol'noi;
Ot ego bessil'ia chasto ia stradaiu,
Chasto taino plachu v tishine nochnoi . . .

(My dear friend, I know, I well know,
That my verse is powerless, pale, and sickly;
I often suffer from its powerlessness,
I often sob secretly in the still of night . . .)

Such poems appealed not only to the sentimental inclinations of intelligentsia readers but also to their civic conscience. Nadson's poetry presents illness as a spiritual dilemma that jeopardizes the potency of the written word—a crucial medium through which the intelligentsia asserted its moral authority in Russian society. In the social and political context of the 1880s his poetry of fatal illness offered consolation to reading members of the intelligentsia, who were increasingly subjected to political injustice and social isolation during the oppressive reign of Tsar Alexander III (1881–1894).

In 1884 Nadson was released from military service for reasons of illness. While working in the editorial offices of *Nedelia,* he received a loan of five hundred rubles from Litfond (The Literary Foundation), a charitable organization supporting Russian scholars, writers, and poets in financial need. The loan was intended to cover the expenses of foreign travel and surgery on the tubercular fistula threatening his life. During most of his journey Nadson was accompanied by Mariia Valentinovna Vatson, whose acclaimed *Ostoumno-izobretatel'nyi idal'go Don-Kikhot Lamanchskii* (The Ingenious Hidalgo Don Quixote of La Mancha, 1907) was the first complete translation of Miguel de Cervantes's *Don Quixote* into Russian; she later became Nadson's biographer and the editor of his collected works. On the advice of Nikolai Andreevich Belogolovyi, who had been the attending physician at Nekrasov's deathbed, Nadson traveled to Nice for a first operation on his fistula. The second operation was performed in June 1885 by the acclaimed surgeon Theodor Kocher in Bern. During a period of recuperation in a sanitorium in Bad Weissenberg, Nadson's condition worsened, and his physician advised him in August 1885 to return to Russia—presumably to die.

While Nadson was abroad, in March 1885, the first edition of his book *Stikhotvoreniia* was published in St. Petersburg. Although the volume received mixed critical reviews, it was an instant commercial success—all 600 copies were sold within three months of publication. In 1886 alone four additional editions were published, and this initial publication success grew into a commercial phenomenon after Nadson's death in January 1887. On the eve of the Bolshevik Revolution of 1917 his book of poetry was available in almost thirty separately published editions, with a grand total of more than 210,000 copies in circulation. The proceeds from the book sales directly benefited the Litfond as dictated by the terms of the poet's final will. Although the earliest editions of Nadson's poems had been divided into sections—the first section went untitled and the remaining ones were given themes—subsequently, the poems were arranged chronologically in two sections, the first encompassing poems published during the poet's lifetime and the second incorporating posthumously published poems. This editorial innovation, in addition to the inclusion of Vatson's medically rich biography of the sick poet and a reproduction of his portrait, invited readers to interpret the poet's suffering in verse in the context of his suffering in life. Vatson also edited the poet's diaries, letters, and fiction for publication in 1912 and his complete collected works in two volumes in 1917.

Nadson's poetry appealed predominantly to an adolescent and young-adult readership, and his unheralded popularity signaled an emerging division of literary taste within the Russian intelligentsia of the 1880s.

The critical establishment, defending the taste for more traditional styles of Russian civic verse, viewed the aesthetic sensibilities of his burgeoning readership as a social pathology that affected the youngest members of the intelligentsia. Aleksandr Mikhailovich Skabichevsky, one critic typifying this trend, attributed the rampant consumption of Nadson's *Stikhotvoreniia* to a mass hysteria afflicting readers: he and others called this social pathology by the neologism *stikhomaniia* (literally "verse mania"). Such sociological interpretations expressing anxiety about the popular taste for Nadson's poetry prefigured the critical assault on Russian decadence in the 1890s.

Soon after Nadson's return to St. Petersburg in 1886, doctors advised the ailing tubercular poet to spend the winter in Kiev. There, he became the object of a cult-like following of youthful admirers. He was carried overhead by enthusiastic members of the audience at a public poetry reading and surrounded by specially selected admirers in his sickroom. Nadson received fan mail in which readers acknowledged the poet worshipfully as their *kumir* (idol); many of these letters are preserved in archives in St. Petersburg. His correspondence with one such fan, who signed her letters pseudonymously "Grafinia Lida" (Countess Lida), was published as the book *S. Ia. Nadson i Grafinia Lida* in 1888 and became part of the larger effort to promote the poet's popular cult after his death. "Grafinia Lida," who wrote Nadson dozens of letters during the last months of his life, represented the ideal Nadson fan. She enshrined a photograph of him like a holy icon and professed to owning several editions of *Stikhotvoreniia,* which she venerated as scripture. Promotion of the sublime passion of the Nadson cult, as specifically exhibited in the epistles of "Grafinia Lida," proved to be a disastrous enterprise. The Russian press subjected the correspondence to uncommon ridicule; in fact, one journalist claimed to have uncovered the "Grafinia Lida" impostor—by identifying the alleged street address of Nadson's pen mate—as a certain "Liuba," who was described as the middle-aged wife of a lowly St. Petersburg bureaucrat. A scandal ensued, leading to the removal of the published correspondence from sale (to this day the book remains a bibliographical rarity).

During his final months, scandalous insinuations about Nadson's private life became the subject of the caustic satires written by the St. Petersburg columnist Viktor Petrovich Burenin. The attacks were intended as a retaliation for remarks, unflattering to Burenin's literary efforts, which Nadson had written in a column for the Kiev newspaper *Zaria* (Dawn) in June 1886. That same month the anti-Semitic pamphlet *Nadsoniada* was distributed free of charge on the streets of Kiev; shortly after Nadson's death the minor Kievan poet Sergei

Aleksandrovich Berdiaev, author of the pamphlet, offered the poem "Mea culpa" (My Fault) as a literary gesture of repentance for writing the offensive mock epic. In September 1886 Nadson arrived in Yalta in frail health, and in November the Russian Imperial Academy awarded him the prestigious Pushkin Prize for his book of poems; this award emboldened adherents of the Nadson cult to insist on the aptness of comparing him to the great Russian Romantic poet, Aleksandr Sergeevich Pushkin. Burenin, meanwhile, devoted five of his weekly columns in *Novoe vremia* (New Times), from November 1886 through January 1887, to satirizing Nadson's poetry and private life. Burenin publicly accused Nadson of fabricating his illness and sponging off others. The columnist further insinuated that an illicit affair had developed between the twenty-four-year-old bachelor poet and his thirty-six-year-old care provider, Vatson, who was married to the well-known social critic Ernest Karlovich Vatson. The public scandal coincided with Nadson's final agonies of tuberculosis: he suffered from partial paralysis one month before his death from tubercular meningitis on 19 January 1887.

Committed readers earnestly promoted the idea of Nadson's great Romantic achievement in death; Burenin was branded a villain who had slandered the great poet and then murdered him in a "duel." Fedor Timofeevich Shtangeev, the respected tuberculosis specialist treating Nadson in Yalta, insisted that scientific truth backed the Romantic claim that the tubercular poet had died an "untimely death"–if only by a few months. In the absence of Burenin's satirical attack, Shtangeev contended, the invalid Nadson "could have lived at least until spring or even autumn." Special attention was given to the fact that Nadson's bodily remains were transported from Yalta to Odessa aboard a steamer named "Pushkin." Speeches, articles, and poems reiterating the tragic realism of the uncanny Romantic analogies were published in 1887 as the single volume *S. Ia. Nadson: Sbornik zhurnal'nykh i gazetnykh statei, posviashchennykh pamiati poeta* (S. Ia. Nadson: A Collection of Journal and Newspaper Articles Dedicated to the Poet's Memory).

After Nadson's funeral and burial in St. Petersburg, fans frequently gathered to perform mass rituals to honor the memory of the tubercular poet. The cultish neo-Romantic atmosphere of the Nadson celebrations is captured in Osip Emil'evich Mandel'shtam's memoir *Shum vremeni* (1922–1923; translated as *The Noise of Time* in *The Noise of Time: The Prose of O. Mandelstam*, 1986). Prerevolutionary "Nadson evenings" often included poetry recitations, speeches in memory of the poet, and vocal performances of his poems set to music by dozens of Russian composers, including Sergei

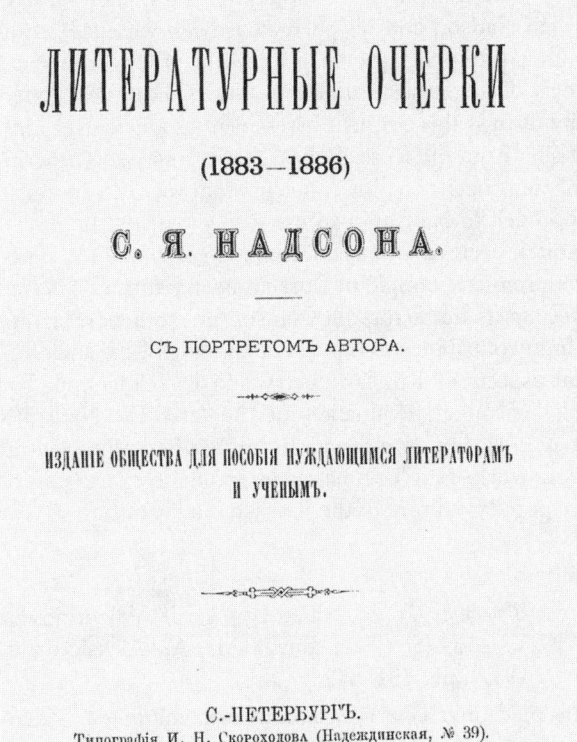

Title page for Nadson's second book of poetry, Literaturnye ocherki (1883–1886) *(Literary Sketches [1883–1886]), posthumously published (Kilgour Collection of Russian Literature, Harvard University Library)*

Vasil'evich Rakhmaninov and Anton Grigor'evich Rubinshtein. At a "Nadson evening" in Yalta in 1917 the archdecadent novelist Mikhail Petrovich Artsybashev delivered the sarcastically titled speech "Tsvetok na navoze" (A Flower Growing on Dung), in which he acknowledged the debt that Russian decadence owed to the Nadson aesthetic. Indeed, the cult of the tubercular poet as it had been practiced in the 1880s can be understood as a cultural bridge to the decadent period of the 1890s. In his novel *Melkii bes* (The Petty Demon, 1907) Fedor Kuz'mich Sologub immortalized the Russian predecadent type in the character of Sasha Pylnikov, an adolescent Nadson fan. Sologub's novel rings true to life, insofar as the juvenile fascination with Nadson proved to be a formative aesthetic experience in the biography of prominent Russian decadent poets who reached adulthood in the 1890s: Merezhkovsky cherished his adolescent friendship with the sick poet; Valerii Iakovlevich Briusov called Nadson his "first youthful infatuation"; and Zinaida Nikolaevna Gippius wrote her earliest poems in Nadson's style.

The posthumous reputation of Semen Iakovlevich Nadson and his poetry has been varied. A committed group of readers places him among the great poets of the Russian tradition. Critics, however, generally dismiss this aesthetic assessment as an exaggeration arising from the Russian mass reader's slavishly uncritical approach to his poetry. Indeed, the popular approach to Nadson, expressed in a "cult of the poet," is often deemed an extended exercise in bad taste, if not the premier example of Russian poetry turned *poshlost'*. Despite its detractors the Nadson phenomenon significantly contributes to our understanding of the sociological aspects of Russian poetry and its readership. For this reason an evaluation of the taste for Nadson's poetry is important within an aesthetically neutral framework—as a legitimate and authentic expression of the popular culture of the Russian intelligentsia.

Letters:

Proza. Dnevniki. Pis'ma, edited by Mariia Valentinovna Vatson (St. Petersburg: M. A. Aleksandrov, 1912), pp. 491–642;

"Pis'ma," in *Polnoe sobranie sochinenii,* volume 2 (Petrograd: A. F. Marks, 1917), pp. 454–575.

Bibliographies:

N. K. Piksanov, ed., "Bibliograficheskie materialy o S. Ia. Nadsone," in *Proza. Dnevniki. Pis'ma,* edited by Mariia Valentinovna Vatson (St. Petersburg: M. A. Aleksandrov, 1912), pp. iii–xii;

N. D. Bernshtein, ed., "Spisok stikhotvorenii Nadsona, polozhennykh na muzyku," in *Stikhotvoreniia,* twenty-ninth edition, edited by Vatson (Petrograd, 1917), pp. 357–360;

Alexander N. Konrad, "Selected Bibliography," in his *The Chord Resounds Still. A Study for the Centennial of Semjon Nadson* (Cleveland: Press of Case Western Reserve University, 1963), pp. 33–38.

Biographies:

Nikolai Petrovich Zherve, *Kadetskie, iunkerskie i ofitserskie gody S. Ia. Nadsona. Po vospominaniiam ego tovarishchei i pis'mam poeta* (St. Petersburg: V. V. Averkiev, 1907);

Mariia Valentinovna Vatson, "Semen Iakovlevich Nadson, (Biograficheskii ocherk)," in *Polnoe sobranie sochinenii S. Ia. Nadsona,* 2 volumes, edited by Vatson (Petrograd, 1917), I: iii–xlviii;

Nadson, "Avtobiografiia," in *Polnoe sobranie sochinenii,* 2 volumes, edited by Vatson (Petrograd: A. F. Marks, 1917), II: 3–6.

References:

S. A. Berdiaev [Aspid], *Nadsoniada. Poema iz literaturnoi zhizni* (Kiev: Petr Barsky, 1886);

V. Khodasevich, "Nadson," *Voprosy literatury,* 9 (1987);

Alexander N. Konrad, *The Chord Resounds Still: A Study for the Centennial of Semjon Nadson* (Cleveland: Press of Case Western Reserve University, 1963);

Vasilii L'vov-Rogachevsky, *A History of Russian Jewish Literature,* edited and translated by Arthur Levin (Ann Arbor, Mich.: Ardis, 1979);

Osip Emil'evich Mandel'shtam, *The Noise of Time: The Prose of O. Mandelstam,* translated by Clarence Brown (San Francisco: North Point Press, 1986);

Dmitrii Sergeevich Merezhkovsky, "Pis'ma k S. Ia. Nadsonu (predisl., publ. i prim. A. V. Lavrova)," *Novoe literaturnoe obozrenie,* 8 (1994): 17–192;

L. N. Nazarova, "Nadson," in *Istoriia russkoi literatury,* volume 9, *Literatura 70–80-kh godov XIX veka,* part 1, edited by B. I. Bursov (Moscow: AN SSSR, 1956), pp. 446–460;

S. Ia. Nadson: Sbornik zhurnal'nykh i gazetnykh statei, posviashchennykh pamiati poeta (St. Petersburg, 1887);

Aleksandr Mikhailovich Skabichevsky, *Istoriia noveishei russkoi literatury (1848–1890)* (St. Petersburg: F. Pavlenkov, 1891); revised and enlarged as *Istoriia noveishei russkoi literatury (1848–1892)* (St. Petersburg: F. Pavlenkov, 1893);

E. P. Tikhancheva, "Briusov o Nadsone," in *Briusovskie chteniia 1973 g.,* edited and compiled by A. V. Aivazian (Erevan: Sovetakan grokh, 1976), pp. 201–216;

Mariia Valentinovna Vatson, ed., "Iz pisem A. N. Pleshcheeva, V. M. Garshina i V. A. Fauseka k S. Ia. Nadsonu," in *Nevskii al'manakh,* volume 2 (Petrograd: Iz proshlogo, 1917), pp. 113–135;

K. F. Vikbulatova, "Russkaia poeziia 80-kh godov," in *Istoriia russkoi poezii,* 2 volumes, edited by Boris Petrovich Gorodetsky (Leningrad: Nauka, 1969), II: 227–252;

Robert Wessling, "Semyon Nadson and the Cult of the Tubercular Poet," dissertation, University of California, Berkeley, 1998.

Papers:

Semen Iakovlevich Nadson's papers are located in "Delovye zapisi M. V. Vatsona," fond 402, at the Institute of Russian Literature (IRLI, Pushkin House) in St. Petersburg, as well as in the Russian National Library (RNB) in St. Petersburg, fond 508, and the Russian State Archive of Literature and Art in Moscow (RGALI), fond 354.

Nikolai Alekseevich Nekrasov

(28 November 1821 – 27 December 1877)

Michael G. Ransome
Bristol Grammar School

BOOKS: *Mechty i zvuki. Stikhotvoreniia N. N.* (St. Petersburg: E. Alipanov, 1840);

Baba-Iaga, kostianaia noga. Russkia narodnaia skazka v 8-mi glavakh, v stikhakh (St. Petersburg: V. Poliakov, 1840);

Stateiki v stikhakh, bez kartinok, 2 volumes (St. Petersburg: K. Zhernakov, 1843);

Tri strany sveta, 2 volumes, by Nekrasov and N. Stanitsky (St. Petersburg: E. Prats, 1849);

Mertvoe ozero, 3 volumes, by Nekrasov and N. Stanitsky (St. Petersburg: E. Prats, 1852);

Stikhotvoreniia (Moscow: K. Soldatenkov & N. Shchepkin, 1856; enlarged edition, St. Petersburg: E. Prats, 1861)—includes "Rodina," "Poet i Grazhdanin," "Shkol'nik," "Kolybel'naia pesnia. (Podrazhanie Lermontovu)," and "Sasha";

Stikhotvoreniia, 5 parts (St. Petersburg: S. V. Zvonarev, 1868–1869);

Moroz, krasnyi nos. Poema (St. Petersburg: N. Nekliudov, 1870);

Stikhotvoreniia (St. Petersburg: V. Pechatkin, 1873);

Stikhotvoreniia, 3 volumes (St. Petersburg: A. A. Kraevsky, 1873–1874);

Poslednie pesni (St. Petersburg: F. Viktorov, 1877);

Stikhotvoreniia, 4 volumes, edited by S. I. Ponomarev (St. Petersburg: A. A. Butkevich, 1879);

Komu na Rusi zhit' khorosho. Poema (St. Petersburg: M. Stasiulevich, 1880); translated by Juliet M. Soskice as *Who Can Be Happy and Free in Russia?* (London: Oxford University Press, 1917);

Stikhotvoreniia (St. Petersburg: M. Stasiulevich, 1881);

Gusi. – Dedushka Mazai i zaitsy (St. Petersburg: Sistematicheskaia biblioteka detskogo chteniia, 1899);

Neizdannye proizvedeniia (St. Petersburg: Peterburg, 1918);

Russkie zhenshchiny. (Babushkiny zapisi) (Berlin: Mysl', 1921);

Neizdannye stikhotvoreniia, varianty i pis'ma (Petrograd: Sabashnikovy, 1922);

Dvadtsat' piat' rublei. (Neizdannye rasskazy) (Moscow & Leningrad: Zemlia i fabrika, 1927);

Nikolai Alekseevich Nekrasov, 1878

Tonkii chelovek i drugie neizdannye proizvedeniia, compiled by Kornei Ivanovich Chukovsky (Moscow: Federatsiia, 1928);

Polnoe sobranie sochinenii i pisem, 12 volumes, edited by Vladislav Evgen'evich Evgen'ev-Maksimov, A. M. Egolin, and Chukovsky (Moscow: Goslitizdat, 1948–1952);

Polnoe sobranie sochinenii i pisem, 15 volumes (Leningrad/St. Petersburg, 1981–1998).

Editions and Collections: *Stikhotvoreniia,* 2 parts (St. Petersburg: K. Vul'f, 1863);

Stikhotvoreniia, 3 parts (St. Petersburg: S. V. Zvonarev, 1864);

Stikhotvoreniia, with illustrations by N. N. Karazin (St. Petersburg: Peterburgskaia kommissiia gramotnosti, 1882);

Polnoe sobranie sochinenii, 2 volumes (St. Petersburg, 1899);

Sobranie sochinenii, 5 volumes, edited by Vladislav Evgen'evich Evgen'ev-Maksimov and Kornei Ivanovich Chukovsky (Moscow & Leningrad: Khudozhestvennaia literatura, 1930);

Polnoe sobranie stikhotvorenii, 3 volumes, Biblioteka poeta, Bol'shaia seriia (Leningrad: Sovetskii pisatel', 1967);

Poslednie pesni, edited by G. V. Krasnov (Moscow, 1974);

Stikhotvoreniia 1856, edited by I. I. Podol'skaia (Moscow: Nauka, 1987);

"Da, tol'ko zdes' mogu ia byt' poetom! . . .": Izbrannoe, compiled by N. N. Paikov (Iaroslavl': Verkhniania Volga, 1996).

Editions in English: *Poems,* translated by Juliet M. Soskice (London: Oxford University Press, 1929);

Russian Poetry under the Tsars, edited by Burton Raffel (Albany: SUNY Press, 1971)–includes "Self-Hate," "Muse of Vengeance," "Muse of Sorrow," "I Feel So Low," and "A Black Day";

"Poet and Citizen," translated by F. D. Reeve and Helen Reeve, *Russian Literature Triquarterly,* 17 (1982): 153–160.

OTHER: "Peterburgskie ugly" and "Chinovnik," in *Fiziologiia Peterburga,* 2 parts, edited by Nekrasov (St. Petersburg: A. Ivanov, 1844, 1845);

"Kolybel'naia pesnia. (Podrazhanie Lermontovu)," "P'ianitsa," and "V doroge," in *Peterburgskii sbornik,* edited by Nekrasov (St. Petersburg, 1846).

Nikolai Nekrasov made a contribution to nineteenth-century Russian literature that was distinctly varied. He was both one of the leading publishers of his day and one of its foremost writers. Over the course of some three decades he edited two journals–*Sovremennik* (The Contemporary) from 1847 until 1866, and then *Otechestvennye zapiski* (Notes of the Fatherland) from 1868 until his death in 1877–and he succeeded in turning first one and then the other into the most progressive monthly publications in tsarist Russia. His work on the journals brought him into close contact with virtually every major figure in the literary world during his lifetime, and he was able to persuade most of these writers

to allow him to be the first to publish at least some of their works.

At the same time, Nekrasov earned for himself the reputation of the first *narodnyi poet* (poet of the people) and arguably the most widely read and ardently discussed poet of mid-nineteenth-century Russia. Nekrasov's literary output covered many genres, but his substantial and enduring reputation was established upon his lyric and narrative poetry. Throughout his later career the writer found inspiration in the theme of the Russian *narod* (folk) and returned to this theme many times in order to present to the reader characters from the broad masses of the people in a way never previously encountered in the literature of his country. His muse was, by his own definition, one of "mest' i pechal'" (vengeance and sadness), and this fact often led to his alienation from many of his contemporaries, who considered that all his works merely repeated the same theme. From his earliest mature writing, Nekrasov portrayed the misfortune of the Russian people, and alone among his contemporaries he was remorseless in the presentation of his message, never heeding the charges of exaggeration frequently leveled against him. His consideration of this favorite theme, however, was also responsible for the production of his *poemy* (long narrative poems), which go beyond a naturalistic presentation of the terrible life of the *narod* and stand out from his other works by virtue of their artistic achievement and continuing interest for the modern reader.

Nekrasov has attracted relatively little critical attention in the West, but in his native land the opposite has been the case. His stature as the leading civic poet of Russia meant that both during his lifetime and after his death he was an author whom scholars could not afford to neglect. After the 1917 Revolution his popularity in Russia became even greater, since he was identified as a progressive thinker whose ideals and beliefs were broadly the same as those of the new Soviet state and the revolutionary tradition that had created it. Nekrasov has generally been viewed in literary criticism as a writer whose aim was primarily to convey a message of social comment and encourage a spirit of optimism in his readers; thus, much of Nekrasov's work was arguably destined to be of interest primarily only to the reading public of the age in which he was writing. However, a few scholars have argued recently that, at its best, Nekrasov's work can also be seen to offer a dimension of weighty philosophical content that is of universal and eternal relevance. All critics agree that at the height of his powers Nekrasov achieved outstanding levels of artistic achievement, meriting his inclusion in the front rank of Russian nineteenth-century literature, but the "message" conveyed in his finest works remains a subject of debate.

Nikolai Alekseevich Nekrasov was born on 28 November 1821 into a minor noble family in the small town of Nemirov in Podol'skii province, where his father, Aleksei Sergeevich Nekrasov, was serving in the army. Aleksei Sergeevich was a vigorous, passionate man and by all accounts quite attractive to women. He made the acquaintance of the daughter of a landowner in Kherson province, Aleksandra Andreevna Zakrevskaia, and quickly won her heart, though her parents were against her marriage to the impoverished and ill-educated army officer. The wedding took place without parental permission, but Aleksandra Andreevna's life did not turn out to be a happy one. Soon afterward Aleksei Sergeevich retired to his Yaroslavl' estate at Greshnevo, which provided Nikolai Alekseevich with many of the experiences of country life in the Volga region of northern Russia that formed his future identity as a writer.

His childhood was far from full of good memories. In addition to his firsthand observations of the harsh lives of Volga peasants—and the boatmen in particular—the young Nekrasov witnessed his father's tyrannical behavior, both within his family and toward his serfs. The boy was close to his cultured mother and keenly felt her suffering. In later life he devoted a series of poems to a depiction of her radiant figure—among them, "Mat'" (Mother, written 1868, published 1869) and "Rytsar' na chas" (Knight for an Hour, written 1860–1862, published 1863). Nekrasov's love for his mother was also arguably reflected in the many positive and sympathetic female figures he depicted as the most memorable characters throughout his literary career.

Nekrasov's path through life was not as easy as might have been predicted for someone of his background. His father's fortunes were steadily eroded by a large family (Nekrasov was one of fourteen children), the neglect of upkeep on the estate, and a series of legal wrangles. Eventually Aleksei Sergeevich was obliged to supplement his income by working as an *ispravnik,* a regional police chief for the tsarist regime. He often took Nikolai with him on his official trips around the province, and the young boy witnessed many examples of the darker side of Russian provincial life that the *ispravnik* was called upon to deal with. In 1832 Nekrasov entered the local *gimnazia* (gymnasium, or high school), where he studied for approximately five years. He was not a particularly successful pupil and was sometimes in conflict with the school authorities, usually because of the satirical verses he was already writing at that time.

Nekrasov's father had always wanted his son to pursue a military career, so in 1838 he decided to send the sixteen-year-old Nekrasov to the St. Petersburg military academy of the Dvorianskii polk (Gentry Regi-

Title page for part 2 of Fiziologiia Peterburga (The Physiology *of Petersburg), which Nekrasov edited early in his career* (*from Liudmila Danilovna Mikitich,* Literaturnyi Peterburg, Petrograd, *1991*)

ment). The entry procedures to the academy were almost complete when Nekrasov by chance met a former school friend, a student called Glushitsky. Through this young man, the unwilling apprentice soldier was introduced to the interesting world of student life at the university in the capital. This experience prompted in the young Nekrasov such a keen desire to study that he defied his father's threat to cut him off without any material support and started to prepare himself to take the university entrance examination. He did not pass it, but he nevertheless joined the department of philology as a *vol'noslushatel',* an occasional student permitted to attend lecture courses without having formal student status.

The years 1838 to 1841 were a difficult period for the aspiring writer and no doubt strengthened his sympathies for the underprivileged in Russian society. He passed these years nominally at the university but spent almost all his time seeking ways of earning an income on which to survive. He suffered extreme need and was not even able regularly to allow himself the luxury of a fifteen-kopeck meal once a day. Likewise, he did not always have somewhere to live. He spent nearly three years in a state of constant hunger; later, he recalled how he sometimes went to restaurants to read their newspapers without ordering anything and, under cover of reading, stole from the bread bowl. His constant malnourishment affected his health, and he fell ill. He had to borrow from his landlord, severely testing the latter's patience because he was unable ever to pay much back. Eventually, Nekrasov returned one night from visiting a friend to find himself locked out. Still sick, he was saved from the cold November night by a passing tramp who took him to a slum dwelling on the outskirts of St. Petersburg. The episode ended well, however, for the aspiring writer was able to earn fifteen kopecks by writing a petition for one of the unfortunates whose shelter he shared.

After this low point, Nekrasov's fortunes improved. The literary skills, practical sense, and business acumen of the future publisher were already in evidence as he set about earning a living by writing reviews and critical articles for various journals, such as *Literaturnye pribavleniia k Russkomu invalidu* (Literary Supplement to the Russian Invalid) and *Literaturnaia gazeta* (The Literary Gazette). He began to give private lessons, compose rhyming alphabet books for publishers of popular literature, and write several minor dramatic works (under the pseudonym Perepel'sky) and pieces of prose fiction. As interesting as the compositions from this period are for the Nekrasov scholar, none of them was sufficient to set the author apart from the many other popular writers of the time. Neither was his first verse publication, *Mechty i zvuki* (Dreams and Sounds), published under the initials N. N. in 1840, a distinguished work. A collection of imitative romantic poems, it was dear to Nekrasov's heart at the time, but it secured at best a few lukewarm reviews and at worst an extremely negative assessment from the leading civic critic, Vissarion Grigor'evich Belinsky. Nekrasov felt this failure keenly, and his reaction was to waste no time in buying up all remaining copies of the collection in order to destroy them. He had become so convinced that they represented an unmitigated literary mistake that he never allowed these poems to be reprinted—even much later in full collections of his works when his reputation was well established.

The early 1840s continued to be a challenging period in Nekrasov's literary development. He joined *Otechestvennye zapiski,* initially in the bibliography department, and then began contributing articles to the journal. In addition to the reviews that earned him his living,

he tried many creative genres as his style evolved toward critical realism. Verse feuilletons and various attempts at vaudevilles taught the emerging author the importance of being in touch with contemporary concerns and issues, as well as dramatic techniques that later became key features of his mature satirical poetry. Vaudevilles were a popular genre at the time, and Nekrasov joined many others both in adapting French originals for Russian audiences and in writing his own pieces, such as *Akter* (The Actor), published in 1841 in *Tekushchii repetuar russkoi stseny* (Current Repertoire of the Russian Stage).

Belinsky and other radical literary critics were urging contemporary writers to champion the underprivileged and promote vigorous social change. Nekrasov's dramatic writings were characterized by their contemporary social content, and he soon earned Belinsky's approval after making his personal acquaintance in 1843. Indeed, Belinsky played a key role in defining Nekrasov's approach to literature, a debt acknowledged by the poet in verse on several occasions, as seen in "V. G. Belinsky" (*Poliarnaia zvezda* [The Northern Star], 1859) and "Pamiati priyatelya" (In Memory of a Friend, *Sovremennik* [The Contemporary], 1855). Belinsky, for his part, realized that Nekrasov's prose talent did not extend beyond that of the average journalistic contributor, but he was lavish in praise of his poetry. Nekrasov responded by becoming a leading proponent of the new "Belinsky tendency" in Russian realism, both as an author and a publisher. In the mid 1840s he edited a collection titled *Fiziologiia Peterburga* (The Physiology of Petersburg, 1844, 1845), which successfully brought together the young realist writers of the *natural'naia shkola* (natural school) who had pledged themselves to Belinsky's line.

The overtly social themes present in Nekrasov's writings during this period sometimes attracted the censor's attention. A case in point was the essay "Peterburgskie ugly" (Petersburg Corners), included in *Fiziologiia Peterburga,* which suffered several cuts. Nekrasov intended "Peterburgskie ugly" to be part of a novel that, though never completed, was published in 1843 in *Otechestvennye zapiski* as *Zhizn' i pokhozhdeniia Tikhona Trostnikova* (The Life and Adventures of Tikhon Trostnikov). He wrote several prose works before and after this piece, including "Tonkii chelovek" (The Thin Man, written 1853–1855, published 1855), and also coauthored some lengthy picaresque novels with his lover, Avdot'ia Iakovlevna Panaeva—who wrote as "N. Stanitsky"—such as *Mertvoe ozero* (The Dead Lake, 1852). By and large, however, these works were unmemorable. Arguably, of most interest to the Nekrasov scholar is *Zhizn' i pokhozhdeniia Tikhona Trostnikova,* although it remained unfinished. This novel was critical of life in the St. Petersburg slums, and one is tempted to believe that, although far from being a wholly autobiographical work, nevertheless it reflected many of the experiences of the young author himself during his early years in St. Petersburg, especially the chapter "Peterburgskie ugly."

From the beginning, Nekrasov had a dual literary career as an author and a publisher. By the mid 1840s he had already published several collections, two of which—*Fiziologiia Peterburga* and *Peterburgskii sbornik* (Petersburg Miscellany, 1846)—brought together the leading proponents of the "Gogolian" tendency in Russian literature (named after the writer Nikolai Vasil'evich Gogol). Focusing on the Petersburg lower classes, these authors highlighted in grotesque detail the sloth, greed, and wretchedness of the "little" people in tsarist society. *Peterburgskii sbornik* was particularly successful, including as it did Dostoevsky's *Bednye liudi* (Poor Folk). Nekrasov's publishing activities had progressed so well that at the end of 1846 he bought the journal *Sovremennik,* which had steadily declined since the death of its founder, the renowned poet Aleksandr Sergeevich Pushkin. Many of Nekrasov's former colleagues at *Otechestvennye zapiski* joined him, including Belinsky. The critic passed on to Nekrasov some of the material that he had been amassing for a collection titled "Leviafan" (The Leviathan) that he was planning, and this guaranteed the success of the reestablished journal. Nekrasov edited and published *Sovremennik* from 1847 until 1866, transforming it into both a major literary journal and also a remunerative concern. He achieved this success despite Belinsky's death and his constant harassment by the censors, especially after the popular uprisings of 1848. After 1856, influenced by its assistant editor, the revolutionary thinker Nikolai Gavrilovich Chernyshevsky, *Sovremennik* began to develop into an organ of militant radicalism. The journal was suppressed in 1866, after the first attempt on the life of Tsar Alexander II, but in 1868 Nekrasov—together with the novelist Mikhail Evgrafovich Saltykov—took over *Otechestvennye zapiski* and remained its editor and publisher until his death. This aspect of his literary career was singularly important in nineteenth-century Russia. The quality of the literary criticism published in Nekrasov's journals was unrivaled. He also published works by the novelists Ivan Sergeevich Turgenev and Ivan Aleksandrovich Goncharov as well as the early works of Leo Tolstoy. Nekrasov himself wrote frequent reviews, and he is credited with reestablishing the reputation of the early- nineteenth-century poet Fedor Ivanovich Tiutchev through his article "Russkie vtorostepennye poety" (Second-Rank Russian Poets), published in *Sovremennik* in 1850.

Nekrasov reached a key stage in the authorial strand of his career by the mid 1840s, when he began to

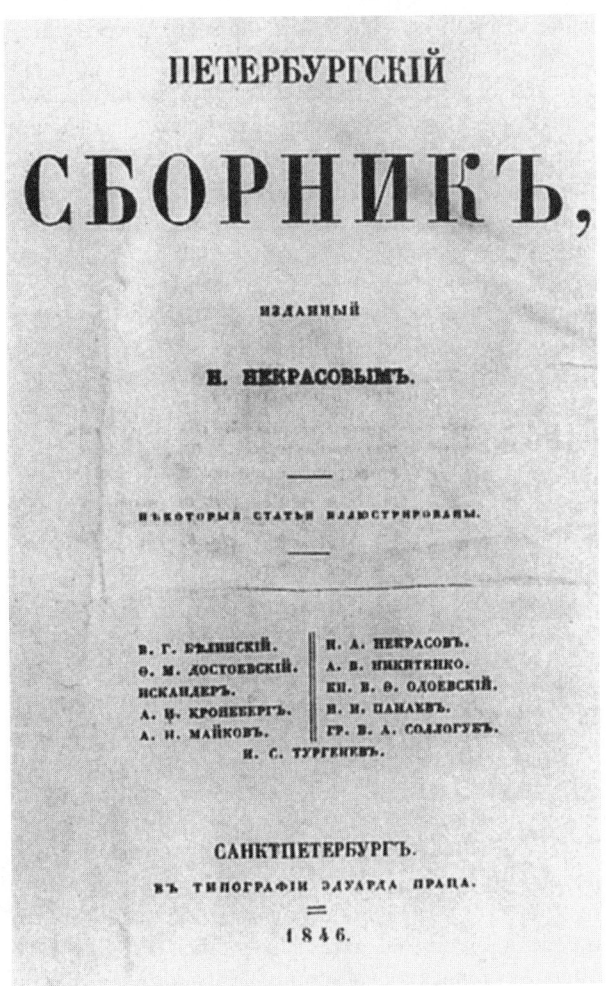

Title page for Peterburgskii sbornik *(Petersburg Miscellany), edited by Nekrasov, which featured stories about the lower class in St. Petersburg (from Mikitich,* Literaturnyi Peterburg, Petrograd, *1991)*

establish his mature poetic style. Poems such as "Rodina" (The Motherland, written 1846, published 1856) told of common folk who had never before been featured so centrally in Russian poetry. As the poet of the faceless masses and of the simple *muzhik* (peasant) in particular, Nekrasov in these years developed an acceptable literary use of the people's vocabulary to present their concerns and experiences to a reading public who, for the first time, had to become used to hearing the voice of the people.

Only in 1856, after some seventeen years of hard and fruitful work, did Nekrasov publish his second collection of poems, *Stikhotvoreniia.* This volume was greeted with a success not seen, his contemporaries believed, since Pushkin's time. On a personal level, however, this period was not a happy one for the poet. In the mid 1850s he fell gravely ill with a throat condition that threatened to end his life. Only a period of convalescence in Italy was able to save him. His serious illness convinced him that his life was coming to an end, and he even titled a series of poems, included in the 1856 collection, "Poslednie elegii" (Last Elegies). Believing that he would soon die, the poet put much effort into the preparation of this volume. Structuring this work carefully, he began with a statement of his poetic beliefs, titled "Poet i Grazhdanin" (Poet and Citizen, 1856), which for many years could be published only with censor's cuts. The rest of the poems fell into sections. One group told of the *narod,* culminating in the optimistic hymn of praise to the Russian peasantry encompassed in "Shkol'nik" (The Pupil, 1856). Another section gave ample expression to Nekrasov's satirical talents, as he depicted forces in contemporary society that, in his view, merited criticism. A particular stir was caused by "Kolybel'naia pesnia. (Podrazhanie Lermontovu)" (Cradle Lullaby. [In Imitation of Lermontov]), whose title made clear that it was intended to echo the poet Mikhail Iur'evich Lermontov's "Kazach'ia kolybel'naia pesnia" (A Cossack Lullaby, 1838). Nekrasov created a scandal by replacing the revered earlier poet's sincere and touching praise of a mother's love with a satirical account of the future that awaits the child in the cradle as a time-serving bureaucrat.

A separate section of the 1856 *Stikhotvoreniia* was devoted to "Sasha," Nekrasov's first *poema* (long narrative poem). Opening with the lyrical song of a Russian traveler's joy on returning to his motherland, this work offers a convincing evocation of 1840s idealism that, in its appeal to the younger generation, predicts Turgenev's novel *Rudin,* which appeared the same year as Nekrasov's 1856 collection. The hero of the *poema,* Agarin, shows many of the characteristics later depicted by Turgenev, while Nekrasov's heroine, Sasha, can be seen as a precursor of the heroine in Turgenev's *Nakanune* (On the Eve, 1860).

A large section of *Stikhotvoreniia* was devoted to lyric poetry. Powerful love poems such as "Kogda iz mraka zabluzhdeniia . . ." (When from the darkness of delusion . . .) and "Ia posetil tvoe kladbishche . . ." (I visited your graveyard . . .) suggested a realistic approach to relationships, a subject that gained full expression in an interesting series of poems prompted by Nekrasov's affair with Panaeva, who eventually became his common-law wife. The Panaeva poems succeeded in conveying the character of not only the hero but also the heroine as they chronicled the frequently stormy development of their relationship. The opening lines of the poems "Ia ne liubliu ironii tvoei . . ." (I do not like your irony . . .) and "Da, nasha zhizn' tekla miatezhno . . ." (Yes, our life has been stormy . . .), for example, immediately suggest the tone of the lovers' relationship.

The 1856 collection appeared at an important time in Russian history: the aftermath of the defeat of Russia in the Crimean War and the ascension of a new tsar to the throne. During this time of hope and expectation of change, with attention focused specifically on the *narod* and its fate, Nekrasov expressed his views in his 1857 *poema* "Tishina" (Stillness), in which he attempted to narrate the heroism of the people during the Crimean War. He continued to seek the essence of the *narod* in, for instance, "V stolitsakh shum, gremiat vitii . . ." (There is a noise in the capitals, orators are thundering . . ., written in 1857 and published in 1861 in *Stikhotvoreniia*) and the *poema* "Razmyshleniia u paradnogo pod"ezda" (Reflections by a Main Entrance), which was published as "U paradnogo kryl'tsa" (By a Main Porch) in 1860 in the journal *Kolokol* (The Bell), managed and edited by Russian exile Alexander Herzen (Aleksandr Ivanovich Gertsen). *Kolokol* rarely published verse but made an exception for Nekrasov's *poema,* which so clearly depicted the social divisions in contemporary Russian society. Prompted by an incident in real life observed by Nekrasov from his window in St. Petersburg, the poem narrates the unhappy visit of some peasants to a sumptuous house (possibly the residence of a government minister) in the capital city. The style of this poem reflects the influence of the Russian folk song and features internal rhymes, repeated word groups, and several examples of folkloric diction.

The year 1861 was key in Russian history. Tsar Alexander II emancipated the serfs, but, crucially, gave them their freedom without any land by which to support themselves. It was also a watershed year in terms of Nekrasov's development as a mature poet. He composed "Korobeiniki" (The Peddlers, published in *Sovremennik,* 1861), the first of his three great *poemy* on the theme of the Russian peasantry that dominate his canon. The artistic achievement of these narrative poems and the richness of their content make them among all his works the most worthy of consideration by the modern reader. They are also of note because they are the only creations by Nekrasov that have been subject to major critical disagreement in the analysis of their message.

"Korobeiniki" was one of many compositions that resulted from the time that Nekrasov spent on his family estate at Greshnevo during the summer of 1861, far away from the pressures that characterized his St. Petersburg life. The close contact he enjoyed with the Russian countryside had, as usual, a fruitful effect on the poet's muse. During July and August he wrote, for example, the poems "Krest'ianskie deti" (Peasant Children), "Pokhorony" (The Funeral), and "Duma" (Meditation), all three of which were published later that year in *Vremia* (Time) and *Sovremennik,* and by the end of August he produced the first draft of the longer work "Korobeiniki." After a further period of revision and completion, the *poema* finally appeared in *Sovremennik*.

Contemporary reviewers were frequently deceived by the authentically folkloric style of "Korobeiniki" into dismissing it as devoid of substantial content. A pleasing evocation of the poetic art of the *narod,* it was Nekrasov's first major work written with the conscious intention that it should be enjoyed not only by the educated classes of Russian society but also by a peasant audience. He dedicated it to his peasant hunting companion, Gavrila Yakovlevich, from whom he originally heard about the real-life incident upon which the *poema* is based. Nekrasov proved his desire for the *narod* to read this new work by publishing it at his own expense in a separate low-priced edition that was sold in Russian villages by peddlers similar to those who are the heroes of the *poema*. Wanting his peasant audience to comprehend what he wrote, he had made more extensive use in "Korobeiniki" of the language and oral tradition of the *narod* than he had done before, or indeed than had ever been attempted in Russian poetry. Not only was he rewarded with Yakovlevich's full approval, but also parts of the text soon became widely known as folk songs that have remained popular to this day.

The *poema* tells a simple tragic tale of two peddlers, Tikhonych and Vania, who are robbed and murdered by an impoverished forester, leaving Vania's beloved, Katia, to wait in vain for his return. Only after the Russian Revolution were Nekrasov scholars willing to look beyond the straightforward narrative and to recognize in "Korobeiniki" a reaffirmation of mid-nineteenth-century revolutionary democratic ideas. Critics of both the East and West, such as Evgen'ev-Maksimov, I. M. Kolesnitskaia, and Michael G. Ransome, have been almost unanimous in their belief that in this *poema* Nekrasov sought to present to his readers a picture of the adversities endured by the broad masses, who likely attributed the blame for their suffering solely to the social order under which the Russian nation was forced to live, and who were encouraged to revolt against this order. These critics believe that Nekrasov offers a positive depiction of the *narod* that affirms faith in the people's long-term well-being. All commentators agree that, as the *poema* progresses, Nekrasov strives to give a panoramic view of mid-nineteenth-century Russia that demonstrates a critical attitude toward particular features of tsarist reality.

The players portrayed in the *poema* might be rogues to varying degrees, but the overwhelming impression left by "Korobeiniki" is that they do not merit their fates. At a late stage in its composition the author rewrote the *poema* to include, among other elements, references to the mythical figure of Gore-Zlochastie (Woe-Misfortune). He took this superhuman force from Russian folklore, where in various depictions it intervenes in human affairs either as condign retribution for wrongdoings or purely as an arbitrary force of malevolence capable of choosing wholly innocent targets for relentless persecution. Nekrasov's conclusion has been argued most recently to follow the latter interpretation.

On many occasions in the *poema* Nekrasov includes elements of unmistakable social criticism that have been widely commented upon. "Korobeiniki" makes reproachful mention of the clergy, minor legal officials, the gentry, the bourgeoisie, and even the tsar himself. These "enemies of the people" do not emerge, however, as the only cause of suffering by the *narod*. Nekrasov chooses to present the collective tragedy of the peasantry, as well as the heroes' individual tragedies, and he achieves such a collective portrait in part through the section of the *poema* that recounts the story of the weaver Titushka and the memorable song he sings, "Pesnia ubogogo strannika" (Song of a Beggarly Wanderer). Nekrasov added this haunting passage to the *poema* during the process of revision. It presented to the reading public a harrowingly brutal image of rural poverty and suffering fewer than nine months after the announcement by Alexander II of his historic Great Reforms to emancipate the serfs. These reforms were greeted enthusiastically among many segments of Russian society, but Nekrasov chose to pass over them in silence when revising his text. The conspicuous absence of any mention of the emancipation suggests that, like other members of the radical intelligentsia, Nekrasov had not been won over by the promise of a significant change for the better in the life of the *narod*.

Artistically quite successful in incorporating the language and rhythms of folklore into the poetic mainstream, "Korobeiniki" is arguably the first of Nekrasov's works to free itself from the confines of its national origin and historical era by offering a commentary on the nature of the human estate that is of timeless and universal relevance. Once he completed this *poema*, Nekrasov wasted little time in beginning work on the second of his narrative poems that can lay claim to this accolade, "Moroz, krasnyi nos" (Frost, the Red-Nosed, published in *Sovremennik*, 1864). One is tempted to conclude that Nekrasov's philosophy was pessimistic at this stage in his life, for the early 1860s were an intensely trying time for him (as for all progressive forces in Russia). His illness had developed during the 1850s and, although the danger presented by his health condition had temporarily diminished, the loss of several people to whom he had been close in the years preceding the composition of his second great *poema* did not allow him to forget the constant presence of death. By the time Chernyshevsky was arrested in July 1862, Nekrasov had already lost the support of the other main figure on the *Sovremennik* editorial board, Dobroliubov, who died in November 1861. He attended the funeral of his young friend and colleague, as he had earlier attended the funeral of the Ukrainian poet Taras Shevchenko, who also died that year. Nekrasov wrote a poem in memory of each of them, an honor that he did not bestow lightly. A year later, in November 1862, he also lost his father, and the death of so close a relative was a further reminder of human mortality. In addition, the years in which "Moroz, krasnyi nos" was written were a traumatic period in the long-standing relationship between Nekrasov and Panaeva, and in 1863 they finally separated.

"Moroz, krasnyi nos" tells about the fate of a young widow who perishes during the Russian winter. Once again the narrative is simple, but the literary prowess is even more significant than in "Korobeiniki." Nekrasov again achieves a seamless amalgam of literary and folk language, but he adds to this mix a greater mastery of the evocation of character and landscape and a subtle and intriguing rearrangement of the chronology of events depicted. The poetic achievement of the *poema* is further enhanced by the frequent rhythmic and metrical modulation of its verse.

Nekrasov's work on revising and developing the *poema* suggests that he became increasingly preoccupied with realities that confront all humankind; purely Russian difficulties assumed a position of secondary importance for him. Unlike "Korobeiniki," which went from initial conception to final publication within a period of a few months, "Moroz, krasnyi nos" was the product of a creative process that continued intermittently over a period of more than two years. Study of Nekrasov's manuscripts has shown that the idea of writing about a peasant family bereft of its male breadwinner first occurred to the poet in 1861. At this time he composed twenty lines of verse, which later became the first two sections of the completed work. By 1862 Nekrasov had expanded his text to some ninety-eight lines. This portion of the *poema* mentioned all the eventual main characters of the work and added to his initial draft scenes describing the dead peasant Prokl's grave and the return home of his old parents; these scenes eventually constituted sections 6 and 7 of the finished *poema*. This extract was the first part of "Moroz, krasnyi nos" to appear in print and was published as "Smert' Prokla" (The Death of Prokl) in the first issue for 1863 of Dostoevsky's journal *Vremia*. The final version of the *poema,* completed by the beginning of 1864, was some three hundred lines longer, including for the first time sections 3 and 4 and the section of the text constituting the major part of the monologue given by Dar'ia, the protagonist (stanzas 20–28). The felicitous conclusion was removed, while the

lines ultimately constituting stanzas 33 and 34, previously included directly before the happy ending, were moved to their present position, leaving stanzas 35 and 36 to bring the *poema* to a close.

A great love of the Russian peasantry and respect for its virtue and fortitude undoubtedly pervade the whole *poema*. Dar'ia, the main character of the work in its final form, is the crowning manifestation of Nekrasov's desire to depict the Russian woman in all her beauty, nobility, and suffering, which repeatedly occupied his attention during his literary career. From her first appearance in the *poema,* when she is silently weeping as she sews her husband's burial shroud, her every feature endears her to the reader. Although the portrayal of Prokl occupies a lesser place in "Moroz, krasnyi nos," his character is likewise beyond reproach.

The Frost is the main aspect of Nekrasov's depiction of Nature in the *poema*. Developing his technique of borrowing from folklore, evident earlier in "Korobeiniki," he uses the figure of Morozko—well known to the *narod* from a famous *skazka* (fairy tale)—but significantly alters his depiction. The popular fairy tale, familiar to every Russian even today, implies the reassuring moral that mortal goodness will be recognized and rewarded by the forces of Nature. Aleksandr Nikolaevich Afanas'ev's *Norodnye russkie skazki* (Russian Folktales), for example, which appeared in its fourth edition in 1858, recounts the traditional story of a virtuous girl, ill treated by her wicked stepmother and left at the mercy of the winter elements in the forest. She is polite to Morozko, who, as a result, takes pity on her and presents her with warm clothes and great wealth. Soviet critics see Morozko as an extension of social injustice and interpret Nekrasov's adaptation of the folk myth to suggest his desire to convey the revolutionary message that meekness and submissiveness do not lead from grief to salvation but only to death. Those arguing for a deeper message in the *poema* suggest that Nekrasov's Dar'ia is not in fact portrayed as submissive and that Morozko goes far beyond implying social injustice to personify the eternal struggle of humans with Nature. Critics espousing this view believe that Nekrasov could see no force at work in the world ensuring that the perfect justice of the fairy tale would ever be repeated in real life. The pessimistic interpretation of the *poema* is in keeping with the universally acknowledged dark mood of the forty-eight-line dedication to the poet's sister, added some years after the main body of the work was written. This dedication was published independently in the 1869 edition of Nekrasov's *Stikhotvoreniia* (Poems) and was combined with "Moroz, krasnyi nos" "on the poet's instructions" in the posthumous edition of 1879.

Never again did Nekrasov consistently reach the artistic heights achieved by "Moroz, krasnyi nos." He was back on more familiar revolutionary democratic ground in 1864 when he wrote "Zheleznaia doroga" (The Railway, published in *Sovremennik*, 1865). This poem is a fairly short but powerful piece in defense of the heroic *narod* that had suffered much in building the railway; it also includes an unflattering portrait of a general who is unwilling to recognize the contribution made by the peasant workers. The office of the censor realized the intent of the piece and ensured that its path to publication was a long and arduous one. Shortly afterward, in 1866, *Sovremennik* was finally closed, though by then Nekrasov was already writing the narrative poem that he intended as the culmination of his work, "Komu na Rusi zhit' khorosho" (*Sovremennik*, 1865; *Otechestvennye zapiski*, 1869–1874; translated as "Who Can Be Happy and Free in Russia?" 1917).

This *poema*, grandiose in design, occupied Nekrasov's attention virtually for the last twenty years of his life and ultimately remained unfinished. It is by far his longest creation, constituting more than 8,500 lines of verse in its final form. Closely linked in theme with both "Korobeiniki" and "Moroz, krasnyi nos," "Komu na Rusi zhit' khorosho" stands apart from these earlier narrative poems in terms not only of overall size but also of form. Unlike the two earlier *poema*, it is a composite work, consisting of a general prologue and four major parts, each of which in turn is split into smaller sections, or "chapters." These parts are largely independent in terms of the stories they recount, although they achieve a general unity in that they all prompt further consideration of the issue raised in the title. The prologue depicts an argument that takes place among seven peasants one day when they meet by chance and begin asking one another who lives well in the Russia of their day. The peasants' odyssey to find the answer to this question provides the fundamental subject matter of the *poema*.

The achievement of "Komu na Rusi zhit' khorosho" is universally recognized as uneven; Nekrasov had been unable to undertake the editing and polishing required before his premature death. The text appeared gradually before the reading public. He had evidently finished the five chapters making up Part 1 by 1865 and included the prologue in the first issue of *Sovremennik* in 1866. The closure of his journal in May of that year and his two-year quest to secure the editorial rights to a new periodical delayed the appearance of subsequent parts of "Komu na Rusi zhit' khorosho," but Nekrasov then used his newly acquired *Otechestvennye zapiski* as the vehicle to publish the rest of his epos. The New Year issue of that journal for 1869 reprinted the prologue and published the first chapter of the first part, "Pop" (The Priest). The following issue included two more chapters, "Sel'skaia iarmonka" (The Village Fair) and "P'ianaia noch'" (A Drunken Night); the final two chapters of Part 1–"Schastlivye" (The Fortunate)

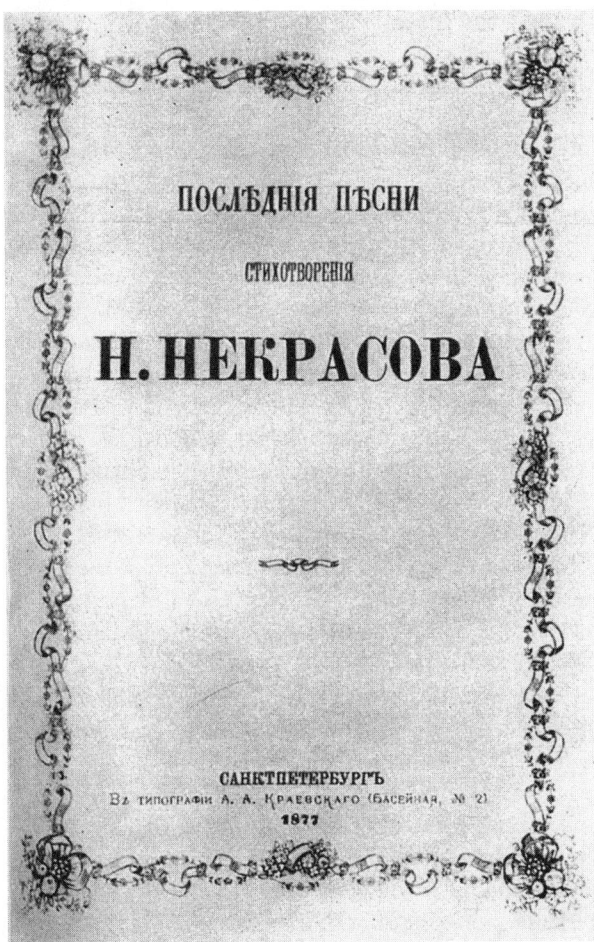

Paper cover for Nekrasov's last major work, Poslednie pesni *(Last Songs), which he wrote while dying of cancer (Nekrasov,* Polnoe sobranie stikhotvorenii, *1967)*

and "Pomeshchik" (The Landowner)–appeared in the second issue for 1870. The second part of the *poema*, "Posledysh" (The Last-Born), was published in 1873, and the fourth part, "Krest'ianka" (The Peasant Woman), appeared in the first issue of *Otechestvennye zapiski* for 1874. The bulk of Nekrasov's final writing for this *poema*, a section titled "Pir–na ves' mir" (A Feast–For All) was completed in 1876, but the poet was unable finally to obtain official permission for its publication before he died. It was printed and distributed illegally in 1879 by the populist Vol'naia russkaia pechat' (Russian Free Press) but became generally known only in 1881 when it appeared, much cut by the censor's office, in the February edition of *Otechestvennye zapiski*. It was included in this same form in the single volume of Nekrasov's poems that came out later that year. While some of the censored material was published in 1908, not until the Soviet period was an attempt made to reconstruct the "full" text of "Pir–na ves' mir." Even following this effort, certain parts of the poem remained the subject of debate.

Critics generally agree that Nekrasov's ultimate concern and achievement in "Komu na Rusi zhit' khorosho" was, broadly speaking, threefold: first, to criticize the emancipation of 1861 and to depict postreform reality in a way that demonstrated the exclusively social causes of peasant suffering; second, to reaffirm faith in the invincible moral and physical strengths of the Russian *narod,* suggesting that its self-awareness was increasing and that its age-old patience was coming to an end; and, finally, to propagandize the optimistic idea that both individual and collective happiness could be achieved by means of a peasant revolution brought about with the help of revolutionary democrats in Russia. Recently, the minority critical view has again been that, far from wishing to create in his audience the mood of unalloyed optimism traditionally identified by critics, Nekrasov consistently sought at the deepest level of the work to render possible the communication of a pessimistic message of universal relevance—a message reminiscent, in spirit, of the messages implied in both "Korobeiniki" and "Moroz, krasnyi nos."

A frequently argued point of contention about "Komu na Rusi zhit' khorosho" among Nekrasov specialists has been the order in which its completed constituent parts should be printed. This problem is clearly one of central importance, for the impression created by the work as a whole is to a large degree dependent on the manner in which this issue is resolved. The controversy began at the start of the Soviet period. In all prerevolutionary editions of Nekrasov's poetry after the appearance of "Pir—na ves' mir" in *Otechestvennye zapiski* in 1881, the constituent parts of "Komu na Rusi zhit' khorosho" were presented in an order that accorded with the chronology of their composition. The first postrevolutionary edition of the poet's works, however, changed the sequence to "end" the *poema* not with "Pir—na ves' mir" but with "Krest'ianka." The editor of the 1881 edition of *Stikhotvoreniia* considered that there was convincing evidence from Nekrasov's manuscripts to suggest that "Pir—na ves' mir" was intended by the author to be the second part of "Posledysh." He argued that this intention was supported by the close similarity in content between the ending of one "chapter" and the beginning of the other and also by the chronology of the seasons portrayed in the completed parts.

Part 1 indeed demonstrates that the emancipation had done nothing to ameliorate the peasants' lot as its supporters claimed it had; this part includes typically satirical depictions of a priest and a landowner. "Posledysh" deepens the critical depiction of serfdom and the landowning class, as does "Krest'ianka." This latter chapter also demonstrates the strengths and goodness of the *narod* in a way reminiscent of "Moroz, krasnyi nos," although with no happier a conclusion and again imply-

ing the malevolent role played by Nature and Chance. "Pir—na ves' mir" intensifies criticism of the social order and suggests a possible means of escape from injustice, thanks to the intelligentsia's emergence from the lower ranks of society, represented in the young protagonist, Grisha Dobrosklonov. To conclude the *poema* with "Pir—na ves' mir" undoubtedly supports the case for an optimistic "revolutionary" interpretation of the *poema* as a whole. The final note struck by "Krest'ianka," on the other hand, leaves little room for anything but a jaundiced closing view. The minority strand of Nekrasov scholarship argues that "Krest'ianka" is indeed an appropriate denouement for the whole *poema.* Throughout the *poema* such critics identify constant reminders that the universe is a place in which prolonged mortal happiness is impossible because of human dependence on the unconstrained arbitrary action of the frequently hostile forces of Chance and Nature that are consistently beyond humanity's capacity to resist.

In addition to "Komu na Rusi zhit' khorosho" Nekrasov also worked on other poems whose unequivocal intentions have not been the subject of debate. In particular he wrote a series of "Decembrist" poems, taking his inspiration from the members of the nobility who participated in the uprising against the tsar on 14 December 1825 and were either executed or exiled to Siberia. The first of these poems, published in 1870 in *Otechestvennye zapiski,* was "Dedushka" (Grandfather), inspired by Prince Sergei Grigor'evich Volkonsky. It offers a positive and straightforward image of a noble old man who, returning from exile, tries to convey to his grandson his understanding that happiness for all is possible if the gentry treat the *narod* decently. Barely avoiding sentimentality on occasion, this poem put Nekrasov firmly back onto the revolutionary democratic line, as did the more substantial *poema* "Russkie zhenshchiny" (Russian Women) that followed, also in *Otechestvennye zapiski,* in 1872 (published as "Kniaginia Trubetskaia" [Princess Trubetskaia]) and in 1873 (published as "Kniaginia Volkonskaia" [Princess Volkonskaia]). "Russkie zhenshchiny" features as its main characters the wives of the Decembrists who showed great courage in accompanying their husbands into exile after they were convicted for participation in the uprising. Basing "Kniaginia Trubetskaia" on an historical source—the anonymous 1870 Leipzig publication *Zapiski dekabrista* (Notes of a Decembrist)—Nekrasov offered his readers an unambiguous and reasonably authentic narrative, though he undoubtedly romanticized his heroine in the portrayal. The first part of the *poema* offers a slightly staccato series of scenes (life in Italy, the uprising on Senate Square) depicted in a way reminiscent of a romantic narrative poem of the 1820s. "Kniaginia Volkonskaia" was based on the actual diaries of Princess

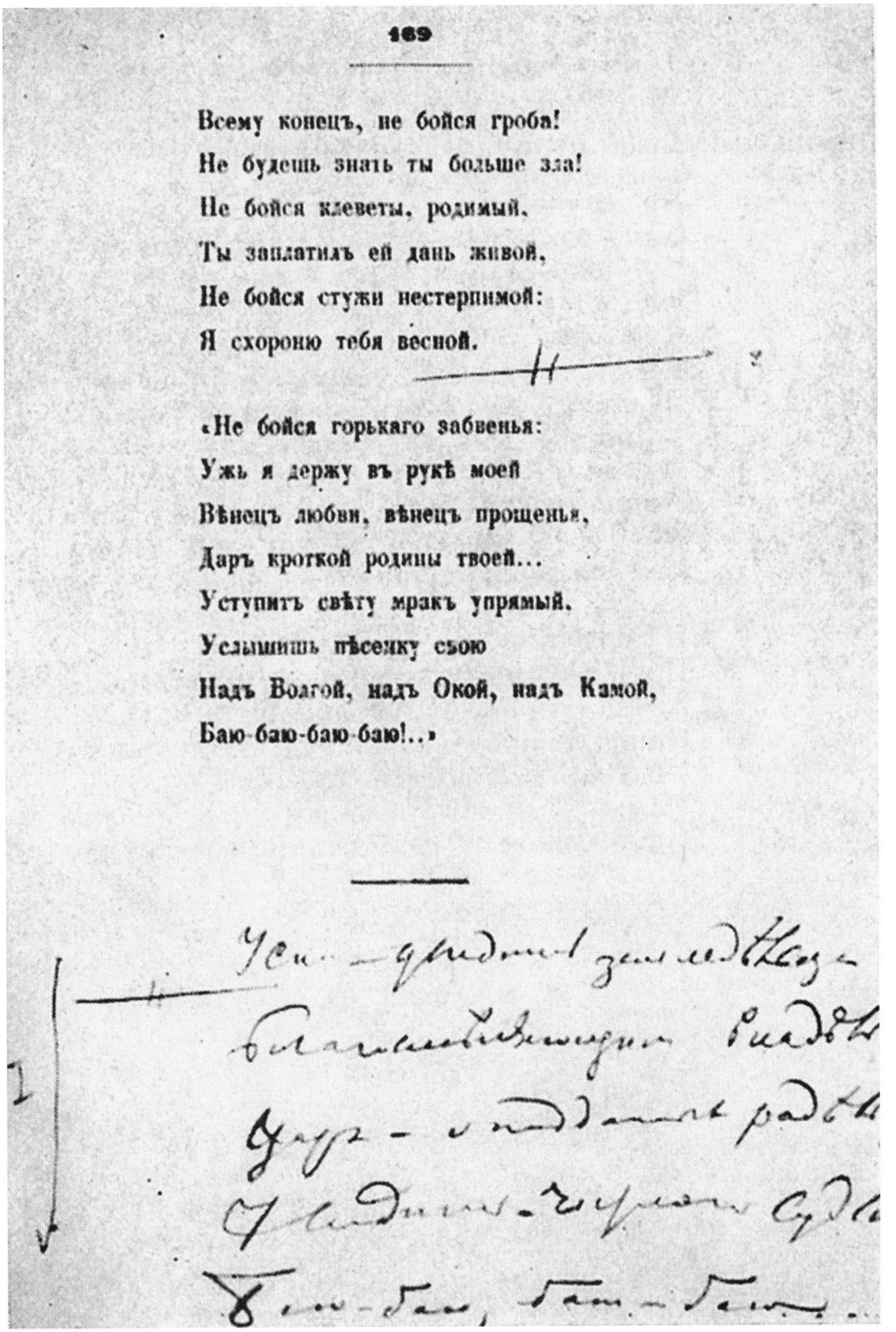

169

Всему конецъ, не бойся гроба!

Не будешь знать ты больше зла!

Не бойся клеветы, родимый,

Ты заплатилъ ей дань живой,

Не бойся стужи нестерпимой:

Я схороню тебя весной.

«Не бойся горькаго забвенья:

Ужъ я держу въ рукѣ моей

Вѣнецъ любви, вѣнецъ прощенья,

Даръ кроткой родины твоей...

Уступитъ свѣту мракъ упрямый,

Услышишь пѣсенку свою

Надъ Волгой, надъ Окой, надъ Камой,

Баю-баю-баю-баю!..»

Inscribed page from Nekrasov's "Baiushki-Baiu" (Bye-Byes, 1877), a poem-lullaby about posterity and remembrance (from Nekrasov, Poslednie pesni, 1974)

Mariia Nikolaevna Volkonskaia, which her son read aloud to the poet in the summer of 1872. These diaries deeply moved Nekrasov, and he turned them into a generally faithful account of the princess's childhood, education, marriage, and subsequent struggle to be allowed to join her Decembrist husband in exile.

At the start of 1875 Nekrasov fell seriously ill with colon cancer. A famous surgeon arrived from Vienna to treat him, but a painful operation brought no improvement in his condition. News of his fatal illness increased his popularity even further, and he received messages from well-wishers from all over the empire. His satirical muse was still capable of pieces of significant impact, such as "Sovremenniki" (Contemporaries, 1875, 1876), but the typical mood of his final period was elegiac. Perhaps inevitably as death approached, his lyric poetry of the 1870s expressed more personal doubts than ever before. He shifted his focus from the Russian peasantry to more global concerns as he tried to generalize and make sense of the world as a whole. A pessimistic assessment of the universal grief of a world set on a fatal path more frequently dominated his verse. The short poem "Utro" (Morning, 1874), written in 1872 or 1873, is one of Nekrasov's most gloomy, as the whole world appears dominated by death, sinful human behavior, and natural disasters such as floods and fires. Nevertheless, he could still strike a more positive note of worthy achievement and defiance, as seen in "Prorok" (The Prophet, 1874), a poem probably inspired by the death of Chernyshevsky but also in memory of all those who, in Nekrasov's words in the final line of the poem, "remind us of Christ." Among his best works of lyric poetry, *Poslednie pesni* (Last Songs, 1877) recounts memories of his childhood, his mother, and his regrets over mistakes he has made in his life. These final poems, all written in the few moments of respite that his fatal illness allowed him, include the cradle song "Baiushki-baiu" (Bye-Byes); in this particularly touching lyric, the narrator hears his mother's voice reassuring him that his songs will continue to be heard in his homeland.

Nikolai Alekseevich Nekrasov died on 27 December 1877. In spite of the frigid weather, a crowd of several thousand predominantly young mourners followed his coffin to its burial in Novodevichii Monastery in Moscow. Nekrasov was a writer who made a key contribution both to publishing and to literature that met the demands of his historical era. Much of his creative output was uneven in quality, but his muse of "vengeance and grief" broke new ground as it focused attention on underprivileged sections of society hitherto ignored by Russian poetry. Modern readers, too, will probably find indifference to Nekrasov's work difficult to maintain. Much of his writing does seem to repeat his central theme of the suffering of the *narod* at the hands of an

unjust social order. Occasionally, however, he wrote poetry that could indeed stand comparison with the work of even the most illustrious of his predecessors in the pantheon of Russian verse. In these instances he can be argued to escape easy categorization as a mere poetic mouthpiece for the ideas of revolutionary democracy.

Letters:

Arkhiv sela Karabikhi: Pis'ma Nekrasova i k Nekrasovu (Moscow: K. F. Nekrasov, 1916);

Pis'ma, volumes 10 and 11 of Nekrasov's *Polnoe sobranie sochinenii i pisem,* 12 volumes, edited by Vladislav Evgen'evich Evgen'ev-Maksimov, A. M. Egolin, and Kornei Ivanovich Chukovsky (Moscow: Goslitizdat, 1948–1952);

Perepiska N. A. Nekrasova: V dvukh tomakh, 2 volumes, edited by G. V. Krasnov, V. A. Viktorovich, and N. M. Fortunatov (Moscow: Khudozhestvennaia literatura, 1987);

Nikolai Alekseevich Nekrasov, *Stikhotvoreniia 1856,* edited by I. I. Podol'skaia (Moscow: Nauka, 1987).

Bibliographies:

Aleksandr Nikolaevich Pypin, "Bibliograficheskii obzor literatury o Nekrasove s ego smerti," in his *A. N. Nekrasov* (St. Petersburg: M. M. Stasiulevich, 1905), pp. 275–321;

L. M. Dobrovol'sky and V. M. Lavrov, "Bibliografiia bibliografii Nekrasova," *Literaturnoe nasledstvo,* 53–54 (1949): 569–572;

Dobrovol'sky and Lavrov, *Bibliografiia literatury o Nekrasove, 1917–1952* (Moscow: Nauka, 1953);

K. P. Dul'neva, G. M. Rudiakov, and L. P. Novikova, "Bibliografiia literatury o Nekrasove za 1953–58 gg.," *Nekrasovskii sbornik,* 3 (1960);

Dul'neva, "Bibliografiia literatury o Nekrasove za 1959–1969 gg.," in *N. A. Nekrasov i russkaia literatura, 1812–1871,* edited by K. N. Lomunov, P. A. Nikolaev, and N. V. Os'makov (Moscow: Nauka, 1971);

N. N. Mostovskaia, "Bibliografiia literatury o Nekrasove. 1970–1974," *Nekrasovskii sbornik,* 6 (1978);

Mostovskaia, "Bibliografiia literatury o Nekrasove. 1975–1986," *Nekrasovskii sbornik,* 9 (1988).

Biographies:

Vladislav Evgen'evich Evgen'ev-Maksimov, *Zhizn' i deiatel'nost' N. A. Nekrasova,* 3 volumes (Moscow: Khudozhestvennaia literatura, 1947–1952);

Charles Corbet, *Nekrasov, l'homme et le poète* (Paris: Institut d'études slaves de l'Universite de Paris, 1948);

M. B. Peppard, *Nikolai Nekrasov* (New York: Twayne, 1967);

Sigmund S. Birkenmayer, *Nikolaj Nekrasov: His Life and Poetic Art* (The Hague: Mouton, 1968);

Nikolai Leonidovich Stepanov, *N. A. Nekrasov. Zhizn' i tvorchestvo* (Moscow: Khudozhestvennaia literatura, 1971);

Vladimir Viktorovich Zhdanov, *Nekrasov,* Zhizn' zamechatel'nykh liudei, seriia biografii, no. 18 (Moscow: Molodaia gvardiia, 1971);

Nikolai Nikolaevich Skatov, *Nekrasov* (St. Petersburg: Nauka, 2001).

References:

Aleksandr Nikolaevich Afanas'ev, *Narodnye russkie skazki* (Moscow, 1858);

Vladimir Andreevich Arkhipov, *Poeziia truda i bor'by* (Moscow: Sovetskaia Rossiia, 1973);

Marietta Boiko, *Lirika Nekrasova* (Moscow: Khudozhestvennaia literatura, 1977);

Kornei Ivanovich Chukovsky, *Masterstvo Nekrasova* (Moscow: Gosudarstvennoe izdatel'stvo khudozhestvennoi literatury, 1962);

Boris Mikhailovich Eikhenbaum, "Nekrasov," in his *O poezii* (Leningrad: Sovetskii pisatel', 1969);

Vladislav Evgen'evich Evgen'ev-Maksimov, *N. A. Nekrasov i ego sovremenniki: Ocherki* (Moscow: Federatsiia, 1930);

Evgen'ev-Maksimov, *Nekrasov kak chevloveck, zhurnalist i poet* (Moscow: Gosudarstvennoe izdatel'stvo, 1928);

A. M. Garkavi, *Lirika Nekrasova i problemy realizma v liricheskoi poezii* (Kaliningrad: Kaliningradskii gosudarstvennyi universitet, 1979);

Garkavi, *N. A. Nekrasov i revoliutsionnoe narodnichestvo* (Moscow: Vysshaia shkola, 1962);

Garkavi, ed., *N. A. Nekrasov i ego vremia. Mezhvuzovskii sbornik,* 7 volumes (Kaliningrad: Kaliningradskii gosudarstvennyi universitet, 1975–1983);

Aleksandr Ivanovich Gruzdev, *Poema N. A. Nekrasova "Komu na Rusi zhit' khorosho"* (Leningrad: Khudozhestvennaia literatura, 1966);

Aleksandr Anatol'evich Iliushin, *Poeziia Nekrasova* (Moscow: Izdatel'stvo Moskovskogo gosudarstvennogo universiteta, 1999);

I. M. Kolesnitskaia, "Khudozhestvennye osobennosti poemy N. A. Nekrasova 'Korobeiniki,'" *Vestnik Leningradskogo universiteta,* 3 (1954);

B. O. Korman, *Lirika Nekrasova* (Voronezh: Izdatel'stvo Voronezhskogo universiteta, 1964);

B. V. Mel'gunov, *Nekrasov–zhurnalist* (Leningrad: Nauka, 1989);

Liudmila Danilovna Mikitich, *Literaturnyi Peterburg, Petrograd* (Moscow: Sovetskaia Rossiia, 1991);

Nikolai Nikolaevich Paikov, *Fenomen Nekrasova: Izbrannye stat'i o lichnosti i tvorchestve poeta* (Iaroslavl': Iaroslavskii gosudarstvennyi pedagogicheskii universitet, 2000);

M. Panchenko, "K istorii posmertnogo izdaniia sobraniia sochinenii Nekrasova," *Literaturnoe nasledstvo,* 53–54 (1949);

Valerian Georgievich Prokshin, *N. A. Nekrasov–put' k epopee* (Ufa: Bashk. knizhnoe izdatel'stvo, 1979);

Michael G. Ransome, "N. A. Nekrasov's Narrative Poetry on the Theme of the Russian Peasantry: A Critical Reappraisal," dissertation, University of Bristol, 1984;

Iurii Nikolaevich Tynianov, "Stikhovye formy Nekrasova," in his *Poetika, istoriia literatury, kino* (Moscow: Nauka, 1977);

Mikhail Fedorovich Vlasov, *O iazyke i stile N. A. Nekrasova: Uchebnoe posobie po spetskursu* (Perm', 1970).

Papers:

The papers of Nikolai Alekseevich Nekrasov can be found in several archives in various locations throughout Russia. The primary collections are located in both Moscow and St. Petersburg. In Moscow, Nekrasov's papers are housed at the Russian State Archive of Literature and Art (RGALI), fond 338; the Russian State Library (RGB, formerly the Lenin Library), fond 195; and the A. A. Bakhrushin State Central Museum, fond 187. In St. Petersburg, collections of Nekrasov's papers are held in the Institute of Russian Literature (IRLI, Pushkin House), fond 202, and in the Russian National Library (RNB), fond 514. Other collections can be found at the Iaroslavl' Memorial Nekrasov Museum in the village of Karabikha, and in the Chernigov Historical Museum.

Ivan Savvich Nikitin

(21 September 1824 – 16 October 1861)

David Vernikov
University of Wisconsin, Madison

and

Yekaterina Vernikov
Indiana University, Bloomington

BOOKS: *Stikhotvoreniia,* with an introduction by Dmitrii Nikolaevich Tolstoy (Voronezh & St. Petersburg: Graf D. N. Tolstoy, 1856);

Kulak. Poema (Moscow: Katkov, 1858);

Stikhotvoreniia (St. Petersburg: Karl Vul'f, 1859);

Sochineniia, 2 volumes, edited, with an introduction, by Mikhail Fedorovich De-Pule (Voronezh: A. P. Mikhailov, 1869; revised, Moscow, 1878; revised and enlarged, Moscow: K. K. Shamov, 1886);

Polnoe sobranie sochinenii, edited, with an introduction, by Mikhail Osipovich Gershenzon (Moscow: A. S. Panafidina, 1912);

Polnoe sobranie sochinenii i pisem, 3 volumes, edited by Aleksandr Grigor'evich Fomin, with an introduction by Iulii Isaevich Aikhenval'd (St. Petersburg: Prosveshchenie, 1913–1915; revised, Petrograd: Literaturno-izdatel'skii otdel Narodnogo komissariata po prosveshcheniiu, 1918)—comprises volume 1, *Stikhotvoreniia* (1913); volume 2, *Stikhotvoreniia. Poemy* (1914); and volume 3, *Proza* (1915);

Sochineniia, edited by Lev Abramovich Plotkin (Moscow: Khudozhestvennaia literatura, 1955);

Polnoe sobranie stikhotvorenii, edited, with an introduction, by Plotkin, Biblioteka poeta, Bol'shaia seriia (Moscow & Leningrad: Sovetskii pisatel', 1965).

Editions and Collections: *Kulak. Poema* (Moscow: K. K. Shamov, 1889);

Izbrannye proizvedeniia, edited, with an introduction and commentary, by Lev Abramovich Plotkin (Voronezh, 1934);

Stikhotvoreniia, edited, with an introduction, by Ivan Nikanorovich Rozanov, Biblioteka poeta, Malaia seriia, no. 35 (Moscow & Leningrad: Sovetskii pisatel', 1936);

Ivan Savvich Nikitin

Sobranie stikhotvorenii, edited, with an introduction, by Plotkin, Biblioteka poeta, Bol'shaia seriia (Leningrad: Sovetskii pisatel', 1947);

Sochineniia, 4 volumes, edited by Ol'ga Vladimirovna Bubnova and L. A. Mashnev, with an introduction by G. Kostin (Moscow: Sovetskaia Rossiia, 1960–1961);

Sochineniia, edited by Plotkin, with an introduction by Oleg Grigor'evich Lasunsky (Moscow: Khudozhestvennaia literatura, 1980);

Stikhotvoreniia. Dnevnik seminarista (Voronezh: Tsentral'no-Chernozemnoe knizhnoe izdatel'stvo, 1986);

Stikhotvoreniia (Voronezh: Tsentral'no-Chernozemnoe knizhnoe izdatel'stvo, 1988).

Edition in English: "Winter Night and Other Poems," translated by Eugene Kayden, *Colorado Quarterly,* 21, no. 4 (1973): 543–560.

OTHER: "Taras" and "Dnevnik Seminarista," in *Voronezhskaia beseda,* 2 volumes, edited by Mikhail Fedorovich De-Pule and P. Glotov (St. Petersburg: Gogenfel'den, 1861).

Ivan Nikitin's early lyrics and, even more, his social origins, have led to comparisons with his predecessor, Aleksei Vasil'evich Kol'tsov, a master of the literary folk song. In addition, Nikitin's realistic poems depicting the lives of the poor–the works for which he is best remembered–are often mentioned in conjunction with the name of his famous contemporary, Nikolai Alekseevich Nekrasov. Nevertheless, Nikitin remains a figure who resists easy classification. His position as one of only a handful of poets who did not belong to the nobility attracted the attention of some of the more radical literary and social critics of his day–but such attention came with expectations about what a *poet-meshchanin* (poet-commoner) and a *poet-obshchestvennik* (civic poet) ought to contribute to a socially relevant literature and was often accompanied by harsh criticism of Nikitin's eclectic talent. At the same time, not merely an impassioned observer, Nikitin saw himself as a product and victim of the ignorance and degradation described in his poems, even though these circumstances clashed with established literary models and with the Romantic poetic ideal that he nonetheless continued to cherish. Out of these extreme personal, social, and literary pressures emerged a poet who remains something of an anomaly in the literature of his time.

Ivan Savvich Nikitin was born on 21 September 1824 to a family of commoners. Thirty-two years earlier, in 1792, his paternal grandfather, Evtikhii Nikitich ("Nikitin syn" [Nikita's son], whence the family surname), retired from the post of deacon at a church in the village of Kazach'e, in Voronezh province. In 1796 he was divested of clerical standing and sent from Kazach'e to Voronezh, the provincial capital, following the complaint of a local priest about his disruptive

behavior. In 1801 Evtikhii Nikitich submitted a petition that his children be divested of clerical standing as well, which was granted. In an 1816 census he was recorded as a merchant of the third guild. The poet's father, Savva Evtikhievich Nikitin, was born in 1796. At the time of his only son's birth in 1824, Savva Evtikhievich owned a quite profitable candle factory and store in the city of Voronezh. He was a cunning merchant, a well-known fistfighter, and a despotic head of the family. Little is known about the poet's mother, Praskov'ia Ivanovna Nikitina, other than that she was quiet and demure.

Likewise, little is known about Nikitin's childhood and early education. He spoke seldom of his early years to his friends, and the theme of childhood is not treated extensively in his poetry. According to his close friend and early biographer, Aleksandr Petrovich Nordshtein, Nikitin's education started when he was six years old, and his first teacher was a shoemaker. Apparently, such instruction proved to be more than adequate, for in 1833 Nikitin entered the parochial school at the second-grade level. One of Nikitin's foremost biographers, Aleksandr Grigor'evich Fomin, interprets this assessment as evidence that Nikitin was better prepared than his peers at the time, and records do show that he was an excellent student at the school. In 1839 he entered the Voronezh seminary, where he began to read extensively and–possibly inspired by the example of Kol'tsov, who had also been a student at the seminary–first tried his hand at poetry. The seminary experience later served as the factual basis for Nikitin's prose work "Dnevnik seminarista" (The Journal of a Seminary Student, 1861). Nikitin's grades declined over the years, and he was expelled in 1843 because of an indifference to the study of theology and inferior marks resulting from his absence in the classroom.

Nikitin's family was also experiencing financial difficulties at this time. He was forced to sell candles in his father's store and even on the streets during church holidays. His mother died that same year, and his father took to drinking heavily, leaving all the work to his son. Nikitin's relationship with Savva Evtikhievich–which had always been strained–deteriorated significantly at this point. He found his father's drinking highly objectionable, which led to constantly recurring confrontations and scandals that continued throughout the rest of the poet's life. In 1844 the Nikitins sold the factory and bought an inn with stables in an attempt to rent it out for profit. The family's financial situation soon became even more desperate, and Nikitin took over the establishment after an unsuccessful attempt to find other employment. He served as a host for the cabbies and started dressing and acting the part, even as he continued to write poetry in his spare time. Still, he was uncertain about the quality of his work, and his first attempt at publication came only in 1849, also the year of his earliest surviving poems. Under the initials I.N., he sent two of his poems, "Les" (The Forest) and "Duma" (Thought), to the newspaper *Voronezhskie gubernskie vedomosti* (Voronezh Province News). The editors thought highly of the poems but could not publish them without knowing the author's name. In the 5 November 1849 issue the newspaper invited the author to identify himself, but Nikitin chose to remain anonymous at the time. "Les" was eventually published in *Stikhotvoreniia* (Poems, 1856) and "Duma" in *Polnoe sobranie sochinenii* (Complete Collected Works, 1912).

Nikitin's literary debut did not occur until 1853, when in two letters dated 6 and 12 November, respectively—the first to Fedor Alekseevich Koni, the editor of *Panteon* (The Pantheon), and the second to Valentin Andreevich Sredin, one of the editors of *Voronezhskie gubernskie vedomosti*—Nikitin offered several of his poems for publication under his full name. Both letters mention his social status as a commoner. Nikitin was immediately sought out by Nikolai Ivanovich Vtorov, another editor at *Voronezhskie gubernskie vedomosti,* who invited him for a visit and recommended him to his friend, Count Dmitrii Nikolaevich Tolstoy. A noted historian, Count Tolstoy was at the time the deputy director of the police department and later the governor of Voronezh province. On 21 November, Nikitin's poem "Rus'" (Russia) appeared in *Voronezhskie gubernskie vedomosti*. A folk stylization written in 1851, "Rus'" trumpets the glory of Russia in her victories against the Tatars, Poles, and Lithuanians. The patriotic enthusiasm of the poem accorded with the general sentiment of the time, a sentiment fueled by the nascent stirrings of the Crimean campaign against Turkey. "Rus'" attracted attention in the capital and was quickly reprinted in *Sankt-Peterburgskie vedomosti* (St. Petersburg News), along with words of praise for the author.

Gradually, Nikitin became a frequent visitor in the Vtorov household and a member of the so-called *vtorovskii kruzhok* (Vtorov circle). This group gathered weekly and included people of various political and literary views united by a common interest in intellectual pursuits. Besides Vtorov, several of the *kruzhok*—such as Anton Rodionovich Mikhailov, a Voronezh merchant, and Mikhail Fedorovich De-Pule, a teacher of Russian and history at the Voronezh Military Academy—became Nikitin's close friends. Mikhailov eventually published some of Nikitin's work, and De-Pule, who later served as the executor of Nikitin's will, was the poet's first biographer and editor. Regular social interaction helped Nikitin become more certain of both himself and his work. He made several important contacts within the literary establishment: he met Nestor

Vasil'evich Kukol'nik—at that time a popular poet, prose writer, and dramatist who resided in Voronezh—and he began corresponding with the well-known poet Apollon Nikolaevich Maikov.

From 1853 to 1854 Nikitin's poetic production increased greatly, as did his popularity. Among his fans was the wife of the governor of Voronezh, Countess Elizaveta Petrovna Dolgorukaia, who was particularly fond of the poem "Molenie o chashe" (Prayer upon the Cup, published in *Sochineniia* [Works], 1869)—which describes Christ's appeal to God on the night before the Crucifixion—and several of Nikitin's other religious verses. While religious themes, along with leitmotivs of nature and creativity, continued as an important presence in Nikitin's poetry, the scope of his subject matter expanded to include everyday life, with his own observations of his customers at the inn playing an especially key role. The poem "Nochleg izvozchikov" (The Cabbies' Night-Lodging), included in Kukol'nik's article "Listki iz zapisnoi knizhki russkogo" (Pages from the Notebook of a Russian) published in *Biblioteka dlia chteniia* (A Reading Library) in 1854, reflects a salient example, since it re-creates in some detail a typical night at the inn. Several of Nikitin's poems appeared in well-known journals such as *Moskvitianin* (The Muscovite), *Otechestvennye zapiski* (Notes of the Fatherland), and *Biblioteka dlia chteniia*. One notable response came from Nekrasov—one of the most influential poets of the period and editor of the literary journal *Sovremennik* (The Contemporary)—who wrote in a review that Nikitin was not without talent, although he was prone to excess and lacked taste. Possibly as a result of these unflattering comments, Nikitin never submitted his work to *Sovremennik* for publication.

Nikitin suffered a debilitating ailment in the summer of 1855. His health had been poor for some time, and his condition was regularly aggravated by long hours of hard work. In April, after swimming in cold water, he caught a severe cold which, compounded by scurvy, left him bedridden for five months. He was unable to write until October.

In 1854 Count Tolstoy had offered to publish a collection of Nikitin's poems, and Nikitin had agreed. His first collection of poetry came out in 1856 under the title *Stikhotvoreniia* and was met with some reserve by the critical establishment. While *Otechestvennye zapiski* and *Biblioteka dlia chteniia* published reviews that were, on the whole, positive, these reviews nevertheless noted the derivative qualities of Nikitin's poetry. Reviews in *Moskvitianin* and *Syn otechestva* (Son of the Fatherland) were less favorable. *Russkii vestnik* (The Russian Messenger) was even cooler in its assessment of Nikitin's work, and Nikolai Gavrilovich Chernyshevsky—an influential radical critic and writer—delivered a scathing review in

Page from the manuscript for Nikitin's Kulak *(The Kulak, 1858), a long narrative poem about a dishonest, tyrannical merchant (State Public Library, St. Petersburg)*

Sovremennik. In spite of some skill for writing poems, Chernyshevsky wrote, Nikitin showed neither talent nor originality in his work. This reception understandably disturbed Nikitin. He wrote a letter (dated 20 August 1856) to Andrei Aleksandrovich Kraevsky, the editor of *Sovremennik,* in which he addressed Chernyshevsky's criticism in detail. In fact, some basis for the critics' objections—if not for their poetic injunctions—does exist, since Nikitin's earlier verses betray their Romantic sources.

In 1857 Nikitin completed work on what became his magnum opus, *Kulak* (The Kulak, 1858)—a *poema* (long narrative poem) that he began writing in 1854—and sent it to the publisher. It appeared as a book in 1858 with surprisingly few censorial elisions. The protagonist, Lukich, is a small-time merchant who makes a living by cheating other merchants and peasants, making minor purchases and sales, or serving as a go-between in larger deals. A despotic patriarch, he also has a proclivity for heavy drinking. Drinking is the source of much of his financial hardship and the cause of his tyrannical behavior toward his wife and daughter; quite likely, Nikitin's own father served as a prototype for Lukich. Lukich forbids his daughter to marry a poor but honest neighbor, whom she loves, and forces her into marriage with a rich suitor—another dishonest merchant, albeit a more successful one. Lukich hopes that having a rich son-in-law will help his own situation, but his hopes are misplaced. His wife dies; his daughter is unhappily married; and he sinks into poverty and alcoholism. By the end of the *poema* Lukich is characterized more as a victim of society than as a petty tyrant. Overall, *Kulak* paints a bleak picture of city life for the commoners. Hardly any character in it does not make a living by cheating, lying, stealing, or taking bribes. In the last stanza of the *poema* Nikitin speaks in the first person; he says that Lukich's fate could well have become his own and that only extremely hard work helped him to escape it. Finally, he speaks of social ills in general: "Thousands all around / Died, like you, under the yoke / Of poverty, ignorance, depravity!" At the end he doubts that humankind will ever be good.

Kulak enjoyed a much more favorable reception from the socially minded critical establishment than had Nikitin's 1856 collection, *Stikhotvoreniia.* Nikolai Aleksandrovich Dobroliubov, another radical critic, reviewed the *poema* favorably in *Sovremennik,* praising the author for his choice, and in-depth knowledge, of the subject matter and for his detailed descriptions of everyday life. The work sold well, and the entire print run was sold out in less than a year. Nikitin received an offer for a second edition and began entertaining plans to change his situation by opening a bookstore in Voronezh.

His goal in opening the store, as he wrote in a 27 October 1858 letter to his old friends from the *vtorovskii kruzhok,* was not only to escape the life he led as an innkeeper but also to provide the reading public with a better selection of books than what was available in the three existing Voronezh bookstores. He also intended to influence the minds of seminary students by putting at their disposal an inexpensive reading library that encompassed all of the best contemporary journals. Nikitin was able to procure the 3,000 rubles necessary to open the store from the St. Petersburg manufacturer Vasilii Aleksandrovich Kokorev, a close acquaintance of Vtorov and a fan of Nikitin's talent. The store opened in 1859, and Nikitin was able to turn it into a rather successful business venture, albeit at the price of further damaging his health. He began suffering from tuberculosis at this time.

Also in 1859 Nikitin published his second collection of poetry, which included not only revised versions of twenty poems from the 1856 *Stikhotvoreniia* but also a selection of work he had written since the first collection. Critical reception for the 1859 *Stikhotvoreniia* was somewhat cooler than that for *Kulak.* Reviewing the book in *Sovremennik,* Dobroliubov noted that Nikitin's work was still derivative and advised him to use his talent to describe experiences based on, and more relevant to, his own life. This suggestion elicited a protest from Fyodor Dostoevsky, who interpreted it as an infringement on the rights of the poet and an expression of brutal utilitarianism. Dostoevsky parodied Dobroliubov's stance in an imaginary injunction to the poet: "Write about your needs, describe the needs and requirements of your class. Away with Pushkin, don't you dare to delight in him. . . ."

By this time Nikitin was generally recognized as a poet of some merit, and Nekrasov extended an invitation to him to publish in *Sovremennik.* Nikitin's earlier admiration of Nekrasov, however, had been replaced by strong dislike, and Nikitin's work did not appear in the journal. In April 1860 Nikitin introduced his poem "Oblichitel' chuzhogo razvrata . . ." (Denouncer of others' depravity . . .) at a public reading; in earlier editions this poem is also known as "Poetu-oblichiteliu" (To a Poet-Denouncer), an explanatory title provided by De-Pule. The consensus among pre-Soviet reviewers holds that this sharply critical poem is directed against Nekrasov. Most Soviet scholarship, however, maintains that, because of shared "revolutionary-democratic" ideology, Nekrasov cannot possibly be the target of Nikitin's criticism.

In 1860 Nikitin became involved in another project. He and De-Pule decided to put together two volumes of an anthology, *Voronezhskaia beseda* (Voronezh Colloquy, 1861). The anthology was edited by De-Pule, who claimed, however, that Nikitin was the heart and soul of the endeavor. For publication in *Voronezhskaia beseda,* Nikitin completed another *poema,* titled "Taras" after its protagonist. The *poema* describes the life of a peasant who leaves his home in search of happiness: "Taras went with a knapsack over his shoulder / To look for happiness and virtue." In an attempt to save a drowning comrade, Taras himself ends up drowning.

Nikitin's most significant contribution to the anthology was, however, the prose work "Dnevnik seminarista," written in the form of a journal, in which the largely autobiographical protagonist of the work, Vasilii Belozersky—a young man who attends the seminary and is compelled by his father to room at the house of his philosophy professor—records his observations. The outlook is once again bleak. Neither students nor professors are the least bit concerned with intellectual or spiritual matters. Original thinking is highly discouraged, and students are expected to learn their lessons by rote. Themselves shown to be uneducated, the teachers are completely uninterested in education. Bribery, debauchery, and drinking are commonplace, and the atmosphere of the seminary is stifling. The only instructor interested in his subject is scorned by his colleagues and becomes progressively more discouraged.

The student who is an exception to such corruptive behavior, Iablochkin, plays an important role in Belozersky's development. He introduces Belozersky to the works of Nikolai Vasil'evich Gogol and Vissarion Grigor'evich Belinsky—authors of the most current literature and criticism in the 1840s—and instills in him the dream of going to the university. After Iablochkin's death from consumption, however, Belozersky's development grinds to a halt, and he becomes resigned to his situation. Iablochkin's deathbed poem, "Vyryta zastupom iama glubokaia . . ." (A deep pit has been dug with a spade . . .), is one of Nikitin's most powerful lyrical pieces. De-Pule, to whom Nikitin read his work, later wrote that only a dying man could have written and recited it in such a way. Indeed, Nikitin's health took a turn for the worse soon after he finished writing "Dnevnik seminarista."

This illness coincided with a period of indecision for Nikitin. He was in love with one of the three daughters of his acquaintance, the merchant Mikhailov, and the feeling was reciprocated. De-Pule writes that had Nikitin proposed marriage, his proposal would have been accepted. Nikitin's cousin and childhood friend, Anna Nikolaevna Tiurina, also mentions that Mikhailov was willing to give his daughter to Nikitin in marriage, thereby indicating that the poet had been considering a marriage proposal, although he apparently never made one. Most biographers mention Nikitin's health as a possible reason. De-Pule writes in

his introduction to *Sochineniia* (1869) that he fully expected a proposal to be made when Nikitin's illness went into remission in the middle of 1860. By that time, however, Nikitin had become interested in Nataliia Antonovna Matveeva, the daughter of a retired general. Their relationship was epistolary for the most part, since Nikitin was not well acquainted with Matveeva's father and thus could not visit her.

In May 1861 Nikitin caught a cold, causing his tuberculosis to worsen. In addition to feeling physically drained, he was burdened psychologically by recurring scandals with his father, who often became drunk and demanded that his son leave him the bookstore in his will. Nikitin had intended to sell the store and donate the proceeds to a charitable cause, but instead he left the money to his remaining relatives, excluding his father. On 16 October 1861 the poet died.

Ivan Savvich Nikitin's writing anticipated some of the dominant poetic trends to come: a general prosaicness of poetry in both theme and diction; the central role of plot in lyrical verse; and the introduction—especially through *Kulak,* with the unidealized, multidimensional portrait of its indigent "hero"—of a wholly new type of poetic protagonist. These trends prevailed in the poetry of the next few decades. Nevertheless, Nikitin's reputation and significance—like that of most figures with roots in the lower classes—tended to be inflated during the Soviet period, and he cannot be placed among the first-rank poets of the nineteenth century. A more sensitive appraisal of his role is provided by the influential turn-of-the-century literary critic Iulii Isaevich Aikhenval'd, who writes in *Siluety russkikh pisatelei* (1994) of Nikitin: "His best poems are distinguished by their musicality and power, and his prose is even elegant in its concision and distinctness of outline; but it is undeniable that as a whole his pages are a human, rather than an artistic document. There was, in Nikitin, definite potential as an artist, but rarely was it realized."

Letters:

"Pis'ma," in Nikitin's *Sochineniia,* edited by Lev Abramovich Plotkin (Moscow: Khudozhestvennaia literatura, 1955), pp. 207–302;

"Ia Rusi syn! . . .": K 150-letiu so dnia rozhdeniia I. S. Nikitina, edited by Oleg Grigor'evich Lasunsky (Voronezh: Tsentral'no-Chernozemnoe knizhnoe izdatel'stvo, 1974), pp. 29–79.

Bibliographies:

A. M. Putintsev, "Kratkii obzor literatury ob I. S. Nikitine," *Filologicheskie zapiski,* 23 (1907): 1–20;

B. N. Kapeliush, "Rukopisi i perepiska I. S. Nikitina," *Biulleten' Rukopisnogo otdela Pushkinskogo doma AN SSSR,* 4 (1953): 99–106;

E. D. Medveditsyna, comp., *I. S. Nikitin. Ukazatel' literatury (1918–1973),* edited by Oleg Grigor'evich Lasunsky (Voronezh, 1974);

Medveditsyna, comp., *I. S. Nikitin. Ukazatel' literatury iubileinogo goda (1974),* edited by Lasunsky (Voronezh: Voronezhskaia oblastnaia biblioteka imeni I. S. Nikitina, 1977).

Biographies:

Mikhail Fedorovich De-Pule, *Biografiia I. S. Nikitina* (Voronezh: V. A. Gol'dshtein, 1869);

F. E. Sivitsky, *I. S. Nikitin. Ego zhizn' i literaturnaia deiatel'nost'. Biograficheskii ocherk* (St. Petersburg: V. I. Shtein, 1893);

Viacheslav Alekseevich Tonkov, *I. S. Nikitin. Ocherk zhizni i tvorchestva* (Moscow: Prosveshchenie, 1968);

Viktor Ivanovich Kuznetsov, *Ivan Savvich Nikitin: kniga dlia uchashchikhsia starshikh klassov srednei shkoly* (Moscow: Prosveshchenie, 1991).

References:

Iulii Isaevich Aikhenval'd, "Nikitin," in his *Siluety russkikh pisatelei,* volume 2 (Moscow: Respublika, 1994), pp. 134–138;

Nikolai Gavrilovich Chernyshevsky, "Stikhotvoreniia Ivana Nikitina," in his *Polnoe sobranie sochinenii,* volume 1 (Moscow: Khudozhestvennaia literatura, 1947), pp. 495–501;

Nikolai Aleksandrovich Dobroliubov, *Polnoe sobranie sochinenii v shesti tomakh,* 6 volumes (Leningrad: Khudozhestvennaia literatura, 1934–1941), I: 383–388, II: 568–586;

Fyodor Dostoevsky, "G-n–bov i vopros ob iskusstve," in his *Polnoe sobranie sochinenii v 30 tomakh,* volume 18 (Leningrad: Nauka, 1978), pp. 70–103;

I. S. Nikitin. Stat'i i materialy. K 100-letiiu so dnia smerti, edited by Viacheslav Alekseevich Tonkov (Voronezh: Izdatel'stvo Voronezhskogo universiteta, 1962);

I. S. Nikitin. Stat'i i materialy o zhizni i tvorchestve, edited by Tonkov (Voronezh: Voronezhskoe oblastnoe knigoizdatel'stvo, 1952);

"Ia Rusi syn! . . .": K 150-letiu so dnia rozhdeniia I. S. Nikitina, edited by Oleg Grigor'evich Lasunsky (Voronezh: Tsentral'no-Chernozemnoe knizhnoe izdatel'stvo, 1974);

Ivan Savvich Nikitin: Ego zhizn' i sochineniia. Sbornik istoriko-literaturnykh statei, compiled by Vasilii Ivanovich Pokrovsky (Moscow: V. Spiridonov & A. Mikhailov, 1911);

I. F. Kamov, *Soderzhanie i kharakter poezii I. S. Nikitina* (Warsaw: Varshavskii uchebnyi okrug, 1901);

Nikolai Alekseevich Nekrasov, *Polnoe sobranie sochinenii i pisem v piatnadtsati tomakh,* volume 11 (Leningrad: Nauka, 1990), pp. 141–162, 185–204;

Aleksandr Petrovich Nordshtein, "Novosti literatury, iskusstv, nauk i promyshlennosti," *Otechestvennye zapiski,* 94, no. 6, part 7 (1854): 57–68;

Poet-demokrat I. S. Nikitin, edited by Sergei Georgievich Lazutin (Voronezh: Izdatel'stvo Voronezhskogo universiteta, 1976);

Tonkov, *Nikitin i narodnoe tvorchestvo* (Voronezh: Voronezhskoe oblastnoe knizhnoe izdatel'stvo, 1941).

Papers:

Some of Ivan Savvich Nikitin's papers are held in Moscow at the Russian State Archive of Literature and Art (RGALI), fond 347, and at the Russian State Library (RGB, formerly the Lenin Library), fond 178. Others are located in St. Petersburg at the Institute of Russian Literature (IRLI, Pushkin House) in the collection of Mikhail Fedorovich De-Pule, fond 569; and at the I. S. Nikitin House-Museum in Voronezh.

Nikolai Platonovich Ogarev

(24 November 1813 – 31 May 1877)

Martha Kuchar
Roanoke College

BOOKS: *Razbor manifesta 26 avgusta 1856* (London: Trübner, 1856);

Stikhotvoreniia (Moscow: K. T. Soldatenkov & N. Shchepkin, 1856)–includes "Druz'iam" and "Fashionable";

Iumor (London: Trübner, 1857);

Stikhotvoreniia (London: Trübner, 1858)–includes "Tiur'ma";

Za piat' let (1855–1860): Politicheskie i sotsialnye stat'i Iskandera i Ogareva (London: Trübner, 1860–1861);

Na novyi god (Moscow: Moskovskii studencheskii kruzhok Zaichnevskogo i Argiropulo, 1861);

Razbor novogo krepostnogo prava (London: Trübner, 1861);

Chto nado delat' voisku? (London: Vol'naia russkaia tipografiia, 1861?);

Essai sur la situation russe: Lettres à un anglais (London: Trübner, 1862);

Nadgrobnoe slovo (Pamiati A. A. Potebni) (London: Vol'naia russkaia tipografiia, 1863);

Finansovye spory (London: Trübner, 1864);

Zemleopisanie dlia naroda, by Ogarev, Lev Il'ich Menchikov, and others (Geneva: Volnaia russkaia tipografiia, 1868);

V pamiati liudiam 14 dekabria 1825 (Geneva: L. Chernetsky, 1869);

Gertsen i Ogarev v Shveitsarii: Ikh poslednie proizvedeniia (Geneva, 1901);

Stikhotvoreniia, 2 volumes, edited by Mikhail Osipovich Gershenzon (Moscow: M. & S. Sabashnikovy, 1904)–includes "Tebe ia schast'ia ne daval dovol'no . . ." and "Exil";

Neizvestnyi Ogarev (Moscow: Ogonek, 1928);

Izbrannye sotsial'no-politicheskie i filosofskie proizvedeniia, 2 volumes, edited by M. T. Iovchuk and Nikolai Grigor'evich Tarakanov (Moscow: Gospolitizdat, 1952–1956);

Izbrannye proizvedeniia, 2 volumes, edited by N. M. Gaidenkov (Moscow: Goslitizdat, 1956)–includes "Buch der Liebe."

Nikolai Platonovich Ogarev

Editions and Collections: *Stikhotvoreniia* (Moscow: K. T. Soldatenkov & N. Shchepkin, 1863);

Rodnye poety, by Ogarev and A. N. Pleshcheev (Moscow: Obshchestvo rasprostraneniia poleznykh knig, 1903);

Iumor. Poema, with a preface by Ia. El'sberg (Moscow & Leningrad: Academia, 1933);

Stikhotvoreniia i poemy, 2 volumes, edited by S. A. Reiser and N. P. Surina, Biblioteka poeta, Malaia seriia (Leningrad: Sovetskii pisatel', 1937–1938)–includes "K moei biografii: Moe nadgrobnoe";

Izbrannye stikhotvoreniia i poemy, edited by Ia. Z. Cherniak (Moscow: Khudozhestvennaia literatura, 1938);

Stikhotvoreniia i poemy, edited by Reiser, Biblioteka poeta, Bol'shaia seriia (Leningrad: Sovetskii pisatel', 1956);

Izbrannoe, edited by G. G. Elizavetina (Moscow: Khudozhestvennaia literatura, 1977);

Stikhotvoreniia i poemy, with an introduction by Viktor Afanas'ev (Moscow: Sovetskaia Rossiia, 1980);

O literature i iskusstve, edited by G. Krasnov (Moscow: Sovremennik, 1988);

O vospitanii i obrazovanii, compiled by V. I. Shiriaev (Moscow: Pedagogika, 1990).

OTHER: Kondratii Fedorovich Ryleev, *Dumy: Stikhotvoreniia,* foreword by Ogarev (London: Trübner, 1860);

Russkaia potaennaia literatura XIX veka, foreword by Ogarev (London: Trübner, 1861);

"Iumor," in *Poliarnaia zvezda,* book 8 (Geneva & Basel: H. Georg, 1868);

"(E. F.) Korshu," in *Pomoshch' golodaiushchim* (Moscow, 1892);

"Profession de foi" and "Tsaritsa moria," in *Russkie propilei. Materialy po istorii russkoi mysli i literatury,* edited by Mikhail Osipovich Gershenzon, volume 2 (Moscow: M. & S. Sabashnikovy, 1916), pp. 111–142.

Nikolai Ogarev was a gifted writer of poems and prose works during the eventful middle decades of the nineteenth century. Beginning his career under the influences of Romantic literature and philosophical idealism, Ogarev evolved over the years from Romantic poet to Realist chronicler of his life and times. Among some of his contemporaries he earned a reputation as a dark and depressing poet. Apollon Aleksandrovich Grigor'ev called him the poet of melancholy, and Aleksandr Vasil'evich Druzhinin described his poetry in an 1856 article for *Biblioteka dlia chteniia* (A Reading Library) as "meek, frail, and sad." Yet, the critic Petr Petrovich Pertsov might have been more accurate when he argued that what sometimes passes in Ogarev's poetry for Romantic malaise is in fact a deeply felt metaphysical anguish, a sad and bitter realization of the absurdity of things. This theme, which runs throughout Ogarev's poetry, occurs when–as in "(E. F.) Korshu" (To [E. F.] Korsh, written 1856, published 1892)–he "dares" the reader not to lie but to admit to the "chaos of life." Ogarev devoted himself to capturing this chaos, most often by scrutinizing his own life as a model of the lives of his generation. His poetry must be seen then as a counterpart to the poems and stories of Aleksandr Sergeevich Pushkin, Mikhail Iur'evich Lermontov,

Alexander Herzen (Aleksandr Ivanovich Gertsen), Nikolai Alekseevich Nekrasov, Ivan Sergeevich Turgenev, and others, who documented the promises and losses of life in the difficult times of nineteenth-century Russia.

If some of his contemporaries saw tragedy in the themes of Ogarev's work, others saw beauty in his craft. The influential critic Vissarion Grigor'evich Belinsky and the novelist Turgenev highly valued his writing, calling it musical, poignant, and sincere. In the twentieth century, commentators have noted a civic strain in Ogarev's work, both in his poetry and especially in his journalism, which he practiced during many years of collaboration with Herzen while living outside of Russia. For example, Mikhail Osipovich Gershenzon described Ogarev as a "poet of quiet courage and of strong resolve," while Victor Terras called him "remarkable." In a poem that Ogarev wrote shortly before his death ("K moei biografii: Moe nadgrobnoe" [Toward a Biography: My Epitaph], written 1874–1876, published 1937–1938), he begins by describing himself in simple terms: "I was a good man, and I wrote my poems." He then goes on to a fuller confession of his artistic credo: "I wrote my poems in a spirit of revolt / Out of a wish to change the people, / For in verse I found joy / And in rebellion virtue." In Ogarev one finds a curious combination: a poet who preferred solitude amid the beauty of nature but whose good conscience compelled him, figuratively and literally, to take to the streets to agitate for change.

Nikolai Platonovich Ogarev was born on 24 November 1813 in St. Petersburg into a wealthy gentry family. After the death of his mother, Elizaveta Ivanovna (née Baskakova) Ogareva, when he was two years old, Ogarev was raised by his father, a high-ranking state councillor, at their estate at Staroe Aksheno in Penza province. Platon Bogdanovich Ogarev was both strict and traditional, and he discouraged his son's creative tendencies. Years later, in a 29 August 1835 letter to Herzen, Ogarev lamented his relations with his father: "I said to him, 'I'm a poet,' and he called me a fool; everything that I live by he called mad." Ogarev felt torn in his feelings toward his father. This ambivalence and a longing for a parental ideal inspire some of Ogarev's best early poetry, as for instance "Ottsu" (To My Father, written 1839, published in *Russkaia starina* [Russian Antiquity], 1889). Ogarev was a sickly and nervous child. Unhappy at home, he sought solace in the countryside and later wrote many poems describing the natural beauty of his boyhood surroundings.

The Ogarev family moved to Moscow in 1820, though they continued returning to the country for periodic visits. Until age seventeen, Ogarev received his education at home. Among his teachers were his sister's governess Anna Egorovna Horsetter and his tutor Karl Ivanovich Sonnenberg, both of whom he described in his unfinished autobiography "Moia ispoved'" (My Confession, written 1860–1862, published in *Literaturnoe nadsledstvo* [Literary Heritage], 1953). From an early age he was exposed to contemporary literature and current ideas. In particular, he admired the writings of Pushkin, Kondratii Fedorovich Ryleev, Jean-Jacques Rousseau, Friedrich von Schiller, Baron de Montesquieu, and John Locke. Perhaps the single most important event of his youth was his meeting on 14 February 1826 with his cousin Herzen. Since his death in 1877, Ogarev's name has survived in the history books primarily because of Herzen. Lifelong friends and associates, Herzen and Ogarev risked danger more than once by working together for social and political change in Russia. This commitment began early. In their writings they describe the vow they made one day shortly after their 1826 meeting. Standing atop Vorob'evye gory (Sparrow Hills) overlooking Moscow, they promised in the name of the Decembrist martyrs to fight despotism with all their strength.

In 1830 Ogarev began attending classes at Moscow University in literature and the natural sciences. More important than his classes was the student group that he and Herzen had organized. This aspect of Ogarev's studies was perhaps the highlight of his life in the early to mid 1830s. The other students in his *kruzhok* (circle)–which included Nikolai Mikhailovich Satin, Nikolai Ivanovich Sazonov, Nikolai Khristoforovich Ketcher, and Vadim Vasil'evich Passek–were interested in the German philosopher Friedrich Wilhelm Joseph von Schelling, especially his *Naturephilosophie,* as well as the "forbidden" works of French utopian authors such as Henri Saint-Simon and Charles Fourier. The group most often met at Ogarev's house on Nikitskii Boulevard. According to Ogarev in his poem "Druz'iam" (To My Friends, written 1840–1841, published 1856), the group was ready "to do battle with reality, without sparing ourselves." In his memoir *Byloe i dumy* (My Past and Thoughts, 1852–1868) Herzen wrote that they "preached hatred toward all compulsion, toward all signs of authoritative abuse." Unlike the outgoing, fiery Herzen, however, Ogarev was taciturn, introspective, and private, as is evident from poems such as "T. N. Granovskomu" (To Granovsky, written 1841, published in *Novyi mir* [New World], 1931), addressed to the Moscow University professor and historian Timofei Nikolaevich Granovsky, or "Ia nakonets ostavil gorod shumnyi" (At Last I've Left the Noisy City, written 1846, published in *Russkii vestnik* [The Russian Messenger], 1856), which is one of the most characteristic poems of Ogarev's early period. Preferring solitude to company, he avoided the kind of

public gaze on which Herzen thrived. While he was sincere in his hopes for social change and angry at the sluggish pace of such change, in his early career Ogarev tended at times toward acquiescence. He described himself thus in an 1841 letter to Herzen, "I'm a man who is full of quiet resignation and unshakable composure. . . . Bear your cross and go forward."

A "poet of reflection," in the words of literary critic and historian Dmitrii Petrovich Sviatopolk-Mirsky, Ogarev began writing verse in the early 1830s, probably before the age of twenty. Influenced by Pushkin, Schelling, Johann Wolfgang von Goethe, and George Gordon, Lord Byron, his poems of the 1830s and 1840s employ Romantic themes and motifs common in his time. One finds in them lyrical explorations of feelings and ideas, reveries and visions of the future, and dialogues with the dead and the forgotten. Ogarev's early verse alternates between melancholy and hope, wistfulness and wrath. His favorite settings include landscapes, often in autumn or winter, and abandoned interiors such as old homes and empty rooms. He was also quite capable of irony and satire. In addition, he employed techniques of folk poetry, from *skaz* (a first-person homespun style of narration) to the *raeshnik* (a humorous rhymed free-verse stanza of varying meter and length) and other folk forms.

In the summer of 1833, partly for his role in leading the student discussions, Ogarev came under police surveillance. On 10 July 1834 he was arrested for singing seditious songs and for corresponding with Herzen on "free-thinking" subjects. He was released after a few days, only to be rearrested on 31 July, ten days after Herzen's own arrest. This time Ogarev spent eight months in jail. On 31 March 1835 he was exiled to his family home in Penza province and put under his father's supervision. Despite their differences Ogarev loved his father and worried about his worsening health. Nevertheless, he could not bear his father's house. The penalty of exile was bad enough, but his father's constant guests, their trivial diversions, the lack of serious conversation, and the constant presence of fatuous social practices and prejudices were beyond his ability to endure. As he describes in his poem "Zhelanie pokoia" (Desire for Peace, written 1839, published in *Russkaia starina,* 1889), Ogarev's solution was to retreat into himself–to take refuge in isolation from other people. For all its distractions, this environment was conducive to private reflection and the writing of poetry. He wrote an estimated two dozen poems and other works during this time.

While staying in Penza province, Ogarev met the woman who later became his first wife. Mariia L'vovna Roslavleva was the daughter of an impoverished nobleman and the niece of the provincial governor, Alek-

Page from Ogarev's musical setting for a poem by Mikhail Iur'evich Lermontov, 1850s
(from Vladimir Aleksandrovich Putintsev, N. P. Ogarev, 1963)

sandr Alekseevich Panchulidzev, in whose home she lived. She seemed to offer a solution to Ogarev's loneliness and, for a while, appeared to be a desirable soul mate. They married in 1836. Soon after, Ogarev realized that her charm had been a deception. Mariia L'vovna had no intention of joining Ogarev in his quest for truth. She just wanted to escape her relatives and enter the beau monde.

Ogarev had suffered from epilepsy since childhood, and now, under the pressures of exile and marital discord, his health worsened. In order to seek therapy, Ogarev requested—and was granted—permission to go abroad. In the summer of 1838 he and Mariia L'vovna traveled to the Caucasus. The trip exacerbated the tensions with his wife but offered him a respite from his other woes. In Piatigorsk, Ogarev met his old friend Satin and, through him, some Decembrists lately transferred from their Siberian exile, including Nikolai Ivanovich Lorer, Mikhail Aleksandrovich Nazimov, and especially Aleksandr Ivanovich Odoevsky, for whom Ogarev developed a deep appreciation. These meetings impressed Ogarev profoundly and reminded him of his vow on Sparrow Hills to avenge the Decembrist heroes. He recorded his impressions in the poem "Ia videl vas, prishel'tsy dal'nykh stran . . ." (I saw you, wayfarers from distant lands . . . , written 1838, published in *Russkaia mysl'* [Russian Thought], 1902) and returned to them again later in life in the poem "Geroicheskaia simfoniia Betgovena" (Beethoven's Heroic Symphony, written 1874[?], published in *Russkaia mysl'*, 1902). With the memory of these encounters fresh in his mind, Ogarev traveled in March 1839, together with his wife, to visit Herzen in his place of exile in Vladimir. They shared an uplifting moment when Ogarev, Mariia L'vovna, Herzen, and his bride, Natal'ia Aleksandrovna Herzen, on bended knee, declared their mutual respect and love for one another and pledged eternal friendship (Ogarev recorded this vow in his poem "Marii, Aleksandru i Natashe" [To Mariia, Aleksandr and Natal'ia]). Once the Ogarevs left Vladimir, however, their troubles returned.

In November 1838 Ogarev's father passed away, leaving his son huge tracts of land and forest and more than four thousand serfs. Over time Ogarev tried instituting reforms on this land. He took steps to build schools and hospitals for the peasants as well as a dress factory and paper factory in order to employ the peasants as paid laborers. Yet, the paper factory burned to the ground, and only a few of Ogarev's plans met with success. After much effort he did succeed in freeing approximately 1,800 serfs who had been living in the Riazan' village of Beloomut—over his wife's objections. In a letter of 1839 he argued with her: "Don't expect me to give up these good, noble, and honest intentions merely for the sake of personal indulgence."

In 1839, with the aid of some influential relatives, Mariia L'vovna secured permission for Ogarev to return to Moscow. Her plans included balls, soirees, and various other aristocratic amusements, but his did not, as evidenced by his satirical poem "Fashionable" (written 1840–1841, published 1856). Attempting to draw Ogarev into the social whirlwind with her, she also tried to break up his alliance with Herzen—who was back in Moscow—and with their former *kruzhok*. She failed, however, and Ogarev began a period of serious study and the writing of poetry in the company of his peers.

The year 1840 was auspicious in the poet's career. He first appeared in print in May in the important journal *Otechestvennye zapiski* (Notes of the Fatherland) with two poems: "Staryi dom" (Old Home) and "Kreml'" (The Kremlin). "Staryi dom," with its themes of transient life and the power of memory, is a favorite among Ogarev's readers. These poems were followed in August by the appearance of Ogarev's translations of poems by Heinrich Heine in *Literaturnaia gazeta*. Beginning in the 1840s he translated literary works by many distinguished poets and writers, including excerpts from William Shakespeare's plays *Hamlet* and *Othello*, excerpts from Goethe's *Faust*, and several other Goethe poems, as well as poems by Heine, Byron, and Adam Mickiewicz. In October 1840 his poem "Derevenskii storozh" (Village Watchman) appeared in *Otechestvennye zapiski*. Thereafter, Ogarev's work began appearing in print regularly, particularly in *Otechestvennye zapiski*. This journal was an important locus for his verse since it attracted the leading writers of the day. With the journalist Andrei Aleksandrovich Kraevsky as its editor and Belinsky as its lead literary critic, *Otechestvennye zapiski* stood at the forefront of liberal debate and literary innovation. Ogarev wrote the majority of his work as a poet during the late 1830s and through the 1840s.

As the Golden Age of Russian poetry (the 1820s and 1830s) passed, enthusiasm for verse subsided during the next decade. Pushkin had died in 1837 and Lermontov in 1841. Nikolai Vasil'evich Gogol, Fyodor Dostoevsky, and Turgenev were publishing prose narratives and paving the way for the great novels of the nineteenth century. A modest poetic revival eventually came with the aesthetic poetry of Afanasii Afanas'evich Fet in the 1850s and the civic poetry of Nekrasov in the 1860s. Ogarev himself wrote some civic poems, a style that has also been called (by Terras) the "poetry of social compassion." In his lyric "Izba" (Peasant Hut, *Otechestvennye zapiski*, 1842), for example, he describes the fate of a girl who must work through the night at her spinning wheel while the rest of the family sleeps. Even in writing civic poetry, Ogarev remained true to his Romantic roots; his touch is light and poignant, and he approaches his subjects with sensitivity and care.

Among Ogarev's poems are many fine love lyrics, written during a time when his relationship with Maria L'vovna was disintegrating. As Herzen reminisced in *Byloe i dumy,* "Ogarev was then at the very height of his powers . . . at moments he seemed to feel that misfortune was at hand, but he could still turn aside and take the lifted hand of destiny for a dream." For a while Ogarev continued to write poems of passion and love for his wife (examples are "K M. L. Ogarevoi" [To M. L. Ogarev], written 1840, published in *Literaturnoe nasledstvo,* 1953) and "Ia pozdno leg, ustalyi i bol'noi . . ." [I went to bed late, tired and ill . . .], written 1840–1841, published in *Poliarnaia zvezda* [The North Star], 1881). The flashpoint came in 1842 when Ogarev returned home to Paris from a visit to Russia and found his wife "living openly with a new lover." Ogarev began to accept that his six-year marriage was over. Yet, he blamed no one except himself, as seen in the poem "Tebe ia schast'ia ne daval dovol'no . . ." (I didn't give you enough happiness . . . , written 1840–1841, published 1904). In "K** [M. L. Ogarevoi]" (To** [M. L. Ogarev], written 1844, published in *Russkii vestnik,* 1856) he prays that Mariia L'vovna will remember him fondly and without reproach.

In addition to poems about his wife, Ogarev wrote a cycle of forty-five love poems between 1841 and 1844. "Buch der Liebe" (The Book of Love), as he titled the cycle, was inspired by his secret feelings for Evdokiia Vasil'evna Sukhovo-Kobylina, sister of the playwright Aleksandr Vasil'evich Sukhovo-Kobylin, and an author in her own right who wrote under the pen name Evgeniia Tur. In the 1840s she hosted a well-known literary salon that Ogarev frequented. He had fallen in love with Sukhovo-Kobylina but kept his emotions hidden. None of the poems of "Buch der Liebe" was published until 1881 so that Sukhovo-Kobylina did not learn of Ogarev's feelings until after his death. In these verses Ogarev admires his beloved's physical and spiritual beauty and compares her to the Madonna. He scrutinizes his feelings, noting their every nuance and every torment. Heine's influence is evident in the poems. At times Ogarev is capable of a finely tuned irony in his poetry as well–as, for instance, in "Proshchanie s kraem, otkuda ia ne uezzhal" (Farewell to a Country I Haven't Left, written 1840, published in *Russkaia starina,* 1889), in which he thanks Russia not only for her beautiful steppes and the opportunities to love but also for his bitter experiences, his prison term, and people's indifference. In the poem "Mladenets" (The Infant, *Otechestvennye zapiski,* 1842) the poet waxes rhetorical as he foretells the adult agonies of

a child he sees who, on closer inspection, turns out to be dead.

From 1841 to 1846 Ogarev traveled abroad for medical reasons to Germany, Switzerland, and Italy. His sojourns were a self-imposed exile from the "idiotic life" in Russia, as he wrote to Herzen in 1840, and, later, from marital troubles. During his absence more than forty of his poems were published in the Russian periodical press. When he returned to Russia in 1846, his reputation as a talented and notable poet had already been firmly established. Belinsky's positive comments about Ogarev, both in published articles and in conversations and letters to friends, had been instrumental in the creation of this reputation.

Ogarev had a lifelong interest in music ("music is love," he wrote in one of his poems). Not only did several of his poems become popular songs–for example, "Derevenskii storozh," "Arestant" (A Prisoner, *Poliarnaia zvezda,* 1857), "Svoboda" (Freedom, *Poliarnaia zvezda,* 1858)–but Ogarev himself composed several musical scores, including settings for two of Lermontov's poems. He also wrote many poems on musical themes and gave such lyrics musically inspired titles such as "I Tempi" (Tempos), "Pesnia" (Song), "Aurora-Walzer," "Scherzo," "Serenade," and "Nocturne." In addition, a certain musical impressionism and the use of understatement and allusion characterize these poems. These traits are possibly what Belinsky referred to when, in his 1842 review in *Otechestvennye zapiski,* he described Ogarev's poetry as full of "deep and quiet feeling," a poetry of indirection which conveys its subject through "inexpressible sensation" and "inadvertent refrains." Similarly, in attributing the idea for his story "Temnye allei" (Dark Avenues, 1943) to Ogarev's poem "Obyknovennaia povest'" (An Ordinary Story, *Otechestvennye zapiski,* 1843)" the writer Ivan Alekseevich Bunin pointed in a 1944 letter to Ogarev's ability in his poetry to keep silent, to refrain from spelling things out: "in this very hesitation [*nedomolvka*], he says much more than words could tell."

While abroad, Ogarev continued to write poetry in a variety of genres: love lyrics such as "Obyknovennaia povest'" and "K pod'ezdu!" (To the Entrance! *Otechestvennye zapiski,* 1842); friendly epistles such as "Druz'iam," "T. N. Granovskomu," and "Iskanderu" (To Iskander, *Poliarnaia zvezda,* 1857); philosophical verse such as the cycle "Monologi" (Monologues, *Sovremennik,* 1847); and longer narrative poems such as "Don" (The River Don, written 1839, published in *Russkaia starina,* 1888) and "Tsaritsa moria" (The Sea Queen, written early 1840s, published 1916). In 1840 he began writing "Iumor" (Humor, parts 1 and 2 published as *Iumor,* 1857), a *poema* (long narrative poem) composed in octaves that received wide acclaim. A map of Ogarev's evolution as a poet and a man, "Iumor" tells the story of life in a Russia that he finds "frightening": "We lack horizons for the mind; we sit, passive and stagnant, in our underground, like condemned men, imaging nothing." Part reminiscence and part philosophical meditation, "Iumor" can be compared to William Wordsworth's *The Prelude, or Growth of the Poet's Mind, an Autobiographical Poem* (1850); both works show how the poet's experiences and observations have shaped his aesthetic and moral sense. Ogarev's "Iumor" is dark, even tragic; its title is possibly connected to the ancient use of the term "humors." This seventy-page *poema* suggests that the poet's life in Russia is out of balance, unhealthy, and perhaps even lethal. Ogarev wrote the first two parts of "Iumor" while living in Russia, and the first two sections focus on conditions within the country and on the dearth of opportunities for energetic, intelligent, sensitive young people. The third and final part of the *poema* was completed twenty-seven years later in 1867, after Ogarev had moved abroad; the work appeared in its entirety in the almanac *Poliarnaia zvezda*, 1868. In this section of the work, nostalgia is mixed with anger as the poet simultaneously longs for his beloved country and realizes that only "war and blood" will free her. A poet's work is valuable when it tells the truth, he asserts. Yet, all the same he wonders in the *poema*, "Have I told enough of the truth? Have I accomplished anything?"

After Ogarev and his wife separated in the summer of 1842, he returned to Russia while she remained in Europe. Because she feared losing her position and income, however, she refused to grant him a divorce. This refusal had several consequences. For one, it contributed to the so-called Ogareva Affair, in which the Ogarevs were swindled. After her separation from Ogarev, Mariia L'vovna legally authorized her longtime friend, the writer Avdot'ia Iakovlevna Panaeva, to act as her agent and, in this capacity, to collect for her some 200,000 rubles in alimony from Ogarev. The transaction took place, but the money never reached Mariia L'vovna; Panaeva and her legal agent Nikolai Samoilovich Shanshiev had received the full amount and spent it. After Mariia L'vovna died in 1853, Ogarev ordered an inquiry, and the embezzlement was uncovered. Panaeva was ordered to return the money, but since it was gone, Nekrasov, then her common-law husband, was forced to pay it for her. The affair served to exacerbate Ogarev's financial problems.

The other problem caused by Mariia L'vovna's refusal to divorce Ogarev involved Ogarev's new love interest. In the late 1840s, after spending some time in Moscow once he returned from abroad, Ogarev moved back to the country—a decision precipitated in part by his break with Granovsky, Ketcher, Vasilii Petrovich

Ogarev and Alexander Herzen (Aleksandr Ivanovich Gertsen) in London, 1860s

Botkin, and others of his close liberal friends on philosophical grounds. (Ogarev's arguments with them covered a variety of subjects, ranging from the historical significance of Maximilien-François-Marie-Isidore de Robespierre to the immortality of the soul, and what emerged was a clear division of worldviews between the liberals' emphasis on gradual reform and the increasingly radical politics of Ogarev, Herzen, and Belinsky.) Living on his Penza estate, a lonely Ogarev befriended the daughter of his neighbor and friend Aleksei Alekseevich Tuchkov, a liberal and an associate of some of the Decembrists with whom he still kept in contact. Tuchkov's elder daughter, Elena Alekseevna, had married Ogarev's friend Satin. Now Ogarev had fallen in love with Tuchkov's younger daughter, Natal'ia Alekseevna Tuchkova. His feelings were reciprocated, and he sought a way to join his lover. As he had with Mariia L'vovna, Ogarev saw in Natal'ia Alekseevna the woman of his radical political dreams. In 1848 in Italy, when she was only nineteen, she marched through the streets carrying a protest banner, and later that year in Paris she tried to climb a barricade during the revolution. In 1849 the couple planned to escape from Russia by following a route through Odessa. Their plan was aborted, but they began living together openly–even though Ogarev was still married to Mariia L'vovna. He and Natal'ia Alekseevna did not legalize their union until after his wife's death in 1853.

Because of his extramarital relationship, a scandal followed. Ogarev faced it boldly, writing about it in his poem "K N." (To N. [A. Tuchkova], written 1850–1852, published in *Poliarnaia zvezda,* 1857). At this time he was accused of not just immorality but also political corruption. In 1850, at the urging of Mariia L'vovna's uncle Panchulidzev, who was still governor of Penza province, Ogarev once again fell under the scrutiny of the Third Section, the government secret police. He was charged with harboring subversive ideas and with engendering a "communist sect." In February he was arrested and taken to St. Petersburg for questioning. By April all charges were dropped, but the unpleasant incident left its mark on Ogarev. He was more eager than ever to leave Russia, that land of "the poor, the beaten, and the forgotten," as he called it in his poem "(E. F.) Korshu." In 1856 he finally secured permission to go abroad, once again for health reasons. Before he left, however, at the age of forty-three–after years of publishing individual poems in Russian periodicals–Ogarev released *Stikhotvoreniia* (Poems, 1856), a collection of eighty-three verses.

This time Ogarev made England, instead of Italy, his destination, and ailing but happy, he arrived in London on 9 April 1856. This journey marked his permanent break with Russia and the start of the second half of his professional career. Ten years had passed since Herzen and Ogarev last saw one another, but the two men immediately renewed their old friendship. With Herzen, Ogarev collaborated in the work of the Free Russian Press, editing and writing for the almanac *Poliarnaia zvezda* and then for the revolutionary newspaper *Kolokol* (The Bell). He wrote dozens of articles, proclamations, leaflets, and reflections on a range of social and economic subjects. Some of his essays appeared as a regular feature under the title "Russkie voprosy" (Russian Questions). He also wrote literary essays on Pushkin, Gogol, Ryleev, Aleksandr Sergeevich Griboedov, Aleksandr Ivanovich Polezhaev, and Aleksei Vasil'evich Kol'tsov. He wrote approximately 200 articles for *Kolokol* alone.

Although busy with editorial work, Ogarev continued to write poems. In 1858 his second book of verse was published in London. It encompassed 106 poems, including parts 1 and 2 of the *poema* "Iumor." He wrote and published many longer poems now,

some of them verse narratives telling stories of social deprivation and injustice. Among these *poema* are "Gospodin" (The Gentleman, 1857) and "Zimnii put'" (Winter Path, published in *Russkii vestnik,* 1856), which many regard as one of Ogarev's finest works. Turgenev wrote in an 1856 letter to the critic Pavel Vasil'evich Annenkov that this poem is "a real *chef d'oeuvre;* in it Ogarev blended all his poetry and himself with a heartfelt and thoughtful charm." Turgenev adds that he and Leo Tolstoy "have already sipped this fine nectar at least three times."

Two other notable publications in which Ogarev was involved include a collection of Ryleev's poems, *Dumy* (Meditations, 1860), for which Ogarev wrote a brief introduction, and a miscellany of taboo literature called *Russkaia potaennaia literatura XIX veka* (Russian Secret Literature of the Nineteenth Century), published in 1861. Ogarev wrote a lengthy introductory essay for this volume in which he highlights the development of Russian poetry. He compares political literature to obscene literature and notes that both reflect a similar freedom: "No matter how strange it is to find poetry with civic aspirations in the same book with indecent poetry, they are connected more closely than it may seem. In essence they are branches of the same tree, and in each indecent epigram you will find a political slap in the face." Ogarev's participation in the publication of this book illustrates one of his central beliefs, which he propounded repeatedly in the latter decades of his life–a belief in the primacy of the word as a weapon of change. He held that in order for real changes to occur in society, speech and writing were necessary, and thus no effective political organization could exist without a publisher at its core.

In the 1860s, in both his writing and his publishing, Ogarev became more politically active than ever before. He helped establish a secret society called Zemlia i volia (Land and Liberty), which consisted of radical thinkers who were eventually successful in several terrorist actions. As historian Stephen T. Cochrane has shown in his *The Collaboration of Nečaev, Ogarev, and Bakunin in 1869: Nečaev's Early Years* (1977), Ogarev also came under the influence of the young radical Sergei Gennad'evich Nechaev and might have helped him formulate plans for anarchist uprisings in Russia. During his involvement with the radical anarchists, Ogarev wrote many essays and proclamations envisioning a widespread revolutionary organization with a base in St. Petersburg. His visions were not realized, but they influenced subsequent revolutionary activities in Russia.

In the meantime Ogarev's marriage to Natal'ia Alekseevna had fallen apart. No sooner had they arrived in London in 1856 than she became involved

*Page from Ogarev's last diary entry, dated 30 May 1877, in which he wrote about
returning to Russia (Russian State Library, Moscow)*

with Herzen. Herzen's own wife, Natal'ia Aleksandrovna, had died in 1852. Tuchkova became Herzen's mistress and then his wife. Ogarev suffered greatly and took even more to drink, which had already contributed to his poor health. Yet, the friendship between the two men did not falter. In April 1865 Herzen and Ogarev moved their families—and the Russian Free Press—to Geneva. In 1868, however, after outliving its usefulness, *Kolokol* ceased publication; Ogarev bids good-bye to it in his poem "Do svidan'ia" (Goodbye, published in *Kokokol*, 1867). Herzen died unexpectedly on 21 January 1870, at the age of fifty-eight.

While in Geneva, Ogarev did not write much poetry. He wrote the third part of his long poem "Iumor" and some autobiographical prose—for example, "Kavkazskie vody" (Caucasian Waters, *Poliarnaia zvezda*, 1861)—and he continued to write essays. He planned several projects (a journal to be called *Obshchina* [The Collective], a biography of Herzen, and his own autobiography), but none of these projects reached fruition. Ogarev left behind many unfinished projects, from poems to prose fiction to essays. Although he never wrote an autobiography, his writings offer many autobiographical elements, and in this regard the following poems are notable: "Vospominaniia detstva" (Memories of Childhood, *Poliarnaia zvezda*, 1858–1861), "Babushka" (Grandmother, 1859), "Exil" (Exile, written 1863, published 1904), as well as the longer poems "Iumor," "Tiur'ma" (Prison, 1858), and "Matvei Radaev" (*Poliarnaia zvezda*, 1859).

Since 1866 Ogarev had been living with Mary Sutherland, a former London prostitute whom he had come to cherish. He helped raise her son, and she proved to be a good and loving companion. Until Ogarev's death the couple lived happily together for more than eighteen years. In the last years of his life, after moving back to England in the summer of 1874, he and Mary settled in Greenwich, on the outskirts of London. Ogarev kept a "poetic journal" at this time and filled it with thoughts, fragments, and quotations on a variety of subjects, particularly his past. On 30 May 1877 he made the last entry. He had been living on a small pension sent to him by the Herzen family and was quite ill. Though happy with Mary and with his decision to live and work productively in Europe, he thought often of his homeland. His final journal entry reads in part, "Just now I dreamed that I had returned to Russia, to my home in the country." He died on 31 May 1877 in the town of Greenwich, England (where he was also buried), in the presence of two people he loved dearly, Mary and Herzen's eldest daughter, Natal'ia Aleksandrovna Herzen. He was sixty-three years old. In 1966 Ogarev's remains were transferred to Russia and interred at the cemetery of the Novodevichii monastery outside Moscow.

At the end of his autobiographical *poema* "Iumor," Nikolai Platonovich Ogarev wonders whether his work has made a difference in his readers' lives. The final lines of the *poema* effect a rhetorical question with an existential ring and call into doubt the value of a poet's work in a land where people stagnate and hopes die unrealized: "Our world gives no joy. It is familiar but stale. / So, after all, is there no hero here?" Deeply sensitive to the mortal wounds inflicted on capable, good citizens by an unjust government and social order, Ogarev is quintessentially the poet of Russian anguish—and ambition. Through his personal example as a reformer and social activist and his work as a reflective and revolutionary writer, he is one of the great poet-heroes of his era. His prose, too, shows glimpses of genius. Appreciation for Ogarev has been growing over the last several decades. In addition to the continuing study of his writing, primarily at Saratov University in southern Russia, he has been the subject of fiction, drama, and motion pictures since the late 1960s, as evidenced by Boris Buneev's 1969 motion picture *Staryi dom* (The Old Home), Lidiia Libedinskaia's 1980 novel *S togo berega. Povest' o Nikolae Ogareve* (From the Other Shore: A Story about Nikolai Ogarev), and Tom Stoppard's 2002 play *The Coast of Utopia: Voyage*. Still largely unexplored, the works of Ogarev represent an underappreciated yet significant contribution to Russian life and letters.

Letters:

Mikhail Osipovich Gershenzon, *Russkie propilei. Materialy po istorii russkoi mysli i literatury*, volume 4 (Moscow: Izdanie M. & S. Sabashnikovy, 1916);

Arkhiv N. A. i N. P. Ogarevykh, edited by Gershenzon (Moscow: Gosudarstvennoe izdatel'stvo, 1930);

"Pis'ma," in *Izbrannye sotsial'no-politicheskie i filosofskie proizvedeniia*, edited by M. T. Iovchuk and N. G. Tarakanov, volume 2 (Moscow: Gospolitizdat, 1952–1956), pp. 253–255;

"Gertsen i Ogarev," *Literaturnoe nasledstvo*, no. 61 (1953): 379–454, 703–909, 910–923; no. 62 (1955); no. 63 (1956): 81–162;

"Lettres d'Ogarev à Natalie Herzen," edited by Michel Mervaud, *Cahiers du monde russe et soviétique*, 10, nos. 3–4 (1969): 478–523;

Lettres inédites: Herzen, Ogarev, Bakounine, edited by Mervaud (Paris: Librairie des cinq continents, 1975);

Lettres inédites à Alexandre Herzen fils, edited by Mervaud (Mont-Saint-Aignan: Université de Haute Normandie, 1978);

"Une lettre d'Ogarev à Bakounine," edited by Mervaud, *Revue des études slaves*, 59 (1987);

"Ogarev et N Tuèkova-Ogareva. Lettres et poèmes inédites," edited by Mervaud, *Revue des études slaves*, 62 (1990);

Gertsen i Ogarev v krugu rodnykh i druzei, edited by L. R. Lansky and S. A. Makashin, volume 1 (Moscow: Nauka, 1997).

Bibliographies:

D. P. Tikhomirov, "Materialy dlia bibliograficheskogo ukazatelia proizvedenii N. P. Ogareva i literatury o nem," *Izvestiia Otdeleniia russkogo iazyka i slovesnosti Akademii nauk,* 12, no. 4 (1907);

V. V. Svitov, *Ogarev v muzyke (notografiia)* (Leningrad, 1939);

Vydaiushchiisia russkii poet-revoliutsioner Ogarev. Kratkii rekomendatel'nyi ukazatel' literatury (Saransk, 1952);

O. F. Grishanova, *Materialy k bibliografii proizvedenii N. P. Ogareva i literatury o nem 1950–1959 gg.: Bibliograficheskii ukazatel'* (Saransk: Mordovskii gosudarstvennyi universitet imeni N. P. Ogareva, 1986);

Grishanova and others, *Materialy k bibliografii proizvedenii N. P. Ogareva i literatury o nem, 1970–1985 gg.: Bibliograficheskii ukazatel'* (Saransk: Mordovskii gosudarstvennyi universitet imeni N. P. Ogareva, 1989);

Liudmila Ivanova Ian'kin and others, *Materialy k bibliografii proizvedenii N. P. Ogareva i literatury o nem, 1917–1949 gg.: Bibliograficheskii ukazatel'* (Saransk: Izdatel'stvo Mordovskogo universiteta, 1991);

I. A. Voronina, *Materialy k bibliografii proizvedenii N. P. Ogareva i literatury o nem 1831–1916 gg.: Bibliograficheskii ukazatel'* (Saransk: Mordovskii gosudarstvennyi universitet imeni N. P. Ogareva, 1999).

Biographies:

Vladimir Aleksandrovich Putintsev, *N. Ogarev: Kritiko-biograficheskii ocherk* (Moscow: Khudozhestvennaia literatura, 1959);

Michel Mervaud, *Socialisme et liberté: La pensée et l'action de Nicolas Ogarev, 1813–1877* (Mont-Saint-Aignan: Université de Haute Normandie, 1984);

Michael Osipovich Gershenzon [Mikhail Osipovich Gershenzon], "Nicholas Ogarev," in *A History of Young Russia,* translated and edited by James P. Scanlan, poetry translated by Edna Lippman Lief (Irvine, Cal.: Charles Schlacks Jr., 1986), pp. 239–280;

G. G. Elizavetina, *N. P. Ogarev: 175 let so dnia rozhdeniia* (Moscow: Znanie, 1988).

References:

"A. I. Gertsen," *Literaturnoe nasledstvo,* nos. 39–40, 41–42 (1941);

Pavel Vasil'evich Annenkov, *The Extraordinary Decade: Literary Memoirs* (Ann Arbor: University of Michigan Press, 1968);

Edward Hallett Carr, *The Romantic Exiles: A Nineteenth-Century Portrait Gallery* (London: Serif, 1998);

Hilary Chapman, "Friendship for a Good Fellow and an Old Man's Passion: The Love Affair of N. P. Ogarev and Mary Sutherland," *New Zealand Slavonic Journal* (1995): 159–171;

Ia. Cherniak, *Nekrasov, Gertsen, Chernyshevsky v spore ob ogarevskom nasledstve: Delo Ogareva-Panaevoi* (Moscow & Leningrad: Academia, 1933);

Stephen T. Cochrane, *The Collaboration of Nečaev, Ogarev, and Bakunin in 1869: Nečaev's Early Years* (Giessen: W. Schmitz, 1977);

Michael Confino, ed., *Daughter of a Revolutionary: Natalie Herzen and the Bakunin-Nechayev Circle,* translated by Hilary Sternberg and Lydia Bott (LaSalle, Ill.: Library Press, 1973);

M. I. Estrina, "Rannee tvorchestvo N. P. Ogareva," *Uchenye zapiski Vyborgskogo gosudarstvennogo pedagogicheskogo instituta,* 1, no. 1 (1957): 139–165;

N. M. Gaidenkov, "N. P. Ogarev–poet," *Uchenye zapiski Moskovskogo gosudarstvennogo politicheskogo instituta,* 115, no. 7 (1957): 111–115;

Mikhail Osipovich Gershenzon, ed., *Obrazy proshlogo* (Moscow: OKTO, 1912);

Aleksandr Herzen, *Byloe i dumy,* in his *Sobranie sochinenii,* volumes 4–7 (Moscow: Pravda, 1975);

Kolokol: Gazeta A. I. Gertsena i N. P. Ogareva, Vol'naia russkaia tipografiia, 1857–1867, London-Zheneva, 11 volumes (Moscow: Nauka, 1960);

S. S. Konkin, ed., *N. P. Ogarev: Problemy tvorchestva. Sbornik nauchnykh trudov* (Saransk: Izdatel'stvo Saratovskogo universiteta saranskii filial, 1990);

Konkin, ed., *N. P. Ogarev v vospominaniiakh sovremennikov* (Moscow: Khudozhestvennaia literatura, 1989);

Boris Pavlovich Koz'min, *Gertsen, Ogarev i ikh okruzhenie. Rukopisi, perepiska i dokumenty* (Moscow: Goslitizdat, 1940);

L. R. Lansky and S. A. Makashin, eds., *Gertsen i Ogarev v krugu rodnykh i druzei,* 2 volumes (Moscow: Nauka, 1997);

Lidiia Borisovna Libedinskaia, *S togo berega: Povest' o Nikolae Ogareve* (Moscow: Politizdat, 1980);

Martin Malia, *Alexander Herzen and the Birth of Russian Socialism, 1812–1855* (Cambridge, Mass.: Harvard University Press, 1961);

N. P. Ogarev v novykh dokumentakh i illiustratsiiakh (Saransk: Ruzaevskii pechatnik, 1999);

E. S. Nekrasova, *N. P. Ogarev* (Moscow: Pochin, 1895);

Tat'iana Passek, *Iz dal'nykh let: Vospominaniia,* 3 volumes (St. Petersburg: A. F. Marks, 1905);

Alexei Pavlov, "Nikolai Ogarev," in *A History of Russian Philosophy: From the Tenth through the Twentieth Centuries,* edited by Valery A. Kuvakin (Buffalo, N.Y.: Prometheus Books, 1994), pp. 231–237;

S. A. Pereselenkov, "Literaturnoe nasledie N. P. Ogareva," in *Literatura,* edited by A. V. Lunacharsky (Leningrad, 1931), pp. 179–194;

Petr Petrovich Pertsov, ed., "N. P. Ogarev," in *Filosofskie techeniia russkoi poezii* (St. Petersburg: M. Merkushev, 1896);

Poliarnaia zvezda: Zhurnal A. I. Gertsena i N. P. Ogareva v vos'mi knigakh, 1855–1869, Vol'naia russkaia tipografiia, London-Zheneva, 9 volumes (Moscow: Nauka, 1966–1968);

I. G. Ptushkina, ed., *A. I. Gertsen, N. P. Ogarev i ikh okruzhenie: Knigi, rukopisi, izobrazitel'nye materialy, pamiatnye veshchi* (Moscow: Gosudarstvennyi literaturnyi muzei, 1992);

Vladimir Aleksendrovich Putintsev, *N. P. Ogarev* (Moscow: Nauka, 1963);

Irina Reshetilova, *V sviatoi tishi vospominanii: Po materialam liriki i pisem Nikolaia Ogareva* (Moscow: Sovremennik, 1990);

Nikolai Grigor'evich Tarakanov, *N. P. Ogarev: Evoliutsiia filosofskikh vzgliadov* (Moscow: Moscow University Press, 1974);

Natal'ia Alekseevna Tuchkova-Ogareva, *Vospominaniia* (Moscow: Goslitizdat, 1959);

Natal'ia Ivanova Voronina, ed., *N. P. Ogarev ot XIX k XXI veku: Materialy i tezisy dokladov XXVII Saranskikh mezhdunarodnykh Ogarevskikh chtenii* (Saransk: Krasnyi oktiabr', 1999).

Papers:

Nikolai Platonovich Ogarev's papers are held in the Russian State Archive of Literature and Art (RGALI), fond 359 (see N. A. Serbova and E. M. Bolotina, *Ogarev. Opis' dokumental'nykh materialov fonda* [Moscow, 1950]) and fond 2197 (the so-called Prague Collection, composed of archival materials from Herzen's and Ogarev's years abroad); in the Russian State Library (RGB, formerly the Lenin Library), fond 69 (see L. Ia. Cherniak, "Fond Ogarev," *Zapiski otdela rukopisei Gosudarstvennoi Biblioteki im. V. I. Lenina,* 12 [1951] and A. V. Askariants, *Opisanie rukopisei Ogareva* [Moscow, 1952]); in the Institute of Russian Literature (IRLI, Pushkin House) (see B. N. Kapeliush, "Rukopisi i perepiski Ogareva," *Biulleten' rukopisnogo otdela Pushkinskogo Doma,* 5 [1955]); and in the Central State Archive of Mordoviia in the city of Saransk (mainly biographical documents), as well as in the State Archives of Penza and Riazan' provinces.

Aleksandr Nikolaevich Ostrovsky

(31 March 1823 – 2 June 1886)

Robert Whittaker

Lehman College, City University of New York

BOOKS: *Svoi liudi sochtemsia* (Moscow: Universitetskaia tipografiia, 1850);

Bednaia nevesta (Moscow: Stepanova, 1852);

Bednost' ne porok (Moscow: V. Got'e, 1854);

Dokhodnoe mesto (Moscow: A. Semen, 1857);

Sochineniia, 2 volumes (St. Petersburg: G. A. Kushelev-Bezborodko, 1859)—includes *V chuzhom piru pokhmel'e* and *Semeinaia kartina;*

Groza (St. Petersburg: N. Grech, 1860);

Vospitannitsa (St. Petersburg: K. Vul'f, 1860);

Koz'ma Zakhar'ich Minin-Sukhoruk (St. Petersburg: Sovremennik, 1862);

Puchina (N.p., Imperatorskaia akademiia nauk, 1866);

Sochineniia, 5 volumes (St. Petersburg: D. E. Kozhanchikov, 1867–1870)—includes *Volki i ovtsy, Bogatye nevesty, Posledniaia zhertva, Voevoda (Son na Volge), Na boikim meste, Na vsiakogo mudretsa dovol'no prostoty;*

Dmitrii Samozvanets i Vasilii Shuisky (St. Petersburg: F. S. Sushchinsky, 1867);

Sobranie sochinenii, 10 volumes (volumes 1–8, St. Petersburg: D. E. Kozhanchikov, 1874; volume 9, St. Petersburg: F. I. Salaev, 1878; volume 10, St. Petersburg: Kekhribardzhi, 1884);

Zhenit'ba Belugina, by Ostrovsky and Nikolai Iakovlevich Solov'ev (Moscow: I. I. Smirnov, 1878);

Na poroge k delu, by Ostrovsky and Solov'ev (St. Petersburg, 1878);

Serdtse ne kamen' (Moscow: S. F. Rassokhin, 1879);

Nevol'nitsy (Moscow: S. F. Rassokhin, 1880);

Svetit da ne greet, by Ostrovsky and Solov'ev (Moscow: S. F. Rassokhin, 1880);

Blazh', by Ostrovsky and Petr Mikhailovich Nevezhin (Moscow: S. F. Rassokhin, 1881);

Dramaticheskie sochineniia, by Ostrovsky and Solov'ev (St. Petersburg: Novoe vremia, 1881);

Talanty i poklonniki. Komediia v 4 deistviiakh (St. Petersburg: S. F. Rassokhin, 1882);

Staroe po-novomu, by Ostrovsky and Nevezhin (Moscow: S. F. Rassokhin, 1882);

Aleksandr Nikolaevich Ostrovsky (portrait by V. G. Perov, 1871; from Russkie Pisatell, 1800–1917: Biograficheskiaei, *volume 4, 1989)*

Polnoe sobranie sochinenii, 12 volumes, edited by Modest Ivanovich Pisarev (St. Petersburg: Prosveshchenie, 1904–1909);

Bespridannitsa (St. Petersburg: Prosveshchenie, 1909);

Bez viny vinovatye (St. Petersburg: Prosveshchenie, 1909);

Polnoe sobranie sochinenii, 16 volumes, edited by Aleksandr Ivanovich Reviakin, Grigorii Ivanovich Vladykin, and V. A. Filippov (Moscow: Goslitizdat, 1949–1953);

Polnoe sobranie sochinenii, 12 volumes, edited by Vladykin and others (Moscow: Iskusstvo, 1973–1980).

Editions and Collections: *Bednost' ne porok. Komediia v 3 deistviiakh* (St. Petersburg: F. Stellovsky, 1861);

Volki i ovtsy (St. Petersburg: Kurochkin, 1875);

Bogatye nevesty (St. Petersburg, 1876);

Posledniaia zhertva (Moscow, 1878);

Polnoe sobranie sochinenii, 8 volumes (St. Petersburg: N. G. Martynov, 1885);

Voevoda (Son na Volge) (Moscow: Zhurnal "Budil'nik," 1890);

Bednost' ne porok. Komediia v 3 deistviiakh (Moscow: I. D. Sytin, 1895);

Sochineniia, 11 volumes, edited by N. N. Dolbov (Petrograd & Moscow: GIZ, 1919–1926);

Sochineniia, edited by N. P. Kashin, with an introduction by A. G. Tseitlin (Moscow: Goslitizdat, 1937);

Izbrannye sochineniia, edited by Grigorii Ivanovich Vladykin (Moscow & Leningrad: Goslitizdat, 1948);

Sobranie sochinenii, 7 volumes, edited by Vladykin and others (Moscow: Goslitizdat, 1959–1960);

Stikhotvornye dramy, edited, with an introduction, by L. M. Lotman, Biblioteka poeta, Bol'shaia seriia (Leningrad: Sovetskii pisatel', 1961);

O literature i teatre, with an introduction and commentary by M. P. Lobanov (Moscow: Sovremennik, 1986).

Editions in English: *The Storm*, translated by Constance Garnett (London: Duckworth, 1899; Chicago: Charles H. Sergel, 1899);

Plays, translated and edited by George Rapall Noyes (New York: Scribners, 1917)–comprises *A Protégé of the Mistress, Poverty Is No Crime, Sin and Sorrow Are Common to All*, and *It's a Family Affair–We'll Settle It Ourselves;*

Bondwomen. A Comedy in Four Acts, translated by S. Kurlandzik and Noyes, *Poet Lore*, 36 (1925): 475–541;

The Forest: A Comedy in Five Acts, translated by Clara Vostrovsky Winslow and Noyes (New York & London: S. French, 1926);

Wolves and Sheep, A Comedy in Five Acts, translated by Inez Sachs Colby and Noyes (Boston: Badger, 1926);

A Last Sacrifice. A Comedy in Five Acts, translated by E. Korvin-Krankovsky and Noyes, *Poet Lore*, 39 (1928): 317–410;

Fairy Gold. A Comedy in Five Acts, translated by Winslow and Noyes, *Poet Lore*, 40 (1929): 1–80;

A Cat Has Not Always Carnival. Scenes from Moscow Life, translated by J. Campbell and Noyes, *Poet Lore*, 40 (1929): 317–372;

The King of Comedy, translated by J. McPetrie (London: Stockwell, 1937);

We Won't Brook Interference, translated by John Laurence Seymour and Noyes (San Francisco: Banner Play Bureau, 1938);

You Can't Live Just as You Please, translated by Noyes, *Poet Lore*, 49 (1943): 203–240;

Easy Money and Two Other Plays, edited and translated by David Magarshack (London: Allen & Unwin, 1944)–comprises *Even a Wise Man Stumbles, Easy Money*, and *Wolves and Sheep;*

The Diary of a Scoundrel, translated by Rodney Ackland (London: Sampson Low, Marston, 1948); republished as *Too Clever by Half, or, The Diary of a Scoundrel*, with an afterword by Daniel Gerould (New York & London: Applause, 1988);

Five Plays, translated and edited by Eugene K. Bristow (New York: Pegasus, 1969)–comprises *It's a Family Affair–We'll Settle It Ourselves, The Poor Bride, The Storm, The Scoundrel*, and *The Forest;*

Artistes and Admirers, translated by Elisabeth Hanson, with an introduction by Lawrence Hanson (Manchester: Manchester University Press, 1970; New York: Barnes & Noble, 1970);

Plays, translated and edited, with an introduction, by Margaret Wettlin (Moscow: Progress Publishers, 1974)–comprises *The Storm, Even the Wise Can Err*, and *More Sinned Against Than Sinning;*

Career Woman. Artistes and Admirers, translated by Hanson (New York: Barnes & Noble, 1976);

Larisa, translated by Michael Green in *The Unknown Russian Theater: An Anthology*, translated and edited by Green and Jerome Katsell (Ann Arbor: Ardis, 1991);

Four Plays, translated by Stephen Mulrine (London: Oberon, 1997)–comprises *The Storm, Too Clever by Half, Crazy Money*, and *Innocent as Charged;*

Without a Dowry and Other Plays, translated and edited by Norman Henley (Dana Point, Cal.: Ardis, 1997)–comprises *Without a Dowry, A Profitable Position, An Ardent Heart*, and *Talents and Admirers;*

Plays 2, translated by Mulrine (London: Oberon, 2001).

PLAY PRODUCTIONS: *Ne v svoi sani ne sadis'*, Moscow, Bol'shoi Petrovskii Theater, 14 January 1853; St. Petersburg, Aleksandrinskii Theater, 19 February 1853;

Utro molodogo cheloveka, St. Petersburg, Petersburg Theater-Circus, 12 February 1853;

Bednaia nevesta, Moscow, Malyi Theater, 20 August 1853;

Bednost' ne porok, Moscow, Malyi Theater, 25 January 1854;

Ne tak zhivi, kak khochetsia! Moscow, Malyi Theater, 3 December 1854;

Semeinaia kartina, St. Petersburg, Aleksandrinskii Theater, 3 October 1855;

V chuzhom piru pokhmel'e, Moscow, Malyi Theater, 9 January 1856;

Prazdnichnyi son—do obeda, St. Petersburg, Aleksandrinskii Theater, 28 October 1857;

Ne soshlis' kharakterami! St. Petersburg, Aleksandrinskii Theater, 1 September 1858;

Groza, Moscow, Malyi Theater, 16 November 1859;

Staryi drug luchshe novykh dvukh, St. Petersburg, Mariinskii Theater, 10 October 1860;

Svoi liudi sochtemsia, St. Petersburg, Aleksandrinskii Theater, 16 January 1861; Moscow, 31 January 1861;

Svoi sobaki gryzutsia, chuzhaia ne pristavai! Moscow, Malyi Theater, 27 October 1861;

Za chem poidesh', to i naidesh' (Zhenit'ba Bal'zaminova), St. Petersburg, Aleksandrinskii Theater, 1 January 1863;

Grekh da beda na kogo ne zhivet, Moscow, Malyi Theater, 21 January 1863;

Dokhodnoe mesto, St. Petersburg, Aleksandrinskii Theater, 27 September 1863;

Tiazhelye dni, Moscow, Malyi Theater, 2 October 1863;

Vospitannitsa, Moscow, Malyi Theater, 21 October 1863;

Shutniki, St. Petersburg, Aleksandrinskii Theater, 9 October 1864;

Voevoda (Son na Volge), St. Petersburg, Mariinskii Theater, 28 April 1865;

Na boikom meste, Moscow, Malyi Theater, 29 September 1865;

Puchina, Moscow, Malyi Theater, 8 April 1866;

Koz'ma Zakhar'ich Minin-Sukhoruk, St. Petersburg, Aleksandrinskii Theater, 9 December 1866;

Dmitrii Samozvanets i Vasilii Shuisky, Moscow, Malyi Theater, 30 January 1867;

Tushino, Moscow, Malyi Theater, 23 November 1867;

Vasilisa Melent'eva, by Ostrovsky and Stepan Aleksandrovich Gedeonov, Moscow, Malyi Theater, 3 January 1868;

Na vsiakogo mudretsa dovol'no prostoty, St. Petersburg, Aleksandrinskii Theater, 1 November 1868;

Goriachee serdtse, Moscow, Malyi Theater, 15 January 1869;

Beshennye den'gi, St. Petersburg, Aleksandrinskii Theater, 16 April 1870;

Ne vse kotu maslenitsa, Moscow, Malyi Theater, 7 October 1871;

Les, St. Petersburg, Aleksandrinskii Theater, 1 November 1871;

Ne bylo ni grosha, da vdrug altyn, St. Petersburg, 20 September 1872;

Komik XVII stoletiia, Moscow, Malyi Theater, 26 October 1872;

Snegurochka, Moscow, Bol'shoi Theater, 11 May 1873;

Pozdniaia liubov', Moscow, Malyi Theater, 22 November 1873;

Trudovoi khleb, Moscow, Malyi Theater, 28 November 1874;

Bogatye nevesty, St. Petersburg, Aleksandrinskii Theater, 28 November 1875;

Volki i ovtsy, St. Petersburg, Aleksandrinskii Theater, 8 December 1875;

Pravda—khorosho, a schast'e luchshe, Moscow, Malyi Theater, 18 November 1876;

Schastlivyi den', by Ostrovsky and Nikolai Iakovlevich Solov'ev, Moscow, Malyi Theater, 28 October 1877;

Posledniaia zhertva, Moscow, Malyi Theater, 8 November 1877;

Zhenit'ba Belugina, by Ostrovsky and Solov'ev, Moscow, Malyi Theater, 26 December 1877;

Bespridannitsa, Moscow, Malyi Theater, 10 November 1878;

Dikarka, by Ostrovsky and Solov'ev, Moscow, Malyi Theater, 2 November 1879;

Serdtse ne kamen', St. Petersburg, Aleksandrinskii Theater, 21 November 1879;

Svetit, da ne greet, by Ostrovsky and Solov'ev, Moscow, Malyi Theater, 6 November 1880;

Nevol'nitsy, Moscow, Malyi Theater, 14 November 1880;

Blazh', by Ostrovsky and P. M. Nevezhin, Moscow, Malyi Theater, 26 December 1880;

Talanty i poklonniki, Moscow, Malyi Theater, 20 December 1881;

Staroe po-novomu, by Ostrovsky and Nevezhin, Moscow, Malyi Theater, 21 November 1882;

Krasavets-muzhchina, Moscow, Malyi Theater, 26 December 1882;

Bez viny vinovatye, Moscow, Malyi Theater, 15 January 1884;

Ne ot mira sego, St. Petersburg, Aleksandrinskii Theater, 9 January 1885;

Voevoda (Son na Volge), revised, Moscow, Malyi Theater, 19 January 1886;

Neozhidannyi sluchai, St. Petersburg, Aleksandrinskii Theater, 1 May 1902.

OTHER: *Neozhidannyi sluchai,* in *Kometa: Ucheno-literaturnyi al'manakh* (Moscow: A. Semen, 1851);

Ostrovsky. Novye mater'ialy. Pis'ma. Trudy i dni. Stat'i, edited by M. D. Beliaev (Leningrad: GIZ, 1924)—includes "Skazanie o tom, kak kvartal'nyi nadziratel' puskalsia v plias, ili Ot velikogo do smeshnogo tol'ko odin shag."

TRANSLATIONS: William Shakespeare, "Usmirenie svoenravnoi," *Sovremennik,* 11 (1865);

Italo Franchi, "Velikii bankir," *Otechestvennye zapiski,* 7 (1871): 109–162;

Dramaticheskie perevody (St. Petersburg: S. V. Zvonarev, 1872);

Dramaticheskie perevody, 2 volumes (St. Petersburg: N. Martynov, 1886).

Considered by many to have been his country's greatest dramatist and the founder of its national theater, Aleksandr Ostrovsky belongs to the nineteenth-century Russian Realist tradition along with novelists Ivan Sergeevich Turgenev, Fyodor Dostoevsky, and Leo Tolstoy. In contrast to those writers' aristocratic, educated, and intellectual heroes confronting vexing philosophical questions, Ostrovsky's plays present merchant and lower-class urban dwellers, largely uneducated and living common lives untouched by European culture.

Aleksandr Nikolaevich Ostrovsky was born on 31 March 1823, in the region of Moscow called Zamoskvorech'e (meaning "beyond the Moscow River"). His father, Nikolai Fedorovich Ostrovsky, a graduate of the Kostroma Seminary and the Moscow Spiritual Academy, chose a career as a civil servant and worked in the Moscow City Courts. His mother, Liubov' Ivanovna (Savvina) Ostrovskaia, the daughter of a communion-bread maker, was the widow of a sexton. Ostrovsky was her third child, born after his two older brothers had died in infancy. The family also included his younger sister, Natal'ia, and two younger brothers, Mikhail (a future prominent government official whose influence assisted his older brother) and Sergei. In his four sketches that make up "Zapiski zamoskvoretskogo zhitelia" (Notes of a Zamoskvorech'e Resident, 1847) Ostrovsky describes this southern region of Moscow, home to merchants and civil servants and colorful in its old Russian and deeply religious traditions. Its characters and their peculiar manners and lifestyle later became the material out of which he fashioned his first plays. His education began at home; several tutors came from seminaries and provided him with little beyond the basics. His childhood was unremarkable, and he wrote little to illuminate it in his later works.

In the fall of 1835 Ostrovsky entered the Moscow Provincial Gymnasium (renamed the First Moscow Gymnasium the following year), where he benefited from the imaginative, talented P. M. Popov, the instructor in language and literature. An average student and mediocre in his achievements, Ostrovsky nonetheless acquired a reputation for independent, idiosyncratic thinking. He neither enjoyed nor respected the "thrice damned" gymnasium, as he wrote in a letter of 27 October 1877 to his fellow classmate, the writer and memoirist Nikolai Vasil'evich Berg (among other noted classmates was the historian Sergei Mikhailovich Solov'ev). The daily trip from Zamoskvorech'e to the gymnasium on the Volkhonka brought the young student into the social and cultural milieu of the upper class, as did changes at home: Ostrovsky's mother died in 1831, and four years later his father married the seventeen-year-old Emiliia Andreevna von Tessin, who came from an impoverished noble family of foreign origin. Among the ancestors of Ostrovsky's stepmother were two generations of imperial architects to the Swedish throne; her grandfather was a renowned diplomat, politician, and litterateur. Emiliia Andreevna brought French and German tutors to the Zamoskvorech'e home (without much effect on the young Ostrovsky), as well as a music tutor, who taught the boy to read music, which proved useful later. The overwhelming influence upon Ostrovsky's general education, however, was his father's extensive library, to which the boy had unlimited access and from which he borrowed and read avidly—classic works of Russian literature, contemporary poetry and novels, and a full selection of the popular journals. However aware he was of the literary currents of his day, Ostrovsky as yet had no contact with the theater.

Graduation from the First Moscow Gymnasium guaranteed entrance into Moscow University; influenced by his father, Ostrovsky entered the Juridical Faculty of Moscow University in the fall of 1840. The university was enjoying its "Golden Age." Revitalized under Count Sergei Grigor'evich Stroganov's aegis, it boasted famous professors such as Petr Grigor'evich Redkin and Nikita Ivanovich Krylov, who taught law; Mikhail Petrovich Pogodin and Timofei Nikolaevich Granovsky, who taught history; and Stepan Petrovich Shevyrev, who taught literature. Ostrovsky observed the conflict between Westernizers and Slavophiles, but unlike some of his fellow students, he did not get carried away with Schellingianism and Hegelianism. At this time his family's fortunes increased: his father acquired several houses in Nikola-Vorob'in, a more fashionable district off the Iauzskii Boulevard (east of the Kremlin). Nikolai Fedorovich's success in the civil service had brought him hereditary noble status, and he became a public solicitor in the Moscow Commercial Court. Ostrovsky passed his first-year examinations with good grades, but in his second year he spent more time in the company of fellow students, was increasingly absent from lectures, and unaccountably missed his final examinations (the excuse was a fever). He chose not to take his exams in the fall and instead repeated his second year of studies (with considerable laxity in attendance), failing Roman Law in the spring of 1843. This failure ended his university career, and he took up a civil service position in the offices of the Moscow court system.

Ostrovsky had discovered his lifelong passion in the traditional entertainment of university students: the Moscow Imperial Theater, whose drama troupe shared the Great Petrovsky (later the Bol'shoi) Theater and the Malyi Theater next door. Two Moscow actors—the tragedian Pavel Stepanovich Mochalov and the comedian Mikhail Semenovich Shchepkin—deeply affected Ostrovsky. Mochalov's best roles were Nino in Nikolai Alekseevich Polevoi's *Ugolino* (1838), Mortimer in Friedrich Schiller's *Maria Stuart* (1801), and Richard III and, above all, Hamlet in William Shakespeare's eponymous plays (published, respectively, in 1597 and 1604). Shchepkin, who also acted in foreign plays (especially the comedies of Jean-Baptiste Molière), excelled in the Russian repertoire, notably as Famusov in Aleksandr Sergeevich Griboedov's *Gore ot uma* (Woe from Wit, 1833)—but Ostrovsky was most impressed by Shchepkin's interpretations of Nikolai Vasil'evich Gogol's classic comedic roles in *Revizor* (The Inspector General, 1836), *Zhenit'ba* (The Marriage, 1842), and *Igroki* (The Gamblers, 1843). Ostrovsky made acquaintances among actors, visited backstage, and frequented the coffeehouses and taverns of the theater crowd, as well as a favorite haunt of students, the tavern Britannia. By the spring of 1843 his interest in studies and a career in law had been replaced by a love for theater, drama, and student social life.

For Ostrovsky, the Moscow courts proved to be both more instructive and a greater source of material than the university. His father arranged for him to serve as a copyist in the offices of the Court of Conscience in Moscow, which functioned to resolve disputes like a combined family, probate, and small claims court, and whose justices were encouraged to resolve cases "according to conscience" rather than by law. The Court of Conscience was located in the municipal buildings just off Red Square and provided a view of the infamous debtors' prison called "Iama" (The Pit). From 1843 to 1845 Ostrovsky observed a colorful pageant of claimants in this court before his transfer to the Commercial Court, where he served until 1851. In the latter, where his father had his law practice, Moscow merchants resolved suits primarily concerning debts and bankruptcy—the subject of Ostrovsky's first play. The courts offered opportunities for material compensation outside the tiny salary (Ostrovsky received less than minimum pay), and although he apparently refrained from taking bribes, he described these practices liberally in works such as *Dokhodnoe mesto* (A Lucrative Post, 1857) and *Puchina* (The Swamp Hole, 1866). If his father had expected regular employment to cure his son of fascination with the theater, the effect was quite the opposite. Ostrovsky's first literary work— "Skazanie o tom, kak kvartal'nyi nadziratel' puskalsia v

plias, ili Ot velikogo do smeshnogo tol'ko odin shag" (Tale of How the Local Policeman Started to Dance, or, From the Sublime to the Ridiculous Is Just One Step, written 1843, published in *Ostrovsky. Novye mater'ialy. Pis'ma. Trudy i dni. Stat'i.* [Ostrovsky. New Materials. Letters. Works and Days. Articles.], 1924)—dates from this period. Not only did the courts provide rich literary material, but the clerk employees took much time off to visit the theaters that were located next door on Theater Square.

Ostrovsky's favorite haunt was Pechkin's Coffeehouse and Tavern—a gathering place for actors and litterateurs established right off Theater Square by Mochalov's father-in-law. Here Ostrovsky was able to observe and meet Moscow actors (Ivan Vasil'evich Samarin, Vasilii Ignat'evich Zhivokini, even Shchepkin, and, of course, Mochalov), as well as notable literary figures, including the vaudeville writer Dmitrii Timofeevich Lensky, the Shakespeare translator Nikolai Kristoferovich Ketcher, the young Alexander Herzen (Aleksandr Ivanovich Gertsen), and the critics and journalists Aleksei Dmitrievich Galakhov and Mikhail Nikiforovich Katkov. Ostrovsky closely observed the actors in the café and made friends with some, notably with the young actor Prov Mikhailovich Sadovsky. At the same time that he met Sadovsky, in 1846, Ostrovsky met the student Tertii Ivanovich Filippov. He and Filippov shared an interest in the writings of George Sand, Charles Fourier, James Fenimore Cooper, and Charles Dickens; in the criticism of Vissarion Grigor'evich Belinsky; and in the journal *Otechestvennye zapiski* (Notes of the Fatherland). Filippov introduced Ostrovsky to a mathematics student, Evgenii Nikolaevich Edel'son, and the three friends formed a literary-philosophical *kruzhok* (circle) that read and discussed not just literature, criticism, and philosophy but also folk songs—of which Filippov was a masterful performer. The *kruzhok* pursued a mixture of national, Slavophile interests and European literature and philosophy.

Influenced by Gogol and the *natural'naia shkola* (natural school) of Belinsky, Ostrovsky's "Zapiski zamoskvoretskogo zhitelia" showed his flair for dialogue, especially conversation characteristic of Zamoskvorech'e. He began a play, titled "Iskovoe proshenie" (The Claim Request), and then before finishing it began another, "Nesostoiatel'nyi dolzhnik" (The Insolvent Debtor), inviting an actor, Dmitrii Gorev, to help him. They worked together briefly in the fall of 1846, then Ostrovsky finished the play himself. In January 1847 the weekly *Moskovskii gorodskoi listok* (The Moscow City Sheet) published *Stseny iz komedii "Nesostoiatel'nyi dolzhnik" (Ozhidanie zhenikha)* (Scenes from the Comedy "The Insolvent Debtor" [Awaiting the Groom]), signed with the initials A. O. and D. G. Ostrovsky returned to

"Iskovoe proshenie," refashioning the work, and read it in February 1847 in the home of Shevyrev at a gathering that was attended by colleagues from the weekly paper as well as by several prominent Moscow intellectuals. The reading was a great success. Shevyrev congratulated those present with discovering "a new dramatic luminary in Russian literature," as quoted by Aleksandr Ivanovich Reviakin in his *A. N. Ostrovsky v vospominaniiakh sovremennikov* (A. N. Ostrovsky in the Recollections of His Contemporaries, 1966), and Ostrovsky considered himself a writer from this time onward. The play, now titled *Kartina semeinogo schast'ia. Kartiny moskovskoi zhizni* (Picture of Family Happiness. Pictures of Moscow Life), appeared in March of the same year in *Moskovskii gorodskoi listok;* then "Zapiski zamoskvoretskogo zhitelia" appeared (in June), and Ostrovsky's career was under way. This success, however, was marred by the theatrical censorship, which in August 1847 forbade Ostrovsky's *Kartina semeinogo schast'ia* from being performed at a benefit for his friend Sadovsky; it premiered only in 1855, under the title *Semeinaia kartina,* and was published in 1859. Ostrovsky then began reworking the play that he started with Gorev into his first full-length comedy, "Bankrot" (The Bankrupt).

In 1848 Ostrovsky's father, consistent with his new noble status, purchased an estate, Shchelykovo, in the Kostroma district, where the family had its origins. That summer the whole family traveled to Shchelykovo, and for the first time Ostrovsky experienced the heart of northern Russia–places that included Sergiev Posad, Periaslavl'-Zalesskii, and Iaroslavl'–and the Volga, regions that provided material for his later works. His father insisted that his eldest son accompany the family to cool the young man's growing affection for Agaf'ia Ivanovna, a local girl of the Iauza region, no doubt of peasant origins, whose surname remains unknown. The next summer, when the family traveled to Shchelykovo, Ostrovsky begged off because of work, but as soon as they departed, Agaf'ia moved into his rooms. Thus began their civil marriage, which continued for eighteen years.

Ostrovsky worked on "Bankrot" throughout the first half of 1849. He retained the basic plot–a rich merchant's plan to dupe creditors by declaring false bankruptcy is foiled by his own clerk, who makes off with the merchant's fortune and his daughter–but developed the language and characteristics of the Zamoskvorech'e merchants. Through typical speech and mannerisms, the dramatist amplified the dull despotism of this merchant version of King Lear–the crude, naive, wild, and intemperate Bol'shov. Ostrovsky never again spent so much time refining and polishing a play. The reactionary response of the government to the 1848 revolution

in France, however, conspired to keep the play off the stage and unpublished. Ostrovsky found an alternative: private readings, which began during the summer of 1849 and were given in the homes of socially and culturally prominent Moscow nobility and intelligentsia such as the Novosil'tsevs, Meshcherskys, and Sheremetevs; of prominent merchant families such as the Karzinkins, Noskovs, and Khludovs; and of Moscow University professors. The sensational effect of these readings was augmented by the abrupt disappearance of striking literary works since early 1848. In the fall Ostrovsky submitted his comedy to the theatrical censorship in a copy with a prominent subtitle, "Svoi liudi–sochtemsia!" (It's a Family Affair–We'll Settle It Ourselves! 1850), but the play was rejected in November. In December 1849 Pogodin, a professor of history and the editor and publisher of the monthly journal *Moskvitianin* (The Muscovite), arranged for a reading at his home, which was one of the centers of Moscow culture. Among the literary and cultural figures present was Gogol, who gave his approval to the young playwright's first full-length comedy. Even more important, Pogodin decided that he must publish this work in his journal, and he set about the considerable task of winning permission from the censorship. Through government connections, his conservative and loyalist reputation, and a shrewd manipulation of approvals from the governor-general and the local censor, Pogodin finally secured permission to publish the play. It appeared in the March 1850 issue of *Moskvitianin* under the title *Svoi liudi sochtemsia.*

The appearance of *Svoi liudi sochtemsia* in print created a sensation, and emboldened by this success, Ostrovsky appealed to the governor-general directly for permission to produce the play. The effect was quite the opposite of what he expected. The censorship committee found the play morally unsatisfactory for its bleak presentation of merchants and its lack of an enlightening effect. According to the committee, *Svoi liudi sochtemsia* undermined the respect of the younger generation for their elders and insulted the honor of the merchant class. Not only was performance of the play forbidden but Ostrovsky was also officially reprimanded, investigated, and placed under secret police watch. He responded by writing the Minister of Enlightenment a respectful letter, which at the same time, however, defended his writing and talent. Instead of quelling the popularity of the dramatist and his new comedy, the reaction of the government served to elevate Ostrovsky in the eyes of his readership and fellow writers.

Temporarily blocked from the stage, Ostrovsky began work as an editor for Pogodin's journal. Although it was the only serious literary journal in the city, *Moskvitianin* was not popular because of its publication of conservative and unexciting literary works and articles (distinctive for their many printing errors). From time to time Pogodin had arranged for various Muscovites to act as its editors, and he succeeded in getting Ostrovsky's assent to co-edit *Moskvitianin,* with the help of the poet Lev Aleksandrovich Mei, beginning in March 1850. Trying to enliven the contents of the journal, Ostrovsky convinced Aleksei Feofilaktovich Pisemsky, with whom he shared Kostroma origins, to publish *Tiufiak* (The Simpleton, 1850), Pisemsky's first major work, in *Moskvitianin.* Ostrovsky, for his own part, attempted to write criticism; his lengthy review of Evgeniia Tur's novel *Oshibka* (The Mistake, 1849) emphasized the role of realistic, national art in exposing truth. This first attempt was Ostrovsky's last, however—save for a short review of *Tiufiak* in 1851—and he returned to drama, contributing a reworked piece from "Iskovoe proshenie" that he titled *Utro molodogo cheloveka* (A Young Man's Morning, 1850). He published another small piece, *Neozhidannyi sluchai* (Unexpected Event, 1851), in an almanac, but both were ridiculed in the St. Petersburg press. After this interlude following his first success, Ostrovsky threw himself into his next comedy, *Bednaia nevesta* (The Poor Bride, 1853; published 1852).

At this time, in the early 1850s, Ostrovsky formed an informal *kruzhok* of acquaintances whose nucleus was made up of his close university friends Edel'son and Filippov, around whom gathered a diverse company of individuals. Beginning writers (Berg, Mikhail Aleksandrovich Stakhovich, Egor Eduardovich Driansky) and established writers (Pisemsky and Aleksei Antipovich Potekhin, who also hailed from Kostroma) belonged to this *kruzhok,* as did other university friends (Boris Nikolaevich Almazov and Arkadii Edel'son, Evgenii's brother) and their friends (Kostia Mal'tsev and Sergei Vasil'evich Maksimov). Actors (Sadovsky, Ivan Egorovich Turchaninov and Sergei Vasil'evich Vasil'ev), merchant friends of Sadovsky (the Koshevarerovs, who introduced the group to their friends, including an assortment of small merchants and traders), musicians (Aleksandr Ivanovich Diubiuk, Otton Ivanovich Diutsh, Nikolai Grigor'evich Rubinshtein), and artists (Nikolai Aleksandrovich Ramazanov, Petr Mikhailovich Boklevsky) composed the rest of the group. This *kruzhok,* which gathered in local taverns and wine cellars, differed from those of the earlier generation in Moscow, whose ideological, philosophical, and political interests remained foreign to Ostrovsky's associates. The times—the *mrachnoe semiletie* (seven gloomy years) of repression after 1848 during the reign of Tsar Nicholas I—were inimical to ideological discussions, and the young people of this period preferred to spend their evenings carousing, enjoying songs, telling folktales and stories, and performing mildly satirical

Prov Mikhailovich Sadovsky, the first actor to perform the role of Liubim Tortsov in Ostrovsky's 1854 play Bednost' ne porok *(Poverty is No Vice)*

improvisations for each other. All of these activities reflected popular, national cultural interests rather than Western philosophical ideas. Ostrovsky and his friends inherited the Moscow Slavophile tradition, but they broadened the movement beyond interests in the rural, steppe peasantry to include the folk culture of the urban middle and lower classes.

Among those who joined Ostrovsky's circle in the 1850s was the critic and poet Apollon Aleksandrovich Grigor'ev, who eventually became the dramatist's most enthusiastic supporter and interpreter. When they met, Grigor'ev (also born and raised in Zamoskvorech'e) already had considerable experience in the literary worlds of St. Petersburg and Moscow. He was engaged at the time in a project of developing nationalist, populist, and urban cultural tastes—much like those of Ostrovsky's *kruzhok,* to which he brought a sophisticated, native, and idealistic romanticism. Ready to embrace the interests of the *kruzhok* in folk singers and performers, Grigor'ev shared as well the group's passionate love for the theater. In Ostrovsky's dramas, moreover, he saw the embodiment of a new national artistic credo. The emotional, unrestrained, and self-indulgent Grigor'ev became renowned for carousing in taverns and visiting the gypsies with this circle of friends. He also began to lead the group in more serious activities, especially journalism, for he also had worked under Pogodin and kept up his relationship with *Moskvitianin.*

Beginning in 1851, Ostrovsky brought his friends into *Moskvitianin* to assist in editing, writing reviews and criticism, and proofreading. Initially he tried to enhance the intellectual level of the journal by inviting prominent Moscow University professors, but all the potential contributors refused because of Pogodin's reputation as a profoundly conservative, stingy, and autocratic editor. Ostrovsky's friends began modernizing the journal, and Pogodin began to object and obstruct. He had never given them actual editorial control, and now he simply called them the *molodaia redaktsiia* (Young Editors), with responsibility for fiction, plays, poetry, criticism, reviews, and humorous commentary. For himself, as senior editor, he retained control over political, historical, and scholarly materials. As a result the journal began to take on a serious literary character, publishing the works of writers such as Pisemsky, Dmitrii Vasil'evich Grigorovich, and Ivan Timofeevich Kokorev and offering polemical surveys of St. Petersburg journals. The *molodaia redaktsiia* rejuvenated the Russophile views of *Moskvitianin* with sympathy for popular, urban folk culture (called "democratism") and by demanding sincerity in literature—*neposredstvennost'* (spontaneity) was their watchword. The young Almazov provided satirical feuilletons under the pseudonym of Erast Blagonravov (this name translates as "Eros Well-behaved"), and in one article he provided a rather transparent commentary on the forbidden play "Bankrot." The views of the *molodaia redaktsiia* produced violent conflicts with Pogodin, which soon exhausted Ostrovsky, as did his long hours in the editorial offices and unending begging for funds to pay authors. In late 1851 Grigor'ev took over as leader of the *molodaia redaktsiia,* writing the major critical articles and taking up arms with the recalcitrant Pogodin over money and ideology, while Ostrovsky (who had left the civil service) turned to his new comedy with feelings of relief and desperation to finish the play and sell it.

While editing *Moskvitianin* in 1850 and 1851, Ostrovsky also spent time at the home of poet and Countess Evdokiia Petrovna Rostopchina, who had the reputation of a Russian George Sand, and whose Saturday evening salons were popular among the Moscow literary and intellectual elite. He was flattered by the attention he received there, and particularly grateful for the Countess's sympathy and support when his sister

fell ill and died suddenly in 1851. Through Rostopchina he met the sisters Sof'ia Vladimirovna Engel'gardt and Ekaterina Vladimirovna Novosil'tseva (whose pen name was T. Tolycheva), themselves minor published authors, whose home became a particular favorite for the warmth and enthusiasm lavished on the young playwright. These upper-class acquaintances, however brief in the career of Ostrovsky, provided him with a glimpse into a world that was otherwise foreign to his own, and allowed him access to material that became useful in his later plays.

While working on his second full-length play, *Bednaia nevesta,* Ostrovsky changed its structure three times. He abandoned the satiric mode and merchant lifestyle, present in his earlier works, and replaced them with a love plot and a positive, even ideal, heroine. The result was a psychological, lyrical comedy. In his central figure, Mariia Andreevna, the classic bride without a dowry, Ostrovsky wanted to confront the ideal, literary image of romantic love with the sober prose of real life, thereby correcting current discussions of *lishnie liudi* (superfluous men) and heroes of their time; his hero, Merich, is an offshoot of Mikhail Iur'evich Lermontov's Grushnitsky from the 1840 novel *Geroi nashego vremeni* (A Hero of Our Time). Ostrovsky found a prototype for the heroine, her mother, and her sisters in the family of the widow Sof'ia Grigor'evna Korsh, whose devotion to settling the future of her five unmarried daughters was well known in Moscow circles. Ostrovsky knew the family well, had gone to school with one of the sons, and was particularly enamored of the youngest daughter, Zinaida, who became the model for his heroine. One of the older daughters, Liubov' Fedorovna, had married the Moscow University professor Nikita Ivanovich Krylov (responsible for the end of Ostrovsky's university career), who was also caricatured in this new play. Other circumstances drew Ostrovsky to the family and its dilemma: Apollon Grigor'ev had fallen in love with one of the sisters, Antonina, and later married her sister Lidiia, with unfortunate results. The character of Khor'kov, who suffers unrequited love for Mariia Andreevna, was partly based on Grigor'ev and partly on the author himself; in addition, Milashin has traits of Filippov. Ostrovsky spent the summer of 1851 at Shchelykovo finishing this final version. In the fall, after reading Pisemsky's new comedy, Ostrovsky polished his own a bit more, finally completing it in December 1851.

As soon as Ostrovsky had finished *Bednaia nevesta,* he began reading the play in Moscow homes—at Rostopchina's, first of all. The intense anticipation was exceeded only by the success of the play, and all found support for their own views: Shevyrev, for example, saw it as an attack on the West, while Rostopchina likened it to a Flemish painting and recent stories by French literary historian and critic Charles-Augustin Sainte-Beuve. The most energetic defender of the play was Grigor'ev, who praised it as the manifesto of a new literary movement. When *Bednaia nevesta* appeared in *Moskvitianin* early in 1852, he hailed the comedy as a "new word," by which he meant *narodnost'* (Russian, or national character). Ostrovsky's *kruzhok* lavishly praised the work, and even liberal Muscovite Westernizers such as Galakhov and Petr Nikolaevich Kudriavtsev reacted favorably—with the exception of the critic Vasilii Petrovich Botkin, who was offended by Merich, the Zamoskvorech'e caricature of Lermontov's Pechorin. Turgenev, whom Ostrovsky admired immensely for his *Zapiski okhotnika* (A Hunter's Sketches, 1852), heard the play at the Engel'gardt salon and praised it warmly. He wrote a respectful review of *Bednaia nevesta* for *Sovremennik* (The Contemporary), which as a rule harshly criticized and ridiculed Moscow Russophiles. Ostrovsky was hailed as Gogol's disciple, and, after the writer's death in February 1852, as his heir and the new leader of Russian theater.

Literary censorship after 1848 had become extremely strict, but theater censorship was even more impossible, with the result that only mediocre, official-nationalist plays dominated the repertoire—which offered only three genuine comedies: two by Gogol, *Revizor* and *Zhenit'ba*, and Griboedov's *Gore ot uma*. In order to see something of his work on the stage, Ostrovsky even translated Shakespeare's *Taming of the Shrew* (1594), but that, too, was forbidden in September 1850. He managed to convince the director of the Imperial Theater in Moscow to accept *Bednaia nevesta* provisionally, on the condition that it be accepted by the censors in St. Petersburg. The play went into rehearsals (Sadovsky was Benevolensky, and Ekaterina Nikolaevna Vasil'eva was Mar'ia Andreevna), but in approving the play the censor so disfigured it that the director refused to produce it. For Ostrovsky there remained only the amateur theaters of private homes (such as that of Sof'ia Alekseevna Panova) and private stages (one, for example, was located in a state textile factory in Pavlov Posad, a suburb of Moscow) to help him gain some practical experience of his plays onstage. Finally, Ostrovsky decided to write a comedy designed to pass the censorship by avoiding satire and social criticism—*Ne v svoi sani ne sadis'* (Don't Bite Off More Than You Can Chew, published in *Moskvitianin*, 1853). A comic melodrama, this light piece describes an aristocratic dandy, Vikhorev, who comes to a provincial town to deceive its simple, good-natured inhabitants in order to marry into money, specifically in the person of a merchant's daughter. The provincial characters—the merchant Rusakov, his daughter Dunia, and the young merchant Borodkin—share broad, open, generous traits, which conflict with the shrewd, calculating cynicism of the city. Almost duped by Vikhorev, Dunia is saved when the dandy's dishonest intentions are unmasked. The simple morality of this melodrama embodied the belief of Ostrovsky and his *kruzhok* in the need for openness and simple directness in literature. The playwright's intention of satisfying the censorship and the theater administration succeeded, although not without timely help from Pogodin through some influential contacts in St. Petersburg.

The premiere of *Ne v svoi sani ne sadis'* on 14 January 1853 was a benefit performance for Liubov' Pavlovna Kositskaia-Nikulina, in which she performed, at the Bol'shoi Petrovskii Theater. Although she was the most popular actress in Moscow, Kositskaia, as she was known onstage, was not universally admired: devotees of European tragic theater, including Rostopchina, found her unrefined—even somewhat simple—and her features too Russian. The play itself, with provincial settings and unstylish characters in Russian middle-class costume, was not typical of the lavish productions usually chosen for a benefit. The curtain opened to show a provincial tavern: itself a novelty, no doubt shocking in its crude realism. Kositskaia as Dunia entered not in a lavish, stylish gown (as would have been expected, no matter what the play), but in a calico dress. The speech sounded more like real life than stage declamations: Sadovsky's Rusakov was based on the merchants that Ostrovsky knew, such as the Koshevarovs; Petr Gavrilovich Stepanov's Malomal'sky, the tavern keeper, amused simply by being natural and recognizable; and Vasil'ev's Borodkin managed to combine the humorous energy of vaudeville with serious dramatic emotion. The premiere and benefit succeeded beyond Ostrovsky's wildest dreams: the play was performed twelve more times in the Bol'shoi and twelve times in the Malyi Theater that season. The critics reacted with equal enthusiasm, and even the skeptical Botkin relented, praising the play as "ennobling the heart." The simple production with realistic sets, costumes, and especially unaffected acting created a sensation. In his "Zapisnaia knizhka 1860–1862 gg." (Notebook of 1860–1862; collected in his *Polnoe Sobranie Sochinenii*, 1972–1988), Dostoevsky later praised Ostrovsky's achievement in *Ne v svoi sani ne sadis'* as the poetry of directness: the play charmed with its "directness" of description, its "immediacy" of emotion, and its absence of guile or manipulation.

Shortly after the premiere of *Ne v svoi sani ne sadis'* in Moscow, Ostrovsky traveled to St. Petersburg to arrange for a premiere in the capital. Fedor Alekseevich Burdin, an old acquaintance from Moscow and the gymnasium, had become an influential member of the

Imperial Theater. He adored Ostrovsky and arranged for the premiere of his earlier work, *Utro molodogo cheloveka,* at the Petersburg Theater-Circus on 12 February 1853. More important was the St. Petersburg premiere of *Ne v svoi sani ne sadis'* at the Aleksandrinskii Theater, for which permission had been granted thanks to Burdin's influence. Ostrovsky found, however, that the St. Petersburg troupe had difficulty abandoning the stylized, overly dramatic, and demonstrative acting developed for European melodramas, and some of the actors openly opposed the work as unsophisticated, provincial, "homespun," and not worthy of a truly sophisticated theater. Nonetheless, the premiere on 19 February was a great success: a leading theater critic, Vladimir Rafailovich Zotov, wrote in *Severnaia pchela* (Northern Bee, 9 March 1853) that "the whole theater wept, and a better review we do not know." The skeptical, severe, and circumspect Director of Imperial Theaters, Aleksandr Mikhailovich Gedeonov, was sufficiently impressed to recommend the play to Tsar Nicholas I, who was especially pleased by the morally uplifting ending. The tsar pronounced that few plays had given him such pleasure, adding "Ce n'est plus une pièce, c'est une leçon" (It is not a play, it is a lesson). Ostrovsky's calculation in creating a morally acceptable play had now succeeded beyond his greatest expectations, and his career was assured. However, he was not in St. Petersburg to experience this personal triumph: three days after the premiere his father died, and Ostrovsky hurried to Shchelykovo for the funeral.

On the heels of his theatrical triumphs, Ostrovsky suffered a major catastrophe. In July 1853 his onetime collaborator Gorev suddenly appeared in Moscow, and soon thereafter rumors began to circulate that Ostrovsky had not written his comedies *Svoi liudi sochtemsia, Bednaia nevesta,* and *Ne v svoi sani ne sadis'* but had stolen them from Gorev. Some rumors to that effect had surfaced in 1851, after the appearance of *Svoi liudi sochtemsia,* and people recalled that scenes from its earlier version, "Bankrot," had indeed been signed by two sets of initials. When Ostrovsky began readings of *Bednaia nevesta,* the accusation clearly seemed baseless. But the same rumors gained currency again, and by the fall of 1853 even Pogodin noted them (which further complicated the already difficult relations between him and the *molodaia redaktsiia*—especially Grigor'ev, who vehemently defended Ostrovsky). The scandal raged, aided by publicly circulated anonymous letters and Ostrovsky's own refusal to bring the matter to a public airing. Finally, Ostrovsky decided to disprove Gorev's claims by creating a new play: he completed *Bednost' ne porok* (Poverty is No Vice, 1854; translated as *Poverty Is No Crime,* 1917) in record time—two months—and gave a reading in November 1853 at the home of Grigor'ev.

Repeated readings throughout Moscow undercut the rumors, and the accusations faded away. Only Pogodin held back and refused to publish the play in his journal, with the result that it appeared early in 1854 in a separate edition, dedicated by Ostrovsky to Sadovsky, who performed in its premiere that January at the Malyi Theater. *Bednost' ne porok* was performed there instead of at the Bol'shoi Petrovskii, which had burned in March 1853.

Ostrovsky's stage triumphs marked a shift from a Romantic to a Realist style in the Russian theater and coincided with a generational change in actors: Mochalov and Shchepkin were replaced by Sadovsky, Vasilii Ignat'evich Zhivokini by Vasil'ev, and the actresses Nadezhda Vasil'evna Repina and Mariia Dmitrievna L'vova-Sinetskaia by Vasil'eva and Kositskaia, among others. *Bednaia nevesta* premiered in August 1853 in the Malyi Theater: Vasil'evna played the title role of Mar'ia Andreevna with simple, direct realism; Sadovsky played the clerk Benevolensky to great effect; and the public adored Vasil'ev as Milashin. Despite the resounding success of the play before the spectators and critics, there was backstage grumbling from actors of the older generation, including the vaudevillian Lensky, who ridiculed the simplicity of language, the lower-class manners, and the lack of culture and fashion in the production.

This conflict escalated with the arrival of Mademoiselle Rachel, the French classical tragedienne of the Comédie-Française. Her performances in Moscow coincided with the premiere of *Bednost' ne porok* in January 1854: matinees of classical French tragedy alternated on the Malyi stage with evening performances of Ostrovsky's play. Devotees of Rachel, notably the Moscow nobility—with Rostopchina most prominent in her adulation—attended in the daytime, while the middle and lower classes, especially merchants, and students took over the evenings. The play itself exacerbated this clash: the plot of *Bednost' ne porok* turns on the conflict of two brothers—the progressive, heartless Gordei Tortsov, a merchant who attempts to anglicize not only his factory but also his lifestyle, and his drunken, feckless brother Liubim, a positive figure who represents Russian sincerity and genuineness. The play brought Russian folk customs of Christmas celebrations to the stage with singing and dancing, which reinforced the national, homey nature of its pro-Russian, patriotic message. Sadovsky played Liubim Tortsov with a realism reminiscent of the *natural'naia shkola* of the 1840s, elevating the "little hero" of that era into an emblem of moral superiority, despite his alcoholism and homelessness. The St. Petersburg press attacked Ostrovsky (Andrei Aleksandrovich Kraevsky in *Otechestvennye zapiski* labeled Liubim an insolent drunkard), while the *molodaia redaktsiia* poured forth praise. Grigor'ev wrote a poem that circulated broadly in manuscript–an "elegy-ode-satire" titled "Rashel' i pravda" (Rachel and Truth)–which ridiculed the French tragedienne's artificiality and praised the "new word" of Ostrovsky's play, describing Liubim as "unfortunate, drunk, and emaciated, but with a pure Russian soul." Grigor'ev's poem was published in *Moskvitianin* under the title "Iskusstvo i pravda" (Art and Truth, 1854). The public voted its support for *Bednost' ne porok* over Rachel by purchasing more tickets for the evening performances at the Malyi Theater.

The *narodnost'* that Ostrovsky's plays elaborated on contrasted strikingly with the official nationalism trumpeted in the press in support of Russian participation in the Crimean War. His popular nationalism was quite unlike the conservative, flag-waving, bureaucratic patriotism that fueled this military debacle. Indeed, Ostrovsky's plays provided scarcely a mention of the war, and he and his friends found themselves much in sympathy with the antimilitary, antiheroic tales of Sebastopol written by the young Tolstoy. By 1854 Ostrovsky was avoiding the salons of high-society Moscow and contemporary ideology, "official" or otherwise. His new play, *Ne tak zhivi, kak khochetsia!* (Live Not As You Would Like, published in *Moskvitianin*, 1855), was far removed from topical concerns; it was set in late-eighteenth-century Moscow, and it demonstratively supported traditional lifestyles. In a whirlwind of pagan and folk elements, music, dance, and carousing, the play contrasts the sanctity of marriage with the destruction caused by the devil in subverting family values. This contrast is impersonated in the conflict between the hero of the play–the passionate, unrestrained, and careless Petr (modeled in part on Grigor'ev)–and the wily, cheerful, and proud Grusha; the setting of the play is the semifabulous, semireal world of Russian folk poetry. The premiere of *Ne tak zhivi, kak khochetsia!* in December 1854 at the Malyi Theater was not a great success: not bold enough for some, the play was too frank and inelegant for others. Though Ostrovsky had managed to squeeze it through the narrow opening afforded by wartime censorship, the result did not approach his earlier triumphs.

The death of Tsar Nicholas I in February 1855 brought a sudden change in atmosphere, accompanied by words such as *glasnost'* (openness) and *ottepel'* (thaw). The censorship relaxed slightly, for both printed matter and–after a six-month mourning period–theaters. Ostrovsky found himself casting about for material, unsure how to gauge the changed circumstances; although he had never been a political writer, he could not escape reflecting the new era. In July he began work on what later became *Bespridannitsa* (The Dowerless

Bride, published in *Otechestvennye zapiski*, 1879) but soon dropped it. He then sketched the plot for a comedy, *V chuzhom piru pokhmel'e* (Your Feast, My Hangover), but abandoned it also. In November he prepared to write *Koz'ma Zakhar'ich Minin-Sukhoruk* (1862), but the next month he returned to *V chuzhom piru pokhmel'e,* which he finished. Though short, this two-act comedy vividly displays Ostrovsky's new direction. The hero is the honest and good-natured Ivanov, an old teacher of classics who worships his daughter. The warmly depicted, strong character of Ivanov disproves the charge that Ostrovsky admired only ignorance. Most significant is the character of the merchant Tit Titych Bruskov, a homegrown despot and the first of Ostrovsky's *samodur* (domestic tyrant) characters. Sadovsky acted in this role in the premiere of the play in January 1856 at the Malyi Theater; his portrayal of the crude force and stubbornness of Bruskov made the moral triumph of the meek Ivanov and his daughter all the more satisfying, as the *samodur* "forces" his son to marry in a happy ending. This image of the *samodur* Bruskov proved hugely successful. It captured the stubborn self-importance typical not only of Zamoskvorech'e merchants but also of powerful landowners, St. Petersburg officials, and all self- righteous, self-indulgent tyrants. The influential journal *Sovremennik* noted Ostrovsky's new approach and praised the play. Although Ostrovsky was still supported by his Moscow friends, the circle of the *molodaia redaktsiia* had begun to dissipate, and the *Moskvitianin* was about to shut down. He published *V chuzhom piru pokhmel'e* in 1856 in *Russkii vestnik* (The Russian Messenger), a new journal edited by Mikhail Nikiforovich Katkov, which later published works by Turgenev, Dostoevsky, and Tolstoy.

Meanwhile, early in 1856 Ostrovsky traveled to St. Petersburg not only to supervise the production there of *V chuzhom piru pokhmel'e* and meet with the censors but also to arrange to participate in an expedition planned by the Ministry of Waterways to acquaint young writers with the seas and rivers of Russia. While waiting in vain for approval from the ministry, he became acquainted with the writers and journalists of *Sovremennik,* which had been trying to attract him as a contributor. Turgenev took the playwright under his wing and introduced him to his friends, and Ostrovsky found a congenial, sympathetic supporter in Nikolai Alekseevich Nekrasov, the editor of the journal. St. Petersburg intellectual and cultural life was energized by expectations of change and new opportunities, and the *Sovremennik* group exemplified this excitement at its gatherings: Turgenev read his new novel *Rudin;* Tolstoy acquainted colleagues with his latest story; and both Nekrasov and Turgenev were editing a collection of Fedor Ivanovich Tiutchev's poetry. Ostrovsky and

Ostrovsky in the 1860s

of Moscow—out of an urban setting—and to renew his artistic energies with the stimulation of travel. He knew the Volga from his travels to Kostroma and visits to Nizhnii Novgorod, and he was fascinated by the simple life of rural Russia along this central artery. Tracking down the origins of the great river held both a literal and metaphorical meaning for Ostrovsky: he not only refreshed his creative life but also found material for future plays on this journey. He set off in April 1856, spent time in Tver', traveled back roads through primitive, impoverished villages, and was impressed by the isolation of Russian provinces. He interrupted his travels in the summer and fall, when he returned to Moscow to heal a broken leg, but returned in the spring of 1857 and ended his travels that summer. He kept methodical notes, compiled a dictionary of Volga dialect, and wrote down folk songs with the assistance of the composer Konstantin Petrovich Vil'boa. Although Ostrovsky wrote only one article for the *Morskoi sbornik,* he was inspired to conceive a cycle of plays, "Nochi na Volge" (Nights on the Volga), which was never realized—save for two works, *Voevoda (Son na Volge)* (The War Lord [Dream on the Volga]), published in 1865 in *Sovremennik,* and *Groza* (The Thunderstorm), which appeared in *Biblioteka dlia chteniia* (A Reading Library) in 1860. The latter reflected his impressions of the promenading in small towns on the Volga and the freedom that young, unattached women allowed themselves, in contrast to the strict, severe image of married women.

After his travels along the Volga, Ostrovsky returned home to Moscow with a new self-confidence. Significantly, he removed himself from the partisan literary politics between Westernizers and Slavophiles, liberals and conservatives, and democrats and nationalists. During 1857 and 1858 he continued work on *Dokhodnoe mesto,* begun in 1856, in which he took up the themes of corruption and bribery. Here, Ostrovsky attempted not a didactic condemnation with moralizing speeches but rather a view of influence-peddling from within, where a gift is not a bribe but an expression of gratitude. Using the stage not as a pulpit but as a mirror, he showed the pervasive nature of corruption, its omnipresence, and the moral price of easy accommodation. The idealistic young couple, Polina and Zhadov, maintain their moral uprightness in the end, but the forces of worldly pragmatism and compromise clearly outweigh them. Many critics were disappointed: the liberals found the play weak; the democrats found the ending unconvincing; and only Tolstoy seems to have responded with enthusiasm. Most important, Ostrovsky in this work had discovered a new social sphere—clerks and the bureaucracy. His next play, *Ne soshlis' kharakterami!* (They Proved Incompatible!), which came out in *Sovremennik* in 1858, opened yet another social

Tolstoy became especially close, perhaps because they were both newcomers to St. Petersburg. The playwright introduced his Moscow friend Ivan Fedorovich Gorbunov, who was beginning to appear at the Aleksandrinskii Theater, to the *Sovremennik* crowd, and Gorbunov delighted the gathering with his stories. In an interesting journalistic innovation, Ostrovsky (along with Tolstoy and Turgenev) signed an agreement to publish exclusively in *Sovremennik* for four years beginning in 1857. This contract marked his transfer from the defunct *Moskvitianin* to the journal that published his plays during the next eight years.

Finally, in March 1856 Ostrovsky received the necessary papers from the Ministry of Waterways, which agreed to send him on an expedition from the source of the Volga River to Nizhnii Novgorod. Like other authors in this program, he was expected to produce descriptions of his travels for *Morskoi sbornik* (Maritime Collection), the journal of the ministry. However, Ostrovsky was motivated by a personal need to get out stratum new to his plays–the nobility. Pol' Prezhnev, an impoverished nobleman, lazy and a spendthrift, plans to marry a merchant widow for her wealth. The widow, however, is reluctant to throw away her money, and the two part company because of incompatibility. What proves to be essentially incompatible, however, are not really the individual characters but the social classes to which they belong–the stingy merchant class and the prodigal gentry. The play is not among Ostrovsky's best; he later returned to this topic–the decline and dissipation of the nobility–in his play *Vospitannitsa* (The Ward, 1863; published 1860), written in a burst of inspiration in only three weeks while he was on one of his regular trips to St. Petersburg in 1858. In *Vospitannitsa,* for the first time Ostrovsky takes the action outdoors, where, despite the airy openness, the world of the landowner Ulanbekova, with her two thousand serfs, is suffocating. Rather than write a tendentious piece on serfdom, Ostrovsky communicated the evil of bondage and oppression through the story of Ulanbekova's ward Nadia, who is forced into a terrible marriage with the drunken manager of the estate.

Dokhodnoe mesto had received preliminary censorship approval and was scheduled to open in December 1857. Its premiere at the Malyi Theater in Moscow was canceled at the last minute, however, by a jittery censorship that feared insulting government clerks. Despite the mood of openness after 1855, the theater censorship remained unpredictable. The print censors were less strict: *Dokhodnoe mesto* had already been published in the Moscow journal *Russkaia beseda* (Russian Colloquy) in January. Two years later, in October 1859, the censorship forbade the performance of *Vospitannitsa* for similar reasons–namely, its insults to the landowning class. Each subsequent year Ostrovsky attempted to get permission to produce these two plays, as well as *Svoi liudi sochtemsia*. The first two plays finally premiered only in 1863. *Svoi liudi sochtemsia,* however, in a version mutilated by the censor, premiered early in 1861–first in St. Petersburg, then two weeks later in Moscow, to a wildly enthusiastic audience in the newly restored Bol'shoi Theater.

Ostrovsky's most acclaimed play, *Groza,* is closely linked to the actress Kositskaia, who eventually played its tragic heroine, Katerina. Ostrovsky had first responded to Kositskaia's request for a benefit play with the ill-fated *Vospitannitsa;* he then created for her the principal role in *Groza,* begun the summer of 1859. During the writing Ostrovsky and Kositskaia became close, and the playwright fell in love with his female lead. The role of Katerina differed from that of the naive, silly ingenue Dunia that she had played in *Ne v svoi sani ne sadis'.* Suffering bitterly from living with an unloved husband, from servility before an evil and envious mother-in-law, Kabanikha (a vicious *samodur* among several in the play), and from the closed, traditional society of provincial life along the Volga, the heroine longs to escape and find beauty. This longing leads to her revolt when her timid husband is gone–to a night of love and then suicide. The *groza* of the title is not just the thunder that accompanies the heroine's confession to her husband; it is also the peculiarly Russian word for threatened terror that is the root of Ivan the Terrible's name, *Ivan Groznyi.* Katerina lives under a threat of destruction, which she accomplishes herself in her final act of revolt. When Ostrovsky finished the play in October, he himself went to win the approval of the censor, who–among other fanciful misreadings– feared that the late tsar, Nicholas I, was being parodied in the character of Kabanikha! Permission was received only a week before the premiere, which took place on 16 November 1859. The great success of the play revived old controversies: the older generation found the realistic depiction of marital infidelity profane– crude, even "dirty"–while younger viewers identified with the heroine's revolt, her need for love, and her self-assertion in the face of oppressive, provincial Russian domestic despotism. The controversy only added to the popularity of *Groza,* and all season it played to full houses. Ostrovsky's affair with Kositskaia continued for a year, until the actress fell in love with a merchant's son–a relationship that ended badly for her but which freed the playwright from his infatuation.

For Ostrovsky, the year 1859 was a watershed not only because of *Groza.* He published his collected works that year: eleven original plays, including *Svoi liudi sochtemsia* (the censor was especially liberal). Among several reviews, an original assessment by a young critic, Nikolai Aleksandrovich Dobroliubov, stood out. In "Temnoe tsarstvo" (The Dark Kingdom), published in 1859 in *Sovremennik,* Dobroliubov noted that Ostrovsky had been judged either for making Russian life seem too dark and degraded, or for making it seem too bright and rosy, and that critics had missed the essence of Ostrovsky's plays– his fidelity to real, actual life. Dobroliubov analyzed not so much the plays as the society they described. In the "dark kingdom" of merchant Russia the *samodur* reigned, fear and hypocrisy ruled, and the power of ignorance smothered individual expression. When Dobroliubov saw *Groza,* he wrote another article for *Sovremennik* in 1860, "Luch sveta v temnom tsarstve" (A Ray of Light in the Dark Kingdom). His metaphor is taken from Katerina's dream, in which she sees a column of light from the church cupola and signifies her spiritual protest against the surrounding darkness of provincial, backward Russia. Dobroliubov viewed Katerina as a powerful female character expressing a popular awakening in

Poster for the first production of Ostrovsky's Volki i ovtsy *(Wolves and Sheep, 1875) at the Malyi Theater in Moscow*
(from Abram L'vovich Shtein, A. N. Ostrovsky, *1962)*

defense of individual rights. He provided a new dimension to Ostrovsky's significance: that of social critic and mirror of the deepest aspirations in society. Up to this point Grigor'ev's view that Ostrovsky's plays re-created the true spirit of Russia onstage, showing her simple, real, popular, and national character, had dominated critics' opinions; Dobroliubov saw in Ostrovsky's works a different realism—more radical and democratic in a political sense. In 1861 Dobroliubov died suddenly of tuberculosis; three years later Grigor'ev died. Ostrovsky suddenly lost his two best, most supportive critics, who, despite the contrast in their approaches, each saw the origins of a truly national Russian theater in his plays.

In need of rest, in the spring of 1860 Ostrovsky accompanied the St. Petersburg actor and founder of the Russian realist school of acting, Aleksandr Estaf'evich Martynov (he had played Tikhon in *Groza*), to the south and the Black Sea, where the latter hoped to recover from advanced tuberculosis. During visits to Tula, Voronezh, and Odessa, Ostrovsky enriched his knowledge of actors and provincial theatrical life. Martynov, however, did not survive the trip, and his death in Khar'kov left the "new Russian theater" and Ostrovsky's future plays without one of their most promising performers.

In 1861, the year of the emancipation proclamation that freed the serfs, Ostrovsky wrote two plays—*Za chem poidesh', to i naidesh'* (You Get What You're Looking For) and *Koz'ma Zakhar'ich Minin-Sukhoruk*—opposites in genre, but each reflecting the temper of the times. The first, subtitled *Zhenit'ba Bal'zaminova* (Bal'zaminov's Marriage) and published in *Vremia* in 1861, is the third in the Bal'zaminov trilogy, which describes the attempts of a Zamoskvorech'e clerk and dandy to find himself a millionaire wife. In the first play of the trilogy, *Prazdnichnyi son–do obeda* (A Holiday Dream Comes True by Noon, published in *Sovremennik*, 1857), the hero turns out not to be a rich daughter's "Prince Charming," and her dream does not come true. The genre of the Bal'zaminov plays is slapstick and vaudeville, with a rich, humorous language. In the second play of the trilogy, *Svoi sobaki gryzutsia, chuzhaia ne pristavai!* (Keep Your Dog Out of Our Dogfight! published in *Biblioteka dlia chteniia*, 1861), the hero accidentally reunites the woman he wants to marry with her true love and again fails in his quest. In the third play Bal'zaminov finds himself not one wealthy bride but two, as this Russian version of the comic loser–a descendant of Gogol's Khlestakov from *Revizor*–succeeds at last. *Koz'ma Zakhar'ich Minin-Sukhoruk*, an historical drama in verse, also examined Russian national character, but in the form of a "chronicle play" based on Russian historical documents. Describing the gathering of a resistance force against the invading Poles in the beginning of the sixteenth century, Ostrovsky presents the merchant-hero Minin as a man of conscience and a high sense of duty, able to rouse the people to heroic feats, although they remain impoverished, downtrodden, and dispirited; they are distinctive only in that they bring forth such a national leader.

In the spring of 1862 Ostrovsky followed the example of Tolstoy and Dostoevsky and traveled to Europe, like many "new" Russians of the reform era. He visited the major cultural centers of Germany, Italy, France, and England, and in May 1862, just before returning home, he visited his fellow Muscovite, Herzen, exiled in London. Less political and ideological than Dostoevsky or Grigor'ev, who reacted with nationalistic negativity to European culture, Ostrovsky felt both enthusiasm and disappointment, together with a sharpened perspective on Russian life. By the end of 1862 he had completed *Grekh da beda na kogo ne zhivet* (Who Is Not Visited by Sin and Sorrow, published in *Vremia*, 1863), a play about forceful, dominating, and destructive characters: a planned adultery by Tania, wife of the merchant Krasnov, comes to light, and he murders her in a passionate rage. Krasnov's tragedy seems Dostoevskian, and the death of the deceitful Tania has none of the sublime overtones of Katerina's suicide in *Groza*. Ostrovsky continued his denunciation of the *samodur* in *Tiazhelye dni* (Difficult Days, published in *Sovremennik*, 1863), which joins the merchant family of *V chuzhom piru pokhmel'e* with a lawyer from *Dokhodnoe mesto* in order to plumb the depths of the moral swamp typified by Zamoskvorech'e. In *Shutniki* (Comedians), which Ostrovsky wrote in 1864 and published the same year in *Sovremennik*, a drama of helplessness unfolds in the face of deceit, as experienced by Obroshenov, who plays the fool–like Dostoevsky's Marmeladov or Snegirev–to protect his own pride, ambition, and vulnerability. Finally, bringing the Zamoskvorech'e theme to a close, Ostrovsky wrote *Puchina* in 1865. In this drama, five to seven years separate each act; the play shows how an idealistic student, romantic and filled with noble ambition, marries a Zamoskvorech'e girl and finds himself drawn down into the depths of oppressive reality, as if through the circles of hell.

By the mid 1860s Ostrovsky was the most successful dramatist in Russia: his *Groza* and *Grekh da beda na kogo ne zhivet* each had won the prestigious academic Uvarov Prize in 1860 and 1863 respectively, and later in 1863 he was elected corresponding member of the Academy of Sciences. Nonetheless, he continually came in conflict with the theater censorship throughout the decade. Although published in 1861, *Za chem poidesh', to i naidesh'* premiered only in 1863; published in 1862, *Koz'ma Zakhar'ich Minin-Sukhoruk* premiered only in 1866. Historical plays by other dramatists were being performed, but not Ostrovsky's. His chronicles of the *smutnoe vremia* (Time of Troubles) period in the early sixteenth century were produced finally: *Voevoda (Son na Volge)* was staged in 1865, and both *Dmitrii Samozvanets i Vasilii Shuisky* (Dmitrii the Pretender and Vasilii Shuisky) and *Tushino* were performed in 1867. These plays were produced with such great difficulty, however, that Ostrovsky contemplated abandoning the theater altogether.

In 1867, after the struggle with his historical plays and disappointment at their lukewarm reception, Ostrovsky turned away from original writing and began translating Italian works and reworking French plays; he also composed two librettos. His life had become increasingly complicated by a liaison with the actress Mar'ia Vasil'evna Bakhmet'eva, which had begun in 1863. In 1864 she bore him a son, Aleksandr, then another in 1866, Mikhail. The affair undermined the health of Ostrovsky's common-law wife, Agaf'ia Ivanovna, who fell seriously ill in the fall of 1866 and died in March 1867. Ostrovsky suffered deeply at the loss of the woman who had provided him companionship, support, and friendship throughout his entire career to date–for almost twenty years. Later in 1867 Mar'ia Vasil'evna moved into Ostrovsky's house, where she bore him a daughter, Mariia. In February 1869 Ostrovsky married her and began the process of legitimizing their children.

When *Sovremennik* succumbed to the censorship in 1866, its editor Nekrasov moved to *Otechestvennye zapiski*, where for the next seventeen years Ostrovsky published a play a year, sometimes two. He experienced a creative resurgence in the fall of 1868 and began drafting two contemporary comedies simultaneously. *Na vsiakogo mudretsa dovol'no prostoty* (Even a Wise Man Stumbles, also known as "Diary of a Scoundrel") premiered that year, and *Goriachee serdtse* (A Passionate Heart) was staged in 1869. In *Na vsiakogo mudretsa dovol'no prostoty* Ostrovsky returned to a portrayal of modern life. This work is unusually biting and satirical; it has a scoundrel as hero and not a single positive figure. Its ridiculing of post-Reform agitation coincided with the views of *Otechestvennye zapiski,* and its wit and sarcasm reflected the new popularity of operettas, such as those of Jacques Levy Offenbach. Ostrovsky presented a pantheon of "wise men." Krutitsky, Mamaev, Gorodulin, and Turusina are each foolish in his own way—the natural fool, the social fool, the habitual fool, and the political fool, respectively—and each has recognizable, real-life counterparts. The one intelligent man, Glumov, is a modern Chatsky (Griboedov's hero in *Gore ot uma*), who dupes them all with deceit and treachery, then falls victim to his own cleverness when his diary is published. When it opened at the Malyi Theater in November 1868, *Na vsiakogo mudretsa dovol'no prostoty* elicited such raves from the audience that it stopped the play and demanded the author appear for an ovation.

In each of his next plays, Ostrovsky changed milieus but kept up the same harsh satire of contemporary life. In *Goriachee serdtse* the action moves to the provinces, where three *samodur* types—Kuroslepov, Gradoboev, and Khlynov—appear in farcical roles in order to ridicule the tyranny that clearly remained a contemporary evil in Russian life. A fairy-tale heroine, Parasha, defeats these "dark forces" with her ardent love and courage. Ostrovsky next wrote *Beshennye den'gi* (Crazy Money, also known as "Easy Money," *Otechestvennye zapiski,* 1870), which satirized nascent capitalism in Russia with its "new" practical Russians and their deals, contracts, stocks, and trading. The aristocratic hero, Vasil'kov, who has made a fortune in the new "dark kingdom," is chosen by Lidiia, who is looking for a rich husband to restore her family's fortune. Both value money over love, find themselves deceived by others, and finally recant and reform—although wealth and nobility seem equally degraded in the end. The forces of capitalism move to the provinces in Ostrovsky's *Les* (The Forest, published in *Otechestvennye zapiski* and performed in 1871), which has become the most frequently produced of his plays. The greedy aristocrat and *samodur* Gurmyzhskaia sells her forest in order to cheat her nephew out of his inheritance, and, in an echo of *Vospitannitsa,* she refuses to pay a dowry so her relative Aksiusha can marry. Gurmyzhskaia, however, is cheated by another *samodur,* the lumber merchant Vosmibratov. The appearance of two wandering actors—the tragedian Neshchastlivtsev (Unlucky), who is her nephew, and his friend, the comedian Shchastlivtsev (Lucky)—after numerous deceptions and unmaskings ultimately brings about the happy union of Aksiusha with her beloved, Petr. Filled with contempt for his aunt, the nephew departs, and the aunt ends up marrying the fool Bulanov. Not only is the nobility discredited, but Ostrovsky's earlier "pure" *samodur* has been corrupted by greed. Also in 1871 Ostrovsky's *Ne vse kotu maslenitsa* (Into Each Life a Little Rain Must Fall) premiered. In this play he sounds his farewell to the *samodur:* Akhov represents the last of this despotic, self-indulgent type, now lost without power or wealth, and without anyone to dominate.

By 1872, the twenty-fifth anniversary of the beginning of Ostrovsky's career, his popularity in St. Petersburg had fallen badly. Tsar Alexander II, who much preferred vaudevilles, was bored by *Ne vse kotu maslenitsa* and rejected any thought of rewarding the dramatist with a state pension. Ostrovsky hoped that *Dmitrii Samozvanets i Vasilii Shuisky* at the St. Petersburg Mariinskii Theater would turn into a celebration of his career, but the play drew little interest. In contrast, Moscow and the Malyi Theater continued their enthusiasm for each new play that he wrote. Ostrovsky's anniversary in Moscow was tremendously popular and continued from the theater to the Moskovskii artisticheskii krug (Artists' Circle), to the Sobranie dramaticheskikh pisatelei (Assembly of Dramatists), to the taverns and restaurants, where actors, fellow writers, intellectuals, merchants, and aristocrats celebrated his career.

Since 1863 Ostrovsky had been spending summers at Shchelykovo, which he bought with his brother from their stepmother in 1867. The rural setting of Kostroma province and Ostrovsky's reflections on Russian folk traditions provided material for his *Snegurochka* (The Snowmaiden), a fairy tale that seemed a sudden departure for a playwright of contemporary social topics. Nekrasov refused to publish the play (though it eventually appeared in *Vestnik Evropy* in 1873), and others were puzzled. However, Petr Il'ich Chaikovsky found the verse drama enchanting (he wrote the music for the production, which included opera and ballet troupes), and later Nikolai Andreevich Rimsky-Korsakov based an opera on it. In addition to its powerful evocation of nature and rich folk motifs in a fairy-tale plot and setting, *Snegurochka* includes recognizable Ostrovskian characters among its ancient Slavs (called the Berendeans).

Ostrovsky settled into a pattern in the 1870s. For the theatrical fall season of each year he churned out a new play on the contemporary social topics of money and morality—with the exception of the last of his chronicle plays, *Komik XVII stoletiia* (Comedian of the

Seventeenth Century, 1872; published in *Otechestvennye zapiski,* 1873), in which he expressed ideas about the theater. Among Ostrovsky's plays staged in the 1870s (all of which were published in *Otechestvennye zapiski*) are *Pozdniaia liubov'* (Late Love, performed 1873; published 1874), set in lower-class society, where a debt and promissory note turn into a dowry; *Volki i ovtsy* (Wolves and Sheep, performed 1875; published 1875); *Posledniaia zhertva* (Final Sacrifice, performed 1877; published 1878), where romantic love succumbs to the power of money; and *Bespridannitsa* (performed 1878) in which the heroine is shot by her fiancé. Tastes had changed under the influence of light opera and sentimental melodrama, however, and Ostrovsky's reviewers became increasingly disparaging; they accused him of repeating himself and having exhausted his talent. Nonetheless, he continued his innovations, and several of his plays from the 1870s have survived the test of time.

The complex plot of *Pozdniaia liubov'* concerning financial transactions, debts, I.O.U.s, and deceit exposed the new reality of the urban petit bourgeoisie in Russia at the time. Not only does the play convincingly depict moral deviousness and corruption, but its technical mastery also makes it one of Ostrovsky's best. The vicious capitalism of land dealing, railroad construction, and industrial building provide the material for *Volki i ovtsy,* one of Ostrovsky's comedies popular for its plot, dialogue, and effective comic roles. The "sheep" are the widow Kupavina—"devoured" by the St. Petersburg financier and "wolf" Berkutov—and her friend, the reluctant bachelor Lyniaev. Lyniaev is "snared" by the wolf Glafira, companion of Murzavetskaia, the woman landowner and forger. There is no retribution in this comedy; the wolves are sated in the end, and the immorality of the corrupt landowner survives as an indictment of her class and the times. In *Posledniaia zhertva* Ostrovsky depicts the new businessmen of Moscow who symbolize new, monied aristocracy and European fashion. Pribytkov, a millionaire, tries to save a young widow, Iulia Tugina, who in exchange for promissory notes has given her entire inheritance to the spendthrift Dulchin, whom she loves; the plot to have Dulchin marry Irina (Pribytkov's grandniece) backfires, however, and Pribytkov marries Iulia, while Dulchin is forced to sell himself in marriage to a rich widow, Pivokurova, in order to pay off his debts. The plot of *Bespridannitsa,* like that of *Pozdniaia liubov',* was based on a crime reported in the newspapers: a young woman was murdered by her jealous lover in Kineshma, near Ostrovsky's summer home. The play pursues familiar topics: the heroine, Larisa, and her former lover Piratov are aristocrats, now impoverished and forced to sell themselves in marriage—the frivolous socialite Larisa to a clerk, Karandyshev, and the indigent ship owner Piratov to a rich heiress.

Piratov humiliates his rival and takes Larisa for one last fling, a night on his steamboat, which he must sell in the morning. A complex heroine and no less powerful than Katerina in *Groza,* Larisa refuses to compromise her freedom for the sake of Karandyshev's repulsive petty materialism and forces him to shoot her—a noble spirit escaping bondage to a businessman.

In the fall of 1877 Ostrovsky moved with his family from the dilapidated house in Nikola-Vorob'in to an aristocratic apartment on the Prechistinka (near the soon-to-be-completed Cathedral of Christ the Savior). The new location, together with the growing needs of the family, increased financial pressures on Ostrovsky to write more and more and to have his plays produced. He became a master at avoiding conflicts with the censorship while still addressing topical themes in his work. He also continued translating plays as an additional source of income: from 1850 to 1886 he completed twenty-two translations, leaving another sixteen unfinished. Some of these he published, such as his translation of *The Taming of the Shrew*—published as "Usmirenie svoenravnoi" (1865)—and translations of Italian plays by Carlo Goldoni, Italo Franchi, Teobaldo Cicconi, and Paolo Giocometti, as well as of ten intermezzi by Miguel Cervantes. Ostrovsky also began assisting young playwrights, of whom the most successful was Nikolai Iakovlevich Solov'ev, in whom he hoped to find a successor and with whom he wrote and published four plays from 1877 to 1882. Ostrovsky participated in the Pushkin Jubilee celebrations in Moscow in 1880—the occasion of famous speeches by Turgenev and Dostoevsky. Ostrovsky also spoke to enthusiastic acclaim, but at an evening dinner, not at one of the public sessions.

Ostrovsky began the 1880s with the play *Nevol'nitsy* (Slave Women, 1880), which continued his exposé of the immorality, cupidity, and cruelty hidden beneath a fashionable civilized surface. When the atmosphere suddenly turned reactionary in March 1881 after the assassination of Tsar Alexander II, Ostrovsky suffered financially when the theaters were closed for six months of mourning, and his own reputation was threatened by his loyalty to *Otechestvennye zapiski,* edited since 1878 by Mikhail Evgrafovich Saltykov, who was more radical and less politic than Nekrasov. The playwright was protected, however, by his brother Mikhail, who had risen to high posts in St. Petersburg and was, in 1881, minister of state properties. Mikhail's powerful protection extended to the journal, where Ostrovsky continued publishing yearly until 1884, when it was finally closed. He was forced to find a new journal for his last play, *Ne ot mira sego* (The Otherworldly), which eventually appeared in *Russkaia mysl'* (Russian Thought) in 1885, the same year that the play premiered. Panned by the critics, this play has

A scene from the 1886 Malyi Theater production of Ostrovsky's revised Voevoda (Son na Volge) *(The War Lord [Dream on the Volga]), originally planned as part of a cycle of plays about life on the Volga*

rarely been performed because of its excessively melodramatic plot, in which a sheltered heroine dies because she is spiritually unable to tolerate the materialistic world of her husband. *Krasavets-muzhchina* (A Handsome Man, premiered in 1882; published in *Otchestvennye zapiski,* 1883) was also panned by critics; yet, its scandalous topic helped it succeed. Delving into the topical question of divorce, *Krasavets-muzhchina* included a scene that depicted a wife caught in flagrante delicto (Tolstoy's novel *Anna Karenina* had been published a few years earlier, from 1875 to 1877).

The other two plays published in *Otechestvennye zapiski* after 1881 are among Ostrovsky's most enduring works: *Talanty i poklonniki* (Talents and Admirers, performed 1881; published 1882) and *Bez viny vinovatye* (Guilty Without Fault, 1884). A play about the provincial theater, its actors, and its managers, *Talanty i poklonniki* (also known as Career Woman) treats not only Ostrovsky's central theme of moral choice, dreams, and practical necessity but also adds a new element to the mix: the love of art. The heroine, Negina, rejects the dreams of the poor student, Meluzov, to whom she is engaged, in order to follow a stage career. Staying true to her talent, however, means taking up with Velikatov, a wealthy, pragmatic estate owner with whom she

leaves for Moscow. In this play the rich variety of characters and depiction of provincial theater life prove more interesting than the plot. As popular as *Les,* Ostrovsky's *Bez viny vinovatye*–which was his penultimate play–combines theater life with the topical theme of unwed mothers and illegitimate children in order to make a humane social statement. Jilted by the father of her illegitimate son–who she believes died in foster care–Kruchinina, now a great actress, finds her son again in the person of the actor Neznamov. The complex plot ends with Kruchinina, who is perhaps Ostrovsky's most unselfish, self-sacrificing heroine, rejecting marriage to Murov, her son's father, because she feels sure that the talented Neznamov will find "legitimacy" with her in a successful stage career.

At the outset of the reactionary reign of Alexander III, the government ironically decided upon theater reform and appointed a Commission to Examine the Position of the Theater. Ostrovsky joined this commission in the fall of 1881 and so began his checkered public career in theater administration, which continued until his death. He prepared two extensive memoranda–one on the state of dramatic art in Russia and another on the needs of the Imperial Theaters–which found sympathetic hearings, but his ideas of significant reform went no further. In contrast, his project for a popular, private theater in Moscow unexpectedly received support and was personally approved by Alexander III in 1882. Just as Ostrovsky was arranging funding for the new theater, however, the government approved the establishment of private theaters throughout Russia. In the face of competition from two additional such projects in Moscow, Ostrovsky withdrew his own proposal. Meanwhile, his financial situation worsened, for his plays were being removed from the repertoire. Thanks to his brother, early in 1884 Ostrovsky was awarded a state pension, albeit quite a small one. He finally agreed to take up government service in the Imperial Theater system, and beginning on 1 January 1886 he became director of repertoire for the Moscow Imperial Theaters and administrator of the Theater School.

He did not enjoy this success for long: after several angina attacks brought on by overwork at his new post, he died at his desk in Shchelykovo of heart failure on 2 June 1886. Ostrovsky was buried in the local churchyard of Nikolo-Berezhki with a simple funeral, unlike the popular, ceremonial affairs of Turgenev and Dostoevsky. Plans to move his coffin to Moscow and the Novodevichii monastery were never realized, and his tomb remains near his family home, Shchelykovo.

Aleksandr Nikolaevich Ostrovsky's belief that he had created a Russian national theater is justified: through his plays he built an entire edifice on a foundation provided by Denis Ivanovich Fonvizin, Griboedov, and Gogol. From his own world of everyday, urban, provincial, and most often Muscovite life, he crafted well-made stage equivalents of the "baggy monsters" written by the great Russian Realist novelists. Combining a comedy of manners with critical realism, Ostrovsky created in the process a satirical examination of various Russian classes and lifestyles. Unlike the novelists, however, he avoided "accursed" philosophical or psychological questions; he preferred moral and social values as lived by simple, "purely" Russian characters of a homely sort, whose foibles he observed with common sense and an optimistic faith in basic humanity. A pragmatic man of the theater, Ostrovsky exploited the traditions, conventions, and advantages of the stage through roles that demanded naturalistic acting; he used dialogue rich in slang and jargon, localisms, and racy colloquialisms (all of which defy adequate translation). Unique in style but classical in structure, Ostrovsky's plays produced a school of realistic actors who later formed the Moskovskii Khudozhestvennyi Akademicheskii Teatr (MKhAT, Moscow Art Theater). He likewise profoundly influenced the realism and naturalism of the plays of Anton Pavlovich Chekhov and Maksim Gor'ky. The significance of Ostrovsky's impact and contribution to the evolution of a national drama and theater has been compared to that of Shakespeare and Molière.

Letters:

A. N. Ostrovsky i F. A. Burdin: Neizdannye pis'ma iz sobranii Gosudarstvennogo teatral'nogo muzeia imeni A. A. Bakhrushina, edited by Nikolai Leont'evich Brodsky, Nikolai Pavlovich Kashin, and Aleksei Aleksandrovich Bakhrushin (Moscow: Gosudarstvennoe izdatel'stvo, 1923);

Aleksandr Nikolaevich Ostrovsky, *Dnevniki i pis'ma. Teatr Ostrovskogo,* edited by Vladimir Aleksandrovich Filippov, commentary by Nina P. Kashina and Filippov (Moscow: Academia, 1937);

Ostrovsky, *O teatre: Zapiski, rechi i pis'ma,* edited by Grigorii Ivanovich Vladykin, commentary by Kseniia Dmitrievna Muratova (Leningrad: Iskusstvo, 1941);

"Pis'ma," edited by A. E. Fridenberg, in *Teatral'noe nasledstvo: Soobshcheniia, publikatsii* (Moscow: Iskusstvo, 1956), pp. 299–305;

"Pis'ma," in Ostrovsky's *Polnoe sobranie sochinenii,* edited by Grigorii Ivanovich Vladykin, volumes 11–12 (Moscow: Iskusstvo, 1979–1980).

Bibliographies:

Rukopisi A. N. Ostrovskogo: Katalog, compiled by Nikolai Pavlovich Kashin (Moscow: Gosudarstvennoe sotsial'no-ekonomicheskoe izdatel'stvo, 1939);

Nikolai Aleksandrovich Golubentsev, *A. N. Ostrovsky v portretakh i illiustratsiiakh* (Moscow: Gosudarstvennoe uchebno-pedagogicheskoe izdatel'stvo, 1949);

Bibliografiia literatury ob A. N. Ostrovskom, 1847–1917, compiled by Kseniia Dmitrievna Muratova (Leningrad: Nauka, 1974);

Kate Sealey Rahman, *Ostrovsky: Reality and Illusion* (Birmingham, U.K.: Department of Russian Language and Literature, University of Birmingham, 1999), pp. 232–247.

Biographies:

Aleksandr Nikolaevich Ostrovsky: ego zhizn' i sochineniia: Sbornik istoriko-literaturnykh statei, compiled by Vasilii Ivanovich Pokrovsky (Moscow: Sklad v knizhnom magazine V. Spiridonova i A. Mikhailova, 1912);

Nikolai Dolgov, *A. N. Ostrovsky, Zhizn' i tvorchestvo 1823–1923* (Moscow: Gosudarstvennoe izdatel'stvo, 1923);

Aleksandr Ivanovich Reviakin, *A. N. Ostrovsky: Zhizn' i tvorchestvo* (Moscow: Gosudarstvennoe uchebno-pedagogicheskoe izdatel'stvo, 1949);

Lev Rudol'fovich Kogan, *Letopis' zhizni i tvorchestva A. N. Ostrovskogo* (Moscow: Gosudarstvennoe izdatel'stvo kul'turno-prosvetitel'noi literatury, 1953);

Aleksei Vasil'evich Mironov, *Velikii charodei v strane beren-deev: Ocherk zhizni i tvorchestva A. N. Ostrovskogo v Shchelykove* (Iaroslavl': Verkhne-Volzhskoe knizh-noe izdatel'stvo, 1973);

Marjorie L. Hoover, *Alexander Ostrovsky* (Boston: Twayne, 1981);

Vladimir Iakovlevich Lakshin, *Aleksandr Nikolaevich Ostrov-sky,* Zhizn' v iskusstve (Moscow: Iskusstvo, 1982).

References:

"A. N. Ostrovsky: Novye materialy i issledovaniia," *Lite-raturnoe nasledstvo,* 88 (1974);

Nikolai Sergeevich Ashukin, Sergei Ivanovich Ozhegov, and Vladimir A. Filippov, *Slovar' k p'esam A. N. Ostrovskogo* (Moscow: Vesta, 1993);

Lidiia B. Chernykh, "*Boris Godunov* Pushkina i *Dmitrii Samozvanets i Vasilii Shuisky* Ostrovskogo," *Russkaia literatura: Istoriko-literaturnyi zhurnal,* 16 (1973): 122–133;

Liudmila Sergeevna Danilova and T. V. Moskvina, comps., *A. N. Ostrovsky. Novye issledovaniia: Sbornik statei i soobshchenii* (St. Petersburg: Rossiiskii institut istorii iskusstv, 1998);

Fyodor Dostoevsky, "Zapisnaia knizhka 1860–1862 gg.," in his *Polnoe Sobranie Sochinenii,* 30 volumes, edited by V. G. Bazanov (Leningrad: Nauka, 1972–1988), XX: 154;

Irene Esam, "A Study of the Imagery Associated with Beliefs, Legends and Customs in *Bednost' ne porok,*" *New Zealand Slavonic Journal,* 11 (1973): 102–122;

Apollon Aleksandrovich Grigor'ev, "Russkaia iziashch-naia literatura v 1852 godu," in his *Literaturnaia Kri-tika* (Moscow: Khudozhestvennaia literatura, 1967), p. 61;

Norman Henley, "Ostrovsky's Play-Actors, Puppets and Rebels," *Slavic and East European Journal,* 14 (1970): 317–325;

Andre van Holk, "The Key Scene in Ostrovskij's *The Thunderstorm:* On the Analysis of Modal Profiles," *International Journal of Slavic Linguistics and Poetics,* 31–32 (1985): 481–493;

Holk, "*The Syntax of the Slovo-er:* On the Thematic Compo-sition of A. N. Ostrovskij's 'An Advantageous Job,'" *Russian Linguistics: International Journal for the Study of the Russian Language,* 8 (1984): 215–250;

Ia. V. Ianush, "Russko-ukrainskie iazykovye sviazi v ukrainskoi klassicheskoi dramaturgii kontsa XIX – nachala XX veka," *Russkoe iazykoznanie,* 19 (1989): 78–84;

Albert Kaspin, "Character and Conflict in Ostrovsky's *Talents and Admirers,*" *Slavic and East European Journal,* 8 (1964): 26–36;

Kaspin, "Dostoevsky's Masloboyev and Ostrovsky's Dosuzhev," *American Slavic and East European Review,* 39 (1960): 222–226;

Kaspin, "A Re-Examination of Ostrovsky's Character Lyubim Tortsov," *Studies in Russian and Polish Litera-ture: In honor of Waclaw Lednicki,* edited by Zbigniew Folejewski, Slavistic Printings and Reprintings, no. 27 (The Hague: Mouton, 1962), pp. 185–191;

Kaspin, "A Superfluous Man and an Underground Man in Ostrovskij's *The Poor Bride,*" *Slavic and East Euro-pean Journal,* 6 (1962): 312–321;

Efim Grigor'evich Kholodov, *Iazyk dramy: Ekskurs v tvorcheskuiu laboratoriiu A. N. Ostrovskogo* (Moscow: Iskusstvo, 1978);

Kholodov, *Masterstvo Ostrovskogo* (Moscow: Iskusstvo, 1963);

Kriticheskie kommentarii k sochineniiam A. N. Ostrovskogo: Khro-nologicheskii sbornik kritiko-bibliograficheskikh statei, 5 vol-umes, edited by Vasilii Zelinsky (Moscow: A. G. Kol'chugin, 1894–1897);

Aleksandr Aleksandrovich Lebedev, *Dramaturg pered litsom kritiki: Vokrug A. N. Ostrovskogo i po povodu ego. Idei i temy russkoi kritiki. Ocherki* (Moscow: Iskusstvo, 1974);

Iurii Vladimirovich Lebedev, "O narodnosti *Grozy,* 'russkoi tragedii' A. N. Ostrovskogo," *Russkaia lite-ratura: Istoriko-Literaturnyi Zhurnal,* 1 (1981): 14–31;

L. S. Litvinenko, "Istoricheskaia khronika A. N. Ostrov-skogo 'Koz'ma Zakhar'ich Minin, Sukhoruk' i tra-ditsii russkoi literatury 'Smutnogo vremeni,'" *Russkaia literatura: Istoriko-literaturnyi zhurnal,* 21 (1978): 147–154;

Lidiia Mikhailovna Lotman, *A. N. Ostrovsky i russkaia dramaturgiia ego vremeni* (Leningrad: Akademiia nauk SSSR, 1961);

Richard Arthur Peace, "A. N. Ostrovsky's *The Thunder-storm:* The Dramatization of Conceptual Ambiva-lence," *Modern Language Review,* 84 (1989): 99–110;

Telesfor Pozniak, "Aleksander Ostrowski w Polsce ne przelomie wieku XIX i XX," *Slavica Orientalis,* 15 (1966): 199–214;

Nikita Ivanovich Prutskov, ed., *A. N. Ostrovsky i literaturno-teatral'noe dvizhenie XIX–XX vekov* (Leningrad: Nauka, 1974);

Kate Sealey Rahman, *Ostrovsky: Reality and Illusion* (Bir-mingham, U.K.: Department of Russian Language and Literature, University of Birmingham, 1999);

Aleksandr Ivanovich Reviakin, *Iskusstvo dramaturgii A. N. Ostrovskogo* (Moscow: Prosveshchenie, 1974);

Reviakin, *Moskva v zhizni i tvorchestve A. N. Ostrovskogo* (Moscow: Moskovskii rabochii, 1962);

Reviakin, ed., *A. N. Ostrovsky v vospominaniiakh sovremenni-kov,* Seriia literaturnykh memuarov (Moscow: Gosudarstvennoe izdatel'stvo khudozhestvennaia literatura, 1966);

Vasilii Grigor'evich Sakhnovsky, *Teatr A. N. Ostrovskago* (Moscow: Moskovskoe obshchestvo narodnykh universitetov, 1919);

Sergei Konstantinovich Shambinago, ed., *Tvorchestvo A. N. Ostrovskogo: Iubileinyi sbornik* (Moscow: Gosudarstvennoe izdatel'stvo, 1923);

Abram L'vovich Shtein, *Master russkoi dramy: Etiudy o tvorchestve Ostrovskogo* (Moscow: Sovetskii pisatel', 1973);

G. V. Starostina, "Traditsii drevnerusskoi literatury v komedii A. N. Ostrovskogo *Bednost' ne porok*," *Russkaia literatura: Istoriko-literaturnyi zhurnal*, 2 (1987): 63–75;

Ulrich Steltner, *Die künstlerischen Funktionen der Sprache in den Dramen von A. N. Ostrovskij* (Giessen: Schmitz, 1978);

Steltner, "Zur Evolution des russischen Dramas: Ostrovskij und Čexov," *Die Welt der Slaven: Halbjahresschrift für Slavistik*, 25 (1980): 1–21;

Janice Marion Stinchcomb, "Aleksandr Ostrovskii: Domestic Drama and National Identity," dissertation, University of Texas at Austin, 1997;

B. S. Svartskopf, "O neizdannom *Slovare k p'esam A. N. Ostrovskogo*," *Izvestiia Akademii Nauk S.S.S.R., Seriia Literatury i iazyka*, 32 (1973): 163–171;

S. Vaiman, "Kliuch, vruchennyi Dobroliubovym," *Novyi mir: Literaturno-khudozhestvennyi i obshchestvenno-politicheskii zhurnal*, 1 (1986): 228–239;

Boris Vasil'evich Varneke, ed., *A. N. Ostrovsky, 1823–1923: Sbornik statei* (Odessa: Gosudarstvennoe izdatel'stvo Ukrainy, 1923);

Grigorii Ivanovich Vladykin, ed., *A. N. Ostrovsky v russkoi kritike* (Moscow: Khudozhestvennaia literatura, 1953);

Robert Whittaker, "The Ostrovskii-Grigor'ev Circle, Alias the 'Young Editors of the *Moskvitianin*,'" *Canadian-American Slavic Studies*, 24 (1990): 385–412;

Nataliia Zhuravkina, "Zhenshchina i 'zhenskii vopros' v p'esakh Aleksandra Ostrovskogo," *New Zealand Slavonic Journal* (1997): 175–191;

Anna Ivanovna Zhuravleva, *A. N. Ostrovsky – komediograf* (Moscow: Moskovskii universitet, 1981);

Zhuravleva, *Dramaturgiia A. N. Ostrovskogo* (Moscow: Moskovskii universitet, 1974);

Irene Zohrab, "Problems of Translation: The Plays of A. N. Ostrovsky in English," *Melbourne Slavonic Studies*, 16 (1982): 43–88;

N. Iu. Zotova, "Formal'no bezekvivalentnaia leksika v p'ese A. N. Ostrovskogo *Volki i ovtsy* i ee perevod na angliiskii iazyk," *Vestnik Leningradskogo universiteta. Seriia 2, Istoriia, iazykoznanie, literaturovedenie*, 2 (October 1986): 81–85.

Papers:

Aleksandr Nikolaevich Ostrovsky's papers are held in five locations in the two major cities of the Russian Federation. In Moscow, Ostrovsky's papers are housed at the Russian State Archive of Literature and Art (RGALI), fond 362; at the Russian State Library (RGB, formerly the Lenin Library), fond 216; at the State Literary Museum (GLM), fond 140; and at the A. A. Bakhrushin State Central Theatrical Museum, fond 200. In St. Petersburg, Ostrovsky's papers can be found at the Institute of Russian Literature (IRLI, Pushkin House), fond 218.

Dmitrii Ivanovich Pisarev

(2 October 1840 – 4 July 1868)

Peter C. Pozefsky
College of Wooster

BOOKS: *Sochineniia,* 10 volumes (St. Petersburg: F. Pavlenkov, 1866–1869);

Dve stat'i, as N. P. (Moscow: A. I. Mamontov, 1868);

Sochineniia, 11 volumes (St. Petersburg: F. Pavlenkov, 1870–1872);

Sochineniia. Polnoe sobranie, 6 volumes (St. Petersburg: F. Pavlenkov, 1894; enlarged, 1900; enlarged again, 1909; enlarged again, 1913);

Polnoe sobranie sochinenii i pisem, 12 volumes (Moscow: Nauka, 2000–   ).

Editions and Collections: *Bazarov* (Kazan': Molodye sily, 1918);

Bazarov—Posmotrim! (Moscow & Petrograd: Gosudarstvennoe izdatel'stvo, 1923);

Izbrannye sochineniia, 2 volumes, with an introduction by Vladimir Iakovlevich Kirpotin (Moscow: GIKhL, 1934, 1935);

Mysliashchii proletariat (Moscow: Gospolitizdat, 1944);

Izbrannye filosofskie i obshchestvenno-politicheskie stat'i, with an introduction by Vladimir Semenovich Kruzhkov (Moscow: Gospolitizdat, 1949);

Sochineniia, 4 volumes, with an introduction by Iu. S. Sorokin (Moscow: Khudozhestvennaia literatura, 1955–1956);

Izbrannye proizvedeniia (Leningrad: Khudozhestvennaia literatura, 1968);

Literaturno-kriticheskie stat'i (Minsk: BGU, 1976)—comprises "Bazarov," "Realisty," and "Iz stat'i 'Promakhi nezreloi mysli'";

Literaturnaia kritika, 3 volumes, with an introduction by Sorokin (Leningrad: Khudozhestvennaia literatura, 1981);

D. I. Pisarev ob ateizme, religii i tserkvi, with an introduction by E. I. Rozenberg (Moscow: Mysl', 1984);

Izbrannye pedagogicheskie sochineniia, with an introduction by V. Bol'shakova (Moscow: Pedagogika, 1984);

Nado mechtat'! with an introduction by I. V. Kondakov (Moscow: Sovetskaia Rossiia, 1987);

Razrushenie estetiki: Izbrannye literaturnye stat'i (Moscow: Sovremennik, 1989);

Dmitrii Ivanovich Pisarev (engraving by I. N. Kramskoi; from Liudmila Danilovna Mikitich, Literaturnyi Peterburg, *Petrograd, 1991)*

Istoricheskie eskizy: Izbrannye stat'i, with an introduction and commentary by A. I. Volodin (Moscow: Pravda, 1989).

Editions in English: *Selected Philosophical, Social, and Political Essays* (Moscow: Foreign Languages Publishing House, 1958), pp. 43–55;

"The Struggle for Life," in *Crime and Punishment and the Critics,* edited by Edward Wasiolek (Belmont, Cal.: Wadsworth, 1961), pp. 134–141;

Excerpts from "Plato's Idealism," "Nineteenth Century Scholasticism," "The Realists," "Thinking Proletariat," in *Russian Philosophy,* volume 2, edited by James M. Edie, James P. Scanlan, and Mary Barbara Zeldin (Chicago: Quadrangle, 1965), pp. 66–108;

"Bazarov," translated by Lydia Hooke, in *Fathers and Sons,* by Ivan Sergeevich Turgenev, translated and edited by Ralph E. Matlaw (New York & London: Norton, 1966), pp. 195–217;

"'Three Deaths': A Story by Count L. N. Tolstoi," translated by Edmund Yarwood, *Russian Literature Triquarterly,* 11 (1975): 186–194;

"Pushkin and Belinsky: Eugene Onegin," in *Russian Views of Pushkin's Eugene Onegin,* edited by Sona Stephan Hoisington (Bloomington: Indiana University Press, 1988), pp. 43–55.

OTHER: "Mysl' Firkhova o vospitanii zhenshchin," in *O vospitanii zhenshchin, soobrazno ee prizvaniiu,* by Rudol'f Virkhov (Moscow: A. & F. Ushakovy, 1865);

"Dnevnik. 1850–1855," in *D. I. Pisarev,* by E. P. Kazanovich (Petrograd: Nauka i Shkola, 1922), pp. 139–191;

"Orden gory. (Son)," edited by Kazanovich, in *Sbornik Pushkinskogo doma* (Petrograd: Gosizdat, 1922), pp. 233–244;

"Perevody iz Geine," translated by Pisarev, edited by L. Speranskii, *Zapiski Otdela Rukopisei Vsesoiuznaia biblioteka imeni V. I. Lenina,* 9 (1940): 50–78;

"Ob"iasnenie.–['Katkoviada']," edited by F. F. Kuznetsov, in *Iz istorii russkoi zhurnalistiki. Stat'i i materialy,* by Aleksandr Vasil'evich Zapadov (Moscow: Moscow University Press, 1959), pp. 222–230; republished as "Dve stat'i Pisareva," in Kuznetsov's *Krug D. I. Pisareva* (Moscow: Khudozhestvennaia literatura, 1990).

SELECTED PERIODICAL PUBLICATIONS–UNCOLLECTED: "Stikhotvorenie na otkrytie pamiatnika Nikolaiu I," edited by B. P. Koz'min, *Krasnyi arkhiv,* 3 (1928): 228–231;

"Didro i ego vremia," edited by E. P. Kazanovich, *Zven'ia,* 4 (1936): 649–700;

"Nameki prirody. Per. C angl. A. Slavtsovoi. Vyp. 1. 1861," edited by E. Rozenberg, *Russkaia literatura,* 2 (1959): 210–218;

"Neopublikovannye zametki Pisareva 'O zhitii igumena Daniila,'" *Trudy Novosibirskogo pedagogicheskogo instituta,* 3 (1962).

Dmitrii Pisarev's literary voice was recognizable for its fluidity, extreme pronouncements, and absurd paradoxes. In iconoclastic essays on themes ranging from student life to anatomy, education, European history, Charles Darwin, and Aleksandr Sergeevich Pushkin to the novels of Fyodor Dostoevsky, Ivan Sergeevich Turgenev, and Leo Tolstoy, he set the agenda for the literary and political polemics of his day. Nonetheless, Pisarev's thought remained influential well into the first decades of the twentieth century. His name occupied an important place in both prerevolutionary and Soviet histories of the radical intelligentsia, social thought, and literary criticism. Several late-twentieth-century Russian-language biographies of Pisarev and the appearance of the first volume of a new collection of his complete writings and letters testify to continued interest in his life and work. Intellectually, Pisarev is most closely associated with nihilism, an extreme form of radicalism of the 1860s. Along with Nikolai Gavrilovich Chernyshevsky and Nikolai Aleksandrovich Dobroliubov, he is considered one of the leading critics of that decade, critical for its contribution to Russian literature and social thought.

Dmitrii Ivanovich Pisarev, the oldest child of Ivan Ivanovich Pisarev and Varvara Dmitrievna (Danilova) Pisareva, was born on 2 October 1840 at Znamenskoe, his father's rural estate in Orel province. The Pisarevs were from an old noble family of modest means. Ivan Ivanovich, like his father before him, had led a short and undistinguished career in the military before retiring to the country. As a landlord he was neither diligent nor talented, and in 1850 he was compelled by debt to sell Znamenskoe and move his family to Grunets, a small estate in Tula province. In spite of their financial troubles the Pisarevs invested much in their only son's education. He was taught by foreign tutors and governesses to speak several languages, to dance, and to conduct himself appropriately in polite society. Although Pisarev was trained to be a gentleman, his parents clearly knew that their son would not be able to support himself in the manner of a gentleman or live in leisure on the income from his estates. Consequently, at the age of eleven, with the financial assistance of a wealthy uncle, he was sent to St. Petersburg to study with the expectation that he would one day enter the diplomatic corps, the most prestigious arm of the civil service.

Pisarev proved to be an outstanding student, with a gift for writing and for foreign languages. He spoke French and German with near-native fluency and excelled in Greek and Latin. In 1856 he graduated second in his class from the Third Petersburg Gymnasium. Later that year he entered the historical-philological faculty at St. Petersburg University, where he impressed his professors and fellow students with his capacity for work and his talent for languages. He found the curriculum tedious, however, and succumbed to several distractions. Some of these distractions were related to the cultural excitement surrounding the thaw that followed the death of the conservative Tsar Nicholas I and preceded the Great Reforms of Russia. In the late 1850s, as the educated public steeped itself in European philosophic and scientific literature, Pisarev read widely, including the works of French enlighteners and socialists, English political economists, and German materialists. Like many of his contemporaries he was inspired by European ideas to question religion and conventional morality and to critique established social hierarchies. He participated in student organizations and on occasion in protests against the university administration.

But Pisarev was not yet a radical. His quarrels with older relatives and his progressive convictions were typical of educated youth at this time; his behavior was dictated more by fashion than by ideology or commitment. During his first years at the university his intimate circle consisted not of activists but of young men from good families—serious students who were engaged in literature and scholarship and who spent their free time at cards, drinking, and billiards. Moreover, as a result of family connections, they were welcomed in fashionable literary salons. Through his acquaintance with Leonid Nikolaevich Maikov, a member of an eminent family that included painters and poets, Pisarev made his first contacts with leading writers, including the novelists Aleksei Feofilaktovich Pisemsky and Ivan Aleksandrovich Goncharov.

In 1859, while still a student, Pisarev began his own literary career by writing a bibliographic column for *Rassvet* (Dawn), a journal for young women. His first articles were critical analyses of novels by Goncharov, Turgenev, and Tolstoy. Pisarev's own parents frowned on his new professional activities. While they understood that journalism provided him with a desperately needed income, they considered literary pursuits unworthy of a nobleman. Pisarev was also diverted from his studies by his feelings for Raisa Aleksandrovna Koroneva. Koroneva, an orphaned first cousin, had been raised by the Pisarevs. She was bright, independent, and energetic and had her own literary aspirations. In childhood the two had planned to marry. While Pisarev studied in St. Petersburg, Koroneva remained with his family at Grunets. Pisarev's mother, however, hoping for a more financially advantageous match for her son, did her best to separate him from Koroneva, while Koroneva herself alternately encouraged and rebuffed his advances. Over several years, periods of formal engagement alternated with periods of estrangement as Koroneva's intentions changed. This complex relationship alienated Pisarev from his parents and tormented him emotionally.

The combination of romantic frustration and parental disapproval to some measure explains the psychological turmoil that Pisarev experienced during his university years. This turmoil culminated in late 1859, when, struggling with depression and paranoia, he sustained a breakdown. In December he was committed by the rector of his university to F. A. Shtein's psychiatric hospital in St. Petersburg, where he suffered from "melancholia" and delusions, attempted suicide several times, and lost all track of time (he perceived his four months in the asylum as a single day). In April 1860 he escaped to Grunets, where he worked diligently in spite of his illness, translating in early summer close to a hundred works by German Romantic poets. In addition he completed a lengthy essay on the fiction of another female cousin, Mariia Aleksandrovna Markovich; under the pen name Marko Vovchok she had established a national reputation for herself with tales that used Ukrainian and Russian folk themes. By the end of the summer Pisarev had reconciled with his mother, resumed his engagement with Koroneva, and recovered his health. He felt in good spirits and was ready to resume his education.

Establishing himself once again in St. Petersburg, Pisarev set to work on a dissertation on the Hellenic mystic Apollonius Tyanus for which, in January 1861, he earned the degree of Candidate and was awarded a silver medal. That fall he abandoned his socially respectable friends to live with student radicals. In addition, dissatisfied with *Rassvet* and its limited readership, Pisarev made overtures to other journals. In October 1860, still a literary unknown, he met Grigorii Evlampevich Blagosvetlov, the editor of *Russkoe slovo* (The Russian Word), the newest of the progressive *tolstye zhurnaly* (thick journals). A prominent Russian radical with a liberal European philosophy, Blagosvetlov had a well-defined worldview that he promoted among his colleagues. He saw individuals as the primary force in history and ignorance as the greatest obstacle to social progress. Russians, from his perspective, needed desperately to acquire a knowledge of European science, politics, and philosophy. Blagosvetlov, however, was less notable for his thought than for his strong abilities as an organizer. He was a founder of Zemlia i volia (Land and Liberty), one of the first underground revolutionary organizations in Russia, and by the early 1860s he had turned the fledgling *Russkoe slovo* into a serious rival of *Sovremennik* (The Contemporary), the leading radical journal of the day.

On his first meeting with Blagosvetlov, Pisarev appears to have made a positive but unremarkable impression. Blagosvetlov commissioned a single book review and a translation of Heinrich Heine's epic poem *Atta Troll* (1847). He quickly recognized Pisarev's gift for the lucid exposition of ideas, however, and for establishing intimate connections with young readers. Blagosvetlov soon became Pisarev's intellectual mentor and confidant. By the spring of 1861 Pisarev was publishing articles in *Russkoe slovo* on a variety of themes, including literature, science, and philosophy. By that fall he had established himself as the most recognizable voice of the journal, Blagosvetlov's chief assistant, and a prominent literary figure in his own right.

Pisarev's writings of 1861 demonstrate two theoretical preoccupations, *osvobozhdenie lichnosti* (the emancipation of personality) and *razumnyi egoizm* (rational egoism). These concepts complemented Blagosvetlov's interest in individualism and enlightenment. Unlike Chernyshevsky and Dobroliubov, the leading writers at *Sovremennik*, Pisarev's immediate concern was the cultivation of a class of physically healthy, critically thinking intellectuals, rather than social questions such as the plight of the poor. His emphasis, however, was based on the belief that the members of this intellectual elite—once they educated themselves and began the process of emancipating themselves from the social mainstream—would dedicate their lives to addressing the problems of the socially oppressed.

In Pisarev's writings the emancipation of personality and rational egoism are closely connected to questions of both aesthetics and science. He believes that the biggest obstacle to the development of free and healthy individuals is aesthetics, by which term he refers alternately to ideal standards of beauty and to widely accepted social norms. In his interpretation the reigning aesthetic standards—the product of religion, tradition, and philosophy—are expressed most strongly in art and literature. He perceives these aesthetic standards (ideal notions of beauty) to be in perpetual conflict with the physiological instincts and impulses that are healthy manifestations of natural human inclinations. Typically, parents and teachers serve as agents of society, repressing these inclinations in the young in order to foster proper social appearance, itself a form of aesthetics. As a result of this pernicious tutelage, children learn how to behave "respectably" as adults but in the process are robbed of their health, happiness, and individuality.

The first step in the "emancipation of personality" from these real but invisible fetters is an understanding of the operations of aesthetics and its idealist foundations. The second step is the establishment of an alternative, materialist code of conduct that will enable enlightened individuals to critique and thereby overcome social convention. Pisarev refers to this code, which was adapted from Chernyshevsky's 1860 essay "Antropologicheskii printsip v filosofii" (The Anthropological Principle in Philosophy), as "rational egoism." While his philosophy was highly individualistic and to some extent epicurean, it was not, as many of his rivals complained, hedonist. In his writings Pisarev does not reject social institutions such as marriage or monogamy per se but calls upon his readers to subject these institutions to critical scrutiny and contest the idea that they require either instinctual renunciation or self-sacrifice. Likewise, he does not see "rational egoism" as justification for the pursuit of riches or sensual pleasures for their own sake. In his view, reason mitigates against wanton or selfish behavior, just as it frequently calls for defiance of the social conventions that deny physiological imperatives. At the foundation of "rational egoism" is respect for impulse, physical health, and individuality, as well as the call for a system of conduct based not on antiquated ideals or social custom but on a utilitarian calculus of pain and pleasure.

From 1861 to 1862 Pisarev articulated these concepts in essays on themes ranging from the popularization of European science and philosophy to contemporary Russian literature. His popular scientific articles for *Russkoe slovo*, such as "Fiziologicheskie eskizy Moleshota" (Moleschott's Physiological Sketches, 1861), "Protsess zhizni" (The Processes of Life, 1861), and "Fiziologicheskie kartiny" (Physiological Pictures, 1862), introduced Russian readers to the work of the European materialists Ludwig Büchner, Jacob Moleschott, and Carl Vogt, while allowing Pisarev the opportunity to illustrate the "medical" dimension of rational egoism and the emancipation of personality. Through descriptions of the central nervous circulatory, respiratory, and digestive systems, Pisarev points to what he perceives as the biological and chemical sources of human happiness, calling attention to the social obstacles that make the achievement of lasting happiness unlikely. His philosophical essays, which include "Idealizm Platona" (Plato's Idealism, 1861) and "Skholastika XIX veka" (Nineteenth-Century Scholastics, 1861), both first published in *Russkoe slovo*, expose what he regards as the weakness of contemporary idealist philosophy, as well as its close relationship to religion and superstition. These two essays, perhaps the most iconoclastic of Pisarev's writings, also define the contours of a radical worldview based on social criticism and physiological materialism as well as the rejection of aesthetic conventions and the patriarchal family.

In his literary criticism of the same period Pisarev reviewed works of fiction by the most eminent authors of Russia, making efforts to demonstrate why this extreme iconoclasm was necessary. Through the analysis of contemporary fiction, he attempts to show in an empirical manner how Russian parents impose aesthetics on their offspring and, in so doing, crush their children's individuality and destroy their health. Essays such as "Stoiachaia voda" (Still Water, 1861), "Pisemsky, Turgenev, and Goncharov" (1861), and "Zhenskie tipy" (Female Types, 1861), all published initially in *Russkoe slovo*, present literary heroes such as Turgenev's Rudin and Goncharov's Oblomov as victims of overzealous parents and teachers, who, in training their children to conduct themselves properly, attenuate the physiological mechanisms that facilitate thought, feeling, and action. If as adults Rudin and Oblomov, well-educated men of high birth with good intentions, fail to manage successfully their personal affairs, to satisfy their social obligations, or to consummate their romantic relations, then the cause is injuries sustained in childhood. In imposing their own ideals and values, Pisarev argues, parents and teachers unknowingly ravage their children's central nervous systems.

Pisarev's most famous work during this time and perhaps of his entire career was "Bazarov" (*Russkoe slovo*, 1862), a review of Turgenev's *Ottsy i deti* (Fathers and Children, 1862). Turgenev's novel describes social conditions in rural Russia on the eve of the emancipation of the serfs and the conflict between two generations of the intelligentsia. The action centers on an enigmatic representative of the people of the 1860s, Evgenii Bazarov, a medical student who, because of his princely arrogance, crude manners, and lack of respect for traditional social ideals and institutions, is referred to as a "nihilist." Bazarov is invited to spend the summer on the country estate of his gentry friend, Arkadii Kirsanov. His hosts, Arkadii's father and uncle, are two representatives of the generation of the 1840s. Bazarov passes the time arguing with them over essential Russian values and pursuing his own scientific research, most notoriously his dissection of frogs.

Because of its clear depiction of the antagonism between old and young, *Ottsy i deti* divided readers and critics along generational lines. Older critics tended to emphasize either the accuracy of the negative portrayal of radicalism or, alternatively, the inaccuracy of an overly critical depiction of the liberal older generation. Young radicals saw Turgenev's representation of a nihilist as an insidious attack on their movement. They disliked the label "nihilist" and were particularly displeased by Bazarov's crude manners, his open acknowledgement of the sexual dimension of romantic love, his simplistic negation of art, and his apparent disdain for the peasantry. In this interpretation, most forcefully expressed by Maksim Alekseevich Antonovich (in his 1862 contribution to *Sovremennik,* where he had succeeded the late Dobroliubov as literary critic), Bazarov was a boor and ignoramus "who poisons everything he touches." In contrast, Pisarev regarded Turgenev as a "true artist" and viewed Turgenev's creation as an authentic depiction of Russian reality. Moreover, he saw his own reflection in the flawed protagonist of the novel and identified with Bazarov's weaknesses as well as his strengths.

While Pisarev did not find Turgenev's picture inaccurate, however, he did find it incomplete. As a representative of the older generation, Turgenev could see but not understand his young hero. In his novel he tactfully refrains from approaching emotions and aspirations that he has never experienced and therefore cannot comprehend. According to Pisarev, *Ottsy i deti* did not attack the young generation but posed the questions "Who are you as people?" and "Why do you behave the way you do?"—questions that Pisarev was eager to answer. In doing so in "Bazarov," he accepts the term "nihilist" as an unfortunate but appropriate label for a cohort of young men and women committed to uncompromising criticism of the status quo. He explains Bazarov's unorthodox conduct in order to defend it from critics of all camps.

As he shows in his essay, Pisarev admires Bazarov's scientific worldview and intellectual independence and believes that his behavior is largely the result of his physiology. As Bazarov explains in the novel, "I adhere to the negating direction . . . by virtue of sensation. I find it pleasing to negate, my brain is constructed in this fashion—and *basta* [enough said]!" Bazarov hopes that his own research on the anatomy of frogs will one day confirm his understanding of the close relationship between neurology and psychology. Another source of Bazarov's apparently unpleasant conduct is his awkward social position. Pisarev suggests that Turgenev's character is not by nature envious or malicious. Possessing new ideas in a society that is not ready for them, Bazarov is faced with a difficult choice. He can either conceal his views or accept that they make others uncomfortable. He chooses the latter course of action, not to give offense but to maintain his integrity.

Pisarev's interpretation of *Ottsy i deti* stood out among other interpretations, in that it warned readers that the antagonisms Turgenev describes in his novel are not as straightforward as they might superficially appear. In "Bazarov" Pisarev points not to the clear division between two generations of intellectuals but to these intellectuals' affinities as *lishnie liudi* (superfluous men). He also emphasizes the disconcerting ambiguities in their relationships to each other and to educated society. Because of its probing exploration of the place of the critically engaged intellectual in society and of the relationship between literature and reality, "Bazarov" came to occupy an important position not only in contemporary polemic but also in the history of Russian social thought and literary criticism.

In his essays of 1861 to 1862 Pisarev drew on many sources, including his broad reading in European thought and Russian literature. But these writings were also derived from his cohorts' experiences as students during the political awakening of the late 1850s and from the works of Chernyshevsky, the leading radical thinker of the day and the editor of *Sovremennik*. While Pisarev was particularly taken by Chernyshevsky's

Feuerbachian materialism, mechanist psychology, and utilitarian ethics, his work diverged from that of Chernyshevsky in important respects. In his writings of this period Pisarev does not entirely subscribe to Chernyshevsky's radical aesthetics, with its subordination of art to more "serious" intellectual concerns; he even chastises Bazarov for taking a philistine approach to poetry. Pisarev saw the best art as a form of materialism in no way inferior to science and, like science, a tool for exploring social questions. In addition, he lacked faith in the revolutionary potential of the peasantry and was not explicitly interested in the questions of social reform and political economy that preoccupied Chernyshevsky. Pisarev's writing focuses less on the welfare of the Russian people as a whole and more on the identity of an educated elite, the group that liberals and conservatives called nihilists and that he later referred to as "realisty" (realists), "mysliashchii proletariat" (the thinking proletariat), or, after Chernyshevsky, "novye liudi" (the new people).

In spite of these differences Chernyshevsky himself must have been impressed by Pisarev. In his revolutionary 1863 novel *Chto delat'?* (What Is To Be Done?) Chernyshevsky explores the question of the identity of the young radicals that Pisarev had raised in "Bazarov." And, following Dobroliubov's death in November 1861, he invited Pisarev to write literary criticism for *Sovremennik*. Pisarev respectfully declined, in part from loyalty to Blagosvetlov and in part to protect the independence that he enjoyed at *Russkoe slovo*.

Between March and May of 1862 Pisarev published almost three hundred pages in *Russkoe slovo* and received considerable attention from journalist rivals on the left and right. The conservative critic Nikolai Nikolaevich Strakhov described him as the most progressive and vital of radical writers, more honest and less dogmatic than either Chernyshevsky or Dobroliubov. Strakhov also ascribed different goals to Pisarev and Chernyshevsky. He saw Chernyshevsky as a builder who sought to construct a new social order and Pisarev as a "saboteur" who hoped to shatter all established ideals and moral conventions. Thus, at the age of twenty-one, Pisarev achieved a measure of fame and prominence.

During those same months, however, Pisarev suffered a series of personal setbacks. In March of 1862 Koroneva announced that she was breaking off their engagement once and for all, and in April 1862 she married Evgenii Gardner. An enraged Pisarev challenged his rival to a duel. Gardner refused; instead, he forced himself into Pisarev's apartment and struck him in the face with a whip. When Gardner declined a second challenge, Pisarev sought revenge. Disguised in a false beard and wearing a coachman's shawl, he

Paper cover for the women's journal Rassvet *(Dawn), to which Pisarev contributed regularly while a student at St. Petersburg University in the late 1850s (from Pisarev,* Literaturnaia kritika, *1981)*

accosted Gardner on the platform of a crowded Petersburg railway station and returned the private blows in public. Subsuquently, the two were detained by the police for disturbing the peace and creating a public disorder. A legal dispute ensued, which ended only when Pisarev promised to leave the newlyweds in peace.

A flurry of radical activity took place in the Russian capital during the winter and spring of 1861–1862, particularly among students. In December, following a series of public demonstrations and the widespread circulation of radical manifestos, the authorities closed St. Petersburg University. In May devastating fires raged in various parts of St. Petersburg. These fires coincided with the appearance of "Molodaia Rossiia" (Young Russia), the latest and most menacing of the manifestos. The public was terrified. Although they lacked evidence, officials at the Ministry of Internal Affairs suspected that the manifestos, student demonstrations, and fires had been orchestrated with the assistance of radical journalists. In response the authorities closed *Sovremennik* and *Russkoe slovo* for a period of eight months. Pisarev was left in despair, without work or income. On 2 July he was placed under arrest in the Peter-Paul Fortress. Chernyshevsky was arrested several days later.

Pisarev was accused of writing an incendiary pamphlet of his own. The pamphlet in question, "O broshiure Shedo-Ferroti" (About Shedo-Ferroti's Brochure), begins with the condemnation of a quasi-official publication attacking Alexander Herzen (Aleksandr Ivanovich Gertsen), the leading Russian socialist thinker. The publication was written by an agent of the Russian government who employed the pseudonym Shedo-Ferroti. "O broshiure Shedo-Ferroti," however, goes beyond a criticism of Shedo-Ferroti and his bureaucratic patrons. It proclaims the "successful overthrow of the reigning Romanov dynasty and the transformation of the political and social structure . . . the only aim and hope of all honest citizens of Russia." For several weeks Pisarev denied any association with the pamphlet, but the evidence against him proved incontrovertible. A typesetter had denounced the pamphlet's publisher, Pisarev's friend Peter Ballod, and under interrogation Ballod had named Pisarev as its author.

The pamphlet was uncharacteristic of Pisarev's thought before or after its publication. He pleaded to investigators that he wrote in despair as a consequence of the financial and romantic setbacks of the previous month. Given the lack of additional evidence linking Pisarev to explicitly revolutionary activities, scholars have generally agreed with his assertion. The prosecutors, however, were not convinced. The affair was turned over to the Senate, which took years to deliberate while Pisarev waited in prison. In November 1864, having already served twenty-eight months, he was sentenced to an additional two years and eight months of imprisonment. Prison, however, did not put an end to Pisarev's career. In April 1863 he was allowed to receive regular visits from his mother, and several months later, as the sole supporter of his gentry family, he was granted permission by the St. Petersburg governor-general to receive books and paper from Blagosvetlov and to publish once again in the newly reopened *Russkoe slovo*. Almost immediately Pisarev began to write. He joined Nikolai Vasil'evich Sokolov and Varfolemei Aleksandrovich Zaitsev, two of his fellow editors, in a vitriolic dispute with *Sovremennik*. The quarrel, christened "Raskol v nigilistakh" (The Schism Among the Nihilists) by Dostoevsky, was followed closely by journalists of the right and center, who were delighted at the dissension within the radical camp.

The dispute began with the disagreement over *Ottsy i deti*. Writers at *Sovremennik* were offended by Pisarev's eager acceptance of the label "nihilist" and of Turgenev's hero as an accurate representation of a rad-

ical. They viewed Bazarov as a mean-spirited parody of their recently deceased colleague, Dobroliubov. While Chernyshevsky was editor of *Sovremennik*, *Russkoe slovo* willingly followed the lead of the rival journal. His absence (Chernyshevsky was still in prison) provided Pisarev and his colleagues with an opportunity to assert their own claims of leadership within the radical community. Pisarev was particularly critical of the person who replaced Chernyshevsky as editor–the satirist Mikhail Evgrafovich Saltykov, whose radicalism, Pisarev felt, was diluted by pragmatism and whose connections to the upper echelons of the civil service made him politically suspect.

In "Motivy russkoi dramy" (Motifs of Russian Drama, published in *Russkoe slovo*, 1864), Pisarev continues his assault on *Sovremennik*. He uses a review of Aleksandr Nikolaevich Ostrovsky's 1859 drama *Groza* (The Storm) to distinguish his own critical realism from the late Dobroliubov's Populism. Ostrovsky's heroine, Katerina, is a simple young woman who lives deep in the provinces as the virtual prisoner of a despotic mother-in-law. Katerina's good-natured but ineffectual husband is unable to protect her. She tries to escape her unbearable predicament–first through fantasy, then through adultery. When both fail, she commits suicide by drowning herself in the Volga River. Dobroliubov, in his 1860 essay "Luch sveta v temnom tsarstve" (A Ray of Light in the Dark Kingdom, published in *Sovremennik*), presents Katerina as a symbol of the heroic capacities of the Russian people. He sees in her passionate pursuit of a better life evidence of the innately progressive spirit of the common people. In Katerina's passion Dobroliubov finds hope for the future of his country. Pisarev, however, considered Dobroliubov's optimism misplaced. As seen in "Motivy russkoi dramy," he does not believe that passion alone can help the oppressed to rise above ignorance and oppression. Liberation requires the cultivation of the intellect and, first and foremost, knowledge of the natural sciences–which, for Pisarev, is the core of an enlightened worldview. He places his own faith not in the common people but in those young people who are already preparing themselves through their education for the task of bettering the lot of the poor.

In "Nereshennyi vopros" (An Unanswered Question), written for *Russkoe slovo* late in 1864 and published the same year, Pisarev establishes his own theory of realism–a variation of the realism espoused by Chernyshevsky and European materialists–which seeks to provide an informal curriculum for those of his readers who aspire to educate themselves and to advance society in this way. Once again, Turgenev's Bazarov serves as Pisarev's model. Pisarev had intended to call his essay "Realisty" (Realists), and he included a dedication to his mother–his best friend and link to the world out-side. A typesetter's error removed the dedication, how-ever, and left the subheading, "Nereshennyi vopros," as the title (the original title and dedication were restored in published collections of Pisarev's work). For Pisarev, the question left "unanswered" by *Ottsy i deti* is how the Bazarov types should live when circumstances conspire to render their actions superfluous.

This essay was addressed not to philosophers or even to Pisarev's literary rivals, but instead to young readers. It does not deal with the question of how to live in a particularly abstract or theoretical fashion. Rather, it explores matters of daily life, of "love, knowl-edge and work," in a concrete, prescriptive manner. According to Pisarev, Russians have two problems: they are "bednye" (poor) and they are "glupye" (stu-pid). Both problems could be solved if the section of society that was stupid but not poor would employ its economic and intellectual resources to develop the wealth and culture of the country. Pisarev's "critically thinking realists" aspired to achieve this ideal through socially constructive work. In his view, this aspiration—so deeply ingrained that it requires no altruism or self-sacrifice—distinguishes them (the realists) from pre-vious generations of Russian intellectuals, whose intro-spection often led to inactivity.

The realists' first task is to educate themselves. To this end, Pisarev discusses the European writers whose works he considers worth reading (they include Johann Wolfgang von Goethe, Heine, and Nikolai Vasil'evich Gogol) and enumerates their various strengths and weaknesses. Even poetry has some merit, although Pisarev advises those poets and writers who are not fully engaged in the task of popular enlightenment to abandon their craft in order to "sew boots" or "bake pies." More important, he advises his readers to study European science and to purchase scientific equipment so that they can conduct their own experiments (in the manner of Bazarov's dissections). Pisarev counsels his readers not to abandon themselves to misplaced ideal-ism or foolish heroism. In particular, he warns them against running off to villages to instruct the common people. For the time being, realists have to "economize their mental forces"–to employ their abilities in the most efficient and meaningful manner possible.

Some of the most impassioned pages of "Realisty" are directed toward the conduct of realists in their per-sonal lives. To the analysis of unreciprocated love found in "Bazarov," "Realisty" adds a prescription for the proper conduct of romance. The essay offers descriptions of social dilemmas and advice for their res-olution, outlining standards of etiquette to guide the thinking realist in a variety of situations. For example, a chapter on the protocol of romance provides the infor-mation that Pisarev believes men need to know to con-duct satisfying relations with women. It begins with a description of the position of women in society and advice on issues such as when to offer them compli-ments. The section ends by suggesting plans for women's liberation. Women, Pisarev observes, have the same intellectual and physical capacities as men, but social practice has kept them in a state of economic ser-vitude, while a preoccupation with the trivial, including household chores, society balls, and shopping, has reduced them to mental dependence. At a critical junc-ture in a woman's life, however, she can be pushed in the right direction. The guidance of a good book or an intelligent man can "immunize" her against the childish attitudes typical of females. Pisarev regrets the sad social fact that the vast majority of women spend their entire lives without experiencing the personal satisfac-tion of practical knowledge and useful work. Realists believed in the obligation of men to educate their part-ners; their romantic relationships were ideally based on a mutual interest in work. For Pisarev, love and work were inseparable.

In *Ottsy i deti* Bazarov was able to find work but not love. Pisarev was moved by Bazarov's tragic loneli-ness, a loneliness that was a result partly of his nature and partly of his worldview. In "Realisty" he dwells at length on Bazarov's courtship of Ekaterina Odintsova, a beautiful widow with progressive views, who initially welcomes Bazarov's advances but later rejects them. Pisarev observes that Bazarov and Odintsova are com-patible both intellectually and physically. All of the "ingredients" of love appear to be present. As Pisarev explains, they do not they fall in love because Bazarov has chosen his own path in life; since he does not couch his romantic feelings in the customary forms, Odintsova can neither understand nor appreciate them. Whereas Pisarev's first essay on *Ottsy i deti* attributed Odintsova's ultimate rejection of Bazarov to the calculation of per-sonal interests, his second essay explains this rejection with reference to "aesthetics." Pisarev adds, "The reader probably thinks that aesthetics is my nightmare, and, in this case, the reader is not mistaken."

In his subsequent work Pisarev continued to develop his theory of realism. His 1865 essay "Novyi tip" (A New Type, published first in *Russkoe slovo;* republished as "Mysliashchii proletariat" [Thinking Proletariat] in editions of Pisarev's collected works), a laudatory review of *Chto delat'?* characterizes Cherny-shevsky's heroes as examples of the emergent Bazarov-type and uses these heroes' lives to continue modeling the appropriate conduct of thinking realists. In other arti-cles of the same period Pisarev examines the relation-ship between realism and aesthetics, his "nightmare," in increasingly antagonistic terms.

Pisarev's rival Antonovich, in an article titled "Sovremennaia esteticheskaia teoriia" (Contemporary Aesthetic Theory, published in *Sovremennik*, 1865), commemorated the publication of a second edition of Chernyshevsky's dissertation "Esteticheskie otnosheniia iskusstva k deistvitel'nosti" (The Aesthetic Relations of Art to Reality, 1853), which had taken the form of a manifesto for a new materialist aesthetics. In the article Antonovich defends Chernyshevsky's assertion that life is superior to the ideal and, therefore, to art, while reaffirming Chernyshevsky's corollary–that life is beauty and that the essential task of art is the reproduction of life. In this role, art serves as a useful substitute for reality, acting as a source both of aesthetic pleasure and of insight into aspects of social reality that are not readily accessible to the reading public. Antonovich takes issue with critics on the right who idealize art as well as with radicals such as Pisarev and Zaitsev, whose latest work calls into question the utility of art and the possibility of a functional aesthetics.

In "Razrushenie estetiki" (The Destruction of Aesthetics), published in *Russkoe slovo* in 1865, Pisarev concedes that Antonovich is right in one sense. Pisarev does in fact disagree with aspects of Chernyshevsky's dissertation, but because, in his opinion, the dissertation does not represent Chernyshevsky's true position. He suggests that Chernyshevsky's dissertation is now obsolete; it is obsolete, however, "not because its author was unable to write something lasting, but because he had been compelled to refute the philistines with arguments borrowed from their own arsenal." He calls attention to a key passage in which Chernyshevsky–having proposed that his new materialist aesthetics, like science, will respect "real life"–had added, "if it is still worth speaking of aesthetics." Pisarev infers that Chernyshevsky spoke of aesthetics for rhetorical reasons, with the intention of undermining it. For this reason, Pisarev can argue that his own rejection of aesthetics represents the natural culmination of Chernyshevsky's superficially more prudent perspective. For Pisarev, there could be no aesthetics whatsoever, as taste was not a normative phenomenon. Pisarev found judgments of beauty useless in both art and life and, consequently, called upon critics to discuss the "content" of literature rather than its form. While Chernyshevsky had sought to establish aesthetics on a materialist footing, Pisarev sought to eradicate aesthetics entirely.

If "Razrushenie estetiki" was Pisarev's most extreme statement about the nature of art and beauty, then "Pushkin i Belinsky" (Pushkin and Belinsky), which came out in *Russkoe slovo* also in 1865, was the most extreme example of his efforts to put those theoretical ideas into critical practice. In this essay Pisarev attempts to knock Pushkin and his verse novel *Evgenii*

Onegin (Eugene Onegin, 1833) from the pedestal on which they have been placed by two generations of critics. Following his own prescriptions in "Razrushenie estetiki," he ignores the style of Pushkin's text in favor of its content. In the process he jeopardizes his own reputation by taking issue with Vissarion Grigor'evich Belinsky, the leading progressive critic of the 1830s and 1840s and the highly respected father of social criticism. Belinsky loved Pushkin and in an 1844 article published in *Otechestvennye zapiski* had praised *Evgenii Onegin*, characterizing it as an "encyclopedia of Russian life" and "an act of consciousness for Russian society." In Onegin's malaise Belinsky had sensed somehow the political awakening of educated society.

By contrast, in "Pushkin i Belinsky" Pisarev sees *Evgenii Onegin* as "nothing more than a vivid and glittering apotheosis of a dreary and senseless status quo"–an apology for the luxury and excess of an idle aristocracy. He acknowledges Belinsky's place in the pantheon of Russian radicalism and recognizes that Belinsky's essays on Pushkin contributed to Russian intellectual development in significant ways. But he also believes that Pushkin's elegant language has led the "excessively trusting and overly impressionable" Belinsky astray. Belinsky did not read Pushkin correctly, Pisarev argues. Rather, he projected his own values onto the shallow hero of the novel. For Pisarev, Onegin's malaise does not reflect political restlessness or unrealized progressive aspirations but a physical response to a truly dissipated lifestyle. He compares Onegin unfavorably to truly progressive literary types, past and present, of whom the latest representatives are the heroes of Chernyshevsky's *Chto delat'?* and Bazarov. Like Onegin, these contemporary figures are bored–but bored for different reasons: "not because their minds are idle, but because the questions long ago resolved in their own minds cannot even be raised in real life."

By the time he wrote "Razrushenie estetiki" and "Pushkin i Belinsky," Pisarev had been imprisoned in the Peter-Paul Fortress for three years. In letters to his family he claimed to be content. Yet, at times he still yearned for the company of his cousin Koroneva, with whom he engaged in a correspondence that was sometimes full of longing, sometimes angry, and sometimes conciliatory. For a brief period in 1865 he abandoned his thoughts of Koroneva and contemplated marriage to a young woman by the name of Lidiia Osipovna Tsvileneva, one of his sister's friends whom he had never met. He wrote to Lidiia Osipovna several times and proposed a marriage based on the principles of critical realism. When Lidiia Osipovna expressed reservations, he lost interest and resumed writing to Koroneva. The activity of writing occupied most of his time and provided him with a sense of comfort. In this state he wrote prolifically on a great variety of themes. In addition to aesthetics and literature he examined the history of European thought, the evolution of the working-class movement, and education. He continued, meanwhile, to be interested in science. His "Progress v mire zhivotnykh i rastenii" (Progress in the Animal and Vegetable World, published in *Russkoe Slovo*, 1864) was one of the first attempts to popularize Darwin's theory of natural selection in Russia.

Pisarev's literary activities were interrupted in late 1865, when a highly negative response by the censor (and author) Goncharov to his essay "Novyi tip" led prison officials to deprive him of paper and books and to limit his visits with his mother. Weeks of idleness followed, during which Pisarev grew discouraged. Fearing a recurrence of his mental illness, he petitioned the governor-general of St. Petersburg and, in January 1866, he was permitted once again to read and write. The next month, however, in response to the publication of several new articles deemed unacceptable by the censorship, the authorities closed *Russkoe slovo* for a period of five months, and in April, following the radical Dmitrii Vladimirovich Karakozov's attempt on the life of Tsar Alexander II, both *Russkoe slovo* and *Sovremennik* were shut down once and for all. Pisarev expected to remain incarcerated through July 1867, but in the fall of 1866, in celebration of the marriage of the crown prince (the future Tsar Alexander III), many prisoners had their terms reduced by a third, and Pisarev was among them. He was released on 18 November of that year. He was twenty-six years old and at the height of his fame. His collected works were already being prepared for publication, a rare honor for a living writer.

Pisarev's first months of freedom, however, were far from his most productive. Unexpectedly, he experienced difficulty reintegrating himself into the world outside prison and began to fear a relapse of his mental illness. Once again he struggled with depression. This condition was exacerbated by a tempestuous affair with his cousin, the writer Markovich. Moreover, the shutdown of *Russkoe slovo* had left him once again in desperate financial circumstances, which added to his anxiety. He contributed sporadically to two journals—*Delo* (The Deed), Blagosvetlov's new publication, and *Otechestvennye zapiski* (Notes of the Fatherland), recently purchased by the progressive poet Nikolai Alekseevich Nekrasov, formerly the publisher of *Sovremennik*. Pisarev feuded with Blagosvetlov, however, whom he believed did not sufficiently respect Markovich and, in addition, found himself in an uncomfortable position at *Otechestvennye zapiski*. While his contributions to *Russkoe slovo* had defined the character of that journal, at *Otechestvennye zapiski* he was merely an appendage. Nekrasov's collaborators—former editors from *Sovremennik*—remained bitter about their feud with *Russkoe slovo* and jealous of Pisarev's fame. They limited the scope of his contributions, while Pisarev withheld his name from articles that he felt did not represent the fullest expression of his thought. Nonetheless, he published several notable essays in the journal, including "Bor'ba za zhizn'" (The Struggle for Life, 1867), a review of Dostoevsky's novel *Prestuplenie i nakazanie* (Crime and Punishment, 1866), and "Staroe barstvo" (The Old Nobility, 1868), a review of the first three parts of the 1868–1869 edition of Tolstoy's *Voina i mir* (War and Peace).

In the spring of 1868, on the advice of his physician, Pisarev applied for a visa to travel to western Europe, where he hoped to receive medical treatment and to recover from the stress of the previous year. When his application was denied, he headed with Markovich for the Baltic resort town of Dubbel'n, where on 4 July he disappeared while bathing. His body was later recovered by fishermen just off the coast. The coroner reported that he had suffered a sudden stroke or seizure, although the unclear circumstances surrounding his drowning have led some scholars to view it as a suicide. News of Pisarev's death spread quickly. His funeral procession was a public event—a large and spontaneous demonstration at a time when few such gatherings were tolerated. The young critic was buried in the Volkov Cemetery in St. Petersburg, across from the graves of the critics Dobroliubov and Belinsky. In August and September 1868 journals and newspapers of all political leanings printed eulogies, most paying him a cordial tribute. Even conservatives praised their late rival for his integrity and his literary gifts.

This sudden end to Pisarev's literary career was, in some sense, a new beginning. In the months immediately following his death, no newer or more striking figure arose to take his place in the radical press and, thanks to the publication of his complete works (the ten-volume *Sochineniia* [Works], 1866–1869), his ideas were spreading beyond the confines of St. Petersburg and Moscow into the provinces. His writings remained of great importance for two types of readers: for leading intellectuals, who used his thought in both positive and negative ways to define their own philosophies, and for educated youth, for whom an acquaintance with Pisarev continued to be a formative experience. Thus, although a second edition of his works, prepared in the early 1870s, was proscribed by the state censorship, several generations of young progressives continued to pass around tattered copies of the first edition as well as the old issues of journals that featured his articles. Following the relaxation of censorship in the 1890s, Russian publishers of the prerevolutionary period released

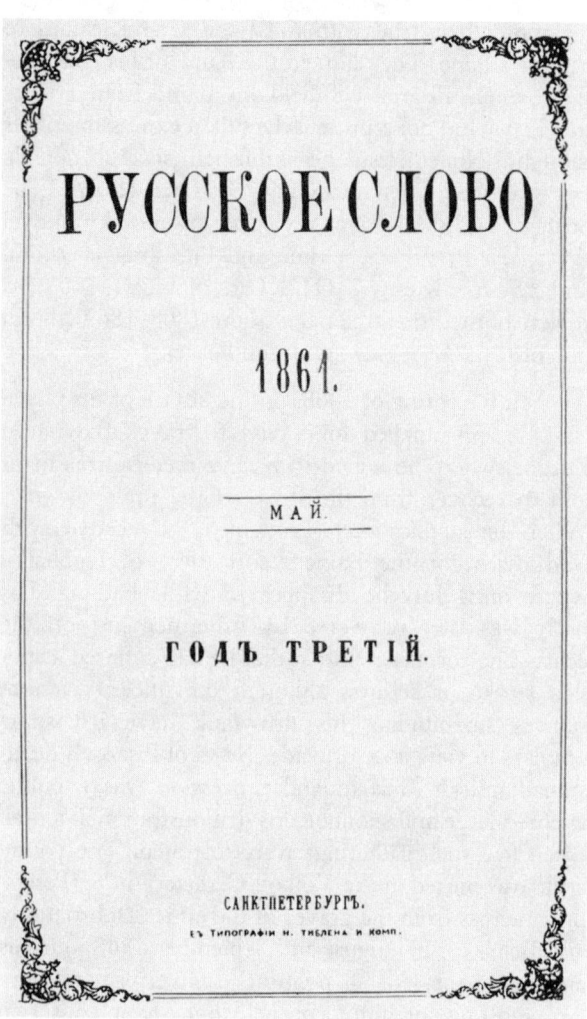

Paper cover for Russkoe slovo *(The Russian Word), the journal that published Pisarev's first significant essays, including "Fiziologicheskie eskizy" (Physiological Sketches), in the early 1860s (from Pisarev,* Literaturnaia kritika, *1981)*

the first biographies of Pisarev along with several new editions of his collected works.

Populist intellectuals of the 1870s and 1880s often derided Pisarev. The critic Aleksandr Mikhailovich Skabichevsky, the publicist Nikolai Konstantinovich Mikhailovsky, and the terrorist Lev Aleksandrovich Tikhomirov all regarded Pisarev's emphasis on self-education, his criticism of conventional morality, and his notion of "the emancipation of personality" as selfish if not immoral and feared that Pisarev's works were continuing to direct the attention of educated Russians inward, away from the people. They attributed what they perceived as Pisarev's excessive individualism to his gentry origins and saw in his aesthetic extremism a lack of intellectual seriousness.

Marxists of the late Imperial period sought to establish their own credentials through links with the radical past in Russia and looked at Pisarev in quite a different manner than did Skabichevsky or Mikhailovsky. In her 1907 essay "D. I. Pisarev" Vera Ivanovna Zasulich discusses Pisarev in a positive light. She observes that his writing had a tremendous impact on provincial youths such as herself. Starved for progressive ideas, they required considerable guidance, which Pisarev generously provided. Pisarev, she remarks, was read differently than other authors—not as an intellectual authority but as a comrade, who articulated in print what his peers were already thinking. For example, in "Realisty" he was the first to speak of the intelligentsia's debt to the people, a notion that had inspired Zasulich's own radicalism and the radicalism of many other representatives of the so-called penitent gentry activists of the 1870s.

Dozens of published diaries and memoirs of eminent scientists, radicals, and members of the artistic avant-garde testify to the validity of Zasulich's observations and the importance of Pisarev's writings for Russian intellectuals through the 1917 Revolution and beyond. Some of these memoirs speak of the existence of a "Pisarevshchina," a movement made up of the ardent followers of Pisarev who modeled themselves after the nihilistic Bazarov-type set forth in Pisarev's essays on *Ottsy i deti.* Vladimir Lenin himself went through a "Pisarev phase," carrying a picture of Pisarev with him in exile and citing Pisarev's thoughts on useful work in his own polemic "Chto delat'?" (What Is To Be Done?), published in 1902. The conservative author Konstantin Nikolaevich Leont'ev saw Pisarev's influence as unfortunate but, nonetheless, among the most profound and lasting of that of all nineteenth-century writers—not that of a succès d'estime but "on a plane with that of Dostoevsky [and] Tolstoy," as quoted by V. Rozanov in his 1903 contribution to *Russkii Vestnik.*

The symbolist A. L. Volynsky (pseudonym of Akim L'vovich Flekser), perhaps the most important Russian critic of the fin de siècle, included several chapters on Pisarev in his *Russkie kritiki* (Russian Critics, 1896). Volynsky describes Pisarev as a genuine literary talent unable to find his real niche because he lacked sufficient philosophical training. Volynsky also believes, however, that Pisarev's early essays on Goncharov, Pisemsky, and other writers showed flashes of genuine brilliance. Pisarev was by nature a gifted critic. From 1862 onward Pisarev's most important intellectual accomplishments were, from Volynsky's perspective, of great cultural significance but entirely negative in their impact. Volynsky is most critical of Pisarev's "Pushkin i Belinsky," which he characterizes as "barbaric . . . a grey scum of unconnected philosophical ideas with a trace of scientific thoughtlessness and the trumpeting of progressive-mindedness." Most significant, from Volynsky's perspective, Pisarev's exceptional talent as a stylist served him well in the literary polemics of the 1860s, helping him to attract a large following and to crush intellectually more sophisticated opponents.

In some ways Volynsky's appraisal is typical of the assessment of Pisarev by leading Russian intellectuals of the late Imperial period. While Pisarev's older contemporaries, such as Chernyshevsky and Dobroliubov, were universally admired by progressives and scorned by conservatives, intellectuals were often ambivalent in their appraisal of Pisarev. Conservatives admired his literary talent and found him more honest and less dogmatic than either Chernyshevsky or Dobroliubov. His aesthetic extremism, however, struck them as childish and destructive. Radicals typically admired Pisarev's commitment to the progressive cause, his critique of Russian cultural backwardness, and his promotion of science, education, and Western ideas. They continued to look to his work as a model of social criticism. Nonetheless, many radicals were embarrassed by his aesthetics, his individualism, and his attacks on Belinsky and Dobroliubov, as well as by what was widely regarded as his focus on a critically thinking elite at the expense of the common people.

The extent of Dmitrii Ivanovich Pisarev's influence was acknowledged, however, by intellectuals of all camps. The last of the major critics of the century, he died at an early age, having played a pivotal role in determining the direction of Russian radicalism in the 1860s and beyond. Pisarev's writings remained popular in the decades following his death but played a different role than they had in the decade in which he lived and wrote. Works such as "Bazarov" and "Realisty" ceased to have an important impact on the dominant tendencies in radical thought but continued to introduce young readers to both Russian literature and radicalism and, in so doing, inspired many to engage in progressive causes.

Letters:

"Pis'ma pokoinogo Pisemskogo, napisannye im iz-pod aresta k raznym litsam," edited by A. D. Danilov, *Russkoe obozrenie*, nos. 1–3, 6, 8, 10, 12 (1893);

O brake (St. Petersburg: Narodnaia pol'za, 1906);

Ivan Sergeevich Turgenev, "Perepiska s D. I. Pisarevym," in *Raduga. Almanakh Pushkinskogo doma*, edited by M. G. Strol'man (St. Petersburg: Kooperativnoe izdatel'stvo literatorov i uchenykh, 1922), pp. 207–225;

"Pis'ma D. I. Pisareva iz kreposti," edited by B. P. Koz'min, *Krasnyi Arkhiv*, no. 5 (1924): 248–253;

"Iz neopublikovannoi perepiski D. I. Pisareva," edited by Koz'min, *Literaturnoe nasledstvo*, nos. 25–26 (1936): 645–654;

N. Bykhovskogo, "D. I. Pisarev v Petropavlovskoi kreposti," *Literaturnoe nasledstvo*, nos. 25–26 (1936): 655–679;

"Pis'ma," edited by E. P. Kazanovich, in *Shestidesiatye gody: Materialy po istorii literatury i obshchestvennomu dvizheniiu*, edited by Nikolai Kir'iakovich Piksanov and Orest Veniaminovich Tsekhnovitser (Moscow & Leningrad: Akademiia nauk SSSR, 1940), pp. 107–172;

"Pis'ma D. I. Pisareva i o Pisareve," edited by Koz'min, *Zapiski Otdela rukopisei Vsesoiuznoi biblioteki imeni V. I. Lenina*, 9 (1940): 19–35.

Bibliography:

Boris Iakovlevich Bukhshtab, *D. I. Pisarev. Ukazatel' osnovnoi literatury* (Leningrad, 1940).

Biographies:

Evgenii Andreevich Solov'ev, *D. I. Pisarev: Ego zhizn' i kriticheskaia deiatel'nost'* (St. Petersburg: Iu. N. Erlikh, 1893);

E. P. Kazanovich, *D. I. Pisarev 1840–1856 gg.* (Petrograd: Nauka i shkola, 1922);

Valerii Iakovlevich Kirpotin, *Radikal'nyi raznochinets D. I. Pisarev* (Leningrad: Priboi, 1929);

Armand Coquart, *Dmitri Pisarev (1840–1868) et l'idéologie du nihilisme russe* (Paris: Institut d'études slaves de l'Université de Paris, 1946);

Lev A. Plotkin, *D. I. Pisarev: Zhizn' i deiatel'nost'* (Leningrad: Khudozhestvennaia literatura, 1962);

Iurii Korotkov, *Pisarev* (Moscow: Molodaia gvardiia, 1976);

Feliks Feodos'evich Kuznetsov, *Nigilisty? D. I. Pisarev i zhurnal "Russkoe slovo"* (Moscow: Khudozhestvennaia literatura, 1983);

G. G. Elizavetina, *Pisarev-kritik: Nachalo puti* (Moscow: Nasledie, 1992);

I. V. Kondakov, ed., *Mir Pisareva*, D. I. Pisarev: Issledovaniia i materialy, no. 1 (Moscow: Nasledie, 1995);

Elizavetina, *Pisarev-kritik: Ispytanie estetikoi* (Moscow: Nasledie, 1999).

References:

Maksim Alekseevich Antonovich, "Asmodei hashego vremeni," *Sovremennik*, 3 (March 1862);

Antonovich, *Literaturno-kriticheskie stat'i* (Moscow: Khudozhestvennaia literatura, 1961);

Frederick Barghoorn, "D. I. Pisarev: A Representative of Russian Nihilism," *Review of Politics*, 10, no. 2 (April 1948): 190–211;

Barghoorn, "Nihilism, Utopia, and Realism in the Thought of Pisarev," *Harvard Slavic Studies,* 4 (1957): 225–236;

Vissarion Grigor'evich Belinsky, "Stat'ia vos'maia," *Otechestvennye zapiski,* 12 (1844);

Edward J. Brown, "Pisarev and the Transformation of Two Novels," in *Literature and Society in Imperial Russia, 1800–1914,* edited by William Mills Todd III (Stanford: Stanford University Press, 1978), pp. 151–172;

Frederick C. Copleston, *Philosophy in Russia. From Herzen to Lenin and Berdyaev* (Notre Dame, Ind.: Notre Dame University Press, 1986);

Abbott Gleason, *Young Russia: The Genesis of Russian Radicalism in the 1860s* (New York: Viking, 1980);

Alexander Herzen, "Eshche raz Bazarov," in his *Sobranie sochinenii,* 30 volumes (Moscow: Akademiia nauk SSSR, 1954–1965), XX: 335–350;

Ronald Hingley, *Nihilists: Russian Radicals and Revolutionaries in the Reign of Alexander II, 1855–1881* (New York: Delacorte, 1969);

Hingley, "Pisarev," in his *Russian Writers and Society, 1825–1904* (London: Weidenfeld & Nicolson, 1967);

Ivan Ivanovich Ivanov, *Istoriia russkoi kritiki: Izdanie zhurnala "Mir Bozhii,"* 4 volumes (St. Petersburg: I. N. Skorokhodov, 1898–1900);

Evgenii Lampert, *Sons Against Fathers: Studies in Russian Radicalism and Revolution* (Oxford: Clarendon Press, 1965);

Mikhail Konstantinovich Lemke, *Politicheskie protsessy v Rossii 1860-kh gg.* (Moscow & Petrograd: Gosizdat, 1923);

Charles Moser, *Esthetics as Nightmare: Russian literary theory, 1855–1870* (Princeton: Princeton University Press, 1989);

Norman Pereira, "Challenging the Principle of Authority: The Polemic Between *Sovremennik* and *Russkoe slovo,* 1863–1865," *Russian Review,* 34 (Fall 1975): 137–150;

Georgii Valentinovich Plekhanov, *Literatura i estetika,* 2 volumes (Moscow: Gosudarstvennoe izdatel'stvo khudozhestvennaia literatury, 1958);

Peter C. Pozefsky, *The Nihilist Imagination: Dmitrii Pisarev and the Cultural Origins of Russian Radicalism (1860–1868)* (New York: Peter Lang, 2003);

Pozefsky, "Smoke as 'Strange and Sinister Commentary on *Fathers and Sons*': Dostoevskii, Pisarev and Tur-genev on Nihilists and Their Representations," *Russian Review,* 54, no. 4 (1995): 571–586;

V. Rozanov, "Iz perepiski K. N. Leont'eva," *Russkii vestnik,* 6 (June 1903): 410;

N. V. Shelgunov, "Neizdannaia stat'ia N. V. Shelgunova: O Dobroliubovtsakh i Pisarevtsakh," *Literaturnoe nasledstvo,* nos. 25–26 (1936): 398–418;

A. L. Shvartzman, *D. I. Pisarev i russkoe estestvoznanie* (Moscow: Sovetskaia nauka, 1955);

Aleksandr Mikhailovich Skabichevsky, *Istoriia noveishei russkoi literatury: 1848–1890* (St. Petersburg: F. Pavlenkov, 1891);

Skabichevsky, *Literaturnye vospominaniia* (Moscow: Zemlia i fabrika, 1928);

Nikolai Strakhov, *Iz istorii literaturnogo nigilizma (1861–1865)* (St. Petersburg: Brat'ia Panteleevy, 1890);

Franco Venturi, *Roots of Revolution: A History of the Populist and Socialist Movements in Nineteenth Century Russia,* translated by Francis Haskell (New York: Knopf, 1960);

A. L. Volynsky, *Russkie kritiki: Literaturnye ocherki,* 2 volumes (St. Petersburg: M. Merkushev, 1896);

Andrzej Walicki, *A History of Russian Thought from the Enlightenment to Marxism,* translated by Hilda Andrews-Rusiecka (Stanford: Stanford University Press, 1979);

Vera Ivanovna Zasulich, "D. I. Pisarev," in her *Sbornik statei,* volume 2 (St. Petersburg: Rutenberg, 1907), pp. 223–310.

Papers:

Dmitrii Ivanovich Pisarev's personal papers and records pertaining to his life can be found in several archival collections. In Moscow these collections are located at the Russian State Library (RGB, formerly the Lenin Library), fond 93 and fond 178 (Museum Collection); the Russian State Archive of Literature and Art (RGALI), fond 415; and the State Archive of the Russian Federation (GARF), fond 95 and fond 112. Additional papers are kept in the records of the Third Section (political police), also in Moscow. In St. Petersburg, Pisarev's papers are held at the Institute of Russian Literature (IRLI, Pushkin House); the Russian State Historical Archive (RGIA), fond 772, fond 776, and fond 777; and the Russian National Library (RNB), fond 326. The collection at IRLI is catalogued under Pisarev's name and is described in K. N. Grigorian's *Rukopisi D. I. Pisareva v sobranii Instituta literatury* (Moscow & Leningrad: Akademiia nauk SSSR, 1941).

Aleksei Nikolaevich Pleshcheev

(22 November 1825? – 26 September 1893)

Alan Kimball
University of Oregon

BOOKS: *Stikhotvoreniia, 1845–1846* (Moscow, 1846)—includes "Vpered! Bez strakha i somnen'ia . . .";

Stikhotvoreniia (St. Petersburg: Smirdin, 1858);

Povesti i rasskazy, 2 volumes (Moscow: M. P. Zakharov, 1860);

Stikhotvoreniia (Moscow: V. Grachev, 1861); enlarged as *Novye stikhotvoreniia* (Moscow: F. B. Miller, 1863);

Angel dobroty i nevinnosti, by Pleshcheev and Viktor Aleksandrovich Krylov (St. Petersburg: G. Shreder, 1873);

Sbornik teatral'nykh p'es dlia domashnikh i liubitel'skikh spektaklei, 3 volumes (St. Petersburg, 1876–1880);

Podsnezhnik. Stikhotvoreniia dlia detei i iunoshestva (St. Petersburg: V. Likhachev & A. S. Suvorin, 1878);

Krestnitsa (St. Petersburg: M. V. Popov, 1880);

Primernaia zhena (St. Petersburg: Kurochkin, 1880);

Zhiteiskoe (St. Petersburg: I. L. Tuzov, 1880);

Zhilets (Moscow: E. N. Rassokhin, 1885);

Stikhotvoreniia (1846–1886) (Moscow: V.M., 1887); enlarged as *Stikhotvoreniia (1844–1891),* edited by Petr Vasil'evich Bykov (St. Petersburg: A. A. Pleshcheev, 1898; enlarged edition, St. Petersburg: A. F. Marks, 1905);

Zhenshchina v XVIII veke: Po Gonkuru (St. Petersburg: A. S. Suvorin, 1888);

Dedushkiny pesni. Stikhotvoreniia dlia detei (Moscow: I. D. Sytin, 1891);

Pesni starogo druga (Moscow: I. D. Sytin, 1891);

Zhizn' Dikkensa (St. Petersburg: I. N. Skorokhodov, 1891);

Rabotnitsa (Moscow: Moskovskii komissariat gramotnosti, 1893);

Povesti i rasskazy, 2 volumes (St. Petersburg: Stasiulevich, 1896, 1897)—includes volume 2, *(1859–1868)*—includes "Dve kar'ery" and "Pashintsev";

Stikhotvoreniia, Biblioteka poeta, Malaia seriia (Moscow & Leningrad, 1937);

Polnoe sobranie stikhotvorenii, edited, with a commentary, by M. Ia. Poliakov (Moscow & Leningrad: Sovetskii pisatel', 1964).

Aleksei Nikolaevich Pleshcheev

Editions and Collections: *Stikhotvoreniia (1846–1891)* (St. Petersburg: A. A. Pleshcheev, 1894);

Podsnezhnik (St. Petersburg: A. A. Pleshcheev, 1895);

Rodnye poety, by Pleshcheev and N. P. Ogarev (Moscow: Obshchestvo rasprostraneniia poleznykh knig, 1903);

Stikhotvoreniia, Biblioteka poeta, Malaia seriia (Moscow & Leningrad, 1937);

Izbrannoe: Stikhotvoreniia, proza (Moscow: Goslitizdat, 1960);

Stikhotvoreniia, with an introduction and commentary by L. S. Pustil'nik (Moscow, 1975);

Zhiteiskie stseny. Povesti, with an introduction and commentary by N. G. Kuzin (Moscow, 1986);

Papiroska. Istinnoe proisshestvie, in the series "Zhivye kartiny. Povesti i rasskazy pisatelei 'natural'noi shkoly'" (Moscow, 1988);

Romansy na slova A. Pleshcheeva: Dlia golosa v soprovozhdenii fortepiano (Leningrad: Muzyka, 1989);

Stikhotvoreniia. Proza (Moscow: Pravda, 1991).

OTHER: *Detskaia knizhka,* compiled by Pleshcheev and Fedor Nikolaevich Berg, with contributions by Pleshcheev (Moscow: Katkov, 1861);

Heinrich Heine, *Vill'iam Ratkliff,* translated by Pleshcheev (Leipzig: C. G. Röder, 1869?);

Na prazdnik: Literaturnyi sbornik dlia detei, edited by Pleshcheev (St. Petersburg: A. Pleshcheev & N. Aleksandrov, 1873);

Obshchestvennaia i domashniaia zhizn' zhivotnykh: Satiricheskie ocherki, edited by Pleshcheev (St. Petersburg: N. P. Karbasnikov, 1876);

Eugène-Marin Labiche, *Povadil'sia kuvshin po vodu khodit',* adapted by Pleshcheev (St. Petersburg: Kurochkin, 1878);

Ludovic Halévy and Henri Meillac, *Liubochka,* adapted by Pleshcheev (Moscow: S. F. Rassokhin, 1884);

Alphonse Daudet, *Zheny artistov: Ocherk nravov,* translated by Pleshcheev (St. Petersburg: A. S. Suvorin, 1886).

Aleksei Pleshcheev made his livelihood as a writer for more than forty years. He was a teenager at the time of his first publications, and he was in his late sixties at the time of his last. His long career stretched from the time of Tsar Nicholas I into the reign of Tsar Alexander III, marking the end of the era of wellborn cultural amateurs and the beginning of a new era of cultural professionalism. Pleshcheev was a journalist and publisher; he also wrote poetry, short stories, and plays and was a pioneer in the writing of children's literature in Russia. He published translations from German, French, and English literature that are consulted to this day. The civic themes of Pleshcheev's writings were matched by an active civic life, all in the defense of his chosen profession—literature. Pleshcheev extolled, perhaps even exaggerated, the virtues and pleasures of an educated but down-to-earth intelligentsia in united action. He celebrated the spontaneous actions of individuals working together in pursuit of careers open to talent rather than to class status and bureaucratic rank.

Aleksei Nikolaevich Pleshcheev was born on or about 22 November 1825 in Kostroma province, northeast of Moscow along the Volga River. His father and mother were noble by formal feudal social designation, both from old aristocratic families, but not wealthy, not even well-off. His father, Nikolai Sergeevich Pleshcheev, was employed in the provincial civilian bureaucracy and thus held a position categorized in the Table of Ranks, the system of military, civil, church, and court promotion introduced by Peter the Great in 1722. His mother, Elena Aleksandrovna (Gorskina) Pleshcheeva, possessed titles to two estates: one in Iaroslavl' province, upstream from Kostroma, and the other in Nizhnii Novgorod province, downstream. These lands were populated by about four hundred male serfs and their families. The title to one of these estates was unclear and contested (therefore frozen). Together, however, the lands and the civil-service job brought little income to the family. Like about half of all Russian gentry landowners, the Pleshcheevs were exceedingly poor. Until near the end of his life, Aleksei Nikolaevich had to work for a living, and through each stage of his life he struggled to make ends meet.

From his earliest years a single set of circumstances worked uniformly to shape Pleshcheev, both as a social being and as a writer: his social class provided him no promise of a better future. Attempting to free himself of both his noble and his state-servitor inheritances, he assumed an active and hostile relationship to imperial traditions. He conceived a better future for himself and, by extension, for all like-minded fellow Russians.

Extremely little is known about Pleshcheev's early years. At age fifteen he enrolled in a St. Petersburg military school, but he later dropped out. Between 1844 and 1849 he transferred to St. Petersburg University, and, without receiving his degree, shifted to a lifelong pursuit of economic, social, and artistic independence from received traditions. His first stories and verse appeared in these years, when he published in *Sovremennik* (The Contemporary), *Biblioteka dlia chteniia* (A Reading Library), and *Otechestvennye zapiski* (Notes of the Fatherland)—the most popular *tolstye zhurnaly* (thick journals), as leading periodicals were called. The first selection of Pleshcheev's verse appeared in *Sovremennik* in 1844, with the signature "A. P-v"; included were the poetic cycle "Nochnye dumy" (Nighttime Musings) and "Pesnia strannika" (Song of a Wanderer).

Both as a social being and a writer Pleshcheev reacted to the cultural policies of Tsar Nicholas I. In 1844 university students were forced to sign a pledge "not to join any sort of organization, however it might be called and of whatever character it might be." Yet, self-organization seemed the only way to a better life. The *kruzhok* (circle), a gathering for discussion, had become a central feature of life among educated Russians who sought to carve out a niche for themselves. Failing feudal social identities and the assignments of state power did not meet their needs. On 8 June 1845 Pleshcheev wrote a letter to the rector of St. Petersburg University and asked how he might complete his degree and prepare himself for honorable, meaningful, and useful work as a member of society. Pleshcheev wished to proceed at his own pace under what his 1846 poem "Vpered! Bez strakha i somnen'ia . . ." (Forward! Without fear or doubt . . .) called "znamia nauki" (the banner of learning), not under the flag of barracks tsar Nicholas. The rector was at a loss for words, even though he had earlier recognized Pleshcheev's literary talent and guided him toward his first publications.

From the beginning Pleshcheev's poems had a way of lodging themselves in the Russian imagination. They were written in memorable, clear, sincere, everyday language. He struck no evident pose and often seemed naive or feckless in his resolute optimism, as in "Vpered! Bez strakha i somnen'ia . . . ," his most popular poem:

Vpered! bez strakhi i somnen'ia
Na podvig doblestnyi, druz'ia!

(Forward! without fear or doubt
To a valiant victory, my friends!)

Pleshcheev's writings never wanted for a readership. From his earliest compositions the central personae of his verse were more often "we" and "us" than "I" and "me." The industrious and enlightened professional who freely interrelates with colleagues was his personal ideal–an ideal that shaped his literary life and defined his audience as well.

Pleshcheev drifted away from the university and into various discussion circles whose members were later given the collective name "Petrashevtsy," after M. V. Butashevich-Petrashevsky, host to one of the groups. Pleshcheev's action was in direct contradiction to the 1844 pledge–indeed, it was perhaps inspired in defiance of the pledge. He now sought a life in literature, a life he always equated with human fellowship. Forbidding open association with fellow members of society, the university in the time of Nicholas I did not provide such a life. Independent, learned people in association with one another seemed to Pleshcheev the quintessence of community and promised a better future for his homeland. Accordingly, working with fellow members of his *kruzhok,* Pleshcheev traveled to Moscow to acquaint himself more closely with conditions of life there and to establish productive literary ties. On 26 March 1849 he dispatched a remarkable report to fellow *kruzhok* member Sergei Fedorovich Durov back in St. Petersburg, describing the civic culture of the old capital. Rich with commentary on organized cultural

life, this letter served as evidence against Pleshcheev after he was arrested later that year, along with the other members of the Petrashevtsy.

As a result of his arrest, one day in Pleshcheev's long life stands out above all others. On a snowy 22 December 1849, on the outskirts of the imperial capital, he was placed before a firing squad. Only twenty-four, he was about to be executed along with other Petrashevtsy members. A fellow convict, Nikolai Sergeevich Kashkin, extended his hand to say goodbye for the last time and, borrowing from Pleshcheev's "Vpered! Bez strakha i somnen'ia . . . ," said to the poet: "We've proceeded under the banner of learning, so in that spirit we will offer one another our hands." The critical concept of *nauka* (scholarship, science, learning) defined a precious commodity in traditional, rural Russia at this time. These journalists, writers, and translators were going to their deaths precisely under the banner of learning: for writing, reading, and listening in groups to the recitation of texts unacceptable to the tsarist state. They were being punished for organizing themselves–in other words, for abandoning their sovereign in favor of voluntary association. Russian law, as expressed in the 1844 pledge, considered volunteerism a desertion of official duty.

In groups of three the prisoners were administered last rites. Pleshcheev's threesome consisted of himself; his close associate Durov, who had recently resigned from state service in the Naval Ministry in order to seek his fortune as a freelance writer; and the recently resigned army officer Fyodor Dostoevsky, who was still at the earliest stages of his literary career. Their eyes were taped shut, and they heard the first words of the infamous command: "Ready, aim . . ." An officer was instructed to intervene at the last moment, however, to announce that the prisoners' sentences had been commuted to exile in distant trans-Volga outposts. Pleshcheev was sent to the edge of the Bashkir steppes in Orenburg for a decade. Throughout most of this time he was sentenced to serve in the military–that is, he was forced back under the banner of the tsar.

He managed nevertheless to keep his hand in literary endeavors during these years of exile. Pleshcheev was never what might ordinarily be called a "political activist." He was an independent-minded, professional writer, an identity that just happened to have serious political implications in his world. Nor were all his writings devoted to civic themes; he wrote affective love lyrics as well. In October 1857, while still in exile, he married Elikonida Aleksandrovna Rudneva, the daughter of a local civil servant, and the verses he wrote to her are among his most tender. For example, "Toboi lish' iasny dni moi . . ." (You alone bring light to my days . . .) and "Kogda tvoi krotkii, iasnyi vzor . . ."

(When your tender, clear gaze . . .), both published in *Stikhotvoreniia* (Poems, 1858), combine two longings–one the love for Elikonida, the other the pain of exile. Pleshcheev's biographer Liubov' Semenovna Pustil'nik draws attention to the close affinity between his socially conscious poetry and his love lyrics. The reader confronts in these otherwise different poems the same simplicity and directness of language, the same motifs and tropes. The two sorts of verse work in the same way.

Pleshcheev thus helped give expression to a characteristic idea or attitude, an inclination of mind often met among educated Russians in the middle of the nineteenth century. At some vital center of individual experience, freedom and love flourished together or were blighted together. Personal and public associations were bonded by a kindred affection. Authentic, honest, sincere friendship and love in pairs or small groups easily contrasted with the contrived formalism of imperial life and prefigured a larger harmonious social order. Poems to Pleshcheev's wife eloquently expressed these compounded qualities of love and civic virtue.

In the mid 1850s students at Kazan' University adopted as their anthem another popular Pleshcheev poem, now set to music. It opened:

Po chuvstvam brat'ia my s toboi,
My v iskuplen'e verim oba,
I budem my pitat' do groba
Vrazhdu k bicham strany rodnoi.

(By instinct you and I are brothers,
We believe alike in redemption,
And to our grave we'll not cease
To resist the scourge of our native land.)

These words signal Pleshcheev's rejection of status by birth or by state imposition. He embraces self-designed and instinctive identity and anticipates a possible redemption (rebirth) of the whole nation via "elective affinities."

In 1859 Pleshcheev was released from exile and was allowed to live and work in Moscow. Like Dostoevsky, who was also freed in these months, Pleshcheev now planned to make a life for himself again in literature and journalism. He scraped together funds and became a partner in a venture to publish the four-volume works of the popular writer Ivan Sergeevich Turgenev. He came into possession of a printing press. His writings again began to appear, and he supplemented his own creations with translations of George Gordon, Lord Byron; Victor Hugo; Heinrich Heine; and Ukrainian poet Taras Shevchenko, as well as other English, French, German, and Ukrainian writers. In another partnership he founded the journal *Moskovskii vestnik* (The Moscow Messenger).

Pleshcheev wrote about what he knew. His short stories–such as "Pashintsev" and "Dve kar'ery" (Two Careers), both written and published in 1859 in *Russkii vestnik* (The Russian Messenger) and *Sovremennik* respectively–concentrate on the theme of good-hearted youths, such as he once was, who are at the beginning of full and productive lives and ready to serve their nation. His heroes regularly meet obstacles. The conventions and habits of imperial life dash their hopes. These themes were highlighted in the most widely read reviews of his work. For instance, in the July 1860 issue of *Sovremennik,* the critic Nikolai Aleksandrovich Dobroliubov accented Pleshcheev's social significance. He was glad to see that Pleshcheev's heroes were not *lishnie liudi* (superfluous men) in the romantic tradition of the day. They were not duplicates of Pechorin, the posturing, tragicomic protagonist in Mikhail Iur'evich Lermontov's *Geroi nashego vremeni* (A Hero of Our Time, 1840). Nor did they emulate Rudin, the defeated dandy of Turgenev's novel of the same name (1855). According to Dobroliubov, characters such as Pashintsev and others in Pleshcheev's stories more clearly exposed the source of Russian stagnation, precisely because they were just ordinary youths prepared to make their way in this life. Dobroliubov expresses the situation with a Pleshcheevan metaphor from daily experience: "On all sides they hear the invitation: come to dinner. And they go. That's all there is to it." They set out in this way, but powerful forces from on high deny them their sustenance. Do not blame the poor dispirited heroes, writes Dobroliubov, but rather look upward to the movers and shapers of Russian life. Dobroliubov was sensitive to the blend of love and civic virtue in Pleshcheev's works. He summed up his critique by drawing on "Dve kar'ery," in which Pleshcheev suggests a parallel between ludicrous Platonic love and dreamy, "romantic" behavior in general. Dobroliubov takes the following lesson from Pleshcheev: what one needs in life, as well as in love, is direct and simple action.

In 1860 Pleshcheev became active in two large volunteer organizations of intellectuals and professionals. The first, Obshchestvo liubitelei rossiiskoi slovesnosti (Society of Lovers of Russian Literature), was in Moscow, where he lived. The second, Obshchestvo dlia posobiia nuzhdaiushchimsia literatoram i uchenym (Society for the Aid of Needy Writers and Scholars), or Litfond for short, was in St. Petersburg, where some of his most important associates lived. Litfond inspired Pleshcheev in life and in literature because it was the largest volunteer association of its kind ever to exist in Russia. Many more hands–a diverse and stable cross section of educated society–now lifted the banner of learning.

Pleshcheev was elected to membership in Litfond at the same time as Aleksandr Andreevich Katenin, a high-ranking state servitor in the Ministry of War and governor-general of both Orenburg (Pleshcheev's place of recent exile) and Samara provinces. In some small way, Pleshcheev felt the world was being set right. In a private letter to the governor of Saratov province, Egor Ivanovich Baranovsky, on 19 February 1860 he described the event with a touch of humor, hinting that it might represent a miniature French Revolutionary victory in Russia:

> A few days ago they elected me and also His Most Esteemed Excellency A. A. Katenin. What sort of equality is this? . . . the most negligible of mortals and one of the most powerful men on this earth–members of one and the same society. . . . Furthermore our names together beautified one and the same column of the newspaper. It was good, however, that my name begins with a "P" or I might unfortunately have been printed higher than him. *Où allons nous, où allons nous* [Where are we headed, where are we headed].

Litfond suited Pleshcheev because it loosened the lingering double grip on Russian life exercised by moribund feudal social estates and the Table of Ranks in civilian, military, court, and church bureaucracies. Pleshcheev's life and work challenged these standard hierarchies, and now Litfond promised a reconstruction of spontaneous and natural social relations. As an organization created by and for public figures themselves, rather than by officials, it promoted independence for learned professionals. In another letter to Baranovsky on 25 April 1860 Pleshcheev bragged about how bold and democratic Litfond was. It granted pensions to the seventy-year-old son of writer Aleksandr Nikolaevich Radishchev, one of the original martyrs under the banner of learning who was exiled for expressing himself freely in the 1790s, and to Baron Vladimir Ivanovich Shteingel, a famous democrat among the Decembrist conspirators of 1825. Pleshcheev noted that money poured into the Litfond treasury for the most part not from the "rich and famous" but from fellow cultural professionals: "The poor are helping the poor." Marching under the banner of learning, they now offered one another a hand.

Pleshcheev himself was one of those poor. When he had a little money, he managed it clumsily. He often offered money to others in loosely enforced loans that he could ill afford. Dostoevsky failed to repay one sizable loan that Pleshcheev offered in order to help him back from Siberian exile. Belles lettres and journalism were not hobbies–not a gentleman's diversion. They were an avocation. Pleshcheev's professional livelihood provided a narrow escape not only from the impoverishment of his noble estate but also from the moral bankruptcy of the whole tsarist social system. The well-

born were positioned on the backs of unfree labor, and even after the emancipation of the serfs in 1861 the Russian political economy discouraged private and public social initiative and left young people few options but to seek government positions and rank in the imperial bureaucracy. The characters in Pleshcheev's stories–like his associates among the Petrashevtsy in his earliest years and in Litfond later–seek new prospects and new identities. The themes of Pleshcheev's life and literary works continued to complement each other.

In the March 1861 issue of *Sovremennik* the poet Mikhail Ilarionovich Mikhailov praised Pleshcheev's inspiring and straightforward appeals to everyday action. Mikhailov contrasted Pleshcheev's poetry with the verse of Apollon Nikolaevich Maikov and Lev Aleksandrovich Mei, whom he called lyrical and dreamy. Pleshcheev's poems written in 1861 (published in *Sovremennik* the same year)–such as "O, ne zabud', chto ty dolzhnik . . ." (O, don't forget that you are a debtor . . .) and "Nishchie" (The Poor)–raise issues of cultural debt to the working classes, to those still impoverished. In these works Pleshcheev expresses with relaxed ease what later proved to be a complicated confrontation between an emerging "public" and the established order of things. His message, which was in clear conflict with dominant imperial social hierarchies, was not easily converted, however, to effective action. Pleshcheev was not as ambitious for massive transformation as were many of his youthful readers. His self-presentation was straightforward; he sought only steady progress against perceived deficiencies of Russian life. Indeed, he fought steadily against the one ubiquitous flaw in the life of the Russian writer: censorship. For Pleshcheev the struggle against censorship was a part of the normal, everyday pursuit of a professional writer and journalist, who, working together with like-minded associates, attempted to overcome the forces that constrained them. Even as emancipation seemed to get the gentry off the backs of peasants, so, too, did Pleshcheev and his associates work to get an oppressive and censorious state system off their own backs.

Pleshcheev also took an active interest in the voluntary literacy movement and the Sunday schools that it supported. These book-hungry schools represented an economic opportunity to him and others in the business of publishing. In 1861 he invested in Nikolai Aleksandrovich Serno-Solov'evich's profitable empirewide publishing and distribution venture. According to Serno-Solov'evich, he sought ways to exercise his talents so as to "do well and do good," that is, to make a living yet simultaneously contribute to the larger process of change initiated by the reform epoch.

Manuscript for Pleshcheev's "Vpered! Bez strakha i somnen'ia . . ." (Forward! Without fear or doubt . . . , 1846),
his most popular poem (Pushkin House, St. Petersburg)

Throughout his life Pleshcheev made fast friends with a wide variety of people. His liberty, equality, and brotherhood were but natural expressions of an attractive and garrulous personality. He was on close terms with Governor Baranovsky of Saratov province, Ukrainian poet Shevchenko, shady student activist Vsevolod Dmitrievich Kostomarov, Moscow entrepreneur Dmitrii Vasil'evich Chizhov, and nearly every member of the Moscow and St. Petersburg theatrical communities. When Pleshcheev assumed the duties of Litfond commissioner in Moscow, he sided with the Litfond liberals against a stodgy and increasingly statist (promonarchical, antiliberal) Moscow cultural elite. He served as a counterpoise to publisher Mikhail Nikiforovich Katkov, who was becoming a hireling of the state, a journalistic promoter of government projects. He also criticized law professor Boris Nikolaevich Chicherin, who took a leading role among academics to resist the university independence movement among students and faculty. In a letter written 6 November 1861 Pleshcheev conceded that the university movement had its foolish side, but he argued that Chicherin should not have addressed the students as he had, offending them with "such flabby fiddle-faddle all dressed up in war-surplus britches, with vague places and twaddle, doctrinal phrases! Is this the living voice of learning–or truth?" The banner of learning carried by Chicherin and his Muscovite associates did not suit Pleshcheev and other Litfond activists.

Yet, the doctrinaire spirit was likewise foreign to Pleshcheev. He praised Litfond activist Nikolai Gavrilovich Chernyshevsky and the other infamous radicals on the staff of the journal *Sovremennik*. His praise was natural enough because Chernyshevsky published Pleshcheev's writing. He devoted the poem "Chestnye liudi, dorogoi ternistoiu . . ." (Honorable people, along a thorny path . . .) to the *Sovremennik* staff. At the same time, though, Pleshcheev praised the grumpy Slavophilic publicist Ivan Sergeevich Aksakov and his obstreperous, eccentric journal *Den'* (Day), which also carried Pleshcheev's work. He liked Aksakov's "profound outlook on life." Relative to lesser Moscow associates, said Pleshcheev, Aksakov and his journal were as remote as the heavenly stars. Pleshcheev's generous and unprepossessing outreach caused him trouble when he sent a letter to Mikhailov in early 1861, recommending Moscow University student Kostomarov. He never forgave himself for facilitating this tragic association. Once introduced to leading Petersburg figures, Kostomarov turned on them. At police dictation, he composed an incriminating letter, ostensibly from Chernyshevsky to Pleshcheev, and suggested falsely that the two were writing and printing inflammatory proclamations. Pleshcheev saved himself from a second arrest and a possible repeat of the 1849 trauma. In the fall of 1862 his face-to-face confrontation with Kostomarov took place before judges in the imperial senate.

This trying confrontation did not save Chernyshevsky, or any other of the scores of leading cultural figures arrested, interrogated, and harassed throughout the second half of 1862. Aksakov's *Den'* was closed on government order in the same wave of reaction that had closed Chernyshevsky's *Sovremennik* the previous summer. There was no (mock) firing squad in store for Pleshcheev this time, but once again the tsarist state came down hard on its most energetic cultural elite, just as it had in Pleshcheev's youth, only now on a vaster scale. Without evidence, the senate found Chernyshevsky and Serno-Solov'evich guilty of several serious state crimes. They were sent into exile, never to return.

Pleshcheev's professional life deteriorated in the months of state suppression that followed these events. His ambitious "joint-stock" publishing enterprise came crashing down when a partner swindled him. His journal failed. Serno-Solov'evich's book-trade business went into a tailspin after his exile, and Pleshcheev lost his investment. Pleshcheev turned to his old acquaintance Mikhailov (who also died later while in political exile) in St. Petersburg to ask for employment on the staff of the vast, multivolume *Entsiklopedicheskii slovar'* (Encyclopedic Dictionary, 1890–1907), a project of leading Litfond figures. Pleshcheev's personal losses echoed his public defeats. His wife died in 1864, leaving him with three young children to care for. The "literature-policeman" Petr Ivanovich Kapnist of the Interior Ministry jumped on the wounded writer. In his annual report for 1865 he accused Pleshcheev of laying down a fog of German Romanticism to camouflage his skulking French socialism. Kapnist wrote that Pleshcheev's poetry represented "a protest against current moral, social and political structures in Russia"; that it asserted "the equality of the poor and the rich"; and that it contrasted "starving poverty with lazy and parasitic wealth."

Pleshcheev was now forty years old. Poems such as "Noch'iu" (At Night, published in *Skladchina* [Common Good], 1874) and "Tak tiazhelo, tak gor'ko mne i bol'no . . ." (How heavy, how bitter it is for me and painful . . ., published in *Teatral'naia gazeta* [Theatrical Gazette], 1893) expressed his mood. He had so far failed to achieve economic security in open journalistic and literary enterprise. His vaster vision seemed a dangerous and infantile dream. The strain of constant financial distress had undermined his health. Yet, he did not give up; on the contrary, in some ways he branched out. He expanded on his long association with the Russian theater, joining playwright Aleksandr Nikolaevich Ostrovsky in 1865 to found the Artisticheskii kruzhok

(Actors' Circle), the first independent professional organization of actors, playwrights, and other theatrical professionals in Russia. He wrote plays that portrayed the pitiful life of provincial gentry, among them "Shchastlivaia cheta" (The Fortunate Couple, published in *Sovremennik*, 1862) and "Poputchiki" (Traveling Companions, published in *Epokha* [Epoch], 1864). César Cui wrote an opera based on Pleshcheev's *Vill'iam Ratkliff* (1876), a translation of Heine's dramatic ballad of the same title.

Financial considerations ultimately forced Pleshcheev to accept an appointment in government service. He served from 1865 to 1875 in the office of State Control as a minor functionary. He was allowed to transfer out of military *chin* (rank), imposed during his exile, into civilian *chin*–but at the lowest rung of the Table of Ranks. At most, his salary might have reached 20 rubles a month. He remarried in the late 1860s; by this time he had already passed his literary prime. He was tired and sickly and, from this point on, wrote little of interest. Nevertheless, his later years were not entirely devoid of literary endeavors.

In 1872 Pleshcheev received a job transfer to St. Petersburg, where, in addition to his government service, he became secretary to the editor of *Otechestvennye zapiski*, one of the first journals to have published his work a quarter of a century earlier. In the 1870s, still curious about the possibilities of expanded literacy in his homeland, he tried his hand at a new genre–children's literature. Previously, he had contributed to a collection of children's poetry, *Detskaia knizhka* (Little Book for Children, 1861); he published a similar anthology in 1873, *Na prazdnik: Literaturnyi sbornik dlia detei* (In Celebration: A Literary Anthology for Children), and a collection of his own verse for children, *Podsnezhnik* (Snowdrop), came out in 1878. In another vein Pleshcheev edited a collection of satirical writings that included translations of works by authors such as Honoré Balzac, George Sand, and Benjamin Franklin; the collection, titled *Obshchestvennaia i domashniaia zhizn' zhivotnykh: Satiricheskie ocherki* (Social and Domestic Life of Animals: A Satirical Account), was published in 1876. During this period he worked with Ostrovsky again in a further effort to win independence from the choking patronage of royal and grandee elites in the theater. In 1874 they formed Obshchestvo russkikh drama-ticheskikh pisatelei i opernykh kompozitorov (The Society of Russian Dramatic Writers and Opera Composers) as well as other professional theater sodalities later. Thirteen of Pleshcheev's plays, written over the course of more than ten years, were staged in the Malyi Theater in Moscow and the Aleksandrinskii Theater in St. Petersburg. His son Aleksandr began to have some success as a theater critic in the 1880s.

In Pleshcheev's last years he achieved for the first time some personal economic comfort and was able to travel abroad. He died in Paris on 26 September 1893. In his will he left 1,000 rubles to Litfond, an amount equal to the loan that Dostoevsky never fully repaid.

Although the legacy of Pleshcheev's banner of learning endures, his civic impulse has not been agreeable to everyone. Soviet-era critic Prince Dmitry Petrovich Sviatopolk-Mirsky (who published as D. S. Mirsky) dismissed Pleshcheev's verse as "flat and tiresome" and considered the poet himself merely "amiable and respectable." Petr Veinberg's sympathetic entry, "Pleshcheev (Aleksei Nikolaevich)" (1898) in *Entsiklopedicheskii slovar'* conceded that Pleshcheev's prose works did not escape the ordinary, "although they do read easily and in addition several are not without interest." In his contribution to *Aleksei Nikolaevich Pleshcheev: Ego zhizn' i sochineniia* (Aleksei Nikolaevich Pleshcheev: His Life and Writings, 1911), Dmitrii Sergeevich Merezhkovsky, the herald of the symbolist era in Russian literature, advised the new generation to make a study of Pleshcheev's "noble simplicity of language" and to consider how "the man and poet were in him so closely twined, so indistinguishable that they cannot be disentangled. In truth it seems sometimes that the life of Pleshcheev was one of his best and most elevated poems." Merezhkovsky added these words of funereal approbation: "Oh, what a gentle, simple and good person this was." Even Dobroliubov damned Pleshcheev with faint praise in his July 1860 review article for *Sovremennik*, stating that he could be read "without displeasure."

Still, Pleshcheev's poem "Po chuvstvam brat'ia my s toboi . . .," which Kazan' University students set to music in the 1850s, was sung well into the twentieth century by a wide variety of Russian intellectuals and professionals at venues ranging from shabby student parties to the comfortable privacy of fine homes. It was a favorite of Vladimir Lenin's father, who was a high-ranking official in the Ministry of Education. The Soviet Revolution did not extinguish the need for this song. Other Pleshcheev poems inspired music, too, especially his lyrical works devoted to love and nature. The great Russian composers Petr Il'ich Chaikovsky, Anton Grigor'evich Rubinshtein, and Modest Petrovich Mussorgsky set several such poems to music. "Moi sadik" (My Little Garden Patch, *Stikhotvoreniia*, 1858), "Noch' proletala nad mirom . . ." (Night soared above the world . . . , *Vremia* [Time], 1862), "Ni slova, o drug moi . . ." (No words, oh my friend . . . , *Vremia*, 1861), and more than one hundred other poems by Pleshcheev received musical settings.

Aleksei Nikolaevich Pleshcheev's work appealed to a wide range of Russian readers. A growing middle-class readership responded with enthusiasm, but his themes also resonated among the refined cultural elite, in both imperial and Soviet times. The authentic expression of love appears not to grow stale too soon, nor does the simple affirmation of brotherhood. Pleshcheev wrote poems that were recited from memory by schoolchildren a century after his death. His creative endeavors saturated the Russian consciousness. He contributed to his national cultural inheritance without reaching to the heights of the great names, such as Aleksandr Sergeevich Pushkin or Leo Tolstoy. He might be thought of as the first major writer of Russian "popular culture," as distinct from "high culture" or "folk culture." In this way he was a thoroughly modern creative figure.

Letters:

Shestidesiatie gody: Materialy po istorii literatury i obshchestvennomu dvizheniiu, edited by N. K. Piksanov and O. V. Tsekhnovitser (Moscow & Leningrad: Akademiia nauk, 1940);

Filosofskie i obshchestvenno-politicheskie proizvedeniia petrashevtsev (Moscow: Gosudarstvennoe izdatel'stvo politicheskoi literatury, 1953), pp. 719–724;

"Pis'ma Pleshcheeva k Chekhovu (1888–1891)," *Literaturnoe nasledstvo,* 68 (1960);

"Materialy po istorii literatury i obshchestvennogo dvizheniia," *Literaturnyi arkhiv,* 6 (1961): 210–213.

Interview:

Vasilii Alekseevich Desnitsky, ed., *Delo petrashevtsev,* volume 3 (Moscow: Akademiia nauk, 1951), pp. 285–315.

Bibliographies:

Petr Vasil'evich Bykov, "Bibliografiia belletristicheskikh proizvedenii A. N. Pleshcheeva," in Pleshcheev's *Poviesti i razskazy A. N. Pleshcheeva,* volume 2 (St. Petersburg: Stasiulevich, 1897), pp. i–ii;

Bykov, "Bibliografiia stikhotvorenii A. N. Pleshcheeva," in Pleshcheev's *Stikhotvoreniia A. N. Pleshcheeva (1844–1891)* (St. Petersburg: A. F. Marks, 1905), pp. 797–813;

Dmitrii Dmitrievich Iazykov, "Pleshcheev A. N.," in his *Obzor zhizni i trudov russkikh pisatelei i pisatel'nits,* volume 13 (Petrograd, 1916), pp. 187–194.

Biographies:

Petr Vasil'evich Bykov, "A. N. Pleshcheev. Biograficheskii ocherk," in Pleshcheev's *Stikhotvoreniia*

A. N. Pleshcheeva (1844–1891) (St. Petersburg: A. F. Marks, 1905), pp. vii–lx;

Vasilii Ivanovich Pokrovskii, ed., *Aleksei Nikolaevich Pleshcheev: Ego zhizn' i sochineniia. Sbornik istoriko-literaturnykh statei* (Moscow: V. Spiridonov & A. Mikhailov, 1911);

I. A. Shchurov, *A. N. Pleshcheev: Zhizn' i tvorchestvo* (Iaroslavl': Verkhnee-Volzhskoe knizhnoe izdatel'stvo, 1977);

Nikolai Kuzin, *Pleshcheev,* Zhizn' zamechatel'nykh liudei (Moscow: Molodaia gvardiia, 1988);

Liubov' Semenovna Pustil'nik, *Zhizn' i tvorchestvo A. N. Pleshcheeva* (Moscow: Nauka, 1988).

References:

Iulii Isaevich Aikhenval'd, "Pleshcheev i Pomialovskii (Sravnitel'naia kharakteristika)," in his *Siluety russkikh pisatelei,* volume 1 (Moscow: Nauchnoe slovo, 1906);

Nikolai Aleksandrovich Dobroliubov, "Blagonamerennost' i deiatel'nost. Povesti i rasskazy A. Pleshcheeva," in his *Sobranie sochinenii,* 9 volumes, edited by Boris Ivanovich Brusov and others (Moscow: Goslitizdat, 1961–1964), VI (1963);

Petr Ivanovich Kapnist, *Sobranie materialov o napravlenii razlichnykh otraslei russkoi slovestnosti* (St. Petersburg, 1865), pp. 56–58;

I. V. Porokh and Nina Mikhailovna Chernyshevskaia, eds., *Delo Chernyshevskogo: Sbornik dokumentov* (Saratov: Privolzhskoe knizhnoe izdatel'stvo, 1968);

Petr Veinberg, "Aleksei Nikolaevich Pleshcheev," in *Entsiklopedicheskii slovar',* edited by I. E. Andreevsky (St. Petersburg: I. A. Efron, 1890–1907).

Papers:

Aleksei Nikolaevich Pleshcheev's papers are held in Moscow at the Russian State Archive of Art and Literature (RGALI), fond 378; the Russian State Library (RGB, formerly the Lenin Library), fond 178; and the State Literary Museum (GLM), fond 145. In St. Petersburg, Pleshcheev's papers can be found at the Institute of Russian Literature (IRLI, Pushkin House); the Russian State Historical Archive (RGIA), fond 1343; and the Russian National Library (RNB), fond 1029, fond 621, fond 608, fond 438 (materials related to Litfond), fond 236, and fond 118 (includes manuscripts of Pleshcheev's poems and a bibliography of his publications).

Iakov Petrovich Polonsky

(6 December 1819 – 18 October 1898)

Karen Evans-Romaine
Ohio University

BOOKS: *Nechaianno* (Moscow, 1844);

Gammy (Moscow: Stepanov, 1844)–includes "K demonu";

Stikhotvoreniia 1845 goda (St. Petersburg & Odessa: A. Braun, 1846);

Sazandar (Tblisi & St. Petersburg: Kantseliariia namestnika kavkazskogo, 1849);

Neskol'ko stikhotvorenii (Tblisi & St. Petersburg: Kantseliariia namestnika kavkazskogo, 1851);

Daredzhana Imeretinskaia. Drama v 5 deistviiakh (Moscow: Stepanov, 1852);

Stikhotvoreniia (St. Petersburg: I. Fishon, 1855; enlarged edition (St. Petersburg: Riumin, 1859)–includes "Kachka v buriu";

Rasskazy (St. Petersburg: Slovo, 1859);

Kuznechnik-muzykant (St. Petersburg: Riumin, 1859; enlarged edition, St. Petersburg: Gogenfel'da, 1863);

Razlad. Stseny iz poslednego pol'skogo vosstaniia (St. Petersburg, 1865);

Ottiski (St. Petersburg: N. Tiblen, 1866);

Sochineniia, 4 volumes (St. Petersburg: M. O. Vol'f, 1869–1870);

Retsenzent "Otechestvennykh zapisok" i otvet emu Ia. P. Polonskogo (St. Petersburg, 1871);

Snopy (St. Petersburg, 1871);

Ozimi, 2 parts (St. Petersburg: V. S. Balashev, 1876)–includes "Mimi" and "Keliot";

Deshevyi gorod (St. Petersburg, 1880);

Na zakate (Moscow: Martynov, 1881);

Krutye gorki (St. Petersburg, 1881);

Pero i karandash (St. Petersburg: V. S. Balashev, 1882);

Stikhotvoreniia 1841–1855 gg. (St. Petersburg, 1885);

Polnoe sobranie sochinenii, 10 volumes (St. Petersburg: Zh. A. Polonskaia, 1885–1886)–includes *Svezhee predan'e;*

Priznaniia Sergeia Chalygina (St. Petersburg, 1888);

Na vysotakh spiritizma (St. Petersburg: Skorokhodov, 1889);

Povesti i rasskazy, supplement to *Polnoe sobranie sochinenii,* 2 parts (St. Petersburg, 1889)–includes "I. S. Turgenev u sebia v ego poslednii priezd na rodinu";

Iakov Petrovich Polonsky

Vechernii zvon (St. Petersburg: A. S. Suvorin, 1890);

Proigrannaia molodost' (St. Petersburg: Rodina, 1891);

Lepta v pol'zu nuzhdaiushchikhsia (St. Petersburg: A. S. Suvorin, 1892);

Sobaki (St. Petersburg: A. Transhel', 1892);

Psikhopatka (St. Petersburg: Rodina, 1892);

Dve propushchennye i naidennye glavy iumoristicheskoi poemy "Sobaki" (St. Petersburg: Russkoe obozrenie, 1893);

Mechtatel'. Iunosha 30-kh godov XIX stoletiia (Moscow: G. O. Nemirovsky, 1894);

Polnoe sobranie stikhotvorenii, 5 volumes (St. Petersburg: A. F. Marks, 1896)–includes *Priznaniia Sergeia Chalygina* and "Zhenit'ba Atueva";

Zametki po povodu odnogo zagranichnogo izdaniia i novykh idei L. N. Tolstogo (St. Petersburg: Sinodal'naia, 1896);

Stikhotvoreniia i poemy, edited, with an introduction and commentary, by Boris Mikhailovich Eikhenbaum, Biblioteka poeta, Bol'shaia seriia (Leningrad: Sovetskii pisatel', 1935);

Stikhotvoreniia, edited, with an introduction and commentary, by Eikhenbaum, Biblioteka poeta, Bol'shaia seriia (Leningrad: Sovetskii pisatel', 1954);

Lirika. Proza, edited, with an introduction and commentary, by V. G. Fridliand (Moscow: Pravda, 1984);

Sochineniia, 2 volumes, edited, with an introduction and commentary, by I. B. Mushina (Moscow: Khudozhestvennaia literatura, 1986)–includes "Dlia nemnogikh," "Moi studencheskie vospominaniia," and "Starina i moe detstvo";

Proza, edited, with an introduction, by E. A. Polotskaia (Moscow: Sovetskaia Rossiia, 1988)–includes "Shkol'nye gody."

Editions and Collections: *Izbrannoe,* by Polonsky, A. K. Tolstoy, and A. N. Apukhtin, with an introduction by N. Kolosova (Moscow: Moskovskii rabochii, 1892);

Stikhotvoreniia, edited, with an introduction and commentary, by Boris Mikhailovich Eikhenbaum, Biblioteka poeta, Malaia seriia (Leningrad: Sovetskii pisatel', 1939, 1957);

Stikhotvoreniia, with an introduction by Vsevolod Rozhdestvensky (Leningrad: Khudozhestvennaia literatura, 1969);

Izbrannoe: Stikhotvoreniia i poema, edited by Vladimir Nikolaevich Orlov (Moscow: Detskaia literatura, 1977);

Stikhotvoreniia (Moscow: Sovetskaia Rossiia, 1981);

Lirika, edited by E. V. Ermilova (Moscow: Sovremennik, 1990);

Stikhotvoreniia (Sverdlovsk: Sredne-Ural'skoe knizhnoe izdatel'stvo, 1990);

Vliublennyi mesiats (Moscow: Letopis', 1998).

Edition in English: Poems by Polonsky, translated by Eugene Kayden, *Colorado Quarterly,* 21, no. 4 (1973): 561–566.

OTHER: *Podzemnye kliuchi,* with contributions by Polonsky, as "P" (Moscow: N. Mansyrev, 1842);

Kuznets Vakula, libretto by Polonsky, music by Petr Il'ich Chaikovsky (Moscow: P. Iurgenson, 1876); revised as *Cherevichki* (Moscow: P. Iurgenson, 1885); translated by Ruth and Thomas Martin as

The Golden Slippers (New York: G. Schirmer, 1955);

"Vladimir Grigor'evich Benediktov," in *Stikhotvoreniia,* edited by Polonsky, 3 volumes (St. Petersburg & Moscow: M. O. Vol'f, 1883–1884); republished as "Biografiia V. G. Benediktova," in Benediktov, *Sochineniia,* edited by Polonsky, 2 volumes (St. Petersburg, 1902), I: i–xxvii;

Literaturnyi sbornik proizvedenii studentov Imperatorskogo gosudarstvennogo Sankt-Peterburgskogo Universiteta, edited by Polonsky, Dmitrii Vasil'evich Grigorovich, and Apollon Nikolaevich Maikov (St. Petersburg, 1896);

"Proizvedeniia o Gruzii," edited by V. Shaduri, in *Russkie pisateli o Gruzii,* volume 1 (Tblisi: Zaria Vostoka, 1948), pp. 303–408, 501–507.

SELECTED PERIODICAL PUBLICATIONS– UNCOLLECTED: "Prozaicheskie tsvety poeticheskikh semian," *Otechestvennye zapiski,* 121 (1867): 717;

"Posmertnye stikhotvoreniia," *Niva,* 34–37 (1917): 517;

"Stikhotvoreniia–Iz staroi tetradi," in *Nevskii al'manakh,* 2, "Iz proshlogo" (Petrograd: Obshchestvo russkikh pisatelei dlia pomoshchi zhertvam voiny, 1917): 189, 195–196;

"Iz dnevnika. Noiabr'–dekabr' 1855. Otryvki iz vospominanii," edited by M. Tsiavlovskii, *Golos minuvshego,* 1–4 (1919): 101–122;

"Aristokratke," edited by I. Rozanov, *Golos minuvshego,* 3 (1923): 116;

"Iz dnevnika [27–30 iiunia 1882]," edited by G. P. Miroliubov, *Zven'ia,* 8 (1950): 230–234.

Iakov Polonsky is considered, together with Afanasii Afanas'evich Fet and Apollon Nikolaevich Maikov, as one of the foremost lyric poets of a generation dominated by great prose writers. The three names were linked together by contemporary critics and remain so to this day; among them Fet is considered the most eminent. Polonsky was a prolific writer and produced works in a vast range of genres, including novels in verse and prose, novellas, short stories, plays in verse and prose, long poems, essays, memoirs, and libretti for operas and other works; yet, today he is known only for his poetry, which in itself comprised five volumes in the virtually complete 1896 edition of his verse, *Polnoe sobranie stikhotvorenii.* Polonsky's poetry is characterized by a mellifluousness and soft lyricism. His strongest genre is the short lyric poem; many of his long poems and larger prose works remained unfinished. His themes range from the intimately personal to the landscapes and portraits of his travels, from the philosophical and religious to the overtly political. Polonsky's love poetry, psychologically charged landscapes, and often gloomy tone reflect the spirit of Romantic longing that typified much poetry of the previous generation in Russia and abroad; because of his themes and lyricism he can be considered a rather late Romantic poet.

For much of his life Polonsky struggled with the demand for politically engaged verse, a demand that prevailed not only in the 1860s and 1870s but also before that time in the works of literary critics, led in particular by Vissarion Grigor'evich Belinsky. Unlike Fet and Maikov, who gradually but solidly moved into the conservative camp, Polonsky established his position as a liberal and thus found himself in the middle of the fundamental literary debate surrounding literature in the latter half of the nineteenth century in Russia; on one side were the leftists, who believed that art must serve a social purpose, and on the other were the defenders of "pure art," who tended to be linked with political conservatives and to publish in their journals. Polonsky's career reflects the development of nineteenth-century Russian literature over six decades: it shows a tendency gradually away from social engagement and toward intimate and philosophical lyric verse. He wrote lyric poems throughout his career, however, and he untiringly defended the freedom of poets to write on all topics that inspired them.

Iakov Petrovich Polonsky was born in Riazan', a provincial town not far from Moscow, on 6 December 1819; he was the eldest son of an impoverished nobleman, Petr Grigor'evich Polonsky. The son of a retired Cossack captain, Polonsky's father was a cold person who disliked poetry. His mother, Natal'ia Iakovlevna (née Kaftyreva) Polonskaia, was from an old noble family; her grandfather was Count Aleksei Grigor'evich Razumovsky, known for his love of music. Natal'ia Iakovlevna was the opposite of Polonsky's father in character: loving and kind, she had a warm appreciation for poetry and kept notebooks of the poetry and song lyrics that she liked. Polonsky was inspired by the folk songs he heard from the servants at the home of his maternal grandmother, whom the family visited weekly at her house in Riazan'. Like his predecessor, the poet Aleksandr Sergeevich Pushkin, Polonsky was also enthralled by the folktales that his nanny Matrena told him, and she appears more than once in his verse.

Polonsky was taught at home beginning at the age of six. When his mother died in 1830, and his father was sent as a tax inspector to the Armenian capital Erivani (Erevan), the boy was enrolled in a local gymnasium and placed in the care of his maiden aunts, the sisters of his deceased mother. At the gymnasium he became acquainted with the poetry of Pushkin and Vladimir Grigor'evich Benediktov, both of whom he immediately admired; he imitated the style of the latter in his early poetic attempts. In 1837 the Romantic poet

Vasilii Andreevich Zhukovsky visited Riazan' with the heir to the throne, the future Tsar Alexander II. The young Polonsky had been assigned to write verses for the occasion. Zhukovsky liked the poetry so much that he asked to meet the young poet, and when he did he rewarded Polonsky with a gold pocket watch. Polonsky graduated from the gymnasium and entered the law faculty of Moscow University in 1838. At his entrance exams he met fellow Moscow University student, writer, and critic Apollon Apollonovich Grigor'ev. Polonsky and Grigor'ev quickly discovered that they were both aspiring writers and became friends. Soon Grigor'ev introduced Polonsky to the poet Fet, his friend and fellow university student, who rented a room in the Moscow home of the Grigor'ev family. At the university Grigor'ev led a student philosophy club, the members of which gently mocked Polonsky for his lack of interest in that subject and in religion. Polonsky responded to their friendly criticism with his poem "K demonu" (To the Demon, 1844), in which he characterizes poetry as a temple in which his beloved poets protect him from the "demon of doubt."

During his student years Polonsky also made an important acquaintance in the person of Mikhail Fedorovich Orlov, a Decembrist and member of the secret societies Soiuz spaseniia (Union of Salvation) and Soiuz blagodenstviia (Union of Welfare). Polonsky befriended Orlov's son Nikolai Mikhailovich Orlov and was a frequent guest at their home, which was a leading Moscow literary salon in the 1840s. There Polonsky met liberal figures who played an important role in his later work, including his future history professor Timofei Nikolaevich Granovsky, the philosopher Petr Iakovlevich Chaadaev, and the young Ivan Sergeevich Turgenev. Polonsky also visited the salon of Avdot'ia Petrovna Elagina, the mother of the Slavophile writers and philosophers Petr and Ivan Vasil'evich Kireevsky; her gatherings were attended by some of the greatest writers and thinkers of the day, including Zhukovsky, Chaadaev, Nikolai Vasil'evich Gogol, and Alexander Herzen (Aleksandr Ivanovich Gertsen), as Polonsky recalled later in his memoristic novel *Deshevyi gorod* (Cheap City, 1880). One of the most important new acquaintances that he made during his university years was Ivan Petrovich Kliushnikov, a friend of Belinsky's and member of the literary *kruzhok* (circle) led by Nikolai Vladimirovich Stankevich. In 1839 Kliushnikov introduced Polonsky to Belinsky, whom Polonsky deeply admired and to whom he sent a letter and some verses. Polonsky later recalled being hurt at the critic's condescending attitude toward him.

In the year 1840 Polonsky made his debut in print: his poem "Sviashchennyi blagovest torzhestvenno zvuchit . . ." (The holy bells ring triumphally . . .)

appeared in the journal *Otechestvennye zapiski* (Notes of the Fatherland). His poems were published there and more often in the conservative *Moskvitianin* (The Muscovite) in the early 1840s. He also published and signed merely as "P" what he later considered immature verse in the student almanac *Podzemnye kliuchi* (Underground Springs, 1842).

Polonsky's first book of verse, titled *Gammy* (Musical Scales), appeared in 1844. The collection received mixed reviews, including a tepid assessment by Belinsky; the poet Nikolai Mikhailovich Iazykov, to whom Polonsky had sent a copy, replied, however, with a friendly epistle in verse. Soon after the appearance of his book Polonsky graduated from Moscow University. His difficult financial situation required that he find work quickly, and he decided, upon the advice of friends, to travel to Odessa in November 1844. Unable to find a suitable post there, he earned his living by giving private lessons. In Odessa he did, nevertheless, meet interesting people—such as Aleksandr Aleksandrovich Bakunin, a lycée teacher with whom he stayed, who was also the brother of anarchist Mikhail Aleksandrovich Bakunin, and Aleksandr Pushkin's brother Lev Sergeevich Pushkin.

In 1846 the second collection of Polonsky's verse appeared. Simply titled *Stikhotvoreniia 1845 goda* (Poems of 1845), it was reviewed harshly by Belinsky. That June, Polonsky left Odessa for the Georgian capital Tiflis (Tbilisi), where Governor-General Mikhail Semenovich Vorontsov was transferred to his new post. Polonsky was one of a group of civil servants who followed the general from Odessa to Georgia, where friends managed to procure a position for him in Vorontsov's office. Polonsky also worked as an editorial assistant at the newspaper *Zakavkazskii vestnik* (The Caucasian Messenger). He spent five artistically productive years in the Caucasus; his literary acquaintances and the general atmosphere in Tiflis helped to broaden his horizons and to strengthen his poetry. Polonsky was drawn into a company of writers, most notable among them the Russian writer Count Vladimir Aleksandrovich Sollogub, as well as of artists and actors, some of whom were in the Georgian capital in connection with Russian state cultural projects there. He also met Georgian and Azerbaijani writers and became interested in the folklore of the Caucasus.

Polonsky's work required him to travel on horseback through the region in order to gather statistical data, and he wrote ethnographic pieces that were published in *Zakavkazskii vestnik* and *Kavkaz* (The Caucasus). The Caucasian setting also inspired him to write poetry: he published a few poems in a newspaper in 1848 and published his third book of verse, a small collection with the Georgian title *Sazandar* (Singer), in Tif-

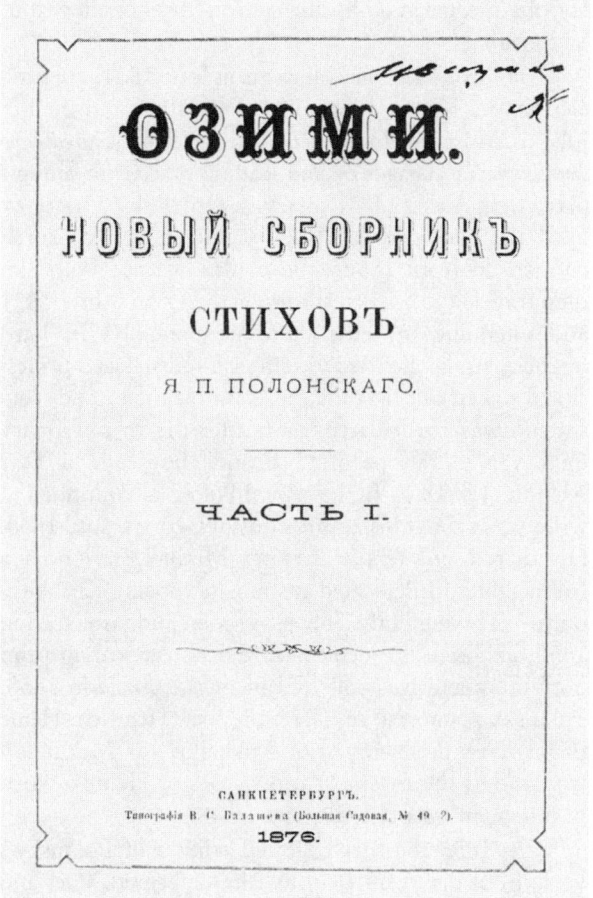

Title page for the first part of Ozimi *(Winter Crop), the verse collection that signaled Polonsky's dedication to writing lyric poetry (Kilgour Collection of Russian Literature, Harvard University Library)*

lis in 1849; the poems in this book were accompanied by detailed notes that reflected his careful study of the region. *Sazandar* was well received, both in Tiflis and in Moscow. This collection is distinguished from Polonsky's other work in its treatment of historical, geographical, and sociopolitical themes. Polonsky's friendly epistle to Lev Pushkin, "Progulka po Tiflisu," in which the poet's "painterly" talents are evident, is one of the pieces that stands out in *Sazandar;* he writes that Tiflis is a "treasure for the painter." The influence of lyric genres prevails even more—many of the verses in the collection are song-like ballads and romances—and the impact of the Romantic poet Mikhail Iur'evich Lermontov's Caucasian verses is apparent. Polonsky published another collection, *Neskol'ko stikhotvorenii* (A Few Poems), in 1851. From 1850 to 1851 he also wrote an historical drama based on the Georgian setting, *Daredzhana Imeretinskaia* (Daredzhana, Imeretian Princess, 1852); although the play was written for the opening of a theater in Tiflis, the censors did not allow it to be staged.

Polonsky left the Caucasus in June 1851. He traveled first to Riazan' to see his ailing father and then in July to Moscow. In Moscow he read his *Daredzhana Imeretinskaia* to Grigor'ev and leading nineteenth-century playwright Aleksandr Nikolaevich Ostrovsky. Grigor'ev liked the play and published it, albeit with censorial cuts, in an April 1852 issue of *Moskvitianin*. Polonsky then traveled to St. Petersburg, arriving on 7 July 1851 and intending to settle there permanently. In hard financial straits, he tried to establish himself as a professional writer, but his timing was unfortunate, since censorship was particularly harsh after the revolutionary upheavals in Europe of 1848 until the death of Tsar Nicholas I in 1855. In the capital Polonsky continued to write verse about his impressions of Georgia until 1853. He shared quarters with poet Mikhail Larionovich Mikhailov and dedicated to him the poem "Kachka v buriu" (Tossing in the Storm), written and published in 1850, although the dedication did not appear in print until the poem was collected in *Stikhotvoreniia* in 1855. Polonsky's interest in German poet Heinrich Heine might have originated with Mikhailov, as Mikhailov was one of the foremost translators of Heine's work in nineteenth-century Russia.

In 1855 the first collected edition of Polonsky's verse from the years 1840 to 1855 appeared. Poet and publisher Nikolai Alekseevich Nekrasov gave *Stikhotvoreniia* (Poems) a positive, albeit unsigned, review in *Sovremennik* (The Contemporary). Polonsky's literary standing gradually improved; he struck up friendships with writers such as Turgenev and Maikov. His financial situation remained unstable, however. Finally, on 26 October 1855 he obtained a civil service job in the office of St. Petersburg governor Nikolai Mikhailovich Smirnov. His new employer soon offered him a position as tutor to his son Misha; Polonsky accepted the post and left the governor's office. Smirnov's wife was the writer Aleksandra Osipovna Rosset, who had served at court and achieved considerable respect as a writer and member of high society. The position of tutor and particularly his dependence on a woman who was well read and highly respected in society were irksome to Polonsky. In May 1857 he left with the Smirnov family for the German resort town of Baden-Baden, where he met Leo Tolstoy; despite this remarkable event, however, Polonsky's impressions of the place were generally negative. After leaving the Smirnovs' employ in August and living in Geneva to study painting (until his money ran out), Polonsky received a letter from Maikov and learned that Count Grigorii Aleksandrovich Kushelev-Bezborodko was organizing a new journal, *Russkoe slovo* (Russian Word). Maikov had recommended Polonsky

as an editor. Kushelev-Bezborodko was then in Italy. Polonsky traveled to Rome, where he stayed with Turgenev and Vasilii Petrovich Botkin, and met with Kushelev-Bezborodko, who invited him to co-edit the journal. He agreed with some hesitation: he wished to stay in Rome to study painting, but his precarious financial position and Mikhailov's advice convinced him to take the position.

Polonsky left for Paris, and there he met Elena Vasil'evna Ustiuzhskaia, the eighteen-year-old daughter of a Russian Orthodox Church sexton. They were married in July 1858 and returned to St. Petersburg in August, when Polonsky began his job with *Russkoe slovo*. The couple stayed with the family of Polonsky's friend, St. Petersburg architect Andrei Ivanovich Shtakenshneider. His next collection of verse, an expansion of his 1855 *Stikhotvoreniia*, appeared in 1859. That same year a collection of his short stories, *Rasskazy* (Stories), was also published; some stories appeared in *Sovremennik* as well. His most successful work of 1859, the long poem "Kuznechik-muzykant" (The Cricket-Musician), came out in *Russkoe slovo;* it is an allegorical piece about the difficult position of an artist in a heartless and mindless society. Polonsky continued this theme in "Dlia nemnogikh" (For the Few, published in *Russkoe slovo*, 1859); in this poem he claimed his position as a poet for the few, who sees visions others cannot see but who does not possess the "satirist's whip" demanded of him by his contemporaries. The poem appeared in the January issue of *Russkoe slovo* but was not included in the 1896 collection of his complete verse.

Despite his prolific literary output at this time, the period from 1859 to 1860 proved difficult for Polonsky. In June 1859 he fell from a carriage and injured his knee so seriously that he had to walk with crutches or a cane for the rest of his life. His son, Andrei, who was born in July 1859, died in January 1860, and within a few months of the baby's death Polonsky's wife fell ill. In addition, his work with *Russkoe slovo* was turning out to be an unsuccessful venture. Displeased with the management of the journal, he left his editorial job there in 1860. On 9 March 1860 he began to work as a secretary at the state committee for censorship of foreign literature, where Maikov and the poet Fedor Ivanovich Tiutchev also worked. The position provided Polonsky with a salary and an apartment. The stability of this new situation provided little comfort, however: his wife died on 8 July 1860. He dedicated to her a cycle of poems, addressing the fear of loss, the moment of her death, and his grief after her departure.

Soon after Polonsky left *Russkoe slovo,* he became associated with the conservative journals *Vremia* (Time) and *Epokha* (The Epoch), edited by Fyodor Dostoevsky and his brother Mikhail Mikhailovich Dostoevsky during the period 1861 to 1865. In 1861 Polonsky went abroad again, this time to the baths in Austria, in an unsuccessful attempt to have his knee treated. That year he began writing a novel in verse titled *Svezhee predan'e* (Fresh Legend), about the literary and philosophical debates of the 1840s. Consisting of six parts out of a planned twenty, the novel was published in *Vremia* (1861–1862). Kamkov, the hero of the novel, is based loosely on Kliushnikov, who had influenced Polonsky greatly during his university years in the early 1840s. Polonsky might have chosen the genre of the novel in verse in order to allow for lyrical and philosophical digressions in which he could convey the atmosphere and ideas of the 1840s, so fundamental to the further development of Russian thought in the latter part of the nineteenth century—and particularly to Polonsky's generation. The authorial digressions in the poem include attacks on the radical writers Dmitrii Ivanovich Pisarev and Dmitrii Dmitrievich Minaev, who had criticized Polonsky in the press for his liberal views.

In 1863 Polonsky was promoted to the position of junior censor at the foreign censorship committee. From 1864 to 1865 he returned to writing socially engaged poetry. That year he published in *Epokha* his drama *Razlad* (Collapse, published as a book in 1865), subtitled *Stseny iz poslednego pol'skogo vosstaniia* (Scenes from the Last Polish Uprising). In 1865 he renewed relations with Nekrasov, damaged in the late 1850s and early 1860s by Polonsky's stance against Nekrasov and civic poetry, and again began publishing poetry in Nekrasov's journal *Sovremennik*. From 1865 to 1870 Polonsky wrote and left unfinished—as he did *Svezhee predan'e*—a semi-autobiographical *poema* (long narrative poem) titled "Brat'ia" (Brothers), about a Russian artist named Ignat Iliushin who leaves Moscow for Rome. "Brat'ia" features scenes of revolutionary uprisings in Rome in 1848, and Polonsky planned in later chapters to have Iliushin imprisoned for revolutionary activity. Completed chapters from the *poema* were published separately in the journals *Zhenskii vestnik* (The Women's Messenger) in 1866; *Russkii vestnik* (The Russian Messenger) from 1867 to 1869; and *Vestnik Evropy* (The European Messenger) in 1870. In 1866 Polonsky met Zhozefina Antonovna Riul'man, a shy orphan who had served as a governess at the home of a family named Bogoliubov in St. Petersburg. They married on 17 July of that year. After their marriage Zhozefina began to sculpt; she became best known for a bust of Turgenev. The couple had two sons and a daughter.

Polonsky soon moved from the novel in verse to prose in *Priznaniia Sergeia Chalygina* (The Confessions of Sergei Chalygin), first published in 1867 in the journal *Literaturnaia biblioteka* (A Literary Library). This unfinished novel takes place during the Decembrist Rebel-

lion of 1825 and depicts the meetings of secret organizations leading up to that event. Polonsky's visits during his student years to the home of the Decembrist Orlov provided him with both material and prototypes for characters in the novel. Some critics considered this novel Polonsky's greatest prose work. Attempting to convey the development of a child's consciousness, it fits into the same genre as Tolstoy's trilogy *Detstvo. Otrochestvo. Iunost'* (Childhood. Boyhood. Youth, 1852–1857). Polonsky did not finish *Priznaniia Sergeia Chalygina* at least partly because he did not see a chance for it to be published in Russia; the novel is marked by a self-censorship of details surrounding the events of 1825.

The first edition of Polonsky's collected poetry and prose appeared in four volumes from 1869 to 1870. It received mixed reviews and became the subject of an intense literary debate. In 1869 an anonymous critic in the Populist journal *Bibliograf* (The Bibliographer) lambasted Polonsky's writing for its outdated Romantic themes. In an 1869 review published in *Otechestvennye zapiski,* critic and satirist Mikhail Evgrafovich Saltykov censured Polonsky as a second-rate eclectic. Turgenev gave encouragement to Polonsky in private correspondence and defended his unique voice publicly in an 1870 letter to the editor of *Sankt-Peterburgskie vedomosti* (The St. Petersburg News). Polonsky's work thus provided leftist critics with a forum to criticize the notion of "pure art," and Turgenev, in turn, provided a forum to defend it. The Turgenev defense put Polonsky in a difficult position, since he did not wish to break relations with Nekrasov. Turgenev's public letter prompted an even harsher response from Saltykov: in a critique of Polonsky's 1871 collection of verse *Snopy* (Sheaves), the critic accused Polonsky of a lack of clarity in his views that rendered his work worthless. This time Polonsky defended himself in a polemical brochure titled *Retsenzent "Otechestvennykh zapisok" i otvet emu Ia. P. Polonskogo* (The *Notes of the Fatherland* Reviewer and Ia. P. Polonsky's Reply, 1871): he brushed aside the criticism as "slander" and "mockery" and affirmed his belief in himself, his literary strength, and his commitment to societal issues. Polonsky's relations with Nekrasov remained complicated; Nekrasov published his *poema* "Mimi" in *Otechestvennye zapiski* in 1873 but rejected his next *poema* "Keliot," on the Greek liberation movement. In 1871 Polonsky wrote a libretto based on Gogol's story "Noch' pered Rozhdestvom" (The Night before Christmas, 1832). The composer Petr Il'ich Chaikovsky used the libretto, *Kuznets Vakula* (Vakula the Smith, 1876), for his opera of the same name.

In 1875 Polonsky reentered the world of journalism by joining the editorship of the weekly *Pchela* (The Bee) and published there that year his satirical poem "Sobaki" (Dogs). After this piece, and especially in the

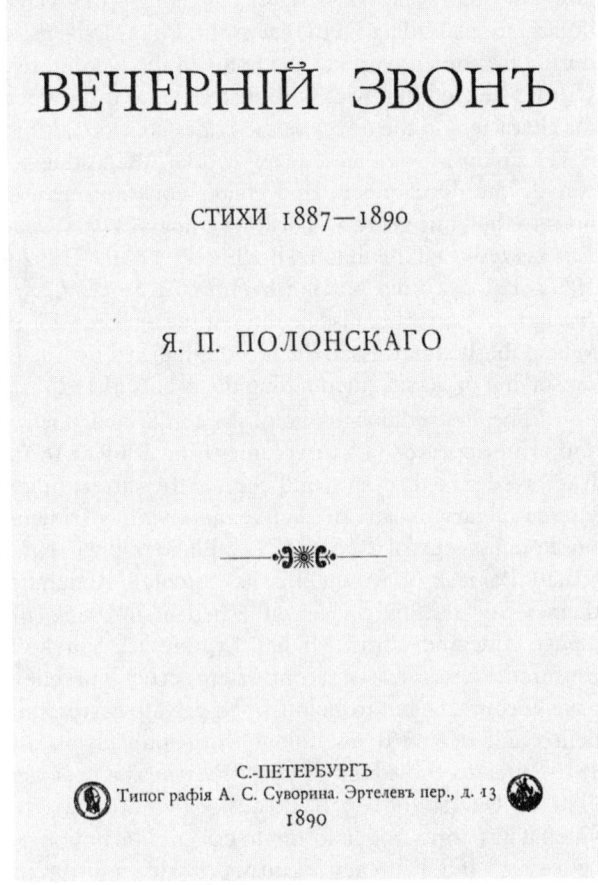

ВЕЧЕРНІЙ ЗВОНЪ

СТИХИ 1887—1890

Я. П. ПОЛОНСКАГО

С.-ПЕТЕРБУРГЪ
Типогрфія А. С. Суворина. Эртелевъ пер., д. 13
1890

Title page for Polonsky's Vechernii zvon (Evening Bell),
a collection of verse written between 1887 and 1890
(Kilgour Collection of Russian Literature,
Harvard University Library)

more conservative 1880s, Polonsky moved away from socially engaged poetry and back more firmly into the "pure art" camp. He dedicated himself to writing lyric poetry. In 1876 there appeared a two-part collection of his verse titled *Ozimi* (Winter Crops), indicative of this change, followed by *Na zakate* (At Sunset, 1881), a book of poetry that he wrote during the period 1877 to 1880. He also published two semi-autobiographical novels during this period: *Deshevyi gorod* in 1880 and *Krutye gorki* (Steep Hills) in 1881. He renewed his friendship with the greatest poetic representative of his generation, Fet. Polonsky, his wife, and their three children stayed with Turgenev on the latter's estate in the summer of 1881, and Polonsky wrote a memoir about Turgenev in 1883, "I. S. Turgenev u sebia v ego poslednii priezd na rodinu" (I. S. Turgenev at His Home during His Last Trip to His Homeland), published in the journal *Niva* (Virgin Field) in 1884.

Polonsky befriended writers of the new generation, including Vsevolod Mikhailovich Garshin, whom he met at Turgenev's estate in 1882; Anton Pavlovich

Chekhov, whom he met in 1887; and the young poet Konstantin Mikhailovich Fofanov. He dedicated many poems to younger writers, including "Pamiati S. Ia. Nadsona" (In Memory of Sergei Iakovlevich Nadson, 1887), "Pamiati V. M. Garshina" (In Memory of V. M. Garshin, 1888), and "U dveri" (At the Door, 1888), dedicated to Chekhov. In 1885–1886 a ten-volume edition of his complete works appeared, and on 10 April 1887 a celebration to commemorate his fifty-year career took place. At the celebration the poets Maikov, Minaev, Fofanov, and others recited congratulatory verses to Polonsky. In 1890 a collection of poems that Polonsky had written since 1887 appeared. Its title, *Vechernii zvon* (Evening Bells), paid homage to Fet's successful *Vechernie ogni* (Evening Lights, 1883–1891); in the summers of 1889 and 1890 Polonsky was a guest at Fet's estate in the village of Vorob'evka.

In his last decade Polonsky returned to the genre of the memoir, which he had first explored in 1883 with his piece on Turgenev. Much of Polonsky's previous work had been partially autobiographical, and his late works evince the development of this trend into pure memoir–his attempt to convey details of his early life in old age. The first set of his memoirs, "Starina i moe detstvo," appeared in *Russkii vestnik* from 1890 to 1891. In 1896 he left his position on the foreign censorship committee and was appointed as a member of the Council on the Press. A continuation of his memoirs, "Moi studencheskie vospominaniia," was published in *Niva* in 1898.

In his last years Polonsky turned his modest St. Petersburg apartment into a Friday evening salon in which he greeted and supported young poets. He did not, however, greet the Russian decadent and Symbolist writers of the 1890s with enthusiasm, according to the memoirs of writer and essayist Petr Petrovich Pertsov. The great Symbolist poet Aleksandr Aleksandrovich Blok, however, was enthralled with Polonsky's manner: in a 1908 contribution to the journal *Rech'* (Speech) he wrote about how the aged poet, a living link with the Romantic past of Russia, "moved hearts . . . with his solemnly outstretched and romantically shaking hand in a dirty white glove."

Polonsky died on 18 October 1898 at the age of seventy-eight; he had been ill and practically blind before his death. Among the people who attended his funeral was Grand Duke Konstantin Konstantinovich Romanov, who published as the poet K.R. and headed the Academy of Sciences. Polonsky's body was moved on 25 October 1898 from St. Petersburg to his native Riazan'. He is buried there at the Spasskii (Savior) Monastery, near his mother. After the poet's death his widow continued to host their Friday evening salon in a different form: it was organized by a newly formed Polonsky Club and held at the Obshchestva arkhitektorov (Architectural Society). The circle continued to meet until 1916.

Iakov Petrovich Polonsky is best regarded today for his lyric poetry and romances; his verses were set to music by leading Russian composers of the nineteenth and early twentieth centuries, including Chaikovsky, Sergei Ivanovich Taneev, Aleksandr Sergeevich Dargomyzhsky, and Sergei Vasil'evich Rakhmaninov. Some of his poems now belong to the realm of Russian folk song. A few critics considered Polonsky's lyric voice weak, whereas other writers found the melodic quality of it congenial; Blok in particular owed Polonsky a debt of gratitude, which he acknowledged even while comparing the poet unfavorably to Fet. Polonsky was fortunate to live long enough to achieve the appreciation of his poetic successors. His work spanned six decades of Russian literary history, half of which were not conducive to the flowering of a purely Romantic talent. To a great extent, because of the homage paid him by the next generation of "pure art" poets in Russia–especially by Blok and Ivan Alekseevich Bunin–Polonsky's voice is known and appreciated today. Recent scholarship on the poet shows that his work continues to attract interest, though there has never been a complete collected edition of his writings.

Letters:
To Anton Pavlovich Chekhov, in *Slovo. Sbornik vtoroi* (Moscow: Knizhnoe izdatel'stvo pisatelei v Moskve, 1914), pp. 223–234;
To Afanasii Afanas'evich Fet, *Novoe vremia,* supplements to 11, 14, 18 January 1914; 29 February 1916, pp. 9–13;
To Nikolai Alekseevich Nekrasov, edited by N. Kozmin, in *Nekrasov, po neizdannym materialam Pushkinskogo doma* (Petrograd: M. & S. Sabashnikovy, 1922), pp. 269–298;
To Fyodor Dostoevsky, edited by Nikolai F. Bel'chikov, in *Iz arkhiva Dostoevskogo: Pis'ma russkikh pisatelei* (Moscow: Gosudarstvennoe izdatel'stvo, 1923), pp. 62–88;
To Vissarion Grigor'evich Belinsky, edited by I. L. Polivanov, in *Venok Belinskomu,* by Nikolai Kir'iakovich Piksanov (Moscow: Novaia Moskva, 1924), pp. 236–242;
To Count Grigorii Aleksandrovich Kushelev-Bezborodko, edited by G. P. Prokhorov, *Zven'ia,* 1 (1932): 296–307, 313–324;
To Aleksandr Nikolaevich Ostrovsky, in *Neizdannye pis'ma k A. N. Ostrovskomu: Iz arkhiva A. N. Ostrovskogo,* edited by M. D. Prygunov (Moscow & Leningrad: Academia, 1932), pp. 437–456;
To Leo Tolstoy, edited by G. Miroliubov, in *L. N. Tolstoy,* 2 volumes, edited by Nikolai Nikolaevich Gusev

(Moscow: Letopisi Gosudarstvennogo literaturnogo muzeia, 1938–1948), II: 210–222;
"Pis'ma," edited by G. P. Miroliubov, *Zven'ia,* 8 (1950): 152–261.

Bibliography:
Ioann Vasil'evich Dobroliubov and S. D. Iakhontov, "Ia. P. Polonsky," in their *Bibliograficheskii slovar' pisatelei, uchenykh i khudozhnikov, urozhentsev (preimushchestvenno) Riazanskoi gubernii* (Riazan': Gubernskaia tipografiia, 1910), pp. 190–194.

Biographies:
Dmitrii Ivanovch Tikhomirov, *A. N. Maikov i Ia. P. Polonsky: Biografii i izbrannye stikhotvoreniia* (Moscow: K. L. Men'shov, 1909);
Aleksandr Vasil'evich Kruglov, *Ia. P. Polonsky: Biografiia i kharakteristika* (Moscow: A. S. Panafinida, 1914);
Pavel Aleksandrovich Orlov, *Ia. P. Polonsky: Kritiko-biograficheskii ocherk* (Riazan': Riazanskoe knizhnoe izdatel'stvo, 1961).

References:
Iulii Isaevich Aikhenval'd, "Polonsky," in his *Siluety russkikh pisatelei,* 2 volumes (Moscow: Terra/Respublika, 1998), I: 174–181;
Aleksandr Aleksandrovich Blok, "Vechera 'Iskusstv'," *Rech'* (27 October 1908);
Igor' Semenovich Bogomolov, *Armeniia v tvorchestve Iakova Polonskogo* (Erevan: Akademiia nauk Armianskoi SSR, 1963);
G. P. Danilevsky, "Pis'ma k Ia. P. Polonskomu," edited by E. V. Sviiasov, in *Ezhegodnik Rukopisnogo otdela Pushkinskogo doma. 1978* (Leningrad: Nauka, 1980), pp. 129–162;
Boris Mikhailovich Eikhenbaum, "Ia. P. Polonsky," in Polonsky's *Stikhotvoreniia,* edited by Eikhenbaum (Leningrad: Sovetskii pisatel', 1954), pp. 5–39;
P. A. Gaponenko, "'Menia garmoniia uchila po-chelovecheski stradat': Zametki o poezii Ia. P. Polonskogo," *Russkii iazyk v shkole,* 4 (July–August 1998): 70–72;
Evgenii Mikhailovich Garshin, *Poeziia Ia. P. Polonskogo* (St. Petersburg: V. V. Komarov, 1887);
Zinaida Gippius, *Zhivye litsa,* volume 2 (Prague: Plamia, 1925);
I. A. Gulkova, "'Svobodnaia obraznost' iazyka': O poetike Ia. P. Polonskogo," *Russkii iazyk v shkole,* 6 (November–December 1999): 52–57;
Iakov Petrovich Polonsky: Ego zhizn' i sochineniia. Sbornik istoriko-literaturnykh statei, compiled by Vasilii Ivanovich Pokrovsky (Moscow: Sklad v knizhnom magazine V. Spiridonova & A. Mikhailova, 1906);

Mikhail Georgievich Khalansky, *Polonsky v ego poezii* (Khar'kov: K. N. Gagarin, 1900);

Aleksandr Ivanovich Lagunov, *Lirika Iakova Polonskogo* (Stavropol': Stavropol'skoe knizhnoe izdatel'stvo, 1974);

N. Mikhailovsky, "Pamiati Ia. P. Polonskogo," *Russkoe bogatstvo,* 11 (1898): 61–62;

Nikolai Alekseevich Nekrasov, "Stikhotvoreniia Ia. P. Polonskogo. SPb., 1855," in his *Polnoe sobranie sochinenii i pisem,* 12 volumes, edited by Vladislav Evgen'evich Evgen'ev-Maksimov (Moscow: Goslitizdat, 1948–1953), IX: 273–275, 724–744;

Iu. Nikol'sky, "Istoriia odnoi druzhby (Fet i Polonsky)," *Russkaia mysl',* 5–6 (1917);

Margarita Odesskaia, ed., "Iakov Petrovich Polonsky i ego piatnitsy," *Voprosy literatury,* 3 (1992): 312–331;

Vladimir Nikolaevich Orlov, "Polonsky," in his *Puti i sud'by: Literaturnye ocherki* (Moscow: Sovetskii pisatel', 1963), pp. 133–178;

Veniamin M. Paradiev, *Ia. P. Polonsky i ego lirika* (Kiev: S. V. Kul'zhenko, 1913);

Petr Petrovich Pertsov, *Literaturnye vospominaniia, 1890–1902 gg* (Moscow: Academia, 1933);

Liudmila Aleksandrovna Pronina, *Polonsky i vremia* (Riazan': Poverennyi, 2000);

Mikhail Evgrafovich Saltykov, "Sochineniia Ia. P. Polonskogo. 2 toma. SPb., 1869" and "Snopy. Stikhi i proza Ia. P. Polonskogo, SPb., 1871," in his *Polnoe sobranie sochinenii,* 20 volumes (Moscow: Khudozhestvennaia literatura, 1937), VIII: 372–376, 422–430, 511, 516–519;

Nikolai Vasil'evich Shelgunov, Luidmila Petrovna Shelgunov, and Mikhail Larionovich Mikhailov, *Vos-pominaniia,* 2 volumes (Moscow: Khudozhestvennaia literatura, 1967);

Elena Andreevna Shtakenshneider, *Dnevnik i zapiski: 1854–1886* (Moscow: Academia, 1934);

Nikolai Matveevich Sokolov, *Lirika Ia. P. Polonskago. Kriticheskii etiud* (St. Petersburg: P. P. Soikin, 1899);

Vladimir Sergeevich Solov'ev, "Poeziia Ia. P. Polonskogo. Kriticheskii ocherk," *Ezhemesiachnoe prilozhenie k Nive,* 2 (1896): 367–379; 6 (1869): 297–312;

Aleksandr Isaevich Solzhenitsyn, "The Ashes of a Poet," in his *Stories and Prose Poems,* translated by Michael Glenny (New York: Farrar, Straus & Giroux, 1970), pp. 248–249;

Nikolai Nikolaevich Strakhov, *Zametki o Pushkine i drugikh poetakh* (Kiev: I. I. Chokolov, 1897);

Sergei Tkhorzhevsky, *Portrety perom: Povesti o V. Tepliakove, A. Balasoglo, Ia. Polonskom* (Moscow: Kniga, 1986);

Ivan Sergeevich Turgenev, "Pis'mo k redatoru 'Sankt-Peterburgskikh vedomostei'," in his *Sobranie sochinenii,* 12 volumes, edited by Iulian Grigor'evich Oksman (Moscow: Khudozhestvennaia literatura, 1956), XI: 193–199, 494–496.

Papers:

Iakov Petrovich Polonsky's papers are kept in St. Petersburg at the Institute of Russian Literature (IRLI, Pushkin House), fond 241 (which includes the unpublished memoir "Koi-chto iz moego bylogo"), and in Moscow at the Russian State Archive of Literature and Art (RGALI), where the unpublished article "O kachestvakh, neobkhodimykh pisateliu, a v osobennosti poetu" can also be found.

Koz'ma Petrovich Prutkov

(11 April 1803 – 13 January 1863)

Barbara Henry
University of Washington

BOOKS: *Polnoe sobranie sochinenii,* edited by Vladimir Zhemchuzhnikov (St. Petersburg: M. M. Stasiulevich, 1884; revised and enlarged, 1885; revised and enlarged, Petrograd: M. M. Stasiulevich, 1916; enlarged, Moscow & Leningrad: Academia, 1933)—includes "Ot izdatelia," "Cherviak i popad'ia," "Romans," "Sheia," "Katerina," "Novogrecheskaia pesn'," "Rodnoe," "Blestki vo t'me," "Pered morem zhiteiskim," "Predsmertnoe: Naideno nedavno, pri revizii probirnoi palatki, v delakh sei poslednei," "Fantaziia: Komediia v odnom deistvii. Soch. 'Y i Z,'" "Srodstvo mirovykh sil: Misteriia v odinnadtsati iavleniiakh," "Vyderzhki iz zapisok moego deda," "Ne vsegda slishkom sil'no," "Biograficheskie svedeniia o Koz'me Prutkove," "Mysli i aforizmy";

Proizvedeniia, ne voshedshie v sobranie sochinenii (Petrograd & Moscow: Raduga, 1923)—comprises "Liubov' i Silin" and "Proekt vvedeniia edinomysliia v Rossii";

Ne vsegda s tochnost'iu ponimat' dolzhno (Novonaidennye proizvedeniia) (Moscow & Leningrad: Zemlia i fabrika, 1926);

Staroe i novoe (Moscow: Ogonek, 1928);

Dosugi (Nizhnii Novgorod: Nizhpoligraf, 1929);

Polnoe sobranie sochinenii, edited by Boris Iakovlevich Bukhshtab, Biblioteka poeta, Bol'shaia seriia (Leningrad: Sovetskii pisatel', 1949)—includes "Ot Koz'my Prutkova k chitateliu v minutu otkrovennosti i raskaian'ia" and "K mestu pechati."

Editions and Collections: *Izbrannye sochineniia,* edited by V. Desnitsky, Biblioteka poeta, Malaia seriia (Leningrad: Sovetskii pisatel', 1953);

Dramaticheskie proizvedeniia (Moscow: Iskusstvo, 1974);

Sochineniia, edited, with an introduction, by V. I. Novikov (Moscow: Kniga, 1986);

Plody razdum'ia (Moscow: Khudozhestvennaia literatura, 1990);

Plody razdum'ia: Mysli i aforizmy. Stikhotvoreniia (Tambov, 1991);

Nikto ne obnimet neob"iatnogo: Samoe izbrannoe (Moscow: Interbuk, 1996);

Glagoly ust moikh, edited by Viacheslav Kabanov (Moscow: Knizhnaia palata, 1997);

Koz'ma Petrovich Prutkov, the imaginary author created by A. K. Tolstoy and Aleksei, Aleksandr, and Vladimir Zhemchuzhnikov (from Liudmila Danilovna Mikitich, Literaturnyi Peterburg, Petrograd, *1991)*

Pukh i per'ia (Moscow: Eksmo-Press, 1999);

Chereposlov (St. Petersburg: Kristall, 2001).

Editions in English: "Twenty Translations from Koz'ma Prutkov," translated by Barbara Heldt Monter, in her *Koz'ma Prutkov: The Art of Parody* (The Hague: Mouton, 1972), pp. 121–138;

Thoughts and Aphorisms from the Fruits of Meditation of Koz'ma Prutkov, with illustrations by Quentin Blake (London: Royal College of Art, ca. 1975);

The Headstrong Turk, or Is It Nice to Be a Grandson? translated and edited by Laurence Senelick in *Russian Satiric*

Comedy: Six Plays (New York: Performing Arts Journal, 1983);

Fantasy, a Farce-Vaudeville in One Act, translated, with an introduction, by Senelick, in *Russian Comedy of the Nikolaian Era,* Russian Theatre Archive, volume 10 (Amsterdam: Harwood Academic, 1997), pp. 59–81;

Fantasy, translated and edited by Michael Green, Jerome Katsell, and Stanislav Shvabrin (Del Mar & El Morro Village, Cal.: Mikastas Press, 1999).

PLAY PRODUCTIONS: *Fantaziia,* St. Petersburg, Aleksandrinskii Theater, 8 January 1851;

Chereposlov, sirech' Frenolog, St. Petersburg, Veselyi teatr dlia pozhilykh detei, 30 March 1909;

Spor drevnykh grecheskikh filosofov ob iziashchnom, St. Petersburg, Veselyi teatr dlia pozhilykh detei, 1911;

Oprometchivyi turka, ili, Priiatno li byt' vnukom? St. Petersburg, Krivoe Zerkalo Theater, 13 January 1913.

SELECTED PERIODICAL PUBLICATIONS: "Nezabudki i zapiatki," "Konduktor i tarantul," "Tsaplia i begovye drozhki," anonymous, *Sovremennik,* 11 (1851);

"Stan i golos," anonymous, *Sovremennik,* 1 (1853);

Dosugi Kuz'my Prutkova, in *Literaturnyi Eralash,* 1 (1854), supplement to *Sovremennik,* 2 (1854); 2 (1854), supplement to 3 (1854)—includes "Nikto neob' iatnogo obniat' ne mozhet" and "Vyderzhki iz zapisok moego deda"; 3 & 4 (1854), supplements to 6 (1854); 6 (1854), supplement to 10 (1854)—includes "Blondy";

"Liubov' i Silin: Drama v trekh deistviiakh," *Razvlechenie,* 18 (1861);

"Proekt: O vvedennii edinomysliia v Rossii," part of "Kratkii nekrolog i dva posmertnye proizvedeniia K. P. Prutkova," *Svistok,* 9 (1863), supplement to *Sovremennik,* 4 (1863);

"S togo sveta," *Sankt-Peterburgskie vedomosti,* 25 March 1876; 8 April 1876;

"Nekotorye materialy dlia biografii K. P. Prutkova: Vziato iz portfelia s nadpis'iu: 'Sbornik neokonchennogo (d'inaché),'" *Sankt-Peterburgskie vedomosti,* 29 April 1876.

Koz'ma Petrovich Prutkov is the only fictional character in Russian literature who is referred to in critical works and bibliographies as if he were a real writer. The joint creation of Aleksei Konstantinovich Tolstoy and his cousins the Zhemchuzhnikov brothers—Aleksei Mikhailovich Zhemchuzhnikov, Vladimir Mikhailovich Zhemchuzhnikov, and to a lesser extent, Aleksandr Mikhailovich Zhemchuzhnikov—Prutkov was "born" in 1850 as a running family joke. As his creators imagined

him, Prutkov was a civil servant and a literary dilettante, a terrible writer who celebrated the tsarist administrative machine in nearly every mode of fiction and nonfiction available to him. Prutkov's character allowed his creators scope for the parody of literary forms and movements and served as an outlet for expressing their animosity toward the tsarist bureaucracy and its cult of obedient conformism. Blithely unaware of his deficiencies as a writer, Prutkov published dozens of hilariously inept works that constitute one of the most sustained examinations of the critical potential of parody in the Russian literary tradition. As his readership grew, his authorial persona acquired a status independent from that of his creators. Prutkov's transformation from an aesthetic phenomenon into a metaphysical one is echoed in twentieth-century critical evaluations of his work. The alogical and defiantly nonsensical character of his verse and prose has been increasingly regarded as a precursor to the nihilistic absurdism of modernist literature itself.

The roles that Prutkov combined—poet and government employee—were familiar to Tolstoy and the Zhemchuzhnikovs. Tolstoy, the only one of the group who could be considered a professional, recognized writer, is best known today as a lyric poet, satirist, and dramatist. He was born 24 August 1817, the son of Anna Alekseevna Tolstaia (neé Perovskaia), daughter of Russian and Ukrainian nobility, and Count Konstantin Petrovich Tolstoy. (Tolstoy's life and works are the subject of a separate entry in the *Dictionary of Literary Biography 238: Russian Novelists in the Age of Tolstoy and Dostoevsky*). Neither an unequivocal Slavophile nor an uncritical Westernizer, Tolstoy demonstrates in his works both an impressive formal range and an equivalent thematic breadth. That the poetaster character of Prutkov should be the partial creation of so serious an artist as Tolstoy is well in keeping with the latter's artistic duality. Both a sincere Romantic and a pitiless self-parodist, Tolstoy's belief in the elevated calling of the artist is consistently deflated in Prutkov's character.

The Zhemchuzhnikovs are remembered in literary histories only through their work as cocreators of Koz'ma Prutkov. Like Tolstoy, they were descended from old Russian nobility and enjoyed a place in the highest Russian society. The eldest Zhemchuzhnikov, Aleksei, was born on 11 February 1821 in Chernigov province to Mikhail Nikolaevich Zhemchuzhnikov and his wife Ol'ga Alekseevna (Perovskaia) Zhemchuzhnikova. Mikhail Nikolaevich was prominent in the government and later became civil governor-general in St. Petersburg, senator, and Privy Councillor. Aleksei was educated at home and then in a St. Petersburg gymnasium and school for jurisprudence. Upon completing his schooling in 1841, he served briefly in the fourth depart-

ment of the senate and in 1844 was appointed Gentleman of the Bedchamber. He left the senate in 1847 to
take up a post in the Ministry of Justice; from 1849 he
served in the State Chancellery, receiving the title of
State Councillor. From 1855 he worked as aide to the
State Secretary of the Government Council.

Aleksei began writing verse and plays while still a
young man. Several early dramatic efforts for the professional stage did not pass muster with the tsarist censor.
In 1850, however, his first play, a verse comedy titled
Strannaia noch' (A Strange Night), came out in *Sovremennik*
(The Contemporary) and was performed at the Aleksandrinskii Theater, where it remained in the repertoire
for more than twenty years. A second verse comedy,
Sumasshedshii (Crazy), was also produced at the Aleksandrinskii in 1853. Reviews of these plays later served as
inspirations for Prutkov's own plays.

Aleksei's first poetry was published in 1851 in
many journals, including *Sovremennik*, *Otechestvennye
zapiski* (Notes of the Fatherland), and *Iskra* (The Spark).
His poetry lacks the technical mastery of his cousin Tolstoy's but addresses a similar theme: the difficulty of rec-
onciling a passionate love of country with the numbing
demands of state service. So vexing proved the clash of
bureaucratic duties with Aleksei's essentially artistic temperament that in 1858 he left government service for
good, as Tolstoy also later did. He settled in Kaluga,
and the following year he married Elizaveta Alekseevna
D'iakova. The remainder of his long life was devoted to
political and literary matters, as he sought to balance his
interest in lyric poetry with an ardent commitment to
social reform and justice. He died in Tambov on 25
March 1908 and was buried in Moscow. His "serious"
work was never as popular as his Prutkovian compositions, a state of affairs that Aleksei himself came to
regard with dismay. As he commented in a letter of
1893 to Mikhail Matveevich Stasiulevich, publisher of
Prutkov's collected works: "I may observe that the
works of Prutkov sell much better than my verses."

Although Aleksei's brother Aleksandr, who not
only collaborated in the writing of two Prutkov plays
and three fables, also wrote many works on his own, he
nonetheless owes his place in literary history entirely to
Prutkov. Unlike Prutkov, he has an uncertain birth
date—cited variously as 13 June or 22 June 1826—and
the inconsistency is not out of keeping with Aleksandr's
character. He had a reputation as both a gifted amateur
actor and an inveterate prankster, usually at the expense
of some high-ranking government official. Aleksandr
received his schooling in Tsarskoe Selo as a member of
the Aleksandrovskii young cadet corps, followed by a
stint in the cadet corps in St. Petersburg. In 1845 he
transferred to the department of jurisprudence at St.
Petersburg University, from which he received a

*Vladimir Mikhailovich Zhemchuzhnikov, one of the writers who
created Prutkov, 1854 (portrait by K. Gorbunov; from
Prutkov,* Polnoe sobranie sochinenii, *1965)*

diploma with distinction in 1850. From 1850 until 1857,
the time of the as-yet-unnamed Prutkov's first compositions, Aleksandr was far from home, serving in the
Orenburg and Samara chancellery, where his uncle,
Vasilii Alekseevich Perovsky, was governor-general.
Despite his waggish reputation, Aleksandr held a series
of important government positions in the Russian provinces until his retirement from the civil service in 1885.

Aleksandr's independently written contributions
to Prutkov's body of works did not always receive the
imprimatur of his younger brother Vladimir, the editor
of Prutkov's writings. Vladimir was wont to exclude
works such as "Liubov' i Silin" (Love and Silin, 1861)
and "Azbuka dlia detei Kos'my Prutkova" (Alphabet for
Kos'ma Prutkov's Children, 1861), although many critics
have subsequently rated these more highly. Aleksandr's
independent creations for Prutkov lack some of the
coherent, consistent idiocy of truly "great" Prutkovian
works, such as the aphorisms. His enthusiasm and affec-

tion for the character, however, was never in any doubt. Aleksandr spent his retirement on his estate, Lobersh, where he died 30 April 1896.

The Zhemchuzhnikov brother who contributed the greatest quantity of Prutkovian works and who oversaw their collection in the 1884 *Polnoe sobranie sochinenii* was Vladimir, born 11 April 1830 in St. Petersburg. Like Aleksei, he was schooled at home, and like Aleksandr, he studied at St. Petersburg University. He failed to complete a degree and in 1854 took up a post in Tobolsk province, where a relative, V. A. Artsimovich, held the position of governor. The following year Vladimir joined the army to serve in the Crimean War; he fell ill and was discharged with the rank of lieutenant in 1857. Between 1864 and 1868 he served in a variety of government ministries; he steadily rose in the civilian service to attain, in 1877, the rank of Acting State Advisor.

Despite Vladimir's success in the civil service and his involvement in the construction of important transportation schemes such as the railway, the life of a government minister held little appeal for him. When he had the opportunity to leave the service in 1881, he did so with few regrets. A good measure of his distaste for tsarist officialdom is observable in Prutkov's most overtly satirical work, "Proekt," which is attributed solely to Vladimir. This demented "plan" for ensuring uniformity of thought gives a good indication of the conflicts that the liberal Vladimir endured in the employment of the stridently absolutist tsarist government. An early version of the "Proekt" was published in the journal *Svistok* in 1863. Vladimir Zhemchuzhnikov then substantially reworked this piece for inclusion in the 1884 *Polnoe sobranie sochinenie* (Complete Collected Words). Censorship concerns prevented the publication of the revised "Proekt," and it did not appear in full until 1933. Vladimir's efforts to publish Prutkov's collected works began as early as 1854, but another thirty years passed before his plan was realized. The publication of the first *Polnoe sobranie sochinenii* came nine years after Tolstoy's death, and just a few months before Vladimir's own death, while abroad, on 6 November 1884.

The incompatibility of state service with the creation of literary works was felt acutely by Tolstoy and the Zhemchuzhnikovs. Even Vladimir, who did not consider himself a writer, felt no great enthusiasm for the work of a tsarist official and gladly abandoned it as soon as he was able. This fundamental incompatibility fueled the subversive spirit that gave rise to Prutkov, who emerged, as Aleksei recalled in a letter of 1 February 1883, "independent of our will and entirely unpremeditated."

Prutkov had his origins in a family fondness for jokes and games, but by the time of his first signed publications, in 1854, he had acquired not only a name but a portrait and a government position as well. He is a *chinovnik* (bureaucrat), and his position in the civil service informs his entire worldview. He believes no calling to be more noble than that of tsarist official, but he nonetheless dedicates his leisure hours to the service of art. The distance and contradictions between his hidebound profession and his lofty artistic aspirations are the source of much of the humor of Prutkov's work, which includes poetry, fables, plays, aphorisms, personal and familial memoirs, and political and philosophical tracts. His salient traits as a writer are a smug bureaucratic mind-set and a complete confidence in his own opinions. This confidence leads to his casual appropriation of vaunted literary forms and themes for his own pedestrian musings on art and politics and on life as a civil servant. His tendency to unify the commonplace with the exalted leads Prutkov to create nonsensical, absurd versions of familiar literary forms, the humorous results of which he is completely unaware. These works reveal his ineptitude as a creative writer even as they parody forms and styles of nineteenth-century Russian literature and drama. His work has always been popular with Russian readers, and his collected works have been reprinted many times since their first publication in 1884.

Prutkov's creators endowed him with a vivid personality and an elaborate fictional biography. The first account of his life appeared as "Kratkii nekrolog i dva posmertnye proizvedeniia Kuz'my Petrovicha Prutkova" (A Brief Obituary and Two Posthumous Works by Kuz'ma Petrovich Prutkov, 1863), published at the time of Prutkov's "death." Aleksandr Zhemchuzhnikov's "Nekotorye materialy dlia biografii K. P. Prutkova" (Some Materials for a Biography of K. P. Prutkov, 1876) has additional insight into Prutkov's character. It was omitted, however, from the first *Polnoe sobranie sochinenii* by Vladimir Zhemchuzhnikov, the editor of the book, who felt that the piece was not entirely in keeping with Prutkov's style. Vladimir Zhemchuzhnikov's own "Biograficheskie svedeniia o Koz'me Prutkove" (Biographical Facts about Koz'ma Prutkov, 1884) was published in Prutkov's first collected works and is regarded as the "definitive" authority on his imaginary life. With its appearance the true identity of Prutkov's creators was at last confirmed.

As a literary fiction that pretends to be a true biography of a character who pretends to be a writer–created by writers who themselves pretend to be characters in the story of their own creation–"Biograficheskie svedeniia o Koz'me Prutkove" manages the Pirandellian feat of simultaneously asserting Prutkov's reality *and* giving credit for his fictional creation. Thus, it treats

Prutkov as a real person, and encounters and conversations are recalled as if they actually took place.

Prutkov was born Koz'ma Petrovich Prutkov on 11 April 1803 at his family estate near Sol'vychegodsk, in the town of Tenteleva. Prutkov's boyhood years were spent with a companion, Pavel Petrovich, under the tutelage of the village priest, Father Ioann Proleptov. Under the guiding intelligence of the priest, Prutkov excelled in the study of arithmetic, grammar, and religion. Such were his scholastic gifts that the boy even took it upon himself to compose verse and prose, attempts that met, however, with little encouragement from either his family or his teacher.

According to "Biograficheskie svedeniia o Koz'me Prutkove," upon finishing his education at the age of eighteen, Prutkov entered the military "only for the dress uniform." After spending a little more than two years in an elite hussar regiment, he took up a position in the Office of Assays in St. Petersburg in 1823 and remained there until his death. At the age of twenty-five he wed Antonida Platonovna Proklevetantova. The couple raised ten children: four daughters and six sons. Prutkov advanced to the rank of Acting State Councillor and ultimately to the position of director of the Office of Assays. He was awarded the Order of St. Stanislav of the First Degree and was generally "extremely satisfied with his work."

Only the reforms of Tsar Alexander II, which included the release of serfs in Russia from bondage, somewhat unhinged Prutkov. An adherent of neither liberal nor radical causes, he was normally entirely untroubled by the *prokliatie voprosy* (accursed questions) that have traditionally been the focus of so much Russian political, philosophical, and literary discourse. When it became apparent that the reforms would be of some duration and influence, Prutkov responded by organizing his own vaguely defined "reforming" projects. Their eventual collapse left him bitter and depressed. The manifold troubles that afflicted Alexander II's own programs for social reform had, however, a beneficial effect on Prutkov's state of mind. His confidence and equilibrium returned with the retreat of the Russian state from its own sweeping change and its return to pusillanimous gradualism. Prutkov undertook a series of more modest "projects," for which he was handsomely rewarded by his superiors.

Prutkov's collapse in January 1863 as he labored at his desk in the Office of Assays was unexpected. The posthumously published "Predsmertnoe: Naideno nedavno, pri revizii probirnoi palatki, v delakh sei poslednei" (Just Before Death: Discovered Recently During an Inspection of the Office of Assays, among the Files of the Latter, 1884) affords a glimpse of the poet's last lucid

moments, as he sat at his desk struggling to finish a final poem:

> Vot chas poslednikh sil upadka
> Ot organicheskikh prichin . . .
> Prosti, Probirnaia Palatka
> Gde ia sniskal vysokii chin,
> No muzy ne otverg ob"iatii
> Sredi mne vverennykh zaniatii!
>
> (Now the final strength gives way
> Due to reasons organic . . .
> Farewell, Office of Assays
> Where I attained high rank,
> But ne'er rebuffed the muse's embrace
> Amidst the work to me entrusted!)

Prutkov's last word was "Akh!" (Ouch!). Alerted by this cry, his co-workers rushed to his side to find him mute and immobilized. He was removed first to a reception room, then to his state apartments, where—as reported in "Kratkii nekrolog i dva posmertnye proizvedeniia Kuz'my Petrovicha Prutkova"—Prutkov died three days later on 13 January 1863. He passed on after "much suffering, in the arms of his tenderly beloved spouse, amid the weeping of his children, relatives, and neighbors, who pressed reverentially about his death-bed. . . ." Prutkov left an "inconsolable" widow and ten children.

The literary activities that secured Prutkov's fame were a late development in his life. Until he made the acquaintance of the Zhemchuzhnikovs and Aleksei Tolstoy in 1850, Prutkov had given little thought to literature or any other public activity. According to "Biograficheskie svedeniia o Koz'me Prutkove,"

> Count A. K. Tolstoy and Aleksei Mikhailovich Zhemchuzhnikov, having no premonition of the serious consequences of their amusing enterprise, took it into their heads to assure Prutkov that they discerned in him a marvelous gift for dramatic creativity. Believing them, he wrote the comedy "Fantaziia" (Fantasy, 1850) under their supervision. The comedy was performed on the stage of St. Petersburg's Aleksandrinskii Theater, in the presence of the highest society, on 8 January 1851, as a benefit for the then-popular actor Maksimov. That same evening, however, the play was removed from the repertoire by a special directive; this can be explained only by the unique character of the play's subject and the inferior performances of the actors.

"Fantaziia," a vaudeville in one act signed by the pseudonymous "Y and Z," so incensed Tsar Nicholas I that he departed the theater midway through the play, offended by its patent absurdity. There can be little disagreement with his assessment. "Fantaziia" concerns the efforts of a group of six suitors to win the hand of Lizaveta,

ПОЛНОЕ СОБРАНІЕ СОЧИНЕНІЙ

КОЗЬМЫ ПРУТКОВА

съ портретомъ fac-simile и біографическими свѣдѣніями.

С.-ПЕТЕРБУРГЪ

1884

Title page for first edition of Prutkov's Polnoe sobranie
sochinenii *(Complete Collected Works), edited by*
Vladimir Zhemchuzhnikov (from Prutkov,
Sochineniia Koz'my Prutkova, *1986)*

ward of the cantankerous Chupurlina. When Chupurlina's beloved pug dog, Fantasy, disappears, the lady promises Lizaveta to the man who recovers the dog. Each man then turns up with what he hopes will prove an adequate substitute dog or, in one case, a plush toy dog. At last the hero, Libental', turns up with the missing Fantasy. He and Lizaveta are affianced, as the unsuccessful suitors castigate Chupurlina and quit the stage. One actor returns, asks to see a program, and then casts aspersions on the play's authors, "Y and Z."

The play pokes fun at the most popular dramatic form on the nineteenth-century Russian stage, the vaudeville. A vaudeville normally consisted of a comic prose narrative punctuated by musical interludes: rhyming *kuplety* (couplets) set to popular tunes. "Fantaziia" replicates the typical vaudeville plot of virtuous love thwarted but transfers the focus of romantic striving to a pug dog. It features extraordinarily inept couplets, nursery-rhyme melodies, colorless romantic leads, and "nonspeaking parts" for a variety of real dogs. While the actor badmouthing the play exclaims, "I really can't even understand how the manage-

ment could allow such a play. It's obviously a lampoon," the satiric intentions of "Fantaziia" were not appreciated by the Aleksandrinskii's audience. After the tsar's departure from the theater, the audience began booing and hissing the work to such a degree that the curtain had to be lowered before the end of the play.

Even after the failure of "Fantaziia," which in addition to being booed was also banned by imperial directive the day after its premiere, Prutkov was not dissuaded from further literary experimentation. With the blessings of Tolstoy and the Zhemchuzhnikovs, he tried to emulate the example of the poet Ivan Andreevich Krylov by writing a series of fables in verse. "Nezabudki i zapiatki" (Forget-Me-Nots and Footboards), "Konduktor i tarantul" (The Driver and the Tarantula), and "Tsaplia i begovye drozhki" (The Heron and the Racing Cart) were published, unsigned, in the eminent literary journal *Sovremennik* in 1851. His first signed works appeared the following year under the general title *Dosugi Kuz'my Prutkova* (The Leisure Time of Kuz'ma Prutkov) in *Literaturnyi Eralash* (The Literary Jumble), the comic supplement to *Sovremennik*. This substantial collection begins with a foreword in which Prutkov proclaims, "I am a poet, a gifted poet! Of this I am convinced; convinced, after having read others: if they are poets, so am I!" *Dosugi Kuz'my Prutkova* includes poems, aphorisms, and a short dramatic scene and makes clear the targets of its parody: would-be Romantics, popular but mediocre poets, and serious literary critics. Singled out for particular attention are second-rate poets Vladimir Grigorievich Benediktov, Aleksei Stepanovich Khomiakov, and Nikolai Fedorovich Shcherbina, as well as the highly esteemed poet Afanasii Afanas'evich Fet and the critic Apollon Aleksandrovich Grigor'ev.

Dosugi Kuz'my Prutkova included the first publication of Prutkov's aphorisms—the works for which he is best known among Russian readers—under the heading "Plody razdum'ia" (The Fruits of Meditation). Prutkov tries hard to make the familiar proverbial form his own, but instead of dispensing time-tested wisdom with laconic wit, his aphorisms are neither wise, nor witty, nor always brief—many run to four or six lines of text. The aphorisms in "Plody razdum'ia," which are numbered rather than titled, report, respectively, the obvious, the bizarre, and the faux oracular: "Chem skoree proedesh', tem skoree priedesh'" (The faster you travel, the faster you'll arrive, 79); "I ustritsa imeet vragov!" (Even an oyster has enemies! 86); and "Pervyi shag mladentsa est' pervyi shag k ego smerti" (A child's first step is a first step toward his death, 33). Some aphorisms recall genuine proverbs: "Ne rastravliai rany blizhnego: strazhdushchemu predlagai bal'zam. Kopaia drugomu iamu, sam v nee popadesh'" (Don't rub salt in your neighbor's wounds; offer a balm to the afflicted. Dig a hole for someone else, and you'll fall into it yourself, 50). This aphorism replicates nearly word for word the Russian proverb "Ne roi drugomu iamu, sam v nee popadesh'" (Don't dig a hole for someone else, you'll fall into it yourself) but embellishes it needlessly with Prutkov's characteristic explanations. So eager is Prutkov for the reader to understand that he repeats himself, as in the famous "Nikto ne obnimet neob"iatnogo" (No one can embrace the unembraceable), which is just slightly rephrased five times in aphorisms 3, 44, 67, 104, and 160.

Not content to limit himself to fables, verse, drama, and aphorisms, Prutkov also turned his attention to history, as seen in "Vyderzhki iz zapisok moego deda" (Excerpts from My Grandfather's Notes, 1862), and politics, as seen in "Proekt: O vvedenii edinomysliia v Rossii" (Project on the Introduction of Unanimity in Russia, 1863). He never allowed a lack of imagination or native intelligence to hamper any of his literary activities. Prutkov's confidence was greatly fostered by Tolstoy and the Zhemchuzhnikovs; as told in "Biograficheskie svedeniia o Koz'me Prutkove,"

> Koz'ma Prutkov was, apparently, a victim of the three aforementioned individuals, who on a whim set themselves up as his guardians or minions. They acted with him like the "false friends" who are put into tragedies and dramas. Under the guise of friendship, they brought out those of his qualities that they wished to ridicule publicly. Under their influence, he acquired traits borne by other successful individuals: audacity, smugness, self-confidence, even insolence, and he came to regard his every thought, his every writing and opinion, as the truth, worthy of proclamation.

For all their questionable influence over Prutkov, Tolstoy and the Zhemchuzhnikovs failed to warp his trusting good nature. He remained, to the end, an innocent—innocent of any conscious attempt to provoke laughter, innocent of his "friends'" malign intentions, and innocently happy in the unexpected fame that his writing afforded him.

In the thirty-year-long interval between the appearance of Prutkov's first signed works (beginning with *Dosugi Kuz'my Prutkova*) and the debut of the collected edition, other writers had begun to adopt the Prutkov name as a pseudonym. This practice undermined both the real authors' copyright and the careful creative control that Vladimir Zhemchuzhnikov exerted over all of Prutkov's works. Scholars conjecture that the usurping of Prutkov's name may have led to the decision to "kill off" the character in 1863. Even this maneuver proved unsuccessful, as Aleksandr Zhemchuzhnikov—independent of his brothers—published in 1876 materials purported to be Prutkov's, as channelled through a spirit medium; these works were aptly titled "S togo sveta" (From the World Beyond, 1876).

Prutkov the bureaucrat was not an unusual character, either in life or in art, but Prutkov the bureaucrat-artist offered scope for satire not only of officialdom but the artistic world as well. Like the works of Joseph Prudhomme, an imaginary French writer created by Henri Bonaventure Monnier, Prutkov's parodies are not directed with any real vehemence at any particular artist or movement. His appropriation of Romantic "Spanish" themes, "Heine-esque" subjects, classical "Greek" motifs, and neoclassical epigrammatic forms does not imply a marked hostility to any of them. Rather, Prutkov's enthusiastic imagining of himself as the poetic master of all these modes provokes hilarity. The Romantic idea of the writer as artistic self-creator is far more often the object of Tolstoy and the Zhemchuzhnikovs' laughter than is the Romantic aesthetic itself. Thus, Prutkov's authors invest him with traits entirely alien to the Romantic spirit. If the Romantic poet is tortured by weltschmerz and *Sehnsucht* (longing), Prutkov possesses unconquerable optimism. If the Romantic poet seeks escape from the quotidian, Prutkov relishes the minutiae of bureaucratic life. If the Romantic poet seeks truth and transcendence in an experience of the sublime, Prutkov courts public adulation and government promotions. Romantic literature emerges from its association with Prutkov relatively unscathed, while the bureaucratic mind-set that guides Prutkov's every thought and action is the object of sustained ridicule.

Prutkov's works technically qualify as parodies: they satirize art through artistic means. If they lack the hostility customarily associated with parody, they do evince the more characteristic attribute of the form—that of imitation. What Prutkov achieves, however, is something rarer than simple parodic merriment and imitation; in many respects his works are genuinely original. They achieve a sustained level of inanity and absurdity that several critics have likened to the works of twentieth-century writers such as the French-Romanian playwright Eugène Ionesco.

Indeed, one contemporary critic, Aleksandr Rafailovich Kugel', attributed the spate of productions of Koz'ma Petrovich Prutkov's plays at the turn of the century to their peculiar consonance with both dissonant modern drama and the dark mood of the times. In 1913, in the journal *Teatr i Iskusstvo* (Theater and Art), the critic and producer Kugel'—whose theater, the Krivoe zerkalo (Crooked Mirror), also staged Prutkov works—noted: "If the spirit of Koz'ma Prutkov is revived today, it is because at this moment we stand on the edge of despair, for there has hardly been a time such as this one that humanity has suffered a more profound fall in idealism." That the deeply banal works of Prutkov should reveal a genuine and dark originality confounds understanding of parody as a derivative and dependent art form. That Prutkov, who began as a merry family joke, a gleeful exploration of the fluid boundaries of the writer's imagined world, in the end achieves an originality that only a "real" writer can, confounds, too, the notion of "reality" itself.

Letters:

Prutkov, *Polnoe sobranie sochinenii*, Biblioteka poeta, Bol'shaia seriia (Moscow & Leningrad: Sovetskii pisatel', 1965), pp. 379–402.

Biographies:

"Kratkii nekrolog i dva posmertnye proizvedeniia Kuz'my Petrovicha Prutkova," *Svistok*, 9 (1863);

"Nekotorye materialy dlia biografii K. P. Prutkova," *Sankt-Peterburgskie vedomosti*, 29 April 1876;

"Biograficheskie svedeniia o Koz'me Prutkove," in Prutkov's *Polnoe sobranie sochinenii*, edited by Vladimir Mikhailovich Zhemchuzhnikov (St. Petersburg: M. M. Stasiulevich, 1884);

Pavel Naumovich Berkov, *Koz'ma Prutkov, Direktor Probirnoi palatki i poet: K istorii russkoi parodii* (Leningrad: Akademiia nauk SSSR, 1933);

Dmitrii Anatol'evich Zhukov, *Koz'ma Prutkov i ego druz'ia* (Moscow: Sovremennik, 1976).

References:

Boris Iakovlevich Bukhshtab, "Koz'ma Prutkov," in Prutkov's *Polnoe sobranie sochinenii* (Moscow & Leningrad: Sovetskii pisatel', 1965), pp. 5–50;

Bukhshtab, "Koz'ma Prutkov," in his *Russkie poety: Tiutchev, Fet, Koz'ma Prutkov, Dobroliubov* (Leningrad: Khudozhestvennaia literatura, 1970);

Nikolai Evreinov, "Koz'ma Prutkov–Pochitaemyi ottsom 'Krivogo zerkala,'" *Vozrozhdenie*, 50 (1956): 101–120;

Frank LeQuellec Ingram, "Koz'ma Prutkov: His Emergence and Development as a Classic of Russian Literature," dissertation, Indiana University, 1967;

A. Kugel', "Zametki," *Teatr i iskusstvo*, 3 (1913);

Barbara Heldt Monter, *Koz'ma Prutkov: The Art of Parody* (The Hague: Mouton, 1972);

A. Morozov, "Parodiia kak literaturnyi zhanr (k teorii parodii)," *Russkaia literatura*, 1 (1960): 48–77;

I. Sukiasova, *Iazyk i stil' parodii Koz'my Prutkova: Leksiko-stilisticheskii analiz* (Tbilisi: Akademiia nauk Gruzinskoi SSR, 1961).

Papers:

The majority of Koz'ma Petrovich Prutkov's papers are held in Moscow in the Zhemchuzhnikov files at the Russian State Archive of Literature and Art (RGALI), fond 639 and fond 214, and at the Russian State Library (RGB, formerly the Lenin Library), fond 101, fond 178, and fond 325. Papers concerning Prutkov are also located at the Russian State Military-Historical Archive (RGMIA), fond 314, also in Moscow. Additional materials of interest can be found at the State Archive of the Tambov Region, fond 112, and in St. Petersburg at the Institute of Russian Literature (IRLI, Pushkin House), fond 274, fond 301, and fond 548; the Russian National Library (RNB), fond 178, fond 391, fond 641, and fond 793; the Central State Historical Archive of the city of St. Petersburg (TsGIA Spb), fond 14; and the Russian State Historical Archive (RGIA), fond 78, fond 102, fond 229, fond 776, fond 780, fond 1021, fond 1162, and fond 1343.

Elisaveta Nikitichna Shakhova

(30 March 1822 – 5 July 1899)

Kathleen E. Dillon
University of California, Davis

BOOKS: *Opyt v stikhakh piatinadtsatiletnei devitsy* (St. Petersburg: Konrad Vingeber, 1837);

Stikhotvoreniia (St. Petersburg: Imperatorskaia Rossiiskaia Akademiia, 1839);

Stikhotvoreniia (St. Petersburg, 1840);

Povesti v stikhakh (St. Petersburg: Konrad Vingeber, 1842);

Mirianka i otshel'nitsa (St. Petersburg, 1849);

Iudif' (Moscow: Leonid Spichakov, 1877);

Sobranie sochinenii v stikhakh, edited by N. N. Shakhov, 3 volumes (St. Petersburg: Ekaterininskaia tipografiia, 1911)—includes "Avtobiograficheskii otzyv iz glushi," translated by Catriona Kelly as "Autobiographical Response from a Provincial Wasteland," in *An Anthology of Russian Women's Writing, 1777–1992,* edited by Kelly (Oxford: Oxford University Press, 1992), pp. 114–117.

SELECTED PERIODICAL PUBLICATIONS– UNCOLLECTED: "Tri vechera u svetskoi priiatel'nitsy," *Sovremennik,* 28 (1842);

"Zhizn' skhiigumenii Staro-Ladozhskogo monastyria Evpraksii; so slov monakhini Avgusty pisano riasofornoi poslushnitsei Elisavetoi Shakhovoi," *Strannik* (1860);

"Pamiatnye zapiski o zhizni igumenii Marii, osnovatel'nitsy Spas-borodinskogo obshchezhitel'nogo monastyria," *Strannik,* 5–6 (1865);

"V nachale zhizni i na poroge vechnosti (Posviashcheno pamiati I. S. Turgeneva)," *Russkaia starina,* 1 (1913): 162–167;

"Sestre-pustynnitse," "Sukhost' serdtsa," "Arkhimandritu Ignatiiu Brianchaninovu (nastoiateliu Sergievskoi pustyni)," "Gimn pokaianiia," *Zhurnal Moskovskoi Patriarkhii,* 12 (1995): 73–74.

Elisaveta Shakhova was the contemporary of prominent Russian women writers such as Elena Andreevna Gan, Karolina Karlovna Pavlova, Evdokiia Petrovna Rostopchina, and Iuliia Valerianovna Zhadovskaia. She is known predominantly as a poet,

although she also wrote essays, a play, and a novel. Fluent in French and Polish, Shakhova was also a skilled translator, as was her elder sister, who instructed her in French. Having entered the convent at the age of twenty-three, Shakhova wrote primarily about religious themes and pious sentiments throughout her life.

Elisaveta Nikitichna Shakhova was born on 30 March 1822 in St. Petersburg to an old and noble family. Her father's ancestors were from Persia. Her great-grandfather (her paternal grandmother's father) had been a leader of a Tatar warring horde and was known for his valor and independence. Her paternal grandfather, Ivan Ivanovich Shakhov, had been a commanding officer of the admiralty during the reign of Catherine the Great. Her father, Nikita Ivanovich, was a naval lieutenant captain of the fleet, and he sailed on the royal yacht. He received a commendation for his participation in a battle with the Swedish rowing fleet in 1808, and, after suffering an injury during a subsequent battle, he was decorated for outstanding service. He died in 1834. Shakhova's mother was Kleopatra Evstaf'evna Shakhova (née Sytina). Her noble surname was conferred on her ancestors, Crimean princes, at the time they accepted Russian citizenship and converted to Christianity. Kleopatra was brought up by her mother, one of the well-known Von Lamsdorfs, according to a strict system of German education.

Under the direction of her mother, Shakhova received the solid education accorded daughters of noble families of that time. Beginning at a young age she manifested exceptional intellectual gifts, especially for poetry. She devoted all the free time available to her after formal lessons to writing, and she commonly greeted visitors and relatives with her own verses. Her father took great delight in her precocious poetic achievement, although her mother was inclined to discourage this activity. After losing her eyesight in 1829, Kleopatra tightened her control over her daughter and restricted her society to that of family members. In 1835, after the death of her husband, Kleopatra took the further step of moving with her daughter to

СТИХОТВОРЕНІЯ

Елизаветы Шаховой.

С. ПЕТЕРБУРГЪ.

Въ Типографіи Императорской Россійской Академіи.

1859.

Title page for Shakhova's Stikhotvoreniia *(Poems), for which
Tsar Nicholas I gave her a diamond necklace and ring
(Kilgour Collection of Russian Literature,
Harvard University Library)*

Spaskoe, the country estate of a cousin in Tula. The pastoral setting nourished Shakhova's youthful thoughts and feelings and inspired her to express them in her poems.

In 1837, the year that the poet Aleksandr Sergeevich Pushkin died, the Imperial Russian Academy—possibly at the prompting of poet Vasilii Andreevich Zhukovsky—published *Opyt v stikhakh piatinadtsatiletnei devitsy* (Works in Verse by a Fifteen-Year-Old Girl). It was a small volume consisting of eight poems that Shakhova had written during the previous year. The first is titled "Dobroi materi" (To My Dear Mother), and several others are dedicated to friends. These adolescent lyrics include themes that endured throughout Shakhova's life: nature, fate, suffering, friendship, sympathy, and God's love. Her precocity was rewarded with a gold medal from the Imperial Russian Academy of Sciences. That same year the journal *Biblioteka dlia chte-*

niia (A Reading Library) reviewed this publication, which included poems that had previously appeared in its issues. The review praised the young author's talent, tastes, and feelings and predicted her future successes when "time and learning would come to the aid of her youthful strengths and inexperience." Other critics praised the purity, innocence, warmth, and inspiration of feminine feeling in these poems.

In 1839 the Academy published Shakhova's second volume of poetry, *Stikhotvoreniia* (Poems), for which she received from Tsar Nicholas I the gift of a diamond necklace and ring. (She later received a gift from Tsar Aleksandr II as well.) While a March 1839 review of the collection in *Sovremennaia bibliograficheskaia khronika* (The Contemporary Bibliographical Journal) praised the poems as quite good, it qualified its approval of the young poet by noting censoriously that her poems embody "genuine feelings, especially when she does not depart from the sphere of women's feelings, in a word where we can see in her a woman, a daughter, a sister." *Zhurnal Ministra narodnogo prosveshcheniia* (The Journal of the Minister of Public Education) applauded the second volume of Shakhova's early poetry as one of those few "which stand out from the stream of ordinary books." Similar acclaim came the same year from *Sovremennik* (The Contemporary). The reviewer at *Sovremennik* not only lauded the talent evinced in Shakhova's present youthful success in the art of poetry but also predicted for her a "future work of astonishing mastery," when maturity of talent would complement her poetic passion.

The tale in verse "Izgnannik i–Epilog" (Exile and–Epilogue, written 1840, published 1842) is representative of Shakhova's earlier work and reflects the refinement expected of upper-class Russian women of the era. It portrays a beautiful female character, Nina, whose beauty is restrained by modesty. Nina is quiet, bashful, and definitively neither passionate nor empowered. Shakhova's epigraph for this text is in French and announces the self-effacing attitude appropriate for a good Christian woman: *Une femme doit trouver du bonheur à souffrir pour celui qu'elle aime* (A woman must find happiness in suffering for the one she loves). There is no hope from the outset for Elena, the heroine of another of Shakhova's early works, "Strashnyi krasavets" (A Terrifying Beauty, written 1840, published 1842): "Her fate was sad, / She did not live, but languished." Elena possesses no trace of agency in her own life: "Alas, Elena, what is the matter? / Are you without protection? / Have you no power over yourself?"

Both "Izgnannik i–Epilog" and "Strashnyi krasavets" were included, along with "Perst' Bozhii" (The Finger of God), in Shakhova's *Povesti v stikhakh* (Tales in Verse), published in St. Petersburg in 1842.

The critic Vissarion Grigor'evich Belinsky gave Shakhova the first pejorative review of her career for this collection. He judged the genre itself "easier to write than to read," and he concluded that "much that is incomprehensible in these lines of poetry would be understood in prose where meaning does not have to be sacrificed for rhyme and meter." Poet and critic Petr Aleksandrovich Pletnev, on the other hand, found that in these verses Shakhova was able to focus her poetic dreams and fulfill them completely rather than in just fragments, as in her juvenilia. He especially admired the graceful sounds, the expressiveness of the lexicon, and the resulting persuasive power of her poems.

During this period Shakhova became a regular contributor to many literary publications, such as *Rossiia* (Russia), *Varshavskii dnevnik* (The Warsaw Daily), *Sovremennik, Severnaia pchela* (The Northern Bee), *Biblioteka dlia chteniia, Syn otechestva* (Son of the Fatherland), *Odesskii al'manakh* (The Odessa Almanac), and *Strannik* (The Wanderer). She also produced prose texts on the topics of society and religion, although most of these writings were never published. Shakhova's family connections permitted her to receive direction in her literary endeavors from eminent scholars, historians, and philologists. She also had at her disposal the valued counsel of some of Russia's great literary critics: Pletnev, Vladimir Ivanovich Panaev, Osip Ivanovich Senkovsky, Mikhail Nikolaevich Zagoskin, and Sergei Timofeevich Aksakov. She considered the Romantic poet Vladimir Grigor'evich Benediktov, who enjoyed a brief but sensational popularity in the 1830s and 1840s, her mentor; to him she had dedicated "Poetu" (To a Poet), written in 1839 and published in 1911 in *Sobranie sochinenii v stikhakh* (Collected Works in Verse).

Despite the brilliance and promise of her early literary career, and despite the efforts of her friends and mentors to persuade her otherwise, in 1845 Shakhova entered the Spaso-Borodinskii Monastery in Moscow. She withdrew from the world fifteen years before the liberating era of the 1860s that so profoundly affected many Russian women writers. Monastic life notwithstanding, Shakhova never discontinued her vocation as a writer. In 1849 she published another book of poems, titled *Mirianka i otshel'nitsa* (The Worldly Woman and the Nun). Strongly committed to dedicating herself to God, she took her vows and the religious name Mother Mariia in 1863. Five years later she was transferred to the motherhouse in Vilna, where she quickly mastered the Polish language. While there she completed various but, as far as is known, unpublished translations. Most of Shakhova's writings from the monastery were published only posthumously in the collected works edited by her great-nephew.

Evidently, Shakhova remained in touch with world events transpiring beyond the cloister. During the 1870s the Balkan states engaged in a series of uprisings against the rule of the Ottoman Empire. In 1876 a brutal suppression of an insurrection in Bulgaria resulted in the involvement of Serbia and Montenegro, leading to a war between Russia and Turkey in 1877. In that same year Shakhova published *Iudif'* (Judith), a biblical poem-drama in five acts. In the spirit of Pan-Slavism she dedicated it to the Orthodox people of Serbia "who in an act of self-sacrifice took up arms in the defense of their oppressed brethren" and fought to defeat the infidels.

The Book of Judith belongs to the section of the Old Testament known as the Apocrypha, a term which in its early usage was applied to writings that were regarded as so important and precious that they must be hidden from the general public. Later, Apocrypha referred to writings that were hidden not because they were too good but because they were not good enough—that is, because they were secondary, questionable, or heretical. Ultimately, Apocrypha became the title of biblical texts that are not considered part of the Hebrew canon. The Book of Judith, which asserts the unequivocal claim to power of a woman of God against the forces of history, is a fitting source for a play written by a cloistered nun about a sensitive political issue.

Iudif' strongly resembles church liturgy in its language and its tone. The solemnity of phrasing underscores the overarching themes of heroism and bravery in the play. This work constitutes a daring departure from the conventional religious poetry of Shakhova's body of works up to this point. The poet's heroine, Judith, speaks in the liturgical refrains that are the sole property of the strictly male church hierarchy. For example, she intones at intervals, "Hosanna! Praise to God in the highest," and she commands the Israelites with priestly authority, "Look, look! Do not close your eyes!" The Amazonian Judith, in stark contrast to the powerless heroines of Shakhova's early poems, is neither meek nor modest about the effect she produces on the Assyrians: "I stunned them with the radiance of my face. . . . They rushed forth and cried out: 'Goddess, daughter of heaven, from whence have you come?'" As for Commander-in-Chief Holophernes himself, Judith again is plainly aware of the instantaneous power she has over him: "I read my triumph in his face . . . and from the very first moment he was my slave." Judith's power does not derive solely from her startling physical beauty. Shakhova endows her heroine with the power of words—the same power that Shakhova herself, in the act of writing this play, uses in order to lend courage to the Serbs. Judith reports the impact of her words on

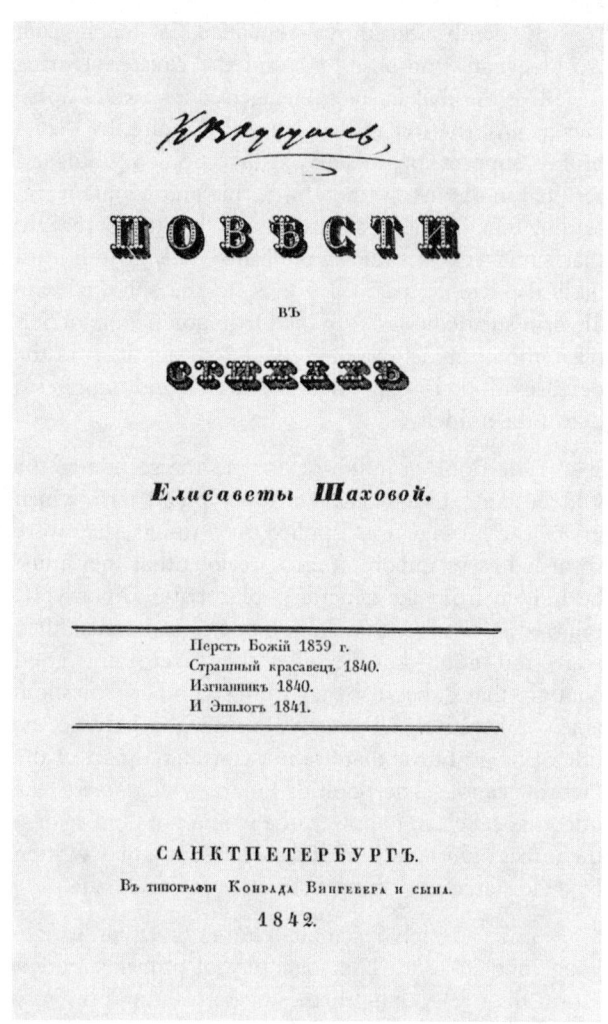

Title page for Shakhova's Povesti v stikhakh *(Tales in Verse),*
which includes "Izgnannik i–Epilog" (Exile and–Epilogue),
about a beautiful upper-class Russian woman
(Kilgour Collection of Russian Literature,
Harvard University Library)

Holophernes: "He heard my speech. It became familiar
to him. But he could not discern the truth from lies."

Judith's virtues are acknowledged by her people,
by the masses and the hierarchy alike. At the beginning
of act 4, Judith reenters the gates of the Israelites' fortress. Josiah, an army commander, shouts, "For shame!
A woman has shown us what heroism is." After Judith
recounts her heroic acts, her slaves address her use of
language, which attributes supernatural qualities to her
and connects her with the power of iconography: "You
are our beloved sovereign! Our angel, our mother! Is it
God who saved you?" At the conclusion of the play the
entire chorus turns to Judith with an encomium full of
echoes of biblical redemption: "Oh, let your praises be
extolled, holy Judith, from generation to generation.
You brought glory to Jerusalem and ennobled us, your

people." The final words of the play belong to Judith.
The stage directions indicate that she raises her arms–a
priest-like stance–and in effect commands a long reach
into history for her heroic efforts. The words are Shakhova's prayer for the Serbs, but they also reflect the
poet's hopes for the whole world. Shakhova's text
extends beyond the biblical story and even beyond the
Balkan crisis that inspired it: "Peace to all people, to the
ends of the earth and for all eternity!"

Iudif', composed in the fifty-fifth year of Shakhova's life and twenty-two years after she became a
nun, is her only explicitly politically motivated work.
Most of her poems evince her devout religious beliefs
and traditional feminine qualities. Dreams and wishes
are more in evidence than reality. Romantic, melancholic tones are intermingled with piety. Nevertheless,
her later works exhibit the poet's increasing affirmation of her talent. In 1865, two years after Shakhova
took her final vows, the poem "Avtobiograficheskii
otzyv iz glushi" (Autobiographical Response from a
Provincial Wasteland, published 1911) pointed to a
shift in Mother Mariia's attitude toward her own writing. In this self-analytical poem, the poet-nun defends
her literary efforts and worth: "A priceless gift, my
cherished songs / I guarded half a century. / They are
my fate, my destiny; / I would not part with them for
anything." Shakhova goes on to unveil her awareness
of the changes in her poetic voice as a consequence of
the radical change in her identity: "Another life–and
other songs! / But I shall go on singing as I have always
done!"

At some point, by order of the Tsarina Mariia
Aleksandrovna, Shakhova was transferred from Vilna
to St. Petersburg to serve as the directress of the Pokrovskaia obshchina sester miloserdiia (Pokrov Society of
the Sisters of Mercy). She found the noise of the capital
city oppressive, however, and quickly retired to the
Uspenskii Monastery in Staraia Ladoga, where she
took the strictest vows of monastic rule in the Russian
Orthodox Church. In the last year of her life, like her
mother, she lost her eyesight. Shakhova, known for
many years as Mother Mariia, died at the monastery on
5 July 1899 and was buried there (Shakhova's papers
have never been officially located, although they are
believed to be among the archives of the Staro-Ladozhskii
Monastery, which are housed at the Russian State Historical Archive in St. Petersburg).

In 1911 Shakhova's *Sobranie sochinenii v stikhakh*
was published in three volumes. The collection was
edited by the poet's grand-nephew N. N. Shakhov, who
also provided a biographical introduction. The appearance of Shakhova's collected works evoked a fitting
tribute to this poetess-nun from a reviewer for *Severnaia
pchela* on 26 May 1912. Her poetry, he wrote, "involun-

tarily calls to mind the pronouncement of Alfred de Musset: 'My glass is not large, but I drink from it.' Shakhova never strove to overburden the harmony of her verse with particular heights or depths of thought, powerful experiences, and clear pictures. She wanted simply—and she had sufficient talent to do it—to love with a guileless love every blade of grass."

One final prose piece by Shakhova, written in 1888, was published posthumously in 1913. "V nachale zhizni i na poroge vechnosti" (In the Beginning of Life and on the Path to Eternity) recounts the occasion long ago when the novelist Ivan Sergeevich Turgenev visited the Shakhov home and praised the young writer's gift. In a prescient moment, after Shakhova's mother declares that "she did not value her daughter's talent for literature as much as her religious convictions," Turgenev retorts jokingly: "Are you headed for the nunnery, then, Elisaveta Nikitichna?" Shakhova's autobiographical essay also records the fact that Turgenev's novel *Dvorianskoe gnezdo* (A Nest of the Gentry, 1859) was the first literary work that she read after concluding her first five years of life as a nun who had "broken all connection with society and with literature."

Elisaveta Nikitichna Shakhova received considerable recognition and adulation as a poet in her own time. Her story is notable among the lives of other renowned women writers of the period because she continued to publish her lyrical work even from the monastery. Her poetry provides a voice for all the women of her age who dedicated their lives to God. Like the better known poet-nun Elizaveta Iur'evna Kuz'mina-Karavaeva who came after her, Shakhova was a feminist ahead of her time. The veil, designed to eliminate a woman's individuality and to signify her submission to God and church authority, became for her a mantle of self-expression. The rediscovery of Rus-sian women writers begun in the late twentieth century has brought critical attention once again to many long-overlooked literary women, Shakhova among them.

Biographies:

N. N. Shakhov, "E. N. Shakhova. Kratkii biograficheskii ocherk," in Shakhova's *Sobranie sochinenii v stikhakh Elisavety Shakhovoi,* edited by Shakhov (St. Petersburg: Ekaterininskaia tipografiia, 1911);

Mary F. Zirin, "Shakhova, Elizaveta Nikitichna," in *Dictionary of Russian Women Writers,* edited by Marina Ledkovsky, Charlotte Rosenthal, and Zirin (Westport, Conn. & London: Greenwood Press, 1994), pp. 571–573;

V. Afanas'ev, "Skhimonakhinia Mariia (Elizaveta Nikitichna Shakhova, 1822–1899)," *Zhurnal Moskovskoi Patriarkhii,* 12 (1995): 72–73.

References:

Anonymous, "E. Shakhova. *Sochineniia,*" *Novoe vremia,* 26 May 1912;

Aleksandr Ivanovich Beletsky, "Turgenev i russkie pisatel'nitsy," in *Tvorcheskii put' Turgeneva: Sbornik statei,* edited by Nikolai Leont'evich Brodsky (Petrograd: Seiatel', 1923), pp. 143–147, 159;

Vissarion Grigor'evich Belinsky, *Polnoe sobranie sochinenii,* volumes 4, 6, 8 (Moscow: Akademiia nauk SSSR, 1953–1959);

Perepiska Ia. K. Grota s P. A. Pletnevym, edited by Iakov Karlovich Grot, volume 1 (St. Petersburg: Tipografiia Ministerstva Putei Soobshcheniia, 1896), pp. 146, 217–218;

Petr Aleksandrovich Pletnev, *Sochineniia i perepiska,* volume 2 (St. Petersburg: Imperatorskaia Akademiia nauk, 1885), pp. 286–287.

Nikolai Fedorovich Shcherbina

(2 December 1821 – 10 April 1869)

Stuart Goldberg

BOOKS: *Grecheskie stikhotvoreniia* (Odessa: L. Nitche, 1850);

Stikhotvoreniia, 2 volumes (St. Petersburg: Eduard Veimar, 1857);

Polnoe sobranie sochinenii N. F. Shcherbiny (St. Petersburg: Tipografiia Ministerstva Putei Soobshcheniia, 1873)—includes "Pesni russkogo na chuzhbine," "Sonnik russkoi literatury," and "Putevye nabroski russkogo lenivtsa i ipokhondrika";

Iz neizdannykh stikhotvorenii N. F. Shcherbiny (St. Petersburg: I. N. Kushnerev, 1907);

Neizdannye proizvedeniia (St. Petersburg: Akademiia nauk, 1910);

Al'bom ipokhondrika: Epigrammy i satiry, edited by R. V. Ivanov-Razumnik (Leningrad: Priboi, 1929)—includes "Al'bom ipokhondrika" and "Satiricheskaia letopis'";

Izbrannye proizvedeniia, Biblioteka poeta, Bol'shaia seriia (Leningrad: Sovetskii pisatel', 1970)—includes *Ifigeniia v Tavride.*

Collection: *Stikhotvoreniia,* edited by I. Ia. Aizenshtok, Biblioteka poeta, Malaia seriia (Leningrad: Sovetskii pisatel', 1937).

OTHER: "Novogrecheskie pesni: Istoriko-kriticheskie issledovaniia i perevody obraztsov pesen," translated by Shcherbina, *Maiak,* 16, nos. 31–32 (1844);

Sbornik luchshikh proizvedenii russkoi poezii, edited by Shcherbina (St. Petersburg: E. Prats, 1858);

Iovo i Mara. Serbskaia narodnaia poema, translated by Shcherbina (Moscow: Katkov, 1860);

Pchela: Sbornik dlia narodnogo chteniia i dlia upotrebleniia pri narodnom obuchenii, compiled by Shcherbina (St. Petersburg: Obshchestvennaia pol'za, 1865; revised and enlarged, 1866; enlarged, 1869).

SELECTED PERIODICAL PUBLICATIONS—UNCOLLECTED:

POETRY

"Novye grecheskie stikhotvoreniia," *Moskvitianin,* 11, no. 22 (1851).

Nikolai Fedorovich Shcherbina, 1867
(Pushkin House, St. Petersburg)

NONFICTION

"Medal'on grafa F. P. Tolstogo v pamiat' osvobozhdeniia krest'ian," *Sovremennaia letopis',* 16 (1861): 10–11;

"Opyt o knige dlia naroda," *Otechestvennye zapiski,* 8 (February 1861);

"O narodnoi gramotnosti i rasprostranenii prosveshcheniia v narode," *Russkii vestnik,* 23 (June
1863): 831–858.

Nikolai Shcherbina, a Russian poet of mixed Cossack and Greek descent, is known first and foremost for
his unusually personal "Greek" poems and his bilious,
malevolent epigrams. He also wrote philosophical and
nature poetry and civic verse (called *iamby,* after the
ancient Greek form dominated by invective against
contemporary ills), collected Russian folk songs, and
published in his later years a much-reprinted collection
of didactic readings for the lower classes. Among contemporaries he was known as a wit and improviser with
a punishing tongue. His roots were in the impoverished
nobility, and his political leanings, though progressive
initially, made a radical turn to the right after the Great
Reforms. Shcherbina was indisputably a poet of some
originality. His Greek poems won him immediate,
widespread–if short-lived–popularity among the Russian reading public. His epigrams and satires were circulated by contemporaries in several handwritten copies.
Shcherbina is generally recognized as one of the better
minor poets of his time.

Nikolai Fedorovich Shcherbina was born on 2
December 1821 into an impoverished noble family on
his mother's estate, Gruzko-Elaninskoe, which lay on
Don Cossack land approximately sixty-five kilometers
from the city of Taganrog on the Azov Sea. His father
was descended from the Ukrainian Cossack nobility of
Khar'kov province, his mother from Don Cossack
nobility and Peloponnesian Greeks. At age eight
Shcherbina was brought to Taganrog by his bankrupt
parents and sent to the parish school, district school,
and then gymnasium. He describes himself as a superb
student in history, geography, and literature, but his
failings at mathematics–he remembered his teacher in
this subject as a particularly oppressive ignoramus–
helped stymie his later attempts to pass the university
entrance exams.

Shcherbina was surrounded in Taganrog by a
largely unassimilated Greek immigrant community. His
own grandmother had arrived in Taganrog from
Morea during the rule of Catherine II. As he explained
in an 1853 letter to the poet Apollon Nikolaevich
Maikov, he grew up daily hearing the sounds of contemporary Greek: "In our house all of the Ukrainian
servant women spoke Greek and sang Greek songs." In
addition to his diligent study of Greek at the gymnasium, Shcherbina took private lessons in ancient Greek
literature. At age ten he was reading Homer's *Iliad*
(circa seventh–eighth centuries B.C.) in the original.

Shcherbina's first poetic work, written at age thirteen, was "Safo" (Sappho), a *poema* (long narrative poem)

that was later destroyed. Also among his juvenilia are
two surviving dramas, "Osada Ipsary" (The Siege of
Ipsara) and "Ksanfo" (Xanthos), both devoted to contemporary Greece. The young Shcherbina was taken
with stories of heroic Greek resistance to the Turks,
including the uprising that had been launched in 1821.
His proclivity for satire was also becoming apparent during his school years. By his own testimony, stated in a letter to Maikov, his schoolmates at the gymnasium dubbed
him "Arkhilokh-nasmeshnik" (Archilochus the Teaser),
and during this time he wrote a lost "comedy from Russian life." Shcherbina complained later that he had been
surrounded in childhood by vulgarity and petty mercan-
tilism and that his literary beginnings were marred by the
lack of a person of taste and refinement who might have
served as his mentor.

In 1838, while he was still at the gymnasium,
Shcherbina's sonnet "K moriu" (To the Sea) was published in the journal *Syn otechestva* (Son of the Fatherland). Shcherbina took heart at this early success, and
in 1839 he left for Moscow to continue his studies and
pursue a literary career. His aim was to enroll in Moscow University, but he was not accepted. The sensitive
young Shcherbina, alone in Moscow without money,
patronage, or position, was surrounded by the dregs of
society and suffered greatly from extreme poverty, degradation, and swindlers. He did meet and win the sympathies of several important Moscow cultural figures,
however, including the writers Aleksandr Fomich
Vel'tman and Mikhail Nikolaevich Zagoskin, and the
ethnographer Vadim Vasil'evich Passek.

After several failed attempts to get into Moscow
University, Shcherbina decided to try his luck in
Khar'kov. He arrived in late 1840 and after four
months with no income left to return to Taganrog. He
found his parents destitute and spent a year living with
them and sharing their difficulties. After this period
came another extremely difficult and penniless one and
one-half years in Khar'kov and another failed attempt
to one and one-half years in Taganrog and more degradation and poverty. Finally, Shcherbina managed to
return to Khar'kov with a fish convoy, and this time
apparently he entered the university–but only for half a
year, after which he was forced to leave for financial
reasons. Whether Shcherbina ever actually enrolled in
the law division of Khar'kov University remains a
point of contention.

Shcherbina earned his living during the following
years as a domestic tutor on the estates of Ukrainian
noblemen and as a teacher at women's boarding
schools. For lack of connections and a societal position,
he was unable to find a job in the civil service. Only
such a position could have given him financial security,
providing him with prospects for marriage in the sphere

of cultured women who appealed to him. In his own words, stated in a letter of 1855, he lived "from time to time in tumble-down shacks with peasants, seminary students, even in a den of beggars."

In Khar'kov, Shcherbina worked hard to further his knowledge of Greek culture. He read much about Greek art and life (using Vissarion Grigor'evich Belinsky's articles on the subject as a point of departure), met like-minded young people, and amassed a library relating to Greece. In and around Khar'kov he wrote the initial body of his Greek poems. He published sporadically. In 1841 his long poem "Klefty" (The Klepts) appeared in *Otechestvennye zapiski*. In 1844 the journal *Maiak* (The Beacon) published his article on new Greek songs together with some translations. During 1843 and 1844 I. E. Betsky, editor of the journal *Molodik* (The Youth), convinced of Shcherbina's unusual talent, published about thirty of his poems under various pseudonyms. In 1846 *Moskvitianin* (The Muscovite) featured two poems, "Noch' v Venetsii" (Night in Venice) and "Ellada" (Hellas, 1844), which begins "Kak ia rad, chto ostavil akropol'! . . ." (How happy I am that I have left the acropolis! . . .)—a pale sibling of the elegant poem of the same name (1846) that ranks as one of Shcherbina's best.

Shcherbina traveled to Odessa in 1849 with plans to accompany a university friend abroad. The trip never materialized, and when he returned to Odessa from Khar'kov a couple of months later, the friend had left for Moscow. Shcherbina found himself once more in dire financial need and was forced to sell his library. Eventually, however, with the help of local acquaintances, he was able to establish himself. In Odessa he began to suffer from the powerful bouts of *ipokhondriia* (melancholic spleen, or depression) that later colored his satire.

Shcherbina's Odessa aquaintances, among them the writers Grigorii Petrovich Danilevsky and Iakov Petrovich Polonsky, pushed him to publish a book despite his personal doubts and his fear of ridicule by the critics. In 1850 his first book of poetry, *Grecheskie stikhotvoreniia* (Greek Verses), came out—a slim, elegantly printed volume of thirty-six carefully chosen poems written between 1843 and 1847. To Shcherbina's surprise, it was highly praised by reviewers of various literary camps; it quickly sold its entire print run—Shcherbina was left without a personal copy—and won him immediate renown. Suddenly, Shcherbina was introduced to circles previously closed to him. He became a frequent guest of Lev Sergeevich Pushkin, brother of the poet Aleksandr Sergeevich Pushkin, who in turn introduced him to the poet Prince Petr Andreevich Viazemsky. The latter took an interest in Shcherbina, despite his skeptical view of the younger generation of writers. Shcherbina's poems were printed

in Nikolai Alekseevich Nekrasov's liberal flagship journal, *Sovremennik* (The Contemporary), the first poetry published in the journal in more than three years. *Moskvitianin* and *Otechestvennye zapiski* also sent requests for submissions. Despite this overwhelming success, however, Shcherbina continued to complain of his psychological illness.

Shcherbina's verse in *Grecheskie stikhotvoreniia* has been lauded for its musicality and plasticity. Many poems are infused with a tense and, at its best, understated eroticism. While the book was initially held up as a paragon of art for art's sake, the situation is in truth more complex. The poems are centered around the cult of beauty in three predominant hypostases: woman (who is usually nude), art, and nature. For Shcherbina, the setting of ancient Greece in the poems was only natural. He saw the eternal in Greece as the ancestor to all contemporary Western culture, and the Greek setting fit his own pantheistic approach to the world.

Shcherbina's later Greek poems, written in the early 1850s, reflect a more metaliterary bent. In these verses his worldview and poetic credo are revealed with particular clarity. His goddess—even before Aphrodite, goddess of beauty and love—becomes Sophrosyne, whom he accords the place of tenth muse. Sophrosyne is an ancient Greek human ideal, an abstract quality (illustrated in the Platonic dialogue "Charmides" [written before 387 B.C.] subtitled "On Sophrosyne"). This ideal was deeply important for the ancient Greeks and represents soundness of mind, moderation, and self-control. Ecstatic passion must give way to calm and psychological health in order for poetry to be written, as Shcherbina points out in "Difiramby" (Dithyrambs, published in full in *Stikhotvoreniia* [Poems], 1857), a poem that combines both extremes. In reality Shcherbina's poetry was the result of meticulous revision.

Grecheskie stikhotvoreniia includes two translations from ancient Greek and several purely anthological verses. Yet, Shcherbina regarded its content as more than simply anthological—that is, imitative of the lyrics of the Greek Anthology and evincing, in Belinsky's words, a "simplicity and unity of thought . . . artlessness and loftiness in tone, plasticity and grace in form." Shcherbina's *Grecheski Stikhotvoreniia* absorbed the influence of all spheres of Greek literatue and culture. Moreover, the Greek poems were not just imitations of the ancients; they also bore the stamp of the author's individuality. As the talented turn-of-the-century critic Iulii Isaevich Aikhenval'd wrote, Shcherbina was not a son but an "orphan of Hellas." From behind the bucolic decorations peers a contemporary lyric persona who suffers for his own and others' degradation. Shcherbina's Greek poems are an expression of the lyric persona's need for the ideal, his thirst for a lost life of unmitigated good and transcendent beauty. They are the flip side of his psychological despondency. The darker side of Shcherbina's lyric persona appears without the bucolic mask in the *iamby* and elegies that he was writing contemporaneously with the Greek poems but that he published in book form only in 1857.

In the fall of 1850 Shcherbina moved to Moscow, where he received a position in the provincial government as assistant editor of *Moskovskie gubernskie vedomosti* (Moscow Province News), thus fulfilling for a while his longtime dream of financial stability. He also tutored girls from Moscow high society. According to a letter to friends, he left his government position as a result of a personal insult but continued with his tutoring. During Shcherbina's time in Moscow his beloved mother died.

In late 1851 Shcherbina published a selection of twelve poems as "Novye grecheskie stikhotvoreniia" (New Greek Verses) in *Moskvitianin*. Aleksandr Vasil'evich Druzhinin, the critic who had written the most expansive article praising Shcherbina's book, found in these poems little that was new, however, and little evidence of continued study of the ancient sources. Under the influence of the Slavophiles associated with *Moskvitianin*, Shcherbina's interest in Russian history, literature, and especially the Russian folk tradition intensified. He began searching for and transcribing Russian folk songs.

In March of 1855, shortly after the death of Tsar Nicholas I, Shcherbina moved to St. Petersburg, where he received the position of personal assistant to Prince Viazemsky, who had recently been appointed Vice Minister of People's Education. Shcherbina was excited by the possibility of reforms and a better civic life for the country in the wake of Tsar Nicholas's death. In 1856 Shcherbina's younger brother died fighting in the Crimean War—an event that deeply shook the poet.

In St. Petersburg in 1857 Shcherbina published a two-volume collection of his poems, which he divided into five conceptual cycles: a first untitled segment, which was to become, in his *Polnoe sobranie sochinenii* (Complete Collected Works, 1873), "Grecheskie stikhotvoreniia" (Greek Verses); "Novogrecheskie melodii" (New Greek Melodies); "Pesni o prirode" (Songs about Nature); "Iamby i elegii" (Iambs and Elegies); and "Iz stikhotvorenii 'Efemeridy'" (From the Ephemerides). He also included among the "Grecheskie stikhotvoreniia" a scene from a tragedy in the ancient Greek manner, *Ifigeniia v Tavride* (*Iphigenia in Tauride*, first published in *Moskvitianin* in 1852). In publishing "Iamby i elegii," his cycle of civic poetry, Shcherbina introduced himself and his "iamb of castigating love"—as he characterizes his talent in the poem "Poetam" (To the Poets, 1856)—to the mainstream of civic-minded Russian poetry of the late 1850s. In his article "Stikhotvoreniia N. Shcherbina" (*Sovremennik*, 1857) the liberal critic Nikolai

Gavrilovich Chernyshevsky praised Shcherbina's great humanity and his poetic gifts but remained dissatisfied; he wondered why a poet of Shcherbina's talent had not written more compelling verse now that he had finally broached contemporary themes. Chernyshevsky's criticisms of the abstractness of Shcherbina's thought in the "Iamby" and the strained invention of many of the newer "Grecheskie stikhotvoreniia" are largely apt. His understanding of Shcherbina's "theory" of poetry is deeply flawed, however, leading him to overlook some fine poetry among these two groups of verse.

Shcherbina's philosophical cycle "Pesni o prirode" has been highly praised. Not coincidentally, in Cheryshevsky's article three of the four examples demonstrating Shcherbina's talent come from this cycle. Lovingly constructed and musical in nature, the poems in "Pesni o prirode" feature the occasional felicitous conceit, although many are eclipsed by the more compelling, and often philosophically similar, nature poetry of Shcherbina's poetic contemporary, Fedor Ivanovich Tiutchev. The early Russian symbolist poet Ivan Konevskoi found in Shcherbina's nature poems his inspiration for an extensive article on the poet's worldview. Not surprisingly, Shcherbina's philosophy attracted a poet of Konevskoi's generation. That philosophy encompassed the unity of man and nature, the spiritual animation of the material world, the ephemerality of human existence before eternity, and a striving for the distant but inevitable achievement of complete truth and love.

In 1858 Shcherbina published *Sbornik luchshikh proizvedenii russkoi poezii* (Anthology of the Best Works of Russian Poetry). In the foreword he stressed the social importance of the development of aesthetic sensitivities among the *narod* (folk). That same year he visited the provinces of Kostroma, Tver', Moscow, and Vladimir, where he traveled from village to village and lived among the people, collecting folk songs and studying Russian history and antiquities. In 1860 he traveled through Russia again, setting out along the Volga River with the composer Milii Alekseevich Balakirev and then tracing an extensive southern route.

Shcherbina wrote the overwhelming bulk of his satires and epigrams beginning in the early 1850s. Those written through 1860 are included in his first satirical cycle, "Al'bom ipokhondrika" (Album of a Hypochondriac), which he signed "The Greek, Nikolaki Omega, Chukhonskie Afiny [Finnish Athens] (Petersburg), 1857." Twelve poems from the cycle appeared in drastically censored form in *Russkaia starina* (Russian Antiquity) in 1873 and in full in 1929 in the collection titled *Al'bom ipokhondrika: Epigrammy i satiry* (Album of a Hypochondriac: Epigrams and Satires). At their best Shcherbina's epigrams are caustic, witty, pointed, and malevolent. They were circulated in numerous handwritten copies and were extremely popular among his contemporaries. Fairness was beside the point. In the author's 1863 foreword to the manuscript for "Al'bom ipokhondrika," titled "Expiatio" (Atonement), Shcherbina wrote that he published these epigrams, rather than destroyed them, as a cruel penance. At times he would write to an editor to ask that a recently submitted epigram not appear since it had been written during an attack of melancholic spleen.

Shcherbina had no strict political affiliation, and his epigrams target a broad range of political and social groupings, publications, writers, and political actors of his day. No one is spared—neither Slavophile nor Westerner, neither friend nor foe. Prior to 1861, however, Shcherbina aligned himself mostly with the liberal camp and wrote many epigrams against the censors, the bureaucracy, Tsars Nicholas I and Peter (known as Peter the Great), reactionary journalists, and writers. While some of the epigrams are flat or excessively bitter, many are excellent, such as "Prevrashchenie Faddeia v 'Novogo Poeta'" (Transformation of Faddei into the "New Poet," 1853), in which writer, essayist, and editor of *Sovremennik,* Ivan Ivanovich Panaev, appears as a pathetic new embodiment of the infamous reactionary journalist Faddei Venediktovich Bulgarin; "Russkaia epigrama (Ne dlia chteniia pri damakh)" (Russian Epigram [Not for Reading before Ladies], written 1854), published in *Al'bom ipokhondrika;* the self-directed "I kakoi ia literator" (And What Kind of Littérateur Am I, written 1857), *Golos minuvshego* (Voice of the Past, 1915); and "Kukol'niku" (To Kukol'nik, written 1859), published in *Russskaia starina* (1872). In the last poem, with wicked precision and economy, Shcherbina brands Nestor Vasil'evich Kukol'nik, a largely forgotten Romantic novelist, dramatist, and poet, who had lived on stolen government funds during the Crimean military campaign and then bragged to an acquaintance that he was now an "ex-bureaucrat and ex-writer":

Khot' teper' ty *ex*-pisatel',
Ex-chinovnik, *ex*-delets
I kazny *ex*-obiratel',–
Vse zhe ty ne *ex*-podlets.

(Even if you are now an ex-writer
Ex-bureaucrat, ex-wheeler-dealer,
And ex-extortionist of the treasury–
Still you are no ex-scoundrel.)

The most noteworthy of Shcherbina's prose satires was the extremely popular "Sonnik sovremennoi russkoi literatury" (Dream Interpretations of Contemporary Russian Literature, *Polnoe sobranie stikhotvorenii N. F. Shcherbiny* [Complete Collected Works of N. F. Shcherbiny]). In this work interpretations of dreams, in which each of a full range of contemporary writers appears, form a gallery of scathing satirical portraits.

In 1861 Shcherbina finally made his long-desired trip abroad to western Europe. He spent roughly six months in Germany, France, Italy, Switzerland, and England. He did not, however, travel to Greece. He brought with him his own two-volume *Stikhotvoreniia* and several collections he had made of Russian folk songs, arranged for voice and piano, wishing to introduce these to western Europeans (these collections were never published). In addition, he sought a meeting with Alexander Herzen (Aleksandr Ivanovich Gertsen) and received from him sympathetic letters, although whether the two writers actually met is not clear. Shcherbina's travels were colored by nostalgia for Russia, shading into an ideological nationalism as well as a general disenchantment with Europe. In Paris he traveled in Russian émigré circles and visited artists such as Count Fedor Petrovich Tolstoy and his family, who were some of his closest St. Petersburg friends. Tolstoy drew illustrations for Shcherbina's *Grecheskie stikhotvoreniia,* and Shcherbina devoted two articles—one written in Paris and published in *Sovremennaia letopis'* (Contemporary Annals) and another placed in the French journal *Le Nord* (The North)–to Tolstoy's medallion in memory of the emancipation of the Russian peasants that year.

The article in *Sovremennaia letopis',* "Medal'on grafa F. P. Tolstogo v pamiat' osvobozhdeniia krest'ian," expressed Shcherbina's joy and high hopes for Russia after the Great Reforms of 1861. These hopes, however, came into conflict with the reality of western Europe, where he found that freedom was illusory in the face of financial and social inequality. Shcherbina saw in Paris "beauty of the external civilization and barbarism of the inner world." In England he was consoled that at least the rainy weather reminded him of home, though he saw in the political system nothing but hollow self-satisfaction. He was rather distantly moved by the ruins of Italy; his previous love for antiquity was now largely eclipsed by his new love for the Russian *narod.* Everywhere in Italy, nature brought nostalgic memories of Russia.

The fruits of this trip were "Putevye nabroski russkogo lenivtsa i ipokhondrika" (Travel Sketches of a Russian Idler and Hypochondriac) and "Russkie pesni na chuzhbine" (Russian Songs on Foreign Soil), Shcherbina's last group of lyric poems. These poems, some of which were published in the Moscow weekly *Den'* (Day) in 1862, vary widely in tone and quality, ranging from precise and intelligent insights to awkward verse and overblown nationalism. After "Russkie pesni na chuzhbine" Shcherbina wrote only epigrams, which shifted radically toward a reactionary stance in the wake of the Great Reforms and betrayed a growing fear of violent revolution. In Shcherbina's second cycle of epigrams, "Satiricheskaia Letopis'" (Satirical Annals, written 1861–1869), the poet bitterly attacks the liberal camp and defends ultrareactionaries such as the publisher Mikhail Nikiforovich Katkov.

In the early 1860s Shcherbina was occupied with the idea of creating a didactic reader for the *narod*. He published articles on the subject in 1861 and 1863, winning the general approval of novelist Fyodor Dostoevsky; he saved from his meager salary to purchase texts that were otherwise unavailable; and he donated thousands of copies after the book was published to benefit country schools, parishes, Sunday schools, and the cause of the Slavs. *Pchela: Sbornik dlia narodnogo chteniia i dlia upotrebleniia pri narodnom obuchenii* (The Bee: An Anthology for Popular Reading and for Use in Popular Education) came out in 1865 and was in its third printing at the time of Shcherbina's death. It included readings from the spheres of theology, history, and literature, as well as practical advice, and was looked upon favorably by the tsarist authorities.

After the reorganization of the Ministry of People's Education, Shcherbina remained without a position for one year. He was then given a job at the Ministry of Internal Affairs, where he was soon commandeered to the Chief Administration for Affairs of Print. There, he compiled a daily "Obozrenie russkikh gazet i zhurnalov" (Review of Russian Newspapers and Journals) for Tsar Alexander II. Shcherbina also evaluated compositions submitted for the Uvarov Prize (a highly prestigious award presented to authors of scholarly works by the Academy of Sciences) and published critical articles and reviews in various journals.

In 1864 Shcherbina fell ill with throat problems. Doctors advised a trip to the south, but despite his worsening condition he put off the journey for several years. Beginning in 1868 Shcherbina was engaged in preparing a new, fuller version of his works, including "Russkie pesni na chuzhbine" and the epigrams. It was published posthumously in 1873 by Mikhail Ivanovich Semevsky as *Polnoe sobranie sochinenii N. F. Shcherbiny*. The epigrams had gone through several stages of censorship; almost all names had been removed, many lines and stanzas excised, and approximately thirty epigrams had been taken out completely.

Not until March of 1869 did Shcherbina begin lobbying for a transfer to Odessa in light of his illness. Prince Viazemsky and the Minister of Internal Affairs, Aleksandr Egorovich Timashev, helped to find him a position and even secured financial support for his move. On 10 April 1869 doctors in St. Petersburg pro-

posed that Shcherbina—who had not yet departed the capital city—undergo an operation to remove a throat polyp that was choking him. Shcherbina refused, and he suffocated the same day. He was buried on 13 April in the New Lazarus Cemetery of the Aleksandr Nevsky Monastery in St. Petersburg.

Shcherbina's popularity among his contemporaries as an anthological poet and a satirist is beyond dispute. In addition, many of his poems were set to music; among such poems, "Moriak" (The Sailor, *Molodik,* 1844) became the basis for a popular song by Aleksandr L'vovich Gurilev; "Primiren'e" (Reconciliation, *Stikhotvoreniia,* 1857) was set to music by Petr Il'ich Chaikovsky; and "Iuzhnaia noch'" (Southern Night, *Molodik,* 1844) was set by several composers, including Aleksandr Sergeevich Dargomyzhsky and Nikolai Andreevich Rimsky-Korsakov. Tiutchev paid tribute to Shcherbina in a powerful and perceptive poem. After a brief window of attention following the poet's death and the publication of *Polnoe sobranie sochinenii N. F. Shcherbiny,* the first wave of significant interest in Shcherbina's poetry came at the turn of the century. Both the neglect and the renewed interest are understandable. His weak civic verse and his strong bucolic poetry were both unneeded in the 1870s and 1880s. In the age of Russian Symbolism, however, a renewed interest in poetry, art for art's sake, spiritualism, and ancient Greek culture produced fertile ground for a new glance. Shcherbina's vision of Russians as rising barbarians in relation to Romans in Europe in poems such as "Na Ostrove" (On the Island, 1861) and "Gladiatoru v kapitolii" (To the Gladiator in the Capitol, 1861) foreshadows one of the central topoi of early-twentieth-century Russian poetry. Moreover, Shcherbina is preoccupied with the form of ancient Greek tragedy in *Ifigeniia v Tavride* in a manner reminiscent of the much later experiments of Viacheslav Ivanovich Ivanov. After the Russian Revolution, Shcherbina was briefly revived as a satirist, among other *oblichateli* (exposers of the evils) of the old regime. Soon relegated to near oblivion, however, both in the West and the Soviet Union, his name emerged almost exclusively for obligatory academic editions, literary histories, or encyclopedia articles. Only in the 1990s was there a renewed, if tentative, interest in his work. Shcherbina's poetry, while of uneven quality, deserves its small, but significant, place in Russian literature.

Letters:

To Sof'ia Vladimirovna Engel'gardt, *Zaria,* 5 (1870): 75–76;

"To my good friends," published by Engel'gardt, *Zaria,* 5 (1870): 78–93;

To F. B. Miller, in Shcherbina's *Polnoe sobranie sochinenii* (St. Petersburg: Tipografiia Ministerstva Putei Soobshcheniia, 1873), pp. 434–438;

To Grigorii Petrovich Danilevsky, *Istoricheskii vestnik,* 1 (1891): 40–53;

To Petr Andreevich Viazemsky, *Istoricheskii vestnik,* 1 (1891): 38–39;

To V. M. Lazarevsky, *Russkii bibliofil,* 4 (1914): 10–19;

To A. N. Ostrovsky, in *Neizdannye pis'ma k A. N. Ostrovskomu* (Moscow & Leningrad: Academia, 1932), pp. 626–628;

To Aleksandr Vasil'evich Druzhinin, with commentary by P. S. Popov, in *Pis'ma k A. V. Druzhininu* (Moscow: Goslitmuzci, 1948), pp. 351–358;

To Aleksander Ivanovich Gertsen (Alexander Herzen), *Literaturnoe nasledstvo,* 62 (1955): 730–734.

Biographies:

Nikolai Lerner, "Shcherbina, Nikolai Fedorovich," in *Russkii biograficheskii slovar'* (St. Petersburg: I. N. Skorokhodov, 1912), pp. 133–144;

I. Ia. Aizenshtok, "N. F. Shcherbina," in Shcherbina's *Stikhotvoreniia* (Leningrad: Sovetskii pisatel', 1937), pp. 5–33;

I. D. Glikman, "N. F. Shcherbina," in Shcherbina's *Izbrannye proizvedeniia* (Leningrad: Sovetskii pisatel', 1970), pp. 5–64.

References:

Iulii Isaevich Aikhenval'd, "Shcherbina," in his *Siluety russkikh pisatelei,* volume 2 (Moscow: Mir, 1917), pp. 46–55;

L. Bel'sky, "Poeziia i zhizn' Shcherbiny," in *Pochin: Sbornik Obshchestva liubitelei rossiiskoi slovesnosti na 1896 god* (Moscow: Russkoe tovarishchestvo, 1896), pp. 516–533;

Boris Iakovlevich Bukhshtab, "Estetizm v poezii 40–50-kh godov i parodii Koz'my Prutkova," in *Trudy Otdela novoi russkoi literatury,* edited by Boris Solomonovich Meilakh (Moscow & Leningrad: Akademiia nauk SSSR, 1948), pp. 143–174;

Nikolai Gavrilovich Chernyshevsky, "Stikhotvoreniia N. Shcherbina," in his *Polnoe sobranie sochinenii,* 15 volumes, edited by B. P. Koz'min (Moscow: OGIZ/Khudozhestvennaia literatura, 1948), IV: 528–544;

Aleksandr Vasil'evich Druzhinin, "Grecheskie stikhotvoreniia N. Shcherbiny," Sovremennik, 21, no. 5, part 3 (1850): 25–50;

Andrzej Dudek, "Poezja Mikolaja Szczerbiny wobec tradycji antycznej," *Zeszyty Naukowe Uniwersytet Jagiellonski Prace Historycznoliterackie,* 80 (1992): 145–158;

Ol'ga N. [Sof'ia Vladimirovna Engel'gardt], "Nikolai Fedorovich Shcherbina," *Zaria,* no. 5 (1870), 67–93;

E. O. Iunge, *Vospominaniia (1843–1863 gg.)* ([Moscow]: Sfinks, 1913?);

Razumnik Vasil'evich Ivanov, "N. F. Shcherbina i ego Al'bom ipokhondrika," as Ivanov-Razumnik, in Shcherbina's *Al'bom ipokhondrika: Epigrammy i satiry* (Leningrad: Priboi, 1929), pp. 5–18;

A. S. Kogan, "Tiutchev i Shcherbina: Motivy antichnosti," *Voprosy russkoi literatury,* 2 [56] (1990): 3–11;

Ivan Konevskoi, "Mirovozzrenie poezii N. F. Shcherbiny," in *Mechty i dumy Ivana Konevskogo* (Berkeley, Cal.: Berkeley Slavic Specialties, 1989), pp. 220–240;

Nikolai Konstantinovich Mikhailovsky, "Iz literaturnykh i zhurnal'nykh zametok 1875 goda," in his *Polnoe sobranie sochinenii,* 5 volumes (St. Petersburg: Russkoe bogatstvo, 1906–1908), II: 600–617;

Barbara Stawarz, "O kontemplacji. Dzielo sztuki antycznej w poezji Mikolaja Szczerbiny i Apollona Majkowa," *Slavia Orientalis,* 44, no. 4 (1995): 473–483;

Stawarz, "Tesknota za bezpieczenstwem. O poezji Mikolaja Szczerbiny," *Przeglad Rusycystyczny,* 3 [91] (2000): 26–36.

Papers:

Collections of Nikolai Fedorovich Shcherbina's manuscripts are held in St. Petersburg at the Russian National Library (RNB), fond 881, and the Institute of Russian Literature (IRLI, Pushkin House) in the "Russkaia starina" collection. In Moscow, Shcherbina's papers can be found at the Russian State Library (RGB, formerly the Lenin Library), fond 178; the Russian State Archive of Literature and Art (RGALI), fond 570; and the State Historical Museum (GIM).

Vasilii Alekseevich Sleptsov

(17 July 1836 – 23 March 1878)

Andrei Rogachevskii
University of Glasgow

BOOKS: *Sochineniia. Rasskazy, ocherki i stseny,* 2 volumes
(St. Petersburg: S. V. Zvonarev, 1866)–includes
"Na zheleznoi doroge," "Mertvoe telo";

Polnoe sobranie sochinenii (St. Petersburg: N. A. Lebedev,
1887; enlarged edition, V. I. Gubinsky, 1903);

Pitomka (Moscow: I. D. Sytin, 1890);

Trudnoe vremia (Berlin, Moscow & St. Petersburg: Z. I.
Grzhebin, 1922);

Sochineniia, 2 volumes, edited by Kornei Ivanovich
Chukovsky (Moscow & Leningrad: Academia,
1932–1933);

Vasilii Sleptsov: Neizvestnye stranitsy, edited by S. A.
Makashin (Moscow: AN SSSR, 1963).

Editions and Collections: *Trudnoe vremia,* edited by
Kornei Ivanovich Chukovsky (Moscow: Khudozhestvennaia literatura, 1949);

Pitomka.–Nochleg (Moscow: Golitizdat, 1956);

Sochineniia, 2 volumes, edited and with an introduction
and commentary by Chukovsky (Moscow: Goslitizdat, 1957); republished as *Proza,* with an introduction by N. I. Iakushin (Moscow: Sovetskaia
Rossiia, 1986);

Trudnoe vremia, with an introduction by V. S. Lysenko
(Moscow: Sovetskaia Rossiia, 1979);

Ocherki. Rasskazy. Povest' (Voronezh: Tsentral'no-
Chernozemnoe knizhnoe izdatel'stvo, 1983);

Izbrannoe. Povest', ocherki i rasskazy (Moscow: Detskaia
literatura, 1984);

Proza (Moscow: Sovetskii pisatel', 1986);

Trudnoe vremia. Ocherki, rasskazy, povest' (Moscow: Sovremennik, 1986).

Vasilii Sleptsov was a controversial figure held in
high esteem by Nikolai Alekseevich Nekrasov, Mikhail
Evgrafovich Saltykov, Leo Tolstoy, and Maksim
Gor'ky and ridiculed, with almost equal ardor, by
Nikolai Semenovich Leskov, Vsevolod Vladimirovich
Krestovsky, and Nikolai Vasil'evich Uspensky. Such a
sharp polarization of opinions with regard to his life and
legacy might be attributed partially to Sleptsov's blatant
revolutionary-democratic agenda. Yet, his personality

Vasilii Alekseevich Sleptsov, 1860s

was deemed interesting enough to serve as a prototype,
friendly as well as unfriendly, in several works of fiction.
The unpublished novel "Na maloi zemle" (On the
Minor Land, 1880 to early 1930s), by Lidiia Nelidova,
still remains an important biographical source on
Sleptsov, who features in it under the name of Sviridov.
Sleptsov's distinguished artistic talent is also beyond dis-
pute. His knack for the accurate rendition of colloquial
speech and his keen sense of humor, manifested in the
short stories "Spevka" (The Rehearsal; published in
Otechestvennye zapiski [Notes of the Fatherland], 1862) and
"Na zheleznoi doroge" (On the Railroad, *Severnaia pchela*

[The Northern Bee], 1862), made even an accomplished humorist such as Anton Pavlovich Chekhov nearly split his sides with laughter. On balance, the story of Sleptsov's life is primarily that of tragically wasted opportunities, which was not atypical for the *shestidesiatniki* (generation of the 1860s).

Vasilii Alekseevich Sleptsov was born in Voronezh to an aristocratic family. His father, Aleksei Vasil'evich Sleptsov, a Tambov landowner, was stationed there with the Novorossiisk Dragoons. His mother, Zhozefina Adamovna (Antonovna), née Vel'butovich-Paplonskaia, Sleptsova was a Polish Catholic who married Aleksei Vasil'evich against his parents' wishes and without a dowry. This situation led to many family tensions; that Sleptsov's family had to share a house in Moscow with Aleksei Vasil'evich's mother for eleven years only exacerbated these tensions. (Sleptsov's family had moved to Moscow after his father retired from the army and started working for the Moscow commissariat.) Only in 1849, after Aleksei Vasil'evich was given his (unfair, some claim) share of the Sleptsov estate, could he afford a house of his own, in the village Aleksandrovka of the Serdobsk district, Saratov province, and he relocated there with his wife and offspring.

Sleptsov, the eldest of six children, was reportedly a sensitive and impressionable boy, torn between his mother and his paternal grandmother, who were not particularly fond of each other. He was at first educated by a private tutor; in 1847 he began attending the First Moscow Gymnasium. Left largely to his own devices, however, he supplemented his education by delving into his grandfather's impressive book collection. After his parents had moved to Aleksandrovka, Sleptsov was transferred to the Noblemen's Institute in Penza, the nearest center of cultural importance. He was one of the best pupils but had to take time off from studies in the spring of 1851 because of the death of his father, who had been suffering from poor health for quite some time; his mother, Zhozefina Adamovna, needed Sleptsov to help her run their estate. He returned to the institute in the autumn of 1852, only to be expelled from it for an act of blasphemy committed in January 1853. The existing accounts of this event are contradictory. One version suggests that he publicly renounced his Christian faith at a service in the institute church; according to another, he entered its altar in the middle of a festive mass; and yet another purports that he swapped the deacon's and the priest's robes during investment. His brother Nikolai maintained that Sleptsov had been looking forward to entering a university, did not want to waste his time at the institute any longer, and quite simply simulated madness. Superimposed upon the accounts of his earlier piety (he had

even worn rusty chains under his garments, as an ascetic of sorts), this episode not only signified Sleptsov's possible disenchantment with religion but also marked one of the first manifestations of the powerful self-destructive trend in his character.

In August 1853 Sleptsov passed entrance examinations and enrolled in the Faculty of Medicine at Moscow University. He left the university soon, however, succumbing to his passion for theater, which had begun developing in his childhood. He was particularly fond of the Malyi Theater, and when its leading actor Mikhail Semenovich Shchepkin confirmed that Sleptsov indeed had a gift (he took part in various amateur productions), his decision to go onstage was made. Sleptsov assumed a pseudonym (Lunin), signed a contract with a theater company in Iaroslavl', and stayed there for the 1854–1855 season, debuting as Khlestakov in Nikolai Vasil'evich Gogol's *Revizor* (1836). His devotion to theater was to last throughout his life and influenced some of his works, such as "Mertvoe telo" (The Dead Body, 1866), "V trushchobakh" (In the Slums, 1866; first published in *Minuta* [A Minute], 1880), "V vagone III klassa" (In a Third Class Carriage, *Kalendar' iskry* [The Spark's Calendar], 1867), "Stseny v politsii" (Scenes at a Police Precinct, *Delo* [The Deed], 1867) and "Stseny u mirovogo sud'i" (Scenes at the Justice of the Peace, *Remeslennaia gazeta* [The Artisan's Newspaper], 1876)—all of which have virtually no narrative, only dialogues and stage directions, and resemble dramatic sketches rather than short stories. In this context, also worth mentioning are Sleptsov's survey of the 1865–1867 repertoire of the Aleksandrinskii Theater in St. Petersburg, titled "Tip noveishei dramy" (On Recent Drama; published in *Otechestvennye zapiski,* 1868), and his review of Aleksandr Nikolaevich Ostrovsky's play *Dokhodnoe mesto* (A Profitable Vacancy, performed 1863, published 1857), which was intended for *Sovremennik* (The Contemporary) but was suppressed by the censors and has survived only in the form of proofs.

A rather handsome man, Sleptsov enjoyed considerable success with women (he even claimed to have seduced nuns in monasteries during his time as a student). Characteristically, his relationships usually did not last long. In 1856 he married the Moscow ballet dancer Ekaterina Aleksandrovna Tsukanova, who died the next year. Soon after that, in 1858, he married Elizaveta Nikolaevna Iazykova, the daughter of a Tver' landowner. Although this marriage produced two children—a son, who died in infancy, and a daughter called Valentina—it was an unhappy union from 1860 until the couple's final separation in 1865.

From 1857 to 1862 Sleptsov worked in the office of the governor of Moscow. During this period his acquaintance with the *kruzhok* circle of the author and publisher Countess Salias de Tournemir, who wrote under the pseudonym of Evgeniia Tur, inspired him to embark on a literary career. He had written poetry in his youth–as well as later in his life–although he had never published it. His first serious literary assignment, however, came in 1859 from the Ethnographic Section of the Geographical Society, through the offices of the famous author, linguist, and ethnographer Vladimir Ivanovich Dal', whom Sleptsov had met when he studied at Moscow University. Sleptsov was commissioned to gather folklore material while traveling on foot through Vladimir province. This trip began in November 1860 and resulted in the appearance of a cycle of eight sketches, *Vladimirka i Kliaz'ma* (The Road to Vladimir and the Kliaz'ma River, 1861), in Tournemir's journal *Russkaia rech'* (Russian Speech), of which Sleptsov was an editor, and in *Moskovskii vestnik* (The Moscow Messenger).

Folk songs, peasant dialects, and other things ethnographic are not given special prominence in *Vladimirka i Kliaz'ma*. The main focus of the cycle is on the hardships of the everyday life of local peasants and factory workers, with occasional forays into the more privileged existence of merchants, innkeepers, factory managers, and provincial clerics. The autobiographical narrator is someone who collects various information about rural customs, old and new. As his business is only semiofficial and his status is unclear–the only mandate he can produce is a letter from Obshchestvo liubitelei rossiiskoi slovesnosti (Society of Lovers of Russian Literature) confirming that he is permitted to "gather songs, proverbs and fairy tales, as well as anything else related to Russian habits, traditions and language"–the owners of the paper mills and spinning factories that he visits treat him with suspicion and, more often than not, give rather unhelpful answers. Although the narrator struggles to project an image of impartiality, his sympathies clearly rest with the workers and poorer peasants, and the reader is bound to come to the conclusion that the owners and managers are being secretive not so much because of the confidentiality of their business schemes but because they do not want to go into detail about how ruthlessly they exploit their employees. The "lower" classes are not idealized either, though, and graphic scenes of women abused by men under the influence of alcohol leave a lasting impression. One of the sketches additionally puts things in perspective through a comparison of the treatment of, and working conditions for, French and Russian laborers, respectively, who are engaged in the construction of a railway bridge over the Kliaz'ma River.

In the late summer of 1861 Sleptsov visited St. Petersburg, where he met Nikolai Gavrilovich Cherny-

shevsky, Vasilii Stepanovich Kurochkin, Aleksandr Nikolaevich Pypin, and Saltykov and began his association with Nekrasov's radical journal *Sovremennik*. With the publication of the first installments of *Vladimirka i Kliaz'ma* Sleptsov earned the reputation of a *sui generis* investigative journalist, and Nekrasov sent him on a fact-finding mission to the town of Ostashkov (in Tver' province) to establish whether it really was a model of liberal reforms in Russia, as had been officially declared, or merely a publicity stunt. After spending October and November 1861 in Ostashkov, Sleptsov returned to Moscow to finish his piece for *Sovremennik* in which he detailed his findings, resigned from his post at the Moscow governor's office, and moved to St. Petersburg. *Pis'ma ob Ostashkove* (Letters about Ostashkov) appeared in *Sovremennik* in 1862 and 1863–not without obstruction on the part of censors–and caused a bit of a scandal. The local authorities in Ostashkov were infuriated to such a degree that they ordered the issue of *Sovremennik* featuring the first part of Sleptsov's work removed from the Ostashkov public library.

Pis'ma ob Ostashkove consists of nine letters that gradually unravel the sinister driving force behind the alleged success of the town. Its public library, common greens, clean streets, exemplary orphanages, and old people's homes–something unheard of in many other contemporary Russian urban settlements–fail to impress Sleptsov as soon as he realizes, contrary to what the dwellers of Ostashkov are led to believe, that all of these wonders are not the result of charitable action and efficient management by the principal rulers and benefactors (the wealthy family of Savins) of the town. On the contrary, these improvements are financed by the public purse via indirect local taxes. The Savins, who had established a bank that promoted individual loans for purchasing luxury items–such as expensive crinoline dresses to flaunt in public gardens and parks–and thus forced the majority of the unsuspecting townsfolk to run into massive debts, claim all the credit, and enjoy the admiration of the rest of Russia. One is somewhat surprised to observe how painstakingly Sleptsov searches for faults in what even now looks like a rather pleasant urban environment; for him, of course, it is only a facade, and he likens Ostashkov to an extremely well-polished boot with a hole in it. On the other hand, in his assessment of the controversial role of banks in modern society, he is quite forward-thinking. As for the cultural life in Ostashkov, to Sleptsov it seems shallow and pretentious–that is, it is dominated by a fad for engravings and coin collecting, which he finds fairly bizarre for unsophisticated provincials. The only consolation for him is provided by the local amateur theater, but even in his appreciation of the inexperienced yet enthusiastic actors he appears to be biased–only this time in a positive direction, out of sheer love for the stage. All in all, Sleptsov is tendentious and patronizing in his approach and consequently too harsh on the inhabitants of Ostashkov, whose existence is actually full of charming and endearing features.

Although *Vladimirka i Kliaz'ma* and *Pis'ma ob Ostashkove* had already demonstrated Sleptsov's intimate knowledge of the values of the lower classes and their means of self-expression, as well as his skill in the art of politically engaged understatement, his first serious success came in 1863 with the publication of his short story "Pitomka" (A Foster Child) in the journal *Sovremennik*. The protagonist of the story is Anis'ia, an illiterate woman from Moscow, who walks through one village after another for miles on end, sometimes without food or drink, searching in vain for her four-year-old daughter whom she had given up for anonymous adoption several years previously. The topic, itself rather maudlin, coincided with a public debate on the right of women to raise so-called illegitimate children themselves, without recourse to children's homes or foster parents, and on the moral ambiguity of concealing the new identities of adopted children from their biological parents. Not by chance did Sleptsov dedicate "Pitomka" to Aleksandra Grigor'evna Markelova, a St. Petersburg "nihilist" who bore a son outside marriage but refused to send him to a children's home.

"Pitomka" evinces an artistic manner that owes a great deal to the genre of sketch; this manner is typical for Sleptsov, who—according to a review in *Razvlechenie* (Entertainment) signed with the pseudonym "Novyi Chelovek" (A New Man)—"reproduces seemingly the most pointless conversations and scenes; however, . . . from the chaos of the minute details of everyday life emerges a profoundly dramatic phenomenon that immerses you in deep thoughts." "Pitomka" earned praise from Ivan Sergeevich Turgenev (in his letter to Vasilii Petrovich Botkin of 21 September 1863), and no less a person than Tolstoy was enamored by it so much that in October 1888, quite some time after its first appearance, he recommended it to the Posrednik publishing house as a possible separate edition "for the people." Remarkably, the issues raised in "Pitomka" still troubled the authorities to such an extent that the first attempt by Posrednik to obtain the imprimatur from the St. Petersburg censors in January 1889 proved unsuccessful. The story came out in book form only in October 1889, with some cuts imposed by the more lenient but nevertheless fairly watchful Moscow censors. The artist Il'ia Efimovich Repin believed that Tolstoy's fascination with "Pitomka" was in no small measure because of the image of a peasant cart driver, who, on his own initiative, gives Anis'ia a lift, offers her

food, and even pretends in public—to prevent undesirable complications—that he is married to her. Sleptsov was not painting the picture of a righteous altruist, though. When his journey with Anis'ia is over, the cart driver demands a drink as a reward for his services, although earlier he had given her the impression that his offer of help was quite selfless and unconditional.

Public readings of this and other short stories by Sleptsov (with the purpose of lending financial support to various good causes, as was common among the St. Petersburg intellectuals at that time) gave him a chance to use his talent as a performer; some contemporaries compared his recitals to theatrical shows. This talent contributed to his growing popularity, and many of his followers were women. He reciprocated their affection and declared himself a vigorous champion of their emancipation. His affairs with Ekaterina Ivanovna Tsenina-Zhukovskaia, Markelova, Vera Zakharovna Voronina, Varvara Aleksandrovna Inostrantseva, and Nelidova (whose real name was Lidiia Filippovna Koroleva-Lamovskaia), to name only a few, seem to be well documented. Sleptsov's desire to link the emancipation of women to the provision of a "foundation for the socialist management of labour" led to the establishment of the so-called Znamenskaia commune (on Znamenskaia Street in St. Petersburg, in the Bekman House), modeled after the sewing shop of Vera Pavlovna in Chernyshevsky's novel *Chto delat'?* (What Is to Be Done? 1863).

Lasting from September 1863 through May 1864, the commune became something of a cult phenomenon and was described in an array of prose and dramatic works: Evgenii Andreevich Salias's short story "12 chasov, voskresen'e" (Twelve O'Clock, Sunday); Mikhail Petrovich Cherniavsky's play "Grazhdanskii brak" (A Civil Marriage, 1866); and the novels *Nekuda* (No Way Out, 1864) by Leskov, *Panurgovo stado* (The Flock of Panurge, 1869) by Krestovsky, and *Povetrie* (The Craze, 1867) by Vasilii Petrovich Avenarius. Descriptions of the commune were found as well in the memoirs of Tsenina, Markelova, Aleksandr Mikhailovich Skabichevsky, and Uspensky. The commune's members were predominantly women; its core was formed by Tsenina, Markelova, Mariia Nikolaevna Kopteva, and Ekaterina Aleksandrovna Makulova—with Sleptsov's brother-in-law Vladimir Nikolaevich Iazykov and the editorial secretary of *Sovremennik,* Apollon Filippovich Golovachev, added for good measure. They planned to make their living out of literary work and translations. In tune with communist principles, income for the commune would be generated "according to aptitude," expenses would be incurred "according to demand," and profits were to be shared equally. In the event of a budget deficit (which was not uncommon) the accounts were supposed to be kept in the black by those who were making more money than the others—that is, almost exclusively by Sleptsov himself, who had to pay the cost of the rent—1,200 rubles per year—out of his own pocket.

An economic system like this one could exist only until its internal resources were drained. Even the reportedly successful series of popular-science lectures for women and literary and musical evenings (which attracted the writers Saltykov and Aleksandr Ivanovich Levitov, the composer Aleksandr Nikolaevich Serov, and the scientist Ivan Mikhailovich Sechenov) could not save the commune from collapse. The situation was aggravated by cultural clashes between the "repentant nobleman" (the aristocrat Sleptsov) and the *raznochintsy* (democratically oriented intellectuals of humble background)—otherwise known as the *burye* (brown)—such as, for instance, Makulova. In addition, the notorious Third Section (secret police) became interested in the Bekman House. Consequently, on 1 June 1864 Sleptsov dismissed the Znamenskaia commune.

The failure of the commune—exacerbated by the crisis of the radical movement as a whole—inspired Sleptsov to create his most significant work, *Trudnoe vremia* (Hard Times, written 1865, published in book form, 1922). Its title alluded, on the one hand, to Charles Dickens's novel of 1854 and, on the other, to lines from Nekrasov's poem "Rytsar' na chas" (Knight for an Hour, 1860–1862): "Zakhvatilo nas trudnoe vremia / Negotovymi k trudnoi bor'be" (Hard times have caught us / Unprepared for a hard struggle). These lines referred to the inability of the radicals to offer a viable alternative to the ultimately disappointing governmental reforms of the 1860s. Superficially familiar with Karl Marx's doctrine, Sleptsov had even discussed in *Pis'ma ob Ostashkove* "the monopolization of capital" and "the despotism of money" and compared the conditions of the workers in Ostashkov to those of workers in Liverpool. In *Trudnoe vremia* he thoroughly examines the conflicts between socialist/communist theory and reality.

The story line of *Trudnoe vremia* focuses on a triangular relationship among the landowner Shchetinin; his wife, Mar'ia Nikolavna; and his friend Riazanov. The frustrated sexual desires of the threesome are either gradually translated into capitalist entrepreneurship (Shchetinin) or boost revolutionary activity (Mar'ia Nikolavna and Riazanov). Most of the novel is set in 1863. At the beginning all three characters are looking for their own way of achieving the socialist ideal. Their heated intellectual arguments are interlaced with expertly written scenes of provincial life, which testify both to the moral corruption of the gentry and to the underdeveloped "class consciousness" of the peasants. Shchetinin would like to give away his land to his serfs

(this part of the story takes place before the 1861 abolition of serfdom). Yet, he encounters skepticism both on the part of the neighboring landowners, who feel threatened by Shchetinin's actions, and of the peasants themselves, who have their own misgivings about the proposed changes—largely because they are too set in their ways but also because of their deep mistrust toward all masters in general. This skepticism seriously upsets Shchetinin's plans and undermines his beliefs, and he finds himself at a crossroads. The writer Riazanov, while on a visit to his friend's estate, forces Shchetinin to admit, by means of ruthless irony and logic, that the principles of socialist farming are virtually impossible to reconcile with private ownership, and Shchetinin finally chooses to make as much money off his land as possible, rather than get rid of it.

Mar'ia Nikolavna is extremely unhappy about her husband's decision. She cannot forgive him for deceiving her and turning her into a housewife, contrary to his earlier promises of involvement in unspecified revolutionary actions. (Any direct mention of a revolution in the making is carefully avoided in the text; Sleptsov refers to revolution as a "great deed that might ruin our lives, and not only ours, but also our friends' lives"). As an alternative she sets her heart on Riazanov, who is especially attractive because he is shrouded in mystery. The true reasons behind his sojourn at the Shchetinins' are never revealed; presumably, he is monitoring the situation in the province and is recruiting reinforcements for the decimated radical movement. Sleptsov makes the most of his preferred artistic device of allusion and insinuation and manages to impress the reader without disclosing much about Riazanov's incendiary activity. Riazanov is also strongly attracted to Mar'ia Nikolavna, but he regretfully stalls their budding romance because as a true revolutionary he must sacrifice his love for the sake of the *obshchee delo* (common cause). Mar'ia Nikolavna nonetheless leaves her husband and heads for St. Petersburg, either to perish there or go into emigration—or, as Gor'ky writes, to go "to the 'common people' and then—into exile, into prison, into a penal colony."

Not by chance did Gor'ky, the founder of Socialist Realism, choose to canonize *Trudnoe vremia* as a precursor of this newly emerged artistic phenomenon. Riazanov is undoubtedly a prototype of the positive hero of Socialist Realism, and many motifs explored in Sleptsov's novel—such as the tragic but life-asserting image of Man struggling with natural elements that are extremely hard to tame, or the conflict between the good and the best (*konflikt khoroshego s luchshim*)—later became Socialist Realist clichés. As for Sleptsov's contemporaries, *Trudnoe vremia* received acclaim from the radical critic Dmitrii Ivanovich Pisarev, who believed that the character of Shchetinin was an accurate description of Russian liberal parasites, and from the revolutionary Petr Nikitich Tkachev, who insisted that Mar'ia Nikolavna should become a role model for Russian women. Less inflammatory critics were also less enthusiastic and reprimanded Sleptsov for the "nebulous and disingenuous plot," consisting mostly of "snapshots [of rural mores], arbitrarily linked together." Riazanov was branded a cynic, and Mar'ia Nikolavna a silly woman. Many Russian women in the provinces read *Trudnoe vremia* as an instruction to follow, and quite a few of them left their families and came to St. Petersburg to seek Sleptsov's advice on what to do next. The philosopher and sociologist Vladimir Ivanovich Taneev recalled that during this time eight or nine different women waited in Sleptsov's living room every day, as if it were a surgery (in this sense, a place where doctors treat patients) and he were a doctor.

As events soon showed, Sleptsov had to endure much more—for toying with revolutionary ideas—than just the unwanted female visitors who exalted him. On 30 April 1866 he was arrested in connection with Dmitrii Vladimirovich Karakozov's attempt on the life of Tsar Alexander II (Karakozov had also studied at the Noblemen's Institute), and from that moment onward everything in Sleptsov's life changed for the worse. Incarcerated for seven weeks, he was released on 18 June 1866 without being charged—although he was put under police surveillance—but his health and career were ruined. In September 1866 he became an editor of the St. Petersburg monthly *Zhenskii vestnik* (The Women's Messenger), but his association with the magazine, whose first issue opened with Sleptsov's editorial "Zhenskoe delo" (The Feminist Cause), was short-lived and ended up in court. The publisher of *Zhenskii vestnik,* Anna Messarosh, claimed that Sleptsov owed her 300 rubles. On 11 March 1867 *Sankt-Peterburgskie vedomosti* (The St. Petersburg News) published a sarcastic account of the court proceedings, titled—in imitation of Sleptsov's manner—"Stseny u mirovogo sud'i" (Scenes at the Justice of the Peace). On 15 March in the newspaper *Golos* (The Voice) Sleptsov announced that he had severed relations with *Zhenskii vestnik* on 1 October 1866. The lawsuit was then withdrawn. As has been suggested in *Vasilii Sleptsov: Neizvestnye stranitsy* (Vasilii Sleptsov: The Unknown Pages, 1963), the case was no more than a ruse to dissociate Sleptsov and *Zhenskii vestnik* publicly in order to make the dealings of the magazine with the Censorship Committee easier. Sleptsov apparently continued to contribute to the magazine anonymously; for example, the feuilleton cycle "Novosti peterburgskoi zhizni: Skromnye zametki" (News from St. Petersburg: Humble Notes, 1867) is attributed to him in *Vasilii Sleptsov: Neizvestnye stranitsy.*

If indeed the lawsuit had been a ruse, the number and significance of Sleptsov's publications substantially decreased in the following years. From this point on he preferred to divide his time between editorial work and theater management. In January 1868 Sleptsov began his job as a secretary for Nekrasov's *Otechestvennye zapiski*—from which he resigned on grounds of poor health in January 1872—and between 1869 and 1874 he served as director for several amateur theatrical groups in St. Petersburg and Tiflis. Of this period, only two works by Sleptsov deserve a brief mention: a piece of topical journalism, "Zapiski metafizika" (Notes of a Metaphysician; published in *Otechestvennye zapiski,* 1868), which centers on the 1867 famine that engulfed Arkhangel'sk, Tver', Kostroma, Orel, and other provinces, and the first five chapters of the novel *Khoroshii chelovek* (A Nice Guy, *Otechestvennye zapiski,* 1871). The chief character of this novel, which was never finished, is the twenty-eight-year-old Sergei Terebenev, who seems to be yet another Russian *lishnii chelovek* (superfluous man) in search of self-realization. In the autumn of 1877 Sleptsov was also working on a novel titled "Ostrov Utopiia" (The Island of Utopia)—"something like *Don Quixote,*" as he described in a letter of 3 November 1877 to Nelidova—but its draft, if it ever existed in any coherent form, has not yet been discovered.

For several reasons Sleptsov could not overcome his writer's block. Some of his friends maintained that the standards he had set for himself as an author were too high. Memoirs of Sleptsov in the last period of his life leave open for speculation whether he suffered from clinical depression. Because he could not do any regular work, he became unable to support himself, and his letters of the time often include requests for more and more money. To make matters worse, in 1873 he was reportedly diagnosed with a rectal ulcer and took a trip to the Caucasus for medical reasons. Although the treatment was quite expensive, in 1876 Sleptsov traveled there again, apparently almost to no avail. In 1877, after consultations with the best doctors in St. Petersburg and an exploratory operation, they established at last that he had intestinal cancer. Sleptsov's ill-wishers, however, claimed that he had fallen victim to the complications of a venereal disease, perhaps the result of the too active part that he had played in women's emancipation. Whatever the cause of his illness, another trip to the Caucasus in July of the same year did not cure him (but did ruin him financially), and in February 1878 he had no other choice but to return home and live with his mother, at the Kurakino estate, near the town of Serdobsk in the Saratov province, where he finally died on 23 March at the age of forty-one.

Vasilii Alekseevich Sleptsov's posthumous reputation owed much to what he had stood for politically. Quite apart from his considerable gift for compact, vivid, memorable descriptions of daily life (with a sharp eye for detail and an admirable sense of humor), his legacy simply was not sizable enough to secure a long shelf life for his works. Had it not been for the October 1917 Revolution, which gave a rather artificial boost to his status, little would be known about Sleptsov today. A large part of what he wrote about was strictly topical and cannot be understood easily anymore without extensive scholarly explanations; the same applies to his occasional, almost esoteric language, which is frequently laden with political allusions that are now difficult to decode. Perhaps a reexamination of Sleptsov's peculiar brand of feminism might spark a renewed interest in his life and work, but he is unlikely to attract little more than academic curiosity.

Letters:

To Ivan Fedorovich Gorbunov, in Gorbunov's *Sochineniia*, volume 3 (St. Petersburg: Imperatorskoe obshchestvo liubitelei drevnei pis'mennosti, 1907), pp. 72–73;

To Zh. A. Sleptsova and To V. Z. Voronina, in *Liudi i knigi shestidesiatykh godov*, by Kornei Ivanovich Chukovsky (Leningrad: Izdatel'stvo pisatelei v Leningrade, 1934), pp. 296–305;

To Nikolai Alekseevich Nekrasov, in "N. A. Nekrasov," edited by P. I. Lebedev-Poliansky, *Literaturnoe nasledstvo*, 61–62 (1949): 493–498.

Biographies:

Nikolai Vasil'evich Uspensky, "V. A. Sleptsov," in his *Iz proshlogo* (Moscow, 1889), pp. 115–128;

Zh. A. Sleptsova, "V. A. Sleptsov v vospominaniiakh ego materi," *Russkaia starina*, 1 (1890): 233–241;

V. S. Markov, "V. A. Sleptsov," *Istoricheskii vestnik*, 3 (1903): 957–976;

E. N. Vodovozova, "V. A. Sleptsov," *Golos minuvshego*, 12 (1915): 107–120;

Grigorii Zakharovich Elisieev, "O romane 'Chto delat'?' i 'Kommune' V. A. Sleptsova," in *Shestidesiatye gody*, edited by Vladislav Evgen'evich Evgen'ev-Maksimov and G. I. Tizengauzena (Moscow & Leningrad: Academia, 1933), pp. 484–493;

A. V. Popov, "Russkie pisateli na Kavkaze," *Materialy po izucheniiu Stavropol'skogo kraia*, 8 (1956): 321–324;

A. L. Korkin, "Peterburgskii period zhizni i deiatel'nosti V. A. Sleptsova: Sotrudnichestvo v zhurnale 'Sovremennik' (1862–1866)," *Uchenye zapiski Piatigorskogo pedagogicheskogo instituta*, 15 (1957): 409–460.

References:

Iulii Isaevich Aikhenval'd, *Siluety russkikh pisatelei*, 2 volumes (Moscow: Nauchnoe slovo, 1908), II: 153–162;

R. R. Alieva, "Ocherki i rasskazy V. A. Sleptsova," dissertation, Leningrad State University, 1967;

Anonymous, "Novyi chelovek," *Razvlechenie*, 34 (1863): 139;

M. V. Avdeev, *Nashe obshchestvo (1820–1870) v geroiakh i geroiniakh literatury* (St. Petersburg: K. V. Trubnikov, 1874), pp. 124–136, 263–277;

Vasilii Grigor'evich Bazanov, *Iz literaturnoi polemiki 60-kh godov* (Petrozavodsk: Gosudarstvennoe izdatel'stvo Karelo-Finskoi SSR, 1941), pp. 118–127;

Anatolii Grigor'evich Bednov, *Tvorchestvo V. A. Sleptsova* (Arkhangel'sk: Arkhangel'skii pedagogicheskii institut, 1958);

William C. Brumfield, "Bazarov and Rjazanov: The Romantic Archetype in Russian Nihilism," *Slavic and East European Journal*, 21, no. 4 (1977): 495–505;

Brumfield, "Sleptsov Redivivus," *California Slavic Studies*, 9 (1976): 27–70;

Kornei Ivanovich Chukovsky, "Tainopis' Vasiliia Sleptsova v povesti 'Trudnoe vremia,'" in Sleptsov's *Sochineniia*, volume 1 (Moscow: Academia, 1932), pp. 15–65;

A. A. Divil'kovsky, "V. A. Sleptsov," in *Istoriia russkoi literatury XIX veka*, edited by Dmitrii Nikolaevich Ovsianiko-Kulikovsky, volume 3 (Moscow: Mir, 1909), pp. 347–356;

Vladislav Evgen'evich Evgen'ev-Maksimov, "O dvukh zabytykh romanakh," *Zhizn' dlia vsekh*, 8–9 (1915): 1,205–1,224;

Maksim Gor'ky, "O Vasilii Sleptsove," in his *Sobranie sochinenii v tridtsati tomakh*, 30 volumes (Moscow: Goslitizdat, 1949–1955), XXIV: 219–224;

Incognito [E. F. Zarin], "Chetyre povesti i odin ponomar'," *Otechestvennye zapiski*, 12 (1865): 703–721;

N. Iordansky, "Raznochinets-prosvetitel'," in Sleptsov's *Trudnoe vremia: Povest'* (Moscow: Gosudarstvennoe izdatel'stvo, 1923), pp. 5–11;

V. Ivanov [V. I. Zasulich], "Krepostnaia podkladka 'progressivnykh' rechei," *Novoe slovo*, 9 (1897): 167–193;

Eva Kagan-Kans, "Vasilij Slepcov: Nihilist Malgré Lui," in *Language, Literature, Linguistics: In Honor of Francis J. Whitfield on His Seventieth Birthday, March 25, 1986*, edited by Michael S. Flier and Simon Karlinsky (Berkeley, Cal.: Berkeley Slavic Specialties, 1987), pp. 102–127;

I. M. Kolesnitskaia, "Problema narodnogo byta i narodnogo tvorchestva v demokraticheskoi literature 1860-kh godov (A. I. Levitov, F. M. Reshetnikov, V. A. Sleptsov)," *Uchenye zapiski Leningradskogo universiteta*, 158 (1952): 266–311;

S. A. Koporsky, "K kharakteristike stilia sochineniia pisatelei-demokratov N. Uspenskogo, V. Sleptsova i F. Reshetnikova," in *Sbornik statei po iazykoznaniiu: Professoru Moskovskogo universiteta, akademiku V. V. Vinogradovu*, edited by Aleksandr Ivanovich Efimov (Moscow: Izdatel'stvo Moskovskogo Universiteta, 1958), pp. 188–213;

Koporsky, "O nekotorykh osobennostiakh leksiki sochinenii pisatelei-demokratov N. Uspenskogo, Sleptsova i Reshetnikova," *Uchenye zapiski Moskovskogo oblastnogo pedinstituta*, 48, no. 4 (1957): 3–42;

Koporsky, "Sobstvennye imena v iazyke pisatelei-demokratov N. Uspenskogo, Sleptsova i Reshetnikova," *Uchenye zapiski Moskovskogo oblastnogo pedinstituta*, 35, no. 3 (1956): 3–68;

N. I. Kubitskaia, "Publitsistika V. A. Sleptsova," *Uchenye zapiski Kazanskogo pedagogicheskogo instituta*, 14 (1958): 119–149;

P. M. Mikhailov, "Zhizn' i tvorchestvo V. A. Sleptsova," *Izvestiia Krymskogo pedagogicheskogo instituta*, 10 (1940): 34–74;

N. K. Mikhailovsky, "Raznochintsy i kaiushchiesia dvoriane," *Otechestvennye zapiski*, 4 (1874): 387–392;

Mikhas Vasil'evich Niakhai, *Russkii demokraticheskii ocherk 60-kh godov XIX stoletiia (N. Uspenskii, V. Sleptsov, A. Levitov)* (Minsk: Izdatel'stvo BGU, 1971);

Derek Offord, "Literature and Ideas in Russia after the Crimean War: The 'Plebeian' Writers," in *Ideology in Russian Literature*, edited by Richard Freeborn and Jane Grayson (London: Macmillan, 1990), pp. 68–74;

Dmitrii Ivanovich Pisarev, "Padrastaiushchaia gumannost'," *Russkoe slovo*, 12 (1865);

L. P. Podluzhnaia, "O khudozhestvennom svoeobrazii rasskazov V. A. Sleptsova," *Uchenye zapiski Kustanaiskogo pedagogicheskogo instituta*, 4 (1959): 133–148;

Andrei Rogachevskii, "Precursors of Socialist Realism: Vasilii Sleptsov's *Trudnoe vremia* and Its Anti-Nihilist Opponents," *The Slavonic and East European Review*, 75, no. 1 (1997): 36–62;

L. A. Sal'kova, "Rannie ocherki V. A. Sleptsova 'Vladimirka i Kliaz'ma' i ocherkovaia literatura 50–60-kh godov XIX veka," *Uchenye zapiski Krasnodarskogo pedagogicheskogo instituta*, 21 (1957): 150–170;

Valerii Nikolaevich Sazhin, *Knigi gor'koi pravdy: N. G. Pomialovskii "Ocherki bursy," F. M. Reshetnikov "Podlipovtsy," V. A. Sleptsov "Trudnoe vremia"* (Moscow: Kniga, 1989);

Mariia Leont'evna Semanova, *Khudozhestvennoe svoeobrazie povesti Sleptsova "Trudnoe vremia"* (Leningrad: Leningradskii gosudarstvennyi pedagogicheskii institut, 1974);

Iu. F. Shal'nov, "Realizm V. A. Sleptsova," *Uchenye zapiski Gor'kovskogo universiteta*, 39 (1957): 43–91;

Ia. Sukhanov, "Razoblachenie tsarstva Savinykh: (V. A. Sleptsov v Ostashkove)," in *Pisateli v Tverskoi gubernii* (Kalinin, 1941), pp. 82–100;

Petr Tkachev, "Podrastaiushchie sily," *Delo*, 9–10 (1868);

E. L. Voitolovskaia, "K voprosu o gogolevskikh traditsiiakh v tvorchestve V. A. Sleptsova," *Uchenye zapiski Leningradskogo pedagogicheskogo instituta imeni A. I. Gertsena*, 198 (1959): 121–142.

Papers:

Vasilii Alekseevich Sleptsov's papers are held at the Russian Center for the Preservation and Study of Documents of Recent History (RTsKhIDNI), fond 95 (manuscript for the unfinished piece of fiction "Zapiski samoubiitsy" [Notes of a Suicide]); at the Russian State Archive of Literature and Art in Moscow (RGALI), fond 479 (letters to Zhozefina Adamovna Sleptsova and Vera Zakharovna Voronina) and fond 331 (letters to Lidiia Nelidova); and in St. Petersburg at the Institute of Russian Literature (IRLI, Pushkin House), fond 9526 (letters to M. A. Markovich [Marko Vovchok]). The manuscript for *Na maloi zemle*, Nelidova's fictionalized memoir of Sleptsov, is kept in RGALI, fond 331.

Konstantin Konstantinovich Sluchevsky

(26 July 1837 – 25 September 1904)

Tatiana Smorodinskaya
Middlebury College

BOOKS: *Iavleniia russkoi zhizni pod kritikoiu estetiki,* 3 volumes (St. Petersburg: V. Golovin, 1866–1867);

Kubiki i nitki. Ucheno-idillicheskaia satira Fadeeva v proze (St. Petersburg, 1867);

Ot potseluia k potseluiu (St. Petersburg: E. Goppe, 1872);

V snegakh. Poema (St. Petersburg: A. S. Suvorin, 1879);

Stikhotvoreniia, 4 volumes (St. Petersburg: A. S. Suvorin, 1880–1890);

Virtuozy. Povest' (St. Petersburg, 1881); enlarged as *Istoricheskie kartinki. Raznye rasskazy* (St. Petersburg, 1894);

Zastrel' shchiki. Posvest' (St. Petersburg, 1883);

Po severu Rossii (St. Petersburg: E. Goppe, 1886–1888)– includes "Po severu Rossii";

Tridtsat' tri rasskaza (St. Petersburg: A. S. Suvorin, 1887);

Dostoevskii. Ocherk zhizni i deiatel'nosti (St. Petersburg: Brat'ia Panteleevy, 1889);

Narva: Ee byloe i nastoiashchee (St. Petersburg: Tipografiia Shtaba voisk gvardii i Peterburgskogo voennogo okruga, 1890);

Vniz po Volge (Moscow: Universitetskaia tipografiia, 1891);

Professor bessmertiia. Rasskaz (St. Petersburg, 1892);

Po severo-zapadu Rossii, 2 volumes (St. Petersburg: A. F. Marks, 1897);

Idol (St. Petersburg: E. Evdokimov, 1897);

Faust v novom pereskaze (Tiflis, 1897);

Virtuozy. Povest' (St. Petersburg: V. V. Komarov, 1897);

Poluskazka (Tiflis, 1898);

Sochineniia, 6 volumes (St. Petersburg: A. F. Marks, 1898)–includes volume 1–includes "Nevmeniaemost'";

Luchi. Rasskaz (St. Petersburg, 1899);

Kostry (St. Petersburg: S. M. Propper, 1900);

Vystrel i drugie rasskazy (Moscow: Universitetskaia tipografiia, 1900);

Dukhovskaia Varvara (Iz moikh vospominanii) (St. Petersburg, 1900);

Gorodskoi golova (Khar'kov: Iuzhnyi krai, 1901);

"Pesni iz Ugolka" (St. Petersburg: A. F. Marks, 1902);

Povesti i rasskazy (St. Petersburg: P. P. Soikin, 1903);

Konstantin Konstantinovich Sluchevsky

Dve babushki i strannitsa Akinfiia (St. Petersburg: Birzhevye vedomosti, 1903);

Novye povesti (St. Petersburg: P. P. Soikin, 1904);

Stikhotvoreniia (St. Petersburg: A. S. Suvorin, 1907).

Editions and Collections: *Stikhotvoreniia,* edited by Andrei Venediktovich Fedorov (Leningrad: Sovetskii pisatel', 1941);

Stikhotvoreniia i poemy, with an introduction by Fedorov (Moscow & Leningrad: Sovetskii pisatel', 1962);

Zabytye stikhotvoreniia, edited by D. Čiževskij (Munich, 1968);

Stikhotvoreniia (Petrozavodsk: Kareliia, 1981);

Stikhotvoreniia, with an introduction by V. G. Perel'muter (Moscow: Detskaia literatura, 1983);

Stikhotvoreniia, edited by V. I. Sakharov (Moscow: Sovetskaia Rossiia, 1984);

Stikhotvoreniia. Poemy. Proza, with an introduction by E. V. Ermilova (Moscow: Sovremennik, 1988);

Po severu Rossii (Vologda: Muzei Diplomaticheskogo korpusa, 2000);

Sochineniia v stikhakh (Moscow: Letnii sad, 2001).

OTHER: *Skladchina,* edited by Ivan Aleksandrovich Goncharov, with contributions by Sluchevsky (St. Petersburg: A. M. Kotomin, 1874);

"Dostoevsky. Ocherk zhizni i deiatel'nosti," compiled by Sluchevsky, in Fyodor Dostoevsky's *Polnoe sobranie sochinenii,* volume 1 (St. Petersburg: A. G. Dostoevskaia, 1889);

"Poverzhennyi Pushkin," in *Pushkinskii sbornik* (St. Petersburg: A. S. Suvorin, 1899), pp. 241–264.

TRANSLATIONS: George Gordon, Lord Byron, "Kogda nash teplyi trup po smerti ostyvaet . . . ," "Ty rasstanesh'sia s zhizn'iu trudnoi . . ."; and Victor Hugo, "Zemlia surovaia, besplodnaia, skupaia . . . ," "So dnia na den' zhivesh', shumish' pod nebesami," *Obshchezanimatel'nyi vestnik,* 3 (1857): 118–120;

Byron, "Stansy," *Obshchezanimatel'nyi vestnik,* 9 (1857): 350;

Auguste Barbier, "Il Pianto Plach," "Smekh," "Chan," *Obshchezanimatel'nyi vestnik,* 9 (1857): 350; 11 (1857): 405; 12 (1857): 424–425;

Martin Opitz, "Pesnia"; Johann Christoph Gottsched, "Iazycheskii mir"; Friedrich Hagedorn, "Chuvstvo vesny"; Novalis (Friedrich Leopold, Baron von Hardenberg), "V grustnyi chas"; and Ludwig Johann Tieck, "Sozertsanie," "Noch'," in *Nemetskie poety v biografiiakh i obraztsakh,* edited by Nikolai Vasil'evich Gerbel' (St. Petersburg: B. Bezobrazov, 1877), pp. 49, 51, 55, 371–372;

William Shakespeare, "Sonnet #14," "Sonnet #31," "Sonnet #32," in *Polnoe sobranie sochinenii,* 5 volumes (St. Petersburg, 1904), pp. 408, 411, 412.

SELECTED PERIODICAL PUBLICATION–
UNCOLLECTED: "On i ona. Real'naia fantaziia," *Nedelia,* 3–4 (1900).

Konstantin Sluchevsky was a prose writer and poet who never received full recognition during his lifetime. The prime of his creative life occurred during the last third of the nineteenth century–a period dominated by a brand of realistic prose ruled by the ideas of materialism, positivism, and nihilism. Neither Sluchevsky's interest in metaphysical and mystical themes nor his heavy, nonmusical, and disharmonious poetic style were timely, and thus his writings were unpopular with his contemporaries. He was a forerunner of the Silver Age poets, and his writings were a bridge between late Romanticism and modernism. Sluchevsky served all his life in a government career, which, unlike his literary endeavors, was quite successful. By the end of his life Sluchevsky was a Privy Councillor; he had been decorated with many orders and awards; and he served as editor in chief of the daily newspaper *Pravitel'stvennyi vestnik* (The Government Messenger).

Konstantin Konstantinovich Sluchevsky was born on 26 July 1837 in St. Petersburg. His father, Konstantin Afanas'evich Sluchevsky, was a nobleman from Ukraine; he was an Actual State Councillor and a member of the council of the Ministry of Finances. In 1836 Konstantin Afanas'evich married Anzhelika Ivanovna Zaremba, the daughter of a wealthy Polish landowner. Although her mother was Russian Orthodox, Anzhelika, like her father, was baptized a Protestant. She was a well-educated woman, fluent in German, French, and Polish, and was also a good singer. Her younger brother, Nikolai Ivanovich Zaremba, became a professor of music and the director of the Moscow Conservatory. There were five children in the Sluchevsky family, among whom Konstantin was the oldest. After her husband's death in 1856, Anzhelika Ivanovna was left with insufficient means to support her children, and in 1865 she moved to Warsaw and became the director there of the Aleksandrinsko-Mariinskii devichii institut (Alexander-Mary School for Girls).

The young Sluchevsky began a military career. He was an excellent student in the First Cadet Regiment. After graduation he served as an officer in the Semenovsky Regiment, and in 1857 he was admitted to the Nikolaev Academy of the General Staff. Like most young educated people of his time, Sluchevsky could not resist the vigorous political and social life just before the Russian reforms of 1861. He was a member of the Semevsky *kruzhok* (circle), which debated the necessity of liberal and democratic changes. At this time Sluchevsky started writing poetic translations. His interest in translation was probably triggered by his acquaintance with Lev Aleksandrovich Mei, a well-known Russian poet and translator. Sluchevsky published his first translations in 1857 in *Obshchezanimatel'nyi vestnik* (The General-Interest Messenger), a radical democratic journal, which was at that time close to the nihilist movement. These were translations of works by the French poets Auguste Barbier and Pierre-Jean Béranger, famous for their poems, songs, and satires highly critical of government, monarchy, and reactionary clergy. Both the choice of poets and the political orientation of the journal demonstrate that, in his youth, Sluchevsky sincerely shared democratic, liberal, and humanitarian political and social views. He also translated the verse of Heinrich Heine, whose influence is prominent in Sluchevsky's early poems. Sluchevsky's translations of Heine, along with his first poems, were published in 1859 in the journal *Illiustratsiia* (Illustration), but they received no attention from the critics.

In 1860 Sluchevsky's friend the poet and writer Vsevolod Vladimirovich Krestovsky brought several of his poems to Apollon Aleksandrovich Grigor'ev. Grigor'ev was excited about the poems and sent them to Nikolai Alekseevich Nekrasov, who was the editor of the most popular revolutionary democratic journal, *Sovremennik* (The Contemporary). Nekrasov, too, liked Sluchevsky's poems, and he published a total of thirteen of them in four issues of *Sovremennik* in 1860. One of the poems Nekrasov selected for publication began thus:

Khodit veter izbochas'
Vdol' Nevy shirokoi,
Snegom stelet kalachi
Baby krivobokoi.

(The wind swirls from side to side
Down the wide Neva River,
With snow rolls pretzels in the sky
Like those the humpbacked woman sells.)

Such complex syntax and daring imagery was not typical for the time but anticipated the poetic innovations of the twentieth century. The tragic motifs, psychological intensity, and alogical metaphors in other poems published in *Sovremennik,* such as "Na kladbishche" (At the Cemetery), "Vecher na lemane" (Evening on the Leman), "Statuia" (The Statue), "Vestalka" (The Fortuneteller), and "Memfisskii zhrets" (Memphis Priest), were later admired by poets of the Silver Age. The publication of his poems in several issues of *Sovremennik* brought Sluchevsky instant fame. Grigor'ev introduced him to Ivan Sergeevich Turgenev, who praised Sluchevsky's poems highly. So did poets Apollon Nikolaevich Maikov and Iakov Petrovich Polonsky and writer Fyodor Dostoevsky. All of them noticed the unusual imagery, originality, and great potential of Sluchevsky's poetry. Yet, Grigor'ev's encouraging enthusiasm provoked the nihilist critics to release a backlash of vigorous attacks and parodies on Sluchevsky's poems, whose unusual themes and innovative poetic imagery made them an easy target for ridicule. Bitter parodies by the radical journalists Nikolai Aleksandrovich Dobroliubov, N. L. Gnut (pseudonym of Nikolai Loginovich Loman), and Vasilii Stepanovich Kurochkin may have prompted Sluchevsky to resign

Sluchevsky in 1855, when he was an officer of the Semenovsky Regiment

from the army. In 1861 he left St. Petersburg to continue his education abroad.

Sluchevsky studied in Paris, then went to Berlin and Leipzig, and finally, after six years, received a doctoral degree from Heidelberg University. He continued to write poetry but did not publish anything under his own name for almost a decade. Sluchevsky stayed in touch with Turgenev; they corresponded frequently and met many times throughout Sluchevsky's time abroad. He sent several poems to Turgenev and received detailed criticism in response. His correspondence with Turgenev clearly reveals that the *poemy* (long, narrative poems) "V snegakh" (Snowbound, published in book form, 1879) and "Tri zhenshchiny" (Three Women), first published as "Kartinka v ramke" (Picture in a Frame) in *Russkii vestnik* (The Russian Messenger) in 1879, along with the dramatic scene "Zemletriasenie" (The Earthquake), first published in *Stikhotvoreniia* (Poems) in 1883, were written during this period. In general the chronology of Sluchevsky's works is rather difficult to establish because he seldom dated his works and frequently changed titles. In

Germany, Sluchevsky met Nataliia Nikolaevna Rashet, an independent-minded woman seven years older than he who was then in the process of divorcing her second husband. Sluchevsky fell in love and proposed marriage to her several times, but Nataliia never accepted his proposal. Sluchevsky introduced her to Turgenev and, after her separation from Sluchevsky, Rashet continued her friendship with the novelist. Turgenev, however, gradually lost interest in Sluchevsky.

Upon his return to St. Petersburg, Sluchevsky wrote three polemical essays in which he harshly criticized nihilistic views and utilitarian aesthetics: "Prudon ob iskusstve, ego perevodchiki i kritiki" ([Pierre-Joseph] Proudhon on Art, His Translators and Critics), "Esteticheskoe otnoshenie iskusstva k deistvitel'nosti" (The Aesthetic Relationship of Art to Life), and "O tom, kak Pisarev estetiku razrushal" (On How [Dmitrii Ivanovich] Pisarev Destroyed Aesthetics). These works were published from 1886 to 1867 as Iavleniia russkoi zhizni pod kritikoiu estetiki (Phenomena of Russian Life under Aesthetic Criticism). Sluchevsky's name became odious to radical and liberal circles, which at that time constituted the core of the reading public in Russia. This negative response of the democratic press was predictable, but Sluchevsky's essays were also denounced by writers who usually sympathized with him—such as Turgenev, Maikov, and Polonsky. Although they agreed with his arguments, they disapproved of his rude style; his rough, unpolished language; and, most of all, the poor timing of his publication. Most of Sluchevsky's opponents had been arrested and exiled (Nikolai Gavrilovich Chernyshevsky), had already died (Dobroliubov), or had been recently released from prison (Pisarev). After this political démarche, Sluchevsky found himself in isolation both as a writer and as a public figure, even as he was embarking upon a successful government career. He began work as a censor in the Press Department in 1867. He never enjoyed the service but considered himself a true Russian patriot, and he continued to fulfill his civic duty throughout his life, despite the hardships and boredom of official business. In 1872 Sluchevsky married Ol'ga Kapitonovna Loginova, a wealthy landowner from Kursk. They had four children, but their family life was not a happy one.

Ten years after his first publication in Sovremennik, Sluchevsky's poems appeared several times in Vsemirnaia illiustratsiia (Worldwide Illustration), although these were either published anonymously or signed with pseudonyms (the initials S., N., or I.). His name first reappeared in 1873 in an anthology edited by poet and translator Nikolai Vasil'evich Gerbel', Russkie poety v biografiiakh i obraztsakh (Russian Poets in Biographies and Images), which included some of Sluchevsky's early poems. From that time on Sluchevsky worked closely with Gerbel' on translations of Western poetry. In 1874 he began service in the Ministry of State Commodities, and in the same year the benefit collection Skladchina (Common Good) included some of his poems signed with his full name. However, Sluchevsky's poetic oblivion truly ended only in 1879, when his poema "V snegakh" was published in Novoe vremia (New Times). Both liberal and conservative critics—in particular Slavophiles—enthusiastically greeted it, but the poem was ignored by radical democratic circles. In "V snegakh" Sluchevsky uses the dactylic meter, typical of stylizations of Russian folk poetry, and at first glance the poema seems to follow Nekrasov's mode of realistic descriptions of peasant life. At the same time, however, it tells the unusual story of a strange old man, a Siberian hunter, and a female pilgrim lost in the midst of a Siberian snowstorm. The poem does not dwell upon any social or political issues, nor does it offer any realistic descriptions of either everyday life or national customs. Instead, Sluchevsky's poema is a meditation on the eternal problems of loneliness, death, faith, sin, and love.

The publication of "V snegakh" was the turning point in Sluchevsky's literary life, and his poems began to appear again in various journals. Dostoevsky recommended Sluchevsky's participation in the celebrations surrounding the 1880 dedication of a monument to poet Aleksandr Sergeevich Pushkin in Moscow. After Dostoevsky's death in 1881, his widow asked Sluchevsky to write a biographical essay about her husband. "Dostoevsky. Ocherk zhizni i deiatel'nosti" (1889) was included in the third edition of the novelist's complete collected works. Dostoevsky had valued Sluchevsky's poetry; he considered its themes and sensibilities close to those of his own writings. In literature the two men shared an interest in the subconscious, irrational side of human nature—the psychological distortions of an individual's inner world. In politics they expressed similar views, denouncing radicalism, nihilism, and violence; they proclaimed the importance of Russian Orthodoxy and embraced the ideas of the pochvennichestvo (Native Soil) movement. Dostoevsky's influence can be observed in many works by Sluchevsky, in particular the poetic cycle "Mefistofel'" (Mephistopheles, published in Stikhotvoreniia, 1881), the poema "Eloa. Apokaticheskoe predanie" (Eloa: An Apocryphal Legend, published in Stikhotvoreniia, 1883), and the short story "Rasskaz-simfoniia" (A Story-Symphony, published in Povesti i rasskazy [Tales and Stories], 1903).

Sluchevsky's poema "Eloa" was rejected for publication by several journals that were concerned with religious censorship; he included the work in the third volume of his collected poems. "Eloa" was a rendition of the apocryphal story about an angel born from a tear that Christ shed over the body of Lazarus. In Sluchevsky's version, Eloa is a female angel who attempts to save Satan through her pity and love. Satan, instead, tries to seduce Eloa, but he fails in his evil mission. In this poema Sluchevsky continues a literary dialogue started by the Russian poet Mikhail Iur'evich Lermontov in his *poema* "Demon" (The Demon, 1829–1839) and the French Romantic poet Alfred de Vigny in his long poem also titled "Eloa." Sluchevsky not only suggests another version of the story but also expresses his views on the metaphysical nature of Good and Evil. According to Sluchevsky, Evil is not an historical or social category but an eternal and necessary part of the world, and there is no distinct borderline between Good and Evil. These same views are expressed in many of his lyric poems. Such ideas were alien to Sluchevsky's contemporaries, but they turned out to be close to those of the Russian Symbolists.

In his lyric poetry Sluchevsky experimented with the articulation of complicated psychological states, ambiguous emotions and feelings, and subtle, elusive spiritual experiences that had not yet been explored in classical Russian poetry. For example, the poem that opened the first volume of his 1898 *Sochineniia* (Works) was called "Nevmeniaemost'" (Irresponsibility) and explored the state of not being responsible for one's actions. One of the best known of Sluchevsky's poems, "Posle kazni v Zheneve" (After an Execution in Geneva, 1881), published in *Stikhotvoreniia,* was obviously written as a tribute to Dostoevsky; this work created a long-lasting, shocking impression on readers for its depiction of the horrors of execution. In many poems Sluchevsky delved into the philosophical issues surrounding the dichotomies of life and death, Good and Evil, eternity and transience. Exotic themes and irrational actions were often at the center of his attention. All of these tendencies were consonant subsequently with those of Russian modernism.

In connection with his official duties Sluchevsky had to do much traveling around Russia. His impressions were reflected in his poetic cycles "Murmanskie otgoloski" (Echoes of Murmansk, 1881–1890), "V puti" (While Traveling, 1880–1881), and "Chernozemnaia polosa" (The Chernozem Region, 1880–1881)—all of which were published in full in *Sochineniia*—and in historical and ethnographical essays, such as *Po severu Rossii* (Around Northern Russia, 1886–1888). Both "V puti" and "Chernozemnaia polosa" consisted of poems depicting nature and the lives of Russian peasants; the verses of "Murmanskie otgoloski" were inspired by the lives of seamen and fishermen in the Russian far north. In 1888 Sluchevsky's official career took yet another turn, when he became a committee member in the Ministry of Education and a council member in the Ministry of Internal Affairs.

In the 1880s and 1890s Sluchevsky was quite active in literary life. He published a four-volume collection of his poetry—*Stikhotvoreniia* (Poems, 1880–1890)—and three collections of stories, *Tridtsat' tri rasskaza* (Thirty-Three Stories, 1887), *Istoricheskie kartinki. Raznye*

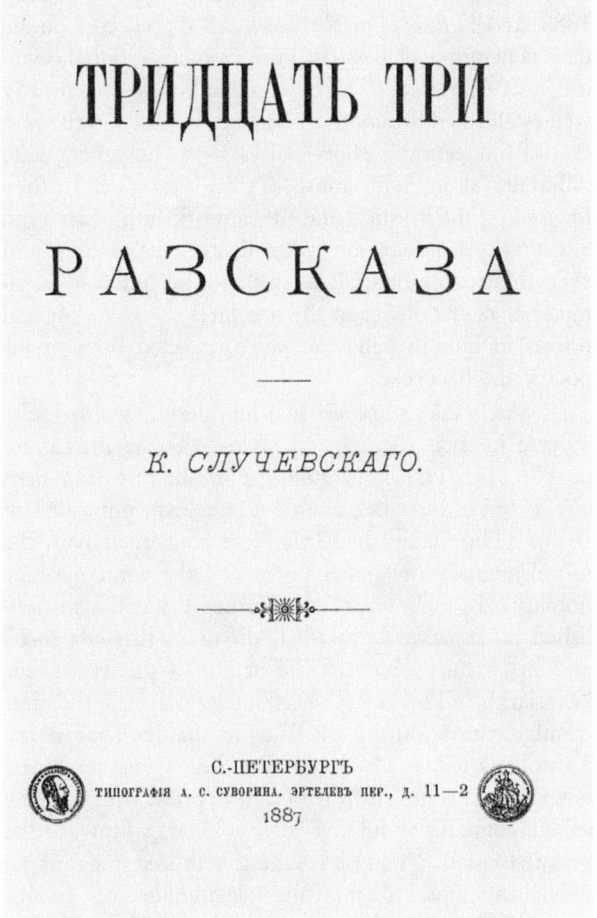

ТРИДЦАТЬ ТРИ

РАЗСКАЗА

——

К. СЛУЧЕВСКАГО.

С.-ПЕТЕРБУРГЪ
ТИПОГРАФІЯ А. С. СУВОРИНА. ЭРТЕЛЕВЪ ПЕР., Д. 11—2
1887

Title page for Sluchevsky's Tridtsat' tri rasskaza *(Thirty-Three Stories), one of three short-story collections that he published between 1885 and 1890 (Kilgour Collection of Russian Literature, Harvard University Library)*

rasskazy (Historical Vignettes. Various Tales, 1894), and *Vystrel i drugie rasskazy* (The Shot and Other Stories, 1900). In addition, separate editions of the stories "Idol" (The Idol, 1897), "Faust v novom pereskaze" (A New Rendition of Faust, 1897), "Poluskazka" (A Half-Tale, 1898), "Luchi" (Rays, 1899), and "Kostry" (Camp Fires, 1900) also came out. On top of all these, he published a six-volume edition of his collected works, *Sochineniia* (Works, 1898), in which three volumes consisted of poetry and three of prose. Sluchevsky's prose was rather unpopular with readers, and it was soon almost completely forgotten. He wrote fantastic stories, historical tales, stories on biblical subjects, stories from the life of Renaissance artists, realistic stories, philosophical etudes, and so on. Most of his prose was not original; "Oko za oko" (An Eye for an Eye), written in 1882 and published in *Russkii vestnik* in 1896, a story describing contemporary life in St. Petersburg, was greatly influenced by Dostoevsky. The *povesti* (long stories) *Zastrel'shchiki* (Pioneers, 1883) and *Virtuozy* (The Virtuosos, 1881) reflected on the new generation of Russian businessmen—rational, cynical, and egotistical. These *povesti* followed the already well-established traditions of Russian Realist novels. Several of Sluchevsky's short stories were, however, quite different: along with most of his lyric poetry, they focused on the mystical and the fantastic in human lives. Sluchevsky's fascination with death, cemeteries, and everything supernatural, as well as his interest in all kinds of deviations from the accepted social and sexual norms in human behavior, were reflected both in his poetry and his prose.

Sluchevsky's *poemy* of this period were quite diverse in their themes and styles. "Tozhe nravstvennost'" (This, Too, Is Morality), published in *Stikhotvoreniia* in 1881, and "Bez imeni" (Nameless), published in *Ogonek* (The Flame) in 1881, were concerned with the moral degradation and hypocrisy of the contemporary nobility. "Byvshii kniaz'" (A Former Prince), also published in *Stikotvoreniia* in 1881, discusses Russia's social and historical problems. The action of the verse epic "Eresiarkh" (The Archbishop) takes place in the thirteenth century during the Russian battles against the Teutonic knights. The *poema* "Pop Elisei" (Father Elisei) describes the inner struggle of a rural priest who is trying to overcome his sinful love for a soldier's widow. In the poem "Larchik" (The Little Chest), a retired low-ranking official attempts to find the illegitimate son of his deceased, beloved wife and digs up her coffin in his desperate search for information. In spite of such a wide range of themes and plots, all of Sluchevsky's *poemy* are united by his heroes' passionate desire to fight their loneliness in this world, and to rebel against any banality of thought or feeling.

By the late 1880s Sluchevsky's name appeared in several anthologies of contemporary Russian verse and in histories of Russian poetry, and he was invited to contribute to many benefit or memorial literary collections. Despite this prominence, however, he was never in the center of literary debates or the focus of national attention. Sluchevsky was known primarily for his lyrical poetry, yet he was never perceived seriously in literary circles. This circumstance resulted only partly from the fact that he was not a professional poet; more important, he had the political reputation of being a conservative monarchist. The popular democratic poet Semen Iakovlevich Nadson published a negative response to Sluchevsky's four-volume collection of poems, denying their value on purely political grounds. The unanimous opinion of contemporary critics, regardless of their political views, was that Sluchevsky's poetry, although indeed quite original in content, imagery, and metaphors, was rough and unpolished in terms of poetic language. Even

favorable critics such as Vladimir Sergeevich Solov'ev, while admiring the "impressionism" of Sluchevsky's poetry, criticized him for writing awkward, difficult, nonmusical verse; selecting strange subjects; and permitting various contradictions in his philosophical statements. Indeed, Sluchevsky sometimes neglected historical accuracy in his prose, and many of his poems were not as musical and harmonious as those by followers of the Pushkinian poetic tradition. But his "awkward verse" was a result of an intuitive search for the new poetic means to express the distorted human psyche. In his verse Sluchevsky employed "professionalisms," official jargon, and scientific terms. He created complex and unusual images, often used an archaic, difficult-to-read syntax, and mixed contrasting styles. Years later, all these devices were developed and employed by the Russian Futurists and many other poets of the twentieth century.

In 1890 Sluchevsky's wife finally granted him a divorce, and he was able to marry Agniia Fedorovna Rerikh, with whom he had been living; their daughter, Aleksandra, had been born approximately five years earlier. Sluchevsky's children from his first marriage, with the exception of his daughter Elizaveta, continued to maintain friendly relations with their father and Agniia Fedorovna. Sluchevsky's son Vladimir was especially close to his father. Vladimir also wrote poetry under the pseudonym "Lieutenant S"; he was killed during the Russo-Japanese War in 1904 after publishing only one small collection of poems. In 1891 Sluchevsky was nominated to be the editor in chief of *Pravitel'stvennyi vestnik*. While in charge of the newspaper, he introduced major changes into its content. He published articles on economics, ethnography, folklore, literature, and theater and turned the formal, boring business paper into a diverse, sophisticated, and intellectual publication.

In 1899 at Polonsky's funeral, Sluchevsky came up with the idea of hosting a Friday literary salon. Thereafter, every Friday many young St. Petersburg poets and writers, as well as writers who were already renowned, visited Sluchevsky's home. The young Valerii Iakovlevich Briusov, Konstantin Dmitrievich Bal'mont, Fedor Kuz'mich Sologub, Dmitrii Sergeevich Merezhkovsky, Zinaida Nikolaevna Gippius, and many others—who in the next century became the leading names in Russian modernism—were frequent guests at Sluchevsky's salon. They called it "the free academy of poetry" and pronounced Sluchevsky "the king of Russian poets." Sluchevsky had some influence on the developing Symbolists, who were particularly fond of his *poema* "Eloa" and his cycle "Zagrobnye pesni" (Songs of the Afterlife). Most poets who attended Sluchevsky's Friday salons admired his *"Pesni iz Ugolka"* (Songs from Ugolok), a collection of lyric poems that was included in his *Sochineniia* (1898) and published in 1902 as a separate edition.

"Ugolok" (Cozy Corner) was also the name of the estate in Finland where Sluchevsky later lived with Agniia Fedorovna and their daughter Aleksandra during the last years of his life.

Despite his poor health in later years Sluchevsky continued to write and publish. In 1899 his play in verse "Poverzhennyi Pushkin" (Defeated Pushkin) appeared in the almanac *Pushkinskii sbornik* (The Pushkin Miscellany), and the following year he published his new *poema* "On i Ona" (He and She) in *Nedelia* (The Week). Neither of these works has been republished since. In 1902 the ailing Sluchevsky retired from his editorial position at *Pravitel'stvennyi vestnik* and decided to devote the rest of his life to poetry. He suffered from various illnesses; he was almost blind and was struggling against nascent cancer. The theme of death and the immortality of the human spirit, which had been of interest to Sluchevsky throughout his life, now became a personal agenda. In his 1892 story "Professor bessmertiia" (Professor of Immortality) he had attempted to prove scientifically the immortality of the human spirit. In the writings of his last years he set out to relieve the tormented human mind even further. His two-part cycle "Zagrobnye pesni" was devoted to the experiences that await people after death; this work was Sluchevsky's poetic attempt to provide rational explanations for the irrational. As a result the cycle was contradictory and so was subjected to censorship by the church. Sluchevsky had trouble finding a publisher, but finally both "Zagrobnye pesni" and its sequel "V tom mire" (In the Other World) were published in the journal *Russkaia mysl'* (Russian Thought, 1902–1903).

Sluchevsky died on 25 September 1904, but his death did not stop the literary salon "Fridays at Sluchevsky's" from meeting until almost 1917. His poetry was admired by the modernist poets Viacheslav Ivanovich Ivanov and Nikolai Sergeevich Gumilev, who attended salon meetings after Sluchevsky's death. Sluchevsky was aesthetically influential, and his mark can be seen in the poetry of Innokentii Fedorovich Annensky, Sologub, Bal'mont, Gumilev, and Briusov, as well as in the early poems of Boris Leonidovich Pasternak. After Sluchevsky's death, however, his name was practically forgotten. In the decades that followed the Bolshevik Revolution, his work was published in the Soviet Union only twice— in 1941 and 1962. His name was mentioned from time to time in the émigré press, but it was known mostly to specialists in Russian poetry. In the 1980s and 1990s several publications of Sluchevsky's works demonstrated that his legacy has begun to revive.

Konstantin Konstantinovich Sluchevsky never arrived at a new theory or formal approach to the problems of poetic expression, but despite that fact he empirically introduced many innovations to verse. His meters were traditional, but his syntax, metaphors, and imagery

Dust jacket for Sluchevsky's "Pesni iz Ugolka" (Songs from Ugolok, 1902), a collection of lyric poems (Pushkin House, St. Petersburg)

were quite innovative. He never developed any coherent philosophical views. While in Germany, Sluchevsky studied not only philosophy but also the natural sciences. As a result of this mix his philosophical views combined contradictory beliefs that were sometimes eclectic and confused. In Sluchevsky's works Charles Darwin's theory of evolution coexisted with theories of the immortality of the human soul, and physical laws stood side by side with mysticism. Along with religious songs for Easter, he wrote rebellious *bogoborcheskie* (God-wrestling) poems. As Briusov wrote in his 1904 contribution to *Vesy* (The Scales) Sluchevsky was "a poet of contradictions." His poetic legacy consists of many weak poems along with several exceptional ones. He was a transitional figure; he composed some truly avant-garde works years before modernism had taken hold in Russia, although in other works he remained trapped in the past. Yet, Sluchevsky's works as a whole were so diverse, original, and heterogeneous that they became an important source of inspiration for poets of the next generation.

Letters:

To Ivan Fedorovich Gorbunov, in Gorbunov's *Sochineniia*, 4 volumes (St. Petersburg, 1904–1910), III: 81;

To K. P. Pobodonostsev, in *K. P. Pobodonostsev i ego korrespondenty*, volume 1, book 2 (Moscow & Petrograd: Gosudarstvennoe izdatel'stvo, 1923), pp. 622–624.

References:

Sergei Arkad'evich Andreevsky, "Vyrozhdenie rifmy," in his *Literaturnye ocherki* (St. Petersburg: A. E. Kolpinsky, 1902), pp. 427–470;

James Bailey, "The Metrical and Rhythmical Typology of K. K. Sluchevsky's Poetry," *International Journal of Slavic Linguistics and Poetics*, 18 (1975): 93–117;

Valery Iakovlevich Briusov, *Dnevniki, 1891–1910* (Moscow: M. & S. Sabashnikovykh, 1927), pp. 54–56, 114, 118;

Briusov, "Konstantin Konstantinovich Sluchevsky," in *Istoriia russkoi literatury XIX veka*, edited by Dmitrii Nikolaevich Ovsianiko-Kulikovsky (Moscow: Mir, 1908–1911);

Briusov, "Poet protivorechii (K. K. Sluchevsky)," *Vesy*, 10 (1904);

Samson Naumovich Broitman, *Russkaia lirika XIX–nachala XX veka v svete istoricheskoi poetiki* (Moscow: Rossiiskii gosudarstvennyi gumanitarnyi universitet, 1997), pp. 197–210;

D. Chizhevsky, "K. K. Sluèevskij als Dichter," in Sluchevsky's *Zabytye stikhotvoreniia* (Munich: Wilhelm Fink, 1968): 9–18;

Chizhevsky, "Stikhotvoreniia i poemy K. Sluchevskogo," *Novyi zhurnal*, 74 (1963): 170–176;

Friedrich Fiedler, *Aus der Literatenwelt: Charakterzüge und Urteile: Tagebuch* (Göttingen: Wallstein, 1996), pp. 241, 246, 306, 610;

Apollon Aleksandrovich Grigor'ev, *Vospominaniia* (Moscow & Leningrad: Academia, 1930), p. 298;

Iu. Ivask, "Sluchevsky," *Novyi zhurnal*, 79 (1965): 270–284;

Apollon Apollonovich Korinfsky, *Poeziia K. K. Sluchevskogo* (St. Petersburg: P. Soikin, 1899);

N. Kotliarevsky, *Sochineniia K. K. Sluchevskogo* (St. Petersburg: Imperatorskaia Akademiia nauk, 1902);

Vadim Valerianovich Kozhinov, *Kniga o russkoi liricheskoi poezii XIX veka* (Moscow: Sovremennik, 1978), pp. 242–257;

Sergei Konstantinovich Makovsky, "Konstantin Sluchevskii. Predtecha simvolizma," *Novyi zhurnal*, 59 (1960): 71–92;

Makovsky, *Na parnase "Serebriannogo veka,"* (Munich: TSOPE, 1962), pp. 63–86;

T. Mazur, "Dostoevsky i Sluchevsky," in *Dostoevsky: Materialy i issledovaniia*, compiled by Georgii Mikhailovich Fridlender (Leningrad: Nauka, 1976–1980), pp. 209–211;

Mazur, "Literaturnye piatnitsy Sluchevskogo," in *Stranitsy istorii russkoi literatury*, edited by Dmitrii Fedorovich Markov (Moscow: Nauka, 1971), pp. 264–270;

G. Meier, "Sluchevsky," *Vozrozhdenie*, 48 (1955): 187–198;

S. V. Sapozhkov, "Semantika vol'nogo iamba v poezii K. K. Sluchevskogo," *Izvestiia AN SSSR. Seriia literatury i iazyka*, 54, no. 2 (1995): 58–63;

V. Smirensky, "K istorii piatnits K. K. Sluchevskogo," *Russkaia literatura*, 3 (1965): 216–226;

L. I. Sobolev, "Pesnia v podzemelii. Poeticheskii stroi liriki K. K. Sluchevskogo," *Russkaia rech'*, 5 (1987): 40–46;

Vladimir Sergeevich Solov'ev, "Impressionizm mysli," in his *Stikhotvoreniia, Estetika, Literaturnaia kritika* (Moscow: Kniga, 1990), pp. 366–371;

Solov'ev, *Razbor knigi K. K. Sluchevskogo "Istoricheskie kartinki. Raznye rasskazy"* (St. Petersburg: Imperatorskaia Akademiia Nauk, 1896);

Elena Arkad'evna Takho-Godi, *Konstantin Sluchevsky: Portret na pushkinskom fone* (St. Petersburg: Aleteiia, 2000);

Semen Afanas'evich Vengerov, "Etapy neoromanticheskogo dvizheniia," in *Russkaia literatura XX veka (1890–1910)*, edited by Vengerov, volume 1 (Moscow: Mir, 1914), pp. 49–50;

S. Zen'kovsky, "Traditsiia romantizma v tvorchestve Konstantina Sluchevskogo," in *American Contributions to the Seventh International Congress of Slavists, Warsaw, August 21–27, 1973*, volume 2 (The Hague: Mouton, 1973), pp. 567–597.

Papers:

In Moscow, Konstantin Konstantinovich Sluchevsky's papers are located at the State Historical Museum (GIM), fond 359, and some of his letters can be found in the Russian State Archive of Literature and Art (RGALI), fond 257, fond 458, and fond 459, as well as at the Russian State Library (RGB, formerly the Lenin Library), fond 171, fond 198, fond 230, fond 249, and fond 331. In St. Petersburg, letters to Sluchevsky and additional letters by Sluchevsky to a variety of addressees are located in the archive of Valery Iakovlevich Briusov at the Russian National Library (RNB), fond 118, fond 248, fond 341, fond 703.

Nadezhda Stepanovna Sokhanskaia
(Kokhanovskaia)
(17 February 1823? – 3 December 1884)

Judith Vowles

BOOKS: *Stepnoi tsvetok na mogilu Pushkina,* as Kokhanovskaia (Moscow: Aleksandr Semen, 1859);

Povesti, as Kokhanovskaia, 2 volumes (Moscow: Bakhmetev, 1863)—comprises "Posle obeda v gostiakh," "Iz provintsial'noi gallerei portretov," "Starina," "Gaika," "Kirila Petrov i Nastas'ia Dmitrova," and "Davniaia vstrecha"; "Posle obeda v gostiakh";

Avtobiografiia, edited by Stepan Ivanovich Ponomarev (Moscow: Universitetskaia tipografiia, 1896); translated by Valentina Baslyk as "Autobiography (Excerpts)," in *Russia Through Women's Eyes: Autobiographies from Tsarist Russia,* edited by Toby W. Clyman and Judith Vowles (New Haven: Yale University Press, 1996), pp. 48–59.

Editions: *Davniaia vstrecha,* as Kokhanovskaia (Moscow, 1862);

Kirila Petrov i Nastas'ia Dmitrova, as Kokhanovskaia (St. Petersburg: A. S. Suvorin, 1885);

Posle obeda v gostiakh, as Kokhanovskaia (St. Petersburg: A. S. Suvorin, 1885);

Starina, as Kokhanovskaia (St. Petersburg: A. S. Suvorin, 1885);

Kirila Petrov i Nastas'ia Dmitrova, as Kokhanovskaia (St. Petersburg: A. S. Suvorin, 1890);

Posle obeda v gostiakh, as Kokhanovskaia (St. Petersburg: A. S. Suvorin, 1890);

Starina, as Kokhanovskaia (St. Petersburg: A. S. Suvorin, 1890);

Posle obeda v gostiakh, as Kokhanovskaia (St. Petersburg: A. S. Suvorin, 1902);

Starina, as Kokhanovskaia (St. Petersburg: A. S. Suvorin, 1902).

Editions in English: *The Rusty Linchpin and Luboff Archipovna,* translated by M. M. Steel and J. L. Edwards (Boston: D. Lothrop, 1887);

"A Conversation After Dinner," translated by Joe Andrew, in *Russian Women's Shorter Fiction: An*

Nadezhda Stepanovna Sokhanskaia (Kokhanovskaia)

Anthology 1835–1860, edited by Andrew (Oxford: Clarendon Press, 1996), pp. 398–459;

"An After-Dinner Visit," translated, with an introduction by Andrea Lanoux, in *Russian Women Writers,* edited by Christine D. Tomei, volume 1 (New York & London: Garland, 1999), pp. 333–347.

PLAY PRODUCTION: *Krazha nevesty,* Moscow, Malyi Theater, 1874.

OTHER: "Slichenie neskol'kikh russkikh pesen'," as Kokhanovskaia, in *Voronezhskaia beseda 1861 goda,* edited by Mikhail Fedorovich De-Pule and P. Glotov (St. Petersburg, 1861), pp. 381–400;

"Pis'mo iz Volynskoi gubernii," as Kokhanovskaia, in *Izvestie o Kirillo-mefodievskom bratstve v g. Ostroge* (Moscow, 1866), pp. 33–37;

"O russkoi pesne. Pis'mo k I. S. Aksakovu," as Kokha-
     novskaia, in *Grazhdanin. Sbornik,* part 1 (St. Peters-
     burg, 1872), pp. 1–14;

"Krokha slovesnogo khleba," as Kokhanovskaia, in
     Skladchina, edited by Kniaz' V. P. Meshchersky
     (St. Petersburg, 1874), pp. 657–686; republished
     as "Slovesnaia krokha khleba," *Russkoe obozrenie,* 2
     (1898).

SELECTED PERIODICAL PUBLICATIONS–UNCOLLECTED:

DRAMA

"Stseny mira (igrannye v sadu, na domashnem teatre).
     Dramatizirovannyi rasskaz," *Syn otechestva,* 1
     (1857);

"Slava bogu, chto muzh lapot' splel. Komediia," as
     Kokhanovskaia, *Zaria,* 1 (1871).

FICTION

"Maior Smagin," *Syn otechestva,* 11–13 (1844);

"Grafinia D.," *Otechestvennye zapiski,* 12 (1848);

"Pervyi shifr,'" *Sankt-Peterburgskie vedomosti,* 154 (1849);

"Sosedi," *Sovremennik,* 12 (1850);

"Vot sluchai!" *Sankt-Peterburgskie vedomosti,* 8 (1851); 10
     (1851);

"Liubila," *Biblioteka dlia chteniia,* 7 (1858);

"Roi Feodosii Savvich na spokoe," as Kokhanovskaia,
     Den', 5–13 (1864); 15 (1864);

"Stepnaia baryshnia sorokovykh godov: Letopisnoe
     skazanie k romanu," *Rus',* 3–6 (1885);

"Soroch'ia kashka: Detskaia pesenka-igra," *Russkoe
     obozrenie,* 1 (1898).

NONFICTION

"Pis'mo iz derevni. (O slukhakh i legendakh o nastupiv-
     shei voine slagavshikhsia i khodivshikh v narode),"
     as Makarovskaia, *Sankt-Peterburgskie vedomosti,* 91
     (1854); 125 (1854);

"Stepnoi tsvetok na mogilu Pushkina: Kriticheskii
     etiud," *Russkaia beseda,* 5 (1859);

"Otvet g. G-vu [Giliarovu-Platonovu] na kriticheskii
     otzyv o povesti 'Iz provintsial'noi gallerei portre-
     tov'," as Kokhanovskaia, *Russkaia beseda,* 6
     (1859);

"Neskol'ko russkikh pesen' (zapisannykh v
     Staro-oskol'skom uezde, Kurskoi gubernii)," as
     Kokhanovskaia, *Russkaia beseda,* 1 (1860);

"Ostatki boiarskikh pesen'," as Kokhanovskaia, *Russkaia
     beseda,* 2 (1860);

"Pis'mo s khutora iz Malorossii," as Kokhanovskaia,
     Den', 3 (1861);

"Cherty iz nashei narodnosti (zapisano v 1850): Kho-
     lera. Kamennye baby," as Kokhanovskaia, *Rus-
     skaia rech',* 41 (1861);

"Pis'mo s khutora," as Kokhanovskaia, *Den',* 13 (1862);

"Zametka ob Ol'ridzhe," as Kokhanovskaia, *Den',* 39
     (1862);

"Iz khutora," as Kokhanovskaia, *Den',* 22 (1863);

"Pis'mo s khutora," as Kokhanovskaia, *Den',* 30 (1864);

"Slava Bogu! Zametka o Belovodskikh staroobriad-
     tsakh," as Kokhanovskaia, *Den',* 38 (1864);

"S khutora. Pis'mo o Sviatykh Gorakh," as Kokhanov-
     skaia, *Den',* 41 (1864);

"Vesti s khutora," as Kokhanovskaia, *Den',* 36 (1865);

"Pros'ba o pozhertvovaniiakh dlia bor'by naroda s
     evreistvom v Iugo-zapadnom krae, ob ustroistve
     bratstv," as Kokhanovskaia, *Den',* 52 (1865);

"Pis'mo v Kirillo-Mefodievskoe Bratstvo iz Makarovki,"
     as Kokhanovskaia, *Sankt-Peterburgskie vedomosti*
     (1866): 125;

"Poezdka na Volyn'," as Kokhanovskaia, *Moskva,* 67–
     68 (1867);

"Chto est' teper' Ostrog?" as Kokhanovskaia, *Moskva,*
     76 (1867);

"Velikii Ostrog," as Kokhanovskaia, *Moskva,* 82 (1867);

"Evreiskaia privillegiia," as Kokhanovskaia, *Moskva,* 84
     (1867);

"Vozmozhno li vosstanie Velikogo Ostroga?" as Kokha-
     novskaia, *Moskva,* 100 (1867);

"Mezhirichi," as Kokhanovskaia, *Moskva,* 134 (1867);

"K delu o evreiskikh privillegiiakh," as Kokhanovskaia,
     Moskvich, 31 December 1867;

"Pis'mo k predsedateliu Rizhskogo russkogo blagotvo-
     ritel'nogo obshchestva," as Kokhanovskaia, *Mosk-
     ovskie vedomosti,* 214 (1870);

"Vopros dnia," as Kokhanovskaia, *Russkii mir* (1877);

"Sevastopol'skie vospominaniia," as Kokhanovskaia,
     Russkii mir, 36 (1877); 37 (1877);

"K delu o vostochnom zaime," as Kokhanovskaia,
     Russkii mir, 252 (1877);

"Pis'mo k redaktoru," as Kokhanovskaia, *Rus',* 21
     (1881); 24 (1881);

"K voprosu o volostnykh sudakh. S khutora
     Makarovki, Khar'kovskoi gubernii," as Kokha-
     novskaia, *Rus',* 39 (1881);

"Khutorskii rasskaz bez kommentariev," as Kokha-
     novskaia, *Rus',* 54 (1881);

"Pis'mo k gr. L. N. Tolstomu po povodu ego *Ispovedi,*"
     Grazhdanin, 8–11 (1884); reprinted as "Pis'mo gr.
     L. N. Tolstomu," *Russkoe obozrenie,* 1–2 (1898);

"Neskol'ko slov *Novomu vremeni,*" *Grazhdanin,* 22 (1884);

"Sumerechnye rasskazy. Staroe vospominanie
     tetushki," *Rus',* 7 (1885);

"Pis'mo v obshchestvo rasprostraneniia Sviashchen-
     nogo pisaniia," *Russkii palomnik,* 4 (1895);

"Ocherk Malorossii," *Russkoe obozrenie,* 1 (1897);

"Golub'-vestnik," *Russkoe obozrenie,* 3–4 (1897);

"Starina (Ded moi rodnoi Grigorii Efimovich)," *Russkoe
     obozrenie,* 1 (1898).

Author of prose fiction, critical essays, autobiography, ethnographical and historical studies, as well as a considerable and substantive literary correspondence, Nadezhda Sokhanskaia became widely known (as Kokhanovskaia) in the late 1850s and early 1860s for her historical and fictional narratives. Deeply religious, with a profound attachment to her native Malorussia (present-day Ukraine), Sokhanskaia maintained close ties with the Slavophiles, who acclaimed her remarkable command and reworking of the Russian language, as well as her skill in depicting the life and people of southern Russia. Written in the last, dark years of Tsar Nicholas I's rule and the early, turbulent years of Alexander II's reign—the age of the Great Reforms—Sokhanskaia's "positive" depictions of the regional and patriarchal life of Old Russia and her defense of the Russian Orthodox Church were attacked by liberal and civic critics. The latter largely defined her subsequent reputation until the present. The project of recovering Russian women's writing has brought a fresh appreciation of Sokhanskaia's literary gifts.

Born on or near 17 February 1823 into a minor, impoverished gentry family in the Khar'kov region in southern Russia, Nadezhda Stepanovna Sokhanskaia was raised by her mother, Varvara Grigor'evna Lokhvitskaia, and aunts after her father, Stepan Pavlovich Sokhansky, died when she was two. At the age of eleven she was enrolled in a "closed institute" (a government boarding school with no vacations, although visitors were allowed) in Khar'kov. A government stipend allowed her to attend the school for girls from 1834 to 1840. In her *Avtobiografiia* (1896), written seven years after she graduated with first-place honors, the former *instituka* (female institute pupil) gave a lively description of the petty difficulties and occasional pleasures of school life. Eager to learn and a passionate reader, she was fortunate in finding schoolmasters who recognized her intellectual abilities and fostered her enthusiasm for Russian literature. Her gift for storytelling emerged in these years in the midnight tales she spun for her classmates. She also wrote verse, heavily influenced by the poetry of her beloved Aleksandr Sergeevich Pushkin and Vasilii Andreevich Zhukovsky, some of which appeared in the institute yearbook. At seventeen Sokhanskaia returned to live with her mother and two aunts at Makarovka, the modest family estate that was a two-day journey over bad roads from Khar'kov, where she made her home for the rest of her life. In her autobiography she recalls her initial shock at the roughness and isolation of her provincial home. She traces her difficult spiritual journey through years of profound depression and apathy before she finally came to accept and embrace her life in the steppe lands. Bouts of depression afflicted her throughout her life, but she found consolation in a deep and abiding faith in God and devotion to the Russian Orthodox Church. Her faith and her love of southern Russia grew stronger over the years,

shaping her as a writer. No less important were the ties of love and affection that she formed anew with her mother and aunt. Years later, in her autobiography, in a letter to Ivan Sergeevich Aksakov (20 April 1860), and in her stories, she recalled her aunt's extraordinary gifts as a storyteller and her mother's knowledge of Russian folk songs. In these two women Sokhanskaia found an endless, living source of material for her own stories.

Extremely poor, but reluctant to give up her freedom to occupy a governess's dependent position, Sokhanskaia embarked on a literary career and became one of the many women who began writing from the provinces at this time, far from the literary centers of St. Petersburg and Moscow. Her first tale, "Maior Smagin" (Major Smagin), appeared in *Syn otechestva* (Son of the Fatherland) in 1844 with a glowing introduction from editor Konstantin Petrovich Masal'sky who praised the originality of her language: "She writes in Russian [*po-russki*]," he declared, "not in European [*po-evropeiski*]." Her second story, "Grafinia D." (Countess D.), was rejected at *Sovremennik* (The Contemporary). However, the well-known critic and writer Petr Aleksandrovich Pletnev, then stepping down as editor, wrote to the unknown author. His letter praised her undoubted poetic gifts, even as it criticized her imitation of the florid style of the popular writer Aleksandr Aleksandrovich Bestuzhev (pseudonym Marlinsky), and recommended that she cultivate the measured prose of Pushkin's novel *Kapitanskaia dochka* (The Captain's Daughter, 1836). Emboldened by Pletnev's words, Sokhanskaia wrote an impassioned reply, begging him to help a young, inexperienced writer and to become her mentor. Pleading her ignorance of the publishing world and her isolation in the provinces, she hoped to appeal to his sense of gallantry. Pletnev, who helped many aspiring writers, both men and women, accepted her proposal. Their personal and literary friendship and correspondence lasted until Pletnev's death in 1865 and was sustained by his wife Aleksandra Vasil'evna Pletneva long afterward.

The immediate result of the friendship between the older critic and the young woman who repeatedly described herself as "a little thing," "almost a child," and "a nobody," and who addressed him in such terms as "great man," "illustrious benefactor," and "venerable father," was Sokhanskaia's autobiography. At his suggestion she wrote her life story as a literary exercise to wean her from the romantic style of Marlinsky and George Sand and—by developing her powers of observation—to practice writing in a realist manner. The autobiography was never intended for publication, nor for an audience larger than this single male reader. Sokhanskaia wrote it during two years (in 1847 and 1848), sending each notebook to Pletnev as it was finished, without keeping a copy. The work appeared in print in 1896, twelve years after her death, but only recently has it attracted critical attention from literary scholars. One of the earliest and relatively few autobiographies by a Russian woman in the first half of the nineteenth century, it is a valuable historical document of Russian girlhood. As a literary work, Sokhanskaia's autobiography has been read by Mary Zirin in her contribution to *Dictionary of Russian Women Writers* (1994) as a "valid female cognate and corrective" to Leo Tolstoy's fictionalized autobiography *Detstvo, otrochestvo, i iunost'* (Childhood, Boyhood, and Youth, 1852–1857). Sokhanskaia merges truthfulness and artfulness in her autobiography as she endeavors to describe an uneventful life apparently devoid of significance or interest. She has learned to be attentive to details, however small or seemingly unimportant.

Sokhanskaia's autobiography tells the story of how she became a writer. It begins tentatively, as she attempts to retain the interest and sympathy of Pletnev—one of the most distinguished and influential critics of the time—who encouraged her to write but who also urged her to respect women's traditional domestic roles as wife and mother. She develops a distinctive and vivid poetic voice that grows stronger and more confident as the autobiography progresses. Intertwining religion and literature in a way characteristic of all her writing, Sokhanskaia recalls learning early on that women were not supposed to be writers, but now, she declares, she has come to realize that her gift as a storyteller is God-given and should not be hidden. She realizes, too, that she does not wish to marry, and she announces her powerful sense of vocation by declaring that she would become a homeless beggar and tell tales to passersby in the street rather than give up storytelling.

Writing, however, was only part of Sokhanskaia's life. She had to satisfy the demands of rural life and running a farm; her early, vivid essay "Ocherk Malorossii" (Sketch of Malorussia, written 1848, published 1897), in which she discusses the problems facing farmers in her area—drought, bad roads, high prices, failed crops, markets—reveals her considerable practical knowledge of farming. She had responsibilities within her community, too, and she was particularly involved in establishing schools for the largely illiterate peasantry. Writing posed its own practical problems. In need of money, Sokhanskaia often lacked the means to buy paper and ink. Her distance from "civilization" obliged her to conduct her literary affairs through an unreliable postal system. Although she eventually acquired some literary acquaintances in distant Khar'kov and occasionally attended philology lectures at Khar'kov University, her refusal to support the development of a national Ukrainian language and literature alienated her from literary circles there. Indeed, she was so isolated in Makarovka that she met another local writer and neighbor, Grigorii Petrovich Danilevsky (pseudonym Skavronsky), only through their mutual acquaintance with Pletnev in St. Petersburg. Despite Pletnev's tutelage

and his generosity in sending books and journals, Sokhanskaia was largely ignorant of the publishing world. She knew little of the politics and factional groupings among literary men and women. She acquired a reputation for being disputatious, demanding, and difficult to deal with, even among those who admired and assisted her. She quarreled with many editors, not always without cause, when she found her stories cut without permission or payment for her work not always forthcoming. Her letters reveal an acute sensitivity to criticism and slights, real and imagined, particularly when addressed condescendingly to a provincial or a woman (or both).

Some of Sokhanskaia's earliest stories ("Pervyi shifr" [First Place, 1849]; "Sosedi" [Neighbors, 1850]; "Liubila" [She Loved, 1858]) attracted little notice, and she later chose not to include these minor pieces in her two-volume collection *Povesti* (Stories, 1863). The most absorbing of these slight works is "Sosedi," a humorous account of village life in Malorussia. A feud occurs between former friends, two female landowners, who wage deadly warfare before they are reconciled by the marriage of their children. Written in vivid, idiomatic Russian with the attention to local color and detail that characterize Sokhanskaia's writing, the story reflects her admiration for Nikolai Vasil'evich Gogol's Ukrainian tales in his collections *Vechera na khutore bliz Dikan'ki* (Evenings on a Farm Near Dikan'ka, 1831–1832) and *Mirgorod* (Mirgorod, 1835). The first of Sokhanskaia's major stories, "Gaika" (The Linchpin), was accepted for publication at *Panteon* (The Pantheon) in 1856. Only the first part of the tale appeared before the journal closed, and "Gaika" remained unfinished until 1860; but it brought Sokhanskaia to the attention of editors of the leading literary journals, who were in search of fresh young talent. She accepted Mikhail Nikiforovich Katkov's proposal to contribute to *Russkii vestnik* (The Russian Messenger), but when her story "Posle obeda v gostiakh" (An After-Dinner Visit; first translated as *Luboff Archipovna*, 1887) appeared in 1858, she was appalled to find that Katkov and the literature editor, Evgeniia Tur, had excised the first twenty-four and the last thirty pages of her manuscript. Nevertheless, the story was a great success.

"Posle obeda v gostiakh" tells a story of thwarted love and unhappy marriage, a common theme among both male and female writers in the 1850s. Sokhanskaia structures her tale as a frame narrative to distinguish it from *svetskie povesti* (society tales). The narrator, an unimportant young lady, and Liubov' Arkhipovna, a lowly, impoverished widow from the minor gentry kept waiting on business, are excluded from the more general conversation of an assembled elegant company of ladies and gentlemen. Longing to join in the highly topical conversation about whether the man or the woman is to blame in a marriage that began in passion and ended in acrimony and separation, Liubov' Arkhipovna speaks her mind to the young lady. Despite their difference in age, social standing, and education, the two women's mutual sympathy and understanding prompt Liubov' Arkhipovna to tell the young lady her life story, to illustrate the truth that the wife is always responsible for marital discord. She relates in a country woman's lively speech how a carefree girlhood, filled with song and merriment, and her love for a young man named Sasha Chernyi come to a harsh end when her mother violently forces her into an arranged marriage. The ritual farewell between Liubov' Arkhipovna and Sasha Chernyi, a handsome youth and a gifted singer but also a penniless orphan, fills some of Sokhanskaia's most poetic and moving pages. The songs that pass between them were much admired and quoted even by critics who otherwise deplored Sokhanskaia's work.

Liubov' Arkhipovna then goes on to tell of the misery of married life and her hatred for her husband, however kindly he treats her—but Sokhanskaia does not allow this conventional ending to stand. Liubov' Arkhipovna has a series of healing conversations with an old pilgrim woman whose simple, religious stories gradually assuage her grief and soften her heart. Eventually she comes to look on her unloved husband with pity and thence to love him, and she lives with him for twenty-three years without a cross word. In answer to her young friend's questioning, Liubov' Arkhipovna tells of Sasha Chernyi's "God-given" fate. She explains that the most beautiful song he had ever sung came from the loss of her, his beloved. Upon his death soon afterward (from a chill he caught while saving a peasant and his horse from drowning), the *narod* (common people) thronged to his burial out of love and gratitude for his songs.

Praised for its moral subtlety and "objectivity," this story was widely acclaimed on all sides for its poetic depictions of Russian provincial life, the author's skillful realization of her characters, and her dazzling command of Russian dialect, as well as her mastery and knowledge of the Russian folk song tradition. Some critics expressed doubts that the story could have been written by a woman and wondered whether "Kokhanovskaia" was a female pseudonym adopted by a man. (Sokhanskaia's adoption of a pseudonym was usual among women writers of the time; her choice of a female rather than a male pseudonym was less common.) Current critics of Russian women's writing have situated Sokhanskaia's narrative firmly among the fiction of writers such as Tur, Avdot'ia Iakovlevna Panaeva, and Nadezhda Dmitrievna Khvoshchinskaia, who shared her interest in the expression of the female voice, the representation of women's conversations and friendship between women, and the treatment of love and marriage in a patriarchal society.

Particularly fervent among Sokhanskaia's admirers were the leaders of the Slavophile movement. Konstantin

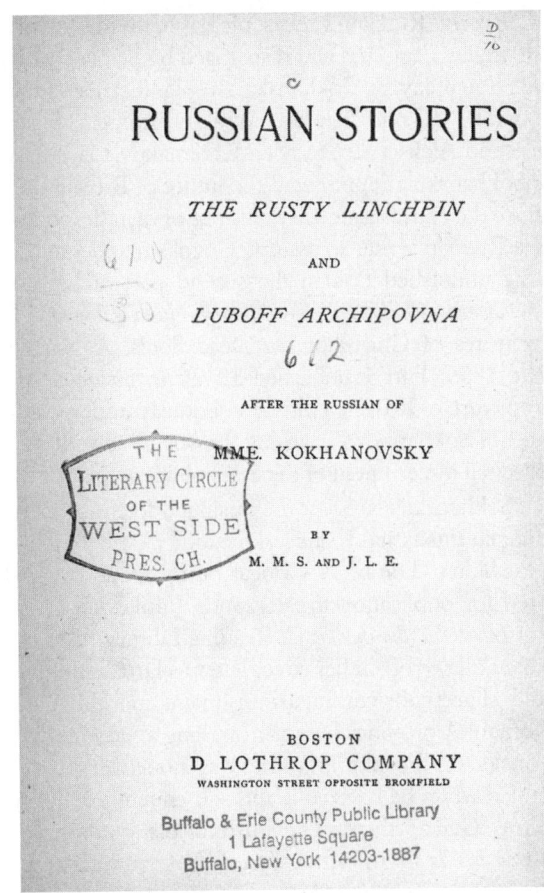

Title page for an English translation of two of Sokhanskaia's stories (Buffalo and Erie County Public Library)

Sergeevich Aksakov's glowing review of her "truly Russian tale" appeared in the Slavophile journal *Russkaia beseda* (Russian Colloquy). His brother, Ivan Aksakov, wrote to the unknown author (uncertain whether he was addressing an old woman, a young lady, or a man) proposing a correspondence, claiming her kinship with the Slavophiles and soliciting her contributions to his journal. This letter marked the beginning of Sokhanskaia's lifelong association with Ivan Aksakov and the Slavophiles. Unlike her letters to Pletnev, in which she appears as a young and grateful student, the ensuing literary correspondence with Ivan Aksakov, which lasted most of their lives, was an exchange between intellectual equals and collaborators. He thought highly of her opinion and asked her advice and assistance on many occasions over the years. Although she disagreed with some of his views and repeatedly insisted on her independence, liberal and "progressive" critics increasingly identified her as a Slavophile, and thus she became associated with conservative writers and thinkers who supported church and tsar, while advocating a retrograde and spurious *narodnost'* (Russian communal heritage).

Recent Russian studies of Slavophilism (a movement largely neglected and disparaged by Soviet scholars) have downplayed Sokhanskaia's significance to the Slavophiles. In this view the Aksakov brothers' fulsome praise and Aleksei Stepanovich Khomiakov's large claim that Sokhanskaia represented the future of Russian literature are the enthusiastic self-delusions of men desperate to find a Russian writer to assume Gogol's mantle and take up the unfinished task in the second part of his novel *Pokhozhdeniia Chichikova, ili Mertvye dushi. Poema* (The Adventures of Chichikov, or Dead Souls. A Narrative Poem, 1855; Part 1 published 1842): to create a "positive" picture of Russia. This view seriously underrates the power of Sokhanskaia's writing, however, as well as the intellectual discernment of the Slavophiles.

Sokhanskaia's essay on Pushkin, "Stepnoi tsvetok na mogilu Pushkina: Kriticheskii etiud" (A Steppe Flower on Pushkin's Tomb: A Critical Study), was originally offered for publication to Aleksandr Vasil'evich Druzhinin at *Biblioteka dlia chteniia* (A Reading Library). Although Sokhanskaia wrote in her cover letter to Druzhinin that "I wholly share your natural astonishment and indignation. A woman! A provincial woman! writing an aesthetic, critical essay on Pushkin!!?", she was nonetheless deeply offended when he rejected it and subsequently refused to publish "Gaika" there. The Pushkin essay appeared in *Russkaia beseda* in 1859, the first of Sokhanskaia's many contributions to Ivan Aksakov's literary ventures. She appreciated his respect for the integrity of her writing and his willingness to publish her work even when he disagreed with her point of view. She wrote "Stepnoi tsvetok na mogilu Pushkina" in response to Pavel Vasil'evich Annenkov's 1855–1857 edition of Pushkin's collected works and his monograph *Materialy dlia biografii Pushkina* (Materials for a Biography of Pushkin, 1855). In her essay Sokhanskaia argues that Pushkin should be understood as a deeply religious writer, and she offers a close reading of five poems she interprets as a cycle, an "epic of the development of the poet's soul." This essay is a significant statement of Sokhanskaia's aesthetic and ethical view of the poet (singer) and his work, in which the Romantic ethos is interwoven with her own religious beliefs. The essay was written at the same time as "Posle obeda v gostiakh," and there are many correspondences between Sokhanskaia's representations of Pushkin and the singer Sasha Chernyi as poets upon whom divine inspiration is bestowed and for whom the act of creation becomes a form of resurrection and eternal life.

Despite her anger at the mutilation of "Posle obeda v gostiakh" and somewhat mollified by Katkov's assurances that her future stories would appear uncut, Sokhanskaia published her next story, "Iz provintsial'noi gallerei portretov" (From a Provincial Portrait Gallery), in *Russkii vestnik* in 1859. Indeed, in this work she followed the editors' suggestion that the excised pages of "Posle obeda v gostiakh" become the basis for a new, separate tale. This transposition was easily accomplished since, as Sokhanskaia's bibliographer Stepan Ivanovich Ponomarev demonstrated years later in his 1898 contribution to the journal *Russkoe obozrenie* (The Russian Review), she characteristically moved large scenes and sections intact from one story to another. In the pages of "Iz provintsial'noi gallerei portretov" the female narrator reflects on the life and character of Anna Gavrilova, a woman of Tsarina Catherine II's time, whose portrait she finds tucked away in a back room because it seems out of place in a westernized Russian home. The lengthy description of Anna's life as a girl in her father Gavril Mikhailov's house reveals Sokhanskaia's fascination with the ways in which the old and the new overlay one another in Russian culture. She lovingly details the intricacies of life on the estate of an eighteenth-century *barin* (lord), with its mixture of traditional Russian ways and newly introduced Western manners and appurtenances.

From the leisurely description of Anna's duties and responsibilities as mistress of the estate, the narrator moves into a plot that gradually quickens into a whirlwind of events, as Anna becomes the object of a struggle between her father, who refuses his daughter's suitor, and the bold young man who steals her away. The narrator relates Gavril Mikhailov's furious and futile pursuit of the young couple as he scours the neighborhood, ransacking homes and interrogating every passerby, intent on hunting down his daughter and her abductor. The family is eventually reconciled when the young couple throw themselves at his feet, and harmony is restored—but only after Gavril Mikhailov has kept his word and given his well-liked son-in-law the severe flogging he had sworn to give the man who stole his daughter. The Homeric, epic feasting that follows their reconciliation is described in lavish detail.

Sokhanskaia was widely praised for her re-creation of eighteenth-century life in this work, which was compared to Sergei Timofeevich Aksakov's novel *Semeinaia khronika* (A Family Chronicle, 1856). The Slavophiles were delighted with the tale for what they saw as its celebration of much that was good in the old ways, and they admired the "epic" nature of Gavril Mikhailov's character and deeds. Nikita Petrovich Giliarov-Platonov, a Slavophile writer and religious philosopher, described Sokhanskaia's accomplishment as the "dawn of the long-awaited literary renaissance" in his review in *Russkaia beseda* in 1859. Other critics, however, found the seductiveness of Sokhanskaia's prose disturbing. On the eve of the emancipation of the serfs, critics were increasingly insistent that portrayals of Russian society serve the interests of social reform; they questioned Sokhanskaia's poetic rendering of the old way of life, her overly sympathetic portrayal of the despotic *barin,* and the meaning of the flogging scene. Sokhanskaia replied to her critics in "Otvet g. G-vu [Giliarovu-Platonovu] na kriticheskii otzyv o povesti 'Iz provintsial'noi gallerei portretov'," which was published in *Russkaia beseda* the same year.

Throughout 1860 Sokhanskaia worked on a variety of projects at Makarovka, delving into her family history for a series of historical studies she had agreed to write for Vsevolod Vladmirovich Krestovsky at *Otechestvennye zapiski* (Notes of the Fatherland), and collecting and transcribing the many folk songs her mother knew. She also completed her unfinished tale, "Gaika," and published it in 1860 in *Russkoe slovo* (The Russian Word) shortly before the journal became radicalized. Applauded, again by the Slavophiles, for its "positive" representation of Russian society and appreciation of truly Russian life, "Gaika" also attracted criticism for its idealization of rural life as well as for its "old-fashioned" plot of love and marriage. In a review in *Vremia* (Time) in 1861, the critic Apollon Aleksandrovich Grigor'ev clearly defined the problem with "Gaika": times had changed, and Sokhanskaia's undoubted talent was not being placed in the service of society as the times demanded.

Like "Posle obeda v gostiakh," "Gaika" tells the tale of a woman's acceptance of an unwanted marriage and takes storytelling and conversation as its central theme. In "Gaika," however, the narrator's voice is more prominent; throughout the story the narrator comments at length on the nature of talk and the circumstances that allow meaningful conversation and mutual understanding. "Gaika" recounts the courtship and marriage of Aleksei Leont'evich—an older man, a landowner who has become prosperous as a "gentry merchant," as he is mockingly called for his entrepreneurial blurring of social ranks—and a young woman who at first rejects him as too old. The young woman, Liudmila Pavlovna (Mila), raised in the home of a wealthy gentry family where she has been educated with the daughter of the house and thus as a lady, has returned to her uneducated, widowed mother's modest home in the steppes and must consider her future. Both of the main characters are displaced, outsiders who—having left and returned to the social world into which they were born—must learn to make a place for themselves in the steppe land. As Mila adjusts to life in the steppes, she gradually comes to appreciate Aleksei Leont'evich's conversation and his tales of his adventures and daily rounds, which she at first found tedious. Although the story begins with a scene of utter misunderstanding and a rift between mother and daughter, it ends with the establishment of harmony and understanding between husband and wife and their reconciliation with Mila's mother—a hopeful marriage of old ways and new.

Sokhanskaia's next publications included "Neskol'ko russkikh pesen' (zapisannykh v Staro-oskol'skom uezde, Kurskoi gubernii)" (Some Russian Songs [Transcribed in Staro-skol'skii district, Kursk province]) and "Ostatki boiarskikh pesen'" (Fragments of Boyar Songs). These two collections of songs with commentary appeared in *Russkaia beseda* in 1860 and were intended to supplement Ivan Vasil'evich Kireevsky's great collections of Russian folk songs. Sokhanskaia viewed the texts as living songs that continued to have meaning in the lives of their singers, rather than as corrupted relics in which one could search for the truth of the original, pure songs of ancient Rus'. She argued this point with Khomiakov and Konstantin Aksakov over songs they wished to exclude because of their content (beatings and a maiden's murder of her lover). Sokhanskaia retorted that she was recording living songs, songs that continued to be sung here and now, and she added sharply in an 1860 letter to Konstantin Aksakov: "Peasant life isn't always a nice little idyll." Nor did she shirk from the unpleasant aspects of Russian history in "Starina" (Olden Days), published in *Otechestvennye zapiski* in 1861. "Starina" is a study of the lawlessness of the region in the olden days, with painstakingly detailed biographies of marauders, murderers, local tyrants, and other unpleasant characters who once populated southern Russia. Sokhanskaia's sources were primarily her mother and aunt, along with an elderly, half-blind Serbian woman with whom she had lived for seven months some years earlier and who had told her stories to while away the long winter evenings. Her narrative emphasizes the importance of women as the keepers of oral family histories and local lore. In Sokhanskaia's view the transmission of such stories is a way of sustaining society and continuity in the unstable life of the steppe lands.

In 1861 she serialized her next story, "Kirila Petrov i Nastas'ia Dmitrova" (Kirila Petrov and Nastas'ia Dmitrova), in Ivan Aksakov's new weekly paper *Den'* (Day). The story relates the life and marriage of Kirila Petrov, an orphaned street urchin raised by a drunken deacon, and the orphaned Nastas'ia Dmitrova, who occupies an awkward position as a ward in a wealthy gentry family that exploits her skill as a fine seamstress. Good and innocent creatures both, they are among the insulted and injured. Kirila Petrov wishes to marry and protect Nastas'ia Dmitrova. The gentry family willingly marries her off, and he finds out after the wedding that Nastas'ia Dmitrova is pregnant by the son of the family—a fact she was prevented from telling him before the marriage ceremony. His misery and inability to love her set him wandering until, like Liubov' Arkhipovna in "Posle obeda v gostiakh," through his faith he becomes able to pity and love both her and the boy born in his absence. Ivan Aksakov was delighted with this story and reported that his readers—including the tsarina, Mariia Aleksandrovna—admired it as well. Sokhanskaia's tale described much that was sordid in Russian life, but its religious aspects and its

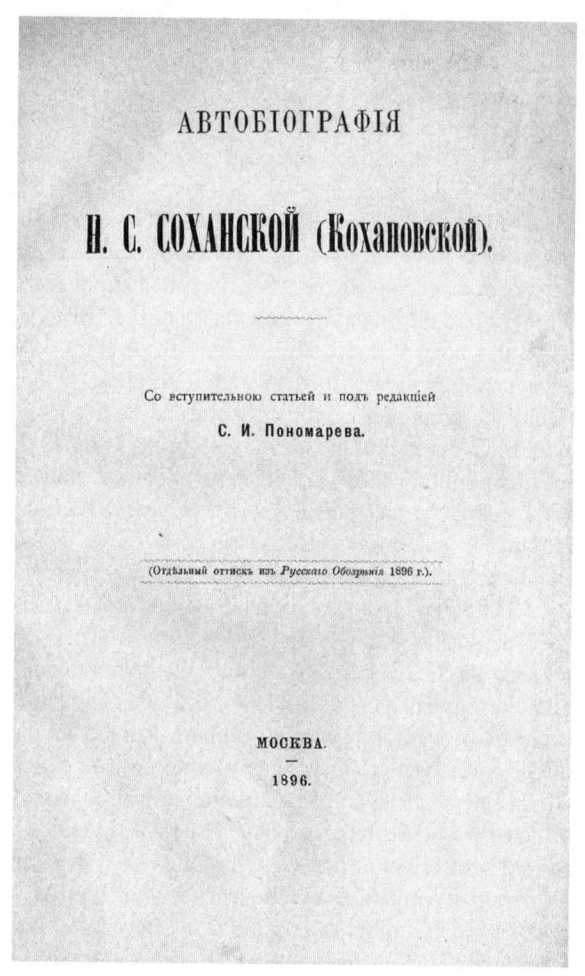

АВТОБІОГРАФІЯ

Н. С. СОХАНСКОЙ (Кохановской).

Со вступительною статьей и подъ редакціей
С. И. Пономарева.

(Отдѣльный оттискъ изъ Русскаго Обозрѣнія 1896 г.).

МОСКВА.
1896.

Front cover for Sokhanskaia's Avtobiografiia *(Autobiography),
written in the late 1840s (after she graduated from a government
boarding school) but published only after her death
(Suzzallo Library, University of Washington)*

"triumph" of innocence through faith were harshly judged by radical critics.

In 1862 Sokhanskaia made her first visit to Moscow and St. Petersburg. She spent only a few weeks in the capital, where she was introduced to the imperial family, before settling in Moscow for two months. She moved mainly in the conservative circles of Ivan Aksakov and his friends and now met many of her correspondents for the first time. She returned to Makarovka in the fall to prepare a collected edition of her works. In 1863 her collection, *Povesti*, appeared in print under her pen name, Kokhanovskaia. The six pieces in the two volumes had all been previously published in periodicals: "Posle obeda v gostiakh," "Iz provintsial'noi gallerei portretov," "Starina," "Gaika," "Kirila Petrov i Nastas'ia Dmitrova" and "Davniaia vstrecha" (A Long-Ago Encounter). "Davniaia vstrecha," printed in *Den'* the previous year, relates Sokhanskaia's own youthful experience of the temptations of reading secular literature (French novels in particular). This reminiscence and the volume itself end

in a profession of faith, not an injunction against secular books—but with the recognition nevertheless that the two greatest books are the Gospels and the "book" of Nature.

Sokhanskaia's *Povesti* was widely and harshly reviewed by many of the leading "progressive" critics, including Nikolai Gavrilovich Chernyshevsky and the satirist Mikhail Evgrafovich Saltykov, whose lengthy review in *Sovremennik* used Sokhanskaia's book to expound the principles of civic criticism. He excoriates the author for obfuscating social ills and serving up her religious faith and *smirenie* (peaceful acceptance) rather than expressing righteous anger and denunciation to force social change and reform. Ironically, Saltykov's influential and decisive review came to be considered one of his best essays, a succinct illustration of the progressive thought of the 1860s, and served to keep Sokhanskaia's name in the history books in the Soviet period. Critics reviewed her book throughout the 1860s. The literary historian Aleksandr Mikhailovich Skabichevsky, for example, contrasted Sokhanskaia's *narodnost'* with that of the *narodniki* (populist) writers such as Fedor Mikhailovich Reshetnikov, whose harsh realism he admired in "Zhivaia struia" (A Living Stream, 1869). Skabichevsky described her as a fanatical Slavophile, whose talent was poisoned by her religion. She entered Russian literary history in his 1891 *Istoriia noveishei russkoi literatury (1848–1890)* (A History of Modern Russian Literature [1848–1890]), listed among the writers of the 1840s. She follows a discussion of Sergei Aksakov, Dmitrii Vasil'evich Grigorovich, Aleksei Feofilaktovich Pisemsky, and Mikhail Vasil'evich Avdeev under the rubric "Zhenshchiny-belletristiki" (Women Writers), together with Khvoshchinskaia, with whom she is unfavorably contrasted.

After 1863 Sokhanskaia turned increasingly to journalism. Although she declined Aksakov's proposal to become the regular Khar'kov correspondent for *Den'*, she did write a number of short articles for the paper about the peasantry, under the collective title "S khutora" (From the Farm). She also published there "Roi Feodosii Savvich na spokoe" (Swarm Feodosii Savvich at Rest, 1864), a tale about a disreputable canon, a variation on the drunken deacon in "Kirila Petrov and Nastas'ia Dmitrova." Much of the critical commentary about this tale focused on the character of her language. She pushed her reworking of the Russian language so far that Ivan Aksakov found it both brilliant and sometimes incomprehensible. He reported to Sokhanskaia in a letter of early 1864, however, that the Moscow philologists were delighted and eager to study her latest work.

Saddened by the deaths of her old friend Pletnev in 1865 and her aunt in January 1866 and depressed by her mother's declining health, Sokhanskaia became more deeply involved in religious work. A number of her articles about the activities of the Cyril and Methodius Society, a group seeking to protect and advance Russian Orthodoxy in western Ukrainian lands to which she belonged, appeared in Aksakov's new paper *Moskva* (Moscow). Several of these articles are tinged with anti-Semitism as well as anti-Polish and anti-Catholic sentiment. Sokhanskaia wrote little between 1868 and 1870, although her letters from that period refer to a long "problem" novel, "Natal'ia Fedoseevna," that she planned to write. She wrote a poorly received play, *Krazha nevesty* (Stealing the Bride), a musical dramatization of her story "Iz provintsial'noi gallerei portretov." She also composed a more successful short story, "Krokha slovesnogo khleba" (A Literary Breadcrumb), for a collection to raise money for famine victims in 1874, but her energies were absorbed elsewhere. She suffered from chronic, painful rheumatism, but she continued to work the farm at Makarovka—a difficult task because, after the emancipation of the serfs in 1861, laborers were hard to hire, and over the years the property had become dilapidated. She cared for her mother until the latter's death in 1873.

Sokhanskaia still lived in the house at Makarovka, although she rented out the farm. A brief trip to the Crimea partially restored her health, and her interest in writing revived in the 1870s. She resumed her lapsed correspondence with Ivan Aksakov and wrote to tell him of Nikolai Nikolaevich Golitsyn's inquiries into her life and work for his bibliography of Russian women writers, and of Golitsyn's request to dedicate this bibliography to her. She told him of the historian Petr Ivanovich Bartenev's interest in her autobiography, which had been found among Pletnev's papers; and she mentioned several requests for her writings from Berlin and Prague. Her letters continued to express her deep religious faith and her commitment to "live not as man wants, but as God commands," as she wrote on 25 April 1871. One of her last essays was an open letter responding to Tolstoy's *Ispoved'* (Confession), urging him to return to the true faith and the Orthodox Church. Sokhanskaia died of cancer soon after writing this essay at her home, Makarovka, on 3 December 1884.

Her death brought her into the public eye again, and some of her writing found its way back into print. Ivan Aksakov published a tribute to his old friend in *Rus'* (Old Russia), reiterating once more her significance as a literary figure and a writer yet to be fully appreciated. He printed fragments of her unfinished novel, "Stepnaia baryshnia sorokovykh godov" (A Young Lady of the Steppes in the Forties) and "Sumerechnye rasskazy: Staroe vospominanie tetushki" (Twilight Stories: An Old Reminiscence by Auntie). "Kirila Petrov i Nasta'ia Dmitrova," "Posle obeda v gostiakh," and "Starina" were all republished in 1885 and again in 1890; both "Posle obeda v gostiakh" and "Starina" appeared once more in 1902. After Aksakov's death in 1886, parts of his correspondence with Sokhanskaia were published by his heirs. Ponomarev, who had been asked by Sokhanskaia's niece to put her papers in order, edited

her autobiographical letters to Pletnev for publication in *Russkoe obozrenie* (The Russian Review) in 1896 (the autobiography was republished in a separate edition later that year). Ponomarev himself published two bibliographical essays on her work, noting that he had received many requests for her fiction but that her *Povesti* was no longer available. Natal'ia Platonova, the daughter of an old friend and neighbor of Sokhanskaia, published a substantial biography of the author in 1909 that remains the basic source of information about her life.

Although since the 1980s Nadezhda Stepanovna Sokhanskaia (Kokhanovskaia) has found new readers, primarily among those interested in Russian women's writing, she has yet to enjoy the full appreciation that Aksakov predicted for her. Despite the efforts of Ponomarev and Platonova, her writing remains largely uncollected and unpublished; much of her extensive correspondence lies unread in the archives. Although there is still much to learn about her life and work, Sokhanskaia's writings clearly exerted a powerful influence over her Russian readers. From her self-chosen isolation in Makarovka she was deeply engaged with the literary, political, and social questions of mid to late-nineteenth-century Russia. She was, for a while, among the most well-known Russian women writers of her time; she played a significant role in Slavophile circles; her writings were studied by scholars and ethnographers documenting the language and culture of Malorussia; and her fictional narratives in particular found a wide readership. Even critics who deplored Sokhanskaia's politics of *smirenie* and her religiosity acknowledged her command of the vernacular and her literary artistry. Among Sokhanskaia's gifts was the ability to draw forth the language and stories of the men and women, peasants and pilgrims, among whom she spent much of her life. Perhaps Sokhanskaia's most striking characteristic and her greatest achievement lay in the brilliance and sheer exuberance of the language that she brought to her own storytelling.

Letters:

"Materialy dlia kharakteristiki russkikh pisatelei, khudozhnikov i obshchestvennykh deiatelei," *Russkoe obozrenie,* 1–3 (1897);

"Perepiska Aksakovykh s N. S. Sokhanskoi (Kokhanovskoi)," *Russkoe obozrenie,* 2–12 (1897); 1 (1898);

"Pis'ma k M. V. Val'khovskoi. Otryvki. 1876–1884," *Russkii arkhiv,* 1 (1900): 108–140.

Bibliographies:

Stepan Ivanovich Ponomarev, "Nashi pisatel'nitsy," *Sbornik otdeleniia russkogo iazyka i slovesnosti imperatorskoi akademii nauk,* 52, no. 7 (1891): 60–71;

Ponomarev, "Rukopisi N. S. Sokhanskoi (Kokhanovskoi) i pis'ma k nei," *Russkoe obozrenie,* 1–2 (1897): 561–568;

Ponomarev, "Opis' bumag, ostavshikhsia posle N. S. Sokhanskoi (Kokhanovskoi)," *Russkoe obozrenie,* 1–2 (1898): 277–312;

Nikolai Nikolaevich Golitsyn, *Bibliograficheskii slovar' russkikh pisatel'nits* (Leipzig: Zentralantiquariat der Deutschen Demokratischen Republik, 1974), pp. 233–236.

Biographies:

A. Pypin, "Novye dannye dlia biografii Kokhanovskoi," *Vestnik Evropy,* 12 (1896): 717–748;

A. E., "Zabytaia pisatel'nitsa (Literaturnyi ocherk)," *Vestnik Evropy,* 2 (1899): 754–776;

Natal'ia N. Platonova, *Kokhanovskaia (N. S. Sokhanskaia) 1823–1884: Biograficheskii ocherk* (St. Petersburg: Senatskaia tipografiia, 1909).

References:

Joe Andrew, "The Matriarchal World in Nadezda Sokhanskaya's 'A Conversation After Dinner'," in *A Centenary of Slavic Studies in Norway: Olaf Broch Symposium: Papers: Oslo, 12–14 September 1996,* edited by Jan Ivar Bjørnflaten, Geir Kjetsaa, and Terje Mathiassen (Oslo: Norwegian Academy of Science and Letters, 1998), pp. 3–22;

Paul Debreczeny, *Social Functions of Literature: Alexander Pushkin and Russian Culture* (Stanford: Stanford University Press, 1997), pp. 49–53;

Ol'ga Demidova, "Russian Women Writers of the Nineteenth Century," in *Gender and Russian Literature: New Perspectives,* translated and edited by Rosalind Marsh (Cambridge & New York: Cambridge University Press, 1996);

Jehanne M Gheith, "Women of the Thirties and Fifties: Alternative Periodizations," in *A History of Women's Writing in Russia,* edited by Adele Barker and Gheith (Cambridge: Cambridge University Press, 2001);

Frank Göpfert, *Dichterinnen und Schriftstellerinnen in Russland von der Mitte des 18. bis zum Beginn des 20. Jahrhunderts* (Munich: Otto Sagner, 1992), pp. 110–114;

Joanna Hubbs, *Mother Russia: The Feminine Myth in Russian Culture* (Bloomington: Indiana University Press, 1988);

Catriona Kelly, *A History of Russian Women's Writing, 1820–1992* (Oxford & New York: Clarendon Press, 1994), pp. 59–78;

Viacheslav Anatol'evich Koshelev, *Esteticheskie i literaturnye vozzreniia russkikh slavianofilov (1840–1850-e gody)* (Leningrad: Nauka, 1984);

Vasilii Ivanovich Kuleshov, *Slavianofily i russkaia literatura* (Moscow: Khudozhestvennaia literatura, 1976);

Andrea Lanoux, "Nadezhda Sokhanskaia," in *Russian Women Writers,* 2 volumes, edited by Christine D. Tomei (New York: Garland, 1999), I: 333–338;

Konstantin Nikolaevich Lomunov, Sergei Sergeevich Dmitriev, and Aleksandr Sergeevich Kurilov, eds., *Literaturnye vzgliady i tvorchestvo slavianofilov: 1830–1850 gody* (Moscow: Nauka, 1978);

Rosalind Marsh, "An Image of Their Own?: Feminism, Revisionism and Russian Culture," in *Women and Russian Culture: Projections and Self Perceptions,* edited by Marsh (New York & Oxford: Berghahn, 1998), pp. 2–41;

Mikhail Evgrafovich Saltykov, "Povesti Kokhanovskoi," in his *Sobranie sochinenii,* 20 volumes (Moscow: Khudozhestvennaia literatura, 1966), V: 368–383, 648–651;

Aleksandr Mikhailovich Skabichevsky, *Istoriia noveishei russkoi literatury (1848–1890)* (St. Petersburg: Pavlenkov, 1891);

Skabichevsky, "Zhivaia struia. (Vopros o narodnosti v literature)," in his *Sochineniia A. Skabichevskogo: Kriticheskie etiudy, publitsisticheskie ocherki, literaturnyia kharakteristiki,* 2 volumes (St. Petersburg: Obshchestvennaia pol'za, 1895), I: 112–143;

Viktoriia Vasil'evna Uchenova, ed., *Dacha na Petergofskoi doroge: Proza russkikh pisatel'nits pervoi poloviny XIX veka* (Moscow: Sovremennik, 1996);

V. A. Viktorovich, "Uroki odnoi sud'by," *Literaturnoe obozrenie,* 3 (1989): 110–112;

Mary Zirin, "Butterflies with Broken Wings? Early Autobiographical Depictions of Girlhood in Russia," in *Gender Restructuring in Russian Studies: Conference Papers, Helsinki, August 1992,* Slavica Tamperensia, no. 2, edited by Marianne Liljeström, Eila Mäntysaari, and Arja Rosenholm (Tampere, Finland: University of Tampere, 1993), pp. 255–266.

Papers:

Nadezhda Stepanovna Sokhanskaia's papers are held in St. Petersburg at the Russian National Library (RNB), fond 14, fond 52, fond 236, and fond 391 (correspondence).

Aleksandr Vasil'evich Sukhovo-Kobylin

(17 September 1817 – 11 March 1903)

Melissa T. Smith
Youngstown State University

BOOKS: *Svad'ba Krechinskogo* (St. Petersburg, 1856); translated by Robert Magidoff as *Krechinsky's Wedding* (Ann Arbor: University of Michigan Press, 1961);

Delo (Leipzig, 1861); revised as *Delo. (Otzhitoe vremia)* (Moscow: L. & A. Snegirevy, 1887);

Kartiny proshedshego (Moscow: Tipografiia Moskovskogo Universiteta, 1869); translated by Harold B. Segel as *The Trilogy of Alexander Sukhovo-Kobylin* (New York: Dutton, 1969);

Raspliuevskie veselye dni (Moscow: F. S. Rassokhin, 1903);

Uchenie Vsemir: *Inzhenerno-filosofskie ozareniia,* edited by A. A. Karulin and I. V. Mirzalis (Moscow: CET, 1995).

Editions: *Trilogiia. Svad'ba Krechinskogo. Delo. Smert' Tarelkina,* edited, with an introduction, by Leonid Petrovich Grossman (Moscow & Leningrad: Gosudarstvennoe izdatel'stvo, 1927);

Trilogiia. Svad'ba Krechinskogo. Delo. Smert' Tarelkina, with an introduction and commentary by Isaak Davidovich Glikman (Moscow, 1955);

Trilogiia. Svad'ba Krechinskogo. Delo. Smert' Tarelkina, with an introduction and commentary by Konstantin Lazar'evich Rudnitsky (Moscow, 1966);

Kartiny proshedshego. Literaturnye pamiatniki, edited by Evgenii S. Kalmanovsk and V. M. Seleznev (Leningrad: Nauka, 1989)—includes "Torzhestvennoe soglashenie batiushki s mirom, ili Tarif na razdrobitel'nuiu prodazu darov dukha sviatogo."

Edition in English: *The Death of Tarelkin and Other Plays: The Trilogy of Alexander Sukhovo-Kobylin,* translated and edited by Harold B. Segel (Amsterdam: Harwood Academic, 1995).

PLAY PRODUCTIONS: *Svad'ba Krechinskogo,* Moscow, Malyi Theater, 26 November 1855; St. Petersburg, Aleksandrinskii Theater, 7 May 1856; Paris, Theatre de la Renaissance, 6 February 1902;

Otzhitoe vremia, Moscow, Malyi Theater, 4 April 1882; St. Petersburg, Aleksandrinskii Theater, 31 August 1882;

Aleksandr Vasil'evich Sukhovo-Kobylin
(Pushkin House, St. Petersburg)

Raspliuevskie veselye dni, St. Petersburg, Literary-Artistic Society, 15 September 1900; produced again as *Smert' Tarelkina,* Petrograd, Aleksandrinskii Theater, 23 October 1917; Moscow, GITIS (State Institute of Theatrical Arts) Experimental Theater, 24 November 1922.

OTHER: "Kvartet," in "Novye materialy o Sukhovo-Kobyline," edited by Konstantin Lazar'evich

377

Rudnitsky, *Ezhegodnik Instituta istorii iskusstv. Teatr* (Moscow, 1955): 290–291.

Aleksandr Sukhovo-Kobylin's literary legacy consists of a single trilogy of plays that ranks along with the satires of Denis Ivanovich Fonvizin, Nikolai Vasil'evich Gogol, and Aleksandr Sergeevich Griboedov as one of the consummate masterpieces of this genre in Russian literature. While Sukhovo-Kobylin considered philosophy his primary vocation, his battles with the censors for the publication and staging of his three plays, *Svad'ba Krechinskogo* (1856; translated as *Krechinsky's Wedding*, 1961), *Delo* (The Case, 1861), and *Smert' Tarelkina* (Tarelkin's Death), first published as *Raspliuevskie veselye dni* (Raspliuev's Merry Days) in *Kartiny proshedshego* (Pictures of the Past, 1869), most effectively stifled his further literary endeavors. The genesis of the plays during the period when he was under investigation for the murder of his mistress, the French seamstress Louise Simone-Dimanche, gave Sukhovo-Kobylin a painfully intimate acquaintance with the Russian legal system, the corrupt bureaucracy that enforced it, and the exquisitely tortuous system of bribery and extortion that existed in Nikolaevan and prereform Russia of the mid nineteenth century. Despite continual critical recognition of his literary and theatrical legacy, an examination of bibliographic material devoted to Sukhovo-Kobylin makes obvious that the question of "did he or didn't he" (murder Simone-Dimanche) has occupied public attention to an at least equal extent.

Aleksandr Vasil'evich Sukhovo-Kobylin was born in Moscow on 17 September 1817 into an aristocratic family whose salons stood at the center of literary and intellectual life in Moscow during his and his parents' generations. While their lineage hailed from the noblest of bloodlines, the family distinguished itself by being more concerned with a correlative nobility of spirit. Early in life Sukhovo-Kobylin not only became conscious of the distinction between his ancient boyar legacy and the newer service aristocracy but also developed a pathological hatred for government bureaucrats, proclaiming his desire to have the motto "he did not serve" as his epitaph.

The family of his father, Vasilii Alekseevich Sukhovo-Kobylin, traced its heritage back to the boyars who helped to establish the Romanov dynasty in Russia; his mother, Mariia Ivanovna (née Shepeleva) Sukhovo-Kobylina, was related to the wealthy landowning family whose ancestors had served Prince Dmitrii Donskoi. A retired army officer who had served in the campaign against Napoleon, Vasilii Alekseevich was a man of strong religious convictions. The dominant force in the family, however, was not this patriarch but Sukhovo-Kobylin's mother, an extraordinary beauty

who possessed a fiery temper and vibrant intellect. Of her three children who survived until adulthood, Sukhovo-Kobylin was the second by birth but first in his mother's eyes and heart and the one who most resembled her in character.

Mariia Ivanovna saw that her children were educated as befitted their social and intellectual position. For tutors to her children, she engaged prominent pedagogues and professors from Moscow University such as Nikolai Ivanovich Nadezhdin, Mikhail Petrovich Pogodin, Mikhail Aleksandrovich Maksimovich, and Fedor Lukich Moroshkin. Under Moroshkin's tutelage Sukhovo-Kobylin began to attend lectures at Moscow University in 1831, when he was just fourteen years old. The boy passed the entrance exams in 1834 and at the age of seventeen enrolled in the division of philosophy and mathematics. In his third year he received a gold medal for his essay "O ravnovesii gibkoi linii s prelozheniem k tsepnym mostam" (The Equilibrium of the Flexible Line and Its Application to Chain Bridges).

The Sukhovo-Kobylin home was a popular meeting place for Moscow intellectuals and literary figures; the critic Vissarion Grigor'evich Belinsky observed that the Sukhovo-Kobylin salon was noted for its erudition, and Pogodin called it "an areopagus of published phenomena," as quoted in Maia Bessarab's *Sukhovo-Kobylin* (1981). Among his early influences Sukhovo-Kobylin counted close family friends Alexander Herzen (Aleksandr Ivanovich Gertsen) and Nikolai Platonovich Ogarev. During his university years Sukhovo-Kobylin shared his passionate interest in philosophy with fellow student Konstantin Sergeevich Aksakov. Soon after, however, his interests shifted. As he became an accomplished sportsman and began winning prizes in equestrian competitions, he became equally drawn to the companionship of his more frivolous and wealthy contemporaries, and he soon parted company with the future Slavophile Aksakov.

Theater was a particular passion of the young Sukhovo-Kobylin. He apparently possessed a great gift of imitation and in particular a sensitivity to linguistic mannerisms and peculiarities of speech—much like his favorite writer Gogol, whose satirical play *Revizor* (The Inspector General) had been the height of the 1836 theater season in Moscow, and who, along with Molière and French vaudeville, were Sukhovo-Kobylin's initial literary models. Frequenting Moscow theaters was not merely a fashionable pastime for Sukhovo-Kobylin, as it was for his aristocratic set. He spent many summers on the estate of the Shepelev family, to which his father had been appointed trustee, and there he took part in amateur theatricals. The theater of the Shepelev estate was considered one of the finest serf theaters in Russia at that time. It had an orchestra of fifty, a chorus and ballet troupe of forty, and regular visits by touring companies. Reportedly, this theater on the Vyksa River could easily rival—and in some respects surpass—the theaters of Moscow and St. Petersburg. Therefore, not surprisingly, Sukhovo-Kobylin's plays have often been cited for the author's apparently deep knowledge of stage practice and have been likened to the well-made plays of his French contemporary, Eugene Scribe.

The Russia of Tsar Nicholas I was renowned for oppressive censorship, particularly in university circles. Informal student gatherings and salons of the well-to-do (such as the Sukhovo-Kobylins) were among the few open for intellectual debate. During the 1830s post-Kantian German philosophy held sway—in particular the ideas of Friedrich Wilhelm Joseph von Schelling, whose proponents included Sukhovo-Kobylin's tutor Maksimovich. During the period 1837 to 1842 the tide turned to favor Georg Wilhelm Friedrich Hegel. Slavophiles and Westernizers alike, the men of the 1840s who were Sukhovo-Kobylin's contemporaries grew out of, and away from, German idealism. Thus, according to Konstantin Lazar'evich Rudnitsky, Sukhovo-Kobylin's lifelong relationship with the German dialectician, which found him "now quarreling with Hegel, now making peace with him," is characteristic of an entire generation of Russian intellectuals.

Upon finishing his course of study at Moscow University in 1838, Sukhovo-Kobylin set out to complete his education through studying with the German luminaries at the Universities of Heidelberg and Berlin. During his years abroad (1838–1842) he traveled throughout the major European capitals—London, Paris, and Rome, where he met frequently with Gogol, who was in self-imposed exile following his disillusionment with the reception of *Revizor* at home in Russia. In Paris at this time Russians had an exotic reputation, and Sukhovo-Kobylin, fluent in French and already an accomplished ladies' man, made quick use of this circumstance. While in a Paris café during his first visit in 1841, he met the woman whose life and death were to provide the critical turning point of his own existence. An exceptionally beautiful twenty-two-year-old, with blonde hair and blue eyes, in the company of an elderly aunt caught Sukhovo-Kobylin's attention; he reportedly introduced himself as a Russian in Paris for the first time and explained that he wished to drink to the honor of French women. The young woman was Louise Simone-Dimanche.

Although later, under official investigation, Sukhovo-Kobylin insisted that their relationship had been platonic, his diaries of the time allude to an early conquest. One entry reports on the evening of their first meeting: "I accompanied Louise home. She wouldn't let me in the house. A visit soon followed—*intimité*." At their

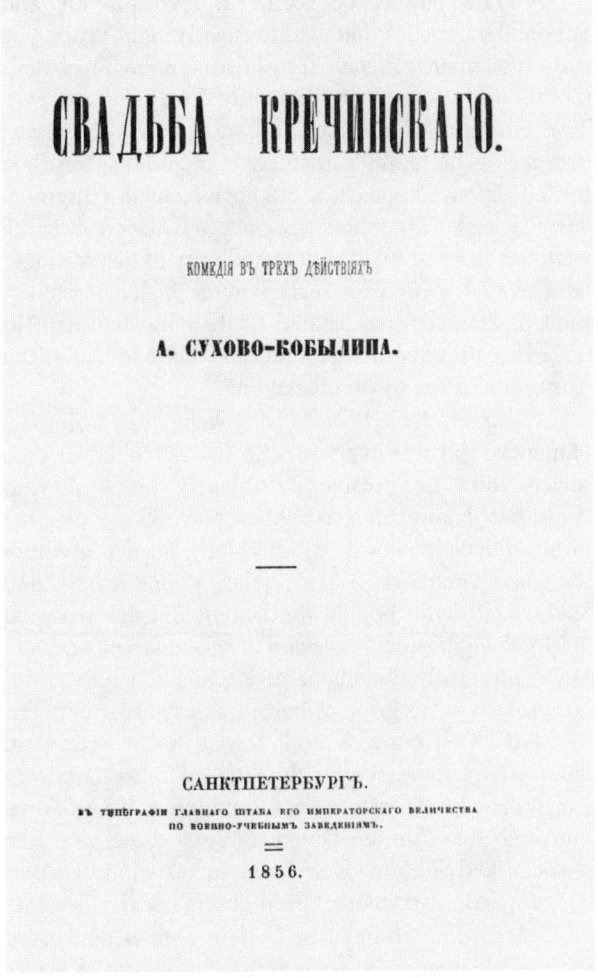

Title page for Sukhovo-Kobylin's Svad'ba Krechinskogo
(The Wedding of Krechinsky), his first play (Kilgour Collection of Russian Literature, Harvard University Library)

first encounter Simone-Dimanche had explained to Sukhovo-Kobylin that she was a seamstress and was having major employment difficulties in Paris at the time. He suggested that she might try her fortunes in St. Petersburg, where he could introduce her personally to the top tailor in the city, Madame Andrie. He gave Simone-Dimanche Fr100 for the journey, and she followed him to Russia in the autumn of 1842. When she arrived in St. Petersburg, Sukhovo-Kobylin first set her up with a wine shop to give her a definite social position as a *vremennaia kupchikha* (temporary merchant woman). Fairly soon her business skills proved less than adequate; her serf-assistants consumed more of the product than they sold, and the shop was closed. She then acquired the position of housekeeper responsible for the marketing of such products as molasses and flour from the Sukhovo-Kobylin estate.

The liaison between Sukhovo-Kobylin and Simone-Dimanche continued for nearly eight years. She was on genuinely friendly terms with Sukhovo-Kobylin's mother and sisters, who frequently dined with the pair. The question of marriage did not arise, of course, because of the family's aristocratic prejudices, but they treated Simone-Dimanche as Sukhovo-Kobylin's common-law wife. The household servants, on the other hand, were less inclined to accept the authority of this foreigner who treated them with such extreme high-handedness. Indeed, the serfs complained of their mistreatment to the Moscow governor-general, and Simone-Dimanche was required to pay an official fine.

Sukhovo-Kobylin's relationship with Simone-Dimanche did not interfere with his active life in high society, and he became passionately involved with Nadezhda Ivanovna Naryshkina. Naryshkina was the rather independent wife of an elderly husband, whom she had married when quite young. In 1849 Sukhovo-Kobylin bought the famous Shigaev mansion in Moscow (Strastnoi Boulevard 9, on Sennaia ploshchad') —evidently with the intent of starting a family, with Naryshkina as his bride. A fierce jealousy arose between the French seamstress and this Russian aristocrat. Simone-Dimanche reportedly "stalked" the parties to which her lover was invited, and once Naryshkina, knowing that Simone-Dimanche was observing the house, asked Sukhovo-Kobylin to open a window. After he complied, Naryshkina kissed him in her rival's sight.

According to reports, Simone-Dimanche herself had been contemplating separation from Sukhovo-Kobylin and a return to France, when her life was cut short under mysterious circumstances that have kept various rumors alive through the years. On the evening of 7 November 1850, while Sukhovo-Kobylin was at a dinner party at the Naryshkins', Simone-Dimanche left him a note with a request for money to cover household expenses, then disappeared. Her absence immediately disturbed Sukhovo-Kobylin, who feared that, because of her habit of stinting on transportation costs, Simone-Dimanche might have fallen victim to the greed of some cutthroat carriage driver. Within twenty-four hours he alerted the police to search for a young woman of her description. On 9 November, Simone-Dimanche's brutally mutilated body was discovered lying in the snow on a road outside of Moscow. Though the body was dressed in elegant clothes, the clothing was arranged somewhat haphazardly and did not include an overcoat. The cause of death was established as asphyxiation.

A distraught Sukhovo-Kobylin received the attentive ministrations of mother, sisters, and a devoted Naryshkina, who stayed with him through the moments of crisis but soon, to put an end to rumors, departed for France. In France she gave birth to the child she was carrying at the time—evidently Sukhovo-Kobylin's—and became first the mistress, then eventually the wife, of Alexandre Dumas *fils*. In France, Naryshkina raised her "adopted daughter," Louise (named in memory of Simone-Dimanche) Weber, to adulthood alongside Ol'ga, her elder daughter by her first husband, Aleksandr Grigor'evich Naryshkin.

From 16 to 22 November 1850 Sukhovo-Kobylin was imprisoned as the major suspect in Simone-Dimanche's murder. The first Moscow court to rule on the case and deliver a verdict of innocence was a divided one, and this fact allowed the case to drag on for seven years, a time frame that included a second period of arrest in 1854. Sukhovo-Kobylin was formally cleared in 1857, but, in a final exercise of power, the then-infamous minister of justice, Count V. N. Panin, released all other suspects as well. The actual findings of police investigators exculpated Sukhovo-Kobylin and pointed to a crime of revenge on the part of the house servants, particularly the cook, Efim Egorov. This evidence was suppressed, however, and it only surfaced when Sukhovo-Kobylin's personal papers were repatriated from France in the 1930s. At the time, commission after commission reviewed the evidence and extorted exorbitant bribes from Sukhovo-Kobylin in the process. Many details of the actual investigation fueled the literary transformations of evidence that appear in Sukhovo-Kobylin's later plays. The writer's own linguistic sophistication provided false clues against him. For instance, playful, rather Freudian references to the vengeance of his "Castillian dagger" in letters to Simone-Dimanche—about whom he publicly made gentlemanly claims of a platonic relationship—provided one of the many versions of the "crime of passion" hypotheses that circulated in Moscow. Indeed, the writer P. Bobrov is reported to have used the Sukhovo-Kobylin/Simone-Dimanche affair as the inspiration for a novel. Sukhovo-Kobylin's final acquittal left him at the mercy of the church to repent his illicit liaison with a Frenchwoman.

This personal catastrophe and the prolonged official scrutiny that followed led Sukhovo-Kobylin to withdraw from his former frivolous society life, and he began to perceive life in a totally new way. "Work, work, and work," as quoted by Bessarab, became Sukhovo-Kobylin's mantra. For the rest of his life he engaged in exacting labors—both physical and intellectual in nature. His diaries document an hour-by-hour scheduling of his time. He rose daily at 6:00 in the morning and intermingled writing, translation, gymnastics, and physical tasks throughout the day until 11:30 at night. The crafting of his literary trilogy occurred simultaneously with his translations of Hegel from German into Russian.

The writing of *Svad'ba Krechinskogo* began as a collective enterprise during the summer of 1852. According to Sukhovo-Kobylin's autobiographical notes, he decided to distract himself by writing, together with his sister Elizaveta Vasil'evna Sukhovo-Kobylina and his officer friend Etienne Sorochinsky, a comedy on contemporary manners; Elizaveta's prose had already received the positive attentions of liberal journalistic circles, and Sorochinsky had a reputation as an excellent raconteur and a theater enthusiast. Sukhovo-Kobylin planned to write the general scenario, and his sister and Sorochinsky would compose the individual scenes. Setting to work immediately, Sukhovo-Kobylin produced both the scenario and the cardsharper Raspliuev's opening monologue in act 2, which his collaborators greeted enthusiastically. The others' efforts at scene writing, however, came to naught. Having plenty of "free time" while being held in Moscow on suspicion of murder, Sukhovo-Kobylin decided to continue the project alone. His second imprisonment, from 7 May to 4 November 1854, provided him the dubious opportunity of working virtually uninterrupted until the completion of the play in October 1854. (The conditions of his imprisonment, as a nobleman, gave him much freer reign than less fortunate prisoners enjoyed.)

Just as the writing process of *Svad'ba Krechinskogo* and its author moved from the witty repartee of the aristocratic Moscow drawing room to darker social experience, so did the play itself acquire a breadth of tragicomic vision that eventually earned it a place in the history of Russian theater alongside Gogol's *Revizor* and Griboedov's *Gore ot uma* (Woe from Wit, 1833). *Svad'ba Krechinskogo,* with the ironic movement typical of Russian comedy, is the story of the protagonist's marriage "plot": a scheme to avoid bankruptcy through marriage to Lidiia (Lidochka) Muromskaia, only child of the wealthy but socially naive landowner Piotr Konstantinovich Muromsky. The plot turns on Krechinsky's "Napoleonically" brilliant scheme (in the mind of his comic foil Raspliuev—whose name, which sounds like *raz pliunut'* [spit once], suggests his readiness for any form of skulduggery) of pawning his fiancée's solitaire diamond brooch just long enough to stave off his creditors' interference in the marriage. The social lion Krechinsky, as he nears forty, finds that the worsening of his finances gradually forces him into spiritual as well as monetary bankruptcy, while the "boiled turnip" Lidochka (as Krechinsky cynically portrays his fiancée) grows in stature. She changes from a young country girl blinded by the glitter of high society to a woman in love, capable of a self-sacrificing gesture to save her fiancé from arrest even after his treachery has been unmasked. At the end of the play the honest Muromsky family, rather than the scoundrel Krechinsky, finds itself forced to flee in shame.

Sukhovo-Kobylin's first attempt at engaging the Malyi Theater actor Prov Mikhailovich Sadovsky for the role of Raspliuev, however, met with rejection. Sadovsky found the initial monologue both unrealistic and unlike Molière, whose work Sukhovo-Kobylin had in fact used as a model for this scene. Somewhat discouraged, the playwright delayed presenting the comedy to other actors, but the script circulated in manuscript form and aroused a great degree of interest in literary Moscow. After a reading held at the Sukhovo-Kobylin estate, Voskresenskoe, on 28 May 1855, the Malyi Theater actor Sergei Vasil'evich Shumsky requested the author's permission to play the role of Krechinsky at his benefit performance. Sadovsky finally agreed to play Raspliuev, and Mikhail Semenovich Shchepkin, the premier actor at the Malyi, acted in the role of Muromsky. That Shchepkin assumed the role of Muromsky, rather than of Raspliuev, has been interpreted as the actor's essential misreading of the cultural significance of Raspliuev's character. Indeed, the character of Raspliuev spawned the diagnosis of a new cultural phenomenon—*raspliuevshchina* (raspliuevitis)—and Raspliuev, along with Krechinsky, had multiple rebirths not only in Sukhovo-Kobylin's later works but also in the satirical sketches of Mikhail Evgrafovich Saltykov. Shchepkin became a good friend of Sukhovo-Kobylin and was later the first member of the theatrical world to hear him read his second play, *Delo*.

The position of the Malyi Theater in mid-nineteenth-century Russia as a "second Moscow University" assured serious consideration of Sukhovo-Kobylin as a major literary figure. However, his lack of adherence to any particular political circle—liberal or conservative—meant that genuine recognition by the dictators of public opinion was delayed. The St. Petersburg premiere of *Svad'ba Krechinskogo* at the Aleksandrinskii Theater, with actor Vasilii Vasil'evich Samoilov in the title role, took place some six months later, on 7 May 1856. While many theatergoers considered Samoilov's performance in the role of Krechinsky his finest, several critics also felt that his interpretation diminished the social significance of the character.

While in St. Petersburg for the Aleksandrinskii premiere, Sukhovo-Kobylin and his mother made overtures to Minister Panin in an attempt to move the Simone-Dimanche case forward. Their interviews, however, resulted in little other than the confirmation of mutual animosity. The friendship of Sukhovo-Kobylin's sister Sofiia Vasil'evna Sukhovo-Kobylina with Tsarina Mariia Aleksandrovna gave an opportunity for imperial intervention. An official pardon from the new tsar, Alexander II, on 3 December 1857 provided final vindication.

Prov Mikhailovich Sadovsky, one of the most popular actors
in mid-nineteenth-century Russia, in the role of Raspliuev,
the protagonist of Svad'ba Krechinskogo
(from Leonid Petrovich Grossman, Teatr
Sukhovo-Kobylin, *1940)*

Concurrently with his literary activities of this period, Sukhovo-Kobylin achieved a measure of success as overseer of the family estates. Appointed to this position by his father in hopes of restoring the family fortunes, Sukhovo-Kobylin made his first official tour of inspection in 1857. The estate of Voskresenskoe was sold to pay debts; the Moscow house was rented out except for one wing retained for visits to the city; and Kobylinka on the Plavishcha River in the Tula province became Sukhovo-Kobylin's refuge. The internal walls of the large wooden structure were unplastered, and he believed that the airy, log-walled interior provided an especially healthful atmosphere. Kobylinka housed the writer's extensive library and several valuable paintings.

Sukhovo-Kobylin earned recognition outside of literary circles, too. For instance, he participated in the founding of the first champagne factory in Russia. He thought of the trees in Kobylinka as members of his family, of whom he was quite protective, and later in life he became exceedingly keen on forestry, planting new trees whenever possible. Attracting the attention of specialists in Denmark, he received a prize from them for his activities in forestry.

Freedom from official scrutiny for Sukhovo-Kobylin came at last in 1858, when he received a passport and was able to travel abroad. He returned to the long-delayed goal of marriage and family and began to seek a bride among the French nobility. Through correspondence he enlisted the aid of a cousin in Paris, Anzhelika Golitsyna. No longer the confident young aristocrat, Sukhovo-Kobylin suffered fears of rejection and conflicting emotions during his months in courtship of a young baroness, Marie de Bourglon. Marie's family, moreover, feared that his financial position was less than suitable and set forth a series of conditions: in a prenuptial agreement Sukhovo-Kobylin had to consent that any of Marie's inherited wealth remain in the country of her birth. Indeed, his marital happiness was short-lived; less than a year after accompanying her new husband back to Russia, Marie died of tuberculosis. Although Sukhovo-Kobylin had, on occasion, noted a certain fragility in his fiancée, the fact that Marie had already contracted the fatal disease in France had been withheld from her suitor.

While in Paris, Sukhovo-Kobylin approached Dumas for assistance in bringing *Svad'ba Krechinskogo* to the French stage. Dumas responded by suggesting that the finale of the play did not correspond to the requirement of the "retrograde" French theater, which called for plays with a clear moral message: evil punished, virtue rewarded. Yet, on the contrary, at the end of the Russian *Svad'ba Krechinskogo,* the heroine Lidochka—who continues to love the man who has betrayed her—insists that Krechinsky's attempt to pawn a paste imitation of her diamond pin was "a mistake." Therefore, the victimizing Krechinsky and Raspliuev get off unscathed, while the victimized Muromsky family are forced to "flee from shame." Sukhovo-Kobylin made changes according to Dumas's suggestions; these did not, however, gain the author a Paris staging at this time.

Encouraged by the extraordinary success in Russia of his first play, Sukhovo-Kobylin set to work on his second in May 1856. As with *Svad'ba Krechinskogo,* he continued crafting his work over a substantial period of time, completing it in April 1861. If *Svad'ba Krechinskogo* bore all the earmarks of a drawing-room comedy, his second play *Delo* was, as he stated in the foreword to its 1862 edition, "not the fruits of leisure . . . , but in all actuality an essential case, ripped out with blood from the realest of life." The text opens with a list of characters, not in order of appearance or importance as dramatis personae, but from the top, "before which everything, including the author himself, is silent," to the bottom—mimicking the social order of the tsarist empire as a whole. The Muromsky family—who, through yet another twist, have ironically ended up the defendants rather than the plaintiffs of their own case—are called "non-entities, or private persons," while the servant Tishka, a serf, is described as a "non-person." Seven years have passed since the action of the previous play. Krechinsky has flown abroad, and on the basis of Raspliuev's evidence, the official world has built a case against the Muromskys that is designed to extort the maximum in bribes and blackmail from the (formerly) wealthy family. The action moves precisely and irrevocably through this "real-life" plot and ends with the pitiful Muromsky—now experiencing the full tragedy of his position as a member of the nobility who had been victorious in the struggle against Napoleon in 1812—being brought to financial and moral catastrophe and losing his life in the bargain. The victorious dark forces are the bureaucrats Varravin (whose name aptly derives from that of Barabbas, the notorious thief in whose place Christ was crucified) and his henchman Tarelkin (from *tarelka* [plate], the dinner plate on which the victim is served).

Although the 1860s began auspiciously, with the completion of *Delo,* a series of personal tragedies colored his life during this time. Indeed, Sukhovo-Kobylin's misfortunes were by no means limited to the death of Simone-Dimanche—a major turning point in his life—and its aftermath. His mother, Mariia Ivanovna, died in 1862, and his sister Sofiia passed away in 1867. The Russian climate proved fatal for both of the playwright's foreign-born spouses. Marie had died in 1860, within a year of marriage. His second wife, an Englishwoman named Emily Smith whom he had married in 1867, survived for an even shorter time. Emily's tender ministrations to her father-in-law, Vasilii Aleksandrovich, at the family estate during the winter of 1868 resulted in her contracting a fatal case of influenza. After Emily's death Sukhovo-Kobylin sold his Moscow home and moved its furnishings to Kobylinka. His father, in ailing health and withdrawn into a world of religious devotion, outlived his wife, daughters-in-law, and one of his daughters. Vasili Aleksandrovich died on 11 April 1873.

As he observed the internal events in Russia in the 1860s, Sukhovo-Kobylin's political views tended to grow more and more pessimistic. The postreform financial crisis and attendant peasant uprisings had forced him to consider moving to France as early as October 1861. As an active participant in the life of his estate, however, he expressed satisfaction in emancipation per se. He was himself a tireless worker and scrupulously honest in his dealings with his peasants, who viewed Sukhovo-Kobylin as strict but fair. They apparently were supportive of him in his times of personal tragedy. His own social hatreds were aimed at governmental officials and clerks.

Sukhovo-Kobylin completed his triad of plays in 1869 with *Smert' Tarelkina,* a "tragi-farcical" synthesis of themes and characters from the first two plays of his trilogy. In this play, yet another seven years have passed. The mechanism of extortion is brought to a conclusion when the petty bureaucrat Tarelkin decides to fake his own death in order to escape his creditors and gain revenge against his superior, Varravin, from beyond the grave (so to speak). The life-and-death struggle of the bureaucrats takes a metaphysical twist when, because of the existence of two death certificates for different individuals and only one dead body in evidence, the police—now under the supervision of Chief of Police Raspliuev—complete their interrogation of witnesses for the purpose of gaining "evidence." Through their powers of reasoning, the police reach the only conclusion possible: the remaining "live" body (belonging to Tarelkin, who has switched identities with his deceased neighbor Kopylov) is actually a vampire. Eventually, of course, Varravin guesses the truth and sets Tarelkin free to wander the world as a beggar.

Sukhovo-Kobylin retained a residence in Moscow for most of his life, but his visits to the city became less frequent and of shorter duration as the years passed. The rare visits do not suggest, however, that he cut himself off from intellectual interaction with the contemporary world. His library at Kobylinka housed more than one thousand volumes; he regularly subscribed to newspapers and magazines published in Russia and abroad. Fluent in French, German, and English as well as Russian, he both read and wrote extensively in these languages. In his younger years Sukhovo-Kobylin's writing showed a marked preference for French; in later life he wrote mostly in Russian, though readers of his diaries claim that his orthography was extremely eccentric. He adopted the German practice of capitalizing nouns when writing in Russian, and he spelled words of foreign origin differently at different times, ignoring the Russian norms.

Sukhovo-Kobylin's youthful attraction to Hegelian idealism persisted throughout his life; among the ancient philosophers, he considered Heraclitus his primary influence. He saw the gymnastic "play" in ancient Greece as essentially intertwined with the development of philosophy. Continually seeking the mathematical corroboration of his ideas, he filled his diaries with mathematical formulae; in his letters to friends he requested books on differential calculus. Indeed, observers have suggested that he was more of a mathematician than a philosopher. Nevertheless, for the latter part of his life, Sukhovo-Kobylin devoted his creative energies to the development of a philosophical tract titled "Vsemir" (All-World). In December 1893 he tried to publish fragments of his treatise in the journal *Russkoe obozrenie* (The Russian Review) but without success. At various times he felt his work on "Vsemir" approaching closure; at other times he admitted to a new gap in understanding of Hegel. Sukhovo-Kobylin's idealism in philosophy was accompanied by contrasting parallel reflections on the degradation of personality in contemporary history. He characterized the Russian gentry as the *staraia obolochka dukha* (old shell of the spirit), which, in the Hegelian movement of the idea through history, was in the process of being cast aside. With great interest, he followed scientific and technical achievements such as Charles Darwin's theories of evolution and the expansion of railway travel. He believed that people of the twentieth century would live significantly better than those of the nineteenth. "Vsemir" remained unknown during Soviet times; fragments of the work, which consists of more than eighteen thousand manuscript pages, were published only in 1995 as *Uchenie* Vsemir: *Inzhenerno-filosofskie ozareniia* (The Teachings of *All-World:* Engineering Philosophical Insights).

In politics Sukhovo-Kobylin parted company with the liberal intelligentsia, at whose center was a literary salon run by his sister Elizaveta, who published under the pseudonym Evgeniia Tur. Tur, whose own fortune had been dissipated by her exiled spouse, edited the literary journal *Russkaia rech'* (Russian Speech) for a brief time. After the thirty-eighth issue of the journal, Tur handed its editorship over to Evgenii Mikhailovich Fedoktistov, one of her brother's major detractors. Within a short period of time *Russkaia rech'* collapsed financially, adding to the Sukhovo-Kobylin family's continually tight financial straits. Tur, under suspicion of harboring political insurgents, was forced into emigration—first to Paris, then to Warsaw.

Sukhovo-Kobylin's further literary career provided major challenges of its own. Years before, although *Svad'ba Krechinskogo* had provoked certain wranglings with the censors, it nevertheless was published in the progressive journal *Sovremmenik* (The Contemporary) under the editorship of Nikolai Alekseevich Nekrasov in 1856. Sukhovo-Kobylin himself turned down Nekrasov's offers of an honorarium in favor of five hundred copies of the journal for personal distribution. The second play, *Delo,* was first published abroad, in Leipzig in 1861, at the author's personal expense; it had a print run of only twenty-five copies, none of which is extant today.

At home in Russia it faced repeated prohibition. The author himself, nevertheless, circulated underground copies of the play in Moscow and St. Petersburg, and it gained a certain number of admirers. Official resistance to his third play, *Smert' Tarelkina,* proved even stronger, and the entire trilogy received approval for publication only when the author bestowed upon it a title, *Kartiny proshedshego* (Pictures of the Past, 1869; translated as *The Trilogy of Alexander Sukhovo-Kobylin,* 1969), which implied to readers that the abuses portrayed belonged to pre-reform (Nikolaevan) Russia. The first edition of the entire trilogy was published by Tipografiia Moskovskogo Universiteta (Moscow University typography) at the author's own expense. At that point, despite his evident physical and intellectual strength and moderate age (he was fifty-two), Sukhovo-Kobylin made the decision to write no more for the stage.

During this period in Russia the publication of one's plays was no assurance of their theatrical production. The censors' accusation that Sukhovo-Kobylin's later comedies evoked "not laughter, but shudders," as quoted in Rudnitsky's biography, clearly points to the raw nerve they obviously touched. Sukhovo-Kobylin repeatedly requested permission for the staging of *Delo* in the 1860s and 1870s. Such requests were formally denied in 1862, 1863, and 1876. The theatrical censors' final approval in 1881 was contingent on several cuts and a change of title—to *Otzhitoe vremia* (Times Gone By). By the time of the premiere of this second play at the Malyi Theater on 4 April 1882, times had indeed changed. Tsar Alexander II died in 1881, and in 1882 the imperial monopolization of the theater came to an end. The Malyi production was closely followed by the 12 April 1882 premiere by the Fedotov troupe at the Russian Theater of Moscow. The Aleksandrinskii premiere took place in St. Petersburg on 31 August of the same year.

The theatrical fate of *Smert' Tarelkina* was even more blighted. In the 1880s Sukhovo-Kobylin developed a friendship with the lead actor of the St. Petersburg Aleksandrinskii Theater, Vladimir Nikolaevich Davydov, who played the roles of Raspliuev in *Svad'ba Krechinskogo* and of Muromsky in *Delo.* Davydov, however, was not able to obtain approval for the third play of the trilogy. Sukhovo-Kobylin's 1882 effort to obtain permission for staging the play met with rejection, as did his second attempt in 1892. This time, however, the motive for censorship had a personal edge: Fedoktistov, former editor of Evgeniia Tur's journal *Russkaia rech',* had been appointed Head of the Main Directorate of Publication Affairs in 1883; he held the post for thirteen years. In making government a career, he had switched allegiance from liberal to ultraconservative, and his vengeance against freedom of the press was the subject of literary epigrams. Only after the end of Fedoktistov's rule did an unlikely supporter for the premiere of *Smert' Tarelkina* turn up: in the person of the reactionary editor of the journal *Novoe vremia* (New Times), Aleksei Sergeevich Suvorin. *Smert' Tarelkina* finally premiered on 15 September 1900 as *Raspliuevskie Veselye dni* (Raspliuev's Merry Days) at the Theater of the Literary-Artistic Society of St. Petersburg.

Although traditional forms of "family happiness" eluded Sukhovo-Kobylin, the last quarter of his life was warmed by his relationship with Louise, the daughter that Naryshkina had borne him. After reaching adulthood, Louise moved from France to live with her father in Russia. In contrast to the haughty manner reported by observers of Sukhovo-Kobylin in earlier periods, his relationship with the young Louise seemed tender. He asked permission of Tsar Alexander III to adopt her officially. Soon after permission was granted, Louise married Count Isidore Failletan. However, Louise, like her father, was not destined for a lengthy married life; within a short period of time in the 1890s she lost both her husband and her son. Thereafter, she remained her father's closest companion. He expressed concerns about providing her with family and fortune in his waning years, even as he outlived most of their nearest relatives: his elder sister, the writer Tur, died on 15 March 1892; Naryshkina passed away on 21 March 1895; and the playwright's younger sister and closest familial confidante, Evdokiia Vasil'evna Sukhovo-Kobylina, known as Dushen'ka, died on 23 January 1897.

Although Sukhovo-Kobylin spent most of the last twenty-five years of his life on his estate at Kobylinka, he made regular trips to St. Petersburg and Moscow, and he actively supported the cultural life of Tula province. Although he dressed simply for work on his estate, a ride into the provincial city of Tula warranted dressing in the latest fashions, and in this respect he remained a dandy throughout his elderly years.

In contrast to many significant authors of nineteenth-century Russia, Sukhovo-Kobylin found no attraction in Russian Orthodox Christianity and considered himself an atheist. He avidly followed European and American developments in liberal Protestantism. Among the authors whose works he translated were contemporary proponents of American Unitarianism. Sukhovo-Kobylin found the writings of American founding father Benjamin Franklin, with his focus on the importance of work in the formation of the human personality, close to his own. Sukhovo-Kobylin's view of the destiny of Russia became increasingly pessimistic over the years. Despite his decision to write no more literary works after his epic struggles to secure public hearings for his plays, two short satirical sketches remain from his last years (albeit in fragmentary form): "Kvartet" (Quartet),

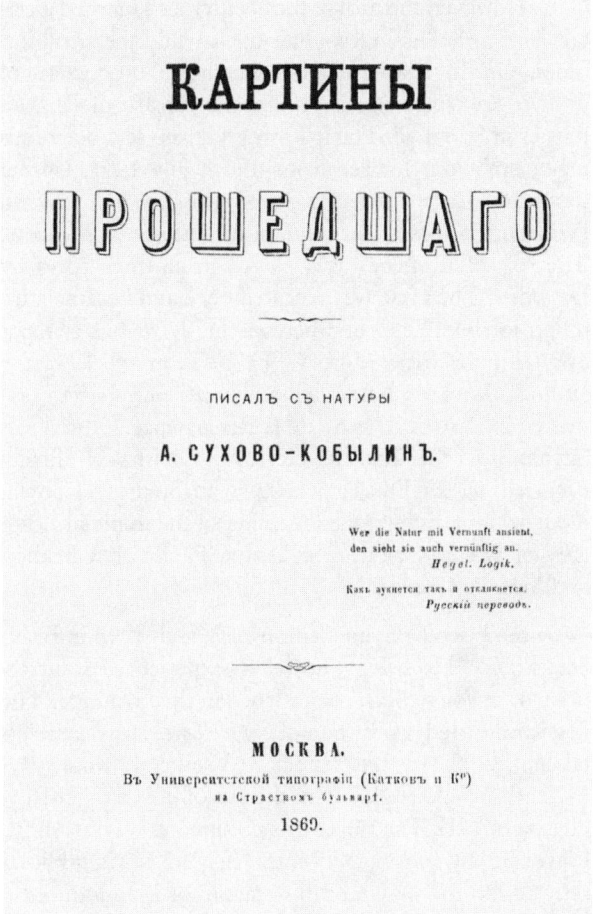

Title page for Sukhovo-Kobylin's Kartiny proshedshego *(Pictures of the Past), in which all three of his plays were collected for the first time as a trilogy (Kilgour Collection of Russian Literature, Harvard University)*

written at the end of the 1870s but first published only in 1955, as Russia became increasingly disillusioned with the "great reformer" Alexander II, and "Torzhestvennoe soglashenie batiushki s mirom, ili Tarif na razdrobitel'nuiu prodazu darov dukha sviatogo" (The Triumphant Agreement between the Priest and the Commune, or the Tariff on the Sale of Fragments of the Holy Spirit), written approximately fifteen years later and eventually published in a 1989 edition of *Kartiny proshedshego*. The former essay—which updates Ivan Andreevich Krylov's eponymous fable (1811), a satire on Tsar Alexander I's new ministerial appointments, to the contemporary era—was at one point intended by its author to follow the fifth act of *Delo* as an apocalyptic scene of a Russian bureaucracy, with none other than the cardsharper-turned-police-investigator Raspliuev at its helm. The latter essay reveals Sukhovo-Kobylin's equal mistrust of hierarchical relations within the Russian Orthodox Church.

However, the turn of the century also marked a certain turn in Sukhovo-Kobylin's literary and theatrical fortunes. On 11 May 1900 he attended a production of *Svad'ba Krechinskogo* at the 150th anniversary of Russian theater in Iaroslavl'. The following year he saw one of his major ambitions fulfilled from 6 to 8 July 1901. During these three days his entire trilogy was produced by St. Petersburg actors at the Aquarium Theater in Moscow. The role of Raspliuev was played in all three plays by Davydov. The cycle was repeated once and became a triumph for both actor and playwright, as well as a major event for theatrical Moscow. On 6 February 1902 the author's own French translation of *Svad'ba Krechinskogo* premiered in Paris at Theatre de la Renaissance. Official recognition by the Russian literary establishment finally occurred on 25 February 1902, with Sukhovo-Kobylin inducted as a distinguished member of the Imperial Academy of Sciences, along with Anton Pavlovich Chekhov and Maksim Gor'ky.

Sukhovo-Kobylin died on 11 March 1903 in Beaulieu, France. His trilogy, however, experienced resurrections of major significance in Russian theatrical life. The first uncensored production of *Smert' Tarelkina* was undertaken by the gifted director Vsevolod Emil'evich Meierkhol'd (Meyerhold) on the eve of the October Revolution of 1917. The run of this production was cut short, however, by ensuing events. In 1922 Meierkhol'd returned to the play, and his staging of it announced a significant new kind of theater: constructivist sets and costumes adorned a production described as a "parade of attractions" by Meierkhol'd's assistant, the future motion picture director Sergei Mikhailovich Aizenshtein (Eisenstein). In the Soviet era *Svad'ba Krechinskogo* again became the only play of the trilogy that was sufficiently palatable to authorities to allow repeated productions; a production of *Delo* by Leningrad director Nikolai Pavlovich Akimov was one of the major events of de-Stalinization in Soviet theater.

In the 1970s and 1980s Sukhovo-Kobylin's trilogy became a vehicle for the successful development of a hybrid Russian American genre, the musical. The first two plays, *Svad'ba Krechinskogo* and *Delo,* were staged by the Leningrad Theater of Musical Comedy from 1978 to 1979 in the first successful Soviet attempt at raising a homegrown version of the American genre to a level worthy of serious consideration. *Smert' Tarelkina,* produced only in 1984, after the death of Leonid Il'ich Brezhnev and the end of the period of *zastoi* (stagnation), moved the musical to the prestigious Tovstonogov Drama Theater in Leningrad. As glasnost came into flower in the late 1980s, the trilogy was staged in Moscow at the Teatr na Iugo-zapade (Theater of the South-West Region). The musical version of *Svad'ba Krechinskogo* has been instrumental in revitalizing the Malyi Theater, the birthplace of the play, on the eve of the twenty-first century.

Critics have often commented on the literary legacy of Aleksandr Vasil'evich Sukhovo-Kobylin as plays of the future; the author himself in many places indicated links between the ironic progression of his dramaturgy and the progress of the Idea, or Spirit, described in Hegelian philosophy. In any case, the periodic resurgence of Sukhovo-Kobylin's name on the stage and in critical literature confirms the distinctive insights of his work into the Russian historical-literary-theatrical experience. Despite a biography fraught with tragedy, Sukhovo-Kobylin's literary incarnation of the Hegelian triad that so fascinated him throughout his life has made the author arguably one of the most prescient explorers of the Russian national psyche.

Letters:

"Pis'ma Sukhovo-Kobylina k rodnym," *Trudy Vsesoiuznoi gosudarstvennoi biblioteki SSSR im. Lenina,* 3 (1934): 185–274;

Vstrechi s proshlym, edited by Natalia V. Volkova (Moscow: Sovetskaia Rossiia, 1978).

Bibliographies:

N. Kashin, "Bibliograficheskii obzor izdanii A. V. Sukhovo-Kobylina i literatury o nem," in Sukhovo-Kobylin's *Trilogiia. Svad'ba Krechinskogo. Delo. Smert' Tarelkina* (Moscow: Gosudarstvennoe izdatel'stvo, 1927), pp. 553–559;

Leonid Petrovich Grossman, "Bibliografiia," in his *Teatr Sukhovo-Kobylina* (Moscow: VTO, 1940), pp. 140–148;

Evgenii Kirillovich Sokolinsky, *A. V. Sukhovo-Kobylin: Bibliograficheskii ukazatel' literatury o zhizni i tvorchestve pisatelia, postanovkakh trilogii* (St. Petersburg: Giperion, 2001).

Biographies:

Dmitrii Dmitrievich Iazykov, *Aleksandr Vasil'evich Sukhovo-Kobylin: Ego zhizn' i literaturnaia deiatel'nost'* (Moscow, 1904);

Leonid Petrovich Grossman, *Prestuplenie Sukhovo-Kobylina* (Leningrad: Priboi, 1928);

Sergei Sergeevich Danilov, *Aleksandr Vasil'evich Sukhovo-Kobylin, 1817–1903* (Leningrad: Iskusstvo, 1949);

Konstantin Lazar'evich Rudnitsky, *A. V. Sukhovo-Kobylina: Ocherk zhizni i tvorchestva* (Moscow: Iskusstvo, 1957);

Isidor Kleiner, *Sud'ba Sukhovo-Kobylina* (Moscow: Nauka, 1969);

Anatolii Gorelov, *Tri sud'by: F. Tiutchev, A. Sukhovo-Kobylin, I. Bunin* (Leningrad: Sovetskii pisatel', 1980): pp. 173–274;

Maia Bessarab, *Sukhovo-Kobylin* (Moscow: Sovremennik, 1981);

Richard Fortune, *Alexander Sukhovo-Kobylin* (Boston: Twayne, 1982);

M. Fekhner, "Aleksandr Vasil'evich Sukhovo-Kobylin," in *Russkie pisateli v Moskve,* compiled by Lidiia Petrovna Bykovtseva (Moscow: Moskovskii rabochii, 1987), pp. 407–420.

References:

Gennadij Yakovlevich Adrianow, "The Importance of Lexical and Socio-Cultural Symbolism in A. V. Sukhovo-Kobylin's Trilogy," dissertation, McGill University, 1976;

Aleksandr Abramovich Anikst, *Teoriia dramy v Rossii ot Pushkina do Chekhova* (Moscow: Nauka, 1972), pp. 631–639;

Iurii Beliaev, "Sukhovo-Kobylin. Delo," in his *Mel'pomena. Sbornik stat'ei* (St. Petersburg: A. S. Suvorin, 1905): 100–115;

Albert Borowitz, *Eternal Suspect: The Tragedy of Alexander Sukhovo-Kobylin* (Kent, Ohio: Kent State University Libraries, 1990);

Nina Brodiansky, "Sukhovo-Kobylin," *Slavonic and East European Review,* 24, no. 63 (June 1946): 110–121;

D. I. Čiževskij, *Gegel' v Rossii* (Paris: Dom Knigi, 1939);

Michael Anthony Curran, "Sukhovo-Kobylin's *Smert' Tarelkina,*" in *Studies Presented to Roman Jakobson by His Students,* edited by Charles Gribble (Cambridge, Mass.: Slavica, 1966);

Curran, "The Theater of Sukhovo-Kobylin and the Tradition of Russian Grotesque Satire," dissertation, Harvard University, 1968;

Vlas Doroshevich, "Delo ob ubiistve Simone- Dimanche," in his *Rasskazy i ocherki* (Moscow: Sovremennik, 1986): 255–260;

Evgenii Mikhailovich Fedoktistov, "Glava iz vospominanii," *Atenei: Istoricheskii-literaturnyi vremennik,* 3 (1929): 110–114;

Feoktistov, *Vospominaniya Za kulisami politiki i literatury, 1848–96* (Leningrad, 1929);

A. A. Golombievsky, "Drama v zhizni pisatelia," *Russkii arkhiv,* 1, no. 2 (1910): 243–290;

Leonid Petrovich Grossman, *Teatr Sukhovo-Kobylina* (Moscow & Leningrad: VTO, 1940);

N. N. Kononov, "Sukhovo-Kobylin i tsarskaia tsenzura," *Uchenye zapiski Riazanskogo pedagogicheskogo instituta,* 4 (1946): 26–36;

Oleg Kudriashov, *Teatr A. V. Sukhovo-Kobylina: Rezhisserskie kommentarii* (Moscow: Sovetskaia Rossiia, 1987);

Nikolai Aleksandrovich Milonov, *Dramaturgiia A. V. Sukhovo-Kobylina* (Tula: Tul'skoe knizhnoe izdatel'stvo, 1956);

Harriet Murav, *Russia's Legal Fictions* (Ann Arbor: University of Michigan Press, 1998);

Stanislav Borisovich Rassadin, *Genii i zlodeistvo, ili, Delo Sukhovo-Kobylina* (Moscow: Kniga, 1989);

A. Rembelinsky, "Iz vospominanii starogo teatrala," *Teatr i iskusstvo,* 5 (1917): 91–93;

P. Rossiev, "A. V. Sukhovo-Kobylin i frantsuzhenka Simone (po povodu stat'i A. A. Golombievskogo 'Drama v zhizni pisatelia')," *Russkii arkhiv,* 2, no. 6 (1910): 316–319;

Konstantin Lazar'evich Rudnitsky, *Meyerhold the Director* (Ann Arbor, Mich.: Ardis, 1981);

Rudnitsky, ed., "Novye materialy o Sukhovo-Kobyline," in *Ezhegodnik Instituta istorii iskusstv. Teatr* (Moscow, 1995);

Iurii Sergeevich Rybakov, *Epokhi i liudi russkoi stseny, 1823–1917* (Moscow: Sovetskaia Rossiia, 1989);

Melissa T. Smith, "A. V. Sukhovo-Kobylin's *Krecinskij's Wedding* on the Russian and Soviet Stage," dissertation, University of Pittsburgh, 1984;

Evgenii Sokolinsky, "Problema groteska v tsenicheskom istolkovanii dramaturgii A. V. Sukhovo Kobylina," dissertation, Leningrad State Institute of Music, Theater, and Cinematography, 1978;

Edmund Wilson, "Who Killed the Frenchwoman?" in his *A Window on Russia: For the Use of Foreign Readers* (New York: Farrar, Straus & Giroux, 1972), pp. 148–160.

Papers:

Aleksandr Vasil'evich Sukhovo-Kobylin's papers can be found in Moscow at the Russian State Archive of Literature and Art (RGALI), fond 438.

Sergei Nikolaevich Terpigorev
(S. Atava)
(12 May 1841 – 13 June 1895)

Kenneth Lantz
University of Toronto

BOOKS: *Oskudenie* (St. Petersburg: F. N. Plotnikov, 1881);

Oskudenie, 2 volumes (St. Petersburg & Moscow: F. N. Plotnikov, 1882)–comprises volume 1, *Ottsy;* and volume 2, *Materi;*

Uzorochnye pestriad', as S. Atava (St. Petersburg & Moscow: F. N. Plotnikov, 1883);

Zheltaia kniga, as Atava (St. Petersburg, 1885);

Zhorzh i Ko., as Atava (St. Petersburg: Ia. I. Liberman, 1888);

Marfin'kino schast'e i drugie povesti, as Atava (St. Petersburg & Moscow: M. O. Vol'f, 1888);

Potrevozhennye teni, as Atava, 2 volumes (St. Petersburg: I. N. Skorokhodov, 1888, 1890);

Istoricheskie rasskazy i vospominaniia (St. Petersburg: I. Gol'dberg, 1890);

Rasskazy (St. Petersburg: A. S. Suvorin, 1890);

Dve povesti (St. Petersburg: Rodina, 1891)–comprises "Bez vozdukha" and "Na starom gnezde";

Dorozhnye ocherki (St. Petersburg: D. A. Naumov, 1897)–comprises "V strane fontanov i kolpakov," "S dorogi," and "Po tikhomu Donu";

Sobranie sochinenii, 6 volumes, edited by S. N. Shubinsky, with an introduction by Petr Vasil'evich Bykov (St. Petersburg: A. F. Marks, 1899).

Editions and Collections: *Oskudenie: Ocherki, zametki i razmyshleniia tambovskogo pomeshchika,* 2 volumes, with an introduction and commentary by N. I. Sokolov (Moscow: Goslitizdat, 1958);

Potrevozhennye teni, edited, with a commentary, by Sokolov and N. I. Totubalin (Moscow & Leningrad: Goslitizdat, 1959);

Potrevozhennye teni, with an introduction and commentary by Iu. L. Boldyrev (Moscow, 1988);

S prostym vzgliadom, edited, with a commentary, by A. A. Shelaeva (Moscow, 1990).

SELECTED PERIODICAL PUBLICATIONS–
UNCOLLECTED: "Otryvok iz vospominanii," *Istoricheskii vestnik,* 39 (1890): 513–536;

Sergei Nikolaevich Terpigorev

"Vospominaniia," *Istoricheskii vestnik,* 63 (1896): 50–65, 401–424, 784–807; 64 (1896): 46–77, 425–454.

Sergei Terpigorev (better known in his lifetime by his nom de plume, S. Atava) has a place in literature as a chronicler of the way of life of the landed gentry and more specifically of the decline of that class in the years following the emancipation of the serfs in 1861. His literary renown came relatively late in life, however, and only after he had established himself as an investigative journalist specializing in sarcastic and humorous exposés of wrongdoing in Russia's provinces. He was nearly forty before he produced his best-known literary work, a collection of sketches titled *Oskudenie* (Impoverishment, 1881). These were fictional vignettes, closely based on fact, of the misfortunes and misadventures of landowners trying but failing to cope with the new economic and social realities that prevailed in the years after major reforms in 1860s Russia. *Oskudenie* was enormously popular in its day, and it has held its value both as a work of literature and as a document of social history. Terpigorev also produced stories and sketches of life in the countryside before the peasant emancipation, as well as some stories about urban life.

Sergei Nikolaevich Terpigorev was born on 12 May 1841 into an old landowning family in the province of Tambov, some three hundred miles southeast of Moscow. His father, Nikolai Nikolaevich Terpigorev, had served for a time in the Ministry of Education. By the standards of his day the elder Terpigorev was well educated, a man of enlightenment who had assembled a good library and who tried to keep abreast of current intellectual issues. Terpigorev's mother, Varvara Ivanovna (née Rakhmaninova) Terpigoreva, had little education, although her goodness and patience had a strong moral influence on her son. The family had fallen on hard times, and the boy was raised on a modest estate in Tambov province, a property of some three hundred acres with a small, decrepit house and thirty serfs, all of which had been purchased with what remained of the family's funds after their debts had been paid. Although his father treated his own serfs humanely, the young Terpigorev witnessed many instances of the brutality of the more typical landowners toward their peasants, and these impressions were later reflected in his writings.

Like virtually all children of his background, Terpigorev was first educated at home and then in boarding school. Although his father took pains to instill in his son his own humane values and love of learning, Terpigorev's home education remained rather haphazard: his father set great store on knowledge of languages and enlisted a Frenchman and a German to tutor his son; but when it came time for the boy to be sent off to school, he was found to be utterly ignorant of basic arithmetic. After some intensive tutoring he was accepted into the third-year class at the Tambov boarding school. He later recalled his school days, and particularly the close friendships he developed there, rather fondly. As he notes in his memoirs, "Otryvok iz vospominanii" (Fragment from Recollections, 1890) and

"Vospominaniia" (Recollections, 1896), however, what preserved him and his schoolmates from scholarly drudgery was the unsystematic pedagogy of the school, which left them enough freedom to learn in their own fashion: "The school itself gave us absolutely nothing, either by way of scholarship or through its official morality. I can imagine the sort of people we would have become and how we might have ended had we taken our teachers as models of virtue and had we listened to the inspector–later, our principal–Bernhard, and had we read only the textbooks from which our teachers taught and then examined us without themselves knowing even those textbooks." Terpigorev goes on to describe Bernhard as a notorious and shameless bribe-taker.

Two exceptions among this group of uninspiring and incompetent pedagogues were the teachers of history and of Russian language, who managed to awaken the students' interest in their subjects and who set personal examples of probity and love for learning. These two encouraged Terpigorev's interest in writing, and during his school years he produced his first literary work. This work was an *ocherk* (sketch), based on his own childhood impressions, of a young peasant woman whose sad lot in life eventually drives her to suicide; a few years later it became his first publication. Most influential in Terpigorev's education, though, was not his teachers but the circle of his friends who, particularly during his last years of schooling, gathered to read and discuss the latest works of Russian literature, criticism, and history.

Terpigorev entered St. Petersburg University in 1860, a time when Russia was about to embark on a period of great reforms that later left the country–and the university as well–fundamentally altered. He intended to study in the Faculty of Philology, where he could devote himself to literature and history, the two subjects in which he had a passionate interest, with the ultimate aim of becoming a professor. On arriving in the city he sought the counsel and support of his maternal uncle, Fedor Ivanovich Rakhmaninov, who was a censor responsible for several newspapers and literary magazines. Rakhmaninov, guided more by a sense of practicality than by his nephew's interests and abilities, persuaded him to enter the Faculty of Law; he reasoned that the great legal reform then imminent would create a demand for people with legal training. Still, Terpigorev's interests remained clearly in literature and journalism, and his uncle's many contacts with writers, critics, and publishers were instrumental in establishing his career. Rakhmaninov was the censor for *Sovremennik* (The Contemporary), the leading radical journal of the day, and it was through him that Terpigorev met the leading figures of *Sovremennik*, which included Ivan Ivanovich

Panaev, Nikolai Alekseevich Nekrasov, and Nikolai Gavrilovich Chernyshevsky.

Terpigorev's student years took place during the golden age of Russian periodicals. After decades of operating under tight government restrictions, the press took advantage of the easing of censorship after the death of Tsar Nicholas I in 1855 to engage in an earnest discussion of issues, which had been taboo only a few years before. The press suddenly acquired an unprecedented influence both in reflecting and shaping public opinion. Readers were caught up by the prevailing mood of reform and were eager to learn of the failings of the old regime, now apparently breathing its last; publishers were delighted to respond to this demand, and journalistic muckraking became the norm.

Terpigorev, who lived with his uncle, was close to the center of this literary and journalistic world. He continued to write while in his first year at university and even began a novel that he tried unsuccessfully to publish. He did have the sketch he had written in school, however, now titled "Cherstvaia dolia" (A Hard Lot); it appeared in the newspaper *Russkii mir* (The Russian World) in late 1861. That newspaper and its satirical supplement *Gudok* (The Whistle) became Terpigorev's first literary home. *Gudok* in particular was eager to publish accounts of scandals and misdeeds in the provinces, and Terpigorev soon became its specialist in exposés from Tambov province, where several school friends were happy to supply him with raw material. His greatest coup was a series of witty and sarcastic articles on the corruption of the governor of Tambov province, Konstantin Karlovich Danzas. These revelations caused an uproar in Tambov; Terpigorev now became both infamous for some and celebrated by others in his home province.

In the autumn of 1861, returning to St. Petersburg after spending the summer in his home province, Terpigorev stopped in Moscow to look up school friends who had entered Moscow University, and only here did he learn that St. Petersburg University had been closed because of student disorders. During the previous year the students had successfully challenged some of the more stringent and archaic regulations instituted by the university administration, and they had managed to win a substantial degree of control over their own affairs. Students had quickly become radicalized, however, and the efforts of some student groups to expand their concerns from academic to political matters alarmed the government. In the fall of 1861 new restrictive regulations were instituted for universities. Student protests in St. Petersburg multiplied until the Minister of Education closed the university for a full year. Terpigorev had not been involved in student movements previously, but on his return to the university he made an effort to acquaint himself with student opinion and student leaders, meeting the students in their homes and at assemblies, in an attempt to understand their movement. Yet, as he recalls in his memoirs, "there was nothing much to understand; it was simply another manifestation of that same spirit that had gripped and invaded a whole society—a society that had undergone the experience of slave owning, had lost faith in it, but, in the end, had become corrupted by it and by its own slavish mentality."

The situation in the university had become so polarized that Terpigorev realized he could continue as a student only if he were to choose sides. He found himself unable to join the student movement, since he respected neither its aims nor its leaders; neither was he willing to ally himself, however, with the defenders of the existing order, whose ways he found pedantic and bureaucratic. The ultimatum of the university administration was that only those who accepted the new regulations would be considered students; the remainder would be expelled. After a good deal of agonizing thought, Terpigorev sent the university his letter of withdrawal. No longer of student status, he was summoned by the police and informed that he must leave St. Petersburg within three days. This sentence was softened somewhat after his uncle interceded with the police; in addition, doctor's notes and guarantees from various influential people enabled Terpigorev to prolong his stay in St. Petersburg until the spring. Shortly before his departure, his tale "Iz zapisok neudavshegosia chinovnika" (From the Notes of an Unsuccessful Civil Servant, 1863) was accepted for publication in the radical journal *Russkoe slovo* (The Russian Word). With his dream of an academic career shattered, he left the capital deeply disillusioned.

Terpigorev returned from the university to spend the summer of 1862—the first after the enactment of the emancipation edict—in the country. He now had no occupation and no idea of what career to undertake. His observations of local landowners, who were trying to reestablish their estates on paid rather than serf labor, led him to conclude that the life of a country squire offered few prospects. He recalls in his memoirs that in the mid 1860s, living on his family's estate, he would spend hours wandering the countryside with his dog and a gun, not so much hunting as simply escaping from the constant lamentations of his own family and their neighbors over the sad state of their affairs caused by the emancipation. Writing had not entirely lost its appeal for him. *Russkii mir,* and with it *Gudok,* had ceased publication at the end of 1862. Terpigorev nonetheless maintained a connection with the enterprising St. Petersburg publisher Andrei Aleksandrovich Kraevsky, who liked his work and urged him to contribute to his newspapers *Sankt-Peterburgskie vedomosti* (The St. Petersburg

News)—also censored by Terpigorev's uncle—and *Golos* (The Voice). Terpigorev began sending items of local news and sketches of local people to *Golos*. In these *ocherki* he applied his particular talent for giving a humorous or satirical twist to accounts of local malfeasance. Such was the power—or at least the perception of power—of the press that many of Terpigorev's neighbors began to regard him as a dangerous person whose role was to inform the St. Petersburg press of their doings. As he told his friend, the writer and bibliographer Petr Vasil'evich Bykov, "I was thrilled that I, a man entirely without means and without position . . . could still be a power of sorts, a power that aroused implacable hatred in those whom I considered vulgar and the keenest, most ardent support and even gratitude in others toward whom I was more inclined."

Soon Terpigorev stumbled on the most important story of his career at this stage. A serious famine had broken out in another province, and the Tambov landowners and merchants joined others across Russia in coming to the aid of the victims. Tambov province was a major grain-growing area, and a sizable amount of grain and flour had been collected in the town of Kozlov (later renamed Michurinsk), located on a newly built railway line. On a visit to the town, Terpigorev was astonished to see an enormous pile of grain as tall as a house; but the grain was simply lying in the open, exposed to the elements, and was already covered in green shoots. He learned that the operators of the railway line, who had received a huge subsidy to construct it, were enhancing their profit by charging an extra commission for shipping grain. Local landowners had little choice but to pay the extra costs for shipping their own produce, but no one had been authorized to pay the commission on the grain for the famine victims. As a result, approximately five thousand tons of grain were spoiling. Terpigorev sent off a stinging account of this affair, attacking the railway concessionaires and accusing them of extortion. Kraevsky immediately published it, accompanied by an angry editorial of his own. The story created a furor when it appeared in *Golos*, and a commission was sent from St. Petersburg to investigate.

Shortly thereafter Kraevsky summoned Terpigorev to St. Petersburg: the operators of the railway line had engaged a leading lawyer, Vladimir Danilovich Spasovich, to sue *Golos* for defamation of character. As publisher, Kraevsky bore the responsibility for what appeared in his newspaper. Without documentary evidence to back up his charges, he stood a good chance of being sent to jail. Terpigorev was sent back to Kozlov but was unable to come up with any documents to prove malfeasance on the part of the railway magnates. The town inhabitants, however, had been delighted with Terpigorev's article and easily persuaded the town

council to compose an official declaration, on behalf of the whole community, thanking Terpigorev for his exposé and attesting that everything in it was absolutely true. When this document was dramatically presented to the court, Spasovich's case collapsed. Kraevsky was not fully acquitted, but he was given a relatively light punishment because of one particularly harsh statement in the published article. Terpigorev notes that the effect of his article on the Kozlov grain scandal convinced him of the power of the printed word. Moreover, the experience motivated him to abandon the lazy, aimless life he had been leading on the family estate. After the trial Kraevsky offered him regular work on *Golos*, and in 1867 Terpigorev returned to St. Petersburg.

Terpigorev contributed several journalistic pieces to *Golos*, and a whole series of feuilletons to the daily *Birzhevye vedomosti* (Stock Exchange News). In 1869–1870 he published two items in one of the leading literary monthlies of the era, the Populist journal *Otechestvennye zapiski* (Notes of the Fatherland). The first of these, a sketch titled "V stepi" (In the Steppe), anticipates Terpigorev's chronicle of the decline of the landowning gentry, *Oskudenie* (Impoverishment), a collection that appeared in print only a decade later. The second work, a comedy titled *Sliianie* (Merging), chronicles the attempts of provincial landowners to come to terms with the emancipation, in this case by trying to "merge" with the peasantry. Both items were signed with the author's new pseudonym, S. Atava (the Russian word *atava* denotes the new grass shoots that in springtime grow out from under the grass cover of the previous year).

Despite his fresh and promising start in belles lettres, Terpigorev virtually disappeared from literature during the 1870s. For ten years he published nothing apart from a few feuilletons in newspapers. Extremely little is known about this period, but he apparently decided that a life as an entrepreneur offered a better income and more security than the uncertainties of writing for a living. He became, among other things, a horse trader—an occupation in which he had much expertise—and a participant in an enterprise that was pioneering the commercial use of electricity. He apparently made a good deal of money in this latter pursuit, then lost it all when he became a contractor supplying firewood. At the end of the decade he returned to literature.

Both the poet and publisher Nekrasov, whom Terpigorev had first met in his student days, and the satirist Mikhail Evgrafovich Saltykov had a high regard for Terpigorev's talent, and they convinced him to return to their journal *Otechestvennye zapiski*. Each of its first eleven issues in 1880 carried one of his sketches under the title *Oskudenie*, subtitled "Ocherki, zametki i razmyshelniia tambovskogo pomeshchika" (The Sketches, Notes, and Reflections of a Tambov Landowner). These are works of fiction but of a fiction rather close to fact: the raw material comes from Terpigorev's own experience in Tambov province or that of his family, friends, and neighbors. From their first appearance the sketches roused great attention and provoked some lively debate; the work as a whole became his best known. The wit, sarcasm, and satirical jibes of Terpigorev's work as Atava led some readers to conclude that they were the products of Saltykov, then the leading satirist in Russia. The great success of this collection is explained not only by the engaging sketches that it comprises but also by its timeliness: Terpigorev's work provided vivid illustrations of the fate of the landowning gentry in Russia—an extremely topical issue in the early 1880s. Many landowners by this time were reacting to the emancipation, arguing that it had served little more than to bankrupt a whole class—one whose members had been able stewards of agricultural resources and capable managers within a patriarchal system of land use that had served Russia well. Terpigorev's sketches clearly demonstrate that such was not the case. As quoted in "S. N. Terpigorev (Sergei Atava)" (from *Istoricheskii vestnik* [The Historical Messenger], 1895), he told his friend Konstantin Petrovich Medvedsky, the poet and critic, "The peasants plowed, the merchants traded, the clergy prayed. And what did the landowners do? They took up any sort of activity or amusement you can imagine—government service, hunting, literature, love affairs; the only thing they didn't do is what they should have done."

Terpigorev writes of landowners who were totally unprepared for the enormous changes brought about by the emancipation of the serfs. After quickly running through the redemption payments made for land they had transferred to peasants, they had gradually become impoverished. Having lived for generations insulated by the work of their peasant serfs from many of the realities of earning a living, they found the prospect of supporting themselves truly daunting. Many were forced to cut down and sell their forests; others mortgaged their estates and then lost them because they were unable to pay the interest charges. Some of the more enterprising tried to modernize and "rationalize" their agriculture by investing in new machinery, but such attempts most often merely hastened the coming of bankruptcy. Others abandoned the land and placed their faith in profits to be reaped from railway concessions; typically, as Terpigorev shows, such landowner-entrepreneurs lacked even basic business acumen and bankrupted themselves along with their investors. In one way or another, most fell victim to the new class of ruthless businessmen.

Encouraged by the success of his 1880 sketches among readers of *Otechestvennye zapiski,* Terpigorev decided to publish them (as *Oskudenie*) in a single volume in 1881; this book sold quickly, and a second,

two-volume edition of the same title followed in 1882. Through the early 1880s his sketches and stories appeared in almost all of the most popular journals and newspapers of the time. Despite his success in *Otechestvennye zapiski,* Terpigorev did not stay with the journal for long. In 1881 Saltykov gave him a warm recommendation as a columnist to Mikhail Matveevich Stasiulevich, who was looking for contributors to his new liberal newspaper *Poriadok* (Order); Saltykov even offered to edit and supervise his protégé's contributions. Terpigorev did contribute some ten feuilletons and then abruptly shifted his allegiance to a newspaper that was Saltykov's ideological archenemy, Aleksei Sergeevich Suvorin's conservative and nationalistic *Novoe vremia* (New Times). The sudden turnabout created a sizeable literary scandal. Saltykov in particular was outraged; he saw Terpigorev's move as an ideological betrayal by a writer whose career he had fostered. Terpigorev, however, was not an ideological writer, and his articles in *Novoe vremia* lean no more toward the conservative nationalism of its publisher than his earlier contributions to leftist publications espoused specifically radical views. His regular Sunday feuilletons were highly popular, and *Novoe vremia* remained his primary literary home for the rest of his life.

During his six years with the newspaper, he published more than six hundred articles and sketches. He was also a frequent contributor to the newspaper *Peterburgskaia gazeta* (Petersburg Gazette) and the monthly *Istoricheskii vestnik* (Historical Messenger). He published another two-volume collection of stories and sketches of landowners as well; it appeared under the title *Potrevozhennye teni* (Phantoms Disturbed, 1888–1890). In this work Terpigorev examines the landowners' way of life in preemancipation days, focusing on their relations to their peasant serfs. He conveys the brutal reality of serfdom, and the mood of the book is far from nostalgic. Several other collections of his writings appeared in the late 1880s. In the last years of his life Terpigorev wrote several short stories and tales in which he abandoned rural life to look at the dispossessed class of St. Petersburg. For example, in works such as "Aver'ian Mikheev i ego zhil'tsy" (Aver'an Mikheev and His Tenants, 1892) and "Kniaz' Ivan" (Prince Ivan, 1894), he sympathetically depicts the tenants of cheap rooming houses in St. Petersburg's slums.

Terpigorev's sudden literary fame never turned his head; in fact, he was overly modest about his talent. As he acknowledged in the preface to the second edition of his *Oskudenie:* "I am, to a certain extent, a literate and observant person, and nothing more. . . . I simply tell of what I have seen." Terpigorev's friends and colleagues are consistent in describing him as affable and sociable. His friend, the writer and journalist Sigizmund Feliksovich Librovich, says of him: "He was an uncommonly jolly, witty and cheerful man, full of *joie de vivre,* a jester and raconteur; his arrival itself was enough to put any gathering into a happy mood." Another friend, the poet and critic Leonid Egorovich Obolensky, sums up the writer's character in much the same way, seeing him as a quintessential Russian landowner who loved eating, drinking, hunting, and entertaining a crowd of guests for whom nothing could be too good.

In the early 1880s Terpigorev had settled in a cottage in Novaia Derevnia on the banks of the Neva River, not far from the center of St. Petersburg. Here he managed to set up a miniature country estate with gardens and an orchard; here, too, he indulged in another passion, the breeding of hunting dogs. His friends from the literary world were regularly invited to partake of elaborate dinners. Terpigorev himself was a great lover of food, and even after doctors had placed him on a strict diet he still enjoyed seeing his friends eat. The writer Nikolai Semenovich Leskov was a close friend and frequent guest. Terpigorev's friend, the writer and journalist Ieronim Ieronimovich Iasinsky (pseudonym Maksim Belinsky), recalls that the author's last words–uttered as he looked out into his garden on the fine morning of 13 June 1895, when he died of heart failure–were: "Ah, how lovely it is!"

Sergei Nikolaevich Terpigorev can claim an honorable if modest place in nineteenth-century Russian literature. He had a genuine gift as a storyteller, and even his works that are closely based on factual events are narrated with humor and verve; his characters, including those modeled on real-life contemporaries, are conveyed with the psychological depth and balance of a perceptive artist. Although his six-volume *Sobranie sochinenii* (Collected Works) appeared in 1899, four years after he died, Terpigorev's writings–with their focus on life in the old regime in Russia–fell out of favor several years later, after the 1917 Revolution and during the Stalin era; his works were referred to only occasionally as illustrations of the evils of serfdom. After the post-Stalin "thaw" of the mid 1950s, however, his major collections of sketches were republished several times. They continue to attract Russian readers for their vivid, if somewhat jaundiced, view of the postreform era in Russia and as appealing works of art.

Letters:

Letter to the Editor, *Novoe vremia,* 14 September 1889, p. 3;

To N. S. Leskov, Anatoly Ivanovich Faresov, *Protiv techenii* (St. Petersburg: M. Merkusheva, 1904), pp. 203–204;

To M. E. Saltykov, *Polnoe sobranie sochinenii,* compiled by Saltykov, volume 19 (Moscow: Khudozhestvennaia literatura, 1939), p. 432;

To A. P. Chekhov, *Arkhiv A. P. Chekhova,* volume 2 (Moscow: Gosudarstvennoe Sotsial'no-ekonomicheskoe izdatel'stvo, 1939–1941), p. 66;

To N. A. Nekrasov, Vladislav Evgen'evich Evgen'ev-Maksimov, *Literaturnoe nasledstvo,* 51–52 (1949): 522–523.

Biographies:

Petr Vasil'evich Bykov, "S. N. Terpigorev: Biograficheskii ocherk," in Terpigorev's *Sobranie sochinenii,* volume 1 (St. Petersburg: A. F. Marks, 1899), pp. v–xxxii;

Dobrinka: Sergei Nikolaevich Terpigorev: 150 let so dnia rozhdeniia, edited by Boris Mikhailovich Shal'nev (Lipetsk: Edinenie, 1991);

Galina Trofimovna Andreeva, *S. N. Terpigorev (Atava): Ocherk zhizni i tvorchestva* (Irkutsk: Izdatel'stvo Irkutskogo universiteta, 1995).

References:

Galina Trofimovna Andreeva, "Fel'etony S. N. Terpigoreva (Atavy) v gazete *Telegraf,*" *Voprosy filologii,* 4 (1974): 140–145;

Andreeva, "Tvorchestvo S. N. Terpigoreva 1860–1870-kh gg.," *Vestnik Leningradskogo gosudarstvennogo universiteta,* 20 (1974);

L. I. Giul'mamedova, *Tvorchestvo Terpigoreva* (Baku, 1972);

I. I. Iasinsky, "Iz vospominanii o S. N. Terpigoreve," *Istoricheskii vestnik,* 102 (1905): 82–97;

Iasinsky, "Neskol'ko slov o S. N. Terpigoreve," *Istoricheskii vestnik,* 61 (1895): 443–445;

Sigizmund Feliksovich Librovich, "'Velikii Mavrikii' i 'Smirennyi Sergei'," in his *Na knizhnom postu: Vospominaniia, zapiski, dokumenty* (Petrograd & Moscow: M. O. Vol'f, 1916), pp. 101–111;

Konstantin Petrovich Medvedsky, "S. N. Terpigorev (Sergei Atava)," *Istoricheskii vestnik,* 61 (1895): 429–442;

Leonid Egorovich Obolensky, "Literaturnye vospominaniia i kharakteristiki," *Istoricheskii vestnik,* 87 (1902): 898–901.

Papers:

Sergei Nikolaevich Terpigorev's papers are held in St. Petersburg at the Institute of Russian Literature (IRLI, Pushkin House), fond 308, and in Moscow at the Russian State Archive of Literature and Art (RGALI), fond 1173.

Gleb Ivanovich Uspensky

(13 October 1843 – 24 March 1902)

Henrietta Mondry
University of Canterbury

BOOKS: *Ocherki i rasskazy* (St. Petersburg: Kukol'-Iasnopol'sky, 1866)—includes "Nravy Rasteriaevoi ulitsy";

V budni i prazdnik. Moskovskie nravy (St. Petersburg: V. E. Genkel', 1867);

Ocherki i rasskazy (St. Petersburg: A. F. Bazunov, 1871);

Razoren'e. Nabliudeniia Mikhaila Ivanovicha. Povest' (St. Petersburg: Biblioteka sovremennykh pisatelei, 1872);

Lentiai, ego vospominaniia, nabliudeniia i zametki.—Pro odnu starukhu (St. Petersburg: A. F. Bazunov, 1873);

Glush'. Provintsial'nye i slolichnye ocherki (St. Petersburg: N. Skaratin, 1875);

Iz starogo i novogo. Otryvki, ocherki, nabroski (St. Petersburg: A. S. Suvorin, 1879);

Iz pamiatnoi knizhki. Ocherki i rasskazy (St. Petersburg: B. G. Iasnopol'sky, 1879);

Liudi i nravy sovremennoi derevni. (Iz derevenskogo dnevnika), 2 parts (Moscow: L. F. Snegirev & M. N. Marakuev, 1879, 1880);

Derevenskaia neuriaditsa, 3 volumes (St. Petersburg: E. Gart'e, 1881–1882)—includes "Krest'ianin i krest'ianskii trud";

Vlast' zemli. Ocherki i otryvki iz pamiatnoi knizhki (Moscow: I. N. Kushnerev, 1882)—includes "Vlast' zemli";

Sochineniia, 8 volumes (St. Petersburg: F. F. Pavlenkov, 1883–1886; enlarged, 1889–1891)—includes volume 2, *Razoren'e* (1883);

Chetyre rasskaza (Moscow: I. D. Sytin, 1893);

Polnoe sobranie sochinenii, 12 volumes (Kiev: B. K. Fuks, 1903–1904);

Polnoe sobranie sochinenii, 14 volumes (Moscow & Leningrad: AN SSSR, 1940–1954).

Editions and Collections: *Nravy Rasteriaevoi ulitsy* (St. Petersburg: A. F. Bazunov, 1872);

Sochineniia, 3 volumes, with an introduction by N. Mikhailovsky (St. Petersburg: F. F. Pavlenkov, 1889–1891);

Polnoe sobranie sochinenii, 6 volumes (St. Petersburg: A. F. Marks, 1908);

Gleb Ivanovich Uspensky

Izbrannye proizvedeniia, edited by A. S. Glinka-Volzhsky (Moscow: Khudozhestvennaia literatura, 1935; Moscow, 1938);

Izbrannye sochineniia, with an introduction by V. P. Druzin and commentary by B. G. Uspensky and M. I. Dikman (Moscow & Leningrad: Goslitizdat, 1949);

Sobranie sochinenii, 9 volumes, with an introduction by V. P. Druzin and N. I. Sokolov (Moscow: Goslitizdat, 1955–1957);

Sochineniia, 2 volumes, edited by N. N. Atanesian (Moscow: Khudozhestvennaia literatura, 1988);

Sobranie sochinenii, edited by T. Aver'ianova, with an introduction by B. Dykhanova (Moscow: Khudozhestvennaia literatura, 1990).

Editions in English: "The Steam Chicken" and "A Trifling Defect," in *The Humor of Russia,* edited by E. L. Voynich (London: Scott, 1895);

"The Power of the Land" (excerpt), in *Anthology of Russian Literature,* edited by Leo Wiener, volume 2 (New York: Putnam, 1903), pp. 408–417;

"Concerning One Old Woman," *Monthly Review,* 17 (1904): 106–122.

Gleb Uspensky was highly politicized during the Soviet era as Vladimir Lenin's favorite *narodnik* (Populist), but in the West and in post-Soviet Russia he is one of the most neglected and least studied nineteenth-century Russian Realist writers. During the 1880s, at the height of the *narodnichestvo* (Populism) movement, Uspensky was immensely popular with truth-seeking youths who found an honest and authentic perception of Russian peasant life in his *ocherki* (sketches). Professional revolutionaries, however, such as Petr Nikitich Tkachev, reproached Uspensky for his lack of stable paradigms and character types. Such revolutionaries criticized his evasive and ever-changing attitude toward peasants. Maksim Gor'ky labeled Uspensky a "hysterical Realist." This categorization reflects a nineteenth-century Russian bias against any indication of infirmity. Uspensky's psychological instability, linked to his clinical schizophrenia, made him unstable; his approach to life was, however, an unbiased one. Today his works retain historical value as documents of ethnological and sociological material, interspersed with the author's impressions and reflections of his own emotional responses to human suffering. This subjective-objective historicity deserves particular interest from contemporary readers.

Uspensky searched for authenticity, believing that there is more than one truth. In his nuanced understanding of human subjectivity, he was significantly ahead of his time. He was one of the first Russian male writers to address gender issues, including physiological and psychological stereotypes of the masculine and feminine. He was also skeptical of ethnic prejudices and expressed this skepticism in his ethnographic travel sketches. Uspensky's writing displays his understanding of the pursuit of various minority cultures for the self-preservation and free expression of their cultural, ethnic, and religious identities. His perceptiveness with regard to the needs of varying cultures is anomalous in nineteenth-century literature and still awaits critical evaluation. Attacks of depression punctuated Uspensky's life and silenced him in his final decade, which he spent incarcerated in mental institutions. His fragmentation of the self is reflected in his writings composed in the 1870s or later, most of which are loosely structured and unfinished. He is best approached for analysis as a publicist rather than a writer of fiction, and his best work is found among his travel notes and impressions.

Gleb Ivanovich Uspensky was born on 13 October 1843 in Tula, where his family was part of the well-established community of officials. Uspensky's father, Ivan Iakovlevich Uspensky, was a member of the clergy; his mother was Nadezhda Glebovna (Sokolova) Uspenskaia. Uspensky's family was extremely loving toward him and introduced him to Russian literature through the works of the great poet Aleksandr Sergeevich Pushkin. In his autobiographical pieces, however, Uspensky claims that he was exposed to government corruption from early childhood and thus became sensitive to the social ills that he saw around him. He witnessed the exchanging of gifts and the acceptance of bribes by members of his own family as well as those of their circle. In addition to encountering the injustices prevalent in peasant life–including the exploitation of illiterate peasants for the purpose of army recruitment–Uspensky also observed prison life on a daily basis. At the end of the street where the Uspensky family lived was a jail. As a boy, Uspensky often watched prisoners marching up his street; sometimes the prisoners were condemned and on their way to execution.

Uspensky's relatives thought he was an impressionable, sensitive child who cared deeply for the poor. According to a family legend still told today, he gave his shirt away to beggars when he was a child. He spent his secondary-school years in Chernigov, to which his family had moved in 1856. As a well-read, perceptive boy, Uspensky knew the works of Alexander Herzen (Aleksandr Ivanovich Gertsen), Vissarion Grigor'evich Belinsky, Nikolai Gavrilovich Chernyshevsky, and Nikolai Aleksandrovich Dobroliubov. These writers and publicists all promoted the development of political awareness in Russian youth of the period, and their writings assisted the rise of a generation of Populists. The writer Nikolai Vasil'evich Uspensky, a cousin, encouraged the young Uspensky's interest in literature. Nikolai Uspensky was a contributor to the democratic journal *Sovremennik* (The Contemporary) and so directed his cousin's literary taste in a similar direction.

Uspensky graduated from the Chernigov secondary school in 1861 and entered St. Petersburg University in the same year. Interested in justice, he enrolled as a law student. His student life was brief: he was expelled from the university in the year of his admittance for his involvement in student unrest. Uspensky then enrolled at Moscow University. He had to interrupt his studies, however, in 1862 because of unexpected financial difficulties resulting from his father's sudden illness. Ivan Iakovlevich's death in 1864 left the burden of supporting his large family to Uspensky.

Uspensky soon gained an income from the publication of his literary sketches. Leo Tolstoy published his first work, "Mikhailych" (1862), in his journal *Iasnaia poliana* (Bright Meadow). Nikolai Alekseevich Nekrasov noted his work and invited him to contribute pieces of writing to *Sovremennik,* the most radical democratic publication circulating in the 1860s. Under Nekrasov's editorship, *Sovremennik* helped established the reputations of Chernyshevsky, Dobroliubov, and Dmitrii Ivanovich Pisarev as leaders of the revolutionary intelligentsia. The first four chapters of Uspensky's renowned work *Nravy Rasteriaevoi ulitsy* (The Manners of Rasteriaev Street, 1872) were published in *Sovremennik* in 1866. As the title of this

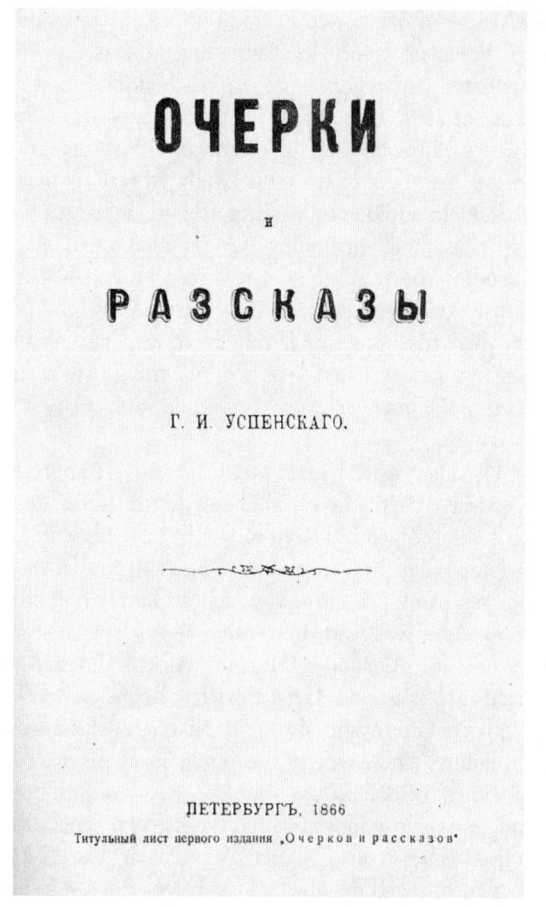

Title page for Uspensky's first book, Ocherki i rasskazy *(Sketches and Stories), which includes the first four chapters of his novel* Nravy Rasteriaevoi ulitsy *(The Manners of Rasteriaev Street), published in 1872 (from* Aleksandr Sergeevich Glinka, Gleb Uspensky v zhizni, *1935)*

work suggests, Uspensky followed in the tradition of the *natural'naia shkola* (natural school) by dissecting the morals and everyday behavior of the Russian middle classes. In *Nravy Rasteriaevoi ulitsy* not only the characters—the inhabitants of Rasteriaev Street—but also the street itself acquires the status of a typological model of the life of Russian provincial towns. The author is concerned both with the low social and economic conditions of the inhabitants of the street and with their low moral and spiritual level. Uspensky links economic disintegration with disintegration of the minds and souls of provincial Russians.

The publication of *Sovremennik* was suspended in 1866 by the authorities, and Uspensky was forced to look for a more stable means of income. In 1867 he decided to sit for professional examinations to qualify as a teacher of Russian language and literature in the rural districts. He successfully passed these exams and took a teaching position at the school in Epifan, a town situated in the province of Tula. A couple of months later he resigned from the position because he found

the atmosphere in the province intolerable. Shortly afterward he accepted a job as clerk to the public prosecutor, Prince Aleksandr Ivanovich Urusov, in Moscow; however, he remained in this position for less than one year.

Uspensky's second important work, *Razoren'e. Nabliudeniia Mikhaila Ivanovicha. Povest'* (Ruin. The Observations of Mikhail Ivanovich. A Novella, 1872), first appeared as "Razoren'e" (Ruin, 1869–1871) in *Otechestvennye zapiski* (Notes of the Fatherland), which had recently reopened; Uspensky also included this work in a trilogy of the same title, *Razoren'e,* in 1883. The theme of the trilogy is the decline of the class of people whose business is founded on their oppression of peasants. The social and economic changes following the abolition of serfdom have brought about the oppressors' financial decline. Uspensky examines the crisis facing those who hold onto the old views and the collapse of family relations and social conventions.

In 1870 Uspensky married Aleksandra Vasil'evna Baraeva. She herself had literary interests and, knowing French well, worked on translations from French into Russian. Although their marriage was happy, it was overshadowed by constant economic worries. The couple had five children.

Uspensky toured Europe in 1872 and from 1875 to 1876. He considered these tours a major watershed in his life and career. He arrived in Paris several months after the fall of the Paris Commune had occurred, and the events that he saw firsthand made a huge impression on him. His recollection of the executions that had taken place in close proximity to his family home during his childhood—and the effect they had on him—were deepened when he witnessed the executions of the Communards. Uspensky met with the exiled leader of the revolutionary *narodniki,* Petr Lavrovich Lavrov, in London. In Uspensky's later writings London exemplifies a capitalist city rife with outrageous social and economic injustices. While visiting London, Uspensky decided to live his life as a *narodnik* and to dedicate himself to the cause of the movement.

Narodnichestvo reached its peak from 1874 to 1875, when *raznochintsy* (non-noble intellectuals) went to the countryside–this movement was called "khozhdenie v narod" (going to the people)–to spread the idea of socialism in hopes of organizing a peasant revolt. Uspensky was drawn to the ideas maintained by Lavrov and other theoreticians of *narodnichestvo.* Like Herzen, Lavrov believed that the future of Russia lay in the hands of Russian peasants. He developed this idea further by arguing that Russia could bypass the capitalist stage of social development; a peasant revolution occurring "in one stroke" would rid Russia of serfdom and the bourgeois system. Such an event would enable Russians to embark on the road to socialism. A mood of disappointment arose after the young educated members of the *raznochintsy* "went to the people," only to discover that the peasants were interested in obtaining land rather than socialist ideals. Uspensky's concept of *vlast' zemli* (the power of the soil) comes from this moment of disappointment and realization. This expression is also the title of one of Uspensky's most important cycles of *ocherki*, "Vlast' zemli" (*Otechestvennye zapiski*, 1882; excerpt translated as "The Power of the Land," 1903).

Uspensky "went to the people" in the summer of 1877. He stayed in the Valdaika junction in the province of Novgorod. Then, from March 1878 until the summer of 1879, he lived in a village near Samara and worked as a clerk in a bank. He was able to buy a small house for his family in Siabrinitsy, situated in Samara province, in 1881. Uspensky's choice of location was influenced by his links with the Populist terrorist organization Zemlia i volia (Land and Liberty). In 1879 an ideological split resulted in the emergence of two separate factions within the organization: Narodnaia volia (The People's Will) and Chernyi peredel (Black Partition). Narodnaia volia became a terrorist organization, while members of Chernyi peredel opposed terrorist activities. The influence of Zemlia i volia on Uspensky is evident in his *ocherki* "Krest'ianin i krest'ianskii trud" (Peasant and Peasant Labor, *Otechestvennye zapiski*, 1880) and "Vlast' zemli." The politics espoused by Uspensky in his *narodnichestvo* period differ from those that he embraced before coming into contact with Zemlia i volia. In *Razoren'e*, Uspensky's protagonist, Mikhail Ivanovich, travels from his village to the large city of St. Petersburg in order to acquire political self-awareness. An opposite trend is evident, however, in Uspensky's cycles of village sketches. In these works Uspensky's hero, the urban *raznochinets*, searches for truth by looking *toward* the Russian village.

The main protagonist of the cycle "Krest'ianin i krest'ianskii trud" is Ivan Ermolaev, based on Leontii Beliaev, a peasant with whom Uspensky was acquainted. In comparing his own life to that of Beliaev, Uspensky ponders the vast difference between how he, an educated man, and Beliaev, a peasant, understand the value of human life. For example, Uspensky remembers that when Beliaev's son fell ill, the family did not call a doctor but instead treated him with home remedies. The child took a long time regaining his health because the obscure remedies did not work. When his horse became ill, however, Beliaev found the money to call a vet. Uspensky expresses concern at the lack of desire for self-improvement among the peasants, who are happy to live in poverty, without material comforts. Peasant culture reflects a total lack of progress: previous generations have not passed any valuable knowledge on to the younger generations, nor have they introduced any technical innovations. In other segments of "Krest'ianin i krest'ianskii trud" Uspensky notes the peasants' complete lack of collective feeling—that is, their failure to understand that more economic success can be achieved through united efforts. He also comes to realize that peasants draw inspiration from their contact with nature and animals, and they develop emotionally and intellectually on the basis of such contact.

In "Vlast' zemli" Uspensky tries to understand how his protagonist, the formerly successful peasant Ivan Bosykh, has deteriorated mentally and physically because of his drinking problems. The peasant has his own theory of why this deterioration has occurred. He argues that the cause of his condition is too much *volia* (freedom)—which he had attained suddenly as a result of his economic success. Bosykh maintains that the mental constitution of city people differs from that of Russian peasants: what is good for city life is bad for village life. To demonstrate his point, he tells a charming story that serves as an allegory of his explanation of the peasant mentality. Once a foreign cow, accompanied by a German doctor, was delivered to his village. The cow was cleaner and bigger than the Russian cows, and she was given a nice clean pen. The animal ate large amounts of feed, but she did not give much milk in return. The German specialist addressed this phenomenon by explaining that the cow was still undergoing a period of adaptation. Time passed, but the cow was still lazy. When a Russian bull was brought in for mating, he ran away at the sight of such a fancy cow. The peasant's point is that a Russian peasant has to work extremely hard and be given extremely little as a reward. Only under these ascetic conditions does he perform well (like a Russian, rather than a foreign, cow). The moment his life becomes easier, he loses his resilience, and his physical and mental faculties degenerate.

Uspensky did not follow blindly the doctrine of the *narodnichestvo*. In his search for truth he expressed profound doubts about the ideas set down by members of the movement. His writings do not constitute a utopian idealization of Russian peasant life; rather, they reflect the actual life lived by Russian peasants. This perspective was aided by his contact with Russian villagers—an experience that supplied him with some bitter disappointments. Uspensky believed that the "erosion" of the poetic relationship between the peasant and the soil resulted from the encroachment of capitalism into the village. The economic implications of this encroachment were in obvious conflict with Populist and Slavophilic ideals. Uspensky shattered the main tenet of the *narodniki*, which classified the peasant as a natural socialist. Yet, he could not relinquish his hope that one day the spiritual needs of poor people would take precedence over their material striving for daily bread.

Indeed, Uspensky believed in the possibility of the emergence of a new type of peasant—one with spiritual and aesthetic needs, such as a yearning for the sublime and a thirst for the beautiful. He expresses this belief in his well-known story "Vypriamila" (She Straightened Out, 1885). Published in *Russkaia mysl'*, "Vypriamila" occupies a special place in Russian literature. A programmatic work that expresses Uspensky's firm belief in the democratic value of art in society, it attempts to emancipate feminine beauty from its objectification by male sexual desire. Robust, versatile, and self-sufficient Russian peasant women made up Uspensky's economic ideal; in "Vypriamila" he applies the same democratic principles to the development of an aesthetic ideal as well.

The narrator of the story, Tiapushkin, is a simple schoolteacher, a *narodnik* whose commitment to the movement has begun to waver. He experiences visions of female images, which include a healthy peasant woman at one with nature; a chaste young maiden searching for a means to sacrifice herself; and a whole succession of enlightened prostitutes from the streets of Paris and London. These visions fill Tiapushkin with joy, but not until he reminisces about the statue of *Venus de Milo,* which he had visited twelve years previously in the Louvre, is he "straightened out"–cured of his apathy and returned to the path of commitment to *narodnichestvo.* This transformation attests to the remarkable power of art, as well as to its democratic range: art is not the sole province of gentlemen and aristocrats, and its meaning is not merely aesthetic but humanitarian as well. Indeed, the *Venus de Milo* in Uspensky's portrayal represents a woman's body freed from the encumbrance of erotic qualities. The statue, with its broken arms, is emblematic of a "crippled" body. Its cropped features, such as its pulled-back and thus shortened hair, produce a peasant-like, masculine appearance, which furthers Uspensky's idea that art appeals universally, irrespective of national and class boundaries, and is therefore capable of serving his ideal of social justice. The *Venus de Milo* is, fundamentally, not female but *human;* it therefore evokes limitless possibilities for the improvement of human society in the imagination of its beholder.

Prostitution is an important theme in "Vypriamila"; Uspensky implicitly challenges the criminal anthropological viewpoint–developed by the Italian scientist Cesare Lombroso and espoused by many psychologists of the time–that prostitutes are innate criminals whose fate is biologically determined. As Tolstoy does in his novel *Voskresenie* (Resurrection, 1889), Uspensky suggests in "Vypriamila" and other works that prostitution is, in fact, a product of economic and social ills.

Uspensky also communicates his objection to gender taxonomies in his travel sketches of the 1880s, in addition to questioning accepted ethnic and racial stereotypes. His travel notes detailing his trip to Siberia in 1888, "Poezdki k pereselentsam" (Journeys to the Land of Migrants, 1888), include descriptions of his meetings with members of various communities. Published in *Russkie vedomosti* (Russian News), Uspensky demonstrates in these *ocherki* an understanding of religious and ethnic diversities that ignores the prevailing stereotypes of the nineteenth century. For example, in one *ocherk* a young Jewish coachman shatters the stereotype of the Jew's visibility in the diaspora by completely blending into the microculture of his profession; he is indistinguishable from his Siberian counterparts in dress, appearance, looks, manner, and speech. The Jewish coachman's ideals, too, are similar to those held by the Russian *narodniki:* he dreams of purchasing land and living out a utopian life on the land, and he believes that peasant labor is the only honest labor. Yet, a *mezuzah* (prayer scroll) hangs in the Jew's house, while the houses of Russians are graced by icons: the Jew retains his religious identity, even as he assimilates to the surrounding culture.

Uspensky's travel notes from his visit to Constantinople in 1886 highlight his second major concern about the life of the rural population–capitalism. While visiting Constantinople, he witnessed the importation of a European economic system into a non-European society. In "V Tsar'grade" (In Constantinople, *Russkie vedomosti,* 1886), he laments the absence of a definite cultural identity in Constantinople–the result, he believes, of the unifying influence of capitalism. He describes the mixed architecture of the St. Sofia Cathedral as emblematic of the hurried and unsuccessful fusion of Christian and Islamic cultures. The restructuring of an Orthodox cathedral into a Moslem temple, according to Uspensky, amounts to an aesthetically unattractive mixture of untidy and unfinished building fragments. He is equally unimpressed by the city life of Constantinople–including the smells of the market streets and the noise of *cafe-shantans* (coffee shops)–and the abundance of brothels that import prostitutes from Russia disgusts him. For Uspensky, Constantinople epitomizes the fate from which he wants to protect Russia at all costs: namely, the encroachment of capitalism onto native, Orthodox soil.

Uspensky's opinion of Karl Marx and the treatise *Das Kapital* (1867) is expressed in his open letter to Marx, titled "Gor'kii uprek" (A Bitter Reproach, written 1888, published 1933). "Gor'kii uprek" was not published during Uspensky's lifetime because of censorship issues. Uspensky was familiar with a letter that Marx had written in 1877 to *Otechestvennye zapiski* that, although it remained unpublished, circulated widely among Russian intellectuals. In his letter Marx writes that his knowledge of the Russian economic system, albeit limited, is sufficient enough to justify this warning to Russia: its inhabitants should beware of encouraging the development of capitalism. He cautions that the only way to save Russia from the pitfalls of the capitalist path is to halt the economic reforms embarked upon in 1861 and maintain the collective structure of village life and work. Marx stops short of expressing a definite opinion about the direction of economic development in Russia, in part because of the enormous peasant class there–a class that could not be considered a counterpart to the proletariat of the developed West. In "Gor'kii uprek" Uspensky remarks on a similarity between Marx's views and the views of the *narodniki,* who liked Marx's writings and believed that the Russian peasants, whom they idealized, would be able to escape the path of capitalism because of the innate power of collectivity. Uspensky believed that the collapse of *narodnichestvo*, the breakup of Narodnaia volia, and the social apathy of the Russian intelligentsia were unavoidable circumstances resulting from the progression of the country toward capitalism.

Uspensky similarly regarded the encroachment of technology into the sphere of agriculture as a negative phenomenon. In his story "Parovoi tsiplenok" (Incubator Chick, *Russkie vedomosti*, 1888; translated as "The Steam Chicken," 1895) he writes that those animals born in conditions where new technology is in use consist of previously nonexistent organic matter. He features a conversation that takes place between peasants, who muse among themselves and discuss questions of a Spinozian nature. Speculating on the intrusion of technology into the field of procreation, they argue that the cessation of the monist continuum of living matter is the Creator's domain. They discuss whether, according to the teachings in the Bible, chickens have souls. One peasant states that a chick raised in an incubator is just a running machine with neither a soul nor the capacity to think, whereas a chick developed by natural means inherits both soul and reason from its mother. This image of an animal as a machine activated by movement closely adheres to the Cartesian concept of an animal and is indicative of Uspensky's familiarity with European philosophical thought. Uspensky's story details the introduction of technological and industrial processes to the field of animal husbandry. This story also raises concerns about the consequences of man's interference with nature.

In his letters to friends, dating from 1888 and 1889, Uspensky frequently mentions the poor state of his mental and physical health. Complaining of physical exhaustion and the poor state of his nerves, he explains that his mental and physical distress renders him incapable of reading and writing. Uspensky's schizophrenia caused him, moreover, to suffer from hallucinatory visions, some of which he shared with Korolenko. According to Korolenko, Uspensky spent hours engaged in imaginary conversations with an imaginary nun, Margarita. This interest in chaste maidens was so strong that Uspensky had visions of women who were pure of thought and flesh whenever he was in a state of neurotic regression.

Uspensky's awareness of his psychological illness is evident in the article that he wrote about the death of Vsevolod Mikhailovich Garshin, author of the renowned story "Krasnyi tsvetok" (The Red Flower, 1883), who suffered from mental illness and committed suicide by throwing himself down a stairwell in March 1888. In "Smert' V. M. Garshina" (The Death of V. M. Garshin, *Russkie vedomosti*, 1888) Uspensky discusses a learned article that identifies Garshin's medical condition as a "paralysis of the will," which manifested itself in the form of muscular paralysis. Interested in the causal link between the physiological and the psychological manifestations of mental illness, Uspensky writes that the genesis of a mental disor-

Uspensky's grave in Volkov Cemetery, St. Petersburg

der is linked to specific social conditions and matters of economic and microcultural environment, as well as to the presence of afflicted organic tissue. Even in the realm of psychology, he thus remains faithful to *narodnichestvo* ideology by refusing to agree with a purely medical approach that attributes the sole cause of mental illness to a fatalistic predisposition and genetic inevitability. In a private letter of October 1889 to his friend, the economist and publicist Aleksandr Sergeevich Posnikov, Uspensky expresses similar sentiments about the death of his cousin Nikolai Uspensky in the same month. Nikolai Uspensky had lived a notorious life of debauchery, and his drunken frenzies had led to his suicide. Once again, Uspensky refuses to believe that genetic and hereditary factors are solely responsible for mental illness. Instead, he blames his cousin's death on childhood influences.

The last ten years of Uspensky's life, from 1892 until his death in 1902, were spent in mental institutions. During his stay at a private mental hospital in St. Petersburg from July to September of 1892, he attempted suicide; after this episode he was transferred to the Kolominskaia mental hospital near Novgorod. There he remained under the observation of the famous psychiatrist Boris Naumovich Sinani until 13 November 1893, when he took a three-month vacation to Nizhnii Novgorod, after which he returned to the hospital. During his stay in the Kolominskaia hospital he began working on his reminiscences of Ivan Sergeevich Turgenev (the two writers had corresponded; Turgenev had liked Uspensky's work for his knowledge of Russian peasant speech) and Vera Figner, whom he viewed as an ideal of feminine self-sacrifice for the good of the Russian people. He failed to complete these memoirs, however, because of the deteriorating condition of his illness. He left the Kolominskaia hospital in March 1900 and entered the Novo-Znamenskaia hospital in St. Petersburg, where he died of a heart attack on 24 March 1902. Uspensky was buried at the Volkov Cemetery in St. Petersburg.

The death of Gleb Ivanovich Uspensky was commemorated by an obituary in Lenin's newspaper *Iskra* (The Spark). The obituary praised Uspensky for his contribution to the initiation of the Russian revolutionary movement. Lenin and Gor'ky referred young writers to Uspensky's exemplary work as a reliable source of information on Russian village life. Indeed, Uspensky's writing remains valuable for his knowledge of peasant language and his ethnographically correct portrayal of the everyday life of the peasant community. His work is also an important repository of peasant vocabulary, beliefs, and superstitions, as well as of peasant views on economics, machinery, animal behavior, and agriculture. Most of this material, however, has failed to arouse the interest of scholars—though Uspensky's writings that include extracts of village speech were studied and copied by writers of *derevenskaia proza* (village prose) in the 1970s and 1980s (notably, Fedor Aleksandrovich Abramov and Viktor Petrovich Astaf'ev). These writers mainly used Uspensky's works as a source of colloquialisms and regional lexis in order to authenticate speech patterns for their peasant protagonists. Uspensky's politically motivated devotion to addressing the needs of the oppressed remained the focus of literary critical studies of his work into the early 1990s, while other aspects of his writing have received no attention at all.

Letters:

Sochineniia i pis'ma v odnom tome, edited by V. V. Bush, N. K. Piksanov, and B. G. Uspensky (Moscow & Leningrad: GIZ, 1929);

"Pis'ma," in Uspensky's *Polnoe sobranie Sochinenii,* 14 volumes (Moscow & Leningrad: AN SSSR, 1940–1954), XIII; XIV;

"Pis'ma," in Uspensky's *Sobranie sochinenii,* 9 volumes (Moscow: Goslitizdat, 1955–1957), IX.

Bibliographies:

V. E. Cheshikhin-Vetrinsky, *G. I. Uspensky* (Moscow: Federatsiia, 1929), pp. 361–380;

R. P. Matorina, "Bibliografiia sochinenii G. I. Uspenskogo," in *Gleb Uspensky. Materialy i issledovaniia,* volume 1 (Moscow & Leningrad: Akademia nauk SSSR, 1938), pp. 678–743.

Biographies:

Nikita Ivanovich Prutskov, *Tvorcheskii put' Gleba Uspenskogo* (Moscow: Akademiia nauk SSSR, 1958);

Nikolai Ivanovich Sokolov, *G. I. Uspensky: Zhizn' i tvorchestvo* (Leningrad: Khudozhestvennaia literatura, 1968);

Prutskov, *Gleb Uspensky* (Leningrad: Prosveshchenie, 1971); translated as *Gleb Uspensky* (New York: Twayne, 1972);

Svetlana Borisovna Mikhailova, *Gleb Uspensky v Peterburge* (Leningrad: Lenizdat, 1987);

Nikolai Aleksandrovich Milonov, *G. I. Uspensky i Tula* (Tula: Interbumaga, 1995).

References:

Dmitrii Aleksandrovich Barabokhin, *Gleb Uspensky i russkaia zhurnalistika, 1862–1892* (Leningrad: Izdatel'stvo Leningradskogo universiteta, 1983);

Iulii Abramovich Bel'chikov, *G. Uspensky* (Moscow: Mysl', 1979);

Grigorii Abramovich Bialyi, "O realizme Gleba Uspenskogo," in his *Russkii realizm: Ot Turgeneva k Chekhovu* (Leningrad: Sovetskii pisatel', 1990), pp. 491–537;

V. E. Cheshikhin-Vetrinsky, *G. I. Uspensky* (Moscow: Federatsiia, 1929);

Berta Sergeevna Dykhanova, ". . . K odnoi tol'ko pravde . . . ," in Uspensky's *Sochineniia,* 2 volumes (Moscow: Khudozhestvennaia literatura, 1988), I: 5–30;

Vladimir Galaktionovich Korolenko, "O Glebe Ivanoviche Uspenskom," in *G. I. Uspensky v russkoi kritike,* edited by Nikolai Ivanovich Sokolov (Moscow & Leningrad: Khudozhestvennaia literatura, 1961), pp. 331–345;

Henrietta Mondry, "How Straight Is the *Venus of Milo*? Regendering Statues and Female Bodies in Gleb Uspensky's *Vypriamila,*" *Slavic and East European Journal,* 41, no. 3 (1997): 415–431;

G. Novopolin, *Gleb Uspensky. Opyt literaturnoi kharakteristiki* (Khar'kov: E. A. Golovkin, 1903);

Georgii Valentinovich Plekhanov, "Nashi belletristy-narodniki: G. I. Uspensky," in his *Literatura i estetika,* volume 2 (Moscow: Khudozhestvennaia literatura, 1958);

Vitalii Borisovich Smirnov, *Gleb Uspensky i Saltykov-Shchedrin* (Saratov: Izdatel'stvo Saratovskogo universiteta, 1964);

Sokolov, ed., *Gleb Ivanovich Uspensky v russkoi kritike* (Moscow: Khudozhestvennaia literatura, 1961).

Papers:

The largest collection of Gleb Ivanovich Uspensky's letters and manuscripts is held in St. Petersburg at the Institute of Russian Literature (IRLI, Pushkin House). Other papers can be found at the Russian National Library in St. Petersburg, and in Moscow at the State Literary Museum (GLM), the Russian State Library (RGB, formerly the Lenin Library), the State Tolstoy Museum, the State Historical Museum (GIM), and the Bakhrushin State Central Theatrical Museum. For a detailed listing of Uspensky's papers, see "Rukopisi G. I. Uspenskogo i ego perepiska," by I. I. Veksler and others, in *Gleb Uspensky. Materialy i issledovaniia,* volume 1 (Moscow & Leningrad: AN SSSR, 1938), pp. 554–675.

Iuliia Valerianovna Zhadovskaia

(29 June 1824 – 28 July 1883)

Karen Rosneck
University of Wisconsin-Madison

BOOKS: *Stikhotvoreniia* (St. Petersburg: E. Prats, 1846);

V storone ot bol'shogo sveta: Roman (Moscow: Katkov, 1857);

Stikhotvoreniia (St. Petersburg: E. Prats, 1858)–includes "Sovremennyi chelovek" and "Sredi bezdushnykh i nichtozhnykh";

Povesti (St. Petersburg: A. Smirdin, 1858);

Zhenskaia istoriia. Roman (St. Petersburg: E. Prats, 1861);

Polnoe sobranie sochinenii, 4 volumes (St. Petersburg: P. V. Zhadovsky, 1885–1886; revised and enlarged edition, St. Petersburg: I. P. Perevoznikov, 1894);

Sochineniia: Stikhotvoreniia i perepiska (St. Petersburg: Dobrodeev, 1886);

Stikhotvoreniia i perepiska (St. Petersburg: Dobrodeev, 1886).

Editions and Collections: *Izbrannye stikhotvoreniia* (Iaroslavl': Iaroslavskoe knizhnoe izdatel'stvo, 1958);

V storone ot bol'shogo sveta. Roman v trekh chastiakh; Otstalaia. Povest' (Moscow: Planeta, 1993).

Editions in English: *Russian Lyrics in English Verse,* edited by Charles T. Wilson, with poems by Zhadovskaia (London: Trübner, 1887), pp. 212–216;

"The Contrast," in *Holy Russian and Other Poems,* edited by Percy Ewing Matheson (London: Oxford University Press, 1918);

The Burden of Sufferance. Women Poets of Russia, edited by Pamela Perkins and Albert Cook, with poems by Zhadovskaia (New York, 1993).

OTHER: *Zhenskaia lirika. Russkie poety XIX veka,* with poems by Zhadovskaia (Moscow, 1960);

Poety 1840–1850-kh gg., edited by Boris Iakovlevich Bukhshtab, with poems by Zhadovskaia (Moscow: Sovetskii pisatel', 1962), pp. 407–426;

Russkie poetessy XIX veka, edited by N. V. Bannikov, with poems by Zhadovskaia (Moscow: Sovetskaia Rossiia, 1979);

"Perepiska," in *Dacha na Petergofskoi doroge. Proza russkikh pisatel'nits pervoi poloviny XIX veka,* edited by Vik-

Iuliia Valerianovna Zhadovskaia

toriia Vasil'evna Uchenova (Moscow: Sovremennik, 1986);

Tsaritsy muz. Russkie poetessy XIX–nachala XX veka, edited by Uchenova, with poems by Zhadovskaia (Moscow: Sovremennik, 1989).

Although contemporary critics often praised her poetry for successfully communicating powerful, unaffected emotion and thought, Iuliia Zhadovskaia's prose frequently elicited indifference or even sharp criticism from reviewers. Her briefly sketched characterizations, simple plots, and tendency to incorporate stylistic features considered more appropriate to poetry frequently baffled critics. Though appealing to readers, her poetry

401

also diverged from contemporary standards and displayed a loose poetic form, inattentiveness to rhyme, and thematic subjectivity, suggesting a greater affinity with earlier Romantic and later modernist writers than with the emerging realistic literary mode of her own age. Zhadovskaia innovatively reworked Romantic stylistic and thematic conventions but also followed the lead of other contemporary writers by experimenting boldly with depictions of the everyday life of common people. Her imaginative refashioning of different literary influences, trends, and subject matter created a valuable link in the development of Russian literature from Romanticism to Realism in the nineteenth century.

Iuliia Valerianovna Zhadovskaia was born on 29 June 1824 in the village of Subbotina in the Liubimskii district of Iaroslavl' province. Born without her left arm and with only three fingers on her right hand, she also suffered from poor eyesight. After the death of her mother, Aleksandra Ivanovna (Gotovtseva) Zhadovskaia, sometime between 1825 and 1826, her civil servant father, Valerian Nikandrovich Zhadovsky, sent his children—Iuliia; her brother, Pavel; and her sister, Klavdiia—to the village of Panfilovo in the Bui district of Kostroma province to live with their grandmother, Anastasiia Petrovna Gotovtseva. Loved dearly by her grandmother, Zhadovskaia apparently flourished in this new environment. She enjoyed unlimited access to her grandmother's library and from an early age included works by François Marie Arouet de Voltaire and Jean-Jacques Rousseau among her favorites.

When Zhadovskaia was thirteen years old, Anastasiia Petrovna sent her to Kostroma to live with her daughter (the sister of Zhadovskaia's mother), Anna Ivanovna Gotovtseva-Kornilova, in order for the girl to obtain a more advanced education. A talented woman, Gotovtseva-Kornilova had published poetry in *Syn otechestva* (Son of the Fatherland), *Moskovskii telegraf* (The Moscow Telegraph), and *Galatea* in the late 1820s and early 1830s. Under the tutelage of her aunt, Zhadovskaia studied French, history, and geography as well as Russian and foreign literatures. After a year her aunt sent her to the nearby Prevo-de-Liumen private boarding school (some sources say Pribytkova boarding school) to continue her education. Zhadovskaia's father withdrew her from the school, however, in 1840 reportedly because of her poor health or discontent there. Returning with her to Iaroslavl', he hired a young teacher named Petr Mironovich Perevlessky from the local gymnasium to continue Zhadovskaia's studies.

Perevlessky, who graduated from the philosophical faculty of the pedagogical institute at Moscow University, encouraged his pupil's literary talent and attempts to write sentimental prose, which she had begun to do earlier in Kostroma in 1840. In 1841

Zhadovskaia's first published work, titled "Pis'mo iz Iaroslavlia o poseshchenii gosudaria imperatora" (Letter from Iaroslavl' upon the Visit of the Emperor) and written in the form of a letter to a girlfriend, appeared in *Moskvitianin* (The Muscovite). Iurii Nikitich Bartenev, a former school director and her aunt's literary mentor, also guided Zhadovskaia's early publishing efforts by introducing her to Mikhail Petrovich Pogodin, the editor and publisher of *Moskvitianin* from 1841 until 1856. The next year, two of Zhadovskaia's poems, "Mnogo kapel' svetlykh" (Many bright droplets) and "Luchshii perl taitsia . . ." (The best pearl remains hidden . . .), were published in *Moskvitianin*.

In time Zhadovskaia and her tutor fell in love, but her father refused to permit his gentry daughter's marriage to a humble Iaroslavl' seminarian. In 1843 Zhadovsky arranged for Perevlessky to be sent back to Moscow; the young man subsequently became a professor of the Aleksandrovskii Lycée in St. Petersburg and published articles on Russian literature. Zhadovskaia saw Perevlessky for the last time in St. Petersburg in the spring of 1858; she continued to correspond with him until his marriage to Ekaterina Aleksandrovna Kolotovaia in 1864. To distract herself from her romantic misfortunes, the nineteen-year-old Zhadovskaia eagerly embraced an opportunity to care for her orphaned eight-year-old cousin, Nastas'ia Gotovtseva. The two later established a close friendship that lasted until Zhadovskaia's death. With the exception of about a year and a half, when Nastas'ia married—and then left—V. L. Fedorov, a professor of the Demidovskii Lycée, the two women remained inseparable throughout their adult lives.

The first collection of Zhadovskaia's poetry appeared in 1846 through the assistance of another mentor, poet, and translator, Eduard Ivanovich Guber. The poems included in *Stikhotvoreniia* (Poems) had already appeared in print, primarily in *Moskvitianin,* between 1840 and 1845—although many of Zhadovskaia's previously published poems were excluded from the collection, particularly those with an explicitly religious content. Nevertheless, the poet's spiritual and sometimes even religious yearning for another, better world shapes this collection as a whole. *Stikhotvoreniia* is organized by a coherent internal logic: the poet's desire to escape reality—the major motif of the volume—especially predominates among the love lyrics, which is the type of poem that appears most often in the collection. A second group of poems, including "Noch'" (Night), "Veter" (Wind), and "Zvezdy" (The Stars), draws on distinctive folk imagery and stylistic devices, such as the frequent use of repetition, typical of the Russian folk song. A third group of poems, represented in the collection by "Mnogo kapel' svetlykh," "Dve sestry"

(Two Sisters), and "Luchshii perl taitsia . . . ," offers philosophical reflections on life, nature, and the changing of generations.

Vissarion Grigor'evich Belinsky reviewed *Stikhotvoreniia* for *Sovremennik* (The Contemporary) in an article titled "Vzgliad na russkuiu literaturu 1846 goda" (A Look at Russian Literature of the Year 1846). In his review Belinsky praised Zhadovskaia's poetic talent, but he regretted that she drew inspiration solely from imagination and dream, rather than from life. Despite his reservations, Belinsky's encouragement powerfully shaped Zhadovskaia's career. In the following years she became attracted to the ideas of the literary radicals. The appearance of her poetry in Iaroslavl' collections from 1849 and 1850 reveals her active participation in the literary life of that city. While she was influenced by Belinsky and the advocacy (by the radical school) of realistic depictions of the common people's daily existence, Zhadovskaia maintained a preference for the distilled emotional intensity offered by lyric poetry. Many poems articulate the pain of personal tragedy and domestic subjugation. The recognition that time will erase the memory of pain contrasts with expressions of bitterness, emptiness, and loss in the present. Her poetry also reveals her passionate love for nature and solitary contemplation.

Several of Zhadovskaia's poems, such as "Ne brosai ty tsvetov" (Don't Throw Flowers, 1847), "Niva, moia niva" (Niva, My Niva, *Syn otechestva*, 1857), and "Tot, kogo liubila" (He Whom I Loved, 1857), became popular songs when set to music. Mikhail Ivanovich Glinka created a musical arrangement for "Ty skoro menia pozabudesh'" (You Soon Will Forget Me, 1845), while Aleksandr Sergeevich Dargomyzhsky wrote music for "Ia vse eshche ego, bezumnaia, liubliu" (Crazy Woman That I Am, I'm Still In Love With Him, 1846). Other composers, including Aleksandr Tikhonovich Grechaninov, Sergei Vasil'evich Rachmaninov, Mikhail Mikhailovich Ippolitov-Ivanov, and Reingol'd Moritsevich Glier, also wrote musical arrangements for her verse. In the 1840s Zhadovskaia published her poetry mainly in *Moskvitianin* and *Biblioteka dlia chteniia* (A Reading Library). Later, she published both poetry and prose in *Syn otechestva, Illiustratsiia* (Illustration), *Moskovskii gorodskoi listok* (The Moscow City Leaflet), *Iaroslavskie gubernskie vedomosti* (Iaroslavl' Province News), *Vremia* (Time), and *Russkii vestnik* (The Russian Messenger).

During the 1840s and 1850s Zhadovskaia lived a lonely life in Iaroslavl', devoting herself both to her ward, Nastas'ia Fedorova, and to her writing. She also corresponded with Bartenev. She came to know the Slavophile poet and idealogue Ivan Sergeevich Aksakov during 1849 to 1851, while he completed military service in Iaroslavl'. Zhadovskaia made infrequent trips to St. Petersburg and Moscow during these years in order to relieve the monotony of her solitary, provincial existence.

Zhadovskaia's prose of the 1840s incorporates aspects of the sentimental epistolary tradition, the Romantic fascination with the supernatural and the theme of tragic love between social unequals, and the Realist focus on civic issues. Motifs of portraits, magic, nature, books, orphans, mirrors, and illness link both her poetry and her prose to the works of earlier Russian writers such as Aleksandr Sergeevich Pushkin. In her prose works Zhadovskaia demonstrates a penchant for parallelism and spare, simply delineated plots and characterizations, as evinced by her 1847 story "Prostoi sluchai" (A Simple Incident). In this story fourteen-year-old Zhozef meddles in the romance of his female cousin and his tutor, Ivan Ivanovich, until the cousin's untimely death from tuberculosis removes her from the lives of both young men. Orphans and wards are a frequent presence in Zhadovskaia's prose; they disrupt the environment of the gentry households depicted in her stories. Zhozef's orphaned cousin, who is never named, recedes into greater passivity and isolation during the course of her illness. Her utterances gradually disappear from the narrative as the diary entries written by Zhozef and Ivan take precedence in the text. The relationship between the two young men is more lasting and heartfelt than the relationship either of them enjoys with the nameless female cousin.

In Zhadovskaia's "Neumyshlennoe zlo" (Unintended Evil, 1847), Vera gives love letters written to her by a young man named Fediusha Mirov to her friend Katia to read. In reducing Fediusha's private correspondence to an object of analysis in order to help her girlfriend "learn about this type of writer," Vera exhibits a detached, purely literary relationship to life. Now married to another man, Vera assures Katia that she had not intended to harm Fediusha. Two years later during a visit, Vera's grandmother points out Fediusha's grave as the two women stroll through the church cemetery. Ignorant of his love for Vera, her grandmother describes him as a crazy boy who caught cold and fell ill. Returning to his grave later that day, Vera again mutters that she had wished him no harm and feels gladdened when she hears echoing strains from the birch thicket. Just as the death of Zhozef's cousin draws the two young men together in "Prostoi sluchai," so, too, do letters written by the now deceased Fediusha promote closeness between Vera and Katia.

In "Otryvki iz dnevnika molodoi zhenshchiny" (Excerpts from the Notebook of a Young Woman, 1848) Mina writes that her husband, Dmitrii, has been romantically involved with an old friend named Vera

Slonskaia for a long time. At Dmitrii's birthday party Mina accidentally overhears his private confession of love to Vera and afterward falls fatally ill. Soon, Dmitrii receives from one of Vera's friends a packet of letters that detail Vera's indifference to him, her disdain for his lack of sensitivity toward Mina, and her desire to punish Mina for stealing a former boyfriend. He then finds Mina's diary, reads of her jealousy, and repents his affair with Vera. When Mina forgives him, he asserts that she will not die but will live for his love. At Mina's funeral, neighbors note that Dmitrii stands like a dead man, while she seems as though still alive. As in other works by Zhadovskaia, women use writing and illness to wield power over others. Mina's illness and death serve poetic justice by punishing Dmitrii for his infidelity.

Katia Pavlovna Zanova also suffers from an unhappy marriage in "Ni t'ma, ni svet: Neskol'ko pisem molodoi zhenshchiny" (Neither Darkness, Nor Light: Some Letters of a Young Woman, *Moskvitianin*, 1848). After relocating with her husband to another city, Katia meets a former admirer at a ball. She feels pleasure at the prospect of this unexpected meeting, but her former lover behaves aloofly, although only three years have passed since they last met. He later visits Katia at home after finishing his business in town. When she tearfully asks if he loves her, he replies that he has not married, nor has he fallen in love; he then kisses her. In a letter to a female friend, Katia characterizes her existence as neither life nor death, neither dream nor reality, and neither darkness nor light. Many of Zhadovskaia's heroines, unlike Pushkin's stoical Tat'iana in the final scenes of his novel in verse *Evgeny Onegin* (Eugene Onegin, 1825–1832), attempt to remain modest, dutiful daughters and wives while simultaneously and energetically pursuing forbidden passion. At the ball Katia views her favorite portrait of a young woman, head tilted backward, eyes lifted upward. An ambiguous image of religious reverence, emotional detachment, or even pleasure, this portrait also symbolizes Katia's striving to combine marital duty, forbidden passion, and chaste spirituality. Although Belinsky criticized Zhadovskaia for relying on dream and imagination for inspiration, her fictional heroines typically struggle to reconcile quite real, contradictory social conventions of feminine behavior.

In "Perepiska" (A Correspondence, *Moskvitianin*, 1849) Ida Nikolaevna, an orphan living with her aunt, Mavra Aleksandrovna, exhibits her mastery of literary convention by skillfully seducing her young mentor, Ivan Petrovich, through a lively exchange of letters filled with animated innuendoes about sex and money. As the relationship blossoms, gossip originating from Ida's servant and the couple's messenger, Fedor Seme-

novich, results in social ostracism for both young people. To avoid scandal Ivan takes a job elsewhere and later marries. They meet twice more in the next ten years, and at the second meeting Ida informs Ivan, now a widower, that she has married. The story features a series of oppositions contrasting student and teacher, art and life, Cain and Abel, reason and feeling, passivity and action, man and woman, and oral and written language.

In "Nepriniataia zhertva" (An Unaccepted Sacrifice, *Moskvitianin*, 1849) Lida, the eighteen-year-old niece and ward of her uncle Aleksei Stoianov, falls in love with a twenty-four-year-old artist named Erov. While Erov paints a portrait (commissioned by her uncle) of Lida by day, her friend Mar'ia Manova, a proponent of women's rights, strives to seduce Erov by night. When Erov refuses payment for the finished portrait and presents it to Lida and her uncle as a gift, Stoianov takes offense. Three days later Lida writes a letter to Erov proposing that they elope, but soon afterward she intercepts a misdirected and tender missive from Mar'ia to Erov. Realizing that Lida now knows about his relationship with Mar'ia and angry at both women, Erov leaves town, followed soon after by Mar'ia. Ten years later Erov receives a commission to paint a portrait of a deceased member of the family of Prince M., his protector. At the funeral, Erov recognizes Lida as the deceased and cries in the arms of his benefactor's son.

The anonymous author of a review of "Nepriniataia zhertva" in *Sovremennik* in 1849 expressed reservations about the quality of Zhadovskaia's prose but nevertheless recognized her talent: "I won't say that Zhadovskaia has no talent for writing: just the opposite." The reviewer especially criticized her tendency to incorporate lyrical asides to the reader more typical of poetry, such as the narrator's admonishment to the heroine of "Nepriniatia zhertva": "Don't cry, Liza." Often considered a flaw by contemporary critics, Zhadovskaia's intrusive lyricism contrasts with the apparent objectivity of her emotionally detached third-person narrators. As in her previous stories, plot parallelisms—such as Erov's paintings of both the living and deceased Lida—appear prominently in "Nepriniataia zhertva." Lida, like many of Zhadovskaia's heroines, also uses illness as a weapon. She successfully thwarts her uncle's marriage plans for her by threatening to become ill and die. Later, her death provides poetic justice by punishing Erov for his infidelity.

Zhadovskaia accumulated a sizable number of literary friendships and acquaintances throughout her career. Critic Valerii Aleksandrovich Blagovo has suggested that the theme of women's oppression in Nikolai Alekseevich Nekrasov's poetry may have originated through Nekrasov's familiarity with Zhadovskaia's works, which include at least one poem dedicated to him—although a meeting between the two writers has never been substantiated. In the late 1850s Zhadovskaia served as an important mentor and friend to the Iaroslavl' poet Leonid Nikolaevich Trefolev. Her other acquaintances in the world of high culture included novelists Ivan Sergeevich Turgenev and Aleksandr Vasil'evich Druzhinin, poet Petr Andreevich Viazemsky, painter Karl Pavlovich Briullov, Goethe translator Mikhail Pavlovich Vronchenko, and economist and professor of Russian history and statistics Iosif Nikolaevich Shill' (a collaborator with the brothers Fyodor Dostoevsky and Mikhail Mikhailovich Dostoevsky on their journal *Vremia*). Zhadovskaia also maintained a correspondence with the poet Evdokiia Petrovna Rostopchina.

Zhadovskaia's prose of the 1850s continued to display characteristics of Romanticism while increasingly incorporating aspects of Realism. In "Sila proshedshego" (Force of the Past, *Moskvitianin*, 1851) Iuliia, Pavel Silin's only child by his first wife, and his stepdaughter Katia live with their aunt, Anna Petrovna, after the death of their parents. When her father was still alive, Iuliia had fallen in love with a young man named Platon Simonsky but was not permitted to marry him. Now, while preparing to marry Voldemar, Platon's friend, Katia asserts that she will avenge Iuliia by toying with Platon's affections. Instead, Katia falls in love with Platon, and they elope. United in their abandonment, Voldemar and Iuliia also marry, and the two couples reconcile. During a summer visit Platon asks for Iuliia's forgiveness, professes his love, and kisses her. When Voldemar informs Iuliia of his intention to return home in three days, she begs to leave with him rather than extend her stay. A reviewer of "Sila proshedshogo" for *Otechestvennye zapiski* (Notes of the Fatherland) in 1851 rejected the narrator's assertion of Iuliia's emotional depth by noting her shallowness in attempting to resolve the complexity of the past "in one kiss." However, the behavior exhibited by both Katia and Iuliia suggests complex motivations of envy, revenge, and competition, as well as the influence of their father, whose name implies the Russian word *sila* (force).

Filled with a fascinating variety of female characters, *V storone ot bol'shogo sveta* (Apart from the Great World, *Russkii vestnik*, 1857) is Zhadovskaia's greatest prose achievement. As the novel opens, Genechka lives with her aunt, Avdot'ia Petrovna, after the death of the girl's parents. When the mother of Genechka's best friend, Liza, hires a tutor named Pavel Ivanovich, Genechka falls in love with him but is not allowed to marry him. Both girls become acquainted with high

СТИХОТВОРЕНІЯ

ЮЛІИ ЖАДОВСКОЙ.

САНКТПЕТЕРБУРГЪ.
—
1858.

Title page for Zhadovskaia's second verse collection,
Stikhotvoreniia *(Poems), which has the same title*
as her first (Kilgour Collection of Russian
Literature, Harvard University Library)

society, Liza marries, and Genechka falls in love with Danarov, a wealthy, artistic, but brooding man. Charmed by Genechka's dissimilarity to his superficial high-society friends, he characterizes her as being "apart from the great world." When he confesses that he is married and asks her to run away with him, she falls ill, and he leaves for St. Petersburg. Shortly afterward, she again meets Pavel but she now loves him only as a brother. At the end of the novel the financially insecure Genechka marries Pavel, although a brief glimpse of Danarov at a performance of William Shakespeare's *Hamlet* (1604) still moves her. She dresses for her wedding, surrounded by the portraits of her relatives. Referred to by radical critic Nikolai Aleksandrovich Dobroliubov as "a wonderful novel," *V storone ot bol'shogo sveta* mirrors aspects of Zhadovskaia's early life at her grandmother's house.

The second collection of Zhadovskaia's poetry, *Stikhotvoreniia* (1858), received a warm review from Dobroliubov for its simple, heartfelt, and sincere lyricism. He rated the book as one of his favorites, asserting, "Not without thought, we have decided to include this book of poetry among the best specimens of our recent poetic literature." The collection also received favorable reviews from Dobroliubov's fellow radical critics Nikolai Gavrilovich Chernyshevsky and Dmitrii Ivanovich Pisarev. In contrast to Zhadovskaia's first collection, this second *Stikhotvoreniia* is arranged not thematically but chronologically by year (with some errors) and divided into three sections. The first section includes poetry published before 1847; however, it omits poems in the style of folk songs, as well as poems directly or indirectly dedicated to Perevlessky. Moreover, although this book on the whole manifests Zhadovskaia's increasing tendency to exclude poems of a religious character from her opus, its first section does feature a few such poems that had been absent from the 1846 volume. The second section of the book, consisting of poems written between 1847 and 1856, displays many of the themes of Zhadovskaia's first *Stikhotvoreniia* and includes translations of verse by the poets Heinrich Heine, Ludwig Uhland, and Ferdinand Freiligrath. At the same time, poems of social protest such as "Sovremennyi chelovek" (A Modern Man) and "Sredi bezdushnykh i nichtozhnykh" (Among the Heartless and Despicable) evidence her experimentation with civic themes, including sympathy for the common people and hatred of oppression. The third section of the volume, composed of poetry written between 1856 and 1858, offers portraits of peasant life and poems that trace the history of romantic relationships. Although Zhadovskaia never published a third collection of poetry, she did not relinquish her intention to do so until 1862.

Zhadovskaia's novel *Zhenskaia istoriia* (A Woman's Story), serialized in *Vremia* and published as a book in 1861, incorporated significant innovations, according to the contemporary critic Aleksandr Mikhailovich Skabichevsky. In his 1886 essay Skabichevsky asserted that in this novel "we see a significant change in the author's worldview toward women's lot." Skabichevsky particularly praised the novel for its depiction of a new kind of heroine in the character of Ol'ga Vasil'evna Martova, a well-to-do woman who shares her life with the peasants and serves them as a doctor. In *Zhenskaia istoriia* Liza relates events from her childhood and young adulthood. Her tough, serious mother, Liubov' Dmitrievna, the wife of a school-district superintendent, hopes her daughter will be smarter than she has been. After her parents die Liza accepts the patronage of a wealthy neighbor named Mikhail Peradov, moves into the home of Mikhail's sister Krinel'skaia, and befriends her daughter, Lidiia, and Lidiia's cousin, Ol'ga. Although Liza gradually falls in love with Mikhail, she continues to pursue her intention of becoming a governess. Finally, Ol'ga marries the aristocratic Latukhin; Lidiia marries a young man beneath her station named Dorel'sky; and Liza marries Mikhail. All three couples stand together in the last scene as if in an enchanted circle. In the end Liza benefits from heeding her mother's warnings about men and money. She acts propitiously to prevent her father's remarriage by absorbing his time and attention, as he cares for her during a deathly illness. She also repeatedly states her intention of becoming a governess to maintain her tenuous position as an outsider in Krinel'skaia's home. Whether egotistical, self-serving and mercenary, or selfless and altruistic, Liza's actions in the novel create the conditions for a number of seemingly successful marriages transcending class barriers and based on love. Although calculating, her actions also create the conditions for her successful marriage to Mikhail, Lidiia's marriage to Dorel'sky, and Ol'ga's marriage to Latukhin.

In Zhadovskaia's *povest'* (novella) "Otstalaia" (The Backward Girl, *Vremia*, 1861) Masha and her best friend, a serf girl named Matresha, have grown up with little supervision or formal education because Masha's father had slighted her mother before his death by entrusting his daughter to the care of a simple peasant, Iakov Orlov. Now, when Matresha reveals her secret trysts with her boyfriend Grisha in the forest, Masha responds with self-righteous indignation, and Masha's mother reacts by sending her daughter to visit thirty-eight-year-old Nenila Nechinskaia. There, Masha meets the intellectual Naletov, who promises to develop her mind, and Arbatov, who plans to develop her heart. When she returns home, Arbatov moves in nearby, and the couple start meeting in the forest after dark. After her mother finds out, Masha runs away with Arbatov and Naletov, asserting that she must pursue life to overcome her backwardness. Several years later she returns married to Naletov. Her mother has since died, and Iakov manages the property. In a tearful encounter Masha and Matresha forgive each other, while Naletov looks on.

Skabichevsky in particular praised the progressive spirit of Zhadovskaia's *povest'*, declaring that "Zhadovskaia's latest prose work, 'Otstalaia,' is even more infused with the new spirit of the times." The writer Nadezhda Khvoshchinskaia (who wrote under the pseudonym V. Krestovsky) advanced a more ambivalent interpretation in an 1862 review, asserting that Masha behaves toward Matresha at the end of the narrative with her characteristic imitation of emotion, displaying genuine emotion only in her defense of a mother's love to Naletov earlier in the novella. Arja Rosenholm has explored the relationship between Masha and Matresha as an expression of sisterhood fraught by the symbolic dichotomy represented by Christian images of the Madonna and Mary Magdalene.

In 1862 Zhadovskaia married a family friend, the doctor Karl Bogdanovich Seven, after the sudden death of his wife. She became a teacher for Seven's children while also caring for her own sick father for five years. From this time on, Zhadovskaia ceased writing literary works. Always modest about her literary talent and good-natured despite her disabilities, Zhadovskaia frequently attributed positive reviews of her writing to condescension. While some critics, including her brother, the writer Pavel Valerianovich Zhadovsky, argued that she stopped writing largely because of readers' lack of interest in her works, her ward and friend Nastas'ia Fedorova asserted in a posthumous essay that Zhadovskaia had loved writing and would have continued but for poor health. Fedorova also asserted, however, that Zhadovskaia once claimed that she stopped writing poetry after the 1860s because "poeziia menia ostavila" (poetry had abandoned me).

Shortly after her father's death in 1870 Zhadovskaia sold her home in Iaroslavl' and bought a modest property in the village of Tolstikovo, seven versts from the small district town of Bui in Kostroma province, not far from where her grandmother had lived. She moved to Tolstikovo in 1873 and lived there until her death. When her husband fell ill and died in 1881, she shouldered the burden of caring for family members alone. As Zhadovskaia's eyesight deteriorated, Nastas'ia Fedorova served as her copyist but also acted as her sight and hands. Among Zhadovskaia's favorite activities in later years were reading the Bible and tending flowers. In March 1883 she began to suffer from painful attacks of constriction in her chest that obstructed her breathing. Her doctor diagnosed these occurrences as benign episodes of angina. The fifth such attack, however, killed her on 28 July 1883. She was buried alongside her husband in the churchyard of the village of Voskresen'e near the town of Bui.

Although Iuliia Valerianovna Zhadovskaia's poetry achieved substantial recognition during her lifetime, her prose proved to be far less successful. In an article published after her death in 1886 Skabichevsky attributed the poor reception of Zhadovskaia's fiction to her cultivation of a narrative subjectivity more appropriate to poetry. Ranking her works behind those of two other contemporary women writers, Khvoshchinskaia and Mariia Oleksandrivna Markovych (pseudonym Marko Vovchok), he argued: "The extreme subjectivity

that composes an integral part of her lyrics remains a failing in her novels and stories; we expect characters, types, and temperaments, but we are disillusioned, finding only the author everywhere among pale, stereotypical portraits." Despite the reservations of critics, both Zhadovskaia's prose and her poetry significantly influenced the works of other contemporary writers such as Nekrasov and Khvoshchinskaia. Her explorations of serfdom, women's emancipation, aesthetics, pride, self-sacrifice, loss, revenge, love, egotism, and betrayal reveal her creative response to the works of earlier and contemporary writers, while casting new light on current strands of intellectual debate and suggesting new directions of literary inquiry. Although Zhadovskaia's reputation as a poet during her lifetime helped to preserve her memory through the twentieth century, her lively and often innovative prose works have only recently begun to attract the attention of readers, translators, and scholars.

Letters:

To Iu. N. Bartenev, *Moskvitianin,* 3, no. 5 (1848): 46–47; *Moskvitianin,* 6, no. 11 (1848): 9–10; *Moskvitianin,* 1, no. 11 (1849): 208–211;

"Pis'ma," in Zhadovskaia's *Polnoe sobranie sochinenii,* volume 4 (St. Petersburg: P. V. Zhadovskago, 1885);

To K. P. Briullov, *Russkaia starina,* 8 (1900): 158–159;

To Bartenev, in *Shchukinskii sbornik,* no. 4 (1905).

Bibliography:

Dmitrii Dmitrievich Iazykov, *Obzor zhizni i trudov pokoinykh russkikh pisatelei,* no. 3 (St. Petersburg: A. S. Suvorin, 1886), pp. 33–34.

Biographies:

Nastas'ia P. Fedorova, "Vospominanie ob Iu. V. Zhadovskoi," *Istoricheskii vestnik,* 30, no. 11 (1887): 394–407;

P. Mizinov, "K biografii Zhadovskoi," *Iaroslavskie gubernskie vedomosti,* 19 September 1889, 22 September 1889;

Mikhail Nikitich Parkhomenko, *Poety-iaroslavtsy* (Iaroslavl': Iaroslavskoe oblastnoe izdatel'stvo, 1944), pp. 44–49;

Bonnie Marshall, "Zhadovskaia, Iuliia Valerianovna," in *Dictionary of Russian Women Writers,* edited by Marina Ledkovsky, Charlotte Rosenthal, and Mary Zirin (Westport, Conn.: Greenwood Press, 1994), pp. 740–742;

Zirin, "Iuliia Zhadovskaia," in *Russian Women Writers,* edited by Christine D. Tomei, volume 1 (New York: Garland, 1999), pp. 371–384.

References:

Andrei Vasil'evich Astaf'ev and Nadezhda Andreevna Astaf'eva, *Pisateli Iaroslavskogo kraia* (Iaroslavl': Verkhne-Volzhskoe knizhnoe izdatel'stvo, 1974);

Valerii Aleksandrovich Blagovo, "Nekrasov i Iu. Zhadovskaia," in *F. M. Dostoevsky, N. A. Nekrasov: Sbornik nauchnykh trudov* (Leningrad: Leningradsky gosudarstvennyi pedagogicheskii institut imeni Gertsena, 1974), pp. 166–174;

Blagovo, *Poeziia i lichnost' Zhadovskoi* (Saratov: Izdatel'stvo Saratovskogo universiteta, 1981);

E. Cheauré, "Zhenskaia literatura XIX veka i literaturnyi kanon," in *Problema avtora v khudozhestvennoi literature,* edited by Galina Vladimirovna Mosaleva (Izhevsk: Izdatel'stvo Udmurtskogo universiteta, 1998), pp. 263–273;

Boris Vladimirovich Mel'gunov, *Vsemu nachalo zdes': Nekrasov i Iaroslavl'* (Iaroslavl': Verkhniaia Volga, 1997);

"P. M. Perevlessky: Pis'ma k Iu. V. Zhadovskoi," in *Literaturnyi Arkhiv: Materialy po istorii russkoi literatury i obshchestvennoi mysli,* edited by Kamsar Nersesovich Grigor'ian (St. Petersburg: Nauka, 1994), pp. 157–187;

Arja Rosenholm, "The New Woman as Sister," in her *Gendering Awakening: Femininity and the Russian Woman Question of the 1860s* (Helsinki: Aleksanteri-instituutti, 1999), pp. 501–542;

Aleksandr Mikhailovich Skabichevsky, "Pesni o zhenskoi nevole," in his *Sochineniia,* volume 2 (St. Petersburg: F. Pavlenkov, 1890), pp. 635–652;

Tat'iana Torgashova, "Iuliia Zhadovskaia: Neizvestnyi avtor izvestnykh romansov," *Kosmopolitan* (November 2000): 167–168;

P. D. Ukhov and A. I. Balandin, "Iu. V. Zhadovskaia," *Literaturnoe nasledstvo,* 79 (1968): 569–572;

Heide Warkentin, "Kak eto prosto, verno i simpatichno! O retseptsii tvorchestva Iulii Zhadovskoi," *Pol, gender, kul'tura,* 2 (2000): 187–204;

Warkentin, *Tod oder Traumhochzeit: Von der Suche nach Identität im Prosawerk von Julija Žadovskaja,* master's thesis, University of Freiburg, 1996.

Papers:

Manuscripts of Iuliia Valerianovna Zhadovskaia's poetry and of her recollections of L. N. Trefolev are held in Moscow at the Russian State Archive of Literature and Art (RGALI), fond 638 and fond 507. Her letters to Pogodin can be found in the Russian State Library (RGB, formerly the Lenin Library). Zhadovskaia's other manuscripts and letters are held in St. Petersburg at the Institute of Russian Literature (IRLI, Pushkin House), fond 273 and fond 448, and at the Russian National Library (RNB), fond 377. They may also be found at the State Archive of the Iaroslavl' Region, fond 213, and at the Bui Local History Museum.

Mar'ia Semenovna Zhukova

(1805 – 14 April 1855)

Svetlana Slavskaya Grenier
Georgetown University

BOOKS: *Vechera na Karpovke,* anonymous, 2 parts (St. Petersburg, 1837, 1838)–comprises "Inok," "Baron Reikhman," "Medal'on," "Nemaia," "Provintsialka, and "Poslednii vecher"; "Baron Reikhman" and "Medal'on" translated by Joe Andrew as "Baron Reichman" and "The Locket" in *Russian Women's Shorter Fiction: An Anthology 1835–1860,* edited by Andrew (Oxford: Oxford University Press, 1996), pp. 145–180, 181–219;

Povesti, 2 parts (St. Petersburg, 1840); republished as *Russkie povesti* (St. Petersburg: V. Poliakov, 1841)– comprises "Sud serdtsa"; "Samopozhertvovanie," translated by Andrew as "Self-Sacrifice" in *Russian Women's Shorter Fiction: An Anthology 1835–1860,* edited by Andrew (Oxford: Oxford University Press, 1996), pp. 220–271; "Padaiushchaia zvezda"; and "Moi kurskie znakomtsy," excerpts translated by Rebecca Bowman as "My Acquaintances from Kursk" in *Russian Women Writers,* 2 volumes, edited by Christine Tomei (New York: Garland, 1999), I: 189–197;

Ocherki Iuzhnoi Frantsii i Nitstsy. Iz dorozhnykh zapisok 1840 i 1842 godov, as M. Zh-k-va, 2 volumes (St. Petersburg: A. Ivanov, 1844)–includes "Rasskazy o iuzhnoi Frantsii" and "Kartezianskii monastyr'."

Edition: *Vechera na Karpovke,* with an afterword by R. V. Iezuitova (Moscow: Sovetskaia Rossiia, 1986).

OTHER: "Chernyi demon, predanie," as M. Zh-k-va, in *Utrenniaia Zaria: Almanakh na 1840 god* (St. Petersburg: V. Vladislavlev, 1840), pp. 123–177;

"Landyshi. Rasskaz starushki," in *Al'manakh Russkoi besedy. Sobranie sochinenii russkikh literatorov,* volume 1 (St. Petersburg, 1841), pp. 3–39;

"Missioner," in *Molodik, na 1844 god, Ukrainskii literaturnyi sbornik* (St. Petersburg: I. Betsky, 1844), pp. 107–122;

"Dacha na Petergofskoi doroge," in *Dacha na Petergofskoi doroge: Proza russkikh pisatel'nits pervoi poloviny XIX veka,* edited by V. V. Uchenova (Moscow: Sovremennik, 1986), pp. 245–322;

Mar'ia Semenovna Zhukova

"Naden'ka," in *Serdtsa chutkogo prozren'em . . . : Povesti i rasskazy russkikh pisatel'nits XIX v.,* edited by N. I. Iakushin (Moscow: Sovetskaia Rossiia, 1991), pp. 172–245.

SELECTED PERIODICAL PUBLICATIONS– UNCOLLECTED:

POETRY

"K N.N. . . . vu," *Otechestvennye zapiski,* 6 (1839): 108.

FICTION

"Oshibka," *Biblioteka dlia chteniia,* 48, no. 2 (1841): 169–244;

"Serdtse zhenshchiny," *Literaturnaia gazeta,* 27–28 (1841): 105–112;

"Dve sestry," *Otechestvennye zapiski,* 30, nos. 9–10 (1843): 3–86;

"Epizod iz zhizni derevenskoi damy," *Otechestvennye zapiski,* 52, no. 5 (1847): 1–116;

Sovremennik, 40, no. 8 (1853): 97–182;

"Naden'ka," *Dve svad'by, Otechestvennye zapiski,* 112, no. 6 (1857): 591–663; 113, no. 7 (1857): 51–138.

A talented author of tales, novels, and a travelogue, Mar'ia Zhukova was quite popular with general readers and highly regarded by critics in the 1830s and 1840s. She made a significant contribution to the development of Russian prose fiction in the period of its transition from Romanticism to Realism. Her portrayal of women and of problems specific to women's lives was noticed and taken into account by the next generation of Russian writers, including Ivan Sergeevich Turgenev, Leo Tolstoy, and Fyodor Dostoevsky. One of the first women to become a professional writer in Russia, Zhukova was among the first to question the position of women in society and suggest expanding their social roles.

Possibly because of her undistinguished background (she was born into a family of small nobility), extremely little is known about Zhukova's life. Zhukova was born Mar'ia Semenova Zevakina in 1805, the eldest of five children in the family of Semen Semenovich Zevakin, an *uezdnyi striapchii* (court official) in Arzamas, in Nizhnii Novgorod province. According to his contemporaries, Semen Semenovich's honesty, intelligence, and education, unusual for someone in his position, gained him the respect of his peers and extraordinary influence in the affairs of the town. Zevakina's mother, Aleksandra Andreevna Zevakina (birth name unknown), is described as an exceptionally warmhearted traditional Russian woman. Semen Semenovich owned an estate not far from the famous Sarov Monastery in Tambov province, and during her childhood and youth the future author divided her time between her father's small estate and the provincial town of Arzamas. Probably because of this background, Zhukova demonstrates in her works a great love for the Russian countryside; a close familiarity with, and certain fondness for, provincial settings; as well as a deep religiosity and an affection for the Orthodox Church and its ritual.

As often happened in those days, Zevakina received her primary education from a local deacon. Most likely, she also received training in the graphic arts at the local Arzamas Academy for painting and fine arts, which was founded by Aleksandr Vasil'evich Stupin in 1812 and was the first such school in the provinces. Later in life she was an accomplished miniaturist and painter of watercolors. According to one of her relatives (quoted by M. Konopleva in her 1913 article on Zhukova), Zevakina supplemented her education abroad. Yet, she did not travel outside of Russia until 1838–although her works, starting with *Vechera na Karpovke* (Evenings on the Karpovka, 1837),

display a broad knowledge of literature and the arts that could hardly have been obtained in her father's house. To explain this discrepancy, Konopleva makes a convincing case that Zevakina must have received most of her education–as do so many of her heroines–in the home of a neighboring rich family. Indeed, she might well have studied alongside the daughter of the Korsakov house, the future Princess Sof'ia Alekseevna Golitsyna, who remained Zevakina's friend and patroness into their adult years and to whom she, as Zhukova, dedicated *Vechera na Karpovke,* her first published work. The figure of a ward, the motif of an emotionally ambiguous ward-benefactress relationship, and meditations on the theme of disinterested charity recur frequently in Zhukova's works and suggest the conflicting emotions that Golitsyna's patronage might have provoked. Another biographer, Petr Vasil'evich Eremeev, conjectures an additional venue for Zevakina's education: after her marriage in 1822, at the age of seventeen, to Razumnik Vasil'evich Zhukov, Zhukova and her husband went to Lipnia, one of her husband's properties in the Ardatov District of the Nizhnii Novgorod province, where she spent a considerable amount of time over the next six years and where she had access to a big library. The estate had belonged to her husband's late mother, Anna Sergeevna (Buturlina) Zhukova, a highly educated woman and published author who had amassed a large and varied collection of eighteenth-century French publications.

One year after marrying, Zhukova gave birth to her only child, her son Vasilii. Razumnik Vasil'evich was an elected district judge in the provincial town of Ardatov during the years 1824 to 1830. According to one of Zhukova's relatives, he was a "gambler and a bon vivant" who conducted their affairs in a disorderly fashion and incurred many debts, some of which Zhukova later had to pay out of her literary earnings. Her husband's poor management of their estate is indirectly corroborated by a letter that Zhukova wrote on 8 August 1829 to Fedor Lukich Pereverzev. She begs Pereverzev, her father's family's benefactor, for help and explains that she and her husband are about to lose two of their properties and become destitute. She mentions her husband's (unspecified) illness, despite which he is about to visit Pereverzev in order to deliver her letter and presumably receive some financial assistance. By all accounts, Zhukova's marriage was an unhappy one. It ended in a separation, which took place no later than 1830. Sometime later her husband died, and, according to V. A. Mil'china, she became the common-law wife of the artist Philippe Berger, who painted her portrait in 1835, accompanied her on her travels, and illustrated her 1844 book *Ocherki Iuzhnoi Frantsii i Nitstsy. Iz dorozhnykh zapisok 1840 i 1842 godov* (Sketches of Southern France and Nice: From Travel Notes of 1840 and 1842).

After separating from her husband, Zhukova was largely responsible for supporting herself and her young son. She became a professional woman–an artist, a writer, and an amateur lawyer, even representing herself in a long-time lawsuit essential to her family's financial security; her experience as a legal supplicant is described in her most feminist tale, "Moi kurskie znakomtsy" (My Acquaintances from Kursk, written 1838, published in *Povesti* [Stories], 1840). According to Zhukova's relatives interviewed by Konopleva, she earned most of her money by copying paintings at the Hermitage Museum in St. Petersburg. Once, while working there, she was noticed by Tsarina Aleksandra Fedorovna and received a commission for a miniature portrait of Nicholas I. In a 25 June 1841 letter to Nikolai Ivanovich Grech mentioned above, Zhukova refers to a gift she received from the tsarina in gratitude for a painting presented to her–probably this miniature of the tsar.

Zhukova spent the years 1830 to 1837 alternating between Saratov, where her father was transferred in 1830, and St. Petersburg, where her son was in school and where she often stayed for long periods of time, sometimes at the house of her childhood friend and patroness Princess Golitsyna. Golitsyna was herself an author and accomplished artist. Being quite wealthy, she sponsored the publication of the Ukrainian miscellany *Molodik* (Young Moon, 1844) to which both women contributed. (In his review of *Molodik* the critic Vissarion Grigor'evich Belinsky highly praised Golitsyna's drawings featured in the miscellany.) In their house on Vladimirskaia Street, Princess Golitsyna and her husband, Vasilii Petrovich Golitsyn, ran a famous salon frequented by poets Aleksandr Sergeevich Pushkin and Petr Andreevich Viazemsky, writer Vladimir Aleksandrovich Sollogub, composer Mikhail Ivanovich Glinka, and, indeed, the rest of the literary and artistic elite of St. Petersburg. Close observation of, and possibly contact with, these creative luminaries probably played an important role in Zhukova's decision to turn to writing. In Golitsyna's salon she also acquired firsthand knowledge of the Petersburg high society within which many of her stories are set.

Zhukova's literary debut took place at the end of 1837, when the first volume of *Vechera na Karpovke* was published anonymously. It quickly sold out, and a second edition appeared in 1838, along with the second volume of the work. This edition was also anonymous, but it had a dedication to Princess Golitsyna that was signed "the authoress," so the critics knew at least the gender of the writer. The book was greeted with many quite positive, even rave, responses. The anonymous reviewer of *Severnaia pchela* (Northern Bee) called *Vechera na Karpovke* "one of the best collections of tales" of the year and predicted it would have a long life. Similarly, critic Nikolai Alekseevich Polevoi considered it the only noteworthy work of Russian belles lettres for 1837; a year later he repeated his praise while reviewing the second volume of the collection and

expressed particular admiration for the historical knowledge that Zhukova exhibited in "Nemaia" (The Mute Girl), declaring it "one of the best historical tales in Russian literature." A reviewer in *Literaturnye pribavleniia k "Russkomu Invalidu"* (The Literary Supplement to the *Russian Invalid*) praised Zhukova–and Russian women writers in general–for their natural, conversational narrative style and expressed his delight that Russian men were finally getting a chance to find out firsthand what was concealed in women's hearts, a matter about which they previously could only conjecture. All critics acknowledged Zhukova's talent, intelligence, powers of observation, and warmth of feeling; the highly moral tone and content of her writing; and her lively, engaging narrative style. As was typical of the gender dynamic during this period, all the reviewers expressed a somewhat exaggerated admiration for her debut–the other side of condescension appropriate for a lady author.

As Belinsky, the premiere critic of the time, wrote in *Moskovskii nabliudatel'* (The Moscow Observer): "We have read *Vechera na Karpovke* with the liveliest pleasure, the liveliest delight." He added that the tales in the collection "are the work of a woman; God grant, however, that we had more men who could write as well." Belinsky quickly denounced such condescension, however, and asserted that bestowing ladies with compliments was already becoming bad form even in salons, while in literature it was "decisively vulgar." In accordance with his stated belief in the same standard of judgment for both sexes in literature–since in intellectual, creative activity "there is no rank or sex"–Belinsky responded to the publication of part 2 and reissue of part 1 of *Vechera na Karpovke* with a lengthy and honest review. Although he lauded many aspects of the work, he ranked Zhukova's talent in the second, not the highest, order; her writings belonged not to the realm of true art–*poeziia* (poetry)–but to that of *krasnorechie* (eloquence). According to Belinsky, truly artistic literature such as "poetry" requires "creative genius," and its main genres are poetry and drama. Categorized in the lower realm of literature, prose fiction necessitates less talent in the creation of successful works in its genres–works that are, by the same token, of less aesthetic value. When Belinsky further developed his concepts of the two types and levels of talents in his 1840 review of Zhukova's collection *Povesti*–her first work to be published under her own name–he baldly stated that women were by nature incapable of "creative fantasy" and that their works were inevitably consigned to the second tier of literary genres.

As a collection of stories united by a "frame" narrative, *Vechera na Karpovke* adheres to a genre that was particularly popular in 1830s Russia. Other examples of this genre, which recalls Giovanni Boccaccio's *Decameron* (written 1348–1351), are Pushkin's *Povesti Belkina* (The Tales of Belkin, 1831), Nikolai Vasil'evich Gogol's

Vechera na khutore bliz Dikan'ki (Evenings on a Farm near Dikan'ka, 1831–1832), and Vladimir Fedorovich Odoevsky's *Russkie nochi* (Russian Nights, 1844). In *Vechera na Karpovke* the unnamed, female authorial narrator introduces to the reader a group of friends who are frequent visitors of a gracious old lady, Natal'ia Dmitrievna Shemilova, and her ward, Liubin'ka, at Natal'ia Dmitrievna's summer residence on the Karpovka river, on the outskirts of St. Petersburg. Since the whole group takes a lively interest in contemporary literature, the elderly hostess exhorts her visitors to add to the corpus of Russian fiction by telling stories of their own experiences or of events they have heard about. Natal'ia Dmitrievna and her guests tell their stories during a series of summer evenings (hence the title of the book). The authorial narrator claims that she collected and published these tales without changing a single word.

Despite certain inconsistencies in the narrative that almost undermine her attempt at "authentic" oral context, Zhukova employs the framing device in an innovative and sophisticated manner. Before presenting the tales themselves, she produces rather detailed portraits of the narrators who tell them. She intersperses the "inner" tales with bits of the "outer" narrative, including little scenes between Natal'ia Dmitrievna and her guests that resonate with the stories that have already been told or are about to be told. Finally, she skillfully unites the "inside" and "outside" narratives in the last tale, appropriately titled "Poslednii vecher" (The Last Evening). The lack of an authoritative narrative voice and the use of multiple narrators possessing various degrees of authority allow Zhukova to create an open-ended text that actively involves the reader in its interpretation.

Zhukova's cycle is representative of the period of transition from Romanticism to Realism in Russian prose. It incorporates several Romantic and transitional genres: an historical tale, "Nemaia"; an historical-ethnographic tale, "Inok" (The Monk); and several society tales—"Medal'on" (The Locket), "Baron Reikhman" (Baron Reichman), "Provintsialka" (A Girl from the Provinces), and "Poslednii vecher" (The Last Evening). All of the tales, even those that feature a man's name in the title, present a woman's perspective on a variety of situations. "Medal'on" captures the plight of a young woman, a ward of a princely family, who is marginalized by society because she is dependent, poor, and—most important—physically plain. In "Baron Reikhman" a young married woman is faced with making a difficult choice between her child and her lover. "Inok" relates the sufferings of an innocent merchant's wife, who is finally murdered by her overly jealous husband on suspicion of adultery.

Within the "inner" tales Zhukova depicts rather dark relations between the sexes: men, representative of "patriarchal authority," always have the upper hand—whether physically, financially, or emotionally—but without deserving such power by any mental or moral advantages. As noted by many critics, Zhukova's male characters lack distinct personalities. The less sympathetic ones, including Prince Z. and Ivan Antonovich in "Medal'on" and Baron Reikhman in the eponymous tale, are sketched by a few satirical traits. Though adequately realistic, they remain two-dimensional and are clearly not the focus of the author's attention. The "heroes"—that is, the objects of the heroines' love, such as Vel'sky in "Medal'on," Levin in "Baron Reikhman," and Aniuta's brother and husband in "Inok"—exist primarily as heroines' ideals, or creations of their imagination; these men usually prove unworthy of the heroines and incapable of appreciating them. Zhukova counterbalances this somber picture of society and of male-female relationships by a radically contrasting presentation of these same topics in the frame narrative. At Natal'ia Dmitrievna's house the reader encounters a group of truly noble characters who are filled with goodwill toward one another and capable of genuine friendship and love. In the lives of Liubin'ka and Vel'sky, the young protagonists of the frame story, a happy ending is achieved through the help of their benevolent elders—Natal'ia Dmitrievna and Pronovsky, who is Vel'sky's uncle and one of Natal'ia Dmitrievna's regular visitors. Zhukova's idealism and the utopian optimism of some parts of the cycle later provoked sharp criticism from Belinsky.

Zhukova continued to develop the themes of women's experience in her second collection, *Povesti,* which consisted of four works (three of which had previously appeared in journals). She revisits the problem of adultery and the moral struggles surrounding feelings of illicit love in "Sud serdtsa" (The Heart's Judgment), although this time the tale is set in Switzerland and Italy and involves a cast of foreign characters (a circumstance that evokes another, albeit mild, rebuke from Belinsky in his 1840 review of *Povesti*). This story, however—along with "Samopozhertvovanie" (Self-Sacrifice), which opens in Baden-Baden—represents Zhukova's first opportunity to share with the reader the many new impressions derived from her travels, impressions that later found their rightful place in her travelogue. "Samopozhertvovanie" picks up another of Zhukova's favorite topics: the complex experience of a poor provincial girl raised by a Petersburg aristocrat. The heroine, Liza, must come to terms with conflicting feelings of anger and humiliation, on the one hand, and love and gratitude, on the other, all of which accompany her abrupt move to her benefactress's mansion in St. Petersburg. She then goes through another humiliating experience upon entering society drawing rooms, where she, a ward, is characteristically neglected because of her low birth. Eventually she sacrifices her already slim chances of a happy marriage for the sake of rescuing her benefactress's reputation and then proudly refuses a marriage of convenience because she loves another. Finally, in a subtly feminist twist of the plot, she ends up supporting herself and her elderly mother through work: she runs a school for girls in the provinces. While Belinsky praised this story, he was less pleased by the more declaratively feminist "Moi kurskie znakomtsy," in which Zhukova polemically defends a woman's right to remain single rather than enter into a loveless marriage; she also asserts women's usefulness to society in other capacities–such as a storyteller–than those of wife and mother. Belinsky disapproved of the publicistic intensity of Zhukova's rhetoric.

Zhukova's second collection, like the first one, was favorably reviewed by several publications. Although Zhukova's name was a relatively new one in Russian literature, Belinsky noted that it was already "honored and famous because of the brilliant talent" it represented. In his review he reaffirms Zhukova as an excellent second-rate writer and reiterates his admiration for her gift of narration and especially for the "fullness of a lively, feminine feeling" that compels one to keep reading even after guessing how the plot will develop. His praise was echoed and magnified by reviewers writing in *Literaturnaia gazeta* (Literary Gazette), *Syn otechestva* (Son of the Fatherland), and *Russkii vestnik* (The Russian Messenger), all of whom spoke of Zhukova's well-established reputation and stressed the authenticity of her portrayal of women. Belinsky's summary assessment of Zhukova's fiction in his article "Sochineniia Zeneidy R-voi" (The Works of Zeneida R-va [pseudonym of Elena Andreevna Gan], 1843) was more critical than his previous essays. He wrote that "the gifted Mrs. Zhukova belongs to the category of authors who depict life not such as it is, therefore, not in its truth and reality, but such as they would like to see it." This sharper criticism resulted from the evolution of Belinsky's demands on literature: he was now putting more value on what he considered to be Gogolian realism and "objectivity" than he had done earlier. He did note, however, that Zhukova's work, under the influence of the "spirit of the times," was developing in precisely that direction–that is, toward a greater sense of realism.

Unfortunately, Zhukova's subsequent works of fiction, all of which appeared in journals, were not commented on by the critics in any substantial way, and her evolution was not reflected in published criticism. She was not ignored, however, by the readers of *Otechestvennye zapiski* (Notes of the Fatherland) and *Sovremennik* (The Contemporary), whose audience certainly included the aspiring authors Turgenev, Tolstoy, and Dostoevsky. In the fall of 1843 Pletnev, editor of *Sovremennik* in the years 1837 to 1847, mentioned in a letter to literary scholar Iakov Karlovich Grot that he had recently read Zhukova's novel "Dve sestry" (Two Sisters, 1843) in *Otechestvennye zapiski* and referred to her as a "fashionable

author" of whom he had wanted to form his own opinion (in the end he did not like her). The young Tolstoy, on the other hand, upon reading Zhukova's *povest'* (novella) "Naden'ka" in 1853 (when it appeared in *Sovremennik*), noted his rather favorable impression and acknowledged the obvious–that women writers have an advantage over men in portraying female characters.

In 1838, because her weak lungs were suffering from the cold, damp St. Petersburg weather, Zhukova was obliged to leave both the northern capital and her son in order to spend almost three years, intermittently, in the warmer climates of southern France and Italy; she usually returned for the summer to visit her son and her publishers in St. Petersburg and her family in Saratov. Her last documented trip abroad took place in 1842. She chronicled her travels in the two-volume *Ocherki Iuzhnoi Frantsii i Nitstsy*, which came out in 1844 to universal acclaim. In his review for *Otechestvennye zapiski* Belinsky praised her animated style, saying that the notes reminded him of Nikolai Mikhailovich Karamzin's *Pis'ma russkogo puteshestvennika* (Letters of a Russian Traveler, 1797, 1801), and adduced a long quotation. The young poet Nikolai Alekseevich Nekrasov wrote in *Literaturnaia gazeta*, "Everyone knows the fine talent of this authoress, who writes so warmly and enticingly. . . . Her tales are always animated by a true and profound feeling, and they constitute some of the favorite reading of the Russian public"; Nekrasov then lamented the fact that Zhukova had been writing less in the past few years. Besides recognizing her graceful and compelling narration, lively intelligence, powers of observation, and wide knowledge of art and history, Belinsky, Nekrasov, and other critics also lauded her distinctive feminine perspective, which enabled her to notice new aspects of foreign life and culture, as well as reveal new facets in sights and situations already observed and written about by male travel writers.

In spite of her nomadic lifestyle, the years 1837 to 1844 can be considered the most productive period of Zhukova's writing career. After the first volume of *Vechera na Karpovke* appeared in print, she placed several tales in the most important literary journals of the period: *Biblioteka dlia chteniia* (A Reading Library), *Syn otechestva*, and–from 1839 onward–the most prestigious and popular of the Russian monthly *tolstye zhurnaly* (thick journals), *Otechestvennye zapiski*, where Belinsky himself was chief critic until 1847. This same journal published her novel *Dve svad'by* (Two Weddings) in 1857, two years after she died. The last tale published in Zhukova's lifetime was "Naden'ka."

Zhukova's *povesti* during this period exhibit a gradual shift away from the poetics of the Romantic tale and toward that of the Realist novel. After 1843 her works become longer and are peopled by a larger cast of characters; their plots develop at a more leisurely pace and rely less on mysterious coincidences or downright supernatural events, such as those figuring in, for example, "Landyshi. Rasskaz starushki" (Lilies of the Valley. An Old Lady's Tale, 1841), "Oshibka" (The Mistake, 1841), and "Chernyi demon, predanie" (The Black Demon, A Legend, 1840). Furthermore, the protagonists in Zhukova's mature works are more psychologically complex, and her writing style is less flowery and emotional than in the earlier works. One of her last purely Romantic works was an extended variation on the theme of Pushkin's poem "Demon" (1824). "Chernyi demon" was warmly greeted by the critics of *Otechestvennye zapiski, Maiak* (The Lighthouse), and *Biblioteka dlia chteniia.* Although her method was changing in her works written during the 1840s (including the two pieces she published in the 1850s, "Naden'ka" and *Dve svad'by*), Zhukova continued to be concerned foremost with women's lives and to develop her favorite topics and plot motifs. She explores the theme of illicit love in "Landyshi," *Dve sestry,* and "Epizod iz zhizni derevenskoi damy" (An Episode in the Life of a Country Lady, 1847). She presents the difficult situation of dependent wards in "Oshibka" and "Epizod iz zhizni derevenskoi damy." She discusses the idea of self-sacrifice in "Oshibka," "Chernyi demon," *Dve sestry,* and "Naden'ka." Throughout all of these works, she dramatizes women's desire for self-expression and the difficulties they encounter in attempting to be seen, heard, understood, and valued by the outside world.

Upon her return from her last trip abroad in 1842, Zhukova lived mostly in Saratov, although she spent considerable periods of time in St. Petersburg, where her son was studying at the university until about 1845. After completing his education he began civil service in Saratov and was, in the late 1840s, the editor of the local newspaper *Saratovskie gubernskie vedomosti* (Saratov Province News). In Saratov, Zhukova became friends with Elena Pavlovna Fadeeva, Gan's mother, with whom she shared interests in literature and botany; there is a chance that Gan and Zhukova met during Gan's stay in Saratov in 1841. Zhukova led an active social life and gathered around herself a group of educated young people, including the future illustrious historian Nikolai Ivanovich Kostomarov, who was in exile in Saratov from 1848 to 1855 and under police surveillance. According to Kostomarov's friend, Ivan Ustinovich Palimpsestov, Zhukova's friendship with the Fadeev family helped improve Kostomarov's standing with the authorities. (Gan's father, Andrei Mikhailovich Fadeev, was then the governor of Saratov.) The future radical journalist Nikolai Gavrilovich Chernyshevsky, also a friend of Kostomarov's, was quite possibly one of Zhukova's young friends and visitors.

Zhukova spent the years 1852 and 1853 in St. Petersburg with her son, and this sojourn in the northern capital appears to have ruined her health completely. She died of complications from tuberculosis in the early hours of 14 April 1855. According to Zhukova's obituary published in *Otechestvennye zapiski* in 1855, in the last years of her life she had devoted herself to painting and natural science, which she practiced "with amazing modesty." While living in Saratov she had collected a sizable herbarium "of interest to any botanist." Her letters, written from Saratov and its environs in the 1840s, to Andrei Aleksandrovich Kraevsky, publisher of *Otechestvennye zapiski,* also speak of her preference for art and botany over writing fiction.

Although Mar'ia Semenovna Zhukova's name was largely forgotten by the public in the second half of the nineteenth century, she was rediscovered and reevaluated by women's historians and feminist critics both in Russia and in the West in the last two decades of the twentieth century. During this period some of her works were reprinted in Russia, and several were published in English. As a result she has now attained—in effect regained—her rightful status as one of the two most prominent women writers (along with Gan) of the mid nineteenth century; indeed, she attracts increasing interest as an important contributor to the development of Russian prose fiction and travel writing as a whole.

Letters:
"Pis'mo E. P. Fadeevoi," excerpt, *Starina i novizna,* 9 (1905): 339.

Bibliographies:
Semen Afanas'evich Vengerov, *Istochniki dlia slovaria russkikh pisatelei,* 4 volumes (St. Petersburg, 1900–1917), II: 384;

Vengerov, "Bibliografiia," in Vissarion Grigor'evich Belinsky, *Polnoe sobranie sochinenii,* 12 volumes, edited by Vengerov (St. Petersburg: M. M. Stasiulevich, 1901), V: 559–560;

S. D. Sokolov, "Zhukova, Mar'ia Semenonva," in *Trudy Saratovskoi uchenoi Arkhivnoi komissii* (Saratov, 1913), pp. 356–357.

Biographies:
M. Konopleva, "Mariia Semenovna Zhukova," *Golos minuvshego,* 7 (1913): 19–38;

M. N. Mezhevaia, "M. S. Zhukova," in *Russkie pisateli v Saratovskom Povolzh'e,* edited by Evgraf Ivanovich Pokusaev (Saratov: Privolzhskoe knizhnoe izdatel'stvo, 1964), pp. 44–49;

Petr Vasil'evich Eremeev, "M. S. Zhukova," in *Zapiski kraevedov,* volume 5 (Gor'ky: Volgo-Viatskoe knizhnoe izdatel'stvo, 1981), pp. 82–91;

V. A. Mil'china, "Zhukova Mariia Semenovna," *Russkie pisateli, 1800–1917: Biograficheskii slovar',* volume 2, edited by Petr Alekseevich Nikolaev (Moscow: Bol'shaia rossiiskaia entsiklopediia, 1992), pp. 277–278;

Giovanna Spendel, "Marija Semenovna Zukova (1804–1855)," in her *Il silenzio delle albe: Donne e Scrittura nell'Ottocento russo* (Torino: Tirrenia Stampatori, 1993), pp. 33–51;

Hugh Aplin, "Zhukova, Mar'ia Semënovna," in *Dictionary of Russian Women Writers,* edited by Marina Ledkovsky, Charlotte Rosenthal, and Mary Zirin (Westport, Conn.: Greenwood Press, 1994), pp. 748–751;

Rebecca Bowman, "Maria Zhukova," in *Russian Women Writers,* edited by Christine D. Tomei, 2 volumes (New York: Garland, 1999), I: 183–189.

References:

Joe Andrew, "The Benevolent Matriarch in Elena Gan and Mar'ia Zhukova," in *Women and Russian Culture: Projections and Self-Perceptions,* edited by Rosalind Marsh (New York: Berghahn, 1998), pp. 60–77;

Andrew, "Mariya Zhukova and Patriarchal Power," in his *Narrative and Desire in Russian Literature, 1822–1849: The Feminine and the Masculine* (New York: St. Martin's Press, 1993; Basingstoke, U.K.: Macmillan, 1993), pp. 139–183;

Hugh Aplin, "M. S. Zhukova and E. A. Gan: Women Writers and Female Protagonists, 1837–1843," dissertation, University of East Anglia, 1988;

Aleksandr Ivanovich Beletsky, "Russkie pisatel'nitsy 1830–60-kh gg.," dissertation, Khar'kov University, 1919, pp. 240–290;

Beletsky, "Turgenev i russkie pisatel'nitsy 1830–1860-kh godov," in his *Sobranie sochinenii,* 5 volumes (Kiev: Naukova dumka, 1965–1966), IV: 273–305;

Vissarion Grigor'evich Belinsky, "Povesti Mar'i Zhukovoi," in his *Polnoe sobranie sochinenii,* volume 4 (Moscow: Akademiia nauk SSSR, 1954), pp. 110–118;

Belinsky, "Vechera na Karpovke," in his *Polnoe sobranie sochinenii,* volume 2 (Moscow: Akademiia nauk SSSR, 1953), pp. 566–575;

Barbara Alpern Engel, *Mothers and Daughters: Women of the Intelligentsia in Nineteenth-Century Russia* (Cambridge: Cambridge University Press, 1983), pp. 33–35;

Svetlana Grenier, "Becoming a Subject: Beyond the Objectifying Male Gaze (Zhukova's *The Locket* and *Self-Sacrifice*)," in her *Representing the Marginal Woman in Nineteenth-Century Russian Literature: Personalism, Feminism, and Polyphony,* Contributions in Women's Studies, volume 185 (Westport, Conn.: Greenwood Press, 2001), pp. 33–61;

Grenier, "'Govorit' ne stesniaias' . . .': Mar'ia Semenovna Zhukova i ee sovremenniki," in *Perom i prelest'iu: Zhenshchiny v panteone russkoi literatury,* edited by Wanda Laszczak and Daria Ambroziak (Opole, Poland: Dariusz Karbowiak, 1999), pp. 58–75;

Hilde Hoogenboom, "The Society Tale as Pastiche: Mariia Zhukova's Heroines Move to the Country," in *The Society Tale in Russian Literature: From Odoevsky to Tolstoy,* edited by Neil Cornwell, Studies in Slavic Literature and Poetics, volume 31 (Amsterdam: Rodopi, 1998), pp. 85–97;

Raisa Vladimirovna Iezuitova, "Svetskaia povest'," in *Russkaia povest' XIX veka: Istoriia i problematika zhanra,* edited by Boris Solomonovich Meilakh (Leningrad: Nauka, 1973), pp. 90–92, 180–182;

Catriona Kelly, "Mariya Zhukova (1804–1855)," in her *A History of Russian Women's Writing, 1820–1992* (Oxford: Clarendon Press, 1994), pp. 79–91;

Wanda Laszczak, "Maria Żukowa–w kregu romantyczności i rzeczywistości realnej," in her *Twórczość literacka kobiet w Rosji pierwszej połowy XIX wieku,* Studia i monografie, volume 208 (Opole, Poland: Wyższa Szkoła Pedagogiczna, 1993), pp. 50–70;

Irina Savkina, "Mar'ia Zhukova: Epizody iz zhizni zhenshchin," in her *Provintsialki russkoi literatury: Zhenskaia proza 30–40-kh godov XIX veka,* Frauen-LiteraturGeschichte, volume 8 (Wilhemshorst: Verlag F. K. Göpfert, 1998), pp. 173–205;

Troy B. Williams, "'Baron Reikhman' by Mariia Semenovna Zhukova," M.A. thesis, Duke University, 1998.

Papers:

Mar'ia Semenovna Zhukova's papers are held in Moscow at the Russian State Library (RGB), fond 32 (letters to I. Iu. Betsky), and in St. Petersburg at the Russian National Library (RNB), fond 391 (letters to A. A. Kraevsky), fond 569 (letter to F. L. Pereverzev), and fond 608 (letter to N. I. Grech).

Books for Further Reading

Aikhenval'd, Iulii Isaevich. *Siluety russkikh pisatelei,* 3 volumes. Berlin: Slovo, 1923.

Andrew, Joe. *Russian Writers and Society in the Second Half of the Nineteenth Century.* Atlantic Highlands, N.J.: Humanities Press, 1982.

Andrew. *Women in Russian Literature, 1780–1863.* Houndmills, Basingstoke & Hampshire, U.K.: Macmillan, 1988.

Belknap, Robert, ed. *Russianness: Studies of a Nation's Identity.* Ann Arbor, Mich.: Ardis, 1990.

Berlin, Isaiah. *Russian Thinkers.* London: Hogarth Press, 1978.

Brooks, Jeffrey. *When Russia Learned to Read: Literacy and Popular Culture, 1861–1917.* Princeton: Princeton University Press, 1985.

Chances, Ellen. *Conformity's Children: An Approach to the Superfluous Man in Russian Literature.* Columbus, Ohio: Slavica, 1978.

Čiževskij, Dmitrij. *History of Nineteenth-Century Russian Literature,* translated by Richard Noel Porter, edited by Serge A. Zenkovsky. Volume 2: *The Realistic Period.* Nashville: Vanderbilt University Press, 1974.

Čiževskij. *Russian Intellectual History,* translated by J. Osborne. Ann Arbor, Mich.: Ardis, 1978.

Clowes, Edith W., Samuel D. Kassow, and James L. West, eds. *Between Tsar and People: Educated Society and the Quest for Public Identity in Late Imperial Russia.* Princeton: Princeton University Press, 1991.

Clyman, Toby W., and Diana Greene, eds. *Women Writers in Russian Literature.* Westport, Conn.: Greenwood Press, 1994.

Cornwall, Neil, ed. *Reference Guide to Russian Literature.* London: Fitzroy Dearborn, 1998.

Crowder, George. *Classical Anarchism: The Political Thought of Godwin, Proudhon, Bakunin, and Kropotkin.* Oxford: Clarendon Press / New York: Oxford University Press, 1991.

Debreczeny, Paul, and Jesse Zeldin, eds. and trans. *Literature and National Identity: Nineteenth-Century Russian Critical Essays.* Lincoln: University of Nebraska Press, 1970.

Dowler, Wayne. *Dostoevsky, Grigor'ev, and Native Soil Conservatism.* Toronto & Buffalo: University of Toronto Press, 1982.

Eklof, Ben, and others, eds. *Russia's Great Reforms, 1855–1881.* Bloomington: Indiana University Press, 1994.

Elizavetina, G. G., and A. S. Kurilov, eds. *Revoliutsionnye demokraty i russkaia literatura XIX veka.* Moscow: Nauka, 1986.

Frank, Joseph. *Through the Russian Prism. Essays on Literature and Culture.* Princeton: Princeton University Press, 1990.

Freeborn, Richard, and Jane Grayson. *Ideology in Russian Literature.* London: Macmillan & The School of Slavonic and East European Studies, University of London, 1990.

Gheith, Jehanne M., and Barbara T. Norton. *An Improper Profession: Women, Gender, and Journalism in Late Imperial Russia.* Durham, N.C.: Duke University Press, 2001.

Gleason, Abbott. *Young Russia: The Genesis of Russian Radicalism in the 1860s.* New York: Viking, 1980.

Gutsche, George J., and Lauren G. Leighton. *New Perspectives on Nineteenth-Century Russian Prose.* Columbus, Ohio: Slavica, 1982.

Heldt, Barbara. *Terrible Perfection: Women and Russian Literature.* Bloomington & Indianapolis: Indiana University Press, 1987.

Herman, David. *Poverty of the Imagination: Nineteenth-Century Russian Literature about the Poor.* Evanston, Ill.: Northwestern University Press, 2001.

Hingley, Ronald. *Russian Writers and Society, 1825–1904,* second revised edition. London: Weidenfeld & Nicolson, 1977.

Holmgren, Beth. *Rewriting Capitalism: Literature and the Market in Late Tsarist Russia and the Kingdom of Poland.* Pittsburgh: University of Pittsburgh Press, 1998.

Iampol'sky, Isaak Grigor'evich. *Poety i prozaiki. Stat'i o russkikh pisateliakh XIX–nachala XX v.* Leningrad: Sovetskii pisatel', 1986.

Istoriia russkoi literatury, 11 volumes. Moscow: Akademiia nauk SSSR, 1941–1956.

Ivanov, I. I. *Istoriia russkoi kritiki,* 4 volumes. St. Petersburg: I. N. Skorokhodov, 1898–1900. Reprint edition, New York: Johnson Reprint Corp., 1970.

Karpovich, Michael. *Imperial Russia, 1801–1917.* New York: Holt, 1946.

Kelly, Aileen M. *Toward another Shore: Russian Thinkers between Necessity and Chance.* New Haven & London: Yale University Press, 1998.

Kelly. *Views from the Other Shore: Essays on Herzen, Chekhov, and Bakhtin.* New Haven: Yale University Press, 1999.

Kelly, Catriona. *A History of Russian Women's Writing, 1820–1992.* Oxford: Oxford University Press, 1994.

Kolerov, M. A., ed. *Rossiia i reformy: Sbornik statei,* 4 volumes to date. Moscow: Medved', 1991–   .

Konovalov, Valerii Nikolaevich. *Literaturnaia kritika narodnichestva.* Kazan': Izdatel'stvo Kanzanskogo universiteta, 1986.

Konovalov, ed. *Russkaia literaturnaia kritika 70–80 gg. XIX veka.* Kazan': Izdatel'stvo Kazanskogo universiteta, 1986.

Kravtsov, N. I., ed. *Istoriia russkoi literatury vtoroi poloviny XIX veka.* Moscow: Prosveshchenie, 1966.

Kuvakin, Valery A., ed. *A History of Russian Philosophy: From the Tenth through the Twentieth Centuries,* 2 volumes. Buffalo, N.Y.: Prometheus Books, 1994.

Lampert, Evgenii. *Sons against Fathers: Studies in Russian Radicalism and Revolution.* Oxford: Clarendon Press, 1965.

Layton, Susan. *Russian Literature and Empire.* Cambridge: Cambridge University Press, 1994.

Leatherbarrow, W. J., and Derek Offord, trans. and eds. *A Documentary History of Russian Thought: From the Enlightenment to Marxism.* Ann Arbor, Mich.: Ardis, 1987.

Ledkovsky, Marina, Charlotte Rosenthal, and Mary Zirin, eds. *Dictionary of Russian Women Writers.* Westport, Conn.: Greenwood Press, 1994.

Levitt, Marcus C. *Russian Literary Politics and the Pushkin Celebration of 1880.* Ithaca, N.Y. & London: Cornell University Press, 1989.

Lotman, Lidiia Mikhailovna. *Realizm russkoi literatury shestidesiatykh godov deviatnadtsatogo veka (Istoki i esteticheskoe svoeobrazie).* Leningrad: Nauka, 1974.

Maegd-Soëp, Carolina de. *The Emancipation of Women in Russian Literature and Society: A Contribution to the Knowledge of the Russian Society during the 1860's,* adapted and translated by Maegd-Soëp and Jos Coessens. Ghent: Ghent State University Press, 1978.

Marsh, Rosalyn, ed. and trans. *Gender and Russian Literature: New Perspectives.* Cambridge: Cambridge University Press, 1996.

Martinsen, Deborah A., ed. *Literary Journals in Imperial Russia.* Cambridge & New York: Cambridge University Press, 1998.

Mendelsohn, Ezra, and Marshall S. Shatz, eds. *Imperial Russia, 1700–1917: State, Society, Opposition.* DeKalb: Northern Illinois University Press, 1988.

Mirsky, D. S. *A History of Russian Literature from Its Beginnings to 1900,* edited by Francis J. Whitfield. New York: Vintage, 1958.

Morson, Gary Saul, ed. *Literature and History: Theoretical Problems and Russian Case Studies.* Stanford, Cal.: Stanford University Press, 1986.

Moser, Charles A. *Esthetics as Nightmare: Russian Literary Theory, 1855–1870.* Princeton: Princeton University Press, 1989.

Moser, ed. *The Cambridge History of Russian Literature,* revised edition. Cambridge: Cambridge University Press, 1992.

Nekhai, M. V. *Russkii demokraticheskii ocherk 60-kh godov XIX stoletiia N. Uspenskii, V. Sleptsov i A. Levitov.* Minsk: BGU, 1971.

Nikolaev, Petr Alekseevich, general editor. *Russkie pisateli, 1800–1917: Biograficheskii slovar',* 4 volumes to date. Moscow: Bol'shaia rossiiskaia entsiklopediia, 1992– .

Offord, Derek. *Nineteenth-Century Russia: Opposition to Autocracy.* New York: Longman, 1999.

Offord. *Portraits of Early Russian Liberals: A Study of the Thought of T. N. Granovsky, V. P. Botkin, P. V. Annenkov, A. V. Druzhinin, and K. D. Kavelin.* Cambridge & New York: Cambridge University Press, 1985.

Offord. *The Russian Revolutionary Movement in the 1880s.* Cambridge & New York: Cambridge University Press, 1986.

Ovsianiko-Kulikovsky, D. N., ed. *Istoriia russkoi literatury XIX v,* 5 volumes. Moscow: Mir, 1911.

Pares, Bernard. *A History of Russia.* New York: Knopf, 1953.

Partridge, Monica. *Revolution and Nineteenth-Century Russian Literature.* Nottingham: University of Nottingham, 1968.

Plotkin, L. A. *O russkoi literature: A. I. Gertsen, I. S. Nikitin, D. I. Pisarev.* Leningrad: Khudozhestvennaia literatura, 1986.

Pomper, Philip. *The Russian Revolutionary Intelligentsia,* second edition. Arlington Heights, Ill.: Harlan Davidson, 1991.

Pypin, A. N. *Istoriia russkoi literatury,* 4 volumes. St. Petersburg, 1902. Reprint edition, The Hague: Mouton, 1968.

Riasanovsky, Nicholas V. *A History of Russia,* sixth edition. New York & Oxford: Oxford University Press, 2000.

Seeley, Frank F. *From the Heyday of the Superfluous Man to Chekhov.* Nottingham: Astra Press, 1994.

Simmons, Ernest J. *Introduction to Russian Realism.* Bloomington: Indiana University Press, 1965.

Skabichevsky, Aleksandr Mikhailovich. *Belletristy-narodniki: F. Reshetnikov, A. Levitov, Gl. Uspenskii, N. Zlatovratskii i drugie. Kriticheskie ocherki.* St. Petersburg: V. S. Balashev, 1888.

Skabichevsky. *Istoriia noveishei russkoi literatury (1848–1890).* St. Petersburg: Tipografiia gazety "Novosti," 1891.

Skatov, N. N., ed. *Istoriia russkoi literatury XIX veka: Vtoraia polovina.* Moscow: Prosveshchenie, 1987.

Slonim, Marc. *The Epic of Russian Literature: From Its Origins through Tolstoy.* New York: Oxford University Press, 1953. Revised edition, 1964.

Slonim. *Modern Russian Literature: From Chekhov to the Present.* New York: Oxford University Press, 1953.

Stavrou, Theofanis G., ed. *Art and Culture in Nineteenth-Century Russia.* Bloomington: Indiana University Press, 1983.

Stites, Richard. *The Women's Liberation Movement in Russia. Feminism, Nihilism, and Bolshevism.* Princeton: Princeton University Press, 1978.

Terras, Victor. *A History of Russian Literature.* New Haven & London: Yale University Press, 1991.

Terras, ed. *Handbook of Russian Literature.* New Haven: Yale University Press, 1985.

Todd, William Mills, III. *Literature and Society in Imperial Russia, 1800–1914.* Stanford, Cal.: Stanford University Press, 1978.

Tomei, Christine D., ed. *Russian Women Writers,* 2 volumes. New York & London: Garland, 1999.

Vengerov, S. A. *Ocherki po istorii russkoi literatury,* second edition. St. Petersburg: Tipografiia Obshchestvennaia Pol'za, 1907. Reprint edition, The Hague & Paris: Mouton, 1969.

Vengerov, and others, eds. *Russkaia literatura XX veka (1890–1910),* 3 volumes. Moscow: Mir, 1914–1916(?).

Venturi, Franco. *Roots of Revolution.* Introduction by Berlin. New York: Knopf, 1960.

Walicki, Andrzej. *A History of Russian Thought from the Enlightenment to Marxism.* Stanford: Stanford University Press, 1979.

Walicki. *The Slavophile Controversy: History of a Conservative Utopia in Nineteenth-Century Russian Thought,* translated by Hilda Andrews-Rusiecka. Oxford: Clarendon Press / New York: Oxford University Press, 1975. Reprint edition, Notre Dame, Ind.: University of Notre Dame Press, 1989.

Wellek, René. *A History of Modern Criticism: 1750–1950.* Volume 4: *The Later Nineteenth Century.* New Haven: Yale University Press, 1965.

Contributors

Radha Balasubramanian . . . . *University of Nebraska, Lincoln*

Luc Beaudoin . . . . *University of Denver*

George Crowder . . . . *Flinders University*

Karla Cruise . . . .

Kathleen E. Dillon . . . . *University of California, Davis*

Wayne Dowler . . . . *University of Toronto*

Karen Evans-Romaine . . . . *Ohio University*

Michael Finke . . . . *Washington University*

John Givens . . . . *University of Rochester*

Stuart Goldberg . . . .

Svetlana Slavskaya Grenier . . . . *Georgetown University*

Barbara Henry . . . . *University of Washington*

Thomas P. Hodge . . . . *Wellesley College*

Alan Kimball . . . . *University of Oregon*

Emily Klenin . . . . *University of California, Los Angeles*

Ann Hibner Koblitz . . . . *Arizona State University*

Martha Kuchar . . . . *Roanoke College*

Kenneth Lantz . . . . *University of Toronto*

Ludmila Shleyfer Lavine . . . . *Pennsylvania State University*

John Mohan . . . . *Grinnell College*

Henrietta Mondry . . . . *University of Canterbury*

Derek Offord . . . . *University of Bristol*

Peter C. Pozefsky . . . . *The College of Wooster*

Michael Ransome . . . . *Bristol Grammar School*

Andrei Rogachevskii . . . . *University of Glasgow*

Karen Kosneck . . . . *University of Wisconsin–Madison*

Donald Senese . . . . *University of Victoria*

Marshall S. Shatz . . . . *University of Massachusetts–Boston*

Melissa T. Smith . . . . *Youngstown State University*

Tatiana Smorodinskaya . . . . *Middlebury College*

David Vernikov . . . . *University of Wisconsin–Madison*

Yekaterina Vernikov . . . . *Indiana University, Bloomington*

Judith Vowles . . . .

Robert D. Wessling . . . . *Stanford University*

Robert Whittaker . . . . *Lehman College, City University of New York*

Judith E. Zimmerman . . . . *University of Pittsburgh, Greensburg*

Mary F. Zirin . . . .

Cumulative Index

Dictionary of Literary Biography, Volumes 1-277
Dictionary of Literary Biography Yearbook, 1980-2001
Dictionary of Literary Biography Documentary Series, Volumes 1-19
Concise Dictionary of American Literary Biography, Volumes 1-7
Concise Dictionary of British Literary Biography, Volumes 1-8
Concise Dictionary of World Literary Biography, Volumes 1-4

Cumulative Index

DLB before number: *Dictionary of Literary Biography,* Volumes 1-277
Y before number: *Dictionary of Literary Biography Yearbook,* 1980-2001
DS before number: *Dictionary of Literary Biography Documentary Series,* Volumes 1-19
CDALB before number: *Concise Dictionary of American Literary Biography,* Volumes 1-7
CDBLB before number: *Concise Dictionary of British Literary Biography,* Volumes 1-8
CDWLB before number: *Concise Dictionary of World Literary Biography,* Volumes 1-4

Delaney, Shelagh 1939- DLB-13; CDBLB-8

Delano, Amasa 1763-1823 . . . . DLB-183

Delany, Martin Robinson 1812-1885 . . . . . DLB-50

Delany, Samuel R. 1942- DLB-8, 33

de la Roche, Mazo 1879-1961 . . . . DLB-68

Delavigne, Jean François Casimir
1793-1843 . . . . DLB-192

Delbanco, Nicholas 1942- DLB-6, 234

Delblanc, Sven 1931-1992 . . . . DLB-257

Del Castillo, Ramón 1949- DLB-209

Deledda, Grazia 1871-1936 . . . . DLB-264

De León, Nephtal 1945- DLB-82

Delfini, Antonio 1907-1963 . . . . DLB-264

Delgado, Abelardo Barrientos 1931- DLB-82

Del Giudice, Daniele 1949- DLB-196

De Libero, Libero 1906-1981 . . . . DLB-114

DeLillo, Don 1936- DLB-6, 173

de Lint, Charles 1951- DLB-251

de Lisser H. G. 1878-1944 . . . . DLB-117

Dell, Floyd 1887-1969 . . . . DLB-9

Dell Publishing Company DLB-46

delle Grazie, Marie Eugene 1864-1931 . . . . DLB-81

Deloney, Thomas died 1600 . . . . DLB-167

Deloria, Ella C. 1889-1971 . . . . DLB-175

Deloria, Vine, Jr. 1933- DLB-175

del Rey, Lester 1915-1993 . . . . DLB-8

Del Vecchio, John M. 1947- DS-9

Del'vig, Anton Antonovich 1798-1831 . . . DLB-205

de Man, Paul 1919-1983 . . . . DLB-67

DeMarinis, Rick 1934- DLB-218

Demby, William 1922- DLB-33

De Mille, James 1833-1880 . . . . DLB-251

de Mille, William 1878-1955 . . . . DLB-266

Deming, Philander 1829-1915 . . . . DLB-74

Deml, Jakub 1878-1961 . . . . DLB-215

Demorest, William Jennings 1822-1895 . . . DLB-79

De Morgan, William 1839-1917 . . . . DLB-153

Demosthenes 384 B.C.-322 B.C. DLB-176

Denham, Henry [publishing house] DLB-170

Denham, Sir John 1615-1669 . . . . DLB-58, 126

Denison, Merrill 1893-1975 . . . . DLB-92

Denison, T. S., and Company DLB-49

Dennery, Adolphe Philippe 1811-1899 . . . DLB-192

Dennie, Joseph 1768-1812 . . . . . . DLB-37, 43, 59, 73

Dennis, C. J. 1876-1938 . . . . DLB-260

Dennis, John 1658-1734 . . . . DLB-101

Dennis, Nigel 1912-1989 . . . . DLB-13, 15, 233

Denslow, W. W. 1856-1915 . . . . DLB-188

Dent, J. M., and Sons DLB-112

Dent, Tom 1932-1998 . . . . DLB-38

Denton, Daniel circa 1626-1703 . . . . DLB-24

DePaola, Tomie 1934- DLB-61

Department of Library, Archives, and Institutional
Research, American Bible Society Y-97

De Quille, Dan 1829-1898 . . . . DLB-186

De Quincey, Thomas
1785-1859 . . . . DLB-110, 144; CDBLB-3

"Rhetoric" (1828; revised, 1859)
[excerpt] DLB-57

Derby, George Horatio 1823-1861 . . . . . . DLB-11

Derby, J. C., and Company DLB-49

Derby and Miller DLB-49

De Ricci, Seymour 1881-1942 . . . . DLB-201

Derleth, August 1909-1971 . . . . DLB-9; DS-17

Derrida, Jacques 1930- DLB-242

The Derrydale Press DLB-46

Derzhavin, Gavriil Romanovich
1743-1816 . . . . DLB-150

Desai, Anita 1937- DLB-271

Desaulniers, Gonsalve 1863-1934 . . . . . . DLB-92

Desbordes-Valmore, Marceline
1786-1859 . . . . DLB-217

Descartes, René 1596-1650 . . . . DLB-268

Deschamps, Emile 1791-1871 . . . . DLB-217

Deschamps, Eustache 1340?-1404 . . . . . . DLB-208

Desbiens, Jean-Paul 1927- DLB-53

des Forêts, Louis-Rene 1918- DLB-83

Desiato, Luca 1941- DLB-196

Desjardins, Marie-Catherine
(see Villedieu, Madame de)

Desnica, Vladan 1905-1967 . . . . DLB-181

Desnos, Robert 1900-1945 . . . . DLB-258

DesRochers, Alfred 1901-1978 . . . . DLB-68

Desrosiers, Léo-Paul 1896-1967 . . . . DLB-68

Dessì, Giuseppe 1909-1977 . . . . DLB-177

Destouches, Louis-Ferdinand
(see Céline, Louis-Ferdinand)

DeSylva, Buddy 1895-1950 and
Brown, Lew 1893-1958 . . . . DLB-265

De Tabley, Lord 1835-1895 . . . . DLB-35

Deutsch, André, Limited DLB-112

Deutsch, Babette 1895-1982 . . . . DLB-45

Deutsch, Niklaus Manuel (see Manuel, Niklaus)

Devanny, Jean 1894-1962 . . . . DLB-260

Deveaux, Alexis 1948- DLB-38

The Development of the Author's Copyright
in Britain DLB-154

The Development of Lighting in the Staging
of Drama, 1900-1945 . . . . DLB-10

"The Development of Meiji Japan" DLB-180

De Vere, Aubrey 1814-1902 . . . . DLB-35

Devereux, second Earl of Essex, Robert
1565-1601 . . . . DLB-136

The Devin-Adair Company DLB-46

De Vinne, Theodore Low 1828-1914 . . . . DLB-187

Devlin, Anne 1951- DLB-245

De Voto, Bernard 1897-1955 . . . . DLB-9, 256

De Vries, Peter 1910-1993 . . . . DLB-6; Y-82

Dewdney, Christopher 1951- DLB-60

Dewdney, Selwyn 1909-1979 . . . . DLB-68

Dewey, John 1859-1952 . . . . DLB-246, 270

Dewey, Orville 1794-1882 . . . . DLB-243

Dewey, Thomas B. 1915-1981 . . . . DLB-226

DeWitt, Robert M., Publisher DLB-49

DeWolfe, Fiske and Company DLB-49

Dexter, Colin 1930- DLB-87

de Young, M. H. 1849-1925 . . . . DLB-25

Dhlomo, H. I. E. 1903-1956 . . . . DLB-157, 225

Dhuoda circa 803-after 843 . . . . DLB-148

The Dial 1840-1844 . . . . DLB-223

The Dial Press DLB-46

Diamond, I. A. L. 1920-1988 . . . . DLB-26

Dibble, L. Grace 1902-1998 . . . . DLB-204

Dibdin, Thomas Frognall 1776-1847 . . . . DLB-184

Di Cicco, Pier Giorgio 1949- DLB-60

Dick, Philip K. 1928-1982 . . . . DLB-8

Dick and Fitzgerald DLB-49

Dickens, Charles 1812-1870
. . . . DLB-21, 55, 70, 159, 166; CDBLB-4

Dickey, James 1923-1997
. . . . .DLB-5, 193; Y-82, Y-93, Y-96;
DS-7, DS-19; CDALB-6

James Dickey Tributes Y-97

The Life of James Dickey: A Lecture to
the Friends of the Emory Libraries,
by Henry Hart Y-98

Dickey, William 1928-1994 . . . . DLB-5

Dickinson, Emily
1830-1886 . . . . DLB-1, 243; CDWLB-3

Dickinson, John 1732-1808 . . . . DLB-31

Dickinson, Jonathan 1688-1747 . . . . DLB-24

Dickinson, Patric 1914- DLB-27

Dickinson, Peter 1927- DLB-87, 161, 276

Dicks, John [publishing house] DLB-106

Dickson, Gordon R. 1923- DLB-8

Dictionary of Literary Biography Yearbook Awards
. . . . . . Y-92, Y-93, Y-97, Y-98, Y-99, Y-00, Y-01

The Dictionary of National Biography DLB-144

Didion, Joan 1934-
. . . . . . DLB-2, 173, 185; Y-81, Y-86; CDALB-6

Di Donato, Pietro 1911- DLB-9

Die Fürstliche Bibliothek Corvey Y-96

Diego, Gerardo 1896-1987 . . . . DLB-134

Dietz, Howard 1896-1983 . . . . DLB-265

Digges, Thomas circa 1546-1595 . . . . DLB-136

The Digital Millennium Copyright Act:
Expanding Copyright Protection in
Cyberspace and Beyond Y-98

Diktonius, Elmer 1896-1961 . . . . DLB-259

Dillard, Annie 1945- DLB-275; Y-80

Dillard, R. H. W. 1937- DLB-5, 244

Dillingham, Charles T., Company DLB-49

The Dillingham, G. W., Company DLB-49

Dilly, Edward and Charles
[publishing house] DLB-154

Dilthey, Wilhelm 1833-1911 . . . . DLB-129

Dimitrova, Blaga 1922- DLB-181; CDWLB-4

Dimov, Dimitr 1909-1966 . . . . DLB-181

Dimsdale, Thomas J. 1831?-1866 . . . . DLB-186

Dinescu, Mircea 1950- DLB-232

Cumulative Index

Hodgins, Jack 1938- DLB-60

Hodgman, Helen 1945- DLB-14

Hodgskin, Thomas 1787-1869 . . . . DLB-158

Hodgson, Ralph 1871-1962 . . . . DLB-19

Hodgson, William Hope
1877-1918 . . . . DLB-70, 153, 156, 178

Hoe, Robert, III 1839-1909 . . . . DLB-187

Hoeg, Peter 1957- DLB-214

Højholt, Per 1928- DLB-214

Hoffenstein, Samuel 1890-1947 . . . . DLB-11

Hoffman, Charles Fenno 1806-1884 . . . DLB-3, 250

Hoffman, Daniel 1923- DLB-5

Hoffmann, E. T. A.
1776-1822 . . . . DLB-90; CDWLB-2

Hoffman, Frank B. 1888-1958 . . . . DLB-188

Hoffman, William 1925- DLB-234

Hoffmanswaldau, Christian Hoffman von
1616-1679 . . . . DLB-168

Hofmann, Michael 1957- DLB-40

Hofmannsthal, Hugo von
1874-1929 . . . . DLB-81, 118; CDWLB-2

Hofstadter, Richard 1916-1970 . . . . . . DLB-17, 246

Hogan, Desmond 1950- DLB-14

Hogan, Linda 1947- DLB-175

Hogan and Thompson DLB-49

Hogarth Press DLB-112

Hogg, James 1770-1835 . . . . DLB-93, 116, 159

Hohberg, Wolfgang Helmhard Freiherr von
1612-1688 . . . . DLB-168

von Hohenheim, Philippus Aureolus
Theophrastus Bombastus (see Paracelsus)

Hohl, Ludwig 1904-1980 . . . . DLB-56

Holbrook, David 1923- DLB-14, 40

Holcroft, Thomas 1745-1809 . . . . DLB-39, 89, 158

Preface to *Alwyn* (1780) DLB-39

Holden, Jonathan 1941- DLB-105

"Contemporary Verse Story-telling" DLB-105

Holden, Molly 1927-1981 . . . . DLB-40

Hölderlin, Friedrich 1770-1843 DLB-90; CDWLB-2

Holdstock, Robert 1948- DLB-261

Holiday House DLB-46

Holinshed, Raphael died 1580 . . . . DLB-167

Holland, J. G. 1819-1881 . . . . .DS-13

Holland, Norman N. 1927- DLB-67

Hollander, John 1929- DLB-5

Holley, Marietta 1836-1926 . . . . DLB-11

Hollinghurst, Alan 1954- DLB-207

Hollingsworth, Margaret 1940- DLB-60

Hollo, Anselm 1934- DLB-40

Holloway, Emory 1885-1977 . . . . DLB-103

Holloway, John 1920- DLB-27

Holloway House Publishing Company . . . DLB-46

Holme, Constance 1880-1955 . . . . DLB-34

Holmes, Abraham S. 1821?-1908 . . . . DLB-99

Holmes, John Clellon 1926-1988 . . . . DLB-16, 237

"Four Essays on the Beat Generation" DLB-16

Holmes, Mary Jane 1825-1907 . . . . DLB-202, 221

Holmes, Oliver Wendell
1809-1894 . . . . . . DLB-1, 189, 235; CDALB-2

Holmes, Richard 1945- DLB-155

The Cult of Biography
Excerpts from the Second Folio Debate:
"Biographies are generally a disease of
English Literature" Y-86

Holmes, Thomas James 1874-1959 . . . . . DLB-187

Holroyd, Michael 1935- DLB-155; Y-99

Holst, Hermann E. von 1841-1904 . . . . . DLB-47

Holt, Henry, and Company DLB-49

Holt, John 1721-1784 . . . . DLB-43

Holt, Rinehart and Winston DLB-46

Holtby, Winifred 1898-1935 . . . . DLB-191

Holthusen, Hans Egon 1913- DLB-69

Hölty, Ludwig Christoph Heinrich
1748-1776 . . . . DLB-94

Holub, Miroslav
1923-1998 . . . . DLB-232; CDWLB-4

Holz, Arno 1863-1929 . . . . DLB-118

Home, Henry, Lord Kames
(see Kames, Henry Home, Lord)

Home, John 1722-1808 . . . . DLB-84

Home, William Douglas 1912- DLB-13

Home Publishing Company DLB-49

Homer circa eighth-seventh centuries B.C.
. . . . DLB-176; CDWLB-1

Homer, Winslow 1836-1910 . . . . DLB-188

Homes, Geoffrey (see Mainwaring, Daniel)

Honan, Park 1928- DLB-111

Hone, William 1780-1842 . . . . .DLB-110, 158

Hongo, Garrett Kaoru 1951- DLB-120

Honig, Edwin 1919- DLB-5

Hood, Hugh 1928- DLB-53

Hood, Mary 1946- DLB-234

Hood, Thomas 1799-1845 . . . . DLB-96

Hook, Theodore 1788-1841 . . . . DLB-116

Hooker, Jeremy 1941- DLB-40

Hooker, Richard 1554-1600 . . . . DLB-132

Hooker, Thomas 1586-1647 . . . . DLB-24

hooks, bell 1952- DLB-246

Hooper, Johnson Jones
1815-1862 . . . . DLB-3, 11, 248

Hope, Anthony 1863-1933 . . . . DLB-153, 156

Hope, Christopher 1944- DLB-225

Hope, Eva (see Hearn, Mary Anne)

Hope, Laurence (Adela Florence
Cory Nicolson) 1865-1904 . . . . DLB-240

Hopkins, Ellice 1836-1904 . . . . DLB-190

Hopkins, Gerard Manley
1844-1889 . . . . DLB-35, 57; CDBLB-5

Hopkins, John (see Sternhold, Thomas)

Hopkins, John H., and Son DLB-46

Hopkins, Lemuel 1750-1801 . . . . DLB-37

Hopkins, Pauline Elizabeth 1859-1930 . . . . DLB-50

Hopkins, Samuel 1721-1803 . . . . DLB-31

Hopkinson, Francis 1737-1791 . . . . DLB-31

Hopkinson, Nalo 1960- DLB-251

Hopper, Nora (Mrs. Nora Chesson)
1871-1906 . . . . DLB-240

Hoppin, Augustus 1828-1896 . . . . DLB-188

Hora, Josef 1891-1945 . . . . . .DLB-215; CDWLB-4

Horace 65 B.C.-8 B.C. DLB-211; CDWLB-1

Horgan, Paul 1903-1995 . . . . .DLB-102, 212; Y-85

Horizon Press DLB-46

Hornby, C. H. St. John 1867-1946 . . . . . DLB-201

Hornby, Nick 1957- DLB-207

Horne, Frank 1899-1974 . . . . DLB-51

Horne, Richard Henry (Hengist)
1802 or 1803-1884 . . . . DLB-32

Horney, Karen 1885-1952 . . . . DLB-246

Hornung, E. W. 1866-1921 . . . . DLB-70

Horovitz, Israel 1939- DLB-7

Horton, George Moses 1797?-1883? DLB-50

Horváth, Ödön von 1901-1938 . . . . . DLB-85, 124

Horwood, Harold 1923- DLB-60

Hosford, E. and E. [publishing house] DLB-49

Hoskens, Jane Fenn 1693-1770? DLB-200

Hoskyns, John 1566-1638 . . . . DLB-121

Hosokawa Yūsai 1535-1610 . . . . DLB-203

Hostovský, Egon 1908-1973 . . . . DLB-215

Hotchkiss and Company DLB-49

Hough, Emerson 1857-1923 . . . . DLB-9, 212

Houghton, Stanley 1881-1913 . . . . DLB-10

Houghton Mifflin Company DLB-49

Household, Geoffrey 1900-1988 . . . . DLB-87

Housman, A. E. 1859-1936 . . . DLB-19; CDBLB-5

Housman, Laurence 1865-1959 . . . . DLB-10

Houston, Pam 1962- DLB-244

Houwald, Ernst von 1778-1845 . . . . DLB-90

Hovey, Richard 1864-1900 . . . . DLB-54

Howard, Donald R. 1927-1987 . . . . DLB-111

Howard, Maureen 1930- Y-83

Howard, Richard 1929- DLB-5

Howard, Roy W. 1883-1964 . . . . DLB-29

Howard, Sidney 1891-1939 . . . . . . .DLB-7, 26, 249

Howard, Thomas, second Earl of Arundel
1585-1646 . . . . DLB-213

Howe, E. W. 1853-1937 . . . . DLB-12, 25

Howe, Henry 1816-1893 . . . . DLB-30

Howe, Irving 1920-1993 . . . . DLB-67

Howe, Joseph 1804-1873 . . . . DLB-99

Howe, Julia Ward 1819-1910 . . . . DLB-1, 189, 235

Howe, Percival Presland 1886-1944 . . . . . DLB-149

Howe, Susan 1937- DLB-120

Howell, Clark, Sr. 1863-1936 . . . . DLB-25

Howell, Evan P. 1839-1905 . . . . DLB-23

Howell, James 1594?-1666 . . . . DLB-151

Howell, Soskin and Company DLB-46

Howell, Warren Richardson
1912-1984 . . . . DLB-140

Howells, William Dean 1837-1920
. . . . .DLB-12, 64, 74, 79, 189; CDALB-3

K

ISBN 0-7876-6021-3

90000

9 780787 660215